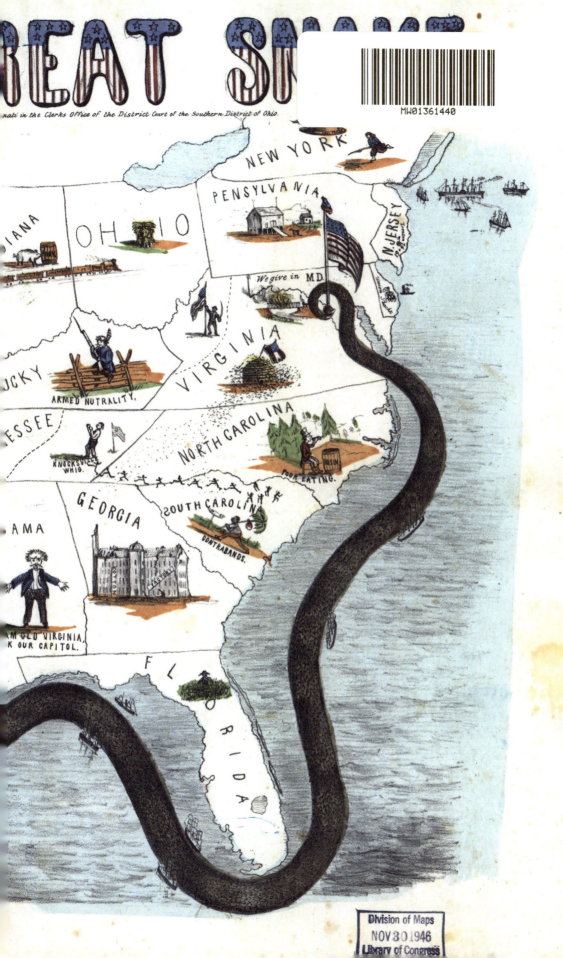

THROUGH THE EYES
OF A SOLDIER

THROUGH THE EYES OF A SOLDIER

A History of the Civil War as Seen by Battery L First United States Artillery 1860–1865

Robert C. Simmonds

Peter E. Randall Publisher
Portsmouth, New Hampshire
2017

Copyright © 2017 by Robert Simmonds.

ISBN: 978-1-937721-36-7

Library of Congress Control Number: 2017944671

All rights reserved. No part of this book may be reproduced or transmitted in any form or by any means, electronic or mechanical, including photocopying, recording, or by any information storage and retrieval system, without permission in writing from the copyright owner.

Published by:

Peter E. Randall Publisher
Portsmouth, NH 03802
www.perpublisher.com

Cover illustration: Gordon Carlisle

Book design: Grace Peirce

Contents

Introduction vii

Chapter 1 1
    *Fort Brown; Record 2/60; Record 4/60; Enlistment;
    Recession; Recruiting; Training; Record 10/60;
    Fort Duncan; Record 12/60; A Pivotal Year*

Chapter 2 27
    *The Texas Surrender; Record 2/61; 1861 Roster;
    Record 4/61*

Chapter 3 51
    *Garrisoning the Florida Forts; Fort Taylor;
    Fort Jefferson; Record 6/61; The Fort Pickens "Truce"; Secret
    Expeditions; The Anaconda Plan;
    Secret Board of Officers; Pickens Armament Complete;
    Battery L to Pickens; Record 8/61; Events Elsewhere;
    The "Truce" Ends; Record 10/61; Sickness;
    Troops to Ship Island*

Chapter 4 103
    *Raid on Santa Rosa; Record 12/61;
    Bombardment of November 22nd & 23rd; Confederate Concerns;
    Record 2/62; 1862 Roster;
    Bombardment of January 1st, 1862;
    Confederate Withdrawals;
    Record 4/62; Reconnaissance on Santa Rosa*

Chapter 5 143
    *The Anaconda Plan: North and South;
    Forts Heiman, Henry, and Donelson;
    The Northern Column; New Madrid/Island No. 10;
    Pittsburg Landing/Shiloh; Louisiana;
    Farragut and Butler; New Orleans; Vicksburg I;
    Corinth; Record 6/62; Occupation of Pensacola;
    Record 8/62; Reassignments; Record 10/62*

Chapter 6 197
    Vicksburg II; The Northern Column;
    Wavering in Washington; Halleck General-in-Chief;
    The Confederacy After Corinth; Return to Baton Rouge;
    Recruitment vs. Draft; The East; McClernand;
    The Department of the Gulf; The Lafourche Campaign; Banks;
    Record 12/62; The Close of 1862

Chapter 7 251
    Review; Record 2/63; 1863 Roster;
    The Nineteenth Army Corps; Engagement at Bayou Teche;
    The Alabama; The Northern Column; Forward!;
    The Yazoo Pass Expedition;
    The Ram Fleet and the Mississippi Marine Brigade;
    Return of the 42nd; Indianola Lost; Banks' Plan;
    Farragut Passes Port Hudson

Chapter 8 307
    The Teche Campaign:
    Record 4/63; Bisland/Irish Bend;
    Queen of the West/Cornie; Chasing the Fox;
    Opelousas; Cooperation with Grant; Grierson's Raid;
    Alexandria, De Russy & Red River, Farragut Departs;
    Turn to Port Hudson

Chapter 9 363
    Record 6/63; Port Hudson; Demonstrations; Plains Store;
    The Wider War; Closing the Ring; May 23rd;
    May 24th; May 25th; May 26th; Easy As 1-2-3;
    Weitzel Advances; Sherman Advances; Augur Advances; Cease Fire

Chapter 10 411
    The Siege Begins; June 10th; June 14th; Paine's Assault;
    Weitzel's Assault; Augur's Feint; Dwight's Assault; June 15th;
    Taylor Again; The Last Days; Finally; Recovery of the La Fourche; "Record" 8/63; The Next Step

Chapter 11 467
    The Sabine Pass Expedition; "Record" 10/63; A Land Route to Texas; The Rio Grande Expedition; "Record" 12/63; The Battle of Grand Coteau; "Record" 2/64; 1864 Roster; "Record" 4/64; The Red River Campaign: Wilson's Farm; Mansfield (Sabine Crossroads & Pleasant Grove); Pleasant Hill

Chapter 12 539
    Withdrawal: April 10th; Grand Ecore; Cane River; Porter's Passage to Alexandria; The Dam at Alexandria; "Record" 6/64; Marksville & Mansura; Canby; Last Days in the Gulf; "Record" 8/64; Camp Barry; Politics & Peace Initiatives; Washington Threatened; The Nineteenth Corps Arrives; After Early; Anecdote

Chapter 13 587
    Sheridan Appointed; The Army of the Shenandoah; First Moves; The Confederate Partisan Rangers; Sheridan Retreats North; The Public Mind; Berryville; Smithfield Crossing; "Record" 10/64; Anderson; Winchester

Chapter 14 643
    Fisher's Hill; The March Up The Valley; Terminated; Tom's Brook/Strasburg/Woodstock Races; Decisions, Decisions; Sheridan's Ride, Cedar Creek

Chapter 15 701
    "Record" 12/64; Mosby, Gilmor &McNeill; "Record" 2/65; 1865 Roster; Sherman's March; Fort Fisher; The Peace Commissioners; Sheridan Leaves the Valley; "Record" 4/65; Events of Note; Sherman; Fort Stedman; Grant Moves; Five Forks; The General Assault; Surrender

Chapter 16 759
    The Remains of the Confederacy Crumbles "Record" 6/65; Full Circle; The Faithful Few; Two Deserters; The 1863 Pensacola Recruits; The Three Cooks; Battery L

Appendix 781
Sources 783
Index 796
About the Author 833

Acknowledgments

Paul Callsen ~ Paul is very special to this book. His great-grandfather, Patrick Donnelly, enlisted in Battery L in the spring of 1860, at about the same time and at the same place, Boston, as did my great-grandfather. As Paul was interested in sharing information that he had discovered, he posted an announcement on a *RootsWeb* message board in 2004. I found it, and responded. Paul revealed that he had obtained nearly all of Battery L's muster rolls for the period of the Civil War, and that monthly reports and regimental records were also available from the National Archives. We arranged to meet in 2006, at the reenactment of the Battle of Cedar Creek, at Middletown, Virginia, one of many battles in which Battery L had fought. The records he had uncovered revealed a wide-ranging and compelling story, really a capsule history of a substantial portion of the Civil War.

Paul has been kind enough to review the manuscript, and in addition has contributed data on the activities of the battery after the war ended. The concept of "the faithful few" in chapter 16 appeared in his writings long before this book was even contemplated.

Ruth Stevens ~ Ruth's brother is an author of several books, all of which she reviewed before publication. Ruth has reviewed these chapters, as they slowly emerged, for at least the last three years. Her advice has been very valuable, particularly as to knowing the desires of the readership regarding an author's opinion. She pointed out that I should not fear commenting on events for fear of "re-writing history." My comments duly appear.

Scott Dearman ~ Scott is Park Manager of the Mansfield State Historic Site, Mansfield, Louisiana. He provided a copy of their map of the Battle of Pleasant Hill, with kind permission to use it. The map is particularly valuable in that it depicts the location of the old village of Pleasant Hill, which has since entirely vanished.

Mike Fraering ~ Mike is Curator of the Port Hudson State Historic Site, near St. Francisville, Louisiana. He provided much background material, particularly a copy of an historic map of the Siege of Port Hudson. It is of particular interest because it bears the markings of Col. I.G.W. Steedman, in describing the Confederate defenses.

Gov. & Mrs. Mike Foster ~ They welcomed the author to tour their home, Oaklawn Manor, the former Porter plantation, in Franklin, Louisiana. It had been where the Yankees had landed in April of 1863, the night before the Battle of Irish Bend, and where a drama between the plantation's elegant mistress and a Yankee general was played out.

Introduction

This is the Civil War odyssey of a small regular army unit: Battery L of the 1st Regiment of Artillery, United States Army. It is based on their service record, which was preserved as a "Record of Events" every two months on their "muster roll."[1] The book follows the same scheme: presenting the Record and personnel updates for the entire war. Everyone in the company is named; perhaps the reader will find an ancestor.

Being a regular army unit, Battery L was in active service prior to the beginning of the war. Thus, it experienced the political upheaval before shots were fired. In their case, they narrowly escaped the Texas Surrender. As may be surmised, the mention of Texas hints that they were located in some remote places not generally focused upon. There is nothing about the famous Battle of Gettysburg in this book, except to note when the troops finally heard about it while they were in Louisiana, days later. However, the story is not solely limited to what Battery L did, because wider political and military events which governed their fate are also presented.

Several of their expeditions involved joint operations with the navy, which both transported them as well as fought in support of them. There was extensive army-navy cooperation during the Civil War, a point that seems to be passed over in popular histories. You will read a lot about the navy in this army history.

The Early Years

The 1st Regiment of Artillery dates from the Act of Congress of March 2nd, 1821,[2] which reorganized the artillery into four regiments of nine batteries. A tenth battery or company (the terms were used interchangeably) was authorized for each regiment on July 5th, 1838. Each battery was designated by a letter from *A* to *K*, omitting the *J*. Batteries L and M were added after the Act of March 3rd, 1847, when experience in the Mexican War (April 25th, 1846–September 14th, 1847) indicated the need.

Battery L was mustered and equipped in 1847 and was sent to Mexico, arriving at Vera Cruz in December. Capt. John S. Hatheway [*sic*] assumed command there on January 17th, 1848. They saw no action, but stationed at the Charity Hospital,

---

1. Preserved at the National Archives as a part of Record Group 391 (Records of U.S. mobile commands) and RG 94 (regular army muster rolls). They were used as references for pension application verification for many years after the Civil War and unfortunately are often worn, torn, taped, and sometimes unreadable; and some are missing. Some monthly and annual returns are available, as well as monthly regimental returns.
2. Rodenbough, T. F., and Haskin, W. L., pp. 302, 303, 305; Haskin, W. L., p. 11.

they remained until the end of July, when they were transferred to Fort Columbus, New York; they were one of the last units to leave Mexico. On November 10th, 1848, they were embarked, with Battery M, on the steamer *Massachusetts*, bound for the newly acquired Oregon Territory. Around the horn and a stop in the Sandwich Islands [Hawaii] delayed their arrival at the Columbia River site of the Hudson's Bay Company, known as Fort Vancouver, until May 13th, 1849. There, they established "Camp Columbia." They remained in the area until March of 1853,[3] when their reduced strength, due to expirations of service, caused the officers and certain picked men to be ordered to New York to be reorganized. The remaining enlisted men were transferred to the 3rd Artillery and the 4th Infantry.

Recruiting for two reorganized companies[4] of 74 men each was begun but not achieved until February 24th, 1854, at Fort Monroe, Virginia. Desertions were substantial – 35 reported, more than at any other time previous – and as a result, the reorganization had taken almost a year. They remained at Fort Monroe until December 12th, when they were embarked on board steamers bound for Key Biscayne, Florida.

Battery L arrived at Key Biscayne on December 26th, 1854, and M three days later. Their assignment was to build a new fort near the site of an older Fort Dallas. Note that much of the work of the army in peacetime years was backbreaking construction. They occupied Fort Dallas, on the north bank of the Miami River, in what is now downtown Miami,[5] on January 15th, 1855, while engaged in the Third Seminole War. Three deaths and two desertions are noted.

On February 15th, 1856, L left on a scouting mission that involved it in the Battle of Big Cypress Swamp on April 7th, 1856. The scouting mission ended at Fort Myers. They returned to Fort Dallas on June 17th. In November, the battery was embarked on the steamer *Suwannee*, destination Fort Brown, Brownsville, Texas, arriving there on November 18th. There were two deaths and five desertions that year.

Their time in 1857 was divided between Fort Brown, Baton Rouge Barracks, Louisiana, and Brazos Santiago, Texas, a series of wharves and storage facilities kept by the army on Brazos Island north of the mouth of the Rio Grande. There were no deaths, but 19 desertions were recorded that year.

In 1858, their time was divided between Fort Brown and Brazos Santiago. The death toll of 39 (more than half the company) while at Brownsville confirms that Battery L did not escape the yellow fever epidemic. Eleven desertions were recorded at Brownsville that year.

In 1859, the company began what can only be described as a long dusty trail odyssey that took them north along the Rio Grande into the Llano Estacado, the

---

3. All following data from "Annual Returns" of the 1st Regiment of Artillery, RG 94, Microcopy 747, rolls 3, 4, and 5; National Archives.
4. Haskin, W. L., pp. 121, 126–128.
5. Personal correspondence from Mr. Paul Callsen.

Staked Plain of West Texas and eastern New Mexico. They were assigned to an expedition to evaluate the use of Egyptian camels in the desert areas of the west. L's participation began on March 22nd at Fort Brown when they were ordered to Fort Duncan, at Eagle Pass, from Brownsville. At Camp Hudson, north of Comstock, they joined an infantry camel caravan, which had originated at Camp Verde, about sixty miles north of San Antonio. As the ranking officer,[6] Capt. Samuel Dawson of Battery L assumed command. The expedition continued to Fort Lancaster, on the Pecos River near Sheffield; and after nearly eight hundred[7] miles, they finally arrived at Camp Stockton on the "Comanche War Trail," now Fort Stockton, on June 12th. Here they remained but two days, when they then began to retrace their steps back to Fort Clark, arriving on June 26th. They remained at Fort Clark until November 10th, when they, with Company M, were ordered back to Fort Brown, arriving on December 6th.

The call to return to Fort Brown was to assist the citizens there in the "First Cortina War."[8] On December 20th, the company left on a scouting mission in search of the Mexican "marauder Cortina," as he was referred to in the L muster roll, that lasted until January 4th, 1860. The strength of the company had dwindled to an aggregate of 39 officers and men. There were seven desertions, with two apprehended, and no deaths.

Prelude to the Civil War

The regular army in 1860 was small, and by most accounts, underfunded and barely able to accomplish its mission of policing the western frontier and the garrisoning of the coastal forts. On December 31st, 1860, the regular army had a total of 16,387 officers and men.[9] It remained very small and even miniscule if compared to the later volunteer force, which did not even come into existence until Lincoln's call upon the states for 75,000 men on April 15th, 1861. By October of 1862, there were 26,255 regulars versus 775,336 volunteers.[10] Sheer numbers, then, help to explain why the volunteers figure prominently in the popular history of the Civil War. Also, events involving "their boys" were scrupulously covered by local newspapers, reporters regularly having been sent to the scene. State politicians and members of Congress did likewise, following their home state regiments. The "regulars" seem to be lost in the shuffle, not only because of the overwhelming numerical statistics

---

6. Haskin, pp. 394–399. See also: www.cr.nps.gov/history/online: Camp Hudson, Camp Verde; Secretary of War; Introductory page by Jefferson Davis.
7. Five hundred ninety-one highway miles today.
8. National Archives RG94 M727 roll 4 *Return of the First Regiment of Artillery*, January 1859. See also www.tshaonline.org: "Cortina."
9. O.R. Ser. III, Vol. 1, p. 23.
10. O.R. Ser. III, Vol. 2, p. 868.

but also because they were not from "somewhere."

In the Civil War they were, in fact, everywhere, supporting, supplying experienced officer material for, and in some cases absorbing recruits from, the volunteers. In fact, during the Civil War, Battery L acquired most of its recruits from the New England and New York volunteer units who were serving alongside them.

The artillery, numbering a total of 210 officers in 1860,[11] alone supplied the Union army with 28 generals over the course of the war. One of those was Richard H. Jackson, formerly of Battery L, who became a brevet brigadier general in command of the 2nd Division of the 25th Army Corps. Another, though not in Battery L, but first associated with it as the engineer officer at Fort Pickens in 1861, was Godfrey Weitzel, who became the commander of the 25th Corps.

At the start of the war, there were four regiments of artillery. A fifth was added under a general reorganization of the regular army on May 4th, 1861.[12] The battery, or company, was the key organization of the artillery. Two, perhaps three, batteries might be assigned to a post or concentrated during a campaign, but no regiment ever took the field. The battery assignments were made directly from Washington through the Adjutant General's Office. Under this arrangement, any battery could have found itself dealt to any of the seven departments of the army: East, West, Oregon, California, Texas, New Mexico, or Utah. Battery dispositions to the various posts within the department were made on orders issued by the commanders of the departments, on instructions from Washington.

Regimental affiliation meant little. The regiment was a paper shuffling entity, which merely managed the monthly returns of its batteries.[13] The regiment had a home address, but it is doubtful if anyone other than the battery officers and the clerk who filled in the muster rolls and monthly returns knew it. In the case of the 1st Regiment, home was Fort Moultrie, Charleston, South Carolina; and when that state seceded, it was moved to Fort McHenry, Baltimore, Maryland, Col. John Erving, commanding. When he retired in October 1861, the command devolved to Col. Justin Dimick, the commander of Fort Warren, Boston Harbor, and later to Battery L's Maj. William Silvey, at Concord, New Hampshire.

An artillery battery, if nothing more, had to be versatile. It could be organized and equipped in one of three ways: as a garrison to a fort, as support to infantry, and as support to cavalry. The army manual for "Instruction of Field Artillery"[14] states: "The employment of field artillery, according to the various conditions of service, . . . varies with the nature of the theater of operations; the character of the enemy's defences; [sic] the composition of his forces . . ." In short, the deployment

---

11. O.R. Ser. III, Vol. 1, p. 22; O.R. 46/III, p. 1037; Adjutant General, 1891, p. 97. Jackson enlisted in the army as a private in 1851.
12. O.R. Ser. III, Vol. 1, pp. 154–157. General Orders No. 15, A.G.O.
13. Rodenbough, T. F., and Haskin, W.L., pp. 305, 308.
14. Board of Artillery Officers, pp. 1–4.

of a battery was whatever satisfied the department commander for the assignment at hand.

The peacetime strength of a battery "for instruction" was 4 guns, 76 men, and 44 horses. "Preparation for service" was the next category, which listed 4 guns, 100 men, and 80 horses. Each of these was to have two stored guns readily available, in the event expansion to "full-war strength" was ordered. This was 6 guns, 150 men, and 110 horses. Additional spare horses were required "for service on the plains."

A battery garrisoning a fort or fixed installation, often without horses, was called a "foot" battery. Batteries supporting infantry or cavalry required horses and were known as "field" batteries; they were either "mounted" if with infantry or "light" if with cavalry. The mounted battery with the infantry had a partial complement of horses sufficient for towing all its guns, caissons, the forge, and supply wagons; but everyone else was on foot. A "light" battery meant that everyone rode a horse. "At an early period of the war," [15] most of the 1st Regiment's batteries were converted to light batteries. As we shall see, Battery L was so converted at the end of 1862.

Today, one might think of how romantic it must have been to be in a light battery: the thundering mounted column of men and six-horse teams riding at full gallop to the battle scene, the sun glinting from the polished harnesses, the order and discipline – *poof!* – end of Hollywood movie. Substitute: blazing sun and dust, or cold rain and mud, and horses that require a great deal of care. On a long march, they became exhausted before a human did. They each require up to 4 or more gallons of water per day, 14 pounds of hay, and 12 pounds of mixed grains. Compare this with the requirements for a soldier: about three pounds per day for his full ration.[16] In a dry area of sparse forage, watering and feeding the horses or mules became a critical item. Worse, having to have extra wagons to carry water and forage became a "catch-22," and the bigger the train grew, the slower it moved, becoming ever more vulnerable to attack. The problem was actually more serious than that of keeping a modern army supplied with fuel because vehicles, at least, do not consume fuel when they are shut down.

---

15. Rodenbough, T. F., and Haskin, W.L., p. 306.
16. Board of Artillery Officers, pp. 33, 34; O.R. Ser. III, Vol. 2, p. 911.

Chapter 1

Fort Brown; Record 2/60; Record 4/60;
Enlistment; Recession; Recruiting; Training; Record 10/60;
Fort Duncan; Record 12/60; A Pivotal Year

Fort Brown

In the winter of 1860, Battery L found itself as part of the garrison of Fort Brown, at Brownsville, Texas (figure 1),[1] having been called there from Fort Clark, Brackettville, Texas, in November of 1859. Their mission was to aid in the chase after the so-called bandit Cortina, who had threatened the Brownsville area and briefly held Brownsville. Cortina's threats were derived from land disputes, he and his fellow Mexicans claiming to have been cheated out of their ancestral holdings by crooked American officials.

FIGURE 1

Brownsville in 1860 was an important trading/smuggling community of some 2,000 people. Across the river was the Mexican town of Matamoros and goods landed at Brownsville would be smuggled across the Rio Grande to avoid the high Mexican tariffs. If the population of the surrounding area, including Brazos

---

1. *Harper's Weekly*, March 23rd, 1861.

Santiago, Port Isabel, the Fort Brown Garrison, and the nearby cavalry camp on the Rio Grande were included, the total would be 5,718.

Record 2/60
31 DECEMBER 1859–29 FEBRUARY 1860, FORT BROWN, TEXAS

"The Co. returned from a scout of 15 days after the marauder Cortina, January 4th."

Samuel K. Dawson   Capt. Commanding.
William Silvey   1st Lt. Reg. Adjutant O. No. 7 Head Qrs. 1st Artillery, Fort Dallas, Fla, Aug. 13, '57. Left Co. April 22, 1854, S.O. No. 62, Head Qrs. New York, April 18, 1854.
James W. Robinson   1st Lt. On leave of absence, left Co. Sept. 5, 1859.
Loomis L. Langdon   2nd Lt. On detached service at Brazos Santiago, in charge of Government stores from abandoned forts. Left Co. Feb. 25, '59.

Strength: 39. Sick: 1.
Detached: 5 enlisted at Ringgold Barracks, Texas.

Note that those present for duty were only 1 officer and 30 enlisted men.

    Captain Dawson, being the senior officer present, was also commanding the fort. Company M, 1st Lt. Bennett H. Hill commanding, was also part of the garrison. As noted, companies L and M were mustered at Fort Monroe in 1847 at the same time and seemed to have crossed paths ever since, from Oregon and Florida and now to Texas, where they had both arrived at Fort Brown on February 18th, 1856. Regarding their "scout" for the "marauder" Cortina, the combined infantry and artillery force caught up with him at Ringgold Barracks, on December 21st, where he was defeated and fled to Mexico.

    The regimental return for January lists Battery L as requiring 50 recruits.[2] As far as resources are concerned, the company had no guns (cannons) or horses,[3] though the men of L carried the model 1855 rifled musket. In fact, only two of the eleven companies in the 1st Regiment had any guns or horses at all. Company I at Fort Leavenworth, Kansas, John B. Magruder commanding, had 4 guns and 63 horses, 1 unserviceable; and Company K, at Fort Clark, Texas, William H. French, commanding, had 4 guns and 24 horses, with 20 unserviceable. Only Company I was in a condition approaching the "preparation for service" category of 4 guns, 100 men, and 80 horses. Ten out of the eleven batteries of the 1st Regiment fell into the definition of a "foot" battery, supposed to garrison a fort. Only some of the batteries scattered around the country were doing duty as anticipated by the definition. Battery A and Battery D were stationed at Fort Monroe, Virginia; B was at Key West Barracks, nearby to Fort Taylor (though the fort itself was unoccupied); C was at Ringgold Barracks, (Rio Grande City) Texas; E and H were at

---

2. The regiment as a whole required 260 (to fill up to a required 960 enlisted).
3. Regimental return for January 1860.

Fort Sumter, South Carolina; and G was at Barrancas Barracks, across Pensacola Bay, Florida, from Fort Pickens, which also was unoccupied.

Thus, we see that few of the batteries of the regiment were actually in a genuine brick-and-mortar fort. The typical Texas "fort" was not a large enclosed structure with guns mounted around the periphery but simply an open cantonment or camp, lucky to have some permanent structures other than tents. By these standards, the majority of the army artillery batteries, including Battery L, at this time were de facto infantry.

Record 4/60
29 FEBRUARY–30 APRIL 1860, FORT BROWN, TEXAS

[No entry in Record of Events]

Samuel K. Dawson	Capt.	In Command
William Silvey	1st Lt.	Reg'l Adjt. O. No. 7 Hdqrs. 1st Arty. Ft. Dallas, Fla. Aug. 13, 1857, Left Co. Apr. 22,'54 S.O. No. 62 Hdqrs. N.Y. Apr. 18,'54
James W. Robinson	1st Lt.	Present
Loomis Langdon	2nd Lt.	Present
Lewis Keller	1st Sgt.	1 Dec.'59, Newport, KY. Transferred to Comp'y L pr. Ord. No. 3, Hdqrs. Gen'l Rect'g Serv. War Dept., Mar. 5, 1860. Appt'd. Apr. 7th 1860, to date from 1st Apr. Appt'd. 1st Sgt. Apr.7th, 1860.
Thomas Conroy	Sgt.	1 Jan.'59, San Antonio, TX, 1st re-enlistment
James Flynn	Sgt.	12 Sept.'59, Fort Clark, TX, 1st re-enlistment
Thomas Newton	Sgt.	13 Dec.'58, Ft. Brown, TX, 2nd re-enlistment
Alexander Livingston	Cpl.	22 Sept.'58, Syracuse, NY, sick
Lewis Lighna	Musician	13 Oct.'58, Ft. Brown, TX
Francis Hagan	"	21 Jan.'59,

Strength: 80, Sick: 1.
Died:
John Murtaugh, Pvt. 10 Oct.'59, NewYork. Joined from General Recruiting Depot, Ft. Columbus, New York, April 15, 1860. Drowned in the Rio Grande, Apr. 27, 1860.

All the battery officers were commissioned prior to 1852. Dawson, Silvey, Robinson, and Langdon were from West Point. Only Robinson was a Southerner, appointed from Virginia.

Captain Dawson was relieved from command of the post by Bvt. Maj. Henry Hunt [Commanding Company M], 2nd Artillery, upon its transfer to Fort Brown.[4]

The transfer of Lewis Keller into the company by the War Department was likely by Keller's request. Having enlisted in 1854, he had served in the Second Seminole War and survived the yellow fever epidemic at Brownsville in 1858. His enlistment term of five years expired on September 11th, 1859, and he had reenlisted on December 1st, 1859. Thomas Newton was an 11-year veteran "severely"

---

4. Newton data from Haskin, W. L., p. 128.

wounded while serving with Battery L at Big Cypress Swamp in 1856. Newton was 32 and on his third tour of duty, having first enlisted on April 12th, 1849, at New York, and assigned to Company K, 1st Artillery, at Fort McHenry. Conroy was 29 and on his second tour. James Flynn was also on his second tour of duty, though he gave his age as 24 in the 1860 census. Fair enough, his parents approved his enlistment at age 19.[5]

All these sergeants were clearly committed to the company. Newton's wife, Ann, was a laundress and their daughter, Mary, was living on the post. Conroy's wife, Elizabeth, also was a laundress. Flynn's wife, Mary, was the hospital matron. Their son, Thomas, and daughter, Emily, lived on the post.

On April 15th, 46 recruits of the 50 called for arrived at Fort Brown from the General Recruiting Depot at Fort Columbus, New York (see table I below). Their first appearance on the muster roll would be at the end of April, and some of them, those listed as "in confinement," had already gotten into unspecified trouble, with unspecified disciplinary action. Most of the recruits in this first group to arrive were foreign born, as obtained from the 1860 census of "Garrison Fort Brown," which was taken on June 25th.

Analyzing the locations from where all the enlisted men in the battery in 1860 had signed up, in addition to the recruits (except where reenlistments were made, which was usually at the duty station), produces a list of mostly Northern addresses: Buffalo, Rochester, Syracuse, and New York; Boston; Philadelphia; Baltimore; Detroit, St. Louis; and Newport, Kentucky, which was across the Ohio River from Cincinnati. Note that the overwhelming majority signed up at either New York or Boston.

NAME	ENLIST. DATE	ENLIST. PLACE	ORIGIN	REMARKS
Anglin, Edmund	19 October '59	New York	Maine	In confinement
Anderson, James	9 November '59	New York	Ireland	
Becker, Julius	12 October '59	New York	Prussia	
Brunskill, William C.	19 October '59	New York	England	
Bissel, John	3 November '59	New York	Ireland	
Brown, William F.	1 November '59	Boston	England	
Baby, Alexander, J.	10 February '60	Boston	Canada	In confinement
Beeler, Andrew J.	9 February '60	Boston	Ireland	
Brook, Thomas	9 February '60	Boston	Massachusetts	
Benjamin, George	13 February '60	New York		In confinement
Casey, John	15 October '59	New York	Ireland	
Cain, Isaac T.	4 October '59	Boston	New Mexico	
Carr, Edward	1 November '59	Boston	Ireland	
Donnelly, Patrick	1 March '60	Boston	Ireland	In confinement
Demarest, William	15 October '59	New York	Maryland	
Dodge, Charles E.	3 November '59	Boston	Massachusetts	
Duffy, Thomas	12 November '59	Boston	Ireland	In confinement

---

5. The age required for enlistment without parental consent was 21.

Flynn, Patrick	3 November '59	New York		
Foley, Christopher	3 November '59	Boston	Ireland	
Friedman, George	7 February '60	New York	Bavaria	
Farrell, Bernard	11 November '59	New York	Ireland	
Golden, James	2 February '60	New York	Ireland	
Hadley, George	1 March '60	Boston	Massachusetts	
Harrison, John	25 October '60	New York	Pennsylvania	
Jaecke, Daniel	11 February '60	New York		
Kenny, Michael	8 February '59	New York	Ireland	
Kinney, Joseph	19 October '59	New York	Newfoundland	
Kutschor, Joseph	13 February '60	New York	Austria	
Morris, John	22 October '59	New York	France	
Myers, John	1 March '60	New York	Baden, Ger.	
Murphy, Michael	8 February '60	New York	Ireland	
Murphy, John	21 February '60	Boston	Rhode Island	
Murtaugh, John	10 October '59	New York		
Nitschke, John G.	6 February '60	New York	Prussia	
Riley, Charles	7 October '59	Boston	New York	
Ryan, James	14 October '59	New York		
Rupprecht, Ludwig	7 February '60	New York	Prussia	
Smith, Joseph	11 October '60	New York	Bavaria	
Schoenfeld, Charles	6 February '60	New York	Prussia	
Straub, Amelius	8 February '60	New York	Baden, Ger.	
Scott, William E.	9 February '60	Boston	England	
Stone, Richard	16 February '60	Boston	Vermont	In confinement
Thayer, Henry B.	9 February '60	Boston	Massachusetts	
White, Michael	7 October '59	Boston	Ireland	
Wicks, David J.	25 October '59	New York	Sweden	
Wilkinson, Joseph	4 February '60	New York	Ireland	

TABLE I

It is striking that there was only one Southerner (though hardly south, St. Louis was in a slave state) in the ranks and none from the Deep South. Do these statistics tell us that for years before the Civil War the country had become polarized to the point that a Southerner would disdain to enlist in the "Yankee" army? There might have been some of that sentiment, but the basic pattern of few Southern enlistments had been true for years. Even when Jefferson Davis of Mississippi was secretary of war[6] (1853–1857), there appears no evidence that the recruitment of Southerners was greater, i.e., more popular. In the report of the secretary of war for 1854, the general recruiting for the army resulted in the enlistment of 2,365 men. Included was a breakdown, as compiled by the adjutant general, which is summarized below:[7]

---

6. *Encyclopedia Britannica*, Vol. 7, p. 867.
7. *Message of the President to the Houses of Congress*, 33rd Congress, Part II, Washington, A. O. P. Nicholson, 1854, p. 68. Whether some of the numbers include reenlistments is not specified.

Eastport, Maine	18	Ohio	25
Boston, Massachusetts	221	St. Louis	134
New York, NY	951	Chicago	87
New York State (remainder)	265	Detroit	1
Pennsylvania	419	Warrington, Florida	1
Maryland	73	Fort Ripley, Minnesota	1
Kentucky	169		

The number from Kentucky included 166 from Newport, suggesting that many of the enlisted would have come from Ohio. Note that most of the enlistments were from two cities – which were major points of entry for immigration, Boston and New York – and many on the list show foreign origin. Clearly, the immigrant was the staple of the "old" army.

A second group of recruits (table II), was requested after the battery experienced a large number of desertions over the course of the summer. On December 5th, 25 arrived at Fort Duncan, Texas, to where the battery had moved that September.

	Enlisted	Place		Enlisted	Place
Ahern, James	18 Oct.'60	Boston	McDonough, Miles	17 Sept.'60	New York
Beglan, James	25 Oct.'60	New York	McGaley, Terence	18 Sept.'60	New York
Burke, John	7 Oct.'60	New York	Olvany, Michael	25 Oct.'60	New York
Craffy, Patrick	27 Sept.'60	Boston	O'Sullivan, Michael	26 Sept.'60	Boston
Creed, William	27 Sept.'60	Boston	Parketton, William	4 Oct.'60	New York
Cummings, Patrick	25 Oct.'60	Boston	Roper, John	22 Oct.'60	New York
Ferrari, Prosper	22 Oct.'60	New York	Schmidt, Heinrick	26 Oct.'60	New York
Flint Charles, A.	22 Sept.'60	Boston	Shaw, Warren P.	26 Oct.'60	Boston
Harkins, James	10 Oct.'60	New York	Stoll, Andrew	24 Oct.'60	New York
Howard, George	25 Oct.'60	New York	Thompson, Wm. V.	13 Sept.'60	Roch. NY
Jackel, Charles	26 Oct.'60	New York	Townsend, Reuben	27 Sept.'60	Boston
McCarthy, James	4 Oct.'60	Boston	William, Henry	28 Sept.'60	Roch. NY
McCoy, Daniel	24 Oct.'60	New York			

TABLE II

The desertions that had taken place are listed in table III, below:

Name and Rank	Enlistment Date	Enlistment Place	Deserted From & Date
Alexander Livingston, Cpl.	22 Sept.'58	Syracuse, NY	Ft. Brown 6 Aug.'60
James Anderson, Pvt.	9 Nov.'59	New York, NY	" 3 Aug.'60
Edmund Anglin, Pvt.	19 Oct.'59	"	" 30 May '60
George Benjamin, Pvt	13 Feb.'60	"	" 1 May '60
John Bissel, Pvt.	3 Nov.'59	"	" 30 May '60
Edward Carr, Pvt.	1 Nov.'59	Boston, MA	" 2 Aug.'60
Peter Cunningham, Pvt.	1 Aug.'58	Ft. Clark, TX	" 11 Mar.'60
Charles E. Dodge, Pvt.	3 Nov.'59	Boston, MA	" 2 Aug.'60
Thomas Duffey, Pvt.	12 Nov.'59	"	" 2 Aug.'60
Patrick Flynn, Pvt.	3 Nov.'59	New York, NY	" 16 Mar.'60
Francis Hagan, Pvt.	21 Jan.'59	"	" 25 Sept.'60
John Harrison, Pvt.	25 Oct.'59	"	" 2 Aug.'60
James Haynes, Pvt.	25 Nov.'57	St. Louis, MO	" 26 June '60

Daniel Jaecke, Pvt.	11 Feb. '60	New York, NY	"	24 Apr. '60
Joseph Kenny, Pvt.	19 Oct. '59	"	"	16 May '60
James McKenzie, Pvt.	23 Sept. '58	Buffalo, NY	"	2 Aug. '60
Francis Merle, Pvt.	30 Sept. '58	New York, NY	"	17 Mar. '60
John Morris, Pvt.	22 Oct. '59	"	"	6 Aug. '60
John Murphy, Pvt.	21 Feb. '60	Boston, MA	"	30 May '60
Michael Murphy, Pvt.	8 Feb. '60	"	Duncan	20 Feb. '60
James Ryan, Pvt.	14 Oct. '59	New York, NY	Fort Brown	16 May '60
Charles Schonfeld, Pvt.	6 Feb. '60	"	"	4 Aug. '60
Robert E. Schlatter, Pvt.	30 Sept. '58	"	"	11 Mar. '60
Richard Stone, Pvt.	16 Feb. '60	Boston, MA	"	3 Aug. '60
Henry B. Thayer, Pvt.	9 Feb. '60	"	"	18 July '60
Richard Walsh, Pvt.	5 Oct. '58	"	[Record obscured.]	
James Williams, Pvt.	22 Oct. '58	New York, NY	Ft. Brown	11 Mar. '60

TABLE III

By the end of the year, there had been 26 desertions. Excepting Livingston, Cunningham, McKenzie, Merle, Schlatter, Walsh, and Williams, 19 were from the group of new recruits that had arrived at Fort Brown on April 15th.

The largest group, five, "went over" on August 2nd. They may have held up and waited for Stone and Anderson, who went on August 3rd, and Schonfeld who went on August 4th. Eight men into thin air – one would think that this large group would have been spotted and reported. The desertion of Cpl. Alexander Livingston, at 29 years of age – perhaps more mature than the rest and a veteran of two years' service – must have raised eyebrows. Did he have a falling out with Keller, the new first sergeant? In any event, the company seems to have been troubled in early 1860, its last year of peace. There were seven court-martial fines handed out to veteran members of the company in March and April alone.

Another observation regarding desertions is the fact that in August the company was likely to have been under orders to move to Fort Duncan, more than four-hundred long dusty miles north.[8] Any potential deserters would thus have known that the company was soon to travel into a remote and hostile area and that surviving after desertion would be even more difficult. The month of August would be now or never. The majority were never apprehended.

The fate of only four of the deserters is known, and that only partially. Edmund Anglin, John Bissel, and John Murphy were apprehended, and rejoined, on June 4th, 1860, after only five days. They were court-martialed and sentenced to six months in confinement with forfeiture of all pay and allowances. They were restored to duty on January 1st, 1861.

Edmund Anglin, though in and out of trouble in the ensuing years, remained to serve out the full term of his five-year enlistment and was discharged on October 12th, 1864. He apparently had had enough at the end of his five years because he

---

8. They left on September 29th. Record of events, 31 August–31 October muster roll.

did not take advantage of the substantial reenlistment bounty offered in July of that war year.

John Murphy also remained on duty but was drowned at Carrollton, Louisiana, on August 1st, 1863.

Francis Hagan turned himself in on January 2nd, 1861, after an absence of three months! He must have presented a convincing argument as he was restored to duty without trial on January 23rd. Bissel and Hagan again deserted on March 10th, 1861, just as the command was leaving Fort Brown to embark at the mouth of the Rio Grande. They were never heard from again.

It is interesting to note that the army thought it could afford to put soldiers in confinement and lose the benefit of their services as useful people. This would change later. During the war, most of the deserters that were apprehended, and only a few were, were only fined. At that time, their services as soldiers were badly needed.

The muster rolls for this period indicate that most of the deserters vanished owing money to the United States, the sutler, and the laundresses.[9] The money owed to the United States was for extra clothing, "camp and garrison equipment," and "ordnance." In 1860, there was a $45.97 allowance for a private's clothing in his first year of service, with lesser amounts in the subsequent four years of his enlistment. Assessments for clothing were for required extra-issue items needing replacement. Assessments for camp and garrison equipment and ordnance were supposed to be only for that which was lost or damaged through neglect. Most of the deserters owed from $2 to $3, or almost three weeks' pay. This would be $250–$380, if calculated in 2009 dollars.[10] Typical debt for clothing was $8 and $3 for camp and garrison equipment. Patrick Flynn owed the most of any individual: $7.70 for clothing, $4.24 for camp and garrison equipment, and $16.91 for ordnance, not to mention 50¢ to one of the laundresses. No doubt, he felt *put upon*, owing rather more than earning, as this was almost four months' pay. No mystery that he deserted on May 16th,[11] and never was heard from again.

---

9. O.R. Ser. III, Vol. II, pp. 615–617. The volunteers were initially allowed $2.50 per month, which was raised to $3.50 on May 18th, 1861, "to allow to the militia . . . the same allowance as is provided for the regular army." This obsoleted the amount quoted above, in that a flat $3.50 per month amounted to $42 per year, or $210 for five years. The complicated table of payments for 1860 only netted an artillery private $187.94, yet a *light* artillery private netted $196.54 because his was a more elaborate uniform. O.R. Ser. III, Vol. I, pp. 153, 213, 234. See also War Department, *Revised Regulations*, 1861, pp. 170, 171. A sutler was a private vendor, given permission to remain with the garrison, who offered for sale supplies not issued as standard by the army. The list of items included women's clothing, canned fruit, and lanterns, essentially everything a general store might offer "back home."
10. In 2009, monthly pay for a private was $1,400. Then it was $11.
11. From the muster roll ending in June 1860. The money owed for ordnance was likely for the 1855 rifled musket, which featured the Maynard tape roll of caps. This feature was proven unsuitable for field conditions and was soon discontinued, though a miserly and unjust Uncle

Enlistment

Why did any young men enlist? There always had been the typical personal reasons, such as escape from a bad family situation or business failure, debts, or crime. Then there were the romantic reasons, such as adventure, the love of soldiering, or to see the frontier; or to fight Indians. However, there may have been a practical reason. After gold was discovered in California, enlistment into the army meant an almost certain free passage to the frontier, where one could desert and head west. Better yet, you might be shipped to the Presidio, or Benicia Barracks, or one of 13 other posts in California.[12]

The economic conditions of the time probably played the pivotal role. If the immigrant couldn't get a job, the army was the fallback course. Although the army had standards for enlistment, such as the ability to speak English, *how well* was not defined. Of course, this caused no problems to the largest group of candidates, those of Irish and English backgrounds. Germans seem to have cleared the hurdle as well.

Patriotism is never heard of, as if it was coined in a later time. Except for the period of the Mexican War, lost to the memories of all but the older officers, and a very few of the enlisted, enlistment in the regular army was in times of peace. There was usually no national crisis to inflame passion. Instead, there were the long simmering regional differences in attitude to the role of the federal government in the affairs of the states. The most intractable social issue was slavery. These differences may have been the topic of conversations among the officers – only they were natives, who, by the appointment process, either directly from civilian life, or after graduation from West Point, were drawn from every corner of the land. In contrast, the mostly immigrant enlisted men, however, were likely ignorant of America's sectional fine points. They were happy to have escaped from Europe. Besides, they were forced to ignore, or accept, all of this, as their priority was sorting out their lives. Finally, the regular army's job had nothing to do with either sectional disputes or slavery; it looked mainly to protect the country's borders and, at this time, keep order in the western territories.

Analysis of the reenlistments in Battery L hints at the idea that most of the recruits had only planned to stay in the army for one "hitch." The muster roll ending in April 1860 shows only three that had reenlisted. A comparison of the 31 December 1860–28 February 1861 muster roll with the 30 June 1865–31 August 1865 muster roll (essentially the beginning of the war through to the end of the war) identifies only 11 men who had remained with the company through to the end of the war. See table IV below, "The Faithful Few," all of whom had reenlisted, albeit under unusual war circumstances.

Sam seems to have blamed the troops for the deterioration of the paper rolls.
12. Atlas, plate 162; O.R. Ser. III, Vol. 1, p. 123.

Name	Rank '60	Rank '65	Name	Rank '60	Rank '65
James Ahern	Pvt.	Pvt.	Philipp H. Schneider	Pvt.	Pvt.
James Beglan	Pvt.	Pvt.	William E. Scott	Pvt.	1st Sgt.
Owen Coyne	Pvt.	Pvt.	Warren P. Shaw	Pvt.	Pvt.
Patrick Donnelly	Pvt.	Cpl.	Wm. V. Thompson	Pvt.	Pvt.
George Hadley	Pvt.	Artificer	Michael White	Pvt.	Sgt.
Lewis Keller	Sgt.	Sgt.			

TABLE IV

Many enlistments into the battery were in late 1859 or in 1860. Hence, the five-year service period gradually expired from late 1864 and throughout 1865. There are 52 discharges alone listed in the August 1865–October 1865 muster roll (the last prior to year's end) when the unit was stationed at Fort Schuyler, New York.

Under the special provisions of the adjutant general's office, circular 47 of June 23rd, 1864, those that had enlisted prior to July 22nd, 1861, "shall have the privilege of re-enlisting" for three additional years for a bounty of $402. The inflation factor calculated previously while discussing ordnance has to be modified slightly because by 1864 pay had increased to $13 per month. Thus, the 2009 value of the bounty calculates to $43,000. The window for this decision was through August 1st, 1864. Most of those who reenlisted in mid-1864 under the new terms should have been on the table IV list.[13] However, many simply had deserted. In fact, Thompson did desert but was only one of two who were apprehended and returned. Thompson thus gained the "Faithful Few"[14] list by a failed attempt at desertion!

It must, however, be stated that several more might have been on the faithful list if it were not for exceptional circumstances, both positive and negative. Combat and accidental death and discharge due to permanent disability from sickness were prominent categories in the loss column. On the happy side, for several of the enlisted, it was promotion to second lieutenant. This opportunity would virtually define itself as their being transferred elsewhere. An officer could accept or reject promotion, but most often acceptance meant assignment to a different unit or even to a different arm of the service, e.g., from the artillery to the infantry, or cavalry – no special training required!

---

13. General Orders No. 66, O.R. Ser. III, Vol. 4, p. 123, and General Orders No. 261, p. 449. One of those listed in Table IV had interrupted service. Keller was discharged on December 29th, 1863, after appointment as a 2nd lieutenant in the Louisiana Volunteer Cavalry. When this temporary duty ended, he reenlisted in the battery as a corporal on October 28th, 1864, in New York.

14. The term "Faithful Few" was coined in the writings of Mr. Paul Callsen and is used here by permission.

Recession

After the end of the Mexican War (1846–1848), which was precipitated over the annexation of Texas, the United States had expanded into New Mexico Territory and California. The dispute with Britain over the northern border of the Oregon Territory had been settled in 1846, and the "manifest destiny" to rule from coast to coast had been achieved. This swelled the national pride, which was soon fueled into wild euphoria with the discovery of gold in California. A get-rich-quick atmosphere ruled. Millions in gold soon flooded the country from the new millionaires of the west, but the downside was inflation. Then President Buchanan, in his 1857 message to Congress, deplored "this paper system of extravagant expansion, raising the nominal price of every article far beyond its real value . . ."[15] Much money had been spent on luxury imports and fashion. Other money went into banks, and they made easy loans to businesses, particularly the railroads, who had lofty expansion plans to meet perceived needs.

Immigration had risen every year, fueled by the Irish potato famine and a failed revolution in Germany in 1848. By 1854, immigration into the port of New York peaked at 319,228 after a steady increase from 129,062 in 1847.[16] This was a boon for the railroads, which transported many of those thousands beyond the Alleghenies to settle in the new west. Actually, the western expansion had been going on since before the Revolution, and the American national pastime of land speculation was still in full force. In the 1830s it had been Michigan, and now it was Kansas. This was just more of the same, but the speculative excess would not help when the crunch came.

The Crimean War was fought between Russia and Turkey from October 1853 to February 1856, and during that time, Russia's grain output was essentially removed from world markets. Shortages loomed, and American farmers stepped into exporting, some for the first time.[17]

August 24, 1857: The New York branch of the Ohio Life and Trust Company reported that it had failed.[18] Note: Erie Railroad stock closed that day at $28.

August 25: One John Thompson failed; his liabilities of $5 million were in the Ohio Life and Trust Company, a large part of whose paper was held by New York banks.

August 26: The failure of seven county banks – scarcity of money.

September 1: Failure of Mechanics Banking Association.

September 3: Rally.

---

15. Appendix to the Congressional Globe, 35th Congress, 1st session, December 8th, 1857, p. 2.
16. "Immigration during 1857," *New York Times*, January 6th, 1858.
17. George van Vleck, *The Panic of 1857*.
18. Members of the New York Press, *A Brief Account of All the Financial Panics and Commercial Revulsions in the United States from 1690 to 1857*, New York: J. C. Haney Pub., 1857.

September 5: All lost from rally. Erie Railroad stock closed at $19.50.

September 17: Report of the sinking of the SS *Central America* in a hurricane off North Carolina; $2.5 million in gold being shipped from the San Francisco Mint is lost, with only $500,000 insured.

September 26: Total suspension of payments by Philadelphia banks. Erie Railroad at $15.

September 29: Chicago banks affected, banks in Louisville suspend payments on October 1.

October 9: Erie Railroad at $9.50.

October 13: All New York banks with the exception of Chemical Bank suspended payments.

October 27: The Liverpool Borough Bank failed; the panic had spread to England.[19]

So the litany continued, exposing an overstrained credit structure and the near-bankrupt condition of the railroads, they having expanded to meet the needs of transporting grain exports that ceased when the Crimean War ended. The boom in immigration had also ceased. The numbers collapsed to 136,233 in 1855, 142,342 in 1856, and 185,847 in 1857.[20] Land speculators lost because their land value had been based on planned rail routes that were never built, or on sales to immigrants that did not appear. Also, Northern manufacturers had lost out to cheaper imported goods allowed by a reduced tariff.

Only the South was uneffected. The value of the cotton and tobacco "form almost the only exceptions to the continued decline which pervades the markets of the world for all other articles of commerce." The value of cotton exports from the United States in 1857 was $131,575,859; and in 1858, it had remained essentially steady at $131,386,661. For 1859, the value of all exports from the North was $45,305,511 versus $193,399,618 for the South; and the value of the cotton exported that year had risen to $161,434,923.[21] Naturally, this only gave support to pro-slavery writers and speakers, such as David Christy and J. A. Hammond, all advocating that "Cotton is King" and that slavery was a superior economic system.

Recruiting

The recession was the atmosphere from which most of the men of Battery L were recruited, transported, and introduced to their remote western station. The recruit was there because he could not find work. The recruiting discussed here was for the regular army. No one would have guessed what was to happen in 1861. The volunteers, who in mere months were to enter the service by the hundreds of

---

19. Evans, D. M., pp. 35, 36.
20. *NY Times*, January 6, 1858; *Encyclopedia Britannica*, Vol. 26, 1911, p. 425.
21. Evans, D. M., p. 112; Elliott, E. N., p. 262.

thousands, were, however, a different group of men; and it is important to note that, like the society from which they came, they may have regarded the regular army with suspicion and disdain. Grant, in his memoirs,[22] notes a distinction between the volunteers, often men of high social standing or wealth who enlisted for the war and risked their life for a principle, and the "regulars" who served in time of peace. The regulars, according to Grant, included, "as a rule, only men who could not do as well in any other occupation." Grant, though a West Point graduate, himself fell into the latter category: *those who could not do as well in any other occupation.*

However, on the western frontier, the job the regulars did was understood and appreciated. They were the only real source of law and order in many of the remote areas.

A retrospective on the recruiting procedure quoted here is from an 1864 report by the Adjutant General's Office:[23] "The officers detailed from the several regiments for recruiting duty are stationed in such localities as give promise of success, and their recruits are sent in parties to the depots, whence they are forwarded to the regiments to which they may be assigned. Besides this, the several regiments recruit their own ranks, as far as practicable, from the country adjacent to their posts."

The enlistee was signed up, and if at a place remote from the depot, he was then held at a "rendezvous" for up to ten days until a "detachment" had gathered, which was finally sent to the depot. The principle depots were Fort Columbus, Governor's Island, New York Harbor[24] and Carlisle Barracks, Carlisle, Pennsylvania. The former was for infantry and artillery recruits and the latter for cavalry and dragoons (mounted infantry), the apparent distinction being that horse-related skills were to be taught at Carlisle. Here, we already see a flaw in the operation in that the artillery, if equipped as a light battery, had a requirement for more horses than the cavalry. There was no equivalent in the cavalry to the six-horse teams required for the gun carriages and equipment of the artillery or the skill to maneuver them. Every man of the light artillery rode a horse and was required to have the same skills as cavalry in caring for the animals. Where was the training for the artillery to take place? In fact, what training was given to an average recruit – or anyone – and for how long?

The recruit, in theory at least, was to spend time at the depot learning basic skills. This had on and off been the subject of many directives and good intentions but never seemed to take hold in a rigidly defined system. The length of stay of the Battery L recruits at Fort Columbus, from an analysis of the dates when the

---

22. *U.S. Grant*, Vol. I, p. 358.
23. O.R. Ser. III, Vol. 5, p. 27.
24. National Archives, "Post Returns," M617, indicate that troops at this station from January 1860 to December 1873 originated from Fort Jay (Columbus was the base, Fort Jay, the barracks).

men of the first group of 46 were recruited, was clearly quite variable. Considering the travel time to Fort Brown to be up to three weeks and the recruits' local travel time including their stay at their rendezvous could be two weeks, those enlisted in March would have been at Fort Columbus not much longer than a week. Those enlisted in early October could have been there for almost five long, boring months.

Their time there at least allowed getting used to the routine of reveille at dawn and retreat at dusk, the questionable diet, and the hours allotted to fatigue duty, roll calls, and drill (without weapons). Guard duty was twice weekly.[25] It is not clear if "setting up drill"[26] (calisthenics) was a part of the routine at this time. A priority in any recruit's earliest available spare time would be visiting the post tailor to have his ill-fitting issue uniform altered.

Isolated on Governor's Island, with no days off, after retreat was the only "sweet" time available.[27] The streets of New York not accessible, there were no strolls downtown to break the monotony or buy some "dainties" (fresh fruit, etc.).

Getting used to the diet, by today's standards, would appear to have been one of the greatest shocks to the new recruit; but then again, little was popularly known about nutrition, and the recruit was often a destitute immigrant. The ration had changed little from that established in 1838. Though it seems that it has always been an item of popular culture to complain about army food, the then-standard ration for the army listed below seems to justify complaint. The rather awkward wording has been retained:

> The ration is[28] three fourths of a pound of [salt] pork or bacon, or one and a fourth pounds of fresh or salt beef; eighteen ounces of bread or flour, or twelve ounces of hard bread [hardtack], or one and a fourth pound of corn meal; and at the rate, to one hundred rations, of eight quarts of beans, or, in lieu thereof, ten pounds of rice, or, in lieu thereof, twice per week, one hundred and fifty ounces of dessicated potatoes, and one hundred ounces of mixed vegetables; ten pounds of coffee, or, in lieu thereof, one and one-half pounds of tea, fifteen pounds of sugar; four quarts of vinegar; one pound of sperm candles, or one and one-fourth pounds of adamantine candles, or one and one-half pounds of tallow candles; four pounds of soap, and two quarts of salt.

In the field, when the cooking had to be done by the private soldier, the

---

25. Meyers, A., p. 157, 160.
26. *Military Training of the Regular Army,* Journal of the Military Service Institute of the U.S., November 1889.
27. Ballantine, G., p. 25.
28. *Revised Army Regulations, 1861,* p. 243. The ration was for one day, and one one-hundredth of it, for example, of the latter category, such as beans, amounted to about about five tablespoons. Clearly, beans were meant for the occasional meal.

division of the bulk quantities of these foodstuffs into individual portions involved some ceremony (figure 2)[29] and some difficulty for the sergeant's arithmetic. On August 9th, 1861, an Act of Congress increased the portions of flour and added potatoes. Yeast and pepper were also added, though they are not in the wording of the law.[30] Thus was added more starch and still no appreciation for the value of sufficient antiscorbutics (fresh vegetables containing vitamin C).[31]

FIGURE 2

Training

The whole concept of training was *unit* based. The company to which he had been assigned was supposed to give the recruit any additional training not accomplished at the depot. If larger-scale firing exercises were to be conducted, or perhaps new technology introduced, an entire battery, or several, might be shipped to Fort Monroe in Virginia, the "home" of the artillery, for practice. As far back as 1824, Secretary of War John C. Calhoun had established an "Artillery School for Practice" at Fort

---

29. Billings, J. O., p. 122; *Frank Leslie's Illustrated History of the Civil War*, p. 493.
30. O.R. Ser. III, Vol. 1, p. 399.
31. This word and spelling is used in *The Personal Memoirs of P. H. Sheridan*, Vol. I, p. 28.

Monroe. However, it was abandoned in 1834.[32] It was revived at Fort Monroe in December of 1857 with Lt. Col. Harvey Brown as its Commander. On May 9th, 1859 the Secretary of War, John B. Floyd, ordered it removed to the frontier post of Fort Leavenworth, Kansas, and Brown was reassigned. Though companies E, F, and M, of the 2nd Artillery arrived at Leavenworth to attend, a chaotic War Department had failed to include their officers, who remained on detached service elsewhere. By now, it was 1860, and Floyd's policies in the administration of the War Department had caused much controversy. The Artillery School seems to have been lost in the shuffle while argument raged over his alleged policy of dispersing the army to remote military posts (to enable their capture by the Confederacy should hostilities break out), corruption, and sales of arms to Southern interests, which is discussed later in this chapter.

It was revived again in 1867. There is no record of Battery L ever being at either forts Monroe or Leavenworth for training prior to 1867.

Thus, given the unpredictable stay and limited facilities at the depot and the philosophy of the approach to training, we have to conclude that the Battery L recruits were ill prepared for duty, never even having fired a musket, let alone a field cannon.

The new commandant of Fort Brown, Henry J. Hunt, West Point class of 1838, had something to say on the issue.[33] In a commentary on proposed organizational changes for the artillery, written on December 16th, 1861, he states:

> The condition of the arm at the commencement of the Mexican War and of this rebellion affords evidence that the bulk of our artillery, as such, has been habitually inefficient, and that there is no remedy under the present system. At Vera Cruz the four regiments which had been in service nominally as artillery more than a quarter century were, with the exception of a few field batteries, wholly uninstructed in their duties, and . . . the men received in the trenches . . . their first lesson in artillery duties, viz.: how to load siege guns and mortars.
>
> This ought to have been sufficient warning, yet within the past two years the artillery has been employed at extreme frontier stations . . . the prominent feature of what is now called the treasonable dispersion of the Army by the late Secretary of War . . .

The "instruction" listed on the muster roll ending on 31 April 1860, notes, "elementary for recruits." The June roll comments: "As light infantry, Good. Progressing rapidly," and the August roll says: "Infantry and in target practice with rifle

---

32. Cullum, G. W.: Harvey Brown, Class of 1818, p. 190; Haskin, W. L., pp. 39, 129, 247; Letters to the Adjutant General, National Archives, Magruder to Cooper, Microcopy M567D, roll 626, image 537; *U.S. Grant*, Vol. 1, p. 226.
33. O.R. Ser. III, Vol. 1, p. 745. Hunt went on to become chief of artillery of the Army of the Potomac.

musket." The roll ending in October, when the unit had arrived at Fort Duncan, says: "Good." Apparently the training was over.

Fort Duncan

Record 10/60
31 AUGUST–31 OCTOBER 1860, FORT DUNCAN, TEXAS

"Company left Fort Brown, Texas, Sept. 29, 1860 (by Steamboat) and arrived at Ringgold Barracks, Tex. Oct. 2nd 1860. Left Ringgold Barracks, Octr. 3rd and marched to Laredo (Ft. McIntosh) Texas, Octr. 8, 1860. Left Fort McIntosh Octr. 9th and arrived at Fort Duncan, Texas Octr. 14th 1860. Distance by steamboat 240 miles and from Ringgold Barracks, to Fort Duncan, Texas about 240 miles more."

Samuel K. Dawson	Capt. Commanding
William Silvey	1st Lt. Reg. Adjt. O. No. 7 Hdqrs. 1st Arty Ft. Dallas, Fla. Aug. 14,'57. Left Co. Apr. 22,'54. S.O. No. 62 Hdqrs. N.Y. April 18,'54
James W. Robinson	1st Lt.

Transferred: Loomis Langdon, by promotion to 1st Lt. Company A, 1st Artillery, Fort Monroe, Virginia
Strength: 61. Sick: none.

When the battery left Fort Brown, they probably left any possibility of discovering the whereabouts of their 23 deserters. They were transported, as noted in the "Record of Events," by shallow draft riverboat to Ringgold Barracks (Rio Grande City, the steamboat terminus) where they disembarked on October 3rd. This left two hundred forty miles of "light infantry" training before they reached Fort Duncan on October 14th. This 11-day march amounted to an average of twenty-two miles per day, excessive compared to the sixteen miles per 10-hour day recommended for artillery. A later recommendation of twenty miles per day was to be considered only if the soldier was fit from proper conditioning.[34]

Fort Duncan, Maj. William H. French commanding, was already occupied by Companies F and K of the 1st Artillery. Ordered abandoned by Secretary of War Floyd in 1859, Fort Duncan was ordered to be regarrisoned by Lt. Col. Robert E. Lee, commander, Department of Texas, in March of 1860. F had arrived from Fort Clark, at Bracketville, sixty miles north, on March 18th, after Fort Duncan's lease from the landowner John Twohig had been signed,[35] and K arrived on August 1st.

Founded in 1849, Fort Duncan was one of the largest posts in the west. It was important in the early fifties because of its location on the California Road

---

34. *Military Training of the Regular Army*, Journal of the Military Service Institute of the U.S., November 1889, p. 614; *Board of Artillery Officers*, p. 34.
35. Notes from displays, and the docent's presentation at the Fort Duncan Commandant's office in 2009.

(for those headed to the gold fields) and as a base for scouting against the Lipan Apache and the Comanche Indians.

A survey map of "Cantonment Duncan" was prepared by the Corps of Engineers in 1853 (figure 3). Shown are five officer's quarters, some with kitchens nearby, and three soldier's quarters; also, a bakery, a quartermaster and commissary store, guardhouse, sutler's store, and a hospital. Described as built in 1849, it remained, along with stables, a magazine, a quartermaster's office, and a commandant's office.[36] The fort had gone from abandoned to a sudden occupancy of some 144 soldiers, not including wives, children, laundresses, cooks, and servants. The arrival of Battery L and then its final 25 recruits from Fort Columbus, New York, would have made up a total of about 234.

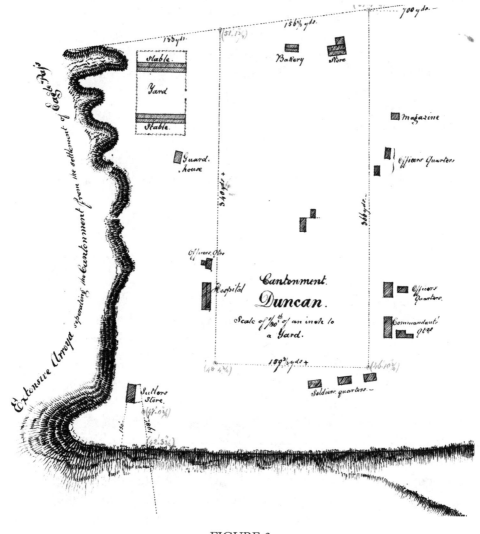

FIGURE 3

36. National Archives. *Cantonment Duncan*, sheet 34; *U.S. Census*, Ft. Duncan, Eagle Pass Post Office, 4th August 1860.

North was the Town of Eagle Pass, population 520,[37] originally established south of the fort on the Rio Grande near the mouth of the Mexican Rio Escondido and opposite the Mexican town of Piedras Negras, a "double row of huts along the river . . . where the men smoked *cigarritos*, and the women made tortillas, and the dogs howled all night long."[38]

The commandant's office is shown in figure 4, as it was in 2009. It has been expanded considerably since 1860, and back then it would have had a thatched roof.

FIGURE 4

The new inhabitants to the area were undoubtedly hoping to make something of a home here; likely, they would be here for five years. Could anyone have guessed what was to happen in a mere four months? Their hope now, with the winter season coming on, was that it would be pleasant without the 100°F summer heat, which had to be endured mostly by rationalizing that "it was dry and there was always a pleasant southwesterly breeze."

Perhaps the fort would once more be the scene of a social life to while away the time as there had been back in 1854 when Phil Sheridan and the cavalry were stationed here. Sheridan's memoirs[39] mention that the area was filled with antelope, deer, and wild turkeys and that hunting was a happy diversion. He also mentions horseback riding, races, and invitations to dances at the home of the Mexican commandant at Piedras Negras.

Sheridan also comments on the diet: "the food was the soldier's ration . . . flour, pickled pork, nasty bacon – cured in the dust of ground charcoal – and fresh beef . . . supplemented with game . . . The sugar, coffee, and small parts of the ration were

---

37. U.S. Census, July 1860.
38. Haskin, p. 352.
39. Sheridan, P. H., Vol. 1, pp. 21, 27, 28. Figure 4, photo by the author.

good, but we had no vegetables and the few jars of preserves kept by the sutler were too expensive to be indulged in. So all during the period I lived at Fort Duncan and its sub-camps, nearly sixteen months, fresh vegetables were practically unobtainable. To prevent scurvy we used the juice of the maguey plant (*agave*), called pulque . . ." He goes on to describe how his company was detailed to ride some forty miles out to cut and gather the stalks, return, and press the mass to obtain the juice. It was then bottled and allowed to ferment, creating a sulfurous-smelling and equally-repulsive-tasting drink. Everyone was required to drink a cup at roll call.

Credit Sheridan and associates with an enlightened view of dietary requirements, recognizing the deficiencies of the army ration and taking action accordingly; though cactus beer was a quaint way to provide it.

Sheridan also cites the general lawlessness of the area.[40]

> The inhabitants of this frontier of Mexico were strongly marked with Indian characteristics, particularly with those of the Comanche type, and as the wild Indian blood predominated, few of the physical traits of the Spaniard remained among them, and outlawry was common. The Spanish conquerors had left on the northern border only their graceful manners and their humility before the cross. The sign of Christianity was placed at all important points on roads or trails, and especially where any one had been killed; and as the Comanche Indians, strong and warlike, had devastated northeastern Mexico in past years, all along the border, on both sides of the Rio Grande, the murderous effects of their raids were evidenced by numberless crosses.

Record 12/60
31 OCTOBER–31 DECEMBER 1860, FORT DUNCAN, TEXAS

[No entry in the "Record of Events"]

Samuel K. Dawson	Capt. On leave, since May 2nd.
William Silvey	1st Lt. Reg. Adj. O. No. 7 hdqrs. 1st Arty, Ft. Dallas, Florida, Aug. 13,'57. Left Co. Apr. 22, 1854. S.O. No. 62 Hdqrs. N.Y. Apr. 18,'54.
James W. Robinson	1st Lt. In temporary Command.

Strength: 87. Sick: 6.

A Pivotal Year

Ever since the founding of our country, people, including the likes of Alexander Hamilton versus Thomas Jefferson, had argued the issue of the power of the federal government versus that of the rights of the states. It took the Civil War for this to be resolved.

---

40. Sheridan, P. H., Vol. I, pp. 33–34.

One of the worst eruptions of the argument up to this time was over the Federal tariff. Early on, the only income of the Federal government was as defined by Section 8 of the Constitution (a permanent income tax did not come along until 1913). The Constitution specifies that Congress shall have the power to lay and collect taxes, duties, imposts and excises; but all duties, etc., *shall be uniform* throughout the United States.

The tariff had long since been applied by Congress for the Federal government's source of income. However, it was recognized that a tariff is, as well, a protection for domestic industry, having the effect of increasing the cost of imported goods, which compete with those manufactured at home. The slave culture of the South had developed no industry, and hence came to feel aggrieved in that only Northern manufacturers benefitted while the South had to pay higher prices for the imported goods demanded by its aristocratic lifestyle. Thus was the Southern claim that the tariff was unconstitutional (not uniform) and as well, was unfair. Failing to, at least, have the tariff reduced or altered to lessen its impact on the South, the right was claimed that any individual state could "nullify" such a Federal law.

After the passage of the Federal Tariff of 1828, which was particularly objectionable, and referred to as the "Bill of Abominations," Southern complaints grew louder. President Jackson favored a reduction of the tariff rate, and a compromise bill was passed in July of 1832. This did not satisfy those in South Carolina. The principle of protection so objectionable to the South had remained. Under the influence of Vice President Calhoun, the spokesman for nullification, and now an enemy of President Jackson, the South Carolina Ordinance of Nullification was passed on November 24th, 1832.[41]

President Jackson swiftly followed with a proclamation on nullification. He declared it to be an "impractical absurdity," which, if given currency, would have dissolved the Union in its infancy. He also denied the right of secession in that the Constitution "forms a government not a league." He sent reinforcements to Fort Moultrie, the sloop-of-war *Natchez* and two revenue cutters to Charleston Harbor, and warned the people of South Carolina that the consequence of their treasonous conduct was military action.

The nation applauded, but the issue was still clouded in South Carolina. Not until the Force Bill (authorizing military intervention), as well as another even lower tariff bill, as proposed by Henry Clay, and passed on March 12th, 1833, did South Carolina back down. However, one point was clear. Andrew Jackson had forever closed the nullification argument. Unfortunately, and shamefully, secession, though declared to be treason by Jackson, remained to be tested.

Given this history, perhaps it was not so incredible to predict that South

---

41. Haskin, W. L., pp. 44, 46; *Encyclopedia Britannica*, 1911), Vol. 19, p. 846, Vol. 26, p. 425, Vol. 27, pp. 696–698; James, M., pp. 610–611; Scott, Winfield, p. 617.

Carolina would choose to revisit its state's rights arguments in the prelude to the Civil War; while a weak president sat in office. Plainly spoken, the differences were over slavery, though many continued to deny it, even after the war.[42]

The 1860 presidential campaign brought the slavery issue glaringly to the forefront. The relatively new Lincoln Republicans were antislavery. The Democrats were divided between proslavery and "popular sovereignty," the idea of leaving the choice of slavery to the inhabitants of those individual states or territories. The Democratic Convention fell apart, with the contending factions retiring to nominate separate candidates. The Southern faction nominated John C. Breckinridge, then the vice president under Buchanan, and the Northern faction nominated Stephen A. Douglas. Split, the Democrats lost the election.

Inflamed by the election of that "Black Republican," Lincoln, the "War of the Southern Rebellion" was launched by South Carolina on December 20th, 1861, with an Ordinance of Secession.

Even before the secession of South Carolina, President Buchanan had taken the paradoxical position, enunciated in his December 3rd message to Congress, that under the Constitution no authority was given for any state to secede, yet the President had no power to prevent any state from seceding. He thus opened the door to South Carolina.

Encouraged by the President's diffidence, Southern secession boldness grew, and his administration began to fall apart. There was increasing agitation on the part of even the Southern members of his cabinet. Jacob Thompson, the interior secretary, remained in office while he accepted a commission from the state of Mississippi to try to convince the state of North Carolina to secede. He finally resigned in January of 1861.

Three cabinet members resigned in December of 1860. Treasury Secretary Howell Cobb of Georgia returned there to promote secession. Secretary of State Lewis Cass, of Michigan, retired in disgust over his inability to convince the President to reinforce the forts in Charleston Harbor. Fortunately, Attorney General Jeremiah S. Black, who strongly held the same views as Cass, stepped into Cass' former position at state, and Edwin M. Stanton became the attorney general. The last to go was Secretary of War John B. Floyd of Virginia. He might have planned to remain to the end, but submitted his resignation after the discovery of financial irregularities in his department, his unequalled flagrant assistance to the Southern states to secure arms, and Buchanan's tardy but resolute decision to reinforce Fort Sumter.[43]

---

42. *Encyclopedia Britannica*, 1911, Vol. XV, p. 109. Taylor, R., pp. 10–12; I. N. Arnold, I. N., p. 156. See also: Logan, J. A., pp. 104–105; *Encyclopedia Britannica, Douglas,* Vol. VII, p. 447, and *Breckinridge,* Vol. IV, p. 847.
43. O.R. Vol. 1, pp. 115–118, 273; The term "Black Republican" is found to have been widely used in Southern correspondence. Nicolay & Hay, Vol. II, 1909, pp. 323, 325, 392, 397; *Encyclopedia Britannica*: *Cobb*, Vol. VI, p. 606, *Cass,* Vol. V, p. 455, *Black*, Vol. IV, p. 18, *Floyd,* Vol. X, p. 573.

An example of Floyd's treason is the following order to transfer arms from Northern arsenals to Southern ones, which was to cause consternation on the part of the North when it was finally uncovered:

> War Department[44] *December 29, 1859*
>
> The Colonel of ordnance will give the requisite orders for supplying the arsenals at Fayetteville, N.C.; Charleston, S.C.; Augusta, Ga.; Mount Vernon, Ala.; and Baton Rouge, La.; with the following arms, in addition to those on hand at those arsenals, viz: 65,000 percussion muskets [caliber .69] and 40,000 altered to percussion [caliber .69] from Springfield Armory; also 6,000 percussion rifles [caliber .54] from Watertown Arsenal and 4,000 percussion rifles [caliber .54] from Watervliet Arsenal. These . . . [details of shipment and storage omitted].
>
> JOHN B. FLOYD
> *Secretary of War*

Floyd continued not only with transfers but with sales to private groups and Southern states for another year. Buchanan finally replaced him (accepted his resignation on December 30th, 1860) following a Senate inquiry[45] and public outcry.

A potential defense of Floyd would note that the guns transferred and the ones sold throughout the year 1860 were mostly obsolete smoothbores, though he had intended to have them rifled but ran out of time before he was forced to resign.[46] None are referred to by name, but the most common .69-caliber weapon was the U.S. model 1822 musket. Thousands of these smoothbores were converted to percussion. The common .54-caliber rifle was the U.S. model 1841 "Mississippi" rifle. Many were later rebored and rifled to .58 caliber to be able to use the same ammunition as the standard "Springfield" rifle. The 105,000 smoothbores noted in the above order were the largest number of any one kind. Regardless of their obsolescence, they could have been used for training and in battle if there were none other, and many of the Confederates who brought personal squirrel guns or shotguns to battles early in the war remind us of extreme Confederate shortages of any modern weapons. As late as 1863, we shall see that most of the Confederate troops at the Battle of Irish Bend in Louisiana had few other than smoothbores, firing buck-and-ball. Even one Union regiment at that battle suffered because of its deficient smoothbores. All of the 10,000 *rifles* mentioned in the order would have

---

44. O. R. Ser. III, Vol. 1, p. 44.
45. O.R. Ser. III, Vol. 1, p. 15, Letter from Sen. Henry Wilson of Massachusetts and letter to the President from concerned citizens of Pittsburgh. See also p. 31, House motion of December 13th, 1860, J. W. Forney, clerk; *Harper's New Monthly Magazine*, Vol. 22, Issue 129, February 1861, p. 406.
46. Taylor, R., p. 13: "The stores of the arsenal [here referring to Baton Rouge] were almost valueless, the arms being altered flint-lock muskets"; Nicolay & Hay, Vol. II, p. 321.

been valuable to anyone regardless of caliber because of greater accuracy.

Statement of arms distributed by sale, by order of the Secretary of War, from January 1, 1860, to January 1, 1861, showing to whom, how, the number, kind, price, and date when sold, and place of delivery.

To whom sold.	How sold.	Number.	Kind of arms.	Price each.	Date.	Place of delivery.
					1860.	
J. W. Zacharie & Co.	Private sale.	4,000	Muskets altered to percussion.	$2.50	Feb. 3	Saint Louis Arsenal, Mo.
J. T. Ames	do	1,000	...do	2.50	Mar. 14	New York Arsenal, N. Y.
Capt. G. Barry	do	80	...do	2.00	June 11	Saint Louis Arsenal, Mo.
W. C. N. Swift	do	400	...do	2.50	Aug. 31	Springfield Armory, Mass.
Do	do	80	...do	2.50	Nov. 13	Do.
State of Alabama	do	1,000	...do	2.50	Sept. 27	Baton Rouge Arsenal, La.
Do	do	2,500	...do	2.50	Nov. 14	Do.
State of Virginia	do	5,000	...do	2.50	Nov. 6	Washington Arsenal, D. C.
Phillips County (Ark.) Volunteers.	do	50	...do	2.00	Nov. 16	Saint Louis Arsenal, Mo.
G. B. Lamar	do	10,000	...do	2.50	Nov. 24	Watervliet Arsenal, N. Y.
State of Mississippi	do	5,000	...do	2.50	Dec. 4	Baton Rouge Arsenal, La.
State of Louisiana *a*	do	5,000	...do	2.50	Dec. 15	Do.

a Of these the State of Louisiana took and paid for 2,500 only.

ORDNANCE OFFICE, *January 21, 1861.*

H. K. CRAIG,
Colonel of Ordnance.

TABLE V

Secretary Floyd authorized the sale of 34,030 percussion muskets in 1860. As can be seen in table V, they went for $2.50 each.[47] They went to a variety of individuals and four Southern states. The largest single sale and one of the last was to a G. B. Lamar of New York, president of the Bank of the Republic, and a front man chosen by Floyd to hide the fact that the arms sold were destined for South Carolina.[48] Note in the table the location of the arms sold to Mr. Lamar: Watervliet Arsenal, New York. His shipments probably followed the same path as an earlier shipment, which had been seized by the New York City Police Department while they were being loaded on board the steamer *Monticello*, bound for Savannah, Georgia.[49] The superintendent of police, John A. Kennedy, then wrote to Joseph Holt, the postmaster general, asking what to do. The police chief also consulted with the district attorney for Southern New York, James I. Roosevelt, and others. It was reluctantly concluded that no law had been broken, and Holt notified Kennedy that, unfortunately, no "legislation on the part of Congress . . . had occurred . . . to relieve the authorities of the embarressments [sic] which they have encountered in the discharge of what they deem an urgent duty of patriotism."[50] The shipment went through.

The arms in question had been seized on January 22nd, 1861, a little more than a month after South Carolina had seceded. No executive order or emergency

---

47. O. R. Ser. III, Vol. 1, p.52.
48. O.R. Ser. III, Vol. 1, p. 7; Nicolay & Hay, Vol. 2, p. 324.
49. O.R. Ser. III, Vol. 1, p.53.
50. O.R. Ser. III, Vol. 1, p.58.

declaration to control such shipments had been made, or would be, by President Buchanan.

By August of 1861, Lamar popped up in Savannah, negotiating the importation of supplies for the Confederate War Department.[51] Lamar is but one example from this transition period into war, of the growing question in the minds of those loyal to the Union: "Whom do you trust?" The tenor of the times is further indicated by a letter of request to Secretary Floyd:

> Springfield, Mass., *November 24, 1860*[52]
>
> Hon. J. B. Floyd
> *Secretary of War:*
>
> My Dear Sir: Please allow me to address a line to you on a matter that deeply interests your State.[53]
>
> Having been engaged in the Springfield Armory for the past fifteen years last past . . . I desire some favors granted to the State of Virginia. I have no hopes of any favors from Colonel Craig, for in conversation with him I found him deadly opposed to the Virginia Armory.
>
> We wish to use some of the armory patterns for the Richmond machinery, and the privilege of taking drawings of fixtures, tools, &c.
>
> I desire that the honorable Secretary issue an order to the superintendants of the Springfield and Harper's Ferry armories to give the master armorer of the Virginia State Armory and Joseph R. Anderson[54] or his agents every facility they may need . . .
>
> I desire to get all the assistance we can from the national armories before our much honored and esteemed Secretary of War vacates his office, for I have no hope of any assistance after a Black Republican takes possession of the War Department.
>
> [Letter continues with details of arrangements.]
>
> Your humble servant,
>
> S. ADAMS,
> *Master Armorer, State of Virginia*

The letter was referred to the ordnance office, and a letter of approval, by Wm. Maynadier, captain of ordnance, was sent. The "patterns for the Richmond machinery" were those that were to allow the Confederacy to produce the "Richmond" rifle, a copy of the model 1861 caliber .58 Springfield rifle, the reliable standard of the Union army. Regardless of Floyd's sales or transfers, this technical espionage may have been the most damaging.

---

51. O.R. Ser. IV, Vol. 1, p. 557.
52. O.R. Ser. III. Vol. 1, pp. 8, 9.
53. Virginia.
54. Of the Tredegar Iron Works, Richmond, Virginia.

Chapter 2

The Texas Surrender; Record 2/61; 1861 Roster; Record 4/61

The Texas Surrender

Hardly having settled into the routine of army life at their new post, events elsewhere were heralding the beginning of the Civil War. Within weeks, orders to the three artillery companies at Fort Duncan would be received with instructions to turn the fort over to the infantry and march out of Texas. On December 6th, 1860, only one day after the last of the new recruits had arrived at Fort Duncan, delegates were elected to a convention called by the governor of South Carolina to consider an ordinance of secession. The "fire eaters" were in control, and on December 20th, the ordinance was adopted unanimously.[55] The people never had a direct say; no popular vote was ever conducted to ratify the action of the convention.

The first act of force occurred on December 30th, with the surrender of the Charleston Arsenal[56] to an armed group of militia directed there on orders from the governor. Though there was mail service to Eagle Pass from San Antonio, it is likely that news of these events did not reach Texas until late January. However, the tenor of the times prompted the new[57] commander of the Department of Texas to write the following letter to the general in chief:[58]

> San Antonio, *December 13, 1860*
> Lieut. Gen. W. Scott, *Commanding U.S. Army, New York:*
>
> > General: I think there can be no doubt that many of the Southern States will secede from the Union. The State of Texas will be among the number, and,

---

55. *Encyclopedia Britannica*, Vol. 27, p. 705, and Vol. 25, p. 501. The convention delegates were "elected" by the legislature. At this time, South Carolina was operating under its Constitution of 1790, which did not require a popular vote to ratify the action of the convention.
56. Fort Moultrie and Castle Pinckney, unoccupied, in Charleston Harbor were occupied by South Carolina troops on the 27th and the Palmetto flag was flown over the Federal Customs House and the Post Office. O.R. Vol. 1, pp. 6, 118.
57. Twiggs assumed command on December 8th, 1860, Nicolay & Hay, Vol. IV, p. 179. The authors speculate that this assignment was part of Floyd's War Department conspiracy to place officers of Southern birth in positions of trust.
58. O.R. Vol. 1, p. 579.

from all appearances at present, it will be at an early day, certainly before the 4th of March next. What is to be done with the public property in charge of the Army?

The arsenal at this place has some ordnance and munitions of war. I do not expect an order for the present for the disposition of them, but would be pleased to receive your views and suggestions. My course as respects myself will be to remain at my post and protect this frontier as long as I can, and then, when turned adrift, make my way home, if I have one. I would be pleased to hear from you at your earliest convenience.

I am, general, with sentiments of respect and regard yours, &c.,

D. E. TWIGGS

The significance of "the 4th of March" was that it was the date of Lincoln's inauguration. The letter lacks the formality of typical correspondence, such as the title under Twiggs' signature: Bvt. Maj. Gen., U.S. Army, Commanding Department. Twiggs and Scott were old acquaintances, Twiggs having served under Scott in the Mexican War.

Scott, born in 1786 and commissioned as a captain of artillery in the U.S. Army in 1808, had personally experienced nearly every military action that had involved the army since the Revolution. By a half century of experience, he had foreseen the events leading up to the current situation. He remembered the resolution on the part of President Jackson in 1832, in quelling the nullification question, and was appalled at the diffidence of President Buchanan on this new challenge from South Carolina. On October 29th, 1860, he violated the chain of command by writing directly to the President. In part, his letter:[59]

> From a knowledge of our Southern population it is my solemn conviction that there is some danger of an early act of rashness proclaiming secession, viz., the seizure of some or all of the following posts: Forts Jackson and St Philip, on the Mississippi, below New Orleans, both without garrisons; Fort Morgan below Mobile, without a garrison; Forts Pickens and McRee, Pensacola Harbor; with an insufficient garrison of one, Fort Pulaski, below Savannah, without a garrison; Forts Moultrie and Sumter, Charleston Harbor, the former with an insufficient garrison and the latter without any; and Fort Monroe, Hampton Roads, without a sufficient garrison. In my opinion, all these works should be immediately so garrisoned as to make any attempt to take any one of them, by surprise or *coup de main* ridiculous.

On October 31st, he requested of the secretary of war Floyd permission to warn those few installations that had garrisons to be alert to attack. Floyd denied permission, and the President did not act.

Scott finally obtained a personal interview with the President on December

---

59. Scott, W., pp. 610, 613, 614.

15th, when he repeated his views, with specific emphasis on reinforcing forts Sumter and Moultrie, but the President said, in substance, that "the time had not arrived for doing so." Scott perhaps did not dare to mention President Jackson's actions with the nullification question; but on reflection, that same night, after the meeting, Scott wrote a note to the President in which he recounted the decisive action President Jackson had taken to reinforce the forts in Charleston Harbor. (At that time, the reinforcements had been under Scott's personal command.)

Thus, the answer to Twiggs' letter came with no surprises. It came from George W. Lay, Scott's chief of staff, dated December 28th, stating in part that "The President has listened to him [Scott] with due friendliness and respect, but the War Department [Floyd] has been little communicative."[60]

Scott's hands were tied as long Floyd's policies ruled. Finally, after a stormy cabinet meeting on December 13th, which had centered on the question of the relief of the Charleston forts,[61] Floyd recommending against, the path to his resignation on December 29th was opened. The postmaster general, Joseph Holt, was appointed as interim secretary on December 31st.[62] The general-in-chief, though ill, now finally had the opportunity to begin the action that he had recommended in October. His action, however, was still to be limited by the caution of Buchanan.

Events at Fort Sumter were a priority. Major Anderson, the commander, later explained that he felt Moultrie was not defensible with its small garrison and that a combined one in Sumter could present a better defense. Thus, on December 26th, 1860, he abandoned Moultrie and occupied Sumter. Anderson's instructions, and his interpretation of them, were the result of a visit to Moultrie by Maj. Don Carlos Buell on December 11th. Buell had carried only verbal instructions from Secretary Floyd, as outlined in a memorandum written after the meeting.[63] The bulk of the advice was what one would have imagined from Floyd's office: "You are carefully to avoid every act which would needlessly tend to provoke aggression . . ." There was, however, one innocent conclusion that turned out to be the source of trouble. "The smallness of your force will not permit you, perhaps, to occupy more than one of the three forts, but an attack on or attempt to take possession of any one of them will be regarded as an act of hostility, and you may then put your command into either of them which you may deem most proper to increase its power of resistance."

Anderson's move offered the new governor of South Carolina a technicality over which to stir the pot. He sent an aide to complain that a previous understanding with the President had been violated in that "no reenforcements [sic] were

---

60. O.R. Vol. 1, pp. 579, 580; see also, pp. 113, 114.
61. Nicolay & Hay, Vol. II, p. 394.
62. O.R. Ser. III, Vol. 1, p. 21.
63. O.R. Vol. 1, pp. 89, 90, 115–118.

to be sent to any of the forts, and particularly this one . . ."[64] As a consequence, the South Carolina militia occupied Fort Moultrie on December 27th, the day after it was abandoned, and on December 30th seized the Charleston Arsenal.

The same day,[65] not knowing of Floyd's resignation, but having long recognized his damaging policies, Scott directly requested of the President that he be allowed to prepare "without reference to the War Department and otherwise, as secretly as possible, to send two hundred and fifty recruits from New York Harbor to re-enforce Fort Sumter." The next day Scott ordered that a force of 200 troops be made ready to board the sloop-of-war *Brooklyn* to be sent to Fort Sumter.[66] The President's fear of armed conflict blunted such boldness. Quoting Scott:[67] "afterward, Secretary Holt and myself endeavored, in vain, to obtain a ship of war for the purpose, and were finally obliged to employ the passenger steamer Star of the West."

By January 5th, 1861, the plan[68] was initiated. The only advantage that the *Star of the West* offered was a cover for its purpose. Because it regularly ran between New York and New Orleans, its departure might not be regarded as a special expedition by ubiquitous Southern sympathizers. Southern spies, unfortunately, took due note of the 200 soldiers that were brought on board and hidden.[69] Forewarned, South Carolina fired upon the unarmed steamer as it approached Charleston Harbor, and it returned to New York.

On January 3rd, and 4th, Scott had the opportunity to take his long since recommended action to occupy other coastal forts. Orders[70] were issued to Lt. A. J. Slemmer, and his Company G, of the 1st Artillery at Barrancas Barracks, to occupy Fort Pickens; to Capt. J. M. Brannan and his Company B of the 1st Artillery at Key West, to occupy Fort Taylor; to Major L. G. Arnold and his Company C of the 2nd Artillery at Fort Independence, Boston, to occupy Fort Jefferson, Tortugas, Florida; and to Major Z. B. Tower to take command of all the facilities "in and about" Pensacola, Florida. These actions were perhaps a few moments past "not a moment too late" but, at least, they were significant directives from whence there had been none. Some parts of a deteriorating situation might now be looked to be salvaged.

---

64. O.R. Vol. 1, p. 3. Report of Robert Anderson.
65. O.R. Vol. 1, p. 114.
66. O.R. Vol. 1, p. 119.
67. Scott, Winfield, p. 621.
68. O.R. Vol. 1, p. 9.
69. O.R. Vol. 1, p. 253.
70. O.R. Vol. 1, pp. 334, 345, 350.

The clouds of secession gathered rapidly:

Jan. 9, 1861	Mississippi
Jan. 10, 1861	Florida
Jan. 11, 1861	Alabama
Jan. 19, 1861	Georgia
Jan. 26, 1861	Louisiana
Feb. 1, 1861	Texas, ratified on Feb. 23

In many cases, even before the ordinances of secession had been ratified, state authorities began the seizure of U.S. property:

Jan. 3	Georgia	Fort Pulaski, Cockspur Island, Savannah River
Jan. 4	Alabama	U.S. Arsenal at Mount Vernon
Jan. 5	Alabama	Fort Morgan, Mobile Point; Fort Gaines, Dauphin Island
Jan. 6	Florida	U.S. Arsenal at Apalachicola
Jan. 7	Florida	Fort Marion, St. Augustine
Jan. 10	Louisiana	U.S Arsenal and Barracks, Baton Rouge
Jan. 11	Louisiana	Forts Jackson and St. Philip, Mississippi River
Jan. 12	Florida	Fort Barrancas, Fort McCree, and Barrancas Barracks, Pensacola
Jan. 14	Louisiana	Fort Pike, Rigolets
Jan. 20	Mississippi	Fort on Ship Island, at sea off the Mississippi River
Jan. 24	Georgia	U.S. Arsenal at Augusta
Jan. 26	Georgia	Ogelthorpe Barracks, Savannah, Fort Jackson, Savannah River
Jan. 28	Louisiana	Fort Macomb, Chef Menteur, and U.S. property at New Orleans
Feb. 16	Texas	Camp Cooper and U.S. Arsenal at San Antonio
Feb. 18	Texas	All U.S. Military Posts in Texas surrendered by Headquarters, Dept. of Texas, U.S. Army

The next wave of secessions followed a month later:

March 16, 1861	Arizona Territory
April 17, 1861	Virginia [divided, as forty-eight Western counties split off to form West Virginia]
May 6, 1861	Arkansas
May 20, 1861	North Carolina
June 8, 1861	Tennessee
October 31, 1861	Missouri [divided, with an unelected pro-Union government]
November 20, 1861	Kentucky [both pro-Union and pro-Confederate factions]

The events[71] bearing on the future of Battery L and its contemporaries in Texas were a study in slow communications and interference by the Texas

---

71. O.R. Vol. 1, pp. 581, 584. Communications took anywhere from 12 to 19 days, from a perusal of Union correspondence. There was a telegraph between New York and New Orleans but apparently not to San Antonio.

authorities. There was not, however, any lack of initiative on the part of either Secretary Holt or General Scott. When Major General Twiggs revealed in a letter to the War Department, dated January 15th, that he would follow the South, he being a "Georgia man," he was promptly relieved by special orders no. 22 dated January 28th, 1861, and replaced by Colonel Carlos A. Waite of the 1st Infantry, stationed at Camp Verde, Texas, some sixty miles from San Antonio.

Though it is not stated in the orders sent out, the choice of artillery companies only as part of an evacuation from Texas makes it clear that General Scott intended them as garrisons or reinforcements for the coastal forts. It is also seems clear that there was not yet a plan for the disposition of the rest of the army in Texas, or if it was felt that there was a need. On January 31st, orders[72] directed the commanding officer of the Department of Texas, San Antonio "to take immediate measures for replacing the five companies of artillery on the Rio Grande . . ." Twiggs, unaware of his having been replaced, duly issued special orders no. 25[73] on February 14th, the same day that the dispatch was received:

I. Companies F, K, and L, First Artillery at Fort Duncan, Company M, First, and Company M, Second Artillery, at Fort Brown, will march, immediately upon receipt of this order, for Brazos Santiago, at which place a steamer has been directed to be in readiness to receive them for transportation out of Texas. The light companies will take their guns, ammunition, and equipments with them, but will leave their horses on embarkation. The other companies will move with their arms and ammunition, and all the companies with such camp equipage as can be transported by the means within their command.

II. Companies C and E, Third Infantry, will move to Fort Brown without delay, to replace the garrison ordered out of Texas, and will take charge of the artillery horses of Companies K, First, and M, Second Artillery, for which purpose details from each company will be made.

III. Company B, Third Infantry, will repair at once to Fort Duncan, and relieve the present garrison of that station.

IV. The troops from Fort Duncan will carry provisions as far as Fort brown.

V. The transportation will be taken from the means at the posts from which the movements will be made.

Twiggs received the news of his being replaced the next day.[74] Colonel Waite did not arrive at San Antonio to assume command until the 19th, only to discover that events in Texas had run faster than anyone in Washington could have

---

72. O.R. Ser. I, Vol. 1, p. 585.
73. O.R. Vol. 1, p. 589.
74. O.R. Vol. 1, p. 590.

contemplated. On the morning of February 16th, the Alamo and other of the facilities of headquarters of the Department of Texas, at the plaza in San Antonio (figure 1) were surrounded by some 1,000 volunteers under the command of Maj. Benjamin McCulloch[75] of the First Regiment of the Texas Mounted Riflemen. On February 18th, Twiggs agreed to give up all Federal property and to withdraw all the 2,684[76] Federal troops stationed in Texas.

FIGURE 1

The news of the surrender[77] of the entire U.S. Army in Texas made Twiggs' name synonymous with "traitor" in the North. However, he had given warning of the direction of events in Texas several times in communications to Washington, as noted. A revealing one is presented here:[78]

HEADQUARTERS DEPARTMENT OF TEXAS
San Antonio, January 23, 1861

Col. S. Cooper,
Adjutant-General, Washington, D.C.:
SIR: Inclosed I transmit a letter from the governor of Texas and my

---

75. He calls himself colonel in his report. O.R. Ser. II, Vol. 1, pp. 34,35. A plaque placed in the plaza at San Antonio honoring the surrender refers to him as major. Figure 1 from *Harper's Weekly*, March 23, 1861, p. 185.
76. O.R. Ser. II, Vol. 1, p.8.
77. O.R. Vol. 1, p. 53, etc.
78. O.R. Vol. 1, p. 582.

answer. As I do not think any one in authority desires me to carry on a civil war against Texas, I shall, after secession, if the governor repeats his demand, direct the arms and other property to be turned over to his agents, keeping in the hands of the troops the arms they now have. I have asked for instructions as to what I was to do after secession four times, viz, on the 27th ultimo, the 2d, the 7th, and the 18th instants, and have received no answer. The troops in this department occupy a line of some twelve hundred miles, and some time will be required to remove them to any place. I again ask, what disposition is to be made of them?

Very respectfully, your obedient servant,

D. E. TWIGGS
Bvt. Maj. Gen., U.S. Army, Commanding Department

He had consulted with Governor Sam Houston as well. His communications with Houston, through Houston's *confidential agent* Gen. J. M. Smith, centered on Houston's concern over how Twiggs would react should an "unauthorized mob" attempt to take control of Federal property before official secession and before Houston could legally act. Houston's letter describing such a mob was dated January 20th. It is of interest to note that on January 22nd, Twiggs issued special orders no. 10 directing reinforcements to San Antonio, one company from Camp Verde and two companies from Fort Clark.[79] On January 28th, Twiggs mysteriously countermanded that portion of the order dealing with the troops from Fort Clark, returning them to their base. This was regarded with suspicion by many pro-Union people, as related by Mrs. Caroline B. Darrow in her *Recollections of the Twiggs Surrender*.[80] The activity that had caused the apprehension of Governor Houston and many of the pro-Union citizens was the planning of a "buffalo hunt" that was begun in December by Capt. John R. Baylor. It was widely regarded as a pretext to gather enough men to surprise and seize the arsenal at San Antonio.

Mrs. Darrow further narrates that suspicion of Twiggs was increased as he frequently consulted with prominent secessionists, "most of them women."

Soon came the hoopla, Mrs. Darrow alleges fraud, involved with the planned Secession Convention and its gathering of delegates on January 28th. Illiterate Mexicans, or those who could not read English, were instructed to vote the ballot with the "longest words" (for secession). "Elected" with less than half of the state having voted, the Austin Convention voted for secession on February 1st, and that action was approved by the legislature on the 4th. Also, on the 4th, the convention voted to assign a commission consisting of four men – Samuel A. Maverick, Thomas J. Devine, Phillip N. Luckett, and James H. Rogers – with power to "demand . . . possession of said arms, munitions, stores, &c" belonging to the

---

79. O.R. Vol. 1, p. 582.
80. *Battles and Leaders...* Vol. 1, p. 33; Nicolay & Hay, Vol. IV, pp. 182, 183.

United States.[81] Traveling from Austin to San Antonio, the commissioners began a series of demands for the property described and the immediate evacuation of all United States troops from Texas.

In response to this, Twiggs appointed his own military commission to treat with the Texas commissioners. This consisted of Maj. D. H. Vinton, quartermaster; Maj. S. Maclin, paymaster; and Capt. R. H. K. Whitley, ordnance department. The two commissions met for the first time on February 11th, when a list of demands was submitted to Twiggs' officers. They answered on the 12th, outlined here:[82]

1. That everything under the control of the general commanding shall remain in status quo until the 2d of March next. [Provisos: orders from Washington to leave, attack by Indians, or attack by "irrepressible parties"].

2. No movement or change of position of the troops shall take place.

3. None of the arms, ordinance, military stores, or other property shall be disposed of.

4. No money in hands of paymaster handed over. Troops to retain their arms, and march out with them and requisite ammunition, clothing, camp and garrison equipage, quartermaster's stores, subsistence, medical and hospital stores, and such means of transportation . . . necessary for an orderly movement . . .

The Texas commissioners replied on the 14th that they objected to any idea that troop movements would be under any control but theirs. They basically agreed to the other points made. It was at this time that Mrs. Darrow overheard a Twiggs' conversation, which included that "the day for the surrender" was fixed. Whether warned by Caroline Darrow or in reaction to the terms he had agreed to as a member of the military commission, Major Vinton removed important papers from his safe and "intrusted" them to Mrs. Darrow's husband, the quartermaster clerk, who hid them in the ashes of an unused stove.

It must be noted here, where it chronologically belongs, that on the 12th, Col. Carlos A. Waite, commanding the five companies of the 1st Infantry that were in Texas, requested Twiggs' permission to concentrate his regiment by joining it with those serving in the Department of the West.[83] Waite was clear in his reading of events, and was trying to save his troops. No response from Twiggs is of record.

On the 15th, in Mrs. Darrow's chronicle of events, it is noted that hundreds

---

81. O.R. Vol. 1, p. 512.
82. O.R. Vol. 1, p. 507.
83. O.R. Vol. 1, p. 522; O.R. Ser. III, Vol. 1, p. 25.

of men (400 in McCulloch's report)[84] had gathered at the stage crossing of Salado Creek, seven miles outside of San Antonio. It seems that Captain Baylor's buffalo hunt had finally materialized, this time under the command of Maj. Benjamin McCulloch. At 4:00 a.m. on the 16th the San Antonio plaza awoke to the screams of negroes to the effect that they were all going to be killed, as men, mounted and on foot, began to fill the area. Coffee, refreshments, and blankets were seen to be being distributed to them "in abundance" by Twiggs' women friends.

As Twiggs left his home for his workday at 6:00 a.m.,[85] he was surrounded, and the demands for surrender were made loud and clear by the commissioners. His answer, at noon, was that he "gave up everything." Thus, let off the hook for the moment, he would be forced to reply *immediately* to a letter from the commissioners on the 17th. By this time, it is evident that the commissioners knew that they were dealing with a lame duck, as the letter was addressed TO THE OFFICER IN COMMAND.

Twiggs' response was to repeat that he would agree to turn over federal property to the commissioners provided that the troops retained their equipment and their means of transportation and arms so as to be prepared for any aggression from any source.[86]

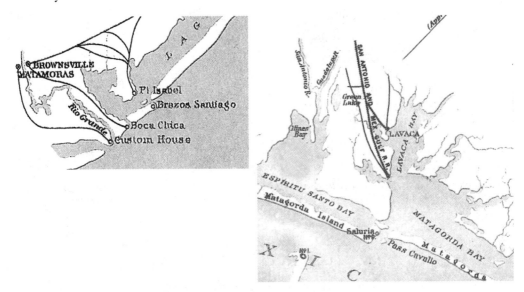

FIGURES 2 and 3

It is interesting to note that in a circular published by the commissioners as a summary of the agreement, dated February 18th, only two light batteries, one at

---

84. O.R. Ser. II, Vol. 1, p. 34.
85. O.R. Vol. 1, p. 513.
86. O.R. Vol. 1, p. 514, 515.

Fort Duncan and one at Fort Brown, were referred to.[87] This confirms our record from chapter 1 that Battery K of the 1st Regiment and Battery M of the 2nd Regiment were the only units with guns, and it was the guns that the Texans wanted.

The circular made it clear that the route that the troops were to take to "leave the soil of the State" was "by the way of the coast." Initially, this meant either Brazos Santiago, at the mouth of the Rio Grande (figure 2) or Indianola, the port south of San Antonio (figure 3).

After the middle of the month of March, the troops were directed only to Indianola, via San Antonio.

Did Twiggs sell out the army? Though he admitted that his allegiance to his state of Georgia came first, a rather peculiar concept from today's perspective, he did what was probably in the best interests of all concerned. At the time, he was 69 years old and had the benefit, at least, of maturity. Nothing is known as to whether he was a scholar or student of military history, but one can imagine that he was well aware of the consequences of an evacuation under hostile circumstances. The troops, accompanied by large numbers of their dependents, would have to trek hundreds of miles through hostile territory, always under the threat of mob or Indian attack; those who could set up and wait in ambush. Malnutrition, bad water (or none at all), exhaustion, and disease – all would take a considerable toll.

Twiggs may or may not have read accounts of disastrous evacuations in military history such as the British retreat from Afghanistan in 1842. There, 4,500 troops and 12,000 dependents who left Kabul in January retreated through the Khyber Pass. While winter weather was a considerable factor, the incessant depredations of the tribesmen left only *one* survivor from the last stand at Gandamak. Clearly, nothing of the sort would have happened in Texas, but why take any chance? Southern chivalry meant get them out in one piece.

Three plans for the withdrawal developed: one put forward by Colonel Waite, one by the commissioners, and one by Washington. The plan from Washington was immediately shattered and unworkable because it was too late, and the one from Colonel Waite, at headquarters in San Antonio, soon became subordinate to the whims of the Texans. At first, the withdrawal was rather orderly and relations between the Texas volunteers and the U.S. Army were correct and courteous. However, as time dragged on, the impatience of the Texans grew. News from elsewhere began to harden their attitude, and some began to regard the Federal troops not so much as departing colleagues but as an escaping group of traitors. On February 25th, Major McCulloch urged that, "This force ought to be disorganized before it leaves this State."[88] He had the audacity to suggest that "the proper bounty" would recruit many to remain and join Texas' service.

---

87. O.R. Vol. 1, p. 516. Figures 2 and 3 are portions of *Atlas*, plate 65, map no. 10.
88. O.R. Vol. 1, p. 609.

Only one day after Battery L and its colleagues received their orders to leave Fort Duncan, the following was sent from Washington (and received on March 1st):[89]

> Headquarters, Department of the Army,
> Washington, February 15, 1861
>
> Col. C. A. Waite,
> *First Infantry, Commanding Dep't of Texas, San Antonio:*
> Sir: In the event of the secession of the State of Texas, the General-in-Chief directs that you will without unnecessary delay, put in march for Fort Leavenworth the entire military force of your department.
>
> [The letter goes on to describe how to accomplish this, in considerable detail, here omitted.]
>
> L. THOMAS
> *Assistant Adjutant General*

The remainder of the letter was moot because the plan was was not what was to be dictated by the Texas commissioners. By February 23rd, the Ordinance of Secession was ratified, and the Texas commissioners took full control – even over Governor Sam Houston.

On March 19th, General Scott at Washington had had another idea. Orders were sent[90] to Col. Waite, to the effect that, if there were still sufficient numbers of troops that had not left Indianola – not less than 500 and preferably 1,200 – they were not to embark but to form "a strongly-entrenched camp at some suitable point convenient to and covering the post of Indianola" to keep a foothold in Texas until the question of secession may be settled between competing factions and "to give such aid and support to General Houston or other head of authority in defense of the federal government as may be within your power. . . ."

"PS. – If on receipt of this duplicate it should be well known that neither Governor Houston nor any other executive authority of Texas has any considerable number of men up in arms in defense of the Federal Government . . . you will consider the foregoing instructions withdrawn."

A special messenger was sent to Sam Houston to discuss the plan. He declined any such assistance,[91] and the perplexed governor then urged: "by all means take no action towards hostile movements . . ."

Scott's order was obsolete the day it was sent. The very same day, March 19th, Colonel Waite had sent a note to headquarters in Washington that he had no choice but to embark the troops as instructed, "under [the orders of] the date

---

89. O.R. Vol. 1, p. 589.
90. O.R. Vol. 1, p. 598.
91. O.R. Vol. 1, p. 551. Houston later refused to swear allegiance to the Confederacy, and on March 16th, the Texas Legislature declared the office of governor vacant.

of the 12th, ultimo"[92] and to proceed to New York. Scott's letter did not arrive at Waite's headquarters until April 1st, and by that time more than 500 U.S. troops had already gathered at Green Lake, near Indianola, prepared for departure.

The idea of a strong foothold, however, did not die. The retention of, and subsequently the taking of, strong footholds at coastal points along the shores of the Confederacy were to become a central strategy in the prosecution of the war. It became known as the "Anaconda Plan."

Record 2/61
31 DECEMBER 1860–29 FEBRUARY 1861, FORT DUNCAN, TEXAS

The Company left Fort Duncan, Texas, February 20 inst. In pursuance of S.O. No. 25, Headquarters Dept. of Texas, San Antonio, Feb. 14 inst. and arrived at Camp Alburquielas, Texas[93] at 1 o'clock today. [29 Feb.]

Samuel K. Dawson	Capt.	Leave of absence for 2 months S.O. no. 4 Dept. of Texas, April 30, 1860 extended For 6 mo. S.O. no. 124, A.G.O. June 20, 1860. Left Co. May 2nd 1860.
William Silvey		1st Lt. Reg. Adjutant O. No. 7 Head Qrs. 1st Artillery, Fort Dallas, Fla, Aug. 13,'57. Left Co. April 22, 1854, S.O. No. 62, Head Qrs. New York, April 18, 1854.
James W. Robinson		1st Lt. Det. svc. on a train to the coast, left co. Feb. 14, 1861.
Richard H. Jackson		2nd Lt. In command of Co. since Feb. 14, 1861.

Detached:
    Wallace Wright Pvt. Escort duty to San Antonio, Texas. Absent from Co. since Febr'y 14, 1861.

Deserted:

Michael Murphy	Pvt.	Deserted near Fort Duncan, Texas,	Febr'y 20, 1861

Discharged:

Henry Hehn	Pvt.	By reason of expiration of service,	Jan. 10, 1861
Henry Lundenberg	Pvt.	" " "	Jan. 25, 1861
Edward O'Donnell	Pvt.	" " "	Jan. 5, 1861
William Robinson	Pvt.	" " "	Jan. 26, 1861

Strength: 83 Sick: 1
Present Sick: none
Absent Sick: Charles Riley Sgt. Sick at Fort McIntosh, Texas. Absent since February 25th 1861.

The muster roll mentions the detached service of 1st Lt. James Robinson who was "on a train to the coast." His mission was the result of a personal note received earlier by the commander of the three batteries at Fort Duncan, Maj. William French. The note came from a friend on the general staff in San Antonio, and it had warned, in part, that: "The matter is arranged. All will be surrendered to the

---

92. O.R. Vol. 1, p. 598.
93. Unknown location, estimated at fifty miles northwest of Rio Grande City. Questionable spelling from handwritten copy.

State, and that in its sovereign capacity."[94]

This provided French with confirmation of the plans of the secessionists. The surrender would soon be announced, and there was no time to be wasted in planning to be ready to move the artillery out. His first move was to get the women and children away.

In peacetime, a soldier could make arrangements for his family to accompany him, largely on the basis of what he could afford. Thus, officers often had their family and servants living on the post. Enlisted families came along if somehow their income could be supplemented, such as by the wife being a laundress, as mentioned in chapter 1. The families of record were Lt. J. W. Robinson and his wife, two sons and a servant; Sgt. Thomas Newton's wife, Ann, and daughter, Mary; Sgt. Thomas Conroy, with wife, Elizabeth; Pvt. Amelius Straub, with wife, Margaret; Pvt. Louis Lighna, with wife, Julia, and son, Louis; and Pvt. James Flynn with wife, Mary, his son, Thomas, and daughter, Emily.

A "train" was put together, consisting of the few available wagons, Mexican carts, and ambulances that could be found, considering that the means of transport had been gradually taken away by the Texas authorities on one pretext or another; clearly their plan being to immobilize them and subject them to threat of capture. The women and children on board, their train set out on February 14th for San Antonio and Indianola, with Lieutenant Robinson in command and Pvt. Wallace Wright as escort.

Twiggs' order for the five artillery companies to move to Brazos Santiago had been issued on the same day. It was rushed to Fort Duncan by "private hand" but did not reach French until February 20th. W. A. Nichols, on Waite's staff at San Antonio, had added a note to it, dated February 16th, 1861: "This order was to be cut off[95] yesterday, move rapidly; the object of the authorities of Texas is to demand the surrender of the guns of the light batteries."

This was all the warning that was needed. The command left Fort Duncan that day. The scarcity of wagons meant that nearly all their personal property was left behind. They moved rapidly, expecting to be intercepted at any of a number of points advantageous for ambush. At Willow Pond, Sgt. Charles Riley was thrown from his horse and his right leg broken in two places. Luckily, the route they had taken led them past Fort McIntosh (Laredo). There was a surgeon at the fort, and he could set the leg. Since Riley could not be moved, he would have to be left behind; and since it was likely that the infantry stationed at McIntosh would soon be forced to leave, a collection was taken up to pay for Riley's keep with a Laredo family, who were allegedly sympathetic to the Union. Bidding farewell on February 25th, the march continued, with Riley left behind in the Fort McIntosh hospital.

---

94. Haskin, W. L., pp. 136–138, 353, 354.
95. Meaning intercepted and kept from circulation; Riley Pension File no. 476558, National Archives.

1861 Roster
31 December 1860–29 February 1861 Muster Roll
FORT DUNCAN, TEXAS

1. Samuel K. Dawson — Capt. Leave of absence for 2 months, S.O. no. 4, Dept. of Texas, April 30, 1860. Extended for 6 mo. S.O. no. 124 A.G.O. June 20, 1860. Left Co. May 2, 1860.
2. William Silvey — 1st Lt. Reg. Adjutant. O. no. 7 Hdqrs. 1st Arty, Ft. Dallas, Florida August 13, 1857
3. James W. Robinson — 1st Lt. Det. Svc. on a train to the soast. Left Co. February 14, 1861.
4. Richard H. Jackson — 2nd Lt. In Command since February 14, 1861.

1. Lewis Keller	1st Sgt.	1 Dec.'59 Newport, KY		1. Julius Becker	Cpl.	12 Oct.'59 New York
2. Thomas Conroy	Sgt.	1 Jan.'59 San Antonio, TX		2. Alexander J. Baby	Cpl.	10 Feb.'60 Boston
3. Thomas Newton	Sgt.	13 Dec.'58 Ft. Brown, TX		3. David J. Wicks	Cpl.	23 Oct.'59 New York
4. Charles Riley	Sgt.	7 Oct.'59 Boston		4. Andrew J. Beeler	Cpl.	9 Feb.'60 Boston

1. Ludwig Rupprecht Musician 7 Feb.'60 New York   1. Isaac T. Cain Artificer 4 Oct.'59 Boston

Privates

1. Ahern, James	18 Oct.'60 Boston	36. Kenny, Michael	8 Feb.'60 New York
2. Anglin, Edmond	19 Oct.'59 New York	37. Kutschor, Joseph	19 Feb.'60 New York
3. Beglan, James	25 Oct.'60 New York	38. Lighna, Louis	18 Oct.'58 Ft. Brown, TX
4. Bissel, John	19 Oct.'59 New York	39. McCarthy, James	4 Oct.'60 Boston
5. Brook, Thomas	9 Feb.'60 Boston	40. McCoy, Daniel	24 Oct.'60 New York
6. Brown, William F.	1 Nov.'59 Boston	41. McDonagh, Miles	17 Sept.'60 New York
7. Brunskill, William C.	19 Oct.'59 New York	42. McGaley, Terence	18 Sept.'60 New York
8. Buckley, John	30 Sept.'58 New York	43. McLaughlin, Edward	30 Sept.'58 New York
9. Burke, John	7 Oct.'60 New York	44. McWaters, James	16 July '57 Newport, KY
10. Carroll, Patrick	17 Dec.'60 Ft. Duncan, TX	45. Meyer, John	1 Mar.'60 New York
11. Casey, John	15 Oct.'59 New York	46. Murphy, John	21 Feb.'60 Boston
12. Connell, Jeremiah	14 Sept.'59 Ft. Clark, TX	47. Myers, Denis	28 Sept.'58 Syracuse, NY
13. Cotterill, Edmond	22 Sept.'60 Boston	48. Nitschke, John G.	6 Feb.'60 New York
14. Coyne, Owen	10 Dec.'60 Ft. Duncan, TX	49. O'Sullivan, Michael	26 Sept.'60 Boston
15. Craffy, Patrick	27 Sept.'60 Boston	50. Olvaney, Michael	25 Oct.'60 New York
16. Creed, William	27 Sept.'60 Boston	51. Parketton, William	4 Oct.'60 New York
17. Cummings, Patrick	25 Oct.'60 Boston	52. Poole, Thomas	4 Nov.'57 Detroit, MI
18. Curran, Robert	6 Oct.'57 Newport, KY	53. Reedy, Michael	1 Jan.'57 San Antonio, TX
19. Demarest, William	19 Oct.'59 New York	54. Roper, John	22 Oct.'60 New York
20. Donnelly, Patrick	1 Mar.'60 Boston	55. Schmidt, Heinrick	26 Oct.'60 New York
21. Farrell, Bernard	11 Nov.'59 New York	56. Schneider, Philip H.	16 Oct.'58 Ft. Brown, TX
22. Ferrari, Prosper	22 Oct.'60 New York	57. Scott, William, E.	9 Feb.'60 Boston
23. Flint, Charles A.	22 Sept.'60 Boston	58. Shaw, Warren P.	26 Oct.'60 Boston
24. Flynn, James	12 Sept.'59 Ft. Clark, TX	59. Smith, Joseph	11 Oct.'59 New York
25. Foley, Christopher	3 Nov.'59 Boston	60. Spangler, Charles	3 Sept.'58 New York
26. Friedman, George	7 Feb.'60 New York	61. Stoll, Andrew	24 Oct.'60 New York
27. Gilroyd, Thomas	26 Aug.'57 Newport, KY	62. Straub, Amelius	8 Feb.'60 New York
28. Golden, James	2 Feb.'60 Boston	63. Thompson, William V.	13 Sept.'60 Rochester, NY
29. Hadley, George	1 Mar.'60 Boston	64. Townsend, Reuben	27 Sept.'60 Boston
30. Hagan, Francis	21 Jan.'59 Ft. Brown, TX	65. White, Michael	7 Oct.'59 Boston
31. Harkins, James	10 Oct.'60 New York	66. Wilkinson, Joseph	4 Feb.'60 New York
32. Hey, Louis	3 Sept.'58 New York	67. William, Henry	28 Sept.'60 Rochester, NY
33. Holland, John	13 Oct.'57 Detroit, MI	68. Wright, Wallace D.	29 Sept.'59 Syracuse, NY
34. Howard, George	25 Oct.'60 New York	69. Wynne, William	9 Oct.'59 Detroit, MI
35. Jackel, Charles	26 Oct.'60 New York		

Record 4/61
29 FEBRUARY–30 APRIL 1861, FORT JEFFERSON, FLORIDA

The Company left Camp Alburquielas on the 1st and arrived at Ringgold Barracks, Texas on the 3rd of March. The Company left Ringgold Barracks, Texas on the 4th and arrived at Fort Brown, Texas on the 9th of March. The Company left Fort Brown on the 10th and arrived at the mouth of the Rio Grande (Brazos Santiago) on the 11th March. The Company left the mouth of the Rio Grande and embarked on board the Steamship "Gen'l Rusk" on the afternoon of the 19th and arrived at Fort Jefferson, Tortugas Island, Florida, on the 24th of March, 1861.

Samuel K. Dawson Capt. Joined Co. from absence with leave Mar. 24, 1861.
William Silvey 1st Lt. Reg. Adjutant O. No. 7 Head Qrs. 1st Artillery, Fort Dallas, Fla, Aug. 13,'57. Left Co. April 22, 1854, S.O. No. 62, Head Qrs. New York, April 18, 1854
James W. Robinson 1st Lt. Joined Company from det. svc. Mar. 9,'61.
Richard H. Jackson 2nd Lt.

Detached:
James Ahern	Pvt.	On det. svc. at Fort Pickens, left Co.	April 14, 1861.
Thomas Brook	Pvt.	" "	"
Wm, F, Brown	Pvt.	" "	"
Patrick Cummings	Pvt.	" "	"
Christopher Foley	Pvt.	" "	"
James McCarthy	Pvt.	" "	"
James McCoy	Pvt.	" "	"
John Meyer	Pvt.	" "	"
Michael O'Sullivan	Pvt.	" "	"
William Parketton	Pvt.	" "	"
Thomas Poole	Pvt.	" "	"

Joined:
Henry A. Ward	Pvt.	From General Recruiting Depot, Fort Columbus, New York,	Mar. 21, 1861
Henry Wilkson	Pvt.	" " "	"
Owen A. Wren	Pvt.	" " "	"

Deserted:
John Bissell Pvt. At Fort Brown, Texas, March 10, 1861
Francis Hagan Pvt. At Fort Brown, Texas, March 10, 1861

Extra Duty with Engineer Dept.: Patrick Craffy, Patrick Donnelly, John Holland, Wm. Scott, Joseph Smith

Strength: 84, Sick: 7

Sick Present: William Brunskill, Bernard Farrell, Joseph Kutschor, Edward McLaughlin, Henry Wilkson, (one not listed).

Sick Absent: Charles Riley Sick at Fort McIntosh, Texas. Absent from Company since Febr'y 25, 1861.

Though the Record never mentions such details, a salute was fired in honor of the inauguration of President Lincoln as they departed Ringgold Barracks at dawn on the 5th.[96] By 11:00 a.m., they had marched twenty-two miles. During the noon halt, an express message came to Major French from Brownsville, with the news that the assistant adjutant general of the army, Maj. Fitz John Porter, had been sent there with instructions for the command and that Porter would await the arrival of the column. The march was then resumed for another seven miles, reaching twenty-nine miles in total – a frantic pace, enough to exhaust both men and animals. On the 6th, they marched twenty-six miles; on the 7th, twenty-seven; and on the 8th, a march of twenty-three miles brought them into Brownsville. Here they joined companies M, 1st Artillery and M, 2nd Artillery, including several infantry companies.

Though the garrison now consisted of two cavalry, five artillery and the infantry companies, they were far outnumbered by the Texas troops that were gathering and organizing in the vicinity. The Texans had previously approached Capt. Bennett H. Hill, commanding, to attempt to enlist him into their cause. He had completely rebuffed them and had replied that he considered it his duty to send traitors to Washington in irons. Thus warned of the gravity of the situation, he had detached 18 men from his small garrison to mount the guns stored at Brazos Santiago. All to no avail, the installation was surrendered on February 21st to several hundred Texas troops sent from Galveston.

FIGURE 4. *DANIEL WEBSTER*, OFF PORT ISABEL, TEXAS

On March 3rd, Porter had chartered the steamer *Daniel Webster* (figure 4) and it was waiting off the bar of the Rio Grande. The command arrived at Brazos on March 11th,[97] whereupon Porter deemed that it was not a secure place to use for

---

96. Haskin, W. L., p. 138.
97. O.R. Vol. 52, p.128; Vol. 1, pp. 587, 588. Additional narrative of departure from Haskin, W. L., pp. 136, 137.

embarkation. He was concerned, not that a shooting incident would occur, but that the undisciplined Texas volunteers and "minute men" would loot the provisions placed there for the use of those awaiting embarkation.[98] In any event, the steamer did not cross the bar and tie up at the wharves. It remained anchored off the mouth of the Rio Grande, enduring high northeast winds and the delay caused by the difficulty of lighters to ferry supplies out to it. Porter's report later hinted that the Texans were using any excuse to make things difficult. Loading did not begin until the 16th.

Major Porter had been instructed by Washington to load additional troops, infantry if available, regardless of prior orders from headquarters at San Antonio. He thus took the initiative to charter an additional steamer, the 750-ton sidewheeler *General Rusk*. Porter's sense of urgency was justified, as later events proved. It was not long after that the *General Rusk*, based at Galveston, was seized by the state of Texas and converted into a gunboat.

Both the *Rusk* and the *Daniel Webster*[99] got off late on the 19th, the *Rusk* to deliver batteries F and K to Fort Taylor at Key West, and batteries L and M to Fort Jefferson. The *Daniel Webster*, with M of the 2nd Artillery and C and E of the 3rd Infantry, continued on to Fort Hamilton, New York, arriving there on March 30th.

A now-distant memory was the fate of Battery L's 22 deserters,[100] those left behind prior to September 29th, when the company left Brownsville for Fort Duncan. Then there was Michael Murphy, who had disappeared on February 20th, the very day that they marched out of Duncan. After deserting at Fort Brown and being restored to duty, one could have hardly imagined that John Bissel and Francis Hagan would again walk away on March 10th, just as the command left Brownsville for the mouth of the Rio Grande.

While the five artillery companies were *ordered* out by headquarters at Washington, company H of the 1st Infantry and companies D and H of the 2nd Cavalry at Camp Cooper, about three hundred miles north of San Antonio, were some of the first to be *forced* to evacuate. On February 14th, the garrison noted that a Texan force was gathering in the area.[101] By the 16th, the camp was surrounded.[102] The situation remained a standoff until the 18th when Col. W. C. Dalrymple, an aide to Governor Houston and commanding the volunteers, warned that he would

---

98. O.R. Ser. II, Vol. 1, p.13.
99. Figure 4, April 13, 1861, *Harper's Weekly*. Port Isabel is located on the Texas mainland (see figure 3). *Harper's* intimation that the troops were embarked at Port Isabel does not agree with the muster roll record.
100. The 1860 muster rolls. The April 13th issue of *Harper's* mentions the Indian danger: "The Indians followed the march of the troops, and committed great havoc among the people, killing some and running off their stock." Murphy had taken a great risk in deserting.
101. O.R. Vol. 1, p. 523.
102. O.R. Vol. 1, p. 542.

demand surrender in 24 hours. On the 19th, the demand was met, and Camp Cooper was abandoned.[103] On the 21st, only one day after French's command had left Fort Duncan, the Camp Cooper garrison moved to Fort Chadbourne, where Col. H. E. McCulloch,[104] a Texas commissioner and now commander of the Northwestern Frontier, gave them orders to proceed to San Antonio.[105] There they received orders for proceeding to Green Lake.[106] Company H arrived there on March 29th and was shipped out to Key West on March 30th. Companies D and H of the 2nd Cavalry arrived at Indianola on March 30th and were shipped out to Washington, DC on March 31st.[107]

One might not understand why Camp Cooper surrendered so easily and undoubtedly before receipt of Twiggs' general orders no. 5 of February 18th,[108] directing all the posts to be abandoned. A quote from a letter Colonel Waite later written to headquarters in Washington[109] explains: "There is not a post in Texas which has the slightest defensive arrangement. They are either camps or open cantonments, and not tenable against a large force."[110]

The abandonments following Cooper were:

Feb. 26	Camp Colorado	Mar. 20 Fort Brown
Mar. 7	Ringgold Barracks	Fort Duncan
	Camp Verde (including 53 camels)[111]	Co. G 2nd Cavalry, Camp on Rio Grande
Mar. 12	Fort McIntosh	Mar. 23 Fort Chadbourne
Mar. 15	Camp Wood	Mar. 29 Fort Mason
Mar. 17	Camp Hudson	Mar. 31 Fort Bliss
Mar. 19	Fort Clark	Apr. 5 Fort Quitman
	Fort Inge	Apr. 13 Fort Davis
		Fort Stockton[112]

On April 23rd, the headquarters of Department of Texas personnel were arrested and held as prisoners,[113] thus bringing the total of the facilities abandoned to twenty. Armed "volunteers" began to interfere with the Federal troop

---

103. O.R. Vol. 1, p. 502.
104. Younger brother of Benjamin.
105. O.R. Vol. 1, p. 544.
106. O.R. Vol. 1, p. 549.
107. O.R. Ser. III, Vol. I, p. 25.
108. O.R. Vol. 1, p. 515.
109. O.R. Vol. 1, p. 540.
110. See chapter 1.
111. O.R. Vol. 1, p. 584.
112. O.R. Vol. 1, p. 502. No date given.
113. O.R. Vol. 1, p. 552.

movements, particularly communications. In a letter[114] dated March 27th, Colonel Waite complains: "Not a line has been received at these headquarters from the headquarters of the Army, or from the War Department, since I entered upon duty as the department commander, except unimportant matters, and I am inclined to believe from inspection of the envelopes that they have been opened, and that all important communications have been withheld."

Regarding communications, a letter[115] from headquarters of the Department of Texas to the Department of New Mexico dated February 24th was apparently never received. It ordered the three companies of the 8th Infantry stationed at forts Fillmore (New Mexico), Breckinridge (Arizona), and the camp at Hatch's Ranch (Nevada) to remain there. They had earlier been ordered by Washington to report to the Department of Texas. Hence, companies B, E, and K of the 8th Infantry filtered into Fort Bliss outside of El Paso between February 18th and the 21st. Fort Bliss was not abandoned until March 31st, with the troops looking at some six hundred miles, or a month's march, to San Antonio and more than a week (one hundred and seventy-five miles) more to Indianola.

By the end of March, the situation in Texas had impressed some of Jefferson Davis' associates that there was the potential to recruit numbers of the "flower of the old army," particularly of the 2nd Cavalry, which had served under both Robert E. Lee and Earl Van Dorn.[116] Van Dorn – formerly in command of Fort Mason but now, as of March 16th, a colonel in the Confederate service – was called upon by L. P. Walker, the Confederate secretary of war, to return to Texas[117] for "securing the U.S. troops for our Army."

Van Dorn arrived at Green Lake on March 26th and almost immediately converted two officers, old associates of his.[118] He optimistically predicted that he would have no difficulty in "securing many of the troops and officers." He was mistaken.

His efforts were later described as having "not succeeded in engaging many of the officers or soldiers to join the Army of the Confederate States." After this assessment, on April 11th Van Dorn was ordered to assume command in Texas and make prisoners of all U.S. troops remaining who refused to espouse the Confederate cause.[119] Now the Confederate government was taking control. This – and two significant events, which followed within days – would increase the difficulties of Colonel Waite.

---

114. O.R. Vol. 1, p. 549.
115. O.R. Vol. 1, p. 593.
116. O.R. Ser. II, Vol. 1, p. 37. Lee, a colonel in the 2nd Cavalry, had assumed command of the Department of Texas on February 20th, 1860. G.O. no. 2 Hdqrs. Dept. of Texas.
117. O.R. Ser. II, Vol. 1, pp. 37, 38.
118. O.R. Ser. II, Vol. 1, p. 38.
119. O.R. Ser. II, Vol. 1, p. 1.

The firing on Fort Sumter and its surrender on April 14th was serious, even electrifying, but President Lincoln's April 15th call for 75,000 volunteers to "suppress" the "combinations" of the seceded states was the straw that broke the camel's back. His proclamation gave 20 days for the people involved in these "combinations" "to disperse and retire peaceably to their respective abodes." Thus, we see why all of the army units that arrived at Indianola before April 13th departed without incident, but after that, there were hard feelings and none of the social delicacies as had been evident in earlier dealings. A war was beginning.

The report of Lt. Col. Gouverneur Morris, commander of Fort Chadbourne, is a study in a rather pompous lack of urgency as well as a spotlight on living conditions in some of the well-established forts. The fort was surrendered on February 28th to the ubiquitous H. E. McCulloch.[120] The transportation requested was for 12 and, at a minimum, 10 wagons to supplement the three available at the post "as there are to be moved one lieutenant colonel, one captain, one assistant surgeon with the rank of captain, one second lieutenant, one chaplain, and their servants, consisting of one man, four women, and three children, Company G, First Infantry, laundresses and children belonging to it, together with a detachment of Company I, First Infantry, with laundresses of same company, and the hospital matron and stores, as [sic] also the records of the post . . ."

Taking too much concern for all of their trappings, they arrived at Green Lake on April 15th, too late for a smooth departure. The steamer *Star of the West*, chartered to take them off, did not appear. They then went looking at Matagorda Bay on April 17th. Returning to Indianola on the 18th, they discovered that the *Star of the West* had been captured. The fact that it was the transport planned[121] for those leaving Texas was no longer of consequence. From now on, everyone not joining the Confederate cause would be taken prisoner. Initially, everyone who wished to leave was required to give his *parole* if an officer or his *oath* if an enlisted man[122] not to bear arms against the Confederate States unless exchanged for other prisoners of war or released from the oath by the President of the Confederate States.

The group from Chadbourne found themselves mixed in with Company K, 1st Infantry from Fort Lancaster; companies A and D, 8th Infantry from San Antonio and Camp Hudson; and three companies of the 3rd Infantry; A from Ringgold Barracks, and F and I from Fort McIntosh, Sgt. Charles Riley's last known location. There was no word as to Riley's fate.

Now under the command of Major Caleb C. Sibley,[123] the group was left to its own devices to find passage and be-damned whether the incident inconvenienced

---

120. O.R. Vol. 1, p. 558.
121. O.R. Ser. II, Vol. 1, p. 39.
122. O.R. Ser. II, Vol. 1, p. 51.
123. O.R. Ser. II, Vol. 1, pp. 39, 40; O.R. Vol. 1, pp. 561–564.

the refugees. Incredibly, Sibley was able to locally charter two small schooners, the *Horace* and the *Urbana*. When they were boarded and ready to sail on the 23rd, the weather turned sour, with high winds. The master of one of the overloaded vessels refused to make sail. They sat out the wind through the 24th and on the morning of the 25th were discovered and taken prisoner off the Port of Saluria by Van Dorn's forces.

They were paroled, and by the 28th, the brig *Mystic*, previously chartered but located at Lavaca, was brought up and the command divided among the three ships. The two schooners cleared Matagorda Bay on April 30th, arriving in New York on May 31st. The *Mystic* being of deeper draft, could not cross the bar until May 3rd, arriving at New York on June 1st.

Having failed to recruit any substantial numbers of the U.S. Army, and with the added blow of Lincoln's declaration of a blockade of the Southern coast, which was announced on April 9th, the Confederate attitude had hardened even further. The change was evident on May 9th when the last column of U.S. troops, the six companies of the 8th Infantry from New Mexico, were apprehended at a place called Adams Hill near San Lucas Springs. The column of 10 officers and 337 men were intercepted by a force of some 1,400 Texans under the command of Earl Van Dorn.[124] The column was surrendered by their commander, Lt. Col. Isaac V. D. Reeve and allowed to march unescorted to San Antonio, where they were disarmed. The officers were promised parole, but the whole group was initially placed in confinement.[125] In early June, the enlisted men were separated from their officers and removed to a camp near Salado Creek, outside of San Antonio.[126] The officers were held for a time at San Antonio and some released on a parole that would allow them to travel anywhere in the Confederate states but not back to the United States. Others were retained as prisoners.[127] A few traveled to Richmond, the machinery of the Confederate government having been transferred there from Montgomery, Alabama, in May.

To be released from the conditions of the parole, you had to wait to be *exchanged*. An agreement on the rules and conditions of exchange was not signed until July 22nd, 1862. It was between Maj. Gen. John A. Dix of the U.S. Army and Maj. Gen. D. H. Hill of the Confederate army and became known as the Dix-Hill Cartel. On January 24th, 1862, the Confederate adjutant general's office ordered all the officers that had been taken prisoner in Texas to be sent to Richmond for exchange. Thus, the exchanges began before the signing of the Dix-Hill agreement. For example, Lt. Zenas Bliss of the 8th Infantry was scheduled to be exchanged for Confederate Captain Tansill, held prisoner at Fort Warren, Boston Harbor. The

---

124. O.R. Vol. 1, p. 571. Van Dorn's and other reports give 2,200 as the size of his force.
125. O.R. Vol. 1, p. 571; Report of Reeve.
126. O.R. Ser. II Vol. 1, p. 69.
127. O.R. Ser. II, Vol. 1, pp. 60, 62.

approval[128] was issued on January 10th, 1862, by Col. Justin Dimick, commander at Boston, but the paperwork moved slowly, and Bliss was not freed from jail in Richmond until April 5th, 1862.[129]

Lt. Edward L. Hartz, with Reeve's command, was listed as released on August 27th and Colonel Reeve on August 20th.[130] A partial list of the officers released was published as general orders no. 118, War Department, adjutant general's Office, Washington DC, on August 27th, 1862.[131]

The enlisted men were moved to Camp Verde[132] and then ordered separated[133] "at different posts" of the Confederate Military Department of Texas. They experienced a total of 20 months of confinement before they were ordered out of Texas[134] to be exchanged at Vicksburg, Mississippi, on December 11th, 1862, even though an exchange had been agreed to the previous October. On March 27th, 1863, 372 were listed as arrived in New Orleans.[135]

As to the success or failure of Confederate attempts to recruit U.S. troops, some quotes are of interest:

1. From the report of Maj. C. C. Sibley, 3rd Infantry, of the surrender of his command at Saluria, Texas, on April 25th, 1861[136]:

    It affords me pleasure, great pleasure, to state the officers and men of my command have shown the most unwavering loyalty to the Government, the men with two exceptions, having taken the oath necessary for their return to the United States . . .

2. Letter from prisoner R. T. Frank[137] from San Antonio, dated August 6, 1861, to a Maj. J. T. Sprague in Albany, New York:

    The men have been removed from our control are in a camp a few miles from town: but few have left, only four out of E Company . . .

3. Letter from Maj. Sacfield Maclin, C.S. Army, acting chief quartermaster, Department of Texas,[138] to his office in Galveston, dated November 16th, 1861 (regarding the prisoners at Camp Verde):

---

128. O.R. Ser. II, Vol. 1, p. 72.
129. Powell, W. H., pp. 67, 491.
130. Cullum, Vol. I, p. 62, no. 830; Reeve, Cullum, Vol. II, p. 628, no. 1700 Hartz.
131. O.R. Ser. II, Vol. 4, p. 437.
132. O.R. Ser. II, Vol. 1, p. 80.
133. O.R. Ser. II, Vol. 1, p. 89.
134. O.R. Ser. II, Vol. 5, p. 783.
135. O.R. Ser. II, Vol. 5, p. 397; Schwartz, S., p. 208
136. O.R. Vol. 1, p.562.
137. O.R. Ser. II, Vol. 1, p. 92.
138. O.R. Ser. II, Vol. 1, p. 93.

They have been solicited frequently to enter our service and have declined. They have manifested much bitterness against our cause.

4. Letter to Gen. Lorenzo Thomas, adjutant general, U.S. Army, from Charles Anderson, Dayton, Ohio, dated February 7, 1862,[139] regarding the prisoners at Camp Verde:

> At this camp, as in town, every kind of exertion was used to get these men to enlist, and with little effect . . .

---

139. O.R. Ser. II, Vol. 1, p. 80.

Chapter 3

Garrisoning the Florida Forts; Fort Taylor;
Fort Jefferson; Record 6/61;
The Fort Pickens "Truce"; Secret Expeditions;
The Anaconda Plan; Secret Board of Officers; Pickens Armament Complete;
Battery L to Pickens; Record 8/61; Events Elsewhere; The "Truce" Ends;
Record 10/61; Sickness; Troops to Ship Island

Garrisoning the Florida Forts

The events of December – the secession of South Carolina and the cabinet shakeup, elevating Holt and Black and adding Stanton, all decisive men and against secession – finally helped President Buchanan to decide that it was his constitutional duty to protect Federal property. His confusion over his power to deal with secession remained, but at least that might be dealt with as a separate issue. It was already very late in the game; on January 4th, Georgia, and on January 5th, Alabama, had begun seizures, as was noted in chapter 2, and it was evident that soon the rebellious states would move to control any remaining Federal property.

    A decision was made to occupy three strategic Florida coastal forts long abandoned, or nearly so:[140] Taylor at Key West, Jefferson at Dry Tortugas, and Pickens at Pensacola. The orders were issued on January 3rd and 4th. The occupation of Jefferson went as planned. The occupation of Taylor did not go as planned, but went smoothly nevertheless, due to the initiative of the officer involved. The occupation of Pickens became a long and complicated drama that would hatch treasonous intrigue on the part of Southern members of Congress, result in a falsely authorized secret naval expedition, cause the stonewalling of the facts before Congress by the Lincoln administration, and generally try the patience and fortitude of everyone. It would initially run parallel to events that led to the fall of Fort Sumter, but its story would not end until the spring of 1862.

---

140. Fort McCree, on Perdido Key, opposite Pickens, was occupied by a lone ordnance sergeant. Haskins, W. L., p. 487.

Fort Taylor

The occupation of Fort Taylor is outlined first because it was accomplished first and its existence in the Union fold allowed it to be used as a key base of supply and support for the subsequent activity at Jefferson and Pickens. Fort Taylor was in the best condition of the three. In a report[141] to the secretary of war dated January 18th, 1861, Colonel of Engineers Joseph G. Totten described it: "Is prepared for its casemate batteries, two tiers; guns enough already in place for efficient action in all directions; in the absence of the projected cover face, not prepared to resist siege by land." In fact, there were fifty 8-inch Columbiads, ten 24-inch flanking howitzers with caissons and four 12-pounder field howitzers, 4,350 projectiles, and 34,459 pounds of powder.[142] There was a deficiency in small arms, however.[143]

Capt. John M. Brannan, commanding Company B of the 1st U.S. Artillery at Key West, had heard of "the recent seizure by unauthorized persons of several forts and arsenals in the Southern States"[144] and in the absence of any answer to a letter he wrote to the adjutant general on December 11th, 1860, asking what action he should take, he acted on his own initiative. In a report dated January 14th, he notes that he has moved his "scanty" force of 44 men from the Key West barracks, located on the northeast side of the island, to the fort, a distance of about two miles. He notes that mail service from the north has ceased and recommends that all mail be sent via Havana through the U.S. consulate.

On January 31st, he blandly acknowledges the receipt, on the 29th, of General Scott's orders of January 4th, which he "had anticipated some time ago."[145]

Brannan's small force was not threatened by the adjacent community. No assemblage of Florida state troops had taken place (which, as we shall see, happened at Pensacola), and Brannan regarded it as his duty to suppress any secessionist activity in the town and keep the pro-Union people protected. He was aided in this by the fact that Key West was relatively small, consisting of fewer than 2,500 people,[146] and was isolated from the Florida mainland. In addition, the people were a diverse group of traders and merchants, were divided on the issue of secession, and were primarily interested more in their business fortunes than outside politics. This same selfish interest will be seen later at New Orleans, a hint that, given a choice without the pressure of their radical peers, many in the wider south – those who owned no slaves and the poorer country folk, who constituted

---

141. O.R. Ser. III, Vol. 1, p. 50.
142. O.R. Vol. 1, pp. 349, 350.
143. O.R. Vol. 1, p. 344.
144. O.R. Vol. 1, p. 342.
145. O.R. Vol. 1, p. 344.
146. Data from August, 1860 U.S. census and *Population of States and Counties . . . 1790 to 1990*, compiled by R.L. Forstall, Dept of Commerce, 1996. There were then 2,913 people, including 431 slaves, in Monroe County, which extended all the way to Fort Myers.

the great majority of the people – would not have approved of secession.[147]

Brannan was concerned about a larger force landing north of the city and advancing on the vulnerable land approach to the fort, but he noted that he was supplemented by some 70 workers, including some who had been employed by the Engineer Department's Captain Hunt. They were willing to "take the fate of it" and assist in the defense. Brannan advised that if his company was "raised to a hundred" and that if a sloop-of-war were stationed there, "there would be no apprehension of an attack at present."

Regarding strengthening his command, he wrote on March 8th to Maj. F. J. Porter, the assistant adjutant general,[148] with the suggestion that Porter leave two companies of infantry coming from the Texas surrender[149] to occupy the barracks and thus protect the upper part of the key, out of the range of the guns of the fort. Porter subsequently saw to it that this was done and companies A and H of the 1st Infantry arrived on April 4th.[150]

On March 13th, Brannan reported to Washington[151] that though the flag of the Confederacy was defiantly flying above some Key West establishments, he was on good terms with the "best portion of the citizens, and all hope there will be no collision."

After delivering batteries L and M to Fort Jefferson on March 24th, the transport steamer *Rusk* dropped off French's command, companies F and K of the 1st Artillery, at Key West the next day. Being the senior officer present, he took command. On the 27th,[152] French had an occasion to write a note to the captain of the steamer *Crusader*, standing in the harbor, which gives us his summary of the conditions at Fort Taylor: ". . . this fort is fully garrisoned with veteran soldiers, and I believe it is entirely within my power to control this island and to prevent a lodgment thereon by any hostile force . . ." He had Brannan's original force of about 116 men, and to that he had brought about 150. Plaudits to French for boldness; the fort was originally designed for a force of 1,000.[153] He may have been anticipating the arrival of the infantry companies from Texas, which would have brought his total manpower to something less than 500.

Congratulations to Captain Brannan for planning and initiative. He would

---

147. *Grant, Memoirs*, Vol. I, p. 223. Nicolay & Hay, Vol. II, p. 309: Letter of the governor of Louisiana, Thomas O. Moore, to the governor of South Carolina, William H. Gist, 26th October 26th, 1860: "I shall not advise the secession of my State, and I will add that I do not believe that the people of Louisiana will ultimately decide in favor of that course."
148. Sent in the steamer *Daniel Webster* to evacuate troops from Texas (chapter 2).
149. O.R. Vol. 52, Pt. 1, p. 127.
150. O.R. Ser. III, Vol. 1, p. 25. Today, only the hallowed ground of the barracks cemetery remains, near Peary Court, on White Street.
151. O.R. Vol. 1, p. 360.
152. O.R. Vol. 1, p. 364.
153. O.R. Ser. III, Vol. 1, p. 48.

go on to become a brigadier general and head of the Department of the South.

Fort Jefferson[154]

To occupy the then-unmanned Fort Jefferson became the object of Maj. Lewis G. Arnold, commander of Company C of the 2nd Artillery, stationed at Fort Independence, Boston Harbor.[155] Acknowledging the receipt of his telegraphed orders, he sailed on January 10th on the steamer *Joseph Whitney* and arrived at Fort Jefferson on the 18th.[156]

Jefferson is located sixty-eight miles west of Key West, on Garden Key in the Dry Tortugas, one of a group of seven (then-named) low-lying sand and brush-covered coral islands, which mark the end of the Florida reef. Discovered by Ponce de Leon in 1513, he named them for the abundant green and loggerhead turtles in the area. "Dry" was later added by mariners to warn that there was no supply of fresh water. Soon after the acquisition of Florida in 1821, the construction of a lighthouse was begun as an aid to the increased shipping between the Gulf ports and the East Coast. Protecting U.S. interests in the Gulf grew in priority during the Mexican War; and after the acquisition of Texas, construction of Jefferson, the "Gibraltar of America," began in 1846. After gold was discovered in California, the location of the fort served to protect the route to the Pacific.

Planned for a garrison of 1,500,[157] the huge brick structure would cover most of Garden Key. It was, however, as of January of 1861, less than half completed. In fact, it would later be abandoned as obsolete before it was ever completed. Capt. Montgomery C. Meigs of the Army Corps of Engineers had been supervising its construction since November 8th, 1860. Eventually rising to a height of 50 feet, the

---

154. Photo by the author, circa 2000.
155. O.R. Ser. III, Vol. 1, p. 23.
156. O.R. Vol. 1, p. 346.
157. O.R. Ser. III, Vol. 1, p. 47.

walls, as Meigs reported, at this time averaged 35 feet and only the 35 embrasures (gun openings) of the lower tier were ready.[158] By January 15th, some 70 to 80 workers had closed 200 openings in the scarp wall and removed several construction bridges across the moat, put up a drawbridge and gate at the postern, and "brought the work into a condition which would enable a small force with guns and supplies to hold it."

There were no guns or barracks, and the water in the cisterns was brackish.[159] By the 25th of January, Meigs reported[160] that the separate cisterns on the parade would hold enough pure water for the 168 persons present, including women and children, to last for 850 days and that the other water would be good for washing and cooking. Though well meaning, Meigs did not contemplate the increased number of troops and prisoners that would eventually be sent there. Condensers for the distillation of seawater eventually had to be brought in. Unfortunately, the storage cisterns allowed this pure distilled product to become so full of "wigglers"[161] that it had to be strained before use. Though this was not technically pollution – and it was then regarded only as an inconvenience – it was far more sinister. The wigglers were mosquito larvae and the source of not only unpleasant evenings but also of malaria and yellow fever, a fact that not a soul understood.

The first action taken by Arnold was to send for some of the guns at Key West that could easily be spared, if not surplus. Six 8-inch Columbiads, with 700 shells, two 6-pounder and two 12-pounder howitzers, and 10,000 pounds of powder were quickly brought back by a barge towed by the *Joseph Whitney* in convoy with the USS *Crusader*.[162] Two steamers, the *Crusader* and the *Mohawk*, had been sent by the navy, at Meig's request, for just such duty as well as to cover the fort while it was defenseless. The guns were all mounted by the 25th.

Unlike Brannan at Fort Taylor, Arnold was totally isolated at Jefferson. There was no land approach to make the fort vulnerable from that direction. The original assumption in the design and construction of these coastal forts was that the threat was from the water. Now, at Taylor – and as we shall see, Pickens – the adversaries were on the land. However, Jefferson was functioning as intended; and with the U.S. Navy virtually ruling the sea, there was little danger of a large-enough force arriving that could be successful in an attack.

---

158. O.R. Vol. 52/I, pp. 4,5.
159. O.R. Ser. III, Vol. 1, p. 691. Dated November 30th, 1861, this report indicates that much of the work of "temporary construction of wooden buildings for storage and shops, and casemates and wooden buildings fitted for barracks and quarters" were constructed after the arrival of the troops. Appropriations for permanent barracks, etc. were requested for the next year. The report also refers to the fact that 79 of the cisterns were "tightened" because of the leakage of seawater into them.
160. O.R. Vol. 52/I, p. 125.
161. Little, H. F., p. 44.
162. O.R. Vol. 1, p. 347.

The work at hand for Arnold at Fort Jefferson was to make it habitable, as well as defensible. There were no barracks, as noted, and with the arrival of batteries L and M on March 24th, the population of the fort would double. Construction was complicated because of the difficulty of procuring and delivering lumber and building materials, all from elsewhere and, now only the North. The quick assignment of five men from Battery L to the Engineer Department (see Record 4/61, chapter 2) testifies to the fact that construction work was ongoing at the time of their arrival.

Record 6/61
30 APRIL–30 JUNE 1861, FORT JEFFERSON, FLORIDA

[No entry in the "Record of Events"]

Samuel K. Dawson   Capt. Sick
William Silvey   1st Lt. Reg. Adj. O. No. 7, Hdqtrs. 1st Arty. Ft. Dallas, Florida Aug. 13,'57 Left Co. Apr. 22,'54. S.O. No. 62 Hdqrs. N.Y. Apr. 18 '54.
Richard H. Jackson   2nd Lt. On detached service Fort Pickens, Florida S.O. No. 24 Hdqrs. Dept of Florida May 29,'61. Left Co. June 11,'61.

Strength: 83, Sick: 5.

Sick Present: Samuel K. Dawson, James Golden, Andrew Stoll, Wallace Wright

Sick Absent: Charles Riley Sick at Ft. McIntosh, Tex. Absent from Company since Feb. 25th 1861

Temp. Attached: M.M. Blunt 1st Lt. June 28th S.O. No. 32 Hdqtrs Fort Jef. Tortugas

Resigned: James W. Robinson 1st Lt. May 15, 1861, as per notice from A.G.O. Washington, June 13, 1861.

On May 29th, 1st Lt. Richard H. Jackson, in command of Battery L at Fort Jefferson, was ordered to be transferred to Fort Pickens. This left the company with no one in command from June 11th, when Jackson left. Capt. Samuel Dawson was sick, and William Silvey, long since assigned as the regimental adjutant of the 1st Artillery, had not been with the company since 1854, and 1st Lt. James W. Robinson,[163] 13th in his class at West Point in 1852 and the next in line for command, had earlier written to the adjutant general's office resigning his commission. His original intention was to join the Confederate service in his native state of Virginia. Though he had changed his mind, probably after the protestations of his Massachusetts-born wife, his resignation was accepted. Hoping to convince the secretary of war that he was loyal and that he wished to continue in the regular army, he had remained at Fort Jefferson. He never was reinstated. He briefly stayed on, however, as a sutler. Finally, on June 28th, Lt. Mathew M. Blunt, an infantry officer and member of Arnold's staff, was attached to command the company.

---

163. Cullum, Vol. I, no. 1548.

Fort Pickens

This huge brick structure was built on the same concept as Fort Jefferson, though situated on the dry sands of Santa Rosa Island, opposite Pensacola. The ravages of time have left the structure in a much poorer condition than Jefferson, and several historic views, keyed to the plan view in figure 1[164], offer the reader a feel for the original structure. In 1861, a person standing at "A" would have seen the view in figure 2, the Sally Port, which faces north. To the right, the northeast bastion, with the flag on it ("E" in the diagram) is no longer standing, destroyed in an accidental explosion of ammunition stored there in 1899. The sloped embankment to the left is a portion of the glacis, the wide shaded area to the right in figure 1, which faces east, toward the only land accessible to attackers. The water in figure 2 is Pensacola Bay, then much closer to the fort, compare with the view in figure 4.

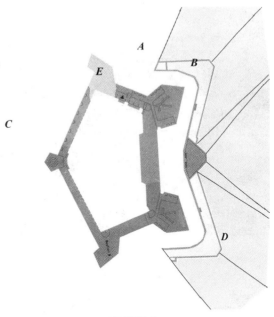

FIGURE 1

FIGURE 2

A person standing at "B" would see the view in figure 3, which is a photo taken in 2010. From left to right, the top of the glacis, the covered way, the counterscarp, and ditch are seen, all of which are still intact today.

---

164. Figure 1, *Atlas*, plate 5, sketch 6, altered by the author; figure 2, *Harper's Weekly*, March 9th, 1861, p. 156.

FIGURE 3

The west walls are shown in figure 4, which would be as viewed from "C." In 1861, the gun ports were seven feet above the ground, but now, sand has drifted in to a depth of some four feet or more. In 1916, extensive modifications were made to the southwest curtain walls at the right. The parapet was removed to clear the field of fire for heavy coastal guns installed on the parade ground in anticipation of World War I.

FIGURE 4

Finally, figure 5 is an old view[165] from position "D," which today is disfigured by an access road. Note that the parapets are at full original height. Perhaps the flagstaff was relocated at some time between when this view (March 1861) and when the Sally Port view was drawn, but the artist may have felt compelled to show that "Old Glory" still flew over Fort Pickens at this tense time. The flag of

---

165. *Harper's Weekly*, April 6th, 1861, p. 213.

a new nation now flew on the opposite shore, and that nation now demanded the surrender of its sovereign territory, the two coastal forts that still remained in Union hands, Florida's Pickens and South Carolina's Sumter. (Claims against Fort Monroe were not made at this time, as Virginia did not secede until April.)

FIGURE 5

Pensacola was the site of three unoccupied forts: Pickens, McCree, and Barrancas. Pickens, begun in 1829 and completed in 1834, was the largest and most important. Located on the outer harbor, it could command the entrance to the harbor and most of the inner harbor, regardless of the lesser two, Barrancas and McCree. Pensacola was also the site of a large naval base, at Warrington, on the mainland of the inner harbor, east of Barrancas (figure 6).[166]

In January of 1861, this entire complex was manned by only one army artillery company (in Barrancas Barracks and understrength at 48 officers and men) and 4 officers, 70 ordinary seamen, and 48 marines in the navy yard at Warrington.[167]

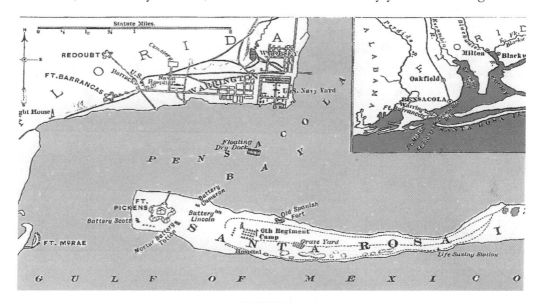

FIGURE 6

---

166. Morris, G., p. 70, revised. The sand batteries and encampments shown were constructed later.
167. Scharf, T., p. 601; O.R. Vol. 1, p. 341; monthly return, 1st Regiment of Artillery, February 1861.

Scott's orders from Washington warning of the danger of seizure, mentioned in chapter 2, went out to Pensacola in two sets on January 3rd.[168] One was sent by special messenger and the other by telegraph, in cipher. The telegraphic message was "stopped" at Montgomery, Alabama, by the Confederates.[169] As a consequence, the hand-carried orders were not received by 1st Lt. Adam J. Slemmer, in command of Company G of the 1st U.S. Artillery, until January 9th. Other orders that had been sent out on January 4th were, as noted, to Maj. Zealous B. Tower, of the Corps of Engineers,[170] to proceed to "Barrancas and assume the command of the troops and forts in and about Pensacola Harbor."

Fortunately, Slemmer, like Brannan at Key West, took the initiative. He had sensed the danger after receiving word of the seizure of Fort Morgan at nearby Mobile on January 5th. On January 7th, he contacted the commander of the navy yard, Cdre. James Armstrong. Like Slemmer, Armstrong had not received orders of any kind. He declined to cooperate with Slemmer, who planned to move stores from the mainland, those at forts Mcree and Barrancas, across the harbor to Fort Pickens. Slemmer correctly viewed the mainland installations to be vulnerable and concluded that the best defense of the area, with his tiny command of 46 men, could only be made from Fort Pickens.

In view of the commodore's decision not to lend assistance, i.e., watercraft to transport materiel across the harbor, on the 8th, Slemmer began to do what could be done to better secure Fort Barrancas. Powder was moved to the inner magazines, the drawbridge was raised, and a guard was detailed. True to Slemmer's fears, a group of some 20 men approached the fort that night with the evident intention of taking possession. The alarm was given; and in the words of Slemmer's second in command, Lt. J. H. Gilman: "The party was fired upon by the guard and ran in the direction of Warrington . . . This, I believe, was the first gun in the war fired on our side."[171]

On the morning of the 9th, the orders from army headquarters arrived. Armstrong also received orders to cooperate on that date, and a plan was quickly developed. The joint plan was that the navy was to furnish a small steamer, the *Wyandotte*, and "all the men he [the commodore] could possibly spare" to help with the dual task of mounting guns within Pickens and removing supplies from Barrancas Barracks and Fort Barrancas.[172] A second ship, the *Supply*, would carry provisions to Pickens and remain anchored nearby so that the provisions could be drawn from as required. The *Wyandotte* would also anchor off the fort to provide

---

168. O.R. Vol. 1, p. 334.
169. O.R. Vol. 52/II, p. 27.
170. O.R. Vol. 1, p. 350.
171. O.R. Vol. 1, p. 334. Slemmer's report, dated February 5th, makes no mention of any gunplay. Gilman, J. H., p. 27, mentions the shooting. He repeats this in Haskin, W. L., p. 488.
172. O.R. Vol. 1, p. 399: 75-man crew.

fire coverage of the land approach. The plan agreed to had it that these two craft would be available by 1:00 p.m. that same day.

By the appointed time there was no sign of the navy. Slemmer, being busy at Pickens, sent Lieutenant Gilman to inquire at the navy yard. The commodore had procrastinated. He now said that he could not support the plan as intended but could only transport the men and supplies. The ships could not remain, as they had other urgent duties. Lieutenant Gilman reported this news to Slemmer, whereupon the two went to the navy yard. Slemmer describes his "immediate" meeting with the commodore:[173] "I stated that I had been deceived by him; that he had promised me men and [the] cooperation of the two vessels of war, besides the mere fact of giving us provisions and taking us over . . ." Slemmer also noted that he had already lost the whole day of the 8th, trying to prepare Fort Barrancas, in light of the commodore's initial refusal of cooperation. He noted that without additional men and the support of the ships, the defense of Fort Pickens would be impossible and that he would never have considered the plan had the commodore not earlier agreed to help. "I should never dream of defending so large a work, calculated for upwards of 1,200 men . . ."

Such a discussion between a 28-year-old lieutenant and a 66-year-old commodore may be not have been unprecedented, but this challenge took courage on Slemmer's part. After the dust had settled, the plan as originally conceived was agreed to be carried out. As if to emphasize his determination, the commodore called into the meeting his subordinates, Cdr. Ebenezer Farrand, Lt. Francis B. Renshaw, and Lt. Cdr. O. H. Berryman of the *Wyandotte*. Before Slemmer, Gilman, and the group, as witnesses, he reiterated the plans. Berryman would now be ready by 5:00 p.m.

Slemmer and his men immediately began preparing for the move by removing essential items from Fort Barrancas and the barracks and placing them on the dock. "Night came, and yet no means of assistance. The company labored until 12 m., when a heavy fog coming in rendered it highly improbable that the steamer would come that night."

At 8:00 a.m. on the 10th, the day that Florida seceded from the Union, the *Wyandotte* and a flatboat appeared, and the goods on the wharf were loaded. Crossing the harbor, they were unloaded at Pickens by 10:00. "On the way over Captain Berryman turned over to me *thirty ordinary seamen*[174] entirely untrained, insubordinate, and of little use . . . without arms or equipments of any kind." Slemmer continues: "We labored all day until night carrying up the stores to the fort, and arranging for its defense . . . The provisions required were, by agreement with the Commodore, to be drawn from the 'Supply' as they were wanted, instead of sending them from the yard; yet, almost the instant we landed the master of

---

173. O.R. Vol. 1, p. 335.
174. These italics appear in the O.R.

the yard came with some small stores in a barge, bringing with him an order from Commodore Armstrong to land the stores immediately. . . . As I was not ready to receive the stores the Supply remained at her anchor that night."

On the morning of the 11th, Captain Walke of the *Supply* reported to Slemmer that he had received another order from the commodore to deliver the stores and return to the navy yard. Berryman reported that he had been ordered to leave for a trip to Cuba. These events resulted in an exchange of notes between the parties with Armstrong conceding that the *Wyandotte* could remain but that the *Supply* must proceed to Vera Cruz (before, the excuse was Cuba; now it was Vera Cruz?) to deliver coal and stores to the home squadron stationed there as had been directed in orders "I have received from the Navy Department . . ."

Fort McCree[175] was abandoned on the 11th and Lt. Henry Erben of the *Supply*[176] destroyed about 23,000 pounds of powder, along with fuses and shot, by rolling it into the sea. Though Erben offered to destroy the navy magazine at Warrington, Commodore Armstrong never granted permission.[177] The guns at Fort Barrancas had been spiked (disabled by driving a rat-tailed file or suitable metal shard into the barrel touchhole) on the 10th.

On the morning of the 12th, word was received that the navy yard was besieged by some 500 Florida and Alabama troops under the Command of Maj. William H. Chase, a Massachusetts native, formerly of the U.S. Army Corps of Engineers and, incredibly, the person who had supervised the construction of the defenses of Pensacola.[178] Soon after 11:00, the navy yard was surrendered to Col. Tennant Lomax and others from Alabama. Armstrong's former colleagues Farrand and Renshaw were in the Lomax party. That Farrand was part of a "fifth column" inside the command structure and the source of the confusion and misunderstandings of the previous several days is clear. Farrand was operating with the rebel command a few days later,[179] and he is referred to as "late of the U.S. Navy" in Slemmer's official report. Renshaw was taken prisoner, but a few days later resigned from the U.S. Navy, as he describes in a letter to the *New York Herald*.[180] It was clear that Armstrong had been betrayed.

The U.S. flag was soon seen to be lowered and replaced by "a flag of thirteen alternate stripes of red and white, and a blue field with a large white star . . ."[181]

---

175. Scharf, T., p. 599.
176. O.R. Vol. 1, p. 341; War of the Rebellion: Official Records of the Union and Confederate Navies, henceforth referred to as "ORN", Ser. I, Vol. 4, pp. 39, 40; Haskin, p. 490.
177. ORN Ser. I, Vol. 4, p. 39.
178. Scharf, T., p. 601; Cullum, Vol. I, Chase no. 150; ORN Ser. I, Vol. 4, pp. 34–38.
179. O.R. Vol. 1, pp. 335–337; ORN Ser. I, Vol. 4, p. 46. Farrand's resignation was received by letter to the Navy Department on January 21st, and was accepted on that date; likewise, Renshaw's was received and accepted on the 22nd.
180. Scharf, T., p. 603; ORN Ser. I, Vol. 4, pp. 60, 61.
181. Scharf, T., p. 602.

Late the same day, a Confederate delegation appeared at the Fort Pickens gate and demanded its surrender. Slemmer refused, and the group "withdrew." An attack was anticipated; and the meager group of 82 officers and men (Slemmer's company and the 31 sailors, plus 2 ordnance sergeants and 1 hospital steward)[182] was distributed around the fort to stand at their guns, ready to fire, all through the long rainy night. Dawn of the 13th came with no attack, but no letup in the frantic efforts to make the fort defensible. There were no embrasure shutters (doors on the gun ports) in the fort. The day prior, Slemmer had directed that any that could be used were to be taken from Fort McRee and that any additional needed be constructed. If the ports were not covered, they would be like open doors where attackers could easily sneak into the fort.

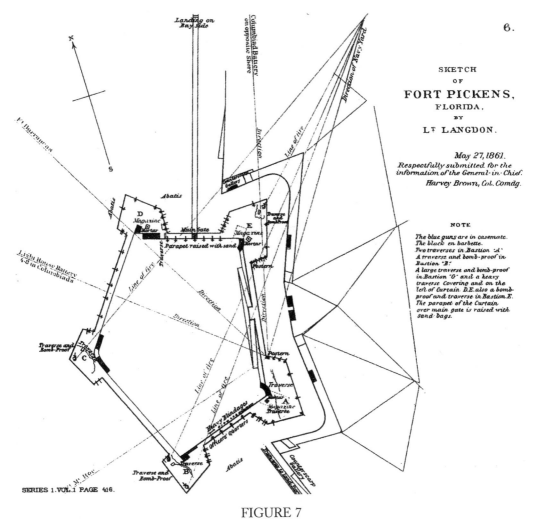

FIGURE 7

---

182. O.R. Vol. 1, p. 341. Note discrepancy: 31 sailors versus 30 in earlier statement.

Sentinels had been placed outside of the fort beyond the glacis (the sloping earthen bank on the land approach, or eastern side of the fort (refer to figure 1) to warn of an attack. The men stood at their guns for a second rainy night. The alert condition paid off. On the night of the 13th, a group of 10 men were discovered, evidently reconnoitering. The strangers fired a shot. The duty sergeant returned the fire, which caused the group to flee. Fort Pickens, January 13th, 1861, the second incident of gunfire in the Civil War?[183]

Continued rain on the 14th evidently dampened activity by the Florida rebels. On the 15th, Colonel Chase, accompanied by Farrand, visited the fort. A letter was handed to Slemmer, which rather begged him to surrender. Slemmer bought some time by indicating that he wished to consult with the captains of the *Wyandotte* and *Supply*, now anchored off the navy yard under a white flag. They had been occupied with trying to rescue the remaining loyal personnel from the base. On the 14th, the *Supply* had taken on board 9 hospital patients, 34 marines, 27 ordinary seamen, and those 11 workers from the navy yard who wished to go. All told, there were 99. On the 15th, the women and children from the fort, including Mrs. Slemmer and Mrs. Gilman, 14 in all, were taken on board.[184] Captain Walke was given parole with the stipulation that all of whom that were permitted to leave would be delivered north of the Mason-Dixon line.[185]

On the 16th the two ships got underway but were signaled by Slemmer, whereupon the anticipated consultation took place, not to mention some tearful good-byes to the women and children. This resulted in the decision of Captain Berryman to remain and support Slemmer and that they send a negative response to Chase's surrender plea of the previous day. Thus, the *Wyandotte* cleared the harbor but anchored nearby.

Walke proceeded to New York with the *Supply*, safely arriving there on February 4th.

Commodore Armstrong, traveling by rail, arrived at Washington on January 25th and requested a court of inquiry, which he apparently felt would exonerate him for the surrender. The court was convened on Friday, February 8th, 1861.[186] In testimony by Josiah Watson (the captain of the marines), Gilman, and others, it became clear that no preparations for defense were made and that no plan to evacuate the navy yard and its stores and join Slemmer in Fort Pickens was contemplated. It also became clear that Farrand was treasonous and insubordinate, including many of the workers of Southern origin. The commodore failed to recognize and control the situation. On February 20th, 1861, the court convened to announce its decision.

---

183. Haskin, W. L., p. 488.
184. ORN Ser. I, Vol. 4, pp. 62, 63, 210.
185. The Southern state line of Pennsylvania, regarded as the demarcation between the North and the South.
186. ORN Ser. I, Vol. 4, pp. 18–55.

The commodore was found "culpable in not taking any precautionary measures for the defense of his post" and "should have induced a resistance" or else "have carried his men . . . to Fort Pickens, and what he could not remove have destroyed." For neglect of duty, disobedience of orders, and conduct unbecoming an officer, he was sentenced to be suspended from the navy for five years, half of that time without pay, and to be reprimanded by the secretary of the navy in general orders.

Colonel Chase, the West Pointer from Massachusetts now in command of the Florida forces, made another request for surrender on January 18th. The answer from Slemmer was the same as before; after consulting with Berryman, they would "hold our position until such a force is brought against us as to render it impossible to defend it . . ."[187] The situation had now developed into a standoff. Chase agreed, on January 26th, to allow the mail that had accumulated at the Warrington Post Office since January 9th, to be delivered. He promised that it would not be interrupted in the future. He also offered to supply fresh provisions on a daily basis and allowed the Company G laundresses to be released. They were transferred to the fort on the 28th.[188]

The Fort Pickens "Truce"

What had happened?

The Confederate government had not yet been formed, and would not be, until after February 4th, 1861, when the Weed Convention met at Montgomery, Alabama, for that purpose. It would be February 12th before the Confederate congress took full official control of war policies, including those regarding the seizure of U.S. government property.[189] Jefferson Davis would be inaugurated president of the Confederate States of America on the 18th.

The diverse seizure efforts that the individual states had earlier taken were so successful that it appeared that anything could be accomplished by brashness with little fear of bloodshed. The passivity of President Buchanan finally had reached a limit when he had allowed plans to go forward for sending reinforcements to Fort Sumter (yet we remember that he had overruled Scott and Holt who wanted a warship to accompany the mission). After the *Star of the West* was fired on as it entered Charleston Harbor on January 9th, it became clear how easily and quickly blood could be shed. It also became clear how ill prepared the seceded states were without a central government and the show of unity and strength that might render their cause successful without a fight. If they had harbored the view that they just might be able to secede and form the Confederacy without a fight, that assumption was now seen to be in peril. Fort Sumter was resisting, as was Fort Pickens. The

---

187. O.R. Vol. 1, p. 338.
188. O.R. Vol. 1, p. 340; Haskin, W. L., p. 500.
189. O.R. Vol. 1, Resolution no. 5, p. 254.

window of opportunity to seize an abandoned Fort Pickens had passed, and an artillery lieutenant had closed it.

Thus, a strategy was formulated by several Southern senators still in Washington to avoid any act on the part of the South that could result in open conflict until a Confederate government could be up and running. In addition, they must remain in Washington as long as possible to blunt the efforts of those in congress or the Buchanan administration to strengthen the military. The U.S. Senator from Florida, David L. Yulee, had urged, on January 5th, to "lose no time about the navy-yard and forts at Pensacola,"[190] but he would now, on the 7th, report of consultations with his colleagues in the Senate that recommended a more calculated approach.

> The idea of the meeting was that the States should go out at once and provide for an early organization of a Confederate Government, not later than 15th February. This time is allowed to enable Louisiana and Texas to participate. It seemed to be the opinion that if we left here, force, loan, and volunteer bills might be passed which would put Mr. Lincoln in immediate condition for hostilities; whereas by remaining in our places until the 4th of March it is thought we can keep the hands of Mr. Buchanan tied and disable the Republicans from effecting any legislation which will strengthen the hands of the incoming administration.[191]

To allow this strategy to develop, senators Stephen R. Mallory of (Pensacola) Florida; John Slidell, and Judah P. Benjamin of Louisiana; Alfred Iverson of Georgia; Clement C. Clay Jr. and Benjamin Fitzpatrick of Alabama; John Hemphill and Louis T. Wigfall of Texas; and Jefferson Davis of Mississippi; composed and sent the following to Governor Perry of Florida:

> Washington, *January 18, 1861*
> We think no assault should be made. The possession of the fort is not worth one drop of blood to us. Measures pending unite us in this opinion. Bloodshed may be fatal to our cause.
> We sent this to Chase today.[192]
> Another dispatch was sent the next day to Governor Moore of Alabama:
> Telegraph not to attack Fort Pickens. Florida Senators and friends think it unwise.
>
> *C.C. Clay, Jr.*
> *Ben. Fitzpatrick*

On January 20th, in another message to Governor Perry, it was explained that the first priority was to get the Confederate government in operation. It concluded with:

---

190. O.R. Vol. 1, p. 442.
191. O.R. Vol. 1, p. 443.
192. O.R. Vol. 1, p. 445 includes the two letters.

The same advice has been given to Charleston, and will no doubt be adopted there.

S.R. Mallory[193]
D.L. Yulee

On the 21st, the senators from Florida, Mississippi, and Alabama resigned from the Senate, with Yulee remaining in Washington. Sometime before they left, Mallory, Fitzpatrick, and Slidell had a personal interview with the President and the then Secretary of the Navy Isaac Toucey, who appears as equally diffident as Buchanan and, as his successor Gideon Welles has written, treasonous.[194] In the interview, the Southern senators were "assured by them that no attack would be made upon Fort Sumter and Fort Pickens, or any excuse given for the shedding of blood, during the present administration, and that they deemed it of great importance that no attack should be made by South Carolina upon Fort Sumter, or by the troops of the seceding states upon Fort Pickens, in the present aspect of affairs . . . It was further explained to Mr. Mallory that a special messenger had been sent by the Secretary of the Navy to the officer in command at Fort Pickens, directing that officer to prevent the ships which had been ordered to Pensacola from entering the bay."

The agreement was imperiled by word that the USS *Brooklyn* had left Fort Monroe on January 24th with "Two companies on board."[195] The telegram, sent by Senator Yulee to Mallory and others at Pensacola, was incorrect in that there was only one company, Capt. Israel Vodges' Company A, 1st Artillery, who on the 21st had been ordered to "re-enforce" Fort Pickens.[196] The news reached Senator Mallory at his residence at Pensacola on the 28th, and he responded with a message to be delivered to President Buchanan by John Slidell: "We hear that the Brooklyn is coming with re-enforcements for Fort Pickens. No attack is contemplated, but, on the contrary, we desire to keep the peace, and if the present status be preserved we will guarantee that no attack will be made upon it, but if re-enforcements be attempted, resistance and a bloody conflict seem inevitable. . . . Impress this upon the President, and urge that the inevitable consequence of re-enforcement under the present circumstances is instant war . . . If the President wants an assurance of

---

193. Mallory had anticipated these letters in telegrams dated the 16th, which he independently sent out to Governor Perry and Major Chase. O.R. Vol. 52/II, p. 9. Charleston, remember, was the site of Fort Sumter.
194. O.R. Vol. 1, pp. 445, 446: Report of Governor Moore of Alabama to Wm. Brooks, President of the State Convention; Welles, Vol. I, pp. 29, 355.
195. O.R. Vol. 52/II, p. 15.
196. O.R. Vol. 1, p. 352. Captain Vodges would be in command, though Major Tower ranked. Standard procedure was to have an engineer officer present to direct how the defensive works of the fort were to be prepared. Seldom was the engineer the ranking officer, thus more confusion for an already complicated situation.

all I say from Colonel Chase, commanding the forces, I will transmit it at once. I am determined to stave off war if possible. Answer promptly."[197]

On January 31st, he received the answer:

> The subject of your dispatch is before the President. Will advise you the result.
>
> D.L. Yulee[198]

The response by the President was faster than the telegram from Senator Yulee. On the 29th, orders from the Secretary of War Joseph Holt were telegraphed to Lieutenant Slemmer to remain "strictly on the defensive," with details to be sent by a special courier. A second message, signed by both the Secretary of War Holt and Navy Secretary Toucey, was directed to the captains of the ships headed for the area, James Glynn of the *Macedonian* and W. S. Walker of the *Brooklyn*, as well as Lt. Slemmer. It began: "In consequences of the assurances received from Mr. Mallory in a telegram of yesterday . . . you are instructed not to land the company [Captain Vodges'] on board the Brooklyn unless said fort shall be attacked or preparations shall be made for its attack." [199]

Thus, the "Fort Pickens Truce" began. It was also honored at Charleston's Fort Sumter, in that food, mail, and essentials were allowed to be delivered. Why not? The Confederates could monitor all of the telegraphic dispatches and hide most of their own buildup, which accelerated. We shall see that the Confederate side was woefully short of supplies, and their strategy of delay was to their own advantage, but attitudes had not changed. The new Congress of the Confederate States passed a resolution on February 15th, "that immediate steps should be taken to obtain possession of forts Sumter and Pickens . . . either by negotiations or force . . ."[200]

Captain Vodges and his company arrived off of Pensacola on February 6th, and "met a telegraphic dispatch from the Secretary of War which instructed the commander of the Brooklyn not to land my company for the present."[201] He, nevertheless, was individually landed at Pickens and "assumed command" but returned to the *Brooklyn* the same day. He reported this in a letter to the adjutant general on February 7th.

His report contains a description of the conditions within the fort as "inefficient" and notes that the artillerymen were "nearly all exhausted with fatigue" so few in numbers and having to be on the alert day and night. He describes the sailors there as being untrained and insubordinate and being of little use in an attack. Only 54 guns were mounted, leaving 57 empty embrasures, some still

---

197. O.R. Vol. 1, p. 354.
198. O.R. Vol. 52/II, p. 16.
199. O.R. Vol. 1, p. 355.
200. O.R. Vol. 1, p. 258.
201. O.R. Vol. 1, pp. 357 and 360.

uncovered, which, being only seven feet above the ground, could be easily entered by any attacker. The guns and carriages were old and nearly unserviceable. There were no bunks for the hospital or for the troops "and but little bedding for the sick." There was no medical officer or engineer officer. (Major Tower of the engineers did not arrive until March 19th, though he was assigned on January 4th.) Vodges reported that: "There are plenty of provisions for the present although I should like some dessicated vegetables and supplies for the officers." He was correct about the vegetables. Eventually, many in Company G were sent away on medical leave suffering from scurvy.

On March 1st, the Confederate government assumed control of the operations in the Charleston area by naming P. T. Beauregard to the command, and on March 7th did likewise for the Pensacola area, by assigning Braxton Bragg.[202] Bragg assumed command on the 11th and was informed on the 14th that a requisition for 5,000 troops from Alabama, Mississippi, Louisiana, Georgia, and Florida had been made by the adjutant general's office. They could be expected within ten days. On March 16th, orders were given by the Confederate war department to the Baton Rouge arsenal to supply General Bragg with an impressive list of thousands and thousands of shot, shell, and related supplies.[203] Bragg soon discovered the effects of the "truce" in that citizens of the area were selling supplies of fuel, food, and water to the Fort Pickens garrison; and on March 14th, he issued orders to put a stop to it.[204] By the end of March, Bragg had an impressive number of troops, as is indicated in his return, figure 8.[205]

Troops.	Present for duty.				Total present.	Aggregate present.
	Infantry.		Cavalry.			
	Officers.	Men.	Officers.	Men.		
General staff						17
First Regiment Alabama, twelve months' volunteers	46	762			839	885
Georgia, twelve months' volunteers	4	106			109	113
Louisiana Zouaves	5	95			97	101
Total	55	963			1,045	1,116

FIGURE 8

Bragg was questioned by the Confederate Secretary of War L. P. Walker as to whether he was prepared to land on Santa Rosa Island. He answered by telegraph that he was prepared only for defense. He exposed his weakness in a follow-up

---

202. O.R. Vol. 1, pp. 259 and 449.
203. O.R. Vol. 1, p. 450.
204. O.R. Vol. 1, p. 451.
205. O.R. Vol. 1, p. 455.

letter on April 6th: "I am[206] not prepared with my batteries for anything more than a feeble defense (see my requisition for ordnance and stores), and that conditions cannot be changed until I get supplies. The only attack which I could hope to make now would be a sudden dash, distracting the enemy by a false attack and scaling the walls in an opposite direction. The weakness of the garrison, and the ardor and *ignorance*[207] of my troops would be strong elements of success . . ."

Here is a commander with 1,100 troops, expecting 1,600 more three days later,[208] discussing a possible attack on a fort defended by 82 men. This inertia has to have an explanation. It seems that Bragg lacked confidence in the discipline of his fresh volunteers. With a shortage of good officers (the state troops having elected their own), Bragg was concerned enough to search out an old friend, a fellow plantation owner from Louisiana and a *civilian* with no military background, to organize and drill his troops. The son of former President Zachary Taylor (for whom Fort Taylor was named) and a student of the military, Richard Taylor was called.[209]

On May 6th, when Bragg again reported to Walker, he sounded confident, except for one other important detail:[210] "My plan for a lodgment on the island is arranged, and will be executed as soon as the means are available. . . . Five thousand sets of infantry accouterments are necessary for the preservation of our ammunition. It is now carried by the men in their pockets, and one day's hard service would destroy it all. A supply of musket cartridges is also a first necessity. Having had no response to my requisition of last March, I shall send an officer to see if some can be had at Baton Rouge. The present supply would last me in an engagement about thirty minutes."

There is nothing in the record to indicate that Bragg had raised any kind of strenuous objections to his lack of supplies or that he had taken any initiatives to remedy his situation for more than a month, including the obvious one he finally suggests (send an officer to Baton Rouge arsenal).

The preceding brings to mind the word *stolid* regarding Bragg. Does this characterize the qualities of a great general? Events will give us an opportunity to make a judgment. Braxton Bragg is destined to play a major role in the Confederacy, and to linger on as the man closest to Jefferson Davis to the very last.

On March 4th, President Lincoln was sworn into office. When briefed on the situation at Fort Pickens, he was apparently taken aback by the "quasi armistice," as he later referred to it in his message to Congress in July.[211] However, he was not

---

206. O.R. Vol. 1, p. 457.
207. Author's italics.
208. O.R. Vol. 1, p. 458.
209. Taylor, R., p. 15.
210. O.R. Vol. 1, p. 465.
211. O.R. Vol. 1, p. 440.

deterred, and, on March 5th, verbally directed General Scott to keep "all possible vigilance for the maintenance of all the places." On March 9th, noting that Scott had done nothing specifically about Pickens, Lincoln put his intentions in writing. By March 12th, the special messenger carrying Scott's orders to Vodges to land his company "At the first favorable moment"[212] was to have delivered it to the USS *Mohawk*, readying to make sail from the Brooklyn Navy Yard. The messenger did not arrive, and the *Mohawk* sailed, by the orders of the commandant of the yard, A. H. Foote, since its urgent destination was to Indianola to pick up some of the last of the U.S. regulars in Texas. Thus, the letter was given to Capt. Thomas Craven of the *Crusader*, which sailed on the 16th.

Vodges had become frustrated at lying offshore at anchor since February 7th and frustrated with Slemmer's reading of the original orders of January 29th, "not to land the company on board the Brooklyn unless said fort shall be attacked, or preparations shall be made for its attack."[213] This order, as previously noted, was addressed to three people: the commanders of the *Macedonian* and *Brooklyn*, Glynn and Walker, and the commander of the fort, Lieutenant Slemmer. Pointedly or not, it was not addressed to Captain Vodges. Thus, Slemmer interpreted it that it would be he alone who would decide when the fort was under attack, or threatened, and that it was he who would signal for the reinforcements to land. In messages dated March 17th and March 21st,[214] Vodges complained to Adjutant Gen. Lorenzo Thomas about the situation. After all, Vodges ranked Slemmer. Regardless of the petty squabble, the March 12th order carried on the *Crusader* would not arrive until March 31st.[215] On March 22nd, the *Brooklyn* left its station on a run for supplies, so Vodges and the "floating artillerists" of Company A were transferred to the frigate *Sabine* under the command of Capt. Henry A. Adams, the senior commander.

On March 30th, Slemmer made a routine report to the assistant adjutant general wherein he states that he estimates that nearly 1,000 men are in Bragg's forces (remarkably not exaggerated, see Bragg's strength report for March in figure 8) with 5,000 expected. He goes on to say that the Confederates have fully armed Fort Barrancas and that guns have been mounted in the navy yard. He mentions that he has protested the continuation of this work, stopped by Chase and reinitiated by Bragg. He mentions that it is important to "be informed of passing events" and that he has had no important communication since February 23rd.[216]

Finally, on March 31st, the *Brooklyn* arrived back on station, having obtained supplies and the crucial order from Scott. It seems that the *Crusader* had called at

---

212. O.R. Vol. 1, p. 360; Welles, Vol. I, p. 29; Nicolay & Hay, Vol. III, p. 393. They incorrectly identify the *Mohawk* as the carrier of the order.
213. O.R. Vol. 1, p. 355.
214. O.R. Vol. 1, pp. 360, 363.
215. ORN Ser. I, Vol. 4, pp. 90, 91, 93, 95, 100, 103, 110.
216. O.R. Vol. 1, p. 365.

Key West, had found the *Brooklyn*, and had transferred the package. Adams finally now had his chance to act. Vodges and A Company were transferred from the *Sabine* back to the *Brooklyn*.[217] Adams refused to disembark the troops, citing the old date of the order, and the "truce" as the reason. His fear of "responsibility for an act that which seems to render civil war inevitable" guided him.[218] With this, he concluded a report of his action to the new secretary of the navy, Gideon Welles, asking for instructions. Adams was so concerned that the action he had taken was questionable that he took the extraordinary step of sending off a messenger, navy lieutenant Washington Gwathmey, with Adams' written report hidden in his belt. He was ordered to travel directly by train to Washington and deliver the confidential message to Welles in person. Gwathmey left on April 1st and arrived at Washington on the 6th.

After reviewing the message with the President, Welles sent his own "special messenger"[219] to Pensacola. Navy Lt. John L. Worden left Washington by rail on the morning of April 7th and reached Pensacola by midnight, April 10th. By previous agreement with Welles, who feared Worden might be challenged and searched as he neared Pensacola, Worden committed the written word to memory and destroyed the letter as he was approaching Atlanta. He was interviewed by Bragg on the morning of the 11th and was asked if he carried dispatches. Bragg was strangely passive to Worden's reply: "not written ones."[220] After some further exchange, Bragg agreed to let Worden proceed and also agreed to allow him to return to Washington via Pensacola but warned that nothing be done in violation of "the agreement existing." Worden was conveyed out to the *Sabine* on the 12th, the delay being that the *Wyandotte* could not safely cross the bar in such rough weather as existed on the 11th. On his return trip, Worden did not stop to see Bragg, who, later the same day, was ordered to intercept him. Worden was taken prisoner.[221] He remained so until exchanged later in the year, in time to be given command of the *Monitor* and fight the famous duel with the *Merrimac*.

Vodges' Company A and 110 marines[222] of the squadron, under the command of Lt. John C. Cash, were landed at 2:00 a.m. on the 13th of April. Adams reported to Welles: "Immediately upon receipt of your order by Lieutenant Worden, on the 12th instant, I prepared to re-enforce Fort Pickens. It was successfully performed . . ."[223]

Adams' earlier action to deny the transfer of the troops was to surface in President Lincoln's July 4th message to Congress. Lincoln probably regretted having

---

217. *Remarks*, Annual Return of the First Regiment of Artillery for 1861.
218. ORN Ser. I, Vol. 4, p. 110.
219. Welles, Vol. I, pp. 29, 30, 31; ORN Ser. I, Vol. 4, p. 111.
220. O.R. Vol. 1, p. 462.
221. O.R. Vol. 1, pp. 459, 460.
222. O.R. Vol. 1, p. 395.
223. O.R. Vol. 1, p. 376.

even mentioned the Fort Pickens "quasi-armistice." Hearing of it, the Senate passed a resolution requesting information concerning the situation, and the President passed the hot potato to the secretary of the navy. Gideon Welles' answer came on July 29th.[224] "The Secretary of the Navy, to whom was referred the resolution of the Senate of the 19th instant, to communicate to the Senate (if not incompatible with the public interest) the character of the quasi armistice to which he refers . . . by reason of which the commander of the frigate Sabine refused to transfer the United States troops into Fort Pickens in obedience to his orders . . . has the honor to report that it is believed the communication of the information called for would not, at this time, comport with the public interest."

Lincoln forwarded this to the Senate on July 30th, and the next day the Senate obliged by entering into the record: "July 31st, 1861 – read, ordered to lie on the table, and be printed."

Slemmer's report[225] of activity in and around the time the troops were landed paints a completely different set of circumstances, which may have obviated the Worden mission. He states that he obtained "private information" that preparations for an attack were being made on the 10th and duly informed Adams. Part of the information Slemmer obtained was from an intercepted letter, posted at Warrington, to a non-com in Fort Pickens by the name of Broady. The envelope contained promises to pay $500 to any private and $1,000 to officers who would join in a plan to betray the fort. The letter concluded with, "I will go over to-night . . . Yours, &c., B." However, a storm prevented any boat movements that night, and Slemmer had Broady removed from his duties and sequestered on the *Sabine*.[226] On the 11th, Adams questioned Slemmer's sources of information, and he replied on the 12th that, "I have deemed my information of such importance that for the last two nights my men have been placed at the guns in readiness to repel an attack. My men and officers are much fatigued, and I deem it absolutely necessary that the fort be re-enforced immediately."

So it seems that if the urgent efforts by so many at Washington had never even been attempted, Bragg's scheme to bribe his way into Fort Pickens would probably have warned Slemmer, then Adams would have heeded Slemmer's warning of an imminent threat, and the reinforcements would have been landed anyway – and on the same date.

Secret Expeditions

It is noted that April 12th was the day that Confederate firing on Fort Sumter began. It fell on the 14th, rendering moot any plans to reinforce it. This story is interwoven

---

224. O.R. Vol. 1, p. 440.
225. O.R. Vol. 1, p. 387, 388.
226. ORN Ser. I, Vol. 4, p. 114.

so closely with the reinforcement of Fort Pickens that it must sorted out.

It soon was evident in Florida that there had been yet other clandestine activity in Washington. Col. Harvey Brown and a large force would appear off the outer beach at Fort Pickens only five days after Vodges had landed. We must step back in time to examine a most bizarre story.

The attempts for the relief of Fort Pickens – begun by the Buchanan administration, as we have seen – were in a state of suspension at the commencement of the Lincoln administration. Taken aback by the revelation of the "quasi-armistice" at Pensacola – and given the advice by General Scott and Commodore Stringham, with strong concurrence in those views by the new Secretary of State Seward, that it was now too late to reinforce Fort Sumter – Lincoln was "much distressed."[227] The exhortations of Postmaster General Blair, however, saved the idea of an expedition to Sumter.

Thus, a split developed between Secretary Seward and the position of Lincoln and the rest of the cabinet. Seward favored more effort at saving Pickens and the complete abandonment of Sumter. "One would be a waste of effort and energy and life . . . while the other would be an effective and peaceable movement." The reinforcements to Sumter would have to fight their way in whereas those to Pickens likely would not. Thus, if the Lincoln administration continued with the Buchanan policy of no reinforcement of Sumter, it would soon be starved out without a fight; and the two parties, Union and Confederate, could be reconciled. As the head of the department of state, he would be in a position to carry out these conciliatory negotiations. Seward should have stopped to realize that this policy was de facto recognition of the legitimacy of the rebels – anathema to Lincoln.

We recall that Lincoln had decided, on March 5th, that regardless of the armistice, Vodges should land, though Scott's order did not even begin its journey to Florida until the 16th. Having the notion that the Pickens issue was resolved, Lincoln returned to the discussion of Sumter. After listening to Blair's declarations that the abandonment of Sumter would be regarded as treason to the country, Lincoln decided to take a firm stand at Sumter as well. Inquiries were made, among them to Gustavus Fox, Blair's brother-in-law.[228] Having served 19 years as a navy officer, though now in private life, Fox had earlier proposed a plan for the relief of Sumter to the Buchanan administration.

Fox was now summoned to plan the task.[229] On March 19th, he was authorized by General Scott to visit Sumter. Fox did so, and returned with the assurance of its commander, Major Anderson, that Sumter could hold out until April 15th, so plans went ahead. At the cabinet meeting of March 29th, Blair, Welles, and Treasury Secretary Chase were in favor of the Fox expedition, with Attorney General

---

227. Welles, G., Vol. I, pp. 8–14.
228. Nicolay & Hay, Vol. VI, p. 383.
229. Welles, G., Vol. I, pp. 14–25; O.R. Vol. 1, pp. 208, 209, 235.

Bates on the fence and Seward and Interior Secretary Smith against. War Secretary Simon Cameron apparently was not in attendance.[230]

On April 4th, transports to deliver subsistence were chartered. Fox was given his instructions from Secretary Cameron on the same day, which said, in part: "If you are opposed in this you are directed to report the fact to the senior naval officer of the harbor, who will use his entire force to open a passage, when you will, if possible, effect an entrance and place both troops and supplies in Fort Sumter." The captains of the *Powhatan*, *Pawnee*, *Pocahontas*, and *Harriet Lane* were given their sealed orders on the 5th.

Fox arrived off the Charleston bar, as planned, on April 12th.[231] However, his most important ship – the fighting portion of the expedition, the *Powhatan* – had not arrived. They waited all the day of the 13th and finally learned "that the Powhatan was withdrawn from duty" *and had been since the 7th*! Nevertheless, Fox decided to "go in" on the night of the 13th. Sumter's commander, Major Anderson, however, had made arrangements on that day to surrender the fort, which was done the next day.

As a part of Secretary Seward's position against the Fox expedition, he had countered that he would "call in Captain Meigs forthwith. Aided by his counsel, I would prepare for war at Pensacola and Texas, to be taken, however, only as a consequence of maintaining the possessions and authority of the United States." Meigs was the engineer, as we remember, who had been in charge of the construction at Fort Jefferson and was present when reinforcements arrived at both Taylor and Jefferson. Now he was in Washington, handily nearby – he was supervising the construction of the new wings of the capitol building – and Seward called him in that afternoon. They met with Lincoln and discussed a possible project for relieving and holding Pickens.

One must remember the background of the meeting. Only a single artillery company, Vodges', had embarked for the relief of Pickens on the 21st of January, and it had accomplished nothing since. Lincoln had given written instructions to Scott to prepare orders to Vodges on March 11th, and now on March 29th, there was no word of a landing. Were Southern sympathizers in the navy subverting the orders?[232] The presence of Bragg and his public show of strength and a recent surprising turn in General Scott's opinion, which included the abandonment of both Sumter and Pickens,[233] seemed to be shocking evidence that Pickens would be lost without rapid and forceful action. As a nervous Seward stood by, Lincoln questioned Meigs as to whether Fort Pickens could be held. "Certainly" was the

---

230. Nicolay & Hay, Vol. III, pp. 429–433.
231. O.R. Vol. 1, pp. 11, 12, 235, 236.
232. Porter, D. D., pp. 13–24.
233. O.R. Vol. 1, pp. 200, 201.

answer. The following passage is quoted from *Abraham Lincoln: A History*:[234]

> The President then asked him whether he could go down there again and take general command of those three great fortresses, Taylor, Jefferson and Pickens, and keep them safe. Meigs answered that he was only a captain, and could not command the majors who were there. Here Seward broke in with: "I understand . . . Meigs must be promoted."

Seward had an answer for everything, and made light of all difficulties. Finally, Lincoln offered to consider the idea and in a few days he would let them know.

On Sunday morning, March 31st, General Scott's military secretary, Erasmus Keyes, called on Meigs and took him to Seward, who requested them to "go forthwith" to Scott, to put a detailed plan on paper, and to have it in the President's hands before four o'clock that afternoon.

Their first stop was at the engineer office to study the charts of Pensacola and the drawings of the fort. This consumed so much time that they were compelled to go directly to the President for the four o'clock meeting without having conferred with General Scott. Having listened to their presentation, Lincoln said: "Tell him that I wish this thing done . . ."

General Scott detailed the plan the same evening. It consisted of the assignment of a senior commander with a force some four, or five, times the size of Vodges' company, which would land on the outer beach at Santa Rosa Island. It would be supported by a powerful naval force, which would steam into the inner harbor and take up a position to prevent the crossing of the Confederate forces to Fort Pickens. In Meigs' handwriting,[235] the orders were approved by Lincoln without reading them. It would entirely bypass the chain of command of the navy. It called for Lt. D. D. Porter to take command of the *Powhatan*, earlier designated as the warship to support Fox in the run into Sumter.

The left hand not knowing what the right hand was doing thus ruined the Sumter expedition.

Welles' explanation:[236] "On the 1st of April . . . Mr. Nicolay, the private secretary of the President, brought to me and laid upon the table a large package from the President . . . Without a moment's delay I went to the President with the package in my hand. He was alone in his office . . . and inquired 'What have I done wrong?'" Having been shown the documents, Lincoln explained that he had left Seward in charge of a "subject which he had in hand," which involved considerable detail.

From Welles: "What, then, were the contrivances which he was maturing with two young officers, one of the army and one of the Navy, without consulting the

---

234. Nicolay & Hay, Vol. III, pp. 435–440.
235. Welles, G., Vol. I, p. 17.
236. Welles, G., Vol. I, pp. 16–21, 25–27, 35.

Secretary of War or the Secretary of the Navy?" The cover of Seward's secret expedition was blown, and the problem was how to pick up the pieces. Time did not allow it. Sent by Seward, the order to restore the *Powhatan* to the Fox expedition was either received too late, or because it was from *Seward*, and not Welles or the President, it was ignored, and the *Powahatan* sailed with a new captain; Seward/Meigs having had the effrontery to displace its assigned commander, Samuel Mercer, with Meigs' fellow confidant, David Dixon Porter.

Worse, Welles suspected Porter as a Southern sympathizer, and it had raised a red flag as to the intent and bogus origin of these orders. Porter and another navy officer, Samuel Barron, were friends and allegedly were part of a "clique . . . who were favorites of Jefferson Davis, Slidell, and other Secessionists, who I had learned, paid them assiduous attention." Porter and friend were opportunists who would have sold out to whomsoever offered them the most self-aggrandizement. The Seward secret expedition had rather bribed Porter to the Union side. Confirming Welles' suspicions, about two weeks later, Barron defected to the Confederate navy. Porter remained in the U.S. Navy, his supreme ego "flattered and gratified" by this special assignment.

Neither Welles nor Lincoln ever forgot the incident, Lincoln complimenting Welles on his use, throughout the war, of Porter's talent, without "resentment."[237]

As to Seward, he never really apologized. However, he admitted that he had better attend to his own business and confine his labors to his own department.[238] The magnanimity and forbearance of Lincoln in keeping his secretary of state on board is remarkable. From Welles: "When he was sworn in to the office of Secretary, he expected and intended to occupy the place of premier, and undoubtedly supposed he could direct the Administration in every Department . . . The incidents . . . the detachment of the Powhatan, the irregular assignment given to Porter . . . convinced him [Lincoln] that he must not give implicit trust to any one . . ."

On April 2nd, Bvt. Col. Harvey Brown, commanding at Fort McHenry, Maryland, received a letter[239] from General Scott, outlining the first part of the plan and endorsed "APPROVED" by Abraham Lincoln. It began: "You have been designated to take command of an expedition to re-enforce and hold Fort Pickens, in the harbor of Pensacola. You will proceed with the least possible delay to that place, and you will assume command of all land forces of the United States within the limits of the State of Florida . . . Should a shot be fired at you, you will defend yourself and your expedition at whatever hazard . . ."

Brown, West Point class of 1818,[240] was a veteran of 43 years of service dating from the Blackhawk War, the Florida War, and meritorious service in the Mexican

---

237. Welles, G., Vol. I, pp. 36, 37.
238. Welles, G., Vol. I, pp. 24, 25.
239. O.R. Vol. 1, p. 365.
240. Cullum, Vol. I, pp. 189–197.

War. He would bring experience, organizing skills, and judgment to the "farce of peace"[241] at Pickens; but he would fail to bring initiative.

The first ship of Brown's expedition, the *Atlantic*, carried two artillery companies, A and M of the 2nd Regiment (M fresh out of Texas); two infantry companies, C and E of the 3rd (also fresh out of Texas); Duane's Engineer Company; and 20 hired carpenters, a total of about 450 men.[242] After the men, equipment, and 73 horses were loaded, the *Atlantic* left the wharf at Fort Hamilton, New York, on April 6th. It remained in the harbor loading more supplies overnight and got underway in the morning. The dock was left covered with equipment to be loaded on the steamer *Illinois*, carrying companies H and K of the 2nd Artillery[243] and due to follow on the evening of the 8th.

The *Atlantic* arrived off Key West on April 12th, and Brown landed on the 13th to consult with Major French and selected local citizens. Brown assigned a project to the engineer at Fort Taylor, Capt. E. B. Hunt, to make a recommendation as to the "field works," which could better protect the land approaches to the fort. (Here was the proper operation of the engineer on-site: an expert but subordinate). Brown authorized French to suspend the writ of habeas corpus if he encountered an insurrection. Hearing of the disloyal behavior of the postmaster, Whalton, he appointed French to the position.[244] He then detached 33 men to his force from the Fort Taylor garrison to make up for deficiencies caused by desertion or absence at New York. Taking some mortars and a field battery, and evidently satisfied with the conditions at Key West, Brown departed for Fort Jefferson.

Brown arrived at Jefferson at 1:00 p.m. on the 14th. He found the armament of thirteen 8-inch Columbiads, with 30 more now being unloaded from a supply ship, plus twenty-four 24-pounder howitzers and 250 barrels of powder, etc., to be sufficient. He complimented Arnold on the "good order" of the fort. He detached 31 volunteers[245] from the garrison to complete the roster of his forces for Pickens and also "took twenty negro laborers" for the Engineer Department. These were skilled workers who had been hired from their owners at Key West. The owners, Southern sympathizers (one of whom was Whalton, the postmaster), made an uproar over this incident, claiming that the transfer was not authorized by them.

Twelve of the volunteers detached were from Battery L, as was seen on the muster roll summary for the period: James Ahern, Thomas Brook, William F. Brown, Patrick Cummings, Christopher Foley, James McCarthy, James McCoy, John Meyer, David Meyers, Michael O'Sullivan, William Parketton, and Thomas Poole.

---

241. O.R. Vol. 1, p. 398; M. C. Meigs.
242. O.R. Vol. 1, p. 399.
243. O.R. Vol. 1, pp. 366, 393, 394.
244. O.R. Vol. 52/II, pp. 51, 53. Examples of communications by the postmaster with the governor of Florida and with L. P. Walker, Confederate secretary of war.
245. Haskin, W. L., p. 400. Nine were from M, 1st Artillery.

Adding four mountain howitzers with prairie carriages, "light and suitable . . . for the sands of Santa Rosa" to the load of material destined for Pickens, Brown and his forces departed. After a stormy passage, they were off Pensacola on the 17th, only five days after the first relief expedition (Vodges) had landed. Unloading across the outer beach, through the surf, began. The signal that an attack was imminent was received from the fort.[246] Though the landing party congratulated themselves on the fact that their arrival prevented the attack, the Confederate torches and hurrahs around Fort Barrancas (at the arrow in figure 9) were probably a celebration of the news of the secession of Virginia, promptly telegraphed to Bragg. We remember that after Fort Sumter fell on April 14th, Lincoln called for 75,000 volunteers on the 15th, Virginia seceded on the 17th, and Lincoln declared the blockade of the southern coast on the 19th. The steamer *Illinois* arrived late on the 19th and began unloading, which lasted into the next day.[247]

Brown found Fort Pickens in "miserable condition" and the guns and carriages that were in place of "indifferent" condition.[248] He overestimated the numbers of the Confederates at 7,000, though their plans only called for 5,000[249]; and at this time, there were only about 2,700 actually in the area. He appreciated that the distances across the harbor, one-and-a-quarter to one-and-one-half miles (figure 10), were beyond the useful range of most of his and the Confederate guns alike, and that the new 42-pounder rifled gun would be a requirement for reducing the rebel forts and the navy yard. He had requested six on April 12th.[250]

FIGURE 9

---

246. O.R. Vol. 1, p. 396.
247. O.R. Vol. 1, pp. 386, 397.
248. O.R Vol. 1, pp. 378.
249. O.R. Vol. 1, pp. 454, 379; figure 9, photo by the author; figure 10 from O.R. Vol. 1, p. 421.
250. O.R. Vol. 1, p. 373.

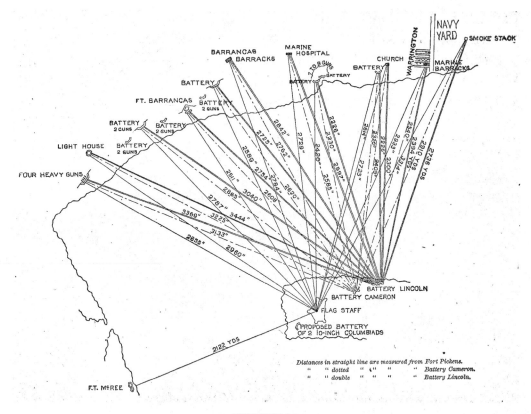

FIGURE 10

He was apprehensive of an engagement with the Confederates. He viewed his forces at this time as too weak and any provocation as inconsistent with his orders. Brown's emphasis that his orders were to remain strictly on the defensive was his interpretation of the following exact statement in Scott's orders: "Should a shot be fired at you, you will defend yourself and your expedition at whatever hazard, and, if needful for such a defense, inflict upon the assailants all the damage in your power within the range of your guns."[251]

As a result, he called off a planned colorful run of the *Powhatan* (Porter was flying the British flag)[252] into the harbor, and thus the second prong of the expedition became a non-event. Meigs, who accompanied the expedition, managed to signal Porter at the last moment, just as the *Powhatan* was heading toward Fort McCree at the harbor entrance. It is easy to speculate that if Porter had not been stopped, the ensuing events would have shown that the Confederates had little ammunition and could not put up a substantial fight. Pensacola would have fallen then and there. Instead, another five months would pass before any event of significance.

---

251. O.R. Vol. 1, p. 366.
252. ORN Ser. I, Vol. 4, p. 132; O.R. Vol. 1, p. 382.

At least one shot was claimed to be fired. This by the egotistical Porter,[253] who notes that on the second day after the *Powhatan*'s arrival, a "flotilla" of Confederate ships, filled with soldiers, approached. Assuming they were bent upon attacking, Porter fired one XI-inch shell whose shrapnel was timed perfectly to "throw up the water in all directions" near the approaching vessels. The flotilla quickly retired.

Ever true to his orders to conduct operations only on the defensive, Brown thought it proper to inform "the secession general" of his arrival and of the defensive posture. The message was delivered by Captain Vodges, who did not obtain a written reply. Bragg merely muttered that the truce had been broken.[254] On the 18th, Brown announced Fort Pickens as his headquarters.

Upon the recommendation of the engineer officers, Meigs and Hunt, the construction of water batteries (batteries external to the fort, on the water's edge) were begun. Also, after a reconnaissance of Santa Rosa Island, a better location to unload supplies, about four miles east of the fort, was found – as was a location for an encampment safely hidden by sand ridges about a mile east. The intent was to minimize crowding in the fort to better maintain sanitary conditions and should it be shelled, the loss of life of those infantry and support people for the fort who did not actually man the guns.[255] By the end of April, there were over 1,000[256] troops under Brown's command, not counting the crews of the various ships of the fleet: *St. Louis*, *Crusader*, *Powhatan*, *Sabine*, *Minnesota*, *Brooklyn*, and *Wyandotte*.

Fort Sumter having fallen, some Confederate troops, including workmen and artillery, were freed by P. T. Beauregard, its new commander, to come to Pensacola. Bragg had recommended a reserve force of 3,000 men be held "on the railroad"[257] between Pensacola and Mobile. On April 20th, Bragg declared martial law in the Pensacola area and declared all intercourse among Santa Rosa Island, Fort Pickens, and the United States fleet prohibited. On May 6th, Bragg[258] wrote to the Confederate Secretary of War L. P. Walker, noting Brown's efforts at the extending of facilities outside of the fort and that: "Every hour will add seriously to the difficulties to be overcome." He added that his "works" for offense or defense were nearly complete but that he still lacked many essentials. "Our best defense against the fleet – shells – cannot be used for want of fuses. Not one has yet reached me." At this rate, it was going to be a long war.

We may look back and think that communications in the Civil War were slow. This was true in the Texas area, as was noted because the telegraph was not available everywhere and the mail was subverted. Here at Fort Pickens, mail

---

253. Porter, D. D., p. 24.
254. O.R. Vol. 1, p. 379.
255. O.R. Vol. 1, p. 398.
256. O.R. Vol. 1, p. 386.
257. O.R. Vol. 1, p. 464.
258. O.R. Vol. 1, p. 465.

brought by ship was indeed slow, though elsewhere, mail by rail and hand-carried by messenger could be nearly as prompt as today. However, in areas where the telegraph was available, news traveled as quickly as the operators could tap it out. The Official Records of the War of the Rebellion are full of verbose telegrams sent without much regard for brevity. Lincoln used to visit the telegraph room at the War Department,[259] and he and Stanton[260] would sit there for hours. Ubiquitous newspaper reporters were avid users of the telegraph, and newspapers were available almost everywhere, whether Confederate or Union. The problem was, as it is today, was the information accurate?

One news story that may have been eagerly awaited from Fort Pickens was the report of the visit of British journalist William Russell and the artist who accompanied him, Theodore Davis. As neutrals writing for the *London Times*, Russell and Davis were allowed to tour *both* Fort Pickens and the Confederate installations on the opposite shore. On May 14th, Russell's tour of the Confederate batteries shook his confidence in American journalism. He had read elsewhere that there was a formidable array of hundreds of guns, "better described as tens" (see figure 11).[261] He toured 10 of the 13 of Bragg's batteries and estimated that there were but five heavy siege guns capable of doing damage to Pickens. Rat holes [bomb proofs] had been, and were, being built to protect from shells from Pickens by working parties from Mississippi and Alabama, "great long bearded fellows with flannel shirts and slouched hats, uniformless in all save brightly burnished arms and resolute purpose . . ." Others were "lying about or contributing languidly to their completion." He noted the inexperience of two officers who were arguing about how to direct the work. "I was quite satisfied Gen. Bragg was perfectly correct in refusing to open his fire on Pickens and the fleet, which ought certainly to have knocked his works about his ears."[262]

Russell's opinion conflicted with the impression that was created in the report of Maj. Josiah Gorgas of the Confederate Ordinance Office for April 1861. Pensacola was listed as bristling with 169 guns and howitzers, 9 heavy mortars, and with: "a good supply of shot, shell, grape, and canister on hand and making at Mobile."

Davis, the artist, was revealed in the June 15th, 1861 issue of *Harper's Weekly*[263] as being employed by their magazine. Russell then issued a statement that Mr. Davis was working for the *Illustrated London News* and denied any connection

---

259. Bates, D. H., pp. 40, 41.
260. Stanton became Secretary of War in January 1862.
261. Miller, F. T., ed., Vol. 5, p. 56. Note that the guns are offset, or "barbet" mounted.
262. Russell, W. H., p. 213.
263. All references here from the June 15th, 1861 issue of *Harper's Weekly*, p. 373, with the exception of Russell's denial, which appeared in the July 20th issue, p. 450.

FIGURE 11

of his or Davis to any "journal in the United or Confederate States . . ." The controversy evidently prevented the issue of any immediate, and damaging, article by Russell as to the true circumstances of the Confederate positions at Pensacola. However, Davis' comments that the gun shown in his sketch (figure 12) forwarded to *Harper's*, was unlikely "to do much injury to the fort, the distance being nearly 1¾ miles."

FIGURE 12

Brown, the "tall elderly man in a blue frock coat with a gold star [sic] on the shoulder," 264 had plenty to do building water batteries which he named Cameron, Lincoln, and Scott, plus a mortar battery facing the south (Totten) and the placing of their guns. Further, the encampment at the east of the fort required entrenching and setting tents and facilities for the horses, not to mention building a plank road to it.

FIGURE 13

Note the interior of Fort Pickens (figure 13) from *Harper's Weekly* of December 14th, 1861, with its barbette-mounted guns (insert) on the parapet of the outer walls.265 Later, they were surrounded with sandbags for the protection of those working them.

The crowded condition and seeming chaos contrasts with Russell's description, but a few weeks would make a difference. As noted earlier, Brown would soon move most of those men not in direct assignment to service the guns to outside the fort, and as well, build a hospital there. The volunteer regiments sent to him later would never be inside the fort for both sanitary and safety reasons, assuming the fort to be the main rebel target.

Russell observed that within the fort the men were engaged in digging deep pits as shell traps266 and adding sand bags to the rear of the casemates several feet in thickness to protect from plunging fire. He noted that the men were the U.S. regulars "not comparable in physique to the Southern volunteers, but infinitely superior

---

264. Russell, W. H., p. 207.
265. Gibbon, J., plate 21, fig. 132, portion.
266. Russell, W. H., p. 217.

in cleanliness and soldierly smartness . . ." He also noted that Fort Pickens seemed more desirable than the rebel camp, being "light, dry, and airy" and probably less prone to yellow fever and dysentery, which the Confederates were "delighted to think the Yankees will get."

Near the end of May, Bragg received a letter from Jefferson Davis which would be most illuminating if it were not lost to history. The information it contained, however, showed that the Confederate leaders were looking east. The capital was being moved[267] from Alabama to Virginia, and Bragg was evidently asked how many troops he could *spare*. This must have come as quite a shock since almost every other communication he had received up to that date had asked the opposite. He responded[268] on the 28th, "I can spare twenty-five hundred men for Virginia and can start them immediately, well armed." If Bragg had not the heart to attack Pickens earlier, he would not do so now. He was still making requests for more troops and ammunition at the end of June.[269]

Though the blockade had been declared on April 19th, no specific action had been taken by the navy squadron standing offshore to enforce it. On May 8th, Brown[270] requested that the navy prevent vessels "loaded with forage or provisions . . . or contraband of war" from entering the harbor. The ever-cautious Captain Adams answered, "I do not know how to proceed towards foreign ships, which by the laws and customs of nations are allowed a certain time to come and go after the declaration of a blockade, nor towards the coasting vessels which exhibit a license from the U.S. Government." Nevertheless, Bragg was given official notification of the blockade on May 14th.[271] Finally, Brown notified Bragg that he would "act on the offensive whenever the interests and honor of my country, in my opinion require it."

The blockade, though declared openly, was a part of a broader plan outlined originally by Gen. Winfield

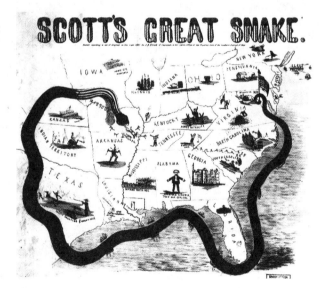

FIGURE 14

---

267. O.R. Ser. IV, Vol. 1, p. 255.
268. O.R. Vol. 1, p. 468.
269. O.R. Vol. 1, p. 469.
270. O.R. Vol. 1, p. 409.
271. O.R. Vol. 1, p. 413.

Scott[272] to secure "posts" at critical points on the coast to deny them to the Confederacy and provide places to support the ships maintaining the blockade. In addition, these were to be places of strength to support possible moves inland. Recall from chapter 2 that Scott had attempted to hold such a post in Texas. This concept of envelopment and coastal occupation, supported by the navy, was Scott's broad strategy for the prosecution of the war. It was eventually dubbed "The Anaconda Plan" or "Scott's Great Snake" by the press, mocking the idea that the Confederacy could be defeated by strangling it as a constrictor snake kills its victim (figure 14).

On May 13th, the "old company", that is, Slemmer's Company G of the 1st Artillery that had been there since the beginning, was ordered out to Fort Hamilton, New York. Almost all were suffering from scurvy; and upon the post surgeon's recommendation, Brown gave the order, noting that a "northern climate" was necessary to restore their health. The absence of desiccated vegetables in the rations supplied, noted earlier by Vodges, had taken its toll. Absent fresh fruit or vegetables, all they needed was some source of vitamin C, not known as such then, but easily available from wild limes growing nearby in the Florida Keys.[273]

In this time of year, May, the modern visitor would find the most pleasant conditions at Pensacola. In fact, with the exception of the depth of winter in prolonged wind and rain, the area is pleasant for "camping out." The camper today would not be weakened by poor diet or would not have to spend the night in a mildewed tent and be greeted by a monotonous breakfast of fried or boiled salt pork, with a bit of ash and wind-blown grit included. He would not have endured the smell of smoke hoping that that condition helped to repel fleas and mosquitoes. He would not be exposed to the sun's glare all day without lotion or sunglasses.[274] He would have known only fresh, bacteria-free water all his life and could not conceive of the consequences of any alternative. He would have always had sufficient sanitary facilities and the use of toilet paper. He would have scorned the idea of waiting months for such meager amenities as soap and candles.

The mosquitoes, as noted by the visiting William Russell, were: "numerous and persecuting . . . no such place known in the world for them as on this coast."[275] The irregular contours of Santa Rosa Island and the mainland were dotted with marshland and numerous seasonal pools of brackish water which were their breeding

---

272. Nicolay & Hay, Vol. IV, pp. 302–307; fig. 14: Elliot, J. B.
273. Vodges reported on January 31st that no desiccated vegetables were available for his troops when they left Fort Monroe. O.R. Vol. 1, p. 356.
274. Supply conditions had improved considerably a year later. Sprague, H. B., p. 46, notes that "green goggles" were used to protect from the sun's glare while they were stationed at Ship Island in April of 1862.
275. Russell, p. 200.

grounds. In fact, nearly everywhere Battery L had been and was destined to go during its assignments in Florida and Louisiana had areas of marsh and accompanying mosquitoes and the danger of yellow fever or malaria. On board the steamer *Luminary* during an inspection tour near Baton Rouge, Louisiana, in 1864, the inspector general of cavalry of the Department of the Gulf noted in his diary: "I had a good stateroom and a nice bed but Oh! Mosketoes! I had no *bar*.[276] I got to sleep, however, and awoke in the night to find my hands and wrists smarting furiously, and my finger joints appearing to be swollen."[277]

A sidelight to the drama of the reinforcement of Fort Pickens is a move made by the Union Defense Committee. A number of private citizens had gotten together to form this group, dedicated to procuring supplies for the Union forces. The chairman of their "Subcommittee for the Purchase of Arms" John J. Astor, had learned of the need for rifled guns at Fort Pickens. He indicated in a letter to Simon Cameron, the secretary of war, that the "requisite" arms were available and could be forwarded to sail for Fort Pickens on May 24th.[278] Cameron rebuffed the offer, but on May 29th, he was back, urgently addressing the chief of ordnance that "a battery of Whitworth guns has been received as a gift to the Government." He was to take immediate steps to have them shipped, along with a long list of other ordnance, to Fort Pickens.[279] The following appears later in the letter: "Fort Pickens appears to be in danger for want of ordnance, called for long since. Where the error lies the Department does not propose to inquire. The present duty is to deal with the question as it stands, and to spare no exertion."

The source of the "error," of course, was Simon Cameron himself, not to derogate the secretary, but to indicate the confusion of fast-moving events at that time of crisis. He would resign in January 1862 and was later censured by the House of Representatives over irregularities involving arms purchases and by following "a policy highly injurious to the public service . . ." In a special message to the Senate and House on May 26th, 1862, Lincoln defended his secretary by saying, in part, that "not only the President but all the other heads of Departments were at least equally responsible with him for whatever error, wrong, or fault was committed in the premises."[280]

Cameron's resignation, however, was actually precipitated by a disagreement over a statement in his annual report for 1861, which dealt directly and realistically with what would become a serious problem. It looked favorably on the possibility

---

276. Netting.
277. Babcock, W. M., Jr., p. 66. Mosquitoes remained such a problem in the Florida Keys that bats were later introduced. Roosts, slatted wooden towers, were built for them. The remains of one still exists on Lower Sugarloaf Key.
278. O.R. Vol. 1, pp. 414, 415.
279. O.R. Vol. 1, p. 422; O.R. Ser. III, Vol. 2, p. 74.
280. O.R. Ser. III, Vol. 2, p. 74. See also Nicolay & Hay, Vol. V, p. 130.

of arming former slaves: ". . . their services against the rebels, under proper military regulation, discipline, and command."[281] Lincoln feared the reaction of the public, particularly those in the border states whom he was still courting for support for the Union cause. Anything so controversial had better be postponed. The only step regarding the status of slaves had been the First Confiscation Act (see *Events Elsewhere*, later in this chapter) and that was enough for now. Cameron's report was recalled and revised to merely point out that there was "a grave question what shall be done with those slaves who were abandoned by their owners on the advance of our troops into Southern territory . . ."

At this time the support for the war in the North was extraordinary and came from every corner of society, even a few former Breckinridge Democrats. Many of the prominent were besieging Washington with offers to raise troops or supplies and offered suggestions for the prosecution of the war. Lincoln's April 15th call for 75,000 volunteers was oversubscribed. One of the first regiments raised, the 6th New York Volunteer Infantry, was allegedly filled that day.[282]

Two politicians from Massachusetts to come forward were Democrat Benjamin Butler and Republican Nathaniel Banks. Centering on Butler, for the moment, a general in the Massachusetts militia, he had earlier taken aggressive action in quelling unrest at Baltimore and was subsequently named to the command of Fort Monroe. This put him in line to be the first participant with the navy in the Anaconda Plan. He was probably the first one in the army who knew that he was part of any plan, and he did not become involved until late August.

The Anaconda Plan

First recommended to the President in a cabinet meeting shortly before Lincoln's call of April 15th, it was enunciated by Simon Cameron as "that plan of the British for subduing the American colonies, which was discussed . . . the previous Saturday," it was, essentially, a blockade.[283] It was more formally laid out as a strategic plan by General-in-Chief Scott in May.

In a letter to Scott dated May 2nd, 1861,[284] George McClellan proposed marching his army of the Ohio Militia straight toward Richmond, presumably ending the war then and there. (We might add that this was uncharacteristically bold for the McClellan that was subsequently revealed when he became

---

281. Nicolay & Hay, Vol. V, p. 126.
282. Morris, G., p. 20. The data in this work must be taken with some "grains of salt" as many of the statistics are grossly exaggerated. Suffice to say, the unit was quickly subscribed. The first five companies were mustered on April 30th, at Staten Island, the remaining by May 25th. Phisterer, F., p. 379.
283. Gilmore, J. R., pp. 25–26. The Saturday referred to would have been April 13th.
284. O.R. Vol. 51, p. 338.

commander of the Army of the Potomac. Lamentably, he proved loath to initiate any bold moves, and after an agonizing time for the President and the then-Secretary of War Stanton, he was replaced.) Scott criticized McClellan's direct attack strategy in an endorsement of McClellan's letter that was, shrewdly enough, sent on to the President. It was only the beginning of an acrimonious relationship[285] that would continue until Scott retired at the end of October. Scott regarded McClellan's proposal as "piecemeal" attacking only one point and, among other deficiencies, being difficult to support, choosing a route deficient of water transport. Scott proposed "enveloping them all (nearly) at once by a cordon of posts on the Mississippi to its mouth from its junction with the Ohio, and by blockading ships of war on the sea-board." In a follow-up letter the next day,[286] Scott mentions launching the Mississippi operation from the North for the reason that the forces could advance as the frost killed the "virus of malignant fever below Memphis." Prescient indeed, the numbers of sick in campaigns in the South would grow to percentages hardly believable. Scott specifically noted the occupation of New Orleans.

The occupation of forts Taylor, Jefferson, and Pickens, we have seen, was a reaction with no evident plan. Harvey Brown's expedition to the relief of Fort Pickens began even before any named plan. The blockade would be the first part of any plan, and the press would mock it.

Though declared on April 19th, 1861, the blockade would take months to go into full operation. The navy had to construct additional ships, and in the words of Navy Secretary Welles, recall far-flung squadrons, enlist seamen, and put into place a plan of how to best conduct patrolling 3,500 river and seacoast miles. Nevertheless, at New Orleans, Cdr. Raphael Semmes, in the process of equipping the Confederate raider Sumter, reported that the USS *Brooklyn* had arrived off Pass a l'Outre, at the mouth of the Mississippi, on May 26th.[287] The blockade had begun.

The form the plan took on the western rivers would be unique. The navy assigned Cdr. John Rodgers to cooperate with the army in the blockade of the Ohio and Mississippi Rivers in May of 1861.[288] He soon purchased three small steamboats for conversion into gunboats.[289] After some controversy as to whether he had exceeded his authority, his purchases were approved and paid for by General McClellan. Rodgers' steamers were modified by adding guns and heavy timbers

---

285. Butler, B. F., p. 245. Butler says that McClellan "quarreled with him and abused him until he got the old general removed from his path to the chief command."
286. O.R. Vol. 1, p. 369.
287. Welles, G., *Galaxy Magazine*, Vol. 12, p. 669; ORN Ser. I, Vol. 1, p. 691.
288. ORN Ser. I, Vol. 22, p. 280
289. ORN Ser. I, Vol. 22, pp. 283, 286.

FIGURE 15

FIGURE 16

for armor. An example is the USS *Tyler* (figure 15), which he later commanded.[290]

Indicative of the growing importance of the mission, Rodgers was replaced by a more senior officer, Capt. A. H. Foote., on August 30th.[291]

Any new construction was specifically for inland waters, such as the navigation of the Mississippi, Ohio, Tennessee, and Cumberland rivers; and it took on a radically different form, an example being the ironclad Cairo (figure 16). The flotilla was unique in yet another way. Though funded by the U.S. Army, through Fremont's Department of the West, it was under the overall command of a navy officer.

Later, a second flotilla consisting of commercial steamers was converted not into gunboats, but into unarmed rams, under the direction of Charles Ellet, who conceived of the idea. These were initially under army control but were eventually transferred to the navy, in a political fight described later.

It is remarkable that Scott's Anaconda Plan remained as the set policy of the war, and by-and-large, it was consistently followed. Control of the Mississippi would be a problem, and it would not be achieved until the fall of Port Hudson, after a sweaty and bloody siege all too familiar to Battery L, on July 9th, 1863. Vicksburg, that objective better known to history, had surrendered five days earlier, more than a year after it was first bombarded by Union gunboats.

Secret Board of Officers

Implicit in the functioning of the Anaconda Plan was the taking of Scott's "posts" for ship supply and eliminating havens for blockade runners. To implement it, a secret board of officers was named and convened by Navy Secretary Gideon Welles on June 25th, 1861. The board consisted of Capts. S. F. DuPont and C. H. Davis of the navy; Prof. A. D. Bache, chief of the coast survey; and Maj. J. G. Barnard

---

290. Figure 15, ORN Ser. II, Vol. 1, p. 226b; figure 16, Miller, F. T., Vol. 1, p. 223..
291. ORN Ser. I, Vol. 22, p. 307.

of the Army Corps of Engineers.[292] They quickly identified Port Royal, South Carolina, and New Orleans; but an attack on the Confederate batteries at Hatteras Inlet, North Carolina, could be launched quickly from Fort Monroe, Virginia, the planned base of operations. Further, it would only require an army contingent of an estimated 860[293] men. Therefore, Hatteras Inlet was chosen as a first trial. On August 13th, General Scott directed the commander of Fort Monroe,[294] Maj. Gen. John E. Wool, to supply the necessary army contingent. Due to the byzantine command arrangements there, this duty would fall to the prominent Democrat and major general of volunteers, Benjamin F. Butler.[295]

Butler, Waterville College (Colby) class of 1838, began a successful law practice in Massachusetts, was elected to the Massachusetts legislature, and was later appointed to the Massachusetts militia. From his position as a brigadier general, he was called upon by Massachusetts Governor Andrew to lead a Massachusetts regiment to Maryland in April of 1861. On April 25th, he was assigned to the temporary command of all of the forces in the Annapolis area.[296] After prominently occupying Baltimore and calling for reinforcements from Pennsylvania – without orders – he was relieved, yet on May 18th he was appointed a major general of volunteers and given the command of the Department of Virginia and the volunteer forces at Fort Monroe.

His first action from Fort Monroe, the first of any of the war in Virginia (the famous Battle of Bull Run, or First Manassas, was to come more than a month later), was repulsed near Big Bethel Church on the Yorktown Peninsula on June 10th, 1861. However, this did not slow Butler's enthusiasm for mounting other operations, though the peninsula area north of Fort Monroe, including the Norfolk Navy Yard, would remain in Confederate hands until May 10th, 1862.[297]

On August 17th, Butler was replaced as commander of the Department of Virginia by General Wool,[298] yet Butler was to remain in control of the volunteer forces in the department exclusive of those at the fort. His command essentially was that of the troops based at nearby Camps Butler and Hamilton. Clearly not satisfied with his place in affairs, he had been angling for a more important command, and on this date he was "cheerfully granted" permission to recruit 5,000 volunteers from Massachusetts and the "Eastern States" by the Assistant Secretary of War Thomas Scott.[299]

On August 26th, a joint amphibious expedition led by Flag Officer Silas

---

292. Welles, G., *Galaxy Magazine*, Vol. 12, issue 5, November 1871, p. 672.
293. O.R. Vol. 4, p. 580.
294. O.R. Vol. 4, p. 579.
295. O.R. Vol. 4, p. 602; *Encyclopedia Britannica*, Vol. IV, p. 881.
296. O.R. Vol. 2, pp. 2, 77–82, 600, 637–639; Butler, pp. 242, 243.
297. O. R. Vol. 11/I, p. 2.
298. O.R. Vol. 2, pp. 641, 642.
299. O.R. Ser. III, Vol. 1, pp. 423, 498.

Stringham carrying General Butler and his troops embarked for Hatteras Inlet. On the 28th, supported by a naval bombardment on forts Clark and Hatteras, Butler's forces landed behind the Confederate batteries. The Confederate garrisons surrendered the next day.[300] It was a resounding success and was received with enthusiasm in the north. The *Harper's Weekly* of September 14th labeled it "brilliant," put Stringham's and Butler's portraits on the cover, and gave a detailed account from the *New York Herald*.

Pickens Armament Complete

It is noted that on May 30th, Lt. Henry W. Closson and Company F, 1st Artillery, arrived at Pickens from Key West.[301] Closson would become commander of Battery L on November 21st, 1861, after his promotion to captain on May 14th, and remain its commander throughout the rest of the war. Graduated from West Point, class of 1854, he remained in the army after the war, eventually achieving the rank of brigadier general. He retired in 1896 and died in 1917. He is buried in Arlington National Cemetery.[302]

On June 12th, the steamers *Star of the South*, the *South Carolina*, and the *Massachusetts* arrived at Pickens with more guns and stores. Brown notes that he had not received orders of any kind since arriving, and given the bombardment and surrender of Fort Sumter, "I do not feel under any obligations to confine myself to defensive measures . . ."[303] On the 14th, he reports: "The weather is now intensely hot, and will probably soon be, to men of Northern constitutions exposed to the miasma of the swamps, very unhealthy. I would not, therefore, throw any large body of troops here until after the September gales are over." He puts forward a scheme for raiding the mainland near Fort McCree with six or eight shallow draft gunboats and another plan for negotiating the channel at the east end of Santa Rosa island. For this, however, he would need gunboats and some 500 more troops.

On June 22nd, Brown notes that he has received seven of the 42-pounder rifled guns, which would be necessary to effectively fire across the bay.[304] He fails to even note the arrival of the 6th New York Volunteers who were on the same steamer, the *Vanderbilt*.[305]

On June 26th, he complained in a letter to the assistant adjutant general of having been ordered to send Barry's Company A and Hunt's Company M of the

---

300. O.R. Vol. 4, pp. 581–587; Butler,, B. F., pp. 282–286; CWSAC no. NC001.
301. O.R. Vol. 1, p. 424.
302. Cullum no. 1638, pp. 580, 581; Powell, W. H., p. 134; Powell W. H., *Army List*, p. 249; www.arlingtoncemetery.net/hwclosson.htm.
303. O.R. Vol. 1, p. 430.
304. O.R. Vol. 1, pp. 432–435, 440.
305. Morris, G., p. 34.

2nd Artillery to New York. He is vexed at now having to accommodate "a regiment of undrilled New York City Volunteers, entirely undisciplined . . ."

At this time, Brown could have experienced few, if any, dealings with the 6th New York Zouaves or Col. Billy Wilson, their colorful commander. It thus seems proven that Brown – the professional, the West Point graduate, and one who had spent his lifetime in the army – was acting on prejudice alone in his opinion of the raucous "roughs" with their Billy Goat mascot[306] and their politically appointed officers, mostly Democrats. They did not wear the gaudy uniform of other Zouave units; in fact, the only hint of Zouave about them might have been that Billy Wilson wore a sash. Rather, they had (figure 17) plain gray shirts and pants, and a brown felt hat. Still, they did not fit in with Brown's sense of military propriety.

FIGURE 17

Brown submitted a table of the armament at Fort Pickens, which he now regarded as complete, though the external water batteries were not. He repeats his complaint, however, that he has been stripped of sufficient officers and enlisted men to efficiently work all the guns.

Battery L to Pickens

To make up his perceived deficiency of men, on July 2nd, Brown ordered: "One of the artillery companies from Tortugas here.[307] I accordingly sent two companies of volunteers to that post. . . They may be expected in about a week, by which time I hope to have the guns and ammunition landed, and will be in a suitable state for offensive or defensive operations."

Thus, the rest of Battery L would join the dozen of its men who had been detached for service at Fort Pickens in April. Companies B and E of the 6th New York were the volunteers referred to that were traded off to Fort Jefferson. At the end of August Brown sent Company A of the 6th to Key West,[308] thus reducing the total numbers of the 6th at Fort Pickens to seven companies, and presumably reducing his having to deal with their foibles.

---

306. Morris, G., p. 35; figure 17 from August 31, 1861, *Harper's Weekly*, p. 552.
307. O.R. Vol. 1, pp. 434, 435, 437.
308. Morris, G., p. 41.

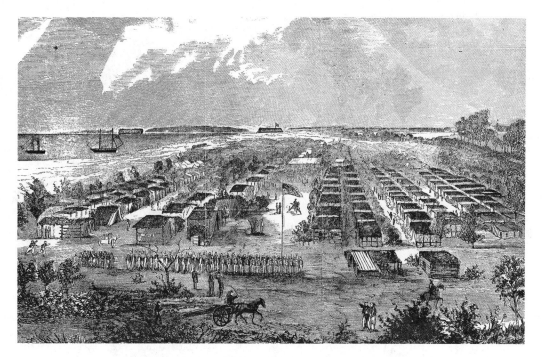

FIGURE 18. CAMP BROWN OF THE 6TH NEW YORK

Fort Pickens is in the distance, flying the flag. Fort McRee is beyond the ships off shore. Note the bowers built over the tents for protection from the intense sun. The troops in formation are still in their Zouave uniforms.
Harper's Weekly, October 26, 1861, p. 678.

Record 8/61
30 JUNE–31 AUGUST 1861, FORT PICKENS, FLORIDA

The Company left Fort Jefferson, Florida on the Steamship State of Georgia on the 5th July and arrived at Fort Pickens, Fla., on the 10th July 1861, per S.O. No. 38 Hdqtrs. Dept of Florida, dated Fort Pickens July 2nd 1861.

Samuel K. Dawson Capt.
William Silvey   1st Lt. Reg. Adj. O. No. 7 Hdqrs. Fort Dallas, Fla. Aug. 13,'57. Left Co. Apr. 22,'54, S.O. No. 62 Hdqrs. N.Y. Apr. 18,'54.
Richard H. Jackson 1st Lt. Joined Co. at Fort Pickens, Fla. (from detached service) July 10th 1861.

Strength: 93. Sick: 19.

Sick Present: Lewis Keller, Isaac T. Cain, Edmund Anglin, Thomas Brook, William C. Brunskill, Patrick Cummings, Christopher Ebel, Charles A. Flint, James Harkins, Joseph Kutschor, Charles F. Mansfield, James McWaters, Morgan S. Shapley, Martin Stanners, William Schaffer, Andrew Stoll, Reuben Townsend, Henry A. Ward.

Sick Absent: Charles Riley Sick at Ft. McIntosh, Texas. Absent from Company since Feb. 25th 1861.

Joined:
Woodruff, George A. 2nd Lt. By Promotion June 24th 1861 (never joined Company).

Joined by Assignment at Fort Pickens, July 15th 1861:

Christopher Ebel	17 Jan.'61 New York,	Franklin W. Richards	6 Feb.'61 New York
Morris Galvan	11 Jan.'61 Boston	Morgan Shapley	10 Dec.'60 Buffalo, NY
James Hanney	8 Jan.'61 New York	Martin Stanners	19 Jan.'61 Boston
John Lanahan	9 Jan.'61 Rochester, NY	William Schaffer	18 Jan.'61 New York
Charles F. Mansfield	16 Jan.'61 New York	John Tomson	9 Jan.'61 Boston
Daniel McSweeney	11 Feb.'61 New York		

Joined from Detached Service at Fort Pickens, July 10th 1861:

James Ahern	Patrick Cummings	Daniel McCoy	Michael O'Sullivan
Thomas Brook	Christopher Foley	John Meyer	William Parketton
William F. Brown	James McCarthy	David Meyers	Thomas Poole

Discharged:
Golden, James Pvt. 2 Feb.'60 New York At Fort Pickens, Fla. By Surgeon's Certificate of Disability, July 11th 1861.

Extra Duty Assignments:

Isaac T. Cain	Carpenter	Robert Curran	Teamster	Miles McDonough	Boatman
George Hadley	Blacksmith	Edward McLaughlin	Teamster	James Harkins	Ord. Dept. Laborer
James McWalters	Teamster	Henry William	Teamster	William Wynn	Ord. Dept. Laborer
Wallace D. Wright	Teamster	William Creed	Boatman		

The large number of those listed as sick is not explained by any special note in the muster roll. Only two of the twelve men detached from the company, Thomas Brook and Patrick Cummings, who had been at Fort Pickens since April 17th were sick. This might be some indication that the conditions at Pickens were better than at Jefferson, with its mosquito-filled cisterns. Five of the eleven that were joined by assignment were sick.

Events Elsewhere

July 3: The Western Department is created, consisting of the state of Illinois and "all of the states west of the Mississippi River and on this side of the Rocky Mountains, including New Mexico" with the colorful "Pathfinder," the trailblazer of the West, and the first Republican candidate for President (1856), John C. Fremont in command, at St. Louis.[309]

July 21: The First Battle of Manassas (Bull Run), Virginia, is fought[310] and is regarded as a great victory for the South. However, this serious setback did not seem to cause panic in Washington. Instead, determination ruled; and Congress continued in session, conducting business in a manner that indicates a certain sense

---

309. O.R. Vol. 3, pp. 390, 406.
310. Nicolay & Hay, Vol. IV, pp. 358, 360, 365–368.

of ultimately prevailing in what was now clearly to be a great struggle.

July 22: Act of Congress authorizes 500,000 volunteers to be raised by the states to serve for three years; to be disbanded at the end of the war.[311] On May 3rd, Lincoln had called for 42,034 volunteers for three years' service, for 18,000 seamen for one-to-three years' service, and 22,714 more men for the regular army, but without any real legal basis. Here, Congress confirmed his action.

July 24: Act of Congress: "The navy may hire, purchase, or contract for, and furnish and arm in the most efficient manner, such vessels as may be necessary for the temporary increase of the navy . . ." No limitation of any kind stated, except the funds appropriated were $3 million.[312]

July 28: The center of attention is now focused even more on the eastern theater, and a request by Bragg to the Confederate War Department for more troops is deflected by asking him how soon "and at what point you wish it to be assembled?"[313]

July 29: Act of Congress authorizes an increase in the regular army by 25,000.[314]

August 6: (1) The first Confiscation Act is signed by the President, confiscating property used for insurrectionary purposes. Thus, it set free any slaves employed by the consent of their masters against the government and lawful authority of the United States.[315]

(2) Lest there be any confusion about any act of the President since his inauguration, another act on this date declared, "all acts, proclamations and orders of the President since March 4, 1861, respecting the army and navy of the United States . . . are hereby approved. . ."[316]

August 10: As the Union "ramped up" to the war, notably after Lincoln's first call for 75,000 volunteers the day after Fort Sumter fell (77,875 volunteered) and his second call on May 3rd, many former officers of the "old army" offered their services. After the Mexican War, many had found careers in civilian life more attractive than in the underfunded army and had resigned their commissions. One such was Ulysses S. Grant, West Point class of 1843. However, his resignation from the army in 1854 had been clouded by allegations that it was to avoid facing disciplinary action by his commander for alcoholism.[317] Another prejudice against Grant was that he was not successful in his time in civilian life, unlike other West Pointers who had cut grand swaths as lawyers, politicians, or business leaders.

Captain Grant offered his services in a letter to the adjutant general on May 24th, 1861. He never received an answer. In fact, the letter was not found until after

---

311. Appendix to *Congressional Globe*, July 18th, 1861, p. 27; *Harper's Weekly*, May 18th, p. 307.
312. Childs, G. W., p. 240.
313. O.R. Vol. 1, p. 469.
314. O.R. Ser. III, Vol. 1, p. 700.
315. *Congressional Globe*, August 6th, 1861, p. 455.
316. Childs, G. W., p. 240.
317. *Encyclopedia Britannica*, 1911; *Harper's Weekly*, August 31sth, 1861, p. 559.

the war, and then by accident. It has since been copied into the Official Records.[318] Undaunted, he began by assisting in the organizing of the Illinois State Militia. Having reintroduced himself to the profession, he was supported by politicians from Illinois when recommendations for appointments for brigadier generals of volunteers were requested by the Lincoln administration. He was confirmed by the Senate on July 31st, 1861, and assigned to the Western Department[319] as commander of the district of Ironton, Missouri.[320]

August 17: A seemingly final blow is handed to Bragg in a letter from the adjutant and inspector general's office at Richmond:

> General: Your requisition for ordnance and ordnance stores, inclosed with letter of 7th August, 1861, has been referred to the Bureau of Ordnance, and returned with report that there are no guns. These guns have been specially in demand for Manassas . . .
> R.H. Chilton, *Assistant Adjutant General*

August 19: McClellan is appointed commander of the Army of the Potomac.[321] George B. McClellan, West Point class of 1846, had resigned his commission in 1857 and had become vice president of the Illinois Central Railroad and then president of the Ohio and Mississippi Railroad. From this prominent position he was appointed a major general to the command of the Ohio militia in April of 1861 and then a major general in the regular army in the occupation of West Virginia. After the Union defeat at First Manassas, he became commander of the Army of the Potomac by order of General Scott. The young (age 35) Napoleon soon clashed with Scott,[322] as predicted by their earlier fundamental disagreement over the strategy for the prosecution of the war. Three months later, General Scott asked to be retired.[323] He was replaced by McClellan on November 1st.[324]

August 30th: Fremont issued an order declaring martial law in Missouri and the confiscation of the property "of all persons who shall take up arms against the United States . . . and their slaves, if any they have, are hereby declared freemen."[325] The fine point was that the slave need not be employed against the Union cause, which was the limitation of the First Confiscation Act. Fremont refused to back away from his sweeping order, and Lincoln then overrode him on September 11th,[326] ordering his

---

318. O.R. Ser. III, Vol. 1, p. 234.
319. O.R. Vol. 3, pp. 390, 406.
320. O.R. Vol. 3, p. 430.
321. O.R. Vol. 5, pp. 567, 575; Cullum, Vol. II, pp 250–254; McClellan was Cullum no. 1273.
322. Nicolay & Hay, Vol. IV, pp. 298–303, 322, 323, 351, 352, 368, 440, 445; *Harper's Weekly*, August 31st, 1861, p. 559.
323. O.R. Ser. III, Vol. 1, p. 611, 613, 614.
324. O.R. Vol. 5, p. 639.
325. O.R. Vol. 3, pp. 466, 467.
326. O.R. Vol. 3, pp. 485, 486.

command to conform to the provisions of the First Confiscation Act only. Lincoln's concern was that Fremont's provision would "alarm our Southern Union friends and turn them against us; perhaps ruin our fair prospect for Kentucky."[327]

The "Truce" Ends

On September 2nd, Brown took the first action of an aggressive nature since his arrival. In May, Bragg's forces had towed a floating dry dock out from the navy yard. The tow line had allegedly parted, and it had drifted to a position off the western shore of Santa Rosa Island near Batteries Lincoln and Cameron (see figure 6, p. 59), where it grounded. For weeks, the Federals watched as the Confederates attempted to refloat it. Concerned that these efforts might be a ruse to construct a floating battery, Brown ordered it destroyed.[328] Lieutenant Shipley of Company C, 3rd Infantry and 11 picked men rowed out to it shortly after 9:00 p.m. Finding no sentries on board, they put in place three "large" Columbiad shells and "combustible material," lit a fuse, and skedaddled. They had rowed "scarcely . . . twenty yards" before flames broke out, followed by the explosion of the shells. No one was injured, and the dry dock was destroyed.

In its turn, the navy conducted a raid on a Confederate schooner, the *Judah*, moored at the navy yard, which was being fitted out as a privateer.[329] Approved by Adm. William Mervine, commander of the Gulf Blockading Squadron, the raid was led by Lt. John H. Russell of the flagship USS *Colorado* in the early morning hours of September 14th. About 100 sailors and marines of the squadron rowed with muffled oars to the schooner. Though they were fired upon by the alert Confederates, they boarded the *Judah* and set it afire. Others of the attackers spiked the only gun in the navy yard, a 10-inch Columbiad.[330]

Bragg later blamed the success of the attack on the conspiracy of nine Confederate marines who had earlier deserted to the Federal side and brought the intelligence of the Confederate preparations. For his part, Brown fully expected retaliation, but none quickly came. Brown was later criticized in a report to the secretary of war, noting that Fort Pickens did not provide covering fire at any time before or during the *Judah* raid and that none of Brown's troops had participated.[331]

---

327. O.R. Vol. 3, pp. 469, 470.
328. O.R. Vol. 6, p. 665; *Harper's Weekly*, October 12th, 1861, p. 655.
329. O.R. Vol. 6, pp. 437, 438; *NY Times*, September 30th, 1861.
330. *Harper's Weekly*, August 3rd, 1861, p. 495. A cast iron, muzzle loaded, smoothbore cannon of a design by Bomford. First used in the War of 1812, they were produced in both eight-inch and ten-inch bores. Modified in 1844 by increasing their length and girth in the hope of increased range, they were found incapable of standing the increased charge used, frequently bursting. They were downgraded to be used as shell guns, which use a lesser powder charge.
331. O.R. Vol. 6, p. 666.

The operation was entirely to the credit of the more aggressive folks in the navy, who suffered three killed and eight wounded, including Lieutenant Russell. The view of the navy was that its duty was the enforcement of the blockade and that it could not countenance the outfitting of a pirate ship.

Record 10/61
31 AUGUST–31 OCTOBER 1861, FORT PICKENS, FLORIDA

[No entry in the "Record of Events"]

Samuel K. Dawson   Capt. Sick since Oct. 1, 1861
Edmund Kirby   1st Lt. Joined by promotion May 14,'61 S.O. No. 64 W. D. Wash. Aug. 22,'61. Abs. on det. ser. Since May 14,'61.
George A. Woodruff   2nd Lt. Joined by promotion June 24,'61 S.O. No. 64 W. D. Wash. Aug. 22,'61. Abs. on det. ser. Since June 24,'61.

Strength: 91. Sick: 7.

Sick Present: Samuel K. Dawson, Patrick Cummings, Michael Olvany, William V. Thompson.

Sick Absent: Thomas Brook, Ft. Hamilton, NY. Left Company Sept. 17, 1861
    William C. Brunskill   do.
    Charles Riley, Ft. McIntosh, TX Abs. since Feb. 25, 1861. Reduced from Sgt. to Pvt. July 12,'61 O. No. 2, Co. L 1st Arty Ft. Pickens, Fla. Subject to the approval of the Commander of the Regiment.

Died: Christopher Ebel, Pvt. Jan. 17,'61 New York, at Ft. Hospital Sept. 27, 1861, of scourbutics.
    James Harkins, Pvt. Oct. 1,'60 New York, at Ft. Pickens Hospital Oct. 8, 1861, of chronic diarrhea.

Transferred:
    William Silvey 1st Lt. Reg. Adj. O. No. 7 1st Arty. Ft. Dallas, Fla. Aug. 13,'57. Left Co. Apr. 22,'54 S.O. 62 Hdqrs. New York April 18,'54. Trans. By prom. As Captain to Co. "A" 1st Arty. To date from Aug. 14,'61. S.O. No. 64, W.D. Adj. Gen'l Office, Wash. Aug. 22,'61.
    Richard H. Jackson 2nd Lt. Trans. By prom. as 1st Lieut. To Co. "B" 1st Arty. To date from Aug.14,'61. S. O. No. 64 Adj. Gen'ls. Office Wash. Aug. 22,'61.

Attached:
    Richard H. Jackson 1st Lt. Since May 14th 1861. In Command of Company since Oct. 1st 1861.

Sickness

The reduction in the number of men sick from 19 on the last roll to the 7 listed here is interpreted to mean that the diet and sanitary conditions had improved, not to mention the weather. Note in the roll that Christopher Ebel died of scurvy and James Harkins of dysentery. Ebel, one of those newly assigned to Battery L, was a healthy young man only six months before when recruited in New York, yet he is listed as sick when he was assigned to Battery L on July 15th. Harkins was with the second group of recruits into Battery L in 1860; he appears in table II, chapter 1. His service was cut short after only a year.

The quick recovery of the rest of the sick is perhaps an indication that the sickness was not due to some one of the more serious lingering diseases like malaria. Health matters were originally drawn to Brown's attention by the surgeon on his staff, Dr. John Campbell, when, as early as May 9th, he noted scurvy "some cases of considerable severity"[332] in Company G [Slemmer's] and had recommended that they be shipped out, as was earlier noted. Brown had agreed, but now seemed to be convinced that the bulk of his command was healthy. Since the surgeon had intervened, it can only be speculated that he had invoked Army Regulation, paragraph 1,079, which states when the surgeon considers it "necessary for the health of the troops, the commanding officer . . . may order issues of fresh vegetables, pickled onions, sauer-kraut, or molasses, with an extra quantity of rice and vinegar." Today we look upon this as only partially correct – skip everything except the vegetables and add fruit. Fresh meat has some value also, but the presence of beef cattle has not appeared in the records from this time at Santa Rosa Island.

In the August 24th, 1861, issue of *Harper's Weekly*, there appears, on page 542, the July 12th report of the recently appointed U.S. Sanitary Commission. Titled "Rules for Preserving the Health of the Soldier," it notes practices that we would today consider obvious to the maintenance of good health, and it concurs with the above army regulation without comment. However, item no. 9 in its list of rules says, in part: "Those great scourges of a camp life, the scurvy and diarrhea, more frequently result from a want of skill in cooking than from the badness of the ration, or from any other cause whatever." Rule no. 13 continues further off the deep end with: "Water should be always drank in moderation, especially when the body is heated. The excessive thirst which follows violent exertion or loss of blood, is unnatural, and is not quenched by large and repeated draughts." This is altogether a rather amazing level of ignorance. Forget common sense, or what the British navy had known about scurvy for years; fill up the soldier with the generous U.S. rations of coffee, gluten, and fat, and he will be in the best of health!

In a June 12th report to the adjutant general in Washington, Brown had written: "My command continues comparatively healthy, there being no serious disease, and the number diminishing." However, just two days later, in another letter to the adjutant general he had written: "The weather is now intensely hot, and will probably soon be to the men of Northern Constitutions exposed to the miasma of the swamps very unhealthy."[333]

Less than two weeks later[334] he announces: "My sick list is heavy and increasing, having this morning upwards of ninety on it . . . [Brown is evidently worried but

---

332. O.R. Vol. 1, pp. 408, 410.
333. O.R. Vol. 1, p. 431.
334. O.R. Vol. 1, p. 432.

then recovers his optimism.] None serious – arising from hard work in the sun and in the water, sleeping in damp casemates, and drinking impure water. We have been nearly six weeks without rain, and with only two light storms since. One of the cisterns leaked and we lost the water, and that of the other has to be used with great economy and only for drinking, water for cooking purposes being obtained by sinking wells."[335] Brown's report of 100 sick "and [oh, yes] 70 volunteers" on August 16th [336] seems to have been the peak of the crisis.

Perhaps some of Brown's optimism was due to the fact that the adjutant general's office had informed him that "provisions for 1,000 men for six months, a cargo of ice and quartermaster stores" were due to be shipped.[337] Ice, but no mention of vegetables, desiccated or otherwise. He also notes that a "temporary" hospital had been built about a mile east of the fort near the beach. This was probably cooler due to the onshore breeze. From the same breeze, it may well have been less haunted by mosquitoes.

The considerable proportions of the sick on the Confederate side is also noted. In June,[338] news was received from an escaped slave that the smallpox was raging. An August 8th letter from Col. S. A. M. Wood, of the 7th Alabama Regiment and a brigade commander at Pensacola, written to the Confederate secretary of war complains: "Perhaps you would like to hear from this place, once of so great importance." He reports of sickness, "In First Regiment three hundred and twenty-four out of nine hundred and seventeen are sick." Further, he talks of the demoralization of the troops from inaction and the evidence that the "field of fight" is to be in Virginia.[339]

Though Brown's theme song was always that he needed more troops in order to properly man the fort and deal with his adversary, he could well have considered the health effects of the numbers of men crowded into this corner of a narrow island with no water supply. There were also almost 100 horses and mules present at this time. With them came flies and sanitation problems, not to mention their requirement for four gallons of water each, per day. More crowding would exacerbate the problem, and another volunteer regiment, the 75th New York, would arrive on December 13th.

---

335. No reference has been found as to the quality of the water in the cisterns of the fort. Hall, H. & J., 75th History, note on page 30 that wells dug in the sand, to the depth of 4 or 5 feet, and lined with barrels, provided fresh water. New ones, however, had to be dug almost continually, because the water became brackish in any of those used for more than a week.
336. O.R. Vol. 1, p. 441.
337. O.R. Vol. 1, p. 428.
338. O.R. Vol. 1, p. 432.
339. O.R. Vol. 1, p. 470.

Troops to Ship Island

On September 10th and 12th, Simon Cameron further defined and expanded General Butler's role. He would command a mission of a volunteer force of six regiments from the six New England states for an expedition along the "eastern shore of Virginia."[340] It is not clear if Cameron knew that the secret board of officers had already decided that the objective was New Orleans. This fact was not revealed even to Butler until mid-January 1862.[341]

On October 1st, the temporary Department of New England was created for Butler, at Boston, as a device for his recruiting efforts.[342] Planning for the Southern expedition now began,[343] and an intermediate location for the troop buildup was chosen as Ship Island, about one hundred miles off the mouth of the Mississippi, which had been occupied by a token force of 170 Union sailors and marines since September 17th, after it had been abandoned by General Twiggs, now commanding the Confederate forces at New Orleans.

Butler aggressively raised troops in parallel with the state machinery designed to meet their previously assigned quotas. In his haste, he offended Governor Andrew of Massachusetts, his former friend and mentor and one of the strongest supporters of the war. Few troops were better equipped than Massachusetts men. The records of the controversy of Butler versus Andrew take up 55 pages in the Official Records.[344] He was accused of interference, insulting behavior, and authorization for the embarkation and sailing of troops that had not been properly mustered. Butler was a man on a mission – like his swift and determined action at Baltimore – a laudable characteristic, but bound to create controversy wherever he went.

On December 3rd, 1861, the first of Butler's Massachusetts and Connecticut troops[345] arrived off Ship Island to begin its real occupation in any numbers.

We shall see that the Confederate authorities refused to believe that this preliminary move to the Union invasion of New Orleans was a threat; and then, when they had to admit that it really was, they would turn away, focus on Union threats in the North, and abandon the coast, with the lone exception of Mobile, which was not attacked by the Yankees until August of 1864. It remained as one of the few ports where Confederate commerce raiders could land to refit and resupply. Their story appears in chapter 7.

---

340. O.R. Vol. 6, p. 677.
341. Welles, Vol. I, pp. 60, 61.
342. O.R. Ser. III, Vol. 1, p. 822; O.R. Vol. 51, p. 491.
343. Welles, *Galaxy*, November 1871, p. 673.
344. O.R. Ser. III, Vol. 1, pp. 810–865.
345. O.R. Vol. 6, p. 466.

Chapter 4

Raid on Santa Rosa; Record 12/61; Bombardment of November 22nd & 23rd; Confederate Concerns; Record 2/62; 1862 Roster; Bombardment of January 1st, 1862; Confederate Withdrawals; Record 4/62; Reconnaissance on Santa Rosa

Raid on Santa Rosa

Brown's abstract for October lists 985 officers and men present for duty,[346] though his "aggregate" strength is listed as 1,203. The difference is those who are sick, on leave, in confinement, on other duty such as hospital attendant, detached[347] for duty elsewhere, sick elsewhere, or not there because of permanent assignment to regimental headquarters. By comparison, an abstract of the field return of the forces under Bragg for October 1st, 1861, totaled 6,533, with 5,247 present for duty.[348] Thus, Brown had about one-fifth the number of effectives as did Bragg. One might therefore ask why Bragg committed only 1,100 men to his raid when he could have potentially overwhelmed Brown.

Bragg's retaliation for the destruction of the dry dock and the raid on the *Judah* came as a raid on Santa Rosa Island. On the night of October 8th, selected troops were detached from Bragg's forces and gathered at the navy yard. Under the cover of darkness, they were boarded on the steamer *Time*, which headed to Pensacola. Under the overall command of Brig. Gen. Richard H. Anderson,[349] the troops were organized into three battalions during the passage. The first, under Col. James R. Chalmers of the 9th Mississippi Regiment, was assigned to advance from the landing place along the north (bay) side of the island; the second, under Col. J. Patton Anderson of the 1st Regiment of Florida Volunteers, was to move along the south (outer or Gulf side) beach; and the third battalion, under Col. John K.

---

346. O.R. Vol. 6, p. 672. Brown mentions 1,300 for November, on page 469, and slightly exaggerates Bragg's strength at 8,000.
347. It is likely that there were none on detached duty at this time, Brown having concern about his strength. Soldiers were given a one-month leave for every year of service, so this would reduce some of the regulars present to something over 1,100. The primary alternate categories remaining, sick and in confinement, could vary widely.
348. O.R. Vol. 6, p. 750.
349. O.R. Vol. 6, p. 460; figure 1, Morris, G., p. 70, altered.

Jackson of the 5th Regiment of Georgia Volunteers, was to follow Chalmers and push through the thickets to the middle of the island and attack Camp Brown, the site of the 6th New York, at the sound of gunfire. A special group of 53 men under Lt. James Hallonquist were lightly armed and carried materials to spike cannon and set fire to buildings and equipment. With a medical staff of 25, the raiding party totaled 1,089 men.

After difficulties with the transfer of some of the men to the steamer *Ewing* and boats and barges to be towed by the smaller steamer *Neaffie*, they got underway at midnight. They had not formed up at the landing site, a little more than four miles east of the fort, near the swampy ground indicated at the extreme right of figure 1, and about three miles from the pickets of Camp Brown, until 2:00 a.m. The dotted lines indicate the tracks of the advance of the three groups.

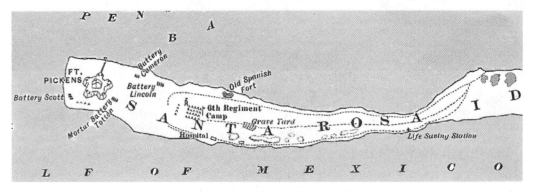

FIGURE 1

After some stumbling through the swampy ground, Chalmers' force of 350 men reached the 6th New York's picket posts at 3:30. Some of the pickets were shot down after a stiff resistance at the site of the old Spanish fort and others at the Gulf beach side, and all were soon driven in by Anderson's force.

The alarm having been given by the firing of the pickets, the 6th New York were rousted from their tents and formed up in what seems to have been in good order.[350] They then fell back toward the water batteries Totten and Lincoln and avoided being surrounded. John K. Jackson's 260 Georgia volunteers were then able to advance into the deserted camp. They, like another group of Confederate attackers Battery L would meet three years later at the Battle of Cedar Creek, Virginia, did not push on immediately, using to their advantage the surprise and confusion of the moment. Instead, they stopped to loot the 6th New York camp. Hallonquist's men then went to work, made easy by the brush construction of the lean-tos and bowers that had been crafted for protection from the sun. By 4:00 a.m. the flames were visible from the fort. The delay

---

350. O.R. Vol. 6, p. 447; report of Col. Wm. Wilson. In fact, if there had been utter chaos, there would have been more prisoners taken.

took the initiative away from any planned Confederate advance.

The largest group of the 6th, about 150 men, commanded by Lt. Col. John Creighton, apparently drifted back to near their campsite after no further advance was made by the Confederates. The men of the 6th, however, took no further action until met at daybreak by Lt. Richard H. Jackson who ordered them to advance.[351] For this lack of initiative, the officers of the 6th were roundly condemned by both Jackson and Brown.[352]

The fort had long since been aroused, the east ramparts manned, batteries Lincoln and Totten prepared, and a force sent out under the command of Maj. Israel Vodges. It included Company E of the 3rd Infantry, 62 men, under Capt. John Hildt, and Company A of the 1st Artillery, 31 men, under 2nd Lt. Franck Taylor. Vodges' little group collected Company G of the 6th New York, under Capt. J. H. Dobie, earlier assigned to Battery Lincoln, as they passed by.

They proceeded up the north beach with Company G deployed as skirmishers on the right flank to a point "some distance above Camp Brown."[353] A group of troops on their right and rear were encountered, which were first confused with their own skirmishers. This was a major part of the Confederate force returning to their boats. Major Vodges, on horseback, rode into them and was captured. His second in command, Hildt, then took over. A Confederate officer who demanded their surrender was shot at, and in the interval, some quick thinking allowed the Hildt group to take cover behind some "rising ground" in their front. Being greatly outnumbered and almost cut off, they withdrew diagonally toward the south side of the island, and to quote Hildt, "as soon as his front was clear, the enemy proceeded along the north beach." It is clear that the Confederates could have soon overwhelmed this small force of 90 men had they wished to retain their foothold on the island.

With word that Vodges had been captured, and his command in trouble, a second group, under the command of Maj. Lewis G. Arnold, was sent out at about 5:00 a.m. It consisted of Company H, 2nd Artillery, Captain Robertson, 48 men, and Company C, 3rd Artillery, Lieutenant Shipley, 64 men. They followed in the footsteps of Hildt's men and found them still engaged with the retreating rebels. Hidden behind the sand ridges along the beach, they fired upon one departing rowboat at about 1,200 yards – long since out of range. Making a further reconnaissance, they discovered the bulk of the rebel force embarking close to their original landing point about four miles up the beach, or about a mile from Robertson's group. At the double-quick, Robertson was able to advance to within 200 to 250 yards of the three Confederate steamers, in no small measure due to the fact

---

351. O.R. Vol. 6, p. 457; report of R. H. Jackson.
352. O.R. Vol. 6, p. 442.
353. O.R. Vol. 6, p. 449; report of J. McL. Hildt. Later analysis put the place at 3,331 yards from the fort, or about a mile beyond Camp Brown. Ibid., p. 442.

that one of the flats in tow was aground.[354] From behind a tree-covered sand hill, the company opened fire on the Confederate flotilla for 15 minutes. In General Anderson's report, he says that the propeller of the *Neaffie* became entangled by a hawser, leading to the incident, which would be comical if it had not been so deadly. It is likely that at this time the greatest number of Confederate casualties were taken. Anderson listed 17 killed, 39 wounded, and 30 prisoners (*his men taken*).[355] Brown listed 4 regulars and 9 volunteers killed, with 20 regulars and 7 volunteers wounded, and 10 regulars and 11 volunteers missing.[356] In contrast, a newspaper seen at Pensacola announced: "It is now certain that 175 in killed, wounded, and missing will more than cover our entire loss, while 250 will barely cover that of the Federalists."[357]

1st Lt. Richard H. Jackson was called out alone to follow Arnold.[358] His duty was to collect any men who had become separated from Arnold's command. He reports collecting about 80 men and 3 officers of the 6th at Camp Brown and Creighton's group nearby. They arrived at the north beach too late to be involved in any action. Jackson is most critical of the 6th New York Volunteers. He states: "I am sorry to have to state that on my arrival at Colonel Wilson's camp, I was greatly surprised to see so many men wandering around, some of them without arms (although there were plenty to be had), and to find . . . 3 or 4 officers, who did not even attempt to organize the men or move forward with them. A great many of the men said that they would have been glad to have gone forward before my arrival if they had any person to organize and lead them."

It is noted that the navy was requested to provide support in terms of firepower and marines, but requesting this by a messenger sent by rowboat proved so slow as to render their subsequent preparations too late for participation in the fight. They conducted a reconnaissance, however, to see if any rebel troops had escaped up the island (none were found).[359] It will be remembered that six months prior, on April 16th, a system of signals[360] in case of an attack on the fort from the east had been agreed upon between Colonel Brown and Flag Officer Adams. If the fort was in danger of attack, it was to send up two signal rockets. As a recognition signal, the navy would answer with two. The fort would then send out a

---

354. This per Robertson's report, O.R. Vol. 6, p. 451. Anderson has it as the steamer *Neaffie*; ibid., p. 462.
355. O.R. Vol. 6, p. 462.
356. O.R. Vol. 6, p. 443.
357. O.R. Vol. 6, p. 442.
358. O.R. Vol. 6, p. 457. Arnold and Company C, 2nd Artillery were transferred to Fort Pickens in September, though no order survives in the O.R. The fort now had six regular artillery companies: A, F, and L of the 1st; A, C, and K of the 2nd; and two regular infantry companies, C and E of the 3rd; plus the 6th New York Volunteers.
359. O.R. Vol. 6, p. 450.
360. O.R. Vol. 1, p. 400.

party equipped with two red lanterns, which they would display on the beach at the place where the marines assigned should be landed. Why Brown did not make use of this protocol is a mystery.

In General Anderson's report,[361] dated October 23rd, he states that after the camp of the 6th New York had been "most thoroughly" destroyed, he reassembled his men "with a view to proceeding against and destroying the batteries . . . but daylight appearing, and there being no longer a possibility of a surprise of the batteries, I directed the signal for retiring to be sounded . . ." He later claims that "large stores of provisions . . . were entirely consumed."

Reports from those on the Federal side dispute Anderson. The report[362] of the engineer officer, Maj. Z. B. Tower, states that about three-fourths of the 6th camp was burned. In Captain Langdon's report,[363] he specifically mentions putting out the fire started in the store shed. Brown[364] admits to 30 tents (half of them), and a dozen muskets destroyed.

The reports Bragg submitted to the adjutant general[365] were exaggerated in almost every statistic, e.g., "600 or 700" was quoted as the strength of the 6th New York (versus 250), and downright controversial in another. He publicly claimed in the *Pensacola Observer* that Confederate wounded had been "massacred" after being captured, something that an offended Brown hotly denied.

The Confederate raid failed by its own admission because Anderson allowed his men to loot and set fire to the camp of the 6th New York. If the camp had been deserted by the 6th, then it offered no obstacle to the overwhelming numbers of Anderson's troops to rush to attack the batteries and disable them. The few men sent piecemeal out from the fort (at first 93, then 112) could hardly have scared away 1,000 Confederates if they were determined to assault the outer batteries.

If the batteries were the objective, would their capture have made Fort Pickens less defensible? Probably not, because the Confederate forces perceived the danger of being shelled out by the blockade fleet had they remained on the island. The argument could be made that the Confederates could have transported enough cannon to the island to both lay siege to the fort and return enough fire to the Federal ships to retain their foothold. However, it must be remembered that Bragg was low on ammunition and had earlier been told that no more guns were available; the field at Manassas having priority.

There is, however, another reason for the restraint. Bragg's command had been expanded on October 7th, to include the "coast and State of Alabama" to be known

---

361. O.R. Vol. 6, p. 460.
362. O.R. Vol. 6, p. 443.
363. O.R. Vol. 6, p. 454.
364. O.R. Vol. 6, p. 442.
365. O.R. Vol. 6, pp. 458, 459, 670, 671.

as the Department of Alabama and West Florida.[366] It is probable that Bragg knew something of the defenses in and around Mobile and that they were weak. If not restrained by this uncertainty, he was well aware of his own weakness, in that, by the end of the year the enlistments of a number of his troops would expire and that recruitment was in a state of chaos. The governors of the individual states were loath to send troops out of the bounds of their state. The politicians were simply answering the cries of their constituents who feared being left defenseless. Thus, one-year state militia were being raised and equipped at the expense of draining volunteers and equipment from the Confederate service, all of whom were to serve for three years or the duration of the war.

Bragg left for an inspection of the defensive preparations in and around Mobile on October 22nd. He met with General Withers on the 23rd and toured the area on the 24th. He found Fort Gaines to be "rapidly approaching a condition for strong defense, but is almost destitute of guns and ammunition." He found Fort Morgan to be in better condition, though not half armed, and with a limited supply of ammunition. Declaring that it was the key to the defenses of Mobile Bay, it must have heavy armament and ample supplies. "I shall at once *reduce my position at Pensacola to one of defense strictly*, and send what can be spared to this point, *though it will be totally inadequate to the wants here*."

The authorities in Richmond must have begun to wonder whether the substantial presence of the Yankees in Pickens and on the sea had trumped their ability to ever take Fort Pickens – even if this was still a worthwhile endeavor. Stalemate, in this remote place, perhaps would be sufficient if the war could be prosecuted with daring elsewhere. In addition to Manassas, success had been bestowed upon the Confederates at Wilson's Creek, Missouri,[367] in August; and again at Lexington, which gave the Confederates control of southwestern Missouri; and again at Ball's Bluff, Virginia,[368] in October, which was a rout of the Union forces that killed Col. Edward D. Baker, a U.S. senator, and had shaken the Washington establishment.

In all, the story of the raid was a story of ineptitude and timidity on both sides. The raid having been beaten back on October 9th, no significant events took place until a general bombardment of the Confederate positions on the mainland would be initiated by Brown on November 22nd, using the combined forces of the army and navy.

---

366. O.R. Vol. 6, p. 751.
367. O.R. Vol. 3, pp. 2, 71–124. Italics added by the author.
368. O.R. Vol. 5, pp. 3, 32, 34, 290, 299, et. seq.

Record 12/61
31 OCTOBER–31 DECEMBER 1861, FORT PICKENS, FLORIDA

The Company was engaged in the bombardment on the 22nd and 23rd Nov.'61 at Fort Pickens, Fla. Corp'l Andrew J. Beeler was wounded in action on the 22nd Nov.'61. Lost his right arm.

1. Henry W. Closson   Capt. Promoted to Co. by letter War Dept. Nov. 21,'61. In Command since Dec. 8, 1861.
2. Edward L. Appleton   1st Lt. Trans. To Co. S.O. no. 321 Hdqtrs. Dept. of the Army, Washington, Dec. 5,'61. Abs. without leave.
3. J.S. Gibbs   1st Lt. Trans. To Co. S.O. no. 321 Hdqtrs. Dept. of the Army, Washington, Nov. 27,'61. Abs. without leave.
4. T. K. Gibbs   2nd Lt.   do.

Transferred:

1. S.K. Dawson   Capt. To 19th Inf. [by promotion to Major] G.O. no. 65, War Dept. A.G.O. Washington, Aug. 23,'61. Left Co. Nov. 3,'61.
2. Edmund Kirby   1st Lt. To Co. "L" 1st Arty. Sp.O. no. 321 Hdqtrs. Dept. of the Army, Washington, Dec. 5,'61. Never joined Co. "L".
3. George A. Woodruff   2nd Lt. Absent on det. svc. since June 24,'61 Person never joined Co. L.

Detached: Richard H. Jackson 1st Lt. Left Co. Dec. 8, 1861.

Strength: 88. Sick: 12.

Sick Present: Andrew J. Beeler, John Buckley, Robert Curran, Michael Hanney, Michael Kenny, William Schaffer, Warren P. Shaw, William V. Thompson, Henry H. Ward.

Sick Absent: Thomas Brook, Ft. Hamilton, NY. Left Co. Sept, 17, 1861.
    William Brunskill   do.
    Charles Riley Ft. McIntosh, TX. Abs. since Feb. 21, 1861. Reduced to Pvt. July 12, 1861.

Died:

1. Thomas Conroy   Sgt. 1 Jan.'59 San Antonio, Killed at Ft. Pickens, Fla. by the accidental explosion of a shell while in the line of his duty.
2. Lewis Hey   Pvt. 3 Sept.'58 New York   do.
3. Thomas Poole   Pvt. 4 Nov.'57 Detroit   do.
4. Michael Reedy   Pvt. 1 Jan.'57 San Antonio   do.

Capt. Henry Closson,[369] West Point class of 1854, first appears here, transferred to the company by his promotion, and the transfer of Samuel Dawson, by promotion to major, and an assignment with the 19th Infantry. Closson had previously been commanding Battery F, which had accompanied Battery L ever since they had arrived at Fort Duncan in 1860. Closson, as was previously noted, would remain in command of Battery L for the rest of the war and beyond; however, his brevet promotion to major on July 8, 1863, would place him in a position to be called away from Battery L for long periods of time. Battery L never saw him from October of 1863 to July of 1864, except as his duties as chief of artillery of

---

369. Cullum, Vol. II, no. 1638.

the 19th Army Corps may have impacted Battery L. Again, during August of 1864, he was detached for service as chief of artillery in the Mobile expedition. Having been promoted to brevet lieutenant colonel, he was again detached in November and December of 1864 as chief of artillery and ordnance of the Cavalry Corps of the Middle Military Division, in the Shenandoah Valley.

This meant that the direct daily command of the battery often fell to the second most senior officer or even the third most senior officer. Since two lieutenants, Kirby and Woodruff, who had been assigned but never joined, a third officer, Edward L. Appleton, was assigned on December 5th, but had not yet arrived. Appleton had been appointed a lieutenant on August 5th, directly from civilian life at Bangor, Maine. He was the second son of the Maine Supreme Court Chief Justice John Appleton. Edward never had any connection with West Point.[370] He apparently was caught up in the popular enthusiasm to join the Union cause several months before his older brother, John, began raising Company H of the 12th Maine Volunteers, which was mustered into Union service in November of 1861. They were assigned to the Department of the Gulf, where Battery L was to find itself in 1863. Thus, by a stroke of fate, the two brothers, one in the volunteers and the other in the regulars, would eventually serve in some of the same campaigns.

Note that Charles Riley, absent since February, has been reduced to private. This was to make way for the promotion of Alexander J. Baby to corporal and Julius Becker from corporal to sergeant.

Bombardment of November 22 & 23

One might ask: Why was there such a long time between the Confederate raid and any retaliation by Colonel Brown? Ever since April 16th, when he first took command, Brown seemed to have interminable excuses why he hesitated to initiate any action even after the "truce" was broken by the navy's burning of the *Judah*. By now, however, Brown was quick to respond to Bragg's raid of October 9th. He quickly consulted[371] with Admiral McKean, and the two had agreed to begin a general bombardment of the Confederate positions on the 16th. Unfortunately, events at the "Head of the Passes," the location at the mouth of the Mississippi where it divides into three branches, caused McKean to advise Brown to postpone the plan. McKean's letter[372] to the Secretary of the Navy Gideon Welles explains:

---

370. Henry, G. V., Vol. II, p. 36; Cleveland, W., pp. 222, 225, 763; Haskin, W. L., pp. 626, 627; Heitman, F. B., p. 168.
371. O.R. Vol. 6, p. 669.
372. ORN Ser. I, Vol. 16, p. 703. William McKean succeeded William Mervine on September 22nd, 1861.

U.S. Flagship Niagara
Off Fort Pickens, October 15, 1861

Sir: The steamer *McClellan* has just arrived with disastrous news from the Mississippi. Our ships have been driven off from the Head of the Passes.

The *Richmond* had several of her planks stove in by the steam ram[373] and all the guns of the *Vincennes* except four have been thrown overboard.

Nothing but the arrival in the *McClellan* of the rifled guns loaned from Fort Pickens saved the vessels from another and, probably, more destructive attack. . . . I shall return to the river immediately in this ship, notwithstanding that every arrangement is made for the bombardment of Pensacola at daylight tomorrow morning. The two ships here, the *Niagara* and the *Colorado*, were to open on Fort McCree, and the adjoining batteries.

A large increase of force and a supply of heavy rifled guns is essential . . .

I shall leave the *Colorado* here to blockade the harbor and to prevent the landing of the enemy upon Santa Rosa . . .

Wm. W. McKean,
Flag-Officer, Commanding Gulf Blockading Squadron

FIGURE 2

The "Battle at Southwest Pass," as it was called in the December 7th issue of *Harper's Weekly*, p. 779, described how, on October 12th, the ships of the Gulf

---

373. The reference to the *Vincennes* throwing its guns overboard was to lighten it. It had become grounded, but this action allowed it to escape the ram *Manassas*, figure 2, from US Naval History and Heritage Command, photo no. NH608.

Blockading Squadron were attacked by Confederate ships, including the iron-hulled ram *Manassas* (figure 2). The *McClellan*, mentioned in McKean's report, was an army transport that had been sent on loan to the Mississippi portion of the blockading squadron by Colonel Brown at McKean's request.[374] It had carried two Parrott rifled guns. McKean had already been aware that the navy did not have many of these new pieces of artillery, and upon his arrival at Southwest Pass on the morning of October 16th, he was dismayed to learn of instances of the affair that showed that the Union ships had been outgunned by the Confederate ships, apparently equipped with rifled guns.

Having cleared up affairs off the mouth of the Mississippi, McKean returned to Fort Pickens on the morning of November 17th.[375] Now plans could go forward for the opening of the guns on the Confederate installations. Fort Pickens, all its outer batteries, and the guns of the two powerful ships of the blockading squadron, the USS *Niagara* and the USS *Richmond*, would now pound Bragg into oblivion, or at least that was the plan.

The delay had been used to advantage, in that, mounted picket outposts were established, which extended far beyond the fort's former picket positions; and to add some strength and flexibility to this outer warning network, Battery L was supplied with four mountain howitzers and ordered to drill as a light battery. No horses being available, mules were substituted.[376] Thus, Battery L was modestly initiated into its eventual official conversion to a light battery a year later.

The mixed organization of the seven batteries of the fort is shown in figure 3. Lieutenant McFarland of the Engineer Corps is in command of a detachment of troops from Company C, 2nd Artillery. The infantry joined in to serve as artillery. Thus, Capt. John Hildt and his men of Company E, 3rd Infantry, acted as a separate battery. Cpl. Alexander Baby of Battery L was assigned to the ditch mortar battery under Capt. Loomis Langdon, and so on. Note that Battery L was in two locations, both under Lt. R. H. Jackson. The future officers of Battery L are all here. Note Franck Taylor, who would not be assigned to Battery L until January 15th, was now serving with Battery A, 1st Artillery. Outside the fort, Henry Closson is noted as assigned to Battery Scott, one of the five outer sand batteries: Lincoln, Totten, Cameron, Scott, and the Spanish fort.

Figure 3 only generally indicates the gun locations at the various positions. Taken from *Atlas*, plate 5, it is altered to show the various troop deployments for the defense of the fort. Since the defensive arrangement is in reverse, the enemy being in the rear, none of the gun positions on the seaside are manned, nor were they able to be; Brown now had less than half of the guns

---

374. O.R. Vol. 6, p. 669.
375. ORN Ser. I, Vol. 16, p. 772.
376. Haskin, W. L., p. 186.

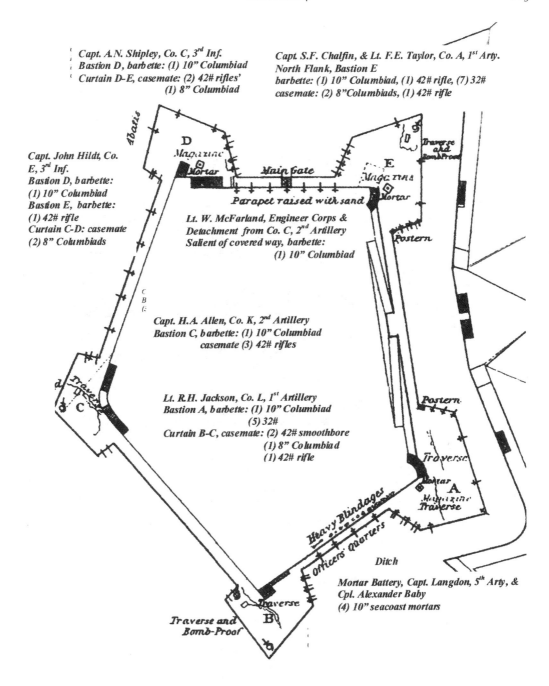

FIGURE 3

that the fort could accommodate. We remember that Barry's and Hunt's batteries had earlier been shipped out, so more guns would be unable to be realistically utilized anyway. The 7 batteries of the fort consist only of a total of 33 guns and 4 mortars.[377] Only 18 are barbette mounted, reaching over the parapet.

---

377. O.R. Vol. 6, p. 667; O.R. Vol. 1, p. 434.

Fifteen guns were mounted in the casemates under the parapet (see figure 4).[378] The casemates on the outer curtain AB, now facing away from the enemy, are of little practical importance and are being used as officer's quarters. Their inner walls had been protected from plunging enemy fire by large timbers leaned against them and on which were layered sandbags. This is indicated by the note "heavy blindages.".

FIGURE 4

The southeast bastion was known as "Hell Row," or "Long Hall," and it was, as Henry Closson remembered,[379] ". . .occupied at this time by a swarm of the younger officers of the garrison, who, when the toils of the day were over, used to congregate in this vicinity and console themselves for their fatigue and isolation with temperate appeals to pipe and cup. The furniture of this apartment consisted mainly of mounted twenty-four pounder howitzers and budge barrels filled with cartridges, which were allotted as seats to the smokers. There were also a few barrels of commissary whiskey, stored in this location for safe keeping, and used only as tables. Army cots filled every corner, and there was even an inflatable india-rubber mattress, introduced of course by the engineer corps, who claimed credit for considerable self-denial in depriving himself of the usual rosewood."

378. Bastion E, Fort Pickens, 2008, photo by the author.
379. Haskin W. L., *Closson's Memoirs*, pp. 356,358; *Langdon's Memoirs*, p. 451. The 24-pounders were useless, as noted earlier, having insufficient range for the current circumstances. Note that the officers smoked while seated on the ammunition barrels. A budge barrel has a leather top, which provided a cushion. Rosewood is assumed to refer to furniture and other comforts, such as the inflatable mattress that the engineers were in a better position to obtain. In the summer of 1861, Godfrey Weitzel was an engineer at Fort Pickens, a name ever familiar to Battery L for the rest of the war.

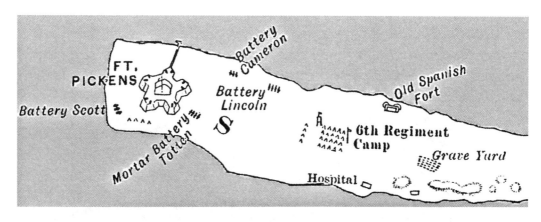

FIGURE 5

The batteries outside the fort were arranged as shown in figure 5 and manned and equipped as listed below:

SCOTT: Capt. R.C. Duryea, Lt. H.W. Closson, Co. F, 1st Artillery
   Barbette: (2) 10" Columbiads, (1) 42 pounder James rifle
   (2) 10" seacoast mortars

TOTTEN: Capt. M.M. Blunt 12th Inf., commanding, manned by Co. C, 2nd Artillery
   (1) 12" and (1) 13" seacoast mortar

LINCOLN: Capt. J.M. Robertson, 2nd Artillery, commanding, manned by Co. H, 2nd Artillery and Dobie's Co. G, 6th New York Vols.

Barbette: (4) 8" seacoast howitzers, (1) 42 pounder James rifle
   (2) 10" seacoast mortars

CAMERON: Capt. J.M. Robertson, commanding, 1st Lt. J.C.M. Pennington, 2nd Artillery, manned by Bailey's Co. I, 6th New York Vols.
   Barbette: (2) 10" Columbiads, (1) 10 pounder rifled Parrott

SPANISH FORT: Lt. F.W. Seeley 4th Artillery, commanding, manned by detachments from Companies A & H, 2nd Artillery.
   (1) 10 pounder rifled Parrott

FIGURE 6

Captain Closson's reminiscences confirm that, "Totten contained the Goliath of the armament, in the shape of a thirteen-inch seacoast mortar,[380] (figure 6), which was the pride of the orderly sergeant of the engineer company, [who] daily polished the bore until it shone like the eye of a cadet's sweetheart."

This monster required a crew of seven, three being required to load the 197-pound shell.[381]

The bombardment began at 10:00 a.m. by the firing of a signal gun located at the flagstaff, bastion A. Those batteries that could be directed at the navy yard, where the *Neaffie*, *Time*, and the gunboat *Nelms* were tied up, opened first, the *Time* being a favorite target.[382] Soon, most of the batteries of the fort were firing; at either the navy yard or Fort McCree, and the sand battery to the west of it.[383] The outer batteries variously opened on McCree, the lighthouse, the navy yard, the steamers, Fort Barrancas, the marine barracks, or the Confederate masked [hidden] batteries as they were discovered by sighting their fire (see figure 10, chapter 3, p. 80). The *Nelms*, though seen to have taken two hits, was backed out from the wharf and made its escape to Pensacola.[384]

---

380. Miller, F. T., Vol. 3, p. 186. Referred to as "The Dictator."
381. Gibbon, J., p. 443.
382. *Harper's Weekly*, December 28th, 1861, p. 827.
383. O.R. Vol. 6, pp. 469–487. Capt. John Hildt, commanding bastion D and curtain CD of the fort, reports it as 9:30; Lt. Francis Seeley, at the old Spanish fort, has it as 8:00; and Capt. James Robertson in command of Battery Lincoln reports the time as 9:30. Problems with variable reports of time plague the historian here, and as will be seen, in future battle actions.
384. O.R. Vol. 6, p. 481, Lieutenant Seeley has three vessels at the wharf: the *Time*, *Neaffie*, "and another armed gunboat." Confederate general Anderson's report, p. 494, only mentions the *Time* removed after dark and the *Nelms*, which "made her escape at once."

About a half hour after the initial firing, the *Niagara* and the *Richmond*, its damage from its encounter with the *Manassas* repaired, stood into a position about two miles south of Fort McCree and commenced firing. Their shells fell short, and after soundings were taken, sufficient depth of water was found to allow them move in closer to about a mile and three-quarters. The *Richmond*, being of lighter draft than the *Niagara*, was able to move into slightly shallower water, closer, and far enough in the rear of Fort McCree and its sand battery so that its guns could not be brought to bear on the ship. The naval gunfire was then resumed at 12:10, and was effective.

The *Richmond* enjoyed its "safe" position briefly until a masked battery in the hills behind Big Lagoon, apparently equipped with rifled guns, opened upon her. At 3:00 p.m., she was damaged by a shell that exploded near her hull some four feet below the surface. Several planks were broken, and a serious leak developed. She was again struck, killing one and wounding seven. At 5:00 she weighed anchor and left the action.[385] The *Niagara* broke off the action at 6:00 when a thunderstorm came up. She had taken two hits as well, reported as "trifling" by McKean. There were no injuries on the *Niagara*.

The barbette guns of Fort McCree were silenced almost immediately after the initial firing from the ships and fort. Per Admiral McKean's report,[386] the sand battery south of McCree was silenced at 3:15. The fire of the casemate guns of McCree slowed gradually, and they were silenced at about the same time. Brown reported that the fire from Barrancas was "reduced very perceptively,"[387] and the fire from the navy yard became silent by dark when the bombardment of the first day tapered off, rain interfering.

No hits from the Confederate guns were sufficient to silence any of Pickens' batteries. Private Cooper of the 6th Regiment of New York Volunteers was mortally wounded by a fragment of a shell that exploded at "about" the center of the fort,[388] and Corporal Andrew Beeler of Battery L was severely wounded in the forearm by a shell fragment while serving one of the barbette mounted 10-inch Columbiads on curtain BC. His forearm was later amputated, and he was eventually discharged on a surgeon's certificate of disability. One private near the barbette 10-inch Columbiad of Company A, 1st Artillery was slightly wounded in the head by a shell that landed and exploded on the parapet in front of the gun.[389]

On the second day, the bombardment was opened by Fort Pickens at "about the same hour." The USS *Niagara* was not able to get within range as a change in the wind had reduced the water depth. Though it was "careened" (tilted by moving

---

385. ORN Ser. I, Vol. 16, p. 779.
386. ORN Ser. I, Vol. 16, p. 775.
387. O.R. Vol. 6. p. 470.
388. O.R. Vol. 6, p. 474.
389. O.R. Vol. 6, p. 483.

guns and ballast) to increase the elevation of its guns, the efforts proved futile. It finally signaled "too great a range" and disengaged. The *Richmond* did not participate. Its damage was being surveyed, and it would likely go to Key West for repairs.[390]

The firing from the Fort Pickens Columbiads and rifled guns was about every 15 minutes and about every half hour from the mortars. Fort McCree did not resume firing, but the sand battery south of it had been repaired overnight and resumed firing. The Confederate guns at Barrancas, a battery on the rising ground to the east of Barrancas, the church battery (in front of the church), from the pier at the navy yard, and the battery known as Wheat's, or Battery no. 2, near the marine barracks, all returned fire. Most were silenced at some time during the day, with the exception of the Fort McCree sand battery and the battery east of Barrancas.

The navy yard at Warrington was "much"[391] damaged according to the report of Brown's executive officer Maj. Lewis G. Arnold, (promoted after Vodges' capture) who had commanded the batteries. The church and parts of the town of Warrington were set afire by midafternoon. Later the fire extended into the town of Woolsey to the northeast. General firing ended at dark, but at 7:00 p.m. was resumed by Battery Cameron, then Battery Lincoln, with mortar fire on the navy yard and surroundings to hamper Confederate efforts to extinguish the flames. Battery Lincoln's 10-inch mortar shells (weighing 87.5 pounds each) had been loaded with a mix of port fire (an incendiary) and regular powder.

All firing ceased at 2:00 a.m. on the 24th. Fort Pickens' damage was minimal. A 10-inch shell entered an embrasure of curtain CD under the command of Capt. John Hildt but did not explode. A shower of brick from the embrasure wounded six of Company E, 3rd Infantry.[392] There were many close calls, but luck prevailed, in that many shells that landed near or in places that could have done serious injury did not explode. One 32-pounder throwing hot shot burst and threw fragments into bastions D and E but did no injury.[393] The mortar battery commanded by Capt. Loomis Langdon, in the ditch in front of curtain AB and protected only with a parapet, had an 8-inch shell drop into its midst. It exploded with no one injured.[394] A 10-inch shell struck the bombproof of Lieutenant Shipley's barbette battery, bastion D, and exploded, throwing sand bags around but without injuring anyone.[395]

The companies of Captains Duffy, Heuberer, and Bailey of the 6th New York were praised for meritorious service. These volunteers, if not all of the 6th, had finally earned Brown's respect.

---

390. ORN Ser. I, Vol. 1, p. 780; also Vol. 16, p. 806.
391. O.R. Vol. 6, p. 475.
392. O.R. Vol. 6, p. 485.
393. O.R. Vol. 6, p. 483.
394. O.R. Vol. 6, p. 485.
395. O.R. Vol. 6, p. 475.

Both 1st Lt. Henry W. Closson and 2nd Lt. Franck E. Taylor, soon to be promoted to Battery L, were mentioned for good service.

Sergeants Keller, Becker, Conroy, and Newton; corporals Beeler, Wicks, and Spangler; and privates Jackel and Hanney, all from L, were mentioned for distinguished service.[396]

Several of the battery commanders reported that the firing accuracy of their rifled guns was inferior to that of the smoothbores. The infantry captains in charge of the batteries obviously did not understand why, but the more detailed reports of the artillery captains reveal certain flaws in the design of the rifle ammunition. Lieutenant Seeley had excellent results with the "most perfect rifled cannon used," his Parrott.[397] However, these results were when he used the Reed projectile and only when firing solid shot, not with time fuses. He observed that the copper disc in the base of the projectile seals too well to ignite the time fuse.[398] Captain Allen observed that some shots fell short, some struck the target, and others passed over it, all with the same careful aim and powder charge. Lieutenant Jackson blames the inaccurate firing of his rifled gun on the James projectile. Jackson, the one regular officer present who was not a West Point graduate and had found his way up through the ranks, gave the perceptive analysis that the lead cover of the James projectile was partially sheared off in the rifling, thus making the trajectory of the round random and erratic.

Thus, we see that the early days of the rifled gun still left some things to be worked out. Brown forwarded these subreports to the adjutant general with a request that they be submitted to the Ordnance Department.

Admiral McKean, however, was so impressed with the range and accuracy of the rifled guns earlier loaned to him by Colonel Brown, in comparison with the performance of his navy XI shell guns, that he was calling for more. Without such guns, he states, any naval bombardment of this type would not be effective "unless shooting from only a few hundred yards."[399] He noted that if Colonel Brown had not supplied him with 20-second fuses (the longest time fuses the navy had were 15), he would not have obtained the two-mile range needed on the first day. Further, he declared that the principle object of interest to him, the destruction of the navy yard, was not accomplished, though he was satisfied that the marine barracks was destroyed.

Bragg[400] lost "21 wounded – 1 mortally" all on the first day. A "defective" magazine at McCree collapsed and killed six others. Col. John B. Villepigue, Fort McCree's commander (West Point class of 1854 and classmate of Henry W.

---

396. O.R. Vol. 6, p. 477.
397. O.R. Vol. 6, p. 482.
398. No flame from "windage," leakage between the projectile and the barrel, could light the fuse.
399. ORN Ser. I, Vol. 16, p. 777.
400. O.R. Vol. 6, pp. 489–493.

Closson), was one of the wounded.

Fort McCree suffered from the combined effects of fire from Fort Pickens and the ships, which "fired with much greater accuracy." It was so badly damaged on the first day that Bragg considered abandoning it and blowing it up. The "defective" structure of McCree prevented it from providing an effective return fire to protect itself. Wooden structures were set afire and the magazines damaged enough to expose the powder to the falling "cinders," which threatened to destroy the whole structure. He reconsidered the abandonment after weighing the effect on morale, and sent an engineer officer and additional workmen to help Colonel Villepigue and his Georgians and Mississippians make repairs overnight.

Bragg complains of Brown turning Pickens' guns on the hospital, which was still flying its yellow flag on the second day, even though it had been evacuated. He does not admit to serious damage to the navy yard, though many houses were struck and damaged. Hot shot and shells landing in Warrington and Woolsey, however, burned "considerable portions of each" (50 buildings were quoted in General Anderson's report).[401]

Bragg waxed eloquent: "For the number and caliber of guns and weight of metal brought into action it will rank with the heaviest bombardment in the world. It was grand and sublime. The houses in Pensacola, 10 miles off, trembled from the effect, and immense quantities of dead fish floated to the surface in the bay and lagoon, stunned by concussion . . ."

He states that he fired "about 1,000 shots, and the enemy not less than 5,000."[402] He notes that he fired the last shot at 4:00 a.m. on Sunday "as a warning that we were on the alert . . ."

The number of shots fired by the two sides is roughly consistent with the number of *useful* guns each had. For the Union side, from the preceding plan view of Fort Pickens, there were 33 guns and 4 mortars. The outside batteries (Scott, Lincoln, etc.) had 13 guns and 6 mortars, to give a total of 46 guns and 10 mortars, including the unforgettable 13-inch "Dictator." The *Niagara* and *Richmond* had provided even more guns, but how many were actually brought into action is not clear, given the difficulties they had with position and range.

As reported on April 20th, 1861, by the Confederate chief of ordnance,[403] Bragg had 169 guns and howitzers and 9 mortars. A more realistic, and current

---

401. O.R. Vol. 6, p. 495.
402. Not too much of an exaggeration. Calculating 55 total guns and mortars, for nine hours, for two days, averaging four shots per hour for the guns, and two for the mortars, results in 3,528. The naval bombardment did not begin until one-half hour later than the fire from the fort, was suspended briefly, and resumed on the afternoon of the first day. It did not continue on the second day but might have, nevertheless, gotten off 1,000 rounds.
403. O.R. Ser. IV, Vol. 1, p. 227.

appraisal, is given by Col. W. S. Lovell in separate testimony.[404] He states that: "When I left Pensacola, about November 5, 1861, there were at least fifteen 8 inch and 10 inch columbiads; also a number of 10 inch and two 13 inch mortars." He does not mention twenty-four 42-pounders, thirty-four 32-pounders, seventy-five 24-pounders and the more than forty smaller guns which were listed in the chief of ordnance's April report. They were ineffective for the range across the bay and therefore not a consideration in Lovell's or any honest man's mind. Confirming Lovell, the November and December muster roll of Company K of the 1st Regiment (Strawbridge's) Louisiana Infantry,[405] stationed at Camp Gladden, Warrington, reports: ". . . were present at the Bombardment from Fort Pickens on the 22nd and 23rd of November 1861, but their guns being of too small a caliber, two 42 and three 32 pdrs. they had to remain inactive."

Thus, Bragg had approximately one-third the number of *useful* guns as did Brown.

Bragg makes two curious statements in the context of the closing of the bombardment: "As they did not renew the action, and drew off with their ships in a crippled condition, our fire was not reopened on Fort Pickens, *to damage which is not our object.*"[406] In a preliminary report,[407] he had stated: "Yesterday and to-day the enemy has not renewed the contest, and, for reasons which the [War] Department will appreciate, *it is not my policy to do so.*" This is entirely consistent with his declaration of the 24th of October of "*defense strictly,*" if he would need to detach troops to reinforce Mobile. Though the Confederate command very realistically expected an assault on Mobile, it would never be made until August of 1864, the Union army and navy being distracted by calls for action elsewhere.

The bombardment revealed the number and position of some enemy batteries that heretofore had not been known, as well as the large caliber of their guns. Therefore, Brown's staff, he says, unanimously recommended contracting his lines of defense. This meant pulling the 6th New York closer to the fort, partially abandoning batteries Lincoln, Cameron, and Totten, and strengthening Battery Scott. He then launches into his usual "inadequate force" warning to the adjutant general,[408] noting that he cannot prevent an enemy landing "at some distance and his erecting batteries against the ships, and, in doing so, with one rifled gun he could drive them all away." Brown is irrational here. The raid of October 9th had the chance to do exactly that – and did not for the reasons previously discussed.

On November 25th, while cleaning up after the bombardment, a fatigue party

---

404. O.R. Vol. 6, p. 599. The record of the court of inquiry for Gen. Mansfield Lovell after the fall of New Orleans.
405. National Archives, Compiled Service Records – Confederate, M861, roll 22, p. 1,261.
406. O.R. Vol. 6, p. 491.
407. O.R. Vol. 6, p. 489.
408. O.R. Vol. 6, p. 472.

was emptying the powder from unexploded rebel shells. Careless handling caused an explosion that killed Sergeant Conroy, privates Hey, Poole, and Reedy, and wounded two others of Battery L, plus one of Battery A, and others of the 3rd Infantry.[409]

We remember that Sergeant Conroy's wife, Elizabeth, had been a company laundress. However, there is no reason to believe that either she or their son was present at the fort as witnesses to this incident. We have a comment from the history of the 75th New York Infantry that the only woman present was the wife of the hospital steward, though this was a month later.[410]

Poole and Reedy had enlisted in L in 1857 and had been survivors of the yellow fever epidemic at Fort Brown in the summer of 1858, which killed 39 of its 78 enlisted men. At the time, Poole was one of three awaiting trial for desertion who were freed in view of the threat of the epidemic on their honor to remain. Poole remained, though the others succeeded in a second desertion. Fate reached them, however, as they were later found dead of the fever at a nearby ranch. Poole had been ever faithful to duty since, being one of the volunteers from Fort Jefferson to accompany Colonel Brown for the relief of Fort Pickens in April.

Brown wrote a note to Admiral McKean on November 29th advising of Bragg's forces firing on a small boat as it tried to enter the harbor.[411] "I suppose Bragg has given a general order to fire on all boats entering the harbor." In his mention of the incident,[412] Bragg defines it as a rowboat, which was abandoned. The significant part of the event, at least to Bragg, was that though several of the Confederate shots passed near Fort Pickens, he seemed relieved to note that no fire was returned.

Confederate Concerns

Sufficient Confederate spies roamed the North to alert the Confederate War Department to the preparations for another Union navy-army expedition[413] but not its destination. Of course, everyone on the Confederate-held coast was put on alert. On November 7th, Flag Officer S. F. DuPont's South Atlantic Squadron struck at Fort Walker, on Hilton Head Island, and Fort Beauregard on Bay Point, on the opposite shore. Known as the Battle of Port Royal Sound, the forts fell after five hours of bombardment. Gen. Thomas W. Sherman then landed some 12,000 men to occupy the area[414] and thus threaten Savannah and Charleston. Another post in Scott's Anaconda Plan had fallen to the Union.

409. Haskin, W. L, pp. 187, 361, 377. Those wounded in the explosion are not specified in the "Record."
410. Hall, Henry & James, *75th History*, p. 32, footnote 7.
411. ORN Ser. I, Vol. 16, p. 796.
412. O.R. Vol. 6, p. 491.
413. O.R. Vol. 6, p. 758.
414. ORN, Ser. I, Vol. 12, pp. 261–319.

On November 28th, Mississippi sent Bragg a regiment of new recruits, his enlistment problems having been somewhat worked out.[415] He noted that he now had four new regiments, or about 3,000 men, though only 600 of them were armed.[416] Bragg's responsibilities were expanded on December 10th to include Pascagoula Bay and "that portion of Mississippi east of the Pascagoula River." Just previous, Wood's 7th Alabama, one of Bragg's best, had been ordered to east Tennessee.[417] Bragg notes that since a railroad had been completed between Mobile and Pensacola (for rapid deployment and the transport of heavy supplies normally sent by ship, but now denied by the blockade) that Wood's departure leaves him with "no apprehension, but it leaves me a large number of men, near 3,000, without arms" – out of a total of 6,000. Having just discussed his weakened situation, Bragg notes[418] that: "The enemy landed about 1,000 men on Santa Rosa Island, and they are now encamped near the fort." This was the 75th New York Regiment of Volunteers, which began landing from the steamer *Baltic* on December 14th.[419]

Bragg[420] not only had supply problems, but recruitment problems, this time due to a recent regulation instituted by the Confederate Congress that there was to be universal suffrage for the troops, meaning that they should elect their own officers. The electioneering and associated disruption had slowed the reenlisting of his one-year men, whose terms were due to expire. To these troubles, add a jurisdictional dispute with the navy. In Mobile, the senior naval officer refused to recognize Bragg's authority on inland waters, though the naval officer at Pensacola had long since done so. The result was that two vessels of use to Bragg had lain idle and caused questions about organization and jurisdiction to be bandied about between Bragg and the Confederate War Department.

On December 27th, Bragg received a letter from Secretary of War Judah P. Benjamin, requesting him to consider the position of commander of the Department of the Trans-Mississippi.[421] The explanation was circuitous, but the sum of it was that the Confederacy was in danger of losing Missouri, and that Gen. A. S. Johnston, whom it had been planned to send there, was detained in Kentucky by the threat of a Union invasion. Benjamin felt that defeat in Missouri was more of a risk than "misfortune" at Pensacola. The Trans-Mississippi Department would encompass Arkansas, Missouri, Northern Texas, and Indian Territory (Oklahoma) (see figure 7).[422] The replacement initially proposed for Bragg was Kirby Smith.

---

415. O.R. Vol. 6, p. 768.
416. O.R. Vol. 6, p. 771.
417. O.R. Vol. 6, p. 777.
418. O.R. Vol. 6, p. 782.
419. Babcock, W. M. Jr., pp. 21, 66.
420. O.R. Vol. 6, pp. 784–787.
421. O.R. Vol. 6, p. 788.
422. *Harper's Weekly*, February 23rd, 1861, p. 124.

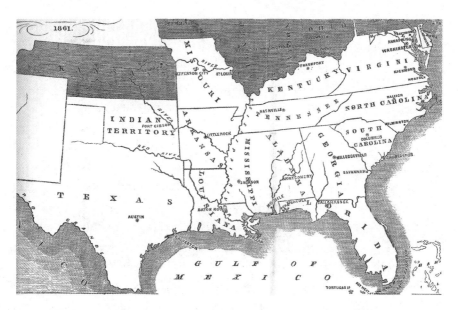

FIGURE 7

On December 31st, forces from the Gulf Blockading Squadron landed at Biloxi, Mississippi. A detachment of marines and a gun's crew, a total of only about 60 men, were put aboard the USS *Henry Lewis*, most useful because of its shallow draft, and were crossed from near Ship Island to the vicinity of the town. They landed and demanded its surrender, which was "acceded" to.[423] There was no fight, probably because it was observed that "the place was found to be almost deserted by the male population, but was crowded by women and children." A sand battery was destroyed and its two guns removed. Though the Union forces left within hours, the Confederates were alarmed, and Benjamin wavered in his thoughts about reassigning Bragg.[424] The push-pull of where to defend the Confederacy was becoming more frantic. However, the scare that the landing on Ship Island had made on December 3rd, and now at Biloxi "puts an end to all idea of assigning you to other duty."[425] This left Bragg's Department of Alabama and West Florida intact for the moment. Earl Van Dorn was assigned to the Department of the Trans-Mississippi.

By mid-January 1862, the scare seemed to pass, Confederate recruitment and reenlistment was picking up, and with the aid of Governor Shorter of Alabama, some 1,000 armed militia could be expected to reinforce Bragg's men. Gen. Jones M. Withers was to be assigned the immediate command of the forces at Mobile, thus freeing Bragg for the broader affairs of the department.

---

423. ORN Ser. I, Vol. 17, pp. 34, 40; O.R. Vol. 6, p. 809.
424. O.R. Vol. 6, p. 794.
425. O.R. Vol. 6, p. 803. Benjamin to Bragg.

Record 2/62
31 DECEMBER–28 FEBRUARY 1862, FORT PICKENS, FLORIDA

The Company was involved in the Bombardment of Jan. 1st, 1862.

1. Henry W. Closson   Capt. In Command
2. Franck E. Taylor   1st Lt. Joined Company by trans. S.O. no. 5 Hdqrts. Dept. of Fla. Jan. 15,'62
3. Edward L. Appleton 1st Lt. Joined Co. from absent without leave, Jan. 6,'62
4. T.K. Gibbs   2nd Lt.   " " " " "   Jan. 6,'62

Transferred:

1. J.S. Gibbs   1st Lt. Left Co. by transfer to Co. "D" 1st Arty. Sp. O. no. 5 Hdqtrs. Dept of Fla., Ft. Pickens, Dec. 15,'62

Discharged:

    1. Andrew J. Beeler Cpl. Feb. 9,'60 Boston, Ma by Surgeon's Certificate of Disability (of wounds received in action) Apr. 5, 1862.

Strength: 88, Sick: 9

Sick Present:

    Julius Becker, Andrew J. Beeler, Michael Olvaney, William Schaffer, Warren P. Shaw, William V. Thompson

Sick Absent:

    Thomas Brook, Ft. Hamilton, NY Left Co. Sept. 17, 1861
    William Brunskill,   do.
    Charles Riley Sick at Ft. McIntosh, Texas. Abs. from Co. since Feb. 25, 1861. Reduced from Sgt. to Pvt. to date from July 12,'61. O. no. 2, Co. "L" 1st Arty, Fort Pickens, Fla.

On January 15th, Lt. Franck Eveliegh Taylor is recorded as being assigned to Battery L, essentially completing its officer makeup, which would survive almost unaltered for the rest of the war. Like Appleton, Taylor had been appointed directly from civilian life on the same exact date: August 5th. He was born in Washington D.C., the son of the prominent bookseller, Franck Taylor.[426] We shall see that for the rest of the war, Taylor and Appleton will be the mainstays in command of the battery, always there while Closson is detached on other duty.

---

426. Henry, G. V., Vol. I, p. 226; Heitman, F. B., p. 632; *Name Authority File*, Library of Congress, *Taylor, Franck*, http://id.loc.gov/.

1862 ROSTER
From 31 December 1861–28 February 1862 muster roll
FORT PICKENS, FLORIDA

1. Henry W. Closson Capt.
2. Franck E. Taylor 1st Lt.
3. Edward L. Appleton 1st Lt.
4. T. K. Gibbs 2nd Lt.

1. Lewis Keller	1st Sgt	1 Dec.'59 Newport, KY	1. David J. Wicks	Cpl.	25 Oct.'59 New York
2. Thomas Newton	Sgt.	13 Dec.'58 Ft. Brown, TX	2. Andrew J. Beeler	Cpl.	9 Feb.'60 Boston
3. Julius Becker	Sgt.	12 Oct.'59 New York	3. Charles Spangler	Cpl.	3 Sept.'58 New York
4. Alexander J. Baby	Sgt.	10 Feb.'60 Boston	4. William Demarest	Cpl.	19 Oct.'59 New York

1. Louis Lighna Musician   13 Oct.'58 Ft. Brown, TX   1. Isaac T. Cain Artificer   4 Oct.'59 Boston

Privates

1. Ahern, James — 18 Oct.'60 Boston
2. Anglin, Edmond — 19 Oct.'59 New York
3. Beglan, James — 25 Oct.'59 New York
4. Brook, Thomas — 9 July '60 Boston
5. Brown, William F. — 1 Nov.'59 Boston
6. Brunskill, William C. — 19 Oct.'59 New York
7. Buckley, John — 30 Sept.'58 New York
8. Burke, John — 17 Oct.'60 New York
9. Carroll, Patrick — 17 Dec.'60 Ft. Duncan, TX
10. Casey, Patrick — 15 Oct.'59 New York
11. Connell, Jeremiah — 14 Sept.'59 Ft. Clark, TX
12. Cotterill, Edmond — 22 Sept.'60 Boston
13. Coyne, Owen — 10 Dec.'60 Boston
14. Craffy, Patrick — 27 Sept.'60 Boston
15. Creed, William — 27 Sept.'60 Boston
16. Cummings, Patrick — 25 Oct.'60 New York
17. Curran, Robert — 6 Oct.'57 Newport, KY
18. Donnelly, Patrick — 1 Mar.'60 Boston
19. Farrell, Bernard — 11 Nov.'59 New York
20. Ferrari, Prosper — 22 Oct.'60 New York
21. Flint, Charles A. — 22 Sept.'60 Boston
22. Flynn, James — 12 Sept.'59 Ft. Clark, TX
23. Foley, Christopher — 3 Nov.'59 Boston
24. Friedman, George — 7 Feb.'60 New York
25. Galavan, Morris — 14 Jan.'61 Boston
26. Gilroyd, Thomas — 26 Aug.'57 Newport, KY
27. Hadley, George F. — 1 Mar.'60 Boston
28. Hanney, James — 8 Jan.'61 New York
29. Holland, John — 13 Oct.'57 Detroit, MI

30. Howard, George — 25 Oct.'60 New York
31. Jackel, Charles — 26 Oct'60 New York
32. Kenny, Michael — 8 Feb.'60 New York
33. Kutschor, Joseph — 13 Feb.'60 New York
34. Lanahan, John — 9 Jan.'61 Rochester, NY
35. Mansfield, Charles F. — 16 Jan.'61 Boston
36. McCarthy, James — 4 Oct.'60 Boston
37. McCoy, Daniel — 24 Oct.'60 Boston
38. Mc Donagh, Miles — 17 Sept.'60 New York
39. McGaley, Terence — 18 Sept.'60 New York
40. McLaughlin, Edward — 30 Sept.'58 New York
41. McSweeny, David — 11 Feb.'61 New York
42. Mc Waters, James — 16 July'57 Newport, KY
43. Meyer, John — 1 Mar.'60 New York
44. Murphy, John — 21 Feb.'60 Boston
45. Myers, Denis — 25 Sept.'58 Syracuse, NY
46. Nitschke, John G. — 6 Feb.'60 New York
47. O'Sullivan, Michael — 26 Sept.'60 Boston
48. Olvany, Michael — 25 Oct.'60 New York
49. Parketton, William — 4 Oct.'60 New York
50. Richards, Franklin W. — 6 Feb.'61 New York
51. Riley, Charles — 7 Oct.'59 Boston
52. Roper, John — 22 Oct.'60 New York
53. Rupprecht, Ludwig — 7 Feb.'60 New York
54. Schaffer, William — 18 Jan.'61 New York
55. Schmidt, Heinrick — 26 Oct.'60 New York
56. Schnieder, Philip H. — 16 Oct.'58 Ft. Brown, TX
57. Scott, William E. — 9 Feb.'60 Boston
58. Shaw, Warren P. — 26 Oct.'60 Boston
59. Shapley, Morgan L. — 18 Dec.'60 Buffalo, NY
60. Smith, Joseph — 11 Oct.'59 New York
61. Stanners, Martin — 19 Jan.'61 Boston
62. Stoll, Andrew — 24 Oct.'60 New York
63. Straub, Amelius — 8 Feb.'60 New York
64. Thompson, William V. — 13 Sept.'60 Rochester, NY
65. Tomson, John — 9 Jan.'61 Boston
66. Townsend, Reuben — 27 Sept.'60 Boston
67. Ward, Henry H. — 8 Nov.'60 New York
68. White, Michael — 7 Oct.'59 Boston
69. Wilkinson, Joseph — 4 Feb.'60 New York
70. Wilkson, Henry — 24 Dec.'60 New York
71. William, Henry — 28 Sept.'60 Rochester, NY
72. Wren, Owen A. — 11 Dec.'60 Boston
73. Wright, Wallace D. — 28 Sept.'58 Rochester, NY
74. Wynne, William — 9 Oct.'57 Detroit, MI

Bombardment of January 1, 1862

On January 1st, 1862,[427] at about 3:00 p.m., a steam tug approached along the sound from the east, and made a landing at the navy yard wharf. This was the first ship to "come within the range of my guns," as Brown put it, since the previous bombardment.[428] As it departed, it did not run straight toward Pensacola but veered into the bay, a man on deck waving the Stars and Bars and attracting the attention of Battery Lincoln. Regarding it as an act of bravado, calculated to draw his fire, Brown obliged. Three shots were directed at the steamer. One shot was returned from a rebel battery in the vicinity which was directed at the gun that fired into the steamer, and one shot was returned from Pickens. There the matter lay for about three-quarters of an hour, when all of the Confederate batteries opened up in a general bombardment. A slow rate of fire was selectively returned from Pickens, only using its heaviest guns, until sundown, and was continued after dark with mortars. In the previous bombardment, the incendiary "port-fire," was noted as being used to put to flame several of the buildings in Warrington. Brown had since ordered and received "rock-fire and carcasses," special shells filled with the incendiary material, designed to set fire to the target.[429]

At about nine o'clock a bright light was seen in the navy yard. By 10:00 p.m "the whole firmament was illuminated, several of the largest buildings being set on fire." Fort Pickens maintained firing until about 2:00 a.m. The Confederates kept it up, despite all their troubles, until 4:00 a.m.

While Fort Pickens probably thought that the dense fog that had rolled in, followed by a drizzling rain,[430] was what had dampened the Confederate enthusiasm; it was actually the precipitate arrival of a fuming Braxton Bragg. Departing for his visit to Mobile, he had left Gen. Richard H. Anderson in command at Pensacola. The wild bombardment was the result of his drunken orders, "so much intoxicated as to be entirely unfit for duty," while Bragg was absent.

Fort Pickens suffered minor damage, few shots even hitting the walls. Brown estimated that the rebels used even more ammunition than they had in the two-day bombardment in November. Two men, one of the 6th New York and one regular in the fort, suffered minor injuries. The entire 75th New York was ordered to leave their camp near the fort and move some two miles east, out of the fire. Bragg admitted to no casualties but fretted over the loss of ". . . a large and valuable

---

427. O.R. Vol. 6, pp. 495–498, ORN Ser. I, Vol. 17, p. 33; Hall, Henry & James, *75th History*, p. 28. Brown's account differs from the *75th History*. The above narrative is an amalgam.
428. The rowboat incident of January 27th was never fully explained. It entered the harbor and was regarded as a provocation by the Confederates and was fired upon by them, not by Fort Pickens.
429. Gibbon, J., p. 329.
430. Hall, H. & J., *75th History*, p. 29.

storehouse" and the "criminal waste of means so necessary for our defense . . ." General Anderson would be relieved as soon as a replacement could be found. "We are sadly pressed for competent officers . . ."[431] Gen. Samuel P. Jones, Provisional Army, took command of the Army of Pensacola on January 27th.[432]

After the distractions of January 1st and 2nd, Bragg had a chance to respond to the adjutant general about the conditions in the Mobile area, saying that the forts (Gaines and Morgan) were in a better condition than when appraised in October and that *with ammunition*[433] they would prevent any entrance to the bay. He went on to say that Gen. L. P. Walker's infantry brigade, stationed some ten to fifteen miles west of Mobile, was in "very bad" condition due to the neglect of their commander. Walker was relieved on January 27th, but the demoralization and sickness made Bragg's job that much more complicated.[434] A crushing reality check had been received from the secretary of war on January 5th, 1862.[435] "I regret the total impossibility of supplying you with arms for your unarmed regiments." Also enclosed was a copy of the regulations "devised" for carrying out the new system of universal suffrage.

Imagine, if you can, the representatives of a government dedicated to the slavery of nearly half of the humanity under its control, worrying about democracy in its military.

Regarding earlier suggestions that Bragg should consider the command of the Trans-Mississippi Department, he responds to Benjamin, on January 6th,[436] that he can best serve by remaining at Mobile. He feels that he has the confidence of the people and does not want to abandon them, now that they are menaced by the Federal troops occupying Ship Island. He then makes an estimate of the situation in Missouri, which was accurate, in hindsight, saying that it was "most unpromising." In fact, the fighting there was to go on and on until the Confederates were soundly defeated at the Battle of Westport on October 23rd, 1864.

Confederate Withdrawals from Pensacola

In a letter to the Confederate adjutant general dated February 1st, Bragg noted that the forces on Ship Island were now estimated at 8,000 or 10,000 "but making no preparation for a decent on us at this time . . . We continue to receive supplies from Havana by small vessels running the blockade, both here [Pensacola] and at

---

431. Vol. 6, p. 802. Benjamin to Bragg.
432. O.R. Vol. 6, p. 816.
433. O.R. Vol. 6, p. 793. Italics by the author.
434. O.R. Vol. 6, p. 815.
435. O.R. Vol. 6, p. 794.
436. O.R. Vol. 6, p. 797. Consecutive events from this time through mid-February are found on pp. 799–826.

Mobile." In the space of a month, Bragg had become relatively transformed in his estimate of the situation, saying: "Should no move be made against us in the next four weeks, I shall look upon their force as merely intended to hold us in check by threatening our positions, and would recommend a withdrawal of a portion of the oldest and best forces in this department for service elsewhere."

Only five days later, he informed Gen. Samuel Jones at Pensacola: "A large naval expedition left Hampton Roads on the 4th with additional land forces for the Gulf; supposed destination Mobile and Pensacola. Suspend all furloughs, and prepare to receive them."[437] This could have mistakenly referred to activity in support the North Carolina Expedition of Gen. Ambrose Burnside, which had sailed from Fort Monroe on January 11th, 1862, and which attacked Roanoke Island on February 7th. It surrendered the next day.[438] Bragg's intelligence that the expedition was headed for the Gulf had been in error, or his spies at Hampton Roads premature in their judgment; the Butler expedition to New Orleans did not leave until February 25th.

The real blow – or, better stated, one that stunned the Confederacy – came with the news of the fall of Fort Henry, on the Tennessee River, on February 6th, 1862, to a joint operation between Gen. Ulysses Grant and the gunboats of Flag Officer A. H. Foote.[439] Bragg was now ordered to "as soon as possible send to Knoxville all the troops you can spare from your command . . ." The number the secretary of war was looking for was "at least" four regiments. Four regiments had already been ordered from Virginia[440] and 5,000 men (six regiments) from New Orleans.[441] Gen. A. S. Johnston was outnumbered, and the next and larger fort, Donelson, was now threatened. Bragg notified Jones at Pensacola that he would likely have to give up the 9th Mississippi Regiment as a part of what was to be sent to Tennessee. However mistaken, Bragg was still convinced that "Farragut and Butler" were going to attack Mobile rather than New Orleans (Butler's buildup on Ship Island was still not complete on March 20th, when he personally arrived there, and the passage of Farragut past forts Jackson, and St. Philip did not occur until April 24th).

As a result of the threat, and the loss of the Mississippi Regiment, Jones was to concentrate his forces at Pensacola. Bragg ordered that Deer Point on "Oak Island," what is today known as Gulf Breeze on Santa Rosa Sound, should be abandoned, except for a small detachment "to act as a mere picket."[442] These movements, necessarily by boat, across the bay to the installations nearer Pensacola

---

437. O.R. Vol. 6, p. 822.
438. O.R. Vol. 9, pp. 72, 74; Butler, p. 336.
439. See chapter 5.
440. O.R. Vol. 6, p. 823.
441. O.R. Vol. 6, p. 825.
442. O.R. Vol. 6, p. 824.

should have been observed by Fort Pickens as an early signal of the eventual Confederate withdrawal, but the record is silent.

On February 15th, Bragg offered[443] the secretary of war some advice, constituting a remarkable reversal of his earlier sentiments. All coastal points except New Orleans, Mobile, and Pensacola should be abandoned. The protection of persons and property should, as such, be abandoned. Only important strategic points should be held. The whole of Texas and Florida should be let go and the enemy allowed to occupy and disperse himself there. As a result: "We could beat him in detail, instead of the reverse." The Confederacy could then concentrate its forces for the delivery of a heavy blow. The point of concentration now had defined itself as Kentucky. (This is the first he mentions of Kentucky, but his belief in its importance never wavered, and he would invade Kentucky in August). He goes on to wistfully note the need for modern rifled guns so as to protect those coastal, or river, "assailable points" from the enemy's shallow draft gunboats.

Bragg had a point; however, he was a bit mistaken about Florida. There was little infrastructure to move goods to supply the Confederacy even if they were landed through the blockade, and Florida's production of goods of interest to the North, particularly cotton, was small, necessarily confined to the northern part of the state. Excepting Key West, south Florida was a wasteland inhabited by fewer than 500 people; hence Florida was ignored by the North. Texas, however, became a nearly fatal obsession; it had cotton, could ship goods passed through the blockade, a population of German and Czech immigrants apparently averse to slavery, and the threat of Napoleon III's army south of the Rio Grande.

The pressure that caused such a radical change of thinking was the result of the activities of the forces of the Union army and navy sent to the Department of the West, introduced in chapter 3, which were another part of the Anaconda Plan. They were the "Northern Column," which must be elaborated on to (1) reveal the field behavior and military initiative of the two key men involved, Halleck and Grant, whose attitudes would directly affect the conditions in which the campaigns in the west would be conducted; and (2) to shed light on how Union western campaigns went from promising to failure in 1862, which, combined with inept Union war efforts in the east, protracted the war.

We shall see how tied together seemingly diverse events really were. The failure to destroy the Confederate army in the west, at Corinth, Mississippi, then caused a resurgence of Confederate fortunes in the south.[444] It would allow the Confederacy to hang on for a much longer period of time, though the outcome of the war was never really in doubt. Thus, Battery L, assigned to the Department of

---

443. O.R. Vol. 6, p. 826.
444. A conclusion reached in W. T. Sherman's memoirs, reviewed in the *Galaxy* magazine, September 1875, p. 334.

the Gulf, would have to sweat through prolonged and mostly futile campaigns in Texas and Louisiana, which would continue until mid-1864.

On February 18th, Bragg notified Benjamin[445] that he was sending the 5th Georgia, 9th Mississippi, 20th Alabama, and 23rd Alabama to Knoxville. That day, he received a telegram in response to his advice of the 15th: "Commence immediately the movement you suggest for aiding General Johnston." It also indicated he would get a policy decision sent by messenger *tomorrow*.[446] Dated the 18th, it arrived on the 27th, the messenger stating that he did not *leave* until the 21st!

The critical policy statement finally having arrived, it went on: the disaster at Fort Donelson, which was taken by Grant only ten days after the fall of Fort Henry, had prompted the Confederate government to agree with Bragg. "Withdraw your forces from Pensacola and Mobile and hasten to the defense of the Tennessee line." In doing so, he was to try to save as much of the artillery and munitions as possible. The orders continued: "It is not proposed to leave any force at all at Pensacola – a weak garrison would eventually be captured – but it is deemed advisable to leave an effective garrison in the forts in Mobile Harbor . . ." The continued occupation of the forts might deter an attack on Mobile, "but the risk of its capture must be run by us." Bragg was to move his troops toward the Tennessee line, and by the time he reached the Memphis and Charleston Railroad, "we will be able to determine towards what point they are to move."[447]

All of the above planning and policy was made without hearing a word from General Johnston, the commander of the Confederate Department of the West. War Secretary Benjamin confessed to have decided the plan from "dispatches in the Northern papers." The North was awash with news,[448] which easily reached Confederate hands. The troops were often accompanied by reporters who, as we shall see, often abused their First Amendment right by revealing army plans.

Taken aback[449] by the magnitude of the withdrawal ordered, Bragg notes: "Heavy movements of troops had already been made as far as our damaged roads would permit; but as your telegram [of the 18th] did not indicate the extent we were to go, no arrangements had been made for abandoning any point." The Confederate War Department also sent orders to move troops out of Texas to supplement those in the Trans-Mississippi Department of Gen. Earl Van Dorn. There was also a long string of demands made on the Confederate general in command at New

---

445. O.R. Vol. 6, p. 894.
446. O.R. Vol. 6, p. 827. Coded messages for the telegraph were in their infancy in the Union army. This would intimate that no Confederate code was used, at least up to this time.
447. O.R. Vol. 6, p. 828.
448. A sidelight to the subjet of newspapers: The *New York Times* published, on July 14th, 1861, a letter of thanks, written by Godfrey Weitzel from the Fort Pickens garrison to the "Ladies Association" for the newspapers, periodicals, and other reading matter they had sent.
449. O.R. Vol. 6, p. 834.

Orleans, Mansfield Lovell, who by now had replaced Twiggs, and on Governor Moore of Louisiana.

On February 27th, 1862, Bragg issued orders to Gen. Samuel Jones to remove the heavy guns, tear up the railroad to its junction with the Mobile railroad, and "burn all from Fort McCree to the junction with the Mobile road." This was to be done at night and in "all the secrecy possible."[450] The next day, Bragg turned over the command of the whole Department of Alabama and West Florida to Jones. Bragg, on his own initiative, diverted some of the troops slated for Johnston, at Nashville, to P. T. Beauregard, at Corinth.[451]

The inconsistency of the order to remove the guns in secret at night, and then to burn resources nearby only in daytime was not lost on Jones. Perhaps flames do not show up in daylight, but smoke from burning the products of a sawmill or from a burning vessel is obvious for miles, and is suspicious. Other factors that would destroy attempts at secrecy were escaping slaves, local Union sympathizers, and even disaffected rebel soldiers, all of whom frequently brought across information to Fort Pickens. Not to be outdone, of course, were the newspapers. Jones hesitated in carrying out the destruction. Other delays were caused by the weather. The shipment of the guns and supplies was delayed by storm damage to the railroad,[452] which was not in operation again until March 4th. Once in operation, the railroad was so overloaded that considerable naval stores were detoured to the steamer *Time*, which was sent up Escambia Bay to Bluff Springs, where they could be transferred to rail.

March 4th, 1862, saw Bragg reassuming command of the Department of Alabama and West Florida with the added command of the troops in north Mississippi and south of Jackson in West Tennessee. He did not explain why until March 28th, then saying it was to gain control of the "means"[453] – that is, the authority to direct where guns were to be sent, overriding demands from every quarter. He noted that he had no intention of interfering with Jones' command of the Department of Pensacola and requested him to resume it.

His short interval of having overall command gave Jones the confidence to take the initiative and propose an alternative to the total and immediate evacuation. He would retain a portion of his command at Pensacola. His reasoning was threefold: First, he asserted that the Union troops on Santa Rosa Island were far fewer than had been believed; second, he would retain only guns that were old and of little value if captured; and third, he had received an offer from the governor of Alabama to recruit 1,000 men "engaged to serve for thirty days." Given the weak garrison of Pickens, the presence of a rear guard force of Col. Thomas

---

450. O.R. Vol. 6, p. 835.
451. O.R. Vol. 6, p. 836.
452. O.R. Vol. 6, p. 838.
453. O.R. Vol. 6, p. 866.

M. Jones' 350 men from the 27th Mississippi Infantry, reinforced by the 1,000 recruits, could be enough of a show of force to convince both those in the fort, as well as the now-panicked citizens of the Pensacola area, that no abandonment was contemplated. The best guns and stores would get to Johnston or Beauregard or Mobile or New Orleans, but the Federals would be held in check, at least for some longer time than could be expected from the original plan. Jones sent a telegram explaining the plan to Bragg on March 5th.

Bragg did not receive the telegram until March 12th,[454] and in his answer he seems to have missed the major point, as he responds that he is confident that everything has been done to carry out his instructions. In despair of ever hearing from Bragg, on March 11th, General Jones had telegraphed the adjutant general of the Confederate army, explaining the plan and asking if he might "make the necessary arrangements to undertake it?" Incredibly, it was received the next day and was approved.

The Confederate side was now in a state of confusion. They looked very weak in Tennessee. Mobile feared invasion, and there was a growing fear of the weakness of the defenses of New Orleans. Poor communications and transportation were hobbling the conduct of the campaign. During March, Secretary of War Benjamin had moved on to become secretary of state and was replaced by George W. Randolph. Suddenly, Robert E. Lee appears in March correspondence. Called in as an adviser by Jefferson Davis on March 2nd, he was charged on March 13th, with the oversight of the Confederate conduct of the war.[455] The Confederacy was badly shaken at this point, and the news that reached the troops at Santa Rosa Island from the Pensacola newspapers prompted Major Babcock of the 75th New York to write: "The news today is glorious. It looks more like success. If *vigorously* carried on the war will approach the beginning of the end by the 1st of April."[456]

Amid all the uncertainty, General Jones finally began to implement[457] the original destruction orders. On March 10th, Jones ordered all sawmills, lumber, and boats that could be found in Escambia and Blackwater Bays to be put to the torch during daylight on the 11th. Finally, on the 15th, Bragg received Jones' letter of the 6th and approved the revised plan.

By March 16th, Deer Point, across Santa Rosa Sound from a point on Santa Rosa Island about seven miles from Fort Pickens, was abandoned and a sham force of 30 men left there with orders to keep enough campfires burning to give the impression that a force of 300 or 400 still remained. Col. Thomas Jones' 27th

---

454. O.R. Vol. 6, p. 854.
455. O.R. Vol. 6, pp. 2,400. Up to that time, Lee was commander of the Confederate Department of South Carolina, Georgia, and East Florida.
456. Babcock, W. M. Jr., p. 106. Newspapers were also brought over by deserters.
457. O.R. Vol. 6, p. 891.

Mississippi and "something over a thousand" volunteers,[458] 300 of whom were now equipped with arms recently sent by the governor of Alabama, remained at Pensacola.

A potential flaw in the Confederate plan to remain with a sham force at Deer Point – or anywhere, for that matter – was the *sound* of a normal camp, both day and night. Certainly, there were the usual bugle calls. It is unknown if the Confederates here had an elaborate structure like a typical Union army camp, with a musician, for the express purpose of calling out the day's routine; however, *no* bugle calls would arouse suspicion. Assembly, reveille, stable call, breakfast, sick, drill, dinner, retreat, and taps were some of those used by the Union; and many were different between the artillery and the infantry.[459]

Night sounds would include the firing of the sentries' guns at the end of their 24-hour duty. A muzzleloader cannot be simply emptied, except by firing. (At one point the ammunition shortage was so acute that any Confederate sentry was ordered to fire at a target after this guard duty as a substitute for regular target practice.) Other firing might be some of the false alarms of nervous pickets. Any sham act would have an impossible task to reproduce what occasionally happened in real life. The firing could occasionally build up to absurd proportions of wild alarm, all false. This happened in both the Confederate and Union camps. A picket would hear a rustle in a bush or see a moving shadow and fire at it. One such event is here excerpted from Babcock[460] of the 75th New York Volunteers:

> One of the most ludicrous of these alarms occurred on January 26, 1862 . . . Several of the officers had been on an excursion down the island [east], partly for a picnic, and partly to see if the Confederates had moved their outposts any closer to the Union position, and they were coming home by boat in the evening. Suddenly a rocket shot up from the Water Witch [one of the Union Navy gunboats on patrol duty off the coast] and in a moment more *Crack! Crack! Crack!* went the muskets of the distant picket line on land, mistaking the signal for a pilot[461] for an alarm from the mounted patrol. The steamer Mississippi lying off shore here answered the signal by another rocket, and *Crack!! Crack!! Crack!!* went the muskets of the pickets again. By this time the mounted patrol down the island took alarm, and sent up a rocket which is a signal that the enemy are on the island. Away went a half dozen shots from the picket guard again. Of course we understood that there was no cause for alarm, but we knew that our absence, coupled with such extraordinary demonstrations would make a terrible excitement in camp, and we hurried in. . . . Meanwhile, Col. Brown and his officers at the Fort understood the

---

458. O.R. Vol. 6, p. 862.
459. Billings, J. D., chapter 9.
460. Babcock, W. M. Jr., pp. 50–53.
461. The patrol vessel apparently wanted to enter the bay, and was signaling for a pilot.

whole thing as we did, but the mounted patrol, excited by the rebel vessels we had seen, the unusual fire over at Pensacola and some little whiskey, kept sending in a messenger at full speed every half hour with new and increasing tales of danger and disaster, until our picket guard was wild with fear and two of them on the beach deserted their posts. 'The pickets had been fired on and one man shot!' 'The enemy were already on the island, and two of the mounted patrol were missing!' The officers of the 75th had been attacked and the Major [Babcock] and Capt. Dwight taken prisoners! (This story came very direct to the Col. about a minute before I got on my horse to join the battalion and report for duty.) And to cap the climax of absurd fright, one of the mounted patrol came down the beach at a full run on his mule, out of breath, shouting to the sentries on the beach as he came along, "Run! G'd d---n you! The enemy are close behind!"

All of this activity, in turn, alerted the Confederate side and the long roll[462] was beaten at McCree and then all along the line for the full four miles of their installations.

Babcock ends by saying: "How the Rebels settled it and when they went to bed, we don't know, but our troops all had 'tattoo' and 'taps' for roll call and lights out at the usual hour."

Another, and dreadful, reason why the sounds of the sham camp would likely not duplicate those of a fully occupied Confederate one was the random occurrence of the shots taken at escaping slaves. Ever since Lieutenant Slemmer had retreated into Fort Pickens, the occasional escaped slave would make it over to the fort, only to be returned to his owner, in keeping with the absurdity of the "truce." This all ended when Brown arrived, vowing never to return the 20 laborers he had taken from Key West.[463] Fortunately, we have "Babcock's Letters" and are informed that, as time went on, Pickens became a magnet for escaped slaves. Brown saw to it that they were received with dignity, given work at $15 per month and one ration per day.[464] The escaped women and children were sent to New York – free people.

All this took place long before Lincoln's Emancipation Proclamation of January 1st, 1863. The authority used by Brown is evidently the First Confiscation Act of August 1861 (which authorized the confiscation of slaves *working for* the Confederate government). Sympathetic Union commanders could interpret this broadly, and it is evident that Brown was one who did. On March 13th, 1862, Congress passed an additional article of war, which prohibited those in the military or naval forces from returning fugitive slaves. Any remaining doubt about how to handle the contraband situation was further enunciated by the Second

---

462. Billings, J. D., pp. 244, 245, 331. The assembly signal to call the unit out in battle order.
463. O.R. Vol. 1, p. 395; Sanger, G. P., Vol. 12, 1863, pp. 354, 589–592.
464. Babcock, W. M. Jr., p. 101.

Confiscation Act of July 17th, which declared that all those former slaves *held by supporters of the Confederacy* that crossed into Union lines were free. Clearly, they must be fed, and to justify that, they must be employed. In a letter to the commander of the southern department's General Saxton, dated August 25th, 1862,[465] Secretary of War Stanton had authorized the number of former slaves that Saxton could hire as 5,000. Further, once mustered, they and "their wives, mothers and children, [are] declared to be forever free."

The rate of pay Stanton authorized came nowhere near the figure Babcock quotes, being $5 for laborers and $8 for skilled workers. The $15 from Babcock may be a misprint, the actual number more likely being the $5 as authorized by Stanton. In any case, we see that the number of contrabands hired and freed unfortunately had a practical budget limitation.

Another vignette from Babcock[466] is the story of "Robert," whose "home" was the plantation of James Abercrombie some forty miles up the Escambia River. Robert told of his escape and his quest to find "de Yankees." Babcock writes: "I asked him a good many questions which he answered with constant grimaces which kept us in a roar of laughter, but finally I put the question, 'Have you got a wife?' The poor fellow's face took a sad look in an instant which touched us all. 'Where is she now?' 'De dogs ketched her massa.'" They had started together and were soon being overtaken by the hounds. He halted, ostensibly to allow her to escape, yet the dogs bypassed him and continued on the scent trail. He had to make the instinctive decision to run in another direction.

His story is eminently believable, though perhaps only to one who has experienced the peculiar behavior of hunting hounds. Out of this vast forest, they have the uncanny ability to find the scent of a raccoon and tree it in minutes. What happens next is the reverse. Having treed the creature, they seem immune to its moves. One has to see it to believe it, but a raccoon will climb to the upper branches of a tree, then swing to an adjacent one and shinny down to earth just a few feet away from the tree attracting the hounds' attention. The raccoon then scampers off, leaving the hounds still "barking up the wrong tree," where the scent trail stops.

At Fort Pickens, the command would soon change hands. On January 29th, 1862, Col. Harvey Brown was directed to turn over the Department of Florida to Lewis G. Arnold, now promoted to brigadier general, U.S. Volunteers.[467] The change-of-command order was apparently not received until February 22nd, 1862, when Arnold finally assumed command. Brown, having been brevetted brigadier general in the regular army, was transferred to New York where he had been

---
465. O.R. Vol.14, pp. 377, 378.
466. Babcock, W. M. Jr., p. 102.
467. O.R. Vol. 6, p. 694. A temporary, or brevet, rank, as Arnold was a still a major in the regular army.

assigned to the command of the defenses of New York Harbor.[468]

Tenth in the West Point class of 1837, Lewis G. Arnold of New Jersey[469] had won distinction in the Mexican War. Babcock's description[470] of Arnold was: "Bred a soldier and having served his country in all sorts of warfare he is fitted by experience for holding an important office . . . He is small . . . his round black eyes very genial . . . He is brave, prudent, ambitious, active and cautious at once . . . He is very popular with all."

The Department of Florida ceased to exist on March 31st, 1862, when it became the western district of the Department of the South. Headquarters of the new department was at Port Royal, South Carolina, and the new commander was Maj. Gen. David Hunter.[471]

Those at Fort Pickens may or may not have observed the smoke of the burning lumber and ships at Blackwater Bay, nearly forty miles distant, on March 11th. However, confirmation[472] of a partial evacuation of the Pensacola area came in mid-March from a party of two whites and two blacks, who came to Fort Pickens from the area of Milton. This prompted Arnold to write to Flag Officer David G. Farragut, commander of the Western Gulf Blockading Squadron, on March 15th. He also wrote to the adjutant general on March 22nd, requesting that his "estimates" to the quartermaster department for a shallow draft steamboat and surfboats be filled without delay. This was necessary before any offensive operations could be initiated, the navy support being now at a minimum (only the sloop *Vincennes*). He requested the support of two or three gunboats to attack Town Point, on the north side of the peninsula opposite Deer Point. The information the visitors had provided indicated that all the guns and most of the 2,000 men had been removed, leaving a force of 400.

It took until April 8th for Arnold's letter to Farragut to arrive at the Head of the Passes, in the Mississippi, and for Farragut[473] to respond, but the answer was no. The very good reason was that he and Butler's forces were "on the eve of attacking New Orleans." The letter was apparently handed over to Butler, who also wrote his regrets.

On April 13th, Arnold turned to Admiral McKean, now commanding the Eastern Division of the Gulf Blockading Squadron, and made the same request. By now, however, he was more specific about the weakness of the Confederate forces, saying that "our recent victories in Tennessee, North Carolina, &c., having caused the rebels to remove most of their best troops from the navy-yard and their whole

---

468. Cullum, Vol. I, p. 189.
469. O.R. Vol. 6, p. 436; Cullum, Vol. I, p. 669; Arnold no. 900.
470. Babcock, W. M. Jr., p. 77.
471. O.R. Vol. 6, pp. 257, 258.
472. O.R. Vol. 6, pp. 704, 705, 711.
473. O.R. Vol. 6, p. 712.

defensive line from Fort McCree to Pensacola . . . With your cooperation, I am confident of taking Pensacola."

Record 4/62
28 FEBRUARY–30 APRIL 1862, FORT PICKENS, FLORIDA

The Company formed portion of an expedition which left Fort Pickens 26 Mar. Went into camp on Santa Rosa Island, 40 miles up the beach, on the morning of the 31st and at dawn shelled and dispersed a rebel force on the mainland. Returned to Fort Pickens April 2, 1862.

1. Henry W. Closson   Capt. In Command
2. Franck E. Taylor   1st Lt. Temp. detached to Command of Co. C 3rd Inf. By virtue of special order no. 19, Hdqrts. Dept. of Fla. Fort Pickens, Feb. 16, 1862
3. E. L. Appleton   1st Lt.
4. T. K. Gibbs   2nd Lt.

Discharged:
    Andrew J. Beeler, Corpl. Feb. 9,'60 Boston, Ma. By Surgeon's Certificate of Disability (of wounds received in action) Apr. 5,'62

Strength: 87. Sick: 7.

Sick Present: Isaac T. Cain, William Henry, William Schaffer, William E. Scott

Sick Absent: Thomas Brook, Ft. Hamilton, NY. Left Co. Sept. 17, 1861
    William Brunskill   do.
    Charles Riley, Ft. McIntosh, TX. Abs. since Feb. 25, 1861. Reduced to Pvt. July 12, 1861.

Reconnaissance on Santa Rosa

Arnold's reading of the signs of the deterioration of the Confederate lines and his impatience to act was indicated by ordering a "reconnaissance in force" on March 27th –31st.[474] Its purpose was to capture or displace what was heard to be a force of rebels some three companies in size who had attacked sailors from the blockading squadron at the Southeast Pass, at the eastern end of Santa Rosa Island. Arnold's force would consist of a detachment from Battery L (see table I), and Company K of the 6th Regiment of New York Volunteers. They would be under the command of Capt. Henry W. Closson of Battery L.[475]

    Carrying rations for five days and with a six-mule team towing a 10-pounder Parrott rifle, they set out on the 27th and camped twelve miles east on the island. They were joined on the 28th by Company D of the 6th New York, led by Lt. Richard H. Jackson (now Arnold's aide and assistant adjutant general) who was accompanied by one of the four rebel "refugees"[476] who had come in to the fort on the 27th. The refugee was to act as a guide. The rebel camp was indicated to be

---

474. The O.R. has the date as the 27th; as can be seen, the muster roll does not agree.
475. O.R. Vol. 6, p. 500.
476. Babcock, W. M. Jr. Babcock says "deserters," p. 55.

on the mainland, about forty miles from the fort. Orders were to make a three-pronged approach, one company passing east past the rebel position, crossing the East Pass onto the mainland, and doubling back. The second group and the rifled gun were to shell the enemy from a position opposite, on the island, and the third was to cross the sound below the enemy camp and approach east along the mainland. Boats were to be furnished by the blockading schooner *Maria Wood*, stationed off Santa Rosa on a line opposite the enemy position.

Capt. Henry W. Closson	John Casey	Joseph Kutschor	William E. Scott
1st Lt. Franck E. Taylor	Jeremiah Connell	Charles F. Mansfield	Warren P. Shaw
1st Lt. Edward L. Appleton	Owen Coyne	James McCarthy	Joseph Smith
2nd Lt. Theodore E. Gibbs	William Creed	Daniel McCoy	Andrew Stoll
Sgt. Lewis Keller	Robert Curran	Miles McDonagh	William V. Thompson
Sgt. Thomas Newton	Patrick Donnelly	Terence McGaley	Reuben Townsend
Sgt. Julius Becker	Prosper Ferrari	Edward McLaughlin	John Tomson
Sgt. Alexander J. Baby	Charles A. Flint	James McWaters	Michael White
Corp. David J. Wicks	James Flynn	Dennis Myers	Joseph Wilkinson
Corp. Charles Spangler	Christopher Foley	John Murphy	Henry Wilkson
Corp. William Demarest	George Friedman	John G. Nitschke	Henry William
Privates:	Morris Galavan	Michael O'Sullivan	Owen A. Wren
James Ahern	George F. Hadley	William Parketton	Wallace D. Wright
Edward Anglin	John Holland	Franklin W. Richards	William Wynne
James Beglan	George Howard	Ludwig Rupprecht	
William F. Brown	Charles Jackel	Heinrick Schmidt	
John Burke	Michael Kenny	Phillip H. Schneider	

Table I. Battery L Members of the Expedition

The expedition went into camp, called Camp Jackson,[477] on March 31st, some thirty-six miles from the fort and four from the supposed location of the rebel camp. The first part of the plan of attack was abandoned because the East Pass was too far from the position for the attack, some ten miles. The schooner was notified to deliver the boats to the point of a signal fire that night, determined by a close reconnaissance of the island by Lieutenants Jackson and Appleton. At sunset, the attacking force of 170 men moved to a point about two miles below the position of the rebel camp, the place where the crossing would be made. The signal fire was lit, and the first two boats arrived at the outer beach at 11:00 p.m. They were

---

477. Referred to as Camp Jackson in Closson's monthly return for March. Twenty-three men of Battery L did not go on this mission: those three listed as "Sick Absent" on the muster roll and one of the "Sick Present": Schaffer. At the time of the mission, Beeler had not been discharged but was listed as sick, as was Cummings, though he was well (not listed as sick on the muster roll) by the end of April. Others remaining at the fort were privates Buckley as hospital attendant, Straub as hospital cook, Cotterill as commissary clerk, the artificer Cain, and the musician Lighna; those on extra duty (not defined): Carroll, Craffey, Farrell, Gilroyd, Lanahan, McSweeney, Meyer, Olvany, Roper, and Stanners. Two were in confinement: Hanney and Shapley.

hauled the eight hundred yards across the island to the inner beach. The third boat did not arrive until 1:00 a.m. The late arrival and the sighting of, and unsuccessful chase after, two rebel spies now "precluded all possibility of surprise," and the plans were changed. The two boats were returned to the outer beach. Company K of the 6th was to return the two miles to Camp Jackson and remain there. Company D and the Battery L men were to proceed to the inner beach opposite the rebel camp, some two miles farther east. With the rifle in position some two hundred fifty yards from it, they waited until early dawn when the huts of the enemy camp could be seen. Lieutenant Jackson was directed to open fire. Quoting Closson: "The shells burst right in their midst." Though a "scattering" volley was fired from the rebel guard, they disappeared along with the rebels in camp, who could be seen running "through the brush in their shirt-tails making rapidly into the back country. After shelling the area thoroughly, I returned to my camp. My supply of rations and forage was nearly exhausted, the mules nearly broken down by a very severe pull of forty miles through the heavy sand of the beach. I therefore sent all my sick men [some 6, two from Battery L: Scott and William] . . . back on the schooner." The command was back at the fort by April 2nd.

A search of the records indicates that the rebel camp was Camp Walton, and was occupied by McPherson's Walton Guards, about 60 men.[478]

The reconnaissance may have satisfied Arnold in that he obtained information on "the character of the upper end of the island," but he made no comment. Certainly, there were no Confederates on the island; they were only camped on what is today known as Fort Walton Beach. It is noted that no prisoners were taken. Though the lack of prisoners precluded that source of information, the lack was soon made up by deserters. On April 4th, Col. Thomas M. Jones at Pensacola sent this message to Gen. Samuel Jones at Mobile: "I am confident the enemy now know my true condition, two men having escaped to Fort Pickens."[479]

---

478. O.R. Vol. 6, pp. 762, 869.
479. O.R. Vol. 6, p. 870.

Chapter 5

The Anaconda Plan: North and South;
Forts Heiman, Henry, and Donelson;
The Northern Column; New Madrid/Island No. 10;
Pittsburg Landing/Shiloh; Louisiana;
Farragut and Butler; New Orleans; Vicksburg I; Corinth;
Record 6/62; Occupation of Pensacola;
Record 8/62; Reassignments; Record 10/62

The Anaconda Plan: North and South

The situation that had originally precipitated the suggested reassignment of Bragg was the fact that on September 10th, 1861, Gen. Albert Sidney Johnston had been ordered to head a redefined Confederate Department No. 2, consisting of the states of Tennessee, Arkansas, and that portion of Mississippi east of New Orleans.[480] It would also be in control of all military operations in Kentucky, Missouri, Kansas, and a portion of Indian Country (Oklahoma). It was now imperative for Johnston to focus on Kentucky and Tennessee to attempt to retain a Confederate foothold there and to counter the increased threat made by Union moves in the area. Gen. Ulysses S. Grant[481] had been assigned to the command of the district of Southeast Missouri on September 1st. Typical of Grant, his moves were decisive. He occupied Paducah, Kentucky, on September 6th, before the Confederates could arrive.[482] Recognizing the threat, Johnston quickly made requests for 30,000 troops from Tennessee and 10,000 each from Mississippi and Arkansas.[483]

The victory of Grant's forces over those led by Gen. Gideon Pillow, at the Battle of Belmont, Missouri,[484] on November 7th, is here regarded as a turning point, and the path to Grant's ascendency, tortuous though it proved to be. Belmont was directly across the Mississippi River from Columbus, Kentucky, to which the Confederates retreated. Columbus then became a strong point at the end of a line in Kentucky that the Confederacy had occupied. The line extended to Bowling

---

480. O.R. Vol. 4, p. 405.
481. O.R. Vol. 3, p. 2.
482. O.R. Vol. 4, p. 196.
483. O.R. Vol. 4, pp. 417, 421, 422.
484. Grant, U. S., Vol. 1, pp. 269–280.

Green and Mill Springs, on the upper waters of the Cumberland River, covering the Cumberland Gap, which leads into Virginia.

On October 24th, John C. Fremont had been relieved of the command of the Department of the West. Military reverses in the department, allegations of pay irregularities, contracts awarded without bids, and Fremont having profited by the purchase of defective arms in Europe[485] were contributing factors; but his ill-timed and unauthorized emancipation proclamation may have been the key to his removal. He was temporarily replaced by Maj. Gen. David Hunter, U.S. Volunteers;[486] but a general reorganization of the Departments of the West, Cumberland, and Ohio gave Maj. Gen. Henry W. Halleck the command of the new Department of Missouri on November 9th.[487] It included the states of Missouri, Wisconsin, Illinois, Arkansas, and that portion of Kentucky west of the Cumberland River. Thus, General Grant fell under the new command of Halleck.

Henry W. Halleck, West Point class of 1839, had served in the Mexican War primarily with the naval forces on the coast of California and Lower California as an engineer for military operations. After the war, he served as the secretary of state of California under the occupation by the U.S. military. He was largely responsible for the draft of the California Constitution. A scholar and author, he became well-known for his many published works, of which we list three: *Coast Defense*; *Elements of Military Art and Science*, and *International Law, or Rules Regulating the Intercourse of States in Peace and War*.

He resigned his captain's commission in 1854 and had become a prominent lawyer in California, director general of the New Almaden Quicksilver Mine, and president of the Pacific and Atlantic Railroad. He was appointed a major general of the California militia in 1860 and reappointed to the U.S. Army as a major general on August 19th, 1861. How could anyone be more qualified to take charge of a department that was in a position to support a major strategic thrust, the "Northern Column," aimed to win control of the Mississippi?

Notwithstanding the "Northern Column," the plan the secret board of officers had put together was still underway, and though it was inadvertently revealed to the new Secretary of War, Edwin M. Stanton, who had been appointed on January 15th, 1862,[488] he embraced it with enthusiasm. From Welles: ". . . Mr. Fox (now the assistant secretary of the navy) made known to General Butler and to Stanton the great object which had occupied the Navy Department for several months . . . Mr. Stanton seized hold of the information with avidity, and gave a hearty support to the movement – the more acceptable because General McClellan, who had known our object and was by express direction of President

---

485. O.R. Vol. 3, pp. 541–544.
486. O.R. Vol. 3, p. 553.
487. Cullum, Vol. I, pp. 733–740, Halleck no. 988; O.R. Vol. 3, p. 567; O.R. Vol. 7, p. 439.
488. O.R. Ser. III, Vol. 1, p. 964; Welles, G., Vol. I, pp. 60, 61.

Lincoln to cooperate with the Navy, appeared indifferent and had little confidence in our success."

McClellan had been briefed[489] on the plan in mid-November by its three most serious proponents: Navy Secretary Welles, Assistant Navy Secretary Fox, and Cdr. David Porter. There is no record of what transpired other than in Welles' later writings. Initially, the plan to attack New Orleans was to support the blockade. It was one of the "points" in the Anaconda Plan. It had been proposed because "the capture of New Orleans itself would be less difficult, less expensive, less exhausting, would be attended with less loss of life, and be a more fatal blow to the rebels, than the most extensive, stringent, and protracted blockade that could possibly be established." McClellan had approved of it when he heard that the 10,000 supporting troops required were only to be there to "garrison the captured forts and hold the city, after the navy had obtained possession . . ."

On January 25th, 1862, McClellan was again asked, this time by Stanton, what he thought of all of this secret navy planning. Giving Stanton a history of the murky origins of the expedition,[490] McClellan outlined his view that there were three "great points" from which operations should be conducted: the Departments of the Potomac, Ohio, and Missouri. The Potomac would face Richmond, the Ohio would oppose the rebels in Kentucky, and the Missouri would clear that state, and then have "for a prime object the control of the Mississippi River and operations against New Orleans." Operations on the seacoast were only to distract the enemy. McClellan estimated that 30,000 to 50,000 men would be required if Butler were to attack from the Gulf – that is, to meet the Missouri "Northern Column." This "new extension of the plan," as he called it, had insufficient troops, and it was his recommendation that General Butler's expedition should be suspended – McClellan the bold!

Brushing McClellan's objections aside, Stanton created the Department of the Gulf on February 23rd, 1862,[491] to "be occupied by the forces of Maj. General B. F. Butler." McClellan now had no choice other than to confirm to Butler his staff assignments and the troops involved. The objective, in support of Admiral Farragut of the navy, was initially to secure New Orleans, but then Baton Rouge and to "open your communication with the northern column [the Department of the Missouri] by the Mississippi . . ."

By February 17th, 1862, the force authorized had grown to 17 regiments of

---

489. Welles, G., *Galaxy*, November 1871, p. 677.
490. O.R. Vol. 6, pp. 677–678.
491. O.R. Vol. 6, pp. 685, 687, 694, 695, 704. Only Chief of Staff Strong and Chief Engineer Weitzel knew the destination. Weitzel was recommended by the board of officers as an expert on the lower Mississippi.

infantry, 3 companies of cavalry, and 6 batteries of light artillery; for a total of 17,945.[492]

Forts Heiman, Henry, and Donelson

In evident recognition of his decisive moves in the occupation of Paducah, Kentucky,[493] on September 6th, 1861, and his recent victory at the Battle of Belmont[494] on November 7th, Halleck added a small force to Grant's command, Gen. C. F. Smith's. His department was renamed the Department of Cairo (Illinois).[495] Grant was apparently to be accepted without prejudice, the memory of his alleged alcoholism forgotten.

Collaboration between C. F. Smith and Grant swiftly hatched the idea of attacking Fort Heiman[496] across the Tennessee River from Fort Henry. On a bluff that overlooked Fort Henry, its capture would almost ensure the fall of Fort Henry. Grant attempted to propose the plan to Halleck by requesting a meeting.[497] At the January 6th, 1862, meeting, he was treated with "so little cordiality"[498] that he failed to utter "many sentences before I was cut short as if my plan was preposterous. I returned to Cairo very much crestfallen."

Halleck, having taken no military initiatives since his November appointment, was ordered by McClellan, on January 3rd,[499] to make a reconnaissance up the Cumberland and Tennessee rivers and threaten the area of extreme western Kentucky, including Columbus, Mayfield, Murray, and Dover. The purpose was to draw attention away from a planned operation by Don Carlos Buell, commanding the Department of Ohio. Buell, with headquarters at Louisville, stood opposite the Confederates under Buckner at Bowling Green.[500] The Department of Missouri's reconnaissance was to prevent troops from forts Heiman, Henry, or Donelson from coming to Buckner's aid. The reconnaissance was assigned to Grant.

Buell's move against Buckner came as the planned advance of Gen. George H. Thomas in the direction of Confederate General George B. Crittenden's winter quarters at Mill Springs, Kentucky, which was situated on both sides of the Cumberland River. Thomas' division was to drive the Confederates across the Cumberland River and break up Crittenden's army. Thomas arrived near Logan's

---

492. O.R. Vol. 6, p. 688.
493. O.R. Vol. 4, pp. 196–198.
494. O.R. Vol. 3, p. 274.
495. O.R. Vol. 7 p. 515.
496. Grant, U. S., Vol. I, p. 286.
497. O.R. Vol. 7, p. 534.
498. Grant, U. S., Vol. I, p. 287
499. O.R. Vol. 7, pp. 527, 528.
500. Grant, U. S., Vol. I, pp. 285–286; CWSAC KY006, Mill Springs.

Crossroads, on the north side of the river, on January 17th, and waited for reinforcements. Though the Union forces had sought to attack, the Confederates did so first on January 19th. The Union counterattacked, and the Confederates were thoroughly beaten, the beginning of a string of good news for the Union in eastern Kentucky.

Grant had moved out on January 13th, and successfully having prevented any Confederate move to aid Crittenden, his forces began their withdrawal on the 18th.[501] An unintended consequence of this reconnaissance was the opportunity for Smith, Grant, and his lieutenant, John McClernand,[502] to revive Grant's proposal to attack forts Heiman and Henry. On January 22nd, C. F. Smith prepared a report of his part in the late reconnaissance, which had been in the vicinity of Fort Henry.[503] He concludes: "I think two iron-clad gunboats would make short work of Fort Henry." Grant now took the initiative to discuss the plan with Flag Officer Foote, whose gunboats were near Cairo, assigned to support the Department of Missouri. Foote agreed, and telegraphed:[504]

Cairo, *January* 28, 1862

Maj. Gen. HENRY W. HALLECK,
St. Louis, Mo.:

Commanding General Grant and myself are of opinion that Fort Henry, on the Tennessee River, can be carried with four iron-clad gunboats and troops to permanently occupy. Have we your authority to move for that purpose when ready?

A. H. Foote,
Flag-Officer

Grant also telegraphed Halleck:[505] "With permission, I will take Fort Henry, on the Tennessee, and establish and hold a large camp there."

At headquarters, St. Louis, January 30th, 1862: Halleck is suddenly in favor of the formerly preposterous plan. Since we have no chronology of that day, we cannot tell the sequence in which several communications were made. One[506] was to McClellan from Buell enclosing a letter to him from "an intelligent and well-informed person I have at Paducah." (C.F. Smith's headquarters). The letter recounts Smith's report of January 22nd to Grant, wherein he had recommended the attack on Fort Henry. Another message, a telegraph,[507] is from McClellan to Halleck, describing the fact that he has received a letter "from an intelligent and well informed person at Paducah." McClellan goes on to say that he believes the

---

501. O.R. Vol. 7, p. 560.
502. Walke, H., *Century Magazine*, January 1885, p. 427.
503. O.R. Vol. 7, p. 561.
504. O.R. Vol. 7, p. 120.
505. Grant, U. S., Vol. I, p. 287.
506. O.R. Vol. 7, p. 572.
507. O.R. Vol. 7, p. 573.

plan is feasible and that he hopes that Halleck will give it a prompt trial.

Halleck to McClellan, January 30: "Your telegraph . . . received. General Grant and Commodore Foote will be ordered to immediately advance and to reduce Fort Henry . . ."

Thus, the approval for the campaign that captured forts Heiman, Henry, and Donelson, was by an intrigue that went over Halleck's head, evidently on C. F. Smith's initiative.

The scenes revealed behind the preparation for the attack on Fort Henry begin to clarify why the momentum of the war was lost several months later. They show Halleck's strange fear of the initiative, habitual overestimation of enemy strength, lack of trust in his subordinates, and an impatient predilection to micromanage – from afar. Halleck was some two hundred fifty miles away at St. Louis and still deluded himself into thinking that it was necessary for him to be in control of Grant's every step.

On February 3rd, Grant telegraphed Halleck from Paducah: "Will be off up the Tennessee at 6 o'clock. Command, twenty-three regiments in all."[508] At this point, Halleck seems not to have been able to control his worry or his extreme caution.

He telegraphed Buell:[509]

St. Louis, February 5, 1862

Our advance column is moving up the Tennessee – twenty-three Regiments. More will soon follow. Can't you make a diversion in our favor by threatening Bowling Green?

If this was necessary, why had he not discussed it with Grant earlier? Buell declines, noting that he will not be that close to Bowling Green for another twelve days.

Halleck then turns to McClellan:[510]

It is reported that 10,000 men have left Bowling Green by railroad to re-enforce Fort Henry. Can't you send me some infantry regiments from Ohio? *Answer.*

Five more telegrams ensue between Halleck, McClellan, or Buell, all on February 5th. Rebuffed, Halleck sends a telegram to the Assistant Secretary of War Thomas A. Scott, reiterating the questionable and possibly fraudulent "10,000 men" story and his need of "reenforcements."

On February 6th, Halleck had not given up, and sent a telegram to McClellan:

---

508. O.R. Vol. 7, p. 581.
509. O.R. Vol. 7, p. 583.
510. O.R. Vol. 7, p. 583–585.

Fort Henry is largely re-enforced from Bowling Green and Columbus. They intend to make a stand there. Unless I get more forces I may fail to take it.... I am sending every available man from Missouri. I *was not ready to move*,[511] but deemed best to anticipate the arrival of Beauregard's force.

Confused by Halleck's exaggerations, Buell and McClellan were now full of recrimination over the fact that Halleck had been allowed to get them into such a mess: "... commenced ... without appreciation – preparative or concert – has now become of such vast magnitude. It will have to be in the face of 50,000, if not 60,000 men."[512]

Confederate General Lloyd Tilghman, in command of the defenders at Fort Henry, had indeed been reinforced – by the 48th and 51st Tennessee Regiments. However, the use of the word *regiment* with regard to the number of men involved here needs clarification. In the Union army, a regiment could consist of up to 900 men. Here, it meant regiments of about 200 men each, or a total of 400. Tilghman's total force at the initiation of the battle was 2,610.[513]

Fort Heiman having been abandoned, Fort Henry surrendered on February 6th, after a gunboat bombardment of an hour and a quarter, to the *unconditional* demand of Flag Officer Foote. Having advanced nearby, Grant took over the fort and its few prisoners about a half-hour later.[514] The remainder of the Confederates escaped toward Fort Donelson.

Regardless of the positive outcome regarding Fort Henry, and the necessary congratulatory telegrams and letters to all (Grant noted that he received warm congratulations from General Cullum, Halleck's chief of staff, but none of any kind from Halleck),[515] the earlier proceedings must have left a bad taste. Grant had exposed Halleck by such a quick and decisive outcome. Rather, Halleck kept up a drumbeat of nonsense, claiming that the enemy was now concentrating troops to regain their lost advantage. Halleck's behavior having begun to be revealed as being out of touch, McClellan then advised him to go to the scene of operations.[516] In fact, he did not leave St. Louis to take command in the field until April, when the Union army was positioned before Corinth, Mississippi.

Busy with his perception that Grant needed almost limitless reinforcements in and about Fort Henry (including entrenching tools, a further revelation of Halleck's mind-set), Halleck never gave Grant any specific orders regarding Fort Donelson. Grant noted that he received word that the entrenching tools had been

---

511. Italics by the author.
512. O.R. Vol. 7, p. 588.
513. O.R. Vol. 7, pp. 140, 145–152.
514. ORN Ser. I, Vol. 22, p. 537.
515. Grant, U. S., Vol. I, p. 317.
516. O.R. Vol. 7, p. 591.

sent to Fort Henry on the day he had arrived "in front" of Fort Donelson.[517]

Thus, by an oversight, Halleck had not put the brakes on Grant. After Fort Henry, Grant had immediately prepared for the move on Fort Donelson, and in what became typical of all of Grant's later moves in the war, he noted that he felt that his "15,000 men on the 8th would be more valuable than 50,000 men a month later."[518]

Any delay in the attack on Fort Donelson was caused by exceptionally muddy conditions. The artillery could not be advanced east across the twenty miles from Fort Henry to Fort Donelson; it, and ordnance, would have to go by transport back down the Tennessee to the Ohio and then up the Cumberland (see figure 1 prepared by the author). For this, and gunboats to support the attack, Grant had to wait until the 11th when Admiral Foote was ready. Grant issued his field orders for the attack on that date.[519] On February 12th, Grant reported to Halleck, "We start this morning in heavy force for Fort Donelson." On the 14th, Grant reported that he had invested the fort despite continual rain, snow, and a temperature of 20°F. The high water would prevent a proper deployment of troops above[520] the village of Dover to cut off reinforcements or to prevent escape of the garrison. Grant sent a second report to Halleck that day, stating that the enemy had been "driven into their works at every point."[521]

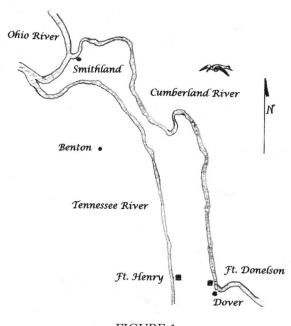

FIGURE 1

---

517. Grant, U. S., Vol. I, p. 296.
518. Grant, U. S., Vol. I, p. 298.
519. O.R. Vol. 7, p. 605.
520. The Cumberland here flows north; hence, "above" is upriver, or south.
521. O.R. Vol. 7, p. 613.

Despite no evidence of a report to substantiate his assertions, Halleck telegraphed to McClellan on the 15th that the garrison at Donelson was 30,000[522] and that the enemy had evacuated Bowling Green and was falling back in the direction of the Cumberland. He must have more troops. "It is a military necessity."

On the 16th, Fort Donelson surrendered to the *unconditional* demand of Grant, taking 12,000 to 15,000 prisoners,[523] though Gen. John B. Floyd, the former secretary of war, and Gen. Gideon Pillow had managed to escape with about 1,000 Virginia men.[524] This time, the surrender was to Grant, rather than to Foote, by the circumstance that Foote had considerable damage to his vessels: 54 killed and wounded, and he had slackened his bombardment after an hour and a half.[525] (Foote was among the wounded, though he made light of it initially. Eventually, its lingering effects would cause his retirement and death.) It is noted that Grant's report opened with: "We have taken Fort Donelson . . ." It is also noted that the phrase "unconditional surrender," so often attributed to Grant, first appears in the February 6th Fort Henry surrender demand of Admiral Foote.

Halleck only saw the victory as part of a continuing crisis whereby the Confederates in the Columbus area (Beauregard) would now attack Fort Henry from the west. He cited the information that 15 steamers loaded with troops from New Orleans had landed at Columbus.[526] Credit McClellan with a response that he felt the steamers had arrived there rather to evacuate Columbus, not for its reinforcement.[527] McClellan was beginning to see through Halleck.

Halleck now blurted to McClellan: "I must have command of the armies in the West. *Hesitation and delay*[528] are losing us the golden opportunity. Lay this before the President and Secretary of War. May I assume command? Answer quickly."[529] Halleck's demand was not approved, but the unfortunate seed was planted.

In his generally strained relationship with Halleck, one thing that was especially damaging to Grant originated from a visit he had made to consult with Buell at Nashville. Communications had always been a problem. As far back as during the preparations for the attack on Fort Henry, Grant had regularly communicated with General Cullum, Halleck's chief of staff, who was then located closer to Grant at Cairo, Illinois. Cullum had been sent there by Halleck (at St. Louis) to ease

---

522. O.R. Vol. 7, p. 616.
523. O.R. Vol. 7, p. 625.
524. O.R. Vol. 7, p. 256. This reference is the Confederate report. Foote's report gave Floyd 5,000 men. O.R.N. Ser. I, Vol. 22, p. 584. Assuming that the Confederate commander knew the correct numbers, compare a rough total of 16,000 to Halleck's allegations of 30,000.
525. ORN Ser. I, Vol. 22, p. 585.
526. O.R. Vol. 7, p. 633.
527. O.R. Vol. 7, p. 640.
528. Author's italics.
529. O.R. Vol. 7, p. 641.

communications and make decisions in his name. This was at the southern end of the telegraph line, and as Grant advanced, a line was being advanced behind him. Grant was sending his dispatches to Cullum by boat, but many of Cullum's messages were sent by the "advancing wire." Halleck had been becoming more and more impatient and dissatisfied with these arrangements, and one event tipped the scale.

After the surrender of Fort Donelson to Grant, and the February 19th surrender of Clarksville, Tennessee, to Foote,[530] Grant went to Nashville – on the heels of the Confederates having abandoned it on February 25th. He felt it necessary to consult with Buell about movements as the troops from Buell's department approached. Hearing this, Halleck raised the question as to whether Grant had reverted to his old habits. "I have had no communication from General Grant for more than a week. He left his command without my authority and went to Nashville. . . . I am worn out and tired with his neglect and inefficiency."[531] Upon receipt of this, McClellan authorized Halleck to arrest Grant if he felt it was necessary. The word spread, and Halleck received an inquiry from the adjutant general as to why Grant had left his command without leave.[532] Fuel to the fire had been added by allegations that property had been illegally removed from Fort Donelson by Grant's troops. (Some steamer captains were Southern sympathizers or opportunist thieves, and cargo was stolen. Other appropriations of stores were by members of the newly formed Sanitary Commission, at the time, largely under no one's control).[533]

The message was clear: do not display any initiative if you are subordinate to Halleck. On March 7th, Grant was so disgusted with Halleck that he wrote: "Every move I made was reported daily to your chief of staff, who must have failed to keep you properly posted . . . I have done my very best to obey orders and to carry out the interests of the service. If my course is not satisfactory remove me at once."[534]

Halleck quickly backed down after the added disclosure that the operator at the end of the "advancing" telegraph line was a rebel sympathizer who had purposely failed to forward requests from Halleck,[535] and Halleck fully exonerated Grant.[536] It was a rather hollow move, considering that it was he who had created the difficulty in the first place. The fact that Halleck had concealed that he was the source of the controversy was not revealed until after the war – in research conducted by Adam Badeau for his history of Grant's campaigns.[537]

---

530. ORN Ser. I, Vol. 22, p. 617.
531. ORN Ser. I, Vol. 22, p. 679–680.
532. ORN Ser. I, Vol. 22, p. 683.
533. O.R. Vol. 10/II, pp. 26, 30, 45, 46.
534. O.R. Vol. 10/II, p. 15.
535. Grant, U. S., Vol. I p. 328.
536. O.R. Vol. 7, p. 683
537. Grant, U. S., Vol. I, p. 328

The Northern Column

The cooperation between the army and the navy continued, and the spirit of the "Northern Column" of the Anaconda Plan lived on. Columbus was occupied on March 3rd by the 2nd Illinois Cavalry under William T. Sherman, after an armed reconnaissance by Foote.[538] Foote indicated to Halleck that he was ready to move to New Madrid on March 12th and was given the go-ahead the next day.[539] Note that the initiative continues to come from the subordinate.

Halleck had created the sub-district of the Mississippi within his department on February 27th, 1862, consisting of that part of Missouri between the St. Francis and Mississippi rivers. Brig. Gen. John Pope was assigned to command.[540] The command was to be used initially to clear the western end of the great Confederate defensive line as it now stood: from New Madrid, Missouri, through Savannah, Tennessee, to Chattanooga – or roughly from the Mississippi to the east–west portion of the Tennessee River.[541] It is also clear that it was to be a part of the Northern Column,[542] as is indicated in a letter from Halleck to Admiral Foote, dated March 21st: "Everything is progressing well on the Tennessee River towards opening your way down the Mississippi. The reduction of these works [Island No. 10] is only a question of time, and we are in no hurry on that point." Apparently Halleck had not *forgotten* about the Northern Column's prime purpose; but in contrast to Lincoln's, Stanton's, Welles', Farragut's, Butler's, and Foote's urgency to complete the opening of the Mississippi, he had the nerve to impose his own priority: *we are in no hurry.*

On March 11th, McClellan was relieved as general in chief, justified by the necessity for him to focus all his efforts as commander of the Army of the Potomac in the forthcoming Peninsular Campaign. A new Department of the Mississippi was created for Halleck, which included Buell's troops in Tennessee.[543] Now, Halleck had what he had earlier demanded.

No replacement was named for McClellan, so Halleck had no direct scrutiny except from the secretary of war in Washington, with information as seen through the eyes of the Assistant Secretary of War Scott, who was initially rather remotely located at Cairo, Illinois. In a message to Scott on March 10th, Halleck says: "Flotilla should go down the [Mississippi] river as far as possible without engaging any batteries below Point Pleasant [near Island No. 10]. Forts Randolph and Pillow will be turned. No use to engage them, but I want the navigation of the

---

538. O.R. Vol. 10/II, p. 651; O.R. Vol. 7 p. 436.
539. O.R. Vol. 10/II, p. 685.
540. O.R. Vol. 53, p. 514.
541. O.R. Vol. 10/II, pp. 16, 24.
542. O.R. Vol. 8, p. 631.
543. O.R. Vol. 10/II, p. 28.

river as far down as possible."544 Here was a brief spotlight on Halleck's approach: turn the forts, do not attack them. He seems to be unable to conceive of anything but surrounding an objective and waiting until it surrendered or until the enemy withdrew without battle.

New Madrid/Island No. 10

Pope had advanced to New Madrid, Missouri, and began to bombard it on March 13th.545 Foote was urged to proceed to attack Island No. 10, opposite New Madrid, and was promised supporting troops.546 The combined threat had its effect, and on March 14th, Pope reported: "To my utter amazement the enemy hurriedly evacuated the place last night, leaving everything."547

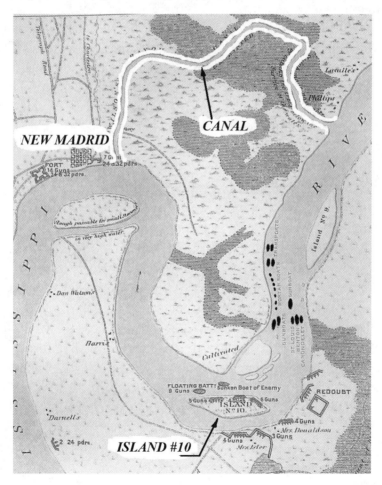

FIGURE 2

---

544. O.R. Vol. 8, p. 603.
545. O.R. Vol. 8, p. 609.
546. ORN Ser. I, Vol. 22, p. 687; O.R. Vol. 8, p. 608.
547. O.R. Vol. 8, p. 608.

The objective was now Island No. 10, and how to get Pope's troops to a suitable point to make an attack. The flooded condition of the countryside had left only the east side of the river dry. Thus, the only approach to the island would mean that Pope would have to cross the swift running river, an impossible task without transports. All the transports were lying upriver from the island and dared not run past its guns. They can be seen, shown in black, along with some of the ironclads, mortar boats, and gunboats of the western flotilla, in the map (figure 2).[548]

A canal to bypass the island to gain access to the transports was proposed by Pope,[549] and it was approved by Halleck on March 21st.[550] See the white highlighted track at the top of figure 2. This massive project passed through a swamp and flooded slough. It had to be dug as well as have trees felled in its path through the flooded forest. The trees had to be cut underwater, leaving their stump tops at least four feet below water level to accommodate the draft of the transports. Some of this clearing activity is shown in figure 3.[551]

FIGURE 3. CLEARING FOR TRANSPORT "*TERRY*"

---

548. Portion of plate no. 150, atlas to accompany the O.R.
549. O.R. Vol. 8, p. 625, 626.
550. O.R. Vol. 8, p. 629.
551. Leslie, Mrs. F., Battle Scenes, p. 98.

At six miles long and fifty feet wide, this herculean undertaking was completed on March 31st,[552] and all of Pope's transports had passed into it by April 2nd. It was, however, of insufficient depth for the passage of Foote's large ironclads, and the decision was made to run the *Carondelet* past Island No. 10's guns on the night of April 4th.[553] It was not hit, and the *Pittsburgh* ran the gauntlet early on April 6th.[554] Pope began crossing troops on the same day, and by day's end, 8,000 had passed.[555]

Island No. 10 was surrendered to Admiral Foote on the morning of the 8th.[556] Pope reported 6,000 prisoners taken by 7:00 p.m. with no Union casualties.[557] One of the Confederate units that surrendered was the 1st Alabama, which Bragg had shipped out from Fort Barrancas in March. The fear of the gunboats and the numbers of Pope's army, 18,500,[558] had overwhelmed the Confederates.

With New Madrid, Island No. 10, and the surrounding area occupied, and the Confederate prisoners directed to Northern prisons, Pope was free to continue pursuing the plan of the Northern Column. He had already issued his orders for just that on April 10th.[559]

Elsewhere, on April 5th, McClellan had begun the Army of the Potomac's Peninsular Campaign by advancing from Fort Monroe to Yorktown.[560]

Pittsburg Landing/Shiloh

On April 6th, Grant had been attacked by General Albert Sidney Johnston at Pittsburg Landing, on the Tennessee River, now called the Battle of Shiloh.

The Confederate secretary of war's urgent calls for troops from Virginia, New Orleans, and from Bragg to reinforce General Johnston, saw a massive buildup near the strategic point of Corinth, Mississippi, the junction of two important railroads and the middle of their defensive line extending to Chattanooga. On March 13th, information was received that the Confederates were concentrating at points along the Memphis and Charleston Railroad and that Bragg had arrived at Memphis.[561] On March 27th, came news that Corinth was being further reinforced - that 13 trains of 20 cars each had arrived.[562] On March 30th, deserters from Corinth

---

552. O.R. Vol. 8, pp. 650, 657; figure 2: Atlas plate 10, portion, revised.
553. ORN Ser. I, Vol. 22, p. 711.
554. O.R. Vol. 8, p. 668.
555. O.R. Vol. 8, p. 671.
556. ORN, Ser. I, Vol. 22, p. 720; McMorries, E. Y., p. 39.
557. O.R. Vol. 8, p. 675, CWSAC MO 012.
558. O.R. Vol. 8, p. 94.
559. O.R. Vol. 8, p. 682.
560. O.R. Vol. 8, p. 665.
561. O.R. Vol. 10/II, pp. 33, 34.
562. O.R. Vol. 10/II, p. 70; O.R. Vol. 10/II, p. 80.

claimed 80,000 men there with few rations and low morale. Grant's Army of the Tennessee was directed by Halleck to follow, but not to engage, until Buell's Army of the Ohio should arrive.[563] The Union buildup took place about twenty miles north of Corinth, at Pittsburg Landing.

The Confederates were presenting a golden opportunity to the Union. They were concentrating in one place where they could be surrounded and beaten. However, General Johnston, aware of the imminent arrival of Buell's 40,000-man army,[564] decided to take the initiative, and launched a preemptive strike on Grant.

Johnston's 44,000-strong Army of Mississippi[565] – organized under Polk, Bragg, Hardee, and Breckinridge as corps commanders – had left their entrenchments at Corinth and marched to Pittsburg. Grant alleges that he was not surprised by the attack, but at the end of the first day, his 33,000-man Army of the Tennessee was driven back about a mile.[566] What intimate knowledge Grant had about the situation, in that he was not surprised, is unexplained. What is known is, at the height of the battle, Johnston was wounded, bled to death on the field, and that his staff waivered. A member of the 1st Tennessee Infantry[567] remembers: "We saw General Albert Sidney Johnston surrounded by his staff and Governor Harris, of Tennessee. We saw some little commotion among those who surrounded him, but did not know at the time that he was dead. The fact was kept from the troops . . . In the very midst of our victory, here comes an order to halt." The halt order was fatal. The hungry Confederates now occupied the Union camp and took the opportunity to loot. (Remember the Confederate raid on the camp of the 6th New York? The situation of hungry and poorly equipped Confederates stopping to loot would show itself again and again.)

The next day, Grant, with the aid of Buell's troops, drove Johnston's army from the field. Grant had been lucky. Perhaps he did not know how lucky, particularly if he was unaware of the Confederate halt order. It is not mentioned in his memoirs. The Union army suffered 13,000 casualties.[568] The sentiment after these numbers was known is reflected in a report the Assistant Secretary of War Scott made to Secretary Stanton on April 10th: "Victory near Corinth has been decisive in our favor, but at terrible cost."[569]

The Battle of Pittsburg Landing – or Shiloh, from the name of a log church

---

563. O.R. Vol. 10/II, p. 41.
564. Grant, U. S., Vol. I, p. 332.
565. O.R. Vol. 10/II, p. 433. Derived from the Confederate return for April 15th. O.R. Vol. 10/II, p. 421, after the battle, but which shows 32,388 effectives. Assuming that 11,000 lost in the battle is correct, (Grant, Vol. I, p. 367) results in the 44,000 quoted here.
566. Grant, U. S., Vol. I, p. 340.
567. Watkins, S. R., p. 33.
568. O.R. Vol. 10/I, p. 108.
569. O.R. Vol. 8, p. 681, CWSAC TN 003.

that stood nearby[570] – was the "severest" according to Grant of any fought in the west.[571] However, it was not decisive because the Confederate army was still powerful despite 10,000 casualties. From all indications, it would continue to be reinforced. Beauregard, Johnston's second in command, and his successor, must be defeated if the will of the Confederates was to be broken. The Confederate army retreated back to Corinth. Their concentration at Corinth, twenty-two miles from Pittsburgh Landing, continued to be an opportunity. Could they be surrounded and forced to surrender after a siege, or would there have to be another Shiloh?

The importance of Corinth to the Confederacy and Beauregard's determination to hold it is reflected in a coded message he sent to headquarters:[572]

CORINTH, *April 9.*

General S. Cooper, *Richmond, Va.:*

All present probabilities are that whenever the enemy moves on this position he will do so with an overwhelming force of not less than 80,000 men. We can now muster only about 35,000 effectives. Van Dorn may possibly join us in a few days with about 15,000 more. Can we not be re-enforced from Pemberton's army? If defeated here we lose the Mississippi Valley and probably our cause; whereas we could even afford to lose for a while Charleston and Savannah for the purpose of defeating Buell's army, which would not only insure us the Valley of the Mississippi, but our independence.

G. T. BEAUREGARD

Halleck apparently agreed, as he had referred to the period prior to Corinth as "the eve of a great battle."[573]

From the perspective at Washington, nothing looked more promising. Since January, there were the victories at Mill Springs, forts Heiman and Henry, Roanoke Island, and Fort Donelson; the occupation of Bowling Green, Nashville, and Columbus; the victory at Pea Ridge (Arkansas); the occupation of New Madrid, Missouri, and New Bern, North Carolina; victories at Kernstown, Virginia; Glorieta, New Mexico; the fall of Island No. 10; and victory, albeit terribly costly, at Shiloh. Halleck's now vast army was viewed to be ready to defeat Beauregard's forces entrenched at Corinth. Farragut and Butler were poised to attack New Orleans. It looked as though May 1862 would undoubtedly be the turning point of the war. In fact, the War Department issued General Orders No. 33 of April 3rd, 1862, directing that all volunteer enlistments be discontinued,[574] and on April 10th,

---

570. Grant, U. S., Vol. I, p. 338.
571. Grant, U. S., Vol. II, p. 356.
572. O.R. Vol. 10/II p. 618.
573. O.R. Vol. 10/II, p. 128.
574. O.R. Ser. III, Vol. 2, p. 2. This was soon realized to be a mistake, and authority to recruit for existing regiments was granted to the "governors of the respective States" by General Orders No. 49, dated May 1st. Ibid, p. 28.

Lincoln issued a Proclamation of Thanks to Almighty God for these "inestimable blessings."[575]

The opinion that the Confederacy was on its last legs was shared widely. In his report for the period of May 23rd, 1861, to August 15th, 1862, the chief engineer of the Army of the Potomac, Gen. John G. Barnard, wrote[576], "At the time the Army of the Potomac landed on the [Yorktown] Peninsula [April 5th, 1862] the rebel cause was at its lowest ebb. Its armies were demoralized . . . and reduced in numbers by sickness, loss in battle, expiration of service, etc. . . . ."

Unfortunately, Halleck would let a substantial strategic victory at Corinth slip from the Union's grasp, and McClellan's Peninsular Campaign would be a total failure. As a result, the country would be doomed to almost exactly three more years of warfare.

Halleck left St. Louis on April 9th,[577] and arrived at Pittsburg Landing on April 12th to conduct operations in person for his first, and last, time in the war. During the lull in communications while Halleck was en route, Secretary Stanton made inquiry about Shiloh.[578] He received the following from the telegraph operator at Cincinnati: "General Halleck gave orders to General Grant some days previous to the battle that in case he was attacked not to pursue the enemy." Grant makes no mention of this in his memoirs but says that he "had not the heart to order the men who had fought desperately for two days" to pursue in the mud and rain.[579] Perhaps Grant did not want to belabor the aftermath of the battle, which had caused so many casualties, in some part because of his failure to take substantial defensive measures, such as entrenching.[580] Grant did, in fact, order W. T. Sherman to follow the rebel rear guard on the 8th, but the two Ohio brigades sent were repulsed, and the pursuit was called off.[581]

At this time, the assistant secretary of war was keeping Secretary Stanton abreast of events, and whether he realized it or not, he was clearing the way for Halleck's fateful decision to remove Pope's army from the Mississippi. As of April 15th, Pope and Foote were within four miles of Fort Pillow, about forty miles above Memphis.[582] Part of Scott's lengthy telegram contained: "I believe the enemy have about 10,000 men in their works . . . If General Pope finds . . . that he cannot capture Fort Pillow within 10 days, had he not better re-enforce General Halleck, immediately, and let Commodore Foote blockade below until forces can be returned . . . by

---

575. O.R. Ser. III, Vol. 2, p. 14.
576. O.R. Vol. 11, p. 129.
577. O.R. Vol. 10/II, p. 99.
578. O.R. Vol. 10/II, p. 104.
579. Grant, U. S., Vol. I, p. 354.
580. Grant, U. S., Vol. I, p. 357.
581. O.R. Vol. 10/I, pp. 263, 268; at Fallen Timbers, Shiloh, CWSAC, TN 003.
582. O.R. Vol. 10/II, p. 106; ORN Ser. I, Vol. 23, p. 5.

General Halleck beating Beauregard and marching upon Memphis from Corinth?" Quite a reasonable proposition, assuming events would continue to unfold as they had been, with the boldness and initiative of Grant, Pope, and Foote.

Halleck's decision to remove Pope from support to Foote was made on April 15th. Foote was left with two regiments of Pope's army under the command of Col. G. N. Fitch, roughly 1,500 men.

Thus, we complete the review of the activity of the Northern Column to April 15th, 1862. We now turn to Louisiana and the Farragut and Butler expedition, and carry their parallel activity to almost the same date in April, and, from there, chronicle how events went awry in May.

Louisiana

Early in April 1861, the governor of Louisiana had made note of the fact that no action to organize a protective force at New Orleans had been undertaken by the Confederate government. What was to happen if the city at the mouth of the strategic Mississippi was threatened? New Orleans was worth less than Pensacola?

Louisiana Governor Thomas O. Moore to L. P. Walker, the Confederate secretary of war, April 10th:

> The news from Washington creates considerable anxiety here. The ships sent from New York are believed to be destined for this place. The forts can be passed. We are disorganized, and have no general officer to command and direct. I doubt the policy of draining this place of troops to be sent to Pensacola. They are all needed here, especially if this place be selected to collect revenues. What can be done with a fleet opposite the custom-house?[583]

The governor would have a year of anxiety before Farragut was, indeed, opposite the customs house; but in April 1861, a desperate Moore, amid his dealings with the Confederate War Department, took the extraordinary action of enlisting men whom he knew the Confederate government would not demand be sent away. They were the men of the free colored population of New Orleans and were accepted into a militia unit known as the 1st Louisiana Native Guards.[584]

The ships Moore had mentioned "from New York" were, of course, Brown's expedition to Fort Pickens, and an explanation to that effect was sent out by Secretary Walker the next day. It was also used to again remind Moore of the urgency of forwarding the remainder of the 1,700 Louisiana troops that had been requested for Confederate service in March. "Either send troops at once to Pensacola or call out volunteers for that service to fill requisition."[585]

---

583. O.R. Vol. 53, p. 669.
584. O.R. Vol. 15, p. 556; O.R. Vol. 53, pp. 669, 670.
585. O.R. Ser. IV, Vol. 1, pp. 134, 135, 175; 700 of the total were to garrison forts Jackson and St. Philip; O.R. Vol. 53, pp. 669, 670.

To answer some of Moore's concerns, the War Department acted to assign Col. Paul O. Hebert to the command of the Confederate troops in Louisiana,[586] and Maj. Martin L. Smith of the Corps of Engineers to advise on the defenses of forts Jackson and St. Philip. As to the forts, Moore was given permission to send "an additional company or two of artillery."

The demands from Montgomery for the recruiting of more troops for Confederate service continued, and by the time Moore had completed raising the 1st Regiment of Louisiana Volunteers, they were ordered to Virginia on April 29th, 1861.[587] The pattern was set. The Confederate government moved to Richmond in late May, and the demands on everyone, from then on, were to ship soldiers to the east or north. We have seen that on May 17th, even Bragg, doing allegedly urgent duty at Pensacola, was asked how many troops he could spare. Thus, three regiments left Pensacola for Virginia.

We saw that the critical Confederate policy decision to abandon the coast, sent to Bragg at Pensacola, was not made until February 18th, 1862. However, the apparent disregard Confederate policy makers had for New Orleans' strategic value soon became obvious. Perhaps the policy was of necessity. Where could the Confederacy's fewer resources be best utilized? Could the Yankees be demoralized by quick victories if they were struck hard in selected places?

The 2nd Regiment of Louisiana Volunteers went to Virginia in May. Moore attempted to reserve the 3rd Regiment, which he had raised in May, for Colonel Hebert and the defenses of Louisiana, but they were ordered to Fort Smith, Arkansas.[588] At least the 4th Regiment, accepted into Confederate service on May 25th, would go to garrison Ship Island.

Also, on the 25th, Moore got his "general officer" Maj. Gen. David E. Twiggs, who, after leaving Texas, was assigned to the command of the Louisiana coastal defenses. Called Department No. 1, it included the "southern portions of Mississippi and Arkansas," including Mobile Bay. Twiggs had offered his services to Jefferson Davis in April.[589] Davis' letter of assignment to Twiggs included a significant phrase: "Hoping that your health will enable you to perform this service . . ." Twiggs[590] was now 71 and in poor health and was the oldest officer in Confederate service. His assignment was questionable, in the light of events, though evidently Jefferson Davis felt that this senior general, known to Louisianans, would be the necessary palliative for Moore.

It was not until July 6th, 1861, that Twiggs had landed 140 men and two guns on Ship Island, the excuse for the delay being the lack of heavy guns.

---

586. O.R. Vol. 53, pp. 668, 669.
587. O.R. Ser. IV, Vol. 1, p. 748.
588. O.R. Vol. 53, p. 685.
589. O.R. Vol. 53, pp. 690, 691.
590. Wilson and Fiske, eds., Vol. VI, pp. 191, 192.

Arrangements were finally made to obtain more from the navy yard at Warrington. By now, some 19 other locations had been lightly manned by a total of about 4,000 troops stretched along the complex Louisiana coast.[591] "City troops" are listed as at Fort Macomb, Bienvenue, Ponce Dupre, Proctorsville, and New Orleans Barracks. Whether the Native Guards were regarded as part of these city troops is not elaborated.

The construction of inner defensive works for the city had been the subject of disagreement between city officials and the Confederate officers Hebert and Smith. Not until August 14th were their recommendations approved, and with $100,000 from the city, and a like amount from the state, the work could begin.[592] Twiggs' suggestion of the use of floating docks as a barrier in the river was also approved.[593]

The navy now demanded the return of the heavy guns "borrowed" from Pensacola, and Twiggs was forced to abandon Ship Island. His order was given on September 13th.[594]

The slow pace of the defensive buildup and Twiggs' poor health now conspired to create demands for his replacement by both the city officials and the governor.[595] The success of Stringham's Hatteras Inlet expedition at the end of August had created renewed fear of New Orleans being the next target. To assist Twiggs, on September 25th, Maj. Gen. Mansfield Lovell was assigned to Department No. 1. He was "charged with coast and other defenses of that department." Brig. Gen. Daniel Ruggles was also assigned to assist. Although it was finally agreed that Twiggs must go, Twiggs asked to be relieved on October 5th, even before Lovell had arrived. On October 7th, Lovell was given command. On the same date, and in separate orders, Department No. 1 was stripped of Mobile and the state of Alabama, and as was earlier noted, they were added to Bragg's command at Pensacola.[596]

By November, Richmond's repeated demands for troops had raised the count of Louisiana regiments mustered for the Confederacy to 19. The 5th through the 8th had left for Virginia in June. Richard Taylor of St. Charles Parish, just northwest of New Orleans, left his assignment with Bragg to command the 9th Louisiana Regiment and had arrived at Manassas in July, one day too late for the battle. The 11th through the 13th regiments were sent to the aid of Johnston, at Columbus, Kentucky. The 14th and 15th and other independent companies, totaling over 3,000 men, were mustered directly into Confederate service. The

---

591. O.R. Vol. 53, p. 711, 712.
592. O.R. Vol. 53, pp. 715, 716, 722, 726, 727. Hebert was transferred to command the Department of Texas the same day. O.R. Ser. I, Vol. 4, p. 98.
593. O.R. Vol. 53, pp. 731, 732.
594. O.R. Vol. 53, p. 718, 739. Completed September 17th (see chapter 3).
595. O.R. Vol. 53, pp. 739, 742–744, 746–748; O.R. Vol. 6, pp. 740, 748.
596. O.R. Vol. 6, p. 643, 751.

newest state units were now at either Carrollton or Camp Moore at Tangipahoa, seventy-eight miles north of New Orleans.[597]

Touring the defensive works, Lovell found that obstructions had not been placed on any of the water approaches to the city. There were no heavy guns, and some of those available were of 40-year-old manufacture, incapable of being charged with heavy shells for long range.[598] On application to the chief of ordnance at Richmond, he was informed, as Bragg had been, that no 8-inch or 10-inch Columbiads were available. Lovell then took the extraordinary step to try to manufacture his own, including powder and small arms cartridges.

He ordered that river obstructions be constructed, the most notable a raft of logs and chains across the Mississippi at forts Jackson and St. Philip. There are myriad water routes into New Orleans, and unlike Twiggs, Lovell recognized that the Union navy would likely approach with deep water ships, and therefore concentrated his defenses accordingly.[599] M. L. Smith was urged to complete an eight-mile-long inner defense line, and independent companies were organized into regiments to man them.

Lovell noted that his department had few boats of any kind available for transport and supply and that there were no gunboats: $2,500,000 for a fleet of gunboats passed by the Louisiana Senate was defeated in the House.[600] Told early on that he could only cooperate with, but not command the naval forces in the area, he could do nothing but hope that the navy preparations would meet the challenge.[601] The navy, or at least those in control at Richmond, particularly Navy Secretary Steven A. Mallory, were pinning all their hopes on three warships: the ram *Manassas* (refer to figure 2, chapter 4), and two massive ironclads, the *Mississippi* and *Louisiana*, now under construction. They were certain to be capable of destroying the wooden Federal ships.

---

597. O.R. Ser. IV, Vol. 1, p. 749; Taylor, pp. 15–17, 111. The 13th Regiment remained at New Orleans until November.
598. O.R. Vol. 6, pp. 558–561.
599. O.R. Vol. 6, p. 512.
600. O.R. Vol. 6, p. 591.
601. O.R. Vol. 6, p. 645, 646.

Abstract from return of Department No. 1, commanded by Maj. Gen. Mansfield Lovell, for January, 1862.

Troops.	Present for duty.		Aggregate present.	Aggregate present and absent.	Artillery.	
	Officers.	Men.			Heavy.	Field.
Forts Jackson and Saint Philip	26	682	838	892	112	5
Fort Pike, La	8	193	245	277	32	......
Fort Livingston, La	9	248	275	294	12	4
Fort at Little Temple, La	3	80	83	96	......	......
Camp Benjamin, New Orleans	204	3,231	4,060	4,520	......	6
Arsenal, New Orleans	2	70	79	81	......	......
Battalion Mississippi Volunteers, New Orleans	11	124	260	291	......	......
Baton Rouge Barracks	1	4	5	5	......	......
Fort Guion	8	93	110	140	2	......
District of Lake Borgne	17	398	484	513	......	......
District of Berwick	42	807	943	1,040	......	......
Fort Quitman	5	137	150	157	......	......
Bay Saint Louis, Miss	34	594	750	1,003	......	......
Handsborough, Miss	24	386	532	896	......	......
Calcasieu Pass, La	2	68	83	91	......	......
Total	396	7,115	8,897	10,296	158	15

FIGURE 4

By January 1862, the weak strength and scattered disposition of Lovell's defense was seen in his return (figure 4).[602] His shortage of boats was apparently answered by his being given the authority to seize 14 private ships at New Orleans, to be converted to rams. The strategy decided upon, perhaps boosted by the limited success of the *Manassas* at the Battle of Southwest Pass, was that a ram was the most effective way to attack the Federal ironclads, such as those that had appeared on the upper Mississippi.[603] Though Lovell was burdened with their conversion, these were not to be for his defense but for an expedition to *meet the Federal flotilla in the north*. The work commenced on January 28th.

In early February 1862, the Confederate War Department needed still more troops, this time, 5,000 for Johnston at Columbus, Kentucky. The War Department had made the policy decision to abandon the coast, which, as we have seen, was discussed with Bragg, and was now finally disclosed to Lovell. The extraordinary explanation was that "New Orleans is to be defended from *above* by defeating the enemy at Columbus; the forces now withdrawn from you are for the defense of your own command . . ."[604]

At the end of the month, Lovell reported that he had managed to comply. A total of eight regiments, two artillery batteries, and a supply of 500 shotguns

---

602. O.R. Vol. 6, p. 819.
603. O.R. Vol. 6, pp. 808, 811, 814, 816, 817.
604. O.R. Ser. I, Vol. 6, p. 823, 832, 847; author's italics.

and 1,000,000 cartridges had been sent. He commented: "People are beginning to complain that I have stripped the department so completely, but I have called upon Governor Moore for 10,000 volunteers and militia for State service." Moore's task would to be compounded by the fact that in January the state legislature had revised the Louisiana militia law. Going into effect on February 15th, it limited the militia to whites only, and the 1st Louisiana Native Guards had to be disbanded.[605]

Imagine a culture, in the face of calamity, being so deranged with prejudice that it could permit such folly.

A clearer picture of the Butler expedition having emerged after it left Hampton Roads on February 25th, Lovell took the same delusionary stance as had Bragg, i.e., that this was not a threat. Lovell's bravado bordered on hallucination: "A black Republican dynasty will never give an old Breckinridge Democrat like Butler command of any expedition which they had any idea would result in such a glorious success as the capture of New Orleans." Governor Moore and the Citizen Defense Committee, recently formed in New Orleans, were, however, not hearing any of this nonsense and were distressed. "I had many unofficial conversations with General Lovell, and none of them inspired me with confidence in the safety of New Orleans, if vigorously attacked by the enemy" (testimony of A. D. Kelley, member of the New Orleans Citizen Defense Committee at the Confederate Court of Inquiry on the capture of New Orleans).[606]

In March, the fortified line of defenses planned and supervised by M. L. Smith was reported as complete. Seven of the riverboats being converted to rams would be ready by the 8th, the rest in a week.

Ever since the end of February, Governor Moore had noted: "Raising war troops is extremely difficult and slow."[607] Militia troops might meet the demands of the Confederate army for short service. State troops raised by Governor Moore agreeing to six months service were now acceptable to the War Department, which had previously insisted on three years service, and they were sent along to Tennessee with the hope (and with pressure applied) that they would enlist for the duration once in the field. The many foreign residents in New Orleans objected to the Louisiana militia law's requirement that they also serve.[608] This was softened on February 16th, by Jefferson Davis who did "not deem it politic to insist their serving outside of the city defenses."

On March 6th, a demand for 20,000 pounds of powder for Richmond brought Lovell's response that: "We have filled requisitions for arms, men and munitions until New Orleans is about defenseless."[609] He had had enough, apparently; and

---

605. Bynum, T., pp. 1, 14.
606. O.R. Vol. 6, p. 645.
607. O.R. Vol. 6, pp. 830, 837.
608. O.R. Vol. 53, p. 786.
609. O.R. Vol. 6, p. 841.

in a defiant letter to the outgoing Secretary of War Benjamin, he indicated that he was going to retain six of the 14 rams for duty at New Orleans.[610]

Martial law was requested by Jefferson Davis on March 13th.[611] The details of its administration were issued in General Orders No. 11 on March 18th. All citizens and aliens alike, above the age of 16, were to register with the Provost Marshall. Lovell also noted: "A city composed of such heterogeneous elements as this . . . is difficult to govern . . ." Its next administrator, Butler, would have been forewarned!

The situation apparently relieved Moore from complying with the militia law and, in Orders No. 426, dated March 24th, 1862, he declared the Native Guards reactivated, and they were to hold themselves prepared "for such orders as may be transmitted to them."[612]

In early April, Lovell had to explain his situation to a new Secretary of War Randolph. The accumulation of drift on the river obstruction installed below Fort Jackson caused it to be carried away at the end of February, and a second one was put in place in March. This, consisting of schooners lashed together, was also materially weakened and scattered by a storm on the night of April 11th.[613] They had a round of discussion about Lowell's need for large guns as well as small arms, which accomplished little. Next came the question of the potential saviors of New Orleans: the ram *Manassas*, and the ironclads *Mississippi* and *Louisiana*. The *Louisiana* would retain (they would not be made available to Lovell) all of its 16 guns, and when ready, soon after mid-April, it was ordered to *leave* New Orleans for Fort Pillow to engage Foote's flotilla.[614]

Now with Farragut's ships in sight below forts Jackson and St. Philip, and his bombardment having begun on April 13th, Governor Moore sent a telegram to Jefferson Davis that it was "suicidal" to send the *Louisiana* up the river. Lovell also protested. Little did Navy Secretary Mallory realize that the deficient *Louisiana*, with its propulsion problems, would have to be towed up the river if it was ever to leave.[615]

By this time, New Orleans had an additional threat: the specter of starvation. A shortage of flour and basic provisions had been caused by the disruption of commerce in the North, the blockade, low water in the Red River, and "the want of communication by rail with Texas."

---

610. ORN Ser. I, Vol. 18, p. 836; O.R. Vol. 6, p. 865.
611. ORN Ser. I, pp. 856, 860, 865, 889.
612. O.R. Vol. 15, p. 557.
613. O.R. Vol. 6, pp. 512, 513, 523, 564.
614. O.R. Vol. 6, pp. 646, 873.
615. O.R. Vol. 6, pp. 877, 878, 879; ORN Ser. I, Vol. 18, pp. 346, 844, 845.

Farragut and Butler

David Glasgow Farragut, born in 1801 near Knoxville, Tennessee, joined the navy at the age of nine and, after more than 50 years of service, rising to captain, found himself at Norfolk at the outbreak of the war. Though a Southerner by birth, he remained loyal and, after serving briefly on the Naval Retiring Board, then specially constituted to rid the navy of unfit or disloyal officers, was given the command of the West Gulf Blockading Squadron on December 23rd, 1861. Ordered to proceed to the Gulf, the expedition to capture New Orleans was his, and General Butler would join him with the supporting army troops.[616]

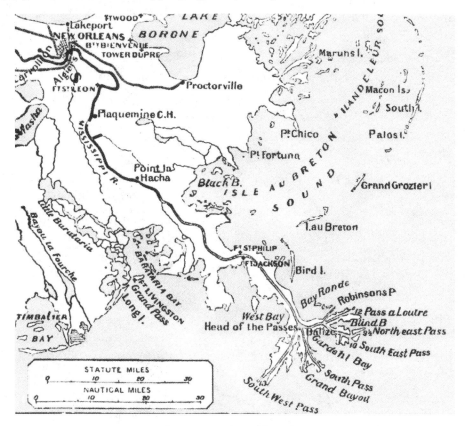

FIGURE 5

On the 25th of February 1862, Butler and a contingent of about 1,400 of his troops left Hampton Roads on the steamer *Mississippi*.[617] After passing through a severe winter storm and running aground off the Cape Fear Lighthouse, which developed a serious leak in the ship's bow, a fuming Butler was not able to assume

---

616. *Encyclopedia Britannica*, eleventh edition, Vol. X (1911), p.187; Welles, *Galaxy*, November 1871, pp. 679–683.
617. O.R. Vol. 6, p. 699.

command at Ship Island until March 20th.[618] By the 30th, even though four regiments and two artillery batteries of his force had not arrived,[619] he announced to Farragut that he could be at the mouth of the Mississippi (figure 5)[620] in 12 hours once notified. Farragut responded[621] from Southwest Pass that only three of his ships had crossed the bar (at which the water depth had been previously estimated by the coast survey to be 19 feet, it was now – despite the high water condition of the river – slightly less than the draft of two of his larger ships, the massive old sidewheeler *Mississippi* and the *Pensacola* (at 19 feet and 18 feet, 7 inches respectively).[622] The USS *Colorado*, the flagship of the Gulf Blockading Squadron when stationed off Fort Pickens, from which was dispatched the raiders on the *Judah*, and which had shelled Fort McCree, never made it into the river. With a 22-foot, 7-inch draft, though lightened by hundreds of tons, a crossing was impossible.

The risk taken here is impressive. It was certain that the river would drop; it was only a matter of time. If these ships were unable to maneuver before the expected onslaught of the formidable Confederate warships, the *Manassas*, *Louisiana*, and *Mississippi*, they would be lost.

Not only the water level at the bar, but fog had also delayed Farragut. Finally, by April 7th, Farragut notified Butler that he had his ships across and was loading supplies at Pilot Town, or Balize, seen in figure 5. Butler was to come ahead at his own discretion.[623] He arrived with eight regiments and three artillery batteries on April 21st.[624]

Farragut had been supplied with extensive information about forts St. Philip and Jackson, which guarded the river about twenty-two miles above the head of the passes.[625] In fact, Fort St. Philip was constructed by Major (now General) Barnard, one of the members of the secret board of officers.[626] In his recommendations, a key point was that the forts were built to "prevent the passage of vessels, not so much to defend themselves." Thus, an aggressive bombardment by Farragut's heavily gunned and maneuverable steamers, in combination with the mortar fleet of Captain Porter, would be unexpected.

The exceptionally high stage of the river – the highest in 25, or perhaps even 50, years[627] – was such that General Lovell was limited in his ability to construct

---

618. O.R. Vol. 6, p. 704. He landed on the 21st; p. 708.
619. O.R. Vol. 6, pp. 706, 707.
620. Leslie, Mrs. F., Battle Scenes, p. 444.
621. O.R. Vol. 53, pp. 517, 518.
622. ORN Ser. I, Vol. 18, pp. 14, 15; ORN Ser. II, Vol. 1, pp. 61, 146, 174.
623. ORN Vol. 18, p. 521.
624. O.R. Vol. 6, p. 710.
625. O.R. Vol. 6, p. 523; O.R. Vol. 15, p. 413.
626. ORN Ser. I, Vol. 18, p. 15–23.
627. O.R. Vol. 6, p. 580.

secondary earthworks and positions where sharpshooters could be stationed.[628] At the Quarantine, about six miles above Fort St. Philip, the Confederate Chalmette Regiment deployed there were forced to move to the other side of the river.[629] At Fort Jackson, the water was up to one and one-half feet deep on the parade ground and in the casemates.[630] Fort St. Philip was nearly as bad.

Though some of Farragut's ships had shelled the forts beginning on the 13th,[631] Porter's mortar flotilla, consisting of 21 schooners and 6 supporting steamers, began a continuous bombardment of Fort Jackson on the 18th.[632] After four days there was no sign of surrender, and Farragut had had enough. On the night of the 20th, a demolition party was sent up to destroy the schooner obstructions across the river. Though the petards[633] set to blow it failed to detonate, in an act of great courage, the sailors manually cut loose enough of the chain to allow the current to open a passage sufficiently wide for the squadron to pass.[634]

New Orleans

Generally, the current and high water worked to the advantage of the attackers. The riverbanks were covered and the water extended to the levees, thus allowing more room for the ships to maneuver. However, on April 19th, the current was so swift and the wind so strong that some of the squadron could barely make headway and were in danger of collision. Farragut decided to delay his planned run.[635]

By April 22nd, Farragut had made up his mind,[636] and after being frustrated that the squadron was not prepared to depart on the 23rd, it was ordered to depart at 2:00 a.m. on the 24th. The 17 steamers of the squadron were moving by 3:30; and by 4:40, 13 had passed the forts, with one, the *Varuna*, sunk, having been rammed by one of Lovell's converted steamers, the *Morgan*.[637] Three others; the *Kennebec*, *Itasca*, and *Winona*;[638] were forced to remain below. They had been a part of the third division of the squadron and the last to make the run through the barrier. By that time, daylight was approaching, and they were slowed by entanglement in remnants of the barrier and were either shot up, such as the *Itasca*, which lost all power, or had sensibly turned back to avoid destruction.

---

628. ORN Ser. I, Vol. 18, p. 563.
629. ORN Ser. I, Vol. 18, pp. 563, 522. Colonel Szymanski's Chalmette Regiment, about 500 men.
630. O.R. Vol. 6, p. 521.
631. O.R. Vol. 6, pp. 876, 877.
632. ORN Ser. I, Vol. 18, p. 357.
633. Demolition charges, electrically ignited.
634. ORN Ser. I, Vol. 18, p. 156.
635. ORN Ser. I, Vol. 18, pp. 134, 135.
636. ORN Ser. I, Vol. 18, p. 144.
637. ORN Ser. I, Vol. 18, pp. 157, 210.
638. ORN Ser. I, Vol. 18, p. 152.

Farragut described the passage of his squadron past the forts as "one of the most awful sights and events I ever saw or expect to experience."[639] Before the war was over, he would have several more such experiences, all connected to Battery L in one way or another.

Figure 6[640] represents the scene before the passage, on April 19th. The barrier across the river can be seen near the top center of the upper image. Upstream (above) the barrier is the Confederate ram fleet. Fort Jackson is on the left and Fort St. Philip on the right. Anchored at the left shore is Porter's mortar flotilla. The lower picture is a closer view of Porter's flotilla from upstream. Eighteen of Porter's 21 boats were anchored on the Fort Jackson side, in a position

FIGURE 6. April 24th, 1862. Top: PANORAMA.
Bottom: ADMIRAL PORTER'S MORTAR FLEET

---

639. ORN Ser. I, Vol. 18, p. 154.
640. Leslie, Mrs. F., Battle Scenes: figure 6, *Panorama*, p. 210; *Mortar Flotilla* p. 274; figure 7, *Passing Fort Jackson*, p. 528.

to shell it. A forested area on the bank partly hid his boats from the gunners in Fort Jackson. As can be seen, the rigging of his boats were dressed with tree foliage as camouflage. Three others, throwing shells at the treeless Fort St. Philip, were draped with aquatic growth to disguise them. Figure 7 gives another view of the passage, the ships abeam of Fort Jackson.

FIGURE 7. FORT JACKSON

The Confederate defenders attempted to maneuver fire rafts against the attackers. The *Manassas* pushed one against the flagship, the *Hartford*, and its starboard side was set ablaze. "Backed with all speed," the flagship's wash was strong enough to drive the fire raft and the *Manassas* into the shore. The *Hartford*'s fire was then heroically extinguished by the crew.[641]

In a letter to his wife, Capt. Thomas Craven of the *Brooklyn* describes how he had lost sight of his course from all the smoke of the firing of the *Hartford*, which he was following, so that he ran completely over one of the hulks in the barrier, crushing it. He then encountered another raft of logs "made of immense trees chained together . . . We ground over them . . ."[642]

The *Manassas* was observed to be making a run at the *Mississippi*, which was signaled by Farragut to "turn and run her down." To avoid the *Mississippi*, the ram turned sharply and ran into the riverbank. The *Mississippi* was then able to pour two broadsides into her. The *Manassas*' crew then abandoned her, and she slid off

---

641. ORN Ser. I, Vol. 18, p. 170.
642. ORN Ser. I, Vol. 18, pp. 196–198.

the bank and drifted downstream in a sinking condition.[643]

The Chalmette Regiment at quarantine surrendered to Captain Bailey in the lead gunboat, the *Cayuga*, and were paroled, so there was no force to oppose Butler when he landed on the bay side near there.

Porter's bombardment then ceased until a surrender demand was sent to Fort Jackson. It was refused, and Porter resumed the bombardment until the end of the day. As events unfolded, there was no necessity to renew it.[644] The Confederate ironclad *Louisiana*, unable to propel itself, and having been towed into place as a floating battery, was unable to move from under the guns of Fort St. Philip and into a position to threaten Porter's mortar schooners.[645] The lull prompted the Confederate defenders to request that wounded be allowed to be removed. They were loaded on the steamer *McRae* and given permission to proceed under a white flag to New Orleans. Heavily damaged, the *McRae* did not get underway until the morning of the 26th. The Confederates then heard the rumor that the city had surrendered. Busy with repairs to Fort Jackson, including remounting the guns so that they could be turned upstream to fire where the enemy now stood, it was clear that the forts were in the process of being surrounded. Porter had spent the time to send two ships around behind Fort Jackson on the western Gulf side. Butler's force, under General Williams, went east to Sable Island on the Gulf behind Fort St Philip. There, their transport steamers grounded and the troops were transferred to yawl boats in which they proceeded up the Maumeel Canal as far as they could go. Then, wading through the muck, they arrived at the Quarantine, five miles above Fort St. Philip, where a detachment was conveyed across the river to the Fort Jackson side by the USS *Mississippi*. The effect of Butler's landing apparently was enough to break the morale of the Fort Jackson garrison, consisting of disaffected impressed troops, many of them resident aliens. On the night of April 27th they mutinied, and about 250 left the fort and surrendered to Butler's pickets. The officers, and the remainder of the garrisons of both forts, surrendered the next day.[646] During the surrender negotiations for the forts, remaining Confederate naval personnel towed the *Louisiana* into the river and set her afire and adrift. Porter claimed the burning hulk was purposely aimed to drift "upon" him, but it blew up before it reached his ship, the *Harriet Lane*.[647]

Lovell's evacuation of the city began on April 24th. He ordered that all the steamboats at the landing be detained until ordnance crews could load them with

---

643. ORN Ser. I, Vol. 18, pp. 154, 157, 175, 303, 358, 529.
644. ORN Ser. I, Vol. 18, p. 433.
645. O.R. Vol. 6, map, p. 546.
646. General narrative from Butler's report: O.R. Vol. 6, p. 503, Lovell's report, ibid. p. 510; Report of Confederate Gen. J. K. Duncan, commanding the coast defenses, ibid., p. 521; Porter's report, Butler, B. F., p. 368; ORN Ser. I, Vol. 18, pp. 356, 433.
647. ORN Ser. I, Vol. 18, pp. 250, 287, 288, 433.

government stores.[648] Those that completed loading left safely and headed upriver to Vicksburg. However, the pilots and crew of nine or 10 of the steamers fled and left their vessels at the levee. "To gratify the people" with a show of a heroic last-ditch effort to fight the enemy, Lovell ordered that 1,000 men be asked to volunteer to man the abandoned boats for a "hand-to-hand fight with the enemy's vessels . . ." "The citizens" then promised to have the men ready by 9:00 a.m. next day. General Lewis, the head of the militia, was requested to cooperate, and the appeal was published in all the city papers. Morning came, and only 140 unarmed men showed up, minus Lewis. Such was the condition of the militia. Largely stripped of men, materiel, and guns, it was a foregone conclusion that the city would be lost. After an initial demand for surrender, General Lovell declined, but he restored the city authorities to power by revoking the martial law in force and evacuated his 3,000 beleaguered troops, only 1,200 of whom were properly armed.[649]

Farragut had arrived off New Orleans soon after noon on the 25th. As soon as his ships were in sight, the Confederate ironclad, the *Mississippi*, unfinished on the ways at Algiers, was put to the torch.[650]

The mayor refused to surrender. Farragut then patiently informed the various interest groups in the city, most notably the consuls of Britain, France, Germany, Spain, Russia, Belgium, Denmark, Portugal, and Brazil, that they and their families, plus some 30,000 of their nationals,[651] were in imminent danger. The fleet would be forced to fire upon the city if the mayor and city officials continued to stall. By the 29th, word was received that the forts had surrendered, and still there was no sign of a capitulation by the mayor. On the 30th, Farragut notified the mayor that he would "terminate our intercourse"[652] considering the mayor's attitude. Having earlier taken possession of the contents of the federal mint, Farragut then ordered a battalion of marines to land and raise the United States flag on the customs house and the city hall. This accomplished, the marines left an occupying force in the customs house.

New Orleans was occupied by Butler on May 1st 1862.[653] Notwithstanding the complications of occupying a chaotic city of some 140,000 people,[654] more than 20 percent of whom were not U.S. nationals, Butler took hold, with a sweeping proclamation of martial law.[655]

Thus, the Confederate policy of defending the city from the north by defeating

---

648. O.R. Vol. 6, p. 568.
649. O.R. Vol. 6, p. 561.
650. O.R. Vol. 6, p. 609.
651. ORN Ser. I, Vol. 18, p. 239.
652. ORN Ser. I, Vol. 18, p. 236.
653. O.R. Vol. 6, p. 717.
654. ORN Ser. I, Vol. 18, p. 234.
655. O.R. Vol. 6, p. 717.

the Northern Column was a total failure. Related evidence indicates that the Confederate authorities really were convinced that New Orleans would never be attacked. The Northern newspapers had always reliably revealed the strategy and plans of the Union army, "where correspondents were generally welcomed and often furnished with every facility to obtain and publish army operations . . ."[656] This time the navy had been in charge, and there were no news leaks of the planned attack.

Our first example of potential press misuse of its First Amendment right was the visit of William H. Russell, the English correspondent, to Bragg's installations near Pensacola, and then to Fort Pickens. Later, General Pope at New Madrid,[657] in March of 1862, is quoted as complaining to Halleck: "I fear to write anything, lest I see it in a day or two in all the newspapers of the country . . . I regret to trouble you with such matters, but if my intentions and movements are published days in advance by persons not under my control I must cease to correspond with the forces above me."

Remember from chapter 4 that Judah Benjamin had ordered the withdrawal of all the troops from Pensacola, with Bragg instructed to move his troops to Tennessee, on the basis of "dispatches in the Northern papers."

We must agree with Gideon Welles, as he wrote after the war, about the navy plans for New Orleans and the Mississippi:[658] "Military plans had been projected from the beginning to obtain control of this national thoroughfare and city near its mouth; but all of these schemes contemplated a combined army and navy movement which should descend from Cairo on the upper waters of the Mississippi. The idea of a naval conquest of New Orleans from the Gulf was not entertained by the army or the administration."

An epilog to the fall of New Orleans appears in the appendix.

Vicksburg I

After the occupation of New Orleans, the next objective for Farragut and Butler's expedition was to "reach the invading forces [the Northern Column] from the upper Mississippi, under the command of Flag Officer Foote and General Halleck."[659] The naïve reasoning was that the only strong point on the river was Vicksburg and that it would be taken quickly. It was not, and a second attempt in 1862 also failed, for far more egregious reasons. At this time, the Northern Column had survived Shiloh but had yet to advance to Corinth, the point that the Confederacy regarded as key to the Mississippi Valley and within possible supporting distance of any attempt on Vicksburg.

---

656. Welles, *Galaxy*, November 1871, p. 672.
657. O.R. Vol. 8, p. 635.
658. Welles, *Galaxy*, November 1871, p. 673.
659. ORN Ser. I, Vol. 18, p. 132.

The story of the two attempts in 1862 affected Battery L only by their failure. The Confederates, freed from Corinth and successful in defending Vicksburg, were then able to fortify another strategic natural feature two hundred miles south; the high bluffs of Port Hudson, Louisiana (figure 8).[660] Though they might lose huge stretches of the Mississippi, by holding that portion between Vicksburg and Port Hudson, the Confederacy would retain control of its junction with the Red River, their avenue of supply from western Louisiana, Texas, and Mexico. The Red was to become critically important as the Union blockade tightened along their coast.

FIGURE 8

Because the two Union expeditions against Vicksburg failed in 1862, the work of opening the Mississippi became ever more complicated, extensive, and costly. It would become the task of Admiral Farragut and General Banks, the new commander of the Department of the Gulf, to which Battery L was soon assigned, to assault, lay siege, and finally capture Port Hudson from the south. From the north, General Grant's massive Army of the Tennessee, assisted by Admiral Porter, would follow a nearly identical procedure against Vicksburg.

---

660. Miller, F. T., Vol. 2, p. 179.

The end of Lovell's defense of New Orleans was in sight on April 24th, when Lovell telegraphed the following to Gen. Samuel Jones at Pensacola:[661] "The enemy has passed our forts. It is too late to send any guns here; they had better go to Vicksburg." Lovell had made the assessment that all was lost for the Queen City,[662] and despite the fact that Vicksburg was in Beauregard's Department No. 2,[663] this was the appropriate strategic point for the defense of the Mississippi Valley, and Lovell planned to send much of the remnants of his force there.

New Orleans' fall and its evacuation[664] on April

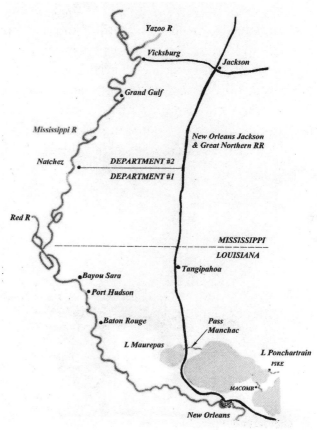

FIGURE 9

25th saw Lovell's forces first directed to Tangipahoa (figure 9), seventy-eight miles north on the Jackson Railroad. All the remaining railroad rolling stock was seized and utilized for the removal of stores from the city. The troops in forts Pike and Macomb, abandoned without Lovell's orders, were soon to be directed to Vicksburg, but a lack of clarity in the plan for their disposition was a later point of rebuke to Lovell. Elements of the Confederate navy also retreated to Vicksburg. The 8th Louisiana Battalion and the 27th Louisiana Volunteers had been there since May 5th, and by May 12th, when M. L. Smith took command, three batteries of its defenses had been completed and a fourth begun.[665]

On May 2nd, Captain Craven in the *Brooklyn* and three other gunboats got

---

661. O.R. Vol. 6, p. 883.
662. Nickname used by Butler; O.R. Vol. 15, p. 610.
663. On May 26, Lovell's Department No. 1 was extended north to the 33rd Parallel (the state line of Arkansas) evidently to give him control of Vicksburg. O.R. Vol. 17/II, p. 624. After Bragg was assigned to the command of Department No. 2 on June 20th its boundaries were redefined to include Department No. 1, which then ceased to exist. Ibid., p. 636.
664. O.R. Vol. 6, pp. 515, 609, 624. Figure 9 drawn by the author.
665. O.R. Vol. 15, p. 6.

underway.[666] Commander Lee in the *Oneida*, accompanied by the *Pinola*, left on the 3rd, destination Natchez.[667] Without a pilot (the pilots were afraid of retribution if they aided the invaders), the *Brooklyn* ran aground some sixty or seventy miles up the river. Finally getting free, she was called back to Baton Rouge, which she had earlier bypassed.[668] Farragut had become worried about the navigation of such large ships on the river, an accurate assessment considering the difficulties to follow.

The *Iroquois* commander, Palmer, had followed, but was instructed to anchor off Baton Rouge. Arriving there on the 7th, Palmer demanded the surrender of the town, which was undefended.[669] He then ordered the arsenal and barracks seized, and the U.S. flag was raised.

Some eight captured river steamers having been turned over to General Butler on May 7th, Gen. Thomas Williams with the 6th Michigan Regiment and six companies of the 4th Wisconsin Regiment, got underway at New Orleans on the 8th.[670] Assigned by Butler to first secure the Jackson Railroad as far as Manchac Pass,[671] Williams did not arrive at Baton Rouge until the 13th.

The *Iroquois* left its anchorage at Baton Rouge on the 10th to join Commander Lee at Natchez. Only now it was learned that the Confederates had begun to fortify Vicksburg.[672] The *Iroquois* overtook Lee and his gunboats and anchored off Natchez at 2:00 p.m. on the 13th.[673] The city surrendered the same day. After taking on coal, the *Brooklyn* and the *Wissahickon* departed Baton Rouge on the 12th, destination Natchez. The necessity of supplying coal to these large ships presented itself. All the vessels could burn wood, but only coal provided a hot-enough fire for some to make headway against the current. The planning for its supply, if none could be found on the way (some was appropriated at Baton Rouge), meant that supply ships such as the *Tennessee*, towing barges of coal, had to be carefully orchestrated.[674] Fortunately, the transports and smaller gunboats negotiated upstream burning wood. These difficulties and that of the navigation of the river with no pilots – Farragut in the *Hartford* had been aground at Tunica Bend from the 14th to the 16th [675] – began to tell upon Farragut.

On May 16th, Commander Lee, in the *Oneida* – accompanied by five gunboats

---

666. ORN Ser. I, Vol. 18, p. 698.
667. ORN Ser. I, p. 700.
668. ORN Ser. I. p. 467.
669. ORN Ser. I, Vol. 18, pp. 473, 474.
670. Stanyan, J. M., p. 95.
671. O.R. Vol. 6, p. 507.
672. ORN Ser. I, Vol. 18, p. 478; O.R. Vol. 15, p. 7. Here it is indicated that they had begun as early as May 2nd.
673. ORN Ser. I, Vol. 18, p. 489.
674. ORN Ser. I, Vol. 18, pp. 477, 519, 520.
675. ORN Ser. Vol. 18, p. 702.

and two steam transports, with General Williams and his meager force of 1,400 troops – departed Natchez for Vicksburg, arriving there on the 18th. Demanding its surrender, they were completely rebuffed by General Smith.[676]

Finally arriving on the 20th,[677] Farragut was disturbed by the situation. First, he blamed Lee for being slow to arrive. He was not happy that Williams' troops had run low on rations. The enemy had received Columbiads from Pensacola or Mobile and placed three batteries below the town and one above, 13 guns in all.[678] (There were six batteries completed by the 18th, per the report of M. L. Smith).[679] The bluffs being two hundred or more feet high, Farragut's guns could not be elevated to fire on them. Further, the rebel tactic of drawing their guns to the edge of the bluff, firing, then drawing them back out of view, made direct fire from the river useless. The mortar fleet would be required.

All of Farragut's ships having arrived in the vicinity by May 24th, a close reconnaissance of Vicksburg was made, which disclosed still more guns and works. A final reconnaissance made by Williams on the 25th concluded that the only suitable place for a landing was at Warrenton, some eight miles below. He could not land and make his way to the batteries on the hill some two hundred to three hundred yards back from the river with his small force, now reduced by sickness, against an estimated 8,000 rebels.[680] To the question of an assault, there was a final unanimous "no" vote of the gathered army and navy officers. Even if they were aware of the position (discussed below) of Halleck's forces at this time – some miles outside of Corinth – or of Admiral Foote, still above Memphis, they would have realized that there was no hope of gaining any support.

Farragut then decided to keep the *Iroquois*, *Oneida*, *Wissahickon*, *Sciota*, *Winona*, and *Itasca* on station as a blockading force, and to harass the enemy by occasional bombardment. The river falling, the large ships and the troop transports would have to return downstream. Williams and the troops were back at Baton Rouge on the 29th. In his report, Williams makes reference to having had to rely on the navy for subsistence for the past three days.[681]

A negative sentiment among the troops under Williams had grown ever since the delays and resultant crowded and filthy conditions, with no facilities for cooking, on the transports that had carried them from Ship Island at the beginning

---

676. ORN Ser. I, Vol. 18, p. 492. In three separate communications, by M. L. Smith, commanding; J. L. Autry, military governor; and L. Lindsay, mayor.
677. ORN Ser. I, Vol. 18, p. 519.
678. ORN Ser. I, Vol. 18, p. 703.
679. O.R. Vol. 15, p. 6.
680. ORN Ser. I, Vol. 18, p. 706. An exaggeration, if taken literally. The total may include those available on short notice, by rail, from Jackson.
681. O.R. Vol. 15, p. 22.

of the campaign.[682] Seventeen days of a repeat experience only served to further exasperate and sicken the troops. In defense of Williams, he had taken issue with Butler and complained that his men had suffered "from insufficiency of transportation cramped and crowded more like livestock than men, without the means of exercise . . . Filth and dirt . . . abounded on vessels and men to a disgusting and of course most unwholesome degree."[683] The whole affair had been a sweaty and exhausting failure, about which, Butler, in his memoirs (*Butler's Book*) makes no mention whatever.

The *Hartford*, with Farragut and the remainder of the squadron, arrived back at New Orleans on May 30th.[684] The six gunboats left behind began their bombardment on May 26th.

Corinth

We left our narrative of the Northern Column – that is, Admiral Foote and General Pope – on April 15th after the fall of Island No.10, when they were within four miles of Fort Pillow, about forty miles above Memphis.[685] Assistant Secretary of War Scott was then suggesting that General Pope's army be sent to reinforce General Halleck at Pittsfield Landing. His innocent phrase "and let Commodore Foote blockade below until forces can be returned . . . by General Halleck" demonstrated, as previously noted, a total misreading of Halleck's personality and subsequent field performance.

The detachment of Pope slowed Foote's progress down the Mississippi, but he persevered despite no evidence of Pope's impending return, finally capturing Memphis in June. Long before that, it would have been reasonable to assume that Corinth would have fallen, and Pope's troops would have been returned to complete the clearing of the Mississippi. The unconscionable performance of Halleck, in taking a month to arrive at Corinth and then letting the Confederate army escape, threw all such anticipation out the window and changed the momentum of the war in the west.

On closer scrutiny, Cullum's biography[686] of Halleck reveals that though he had served in the Mexican War, he did not serve anywhere in General Winfield Scott's command or in any of the major battles. At the outset, he was shipped from New York to California, and that alone took seven months. He did not arrive there until late in the year 1847 and was not involved in any fighting until November. As a 1st Lieutenant, he was involved in four skirmishes as the aide-de-camp of

---

682. Bacon, E., p. 21.
683. O.R. Vol. 15, p. 23.
684. ORN Ser. I, Vol. 18, p. 519, 707.
685. O.R. Vol. 10/II, p. 106; ORN Ser. I, Vol. 23, p. 5, states two miles.
686. Cullum, Vol. I, no. 988, pp. 733–740.

Navy Cmdre. W. B. Shubrick, during operations on the Pacific coast of Mexico. Subsequent assignments were all as staff positions, most notably under the military governorship of California, where, as was previously noted, he was involved in writing its constitution. His career prior to as well as after his resignation from the army can only be defined as one of visible renown – as a scholar. This man had never been in the field of battle and had never proven himself as a field commander in a war setting. His subsequent management of the advance to Corinth proved his lack of battle sense.

Further, we remember the description of Halleck's participation in the events in and subsequent to the fall of forts Henry and Donelson. He never took the initiative; Grant and Foote did. He was paranoid about any danger the enemy posed, always exaggerating their size and capability.

Upon his arrival[687] at Pittsburg Landing from St. Louis on April 12th, which would be his first time at any frontline location, Halleck declared that Grant's army, after the battle of Shiloh, was incapable of *resisting an attack*[688] and that it must be reorganized to make up deficiencies in men and equipment. No orders were issued to indicate his broader plans and objectives. First, Halleck had to make everything perfect according to his interpretation of military theory. In retrospect, we note that this behavior was remarkably similar to McClellan's.

Halleck's fateful decision to move the bulk of Pope's army away from the Mississippi[689] and thus remove the right arm of Admiral Foote's flotilla was made on April 15th. Pope did not arrive near Pittsburg Landing until April 21st. The interval was taken up with reorganizing and drilling the troops.[690]

Grant describes the period up until April 30th as one of extensive preparation: "The roads toward Corinth were corduroyed and new ones made; lateral roads were constructed . . . [for mutual support between units]. All commanders were cautioned against bringing on an engagement, and informed in so many words that it would be better to retreat than to fight."[691] Finally, the advance of the three armies – Grant's 50,554 strong Army of the Tennessee, Buell's 48,108 Army of the Ohio, and Pope's 21,510 Army of the Mississippi[692] – began on April 30th.[693]

From Grant: "The movement was a siege from start to close. The National troops were always behind entrenchments, except of course the small reconnoitering parties sent to the front to clear the way for an advance. Even the commanders of these parties were cautioned, 'not to bring on an engagement.' The

---

687. O.R. Vol. 10/II, p. 99.
688. O.R. Vol. 10/II, p. 106.
689. O.R. Vol. 10/II, p. 107. O.R.N. Ser. I, Vol. 23 p. 6.
690. O.R. Vol. 10/II, p. 109.
691. Grant, Vol. I, p. 372, 373.
692. O.R. Vol. 10/II, pp. 146, 148, 151 (aggregate present).
693. Grant, Vol. I, p. 376.

enemy were constantly watching our advance, but as they were simply observers, there were but few engagements that even threatened to become battles. Roads were again made in our front and again corduroyed; a line was entrenched, and the troops were advanced to the new position."[694]

The investment of Corinth was not begun until May 28th. This vast Federal army had taken a month to advance the twenty or so miles from Pittsburg Landing to Corinth.

Beauregard had decided, however, to evacuate on the 26th. It was begun on the 29th and was completed on the 30th.[695] The Confederate army left "not a sick or wounded man . . . nor stores of any kind." Notwithstanding, on that day, Halleck announced in orders that there was the danger of a Confederate attack on Pope's front.

Beauregard's retreating army was chased by a detachment from Pope's forces, which consisted of the 2nd Iowa Cavalry and the 2nd Michigan Cavalry under the command of Col. W. L. Elliott, which briefly occupied Boonville, Mississippi, about twenty-two miles south of Corinth, on May 29th. They destroyed a portion of the Mobile and Ohio Railroad track which passed through Boonville, and burned some of its cars, which contained 10,000 stand of arms. They took some 2,000 "convalescent and sick of the enemy" into brief custody and "500 to 700" infantry prisoners, plus some 30 to 40 of their officers.[696] Learning that a large force of the enemy from Corinth was approaching Baldwyn and Guntown, they departed in haste without paroling the infantry prisoners and took away only the mounted officers.

An obviously impatient Pope was never directed to chase after Beauregard's army "along the road to Columbus for 60 miles in no condition for service anywhere."[697] Sheridan's 2nd Michigan Cavalry (Col. P. H. Sheridan, later to become the general in command in the Shenandoah Valley, and under whom Battery L would serve) remained encamped a few miles south of Corinth with the rest of Pope's army, "along the plateau from Ripley to Tuscumbia, covering the railroad to Decatur."

Remote as he was, at Corinth, Halleck could embellish the facts in his reports to Washington much as he had done earlier from St. Louis. Though we have noted that McClellan had suspicion of this, no one else had the time to challenge him. McClellan had been relieved on February 11th, and since then Lincoln and Stanton were attempting to manage the war without a general-in-chief.

After the war was over, Pope raised a question about a report attributed to him

---

694. Grant, Vol. I, pp. 376, 377.
695. Grant, Vol. I, p. 380.
696. O.R. Vol. 10/I, Elliott's and Sheridan's reports, pp. 862–865; Sheridan, P. H., Vol. I, pp. 147–149.
697. O.R. Vol. 16/II, pp. 13, 14.

for the time period shortly after Corinth had been evacuated. Tucked away in the back of Series I, Volume 10, Part II, of the O.R. is a letter dated July 3rd, 1865. It is from Pope to Halleck requesting that alleged reports that he made be furnished to him.[698] It seems that the newspapers of the time were given a story that went: "General Pope is 30 miles south of Corinth, pushing the enemy hard. He already reports 10,000 prisoners and deserters and 15,000 stand of arms captured." Halleck responded by denying giving such information to the papers or the Secretary of War.[699] Pope's retort in part: ". . . when you left the West you ordered that portion of the dispatches and reports concerning the operations around Corinth which bore upon this question to be cut out of the official books and brought with you to Washington, leaving the official records in St. Louis mutilated and incomplete."

The official records, however, have since published those dispatches received by the War Department on this subject and the misleading one referred to by Pope, dated June 4th, 1862, is from Halleck to Stanton.[700] Pope's report to Halleck of June 1st repeats the facts as quoted by Colonel Elliott: 10,000 arms destroyed and 2,000 prisoners taken. The only error in Pope's report is that the prisoners were not paroled but released. Thus, history must record that 50,000 Confederate troops had escaped Corinth and but "30 to 40" were taken prisoner, not 10,000.

On June 10th, Buell was ordered east toward Chattanooga and was making slow progress while repairing the Memphis and Charleston Railroad as he went. Grant's 50,000 were building extensive defensive works around Corinth and were scattered between Memphis and Columbus and "driving guerilla parties out of West Tennessee."[701]

Comments on operations at Corinth:

From Grant: "For myself I am satisfied that Corinth could have been captured in a two day's campaign commenced promptly on the arrival of reinforcements after the battle of Shiloh." There was a pursuit of the retreating rebels, but it did not result in the capture of any numbers. It was back at Corinth by June 10th.[702]

From Sheridan: "General Beauregard's evacuation of Corinth and retreat southward were accomplished in the face of a largely superior force of Union troops, and he reached the point where he intended to halt for reorganization without other loss than that sustained in the destruction of the cars[703] and supplies at Booneville . . . the enemy was considerably demoralized. Under such circumstances, an energetic and skillfully directed pursuit might not have made certain the enemy's destruction, but it would largely have aided in disintegrating his forces,

---

698. O.R. Vol. 10/II, p. 635.
699. O.R. Vol. 10/II, p. 636.
700. O.R. Vol. 10/I, p. 774.
701. O.R. Vol. 16/II, p. 33, 62, 63.
702. O.R. Vol. 16/II, p. 33, Grant, U. S., Vol. I, pp. 381–383.
703. Railroad cars.

and I never could understand quite why it was not ordered."[704]

In defense of Halleck, on June 8th, his Department of the Mississippi had been expanded by the War Department to include the states of Kentucky and Tennessee. Stanton may have used this department realignment as a device to have Halleck join in consideration of the allegedly dire straits of those states. In a letter to Buell, the secretary of war had lent weight to the idea that "much alarm and insecurity continues to be manifested in that State and also in Tennessee."[705] Buell had already disclosed his opinion to Stanton that "concentrating a heavy force at Corinth almost denuded Kentucky, and left barely a sufficient force for an active defensive position in Middle Tennessee . . ." Lincoln had received warnings as to the state of affairs in Kentucky,[706] which could have been key in influencing the policy decision to break up the army. Nearly a year earlier,[707] he had expressed the concern that to lose Kentucky would precipitate the loss of Missouri and Maryland and "the whole game."

Sadly, the "grand army" was thus broken up, with Grant, Pope, and Buell ordered to resume the command of their separate army corps on June 10th.[708] Buell, as noted, was ordered to move elements of his force to Chattanooga *but* was told to: "Repair the Memphis and Charleston Railroad from Corinth to Decatur [Alabama] and put it in running order, as a line of supply" as he advanced.[709] These instructions were "oral."[710] The closest written evidence of the instructions given to Buell is found in a report by Halleck to Stanton dated June 9th. Here he reveals that: "Buell, with four divisions, has been directed to move east, to form a junction with Mitchel. The destruction of the railroad and bridges will make his movement slow."[711]

It was precisely his slow movement that caused him to be beaten to Chattanooga by Bragg, and the fallout was the early success of Bragg's Heartland Campaign, which is discussed in the next chapter. The result of Buell's performance would lead to his being investigated by a military commission which was convened on November 27th, 1862. The lack of specific written instructions from Halleck protected him at Buell's expense. The commission concluded that Buell had been given "discretionary power" and that he should have recognized the "hopelessness and absurdity" of the assignment of both repairing the railroad and arriving at Chattanooga in a timely fashion.[712] It ultimately found no charges against Buell.

---

704. Sheridan, Vol. I, p. 152.
705. O.R. Vol. 10/II, p. 285.
706. O.R. Ser. III, Vol. 2, pp. 252, 266.
707. Stephenson, N. W., p. 259.
708. O.R. Vol. 10/II, p. 288.
709. O.R. Vol. 16/I, p. 9.
710. O.R. Vol. 16/I, p. 13.
711. O.R. Vol. 10/I, p. 670, 671.
712. O.R. Vol. 16/I, p. 6, 7, 12, 13; Buell, West Point class of 1841. Cullum, Vol. II, no. 1030

He was never given a new assignment, and resigned from the army in 1864; a sad ending for one who had followed Halleck's absurd order to the letter.

Instead of the surrender of Corinth with the capture of upward of 50,000 prisoners, Halleck had burdened his army with occupying some real estate in a hostile territory, a fact little understood in Washington. There, the concern was for the safety of the city itself, after the failure of McClellan's Peninsular Campaign, and the successes of Confederate General Stonewall Jackson in the Shenandoah Valley, which is discussed in the next chapter. Lincoln and Stanton were looking for more troops to be sent east, and initially Halleck had stoutly resisted detaching any additional, having already sent away Buell. However, after Halleck's elevation to general-in-chief and his being called to Washington, the calls for troops came from Halleck.

All of this gave the Confederacy a pass to reorganize, recruit, and make trouble. Thus, the fall of Corinth would prove to be a tactical non-event and a strategic liability. Grant's weakened Army of the Tennessee was assigned to the job of occupation, and the embarrassment of collecting all of the cotton possible. Referring to his time here, Grant writes:[713] "The most anxious period of the war, to me, was during the time the Army of the Tennessee was guarding the territory acquired by the fall of Corinth. . . South . . . was Van Dorn with . . . a force of thirty-five to forty thousand men" who could attack Grant's equivalent but scattered forces at any point. "I was put on the defensive in a territory whose population was hostile to the Union . . ."

The Confederacy had begun to recover, and to react. Maj. Gen. Earl Van Dorn assumed command of the Department of Southern Mississippi and East Louisiana on June 20th, and Maj. Gen. Sterling Price had assumed command of the District of Tennessee on July 25th. Price, in late July, and again in August, then proposed to Van Dorn that they combine their forces to attack Grant.

In August, Van Dorn was occupied in attacking Butler at Baton Rouge, which is covered in chapter 6, but by September, he had agreed to join Price, who had occupied Iuka, Mississippi, on September 13th. Before Van Dorn arrived, Price attacked Grant's forces, commanded by Maj. Gen, E.O.C. Ord and Maj. Gen. William S. Rosecrans, on the 19th. Known as the Battle of Iuka, it was a clear Union victory, but Rosecrans, though ordered to pursue the defeated Confederates the next day, did not, allowing them to concentrate still more forces outside of Federal-held Corinth. On the 3rd of October, Van Dorn attacked, he being the senior officer present. By the end of the day, it appeared that he had won, and by evening he called a halt, planning to resume the battle at daybreak, but he was then repulsed "with great slaughter."

---

713. Grant, U. S., Vol. I, pp. 395, 397, 398, 399, 401, 406, 412, 413, 416, 417; O.R. Vol. 15, p. 1; O.R. Vol. 17/I, pp. 119-121; Iuka, CWSAC MS 001; Corinth, CWSAC MS002.

Once again, Rosecrans failed to pursue, but Ord caught Van Dorn at Hatchie Bridge, outside of Corinth, on the 5th, and inflicted even more losses on the retreating Confederates.

Grant writes: "The battle relieved me of any further anxiety for the safety of the territory within my jurisdiction, and soon after receiving reinforcements, I suggested to the general-in-chief a forward movement against Vicksburg."

Grant's reinforcements were to come, not from any plan by Halleck, but from John C. McClernand, whose efforts to restore the lost initative are covered in chapter 6.

Record 6/62
30 APRIL–30 JUNE, 1862, PENSACOLA, FLORIDA

The Company was engaged in the bombardment of the rebel lines on the night of May 9th. Left Fort Pickens on May 10th, 1862 with the command, which recaptured Fort Barrancas. Marched on Pensacola – 9 miles – May 12th and went into quarters in the city.

1.	Henry W. Closson	Capt. In Command of Company
2.	Franck E. Taylor	1st Lt.
3.	E. L. Appleton	1st Lt.

Detached:
> T.K. Gibbs 1st Lt. Prom. By virtue of letter A.G.O. Wash. April 21, '62. Assigned to duty with Co. A 1st Arty. Left Co. May 30,'62
> George Friedman Pvt. On det.svc. (as artillerist) at N.O. S.O. no. 11, West. Dist. Dept. of the South, Pensacola, Fla. May 24, 1862.

Strength: 86. Sick: 13.

Sick Present:
> Julius Becker, William Demarest, Robert Curran, Christopher Foley, Thomas Gilroyd, Dennis Myers, Michael Olvaney, John Roper, William Schaffer, Joseph Smith.

Sick Absent:
> Thomas Brook, Ft. Hamilton, NY, Left Company Sept. 17, 1861.
> William C. Brunskill   do.
> Charles Riley, Ft. McIntosh, TX Abs. since Feb. 21, 1861. Reduced to Pvt. July 12, 1861.

It is noted that the roll seldom indicates what the sickness was. To this point in time, we only know of "scourbutics" and dysentery as a cause of death, one in each case. However, the increase in the number of sick from the previous roll would indicate the onset of warm weather related problems or perhaps indications that the water supply was becoming tainted on overcrowded Santa Rosa Island. Soon, the men would be relieved to be able to move to the healthier environs of Pensacola.

Occupation of Pensacola

On April 9th, Robert E. Lee ordered Gen. Samuel Jones to report to P. T. Beauregard at Corinth, Mississippi, and to transfer the command of the Department of Alabama and West Florida to Brig. Gen. John H. Forney.[714] Forney was recovering from a wound and could not immediately take over the command. In the interval, Bragg ordered Jones to join him; and several telegrams passed between the parties, only adding to the confusion of events, which were fast spinning out of control. As previously noted, one ominous telegram Jones received on April 24th was from Gen. Mansfield Lovell, commanding at New Orleans: "The enemy has passed our forts. It is too late to send any guns here; they had better go to Vicksburg."

On the 27th, Lee advised Jones to remove everything from Pensacola "not necessary for service." On May 6th, the secretary of war sent the message: "In case you have to evacuate Pensacola, destroy cotton, tobacco, and military and naval stores, but avoid the destruction of buildings and other private property as much as possible."[715]

The Confederate defeat at Shiloh plus the news of the surrender of Fort Pulaski, Savannah, Georgia, on April 11th, and the crushing news of the surrender of New Orleans had scotched any Confederate equivocation about Pensacola.

FIGURE 10

On the night of May 9th, Fort McCree, buildings in the navy yard, the hospital, the barracks, and two steamboats, the *Mary* and *Helen*, were observed to be on

---

714. O.R. Vol. 6, p. 881.
715. O.R. Vol. 6, p. 890.

fire.[716] Lumber had been piled in the casemates of McCree and set on fire rather than use precious gunpowder to blow it up. The same was allegedly done to Fort Barrancas (figure 10), but the fort suffered little, and survives intact to this day.[717]

To try to prevent the rebels from continuing with their work of destruction, Arnold opened a bombardment "with a very happy effect." Lt. Richard H. Jackson, now Arnold's assistant adjutant general, was sent over to Pensacola on the schooner *Maria Wood* to seek out the mayor and "summon the city . . . to surrender," which was done. In the early morning, Cdre. David D. Porter arrived in the gunboat *Harriet Lane*. The *Lane* and the schooner were soon transporting numbers of troops from Pickens across the bay. The sloop-of-war *Vincennes* and the steam propeller *General Meigs* were soon sent to Arnold's support.

Close examination confirmed that Fort McCree was in a seriously damaged condition and that several storehouses in the navy yard were burned. Barrancas Barracks was in good condition. The once-imposing, three-story brick structure of the marine hospital was reduced to a heap of rubble, strangely out of place in the surrounding acres of green lawns and magnolia and orange trees.[718] Fort Barrancas was made the temporary headquarters.

On the morning of May 12th, a column consisting of the 6th New York led by their "Billy" goat mascot, labeled in red paint, five companies of the regulars, and the 75th New York was formed up at the outskirts of Pensacola. With the 75th Regimental Band at the head of the column, "the thrilling strains of Yankee Doodle"[719] were struck up, and a full dress marching entrance, white gloves and all, was made.

The city was described by Arnold as orderly and quiet and acting mayor Brosenham[720] "zealous and apparently loyal." About half of the buildings were burned, and many dwellings were deserted, the more militant of the inhabitants having fled along with the Confederate troops. "A good portion of the population that remained were loyally disposed Dutch."[721]

The troops were delighted to be able to stand in the shade of pleasant flowered trees for the first time in months or to drink from a fresh water stream. Tents were

---

716. O.R. Vol. 6, p. 658, 660, 661; ORN Ser. II, Vol. 1, p. 89. The old side-wheeler, the *Fulton*, laid up at the navy yard at the time, was also destroyed. She had been considered for use by the Confederate navy but never fitted out.
717. Figure 10 photo by the author, 2008.
718. Hall, Henry & James, *75th History*, p. 39.
719. Hall, Henry & James, *75th History*, p. 41. Henry Closson, (Haskin, W. L., p. 362), confirms the 6th New York leading, the regulars in the center, and the 75th taking up the rear.
720. O.R. Vol. 6, p. 659. From the diary of Mary E. Caro (display at the Wentworth Museum at Pensacola), it is noted that Mayor Bobe had fled to Alabama on the 10th, and Union officers came as early as the 9th to raise the Union Flag. Porter, in his *Anecdotes and Incidents of the Civil War*, pp. 41–42, describes the "Mayor" as a cynical opportunist, earlier a close friend of Bragg's and today a true loyalist.
721. Hall, Henry & James, *75th History*, p. 48.

pitched on fine wooden floors made from the "immense quantities of oak and pine lumber"[722] not destroyed by the retreating rebels. Battery L was located at the plaza at the city center, Captain Closson soon to be in charge of the defenses of the city.

The 91st New York arrived on May 20th, having been transferred from Fort Taylor.[723]

The arrival of the Union army had to have been welcomed for the reason that they had money to spend. It was soon funneled to purveyors of food, clothing, liquor, and vice. Major Babcock of the 75th became provost and had the opportunity to describe drunken riots, assaults, and muggings, many by the members of the 6th New York. He comments: "With all of the raving passions of these soldiers, brutal enough for anything, there has not yet been a complaint of rape . . . If you should come into Pensacola on a Sunday, or at parades, you would be struck by the gay costumes of the black belles, but the new dresses, $15, $20, $30, have all been bought with the money of soldiers, and the dresses were brought here by the army sutlers."[724]

If the foregoing offered too rough a view of Pensacola, the following is quoted for balance: "The good conduct of the Union soldiers helped to do away with the bitter hostility of the leading people of the city . . . Nobody stays at home out of spite toward us, and the list of ladies who attend the ministrations of Father Nash of the 6th Regt. comprises many pretty ones."

Arnold quickly asked for more troops, particularly a regiment of cavalry, for scouting and picket duty "and to carry on other important military operations that I have in view."[725]

The rebel troops had evacuated to the railroad, at Oakfield, six miles north. Five companies of Confederate cavalry were detached there to stay in the area and "watch the enemy's movements."[726] This band of Alabama volunteers, or a part of it, remained on the outskirts of Pensacola for months. Seldom seen, they never attacked, but a number of reconnaissances were sent out to determine their strength and to engage them if possible. In late May, a party commanded by Lieutenant Colonel Merritt of the 75th New York took a prisoner who divulged the rebel cavalry strength as about 100 men.[727] Other reconnaissances went up Escambia Bay and found some naval stores and lumber. One, by the 6th New York, went up Blackwater Bay to Milton, captured three rebel soldiers and "3 citizens of Milton and 2 negroes."[728] An expedition to Bagdad, that lasted from August 7th to

---

722. Hall, Henry & James, *75th History*, p. 42.
723. O.R. Vol. 15, p. 459.
724. Babcock, W. M. Jr., pp. 79, 90, 109.
725. O.R. Vol. 6, p. 659.
726. O.R. Vol. 6, p. 662.
727. Hall, Henry & James, *75th History*, p. 43.
728. O.R. Vol. 15, p. 108–110.

August 10th, met four families who were delighted to escape the "tyranny of their oppressors," and were apparently taken back to Pensacola.[729] The tyranny alluded to might have consisted of demands for, or the theft of, food and forage by roaming "marauders" or "bushwhackers" pretending to be affiliated with the Confederate army. A considerable factor in this regard was the first Confederate Conscription Act of April 1862. Under this act, all white men 18 to 35 were required to serve. The age limit was soon raised to 45. In desperation for able-bodied men, the Confederate government allowed the conscription methods used to deteriorate into on-the-spot impressment. From the start, there had been rather lukewarm sentiment for the war among poor backwoods whites who had no slaves, and who had little connection with official government, whether State or the Confederacy. The families of these subsistence farmers would suffer if the men were dragged away, by the "gangs that . . . infest the country for the purpose of plunder and . . . enforcing . . . the Conscription Act."

Other reconnaissances accomplished little militarily, but what was discovered delighted the troops, such as "unguarded" watermelons, peaches, figs, and cattle.[730] Looting of the many abandoned houses in and around Pensacola is not mentioned until later, after Gen. Neal Dow took over the command in October 1862.[731] Then, Dow authorized the removal of furniture for his and other officer's use and for the hospital.

Record 8/62
30 JUNE–31 AUGUST, 1862, PENSACOLA, FLORIDA

[No Entry in the Record of Events]

1. Henry W. Closson   Capt. In Command.
2. F.E. Taylor   1st Lt.
3. E. L. Appleton   1st Lt. On special duty as Bat. Adj. by virtue of O. no. 31 Hdqrts. Reg. Bat., Pensacola, Fla. Aug. 22, 1862

Detached:
    George Friedman Pvt. On det. svc. (as artillerist) at N.O. S.O. no. 11, West. Dist. Dept. of the South Pensacola, Fla. May 24, 1862.

Died:
    Patrick Carroll Pvt. Dec. 17,'60 Ft. Duncan, Tx. At Ft. Pickens, Fla. Aug. 19th 1862, of consumption.

Discharged:
    James McWaters Pvt. July 16,'57 Newport, Ky. By exp. of svc.; at Pensacola, July 16, 1862.
    Thomas Gilroyd Pvt. Aug. 26,'57   do.   Aug. 26, 1862.

---

729. O. R. Vol. 15, pp. 126, 503; O.R., Vol. 16, p. 789.
730. Hall, Henry & James, *75th History*, pp. 44–47.
731. O.R. Vol. 15, p. 585.

Strength: 82. Sick: 6.

Sick Present: John Tomson

Sick Absent: Thomas Brook Ft. Hamilton, NY. Left Company Sept. 17, 1861, discharged on Surgeon's Certificate of Disability, July 25, 1862 (thus, he is counted as both sick, and discharged.)
William C. Brunskill Ft. Hamilton, NY. Left Co. Sept. 17, 1862.
Joseph Kutschor Ft. Pickens, FL. Left Company Aug. 3, 1862.
Charles F. Mansfield Ft. Pickens, FL. Left Company Aug. 12, 1862.
Charles Riley Ft. McIntosh, TX. Abs. since Feb. 21, 1861. Reduced to Pvt. July 12, 1861.

The drop in sickness since relocating to Pensacola is noted, but we must add another kind of disease to the list: tuberculosis. The list of those who have been transferred out due to serious long-term sickness and needing treatment in the north keeps edging up.

Reassignments

The occupation of New Orleans by General Butler's forces soon affected one of Battery L's men, Pvt. George J. Friedman. The 23-year-old goldsmith – an emigrant from Baden to New York, who joined Battery L in 1860 – was detached on May 24th, 1862. Sent to New Orleans as an "artillerist," he undoubtedly helped to fill Butler's need for people to train his green New England volunteers and additional units that would soon be recruited in New Orleans. The 1st Regiment of Louisiana Infantry (white) would begin recruitment in July, the Native Guards (free black) in August, and recruiting for the 1st Regiment of Louisiana Heavy Artillery (former slaves) had begun by the fall.

Friedman left Pensacola and never returned. He was not formally transferred out of Battery L until July 3rd, 1864,[732] when arrangements had been made to assign him as a second lieutenant in Company F of the 10th Regiment, U.S. Colored Heavy Artillery. He was mustered in on August 19th, 1864. He was promoted to first lieutenant on November 19th, after the 77th Colored Infantry was consolidated into the 10th Regiment, and he was transferred to Company H. He had achieved the rank of brevet captain before being mustered out when the regiment was decommissioned on February 22nd, 1867. He and his regiment had served entirely in the defenses of New Orleans.

Arnold's requests for reinforcements were initially honored by the Department of the South. General Brannan at Key West had been ordered to transfer the 91st New York Infantry Regiment to Pensacola in May, as was previously noted.

---

732. Pension record application no. 836550, National Archives; S.O. 200, A.G.O. Department of the Gulf. He is listed as being from Bavaria, according to his wife, who spelled her married name as Freeman.

However, the Army of the Potomac had better use for the regulars of the 3rd Infantry. Both Companies C and E were shipped out in June.[733] Arnold's request for a small steamer for transport between his supply base at Pickens and the mainland was honored when the *Creole* arrived on July 19th.[734] It came from the Department of the Gulf: General Butler. However, the flow of requests would quickly reverse. Butler was searching for reinforcements after the second disaster at Vicksburg, which is covered in the next chapter, as he feared an attack on Baton Rouge or New Orleans, or both. As it was, Butler's anticipation of an attack on Baton Rouge was correct. It came on August 5th, and is also covered in the next chapter.

On August 8th, the Western District of the Department of the South became a part of Butler's Department of the Gulf.[735] Halleck, general-in-chief since July 11th, had given Butler Pensacola in lieu of any additional reinforcements, which he claimed were not available. Butler immediately called upon Arnold to consult with him as to what troops he could spare from Pensacola. Needless to say, as the result of Arnold's and Butler's "consultation," the 75th New York Infantry embarked on the *Ocean Queen* at Pensacola on August 30th, 1862, and arrived at New Orleans on September 2nd.[736] As somewhat in recompense, the 15th Maine Infantry Regiment was transferred from Camp Parapet, near Carrollton, above New Orleans, to Pensacola on September 11th.[737]

In the *Story of the Maine Fifteenth*, the chapter describing the transfer to Pensacola is titled "The Fifteenth Recuperates in Western Florida." They were delighted to be there after malaria and heat-related sickness had decimated their ranks over the past summer in Louisiana.

In the days soon after the occupation of Pensacola, Battery L's commander, Henry Closson, was named chief of artillery and given charge of planning and supervising the construction of the defenses of the city. However, as the work of construction ground on through the summer, the troops must have seen that Pensacola was to become a backwater in the strategic plan of the war. Pensacola was now a mere outpost of the Department of the Gulf rather than being the jumping-off point for a land thrust at Mobile, or a link-up with Union forces thrusting south. It was to be occupied initially simply to deny the Confederates the use of the harbor and to retain the Union hold on the navy base. However, after inspecting the base on June 2nd, the commander of the mortar flotilla, David D. Porter, wrote to the Secretary of the Navy Gideon Welles: "This place is so far superior to Ship Island that I would respectfully recommend removal of all naval property to this

---

733. They appear at White Post, Virginia, on June 19th, 1862. O.R Vol. 11/I, p. 1,032.
734. O.R. Vol. 15, p. 526.
735. O.R, Vol. 15, p. 544.
736. Hall, Henry & James, *75th History*, p. 56.
737. Shorey, H. A., p. 28.

place."[738] The navy soon had ships and supplies back at the base. By mid-June, 33 schooners of the mortar flotilla were counted moored in the bay.[739] Imagine hundreds of sailors on shore leave at Pensacola.

Captain Closson's work of preparing the defenses was completed on September 13th and he issued a report.[740] It is reproduced here, allowing the original words of Battery L's commander to explain the huge effort that went on through the hot summer months of 1862 (and possibly the reason he is reported as sick on the next muster roll). The narrative at least informs us that Battery L was now mounted, though no official order had designated it a *light* battery, and that it was equipped with the most desired of guns, the new lighter Model 1857 12-pounder, a copy of the *canon-obusier* of Louis Napoleon III.

OFFICE OF CHIEF OF ARTILLERY,
Pensacola, Fla., September 13, 1862.

Brig. Gen. Lewis G. Arnold,
United States Volunteers, Pensacola, Fla.:

GENERAL: In obedience to your instructions I submit a report upon the means adopted for the defense of Pensacola, as follows:

Woods and thick undergrowth sweep well up to the town on every side, except where cleared away for our own fire or on the different lines of approach. Generally the line of defense, including the principle portion of the city within its limits, is A-shaped, the flanks resting on the beach east and west and a redoubt at the apex to the north, which in conjunction with gunboats lying off the prolongation of the lines afford ample security.

On the east beach the mill has been surrounded with abatis, loop-holed,[741] and otherwise arranged so as to be serviceable for and against musketry and field artillery. The swamp to the front and left has been diked and overflowed across the approaches leading in west of the swamp. A breast-height has been thrown, embrasured for one gun (12 pounder field howitzer), and flanked by rifle trenches. A line of abatis runs from this point to the cotton-press, the 8 foot fence around which is loop-holed for a rifle trench and platformed for another tier of musketry. The brick wall forming part of the north side has been loop-holed and embrasured for one gun (12 pounder howitzer), which

---

738. ORN Ser. I, Vol. 18, p. 481–482.
739. Hall, Henry & James, *75th History*, p. 51.
740. O.R. Vol. 15, pp. 569–570.
741. Abatis are tree branches laid in line with their butt or thick ends anchored in the ground. The smaller branches, facing outward, are sharpened. Loop holes are protected windows for riflemen to fire through, constructed of logs and sandbags. Breast height: earthwork, or log/sandbag embankment, or wall; breast high. Embrasured: openings cut at intervals in the earthwork for guns to fire through. Half-bastion: one side only of a bastion, which is a projection from the fort wall from which a gun mounted parallel to the wall can sweep fire along the wall. This prevents the approach of an enemy intending to scale it.

bears up the line of the railroad. Abatis connects this point with the rebel Ex-Senator Mallory's house, now the headquarters of Colonel Wilson, the fence around which is loop-holed and trenched, and a gun (12 pounder field howitzer) placed in position on the northeast corner, which flanks the abatis to the east, and also a line of the abatis running up the redoubt. A stockade crosses the road leading into the town past Colonel Wilson's headquarters.

The redoubt is built on the site of the old Spanish Fort San Miguel, an eminence which commands the town and vicinity; is a half bastion, with flanks and wings running back to meet the abatis on each side; is furnished with two 30-pounder Parrott rifles, one 10-pounder Parrott rifle, two 12-pounder field howitzers, and two roomy magazines; is closed at the gorge[742] and flanked by its own fire as well as that from positions occupied within the lines. Abatis runs from this point to the plateau west of the town, where another work has been thrown up, commanding the Mobile approaches, and consisting of a ditch and breast-height embrasured for four 12-pounder field how-itzers. There is also at this point a battery of two mountain howitzers, to be used as required. From this point to the west beach the line consists of abatis, swamps, and rifle trenches, and is throughout its whole extent arranged for a close flank fire of musketry.

The Fifteenth Maine Regiment now holds the east of the town as far as the cotton-press, which is garrisoned by three companies of the Sixth Regiment New York Volunteers. Colonel Wilson's headquarters are held by two companies of the Sixth; the Lyon house, just northward and within the lines, by one company of the Sixth. There is here a battery of two mountain howitzers, to be used as required. The Hyer house, just in rear of the redoubt, is held by one company of the Sixth. Two companies of the Ninety-first New York are camped between this point and the redoubt, and one company of the Sixth garrison's the redoubt. Four companies of the Ninety-first hold the work on the Mobile plateau, and four companies of the same regiment are quartered on the lines by the bay in the southwest part of the town. My own company, mounted, with a battery of four Napoleon guns, occupies the center of town.

I am general, very respectfully, your obedient servant,

HENRY W. CLOSSON
Captain, Chief of Artillery.

---

742. Rear.

Record 10/62
31 AUGUST–31 OCTOBER 1862, PENSACOLA, FLORIDA

[No entry in "Record of Events"]
1. Henry W. Closson   Capt. Sick
2. Franck E. Taylor   1st Lt. In temp. Command of Co.
3. Edward L. Appleton 1st Lt. Absent with leave at N.O. Left Co. Oct. 21,'62.
4. James A. Sanderson 2nd Lt. App. To Co. by prom. vice Gibbs G.O. no. 73, War Dept. A.G.O. Washington, July 4, 1862 (never joined Co.)

Detached: George Friedman Pvt. On det. svc. (as artillerist) at N.O. S.O. no. 11. West. Dist. Dept. of the South Pensacola, Fla. May 24, 1862.

Discharged:
  Thomas Brook Pvt. Feb. 9,'60 Boston. Ma. by surgeon's list of disability at Fort Hamilton, New York, July 25, 1862.
  William Schaffer Pvt. Jan. 8,'61 New York by surgeon's list of disability at Fort Hamilton, New York, Nov. 6, 1862.
  Robert Curran Pvt. Oct. 6,'57 Newport, Ky. By exper. of service, at Pensacola, Fla. Oct. 6, 1862.
  John Holland Pvt. Oct. 13,'57 Detroit, Mich. By exper. of service, at Pensacola, Fla. Oct. 13, 1862.

Temp. Attached:
1. William Bruce   Pvt. June 30,'58 Ft. Independence, Ma. S.O. no. 73, Hdqrts. Troops in West Fla. Dept. of the Gulf, Pensacola, Fla. Aug. 30,'62
2. Sigmund Loeb   Pvt. Dec. 5,'57 Ft. Snelling   do.
3. Christian Allendorf Pvt. Sept. 29,'58 New York, NY   do.

Strength: 80. Sick: 13.

Sick Present: Henry W. Closson, James Ahern, William Brown, Bernard Farrell, Charles F. Mansfield, James McCarthy, Daniel McCoy, Thomas Newton, William E. Scott, Reuben Townsend, Michael White.

Sick Absent: William C. Brunskill, Ft. Hamilton, NY. Left Co. Sept. 17, 1861
  Charles Riley Ft. McIntosh, TX Absent since Feb. 12, 1861. Reduced to Pvt. July 12, 1861

The increase in the number of sick may indicate seasonal related sickness, e.g., malaria, and sanitation problems with a now-more-crowded Pensacola. Regarding discharges, note that Robert Curran was the last of the three who had been recruited in 1857 at Newport, Kentucky. McWaters and Gilroyd left in July and August, respectively. Holland was another from the midwest who was apparently not interested in this war. The three may have missed the notification of the operation of General Orders No. 74 issued on July 7, 1862, and General Orders No. 154, issued on October 9th, offering an additional $100 bounty for new recruits as well as reenlisting soldiers.[743]

General Arnold was transferred out of Pensacola at the end of September to

---

743. O.R. Ser. III. Vol. 2, pp. 187, 206, 654, 687.

be the military administrator of New Orleans and Algiers. He was briefly replaced by the next highest-ranking officer, Col. William "Billy" Wilson of the 6th New York, who duly moved into the commander's quarters, the mansion of the ex-senator from Florida, Stephen R. Mallory, now the Confederate secretary of the navy.[744] Wilson was soon displaced by another commander, Gen. Neal Dow, who arrived in October.[745] The 7th Vermont Infantry arrived on November 14th. It had sweated and suffered in Louisiana the previous summer.[746] Another unit for the Pensacola rest camp.

On November 16th, the 6th New York boarded the steamers *Nassau* and *Creole*, bound for New Orleans. They were initially assigned to Thomas W. Sherman's division at Carrollton.

---

744. Morris, G., p. 82. All references to the 6th here on pp. 80–84. There is reason to question this source. Babcock states, p. 63, that the commander's quarters were at the plantation of Major Chase.
745. Shorey, p. 28.
746. Benedict, G. G., *Vermont in the Civil War*, Burlington: VT Free Press Association, 1888.

Chapter 6

Vicksburg II; The Northern Column;
Wavering in Washington; Halleck General-in-Chief;
The Confederacy After Corinth; Return to Baton Rouge; Recruitment vs. Draft;
The East; McClernand; The Department of the Gulf; The Lafourche Campaign;
Banks; Record 12/62; The Close of 1862

Vicksburg II

Upon Farragut's May 30th return to New Orleans from the Vicksburg I episode, to his chagrin, he was met by a message of such urgency and import that the secretary of the navy had sent copies of it on three separate ships to guarantee that it would reach him. Dated the 19th of May, it said: "The President of the United States requires you to use your utmost exertions (without a moment's delay) to open the river Mississippi and effect a junction with Flag Officer Davis, commanding pro tem, the Western Flotilla."[747]

Next day, an apprehensive Farragut notified Porter to bring from six to ten of his mortar boats up from their anchorage at Pensacola. After all, the river was falling. His view was that his ships had barely escaped from the last trip. Porter responded on June 3rd that he was underway.[748] Porter, in his own remarkably candid way, continues with the opinion that the whole expedition is better off being given up. He presciently predicts: "General Butler has not men enough to protect New Orleans in case Beauregard is defeated and retreats south, for he has nowhere else to go, and I think that he, Butler, had better give this thing up. As you say, we must do our duty, and I am on the way and going to do all you tell me to, but at the same time don't you think it our duty to point out to the Government what they don't know?"

On June 1st, Butler issued new orders to General Williams to the effect that three additional regiments were being sent to him – the 30th Massachusetts, 9th Connecticut, the 21st Indiana, and the 2nd Massachusetts Battery (Nims') – making a force of about 4,500 men. An initial object was to secure Baton Rouge by making

---

747. ORN Ser. I, Vol. 18, p. 502. Foote was temporarily replaced by Davis on May 9th and permanently on June 17th, ORN Ser. I, Vol. 23, pp. 86, 213.
748. ORN Ser. I, Vol. 18, p. 576.

a "demonstration" on Camp Moore at Tangipahoa, to where General Lovell had fled after the fall of New Orleans. This was to be completed by June 8th, "so as to assist in ulterior movement." By June 6th, Butler concluded that Camp Moore had been sufficiently broken up and that he was adding the remainder of the 6th Massachusetts Battery (Everett), the 31st Massachusetts Regiment, the 7th Vermont Regiment, and Magee's Cavalry to General Williams' force.

The June 7th entry of the diary of navy commander H. H. Bell[749] notes: "Troops went up the river to join those at Baton Rouge, for the combined attack upon Vicksburg. Talk of General Butler going up. Considered rash to take troops from city while those sent, 5,000 in all, are considered insufficient for the work. Mortar fleet arriving."

Plaudits to Farragut and Butler – they were doing everything they could, but they would ultimately be let down.

If Butler realized that the troops being sent were insufficient to capture and hold Vicksburg, a canal would bypass it; thus, the Mississippi would be opened anyway. Williams' task upon arrival at Vicksburg was: "You will send up a regiment or two at once and cut off the neck of land beyond [opposite] Vicksburg by means of a trench across, thus . . ." He included a sketch in his written order. A later drawing appears as figure 1.[750] The first mention of the Vicksburg canal appears in this directive, dated June 6th.[751] It also appears in navy correspondence on June

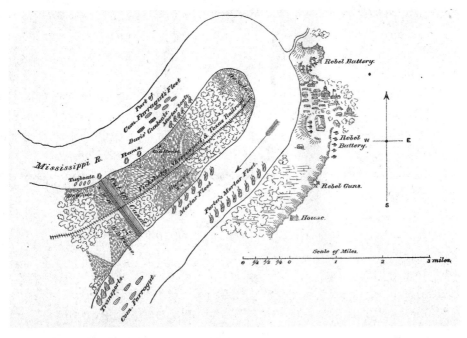

FIGURE 1

---

749. ORN Ser, I, Vol. 18, p. 708.
750. O.R. Vol. 15, p. 29.
751. O.R Vol. 15, p. 25.

14th, and is worded almost as if it was the independent idea of Commander Bell.[752] Another note from Gideon Welles dated June 25th, asks Flag Officer Davis to look into the scheme, with not a word of reference to Butler's plan or to the origin of the idea, the seed of which was likely the successful New Madrid Canal.[753] No one, it seems, considered that the conditions here or the number of troops available were not the same. The New Madrid Canal was dug with, or backed by, an army of 18,500 in cool weather, uncomfortable perhaps, but not with the threat of heat related maladies, including malaria. Then, the river continued to rise and helped to open any clearing made. Now, it was the opposite. The river was continuing to drop, the weather was steaming, and there were less than one-third the numbers of troops available. The result would be a notable failure.

Farragut's flotilla had begun the repeat struggle to get upriver with the departure of the *Hartford* and the *Brooklyn* from New Orleans on June 8th. There was plenty to think about: possible grounding at every bend, Confederate batteries now established at Port Hudson and Ellis Bluffs, and a militia battery at Grand Gulf that had fired on the fleet as it retreated in May. Supplies of coal were critical, and of course, the river continued to fall.[754] Then there was the *Arkansas*, the Confederate ram being constructed on the Yazoo River, a tributary that enters the Mississippi above Vicksburg, which was greatly feared, despite the poor showing that similar craft, such as the *Manassas* and *Louisiana*, had made at New Orleans.

Williams' troops, consisting of the 30th Massachusetts, the 9th Connecticut, the 8th Vermont, the 4th Wisconsin, the 2nd Massachusetts Battery, (Nims', see figure 2) and two sections of the 6th Massachusetts Battery, began embarking at Baton Rouge on the 18th.[755] They got underway on the 21st.[756]

By June 25th, almost the entire expedition, including Porter's 16 mortar boats, had anchored seven miles below Vicksburg. Williams had been detained by stopping at Ellis Bluffs to attack the rebel battery there, and at Grand Gulf to rout the militia out of the town and burn it. His troops were landed on Burey's Point,

---

752. ORN Ser. I, Vol. 18, p. 582.
753. ORN Ser. I, Vol. 18, p. 585.
754. ORN Ser. I, Vol. 18, pp. 708–712; O.R. Vol. 15, p. 27.
755. O.R. Vol. 15, p. 26.
756. ORN Ser. I, Vol. 18, p. 710. Picture from Miller, F. T., Vol. 2, Pt. II, pp. 180, 181, digitally restored. The original caption describes the picture as showing the 2nd, 4th, and 6th Massachusetts Batteries. The 4th and 6th Batteries were equipped with mixed types of guns, and only the 2nd Battery had "six bronze guns which had been rifled . . . and fired a 10 ½ pound Schenkel shell . . ." This picture, showing six identical light-colored (bronze) guns, defines it to be that of the 2nd Battery; as described in *Massachusetts Soldiers Sailors and Marines in the Civil War* by the Massachusetts adjutant general, Vol. V, 1930, pp. 355, 383, 412. After Battery L's arrival at Baton Rouge at the end of the year, the two batteries, one volunteer and one regular, would go on to serve nearly side by side for the rest of the campaign in the Gulf. No equivalent "portrait" of Battery L has been found.

FIGURE 2. NIMS' BATTERY AT THE PENTAGON BARRACKS, BATON ROUGE

where the proposed trench was to be dug, and the two artillery batteries were mounted further east to support Farragut's run past to link up with the Northern Column, proposed for the 28th.[757]

At 3:00 a.m. on the 28th, the squadron weighed anchor and began its run past Vicksburg. Supported by the mortar boats and fire from Nims' and Everett's batteries, eight of the eleven ships had made it past by 5:30 a.m. The slightly damaged *Brooklyn*, the *Katahdin*, and the *Kennebec*, by a mistaken interpretation of Farragut's signals, remained below. Above, Farragut met the army's new ram fleet under the command of Col. Charles Ellet, described below, who had been hunting the *Arkansas*. Dispatching a letter to Davis and to Halleck, Farragut reported his having run past Vicksburg, noting that the enemy now had "Van Dorn's division of Beauregard's army" there, "some eight or ten thousand troops,"[758] making any landing on the east side of the river impossible for Williams.

The Northern Column

We have already noted that Flag Officer Foote, after Halleck's April 15th decision to remove Pope's army from his support, was left with only two regiments under Col. G. N. Fitch, roughly 1,500 men.

On April 19th, Foote sent a report to the Navy Secretary Gideon Welles, which was a summary of the events since Pope left.[759] He is emphatic that if Pope had not been withdrawn that Fort Pillow would have fallen in four days and

---

757. ORN Ser. I, Vol. 18, pp. 711, 712.
758. ORN Ser. I, Vol. 18, Farragut's Report, p. 590; Davis' Report, p. 592. Beauregard had been replaced by Bragg on June 20th.
759. ORN Ser. I, Vol. 23, pp. 5, 11; O.R. Vol. 10/ II, p. 120. In May, his friend, D. D. Porter, sent him some "magic oil" to treat his wound. We shall see that it did no good. ORN Ser. I, Vol. 22, p. 731.

Memphis two days later. "I am greatly exercised about our position here . . ." He would remain stationed near Fort Pillow and keep working with Fitch to find a landing for the troops, which would be essential in an attack on the fort.

In a personal note, he refers to an interview that he had with Mrs. Simon Buckner, evacuated from Columbus (whose husband surrendered Fort Donelson) about events shortly after the fort's fall: ". . . they feared the gunboats, and only the gunboats . . . The rebel papers and prisoners all say that the gunboats demoralize their army." He also mentions being miffed at Halleck's report on the capture of Clarksville: "General Halleck refers to General Smith taking possession . . . and says not a word about gunboats, whereas three days before I took possession . . ." He reveals his disdain for Halleck and is fed up not only with recent events but also with his health. His wound from the attack at Fort Donelson had continued to bother him. With the dreadful medicine of the time, it is small wonder that in a month's time, his leg, which was swollen and inflamed, and required him to use crutches, and would cause him to request temporary leave.

On April 20th, Fitch reported many details of his and Foote's moves to Pope and added: "Could you have remained, I am confident that Fort Pillow would have been in your possession today or to-morrow."[760] Fitch continued to try to find a place where his few troops could land and make an effective move on the fortifications, and the mortar boats continued to bombard the Confederate positions; to little avail. By April 30th, it was reported that 13 rebel gunboats were below the fort and that it might be advisable to take the initiative to attack them, considering that they might come upstream and initiate a surprise attack.

It is important to note that gunboat tactics were driven by the strong river current. Any gunboat damaged above the fort might drift helplessly downstream past its guns and could be destroyed in the process.[761] Only a small loss of power, for example, would cause it to fail to stem the rapid current and hence maintain steering control.

On May 9th, Foote left the flotilla for home at Cleveland, Ohio, for what he thought would be a temporary leave (he intended to be gone for only two weeks) for his recuperation.[762] He assigned Cdre. Charles H. Davis to the command, remembered as one of the members of the secret board of officers originally gathered to plan the execution of the Anaconda Plan.

As fate would have it, the very next day, eight of the Confederate gunboats came "handsomely" steaming upstream with eight ironclads and attacked the new flag officer's flotilla. Three of the Confederate vessels were sunk, and the remainder fled to the protection of the guns of the fort. Only six of Davis' gunboats were

---

760. O.R. Vol. 10/ II, p. 116.
761. ORN Ser. I, Vol. 23, p. 12.
762. ORN Ser. I, Vol. 23, p. 86.

engaged, and only the *Cincinnati* and *Mound City* sustained damage, though repairable. The action only lasted an hour.[763]

On May 16th, Gen. I. N. Quinby, in command of the troops occupying Island No. 10, visited Davis, with the object supplementing Fitch in a combined operation against Fort Pillow.[764] Quinby's force arrived on May 22nd and a reconnaissance was begun. It was discovered, attacked, and driven back. The action was sufficient for Quinby to estimate that some 5,000 troops occupied the fort. Coupled with the word of a threatened attack on Hickman and Columbus in the north, Quinby withdrew.[765]

Fortunately, another source of aid to Davis appeared on June 3rd. This was the ram fleet of Col. Charles Ellet, Jr. Ellet, a civil engineer, had proposed to the War Department the idea of quickly converting riverboats into rams to breach the hulls of the rebel gunboats. As his theory went, the rams would be unarmed and therefore would not need trained gunnery crews. Secretary Stanton approved of the conversion of seven small steamers, including three coal towboats, on March 27th.[766] The first were the *Lancaster No. 3*, the *Switzerland*, and *Queen of the West*. The latter two were inspected and approved for purchase by April 11th.[767] The army had created its own navy, under Ellet's command, Stanton commissioning him a colonel, and his brother Alfred a lieutenant colonel.[768]

They were on their first mission when they showed up at Fort Pillow, much to the surprise and slight consternation[769] of Davis. Ellet made it clear that he was there to help, and he would desist in any independent action if Davis considered that it would jeopardize his "general operations."

Davis finally approved of Ellet's participation, and a small party of Ellet's and Fitch's men was sent out to scout the approach to, and the location of, a target rebel gunboat. They instead observed that Fort Pillow was being evacuated.

The fort was occupied on June 5th by Colonel Fitch's troops, who found that the guns and stores had been destroyed. Fitch concluded that the fort could not be properly garrisoned without new armament and a "corps of artillerists," and that "for all practical purposes one or two gunboats would be more effective than my command of infantry." He then proposed leaving gunboats to hold the fort and for his command and the rest of the flotilla to move on to Memphis that

---

763. ORN Ser. I, Vol. 23, pp. 13, 14.
764. ORN Ser. I, Vol. 23, pp. 22, 24.
765. ORN Ser. I, Vol. 23, p. 30.
766. O.R. Vol. 10/II, pp. 621, 622.
767. O.R. Ser. III, Vol. 2, pp. 9, 15, 835. Modifications to all were completed by September 20th, 1862.
768. O.R. Vol. 10/II, p. 130.
769. ORN Ser. I, Vol. 23, pp. 42, 43.

night.[770] Ellet then joined Davis and the two moved south.

The combined forces arrived off Memphis at 9:00 on the night of the 5th and anchored above the city. Early on the morning of the 6th, they discovered eight Confederate rams and gunboats lying at the levee. Davis and Ellet attacked at 5:30, and by 7:00, seven of the Confederate vessels had been captured or destroyed after a running fight. Only one escaped, believed to be the *Van Dorn*, by her superior speed.

The mayor of Memphis, John Park, surrendered the city at 11:00 a.m., and Colonel Fitch took possession.[771] Colonel Ellet was the only man wounded in the battle, suffering a pistol shot in the knee. He died of complications from this on June 21st.[772]

Flag Officer Foote finally recognized that his health was not improving, and his departure from the Western Flotilla would have to be permanent. He was relieved from command at his request on June 17th, and Davis was named in his place.[773]

On June 28th, Davis, still at Memphis, received the request from Farragut from below Vicksburg, to aid him in the "reduction of that city."[774] He would leave "at the earliest possible moment," which was the next day.

Davis hove into Farragut's sight at 8:00 a.m. on July 1st. The difference between the two flagships, Farragut's *Hartford* (figure 3) and Davis' *Benton* (figure 4)[775] pointed up Farragut's risk of a falling river. Though the two vessels were of similar length, the *Hartford* at 225 feet and the *Benton* at 202 feet, all similarity ended there. The draft of the *Hartford* was 17 feet and that of the *Benton* was only 9. An ocean-going ship likely had never been there before.

FIGURE 3. USS *HARTFORD*

FIGURE 4. USS *BENTON*

---

770. ORN Ser. I, Vol. 23, pp. 45–48.
771. ORN Ser. I, Vol. 23, pp. 118–122, 213.
772. ORN Ser. I, Vol. 23, p. 275.
773. Additional reading: Walke, H., The Century, January 1885, p. 434; Welles, Vol. 1, pp. 316, 335, 345. Foote died on June 26th, 1863.
774. ORN Ser. I, Vol. 23, pp. 231, 232.
775. Figure 3, *Hartford*; Leslie, Mrs. F., Battle Scenes, p. 440; figure 4, *Benton*, ORN Ser. II, Vol. 1, p. 44a.

Farragut mentioned that it was the furthest away from the ocean his ship had ever been.

Spirits were high for a few moments until it was disclosed that Davis brought no troops – had none to bring – and that Farragut's strength, with Williams' force of 5,000, was insufficient even if it were not already depleted by sickness.

On June 30th, Farragut sent another message, directed through Memphis[776] to Halleck, which said that it was "absolutely necessary to have additional troops to occupy Vicksburg after the batteries are silenced."[777] On July 3rd, Halleck responded that: "The scattered and weakened condition of my forces renders it impossible for me at the present to detach any troops to cooperate with you at Vicksburg." This was the man who had occupied Corinth without a fight on May 30th, with the largest army ever seen in the west: 120,171.[778] It was now, indeed, scattered and weakened, with Buell's 48,000 headed toward Chattanooga, though there were still more than 70,000 of Grant's troops in the area at that time.

Back at Vicksburg, General Williams had pressed into service some 1,200 or more slaves taken from plantations in the surrounding countryside, in addition to the labor of his own troops. Now, in one of the most unpleasant and unhealthiest months of the season, the digging began.[779] The average depth of the cut was about seven feet on July 4th. Regardless, this was not deep enough to let in the falling river. By July 11th, the depth of the cut had reached thirteen feet and was about eighteen inches below the river level whose fall had begun to slow. However, at this point, the banks of the cut began to cave in. Williams then suggested that he be allowed to add to his force of laborers and dig "a real canal" to a depth of perhaps forty feet, which would take three months.[780] He need not have been concerned, for an order from Butler dated July 16th, told him that he was needed to return to protect Baton Rouge. The Confederates were reforming and would likely attack Baton Rouge and threaten New Orleans.

Wavering in Washington

As far back as May 22nd, Farragut had received an inquiry as to whether the mortar fleet could better be used at Mobile.[781] He had to patiently explain, in his answer of June 30th, the importance of having it at Vicksburg. Now, on July 5th, he was ordered to send 12 of Porter's schooners to Hampton Roads.[782] Those

---

776. Grant, U. S., Vol. I, pp. 385, 386.
777. ORN Ser. I, Vol. 18, p. 593.
778. O.R. Vol. 10/II, pp. 146, 148, 151.
779. O.R. Vol. 15, p. 30. Profile of canal across Burey's Point opposite Vicksburg.
780. O.R. Vol. 15, p. 31; ORN Ser. I, Vol. 23, pp. 249, 250.
781. ORN Ser. I, Vol. 18, p. 591.
782. ORN Ser. I, Vol. 18, p. 629.

in Washington had become alarmed for the safety of the city after the failure of the Peninsular Campaign and the successes of now-famous Confederate General Stonewall Jackson in the Shenandoah Valley. "How strange . . ." Farragut noted, sending some two thousand miles for mortar boats.[783] Further, he was still on the north side of Vicksburg and was worried about again running the gauntlet and extricating his ships from a river that had been falling for the past six weeks. On July 13th, he sent the following curt telegram (via Cairo on the 17th) to Gideon Welles: "In 10 days the river will be too low for the ships to go down. Shall they go down, or remain up the rest of the year?"[784] Apparently, Welles had anticipated his concern, and Farragut had been ordered down on July 14th, four days before his telegram left Cairo. Davis' flotilla was to remain.

Note that Welles ordered Farragut to break off the attack only two days before Butler ordered Williams back to Baton Rouge. There is no evidence that these two orders were coordinated in any way, but like minds were created accidentally by totally different circumstances.

So much time and opportunity had passed. Washington had now forgotten about the 19th of May order to Farragut: "The President of the United States requires you to use your utmost exertions (without a moment's delay) to open the river Mississippi and effect a junction with Flag Officer Davis . . ." By the end of June, it was clear that events elsewhere would cause the President and the cabinet to refocus their attention. "Elsewhere" was a few miles outside of Washington itself, the imminent failure of McClellan's Peninsular Campaign.

The fate of the Peninsular Campaign that was planned and finally launched by McClellan is often referred to as commencing with the Battle of Hampton Roads, the *Monitor* versus the *Virginia* (*Merrimac*), on March 8th–9th. Though this was technically historic, it had little bearing on the land campaign. The Army of the Potomac had moved from Fort Monroe in late March, appearing before Yorktown to face Confederate General J. B. Magruder. Fearful of making a direct attack on what he conceived as a powerful Confederate force, McClellan laid siege. This lasted from April 5th to May 4th when the Confederates slipped away toward Williamsburg. The Peninsular Campaign,[785] McClellan's advance to Richmond, continued with engagements at:

2. Williamsburg	3. Eltham's Landing	4. Drewery's Bluff	5. Hanover Court House
6. Seven Pines	7. Oak Grove	8. Beaver Dam Creek	9. Gaines' Mill
10. Garnett's Farm	11. Savage's Station	12. Glendale	13. Malvern Hill

Many of these were inconclusive, including the large battle (84,000 troops,

---

783. ORN Ser. I, Vol. 18, p. 632.
784. ORN Ser. I, Vol. 18, p. 594.
785. Williamsburg, May 5th – Malvern Hill reoccupied August 8th; O.R. Vol. 11/I, pp. 1–3. Seven Pines CWSAC VA 014, Gaines' Mill CWSAC VA 017, Malvern Hill CWSAC VA 021.

total) at Seven Pines. The Confederate victory at Gaines' Mill on June 27th turned the tide, convincing McClellan to discontinue his advance. The final engagement, Malvern Hill, was fought on July 1st, 1862; and though technically a Union victory, it really only served to protect McClellan's withdrawal.

Concurrent with the Peninsular Campaign was Stonewall Jackson's Shenandoah Valley Campaign, with the Union army being driven out of the valley after being defeated at Winchester on May 25th, and again at Cross Keys and Port Republic in early June.

The letters home from Willoughby Babcock at Pensacola indicate the prevailing public reaction: "We have . . . a N.Y. Times of the 3rd of July, and enough seems to have become certain to assure us that the energy and military science of the South have proved superior . . . One of the commonest matters of strategy is to have superior numbers at the point where serious work is possible, but McClellan has dallied away eleven months in Virginia, has had every wish and request gratified, has had wonderful means at his disposal, and yet has allowed the enemy to put two men to his one on the point of attack and thus beat him . . . We knew here, and he has had the means of knowing, that the Army of the South dispersed at Corinth, was being sent to Richmond." [786]

Yes, Confederate troops east to Richmond, Van Dorn to Vicksburg, and eventually Bragg's whole army on an ill-advised campaign into Kentucky.[787] Regarding troops to Richmond, note the extraordinary reaction of Halleck. On June 28th, Halleck received a telegram from Secretary of War Stanton: "Absolutely necessary, in the opinion of the President, for you immediately to detach 25,000 of your force and forward it . . . by way of Baltimore and Washington to Richmond."[788] Lincoln's concern was the same as when he had ordered Porter's mortar boats detached from Farragut. It was for the safety of Washington. After the Peninsular Campaign had ended, Lee was free to begin his Northern Virginia Campaign. Halleck sounds miffed after making threats to Washington that if the order were carried out, "we should have been defeated or forced to retreat."[789] The President repeated the order, this time more as a request, on June 30th: "Would be very glad of 25,000 infantry . . ."[790] Halleck replied in a long telegram dated July 1st that concluded: "I am . . . satisfied that a detachment of 25,000 from this army at the present time will result in the loss of Arkansas and West Tennessee, and perhaps both."[791] Flouting the President's contention, he claimed, "All scouts, spies, deserters, and prisoners without a single exception report that no troops have been sent from here east."

---

786. Babcock, W. M., pp. 106, 107.
787. Wheeler, J., Vol. III, pp. 1–25.
788. O.R. Vol. 16/II, p. 70.
789. O.R. Vol. 16/II, p. 82.
790. O.R. Vol. 16/II, p. 77.
791. O.R. Vol. 16/II, p. 81.

Stanton suspended the order the same day.[792] Nevertheless, Lincoln sent out his own response[793] on the subject the next day: "I did say and now repeat, I would be exceedingly glad for some re-enforcements from you." Lincoln goes on to humble himself by adding: "Still do not send a man if in your judgment it will endanger any point you deem important to hold or will force you to give up or weaken or delay the Chattanooga expedition." Lincoln did not give up. On July 4th, he sent another telegram to Halleck asking for 10,000 infantry. "Can you not? Some part of the Corinth army is certainly fighting McClellan in front of Richmond. Prisoners are in our hands from the late Corinth army." [794]

This is one of the rare times where Halleck appears resolute. He seems convinced that after sending Buell east, a further weakening of the Army of the Tennessee would be dangerous, an opinion held by Grant as noted in chapter 5. However, after Halleck was called east to become general-in-chief, his resolve weakened, or rather he fell in with the prevailing view at Washington, and we recall that five divisions were transferred from Grant during August and September.

Halleck General-in-Chief

It is perhaps significant that on the 26th of June, Pope had been promoted and reassigned to the command of the Army of Virginia to oppose Lee.[795] Clearly, he had done so spectacularly well at New Madrid and Island No. 10 that no one could deny that he deserved it. Of course (from the diary of Gideon Welles),[796] it helped that he was "a connection of Mrs. Lincoln and was somewhat intimate with the President, with whom he came to Washington in 1861. There were some wonderful military operations on the Mississippi and at Corinth reported of him just before he was ordered here, and which led to it, that have not somehow been fully substantiated. Admiral Foote used to laugh at the gasconade and bluster of Pope."

Now in Washington, Pope began to sing the praises of Halleck. From Welles: "On one or two occasions I heard him express his admiration of the extraordinary capacity of Halleck and his wish that H. could be on this field where his great abilities could comprehend and successfully direct military operations . . . The President listened, was influenced, and finally went to West Point and saw General Scott." Old "fuss and feathers" apparently approved, and Halleck was assigned to

---

792. O.R. Vol. 16/II, p. 82.
793. O.R. Vol. 16/II, p. 88.
794. O.R. Vol. 16/II, p. 95.
795. O.R. Vol. 12II, p. 435.
796. Welles, G., Vol. 1, p. 120.

the command of the Armies of the United States on July 11th, 1862.[797]

As a result of the fact that Grant was the senior officer in line in the Department of Mississippi, Halleck sent for him to report to headquarters at Corinth. No reason was given, as if it was too much for Halleck to even mention the thought of Grant in command. Their strained relationship was apparently undiminished. When Grant[798] asked if he should take his staff, Halleck replied: "This will be your headquarters. You can judge for yourself." When Grant arrived at Corinth on the 15th of July, he was ignored; and when Halleck left on the 17th, he had not told Grant why he had been called. Grant notes: "Practically I became a department commander, because no one was assigned to that position over me and I made my reports direct to the general-in-chief; but I was not assigned to the position of department commander until the 25th of October."[799]

The Confederacy After Corinth

Beauregard temporarily transferred his command to Bragg on the advice of two Confederate army surgeons.[800] He was quickly and permanently replaced by Braxton Bragg, per order of Jefferson Davis, on June 20th, 1862.

The dispersal of Halleck's forces at Corinth most notably included sending Buell's army east. As noted, a flaw in Halleck's order to Buell was that he was to repair the Memphis and Charleston Railroad along the way. Guerilla attacks on his efforts, and the resulting slow progress, were duly noted in Confederate circles. Most significantly, many prominent citizens of Kentucky came forward to stress to Bragg their loyalty to the South and that "as soon as they were given an opportunity, it would be proven."[801] Bragg then succumbed to the siren song of a campaign into eastern Tennessee to win back Kentucky. The Confederacy thus copied Washington's wishes, and also dispersed their forces. Thus, by weakening their position in the Mississippi Valley, the Confederacy gave the Union (Grant and Butler) a reprieve. It also gave life to Confederate internal contention as to leadership and policy. This was the beginning of the end, if anyone in Jefferson Davis' inner circle dared to think.

A commentary on the situation, written after the war by Gen. Joseph E. Johnston,[802] is quoted here: "Their [the Union's] wide dispersion put them at the mercy of any superior force, such as the Confederacy could have brought against them readily; but this opportunity, such a one as has rarely occurred in war, was put aside

---

797. O.R. Vol. 16/I, p. 1.
798. Grant, U. S., Vol. 1, p. 393.
799. O.R. Vol. 17/I, p. 4, gives October 16th as the date.
800. O.R. Vol. 17/II, pp. 601, 614, 623.
801. Urquhart, D., Vol. III, p. 600.
802. Johnston, J. E., North American Review, December 1866, p. 585.

by the Confederate Government, and the army which, properly used would have secured to the South the possession of Tennessee and Mississippi was employed in a wild expedition into Kentucky, which could have had only the results of a raid."

On June 19th, Earl Van Dorn was assigned to the command of the Department of Southern Mississippi and East Louisiana (Lovell's Department No. 1) without a word as to Lovell's fate.[803]

After marginal success in Texas in 1861 (few recruits, but the capture of Sibley's and Reeve's commands) and failure in command of the Army of the West, with a loss at the Battle of Pea Ridge in Arkansas in March of 1862, the impulsive Van Dorn had been given another chance. Then, Jefferson Davis had second thoughts. On June 25th, Bragg's Department No. 2 was expanded to include Department No. 1, which disappeared.[804] Uncharacteristic of Bragg – who, as the war wore on, was seen as a martinet who openly displayed little faith in his subordinates – he appointed Van Dorn to half of the new department, which was split into two districts: the Mississippi under Van Dorn and the Gulf under Forney.[805]

Now convinced of the opportunity to regain Kentucky and eastern Tennessee, on July 21st, Bragg ordered his Army of Mississippi east to Chattanooga from its base in Tupelo. Having the Confederate advantage of internal rail lines through friendly country, he arrived in Chattanooga on July 29th, long before Buell, to begin what has become known as the Heartland Campaign.

In late July, Van Dorn, at Jackson, still retaining Bragg's confidence, was advised by Bragg to "do all things deemed needful without awaiting instructions from these headquarters."[806] The impulsive Van Dorn soon ordered Breckinridge to attack Baton Rouge.

Return to Baton Rouge

On July 15th, the *Arkansas* – "a heavy, clumsy, rusty, ugly flatboat with a great square box in the centre, while great cannon put their noses out at the sides, and in front," figure 5[807] – made its move down the Yazoo. It engaged the three Union vessels sent there on a reconnaissance: Davis' ironclad *Carondelet*, the converted "timber-clad" side-wheel steamer *Tyler*, and

FIGURE 5. CSS *ARKANSAS*

---

803. O.R. Vol. 17/II, pp. 612, 613, 616, 617. In this new assignment, he was forced to relinquish command of the Army of the West.
804. O.R. Vol.17/II, p. 624. It was enlarged later to include Alabama and Florida.
805. O.R. Vol.17/II, p. 636. Price then assumed command of the Army of the West, p. 655.
806. O.R. Vol.17/II p. 656, 657.
807. Dawson, S. M., p. 145; figure 5, ORN Ser. I, Vol. 19, frontispiece.

Alfred Ellet's flagship, the *Queen of the West*.[808] Forty-two of General Williams' troops were assigned on board as sharpshooters, 21 each from the 4th Wisconsin and the 30th Massachusetts, and were engaged in a running battle that followed along the Yazoo for ten miles – out to the Mississippi. Six of the sharpshooters were killed and five wounded.[809] The apparently damaged *Arkansas* then slowly proceeded right through Farragut's nonplussed squadron and anchored under the guns of Vicksburg before any of Farragut's powerful ships could get up steam to engage.[810] Farragut, "with deep mortification," reported it to Secretary Welles on the 17th.

Upon hearing the news, both Davis and Farragut were chastised by Welles in nearly identical separate letters[811] written on August 2nd. "I need not say to you that the escape of this vessel and the attending circumstances have been the cause of serious mortification to the Department and the country. It is an absolute necessity that the neglect or apparent neglect of the squadron on that occasion be wiped out . . . which I trust will be accomplished before this reaches you. I have omitted writing since the receipt of your official report in the confident expectation that we should have advices that you should have overcome her."

To Davis, he closed with: "I cannot suppose that Admiral Farragut would leave Vicksburg until this is accomplished." To Farragut, he closed with: "It is not to be supposed that you will leave Vicksburg until this is accomplished." Thus, Farragut, with his deep draft ships, was expected to delay his departure and risk his whole squadron to becoming trapped by the falling river.

Farragut's first move was a decision to run down past Vicksburg, bombard the *Arkansas* as he went, and accomplish getting in a position to leave. This was done on July 16th and it was successful in getting his ships through, including Davis' ram *Sumter*, which was assigned to remain with Farragut.[812] However, the squadron failed to inflict any damage to the *Arkansas*, and it remained to Davis and Farragut to put together a plan to attack it.

It was not until the 20th that Davis decided to send down his newest and most powerful ironclad, the *Essex*, commanded by W. D. Porter, David D. Porter's older brother,[813] to be accompanied by Alfred Ellet, in the *Queen of the West*. They would ram the *Arkansas* and then pass on down the river and remain south of Vicksburg. Davis' squadron would stay north of Vicksburg permanently, giving his reasoning that "it would be an inexcusable sacrifice of the greatest interests of the country

---

808. He replaced his brother Charles, who died after being wounded in the knee at Memphis.
809. O.R. Vol. 15, pp. 31–33.
810. ORN Ser. I, Vol. 19, pp. 3, 4, 6.
811. ORN Ser. I, Vol. 19 pp. 5–7.
812. ORN Ser. I, Vol. 19. pp. 8–10, 13, 62.
813. The *Essex* had just entered service. ORN, Ser. I, Vol. 23, p. 247.

to abandon the possession of the upper Mississippi . . ."[814] He would position his vessels so as to bombard the upper works of Vicksburg while Farragut would advance and bombard the lower. All this was to cover the *Essex* and the *Queen* as they ran in to attack the *Arkansas*. The *Sumter*, on signal, was to steam north and attack as well. The plan was carried out, or better described as miscarried, on July 22nd.[815]

The *Essex* went down without coordinating its move with Ellet. It failed to ram the *Arkansas* but instead grazed it, and then ran aground. In this situation, by accident, it was able to fire its IX-inch guns into the *Arkansas* at point-blank range – 10 or 12 feet – before proceeding downriver. A later Confederate report indicated that the *Essex*'s shots were determined to have torn a "long hole" in the *Arkansas*, and that there had been six of the crew killed and six badly wounded.[816]

The *Queen* also managed to ram the *Arkansas*, but as Ellet relates, "I could not reach her vulnerable side without rounding [turning] partly, and thus losing much headway." The *Queen* was shot up badly. It was with difficulty that she returned to her anchorage upriver, and she would have to be sent "north to be repaired."

The *Sumter* did not see its signal and did not even enter the fight.

On July 23rd, Farragut had completed arrangements for convoying Williams' transports downriver, conscious that he had failed regarding the *Arkansas*. He and Davis had agreed that Commander Porter would "take charge of the lower part of the river with the Essex and the Sumter" in the hope that if the *Arkansas* dropped downriver, it could be destroyed. Farragut planned to leave only the *Pensacola*, *Mississippi*, and *Portsmouth* permanently at New Orleans for the protection of General Butler and his troops.[817] After that, he planned to pull his remaining squadron out of the Mississippi and head for Pensacola.

Note that Mobile, Alabama, remained in Confederate hands. Despite all the Union activity nearby, Farragut had not the chance to organize an attack and made no mention of any plans at this time. Mobile was destined to go undisturbed for another two years.

Williams and his worn troops were back at Baton Rouge on the 26th.[818] The martinet having forbidden the troops to land until he personally had stepped off: "At length the General . . . steps on the plank and then on the land . . . Next, comes Nims' Battery . . . the gaunt skeleton horses . . . Even the worn and cracked harness seems too much to carry. The Ninth Regiment of Connecticut Volunteers, the Fourth Regiment of Wisconsin, and the Seventh Regiment of Vermont, are beginning to

---

814. ORN Ser. I, Vol. 19, p. 15; ORN Ser. I, Vol. 23, pp. 237, 238.
815. ORN Ser. I, Vol. 19, pp. 17, 18, 45, 46, 48–50, 96–98.
816. ORN Ser. I, Vol. 19, p. 70. The total of Confederate killed and wounded from this and the previous Yazoo action was 42.
817. ORN Ser. I, Vol. 19, pp. 19, 48, 49, 97.
818. ORN Ser. I, Vol. 19, p. 33.

land as the heat of the day comes on. The faces of the officers are changed, as if by 10 years of care and trouble. The men appear like wretches escaped from the dungeons of the Inquisition every face and form shows the effect of long continued exercises in torture . . . This day the surgeon's command outnumbers that of the General . . ."[819] Barely 800 of the 3,200 sent up were fit for duty (21 of 140 in Nims' battery). They would have less than 10 days to recuperate before the fight of their lives[820] (figure 6).

FIGURE 6. UNION CAMP AT BATON ROUGE, SOON THE BATTLEFIELD
To the extreme left, the three-story structure is the penitentiary, the future home of Battery L.

After the Union attempt on Vicksburg had failed, Van Dorn had resolved to attack Baton Rouge as part of a plan to secure the Red River and recapture New Orleans. He sent Gen. John C. Breckinridge and his Kentuckians to unite with a small force under Gen. Daniel Ruggles at Tangipahoa, and then proceed, on July 30th, to attack Baton Rouge.

Due to "appalling" sickness, the actual strength of Breckinridge's force was reduced from about 4,000 to 2,600 on the early morning of August 5th, when the attack began.[821] It was repulsed by the hard, face-to-face, often at forty yards or less, fighting of the units of the garrison, some 2,500 in number. They held off the

---

819. Bacon, E., pp. 5, 6; Massachusetts AG Report, Vol. V, p. 355.
820. Williams, from West Point, is claimed to have hated the relatively sophisticated volunteers of the 6th Michigan, who often questioned Williams' orders and were accused of mutiny. See Bacon, pp. 20–32. Figure 6: Miller, F. T., Vol. II, p. 133.
821. O.R. Vol. 15, p. 77, Pirtle, J. B., *The Battle of Baton Rouge*, Southern Historical Society Papers, Vol. 8, pp. 327, 328. The quote "appalling" is Breckinridge's comment. The force began with 4,000 men, about one-third of them with no shoes. Water on the march from Tangipahoa was scarce and the heat intense. Irwin, R. B., *Battles and Leaders: Military Operations in Louisiana*, Vol. III, pp. 582–583.

attackers despite their sickness (many left the hospital to fight) and General Williams' poor defensive preparations (regiments beyond supporting distance from one another and few preparations such as earthworks or rifle pits).[822]

Toward the end of the battle, General Williams was killed by a Minie ball through the heart,[823] and Col. Thomas W. Cahill of the 9th Connecticut took over the command.[824]

Shelling from the navy gunboats *Kineo* and *Katahdin* was directed with good effect from an officer in an overlook in the statehouse.[825] The *Arkansas*, ordered to advance downriver to the support of the Confederate attack, according to Van Dorn's report, "Broke machinery five miles above Baton Rouge. On way down was attacked by enemy. In this condition fought well, inflicting great damage to gunboats, and was then blown up by crew, all of whom escaped."[826] Failure of the *Arkansas* to support the attack was concluded by the Confederate side as the as the reason for the failure of the attack.

Farragut wrote: "It is one of the happiest days of my life that I am able to report to the Department of the destruction of the Arkansas . . . As soon as the enemy was repulsed, Commander Porter, with the gunboats, went upstream after the ram Arkansas, which was lying about 5 miles above, apparently afraid to take her share of the conflict . . . as he came within gunshot he opened upon her, and probably disabled some of her machinery or steering apparatus for she became unmanageable, continuing, however, to fire her guns at the Essex . . ."[827] Commander Porter says . . . 'After his first discharge . . . a gush of fire came out of her side, and from that moment it was discovered that she was on fire . . .' They backed her ashore and made a line fast, which soon burned, and she swung off into the river, where she continued to burn until she blew up . . ." W. D. Porter's report was later criticized for its inaccuracy, which seemed to live up to Welles' opinion: "given to exaggeration," "a Porter infirmity."

Compare this with the Confederate report, which says: "at the critical time, when the Arkansas was headed for the Essex . . . with the intention of running her down . . . the larboard engine suddenly stopped." The crew was then "ordered ashore and the vessel fired."

---

822. The sharpshooters of the 6th Michigan, though limited in their traditional role by the morning fog, may have made a surprise impression on the close action by bringing to bear their Henry repeating rifles, able to fire 15 shots in as many seconds. McGregor, C., p. 422. Most of the infantry carried Springfield muskets. McGregor's specific quote refers to the 6th Michigan while at Port Hudson, but evidence of the gradual introduction of modern weapons.
823. Bacon, E., p. 28, claims that his head was shot off by a cannonball.
824. O.R. Vol. 15, pp. 55–58.
825. ORN Ser. I, Vol. 19, p. 116.
826. O.R. Vol. 15, p. 14.
827. ORN Ser. I, Vol. 19, pp. 115, 116, 130–136; Welles, Vol. I, p. 157.

Baton Rouge was saved for the moment, but the result was less than satisfactory. Driven off, Breckinridge followed Van Dorn's general directive "to secure a strong position on the Mississippi below the mouth of the Red River . . ." He then moved the Second Division of his command, under General Ruggles, to Port Hudson, twenty miles upriver.[828] Breckinridge concluded: "Port Hudson is one of the strongest points on the Mississippi, and batteries there will command the river more completely than at Vicksburg."

Breckinridge was not exaggerating, if one interprets his remark to mean that once Port Hudson was fortified, it being below the Red River, and Vicksburg above, the mouth of the Red would be inaccessible to Union navy gunboats. Hence, this major Confederate supply route would be secure. War materiel bound for as far away as the Virginia battlefields could still avoid the blockade by being received in Mexico and Texas, and then transported via the Red River to the Mississippi. It would then cross at that secure section between Vicksburg and Port Hudson, some two hundred miles long, which provided multiple landings on the east side, such as Natchez.

FIGURE 7

Butler's fear of another attack drove frantic efforts to improve the defenses of the town, and this caused considerable additional damage. New defensive lines were brought closer to the center. To clear fields of fire, houses were destroyed and trees cut (figure 7).[829]

---

828. O.R. Vol. 15, pp. 76, 77, 80, 81. Van Dorn's order to move there reached him the next day, August 13th; ibid., p. 797.
829. Bacon, E., p. 30; figure 7, Miller, F. T., Vol. II, p. 136; Clark, Orton S., p. 54.

Rifle pits and breastworks were thrown up, which turned the area around the arsenal grounds into a small fort. The two-week interval during which all this activity took place had allowed Butler to decide that Breckinridge's attack was but a prelude to an attack on New Orleans and that the troops at Baton Rouge were better utilized as reinforcements for the defense there. On August 16th, he ordered Baton Rouge to be destroyed and evacuated. However, on the 19th, he countermanded that portion of his order to destroy it when he found out that by destroying the town he would destroy the means of support for the orphanage, the insane asylum, and the penitentiary.[830]

The then-commander at Baton Rouge, Col. Halbert Paine of the 4th Wisconsin Infantry, and the person who brought the plight of these institutions to the attention of General Butler, carried out the order to evacuate. The evacuation was completed on August 21st. A last act was the opening of the penitentiary gates, setting free several hundred prisoners, with the obligation to those who were fit to join the Union army.[831]

Two gunboats remained stationed off the town and threatened to shell it if the Confederates reentered. Regardless, from the wording of General Ruggles' report of the battle, it is clear that they initially reoccupied the "suburbs,"[832] and later drifted back into the town.

Having fled the battle, Sarah Morgan returned to her home in Baton Rouge on August 28th to find it looted. On passing the penitentiary, she noted that it was "occupied by our men." There were 182 Confederates there: 136 men of the 9th Louisiana Infantry, and one section, or 46 men of Fenner's battery.[833]

Butler's successor, Banks, ordered General Grover to reoccupy Baton Rouge, and on the morning of December 17th, as Grover's force of 4,500 men approached, "the enemy . . . (probably 500 strong) . . . fled immediately."

Recruitment vs. Draft

Congress passed public law no. 166 on July 17th, 1862, which was an extensive amendment of the militia law of 1795. Its main thrust was to restore flagging recruitment, and it called for 300,000 states' militia. This was in addition to the previous 300,000 volunteer three-year enlistments that had already been called for. Militia service had always been required, and Congress used the old law to avoid passing a specific new draft law. The term of service was extended to nine months from three. Provisions were made for the central government to make all the rules as to its operation, and the states were each issued quotas, which they had to fill by the absurdly short deadline of August 15th.

---

830. O.R. Vol. 15, pp. 552, 553.
831. O.R. Vol. 15, p. 130; Bacon, E., p. 31.
832. O.R. Vol. 15, p. 92.
833. O.R. Vol. 15, pp. 191, 841; Dawson, S. M., p. 198.

This nonsense undoubtedly fooled no one, yet grated on the public mind, and the midterm congressional elections in November threw out many Republicans in the House; the Democrats gaining 28 seats. The administration would have to function with only 85 Republicans versus 72 Democrats, with 16 Unconditional Unionists, 9 Unionists, and 1 independent. Briefly, the Unionists maintained a spectrum of opinions, and though committed to the preservation of the Union, they were willing to listen to compromises on the issues. As Grant puts it in his memoirs, they were not necessarily "for the prosecution of the war to save the Union if it took the last man and the last dollar."[834]

Buried in the verbiage of the new law, at section 23, the President was authorized "to receive into the service of the United States, for the purpose of constructing entrenchments, or performing camp service, or any other labor, *or any other military or naval service for which they may be found competent, persons of African descent* . . ." Here, Congress was moving faster than Lincoln.

In dire need of more troops after the depletion of Williams' ranks at Vicksburg II and the attack on Baton Rouge, Butler had taken some decisive steps of his own. In July, he had authorized the recruiting of Southern white volunteers for Louisiana Regiments. Major Richard E. Holcomb of the 13th Connecticut Volunteers opened a recruiting station in New Orleans for the 1st Louisiana Regiment,[835] and Charles J. Paine of Butler's staff began raising the 2nd Louisiana Regiment.[836]

On August 8th, the very day that the Western district of the Department of the South was transferred to his command,[837] Butler ordered troops from Pensacola, as was noted in the previous chapter. At this moment in time, it is clear that he would not have received general orders no. 94 and no. 99 from the adjutant general's office dated August 4th and August 9th respectively, which quoted the new militia law and its operational regulations (which were silent on the matter of drafting colored men, free or otherwise). Regardless, Halleck would soon inform him that he could expect no reinforcements. Recruiting had become difficult as the public perception of the prosecution of the war had turned sour, and Butler needed troops *now*.[838]

Butler was intensely aware of the fear Lincoln had of arming the slaves. (This was before the preliminary Emancipation Proclamation of September 1862, and Lincoln was still entertaining the fond hope that the South would return to the

---

834. Grant, U. S., Vol. 1, p. 443. Sanger, G. P., Vol. 12, pp. 597–600.
835. Sprague, H., pp. 71, 72.
836. Irwin, R. B., *Battles and Leaders*, Vol. III, p. 582; O.R. Vol. 15, p. 254.
837. O.R. Vol. 15, p. 544.
838. O.R. Ser. III, Vol. 2, pp. 291, 292, 333–335; O.R. Vol. 15, p. 555. He received his answer on November 20th, O.R. Vol. 15, p. 601, that the whole matter was left up to his "judgment and discretion . . ."

fold. He did not want to offend the slaveholders.)[839] Wishing to avoid a repeat of the controversy that had resulted when one of his Vermonters, General Phelps, had proposed to organize and arm fugitive slaves,[840] the clever Butler found his way around the "vexed question." His fine point of reasoning was that the group of blacks he had in mind had been free from the beginning, and were not freed slaves. They were the Native Guards, the Confederate militia unit raised by Governor Moore in 1861 and, as we have seen, left behind at the fall of New Orleans.

On that busy day of August 8th, he invited some 20 of the former militia officers to a conference in which it was determined that there was great enthusiasm for recruiting for a Union Native Guard organization. The meeting broke up with the promise that two regiments could be raised in 10 days. Butler gave them "a fortnight." On August 22nd, at the designated Touro Charity Building, Butler "saw such a sight as I never saw before: Two thousand" men in white "biled shirts" were on hand ready to be mustered into the Union army.[841] Before the end of his tenure, Butler had raised the 1st and 2nd Louisiana Infantry Regiments; Barrett's, Godfrey's, and Williamson's troops of cavalry; the 1st and 2nd Regiments of the Native Guards Infantry; and the 1st Louisiana Native Guards Heavy Artillery.[842] He proudly noted that, altogether, his forces were now 3,000 stronger than when he began the campaign.

As previously noted, the question of recruiting from those of African descent had come to a head almost simultaneously elsewhere, as has been briefly noted. On August 25th, 1862, Secretary of War Stanton had given authority to Gen. Rufus R. Saxton, in the Department of the South, "to arm, uniform, equip, and receive into the service of the United States such number of volunteers of African descent that you deem expedient, not exceeding 5000 . . ."[843]

---

839. Nicolay & Hay, Vol. VI, p. 145: Letter to Reverdy Johnson, July 26th, 1862: "they [the South] are annoyed by the presence of General Phelps. They also know the remedy – know how to be cured of General Phelps. Remove the necessity of his presence . . . to take their place in the Union upon the old terms."
840. Butler, B. F., pp. 488, 489. Phelps resigned on August 22nd. O.R. 15, p. 555; Wilson, J. T., pp. 183–193.
841. O.R. Vol. 15, pp. 556–557, 559; Butler, pp. 492, 493; Wilson, J. T., pp. 194, 195.
842. The 1st Regiment Native Guards was mustered into service on September 27th, 1862, and the 2nd on October 12th. The 1st Regiment Native Guards Heavy Artillery was mustered on November 19th, 1862. The 3rd Native Guards Infantry was mustered on June 6th, 1863, under Banks; Williams, G. W., p. 99; O.R. Vol. 15, pp. 711, 713.
843. Saxton had been assigned to run the abandoned plantations in General Hunter's Department of the South (South Carolina, Georgia, and Florida, until Florida was transferred to the Department of the Gulf on August 8, 1862). The 5,000 to be armed was in addition to 5,000 laborers authorized. O.R. Vol. 14, pp. 189, 190–193, 369, 377; O.R. Vol. 15, pp. 158–161. A Kansas colored regiment had been organized in August, but was not mustered into Federal service until January 13, 1863; Fox, W., p. 53.

By September, Butler had seen rumors of his replacement in the "secession newspapers";[844] and perhaps what he had done, or would do, in his future short tenure would be moot. In any event, in November, Butler again brought up the recruitment issue to Halleck, noting that "more than seventy days since"[845] he had called attention to his action and that he now assumed that, by the lack of response, it had been approved.

Saxton's 1st South Carolina Volunteers went into action on the 13th of November, but it was Butler's 1st Louisiana Native Guards who were sent into action in the Lafourche Campaign, west of New Orleans, on October 26th. Thus, we have to credit Benjamin Butler with being the first Union general to organize and deploy troops of African descent, former slaves or otherwise. A further point regarding Butler's Native Guards was the promise that they would have colored line officers (those up to major). They expected the same rights from the Union as was granted by the Confederacy (!), namely, black officers (figure 8).[846]

FIGURE 8. LINE OFFICERS OF THE 1ST LOUISIANA NATIVE GUARDS

Though the Native Guards were to be recruited only from free blacks, who was to question any healthy black man who appeared before the recruiting officer?

---

844. O.R. Vol.15, p. 558
845. O.R. Vol.15, p.162.
846. *Harper's Weekly*, February 28th, 1863, p. 143; figure 7, p. 133. Typical of many of the newspaper reports of the time, the information is apocryphal. None of those named in the picture appear in the subsequent roster published in the *Black Phalanx*, J. T. Wilson, p. 176.

Thus, some in the 1st, and many in the 2nd Regiment were former slaves, including those recruited by Capt. F. E. Dumas, himself black and a slaveholder, who had organized a company of his own slaves.

The East

Pope's Army of Virginia was tested in the Battle of Cedar Mountain and brought to a standstill on August 9th. One of Pope's corps commanders was Gen. Nathaniel P. Banks.

Stonewall Jackson's shrewd moves forced Pope to retreat, first to the line of the Rappahannock River and then beyond, in the opening battles of Lee's Northern Virginia Campaign. Pope was then decisively defeated at Second Manassas on August 28th–30th, and he retreated toward Washington. He suffered another loss at Chantilly on September 1st. Lee was now free to invade Maryland. Pope's army and the Army of the Potomac were then consolidated, with McClellan in command.[847]

Lee now attempted to cross the Blue Ridge Mountains at the gaps at South Mountain and was repulsed on September 14th. However, Harper's Ferry fell to the Confederates the next day, all 11,000 of the garrison surrendering.[848] Lee's main force then retreated behind Antietam Creek near Sharpsburg, Maryland. Here, McClellan assaulted on the morning of September 17th, with 70,000 troops versus Lee's 40,000. A classic blunder was made by McClellan in that he did not commit all his force in a coordinated manner. McClellan's force suffered 12,400 casualties in the battle, called Sharpsburg by the Confederates, and Antietam by the Federals. It proved to be the bloodiest in any single day of the war.[849] Lee suffered 10,300, certainly a very high percentage compared to the Union. Lee's strong rearguard action at Shepherdstown on September 19th–20th allowed him to safely cross the Potomac and return his battered army back into Virginia. Despite the fact that Antietam was inconclusive, the South had failed to invade the North, and Lincoln was convinced that now was the time to pursue a subject that had been broached back in July: removing the *necessity* for the war.[850] He would bring the subject of the Emancipation Proclamation before the cabinet.

McClellan then returned to his old ways. He refused to follow Lee on grounds that his army needed reorganization and was ill equipped: not enough shoes, horses, and clothing.[851] He did not move from the north side of the Potomac until

---

847. O.R. Vol. 19/ II, pp. 183, 188; Cedar Mountain CWSAC VA 022; Second Manassas CWSAC VA 026; Chantilly CWSAC VA 029.
848. O.R. Vol. 19/I, p. 148.
849. O.R. Vol. 19/I, pp. 189–200, 811–813; Nicolay & Hay, Vol. VI, pp. 131–146; CWSAC, MD 003.
850. Nicolay & Hay, Vol. VI, p. 151.
851. O.R. Vol. 19/I, pp. 68–85; Vol. 19/II, pp. 397, 424, 442, 464, 485, 490.

October 26th.[852] An exasperated Lincoln replaced him with Ambrose Burnside on November 5th, 1862.[853]

Recognizing the need, and undoubtedly pressured to do something quickly, Burnside issued plans on November 7th,[854] for an attack on Richmond via Fredericksburg; the resulting Battle of Fredericksburg, which lasted from December 11th to December 15th, saw the 100,000-man Union Army make a series of futile frontal assaults on 72,500 entrenched Confederates. The result could have been easily predicted, given Burnside's barren strategy. After 13,000 casualties, compared to the 4,500 of the Confederates, Burnside withdrew.

The attitude of the people of the north at the close of 1862, if the midterm elections had not already shown it, may be able to be summed up with a quote from Gideon Welles' diary for Monday, December 29th, 1862:[855]

> There is discontent in the public mind. The management of our public affairs is not satisfactory. Our army operations have been a succession of disappointments. General Halleck has accomplished nothing, and has not the public confidence. General McClellan has intelligence but not decision; operated understandingly but was never prepared. With General Halleck there seems neither military capacity nor decision. I have not heard nor seen a clear and satisfactory proposition or movement on his part yet.
>
> Information reaches us that General Butler has been superseded at New Orleans by General Banks. The wisdom of this change I question. . . . I have reason to believe that Seward has effected this . . . and that he has been prompted by the foreigners to do it.

The reason would never become public, even to Butler, though he later correctly named his nemesis as Seward, who feared offending France.[856]

McClernand

On August 25th, 1862, General Grant, at Cairo, Illinois, received the following telegram from Halleck:[857]

> Gen. J. A. McClernand will repair to Springfield, Illinois and assist the Governor in organizing volunteers.

John A. McClernand – a war Democrat from Springfield, Illinois, and

---

852. O.R. Vol. 19/II, p. 497.
853. O.R. Vol. 19/II, p. 545.
854. O.R. Vol. 19/II, pp. 552, 555; CWSAC, VA 028.
855. Welles, G., Vol. 1, pp. 209, 210.
856. Butler, p. 530. It was eventually disclosed to Gideon Welles, (*Diary*, p. 304), as "a necessity to appease France."
857. O.R. Vol. 17/II, p. 187.

Lincoln's colleague and rival when he served in the House of Representatives – had volunteered his services to the Lincoln administration while serving in the 37th Congress and was appointed a brigadier general on May 17, 1861, the same day as Grant, Sherman, Pope, and others.[858] On September 4th, 1861, he was appointed the commander of the post at Cairo[859] in the Western Department by Grant, then the commander of the Military District of Southeast Missouri.

Under Grant, McClernand had participated in the battles of Belmont, forts Henry and Donelson, and Shiloh. At Belmont, both he and Grant had their horses shot out from under them, and Grant issued a congratulatory order to all the troops for their "gallant" behavior.[860] No suspicion of McClernand was evident, except Grant may have been curious to note that McClernand addressed a separate report of the battle to General McClellan in addition to his verbose report to Grant.[861] In the events preceding Grant's attack on Fort Henry (chapter 5), McClernand had led the reconnaisance into Kentucky in the direction of Columbus, and though Grant had ordered the move and remained in overall command,[862] McClernand's report was addressed to Halleck.[863]

Even if his 1st Division did not have any actual contact with the enemy at the attack on Fort Henry, McClernand nevertheless took the spotlight and renamed it Fort Foote. Fair enough, that gallant naval officer deserved the compliment, but the political McClernand had initiated the move. The attack on Fort Donelson saw McClernand's command in the thick of the battle, and no aspersions had been cast as to his determination or heroism, but his *twelve-page* report of his exploits had to be called out as "highly colored" by Grant.[864]

After Shiloh, McClernand supplied a separate report to Lincoln, which was unabashedly self-laudatory.[865] McClernand's excessively verbose report to Grant, consisting of nine pages, was criticized by Grant for its inaccuracy, particularly for events covered which were not a part of the actions of McClernand's 1st Division. McClernand was revealing the behavior for which he became well-known: his pretentiousness and a resentment of Grant, and the cultivation of Lincoln and Stanton for a more prestigious assignment. A westerner, he appreciated the value of the Mississippi to the economies of the western states, and had his eye on the

---

858. *Encyclopedia Britannica*, Vol. 13, 1911, p. 202; Nicolay & Hay, The Century, February 1887, p. 532.
859. O.R. Vol. 3, pp. 145 and 470; Walke, H., The Century, January 1885, p. 426. Wilson, J. H., The Century, October 1885, pp. 949, 950.
860. O.R. Ser. I, Vol. 3, p. 274.
861. O.R. Vol. 3, To McClellan, p. 277; to Grant, pp. 277–283.
862. O.R. Vol. 7, p. 541.
863. O.R. Vol. 7, pp. 68–72.
864. O.R. Vol. 7, pp. 170–182.
865. O.R. Vol. 10/I, pp. 113–114. Report to Grant, pp. 114–122. Grant's remarks, p. 114.

drive against the most important strategic point left in the west: Vicksburg.

As the buildup of Grant's army of the Tennessee progressed, thanks to McClernand's recruiting efforts, more staff was needed. It was fortunate that Gen. James H. Wilson was named as Grant's engineer officer. Arriving from Washington in October, he informed Grant about the intrigues there. "I became satisfied that the honors of his command would be given to McClernand, if the President and Secretary of War could manage it without a public scandal."[866] The cloud of doubt about Grant since Donelson had not gone away, but Lincoln was cautious. McClernand would be promoted to a position that should satisfy him, and Grant would be retained, for the time being, at least.

Grant was given the command of the newly constituted Department of the Tennessee on October 16th, 1862,[867] and the 13th Corps was constituted on the 24th, with Grant given the command of both.[868] Grant made his first move toward Vicksburg by marching south toward La Grange, Tennessee, on November 2nd, with troops from Bolivar and Corinth. He reports: "If found practicable, I will go on to Holly Springs, and maybe Grenada . . ." Given clear permission by Halleck on November 11th to conduct matters in his department as he saw fit, and with many of the units that had been recruited by McClernand having arrived, Grant, never idle, got busy. He wrote to W. T. Sherman[869] on the 14th, "I think it advisable to move on the enemy as soon as you can leave Memphis" to Tallahatchie, thus forming the right wing of Grant's forces, with Grant then moving to Holly Springs. Sherman marched on November 25th, 1862.[870]

Grant was again tipped off about moves in Washington to put McClernand in command of the river expedition to Vicksburg, this time by his mentor, Rep. Elihu Washburne of Illinois. He immediately detached Sherman from his march to Vicksburg, and sent him back to Memphis to take command there. The purpose was to co-opt the Vicksburg expedition, with Sherman in command.[871] Grant then, mistakenly, on December 14th, 1862, confided to Halleck,[872] in part:

> I am sorry to say it, but I would regard it as particularly unfortunate to have either McClernand or Wallace sent to me.

This was to no avail. On December 18th, Grant's troops and the numbers recruited by McClernand and sent into Grant's department were directed to be reorganized[873] as the:

---

866. Wilson, J. H., The Century, Jan. 1885, p. 950.
867. O.R. Vol. 17/I, p. 4; O.R. Vol. 16/II, pp. 641–642.
868. O.R. Vol. 17/II, p. 469. Grant's move: Vol. 17/I, p. 466.
869. O.R. Vol. 17/I, p. 347. To Sherman: Vol. 17/II, pp. 347, 348.
870. O.R. Vol. 17/II, p. 361.
871. Grant, U. S., Vol. I, p. 428–431.
872. O.R. Vol. 52/I, p. 314.
873. O.R. Vol. 17/I, pp. 4, 5, 476.

13th Corps, McClernand
15th Corps, Sherman
16th Corps, Hurlbut
17th Corps, McPherson

By this move Lincoln probably believed that his debt to McClernand and the western governors – Yates of Illinois, Morton of Indiana, and Kirkwood of Iowa, who, though Republicans all, had heartily welcomed and supported McClernand – was fulfilled.[874]

McClernand, regardless of his faults, had been a gift to the Lincoln administration. He was there to witness the lapse in the Union initiatives in the west and, being from the area, he understood the economic impact that the closure of the Mississippi River had. Shipments of grain and livestock to the east were disrupted. They were now limited to the lake routes that were closed in the winter and to a railroad of limited capacity and which had raised rates to prohibitive levels. There was great popular sentiment for the opening of the Mississippi. A well-known politician from the home area was welcomed when he had proposed his expedition to Vicksburg and had met with eminent success when he requested troops "outside the call" – that is, above the previously established quotas.[875] In all, by December 12th, 1862, he had raised more than 40,000 troops,[876] probably more than could have been done in the same time frame by a stranger appointed by the administration, mired as it was in the latter stages of the Peninsular Campaign and, as Gideon Welles notes, with a general-in-chief who has "shirked responsibility in his present position" and is "in short a moral coward worth but little except as a critic and director of operations."[877] Lincoln should have thanked his lucky stars that there was someone like McClernand in the right place at the right time.

The Department of the Gulf

When Butler first took over New Orleans, it was in desperate condition; the people were starving. The blockade had reduced commerce, and food was scarce. Butler was swift and determined in his humanitarian actions, on May 3rd authorizing safe conduct to a shipload of flour to come from Mobile, the safe conduct of supplies on the Opelousas Railroad, and safe conduct to supply boats known to be at the junction of the Red and Mississippi rivers, and all those with cargoes of cotton and sugar.[878] On May 8th, he wrote to Secretary of State Seward, asking if the blockade

---

874. O.R. Vol. 17/II, pp. 332–334; O.R. Ser. I, Vol. 52/I, p. 431.
875. O.R. Vol. 17/II, pp. 282, 300, 308.
876. O.R. Vol. 17/II, pp. 401, 415.
877. Welles, G., Vol. 1, p. 180.
878. O.R. Vol. 7, pp. 720–722.

could now be lifted, which was done by Lincoln's proclamation of May 12th.[879] This also freed commerce at Beaufort and Port Royal, long since in Union hands.

Initially, there was danger of disease from filthy conditions due to disorder and neglect, and on May 9th, he requested the mayor to employ the starving to clean up the city.

In a May 16th letter to Secretary of State Seward, Butler notes his suspicion of the actions of some of the foreign consuls, whom he would soon require to take an oath of neutrality and to surrender their arms. His men discovered "a large amount of Confederate specie," subsequently disclosed as $800,000 in Mexican coin, "bearing the mark of the Citizens Bank of New Orleans,"[880] in the liquor store of the Netherlands consul. It had been prepared for shipment out, suspected to the Confederacy. This was but one of many irregularities suspected of the consuls. He discovered that the "British Guard" had sent their arms and equipment to Beauregard after New Orleans had fallen, etc. Investigating and putting a stop to these sorts of activities nevertheless involved him in contention with the State Department and Secretary Seward's fear of offending any of the foreign powers who might find cause to interfere in the war. A State Department representative, Reverdy Johnson, "that Baltimore secessionist," was later sent to look into some of the complaints. He caved in, "in every case" reversing Butler.[881] It was a signal of the beginning of the end for Butler.

Butler's administration of New Orleans was going to be tough, but efficient, as promised in his declaration of martial law on May 1.[882] Some of the controversy was created by die-hard Confederate sympathizers that would try to blunt every move and make trouble for any Yankee, such as the feigned outrage that resulted from his infamous General Orders No. 28, of May 15th, in which he declared,[883]

> As the officers and soldiers of the United States have been subject to repeated insults from the women . . . of New Orleans . . . it is ordered that hereafter when any female shall by word, gesture, or movement shall insult or show contempt . . . She shall be regarded as a woman of the town plying her avocation.

Another special order was exceedingly harsh. On June 5th, William Mumford, "having been convicted before the military commission of treason and an overt act thereof, tearing down the United States flag from a public building [the U.S. Mint]. . . It is ordered that he be executed . . . on Saturday, June 7 . . ."[884]

---

879. O.R. Vol. 7, p. 723; O.R. Ser. III, Vol. 2, p. 31.
880. O.R. Vol. 7, p. 723; Vol. 15, p. 422; O.R. Ser. III, Vol. 2, p. 116–125.
881. Butler, B. F., p. 522.
882. O.R. Vol. 7, p. 717.
883. O.R. Vol. 15, p. 426.
884. O.R. Vol. 15, pp. 465, 469.

More people were sent from Washington to look over Butler's shoulder, notably by the Treasury Department. At the end of a long letter from Secretary Chase, dated June 24th, which sternly opined on the consequences of illegal trading, then meandered about with platitudes, and finished with:

> Permit me to commend to your support and confidence my two special agents Messrs. Denison and Bonzano, and express the hope that they may be useful to your arduous duties.
>
> Yours,
S.P. CHASE[885]

We have seen that official observers had been on to the scene elsewhere. Assistant Secretary of War Scott was present in Halleck's department at the time when Pope's army was diverted from the support of Admiral Foote in April (chapter 5). Perhaps Chase's people were really sent as help, and were innocent of motive, but in fact, combined with Seward's fear of France, they helped to spell the end for Butler. In future, we shall see that another observer, Charles Dana, sent by a suspicious Stanton into Grant's Northern operations, resulted in the reverse: he became Grant's advocate.

George S. Denison's first letter to Chase is dated June 28th, at New Orleans.[886] He follows on July 19: ". . . the military rule here . . . is not severe enough." He strangely has not yet fallen in with the popular opinion that Butler was a "Beast" after his General Orders No. 28 and the execution of Mumford.

Then there was the oath. On June 10th, Butler had issued General Orders No. 41,[887] requiring all officials, "Judges, justices, sheriffs, attorneys, notaries, and all officers of the law whatever, and all persons who have ever been or who have ever claimed to be citizens of the United States in this Department"; plus, anyone looking for a passport or official action of almost any description, must take and subscribe to an oath of allegiance before their request could be heard. The oath was: "I do solemnly swear (or affirm) that I will bear true faith and allegiance to the United States of America and will support the Constitution thereof."

An oath of allegiance was nothing new, Major French had ordered it at Key West[888] back on September 6th, 1861, and on the Confederate side, General Lovell had ordered it at New Orleans in March of 1862.[889]

September 9:

> . . . for while all admire his great ability, many of his soldiers think him

---

885. O.R. Ser. III, Vol. 2, p. 174.
886. Chase, S. P., Vol. II, pp. 310–342.
887. O.R. Vol. 15, pp. 483, 484. A modified one was required of all foreigners.
888. O.R. Vol. 6, pp. 665, 666. This was authorized by Lincoln on May 10th, 1861; see O.R. Ser. II, Vol. 2. p. 577.
889. O.R. Vol. 6, pp. 665, 666, 860, 861.

selfish and cold hearted, and many . . . think he is interested in the speculations of his brother (Col. Butler) and others . . . Notwithstanding the impression above mentioned it would be difficult to find a man capable of filling Gen. Butler's place . . . The city is very healthy, and the Yellow Fever is no longer feared.

September 24:

Gen. Butler does more work than any other man in Louisiana. Every thought seems to be given to the interest of the Government, and his powers of endurance are remarkable . . . It is to be regretted that his brother does business here, but I do not think that the General is interested in his brother's speculations.

On the 5th October your regulations of August 28th reached me. I immediately stopped all trade with the enemy, [Denison was now Collector of Customs] and as this brought me in contact with the persons who have been conducting the trade, I acquired much information. Almost all of the information to be given in this letter has been collected this week.

A brother of Gen. Butler is here, who is called Col. Butler, though he occupies no position in the army . . . [He] has made between one and two million dollars since the capture of the city.

There are two channels of trade with the rebels – the River and Lake Pontchatrain . . . River trade must be conducted by steamboats. There are eight or nine riverboats here, all seized and in the hands of the military authorities. Col. Butler has used these boats as he pleased, for carrying up and bringing down freight . . . Of late, frequently, one or two infantry companies would accompany a boat taking up cargo and bringing back produce . . .

The lake traffic was conducted by private schooners, laden with salt for the Confederate army. Two dollars per sack was the price of a permit to ship it. One thousand sacks were on a single shipment that Denison had seized. Denison estimated that 10,000 had been sent recently and traded for cotton at the rate of 10 sacks per bale.

October 10: (Private and Unofficial)

Ever since the capture of this city, a brisk trade has been carried on with the rebels, by a few persons, under military permits, frequently with military assistance and as I believe, much to the benefit of some of the principal military commanders of the Department . . .

October 27: At the end of a long letter on other subjects, Denison says:

I know of but one fault to be found with Gen. Butler. He has (in my opinion) been altogether too willing to permit his friends to make fortunes.

December 10:

>An occurrence has just taken place which causes me to feel much indignation and some chagrin. Col. Butler has three or four men in his employ who manage his business for him. The principal one is a Mr. Wyer. Some days ago Wyer loaded a vessel for Matamoras. She was loaded in the New Basin, and when she got into the Lake, ran into Ponchitoula . . . I am satisfied that it was a predetermined plan to take the cargo to . . . the rebels . . . I am also satisfied that Col. Butler was the sole owner . . .

December 23:

>I do not know your opinion and wishes concerning Gen. Butler, but it is certain that his removal gives great satisfaction to all classes including officers, soldiers and citizens.

The military developments that ran parallel with the above chronology, from after the evacuation of Baton Rouge until the end of the year, is difficult to characterize in one general statement, except, perhaps, to say "regrouping for another fight." Butler, retrenching and trying to strengthen his command, found himself facing Confederate forces that were also rebuilding. On August 20th, Maj. Gen. Richard Taylor was assigned to the command of the District of Louisiana. Opposite Grant, Van Dorn had been relieved after his defeat at the second Battle at Corinth, and on October 1st, Maj. Gen. John C. Pemberton took over at Vicksburg, heading a up new Confederate Department of Mississippi and East Louisiana. He would take no new initiatives toward New Orleans, being satisfied with the occupation of Port Hudson;[890] but Butler could not have been sure of that in August.

Taylor stepped into what was the relative vacuum of the Western Louisiana district of the Confederate Trans-Mississippi Department. Described by Governor Moore and Gen. A. G. Blanchard (who was sent to evaluate the condition of the district) as destitute of arms (the small number of which had been seized by Van Dorn in June, another of his missteps) and generally abandoned by the Confederacy when Lovell left.[891] There were only two regiments and one battalion of six companies of volunteer troops, only partially armed with shotguns, in the district in July.

Taylor's first directive from the War Department was for "carrying out the enrollment act in western Louisiana, in hastening forward recruits to fill the

---

890. O.R. Vol. 15, pp. 2, 174. In Taylor's words, his problem on the western side of the river was "a difficulty which was greatly augmented by the withdrawal of a considerable portion of the forces menacing New Orleans on the eastern side of the river about the period of my arrival here."
891. O.R. Vol. 15, p. 766, 779. Examination of Taylor's *Destruction and Reconstruction*, pp. 108–110, seems to confirm a total of about 2,000 troops, though the definition of a regiment can be misleading, as noted in chapter 5, where Tennessee "regiments" at Fort Henry only totaled 200 men each.

regiments of the Louisiana Brigade serving in northern Virginia, and in assembling conscripts for further assignment or for future organization of the reserve."[892] The Confederate government was still apparently in the same mind-set as before the fall of New Orleans: more interested in the eastern campaigns. After some reconsideration, a more detailed set of instructions were sent to Taylor two days later which would give him cause to regard his mission as more important, and more daunting, than mere recruiting. He was to prevent the use of the rivers and bayous of "that region of country to the occupiers." He was to "embarrass the enemy in the navigation of the Mississippi River . . . organize and equip light batteries . . . at points suitable for the attack on passing vessels of the enemy," and he was to "confine the enemy to the narrowest limits and recover lost ground, if possible."

Butler would, of course, try to maintain a presence as far beyond New Orleans as possible until he could build up his forces, and Taylor would conduct guerilla raids on the Yankee outposts until he could mount a large enough operation to recover lost ground. The navy would greatly aid Butler. Still patrolling the river after the Battle of Baton Rouge, Farragut had bombarded Donaldsonville on August 9th, and on August 10th, the *Essex* raided Bayou Sara, above Port Hudson. The navy landed and seized some hogsheads of sugar, meeting no resistance. The Confederate report of the incident notes that their rangers were "either at the Atchafalaya 45 miles above, or gone to Opelousas . . ."[893] Opelousas, on the western side of the river, was now the seat of the Moore government.

From the north, the gunboat flotilla of Flag Officer Davis, in the company of Ellet's rams, with two regiments from the Army of the Southwest, was showing its presence above Vicksburg. An expedition under Lt. Commander S. L. Phelps captured the rebel steamer *Fair Play* with a cargo of 1,200 Enfield rifles and 4,000 muskets, at Milliken's Bend on August 18th.[894] Pressure from this direction helped to keep arms out of the hands of the Confederates, but it was limited, and Gideon Welles had come to believe that a younger and more energetic man was needed. D. D. Porter would be named to replace Davis in October.[895]

The presence of Confederates near St. Charles Courthouse and Boutte Station, only twenty-four miles west of New Orleans, on the New Orleans, Opelousas, and Great Western Railroad, led Butler to order a raid on August 29th. It was conducted by elements of the 8th Vermont Regiment and the 2nd Massachusetts Cavalry. A handful of prisoners were taken.

On September 4th and 5th, Taylor made his first move in retaliation. Taylor

---

892. O.R. Vol. 15, pp. 789, 791.
893. O.R. Vol. 15, p. 129.
894. ORN Ser. I, Vol. 23, pp. 241, 242, 296, 297; O. R. Vol. 13, p. 241, 242; Welles, G., Vol. I, pp. 157, 158, 167.
895. Welles, G., Vol. I, pp. 157, 158.

was particularly familiar with the area. His family plantation, "Fashion" was here.[896] The post of a detachment of the 8th Vermont, near Bayou des Allemandes Station, to quote Taylor, "as being the especial center from raid on which the helpless inhabitants were undertaken" was targeted (figure 9). He assigned Colonel Waller's battalion of the 13th Texas Cavalry,[897] who had recently joined him, to the raid. Being a lifelong resident of the area, he was able to carefully instruct them as to the "roads and paths through plantations and swamps" that could be used to approach the outpost without detection. Moving by night, with local guides, Waller's troops "gained the enemy's rear, advanced on his camp, and, after a slight resistance, captured two companies of infantry and the guns."

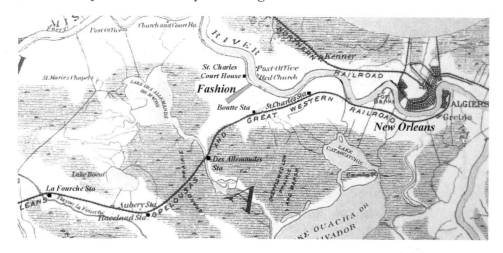

FIGURE 9

Butler's report and that of Col. Stephen Thomas[898] of the 8th Vermont differ harshly and substantially from Taylor's. Butler and Thomas had it that Waller's men hid by the railroad tracks at Boutte Station, east of Bayou des Allemandes Station, and intercepted a train headed for Algiers for supplies. The tracks had been switched, causing the train to run onto a siding. Numbers of the 8th, riding in flatcars, were shot before and after the train collided with an empty passenger car standing on the siding. Prisoners taken were later used as hostages under a flag of truce to attract those members of a security force, on a second train, which had

---

896. Figure 9, altered portion of Atlas plate 156. Location of "Fashion" from Persec's 1858 map showing landowners on the lower Mississippi; Library of Congress.
897. Taylor, p. 110. Taylor included Gen. John Pratt and the Louisiana militia in the raid though makes only a deprecating reference to them: "One or two companies of mounted men, armed with fowling pieces, had been organized under authority from Governor Moore, and Colonel Waller's battalion of mounted riflemen had recently arrived from Texas. These constituted the Confederate army in this quarter." Pratt had been called into service by Governor Moore on May 8th (O.R. Vol. 15, p. 742).
898. O.R. Vol. 15, pp. 132–134; Taylor, p. 111. Taylor specifically refers only to Waller.

set out to escort the first train into Algiers. Surprised by this lawless ruse, they also surrendered. The ugly results that the dead or the dying wounded and prisoners were robbed and slashed by sabers was reported by a relief force, which did not arrive in time to engage the rebels.

The result of the work was 9 killed, 27 wounded, 155 missing, and the loss of enough good weapons to equip Waller's men, who threw away their "worthless altered flintlocks" and then fled north toward the river, in the direction of Fashion. Taylor wrote in his memoir: "This trifling success, the first in the state since the fall of New Orleans, attracted attention . . ."

On the 7th, Butler sent out an expedition, including the 21st Indiana Regiment, looking for the attackers. It departed New Orleans by boat, in two groups, with the intent of one landing below and one above where the attackers were thought to be; about twenty miles out. They appeared to have trapped Waller's men between the Mississippi to the east and the swamp of Lake Des Allemandes to the west. Never mind, the Texans escaped by abandoning literally everything and wading through the swamp. Their horses were left in the swamp tied to trees in waist-deep water. Two hundred or more were recovered that day, and on the 8th, 50 more. A few more had to be destroyed.[899] Col. J. W. McMillan of the 21st Indiana concluded his report of the event with: "We captured over 50 prisoners . . . found but two dead and three wounded . . . captured about 300 horses and saddles, 2 rebel flags, 1 French flag, shot guns, pistols, and, indeed, nearly everything they had with them, even their spurs."

These actions confirmed two things. Taylor's strength was growing, and the level of desperation and duplicity of which war had made some men capable.

Of course, the navy was actively keeping up the coastal blockade throughout this time. Of interest were the Sabine and Neches rivers in Texas and their use as a supply route to western Louisiana. The navy captured the town of Sabine City on September 25th, and kept up operations between there and Lake Calcasieu through October 12th.[900]

During these operations, the importance of the Sabine to the Confederacy was confirmed in that the quantity of goods that had passed through the blockade into the area was described as "enormous, and large quantities of cotton have been exported." Eight ships, four of British registry, and four of Confederate, were taken as prizes. On board the British schooner *West Florida* was found a most controversial and damaging pass attributed to Butler. The letter, dated September 24th, and marked "confidential," gave permission to the ship to proceed from New Orleans to Matamoros but to exchange her "present cargo" for cotton at Sabine Pass. The

---

899. O.R. Vol. 15, pp. 135–137. This action is referred to as the battle at Bonnet Carre. Noel, T., *A Campaign...* p. 45. It reports: lost 2 killed, 21 prisoners, and 256 horses.
900. ORN Ser. I, Vol. 19, pp. 217–236. Butler pass, p. 227, to Welles from Farragut, p. 230, rebuke from Stanton, p. 231.

cargo was salt, a commodity desired by the Confederacy, which had plenty of cotton to exchange. A copy of the letter was forwarded to Farragut, who reported it to Gideon Welles by letter, which was delayed until October 28th, after he had returned to Pensacola. Welles informed the President. Butler got off with a rebuke from Stanton dated November 11th. It was mild: ". . . that you will not issue similar passes without further instructions from this department." Stanton probably did not make as much of the issue as he might have because it was clear that Butler's regime was already history. General Banks had received his orders replacing Butler three days before.

Butler began reorganizing for a new campaign at the end of September, and elements of what was called the Reserve Brigade[901] were assigned. It was to consist of the 12th and 13th Connecticut Volunteers, 75th New York, 1st Louisiana, 7th Vermont, Carruth's 6th Massachusetts Battery, Thompson's 1st Maine Battery, Perkins' 2nd Massachusetts Cavalry, and the three newly recruited companies of Louisiana cavalry – Barrett's, Godfrey's, and Williamson's – all under the command of Godfrey Weitzel.

Weitzel had been promoted to brigadier general from a position as a lieutenant on Butler's staff on August 29th. Battery L had known him from his brief stay as engineer officer for the defenses of Fort Pickens from the time of the landing on April 19th to September 17th, 1861.[902]

Weitzel's earlier career had placed him in a position to be a major strategist for Butler. After graduating from West Point in 1855 and assigned to the engineers, he had worked on the construction and repairs of the defenses of the lower Mississippi for four years. J. G. Barnard of the secret board of officers had recommended Weitzel to accompany Butler on the expedition to New Orleans, and he had been appointed the chief engineer on Butler's staff. He is credited with having planned Butler's land attack and then accompanying it with a group of pioneers.

The Lafourche Campaign

This, the last campaign in the department under Butler, successfully brought the area west of New Orleans under Union control to its farthest extent: eighty miles, as far as Berwick Bay, a wide portion of the Atchafalaya River which separated Berwick City and Brashear City. Up until July of 1863, when the siege of Port Hudson ended, this fertile region would be sharply contested and briefly recaptured by Richard Taylor, who had set his sights on the recapture of New Orleans.[903]

---

901. O.R. Vol. 53, pp. 537, 538. Details of training: Sprague, pp. 74, 75.
902. Cullum, Vol. II, p. 606, no. 1678.
903. O.R. Vol. 6, pp. 685, 704, 705. Brashear City is now Morgan City.

Weitzel's Reserve Brigade, with the 7th Vermont having been replaced by the 8th New Hampshire,[904] began training on September 30th at Carrollton, some five miles upriver from New Orleans, at what was christened Camp Kearney. They drilled, practiced skirmishing, and conducted target shooting until a grand review was held on Canal Street on October 18th. On the 24th, they were embarked on transports at Carrolton and headed upriver, arriving below Donaldsonville the next morning, where they met no opposition. The plan[905] of the expedition was to have Weitzel's brigade drive the enemy down Bayou Lafourche, which runs south from Donaldsonville, labeled (1) in figure 10, into the 8th Vermont and the 1st Louisiana Native Guards, who would work their way west along the New Orleans and Opelousas Railroad from Boutte Station.[906] They would link up in the vicinity of the Lafourche rail crossing three miles below Thibodaux (2). The 21st Indiana, in the transport *St. Mary's*, supported by four gunboats under the command of navy lieutenant commander Thomas Buchanan,[907] were to enter the Atchafalaya River and proceed up the river to Brashear City (3) to trap any Confederate retreat across Berwick Bay.

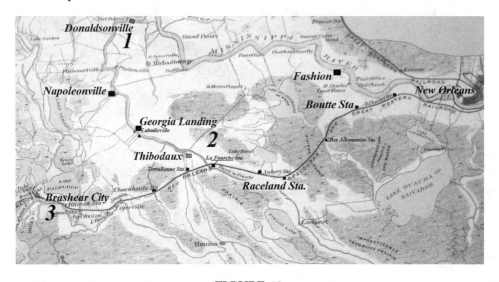

FIGURE 10

The total force for the campaign is estimated at 5,500, given the average strength of 600 to 700[908] for each of the seven regiments and supporting cavalry

---

904. Benedict, G. C., Vol. II, pp. 46, 47. The regiment was transferred to Pensacola on November 13.
905. Sprague, H. B., p. 78; Stanyan, J. M., p. 140; figure 10, Atlas, plate 156, altered.
906. The railroad had been secured to that point but was enemy held at Des Allemandes Station; O.R. Vol. 15, pp. 160, 161.
907. The "light-draught" steamers were built with Butler's funds and manned by the navy. O.R. Vol. 15, pp. 160, 167; ORN Ser. I, Vol. 19, pp. 326–329. Report of Lt. Cdr. Buchanan.
908. Sprague, H. B., p. 89.

and artillery. It was the largest force sent out by Butler since Vicksburg II. It would meet Taylor's small force under Mouton, with a strength of 1,392 men, plus scattered militia of 500 or so more.[909]

Leaving Holcomb's 1st Louisiana to garrison the place, Weitzel started out from Donaldsonville on October 26th. Driving south on both sides of the Lafourche, Weitzel's troops were shadowed by about 500 of Taylor's cavalry, clearly intending to avoid an engagement until Mouton's troops could concentrate at some strong position.[910] Weitzel bivouacked above Napoleonville, got off again next day, and soon made contact with Mouton's pickets above Georgia Landing, about a mile above Labadieville. There, extensive rifle pits and embrasures had been dug into the levee at a bend in the river.

A frontal attack was driven home, the overwhelming numbers of the 12th Connecticut, the 8th New Hampshire, and the 13th Connecticut causing a break in the Confederate line when one of its artillery batteries ran out of ammunition. With its captain wounded, it fell back.[911]

Weitzel listed 97 of his men killed, wounded, and missing while taking 166 prisoners that day and 42 later.[912] Mouton listed 5 killed, 8 wounded, and 186 missing, though he notes an even larger number of conscripts captured who had "lagged behind." Compare this with the report of Lt. D. W. King of the 8th New Hampshire, who wrote that 17 Confederate dead were counted "along the line of our advance" and that they alone had taken 170 prisoners.

The 8th Vermont and the Native Guards made it out to near Raceland Station about twelve miles short of their goal, but sufficient to link up with a detachment sent out by Weitzel on the 29th. The delay was caused by the fact that they had to repair a burned bridge, culverts, and clear the "rank grass" on the track bed, which was so thick it impeded the locomotive.

The naval force sent around to the Atchafalaya did not arrive at Brashear City until November 1st, two days after Mouton's force, the Lafourche Militia Regiment, and others, had passed west over into the Teche country. The report[913] of Lt. Cdr. Thomas Buchanan is filled with tales of woe regarding the difficulties encountered in bringing up the transport *St. Mary's* and his four gunboats, the *Calhoun*, *Diana*, *Estrella*, and *Kinsman*. They had departed Lake Ponchartrain on October 25th but had breakdowns and groundings, even before leaving the mouth of the Mississippi. The channel markers in shallow Atchafalaya Bay had been removed by the Confederate defenders, and Buchanan's boats had repeatedly grounded, both at the bar and in the bay. Buchanan succeeded, however, in trapping Taylor's gunboat, the

---

909. O.R. Vol. 15, p. 176.
910. O.R. Vol. 15, pp. 167–174; Sprague, pp. 79–91.
911. O.R. Vol. 15, pp. 176–180; Stanyan, pp. 142–144.
912. O.R. Vol. 15, pp. 169, 172, 178.
913. ORN Ser. I, Vol. 19, pp. 326–333.

Cotton, about three miles up Bayou Teche. The threat it posed was a measure of the unfinished business of the campaign. Its destruction would be an important goal. The campaign ended on this note.

Butler offers no recrimination in a report on the campaign that he made to Farragut. Construction of the gunboats had only been completed in mid-September, and the volunteer crews had only a short time to mount guns and prepare. Everyone seemed happy that the parishes west of New Orleans were, at last, secure. An eighty-mile fertile area could now be brought under supervision to bring in its crops and, in the process, provide employment for thousands of displaced former slaves. The job of feeding and employing these masses was more urgent than capturing the enemy.[914]

There was considerable recrimination, however, on the Confederate side. A letter written by Governor Moore to Jefferson Davis dated December 1st, 1862, stated, in part:

> I am compelled by the lamentable condition in which Louisiana is now placed to . . . demand, if our own troops cannot be returned to fight for their homes, that at any rate others may be forwarded to prevent the utter ruin of this state. I have hitherto imposed no obstacle to the Confederate Government in obtaining men from this State. Every requisition made upon her has been more than filled, but how can I excuse to my people this depletion of their strength to furnish soldiers to States not more exposed than she is, nor of as much value materially to the country at large, when she is not only invaded, but the occupation of her soil is being extended every day and a mere handful of troops here to resist them. Over 50,000 slaves are now in the possession of Butler's army. Immense sugar plantations are being at this moment worked by his troops that were deserted by their owners on the approach of a force that they could not resist.[915]

Weitzel went into camp one mile below Thibodaux, which he named Camp Stevens. Food was foraged from the plantations of the area including that of Leonidas Polk, now a general serving under Bragg, and at Bragg's plantation, Greenwood, across the bayou from Polk's, four miles north.[916]

This note ended the military initiatives of the Butler administration – rather a success, regardless of all the controversy.

---

914. O.R. Vol. 15, p. 162.
915. O.R. Vol. 53, pp. 836, 837. The number of escaped slaves was also estimated to be 50,000 by the chief quartermaster of the Department of the Gulf, Col. Shaffer: O.R. Ser. III, Vol. 2, pp. 807–808.
916. Sprague, pp. 93, 94; Wm. B. Woods, p. 210; Bragg's plantation was seized by Public Law No. 160, the Confiscation Act, approved by Congress on July 17th, 1862. See O.R. Ser. III, Vol. 2, pp. 275, 276; Sanger, G. P., pp. 589–592.

Banks

The now-successful recruitment of troops by McClernand had assured that the "Northern Column" was revived, and it was felt that a renewed and reinforced effort from the south should meet it. Politics, however, dictated that it would not be commanded by Butler, but by Banks.

Nathaniel P. Banks[917] was born in Waltham, Massachusetts, in 1816. Receiving only a common school education, he began work as a bobbin boy in the Lowell, Massachusetts, cotton factory where his father was superintendent. He studied law and was admitted to the bar. Becoming involved in politics, he was elected to the Massachusetts House and then to the U.S. House, as a coalition candidate of Democrats and Free Soilers. He soon identified with the Republican Party, and when he became Speaker in 1856, his installation was regarded as the first on the national scene for any Republican. He became governor of Massachusetts in 1858 and later succeeded George B. McClellan as President of the Illinois Central Railroad. Thus, he was known to Lincoln.

He was one of the first to offer his services to the President and was appointed a major general on May 16th, 1861. First in command at Annapolis, he was credited with keeping Maryland in the Union, though we know from chapter 3 that Butler had also taken significant and decisive actions there at Baltimore. Banks then commanded two divisions in the Shenandoah Valley in the spring and summer of 1862. Beaten by Stonewall Jackson at Winchester on May 25th, he was driven north across the Potomac. In command of the 2nd Corps of Pope's Army of Virginia, he met Stonewall again at Cedar Mountain on August 9th, and facing superior numbers (US 8,000, CS 16,800), he attacked rather than wait, as ordered.[918] The attack was carried on "with such vigor and impetuosity that he came near defeating Confederate Gen. A. P. Hill. Though finally repulsed, he inflicted such a blow upon Jackson as to give him an exaggerated idea of his numbers, and hearing two days afterward that Banks had been reinforced, Jackson thought it best to retire to the Rapidan."[919] Banks received "injuries," though not specified.[920]

When Pope's Army of Virginia was consolidated with McClellan's Army of the Potomac on September 5th, Banks was given the command of the defenses of Washington. He was also named as commander of the 12th Corps, though Brig. Gen. Alpheus Williams is listed as serving in Bank's place.[921] Under Banks' brief tenure, order was restored in Washington with thousands of wounded, convalescents, and stragglers placed appropriately, in a full army corps, which was sent to

---

917. *Encyclopedia Britannica*, Vol. 3, 1911, p. 333.
918. O.R. Vol. 12/II, p. 133; CWSAC, VA 022.
919. Nicolay & Hay, *Abraham Lincoln: A History*, Vol. VI, New York: The Century Co., 1890, p. 6.
920. Irwin, R. B., *19th Army Corps*, p. 55.
921. O.R. Vol. 19/I, pp. 1,157.

the field. The fortifications were completed, etc. This all attributed to a man still recovering from injury.

On October 27th, he was relieved and ordered on a confidential assignment to New York, where he made his headquarters. The pattern of recruitment for a special expedition, much as those of Butler and McClernand, was followed. Banks was to lead a "southern expedition"[922] to renew the effort to open the Mississippi from that quarter. Well-known and politically well connected, he had succeeded by early November, aided substantially by Stanton's instructions to the governors. For example, to the governor of New York: "All troops in your state not otherwise appropriated are placed at his command . . ."

On November 8th,[923] he was assigned to the command of the Department of the Gulf. Banks' first instructions from Halleck, the day after he was assigned,[924] were to open the Mississippi River: "A military and naval expedition is organizing at Memphis and Cairo to move down the Mississippi and cooperate with you against Vicksburg and any other points which the enemy may occupy on that river." After the capture of Vicksburg, Banks was to, first, destroy the railroads east of there to cut off all connection by rail to Mobile and Atlanta and, second, ascend the Red River as far as it was navigable and "thus open an outlet for the sugar and cotton of Northern Louisiana." This would be a good base for operations in Texas, for Banks was to command not only the Department of the Gulf, but Texas as well.

The governors of the New England states and New York had been remarkable in their cooperation and alacrity in raising the troops required, either forced or aided by the new militia law, but the flaw in this was that many of Banks' regiments were enlisted only for nine months. From another quarter, Banks had received help in the chartering of transports and inspecting them from "Commodore" Vanderbilt the shipping magnate, among others.[925]

By November 1st, Banks reported that he now had three Maine regiments, that Governor Andrew of Massachusetts had assigned the 41st Massachusetts and seven other nine-month militia regiments to the expedition, and that three New York regiments had been assigned, including Corcoran's brigade.[926] On the 7th of the month, 10,000 troops assembling at Fort Monroe were assigned to Banks by Halleck. By November 16th, Halleck told Banks to send the troops from Fort

---

922. O.R. Vol. 19/I, p. 3; O.R. Ser. III, Vol. 2, p. 691.
923. O.R. Vol. 15, pp. 3, 610–613; Irwin, R. B., pp. 59, 60. Note that Butler was relieved only two days after the fall elections. McClellan had been relieved on the 5th. Both he and Butler were Democrats, the fact of which many of Lincoln's critics took note. In Butler's Book, p. 549, Butler gives his opinion of why he was recalled, gracefully laying no political motives at Lincoln's door. Lincoln would soon have misgivings.
924. O.R. Vol. 15, p. 590.
925. O.R. Vol. 15, p. 713; ORN Ser. I, Vol. 19, p. 420.
926. O.R. Vol. 15, pp. 705, 706, 712, 713, 784, 879, 913, 955.

Monroe without waiting for those from New York. Banks finally announced he would sail on Wednesday, December 3rd, and though everyone was on board, they could not sail until the next day due to weather. The troops from Fort Monroe had sailed on December 2nd, as a separate "convoy." All those troops that had not yet arrived were then directed to rendezvous at Fort Monroe for later embarkation.

Underway, sealed orders were opened, and the destination of this immense fleet was revealed as Ship Island. Banks carried with him[927] Gen. Andrew J. Hamilton who had been appointed as the military governor of Texas, whose task was to "re-establish the authority of the Federal Government in the State of Texas" and who was authorized to raise two regiments of Texas Volunteers. Banks was to support him "by a sufficient military force, to be detailed by you from your command . . ."

Was there any thought given by the War Department to the possibility of one or both of two new Confederate commerce raiders creating havoc among the undefended transports? The answer was a definite yes. In another of the relatively unnoticed dramas of the U.S. Navy in this war, the navy secretary had become concerned. The *Alabama*'s first victim, on September 5th, was the capture and burning of the *Ocmulgee*, a whaler out of Edgartown, Massachusetts, near the Azores.[928] By the end of November, the *Alabama*'s victims numbered 23. On November 4th, Gideon Welles noted in his diary: "Further news of the depredations by the Alabama."[929] Hull number 290 had been built under private contract for the Confederacy at Liverpool, England. The unarmed 290 or the *Enrica*, as she was initially known, with a British crew, steamed out of the Mersey on August 29th, 1862. She departed amid a flurry of diplomatic activity by the United States in trying to stop her, it being suspected that she was to be used as a Confederate raider: a newer and faster one than an earlier, and less well-known one, the *Sumter*.[930] The *Enrica* evaded the USS *Tuscarora*, hovering off the west coast of England, and made her way to the Azores, where she rendezvoused with a supply ship loaded with her armament, and where she was renamed the *Alabama*. Welles' diary continues: "Ordered Dacotah, Ino, Augusta, etc. on her track." Here he was referring to the fact that he had created a separate command on September 8th, only three days after the *Alabama* had captured and burned the *Ocmulgee*. This was designated as the West India Squadron, specifically to search out and either capture or destroy the threat.[931]

The second of the raiders purchased by the Confederate government at this time was the *Oreto*, renamed the *Florida*, and was not a threat to Banks' fleet. With its armament incomplete, and its crew wracked with yellow fever, it had dodged

---

927. O.R. Ser. III, Vol. 2, pp. 782, 783, 913.
928. ORN Ser. I, Vol. 1, pp. 787, 780, 480.
929. Welles, G., Vol. 1, p. 179.
930. ORN Ser. I, Vol. 1, pp. 414, 775, 777, 778.
931. ORN Ser. I, Vol. 1 pp. 470, 471.

the blockade and run into Mobile.[932] On November 24th, Welles, in addition to all his other precautions, ordered the USS *Augusta* to make arrangements to convoy the steamers of Banks' expedition.

It was anticlimactic that the *Alabama* was never seen nor heard from, yet Capt. Raphael Semmes had every intention of attacking Banks. At his anchorage in the Arcas Keys, he entered in his log: "I must get to sea on Tuesday, though I fear I might not be quite done caulking. But the Banks expedition must be assembling off Galveston, and time is of importance to us if we would like to strike a blow at it before it is landed."[933] The Tuesday to which he was referring was January 6th, 1863, but the mention of Banks' destination as Galveston gives evidence of either a successful ruse by the Federals or of a huge miscalculation on Semmes' part.

In the *Century* magazine, issue 6, April 1886, Semmes' Executive Officer John M. Kell notes: "Our prizes gave us regularly the mails from the United States; from which we gathered the fitting out of the army under General Banks for the attack on Galveston and the invasion of Texas, and the day on which the fleet would sail."[934] We note that the last ship that the *Alabama* captured was the U.S. Mail steamer *Ariel*, outward bound from New York to California. It was captured off Cape Maysi, Cuba, on December 7th, which means that any mail it had on board could not have been dated more recently than the end of November. If anything, Semmes could have only learned that Banks' fleet had not yet sailed. Semmes did not finish his business with ransoming the *Ariel* until the 9th, and then mentioned having to take three days to repair his engine while hove to off the north coast of Jamaica. At this location, the *Alabama* would have been more than a thousand miles away from Ship Island.

We cannot but assume that the mail Semmes read was from some of the horde of speculators,[935] the "friends" of the presumptive governor of Texas, Hamilton, who accompanied the expedition. Hamilton was to occupy Galveston, which had been captured and occupied by the navy since October 5th.[936] Since absolute secrecy had been maintained by Banks – only a few of his staff knew that the final destination was New Orleans – the only information anywhere abroad was that Hamilton was headed for Galveston. In fact, when Banks arrived at Ship Island and disclosed that the destination was New Orleans, "those connected with him [Hamilton] became very violent, and denounced unsparingly the Government and all connected with the expedition for what was called bad faith in its management."

---

932. ORN Ser. I, Vol. 1, pp. 761, 770.
933. ORN Ser. I, Vol. 1, pp. 816, 817; the Arcas Keys are off the coast of Mexico.
934. Kell, J. M, The Galaxy, p. 913; *Recollections of a Naval Life* Washington: Neale Co., 1900, pp. 208, 209; ORN Ser. I, Vol. 1, pp. 779, 782.
935. O.R. Vol. 15, p. 201. They undoubtedly had their eye on the potential millions to be made in smuggling and illegal commodities trading with the Confederacy, made notorious by Butler's brother.
936. ORN Ser. I, Vol. 19, p. 254.

Banks' fleet had been warned of the *Alabama* danger, and they were on the lookout. A. J. H. Duganne of the 176th New York Infantry remembers, as they sat on deck, there was "conjecture as to the latitude of pirate Semmes and his ubiquitous Alabama."[937] The 114th New York, in the steamer *Thames*, were so badly tossed about in the gale through which some of the fleet had to pass that they barely reached Hilton Head. There, the steamer was condemned, and they were transferred to the sailing bark *Voltiguer*. Not underway again until December 17th and blown way off course, they swore that they had spotted the *Alabama* off Abaco Island on the evening of December 20th. "Quite a sensation was created. Finally, she disappeared from our sight."[938] They did not reach Ship Island until December 28th.

FIGURE 11. ARRIVAL OF BANKS AND STAFF AT NEW ORLEANS ON THE NORTH STAR

Only two ships had been lost, one having run up on a reef and the *Thames* condemned, though many were dispersed.[939] At Ship Island, Banks gave instructions to the fleet to proceed to New Orleans. Banks and the transports left on Sunday, December 14th, arriving that evening (figure 11).[940] He immediately met with Butler and delivered Halleck's order relieving him of command. Butler issued his gracious farewell address the next day.

---

937. Duganne, A. J. H., p. 10.
938. Pellet, E. P., p. 37.
939. ORN Ser. I, Vol. 17, p. 332; Vol. 19, p. 429; Vol. 13, p. 459, 460.
940. O.R. Vol. 15, pp. 613, 191, 609. Figure 11 from *Harper's Weekly*, January 10th, 1863, p. 21.

Banks delivered an introductory letter from President Lincoln to Farragut on the morning of the 15th, noting that he was delighted with Farragut's cordial promise of cooperation in the enterprise that had been outlined by Halleck's orders.[941] Farragut's report of the meeting notes that it was he who had recommended the occupation of Baton Rouge, which was agreed to by Banks, who assigned the 4,500 effectives of Grover's command to the task. Commander Alden of the *Richmond* and two gunboats were to convoy the six transports of Grover's command and support the landing. They got off on the 16th without disembarking at New Orleans.

Arriving at daybreak on the 17th, four companies of the 26th Maine Regiment were the first to land "and drive the rebs out of the city."[942] They captured several prisoners and put them in the State House. The few rebels present who, as Sarah Dawson noted, were using the penitentiary for a barracks, fled. The threat of shelling by the *Essex* and Gunboat No. 7, which had been stationed off the town,[943] had proven to be little deterrent to Ruggles' troops, the occasional shelling only serving to drive out some of the civilian population and leave the town open to looting.

Thus, Banks' first military initiative was a complete success. The second, to Galveston, spoiled the initiation. Never mind that Hamilton was impatient to get to Galveston; Farragut was also interested. He had requested troops from Butler to reinforce it soon after its capture;[944] and with the threat of it being attacked by the aggressive new Confederate commander of the district of Texas, New Mexico, and Arizona, John B. Magruder, he was more concerned than ever. After consulting with both Farragut and Butler, Banks agreed to send troops. The lead group, consisting of three companies, a total of 15 officers and 249 enlisted men of the 42nd Massachusetts Infantry, had already arrived at New Orleans and encamped at Carrollton, but were ordered away and landed at Galveston on the 24th.[945]

Early on the morning of the first of January, they were attacked by a force commanded by Magruder that was estimated at 3,000 or more. The supporting troops for the 42nd, arriving on another steamer the next day, were too late. The entire detachment of the 42nd had surrendered. Being hurried out from New Orleans, they were ill equipped and too few. Of the gunboats of the fleet, the *Harriet Lane* had been boarded and captured, and the *Westfield* had been grounded and then abandoned and blown up, killing Commodore Renshaw and four others.[946]

---

941. ORN Ser. I, Vol. 19, pp. 342, 409, 415, 417, 418.
942. Maddocks, E. B., pp. 18, 19; Tiemann, W. F., p. 17.
943. O.R. Vol. 15, pp. 130, 131.
944. ORN Ser. I, Vol. 19, pp. 300, 319. Magruder: assigned October 10th; O.R. Vol. 15, p. 826. Assumed command November 29th, p. 880.
945. O.R. Vol. 15, pp. 200–211; O.R. Vol. 26/I, pp. 5–7; Bosson, C. P., pp. 63, 72, 74, 86, 109.
946. ORN Ser. I, Vol. 19, pp. 458, 460.

That Butler had not sent troops to occupy Galveston[947] in the weeks since its capture is recorded in the official records of the navy. Butler had promised the 21st Indiana[948] to Farragut, but the Lafourche campaign had delayed sending them. Farragut had to admit that: "The general has really not half troops enough . . ." Farragut had been incensed when he heard in early December the frank words from Commodore Renshaw, patrolling off Galveston, that the place might have to be abandoned, given evidence of preparations by Magruder.

Banks did not officially announce taking command of the Department of the Gulf until the 17th, when his staff assignments were announced. The organization of the units in the department as of the end of December 1862 is shown in the table I.[949] Those shaded were newly arrived as a part of the expedition. The remainder were Butler's old units or those recently raised by him. The 1st Texas Cavalry and Louisiana Artillery are listed, raised by Butler in New Orleans too late in November to be involved in the Lafourche campaign or in the reinforcement of Galveston.

GROVER'S DIVISION

13th Connecticut	52nd Massachusetts
24th Connecticut	6th New York
25th Connecticut	91st New York
2nd Louisiana	131st New York
12th Maine	133rd New York
22nd Maine	159th New York
26th Maine	161st New York
41st Massachusetts	173rd New York
174th New York	2nd Massachusetts Battery
4th Wisconsin	1st U.S. Artillery, Battery L
1st Louisiana Cavalry, Co. C	2nd U.S. Artillery, Battery C
2nd Mass. Unattached Cavalry, Co. B	

W. T. SHERMAN'S DIVISION

26th Connecticut	114th New York
14th Maine	156th New York
31st Massachusetts	160th New York
42nd Massachusetts	162nd New York
6th Michigan	2nd Massachusetts Cavalry, Co. A
15th New Hampshire	18th New York Battery
16th New Hampshire	1st Vermont Battery
110th New York	

---

947. ORN Ser. I, Vol. 19, p. 404; see also 344, 346, 347, 384.
948. Butler, B. F., p. 531.
949. O.R. Vol. 15, pp. 627, 628.

RESERVE BRIGADE

12th Connecticut
1st Louisiana
75th New York
1st Louisiana Cavalry, Co's A & B

2nd Massachusetts Cavalry, Co. B
1st Maine Battery
6th Massachusetts Battery

DEFENSES OF NEW ORLEANS

9th Connecticut
26th Massachusetts
30th Massachusetts

1st U.S. Artillery, Batteries A & F
5th U.S. Artillery, Battery G

DISTRICT OF PENSACOLA

28th Connecticut
15th Maine

7th Vermont
2nd U.S. Artillery, Batteries H & K

INDEPENDENT COMMANDS

23rd Connecticut
21st Indiana
1st Louisiana Native Guards
2nd Louisiana Native Guards
3rd Louisiana Native Guards
13th Maine
8th New Hampshire

128th New York
165th New York
177th New York
8th Vermont
1st Texas Cavalry
Louisiana Artillery (one company)
4th Massachusetts Battery

TABLE I

Counting regiments only, Banks had brought, up to this date, 25, more than doubling the strength of Butler's old command. More units, both veteran and freshly recruited, would continue to arrive in the next few weeks. The final tally of the reinforcements for the department would total 39 infantry regiments, six artillery batteries, and three cavalry units.[950] Note that Battery L appears as assigned to General Grover.

Record 12/62
31 OCTOBER–31 DECEMBER 1862, BATON ROUGE, LOUISIANA

Embarked Battery on board steamer "Che Kiang," left Pensacola Dec. 24th – reached New Orleans Dec. 25th and received orders to proceed to Baton Rouge. Reached that place Dec. 27th and took up quarters in the State Penitentiary. Company serving as Mounted Artillery with Battery of: 4 light twelves, 2 ten lb. Parrot rifles[951]

---

950. O.R. Vol. 15, pp. 712–714. The 18th New York, 2nd Rhode Island, and a detachment of the 14th New York.

951. Full war organization; see p. 4, *Field Artillery Tactics*, U.S. War Dept., 1864 (6 guns, 150 men, and 110 horses).

1. Henry W. Closson   Capt. In Command
2. Franck E. Taylor   1st Lt.
3. Edward L. Appleton   1st Lt. Absent on det. svc. At Pensacola – left Co. Dec. 24,'62
4. James A Sanderson   2nd Lt. App. to Co. by prom. vice Gibbs G.O. no. 73 War Dept. A.G.O. Washington July 4, 1862 (never joined co.)

Detached:

Edmond Cotterill   Pvt. Abs. on det. svc. at Pensacola. Fla. As clerk in A.G.O. Abs. from Co. since Dec. 24, 1862.

George Friedman   Pvt. Abs. on det. svc. at N.O. (as artillerist). Left Co. May 24, 1862.

Franklin W. Richards   Pvt. Absent, confined at Ft. Pickens, Fla. Since Nov.10, 1862.

Transferred:[952] Charles Riley, Pvt. Trans. (from abs. sick) to Co. F 1st Art. U.S.A New Orleans, La.

Discharged: William Wynne, Pvt. Oct. 9, 1862 By Expiration of Service
Michael Harrington Pvt. Dec. 23,'62 Pensacola, Fla. Discharged as a minor and returned to his Company "I" 15th Me. Vols.

Strength: 126. Sick: 8.

Sick Present: Charles A. Flint

Sick Absent: William C. Brunskill Ft. Hamilton, NY. Left Company Sept. 17, 1861.
Charles F. Mansfield Left sick at Pensacola since Dec. 24, 1862.
Wallace D. Wright Left sick at Pensacola since Dec. 24, 1862.

The ratio of those sick to total strength is noted as being the lowest since leaving Texas.

Horses: Serviceable: 88, Unserviceable: 0

Temporarily Attached: not included in Strength:

William Bruce,	Extra Duty – Ord. Dept.	Co. C, 2nd Arty.
Sigmund Loeb,	" " " "	Co. A, 1st Arty.
Christian Allendorf	" " " "	Co. F, 1st. Arty.

Joined:
47 Volunteer unit Privates enlisted in Battery L at Pensacola, 30 in November and 18 in December. $100.00 Bounty Due.

1. Allen, James H.	A 91st New York	25. McEnearny, Cornelius	A 91st New York
2. Baker, John	A 91st New York	26. Mahoney, Thomas	F 15th Maine
3. Card Rowland	A 91st New York	27. Moore, Churchill	H 91st New York
4. Campbell James	F 15th Maine	28. Meese, Christian	A 6th New York
5. Champion, Henry	H 91st New York	29. Miller, John	A 6th New York
6. Comfort, James	B 6th New York	30. Montgomery, Solomon	V I 91st New York
7. Crowley, William	I 15th Maine	31. Morgan, Frank	H 91st New York
8. Chase, George	A 91st New York	32. Orcutt, Ephraim	H 91st New York
9. Deering, John	F 15th Maine	33. Parks, William	F 15th Maine

---

952. The muster roll record is unreadable, though the "Strength" section lists one private transferred. Sick at Ft. McIntosh, Texas, February 25th, 1861, reduced to Private October 1st, 1861, at Fort Pickens, Florida; last paid December 31st, 1860. This additional information is contained in the monthly report for December 1862.

10. Deal, Charles	C 91st New York	34. Pelky, Henry	C 91st New York
11. Flynn, Arthur	A 6th New York	35. Parslow, Joseph	I 15th Maine
12. Fudge, William	C 15th Maine	36. Ranahan, Michael	F 15th Maine
13. Gibbon, Patrick	I 91st New York	37. Stewart, William	I 15th Maine
14. Hubbard, Hiram	H 91st New York	38. Smith, Hiram	A 15th Maine
15. Hall, Benjamin O.	H 15th Maine	39. Smith, James H.	C 15th Maine
16. Harrison, George	C 91st New York	40. Smith, William H	A 15th Maine
17. Jessop, Francis	B 6th New York	41. Walton, Charles E.	6th New York
18. Kilburne, Sirenus T.	I 7th Vermont	42. Welsch, Peter	H 91st New York
19. Kelly, George	A 91st New York	43. Wilder, Joshua E.	H 7th Vermont
20. Kelly, John	A 91st New York	44. Wilson, Thomas W.	C 91st New York
21. Lewery, John	A 15th Maine	45. Winn, Abram F.	A 91st New York
22. Lashner, Joseph	H 91st New York	46. Winn, Joel T.	A 91st New York
23. McKenney, John	I 15th Maine	47. Woods, John C.	A 91st New York
24. McGinnis, Angus	F 15th Maine		

When Enos Deal, of C company, 91st New York, stepped up to Lieutenant Appleton, Battery L's recruiting officer, he may have been hoping for a new beginning. He gave his name as Charles, see No. 10 in the list. The "new" Deal did not last long; he deserted on September 15th, 1863, just as Battery L was leaving New Orleans.

The large number of recruits from the volunteer units is of note. All were due a $100 bounty, which had been originally planned to be paid upon their honorable discharge.[953] Recognizing that this incentive was too distant in time to be effective, many, including most of the state governors, proposed that one-fourth of the bounty be paid up front. This was so ordered on July 1st, 1862, but additional recruits taken into Battery L at Baton Rouge in February of 1863 were not paid up front, despite this order.[954]

Regular army recruiting of those already serving in volunteer units was specifically authorized by the issuance of General Orders No. 154 dated October 9th, 1862, by the adjutant general's office.[955] It ordered that all batteries, battalions, and regiments appoint "one or more recruiting officers, who are hereby authorized to enlist, with their own consent, the requisite number of volunteers to fill the ranks of their command to the legal standard." The day previous to the day the volunteer enlisted in the regular army, he was to have been considered as honorably discharged from his volunteer unit. The volunteer unit commander had no choice in the matter, which was objected to by the state governors.[956]

---

953. O.R Ser. III, Vol. 1, p. 382, Act of Congress, July 22nd, 1861. Name spelling and company designation has been changed in several cases to agree with Shorey's *History of the Maine Fifteenth*.
954. O.R. Ser. III, Vol. 2, p. 187.
955. O.R. Ser. III, Vol. 2, p. 654.
956. O.R. Ser. III, vol. 2, pp. 694, 737.

Was the bounty a major factor in their decision to join, or was Battery L attractive for other reasons? As a basis for calculating a current value of the bounty, the ratio of the lowest army pay grade for 2009 to the pay of a new private in 1862 is 1,400:13.[957] On this basis, the bounty was worth $10,700. The one quarter paid up front calculates as $2,675. A goodly sum to grab and desert, which some did.

The mysterious case of Sgt. Charles Riley must now be closed. Carried on the rolls as "sick at Fort McIntosh, Texas; Absent from Company since Feb. 25, 1861" for almost two years, and in the interval reduced to a private, he now appears as having been transferred to Company F of the 1st Artillery at New Orleans.

Fort McIntosh was abandoned on March 12th, 1861, according to the report of the commander, Maj. C. C. Sibley. The report refers to a post return, which had been "herewith, inclosed,"[958] but is missing from the official records. The post return is, however, available from the National Archives.[959] Examination of the February return shows under "Those Casually at Post" Riley, Charles, Sgt. 1st Arty L 26 Feb'y 1861. He does not appear on the final, or March return, cut short, as it was, to the 12th. This means that he was shipped out before the fort was abandoned and was therefore not a part of Sibley's command when it left.

Riley's pension record[960] has supplied some answers. Riley did not apply for a pension until 1882. Because the time interval from the event to the time the pension application was made had been 22 years, memories had faded and people had died. Affidavits were required by the Pension Bureau for proof of service. The adjutant general's office confirmed his enlistment and service in Batteries L and F and his prisoner-of-war record. Col. Richard C. Jackson, who commanded Battery L at the time of the march out from Fort Duncan, couldn't remember Riley at all, much less the incident at Willow Pond, Texas, where Sergeant Riley was thrown from his horse, resulting in a severe multiple fracture of his right leg and injury to his ankle. Fortunately, the Fort McIntosh post surgeon, Lt. Charles C. Byrne, remembered Riley's arrival there and that he had set his leg. "Flat on his back," Riley was not abandoned at the fort; but after a private collection from members of the battery, he was left with provisions and money for his support, in the care of an apparently loyal private family in Laredo. All this was to no avail; he was taken prisoner on April 15th, 1861.

As was described in chapter 2, those enlisted men taken prisoner were sent to Camp Verde and then ordered separated at different posts. Riley mentions being at Ringgold Barracks and Camp Cooper, as well as Verde. He remained a prisoner

---

957. O.R. Ser. III, Vol. 1, p. 402. An act of Congress approved August 6th, 1861, raised a private's pay to $13 per month.
958. O.R. Vol. 1, p. 560–561.
959. National Archives Microfilm Publication M 617, Returns from U.S. Military Posts, 1800–1916, M 671D, roll 681.
960. Case no. 476558 National Archives, Civil War Pension Files.

until his "escape" on October 19th, 1862. He gave no details of his return to New Orleans, though a prisoner exchange took place at Vicksburg in December. He was assigned to Battery F at the end of October, and Battery L records finally caught up with that fact in December. He was described as "lame" by one witness. He had been partially disabled since his accident. Nevertheless, he was accepted into service in Battery F upon his return from prisoner of war status, as he wrote, "for the reason that any man who could mount a horse was not sent to hospital."

A subsequent report of the involvement of Battery F in the engagements at Fort Bisland and at Jeanerette, Louisiana,[961] in April 1863, gives mention of those who were distinguished in battle. Sgt. Charles Riley is among those listed.

For those at McIntosh who had been solicitous of Riley, judging it best to take up a collection to provide for his care and to leave him with a "loyal" family, in hindsight, was a mistake. Remember from chapter 2 that the Fort McIntosh command and others under Major Sibley were taken prisoner, but paroled, and left Texas at the end of April. If they could have only predicted the deprivations and exposure that the still-injured Riley would suffer as a prisoner for 19 months, they might have caused him to suffer the jolts and jounces of their travel to be rid of Texas promptly.

The Close of 1862

The "record of events" section statement closes the history of Battery L at Pensacola. The *Che Kiang*, a relatively new side-wheeler built for the China trade,[962] had arrived from New Orleans on December 22nd, bringing the 28th Connecticut Regiment for duty to replace the 91st New York. Embarking on the 24th, Battery L, along with the 91st New York, would have arrived at Balize, on the passage up the Mississippi, on Christmas morning. As it happened, this was the same day that the 15th New Hampshire Regiment, one of Banks' drafted nine-month militia units, passed up the river. Their observations and those of another volunteer unit, the 49th Massachusetts, provide us with impressions of the scene:[963] ". . . dawn found us on deck, gazing at Secessia" ten feet below them from the height of the levee. As they passed forts Jackson and St. Philip, they were "greeted with songs by the colored people on the shores and the waving of bandannas." They marveled at the rice, cane and cotton fields, the magnolias, and the "prolific orange . . . groves, bending with their golden fruit" that they saw near Quarantine. "Now, green fields . . . palatial mansions, and slave cabins fully occupy our attention." It was a pleasant time of the year. The weather made things upbeat, except for "the sight of the contrast between

---

961. O.R. Vol. 15, p. 337.
962. *New York Times*, November 9th, 1862. Compiled Service records, 91st New York, National Archives, M594, roll 128, p. 21.
963. McGregor, C., pp. 197; Johns, H. T., p. 135.

the homes of the planters and of their laborers is suggestive of the fact that, in the everduring struggle between the privileges of the few and the rights of the many, victory had here crowned the wrong."

Captain Closson remembers that upon arriving at New Orleans at 4:00 p.m. on the 26th that they had lain on board at the foot of Canal Street "looking up its long vista of lights."[964] In contrast, a member of the 49th Massachusetts saw nothing but "deserted rotting levees, frowned on by numerous gunboats, everything to denote war and its destructiveness, nothing to convince us that we were before the great metropolis of the Southwest. Divers pieces of calico and a few carriages reminded us of the friends and comforts of the North. Peddlers brought us pies, apples and oranges: of the latter you could get three as large as pound apples for 10 cents. You had better believe that those who had any money left rapidly invested it in this inviting stock."

L and the 91st soon received word to proceed to Baton Rouge, the state capital. Approaching on December 28th, from miles away, they could see this "beautiful Southern capitol . . . situated on . . . a plateau, the first bluff above the Head of the Passes." The capitol building[965] presented "a fine appearance . . . its massy snow white-walls and towers remaining intact . . ." (see figures 12 and 13).

FIGURE 12. CAPITOL, 1862

---

964. Haskin, W. L., *Closson's Memoirs*, p. 363; Johns, H. T., p. 136.
965. Leslie, Mrs. Frank, Battle Scenes, p. 476; author's photo, 2009.

FIGURE 13. CAPITOL, 2009

The 110 members of Battery L aboard the steamer *Che Kiang* that day were among the last to see it in its nearly original condition for 20 years.[966] Late in the afternoon, it caught fire and was gutted, only the walls remaining. An investigation revealed that the cause was a defective flue, not the action of the Union troops.

FIGURE 14

---

966. O.R. Vol. 15, pp. 630–633. The capitol building was restored in 1882 and again in the 1970s. It is now a museum. Maddocks, E. B., p. 19.

Disembarking across the derelict steamer *Natchez*, which was used as a wharf, Battery L took up residence in the state penitentiary (figure 14).[967]

When General Banks took over the command of the Department of the Gulf, he initiated a review of the troop dispositions at Pensacola. A recommendation was made to abandon the city and withdraw to the peninsula on which stood the small communities of Woolsey and Warrington, the navy yard, and Fort Barrancas. Bounded by Bayou Grande to the north, and Pensacola Bay to the east and south, the only access to it was a road bridge from Pensacola (noted by the arrow in figure 15) or the land approach from the west.[968] If the bridge was destroyed, a defensive line from Fort Barrancas to the advanced redoubt was considered adequate. Constructed between 1845 and 1870, the redoubt was essentially another fort like Barrancas. It was in good condition because it was never a factor in any of the previous bombardments.

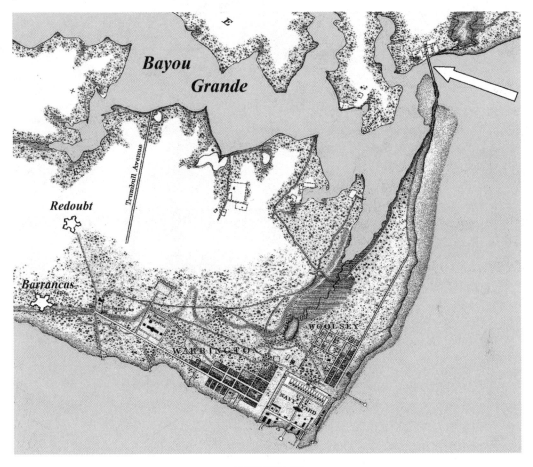

FIGURE 15

---

967. Tiemann, W. F., p. 17; figure 14, G. H. Suydam Collection, Mss. 1394, Louisiana and Lower Missisippi Valley Collections, LSU Libraries, Baton Rouge, La.; figure 15, portion of NOAA Historical Chart 490-00-1858, altered.
968. O.R Vol. 15, p. 677, 1,109.

After Halleck had approved, the plan was carried out. The evacuation took place between March 17th, and March 23rd, 1863.[969] Of the 1,100 or so residents, about 1,000 Union sympathizers who feared Confederate retribution, or conscription, were transported out. The Spanish consul, Francesco Moreno[970] remained, and under his "flag of neutrality," the 70 or so remaining citizens hoped to be afforded protection from the "marauders" alluded to in chapter 5.[971]

---

969. O.R. Vol. 15, p. 699.
970. O.R. Vol. 15, p. 1,036. Moreno was the father-in-law of the Confederate Secretary of the Navy Stephen A. Mallory.
971. Shorey, H. A., pp. 33, 34.

Chapter 7

Review; Record 2/63; 1863 Roster;
The Nineteenth Army Corps;
Engagement at Bayou Teche;
The Alabama; The Northern Column; Forward!;
The Yazoo Pass Expedition;
The Ram Fleet and the Mississippi Marine Brigade;
Return of the 42nd; Indianola Lost; Banks' Plan;
Farragut Passes Port Hudson

Review

At the end of his tenure, Butler's Department of the Gulf and the environment into which Battery L was thrust, might best be summarized by reference to the background of the Emancipation Proclamation. On September 22nd, 1862, the President issued a proclamation,[972] which might fairly be called the emancipation warning. In it, he called attention to the March 13th and July 17th acts of Congress[973] that (1) forbade anyone in the military or naval service from returning fugitive slaves who had escaped from masters who were in rebellion against the government, (2) declared them to be free, and (3) provided that any claim by an owner of a fugitive slave would only be considered if the owner first came forth with an oath of allegiance to the Union.

The President went on to say that on January 1st, 1863, he would declare free all slaves held within any state or designated part of a state still in rebellion. He added that *compensation for loss of property*, "including the loss of slaves," to citizens that had remained loyal, would be recommended at a future date. Thus, Lincoln tread the fine line of his duty to the Constitution, his fear of losing support in the slaveholding border states of Kentucky,[974] Tennessee, Missouri, Maryland, and Delaware, and his personal belief that "if slavery is not wrong, nothing is wrong."[975]

Apparently, the public never misunderstood the message. A letter home from a

---

972. O.R. Ser. I, Vol. 15, pp. 621–622.
973. Sanger, G. P., pp. 354, 589–592.
974. Stephenson, N. W., p. 259.
975. http://memory.loc.gov/ammem/alhtm/almass/ln001.html. Letter to Albert G. Hodges, April 4th, 1864. Lincoln also expresses: "I believed the indispensible necessity for military emancipation, and arming the blacks would come."

soldier in the 49th Massachusetts Volunteers at Camp Briggs, Massachusetts, dated September 29th, 1862, put it this way: "Look here! rebels! I give you one more chance to repent. I dislike slavery but I dislike disunion and war more. I have offered to buy back your slaves . . . but mark me, if you are not in the Union by the first of next January . . . I will not only declare your slaves free, but I will put arms into every one of them willing to use them . . ."[976] This recruit had it clearly, but he had made the leap that Lincoln was dearth to enunciate – that the slaves would be armed.

As earlier related, Lincoln had repudiated generals Fremont in Missouri and Hunter in the Department of the South on their initiatives regarding emancipation. However, in the experience of the 49th Massachusetts Regiment at Carrollton in February, it was observed that every slave remembered Fremont, and that he was "the standard-bearer" in the emancipation campaign. Further, "the North Star brought down to the Gulf, their first and enduring love."[977] The *North Star* was of course the ship that brought Banks to New Orleans. The subtle point being that Banks was the first Republican to come to the Gulf and the astute slave population closely identified him with Fremont, the first man to issue an Emancipation Proclamation.

The subject of freed slaves as soldiers was an even more potent one. Lincoln had recalled Secretary Cameron's 1861 annual report which had mildly suggested it. He still avoided the subject in September of 1862 as though he was apprehensive about publicity regarding the recent actions of Butler and the secretary of war's specific instructions to Saxton for the enlistment of persons of African descent, slave or otherwise. Finally,[978] on January 1st, 1863, the Emancipation Proclamation was issued, and it further declared that the newly freed slaves "will be received into the armed service of the United States . . ."

It would seem clear that all slaves were now free and could join the army or the navy if they wished. Not quite, or better described as *perhaps*. The proclamation only applied to: "Arkansas, Texas, Louisiana (*except the parishes of Saint Bernard, Plaquemines, Jefferson, Saint John, Saint Charles, Saint James, Ascension, Assumption, Terre Bonne, Lafourche, Saint Marie, Saint Martin, and Orleans, including the city of New Orleans*), Mississippi, Alabama, Florida, Georgia, South Carolina, North Carolina, and Virginia . . ." The 48 counties to be known as West Virginia were also exempted as were the Virginia cities of Norfolk and Portsmouth, and eight counties nearby.

Thus, owners of slaves who lived in those states or parts thereof still in the Union, were exempted from the provisions of the proclamation. The Constitution still ruled the Union, and Lincoln could not make a declaration that would illegally confiscate the property of any citizen. He could only make a pronouncement about those *enemy areas in rebellion*.

---

976. Johns, Henry T., pp. 43, 44.
977. Johns, Henry T., p. 141.
978. O.R. Vol. 15, pp. 667–669.

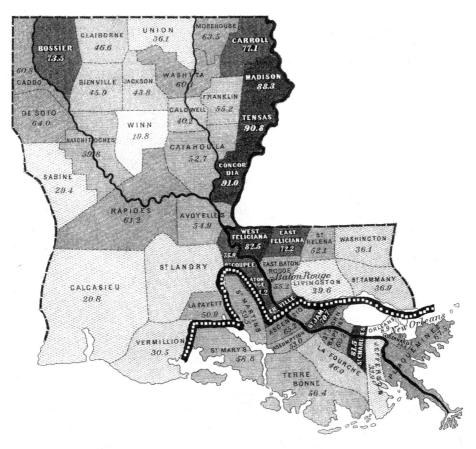

FIGURE 1. LOUISIANA AT THE CLOSE OF 1862

The Lincoln administration had apparently concluded that the exempted areas, and particularly those thirteen Louisiana parishes, were either loyal or could be claimed as being so, as they were under Union military control. They were all in the southeast corner of the state and are shown separated from the remainder of the state by the heavy dotted line in figure 1.[979] Though Governor Moore was in despair about the situation, the map supports the impression that little of Louisiana had fallen to the Yankees.

Allowing slavery to remain in areas under Union control would seem to have been a hypocritical and immoral deed to anyone, especially those slaves expecting freedom; but from a practical point of view, many had long since escaped their masters and were free by earlier rules. The 1860 census data indicates 11,455 slaves in the affected parishes. Statistics of how many were now free in occupied Louisiana, some 50,000 were briefly outlined in chapter 6. They were planned to be employed by the Butler administration and not returned. Furthermore, most officers were loath to honor claims by slave owners, and the latest instructions from

---

979. Figure 1. NOAA Map 3033-09-186, portion, altered.

Banks officially concurred. General Orders No. 12,[980] headquarters, Department of the Gulf, dated January 29th, 1863, noted: "The laws of the United States, however, forbid officers of the Army and Navy to return slaves to their owners or to decide upon the claims of any person to the service of another... Officers and soldiers... cannot compel or authorize their return by force." We conclude that most slaves who were able to flee to Union controlled areas remained, and were beyond the control of their former masters, regardless of the exemptions to the Emancipation Proclamation. On the flip side of this, in November, Butler had made "arrangements" to have the *loyal* owners of slaves pay them, if they remained on the plantations, and out of trouble.[981]

Record 2/63
31 DECEMBER 1862–28 FEBRUARY 1863, BATON ROUGE, LOUISIANA

Record of Events: [This portion of page missing].
1. Henry W. Closson — Capt. Commanding
2. Franck E. Taylor — 1st Lt. sick
3. Edward L. Appleton — 1st Lt. Joined from det. svc. Feb. 22, 1863 (Acting Ordnance Officer, Pensacola since Dec. 24, 1862)
4. James A. Sanderson — 2nd Lt. Appointed to Co. by promotion/ Gibbs prom. G.O. no. 73, War Dept. Washington July 4, '62 (never joined Co.)

Joined: Edmond Cotterill Pvt. From det. svc., Jan. 13, 1863 (as clerk in A.G.O. Pensacola, since Dec. 24, 1862)

Detached: George Freidman Pvt. On det. svc. (as Artillerist) at N.O. S.O. no. 11, Hdqtrs. West. Dist. Dept. of the South, Pensacola, Fla. May 24, 1862

Strength: 149. Sick 14

Sick Present: Franck E. Taylor, Charles A. Flint, Benjamin O. Hall, George Harrison, Daniel McCoy, Denis Myers, Angus McGuiness, John G. Nitschke, Ephraim Orcutt, Joshua E. Wilder, Thomas M. Willcox.

Sick Absent:
William C. Brunskill, Fort Hamilton, NY Left Company Sept. 17, 1861
Charles F. Mansfield, Sick at Pensacola, Fla. since Dec. 24, 1862
Wallace D. Wright   do.

Horses: Serviceable: 86 Unserviceable: 8

Volunteer unit Privates enlisted at Baton Rouge in February, 1863; $100. Bounty due:[982]

---

980. O.R. Vol. 15, pp. 666, 667.
981. O.R. Vol. 15, p. 162.
982. O.R. Vol 15, p. 678. The men were enlisted for three years, or the war. Those enlisted at Pensacola were paid $25 up front, with $75 due on expiration of service. Those enlisted at Baton Rouge were promised their bounty at expiration of service, which was at odds with then current policy.

1. O'Brien, Sholto	Co. B, 13th Conn. Vols.	13. Kenny, Theodore W	Co. C, 131st New York Vols.
2. Breen, Michael	Co. G, 174th New York Vols.	14. Kastenbader, John M.	Co. F, 13th Conn. Vols.
3. Bieber, Peter	Co. K, 13th Conn. Vols.	15. Leonard, George F.	Co. D, 174th New York Vols.
4. Brooks, William	Co. G 174th New York Vols.	16. Lowry, John	Co. F, " " "
5. Clinton, Thomas	Co. K, 13th Conn. Vols.	17. Mansfield, Herbert B.	Co. H, 13th Conn. Vols.
6. Cook, Charles	Co. B, " " "	18. Moore, Daniel	Co. B, 174th New York Vols.
7. Dickson, Clark	Co. B, " " "	19. Mint, William	Co. F, 13th Conn. Vols.
8. Eisle, Joseph	Co. K, " " "	20. Moran, John H.	Co. H, 2nd Louisiana Vols.
9. Foote, Edward A.	Co. B, " " "	21. Pfiffer, George	Co. F, 13th Conn. Vols.
10. Harrington, Jas. R.	Co. E, " " "	22. Tieghe, Michael	Co. F, " " "
11. Howard, Daniel	Co. C, " " "	23. Woodruff, Lyman	Co. E " " "
12. Hughs, Benjamin	Co. B, " " "		

As to their health while at Baton Rouge, both Battery L and Nims' 2nd Massachusetts Battery could look to the services of Assistant Surgeon William Y. Provost of the 159th New York Regiment.[983]

Having absorbed 70 new recruits since the end of October, Battery L had reached its highest strength ever, achieving close to "Full War Organization," with six guns (two 10 pounder Parrots and four 12 pounder Napoleons), and 86 horses. The addition of the horses required new "Extra Duty" assignments. Luckily, the skills required were found in the newly recruited members, who were from mostly rural locations:

1. Henry Champion, blacksmith since Feb. 5th, 1863, recruited from the 91st New York Infantry, Company H, which he had joined at Hillsdale, New York, on October 5th, 1861.

2. John Deering, artificer since Dec. 24th, 1862, recruited from the 15th Maine Infantry, Company F, whose men hailed from either Cumberland or Aroostook counties. Deering's position as artificer was additional to that of Isaac T. Cain, who remained separately listed as artificer on the muster roll.

3. George F. Hadley, blacksmith since Dec. 24th, 1862, the only original "Regular."

4. Sirenus T. Kilburne, blacksmith since Jan.1st, 1863, recruited from the 7th Vermont Infantry, Company I, which he had joined at the picturesque south-central town of Manchester, on February 7th, 1862.

5. Frank Morgan, saddler since Nov. 14th, 1862, named the same day that he was recruited from Company H of the 91st New York Infantry; which he had joined at Albany, New York. His quick appointment indicates that his skills, and at age 32, his maturity, were desirable assets. (Referred to as Harness Maker in the December 1862 Monthly Report.)

---

983. Tiemann, W. F., p. 19.

The preparation required for officially converting Battery L from a foot battery to a light battery had been expensive and involved, even down to the enlisted man's uniform, figure 2, which was changed to a red-trimmed dark blue coat of twelve buttons versus nine, with red-striped, sky-blue trousers.[984] Also, the greatest of care and expense would involve the maintenance, health, and training of the horses. To respond to the reins, the six-horse teams that were fundamental to the transport of the guns and caissons would require precious training time not only for the horses but for the men. The whole look and daily routine of the company was different from a foot company.

FIGURE 2

BATTERY L
1863 ROSTER

From 31 December 1862–28 February 1863 muster roll
BATON ROUGE, LOUISIANA

1.	Henry W. Closson	Capt.
2.	Franck E. Taylor	1st Lt.
3.	Edward L. Appleton	1st Lt.
4.	James A. Sanderson	2nd Lt.

1. Lewis Keller	1st Sgt.	1 Dec.'59 Newport, KY	1. David J. Wicks	Cpl.	25 Oct.'59 New York
2. Thomas Newton	Sgt.	13 Dec.'58 Ft. Brown, TX	2. Charles Spangler	Cpl.	3 Sept.'58 New York
3. Julius Becker	Sgt.	12 Oct.'59 New York	3. William Demarest	Cpl.	19 Oct.'59 New York
4. Alex. J. Baby	Sgt.	10 Feb.'60 Boston	4. James Flynn	Cpl.	12 Sept.'59 Ft. Clark

1. Ludwig Rupprecht Musician 7 Feb.'60 New York 1. Isaac T. Cain Artificer 4 Oct.'59 Boston

Privates

1. Ahern, James	18 Oct.'60 Boston	69. Mansfield, Herbert E.	24 Feb.'63 Baton Rouge
2. Allen, James H.	17 Nov.'62 Pensacola	70. McCarthy, James	4 Oct.'60 Boston
3. Anglin, Edmond	19 Oct.'59 NewYork	71. McCoy, Daniel	24 Oct.'60 New York
4. Baker, John	15 Nov.'62 Pensacola	72. McDonagh, Miles	17 Sept.'60 New York
5. Beglan, James	25 Oct.'60 New York	73. McEnearny, Corneilus	16 Dec.'62 Pensacola
6. Bieber, Peter	24 Feb.'63 Baton Rouge	74. McGauley, Terence	18 Sept.'60 New York
7. Breen, Michael	24 Feb.'63 Baton Rouge	75. McGuiness, Angus	14 Nov.'62 Pensacola
8. Brooks, William	27 Feb.'63	76. McKinney, John	14 Nov.'62 Pensacola
9. Brown, William F.	1 Nov.'59 Boston	77. McLaughlin, Edward	30 Sept.'58 New York
10. Brunskill, William C.	19 Oct.'59 New York	78. McSweeny, Daniel	11 Feb.'61 New York

---

984. Army of the United States, *Revised Regulations*, War Department, 1861, p. 477; figure 2, portion of Atlas, plate 172.

11. Buckley, John — 30 Sept. '58 New York
12. Burke, John — 17 oct. '60 New York
13. Campbell, James — 15 Nov. '62 Pensacola
14. Card, Rowland — 12 Nov. '62 Pensacola
15. Casey, John — 15 Oct. '59 New York
16. Champion, Henry — 12 Nov. '62 Pensacola
17. Chase, George — 11 Dec. '62 Pensacola
18. Clinton, Thomas — 24 Feb. '63 Baton Rouge
19. Comfort, James — 12 Nov. '62 Pensacola
20. Connell, Jeremiah — 14 Sept. '59 Ft. Clark, TX
21. Cook, Charles — 24 Feb. '63 Baton Rouge
22. Cotterill, Edmond — 22 Sept. '58 New York
23. Coyne, Owen — 10 Dec. '60 Ft. Duncan
24. Craffy, Patrick — 27 Sept. '60 Boston
25. Creed, William — 27 Sept. '60 Boston
26. Crowley, William — 17 Nov. '62 Pensacola
27. Cummings, Patrick — 25 Oct. '60 new York
28. Deal, Charles — 20 Dec. '62 Pensacola
29. Deering, John — 15 Nov. '62 Pensacola
30. Dickson, Clark — 23 Feb. '63 Baton Rouge
31. Donnelly, Patrick — 1 Mar. '60 Boston
32. Eisele, Joseph — 24 Feb. '63 Baton Rouge
33. Farrell, Bernard — 11 Nov. '59 New York
34. Ferrari, Prosper — 22 Oct. '60 New York
35. Flint, Charles A. — 22 Sept. '60 Boston
36. Flynn, Arthur — 12 Nov. '62 Pensacola
37. Foley, Christopher — 3 Nov. '59 Boston
38. Foote, Edward A. — 24 Feb. '63 Baton Rouge
39. Freidman, George — 7 Feb. '60 New York
40. Fudge, William — 14 Nov. '62 Pensacola
41. Galavan, Morris — 14 Jan. '61 Boston
42. Gibbons, Patrick — 16 Dec. '62 Pensacola
43. Hadley, George F. — 11 Mar. '60 Boston
44. Hall, Benjamin O. — 15 Oct. '62 Pensacola
45. Hanney, James — 8 Jan. '61 New York
46. Harrington, James R. — 27 Feb. '63 Baton Rouge
47. Harrison, George — 25 Dec. '62 Pensacola
48. Howard, Daniel — 24 Feb. '63 Baton Rouge
49. Howard, George — 25 Oct. '60 New York
50. Hubbard, Hiram — 19 Nov. '62 Pensacola
51. Hughes, Benjamin — 27 Feb. '63 Baton Rouge
52. Jackel, Charles — 26 Oct. '60 New York
53. Jessop, Francis — 12 Nov. '62 Pensacola
54. Kastenbader, John M. — 24 Feb. '63 Baton Rouge
55. Kelly, George — 16 Dec. '62 Pensacola
56. Kelley, John — 25 Dec. '62 Pensacola
57. Kenny, Michael — 8 Feb. '60 New York
58. Kenny, Theodore W. — 23 Feb. '63 Baton Rouge

79. Meese, Christian — 12 Nov. '62 Pensacola
80. Meyer, John — 1 Mar. '60 New York
81. Miller, John — 12 Nov. '62 Pensacola
82. Mint, William — 24 Feb. '63 Baton Rouge
83. Montgomery, Solomon J. — 14 Nov. '62 Pensacola
84. Moore, Churchill — 19 Nov. '62 Pensacola
85. Moore, Daniel — 24 Feb. '63 Baton Rouge
86. Moran, John H. — 28 Feb. '63 Baton Rouge
87. Morgan, Frank — 14 Nov. '62 Pensacola
88. Murphy, John — 21 Feb. '60 Boston
89. Myers, Denis — 25 Sept. '58 Syracuse
90. Nitschke, John G. — 6 Feb. '60 New York
91. O'Brien, Sholto — 24 Feb. '63 Baton Rouge
92. O'Sullivan, Michael — 26 Sept. '60 Boston
93. Olvany, Michael — 25 Oct. '60 New York
94. Orcutt, Ephraim — 19 Nov. '62 Pensacola
95. Parketton, William — 4 Oct. '60 New York
96. Parks, William — 17 Nov. '62 Pensacola
97. Pelky, Henry — 25 dec. '62 Pensacola
98. Parslow, Joseph H. — 15 Dec. '62 Pensacola
99. Pfiffer, George — 24 Feb. '63 Baton Rouge
100. Ranahan, Michael — 14 Nov. '62 Pensacola
101. Richards, Franklin W. — 6 Feb. '61 New York
102. Roper, John — 22 Oct. '60 New York
103. Schmidt, Heinrick — 26 Oct. '60 New York
104. Schneider, Phillip H. — 16 Oct. '58 Ft. Brown
105. Scott, William E. — 9 Feb. '60 Boston
106. Shapley, Morgan L. — 18 Dec. '60 Buffalo
107. Shaw, Warren P. — 26 Oct. '60 Boston
108. Smith, Hiram — 15 Dec. '62 Pensacola
109. Smith James H. — 16 Dec. '62 Pensacola
110. Smith, Joseph — 11 Oct. '59 New York
111. Smith, William H. — 16 Dec. '62 Pensacola
112. Stanners, Martin — 19 Jan. '61 Boston
113. Stewart, William — 12 Nov. '62 Pensacola
114.. Stoll, Andrew — 24 Oct. '60 New York
115. Straub, Amelius — 8 Feb. '60 New York
116. Thompson, William V. — 13 Sept. '60 Rochester
117. Tieghe, Michael — 25 Feb. '63 Baton Rouge
118. Tomson, John — 9 Jan. '61 Boston
119. Townsend, Reuben — 27 Sept. '60 Boston
120. Walton, Charles A. — 12 Nov. '62 Pensacola
121. Ward, Henry H. — 8 Nov. '60 New York
122. Welsch, Peter — 19 Nov. '62 Pensacola
123. White, Michael — 7 Oct. '60 Boston
124. Wilder, Joshua E. — 19 Nov. '62 Pensacola
125. Wilkinson, Joseph — 4 Feb. '60 New York
126. Wilkson, Henry — 24 Dec. '60 New York

59. Kilburne, Sirenus	17 Nov.'62 Pensacola	127. Wilcox, Thomas M.	15 Dec.'62 Pensacola
60. Kutschor, Joseph	13 Feb.'60 New York	128. William, Henry	28 Sept.'60 Rochester
61. Lanahan, John	9 Jan.'61 Rochester, NY	129. Winn, Abram P.	16 Dec.'62 Pensacola
62. Lashner, Joseph	16 Dec.'62 Pensacola	130. Winn, Joel T.	20 Dec.'62 Pensacola
63. Leonard, George F.	24 Feb.'63 Baton Rouge	131. Woodruff, Lyman	27 Feb.'63 Baton Rouge
64. Lewery, John	14 Nov.'62 Pensacola	132. Wood, John C.	16 Dec.'62 Pensacola
65. Lighna, Louis	13 Oct.'58 Ft. Brown	133. Wren, Owen A.	11 Dec.'60 Boston
66. Lowry, John	24 Feb.'63 Baton Rouge	134. Wright, Wallace D.	28 Sept.'58 Rochester
67. Mahoney, Thomas	14 Nov.'62 Pensacola	135. Wynne, William	9 Oct.'62 Pensacola
68. Mansfield, Charles F.	16 Jan.'61 Boston		

The Nineteenth Army Corps

Through the month of January, Banks' fresh new regiments continued to arrive; and the 19th Army Corps, as his force was designated, was, as seen, organized into four divisions, consisting of three brigades each, under Generals Augur, Thomas. W. Sherman, Emory, and Grover.[985] The last to be announced was Sherman's on January 13th, and it was assigned to the defenses of New Orleans. Augur was to command at Baton Rouge.

On January 7th, Banks reported to Halleck that correcting matters regarding the abuses of trade by private parties under Butler had occupied much time, which had interfered with military matters. He noted that the troops are "not in condition for immediate service." Banks also noted that he had no heavy guns, as would be required to assault Port Hudson, "whose works . . . have been in progress many months and are formidable." On that date, there were reported to be 10,700 Confederate effectives at Port Hudson, counting Gregg's Brigade, which had been ordered to report to General Gardner. Gardner had replaced Ruggles in command there on December 29th.[986]

A substantial difficulty was a lack of sufficient transport steamers to take advantage of the flooded condition of the country north and west of New Orleans and pursue any plan to approach Port Hudson from the river systems on the west side of the Mississippi. Only seven steamers were available by February 12th, when plans for a campaign were outlined to Halleck.[987]

Banks' command was not completely manned until February 11th. Having taken so much time to be mustered, equipped, and transported to the scene of operations, some of the nine-month regiments would have only until May 1863 before the expiration of their service. All of those 22 regiments whose service term was nine months would have expired by August. Thus, Banks was under pressure to accomplish his mandate to open the Mississippi in short order. He appreciated

---

985. O.R. Vol. 15, pp. 636, 626, 634, 645-647.
986. O.R. Vol. 639-641, 933, 913.
987. O.R. Vol. 15, pp. 24, 241.

the dilemma, and as early as April, he began to request replacements.

Examples of administrative problems in the Department surfaced by mid-January; horses and even food, shoes, and clothing, were scarce; and Banks felt that he needed more cavalry.[988]

Back on November 22nd, Lincoln had warned Banks about the "catch 22" of horses and of the danger of employing too much "*impedimenta*," which "has been, so far almost our ruin, and will be our final ruin if it is not abandoned . . . You would be better off anywhere, and especially where you are going, for not having a thousand wagons to feed the animals that draw them, and taking at least two thousand men to care for the wagons and animals who otherwise might be two thousand good soldiers."[989] This was a rare example of an angry Lincoln. Before he left, Banks had made requisitions for such a large amount of supplies that Lincoln felt it could not be filled "for an hour short of two months. I enclose you a copy . . . in some hope that it is not genuine – that you have never seen it."

Banks' whining seems to have prompted Lincoln to wonder if he had made a mistake in relieving Butler. Butler's commission as a major general had not been revoked, and the issue of his replacement was still apparently a topic at Washington. On January 8th, Senator Sumner, the Republican from Massachusetts, wrote to Butler[990] that he had seen the President, who had said that "he hoped very soon to return you to New Orleans." A letter from Lincoln to Stanton on the 28th suggested it.

All this was followed by a formal offer on February 11th, for Butler to return to New Orleans "at my request, for observation." Butler did not have to refuse, he alleges,[991] because Seward had tendered his resignation over the matter, and Lincoln had to back down.

Any lapse in military matters ended, however, as Weitzel, on January 6th, called attention to the unfinished business of the Lafourche campaign. Taylor's forces had fallen back across Berwick Bay to an earthwork called Fort Bisland. They had beaten the naval force sent to trap them, as outlined in chapter 6, and had taken the steamer J. A. Cotton, mounting 2 twenty-fours and a field piece – protected by cotton bales and some railroad iron – up Bayou Teche.[992] Buchanan's gunboats

---

988. Tiemann, W. F., p. 21. They were on short rations for two weeks. O.R. Vol. 15, pp. 618, 619, 647, 671, 688, 691, 1,099–1105. To supplement cavalry horses received from the north, the countryside was searched, and only 129 brought in as of January 16th. Five hundred were finally arranged to be shipped from New York in March. Later, it would be discovered that many horses were available in the surrounding country, though they had been well hidden by their owners.
989. Nicolay & Hay, Vol. VII, Ch. XI, pp. 312, 313. One of the rare references voicing worry about the cost of the war.
990. O.R. Vol. 53, pp. 546–548.
991. Butler, B. F., pp. 569, 570.
992. Taylor, R., p. 120.

had remained in the bay since, and had "rendered efficient service in clearing the bay and the highly important adjacent waters of rebel craft, and have securely and effectually protected my left flank." Now, however, news of the July 16th, 1862, Act of Congress transferring the river gunboats from army control to navy control had finally filtered down.[993] Farragut was planning to remove two, for service at Galveston.[994] He had lost two there, the *Harriet Lane* and the *Westfield*, on January 1st, and the blockade had been interrupted. A proclamation issued by Magruder was a stinging announcement of the setback. On January 5th, Magruder proclaimed: "Whereas the undersigned has succeeded in capturing and destroying a portion of the enemy's fleet and in driving the remainder out of Galveston Harbor . . . thus raising the blockade . . . He therefore proclaims to all concerned that the harbor of Galveston is open for trade . . ."[995]

If Banks had not the opportunity to form a judgment as to the strategic value of various points in southwestern Louisiana, he here was given a quick tutorial by Godfrey Weitzel.[996] By denying these water routes to the Confederates, "numerous light-draught boats now hidden in the adjacent bayous and streams" would be prevented from making frequent raids, and the Confederate "line of communication from Port Hudson westward to Opelousas and Texas" would be denied. Weitzel went on to warn that if the naval presence on the Mississippi above New Orleans and on Lake Pontchartrain were removed, the city would be vulnerable. He noted that this "compels me also to give you some information on the system of defense and security of New Orleans which I suggested on our arrival in the city to General Butler, and which has ever since been followed."

The strategy had been for the land forces to occupy forts Jackson and St. Philip, forts Pike and Macomb on Lake Pontchartrain (see figure 3 prepared by the author), and maintain a "sufficient" force behind the old Confederate defensive lines at Carrollton (Camp Parapet) with a minimal force in the city to maintain order. The navy would protect the flanks, i.e., the Mississippi to the west and Lake Pontchartrain to the east. The steamer *New London* had been stationed continually on Lake Pontchartrain and the *Portsmouth* had been permanently stationed on the river, but the water courses to the west were still open to Taylor.

---

993. O.R. Ser. III, Vol. 2, pp. 227, 644; Ellet's ram fleet was initially exempted, O.R. Vol. 17/II, p. 282. Porter argued for and obtained control of Ellet's brigade on November 7th, 1862, by order of the President. ORN Ser. I, Vol. 23, p. 469.
994. O.R. Vol. 15, pp. 637, 638.
995. O.R. Vol. 15, p. 931.
996. O.R. Vol. 15, pp. 636–638.

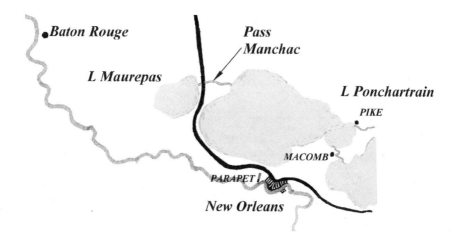

FIGURE 3

Weitzel closed with: "I consider it . . . my duty to call the admiral's attention through you to this fact, which I fear he has lost sight of . . . This disposition, which thus far has held it, requires a force not large for the service it performs, has given us a secure base, and thus enabled us always to employ our remaining land and naval forces for other operations without fear of losing our base and depots." Weitzel's tone of urgency was the result of a warning he had received the day before from Banks' assistant adjutant general about a build-up of Taylor's forces.[997]

As seen in figure 1, eight months of Union occupation had made little impression on the greater part of the state, and Taylor's forces were able to range freely wherever they pleased in the north and west. As of January 1863, Taylor reported his strength as an aggregate of 7,233.[998] This was very small, but the state had been drained of men long before, as was described in Lovell's problems recruiting for the defense of New Orleans.

Writing to the Confederate adjutant general at the end of December, Taylor reports having enrolled 3,000 men, 1,000 of whom were now serving at Port Hudson. Recently, the number of conscripts brought to his camps of instruction were described as "small, and these have to be hunted down by detachments from the small command which I have at my disposal and brought in tied and sometimes ironed" - an embarrassing revelation about the lack of enthusiasm of the people of the Attakapas country for the war.

Taylor had been constructing a series of forts, Bisland, Burton, DeRussy, and Beauregard (figure 4, prepared by the author), for the purpose of denying the navigable watercourses west of the Mississippi to the Federals and protecting the Confederate supply routes from Texas, particularly the Red River. These "forts"

---

997. O.R. Vol. 15, pp. 636, 637.
998. O.R. Ser. IV, Vol. 2, p. 380; O.R. Vol. 15, pp. 874, 919.

were earthen water batteries, manned by small crews. There were 60 men at Butte-la-Rose, and at Beauregard and DeRussy there were from 50 to 100. The largest was Fort Bisland, on Bayou Teche, which was supported by the gunboat *Cotton*.

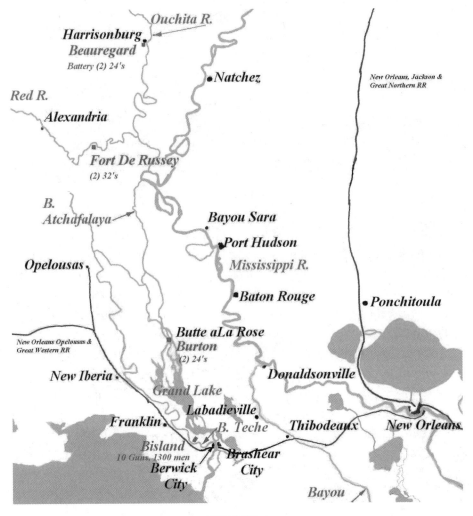

FIGURE 4

At all but Bisland, which had ten, there were but two guns, all salvaged from the waters of Barataria Bay and Berwick Bay, where they had been thrown after the fall of New Orleans.

Taylor had succeeded in recovering from the Lafourche setback. Few of Mouton's troops had been lost; they merely had withdrawn behind Fort Bisland. Though it was vulnerable, Taylor felt that, for the moment, its presence served to raise the spirits of the locals.[999]

---

999. Taylor, R., pp. 120, 118.

Engagement at Bayou Teche

Weitzel's arguments resulted in his receiving more reinforcements. Previously, the 8th Vermont, the 21st Indiana, and the 1st, 2nd, and 3rd Louisiana Native Guards had been added to his command; now the 116th and 160th New York, 23rd Connecticut, 6th Michigan, and two sections of Bainbridge's Battery A, 1st U.S. Artillery were added.[1000] A strengthened Lafourche District, coupled with the completion of fortifications at Brashear City and Donaldsonville,[1001] would ensure the safety of New Orleans' approaches while Banks' main force at Baton Rouge focused on attempts to open the Mississippi, which had now run up against the new reality of the Confederate fortifications at Port Hudson.

Hearing of Mouton preparing an attack on him, Weitzel decided on a pre-emptive strike. On January 13th, at 3:00 a.m., Weitzel's troops, consisting of six of his volunteer regiments, elements of four batteries of his artillery, and Barrett's Company B of the 2nd Louisiana Cavalry, began being ferried across Berwick Bay by the navy. The whole force was disembarked and formed up at Pattersonville. After waiting for the gunboats to make a reconnaissance, they advanced upstream about two miles to Lynch's point and went into camp under the cover of the gunboats. They were just within sight of the *Cotton*, lying a short distance above the earthworks of Fort Bisland and above a floating bridge, where obstructions and torpedoes had been placed in the Bayou near the Cornay residence (figure 5).[1002]

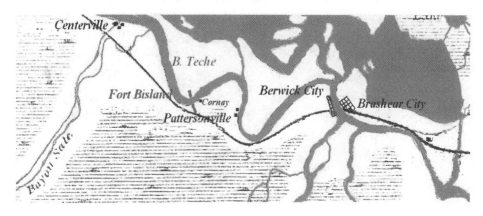

FIGURE 5

1000. O.R. Vol. 15, pp. 646, 647, 634.
1001. Fort Butler, constructed by Holcomb's 1st Louisiana Regiment, had occupied it since October 25th, 1862, during the Lafourche campaign. O.R. Vol. 15, p. 174. It was not completed, with guns mounted, until January 31st, 1863, pp. 163, 240. The fort at Brashear City was named for navy Lieutenant Commander Buchanan, killed in the Teche engagement. O.R. Vol. 26/I, p. 215.
1002. Figure 5, Atlas, portion of plate 156. O.R. Vol. 15, p. 234–237; Taylor, R., pp. 120, 121; ORN Ser. I, Vol. 19, pp. 337, 516.

Notably absent from the expedition were the Native Guards. Weitzel had objected to their being assigned to his command back in November.[1003] Butler had tolerated his bizarre views at the time, and Weitzel was convinced to retain them, though their only employment up to this time had been as guards for the railroad.[1004]

Next morning,[1005] 60 volunteers were assigned from each of the 8th Vermont and the 75th New York to act as sharpshooters, who were to move up to the *Cotton* and shoot down her gunners. The regiments were then to follow. Navy Lieutenant Commander Buchanan's supporting gunboats, led by the *Kinsman*, moved upstream with the advance of the regiments; and with enfilading fire from Bainbridge's, Carruth's, and Bradbury's artillery, the enemy was driven from his positions, first on the west side and then on the east. The gunboats continually fired into the *Cotton*, which withstood the onslaught "for some time" until it backed out of range. It returned, only to back out of range once again.

The *Kinsman* had a torpedo explode under her stern, causing her to back out of the action. Buchanan was killed by a rifle bullet from shore as the *Calhoun* advanced forward to replace the *Kinsman*. All told, the gunboats suffered 3 killed and 7 wounded: 3 killed and 6 wounded on the *Calhoun* and 1 on the *Kinsman*, none on the *Estrella* or the *Diana*.[1006] Weitzel reported 6 killed and 27 wounded.

Next morning, the *Cotton* was seen to be on fire, swung across the bayou as to form an obstruction. At this, Weitzel ordered the entire expedition returned to Camp Stevens near Thibodeaux. A successful result might have fairly been predicted considering that Weitzel brought some 6,000 men, 18 field guns,[1007] and a company of cavalry – all supported by gunboats – against 1,300 men behind the Confederate works. However, Mouton did not retire, and the *Cotton*'s 2 twenty-fours were salvaged and mounted on the west side of the Teche. Mouton's line of earthworks were strengthened, and some recruits were added to his force.[1008]

Banks quickly wrote to Halleck "of the complete success of the expedition,"[1009] and it was gratifying news to receive, following on the heels of the Galveston episode. However, it accomplished little, Mouton was still there, was reinforced,

---

1003. O.R. Vol. 15, pp. 164–166, 171, 172.
1004. When the Teche engagement was over, the 1st and 2nd Regiments of the Louisiana Native Guards were sent, on January 21st, to garrison forts St. Philip, Jackson, Macomb, and Pike, effectively getting them off of Weitzel's hands. *Harper's Weekly*, February 28, 1863, p. 143, O.R. Vol. 53, p. 546. The inspector general's report of January 15th, 1863, had reported the "sadly neglected" condition of these posts, O.R. Vol. 15, p. 649.
1005. O.R. Vol. 15, pp. 234, 235.
1006. ORN Ser. I, Vol. 19, pp. 517–520.
1007. O.R. Vol. 15, p. 234: (4) of Battery A, 1st Arty, (2) of the 4th Massachusetts, all of the 1st Maine, and all of the 6th Massachusetts (each having 6 guns if properly equipped).
1008. Taylor, R., p. 120, 121.
1009. O.R. Vol. 15. pp. 233, 234. Dated January 16th.

and would fight another day. Nonetheless, this was an aggressive action for a department that was still receiving its troops, still trying to strengthen the defenses of the city, and generally trying to organize.

Farragut learned of the action and the death of Lieutenant Commander Buchanan on January 14th, from a telegram from the captain of the *Estrella*.[1010] Impressed by the severe action, he dropped plans to redeploy the gunboats.

By mid-January, Camp Weitzel, at Donaldsonville, as it was called, was ready to receive its guns, and Perkins' cavalry had pushed up as far as Plaquemine. Pickets extended out as far as Grand Bayou to observe any enemy movement south.[1011] Now would begin an exploration of the water routes in the country west of Port Hudson, as a way to skirt around Port Hudson to unite with Grant above, and then turn to the reduction of Port Hudson. At least, this is what Banks had in mind at the time.

The Alabama

On the 11th of January, the *Alabama* finally appeared off Galveston. Semmes had arrived there as he had calculated, "but instead of sighting General Banks' fleet of transports we sighted five vessels of war at anchor, and soon after, our lookout reported a steamer standing out for us."[1012] This was the *Hatteras*, which gave chase and challenged the "suspicious" vessel flying the British flag. The *Alabama* then followed its usual tactic and hove to, broadside guns hidden and at the ready. Hailed by Captain Blake of the *Hatteras*, the *Alabama* identified herself as "Her Majesty's Steamer Spitfire."[1013] Shortly, the *Hatteras* sent out a rowboat with a party to board the stranger. Hardly had the rowboat shoved off when the *Alabama* lowered the British flag, ran up the Confederate, and opened fire with three broadside guns, all at a distance of a hundred yards or less. The men in the rowboat then observed a running battle which continued for some 15 or 20 minutes until the *Hatteras* was observed to be "blowing steam." They then rowed to the squadron to report the incident.

The next morning, the *Hatteras* was found sunk, upright, in shoal water, her mastheads visible, about twenty miles south of Galveston light, the *Alabama*

1010. ORN Ser. I, Vol. 19, pp. 515, 518, 519, 525, 526.
1011. O.R. Vol. 15, p. 655.
1012. Kell, J. M., *Cruise and Combats of the Alabama*, p. 913. Kell has the *Hatteras* as sunk in thirteen minutes; Semmes, R., pp. 153, 154.
1013. The name with which the *Alabama* took for its phony identity apparently was random and so often varied that the memory of witnesses accordingly varies. A second witness remembers the name used as "Petrel." From *Our Cruise in the Confederate States War Steamer Alabama*, attributed to George T. Fullam.

nowhere in sight.[1014] The crew of the *Hatteras* had been taken on board the *Alabama*. They were eventually brought to Kingston, Jamaica, and there paroled on January 23rd.[1015]

The Northern Column

Remembering his instructions that his first priority was the opening of the Mississippi River in cooperation with the "military and naval expedition . . . organizing at Memphis and Cairo," Banks wrote, in a December 24th dispatch to Halleck, saying: "We have no news from Vicksburg yet." [1016]

Indeed, the communications were poor. Any communication from Grant could not come by telegraph. Two hundred miles of enemy territory intervened. No communication by courier or by riverboat could be contemplated for the same reason. Grant could communicate from Memphis to Washington by telegraph, but Banks' communications with Washington were by steamship. Thus, any messages between them would be delayed by from 10 days to two weeks.

On January 4th, Halleck advised Banks: "You will learn from the *newspapers* that our last advices General W. T. Sherman has his hands full at Vicksburg." What was going on? What basis for planning did this information provide?

Our narrative in chapter 6 last left Grant fully reinforced, courtesy of McClernand's recruiting efforts. He had begun a land approach south toward Vicksburg on the east side of the Mississippi. Leaving Jackson, Tennessee, on November 2nd, he headed through Grand Junction by way of the Mississippi Central Railroad toward Holly Springs, Mississippi, aiming at Pemberton there, and Confederate entrenchments further south, behind the Tallahatchie. W. T. Sherman, Grant's right wing, advanced from Memphis toward the Tallahatchie on November 25th. On Grant's approach to Holly Springs, Pemberton fell back behind the Tallahatchie. By the 30th, Grant had crossed the Tallahatchie and was at Oxford, with a flustered Pemberton planning to retreat behind the Yalobusha (figure 6, prepared by the author).[1017] Grant adds,[1018] that he was delayed at Oxford "repairing railroads" and bringing up supplies of food, forage, and ammunition. It was here that he learned that "an expedition down the Mississippi was now inevitable . . ." This was a tip

---

1014. ORN Ser. I, Vol. 19, pp. 504–509.
1015. *Harper's Weekly*, February 28th, 1863, p. 13. Raphael Semmes, the captain of the *Alabama*, usually saw to it that the survivors of any ship he had taken were rescued. This was feasible if you took on board the prisoners of one victim at a time (often numbering more than the entire crew of the *Alabama*) and could then land them at a convenient port. Had he caught Banks' fleet, easily tearing into and sinking multiple unarmed transports, thereby throwing thousands of soldiers into the winter water, is fortunate to be left only to the imagination.
1016. O.R. Vol. 15, pp. 618, 636.
1017. O.R. Vol. 17/II, p. 717.
1018. Grant, U. S., Vol. I, p. 427–429, 432.

he had received from Illinois Congressman Elihu Washburne, and the subsequent notice that his forces were to be reorganized into four corps, with McClernand in command of the 13th.[1019] It would be given the assignment of the Vicksburg River Expedition. Having already expressed his negative opinion of McClernand to Halleck, he nevertheless had been overruled, and "desiring to have a competent commander in charge," he ordered Sherman, on December 8th, to break off and return to Memphis. There, Sherman was to assume command of all the forces, and as soon as possible, move "down the river to the vicinity of Vicksburg, and with the cooperation of the gunboat fleet under command of Flag Officer Porter, proceed to the reduction of that place . . ." By now, everyone in

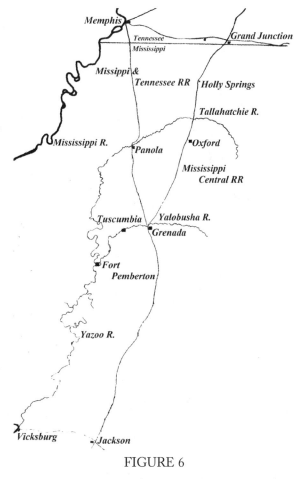

FIGURE 6

Washington was committed to the idea of a river expedition, giving little thought to any alternative. The Anaconda Plan, forgotten in name, had become ingrained in the strategic thinking.

Grant's delay and Pemberton's retreat behind the Yalobusha had briefly stabilized the situation, and Grant adds that he did not want to press Pemberton so hard that he would fall all the way back to Vicksburg before Sherman could arrive.[1020]

This pause allowed Van Dorn to execute the most memorable action of his brief career. On December 20th, with eight regiments of cavalry, he conducted a daring and spectacularly successful raid on Grant's supply base at Holly Springs, capturing the garrison and utterly destroying the place. This caused Grant to abandon any further attempt at an overland supply, and he gave orders to depend on seizing supplies from the countryside. In his memoirs, Grant insists that he never intended driving south of the Yalobusha; his main thrust was intended to be via Sherman's river approach. Thus, he claims, Van Dorn's raid had little or no

---

1019. O.R. Vol. 17/ I, pp. 4, 474, 475, 601.
1020. Grant, U. S., Vol. I, pp. 431, 432; O.R. Vol. 17/II, pp. 444, 448.

effect on his plans. Celebrants of Van Dorn insist that it halted Grant's overland thrust, which is true beyond a doubt. Grant notes,[1021] however, that "Pemberton got back to Vicksburg before Sherman got there," and Sherman was then repulsed.[1022]

The net result was that Grant returned to Memphis. He did not arrive until the 10th of January.[1023] There, he received reports of Sherman's attack on Vicksburg, south of Chickasaw Creek, on December 29th,[1024] and Sherman's description of its outcome: "I reached Vicksburg at the time appointed, landed, assaulted and failed." (Try to find this laconic honesty anywhere – then or now.)

Grant was also given details of Sherman having been displaced by McClernand on January 4th, and their mutual hatching of an attack on Fort Hindman at Arkansas Post. "Re-embarked my command unopposed and turned it over to my successor, General McClernand."

At his meeting with Sherman, McClernand brought the news that Grant had fallen back from the Tallahatchie. Sherman then reports: ". . . and as we could hear not a word of General Banks below, instead of remaining idle I proposed that we should move our entire force in concert with the gunboats to the Arkansas, where 7,000 of the enemy are entrenched, and threaten this river."

The attack was begun with a bombardment by Porter's fleet, which went on from the 10th until, surrounded, Fort Hindman surrendered on the 11th. In all, 4,791 prisoners and 17 guns were taken.[1025]

Grant at first disapproved of this "side movement," which seemingly had no bearing on the objective of attacking Vicksburg, but he had to admit that 5,000 Confederate troops in the rear of his operations could have posed a problem and that the resultant success was "very important."

At this point, the specter of McClernand's incompetence came to the fore. As Grant explains it, upon arriving from Memphis, on the 17th of January, he had a meeting with "McClernand and his command at Napoleon" at the mouth of the Arkansas river.[1026] "It was here made evident to me that both the army and the navy were so distrustful of McClernand's fitness to command that . . . this distrust was an element of weakness." Grant lets it slip that Porter had written to the secretary of the navy on the subject, "with a request that what he had said might be shown to the Secretary of War." Grant then decided that the way out of the dilemma was for him to take the direct command of the "Army of the Mississippi" as McClernand had self-styled the 13th and 15th Corps of the Army of the Tennessee.

1021. O.R. 17/II, p. 437; Johnston, J. E., pp. 588, 589.
1022. O.R. Vol. 17/II, pp. 676, 800; Vol. 52, p. 399. Bragg was ordered to send Maj. Gen. C. L. Stevenson's 9,000 troops, which left Chattanooga on December 23rd.
1023. O.R. Vol. 1, p. 438.
1024. O.R. Vol. 17/I, pp. 601–610, 613, 614.
1025. O.R. Vol. 17/ I, p. 711; Grant, Vol. I, pp. 439, 440; Sherman, W. T., pp. 323–325.
1026. Grant, U. S., Vol. I, pp. 440, 441; O.R. Vol. 24/I, pp. 1, 8, 9, 11.

Grant then completed his arrangements to abandon the territory along the Mississippi Central Railroad and, on the 29th, returned to where his command was encamped along the Mississippi River, viz, from Milliken's Bend to Young's Point, above Vicksburg. McClernand was superseded the next day, still assigned to the command of the 13th Corps, but no longer in command of a specific Vicksburg River Expedition.[1027]

Sherman's memoirs shed no light on other sources of distrust for McClernand, except to mention that Porter was "curt" in the meeting of the three, while they planned the Arkansas Post expedition. When Porter was taken aside by Sherman and asked about McClernand, he merely stated that "he did not like him." Porter, in his *Incidents and Anecdotes of the Civil War*,[1028] relates as being miffed over being summoned to meet with McClernand and offers nothing substantive, except to hint at the fact that he simply resented that Sherman had been superseded. Intensely political, and, as we have seen, having survived at pushing the limits of the chain of command in the Seward-Meigs episode during the relief of Fort Pickens, had Porter's swelled head come to a prejudiced conclusion? He had been very prematurely appointed acting rear admiral the previous October, coincident with the reorganization of the "Western Gun Boat Fleet"[1029] despite the misgivings of Gideon Welles:[1030] "Relieved Davis and appointed D. D. Porter to the Western Flotilla which is hereafter to be recognized as a squadron. Porter is but a Commander. He has, however, stirring and positive qualities, has great energy, excessive and sometimes not over-scrupulous ambition, is impressed and boastful of his own powers, given to exaggeration in relation to himself – a Porter[1031] infirmity – is not generous to older and superior living officers whom he is willing to traduce . . . This is an experiment, and

---

1027. A satisfying turn of events for William Tecumseh Sherman. He had been deeply offended at being displaced by McClernand. His official reports do not contain any hint. However, in a letter to his brother, Sen. John Sherman of Ohio, dated January 17th, he says: "I never dreamed of so severe a test of my patriotism as being superseded by McClernand, and if I can keep down my tame spirit and love, I will claim a virtue greater than Brutus'." Century, January 1893, p. 434.
1028. pp. 130–131.
1029. ORN Ser. I, Vol. 23, p. 429; O.R. Ser. III, Vol. 2, pp. 227, 644, 793.
1030. Welles, G., Vol. I, pp. 157, 167.
1031. Here Welles was referring to Porter's older brother navy Commodore William D. Porter, who had commanded the *Essex* during its engagement with the *Arkansas* and who was censured for his boastful and inaccurate reporting of that event, as well as for a disrespectful letter to the secretary of war. ORN Ser. I, Vol. 19, pp. 122, 123. The Porter family had served in the U.S. Navy ever since the revolution. David Dixon's father had commanded the frigate *Essex* in the War of 1812 and in a later event, which involved an insult to the Spanish authorities at Puerto Rico, was court-martialed. He subsequently resigned. Yet another brother, H. O. Porter, was the executive officer of the *Hatteras* when it was sunk by the *Alabama*. He died of wounds received.

the results not entirely certain." There was, essentially, no another naval officer available with the aggressiveness required.

It was now the end of January, and Grant had little to show for the three months of effort since the November beginning of his campaign. He feared for the general mood of the country. "The elections of 1862 had gone against the party which was for prosecution of the war to save the Union if it took the last man and the last dollar[1032] . . . Voluntary enlistments had ceased throughout the greater part of the North, and the draft had been resorted to . . ." This was the Militia Act of 1862 (see chapter 6).

From the north, the approaches to Vicksburg on the west side of the Mississippi were lowland, cut up by narrow bayous, most not navigable, except for such as canoes or flatboats. There was widespread flooding from continuous rain and by breached levees not now maintained by either of the states of Mississippi, Alabama, or Louisiana, which, in this time of war, had no priority for infrastructure. Marching through these areas was nearly impossible. The higher dry land on the east side of the river was the "strategical way according to the rule" with Memphis established as a secure base of supplies. Nevertheless, Grant did not continue on the expected approach for sagacious reasoning that is revealing. "It was my judgment at the time that to make a backward movement as long as that from Vicksburg to Memphis, would be interpreted, by many of those yet full of hope for the preservation of the Union, as a defeat, and the draft would be resisted, desertions ensue and the power to capture and punish deserters lost. There was nothing left to be done but to *go forward to a decisive victory*."

Forward!

Unfortunately, *forward* would consume three months of Sisyphean effort. It had, nevertheless, two positives for Banks' Department of the Gulf. It kept the Confederate focus on the north and away from Banks' predominantly green militia troops, who still required training. It also allowed time for Banks to try to clear up matters regarding the neglected state of the forts defending New Orleans, such as Macomb and Pike. Another problem was the depleted condition of the old regiments under Butler and the "miserable" arms issued to some of his new troops.[1033] For example, the 15th New Hampshire had been issued old flintlock

---

1032. Grant, U. S., Vol. I, pp. 443–447. Troop strength inferred from memoirs, pp. 423, 430; and O.R. Vol. 24/III, pp. 74, 75 (February returns, 13th, 15th, and 17th Corps). The 16th Corps occupied Memphis, Columbus, Kentucky, Corinth, Mississippi, and other points in western Tennessee, and were not directly engaged. At this time, Grant's forces – at 116,000 aggregate present – were larger than those of the combined army under Halleck, at Corinth, the previous May.

1033. Report of the inspector general, January 15th, 1863. O.R. Vol. 15, p. 648, 649.

muskets altered to percussion, an arm considered obsolete since before the war. The 47th Massachusetts had been issued the "badly constructed" Austrian rifle. Out of 800 inspected, less than 100 were considered serviceable.

The high water confined those portions of the 13th, 15th, and 17th corps involved in Grant's move on Vicksburg to the levees along the river stretching for seventy miles; from Lake Providence down to Young's point opposite the mouth of the Yazoo River, above Vicksburg. There were few options for movement before dryer weather at the end of March, but "it would not do to let almost 60,000 troops . . . lie idle all this time . . . Then commenced a series of experiments to consume time, and divert the attention of the enemy, of my troops, and of the public generally."

There were five experiments, guided by Grant's opinion that Sherman's December assault on the fortified high bluffs of Vicksburg, known as the Walnut Hills, was "very unfortunate" and "necessarily unavailing." "The rebel position was impregnable against any force that could be brought against its front[1034] . . . a front attack was therefore impossible, and was never contemplated; certainly not by me."

Three of the experiments were intended to bypass the six miles of guns on the bluffs on the eastern side of the Mississippi. They would attempt to create useable waterways on the western side. Once past the guns, this would enable a crossing of the Mississippi to the relatively dry eastern bank below the bluffs at Warrenton to enter an area perceived to be a less formidable place to make an assault. The other two experiments consisted of approaching the right flank (northeast) of Vicksburg along tortuous river routes, to avoid the Walnut Hills fortifications, which now extended along the Yazoo River to Haynes Bluff (figure 7, prepared by the author).

First, the Army of the Mississippi (McClernand remained in command of the 13th and 15th corps until January 30th) was ordered to initiate the widening and deepening of the old bypass canal on Burey's Point, opposite Vicksburg, which we remember as having been ordered by Butler and begun by General Williams' sweating troops in June of the previous year.[1035] As early as January 10th, Grant had sought advice on how to proceed. He engaged Col. Josiah W. Bissell of the Engineer Regiment of the West to consult in person with Admiral Porter[1036] as to the feasibility of resuming the effort. A blustering Porter condemned the earlier effort as being located incorrectly. The existing entrance was in an eddy and the outlet vulnerable to the Confederate guns on the bluffs below. By relocating the inlet one-half mile farther upstream and the outlet two miles farther downstream, it would stand a chance of success. Never mind that it would be three times as long, Porter's estimate was that it could be completed in twelve days. Those in Washington were so enamored with it that as early as January 19th, Secretary Welles had informed

---

1034. Grant, U. S., Vol. I, pp. 436, 445-447.
1035. O.R. Vol. 24/III, pp. 6, 7, 9, 12, 13.
1036. O.R. Vol. 17/II, p. 551; ORN Vol. 24, pp. 149, 181, 204, 205.

FIGURE 7

Porter that: "The President is exceedingly anxious that a canal from which practical and useful results would follow should be cut through the peninsula opposite Vicksburg." Grant reported to Halleck on January 20th,[1037] that the work would proceed, and Halleck telegraphed to Grant on the 25th confirming the President's interest. McClernand's troops were on the site by the 22nd.[1038]

The second experiment was at Lake Providence. On January 30th,[1039] Grant had written to Porter: "Through inquiry, I learned that Lake Providence which connects with the Red River through Tensas Bayou, Washita [Ouachita] and Black Rivers is a wide and navigable way through. As some advantage may be gained from this I have ordered a brigade of troops to be detached for this purpose."

The project would involve digging a canal approximately a mile long from the

---

1037. O.R. Vol. 24/I, pp. 9, 10.
1038. O.R. Vol. 24/ III, p. 7.
1039. Grant, U.S., Vol. I, pp. 448, 449; O.R. Vol. 24/I, pp. 14–18, 45.

Mississippi to Lake Providence, an old arm of the Mississippi seventy miles north of Vicksburg, which would open access to the river system mentioned, and back again to the Mississippi, where the Red enters it below Vicksburg. It would run a course of more than four hundred seventy miles.

A few days later, upon inspecting the project, Grant noted that he felt that: "There was scarcely a chance of this ever becoming a practicable route for moving troops through an enemy's country." Yet he let the work on this, and the other schemes go on, as he notes, their having "had the effect of making the enemy divide his forces and spread their big guns over a great deal of territory."

The third experiment would attempt to approach Vicksburg's right flank from the northeast. Though the obvious route was by entering the Yazoo from the Mississippi just above Vicksburg, the Confederates had fortified and blocked it at Haynes Bluff. Any entry into the Yazoo and the interior above Vicksburg would have to break the raft and run past the guns. Thus, Grant chose to open an old riverboat route through a cut called Yazoo Pass, some two hundred fifty miles to the north, at Delta, eight miles south of Helena, Arkansas. Closed off since 1853 when the state of Mississippi built a new levee there, this pass route followed the Coldwater River to the Tallahatchie, the Yalobusha, and finally the Yazoo. The initial route can be seen in figure 8,[1040] and the entire route in figure 9 (prepared by the author).

Details of this operation are given here because it is the only "experiment" that involved substantial shooting; and had it been successful, it might have become Grant's main attack route. Unfortunately, it was a sorry effort that failed, and resulted only in recrimination and political spin by the navy. A point of note is that modern heavy artillery had finally fallen into the hands of the Confederates. The rifled cannon was employed here and was found capable of wreaking havoc on the Federal gunboats, shaking Porter's faith in their future.

The Yazoo Pass Expedition

Under the supervision of Lt. Col. J. H. Wilson, the engineer on Grant's staff, the cut of the levee below Helena was completed by thousands of shovels, followed by explosives, on February 3rd, the day after it was begun.[1041]

The water rushed into the cut, and by February 7th, it had widened, and the water level in the old arm of the Mississippi known as Moon Lake had risen about 8 ½ feet, equal to that of the river. Now, all that was required was to clear the growth out of the fourteen miles of the old pass.

1040. ORN Ser. I, Vol. 20, p. 8, indicates it is Grant's idea; ORN. Ser. I, Vol. 24, p. 321, Porter claims it as his proposal. Figure 8, O.R. Vol. 24, p. 372.

1041. ORN Ser. I, Vol. 24, pp. 228, 249–250; O.R. Vol. 24/I. pp. 372–373, 377, 389; O.R. Vol. 24/III, pp. 55, 56.

This enormous task, begun on the 10th, was completed on the evening of the 21st by an army force that had grown to some 2,000 men.[1042] On the 22nd and the 23rd, the steamers *Henderson* and *Mattie Cook*, with a regiment of troops on board, entered the Coldwater River (figure 9), and descended it about fourteen miles. Finding it navigable, they returned. In the meantime, Admiral Porter had readied the ironclads *Chillicothe* and *De Kalb*, six tin-clads and a mortar boat, plus the 12th and 17th Regiments of Missouri Infantry from W. T. Sherman's 15th Army Corps, to go along as sharpshooters. All were under the command of navy lieutenant commander Watson Smith. Porter did not plan on any additional army support, but everything looked so favorable that Grant then called for 5,000 more troops to follow. The great object of severing the railroad supply routes to Vicksburg from the north, destroying the Confederate river fleet on the Yazoo, and lodging an attack from the northeast, seemed very promising.[1043] It was, after all, the environs into which he had marched back in November and still was "the strategical way according to the rule . . ."

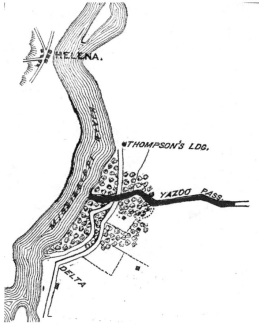

FIGURE 8

The additional army troops consisted of nine regiments of the 13th Division of McClernand's 13th Army Corps, all under the command of Brig. Gen. Leonard F. Ross, of the 17th Illinois Volunteers, accompanied by Lt. Col. Wilson. It took some time to gather the scarce troop transports necessary, and they did not arrive at Moon Lake until the 25th.

Unfortunately, nothing on such a scale could be kept secret from the Confederates, and Pemberton, now in command of the Department of Mississippi and East Louisiana, had been warned as early as February 9th.[1044] A dispatch forwarded on the 14th read: "The enemy have driven us off from the works on the Pass, and are coming through." The Confederates had occupied their time up to this point by felling trees and otherwise attempting to block the pass. This effort having failed, an alarmed Pemberton ordered guns intended for Gen. Richard Taylor diverted

---

1042. O.R. Vol. 24/I, pp. 374–376, Wilson's Report; ORN Vol. 24, p. 255.
1043. O.R. Vol. 24/I, pp. 10, 18, 45; ibid., Pt. III, p. 56, 62; ORN Ser. I, Vol. 24, pp. 258–268, 292, 293.
1044. O.R. Vol. 15, p. 2; O.R. Vol. 24/III, pp. 629, 630; ORN Ser. I, Vol. 24, pp. 263, 271, 294.

to Yazoo City, and on the 17th, Col. T. N. Waul and his Texas Legion were ordered to "establish batteries at the mouth of the Yalabusha . . ." The *Mary Keene*, *Saint Mary*, and Ellet's ram *Star of the West*, which had been captured on February 14th,[1045] were reported as being fitted out by Commander I. N. Brown of the Confederate navy, all for use in the defense against the Yankee expedition.

Underway after the clearing work was completed, the expedition made painfully slow progress, due to the unfortunate mind-set of its navy commander, Watson Smith, who was apparently on the verge of a nervous breakdown.[1046] Typically, rather than moving at dawn, the navy did not complete coaling each day before 7:00 a.m. and "on several occasions . . . stopped and lay to an hour for dinner."[1047] The difficulty that the gunboats and

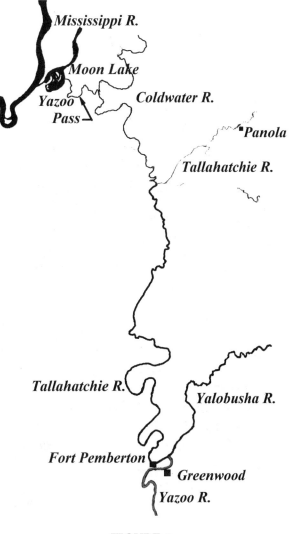

FIGURE 9

transports had at negotiating the narrow channels limited the expedition to moving only in daytime. However, the ironclads, having twin side-wheels, independently driven, were able to negotiate the channels with greater facility, yet they were held back and waited for the rest.[1048]

Porter received a report from Smith on the 12th, informing him that the expedition had reached the Tallahatchie on the 7th. Porter passed on the information to

---

1045. The story of the capture appears later in this chapter.
1046. ORN Ser. I, Vol. 24, pp. 259, 261, 262, 280, 281, 284–286; O.R. Vol. 24/I, p. 388, 390, 391, 415.
1047. O.R. Vol. 24/ I, pp. 379, 380, 394, 399, Wilson's Reports. ORN Ser. I, Vol. 24, p. 292. Ross' report.
1048. Most of the tinclads were sternwheelers. To steer around sharp turns, they had to back against their rudders, slowing them and wasting coal.

Secretary Welles,[1049] adding the blustering non sequitur "which gives us control of the heart of Mississippi." He goes on: "The vessels had to work their way through a narrow creek for over a hundred miles, while two vessels cannot pass each other . . . But for our newspapers, this would have been a surprise; but the rebels heard of it in time to be able to delay the progress by felling trees across the stream . . . This was to be a naval affair altogether,[1050] only I borrowed 800 men from General Grant to fill up our crews. At the last moment (and without my knowing it) 6,000 soldiers were ordered to join the expedition. Six days were lost waiting for them . . ." He had to admit, though, that the men "worked like heroes in clearing away obstructions . . . Indeed, I do not know how the expedition could have got through without them."

The wait Porter refers to is typical Porter theater.[1051] His motive seems to be aimed at excusing its ultimate failure, caused in no small part by his choice of the cautious Smith as commander. The army completed the clearing on the 21st. Wilson went down into the Coldwater on the 22nd and 23rd and, finding the route open, returned. The mission could thus have gotten underway on the 24th, or earlier, but it was Smith's decision to wait for the army troop transports until they arrived on the 25th. Further, once underway, Smith followed a plan of waiting for the slowest vessels to catch up – his own gunboats – which as mentioned, had difficulty negotiating the frequent turns in the narrow and tortuous stream. The more maneuverable ironclads – which, by normal naval attack doctrine were expected to "go in" first anyway – were not allowed to dash ahead, though the ironclad captains, Foster of the *Chillicothe* (figure 10), and Walker of the *Baron De Kalb* (figure 11),[1052] as well as Ross and Wilson, had urged Smith to do so.

FIGURE 10

FIGURE 11

1049. ORN Ser. I, Vol. 24, pp. 264, 265.
1050. We remember that Grant conceived of the idea. ORN Ser. I, Vol. 20, p. 8.
1051. ORN Ser. I, Vol. 24, Smith: pp. 258, 259, 262, 263; O.R. Vol. 24/I, Wilson: pp. 386–390. O.R. Vol. 24/III, pp. 640, 644.
1052. Figure 10, http://www.history.navy.mil/danfs/c8/chillicothe.htm; figure 11, Miller, F. T., Vol. 9, p. 271.

The Confederates had been working on the construction of a defensive position at the mouth of the Yalobusha, near Greenwood, since Waul's Texas Legion had been ordered there on February 17th. Also, the Second Texas Infantry, destined for the fort, had left Vicksburg on the 15th. By the 25th, Maj. Gen. W. W. Loring, in command, reported that he had two regiments, a field battery, and four heavy guns: "If we have five days more time; defenses and raft will be formidable."

General Ross stated in his final report that if they had been "allowed to proceed without waiting for the rest of the fleet, they could have reached Greenwood probably in two days after leaving the pass." This could have been February 28th. As it was, the expedition did not arrive near the Confederate fort, now called Pemberton, until March 10th. Long since, an earth and cotton-bale structure[1053] had been thrown up and was well armed and manned. On the 11th the Confederates swung a log raft into place across the Tallahatchie. The expedition would now have to fight and ram its way past to gain the Yazoo.

In retrospect, it would seem that all the argument regarding the pace of getting there was moot. The fort was armed and manned before March 2nd, and no one proved that the expedition could have arrived more than two days sooner under any circumstance.

On the morning of the 11th, the *Chillicothe* approached the fort "to reconnoiter." She was fired upon 25 or 30 times and struck twice, once in the iron plating above the hull and once in the turret. Neither shot penetrated, but the iron plating was fractured, and the turret framing was smashed behind where the shot struck. After only 20 minutes, she backed out of range, with one man slightly wounded. Forward of the turret was then covered with cotton bales, and in the afternoon, she again went in to attack. In this action, a chance shell penetrated her port gun slide and exploded. As luck would have it, this was just as the *Chillicothe's* no. 2 gun was being reloaded. A shell in the muzzle was ignited, exploded, and the gun "rendered perfectly useless," 3 men were killed, 1 mortally wounded, 10 seriously wounded, and "5 of the gun's crew had their eyes filled with powder." There was extensive damage to the turret slides, framing, and armor.

Lieutenant Commander Foster, the *Chillicothe's* captain, reported: "It is to be regretted that from the ease with which the enemy's shell, in weight not to exceed 68 pounds,[1054] penetrates the armor of the Chillicothe that she is almost a failure and will remain so until alterations are made in the backing of the turret." Fort Pemberton had been equipped with a 6 ½-inch rifle, and had used conical projectiles. It had, in addition, an 8-inch gun, among others. The rifle had added a new dimension to the severity of gunfire, a development not appreciated when the *Chillicothe* was built. Lieutenant Colonel Wilson described the *Chillicothe* as

---

1053. The fort was reported to be 15 bales thick covered with earth. ORN Ser. I, Vol. 24, p. 509.
1054. A solid ball from an 8-inch gun weighed 68 pounds.

"a great cheat and swindle upon the Government. Her plating is laid against a backing of only 9 inches of pine wood, and fastened by 6 inch spikes . . . instead of bolts . . ."[1055] Bolts had been used in earlier ironclads, such as the *De Kalb*.

That night, Wilson established a cotton-bale battery about seven hundred yards from the fort, on the only dry land available, and armed it with a naval 30-pounder, with the intent of silencing the offending rebel guns. Another 30-pounder and a 12-pounder howitzer were added the next day, the 12th.[1056]

A general attack with the land battery – the repaired *Chillicothe*, the *De Kalb*, and the mortar boat – was made on the 13th. The *Chillicothe* remained in the action for an hour-and-a-half, and though having been struck 38 times, she got off 54 shots of her own, enough to exhaust all of her five second fuses, so she then withdrew. The *De Kalb* remained until dark. Walker, the *De Kalb* captain, noted that: "The enemy fired but few shots after 2 p.m." This was significant. The fort was low on ammunition. An 8-inch gun from the *De Kalb* was added to the land battery on the 15th.

Repairs made, both the *Chillicothe* and the *De Kalb* were sent in on March 16th, with the intention of "going in . . . upon the well established principle of gunboat warfare, . . . close quarters and quick work." The *Chillicothe* was hit eight times, four on her gun ports, both by 8-inch solid shot and the powerful rebel 6 ½-inch rifle. As a result, her gun ports were distorted sufficiently to prevent their opening. She was forced to retire in less than 15 minutes. The *DeKalb* was also "drawn out."[1057] Nevertheless, Wilson makes the point that Fort Pemberton had been well hammered by the combined efforts of the gunboats and the now reinforced land battery, which fired until "night, and with so much effect that, I am convinced the two boats assisting it would have had a better chance than at any other time. I urged that the De Kalb alone should try it at close quarters, but it was not done." His calculation that the enemy was low on, or out of ammunition was ignored, though the fact was later confirmed by deserters and prisoners.

Now the fatal flaw of the expedition raised its ugly head. Lt. Cdr. Watson Smith was in command of the expedition and the army troops were merely attached. Strategy was determined by the commander, and pleas from the army were ignored. As delay and the potential failure of the expedition crept into the air, the basis for recrimination was laid.

Wilson repeatedly condemned Smith in official reports to Grant. "I have no confidence in the snap or activity of the present naval commander . . . and don't

---

1055. O.R. Vol. 24/ I, pp. 380–383, 385, 386; Wilson's reports. ORN Ser. I, Vol. 24, pp. 270–274. Smith reported that the *De Kalb*'s nine-inch guns fouled their vents, and as they had to be cleaned, it slowed their rate of fire. The *Chillicothe* had eleven-inch guns.
1056. ORN Ser. I, Vol. 24, Ross: p. 279. Walker of the *De Kalb*: p. 275.
1057. ORN Ser. I, Vol. 24, pp. 276, 277; Foster. O.R. Vol. 24/I, p. 383, Wilson. The embarrassing 15 minutes is in Wilson's report, not Foster's.

hesitate to say I regard him entirely responsible for the failure to take this place without a fight." In a semi-official letter to Grant's Chief of Staff John Rawlins, Wilson was more candid. On March 13th, he wrote: "One good gunboat can do the work, and no doubt; the two here are no great shakes." On the 15th, he reports: "Smith you doubtless have understood by this time, I don't regard as the equal of Lord Nelson." In a March 18th letter to Rawlins, he is angry: "We have thrown away a magnificent chance to injure the enemy, and all because of the culpable and inexcusable slowness of the naval commander in the first place, and his timidity and caution in the second."

On March 17th, Smith declared that he was too ill to continue in command and asked to be relieved.[1058] Lt. Cdr. James P. Foster of the *Chillicothe* then took command.

The naval force ineffective, and the fort surrounded by water, the army (Ross and Wilson) concluded it could not launch an attack. The widespread flooding that the levee cut at Delta had created, though allowing the expedition vessels to be able to get there, now functioned to save the fort! A second cut in the levee, above the first, suggested by Wilson, and then requested by Ross, was made. The small flood rise that resulted was insufficient to *drown* the Confederates out.

The land battery built by the army that had tried to silence the guns that were so devastating to the ironclads was ineffective because it could not be located so as to enfilade the fort, or close enough to dismount its guns by direct fire. Short of ammunition and food, on the 20th, the expedition decided to withdraw.[1059] On the 21st, on its way out, it was met by a relief force, the 7th Division of the 17th Army Corps, under Gen. Isaac N. Quinby. Senior to Ross, Quinby ordered him to join him in a renewed attack. (Foster, having replaced Smith as the navy commander, *agreed* to join.) Quinby reconnoitered the area and decided on an attack that would require bridging either the Yalobusha or the Yazoo in order to attack the fort from the rear.

On the 23rd, while Quinby was waiting for the bridging materials, Grant ordered the army force withdrawn. He had learned of the failure of yet another expedition led by Admiral Porter, through Steele's Bayou. Just the day before, he had concluded that: "The party that first went in have so delayed as to give the enemy time to fortify. I see nothing for it now but to have that force return the way they went in. I will let them try . . . a short time longer."[1060] It is evident that the order to withdraw did not soon reach Quinby, and, only then, it was received verbally through Wilson on the 31st. Prior to this, Quinby had been confronted with the decision by the navy to pull out "on or before the 1st proximo." If this were

---

1058. ORN Ser. 1, Vol. 24, pp. 280–282; O.R. Vol. 24/I, p. 45.
1059. O.R. Vol. 24/I, pp. 397–398, 407–408; O.R. Vol. 24/III, p. 124.
1060. O.R. Vol. 24/III, pp. 127, 151, 159, 183; ibid., Pt. 1, pp. 21, 23, 46, 68; ORN Ser. 1, Vol. 24, p. 694.

to happen, Quinby would have been left "in a very precarious position, with nearly 200 miles of unguarded water communications" between him and the Mississippi. At this, Quinby comments: "It is one of the great evils of our service that the land and naval forces are left, in a great measure, independent of each other." The entire expedition was back at Helena by April 8th, their position at Greenwood having been evacuated on the 5th.[1061]

The failed fourth expedition, Steele's Bayou, was really a corollary of the Yazoo Pass expedition. It was conceived by Porter[1062] to open a route to the upper Yazoo via Steele's Bayou, which he had prospected on March 14th. If this had been successful, it would have reached Fort Pemberton from the rear, and thus have relieved the Yazoo Pass expedition. Porter personally took charge,[1063] and even before an army force of pioneers from W. T. Sherman had arrived to help clear the way, he set off on March 15th, smashing his ironclads – the *Louisville*, *Cincinnati*, *Carondelet*, *Mound City*, and *Pittsburgh* – plus four mortar boats and two tugs, through the ever-narrowing bayous. From the lower Yazoo, he went upstream into Steele's Bayou[1064] and then into Black Bayou. There, "the crews . . . had to clear the way, pulling up trees by the roots or pushing them over with the ironclads . . ." They continued up Deer Creek, to Rolling Fork, which was little more than a flooded ditch. Here, they were halted by dense tangles of willows. Soon, groups of rebels were felling trees in their rear. At this point, Porter decided to retreat. A relief force under Sherman arrived in the nick of time and rescued him from a gathering attack. Porter was back out by the 24th.

Charles A. Dana, Secretary Stanton's special commissioner, reports[1065] of the incident: "I learn that when Admiral Porter was entrapped by the rebels at Deer Creek . . . His situation was so desperate that when Sherman's forces arrived . . . they found he had already smeared his gunboats with turpentine preparatory to abandoning them and setting them on fire."

Porter seems to have forgotten his own recommendations for Ellet's marine brigade (see below), as well as what admirals Foote and Davis knew, viz, that the ironclads need a supporting land force and vice versa. They had been successful at forts Henry and Donelson when accompanied by Grant's forces. They had succeeded at Fort Pillow after Pope's army had been ordered away only because the fort had been abandoned. Porter seems not to have credited the value of the army at the capture of Arkansas Post, his only recent experience. Almost a year prior, his ego let him believe that forts Jackson and St. Philip had surrendered to his

---

1061. O.R. Vol. 24/I, p. 401.
1062. ORN Ser. I, Vol. 20. pp. 7– 9.
1063. ORN Ser. I, Vol. 24, pp. 474–478; O.R. Vol. 24/III, pp. 112, 113.
1064. There are two Steele's bayous. The one referred to enters the Yazoo at "the ruins of Johnson's plantation . . ."
1065. O.R. Vol. 24/I, p. 72.

mortar flotilla, when what actually caused their decision to surrender was the sight of Butler's troops having flanked them.[1066]

A shaken Porter closes his report of the affair, which ended any attempt to approach Vicksburg from the northeast, with a confidential section to Secretary Welles: "As to harm the gunboats can do at Vicksburg, it is not to be taken into consideration at all . . . The batteries at that place could destroy four times the number we have here and not receive any damage in return."

The *Chillicothe* had sustained serious damage at Fort Pemberton from the Confederate 6½-inch rifle, a modern weapon. How many of tinclads were so poorly constructed? Its commander, Foster, had declared her "almost a failure." Porter laid the blame for the poor construction on the doorstep of "Mr. Hartt," the naval constructor.[1067] A significant factor, perhaps, was that the Confederate fear of gunboats was gone. The rifled gun and the sharpshooter, it seems, had learned to deal with the gunboat. He was shaken. Here he discounted the worth of his own service; yet in the same letter, he soon recovers his typical grandiloquence: "There is but one thing now to be done, and that is to start an army . . . from Memphis via Grenada . . . had General Grant not turned back when on the way to Grenada he would have been in Vicksburg before this." The whole big mess was Grant's fault.

In the official records of the navy,[1068] there appears: "Memorandum regarding the operations of the Mississippi Squadron, under Acting Rear-Admiral Porter, U.S. Navy, from October, 1862 to May, 1863." Here the myth that the army delayed the Yazoo Pass expedition is put forth fully embellished.

> The expedition was to have been a surprise, or to have reached the different points on the Tallahatchie before the enemy could have time to fortify them; this they would have done but for the change in the programme, about which Admiral Porter had not been consulted. The navy plans so far had succeeded admirably, aided as the vessels were by the troops in removing the obstructions, and the naval officer in command felt that he was duty bound to wait until the army was ready at all points to move. There was a delay of six or seven days, which enabled the enemy to fortify sufficiently to arrest the progress of the expedition until it could be ascertained what its object should be. They seem to have divined it very well, and no doubt had been well informed by traitors (an abundance of whom there were accompanying our army) exactly what the expedition intended to do, and they made their preparation so well that the expedition was unsuccessful.

1066. O.R. Vol. 6, pp. 505, 531, 532.
1067. ORN Ser. I, Vol. 24. p. 281, 322. Edward Hartt, Naval Constructor, Philadelphia Navy Yard. Much of Hartt's work took place under Davis. ORN Ser. I, Vol. 23, p. 305.
1068. ORN Ser. I, Vol. 23, pp. 395–416; *Encyclopedia Britannica*, 1911, Vol. 28, p. 506.

Wary old Gideon Welles would never have allowed such nonsense to find its way into the official record had he been alive. That portion of the ORN was not printed until 1910, 32 years after his death.

Ross' report had been respectful of the two subordinate navy commanders, only mentioning such things as "I urged the necessity of greater rapidity of movement . . . I was ably seconded by Lieutenant-Colonel Wilson. Lieutenant Commanders Foster and Walker also concurred in these views, and were very desirous to be permitted to push forward."[1069]

Foster spoiled his otherwise factually accurate April 13th report by concluding with a flagrant statement that is far removed from the original context of mutual understanding and is a patent falsehood: "In conclusion . . . had the expedition been carried out as it was originally planned, and had not the army detained us by the slowness of their movements, the expedition would have been a complete success." Given the atmosphere created by the intensely political Porter, this sentence appears to have been Foster's calculated afterthought – made under pressure. Anyone who has ever been in any of the armed services would understand the cultural cynicism. A maxim for any career officer always has been: "Do not run afoul of the popular party line . . . or of the commanding general . . ."

An apparently disgusted Ross resigned from the army in July.[1070] Watson Smith was sent on leave to recuperate, and later returned to the service to participate in the Red River Campaign. Porter again gave him the command of the *Chillicothe* on April 7th, 1864, but his health once again failed. He was relieved on June 8th, and Porter granted him leave, revealingly mentioning his "mental faculties." Smith died at Trenton, New Jersey, on December 19th, 1864.

As to the Williams canal opposite Vicksburg, the dam holding the river from entering at the upper end broke on March 7th, flooding it.[1071] Dana reported to Stanton that "The canal . . . has broken through at its upper end. The river, entering with great force, strikes the railroad embankment . . . which diverts the current . . . and floods the land without cutting the channel. A pile driver was sent . . . to bar the opening into the canal, so that digging may be resumed, but by the time it is successfully completed, the lower approaches to Vicksburg will no doubt be as strongly defended as from above." On March 24th, Dana notes: "The water is now flowing freely through the whole length of the canal . . . but produces no effect in wearing away the compact clay soil, which in the lower half of its course is especially tenacious. The dredging machines are inadequate to complete the excavations, and the water, though too shallow for the boats, is too deep for men to dig in."

1069. Ross: O.R. Vol. 24/ I, p. 399, Wilson: p. 391. Foster: ORN Ser. I, Vol. 24, pp. 282–284.
1070. Ross was a volunteer; O.R. Vol. 24/ I, p. 577; ORN Ser. I, Vol. 26, pp. 777, 779, 444, 445. www.usna.edu/Library/SpecialCollections/findingaids/watsonsmith.html.
1071. O.R. Vol. 24/ I, pp. 19, 23, 64, 65; Capt. F. E. Prime's report, p. 122. The water let out of the Mississippi at Yazoo Pass and Lake Providence diverted water from the Williams Canal.

As to the Lake Providence scheme, Dana says: "the cutting is perfectly successful, but Bayou Macon is full of snags, which must be got out before the Tensas will be accessible." In his memoirs, Grant notes that the work on both Lake Providence and the Williams Canal was abandoned on March 27th.[1072] He mentions in a report to Halleck that: "The [Williams] canal may be useful in passing boats through at night . . . but nothing further." The reason was that the greatly increased range of the guns the Confederates had set up since work began could now hit every vessel passing through it.

On the return of Sherman and Porter from Steele's Bayou on the 28th, Grant was reported by Dana to have confidentially stated "that he had now tried unsuccessfully every conceivable indirect means of attacking Vicksburg, and that nothing but a direct assault on the . . . works remained."[1073] However, at this time Dana was still in Memphis, reporting rumor. Based perhaps on a fleeting comment, Dana had speculated even further, reporting to Stanton that Grant "is about to move the bulk of his army back up the river." How could Dana have so misread Grant? Grant was not one to quit, and on April 2nd, Dana had to report that yet another experiment was already underway. On March 29th, Grant had ordered McClernand's corps to "take up its line of march . . . for New Carthage, the Fifteenth and Seventeenth Army Corps to follow . . ."[1074] Grant was still going *forward*.

On April 1st, Grant had a final look at Haynes Bluff.[1075] "I am satisfied that a direct attack . . . would be attended with an immense sacrifice of life. This, then, closes out the last hope of turning the enemy by the right." Recognizing that the falling Mississippi was changing the possibilities, a fifth experiment, a dual canal-road scheme, had already begun. If the water fell, the road would be used, and a fortuitous outcome might result in both a road and a watercourse.

Hence, on March 31st, Col. Thomas W. Bennett, commanding the 69th Indiana Infantry and a detachment of the 2nd Illinois Cavalry, marched off with orders from McClernand to make a reconnaissance south to Richmond, Louisiana, with the object of examining the "practicability of a road connection between Richmond and New Carthage, La."[1076] The canal work was begun the same day. It would consist of cutting a three-mile channel through the levee at Duckport Landing (figure 12), connecting into Walnut Bayou and the series of bayous that lead south and west to Richmond and New Carthage, some thirty-seven miles, a route suggested by Col. G. G. Pride.[1077] The route was narrow, and any of the earlier grandiose ideas of

---

1072. Grant, U. S., Vol. I, p. 456; O.R. Vol. 24/I, pp. 23, 26, 123.
1073. O.R. Vol. 24/I, pp. 69, 70.
1074. O.R. Vol. 24/I. p. 46.
1075. ORN Ser. I, Vol. 24, pp. 520, 521. O.R. Vol. 24/I. p. 24–26, 44, 46.
1076. O.R. Vol. 24/I, pp. 490–495.
1077. O.R. Vol. 24/I, pp. 45, 47, 70–72, 74, 76, 123, 125; figure 12, portion of Atlas plate 36, map no. 1, altered.

riverboats entering had been dropped. Now only supply barges were contemplated. The water from the Mississippi was let into the cut at the levee, dug by 3,500 hands, on April 14th, and dredges that had been made available then entered and commenced the work of widening and deepening the passage.

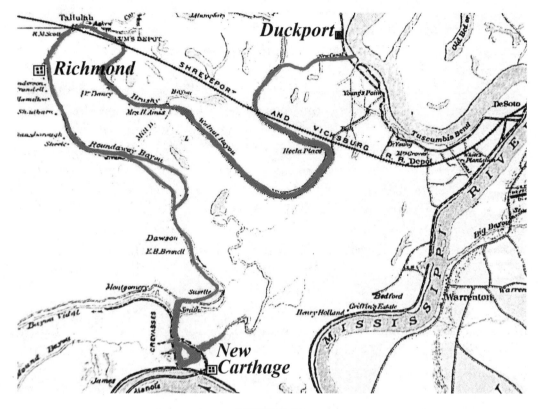

FIGURE 12

However, it took W. T. Sherman to burst the bubble of this final canal concept. On April 26th, he reported to Grant that portions of the canal were only one foot deep and that he estimated that 50 days' work would be required to complete a canal eight feet deep, sufficient for the passage of the army tugs.[1078] The continued dropping of the river had signaled the end of the canal. By May 4th, the engineers were lucky enough to rescue two of the dredges from the canal entrance, but the two others were stranded, along with 20 barges. Grant's army would have to move south on the road, on bridges, and along the levees, which had been reported as feasible by McClernand as early as April 1st.[1079] The heavy supplies would be floated past Vicksburg on unmanned barges and only at night. The way south had finally been found: the army would march.

1078. O.R. Vol. 24/III, p. 235.
1079. O.R. Vol. 24/III, pp. 164, 170, 171.

Dana

Three months had passed since Banks had arrived at New Orleans, and any attempt to follow Halleck's original directive of cooperating with the "military and naval expedition . . . organizing at Memphis . . . to open the Mississippi River"[1080] had been entirely frustrated. Likewise, Grant had totally failed to move upon, or past, Vicksburg. By April, Halleck related to Grant that the President "seems to be rather impatient about matters on the Mississippi . . . Your forces and those of General Banks should be brought into co-operation as early as possible . . . As the season when we can do very little on the lower Mississippi is rapidly advancing, I hope you will push matters with all possible dispatch."[1081]

Several times prior, we have referred to reports to Washington by Charles Dana. Stanton had originally assigned Dana to spy on Grant, and as it turned out, this may have been the turning point in Grant's career. Though Stanton's motive was suspicion, Dana turned out to be Grant's ally. A well-connected Republican, known by Chase and Seward, and the former editor of the *Chicago Tribune*, Dana had editorially supported Stanton ever since his appointment as the Secretary of War in January of 1862. This led to a correspondence between them, and the eventual assignment of Dana to investigate and audit unsettled claims against the Quartermaster's Department at Cairo in June.[1082] In the course of this work, he met both Grant and his adjutant general, Rawlins, for the first time. He was favorably impressed. His work completed in August 1862, he returned to New York.

In New York, he went into a partnership for the purpose of joining others he had observed making fortunes in cotton speculation in the newly occupied Mississippi Valley. It was not long before he had changed his mind. He saw the extent to which the mania was corrupting and demoralizing the army and resolved to expose it to Stanton, along with his recommendations as to how it could be reformed.[1083] Impressed, Stanton again summoned Dana to Washington, this time to look into the inner condition of Grant and his command, given the suspicions that had been again raised as to his competence (by McClernand's friends) and drinking habits (by the temperance movement).[1084] It was at this time that Lincoln had remarked: "Can you tell me where Grant buys his liquor? For I would like to distribute a few barrels of the same brand among my other major-generals."

1080. O.R. Vol. 15, p. 590.
1081. O.R. Vol. 24/ I, p. 25.
1082. Wilson, J. H., pp. 182–192.
1083. Wilson, J. H., pp. 195–198. O.R. Vol. 52, p. 331; O.R. Vol. 24/I, pp. 63–64. We note here that the navy continued to operate under the old system of prize laws. If the navy captured an enemy ship, it was a prize, and a prize court adjudicated shares of its value to the sailors. This later caused much dissention between the army and the navy when cotton, mules – sometimes even army ones – and other supplies were taken by Porter's Mississippi squadron.
1084. Wilson, J. H., pp. 200, 201.

Assigned as a "special commissioner of the War Department to investigate and report upon the condition of the pay service in the Western armies," he returned to Memphis in March 1863 to spy on Grant and the Vicksburg campaign, as everyone on Grant's staff already suspected.

We credit Grant with the decision to welcome him into his inner circle and allow him free access to all policy decisions and information. Dana soon fell into sympathy with the moves Grant was taking. His frequent and detailed reports to Stanton, initially based on hearsay, kept the telegraph room at the War Department filled with optimistic information.[1085] These were a great palliative, which had excused Grant's floundering "experiments." It seems Dana could make a positive interpretation of the most obscure news. One example is from March 24th, at Memphis: "The cutting of the Mississippi levees has flooded the whole country, and their [Pemberton's forces] only avenue of supplies or escape is now the Jackson Railroad." This was only partially true. Vicksburg was receiving adequate supplies via the Red River. When Dana finally arrived at Grant's headquarters after March 30th, his reports became more accurate, yet the optimism remained, viz, April 8th, at Milliken's Bend: "Everything is going on cheeringly."

Banks could have used another like Dana. There was no equivalent, however; and later in 1864 when things began to go badly, his reputation might have emerged less stained, had he such a defender.

Another thing going for Grant was Halleck's altered stature in the War Department. He was now, as Gideon Welles had frequently noted, merely a clerk,[1086] his prejudice against Grant apparently finding no audience. After so much experimentation with generals, thoughts about replacing Grant were beginning to fade, no doubt displaced by the events Lincoln and Stanton had to manage in the east. They had relieved McClellan as commander of the Army of the Potomac on November 5th, 1862, and had invested their hopes in General Burnside, whose moves against Lee proved disastrous. As was noted, Burnside was repulsed in December at Fredericksburg with 13,000 casualties to Lee's 4,600. Burnside's ill-conceived next move came in late January 1863, which was called the "Mud March" up the Rappahannock. This failure forced Lincoln to replace him with Hooker.

Even Union victories in the east were expensive and tenuous. In Tennessee, at Stones River, from December 26th, 1862, to January 5th, 1863, Rosecrans forced Bragg to retreat, at the cost of 13,000 Union casualties to Bragg's 10,000. There was little consolation[1087] in the notion (though true) that Bragg could not afford such losses.

Back at Vicksburg, it was Porter, with the Mississippi Squadron and the Ram Fleet, that now made some offensive moves. This was the result of his conviction

---

1085. O.R. Vol. 24/I, pp. 64, 65, 71.
1086. Welles, G., Vol. 1, p. 180; O.R. Vol. 19/II, p. 545.
1087. Nicolay & Hay, Vol. VI, pp. 273–296; O.R. Vol. 20/I, p. 215; O.R. Vol. 20/II, p. 446.

about the importance of the Red River as a supply route to the Confederacy, an opinion that he had held ever since July of the previous year.

We may remember from chapter 6 that most of Porter's mortar flotilla had been ordered to leave Vicksburg on July 5th, 1862, to proceed east to Hampton Roads. In passing down the Mississippi, Porter anchored at the mouth of the Red. Here, he was impressed with the evidence of Confederate activities. In a report to Farragut dated July 13th, 1862, he made the statement: "I am convinced that this war will never end while the Red River is open, with the Atchafalaya Bayou also opening into the sea." The report was almost a treatise on the necessary prosecution of the war in this theater.[1088] He even suspected or anticipated Taylor's construction of Fort DeRussy: "I have an idea that they are putting a battery about 10 miles up the river . . ." It went on: "Up the Red River and Ouachita they have about twenty steamers . . ." Porter took the liberty of forwarding a copy to Welles, even though Farragut had done so.[1089] Welles then sent an extract to Stanton. At that time, the resources and the opportunity to act had passed out of the picture; and it was only now, seven months later, that anyone could begin to act. It was D. D. Porter who was left to carry into execution his own recommendations.

The Ram Fleet and the Mississippi Marine Brigade

One matter remained to be cleaned-up however. Following the October 1862 transfer of the army river vessels to the navy,[1090] Secretary Stanton resisted the inclusion of Ellet's ram fleet and specifically advised Alfred Ellet, on October 20th, that he was to retain command of it until further orders. After some heated negotiations in a November 7th, 1862, cabinet meeting among Stanton, Welles, and Assistant Navy Secretary Fox, the President made it clear that the ram fleet would be a part of the navy; and in addition, an earlier proposal of Porter's would be implemented, that of adding a support unit to the ram fleet, to be called the Marine Brigade. It would have a total of 1,500 men, consisting of infantry, artillery, and cavalry, all under the command of Alfred W. Ellet, reporting to Porter.[1091] It was not completely manned and equipped until March 24th, 1863, but other operations of the ram fleet did not wait.

On February 1st, 1863,[1092] Ellet's ram, the *Queen of the West*, was ordered by

---

1088. ORN Ser. I, Vol. 18, pp. 678–681.
1089. ORN Ser. I, Vol. 18, pp. 645, 101, 95, 96; O.R. Vol. 15, pp. 530–532.
1090. O.R. Ser. III, Vol. 2, pp. 227, 644. ORN Vol. 23, pp. 427–429, 430. Porter threatened to detain the ram fleet if they continued to operate on the river without it under his command.
1091. ORN Ser. I, Vol. 23, pp. 396, 469. Charles Ellet, the originator of the idea for the ram fleet and its first commander, was wounded at the Battle of Memphis and had died, as mentioned in chapter 6. Alfred, his younger brother, had succeeded him.
1092. O.R. Vol. 24/I, pp. 336, 337.

Porter to proceed to Vicksburg and "destroy the [Confederate] steamer [City of] Vicksburg,[1093] lying off that place; after which you will proceed down the river as far as our batteries, below the [Williams] canal, and report to me."

The assignment was given to Alfred's nephew, Charles Rivers Ellet, the late Charles Ellet's son. It was a replay of the run the *Queen* had made on the *Arkansas* the previous July. The *City of Vicksburg* lay anchored in nearly the same position, under the bluff of Vicksburg, and Ellet frankly reported that: "The same causes which prevented the destruction of the Arkansas then saved the City of Vicksburg this morning. Her position was such that . . . we were compelled to partially round in order to strike." The *Queen* lost speed, and the collision lacked the force hoped for. However, Ellet had suspected such a result, and carefully following Porter's instructions, had the starboard bow gun "shotted" with turpentine balls. The *Vicksburg* was set on fire, but it was extinguished. All the while, the *Queen* had been taking heavy fire, being struck twelve times, and some of the 250 cotton bales used for her protection had been set on fire. Ellet judged he could not continue and fell downstream to the landing below the Williams canal to continue with the second portion of the mission, which was to: "Destroy all vessels he met with."

On February 2nd, running the gauntlet of the rebel batteries at Warrenton, where the *Queen* was struck twice, they passed Natchez and went about fifteen miles below the mouth of the Red River. There, they met the steamer *A. W. Baker*, which, having delivered a cargo to Port Hudson, was returning for another. It was taken captive along with seven Confederate officers and "a number" of civilians.[1094] Shortly, they took the steamer *Moro*, coming downstream for Port Hudson, laden with salt, 110,000 pounds of pork, and some 500 hogs.

While releasing his prisoners at a plantation near the mouth of the Red River, Ellet observed the steamer *Berwick Bay* coming out and seized it. It too had a cargo for Port Hudson. Leaving his prizes in the custody of a guard, Ellet proceeded fifteen miles up the Red, hoping for more victims. Finding none, he returned to the Mississippi and headed upstream with the three prizes following. The progress of the three was so slow that Ellet determined to destroy them rather than risk the *Queen*, which was running low on coal. The *Queen* was back at the landing below Vicksburg on the morning of the 5th.

Grant's first news of Banks' situation was from the prisoners Ellet had taken. Banks was (inaccurately) reported to be seven miles from Port Hudson and that "a severe engagement had taken place a few days ago. The rebels withdrew, and went back to the fort . . ." This vague reference may have been to the engagement of Perkins' and Williamson's cavalry with the enemy at Indian Village near

---

1093. ORN Ser. I, Vol. 24, pp. 220–223. The *City of Vicksburg* was a large Confederate supply steamer, "the strongest . . . on this river."
1094. ORN Ser. I, Vol. 24, pp. 223–225.

Plaquemine on January 28th.[1095] In any case, the presence of Banks' army somewhere near Port Hudson was at least confirmed.

Regarding the fate of the steamer *City of Vicksburg*, Porter redeemed Ellet in a report a week later, after he was informed that she was only being kept afloat by coal barges lashed to her side, and that: "Her machinery has been taken out, and she will likely be destroyed." Porter then ordered a coal barge to be floated down to Ellet to supply him with enough coal to continue with his depredations.[1096]

Having acquired the needed coal and having borrowed the small steamer *De Soto* and two 30-pounder Parrotts, one for the *De Soto* and one to be added to the four smaller pieces on the *Queen*, Ellet got off on the evening of February 10th.[1097] Informed that Porter was going to order the ironclad *Indianola* to join him in a few days, he ranged up the Red to the Atchafalaya, and down to Simmesport, destroying skiffs, flatboats, and wagons and stores found on shore. Returning to the Red, he surprised and seized the steamer *Era No. 5* on the 14th, about fifteen miles above the mouth of the Black. Hearing of other steamers thirty miles farther upriver, at Gordon's Landing,[1098] the site of Richard Taylor's Fort DeRussy, he did not attempt to join the Indianola. The *Era* was left under guard; and the *Queen*, with the *De Soto* following, headed upriver, reaching a sharp bend below Gordon's Landing just before dusk.

The *Queen* was fired upon on the moment she slowly crept past the point of the bend and into the view of the fort's gunners. After three shots, Ellet ordered the pilot to back out of sight. In doing so, the *Queen* grounded, where she remained a sitting duck. She was disabled by a shot through her steam pipe. She had to be abandoned, some of the crew escaping to the *De Soto*, though Taylor's men found 13 still on board, who were taken prisoner. Nine of those who had escaped by floating downriver on cotton bales were later made prisoners by the Confederate gunboat *Webb*. Having left Alexandria, the *Webb* continued to chase the *De Soto* and the *Era* all the way into the Mississippi.

Escaping downriver into a dense fog, the *De Soto* ran into the riverbank and lost her rudder but was able to drift back down to the *Era*. There, the *De Soto* and its coal barge were scuttled and burned. Ellet and crew continued downstream in the *Era*, reaching the Mississippi at dawn of the 15th. Proceeding upriver, they met the *Indianola*, Capt. George Brown commanding, about eight miles below Natchez

---

1095. O.R. Vol. 15, pp. 239, 240.
1096. ORN Ser. I, Vol. 24, p. 222 and Vol. 20, p. 36.
1097. ORN Ser. I, Vol. 24, pp. 383–386; O.R. Ser. I, Vol. 24/I, pp. 341–348. Note that Charles Ellet's original concept of the ram fleet being unarmed (chapter 6) was no longer practical.
1098. Fort De Russy, figure 1, is the "Fort Taylor" referred to by both Ellet, Porter, and in some Confederate correspondence. To add to the confusion, it was also referred to as Norman's Landing. ORN Ser. I, Vol. 24, p. 378.

on the morning of the 16th.[1099] Ellet and Brown then decided to continue with their assignment and "as soon as the Era could be put in running order" they proceeded back down the river. At 5:10 p.m., less than an hour after getting underway, they met the *Webb*. The *Indianola* fired two shots, and the *Webb* turned around and fled, all the way to Gordon's Landing. Brown then decided to continue to patrol the Mississippi to blockade the Red, and Ellet chose to return to Vicksburg and report to Porter.

In a report to Welles dated February 22nd, Porter called the loss of the *Queen* "a serious disappointment to us all here, as we calculated certainly on starving out the garrison at Port Hudson . . ." He chastised the young colonel[1100] for not waiting "patiently" for support from the *Indianola*, which had been detained by the fog, before proceeding to the attack at DeRussy. "I can give orders, but I can not give officers good judgment." Porter's dismay extended to the *Indianola*, which was now alone and in possible danger from the likes of the *Webb*. "Whether the commander will have the good sense not to be surprised, remains to be seen. He should return for the present."

Return of the 42nd

Ellet's adventure briefly interrupted the return of the three companies of the 42nd Massachusetts Regiment, those sent by Banks to occupy Galveston, and who been taken prisoner on January 1st, 1863 (chapter 6).

The day after their surrender, they were transported, along with the navy prisoners taken from the *Harriet Lane* in the same incident, to Houston and confined. Ordered out on January 22nd, to be paroled or exchanged at Vicksburg, they arrived by rail at Beaumont on the 23rd and on the 29th embarked on a steamer headed up the Sabine River to Burr's Landing, Louisiana, on February 4th. From there they marched to Alexandria, arriving on the 13th. On Sunday, February 15th, news that the *Queen of the West* was headed toward Alexandria gave the Confederates "a great scare." The prisoners were loaded on board the steamer *General Quitman*, which joined a river full of boats "skedaddling in perfect panic." They headed up river for about five miles until word was received that the *Queen* had been captured, when they then reversed course and made all haste back to Alexandria.

Their trip resumed the next day only to be interrupted again. Hove-to south of Alexandria, they had to await a transport loaded with 278 men of the 8th Infantry, with wives and children, those who had been surrendered in Texas in 1861, and 21 of the crew of the *Queen*. Everyone having been "conditionally" paroled on the 18th and 19th, the *General Quitman* finally departed on the 23rd after a dispute among the Confederates as to which of their steamers would be allotted their wood

---

1099. ORN Ser. I, Vol. 24, pp. 378, 379, 393.

1100. ORN Ser. I, Vol. 24, pp. 382, 383. Charles Ellet was only nineteen years of age.

fuel supply. Their destination was changed from Vicksburg to Port Hudson, and finally to Baton Rouge where they arrived on the 24th.[1101] The black members of the crew of the *Harriet Lane*, were kept in captivity until the end of the war, and treated as convicts, remained at the Texas state prison at Huntsville.[1102]

Indianola Lost

We have twice before credited Porter with prescience: before New Orleans, and for his "treatise" on the value of the Red River. Here again he was prescient, or clairvoyant. The fearsome Union ironclad, the *Indianola* (figure 13), would be sunk on February 24th.[1103] It would be attacked by a repaired *Queen of the West*, acting with the *Webb*, and two cotton-clad steamers carrying troops acting as sharpshooters and boarders. Though an ironclad, and not vulnerable to the light guns of the Confederate ships, she was towing two coal barges, which slowed her, and thus made her vulnerable to ramming. Rammed seven times, she was in an "almost powerless condition" when she ran into the west bank of the Mississippi below Warrenton and surrendered.[1104]

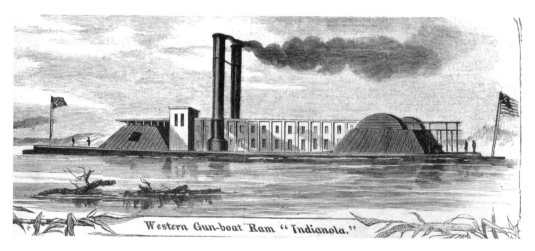

FIGURE 13

By the afternoon of March 2nd, Porter's initial telegram, sent on the 27th from Memphis, had reached Welles. It mentioned only that the *Indianola* "had fallen into the hands of the enemy."[1105] The reaction was sober:

> The disastrous loss of the Indianola may, if she has not been disabled, involve the most serious results to the fleet below. Without due knowledge of

---

1101. Bosson, C. P., pp. 173–193.
1102. O.R. Ser. II, Vol. 5, p. 397.
1103. ORN Ser. I, Vol. 24, pp. 390, 393.
1104. Figure 13, *Harper's Weekly*, February 7th, 1863, p. 84.
1105. ORN Ser. I, Vol. 24, p. 388.

all the circumstances under which you are placed at Vicksburg, the Department is not prepared to give a positive order, but rather suggests that a sufficient number of ironclads be sent to destroy her or ascertain her fate. She is too formidable to be left at large, and must be destroyed unless the attempt, in your judgment, involves still greater risks. The Department has no means of notifying the fleet at New Orleans.

The "no means of notifying" is a clue as to how upset Welles was. There was, of course, the same means as always, by ship - 10 days or more – clearly unthinkable. Nevertheless, Welles got off a warning to Farragut on March 3rd.[1106] Control of the Mississippi from Vicksburg to Port Hudson had once more passed into the hands of the Confederacy, and the urgent focus of the navy had now shifted to the south, viz. Farragut and Banks.

Banks' Plan

Before he had departed from the department in December, Butler had advised Banks to occupy the Lafourche with the "nine-months' regiments that had come down"[1107] and to then use Weitzel and his experienced troops "under cover of the fleet, to ascend the river and take possession of the west shore opposite Port Hudson . . ." The remainder of the troops, those at Baton Rouge, would then move to the rear of Port Hudson.

The plan Butler had originally suggested, and what Banks would outline to Halleck were essentially the same: render Taylor ineffective so that the breadbasket of the Lafourche and Union communication with New Orleans was secure, then surround Port Hudson, and try to starve it out. If this failed, an assault would be considered, though he wrote: "Their works are too strong for a direct attack by men who have never fired a gun. Such an attempt would result as at Fredericksburg and Vicksburg having become synonymous with excessive casualties."[1108]

As earlier noted, the 19th Corps division assignments and their brigade organizations were completed by mid-January – 1st Division Christopher C. Augur, 2nd Division Thomas W. Sherman, 3rd Division William H. Emory, and 4th Division Cuvier Grover – though it was not until February 11th, 1863, that the remainder

---

1106. ORN Ser. I, Vol. 19, p. 645.
1107. Butler, B. F., p. 531.
1108. O.R. Vol. 15, pp. 240, 241. At Fredericksburg, the past December 11th–15th, Burnside had mounted a series of frontal assaults on Lee's entrenched positions. The excessive casualties referred to earlier caused Burnside's replacement. His other reference was to Vicksburg, at Chickasaw Bayou, the past December 26th–29th, where Sherman was repulsed by Pemberton after making a frontal assault on the Walnut Hills. The Union suffered 1,700 casualties to the Confederate 200.

of the troops and two generals, Dwight and Andrews, had arrived.[1109]

Having completed his organization, the next day Banks wrote to Halleck giving the details of his broad plan of attack. It would consist of a large force sent north through the watercourses to the west of the Mississippi, the Atchafalaya, and Bayou Plaquemine to attack Taylor's fort at Butte la Rose and gain control of the country opposite Port Hudson. Then, Admiral Farragut "will attack the works on the river, and will probably run the batteries with one or more vessels, placing us in communication with the forces above." The land force at Baton Rouge would then attack Port Hudson from the rear.

Unfortunately, reconnaissance found that the proposed watercourses west of Plaquemine were blocked by miles of drift, and a revised plan, described in a letter to Halleck dated February 21st, used an altered route "via Berwick Bay and Grand Lake."[1110] All was set, and the troops that had been drilling for weeks were ready to step out on the grand mission for which they were sent to Louisiana. However, only six days later, all the preparation for Banks' plan was on hold. After hearing the news of the sinking of the *Indianola*,[1111] Banks again succumbed to Farragut's entreaties and postponed his own plans.

Farragut Passes Port Hudson

Admiral Farragut had learned of the disaster from "secesh" newspapers. He had been moored off New Orleans since returning from Pensacola on November 13th,[1112] at that time, concerned about Butler fulfilling his promise to hold Galveston, captured by the navy on October 5th. His presence at New Orleans[1113] had allowed close consultation with Butler and now with Banks, and he was therefore on top of the local news.

The West Gulf Blockading Squadron would once again step into the Mississippi above Port Hudson. In a report to Welles dated March 3rd, Farragut announced that he was "all ready to make an attack on or run the batteries at Port Hudson, so as to form a junction with the army and navy below Vicksburg[1114] . . . The army of General Banks will attack by land or make a reconnaissance in force at the same time that we run the batteries." Banks' force would divert the attention

---

1109. O.R. Vol. 15, pp. 241, 650, 714.
1110. O.R. Vol. 15, pp. 242, 243, 248, 249, 1,104; Taylor, R., p. 127.
1111. O.R. Vol. 15, pp. 1,104–1,106. Banks had little choice. The navy was a critical element in the security of New Orleans, and without close and friendly cooperation – recall Weitzel's earlier concern about Farragut removing the gunboats from Berwick Bay – life would have been infinitely more difficult.
1112. ORN Ser. I, Vol. 20, p. 6.
1113. ORN Ser. I, Vol. 19, pp. 255–260, 344; O.R. Vol. 15, p. 201.
1114. ORN Ser. I, Vol. 19, p. 644

of the Port Hudson garrison and reduce – or eliminate – its fire on Farragut.

Farragut justified his move by Welles' original order to him of October 2nd, 1862, viz: "Whilst the Mississippi River continues to be blockaded at Vicksburg, and until you learn from Commander D. D. Porter, who will be in command of the Mississippi Squadron, that he has, in conjunction with the army, opened the river, it will be necessary for you to guard the lower part of the river, especially where it is joined by the Red River, the source of many of the important supplies of the enemy."[1115] It was an emotional thing for Farragut. As Irwin,[1116] says, "Farragut took fire." The wisdom of his move was questionable, and he later would have to describe it as a disaster. For Banks, the delay would sap yet more days from the enlistment period of his nine-month men and thus put fatal pressure on the schedules of his subsequent campaigns.

Banks' plan for supporting Farragut's run was to leave Thomas W. Sherman's 3rd Division to cover New Orleans, with Weitzel's Reserve Brigade to hold the Lafourche. Every other unit was to concentrate at Baton Rouge. A demonstration, as Banks referred to it, on Port Hudson would serve to distract the Port Hudson garrison and thus allow Farragut to run past.

Battery L had been assigned as one of the three mounted batteries of Grover's 4th Division. They would be under the command of the division's chief of artillery, Battery L's own captain Henry Closson, named to that position on March 13th. The other two artillery batteries of Grover's division were the experienced and respected 2nd Massachusetts Battery (Nims'), which had suffered in the summer heat of the first and second Vicksburg expeditions under Williams, and Battery C (John Rodgers') of the 2nd U.S. Artillery, with whom Battery L had been serving nearly continuously since their days at Fort Jefferson.

Baton Rouge and the surrounding country was now one vast camp; for days the troops of Augur's division had been arriving from New Orleans. The journal[1117] of the *USS Richmond*, one of the four major warships Farragut had been able to gather for the planned run, notes: "February 25 – New Orleans. Two regiments and one light battery went up to Baton Rouge to-day. Steamer loads of provisions and stores are going up every hour in the day . . ." The journal continued daily with similar commentary ("mules," "wagons," "troops") every day, right through to the last minute: "March 9 – New Orleans. Ten or twelve steamers and transports came down from Baton Rouge last night to take up more troops and provisions . . . At 10 A.M. we stood up the river; the flagship and the *Monongahela* followed us." The last of the troops arrived at Baton Rouge on the 12th.

The drudgery of organizing, equipping, and the drilling of the troops in company formation in the morning, and in brigade formation in the afternoon,

---

1115. ORN Ser. I, Vol. 19, pp. 245, 318.
1116. Irwin, R. B., p. 76.
1117. ORN Ser. I, Vol. 19, pp. 767, 768.

had been suspended on February 22nd and a "holiday" given on the 23rd. On the 26th, General Augur, the old West Pointer, was assigned to the command at Baton Rouge.[1118] Close inspections followed, which resulted in an order from headquarters commenting "severely" on the condition of most of the troops, but which singled out the 116th New York and the 38th Massachusetts Volunteers as the objects of "emulation" of the department.

On March 7th, 8th, and 9th, the troops had been placed under marching orders; those first to depart were the first notified. All extra baggage was to be stored, including their Sibley tents. Shelter tents were issued, but apparently not to all, as the 13th Connecticut remembered having none, and having to sleep under no shelter at all for the next five months.[1119]

All were to be ready to leave at a moment's notice with three days' cooked rations. The word of the admiral that the fleet was prepared would be the signal to move. On the 11th and the 12th, a grand review by Augur, Banks, and Farragut was held at the racecourse. "Gen. Banks comes up with a multitudinous staff. Now is the time for splendid steeds . . . arching necks, prancing limbs . . . bays, blacks and grays, prancing and rearing . . ." Farragut and staff appear. "See the bluff captains and commodores from the fleet! Bump, up and down! Winnowing the air may be graceful work for . . . a swallow, but not for the elbows of a commodore. Trip goes a horse into a ditch and an aide goes down."[1120]

Farragut and the elements of the blockading squadron that could be spared for this exploit had arrived off Baton Rouge on the 11th, but last-minute preparations were still being made. On the *Richmond* (figure 14),[1121] for example, the work involved "sending down the running rigging and putting up splinter netting on the starboard side" and mounting two more guns, which consumed all that day, the next, and into the 13th. While underway to their anchorage for that night, about fifteen miles above Baton Rouge, below Profit Island (figure 15), one of the final preparations was the whitewashing of the decks and gun carriages. This increased the visibility for the gun crews for night action and is an indication that Farragut may have already altered his thinking about the original plan, which was that the attack would be made in "the grey of the morning."

1118. O.R. Vol. 15, p. 1,104; Clark, O. S., p. 55; Hanaburgh, D. H., p. 30.
1119. Sprague, H. B., p. 101. Tiemann, W. F., p. 23; Irwin, R. B., p. 77; Johns, H. T., p. 174; Maddocks, E. B., pp. 19–20.
1120. Johns, H. T., p. 174; Tiemann, W. F., p. 23; Maddocks, E. B., p. 19; Pellet, E. P., pp. 54, 55; Sprague, H. B., p. 101; Irwin, R. B., p. 77; Hosmer, pp. 80, 81.
1121. Figure 14, Miller, F. T., Vol. I, p. 227; figure 15, Persec map, portion. Note Judah P. Benjamin's plantation below Port Hudson.

FIGURE 14 USS *RICHMOND*

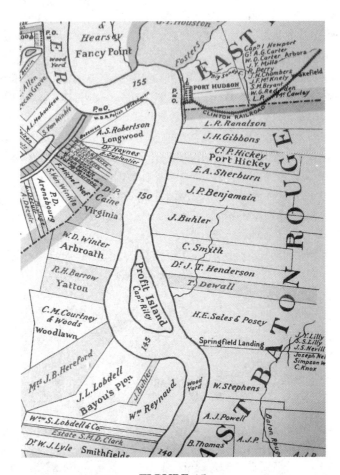

FIGURE 15

The land force,[1122] on the afternoon of Friday the 13th, with Grover's 4th Division as the advance guard flying its red flag with the white star in the center, marched out on the Bayou Sara Road. The brigades followed by number, baggage wagons sandwiched between. First rode the yellow-trimmed cavalry. The artillery, including Battery L, was sprinkled through the column, brightening the scene with their red trim. Included was a small detachment of signal corps officers and flagmen, assigned to open communications with the fleet. The weather was "grand." The road was "just what it should be, not muddy, not dry enough to be dusty; but smooth and soft enough for the foot to feel like a cushion . . ." They were shielded from the sun by a tall Magnolia forest. Not everyone, though, was happy. The day before, James A. Allen, feeling that he had been ill-used, had deserted from Battery L while at Baton Rouge. Enlisting at Hillsdale, New York, on September 28th, 1861, he had served a little more than a year in the 91st New York before he had transferred to Battery L at Pensacola on November 17th, 1862.

Allen was never heard from again by anyone in Battery L, but he continued his service in the war, a most peculiar story. Perhaps to avoid the coming campaign, he joined the 47th Massachusetts Infantry, one of Banks' nine-month militia units, using the alias James Warren, on March 25th. They remained stationed at Camp Parapet until mustered out on September 1st, 1863. Now back in Massachusetts, again calling himself James Allen, he enlisted in the 27th Massachusetts Infantry, a three-year unit, on December 14th, 1863, which was then stationed at Norfolk, Virginia. It remained there on Provost duty until March 22nd, 1864. It was then sent into active service with the Army of the James, and at the Battle of Drewry's Bluff, on May 16th, Allen was taken prisoner. He was sent to Camp Sumter, Andersonville, Georgia, perhaps the most infamous Confederate prison of all, and remained there until he was exchanged on December 24th, 1864. He was discharged on June 26th, 1865.[1123]

A provisional brigade consisting of a section of Nims' battery, Company E of the 1st Louisiana Cavalry, three companies of the 26th Maine, and the 159th New York, all under the command of Col. E. L. Molineaux, marched up the Clinton Plank Road toward the rear of Port Hudson. Emory, with the 3rd Division, followed Grover's route the same day. Augur's 1st Division brought up the rear on the 14th.

1122. O.R. Vol. 53, pp. 548–551. Irwin, R. B., pp. 66, 77, 78, 79; Tiemann, W. F., p. 23; O.R. Vol. 15, pp. 252, 253. Banks gives his force at Baton Rouge as 17,000. The security force that remained at Baton Rouge consisted of the 41st Massachusetts, the 173rd New York, the 175th New York, the 3rd Louisiana Native Guards, the 18th New York Battery, and Company F of the 2nd Rhode Island Cavalry, about 3,000 men. Other detachments were used as guards at various points. If these numbers are subtracted from the 17,000, the numbers reasonably reconcile a force of 12,000. Description of the order of march taken from Johns, H. T., pp. 84–89; Sprague, H. B., p.102, McGregor, C., p. 249; Moors, J. F., pp. 76–79; Johns, H. T., pp. 183, 184; Stanyan, J. M., pp.189, 190; Clark, O. S., p. 55.
1123. Pension file nos. 623878, 2467320; Massachusetts Soldiers Sailors and Marines in the Civil War, Vol. III, 1931, pp. 129, 424; CWAC VA 053.

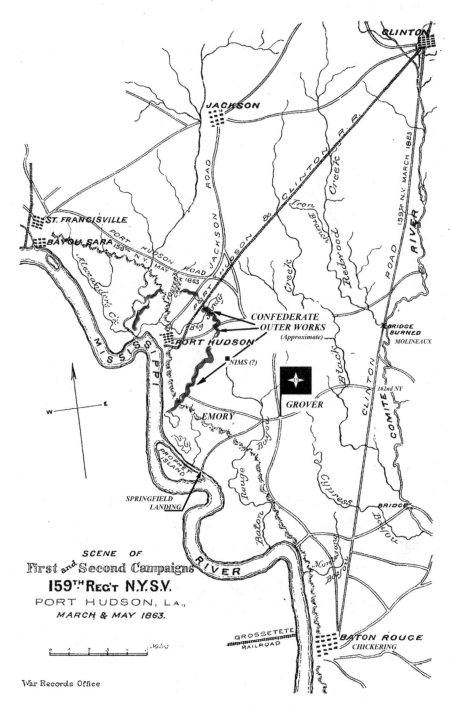

FIGURE 16

By 8:00 p.m. Grover had reached Green's Plantation, about eight miles from Baton Rouge, and halted for the night. Resuming the march on the next day, described as "beautiful," the column was now out of the shade. Soon the sun began to burn, and the road had become dusty. Men began to fall out. The sweaty 4th Division reached Barnes' Crossroads, about four miles from Port Hudson, at noon. Here, the division went into camp, and the signal detachment was sent off to Springfield Landing to open communications with the fleet. Nearby, Grover's headquarters was established, the flag in figure 16. Emory's division formed on the left of Bayou Baton Rouge covering the road to Ross Landing. Augur formed in the rear. The total mobile force was about 12,000.[1124]

The detachments continued their advance: Molineaux up the Clinton Plank Road (figure 16), with the 52nd Massachusetts Regiment pushed up to the rebel pickets just outside of the Port Hudson earthworks.

It was during one of these reconnaissances that Colonel Clark of Banks' staff had his horse shot out from under him and the fall had broken his leg. Though the wounded and dead horses of the cavalry lying about were evidence of some sharp action, he was one of the few injured. They had run into a portion of the Confederate cavalry under Gen. Albert Rust, which was picketed outside of the Port Hudson works.

At 1:30 p.m. on the 14th, a message was "sent off" according to the signal officer Lt. Joseph L. Hallett[1125] from Banks to Farragut: "My command is at Barnes' Cross-roads, and occupies the road to Ross Landing, on the flank and rear of the rebel batteries. When will you open fire? We shall be ready this evening."

At 5:00 a.m. that day, the flagship, the *Hartford*, had made signal to get underway from its anchorage off Springfield Landing, it being cloudy with a "heavy mist" hanging over the river.

By 8:00 a.m., the fleet had come to anchor within sight of Port Hudson, and at 10:00, Farragut signaled for all of the commanders to "repair on board the flagship" for a council of war. The decision was to make the attempt that night, not as planned, in the grey of the following morning. Thus, Farragut answered Banks, by a dispatch received at 5:00 p.m., that though he had earlier been delayed by the failure to complete the repairs to the engines of the *Winona* and the *Essex*,[1126] he would move at eight o'clock that evening and expected to be past the batteries by midnight.

There is the hint that Farragut was exasperated by the delay mentioned and had long since resolved to make up for it by scuttling the plan to pass Port Hudson

---

1124. Figure 16, Tiemann, W. F., insert, pp. 22–23, modified to add captions showing approx. troop locations. A more detailed map is available: "Baton Rouge to Port Hudson; Showing Position of 119th Army Corps, Maj. Gen. N.P. Banks Com'd'g. On the 14th March 1863," a copy of which was obtained, courtesy of the Port Hudson State Historic Site, Jackson, Louisiana. It was used as a reference for the preparation of the much less detailed map shown here. See also O.R. Vol. 15, p. 1,113.
1125. O.R. Vol. 15, pp. 260–262.
1126. O.R. Vol. 15, pp. 251–256, 1,112–1,114; Tiemann, W. F., p. 23; O.R., Vol. 19, p. 768.

in daylight. Whatever the case, Farragut's arbitrary decision to move that night was too quick for Banks to finalize the positions of his forces. He took it rather blandly: "I immediately directed the best disposition of our forces that circumstances would admit of, in view of the fact that our maps were in many important respects very unreliable. Of the enemy's position we had not the information necessary to enable us to approach it with confidence, and had no time to obtain this information." Add to this the fact that Banks was made cautious in that he believed that Gardner had "not less than 20,000 men."[1127] This was quite accurate. General Gardner reported 15,572 aggregate present for the month of February, and Rust arrived on March 7th, with 2,771 men. The 6th Mississippi Regiment was expected.[1128] Gardner's March return shows 20,388 aggregate present.

In a later report, Banks noted: "Had the original purpose been carried out my batteries would have been in position before morning." This may have been true, but it is of note that the guns of his heavy artillery would likely have better gained the attention of the Port Hudson garrison, and 1st Indiana Heavy Artillery does not appear in any of the marching orders. They, in fact, remained at Baton Rouge.[1129] As it happened, the fire from the light batteries accompanying the 3rd and 4th Divisions, and the cavalry skirmishing that had taken place as it had advanced, would be the full extent of any engagements on the land. The diversion would prove to be ineffective – in fact, useless.

Only those sections of Nims' battery not with Molineaux were later sent forward to shell the fort.[1130] It is presented in their history as a farce; they did not know where they were, and hardly knew in which direction to fire. "We arrived at a certain point on the road and having passed through the woods, were ordered to halt, unlimber and go into battery. Said the lieutenant to the guide: 'Where is Port Hudson?' 'Right ober dar.' Was the reply. 'Which way is that?' 'Right ober dat away.' 'How far is it?' 'Oh right smart aways.' The gunners then elevated their guns, and each fired a few shots, after which "all was still and dark as before . . . Then we limbered up, thinking of our tents and stole away back to camp and turned in."

Regardless of the forward positions of the few detachments mentioned, the vast body of Banks' forces were never much closer than five miles from the Port Hudson outer works. The monthly report of Battery L mentions having marched twenty-five miles as a part of Grover's Division; having marched twelve-and-a-half miles from Baton Rouge, they never fired a shot, stopping on the Bayou Sara Road some seven or eight miles from the fort.

1127. O.R. Vol. 15, pp. 255, 678.
1128. O.R. Vol. 15, pp. 1,000, 1,005, 1,032.
1129. Ewer, J. K., p. 64.
1130. Hosmer, J. K., p. 96; Moors, J. F., p. 76; Whitcomb, C. A., p. 44. Unfortunately, no specific mention of Battery L has been found.

The positions Farragut's ships took appear in figure 17.[1131] Note that a gunboat has been lashed to each of the three forward warships. This was to protect the gunboats as well as to provide potentially more speed and maneuverability to the combination. For example, the *Genesee*, the fastest gunboat, was lashed to the *Richmond*, the slowest warship. In making the turn past Port Hudson, the gunboat could back (power in reverse) while the steamer could drive forward for a more effective turn. The old frigate *Mississippi* was not given a gunboat because it was a sidewheeler, and there were only three gunboats available anyway.

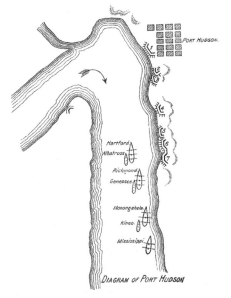

FIGURE 17

Six mortar boats and the *Essex* and *Sachem* were positioned below, above the head of Profit's Island, behind a slight bend in the river, to provide enfilading fire upon the lower of the Port Hudson batteries. They began firing their single "Dictators" (13-inch mortars) at 4:00 p.m. with the intention of keeping up the firing until the fleet had passed. On this beautiful clear afternoon, the booms were heard one hundred miles away at Camp Parapet.[1132]

The fleet got underway, and reached a position at 11:20 p.m. where the Port Hudson lower batteries opened upon the *Hartford*. The river depth was such that the fleet had to pass close to the Port Hudson shore – so close, in fact, that the voices of General Gardner's gunners could be distinguished above the clank and hiss of the *Hartford*'s steam engines.

The numerous guns on the bluff opened upon the fleet as they moved further upriver at their painfully slow pace, less than three miles per hour, their net forward speed being reduced by the speed of the current. Soon, the smoke from the Confederate guns, the ship's guns, and their smokestacks – their coal-fired boilers straining at maximum power – had, in this still, damp evening, settled upon the river to a degree that made it almost impossible to distinguish anything of the action. The *Hartford* had the advantage of being in the lead, running clear, but leaving those to follow in difficulty.

Continuing the narrative, now from the log of the *Richmond*:

> The rebel sharpshooters opened on us, but they were soon silenced. The

---

1131. Figure 17, ORN Ser. I, Vol. 19, p. 669; ibid pp. 697, 698, 700, 709, 769. Various reports state the time as anywhere from 11 to 11:30. The log of the *Hartford* is here the authority. Note that, all of the ships are shown close to the eastern shore, very close to the Port Hudson guns.

1132. McGregor, C., p. 248; Hosmer, J. K. p. 80.

engagement now became terrible. The rebel's guns raked us as we came up to the point. The lower batteries were all silenced as we passed, but misfortune now befell us: as we were turning the point almost past the upper batteries we received a shot in our boilers, and almost at the same time the Genesee got a shot in her machinery and a fire broke out in her, and another shot went through our steam drum. Our steam was all gone; we could not steam up against the current with one boiler. Torpedoes were exploding all around us, throwing water as high as the tops [figure 18]. We were, for a few minutes, at the rebels' mercy; their shell were causing great havoc on our decks; the groans of the wounded and the shrieks of the dying were awful. The decks were covered with blood . . . We turned her head downstream.

The admiral and the Albatross were the only vessels that succeeded in passing up the river. . . . The Mississippi got aground and could not be got off, and the rebel shell were tearing her to pieces. The crew left her in boats, some coming down the river and some going ashore. After they deserted her they set fire to her . . . The Monongahela and Kineo were pretty badly cut up; they got down safe again.

FIGURE 18. FARRAGUT PASSING PORT HUDSON

An engraving from *Harper's Weekly* of April 18th, 1863, pp. 248–249. The artist has forgotten that the ships were forced to pass close to the Port Hudson side where there was adequate water depth. Where shown, all would have run aground, as has the *Mississippi*, the last in line and now in flames.

At about 4:00 a.m. the sky was lit, and a dull roar, "resembling distant thunder," shook the ground where the 26th Maine Regiment was standing, four miles away from the river.[1133] It was the *Mississippi*'s magazine, which demolished

---

1133. Maddocks, E. B., p. 25.

the venerable veteran, the flagship of Commodore Perry when he had entered Tokyo Bay in 1853.[1134]

At 6:00 a.m., Signal Officer Hallett sent off a message to Banks, indicating details of the disaster and that only the *Hartford* and the *Albatross* had passed Port Hudson. The action was ended. Orders to Banks' troops were soon sent out that the object of the expedition had been achieved, and that they should be ready to march. "Much wondering at this Delphic announcement, not yet knowing that Farragut had successfully passed the batteries . . . we marched at daybreak."[1135] Given these orders to retreat in apparent disgrace, without firing a shot, and in ignorance of the purpose of the plan, the troops were sullen.[1136]

In the afternoon it began to rain in torrents, the dry pleasant weather of the previous week forgotten. Then, there was straggling and complaining about the insufferable heat and the casting aside of various pieces of their equipment. Now, the complaint was where to find shelter and cook supper. An area previously chosen for their bivouac was now a swamp, but they must obey orders. Many spent the night standing in water from a few inches to a foot deep. No supper, no breakfast.

Despite the spectacular nature of the "disaster" as Farragut referred to the affair,[1137] the numbers of navy casualties were small. The preliminary reports of the casualties were (K [killed], W [wounded]):[1138]

	HARTFORD	ALBATROSS	RICHMOND	GENESEE	MONONGAHELA	KINEO	MISSISSIPPI
K	1	1	3	0	6	0	25
W	2	2	12	3	21	0	9

As a measure of the activity on land, Confederate losses were reported as one killed and nineteen wounded.[1139] The only reference Banks makes to casualties is to those of the navy; General Dwight, 1st Brigade, Grover's Division, reported no losses.

Some of the regiments were ordered directly back to Baton Rouge. Others were detained for several days to escort wagon trains carrying cotton confiscated from the area.[1140]

1134. ORN Ser. II, Vol. 1, p. 146.
1135. Sprague, H. B., p. 104. The 52nd Massachusetts (Hosmer); 26th Maine Regiments (Maddocks) list noon (p. 99) and 3:00 p.m. (p. 27), respectively. The 26th was the rear guard. O.R. Vol. 15, p. 262.
1136. Hosmer, J. K., p. 100.
1137. ORN Ser. I, Vol. 9, pp. 667, 670, 676, 680, 683, 688, 689, 693–695.
1138. The number of missing for the *Mississippi* was listed on March 20th as 76, with an initial count of 233 saved. The numbers shown are those reported by the surgeon of the *Richmond*.
1139. O.R. Vol. 15, pp. 252, 265, 278.
1140. Moors, J. F., p. 92; Morris, G., 6th New York, p. 89.

The historian of the 6th New York commented: "Altogether this raid was valuable training, as accustoming everybody to be cheerfully uncomfortable, but it affected little in the way of suppressing the rebellion, and when the Sixth settled back into its camp, cleaned its trousers, and got itself into shape, it had an internal feeling that perhaps the high military authorities of the Department of the Gulf were not so much wiser than the rest of the world as they would have desired other people to believe."

The soldier's view about not suppressing the rebellion was a misunderstanding, as Irwin, in his *History of the Nineteenth Army Corps*, maintains. Irwin's optimistic view (also Farragut's) was that as the result of Farragut's presence above Port Hudson, the Confederacy was denied the use of the Red River to carry supplies across the Mississippi, "save in skiff-loads." The Confederate supply road from Galveston and Matamoros was closed. Also, of course, the operation resulted in the army gaining "some facility of movement, some knowledge of its deficiencies, and some information of great future value as to the topography of the unknown country about Port Hudson . . ."[1141]

Irwin seems to have forgotten that only two of Farragut's ships had managed to pass Port Hudson – his flagship, the *Hartford*, and the *Albatross* – and that to accomplish anything in terms of future patrolling of the Red River, he had to ask the assistance of the Mississippi Marine Brigade, as is discussed in the next chapter.

The fact that General Gardner, the Confederate commander at Port Hudson, did not move out and attempt to crush Banks' lesser force, as was suggested to him on March 9th and 10th by Pemberton, was perhaps because Gardner had overestimated Banks' strength at 30,000 and Pemberton, at Vicksburg, had advised him that, "I am too much pressed on all sides to give you more troops."[1142] Grant's "experiments" were working, keeping the Vicksburg defenders occupied; and by the end of April, when Grant finally crossed to the east side of the Mississippi and began his assault, Pemberton would be overwhelmed and unable to operate on the west side of the Mississippi, to aid Richard Taylor, as Kirby Smith would request.

Banks' letter to Grant describing the diversion, dated March 13th, had been carried on the *Hartford* and therefore was able to be delivered promptly. Farragut's passage may or may not have accomplished the closing of the Red River, but it is certain that it had, at least, opened communications between Grant and Banks, then regarded as significant. Unfortunately, Grant's initial response was confusing.[1143] One note was addressed to Banks, and another was to Farragut, dated the same day, March 23rd. In this, Farragut was requested to "inform the general of the contents of this."

In the note to Banks, Grant outlines his recent "experiments" at trying to

---

1141. Irwin, R. B., p. 81.
1142. O.R. Vol. 15, pp. 269, 303, 692, 693, 1,044.
1143. O.R. Vol. 15, pp. 300, 301.

pass Vicksburg. He mentions the Yazoo Pass expedition and Commodore Porter's attempt at its rescue from Steele's Bayou, which, at that date, was still unresolved. "This experiment failing," he would be left with no other option than to attack Haynes Bluff. He ends the letter with: "The best aid you can give, if you cannot pass Port Hudson, will be to hold as many of the enemy there as possible. If they could be sent, I could well spare one army corps, to enable you to get up the river. My effective force, including all arms, will be between 60,000 and 70,000, if I bring all from Memphis that can be spared in an emergency. An attack on Haines' Bluff [sic] cannot possibly take place under two weeks, if so soon. My forces are now scattered and the difficulty of getting transportation is very great."

The size of Grant's force must have astonished Banks, and the "experiments" he described must have mystified him, not to mention Haynes Bluff, which likely had no context whatever.

The letter to Farragut must have been an attempt at clarification. In this, Grant mentions the Lake Providence scheme and that it would provide a route to the Red River. In somewhat of a *faux pas*, he says:

> This is now reported practicable for ordinary Ohio River steamers. I sent several weeks ago for this class of steamers and expected them before this. Should they arrive, and Admiral Porter gets his boats out of the Yazoo, so as to accompany the expedition, I can send a force of, say, 20,000 effective men to cooperate with General Banks on Port Hudson . . . This force certainly would reduce Port Hudson and enable them to come up the river and maintain a position on high land near enough to Vicksburg until they could be re-enforced from here sufficiently to operate against the city.

On the very same day, Grant had ordered General Quinby to withdraw from the Yazoo Pass, making the reference to it in the first letter irrelevant; and though when he initiated the Lake Providence experiment on January 30th, he had commented that it had scarcely a chance of success, yet he had here prematurely counted it as successful. As we have seen, Grant had ended up abandoning both the Lake Providence experiment and the Williams canal on March 27th. The steamers requested by Grant never came, their seizure being vetoed by Halleck.[1144]

Unfortunately, Banks did not receive Grant's letter until April 21st and, until then, only heard an oral summary of a letter from Grant to Farragut by Farragut's secretary Gabaudan, who arrived at Brashear City on April 10th, long after Banks had begun the Teche campaign, described in chapter 8. This initial presentation falsely gave the impression that Grant would send reinforcements via the Lake Providence route to join Banks.

With that false but positive note, Banks took the risk of pulling substantial numbers of troops out from the area adjacent to Port Hudson and redirected them

---

1144. O.R. Vol. 23/II, p. 151; O.R. Vol. 24/III, pp. 120, 121.

to begin his postponed campaign up the waters to the west of the Mississippi, namely the Atchafalaya River and Bayou Teche. The garrisons at Baton Rouge and New Orleans would have to "hold the fort" as the saying goes.

Chapter 8

The Teche Campaign:
Record 4/63; Bisland/Irish Bend;
Queen of the West/Cornie; Chasing the Fox;
Opelousas; Cooperation with Grant; Grierson's Raid;
Alexandria, De Russy & Red River, Farragut Departs;
Turn to Port Hudson

Record 4/63
28 FEBRUARY–30 APRIL 1863, BARRE'S LANDING, BAYOU CORTABLEAU

Battery with Gen. Grover's Division, left Baton Rouge the 13th. Marched toward Port Hudson. Remained in the field until the 20th and returned. Left Baton Rouge on Steamer "Laurel Hill" & arrived at Donaldsonville, La., on the 27th. Took up line of march and camped at Assumption Parish, La., 31st, 15 miles. Took up line of march April 1st for Brashear City, La.,[1145] and arrived April 9th, distance 80 miles. Embarked on Steamers and Flats, night of the 11th, disembarked, morning of the 13th on Madame Porter's plantation / Grand Lake. The Battery was thrown to the front at 6 a.m. Appleton's sections detached each to secure and hold bridges across the Teche Bayou. This was accomplished, and at the left bridge, by Appleton's section, under a very annoying fire from 4 guns of the Rebel artillery and his Sharpshooters. Casualties two horses wounded. During the fight of the 14th the Battery was held in reserve. On the 15th, took up line of march and reached Vermillion River the 17th, estimated distance 45 miles. At Vermillion Bridge, Taylor's section of the Battery was opened upon by Sharpshooters and the Rebel artillery of 4 guns from the cover of the opposite bank. Casualties 2 horses killed, the remainder of the Battery in action soon shelled the Rebels out. On the 20th marched into Opelousas, an estimated distance from Grand Lake landing 60 miles. On the 26th inst. Marched from Opelousas and encamped same day at Barre's Landing,[1146] Bayou Courtableau, La. distance from Opelousas, 8 miles.

Henry W. Closson	Capt. Commanding Battery and Chief of Artillery Grover's Div. 19th Army Corps.
Franck E. Taylor	1st Lt. Ass't. Comm'y Of Musters S.O. no. 16 Hdqrts Dept of the Gulf 19th Army Corps Apr. 9, 1863
Edward L. Appleton	1st Lt.
J.A. Sanderson	2nd Lt. Appointed to the Co. by promotion: vice Gibbs promoted War Dept. A.G.O. Wash. July 4, 1862 (never joined co.)

1145. Now Morgan City.
1146. Now Port Barre.

Detached: George Friedman	Pvt. On Det. Svc. at N.O. as Artillerist. Left Co. May 24,'62.
Amelius Straub	Pvt. Absent on Ex. Duty as Cook in Gen. Hosp. Baton Rouge since Mar. 14,'63.
Martin Stanners	Pvt. Absent on detached serv. At Bayou Boef, La., since April 7, 1863.

Strength: 143. Sick: 15

Sick Present: Julius Becker, John Baker, John Burke, Edward A. Foote, Edward McLaughlin

Sick Absent: William C. Brunskill, Fort Hamilton, NY, Left Company Sept. 17, 1861
     Isaac T. Cain Brashear City, La. since Apr. 22, 1863
     George Chase Brashear City La. since Apr. 22, 1863
     William Crowley Absent sick in General Hospital, Baton Rouge, La. since Mar. 27, '63.
     Joseph Eisele In Hosp. at Franklin, La. since April 15 ,'63
     Benjamin O. Hall Abs. sick at Baton Rouge, La. since Mar. 27,'63
     Michael Kenny In Hosp. at Franklin, La. since April 15,'63.
     Charles F. Mansfield sick at Pensacola, Fla. since Dec. 24,'62
     Joseph Smith Brashear City, La. since April 22,'63
     Wallace D. Wright sick at Pensacola, Fla. Since Dec. 24,'62

Horses:	Serviceable: 96 Unserviceable 8.
Died:	Daniel McCoy Pvt. 22 Oct. '60 New York, at Gen. Hosp. Baton Rouge, La. Mar.4,'63
	Charles A. Flint Pvt. 22 Sept. '60 Boston, " " " April 13,'63
Deserted:	James A. Allen Pvt. 17 Nov. '62 Pensacola. From Baton Rouge, La., on Mar. 12,'63
	James R. Harrington Pvt. 27 Feb. '63 Baton Rouge. From Camp at Thibodeaux, La., April 17,'63
	Abram P. Winn Pvt. 16 Dec. '62 Pensacola " " "
	Joel T. Winn Pvt. 26 Dec '62 Pensacola " " "

  The sick list is long, and two deaths due to it appear. The cause of death is not listed, and that portion of Danield McCoy's service record is unreadable. Substantially more information has been found in Sarah Flint's application for a mother's pension. She cites the surgeon's report that lists Charles as having died of "Typho Malarial Fever." Her file also contains a personal letter from Captain Closson, which is reproduced here (figure 1).

  It is the only one that has been found from the many records examined relating to deaths in Battery L. There was apparently no official requirement that the company commander write such a letter or that it pass through channels. The only official requirement was that "final papers" be made out as for a typical discharge. Enumerated were pay adjustments that we have seen before; those that may have been owed to the sutler, laundress, or for "camp and garrison equipment."

  It is believed, however, that either Henry Closson or Franck Taylor wrote a letter in every case of a Battery L death, because an affidavit in yet another pension application, that of Clarissa Parslow, makes reference to such a letter: "Said Joseph

H. Parslow died in battle as his colonel wrote my husband . . ." Parslow died at Smithfield, West Virginia (chapter 13)[1147].

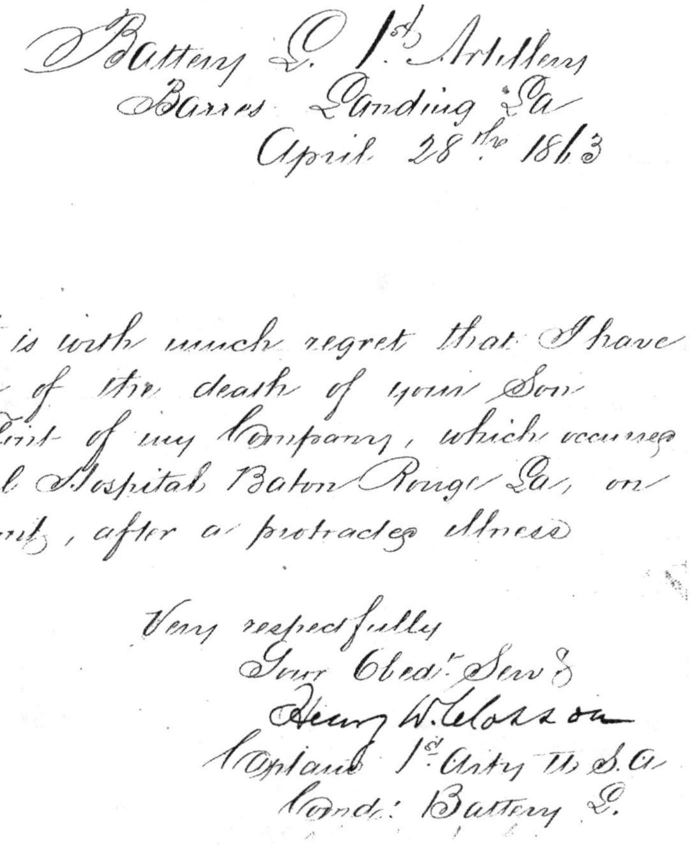

> Battery L 1st Artillery
> Barres Landing La
> April 28th 1863
>
> Madam
>
> It is with much regret that I have to inform you of the death of your Son Charles A. Flint of my Company, which occurred at the General Hospital Baton Rouge La, on the 13th instant, after a protracted illness
>
> Very respectfully
> Your Obed" Serv'
> Henry W. Closson
> Captain 1st Arty U.S.A.
> Comd: Battery L.

FIGURE 1

Allen had enlisted from Company H of the 91st New York Regiment and the Winn brothers from Company A. Harrington was from Company E of the 13th Connecticut.

The muster rolls, as earlier mentioned, were used to verify service for pensions granted long after the end of the war. This repeated usage resulted in many of the rolls being in poor condition. Corrections and status changes as may have been effected by laws subsequently enacted by Congress were simply overwritten into the original document. This roll is an example. Above Allen's name, there appears an overwrite: "Also, under prov. of Act of Congress approved March 2, 1889, charge of desertion is removed, vide AG 1741499."[1148] His story, covered in

---

1147. Flint file no. 43709, Parslow file no. 147787; National Archives.
1148. The number is the adjutant general's file number. This decision was made on April 13, 1911. The law referred to is recorded in the 1890 Annals of Congress, 50th Congress, ch. 390, pp. 692–694.

the last chapter, explains why – he reenlisted sooner than the required four months limit stated in the law.

There are numerous overwrites on the names of the two Winns, which are nearly illegible. Below the original entry, there appears this new entry:

> #Abram P. Winn} See Prisoner of War records for report of capture May 16/63, subsequent parole and desertion.
> # Joel T. Winn}   do.   do.

Though the subject of prisoner parole and exchange had had a checkered history right from the beginning, it was at least operating up to 1863, as we have seen regarding the troops in Texas, and the exchange of Sergeant Riley. The Dix-Hill Cartel was agreed to, as mentioned earlier, on July 22nd, 1862. The following February, noting that the Confederacy was violating the terms of the cartel, caused the War Department to issue new instructions[1149] in the form of General Orders No. 49, dated February 28th, 1863, to guide commanders on how to handle prisoners. The final rules for the parole and exchange of prisoners were not worked out until April of 1863 and were issued as General Orders No. 100[1150] on May 20th, 1863. However, this strict construction was suspended on May 25th, by Halleck in the case of Confederate officers who, henceforth, were not to be paroled and were to be confined until further orders. The case of the Winn brothers tested the system with a rather strange twist.

Having deserted at Thibodeaux, on April 17th, as Battery L was marching to Berwick City, the Winns managed to reach Jackson, Mississippi, by May 16th, where they were taken prisoner. They had tried to cut through Confederate territory to get home to Vermont! Transported to Richmond, Virginia, they were paroled, with the remark "deserter," at City Point, Virginia, on June 13th. Sent to

---

1149. O.R. Ser. II, Vol. 5, p. 256, 306, 307. The whole issue of dealing with the Confederacy as an honest and civilized entity was brought into question by Jefferson Davis' proclamation of December 24th, 1862 (O.R. Ser. II, Vol. 5, pp. 795–797). In a reaction to the hanging of William Mumford at New Orleans, Davis declared Benjamin Butler a "felon deserving of capital punishment" and that if captured he would be put to death by hanging. More important was Davis' declaration regarding former slaves serving in the Union army. If captured, they would: "At once be delivered over to the authorities of the respective States to which they belong, to be dealt with according to the laws of said States." These were code words for execution because an escaped slave under arms was in "armed insurrection" punishable by death. Proof of the extreme Confederate attitude is found in a letter to Richard Taylor from his superior E. Kirby Smith, dated June 13th, 1863. Smith, in part, says: "I have been unofficially informed that some of your troops have captured negroes in arms. I hope that this may not be so, and that your subordinates who may have been in command . . . may have recognized the propriety of giving no quarter to armed negroes or their officers," O.R. Ser. II, Vol. 6, pp. 21, 22.

1150. O.R. Ser. II, Vol. 5, pp. 671–682, 696; Abram Winn, pension file no. 766906; Joel Winn, file no. 957542.

College Green Barracks, Maryland, they were examined at hospital and then sent to Camp Parole, Maryland, on the 22nd, arriving there on the 23rd. There, they again deserted, and never returned to Battery L.

As the criteria for an invalid pension was eased by a sucession of laws after the war, both applied for pensions. Both were denied. After Joel's death in 1877, his wife Mary repeatedly applied for a widow's pension, a process she carried on for some forty years. Finally, after a Special Act of Congress, dated December 23rd, 1923, she was granted $30 a month.

Bisland/Irish Bend

The campaign would begin at the lower waters of the Atchafalaya and follow the Teche, where Longfellow's Father Felician had acted as guide to Evangeline.[1151] Heading north along the Teche (figure 2), it would clear Taylor out of the Attakapas (which today comprises St. Martin, St. Mary, Lafayette, Vermilion, and Iberia parishes), and the western bank of the Mississippi opposite Port Hudson, as far north as Opelousas.[1152] At that point, the plan, as Banks outlined to Grant in a letter dated April 10th, 1863, was to return to Baton Rouge to "cooperate with you against Port Hudson."

The plan would step off in a move essentially identical to what Weitzel had made the previous January when the Confederate steamer *J. A. Cotton* was destroyed. Weitzel's reinforced brigade, separated from Augur's division, would be transported from Brashear City across Berwick Bay to be landed near Pattersonville to again attack a revived Fort Bisland, which once again had a gunboat, the recently captured *Diana*, to support it.[1153] This time, however, Weitzel would be followed and supported by Emory's division; and as part of a classic flanking movement, Grover's division would be transported up Grand Lake to a point

FIGURE 2

1151. Longfellow reference: Ewer, J. K., p. 68.
1152. ORN Ser. I, Vol. 20, p. 50; Sprague, pp. 108, 109; Irwin, R. B., pp. 80 (figure 2), 104, 105.
1153. Taylor mentions having brought the USS *Diana* to the fort, where "her 'Parrott' became a valuable adjunct to our line of defense." It had been captured on the Teche on March 28th. Taylor, R., p. 128; ORN Ser. I, Vol. 20, pp. 109, 110, 113.

above Franklin (figure 2), where the shore of Grand Lake lies close to one of the bends in the Teche. There, he would land in the rear of Taylor's forces, seize the road, and cut off any possible avenue of retreat. At least, that was the plan.

Augur was left to defend Baton Rouge with his 1st and 3rd brigades, and T. W. Sherman was in command of the defenses of New Orleans and the Lafourche. Having been warned from headquarters to be ready to move at a moment's notice, marching orders were issued to the troops on March 25th, the day after Banks had returned to New Orleans from Baton Rouge.[1154]

FIGURE 3

Grover's division was ordered to move on transports to Donaldsonville and to march from there to points on the Great Western Railroad. Emory's division would be transported to Algiers as soon as the transports were released from Grover to move to Brashear City by rail. Battery L boarded the transport steamer *Laurel Hill* (figure 3), on the 27th and arrived at Donaldsonville, some 90 miles south of Baton Rouge, next day.[1155] Some of Battery L's colleagues from the days at Pensacola, Billy Wilson's 6th New York, found whiskey on board their steamer, the *Morning Light*, got very drunk, and a part of the resulting shenanigans was an attempt to throw General Dwight overboard.[1156] Whether Dwight was a part of the affair, or

---

1154. Irwin, R. B., p. 88; Sprague, H. B., p. 106; O.R. Vol. 15, p. 258.
1155. Figure 3, March 21st, 1863, *Harper's Weekly*, p. 21; the steamer was rated at a capacity of 1,000 troops. O.R. Vol. 15, p. 1,102; Haskin, W. L., p.189; O.R. Vol. 15, p. 365, Closson's report; pp. 380, 381, Day's report.
1156. Bissell, G. p. 26.

was merely asked to quell it, is not reported; however, woe unto those officers, Billy Wilson among them, and the 24 enlisted men who were involved. Dwight saw no humor in the incident. They were all disarmed and arrested.

Who was this Dwight?

Born in Massachusetts, he attended West Point from 1849 to 1853 but resigned to enter private business in Boston. He entered the army as a captain of the 13th Infantry on May 4th, 1861, but in June was appointed a lieutenant colonel of the 70th New York Volunteer Infantry. At the Battle of Williamsburg – where the 70th lost half of its men killed, wounded, or missing – Dwight was twice wounded and left for dead on the field. He was taken prisoner and was eventually exchanged and promoted to brigadier general on November 29th, 1862.[1157]

There are "different strokes for different folks," and Dwight's experience could have resulted in a personality of sage patience, and a sunny attitude, overlooking minor events. Another type might have emerged with a deadly serious attitude of disgust with human frailty and a no-nonsense approach to life. Billy Wilson's men tested Dwight and evidently discovered the latter.

Though most of Grover's infantry marched south from Donaldsonville to take the railroad at the Lafourche or Terrebonne stations, Battery L, being fully mounted, and towing heavy cannon, marched all the way to Brashear City. On Wednesday, April 1st, with a cool northeast wind blowing, Battery L set out. The weather remained clear and cool, only warming on Sunday the 5th. There had been no rain, and the ground was dry. It was an easy pace of about ten miles per day – nothing like the urgency of the march out of Texas or the pull in the sand during the reconnaissance on Santa Rosa. Memories were accumulating and were attaining the usual rosy glow. All of that would soon pale before what was in store for them in the coming campaign.

Following south along the banks of the Lafourche[1158] to Thibodeaux, they entered an area where there were some of the first settlements of the Acadians, the Louisiana described by Longfellow. It was here, with easy access to the railroad to New Orleans, that the Winn brothers and James Harrington deserted. Strangely, they headed north, into Confederate territory, and as was noted, they were captured.

Battery L reached Bayou Boeuf, just east of Brashear City on April 9th, where Grover's division had been encamped since the 4th. That day, the whole division moved on to Brashear City as part of the beginning of the campaign.

Weitzel began to cross the mile-wide Berwick Bay at about 10 o'clock on the morning of the 9th, the navy gunboats *Estrella*, *Clifton*, *Calhoun*, and *Arizona*

1157. Johnson, R., Brown, J. H., eds., *Biographical Dictionary*, Vol. III.
1158. Today, the Lafourche is nothing like the free-flowing stream witnessed by Battery L, having been sealed off from its Mississippi source by a dam built in 1905. Weather references from McGregor, C., pp. 258–266.

adding to the ferrying capacity of the transports, the *St. Mary's*, *Laurel Hill*, and *Quinnebaug*.[1159] Emory followed, and the four brigades – some 12,000 officers and men – were bivouacked near their landing place that night. The short distance across Berwick Bay had allowed many round trips, the landing points were clear, and the vessels could be loaded without regard to crowding, the criterion being merely that the vessel remained afloat for the short trip. Banks and staff arrived at Brashear City that evening.

For Grover's force, consisting of thirteen regiments, three artillery batteries, and one cavalry company – more than 4,000 officers and men – the situation was different. The only available vessels[1160] had to be loaded for a one-way twenty-mile trip up to the planned landing on Grand Lake. There could be no return for supplies if this was to be a surprise operation. The situation taxed the vessels and the constitution of the troops to the extreme.[1161] For example, the crowding on the *St. Mary's* – formerly a New York and Galveston ocean liner, "a beautiful vessel" built to carry 500 passengers at a pinch – was extreme. Loaded with the 52nd Massachusetts, the 25th Connecticut, the 12th Maine (Lt. Appleton's brother's unit), the 24th Connecticut, and a portion of Nims' battery – some 2,500 men – conditions, were described by J. F. Moors of the 52nd Massachusetts as "full to overflowing, so that the men appear to lie two to three deep on deck; while some hang up in the shrouds, and others stand leaning against or crouching on the bulwarks. We are literally as thick on board as three in a bed." Of course, there was no room for cooking; and when the planned day trip had dragged on to 40 hours – one day, two nights, and part of another day – the sanitary conditions had become terrible, the troops had had little sleep or food, and they were hardly ready to be thrown forward into battle.

The little flotilla had to be supplemented in its capacity by towing flatboats (figure 4),[1162] or scows, as they were labeled by the navy,[1163] which were "picked up along the bay."[1164] Portions of Rodger's and Nims' batteries, as well as Battery L, their guns, caissons, and some of their horses, were assigned to the flats. Add in the

---

1159. Sprague, H. B., p. 108. A fourth small steamer, the *Sykes*, was in the area but was retained by Weitzel to transport troops across the Teche as part of his advance on Fort Bisland; O.R. Vol. 15, p. 355.

1160. Commodore Morris in command at New Orleans in Farragut's absence had dispatched the *Sachem* to support Banks in addition to the *Clifton*. It sprung a leak and had to return to base in a sinking condition. ORN Vol. 20, p. 106; O.R. Vol. 15, p. 383.

1161. Irwin, R. B., p. 90, 104; Ewer, J. K., p. 69; Tiemann, W. F., p. 27; Moors, pp. 111, 112; Hosmer, J. K., p. 125; Bissell, G., McManus, T., *Battlefields*... pp. 33, 34; O.R. Vol. 15, p. 382; Grover's force level: O.R. Vol. 15, p. 712; Berwick Bay & reports: O.R. Vol. 15, pp. 294, 326, 364, 365; Taylor, L. R., p. 129.

1162. Leslie, Mrs. Frank, Battle Scenes, p. 362; O.R Vol. 15, p. 294; Irwin, p. 91.

1163. ORN Ser. I, Vol. 20, p. 134; Leslie, Mrs. Frank, Battle Scenes, p. 362.

1164. Vol. 15, p. 358, 359.

cavalry and various stores, and the loading process could not be completed until the night of the 11th, though the original plan was to have Grover at his landing point that morning.

The use of the flats to supplement transport, if not routine, was known, as is shown in figure 4, which depicts Weitzel's wounded being towed home after his engagement in January. Why more flats were not built or seized while planning for this campaign is not explained, yet Banks had noted that they would be a key component in landing Grover's force as the transports could not approach closer than an estimated mile or more from shore in muddy and shallow Grand Lake.

FIGURE 4

Weitzel had made a reconnaissance to the landing area in February and noted even less favorable conditions for the landing – that a steamer drawing six feet of water could get no closer than three miles from shore. Essential for the landings, more flats could have speeded the departure, since they could, as well, have been preloaded with Grover's stores while the transports were busy with Weitzel and Emory.

None of this is mentioned in Irwin's *History of the Nineteenth Army Corps*. As assistant adjutant general, and a member of Banks' staff, Irwin may be less critical of what here was clearly a flaw in the planning. It had always been evident that there was a lack of water transport, a fact since Butler had requested twelve light draft transports from the War Department in February of 1862. We remember that he got none.[1165]

To compound Grover's problems, a fog developed on the night of the 11th,

---

1165. Butler, B. F., p. 477; O.R. Vol. 15, p. 244.

which did not clear until 8:00 the next morning. Only then did the flotilla finally get underway. This was yet another flaw in the plan. Fog was common in this country at this time of the year and should have been taken into account.

The operation was soon spotted by Taylor's scouts, and Taylor ordered Vincent, with the 2nd Louisiana Cavalry and a section of Cornay's Battery, to Verdun Landing near Centerville to observe and oppose the movement. A second section of Cornay's battery was sent later in the day, and on the morning of the 13th, Reily's 4th Texas was sent out to oppose the landing. There is no evidence that any of these troops fired upon the flotilla while it progressed up Grand Lake.

Taylor had long realized that his little fort at the Bisland Plantation was vulnerable to this sort of flanking movement[1166] and with the "Increased activity of the enemy at Berwick's Bay" had ordered Fuller, the former captain of the *J. A. Cotton* to Alexandria to repair the *Queen of the West* and to prepare "one or two other steamers as gunboats." Fuller had done so, and had then brought the *Queen* to Butte la Rose, where he now looked for the arrival of his two other steamers, the *Grand Duke* and *Mary T*, delayed awaiting their guns. If Fuller could arrive in Grand Lake before Grover's troops could be disembarked from their overloaded transports, there was potential for an attack resulting in hundreds of drowned men.

At 11:30 a.m., the *Arizona* grounded near Cypress Island. In order to lighten it, to try to raise it out of the mud, 400 men of the 41st Massachusetts were transferred to the flagship, the *Clifton*, which already had the 1st Louisiana on board.[1167] This was to no avail, and leaving the *Arizona* to continue the attempt to extricate itself after four hours of fruitless effort,[1168] Grover and the rest of the flotilla departed. It finally was freed and arrived at the landing the next day.

Arriving at Hutchin's Point,[1169] opposite the Porter plantation, in darkness, a detachment of Holcomb's 1st Louisiana under Fiske was sent out on a reconnaissance. It was 9:30 p.m. before they returned with the news that the shell road planned as the landing point, which gave access to Irish Bend, was under water. The flotilla again got underway and anchored about six miles farther north opposite the McWilliams Plantation at Indian Bend, where a second road west was known. At 1:00 a.m., a detachment of the 6th New York, and two of Dwight's staff, were sent out on a reconnaissance which revealed that there was a "practicable" plantation road leading to the Teche, and debarkation began at daybreak, figure 5.[1170]

1166. Taylor, R., p. 127–129.
1167. O.R. Vol. 15, p. 377.
1168. Taylor, R., p. 129; Ewer, p. 70; Irwin, R. B., p. 104–107; All times are per Grover's report, Vol. 15, p. 358; ORN Ser. I, Vol. 20, p. 822.
1169. Irwin calls it Miller's Point. We defer to Taylor, p. 130, Tiemann, W. F., p. 27, calls it Hudgin's point. Present-day Grand Lake has filled in and been altered to the point that these landmarks are no longer recognizable, if extant.
1170. O.R. Vol. 15, p. 371; figure 5, Irwin, R. B., portion of p. 112a.

The position of the flotilla having been reported to Taylor on the evening of the 12th, Vincent's 2nd Louisiana Cavalry, and two sections of Cornay's battery were ordered there. Vincent failed to obey Taylor's orders, assigning only pickets at the landing, with his main force encamped west of the Teche. Thus, the small force at the landing was only able to establish "a scattering fire" on the landing. The 1st Louisiana, on the *Clifton*, was the first to land and was "at once opened upon by . . . the enemy's artillery, supported by . . . sharpshooters."[1171] Colonel Fiske and four men were wounded.

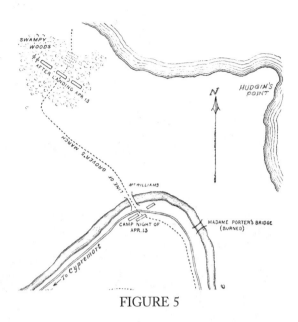

FIGURE 5

The heavy guns of the *Clifton*, a converted Staten Island ferry,[1172] guided by signal flags on the *Laurel Hill* "sent out, now a solitary puff, now three or four nearly together; while in the pauses of these heavier firings, came from the shore the fainter fusillade . . . At length it ceased."[1173] Cornay's field pieces were no match for the IX-inch bow gun of the *Clifton*, its fire directed by signal corps officers assigned to it, and the *Estrella*. The 1st Louisiana advanced, and Vincent's pickets retreated.

The second and third units to land were the 13th Connecticut and the 159th New York. They were both on the same transport, the *Laurel Hill*, which had shallow draft, allowing it to come in close to shore. Grover, "vigorously puffing" on his cigar, was there to greet them; and by 9:00 a.m., they were detached from Birge's 3rd Brigade and loaned to Dwight's 1st Brigade to reinforce the 1st Louisiana. By 10:30, Battery L and Barrett's cavalry, on flats, had disembarked and were assigned by Grover to Dwight. Dwight now ordered an advance.[1174] Grover had granted him permission to detach this force to "prevent the destruction of the

---

1171. O.R. Vol. 15, p. 363. Report of the signal officer on board the *Clifton*. He also states that the fire direction was from his colleague Lieutenant Hall on board the *Laurel Hill*. Hosmer's quote has been retained, though we remain wary of many observations in volunteer unit histories, written long after. However, Hosmer wrote this in 1863.

1172. Bosson, C. P., p. 70.

1173. Hosmer, J. K., p. 127; Irwin, R. B., p. 107; O.R. Vol. 15, pp. 363, 390, Bissel, G./McManus, p. 35.

1174. O.R. Vol. 15, pp. 359, 371; Tiemann, W. F., p. 27; Sprague, H. B., p. 108; figure 6 photo by the author.

bridges across the Teche, which would be almost indispensible to our crossing." Without the bridges, or at least one of them, the attack could have been seriously slowed, making it tardier than it was already. The Teche is too deep for troops to easily ford and would have been impossible for the artillery. The bayou runs for miles, remarkably like a man-made canal (figure 6). It has remained relatively unchanged by mother nature, industrial development, or flood control, and is estimated to be about one hundred fifty feet wide here.

FIGURE 6

The rest of the artillery had to wait for the assembly of a bridge of flatboats to disembark its heavy guns and caissons, and it was not until 4:00 p.m. that the whole division had disembarked, the *Saint Mary's* not being able to approach closer than a half mile from shore.

The enemy cavalry had withdrawn behind a sugarhouse on the McWilliams plantation, but when Holcomb's 1st Louisiana skirmishers pushed forward and Barrett's cavalry advanced along the road, the Confederate cavalry, now reinforced with "some" infantry sharpshooters, reappeared and opened with their long-range rifles. Supported by the 159th New York and 13th Connecticut, the 1st Louisiana arrived at the McWilliams Bridge, about five miles distant from the landing, by noon. By now, the Confederates had withdrawn out of range, simply observing. The McWilliams bridge was found to be partially destroyed by fire, which was extinguished, and slaves from the Porter plantation were used to repair it.[1175]

While those sections of Battery L that remained under Lieutenant Taylor (Captain Closson was division chief of artillery and Lieutenant Sanderson had not yet reported) were detached to help secure the upper bridge, Appleton's section, along with Barrett's cavalry and two sections of Rodger's battery, galloped south to Madame Porter's bridge, about a mile or so below. Under the "very annoying fire of 4 guns of the Rebel artillery, and his Sharpshooters," it was, nevertheless, seized. The 131st New York, the 22nd Maine, and a detachment of the 6th New York were then sent to support the 1st Louisiana in holding it. Casualties were two men of

---

1175. O.R. Vol. 15, pp. 366, 367, 379–381.

the 1st Louisiana killed, four men of the 131st New York wounded, one mortally, and one of Battery L's horses wounded.[1176]

Colonel Day of the 131st included an echo of a past problem in his report of the action: "We found by this day's experience that our pieces were very defective and exceedingly short of range." He does not state what type of weapon had been issued to his men, but apparently, the inspector general's examination in January and the report of his findings of many defective and "worn"[1177] weapons had not been fully acted upon. Here it is April of 1863, after two full years of war, and the Union army still has defective weapons.

Having approved of the detachment of the force to seize the bridges, Grover became cautious. He reports that he was unsure enough of the strength of the enemy in his front that he did not wish to "expose a large force to the enemy until the whole division was in readiness to cut its connection with our point of landing."[1178] That said, he had seized the road – that is, the road along the Teche, leading north to Cypremort and New Iberia – and the trap was closed, at least as far as he understood.

The slow pace of the landings allowed the 13th Connecticut to relax a bit.[1179] "In perfect silence we passed a mile through the dense woods in pursuit of the enemy, who retreated to Madame Porter's plantation. Emerging from the woods, we saw a few of their cavalry a mile distant . . ." Following Grover's orders not to engage, they rested. "While the other regiments and batteries were coming up, we improved the opportunity to take a lunch. Crossing the bayou bridge . . . near the beautiful mansion of Madam Porter (Oaklawn Manor, figure 7)."[1180] They helped themselves liberally to sugar from the large mill that stood next to the bridge.

Aboard the *Saint Mary's*, and consequently one of the later regiments to land, the 25th Connecticut noted that all the commotion had drawn the plantation inhabitants and its mistress outside to witness their passing. "This stately, handsome lady, surrounded by scores of fat, happy looking and well clad slaves, stood in front of her elegant home and sadly watched as we passed. No farm in Connecticut, however carefully supervised, could show better evidence of wise management . . ." Oaklawn Manor still survives intact, and its current picture fits well into the description given in 1863: "The elegant mansion, the delightful grounds, the fences, granaries, fields, slaves and everything, were in perfect order . . . and Madame Porter herself, a splendidly beautiful woman, all looked lovely as peace itself in contrast with the ugliness of war."

1176. O.R. Vol. 15, p. 381. The record of events lists two horses wounded.
1177. O.R. Vol. 15, pp. 648, 649.
1178. O.R. Vol. 15, p. 359.
1179. Sprague, p. 109, 110, 122; Bissell G., (McManus), p. 35.
1180. Picture taken in 2012 by the author with the kind permission of Governor & Mrs. M. J. Foster.

FIGURE 7

While halted at the bridge crossing, Grover was approached in haste, and in much agitation, "by a very stately lady . . . a matron of fine bearing, elegantly attired, her face full of character; she is bareheaded . . . She sweeps by us hastily, with the majesty of a noble mother of Rome, and stops at the stirrup of Gen. Grover. . . . She has come to intercede . . . for her son, [Alexander, age 17] who has just been taken prisoner – a fine fierce boy . . . who stands, haughty and tall, close by, among a group of captive rebels."[1181] This was Mary Porter, 40, the second wife and widow of James Porter, and proprietress of one of the largest plantations in Louisiana – the 1860 federal slave census listing 297. She, her son, two daughters, and personal staff were well-known residents "in former seasons"[1182] of the exclusive social colony at Newport, Rhode Island, and had now been swept up into this maelstrom of war, her son a suspected partisan.

She pleaded, "Do let him go, general; he is all I have" many times. Fortunately, Capt. Homer Sprague of the 13th Connecticut Volunteers, himself a prisoner before the war was over,[1183] ends the drama for us by noting in his diary: "Her young son was taken prisoner, but soon released."

There was no incident of pillage to the Porter plantation, perhaps for the reason that the troops were focused on the mission, under the threat, as they were, of Vincent's cavalry. Another factor may have been the close supervision of the officers of the command, who, except staff, were quite literally on the ground. All

---

1181. Hosmer, J. K., p. 130. Hosmer was a corporal in the 52nd Massachusetts Volunteers, also aboard the *St. Mary's* and passing in the same time frame. Additional details of the plantation at that time are given in the February 6th, 1864, issue of *Frank Leslie's Illustrated Newspaper*. Today the plantation remains open to visitors.
1182. Duganne, A. J. H., p. 103. Data from 1860 federal census of Newport, Rhode Island.
1183. Sprague, H. B., p. 122.

the other officer's horses and baggage had been left behind.[1184] Another factor was that Mary Porter had not fled from her property, an act regarded as an almost sure sign that the owner was a rebel sympathizer. She was there to insist that she was loyal, a declaration, whether sincere or not, which would preserve her rights as a slave owner. *This, after all, was St. Mary's Parish, one of those exempt under the terms of the Emancipation Proclamation.* In any event, the troops were simply in awe of and full of respect for her and her plantation.

Having completed its landing at 4:00 p.m., the remainder of the division could not march out until 6:00. It had few wagons, and as much food that could be carried in individual haversacks had to be issued, along with ammunition. Any excess was left behind on the boats. The last units of the division did not arrive at the plantation bivouac area until after sunset.[1185] "We marched a short distance further and then bivouaced our regiment [the 13th Connecticut] being thrown out as advanced guard. At intervals during the day we had heard Weitzel thundering at the gates of Franklin."

Grover had feared that there was a strong enemy force in the woods to his front and concluded that the night was too dark to "dislodge or even find his position, or for our own skirmishers to keep up the connections." The delays of the day had taken their toll, and Grover's caution and, as noted earlier, his apparent satisfaction at having captured the road decided the matter; they would bivouac for the night.[1186] Grover's attitude is revealed by this statement in the history of the 25th Connecticut Regiment: "Our generals had believed, and we had hoped, that as soon as Taylor would find this large force . . . suddenly occupying the road in his rear, he would submit to the inevitable and surrender . . ."

Unfortunately, Grover was ignorant of the fact that there was a cut-off road on a causeway across the swamp about three miles to the west of his bivouac (see figure 9). It was the one critical to Taylor's escape. If he had sent out Barrett's cavalry, or a few of the staff (those few of the troops that were mounted), as scouts on a reconnaissance along the northern arm of the bayou road, they would have discovered the cut-off road in 15 minutes. Little did Grover know that it was only Vincent's cavalry that opposed him. Reily's troops were encamped at Franklin, and would soon be asleep; Clack's battalion, called by Taylor from the salt works at New Iberia, had not yet arrived.[1187] Grover then called in Appleton, Rodgers, and Barrett, the detachment that had saved the lower bridge; and with that, the 1st Louisiana and its attached force of portions of the 131st New York, the 6th New York, and the 22nd Maine were ordered to burn it and retire.

1184. Bissell, G., (McManus), p. 36; Duganne, A. J. H., pp. 103, 104.
1185. Sunset was at 6:27. Sunset times are taken from tables published by the U.S. Naval Observatory, or NOAA.
1186. Sprague, H. B., p. 110; Grover's report, O.R. Vol. 15, p. 359; Bissell, G., (McManus), p. 36.
1187. Taylor, R., p. 132. Clack's "battalion" consisted of 90 men.

Grover's orders were to advance to Franklin, and it was upon that direction only that he had remained focused.

Who was this Grover? Graduated from West Point in 1850, he had been in continuous service in the army ever since: at Fort Leavenworth, Kansas, involved with the Northern Pacific Railroad exploration; in garrison duty at forts Crawford and Snelling, in the Utah Expedition of 1857–1858; and, rising to captain in the 10th Infantry, at Fort Garland, Colorado, and forts Union and Marcy, New Mexico, through 1861.

Much like many others in the early months of the war, Grover, a captain in the regulars, was vaulted up to become brigadier general of volunteers in April of 1862. He served in the Army of the Potomac during the Peninsular Campaign, in the battles of Yorktown, Williamsburg, Seven Pines, Savage's Station, Glendale, Malvern Hill, and the skirmish at Harrison's Landing. In the Northern Virginia Campaign, he was at Bristoe Station and Second Manassas. He was brevetted lieutenant colonel for meritorious service at Williamsburg and colonel for meritorious service at Seven Pines.[1188] As we have discussed before, background was a poor predictor of success in this war, Halleck versus Grant the prime example.

Weitzel "thundering at the gates of Franklin" as was heard by the 13th Connecticut, was the little that was known of Banks' attack at Bisland. Weitzel's and Emory's troops had remained encamped near their landing on the 10th because it was Banks' intent not to attack in force until something of Grover's progress was learned.

At noon on the 11th, Weitzel had begun a halting advance on Bisland.[1189] By six o'clock they had advanced ten miles and bivouacked about a quarter of a mile beyond Pattersonville, opposite Sibley's Texas men. Emory followed with the 3rd Division and went into bivouac on Weitzel's left.

Finally, early on the morning of the 12th, Banks gained the word that Grover was underway. It was now necessary to occupy the enemy, "yet not too strongly, lest he abandon his position too soon and suddenly spoil all."[1190] Weitzel pushed forward, stiffly resisted by the rebel cavalry, which was supported by two regiments of infantry. By 4:00 p.m., the advance, consisting of a line of battle made up of the 12th Connecticut (the "Wooden Nutmegs") on the left; the 160th New York and 75th New York at the center, with the 114th New York and the 8th Vermont (the Green Mountain Boys) on the right, had traversed through three miles of rough cane fields coursed with muddy trenches. Contested all the way by the enemy skirmishers, they finally reached just short of the range of the guns of Brig. Gen. H. H. Sibley. Here was observed a row of cane shocks "arranged with careful negligence parallel with and about half to three quarters of a mile from the plainly visible

---

1188. Cullum, Vol. 2, no. 1453, p. 256, 257. Seven Pines was also known as Fair Oaks.
1189. O.R. Vol. 15, pp. 294, 324–325; Hall, H & J, *75th History*, pp. 90–92.
1190. Irwin, R. B., p. 91.

works." To Weitzel's discerning eye, these had been placed to sight and range the rebel guns, and he halted the command. He then sent word to Banks that he was just outside of the enemy's range and asked to open his artillery before making any further advance on the fort.

Banks' reply was to advance. The order was obeyed, and in less than five minutes, Weitzel's suspicions were verified. The rebels opened a "quite severe" fire. Two men of the 75th New York were killed and three wounded. The "bobbin boy" was thus taught his lesson, and he ordered a cease to the advance, with the troops to lie in the trenches of the cane field. Bainbridge's battery on the right and Carruth's battery on the left were brought up and opened a return fire, which lasted until sunset, when the troops were withdrawn about a mile; to pass a night "besieged with mosquitoes from the adjacent swamp."

Finding Mouton in his recently-thrown-up and only-partially-completed works on the east side of the Teche too strong for the cavalry, Banks ordered Emory to reinforce it with the 31st Massachusetts and the 175th New York, along with a section of the 1st Maine Battery. They were deployed, and with Gooding in command, they were ordered to observe and conform to the advance of the main line (figure 8).[1191]

Banks had waited for the sound of Grover's guns, and none having been heard, Banks gave orders to continue the assault the next day, thus risking the potential for Taylor withdrawing before Grover was ready.[1192]

It was at this time that Taylor had received word of the position of Grover's flotilla, off Hutchin's Point, and he had sent Vincent's regiment to oppose it. A few hours later, Taylor left Fort Bisland to visit Vincent, leaving behind orders with General Sibley to prepare for a bold plan. Taylor had no thought of a withdrawal.

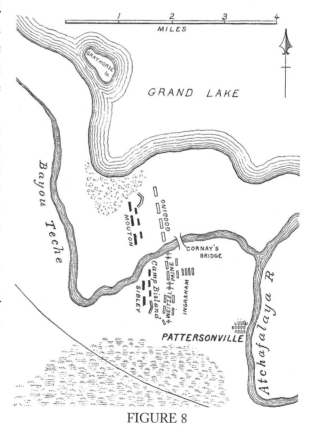

FIGURE 8

1191. Irwin, R. B., p. 97.
1192. O.R. Vol. 15, pp. 296, 297.

Instead, Sibley was to prepare for an attack on Banks the next morning. Taylor had calculated that the result would be that Banks would recall Grover for reinforcement.[1193] Returning at daylight, Taylor was angry to discover that Sibley had failed to organize for the attack, considering it impractical.[1194]

The dense fog that so characterized that time of the year – which had delayed Farragut at Port Hudson and, yesterday, Grover – had prevailed during the evening, but it lifted on the morning of the 13th to reveal a bright sunny day. Banks' attack was resumed with the whole line returning to within musketry range.[1195] Banks ordered the right strengthened, sending the remainder of Gooding's brigade – the 38th Massachusetts, the 53rd Massachusetts, the 165th New York – and the remaining sections of the 1st Maine battery, to the east side of the Teche.

Taylor then brought the gunboat *Diana* well out in front of his earthworks to provide enfilading fire on the advancing Yankee line, but it was silenced by a fortunate shot from one of the 30-pounder Parrotts of the 1st Indiana Heavy Artillery. It was then observed to withdraw up the bayou and out of the fight. This risk removed, the artillery engagement became general.

By afternoon, when the Union forces had reached advanced positions in front of the works, Banks began to believe that something had gone awry with Grover. He feared losing an opportunity to defeat Taylor then and there. Somewhat in desperation, he gave discretionary orders to Weitzel and Emory to form a plan to storm the Confederate works if a favorable opportunity presented itself. Weitzel and Halbert Paine of the 4th Wisconsin, commanding Emory's 2nd Brigade, conferred, and then concluded to attack. Gooding, on the west bank, as already ordered, would conform to whatever took place on the east bank.

Every preparation having been made, the generals waited for Banks to give approval. It was already past 4:00 p.m., and the opportunity was passing. Banks was still anxiously waiting, weighing the cost of the assault versus the chance of news from Grover.

Suddenly, a shell was seen to travel high over their heads, which burst on the Confederate works. Then followed the deep roar of the *Clifton*'s IX-inch bow gun. Having covered Grover's landing, it had been dispatched back to the Teche, with the news so long awaited. Relieved, and assuming Grover to be in place, Banks cancelled any further operations for the day and withdrew his front line out of the range of the Confederate musketry. The trap was closed, and the full assault could begin the next day.

After dark, signal rockets sent up by Grover confirmed the news.

At one point in the day's attack, Taylor had worried that some of his green troops had been shaken sufficiently that Weitzel might have broken through.

1193. O.R. Vol. 15, p. 389, 390.
1194. O.R. Vol. 15, pp. 1,093–1,095.
1195. O.R. Vol. 15, p. 296; Irwin, R. B., pp. 93–103; Bissell, G. (McManus), p. 35.

However, he claims, he had steadied his men toward the end of the day to a degree that he was looking forward to any assault "feeling confident of repulsing it."[1196] The *Diana* was expected to be repaired, and behind the breastworks "we had suffered but little." We must question this as bluster, written as it was in 1879. According to a former member of Taylor's staff, Taylor "was the most anxious man in the Southern Confederacy, when . . . he learned that Grover's division had landed by way of Grand Lake . . ."[1197]

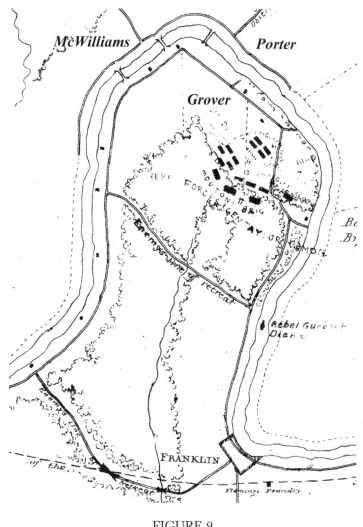

FIGURE 9

However, at 9:00 p.m., all that quickly changed. Reily appeared with the news that, yes, Grover had landed and advanced to the Porter plantation but had not entered Franklin. The indication was that the cut-off road to New Iberia was open (figure 9). From Taylor: "Here was pleasant intelligence! There was no time to ask

---

1196. Taylor, R., pp. 132, 133.
1197. McManus, T. P., *Battlefields of Louisiana*, p. 17.

questions." Mouton was directed to withdraw to Franklin, starting the artillery – one section to reinforce at Irish Bend – followed by the trains and the infantry.[1198] Green, with the 5th Texas Regiment, Waller's battalion, and the rifle section of Semmes' battery constituted the rear guard. Semmes[1199] was ordered to get the *Diana* to Franklin by dawn. Taylor then rode for Franklin with Reily and arrived at his camp above the village at about 2:00 a.m. The sleeping men were awakened and sent off to position themselves in Nerson's Wood, near where Grover was camped.[1200]

Taylor now rode farther on and discovered Clack and his men camped along the cut-off road. Originally ordered by Taylor to reinforce him at Bisland, Clack had stopped for the night. They were near the Yokely Bridge, almost within sight of the Federal campfires, though few there must have been, considering the drenching rain. It had been no cooked supper for most of the Federals; that night they were limited to the hard tack and salt pork that they carried.[1201]

The road and the causeway bridge were safe. Taylor's comment: "It was a wonderful chance. Grover had stopped just short of the prize. Thirty minutes would have given him the wood and bridge, closing the trap on my force." Taylor is quite right. Grover was camped about three miles away, about a half hour at the quickstep.

With his main force still south of Franklin, Taylor would evacuate Bisland and meet Grover here at Irish Bend to prevent his closing of the cutoff road by the destruction of the bridge at Yokely Causeway.

Back at Bisland, Halbert Paine, commanding Emory's 2nd Brigade, noted in his diary: "At 1:00 a.m., a messenger from the picket line reported the moving of artillery. A personal observation upon the picket line failed to satisfy me whether a general evacuation was going on or only a transfer of guns from one part of the fortification to another. . . . Soon Gen. Emory ordered me to go into the works if I could. A like order came from Gen. Banks . . . The 8th New Hampshire being deployed as skirmishers along my entire front, marched to the entrenchments. As I took and planted the flag of the 8th New Hampshire on the breastworks, they all bounded in with three loud cheers." [1202]

An immediate advance was ordered. Quoting from the *History of the 114th New York Regiment* [Pellet]:

> At four o'clock a.m. of the 14th, we advanced on the works. Not a shot was fired. We moved almost breathlessly. Soon we saw one of our flags waving from the parapet of the works. The cause was apparent. The enemy had fled. Such was the battle of Fort Bisland.

1198. O.R. Vol. 15, p. 1,092.
1199. Son of the *Alabama* captain.
1200. Figure 9, portion, Chief Top. Eng. Dept Gulf, undated, National Archives RG 77, map 111. Grover, Porter and McWilliams captions by the author.
1201. Bissell G., (McManus), p. 35.
1202. Stanyan, J. M., p. 199; Pellet, E. P., p. 69; order of march: O.R. Vol. 15, p. 384.

As we have related, the "battle" was a mini-siege, relying on artillery. Banks' forces never made an assault.

Fifteen miles or so to the north, it was dawn at Grover's encampment at Irish Bend when the troops of Birge's 3rd Brigade fell into line and headed south along the bayou road toward Franklin. It having rained during the night, they had had little sleep, lying on the freshly plowed ground of Mrs. Porter's cane field "drenched to the skin, and covered with the red soil of Louisiana, we looked like a moving brick yard."[1203] Five companies of skirmishers of the 25th Connecticut led off, followed by five companies in reserve. Next, came two companies of the 26th Maine, Bradley's section of Rodger's battery, eight companies of the 26th Maine, the 159th New York, the other two sections of Rodger's battery, and, finally, Birge's own: the 13th Connecticut. Dwight's brigade and Battery L were next in the column, followed by Kimball, with Nims' battery.

Figure 10 provides an introduction to the battlefield.[1204] Note that the impassable swamp surrounding Yokely bayou in the center, and Nerson's Woods south of it, confine the battlefield to the open cane fields and the small section of woods between the fields and the bayou to the east and south. As to scale, the distance along the bayou road from the sugarhouse access drive to the fence along the east edge of Nerson's Woods is about a mile.

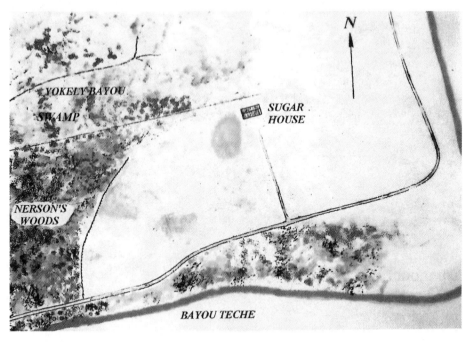

FIGURE 10

1203. Maddocks, E. B., p. 354.
1204. Figure 10. An interpretation, drawn by the author.

Marching south from their bivouac on the Porter plantation, the skirmishers of the five companies of the 25th Connecticut were spread across their entire front – from the Teche on the left, to the swamp on the right. After about a half hour, they passed a sugarhouse on their right. They had left the Porter plantation and entered McKerall's,[1205] a position about "40 rods" (one-eighth of a mile) from the sharp bend in the road where it makes its turn to the southwest.

Leading to their right, or west, they entered "an immense cane field, its furrows in line with the road. On the west the field was bounded by a rail fence, beyond which arose a dense wood of magnolias, cottonwood and semi-tropical trees looking like a long green wall . . . near to the ground this forest was absolutely impenetrable to the sight, by reason of the suffocating briars, vines, palmettos and underbrush. We ought to have occupied these woods the night before . . ."[1206]

The 25th Connecticut was now poised to advance into the cane field, as is shown in figure 11, Grover having expressed the thought that there was "nothing more than a picket" in the woods – quite a change in attitude from the night before.

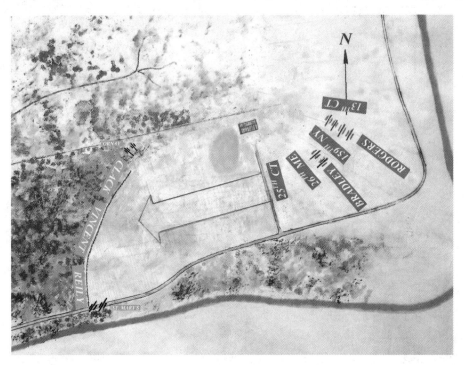

FIGURE 11

1205. O.R. Vol. 15, p. 391, 392. Taylor's official report in the O.R. differs substantially from his account in *Destruction and Reconstruction*. Since Taylor's official report is more in line with those of Birge, McManus, and others, one element of the account in *Destruction* is omitted. Specifically, Taylor has his troops charging out from the woods at the time of initial firing. We credit elements of his force, probably Clack's men, with having taken advanced positions beyond the brush in front of the ditch behind the sugarhouse, to which they soon retreated.

1206. Bissell G., (McManus), p. 36.

Of course, in place, and unseen at the edge of the woods, were the dismounted cavalry of Reily and Vincent, and Clack's battalion. Compare this situation with that of Weitzel at Bisland and Banks' order to advance without a preliminary bombardment. The result then was casualties; and Banks, realizing his mistake, allowed Weitzel to withdraw. Then, according to accepted tactics, Weitzel brought up the artillery. As the 25th Connecticut's skirmishers marched forward, they were greeted by "a puff of smoke from the green wall in front of us and a second or two later the crack of a rifle." Next, it would be the shells from a section of Cornay's *St. Mary's Cannoneers*, placed as they were at the edge of the woods, by the road, and the other two guns of Cornay, shown at the edge of the upper portion of the woods.[1207] The skirmishers were now called in, and the regiment changed to the right "front forward on first company."

FIGURE 12

Those few rifle cracks of Taylor's skirmishers could have been effective when the 25th was some five hundred yards from the edge of the "green wall," but the majority of Taylor's force still carried smoothbore muskets, guns regarded as obsolete when they were transferred to Southern arsenals by Secretary Floyd in 1859 and 1860. These would not be effective until the 25th marched much closer; to less than fifty yards, if they were to continue to advance.[1208] They did, marching erect and in plain sight of the enemy – something out of the tactics of the wars of Napoleon. See figure 12, taken from the May 6th, 1863, issue of *Harper's Weekly*, p.

1207. O.R. Vol. 15, p. 391. Cornay had six guns. One was destroyed at Bisland (Taylor, R., p. 134), and the fifth was brought here by Cornay and the 4th Texas Regiment (Noel, T., p. 47). No record has been found as to where it was placed.

1208. McMorries, E. Y., pp. 62–63. "Our arms were the old flintlock musket (but they were a sure fire) not effective over forty yards . . ."

316, which clearly depicts the typical close order formation.

By now, (it is estimated that the time was 6:45 a.m.) the 25th had advanced more than 800 yards, loading and firing as it went, and it became evident that there were more than a few skirmishers in the woods. They were opened upon with buck-and-ball "four shots to our one in return . . ."[1209] Soon shells began to burst overhead. The 25th was ordered to lie down in the furrows of the cane field, a difficult position from which to reload their Enfield rifles. They were initially alone on the field. "An unexpected force of the enemy having thus developed, Grover then ordered up the rest of Birge's brigade," (figure 13). Instead, it would have been the time to order his artillery to shell Taylor's positions before sending in more troops to the slaughter.

The 26th Maine was ordered forward and took position to the left of the 25th Connecticut. They were also ordered to lie down and fire "when the enemy could be seen." Bradley's section of Rodgers' battery B, was ordered forward by Birge, and placed in the interval between the 25th Connecticut and the 26th Maine, about five hundred yards from the woods.[1210]

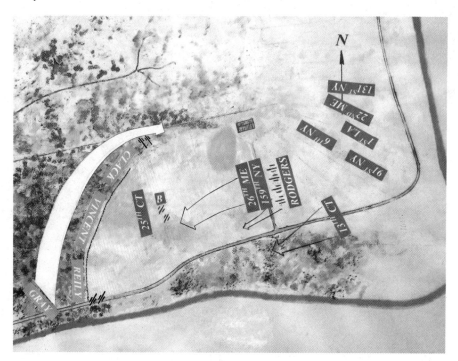

FIGURE 13

At about 7:00 a.m., the 28th Louisiana, under Gray, reported to Taylor from Franklin, and unseen behind bushes and canebrake, had begun deploying along the ditch at the northern portion of the field (the white arrow in figure 13). Grover

---

1209. Bissell G., (Ellis), p. 30; Bissell G., (McManus), p. 37.
1210. O.R. Vol. 15, pp. 366, 384.

would soon have a surprise flanking attack to deal with, Gray nearly doubling the strength of the force Taylor had initially deployed.

Then, the "peculiar whistle of a Parrott shell was heard, and Semmes appeared with the *Diana*[1211] . . . Roger's battery was brought up to reply to the rebel artillery and also to the *Diana*, whose guns now swept the field."[1212] One gun was placed eight hundred yards away and another, some four hundred yards in advance, *R* in figure 14.

In the meantime, the 13th Connecticut, remaining south of the road, had advanced in the woods between the road and the bayou. Company A's skirmishers led the advance at the double-quick. The cover of the trees allowed them to quickly advance without firing until they reached a stretch of open ground close to where the guns of Cornay's *St. Mary's* Cannoneers were in battery. Crossing the 300-yard open stretch, they had the advantage of their skirmishers being equipped with Sharps repeating rifles and like the 25th Connecticut, they had received training to load and fire their Springfields while advancing.[1213] This steady barrage added up to their quickly overpowering Cornay's position.

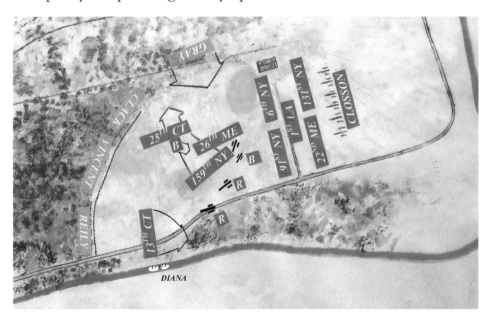

FIGURE 14

At this point, the 13th was far in advance of the rest of the division, and they knew that a furious battle was taking place to their right and rear. They were withdrawn to the edge of the woods as shown in figure 14, where they posted sharpshooters to try to pick off the *Diana*'s gunners and stood ready to support the

---

1211. Taylor, R., p. 133.
1212. Sprague, H. B., p. 112, 117, 118.
1213. Note the variety of weapons.

159th New York. When the 13th withdrew, the 4th Texas Cavalry came to the aid of Cornay's Cannoneers, and they were able to make off with their most important possessions: their guns. Nevertheless, the 13th retained some 50 to 60 prisoners, 2 caissons, a limber, and the Cannoneer flag.[1214]

Disorder briefly reigned[1215] when Gray's infantry opened, concealed as they were behind the brush and canebrake. It is likely that at about this time the actions that he took to reform the line of battle, while under this intense fire, that the sergeant major of the 25th Connecticut William E. Simonds was cited for, and ultimately received the Medal of Honor. The 26th Maine had originally formed to the left of the 25th Connecticut, but, now in the position shown, had the 159th New York, marching at the double-quick, move through its left and then through the depleted 25th Connecticut, shown turned to meet Gray's threat. Firing as they had been, for more than an hour, the ammunition of the 25th was beginning to run out, and the number of men wounded had significantly depleted their ranks. Those wounded that were able crawl, retreated.

It was fortunate that the 159th had arrived because the 26th Maine was having troubles of a different kind. Its old Harper's Ferry muskets, firing buck-and-ball, were fouling after becoming heated from repeated firing. Their rate of fire was dropping off because their weapons, one by one, were becoming useless. Their rammers began sticking in their barrels, which could only be cleared by firing. This would briefly treat the enemy to a ramrod missile, followed by three buckshot and a ball.[1216] They were in desperate straits, looking for available guns left by the wounded, all the while lying down under the increased fire from the 28th Louisiana. They suffered significant numbers of wounded. Philip Holmes remembers having found a Belgian rifle near one of the dead of the 159th, and, while reaching over him to obtain the contents of his cartridge box, was wounded by three almost simultaneous shots. He was helped to the rear by a comrade.

The response of the 159th faltered when its colonel, Molineux, was struck in the mouth by a ball and fell, just as he had raised his sword to order a charge. Soon, Gray's whole line drove forward, led by a mounted Taylor and members of his staff.[1217] This shattered the Yankee troops, who ran to the rear in disorder, abandoning Bradley's battery, which was forced to withdraw to a new position. In the process, he had 8 men and 6 horses wounded.[1218] Seeing this, Rodgers briefly

---

1214. Noel, T., *Autobiography...* pp. 92, 93; Sprague, H. B., p. 118.
1215. This is a conclusion inferred from the record of the award of the Medal of Honor to Sgt. William E. Simonds of the 25th Connecticut. www.history.army.mil./html/moh/civwarmz.html, p. 35.
1216. Maddocks, E. B., pp. 354, 355; O.R. Vol. 15, p. 384, Birge's report.
1217. Tiemann, W. F., p. 29; Taylor, R., p. 133. Here, Taylor recounts his charge as happening earlier. Taylor's report in O.R. Vol. 15, p. 392, places it along with Gray's charge.
1218. O.R. Vol.15, pp. 367, 392, 393. Subsequently altered to 1 killed and 7 wounded.

waited for orders to turn his guns toward Gray and finally fired over the heads of the Union line to cover "the retrograde movement as well as possible."

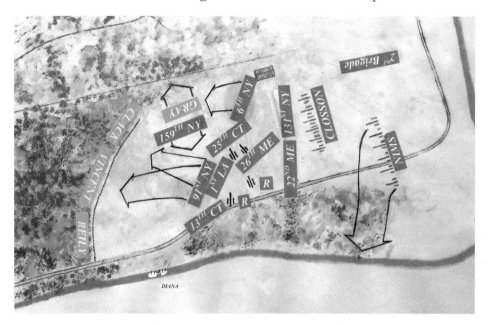

FIGURE 15

From Taylor: "The enemy then displayed a much larger force . . ." This was Dwight, (figure 15), with the 1st Brigade, which had been the next brigade in the marching column, along with Battery L. Dwight's regiments had been ordered forward while Battery L and the remainder of the artillery, 14 guns, stood in reserve. With that, Gray fell back, and the general withdrawal that had been the core of Taylor's plan was set in motion.

Taylor reports that all his wagons and troops from Bisland had passed through Franklin by 9:30 a.m. Green's rear guard was necessarily somewhat later. Fear of Banks' force from Bisland arriving in his rear, it was only the final course of the battle that would set Taylor's withdrawal time. Now, Taylor had to wrap it up quickly.

Nims' battery had come up with the 2nd Brigade; initially posted by Captain Closson near the road, it was shifted to the edge of the bayou to meet the *Diana*, should it move farther up. It did not, but it kept firing for some time while Dwight advanced. Semmes had been instructed to work the *Diana's* gun to the last moment, then get ashore with his crew and blow up the boat. Fortunately for Grover's troops, many of its shells failed to explode.[1219]

When Dwight's regiments arrived at the edge of Nerson's Woods (figure 16), they were ordered to halt, Grover fearing that Taylor had massed his troops for a counterattack. From Dwight: "The character of the wood, and of the ground on our

---

1219. O.R. Vol. 15, p. 365, 367; Taylor, R., p. 134.

right flank made it difficult, if not impossible, to tell what the enemy was doing in that direction, and the constant reports from my front in a great degree confirmed the reports from the front of the Third Brigade that the enemy were massing their troops on our front and right for the purpose of making an attack." He then complains that: "For one and a half hours this brigade held all of the positions of the enemy unsupported by any portion of the Third Brigade."[1220]

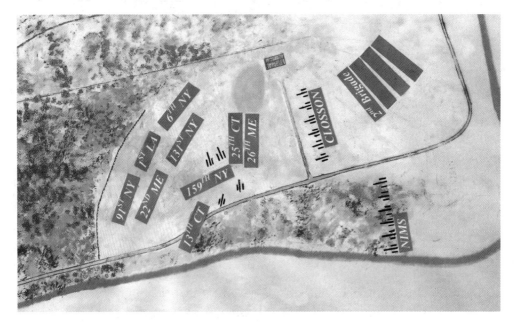

FIGURE 16

There are two estimates of time in the official reports other than Taylor's mention of 7:00 a.m. when Gray arrived, and 9:30, when his main force had passed through Franklin. One is in Rodger's report – "the whole engagement, from 8:00 a.m. until 2:00 p.m." – and the other is in Birge's report: "About 2 p.m., was ordered by General Grover to advance . . . to feel the enemy. Before this order could be executed he suddenly withdrew, and the Diana was discovered to be in flames."

Subtracting Dwight's "one and a half" hours from 2:00 p.m. gives 12:30 p.m. as when shooting had ended.[1221] Given that the *Diana*'s crew were captured, they being the last to retire, and allowing time for Semmes to back out of his position, abandon the *Diana*, and then set it on fire, it is concluded that the last of Taylor's force (Mouton's) had crossed the burning Yokely Bridge by about 11:30 a.m.[1222]

Dwight heaped abuse on the 3rd Brigade for the "embarrassing" retreat of the 25th Connecticut, but the casualty figures show that by the time his brigade had

---

1220. O.R. Vol. 15, pp. 367, 373, 385.
1221. Tiemann, W. F., p. 30: "The fight lasted until noon." O.R. Vol. 15, p. 399: "midday."
1222. O.R. Vol. 15, p. 393.

made its advance it met only token resistance.[1223] The killed and wounded in the respective regiments of the 3rd Brigade were: 25th Connecticut, 86; 26th Maine, 61; 159th New York, 97; and the 13th Connecticut, 54. These numbers approach 20 percent. In contrast, Dwight's 1st Brigade reported a casualty total of 16, with none in the 6th New York or the 1st Louisiana. The total battle casualties were 49 killed, 274 wounded, and 30 captured or missing, a total of 353.

It is clear that by the time of Dwight's arrival, Taylor had turned the page of the playbook, and had begun his skillful withdrawal. Nevertheless, Dwight congratulated his brigade and took pains to mention the good conduct of the 6th New York, apparently justifying his "ridding this regiment . . . of certain officers and soldiers."[1224]

A timeworn story was played out at this battle and is reminiscent of the "what ifs" of this and many other battle actions in U.S. history. If out of ammunition, what should the men of the 25th have done? Should they have fixed bayonets, charged, and essentially committed suicide? Or, were they wise to have saved themselves for a future action in which it would be hoped skilled generalship would conduct the battle, and accomplish the destruction of the enemy by a thoughtful attack? The circumstances give the answer. Remember that Battery L and Nims' 2nd Massachusetts Battery, plus two of Rodger's guns, were never brought into action, though these 14 guns had the potential to shell Taylor's men into oblivion.

Irwin concludes his account of the battle with this mild censure of Grover: "Bold adventures must be conducted boldly to the end."[1225]

McKerrall's sugarhouse, which was used as a hospital, was now filled with over 250 "Union and rebel" subjected to the medieval medical procedures of that era by only three or four overwhelmed surgeons. Passing "a pile of legs, feet, arms, hands beside the table" while searching for over an hour for his wounded men, Capt. Homer Sprague of the 13th Connecticut detailed a man to provide for them, and only then left; "sick at heart of war and all its surroundings."[1226]

1223. O.R. Vol. 15, p. 319, revised casualties. There is a discrepancy of one if the total of the individual regiments is compared with the revised total reported here. Birge's original report, ibid., p. 385; Dwight, pp. 372, 373. As to percentage of loss, the size of these regiments averaged less than 400 men. For example, Bissell, p. 7, lists 350 and on p. 30 lists 380. Tiemann also mentions, p. 35: "Most of the missing returned to the regiment within a week, those captured having been paroled by the rebels."
1224. O.R. vol. 15, p. 374.
1225. Irwin, R. B., p. 118.
1226. Sprague, H. B., p. 120.

Queen of the West/Cornie

The final engagements related to the Battle of Irish Bend involved two steamers. One action resulted in the destruction of Ellet's venerable ram, the *Queen of the West*, now flying the "Stars and Bars," and the other involved the surrender of the Confederate transport *Cornie*.

After discharging Grover's division, the *Estrella*, *Arizona*, and *Calhoun* had remained at Indian Bend holding Grover's surplus of supplies. At about 2:00 a.m. on April 14th, the lights of steamers were occasionally seen headed south from Chicot Pass. At daylight, a "large black steamer and a white river boat" approached; and the navy opened on the black one, the *Queen*, which looked to be readying to ram the *Arizona*. The rifled 30-pounder Parrott bow guns of the navy overwhelmed her, and she was soon observed to be on fire. Her riverboat consort[1227] then turned and, having lighter draft and greater speed, fled through waters in which the navy could not follow. Captain Fuller and 90 men were pulled from the water, and the *Queen* was left a burning wreck.[1228]

The *Cornie* fled into Union hands by the actions of General Sibley, who seems to have possessed a congenital inability to follow Taylor's orders. Having provided sufficient ambulances to evacuate his wounded from Irish Bend, Taylor had ordered the destruction of all his river transports, including the *Cornie*. Instead, Sibley decided to transport the wounded on the *Cornie*, calculating that Grover would let a hospital boat pass up the Teche. The *Cornie* was apprehended, and two Union officers that had been taken prisoner when the *Diana* was captured were found on board. This deceit removed any sympathy for it as a hospital, and it was seized.[1229]

Charges related to Sibley's failure to organize the attack at Bisland, the *Cornie* incident, and that Sibley had caused the capture of Semmes and the crew of the *Diana* by prematurely ordering the burning of the bridge across the causeway at Yokely Bayou were later brought against Sibley.[1230] He was found not guilty.

Sixteen years later, in his memoir, *Destruction and Reconstruction*, Taylor seems to have reconsidered, and says that Semmes remained too long near the *Diana* to witness the explosion that he had arranged; and for that reason, he was captured. It was not the result of Sibley's actions.[1231]

1227. Irwin, R. B., p. 121, identifies it as the *Mary T*.
1228. ORN Ser. I, Vol. 20, p. 135.
1229. Ewer, J. K., p. 74.
1230. O.R. Vol. 15, pp. 1,093–1,096. The court found that (1) "disobeyance" of orders was not deliberate, (2) use of the *Cornie* was the only possible means to save the wounded, and (3) Sibley misconstrued the orders of his superior.
1231. Taylor, R., p. 134.

Chasing the Fox

Banks' forces entered Franklin on the heels of Taylor's forces leaving via the cutoff. Grover having failed to trap Taylor, there was nothing left to do for Banks other than begin a fruitless month-long march, toward Alexandria (figure 17), much like the proverbial fox and hounds. The fox was always ahead and just out of reach.

Taylor never published a casualty list, but bemoaned the fact that his force began to fall apart on the march north, a fact that he fails to mention in his postwar memoir. "Nearly the whole of . . . Fournet's battalion, passing through the country in which the men had lived before joining the army, deserted with their arms . . ."

Theophilus Noel,[1232] a member of the 4th Texas Cavalry, remembers: "We started for the rear; those under command toward Alexandria and those in desperate want of home comforts toward Niblett's Bluff, Texas; very few of whom ever afterward heard the sound of their own reveille toot-horns, much less Yankee cannon or musketry." The ability of the Texans to disappear into the vastness of Texas was to be repeated in 1865. Rather than surrender, their numbers would be seen to have just melted away, encouraged by E. Kirby Smith, who fled to Mexico.

Taylor's superior, E. Kirby Smith, commanding the Department of the Trans-Mississippi, offers the estimate of Taylor's loss as one-third from

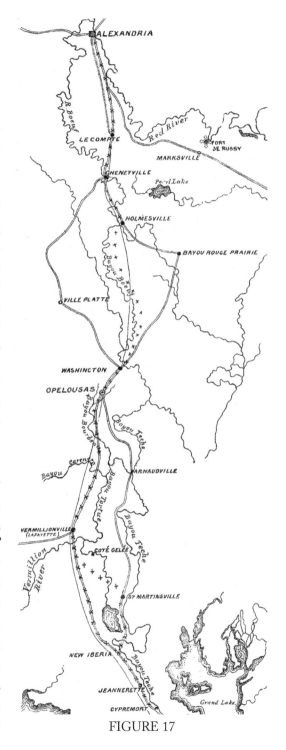

FIGURE 17

1232. O.R. Vol. 15, pp. 393–396, 387; figure 17, Irwin, R. B., pp 80a, 80b; Noel, T., *Autobiography*, p. 93. The road west to Niblett's Bluff left from Vermilionville, now Lafayette.

"straggling and desertions." Few were killed, and with their arms, they could – and they would – be put back together again.

Duryea's Battery F of the 1st U.S. Artillery, which accompanied Weitzel's brigade, took the lead in chasing Taylor as he retreated. There was a skirmish at Jeanerette, where Taylor had encamped, as the artillery of Green's rear guard faced Battery F. It was at this action that Sgt. Charles Riley, among others, was cited for coolness and accuracy in sighting their guns, which drove Green's guns back.[1233]

On the 15th, Taylor stopped at New Iberia, long enough to discover that the gunboat *Stevens* was not ready for service, and he ordered it sunk as far down the Teche as possible to block the Union boats from ascending. Again, his orders were not diligently carried out; the Confederate navy lieutenant in command only going down the river about two miles before scuttling it. The retreat then continued, stopping only for the night. Banks' forces entered New Iberia that afternoon.

Taylor's first prolonged stop was at his first defensible position, Vermilion River, which he reached on the afternoon of the 16th. After they crossed, the bridge was burned, and his troops were allowed to rest until midday on the 17th, when Grover's division caught sight of Green's Texans, posted so as to prevent its reconstruction. Dwight's skirmishers were then deployed on either side of the road in support of Battery L and Nims' battery, which "shelled the Rebels out."

Battery L's record of events gives an unusually detailed account of the action that took place when Grover's division arrived: "On the 15th took up line of march and reached Vermillion Bayou on the 17th estimated distance 45 miles. At Vermillion bridge, Taylor's section of the Battery was opened upon by Sharpshooters and the Rebel artillery of 4 guns from the cover of the opposite bank. Casualties 2 horses killed, the remainder of the Battery in action soon shelled the Rebels out." Battery L had remained with Grover's division as did two sections of Nims' battery, which also participated, under Closson's direction.[1234] Grover had proceeded directly to that point while Banks, with Weitzel and Emory, had branched off the main road at New Iberia and headed to Saint Martinsville.

Longfellow's St. Martinsville:[1235]

> On the banks of the Teche, are the towns of St. Maur and St. Martin . . .
> Beautiful is the land, with its prairies and forests of fruit trees;
> Under the feet a garden of flowers, and the bluest of heavens
> Bending above, and resting on its dome on the walls of the forest.
> They who dwell there have named it the Eden of Louisiana.

The purpose of the diversion was to capture or destroy five more of Taylor's rivercraft, but it was learned on the 18th that four had been destroyed by Taylor's

---

1233. O.R. Vol. 15, pp. 335–337, 393.
1234. O.R. Vol. 15, p. 365; Irwin, R. B., Action at Vermilion Bridge, p. 124.
1235. Longfellow, H. W., *Longfellow's Poems*, p. 115.

men. Upon hearing of Grover being stopped at Vermilion River, Banks ordered the expedition to return.

A detachment sent from New Iberia to the Avery salt works on Petit Anse Island, about sixteen miles to the southwest, was more successful. Left unguarded by Clack's departure, the 41st Massachusetts, the 12th Maine, a part of the 24th Connecticut, and a section of Nims' battery met no opposition. The buildings were burned, the machinery was destroyed, and about 200 horses were confiscated.[1236]

It was at this time that confiscation of the resources of the area began in full swing, and initially, at least, they swung out of control. Though some 200 cattle had been rounded up at Irish Bend by the 26th Maine and slaughtered for rations on the night of the 14th, a wider swath of confiscation now began. There was disorder in the ranks, and as a blunt Dwight reports,[1237] the "pillage on these two day's march were disgraceful . . . Houses were entered and all in them destroyed . . . Ladies were frightened into delivering their jewels and valuables . . . by threats of violence . . . Negro women were ravished in the presence of white women and children." Shortly, Dwight would take extreme action to curb this plundering, as it was called, by ordering the summary execution of Henry Hamill of the 131st New York as an example to the rest of the brigade.[1238]

Official confiscation of supplies needed for the sustenance of the army or of that authorized by the War Department, such as cotton, continued. Any materials in excess of the army's needs were turned over to the quartermaster to be sold at auction at New Orleans. The war had to be paid for, New Orleans had to be fed, and confiscation of rebel property had long since been authorized.

The problem was, who was a rebel? In one case, at least, the 26th Maine history notes: "We came in sight of a rebel flag flying over a set of buildings and at once the match was lighted and . . . that house and outbuilding were burned to the ground."

The facility with which Taylor's forces, many mounted, had kept ahead of Banks' footsore troops had highlighted the issue of cavalry. True, many of Taylor's troops were mounted, but many were not, but by their background and long service were simply inured to these tough marches. In any event, Banks had been looking for horses to convert some of his infantry to cavalry ever since he had arrived in the department, having been rebuffed and lectured by Lincoln for having made

---

1236. O.R. Vol. 15, p. 382; Ewer, J. K., p. 76; Irwin, R. B., pp. 123, 124.
1237. O.R. Vol. 15, p. 373.
1238. O.R. Vol. 15, p. 1,119. This extreme action initially may have engendered fearful respect, but later, Dwight's alleged drunken arbitrary orders were received with derision. Bacon, pp. 156, 157, 208. Banks never took action against Dwight, though the execution without trial was a serious breach of army doctrine. Banks' subsequent handling of Dwight was ever held in suspicion, it being alleged that Banks was a debtor to Dwight's wealthy Boston family; Irwin, p. 134.

too many requisitions (see chapter 7). Back in February, the commander of the 1st Louisiana Cavalry (Union) had complained that the scarcity of horses would limit his ability to raise more companies for his regiment or the Texas cavalry as planned.[1239] Urged to scour the countryside, he had failed. In March, Banks had written to Halleck about the deficiency of cavalry, especially regretting the fact that the 2nd Massachusetts, originally raised by Governor Andrew for the Banks expedition, had instead been sent to Virginia. Now, on April 18th, Banks sent a telegram to Halleck again requesting that the 2nd Massachusetts be sent to him.

Banks finally took his own initiative in view of the large new prairie area he had just occupied. The 114th and the 159th New York, having arrived at Vermilion Bayou, were ordered to proceed back down the country and collect all the horses and cattle they could find, and deliver them to Brashear City. After a day's rest, which allowed the men to wash their clothing, which was "blackened with dust, and to care for their feet, which were in wretched condition," they set off on the 19th.[1240] He also ordered Gen. T. W. Sherman at New Orleans "to collect all of the saddles and bridles in the city . . ."

Earlier, the locals had successfully hidden horses and supplies from the Yankee invaders; not so this time. A bible passage comes to mind: "… the land is as the Garden of Eden before them, and behind them a desolate wilderness: yea and nothing shall escape them."[1241] The 114th arrived at Berwick City on the 28th with 3,000 head of cattle and 800 horses; the 159th arrived the next day, having spent the extra time to destroy the earthworks at Bisland. They had collected "about five thousand head, as well as a number of horses and mules . . ."

Opelousas

The bridge at Vermilion Bayou repaired, Grover's force crossed and proceeded in rain and mud to Carrion Crow Bayou. The next day, April 20th, they arrived at Opelousas, to where the government of Louisiana had initially fled after the fall of New Orleans[1242] and from which it now had fled to Shreveport. Opelousas was as far as Banks had originally intended to go, and here his headquarters remained until May 4th, to sort out his situation regarding cooperating with Grant, and to make several other significant decisions:

1. The number of horses already confiscated allowed the creation of more cavalry. The 41st Massachusetts, the 4th Wisconsin, and Company G of the

---

1239. Maddocks, E. B., p. 34; O.R. Vol. 15, pp. 653, 1, 103. 2nd Cav. Refs.; O.R. Vol. 15, pp. 259, 702, 703.
1240. Pellet, E. P., pp. 73, 74; Tiemann, W. F., p. 36; O.R. Vol. 15, p. 703.
1241. King James Bible, Joel 2.3
1242. O.R. Vol. 15, pp. 735, 307.

8th New Hampshire were designated as mounted. Eventually, the name of the 41st was changed to the 3rd Massachusetts Cavalry, though on May 17th, it had become the "Mounted Rifles."[1243]

2. General orders no. 35, Department of the Gulf,[1244] dated April 27th, 1863, required registered enemies of the United States to leave the department "before the 15th day of May proximo. The provost-marshal-general is charged with the peremptory execution of this order."

Butler had first required the oath on June 10th, 1862. That those who had refused to take it were still there is telling. Banks had first tried reconciliation when he arrived, calculating that Butler's harsh measures had only alienated the citizenry. Not true. Reconciliation had not worked. These declared enemies would cause trouble if the city's security was weakened by drawing off forces to Port Hudson; and they could no longer be tolerated, in view of the fact that there were as many, or more, hypocrites who were not willing to sacrifice their personal interests and had declared themselves loyal.

The June 6th, issue of *Harper's Weekly* (p. 363), noted: "You can readily imagine what a flutter this has caused in the ranks of the Secesh . . . a Secesh told a friend of mine the other day, when asked what he was going to do – take the oath or leave – Oh, just as all the rest have done; take it over the left . . . It is really quite amusing to spend an hour at the [provost marshall's office]. People – principally ladies – are constantly flocking in to try if there is no possible way of avoiding the dreadful alternative of starvation in Dixie or bowing to the horrible Yankee flag."

The latter was precisely the story of Sarah Dawson, an avowed Confederate. She, her sister, her servant, and her mother had all moved to New Orleans at about this time to join her brother. They were starving while in the Confederate realm.[1245] Others were fleeing Mobile for fear of an attack on that port city, the only one in the central Gulf still in Confederate hands.

Later, when Emory was in charge of the defenses of New Orleans, he warned of the attitude in New Orleans, which prevailed up until the last moment before the siege of Port Hudson had ended: "The attempt to raise troops here is futile. There are at least 10,000 fighting men in this city (citizens), and I do not doubt, from what I see, that these men, at the first approach of the enemy will . . . be against us to a man."

3. General Orders No. 40, Department of the Gulf, dated May 1st, 1863,

---

1243. Stanyan, J. M., pp. 209, 211; Ewer, J. K., p. 79.
1244. O.R. Vol. 15, p. 710.
1245. Dawson, S. M., pp. 343, 344, 366, 386–388; O.R. Vol. 26/I, p. 51; ORN Ser. I, Vol. 20, p. 181.

proposed the "Corps d' Afrique."[1246] It would consist of 18 regiments of former slaves. Officers for these units were to be obtained from "the nomination of fit men from the ranks and from the lists of non-commissioned, and commissioned officers . . . respectfully solicited from the generals commanding . . ." All officers were to be white, a blow to the faithful free blacks who had volunteered for the Native Guards, and a reversal of "Beast" Butler's promise.

The general chosen to raise, equip, and command former slaves in Louisiana had already been assigned by the War Department back on January 13th.[1247] This was confirmed on March 24th, and on the 25th, Daniel Ullmann was ordered to report to Banks "at New Orleans" and then to Baton Rouge where he was to: "Proceed to fill up your command with colored troops as rapidly as possible." At the time, the size of the force for Ullman contemplated by Stanton was a brigade, but now, Banks was proposing more than four times that number.

This, we shall see, opened up opportunities for the enlisted men of Battery L. In fact, we have already had a preview of one, disclosed in the record of Charles Riley in chapter 6.

On April 20th, Lt. Commander Cooke, commanding the *Estrella*, and his three other gunboats – the *Arizona*, *Clifton*, and *Calhoun* attacked Taylor's Fort Burton at Butte-la-Rose (see figure 4, chapter 7). A detachment of six companies of the 16th New Hampshire were on board as sharpshooters and were to occupy the fort if it fell.

The *Clifton*, with the heaviest armament, pushed ahead, followed by the *Arizona*, the *Calhoun*, and the *Estrella*. After "two or three" shots, "the fort immediately ceased firing and surrendered." The *Clifton* and *Arizona* gave chase to the *Mary T.* and the *Webb*, the two Confederate gunboats present. The fastest of Cooke's boats, the *Arizona*, led the chase, but its pilot taking it into the wrong channel allowed the Confederates to escape. There was some suspicion that the pilot had Confederate sympathies.

About 60 of the garrison were taken prisoner, the few remaining having escaped on the *Webb* and *Mary T.* A large quantity of ammunition and stores was captured.[1248] Only four of the 16th New Hampshire men were casualties, with two dead and two wounded.

Stepping ashore, the conquerors were greeted by the Confederate commander, with the pregnant statement: "You will be doubtless glad to get here, but you will be gladder when you leave . . ." Next, we quote from the author of the *History of*

1246. O.R. Vol. 15, pp. 716, 717.
1247. O.R. Ser. III, Vol. 3, pp. 14, 99–103; ORN Ser. I, Vol. 17, p. 422.
1248. ORN Ser. I, Vol. 20, pp. 153–155; Townsend, L. R., pp. 152, 159, 166, 196; Irwin, R. B., pp. 126, 127.

the Sixteenth New Hampshire Volunteers (Townsend), who penned: "No prophet of early times ever has offered a truer prediction."

Fort DeRussy, further north on the Red River, would be the next target for the navy, so the New Hampshire men were left at Burton. They were basically forgotten, without sufficient supplies for their 600, in the center of a malarial swamp. Arrangements were finally made for the fort's abandonment on May 30th, but from privations due to a lack of rations, overcrowding, and disease, there were but 150 effectives that day.

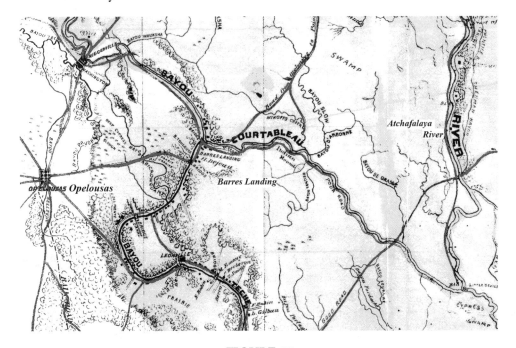

FIGURE 18

Barre's Landing, at the junction of the Teche and Courtableau which entered the Atchafalaya to the east (figure 18),[1249] was taken on the 22nd. Here, the steamer *Ellen* was captured, along with 300 bales of cotton and 100 horses. This now opened water communication back to Brashear City by the Atchafalaya, as well as the Teche, and of course, it allowed direct passage to the Red River past Simmesport and to the Mississippi. The alternate passage past Port Hudson, so long sought, was now in Banks' hands, though falling water would soon render it useless.

Barre's Landing became a suburban camp to Opelousas, eight miles west. Battery L, still with Grover's division, arrived there on the 26th and did not leave until ordered to march to Alexandria on May 5th.

The days spent at Barre's Landing are remembered as "exciting" for those of

---

1249. O.R. Vol. 15, p. 313, 338, 714; Ewer, J. K., p. 79; figure 18, portion of NOAA Historical Map CWAB, Atchafalaya Basin, 1863.

the 41st Massachusetts, who remained until they were designated, as previously noted, "Mounted Rifles" on May 17th. Here, many learned to ride a horse for the first time.[1250] One member of the regiment wrote:

> I was given a horse who evidently had never been ridden much. He objected to the bridle, saddle, and indeed, to about everything I showed him. He seemed to have some conscientious scruples about joining the Union Cavalry . . . the first time I tried to mount . . . I got off as soon as I got on. I usually got off more rapidly than I got on. It is wonderful how quickly a man can get off a horse . . . At last I conquered the beast, and felt proud of the operation. I began to enjoy riding . . . I should now be free from sore feet and weary bones when on the march. After I had ridden . . . about two weeks, I changed my mind. I was naturally tender-hearted; while in the infantry I was tender-footed; but now I was tender 'all along the line.' I often heard my comrades say their saddles were covered with 'raw hide' and filled with the same material.

Though most of Grover's force moved out on the 5th, it was regarded that the important work of seizing the products of the countryside be carried on, as well as "receiving and guarding Gen. Butler's historic 'contraband of war."[1251] Here, an unusual plantation story arose:

Colonel Greenleaf of the 52nd Massachusetts was named the commandant of the post, and six companies of the regiment were assigned as a part of the post command. Soon after taking command, the colonel had his attention drawn to a planter who professed to be a Union man. He had voluntarily delivered his cotton, sugar, and molasses, hauling it to the steamboat himself, and taking the quartermaster's receipt. It was also learned that this Mr. Gantt had on one occasion saved the quartermaster by warning him of an enemy ambush. All that Gantt had asked in return was that he be protected "from molestation."

Soon, the planter introduced himself to the colonel, invited him to visit the plantation, and once assured that he would be protected, Gantt departed. Quoting the colonel:

> A few days later a delegation of negroes – intelligent, healthy, hearty looking fellows – waited upon me, as they said to 'advise with me about the situation.' They had noticed . . . their people flocking to the post by the thousand, and that they were protected and fed . . . They wanted my advice with regard to their own coming, also, with their families. I asked them whence they came and to whom they belonged. They answered that they came from a plantation about two miles away, and that they belonged to 'Massa Gantt' – our Union friend and planter.
>
> I then asked them if . . . Gantt was kind to them. They said he was. If they

---

1250. Ewer, J. K., pp. 79, 80.
1251. Moors, J. F., pp.131, 132, 141, 142.

fed and clothed them well. They said he did; that they had no fault whatever to find with his treatment of them, but they 'wanted to be free.' I answered them that they could come within our lines, with their families, and that, if they came they would be protected the same as the others; but that from what I had learned of 'Massa Gantt' before, and what they had just told me, my advice to them would be to remain, for the present, just where they were, explaining that 'I had little doubt' that they all would be free when the war was over, but that if they undertook to follow the fortunes of the army . . . I feared but few of them would live . . . The death rate from disease in the great congregations in the camps had proven to be large.

They thanked him and departed.

"A week or two later," the colonel accepted Mr. Gantt's invitation to visit the plantation. Seeing the conditions under which Gantt's slaves were living, Colonel Greenleaf was confirmed in the opinion that he had given them wise counsel.

On May 21st, the same slave group was seen in the refugee column that had evacuated Barre's Landing. Despite Colonel Greenleaf's advice, the promise of freedom had overcome all else.

Cooperation with Grant

As earlier noted, at the last moment, before the beginning of the Teche campaign, Farragut's secretary Gabaudan had arrived at Banks' headquarters at Brashear City with the substance of a letter from Grant to Farragut dated March 23rd, with instructions to: "Please inform the general of the contents of this, and much oblige your obedient servant." Gabaudan had memorized the letter in order to prevent its contents from falling into Confederate hands, should he be captured. At 8:00 p.m. on April 7th, he had left the *Hartford* in a skiff covered with bushes, accompanied only by "a contraband," as was described his guide, intending to float down the river to below Port Hudson. He was picked up by the crew of the *Richmond*, which was lying off Baton Rouge, at 2:00 a.m. on April 8th. Though seen and hailed by the Confederates, the disguise was sufficiently akin to a piece of drift to allow them to have passed unmolested. Finally, Gabaudan reached Banks on the morning of April 10th.[1252]

In the original letter, Grant had noted that his Lake Providence experiment was expected to be successful and that: "This will give navigable water through by that route to the Red River." Further, assuming that transports would become available, and if "Admiral Porter gets his gunboats out of the Yazoo," Grant could send 20,000 "effective men" to cooperate with Banks "on Port Hudson."[1253] Though

---

1252. ORN Ser. I, Vol. 20, pp. 765, 788; O.R. Vol. 15, pp. 294, 295; O.R. Vol. 24/III, p. 225; Irwin, R. B., p. 135.
1253. O.R. Vol. 24/III, pp. 131, 182, 183.

there were two big ifs in the original, Gabaudan may not have stressed them. In any case, Banks sent the secretary back with a letter, which he was ordered to memorize and destroy, with the answer that he, Banks, could be at Baton Rouge "to cooperate with you against Port Hudson. I can be there easily by May 10." Significantly, this was not received by Grant until May 2nd.[1254]

The thought of cooperation had buoyed Banks during the entire Teche campaign. Now, at Opelousas, on April 23rd, he wrote to Grant,[1255] giving a summary of his situation. Taylor's forces were dispersed. One portion, Sibley and Mouton, were on the road to Texas, and Taylor's artillery and some cavalry were on the road to Alexandria.

Grant's commitment to the idea of cooperating with Banks had been solidified by his April 12th assignment of McClernand's 13th Corps to move down the river to Bayou Sara after the capture of Grand Gulf. "From there you can operate on the rear of Port Hudson, in conjunction with Banks from Baton Rouge."[1256]

In the interval between March 23rd and May 2nd, Grant had known nothing of Banks' situation. On April 30th, Grant's forces had begun crossing the Mississippi, landing at Bruinsburg and moving immediately toward Port Gibson.[1257] His long-planned southern attack on Vicksburg was finally in motion. The last of Grant's experiments, the Duckport Canal, had proven too shallow due to the drop of the Mississippi, though the effort had revealed that the countryside through which it passed was passable if roads were improved and bridges were constructed. The way around Vicksburg had finally been found: from Milliken's Bend via Richmond to New Carthage. As early as April 19th, two divisions of McClernand's corps had made it to New Carthage, and Porter's fleet was lying offshore. Grant reminded Halleck that he had earlier offered McClernand's corps to Banks, but now, he said, "This will be impossible."[1258]

There was no turning back, and in the middle of an assault that had been impatiently anticipated by everyone looking over Grant's shoulder, from Lincoln on down, Grant did not feel that he could send troops to Banks. Thus, the sincere promise of 20,000 troops for Banks that Grant had made in his letter to Farragut ultimately went unfulfilled; its time had passed – altered since the Lake Providence scheme was abandoned on March 27th and cancelled on April 19th.

1254. ORN Ser. I, Vol. 20, p. 71; Irwin, R. B., p. 139. This shows it in Farragut's hands on the 1st. Irwin noted Grant received it on the 2nd. In fact, Gabaudan did not destroy it but carried it in his mouth when chased by enemy pickets as he hiked across the peninsula opposite Port Hudson. The Confederates had flooded the peninsula at the time of his downward passing, hence the floating drift scheme.
1255. O.R. Vol. 15, pp. 304, 305; O.R. Vol. 24/III, p. 225.
1256. O.R. Vol. 24/III, pp. 188, 189.
1257. O.R. Vol. 24/I, p. 34.
1258. O.R. Vol. 24/I, p. 30.

As late as April 14th, Grant had sent the following to Banks: "I am concentrating my forces at Grand Gulf. Will send an army corps to Bayou Sara by the 25th to cooperate with you on Port Hudson. Can you aid me and send troops, after the reduction of Port Hudson, to assist at Vicksburg?" Banks did not receive this until May 5th.[1259] On May 3rd, from Opelousas, he had sent word to Grant that he would move on toward Alexandria "to-morrow morning" and again proposed: "If you can forward by the Black River the corps mentioned in your dispatches . . ."[1260] Thereupon, Banks' ordered his army to march out from Opelousas, destination Alexandria, on the 5th of May, after 13 days of hesitation, planning and negotiation, but with the good news from Admiral Farragut that Admiral Porter would meet him there, that Grierson had arrived at Baton Rouge, and that Grant was sending a corps via the Black River.

This is a measure of how confused was Banks' knowledge of Grant's current status. The Black River route was a part of the Lake Providence experiment, and work on it had ceased. Further, he misunderstood the "25th" in Grant's note to mean the 25th of May and responded on Wednesday, the 6th of May, with: "By the 25th, probably, by the 1st, certainly, we will be there." Note that communications finally became faster since Farragut had established the protocol that he would descend the Mississippi with the *Hartford* every Thursday to send and receive flag signals across the point opposite Port Hudson, masthead to masthead, to Alden, in the *Richmond*, below. Consequently, Grant received this signal from Banks on Monday, May 10th.[1261] Banks followed up on the 8th, with the news that the 25th was a good number after his being successful at arriving at Alexandria on the 7th.[1262]

Finally, on the 10th of May, Grant put an end to the negotiations, for the lack of a better description. It may be useful to quote his note in some detail. After describing that his advance was far along, he said:

> It was my intention, on gaining a foothold at Grand Gulf, to have sent a sufficient force to Port Hudson to have insured the fall of that place with your co-operation, or rather to have co-operated with you to secure that end . . . Meeting the enemy, however, as I did, south of Port Gibson, I followed him to the Big Black, and could not afford to retrace my steps. I also learned, and believe the information to be reliable, that Port Hudson is almost entirely evacuated . . . I would urgently request, therefore that you join me or send all the force that you can spare . . . Grierson's cavalry would be of immense service to me now, and if at all practicable for him to join me, I would have him do it at once.[1263]

1259. O.R. Vol. 24/III, p. 192.
1260. O.R. Vol. 15, p. 265; Irwin, R. B., pp. 137,138.
1261. O.R. Vol. 15, p. 276.
1262. O.R. Vol. 15, p. 281.
1263. O.R. Vol. 24/III, pp. 288, 289.

Banks received this early on the morning of May 12th. It had been hand carried. Finally, the two generals had knowledge of each other's status that was something akin to current. Banks responded[1264] that he had no water or land transportation to:

> . . . be of service to you in any immediate attack . . . The utmost I can accomplish is to cross for the purpose of operating with you against Port Hudson . . . Were it within the range of human power, I should join you, for I am dying with a kind of vanishing hope to see two armies acting together . . .
>
> The only course for me, failing in co-operation with you, is to regain the Mississippi, and attack Port Hudson, or to move against the enemy at Shreveport. Port Hudson is reduced in force, but not as you are informed. It has now 10,000 men and is very strongly fortified. I regret . . . my inability to join you. I have written Col. Grierson that you wish him to join you, and have added my own request to yours.

The famed Grierson is discussed below.

The decision on immediate cooperation had been made. The words "immediate cooperation" are used for the fact that if Banks turned toward Port Hudson and kept a considerable number of the forces of the enemy occupied by his attack, he would be de facto cooperating with Grant. Given that Banks had heard that 7,000 Confederate troops had left Arkansas to join Kirby Smith at Shreveport, and that a Texan column was coming to join Taylor at Grand Ecore, Taylor might then succeed in reconstituting some of his army and potentially the whole effort of the Teche campaign would be lost. Should he chase after them?[1265] Clearly, this would be nothing but the continuation of a fruitless campaign. Though Banks' reports were filled with the numbers of prisoners and the immense amount of confiscated goods taken, he mentions nothing of the basic failure of the Battle of Irish Bend and the consequent lost opportunity to trap Taylor.

On the same day, May 12th, Banks turned from being beaten in his attempt to have Grant join him, to a decision to retreat back to New Orleans, and start again for Baton Rouge and Port Hudson. Orders to that effect were issued.[1266] The next day, however, his engineers having reconnoitered the area, it was determined that it would be feasible to march to Simmesport and board any watercraft available there to be transported to Grand Gulf. Banks decided on this course. The orders of the previous day were countermanded, and messages then sent to both Farragut and Grant that his headquarters was being moved to Simmesport as the first stage of the move.

1264. O.R. Vol. 24/III, pp. 298, 299.
1265. Irwin, R. B., p. 149–151; O.R. Vol. 26/I, pp. 494, 495, 500; O.R. Vol. 26/I, pp. 6–21 (Banks' final report, April 6, 1865).
1266. O.R. Vol. 15, pp. 729, 730.

The plan was to enter the Mississippi from the Red, near Simmesport, and then head north to join Grant. Later in the day, however, unshakeable in his obsession, Banks sent Grant another message, trying to sell the idea of a combined attack on Port Hudson.[1267] This was carried by Dwight, duly escorted by 28 of the few healthy men left from the 16th New Hampshire's recent trial, with instructions to urge Grant's consideration of Banks' views. (Compare Dwight's entourage with that of Farragut's man Gabaudan.) Dwight proceeded to Grand Gulf by steamboat, and riding forward toward Grant's location, he was just in time to witness the Battle of Champion's Hill on the 16th of May. Dwight sent back the promise "to secure the desired cooperation" but urged Banks not to wait for it. This was apparently only Dwight's opinion and was no real assurance whatever, and the offer was reduced to 5,000 troops. However, Banks took it as a positive, and thus set his final course to Port Hudson, not Grand Gulf.

On May 25th, Grant sent a staff member to Banks to explain that he now had all of his available force at Vicksburg, which was fully invested. He was concerned about a reported force of the enemy "now about 30 miles northeast of here." This was Joseph E. Johnston (see chapter 9). He was asking for 8,000 to 10,000 men from Banks and again asked for Grierson.[1268] The circumstance that Grierson's cavalry was with Banks is the result of a raid planned by Grant and is explained below. It would prove to be the only transfer or contact of any troops of any kind between Grant and Banks.

Postscript:[1269] In his report to the adjutant general, summarizing the operations of the Army of the Tennessee through July 6th, 1863, Grant notes: "I received a letter from General Banks, giving his position west of the Mississippi River, and stating that he could return to Baton Rouge by May 10; that by the reduction of Port Hudson he could join me with 12,000 men. I learned about the same time that troops were expected at Jackson [Mississippi] from the Southern cities, with General Beauregard in command. To delay until May 10, and for the reduction of Port Hudson after that, the accession of 12,000 men would not leave me relatively so strong as to move promptly with what I had."

This was pure Grant. Here, he displays the decisiveness that he had not had a chance to use since Fort Donelson, as was noted in chapter 5: "15,000 men on the 8th would have been more valuable than 50,000 men a month later . . ."

1267. O.R. Vol. 15, pp. 731, 732; Irwin, R. B., pp. 157, 158; O.R. Vol. 26/I, pp. 12, 489; Townsend, L. R., p. 172.
1268. O.R. Vol. 24/III, p. 347; Irwin, R. B., p. 159.
1269. O.R. Vol. 24/I, pp. 49, 50.

Grierson's Raid

Grierson's Raid[1270] and a demonstration by Gen. W. T. Sherman before Haynes Bluff, was planned by Grant as a diversion for his long-awaited crossing. There were two lesser raids from points in Tennessee, all well calculated to confuse the Confederate command, including Pemberton, Gardner, Johnston, and even Bragg, two hundred and fifty miles away, in Chattanooga. One was a combined attack on the Confederate 5th Military District, commanded by Gen. J. R. Chalmers. This was a column of 1,500 infantry and an artillery battery under Gen. Sooy Smith, which left La Grange, Tennessee, by railroad to Coldwater, Tennessee, on April 17th, with orders to push to between there and the Tallahatchie River to flank Chalmers.[1271] Another force consisting of three regiments, an artillery battery, and 200 cavalry, under Col. George Bryant of the 12th Wisconsin, left Memphis on the 18th to make a frontal attack on Chalmers.

Yet another raid acted as a dual diversion for Grierson's raid, as well as that of a planned move by Rosecrans, in the Department of the Cumberland, known as Streight's Raid. This was intended to cut the railroad from Chattanooga to Atlanta south of Dalton, Georgia, to prevent reinforcements from reaching Braxton Bragg's army in Tennessee. The diversionary force was a part of Grant's 16th Army Corps and was conducted by Col. Grenville Dodge and his command from the District of Corinth. The expedition left Corinth on the 15th of April. It proceeded to Iuka, Tuscumbia, and finally as far as Town Creek, Alabama.[1272]

Grierson's force consisted of his own, the 6th Illinois Cavalry; the 7th Illinois Cavalry, under Prince; and a brigade of the 2nd Iowa Cavalry, under Hatch. Supplemented by a battery of artillery, the total force came to 1,700 men. It was intended to break up Pemberton's communications with Johnston to the east, and it caused Pemberton to order all his available cavalry, and even some infantry, chasing after it. An item in favor of Grierson was that Pemberton had few cavalry. It had been assigned to Van Dorn, and he had been sent to Bragg in Tennessee.

Leaving La Grange, Tennessee, on the morning of the 17th (see figure 19)[1273] and heading south "without material interruption," the three units traveled parallel to one another, about two miles apart, crossed the Tallahatchie on the 18th, and then encamped. On the 19th, detachments were sent east and west to disguise the true course of the raid. An engagement with 200 of the enemy took place at New Albany. Here, Hatch's command joined the column and reported a skirmish with an equal number farther east.

1270. O.R. Vol. 24/ III, pp. 49, 50; O.R. Vol. 24/ I, pp. 519–531.
1271. O.R. Vol. 24/ I, pp. 253, 554–556, 561–564.
1272. O.R. Vol. 23/ I, pp. 241–246, 281, 289–292. Nathan Bedford Forrest captured Streight's whole command after several running battles on May 3rd.
1273. *Harper's Weekly*, June 6th, 1863, p. 358. Corrections/additions have been made by the author.

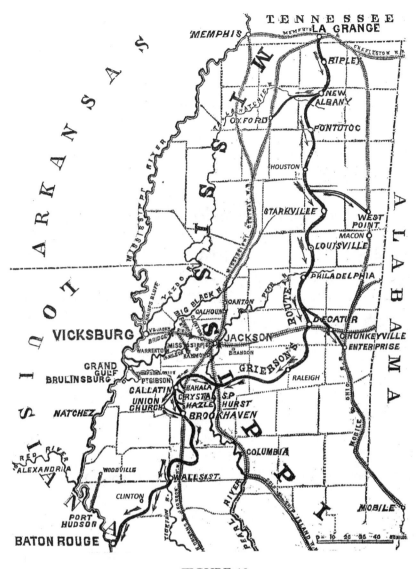

FIGURE 19

They reached Pontotoc that evening, where they clashed with guerillas; destroyed their camp, a mill, and other stores; then moved south five miles and encamped.

At three o'clock the next morning, to confuse the enemy and to return prisoners, the sick and captured property, a detachment of 175 men was ordered north to La Grange. Marching north through Pontotoc before daylight, it was hoped to create the impression that the whole raid was retracing its steps. A single scout was sent to cut the telegraph wires at Oxford. The main column then moved south toward Houston, passing around it and encamping south of it, on the road to Starkville.

The following morning, they proceeded south, to the road to Columbus, where a detachment of the 2nd Iowa was sent east to destroy the Mobile and Ohio Railroad and the telegraph wires near West Point. They were to continue as far south as Macon, thirty-eight miles, and then double back to Columbus, destroy the place, and return via Okolona, again hitting the railroad and finally escaping by any route possible back to La Grange. Grierson considered this useful as yet another diversion even if the Iowans encountered difficulty destroying so many miles of rail track.

With the remaining 950 men of his force, Grierson headed south on the Starkville road, arriving there at 4:00 p.m., he destroyed "a mail and a quantity of Government property . . ." Four miles farther, through a dismal swamp and violent rain, they halted, and a detachment was sent to a tannery and shoe factory. All its machinery and a shipment of boots and shoes destined for Port Hudson were destroyed. They even captured the Port Hudson quartermaster. The trek was resumed toward Louisville, through Noxubee Bottom, often swimming the horses. The column moved through Louisville without incident; "not a thing was disturbed." There was no Confederate property there to destroy. They encamped about ten miles south.

April 23rd, the march resumed on the road to Philadelphia; finding the bridge across the Pearl River intact, they crossed and moved through the town, the resistance planned by the citizens having collapsed. After resting at a point five miles east until 10:00 p.m., an advance was sent along the Enterprise road through Decatur to the hit the Mobile and Ohio Railroad once again. Two trains at Newton Station – a total of 38 cars loaded with ties, machinery, commissary stores, and ammunition – were destroyed. The locomotives were blown up and 500 stand of arms were destroyed. The 75 prisoners taken were paroled. Bridges and trestlework to the east, across the Chunky River, were destroyed. Exhausted, they moved four miles south and "fed men and horses."

From captured mail and his scouts, Grierson confirmed the obvious, that "large forces had been sent out to intercept our return . . ." He decided to head back through Alabama or strike out for Baton Rouge, whichever seemed best when the time came. They now resumed the march to Garlandville, where a slight resistance had been organized by the citizens, "many of them venerable with age." One of Grierson's men was wounded, and the resistance was charged upon; "several" being captured. They were then disarmed and freed. This treatment rather reformed their opinion of Yankees, and one volunteered as a guide. Significantly, Grierson here notes that all along the way, he had seen "Hundreds who are skulking and hiding out to avoid conscription, only to await the presence of our arms to sustain them . . ." They now moved on ten miles and camped two miles west of Montrose.

April 25th, at an easy pace necessary for exhausted men and horses, they moved southwest toward Raleigh. A single scout was sent north to cut the telegraph at the Southern Railroad. Disguised as a citizen, he came upon a cavalry regiment from

Brandon that was hunting for the raiders. Misdirecting them, he returned to camp. This was a close call. Hearing that this area had been reinforced with infantry and artillery and that a battle was expected at Grand Gulf and Port Gibson, Grierson decided to make haste to the Pearl River; strike the New Orleans, Jackson, and Great Northern Railroad at Hazelhurst; and thereafter, gain the area near Grand Gulf, the flank of the enemy; and cooperate with Grant.

April 26th, crossing the Leaf River, burning the bridge, and passing through Raleigh, Grierson sent a detachment forward to secure the Pearl River ferry and landing. They succeeded in capturing a courier who had brought information on Grierson's approach with instructions to destroy the ferry. They succeeded in crossing by 2:00 p.m. Reaching Hazelhurst, they found cars loaded with shells and stores intended for Grand Gulf and Port Gibson, which were destroyed, "and as much of the railroad and telegraph as possible." They then left for Gallatin and encamped.

April 27th, upon leaving Gallatin, a 64-pounder gun and a load of ammunition and equipment were captured. All the equipment was destroyed and the gun spiked. A heavy rain began, and the march was discontinued.

April 28th, they moved westward, a battalion detached to move back to the railroad at Bahala, to destroy all the enemy property that could be found. The rest of the command moved toward Union Church, where they skirmished with a "considerable force" of Wirt Adams' Mississippi cavalry, driving them through the town. Holding the town, they bivouacked for the night. At about 3:00 a.m. the Bahala detachment returned, drawing up against Adams' rear. He had remained outside of town intending to attack, but the appearance of the detachment drove him off on the road to Port Gibson.

Making a feint toward Port Gibson, Grierson reversed direction, toward Brookhaven. There, a large camp of instruction was broken up and some 200 prisoners taken. Destroying railroad property and the telegraph, they camped eight miles south of the town. The following morning they followed the railroad south, destroying all the bridges and trestlework on the way, to Bogue Chitto Station, where the depot and 15 freight cars were burned. Thence, they passed on to Summit, burning bridges and water tanks. At Summit, 25 freight cars and a large quantity of sugar were destroyed. "We found much Union sentiment in this town, and were kindly welcomed and fed by many of the citizens."

Here, Grierson concluded to make for Baton Rouge and thus started out on the Liberty Road, only then halting until daylight.

On the morning of May 1st, leaving the Liberty Road, they avoided Magnolia and Oyska, where "large forces were concentrated to meet us . . ." Taking a course due south, through woods, lanes, and by-roads, they struck the road leading from Clinton, Louisiana, to Osyka. They quickly ran into a detachment about a hundred men of the 9th Louisiana Battalion, Partisan Rangers, (Wingfield's Cavalry) guarding Wall's Bridge over the Tickfaw River. "We captured their pickets [26] and attacking them, drove them before us . . ." Here, one man was killed, and Col. William D. Blackburn and four others were wounded.

Pressed to move immediately, the raiders had to leave behind Colonel Blackburn, who was in no condition to be moved. He was left in the care of the sergeant major and the surgeon of the 7th Illinois. The scene as the troops departed is a memorable one from the 1959 John Ford movie production *The Horse Soldiers*. Accurately portrayed, with the bridge in the background, William Holden was the surgeon and John Wayne was Colonel Grierson.[1274]

Moving south, on the Greensburg road, they soon met another rebel cavalry column, which they were able to drive off. "The enemy were now on our track in earnest." The wide and rapid Amite River had to be crossed, which was "in exceedingly close proximity to Port Hudson." Secured by an advanced guard, it was crossed at midnight. They pushed on to Sandy Creek, just north of the town; and at dawn on May 2nd, they surprised the encampment of Hughes' cavalry, capturing "a number of prisoners." Their camp of about 150 tents and all its equipage and ammunition were destroyed, with the raiders immediately heading south on the road to Baton Rouge.

Arriving at the Comite River, "we utterly surprised Stuart's cavalry . . . capturing 40 . . . with their horses, arms, and their entire camp." Fording the Comite, they halted within four miles of Baton Rouge to rest and feed the horses. A lone member of the 7th Illinois could not wait and forged ahead. The following is an edited narrative from the history of the 50th Massachusetts Regiment.[1275]

> At about 10 o'clock a.m. a cavalryman put in an appearance in front of the picket post . . . The stranger approached, bid us all good morning, tied his horse to a tree, sat down on a log and told his story. The first announcement was received with some distrust, but clouds of dust in the distance soon dispelled the doubt, and all were filled with enthusiasm as they beheld the travel-stained array of horsemen entering the city escorting many prisoners, and accompanied by a numerous procession of contrabands . . .

Augur, now alerted to Grierson's arrival in the area, sent out Godfrey's cavalry to meet them (figure 20).

They had covered some six hundred miles in less than 16 days, often going without food or sleep; the last march up to Baton Rouge was 28 hours without food or rest. All the many detachments sent out along the way, from individuals to the 500 Iowans sent to West Point, safely returned, though Hatch was attacked and never

---

1274. O.R. Vol. 24/I, p. 549. The Confederate report claimed two killed and 14 wounded. Hollywood found it necessary to alter the scene slightly; the sergeant major was replaced by Constance Towers.

1275. Stevens, W. B., pp. 98, 99. Figure 20 from Miller, F. T., Vol. 4, p. 130.

did tear up any of the railroad at Macon. All told, losses were 3 killed, 7 wounded, 9 missing, and 5 left en route sick, including the sergeant major and the surgeon of the 7th Illinois who stayed behind to care for Lieutenant Colonel Blackburn.

FIGURE 20

Regarding the raid, the laconic Grant allows one of his rarest and most extraordinary comments.[1276] "Colonel Grierson's raid from La Grange through Mississippi has been the most successful thing of the kind since the breaking out of the rebellion. . . . The Southern papers and the Southern people regard it as one of the most daring exploits of the war. I am told the whole state is filled with men paroled by Grierson."

Returning to the drama unfolding at Vicksburg, Pemberton reveals that Admiral Porter's presence on the Mississippi below Vicksburg, which he had run past on April 16th, had had a powerful effect in aiding the success of Grant's moves in the New Carthage area and his subsequent crossing.[1277] An April 17th message that Pemberton requested be forwarded to either Kirby Smith or Richard Taylor read as follows: "For the want of the necessary transportation I cannot operate effectually on the west bank of the river; the enemy is now in force at New Carthage and Richmond. I beg your attention to this matter." In an April 18th, message, and a subsequent one on the 22nd, Pemberton declared, "The enemy are cutting a passage from near Young's Point to Bayou Vidal, to reach the Mississippi River near New Carthage. Without co-operation, it is impossible to oppose him. Inform me what action you intend to take."

There was great pressure by the Confederate authorities on Kirby Smith "to

---

1276. O.R. Vol. 24/ I, pp. 33, 34.
1277. O.R. Vol. 24/I, p. 252, Grant, U.S., Vol. I, pp.461–464.

do something,"[1278] and Taylor was reinforced by Walker's Texas Division, 4,000 strong, which marched from Arkansas. Taylor was directed to use Walker in some attempt to relieve Vicksburg. Of the remnants of Grant's army still remaining on the west bank of the Mississippi, the camps at Milliken's Bend and Young's Point were attacked on June 7th and at Providence on June 9th. Driven back to the protection of the gunboats on the river, they held; though with bloody losses and prisoners taken. The fighting continued to Richmond, Louisiana, as Grant's defenders reacted in force. Porter even called in Ellet's Mississippi Marine Brigade.

The result is summarized in an endorsement on Richard Taylor's report of the action to the Confederate Secretary of War. It was by Gen. W. R. Boggs, Kirby Smith's chief of staff, and was dated June 11th. He discloses that Taylor will henceforth focus on Banks. "This report contains a clear statement of the expedition against Milliken's Bend by General Taylor, which awakened so much hope, and which is here shown to have been abortive."

Taylor – and as we shall see, Johnston – saw that to try to hold Vicksburg was a mistake and that: "The problem was to withdraw the garrison, not to reinforce it . . ."

Pemberton received an acknowledgment of the receipt of his call for help of April 22nd, dated May 20th, which only reached him on July 4th after the capitulation of Vicksburg.

Alexandria, DeRussy and Red River – Farragut Departs

The last of the Teche campaign was played out at Alexandria. After passing up the Mississippi past Port Hudson, Farragut was embarrassed to find himself with only the *Hartford* and the *Albatross,* insufficient to patrol the river. Uninformed of Porter's involvement with the Yazoo Pass Expedition, or of his wild and foolish Steele's Bayou escapade, Farragut sent off a message on March 20th to Porter requesting help, and in a message to Grant, requesting coal, he mentioned: "I do not know what Admiral Porter would suggest if he was here, but I think he might spare one or more of his rams."[1279]

Word of Farragut's request got out to Alfred Ellet of the Mississippi Marine Brigade, and on the 23rd, the innocent Farragut invited Ellet on board the *Hartford* for a consultation. He and Ellet then agreed that Ellet would run the Vicksburg batteries on the night of the 24th, to bring Ellet's two rams, the *Switzerland* and the *Lancaster,* down to Farragut. Leaving later than planned, the two boats were caught in dawn light and shot up to the extent that the *Lancaster* was sunk and the *Switzerland* was lucky to drift past the remaining batteries after having her center

---

1278. Taylor, R., pp. 137, 138; Blessington, J. P., pp. 95–109; O.R. Vol. 24/II, pp. 446, 453, 454, 457–461, 462–465.
1279. ORN Ser. I, Vol. 20, pp. 6–23.

boiler shot through.

Informed of the disaster, the political Porter promptly reported it to Welles. Ellet was in big trouble for not getting Porter's permission, and especially so, given the result. Porter threatened to have him tried by court-martial.[1280] Remember that Ellet and the Mississippi Marine Brigade had been assigned to Porter's command the previous November. Farragut had stepped into Porter's private domain, and Ellet volunteering to cooperate with him without Porter's blessing was more than Porter could countenance. Never mind that he had been incommunicado in Steele's Bayou.

Finally remembering his place (Porter was an *acting* vice admiral) he asked Farragut to keep the *Switzerland*, which, it turned out, could be easily repaired. Porter then confessed that he had no ironclads to send, considering their condition since the Yazoo Pass and Steele's Bayou debacles. Another reason – clearly a stretch – was that the "fight at Haynes' Bluff must come off soon." This was written on March 26th, 22 days before he would run past the batteries at Vicksburg and a month before Grant would need his support in the crossings from New Carthage.

In any case, Farragut promptly made use of what he now had – the *Hartford*, the *Albatross*, and the *Switzerland* – by attacking the Confederate guns at Grand Gulf and Warrenton. He then proceeded to the mouth of the Red River to initiate its blockade on April 1st.[1281] On the 8th, he captured the Confederate steamer *J. D. Clarke*, which had on board a major from the Confederate Commissary Department, who had been making "extensive arrangements" for the crossing of cattle to the eastern shore of the Mississippi. On the 15th, he dropped down with the *Hartford* to the point above where the *Hartford* and the *Richmond* could exchange their masthead to masthead signals, a protocol, as previously noted, he had repeated once a week. It was April 22nd when he first learned of the capture of the fort at Butte-la-Rose, which opened the Atchafalaya, and he promptly speculated to Commodore Morris at New Orleans that the *Queen of the West*, the *Arizona*, and the *Clifton* could be sent up to join the blockade. Farragut did not know, of course, of the capture and subsequent destruction of the *Queen*.

However, as result a of Farragut's suggestion, the commander at New Orleans, Morris, ordered the *Estrella*, the *Arizona*, and the *Sachem* to proceed up to Farragut. On April 29th, Farragut ordered the *Switzerland* to make a reconnaissance up to Fort DeRussy. From this, he learned that its guns, including those salvaged from the Indianola, had been removed for the defenses at Alexandria. On May 3rd, Farragut ordered the *Albatross*, *Estrella*, and *Arizona* on a reconnaissance up the river; but on the 4th, Porter appeared off the mouth of the river, and in a note to Banks, Farragut declared: "As soon as Alexandria falls, I wish to be at work below

---

1280. ORN Ser. I, Vol. 20, pp. 28, 29, 31, 37.
1281. ORN Ser. I, Vol. 20, pp. 35, 36, 47–49, 54, 59, 67–69.

Port Hudson."[1282] Indeed, Porter had received a confidential telegram from Gideon Welles, dated April 15th, 1863, stating: "The Department wishes you to occupy the river below Vicksburg, so that Admiral Farragut may return to his station."

The reconnaissance ordered by Farragut did not get underway until May 4th and when it arrived at Gordon's Landing, on the Red River, the site of Fort DeRussy, it surprised the Confederate steamers *Grand Duke* and *Mary T* in the process of removing of the guns from the fort. One of the guns was an XI-incher from the Indianola. On May 1st, an expedition under Dwight had attacked the Confederate outposts at the junction of bayous Boeuf and Cocodrie. Though more than fifty miles from Fort De Russy, their fall, following the fall of Fort Burton at Butte La Rose, evidently precipitated Taylor's decision to abandon De Russy. As he recounts: "Threatened in the rear, Fort De Russy was untenable; so the place was dismantled and the little garrison withdrawn."[1283]

The *Albatross* attacked and, failing to be supported by the *Arizona* and the *Estrella*, was severely damaged and backed out of the action.[1284] All three concluded to return downriver, though it was later learned that the two Confederate steamers had been ready to surrender. On the way down, they met Porter and his Mississippi squadron coming up, who then ordered the *Arizona* and *Estrella* to join him. The chase, with the addition of Porter, would now continue to Alexandria, the very destination, on the very day, that Banks had ordered his army to march.[1285]

Leaving Washington on the 4th, Dwight's brigade of Grover's division was followed by Weitzel, who left Opelousas at 5:00 p.m. Emory's division, temporarily under Weitzel's command, left Opelousas on the 5th. Grover, who had to cover the ninety-five miles from Barre's Landing, also left on the 5th, "a four days march," as is noted in Battery L's April 30th–June 30th muster roll.

Bunkie, just below Cheneyville, had been tramped past by these thousands en route to Alexandria. Here, Major Elias P. Pellet, of the 114th New York, seems to have been one of the few who connected with the historic significance of the Epps Plantation.[1286] "We passed the Epps plantation, famous as being the home of Solomon Northrup, [sic] whose book made such a sensation in anti-slavery circles some years ago. Old Mr. Epps yet lives, and told us that a greater part of the book was truth . . ."

The past weeks, with everyone having been plunged into the plantation culture of the south, may have brought to mind memories of the popular 1852 novel *Uncle Tom's Cabin*. So popular was it that the author, Harriet Beecher Stowe, has been

---

1282. ORN Ser. I, Vol. 20, pp. 74, 75, 56; O.R. Vol. 24/I, pp. 684–686.
1283. O.R. Vol. 26/I, p. 11; Irwin, R. B., p. 132, 147; Taylor, p. 136.
1284. ORN Ser. I, Vol. 20, pp. 79–83, 294, 295.
1285. O.R. Vol. 15, p. 306, 307. Emory, with "severe illness," was given leave to rest at New Orleans; Irwin, R. B., p. 144.
1286. Pellet, E. P., p. 77; Northup, S., *Twelve Years a Slave*.

referred to as one of those "who laid the foundation for the liberation of the slave"[1287] Not so recognized was Solomon Northup. The story of Northup was no novel. He had lived in slavery here at the Epps plantation and, after escaping, had published his autobiography, *Twelve Years a Slave*, in 1853. The beatings, and dawn-to-dark work that he described were now confirmed by none other than his owner.

The rest at Opelousas had recuperated the troops, and "there was not the least appearance of straggling or disorder in any portion of the command." No opposition was met.[1288] Porter had destroyed the casemates at the unoccupied Fort DeRussy, removed the raft that had been placed across the river, and arrived off Alexandria on May 7th. Banks arrived that night, ahead of his infantry.

Hearing that Banks was in Alexandria and Grant was in Jackson, Mississippi, caused great dissatisfaction at Washington.[1289] In a letter dated May 19th, Halleck reminded Banks that:

> . . . the Government is exceedingly disappointed that you and General Grant are not acting in conjunction. I thought to secure that object by authorizing you to *assume the entire command* [Note that even at this juncture, Banks was regarded as more fit to command than Grant.] . . . The opening of the Mississippi River has been continually presented as the first and most important object to be attained. Operations up the Red River, toward Texas, or toward Alabama, are only of secondary importance, to be undertaken after we get possession of the river . . .

True to his word, Farragut departed. The May 8th log of the *Hartford* reads: "At 4:40 a.m. the following officers left the ship, on board the Sachem, for passage to New Orleans: Rear-Admiral D.G. Farragut . . ." Of the six named, one was Farragut's secretary Gabaudan; another was the army signal officer Lt. S. M. Eaton, who had been aboard the *Hartford*, Farragut's flagship since its run past Port Hudson, and who had been involved in the mast-to-mast protocol.

Turn to Port Hudson

The tortuous decision process regarding cooperation with Grant settled, Banks ordered a recall. Dwight's and Weitzel's troops, who had gone forty-one miles farther beyond Alexandria toward Grand Ecore, would be the rear guard and would remain in Alexandria until May 17th.[1290] A portion of the troops would march to Simmesport, cross the Atchafalaya, remain there briefly, and from there,

---

1287. *The American Missionary*, Editorial, "Leaders," pp. 244–245.
1288. O.R. Vol. 15, p. 313; ORN Ser. I, Vol. 20, p. 42.
1289. O.R. Vol. 26/I, pp. 494, 495, 500; ORN Ser. I, Vol. 19, p. 699, 700; ORN Ser. I, Vol. 20, p. 767.
1290. O.R. Vol. 26/I, pp. 11, 12; O.R. Vol. 15, p. 325; Tiemann, W. F., p.37; Irwin, R. B., p. 152.

be transported up the Atchafalaya to the Red, then down the Mississippi to Bayou Sara. Landed there, they would march on Port Hudson. However, on the 19th, the water level of the Mississippi having dropped, a land route to Morganza was found,[1291] so some of the troops or trains would divert to Morganza on the Mississippi (see the arrow in figure 21), and be ferried across to Bayou Sara by whatever water transport that could be made available.

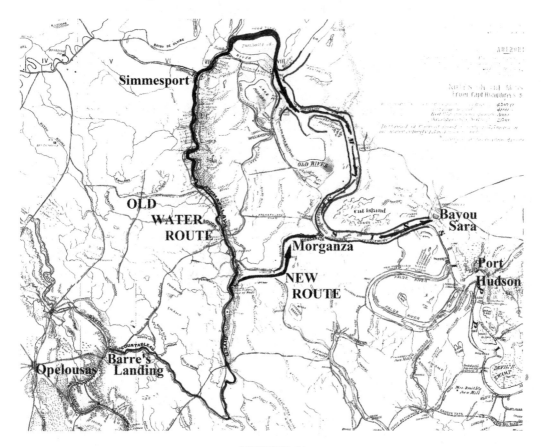

FIGURE 21

The 159th New York, part of Grover's division, never quite reached Alexandria. From their encampment twelve miles below, their history records: "May 14th, we again started on the march, partially retracing our route, passing Cheneyville and Enterprise; to the Bayou Rouge and along the Bayou de Glaise, reaching the west bank of the Atchafalaya River [Simmesport] on May 17th, a march of sixty miles in four days, and were transferred across the river on large flatboats rowed by negroes . . . on the afternoon of May 18th." Battery L's laconic Record agrees (see chapter 9), except that they started on the 15th. Grover's troops were still crossing on the 19th.

Some troops remained encamped at Simmesport until the 21st, long enough

---

1291. O.R. Vol. 26/I, pp. 493, 495, 502. Figure 21, NOAA CWAB, portion.

to explore and visit. Colonel Warner and several other officers of the 13th Connecticut were cordially greeted by Mrs. Bennet Barton Simmes at White Hall plantation. Mrs. Simmes entertained at the piano, one song being "The Bonnie Blue Flag." She broke down at the first line of the second stanza: "As long as the Union was faithful to her trust." Recovering, she bemoaned the fact that we were now "a northern nation and a southern nation!" To this, one of the officers replied, "That second nation you so beautifully allude to, is a mere imagi-nation!" The regimental history goes on to report that, remarkably, "This convulsed the listeners with merriment and restored good feelings at once." Mrs. Semmes [sic] recovered enough to ask, "What's the real object of this expedition?" "The real object of this expedition," replied the chaplain of the regiment, "is to protract the expedition until the quartermasters and the contractors all get rich."[1292]

The flavor of cynicism here noted, sprinkled as it was, into the history of the 13th, reveals a suspicion of dishonest private profiteering regarding the "authorized" confiscations by those in the quartermaster department, as well as the questionable activities of the navy regarding the prize law. Apparently, it was widespread. For example, the title of the history of the 6th Michigan Regiment by its author, Edward Bacon, was, of course, *Among the Cotton Thieves*.

The suppliers to the government got rich simply by the immense increase in the business of supplying the army, and the increased prices that the war had created. What grated on many a mind, however, was the poor-quality, or "shoddy," goods, which, too often, were supplied.[1293]

The decision to move to Port Hudson meant abandoning the Teche country. Banks' small force could not both hold this area and conduct operations against Port Hudson or whatever might develop on the east side of the Mississippi. One of the concerns Banks had was that: "The force west of the Mississippi, which I had dispersed, would reorganize by re-enforcements from Texas, and move directly upon the Lafourche and Algiers . . . both of which were nearly defenseless."[1294] Retreating south and back across Berwick Bay to more defensible positions was a necessity. Essentially, this was an admission that the Teche Campaign was a failure. If Grover had captured Taylor and his force at Irish Bend, the options now would be less bleak. In fact, Taylor soon returned to Alexandria from Natchitoches, where the "fox" had stopped at the end of the "hound's" chase. In a few days, he was informed that Walker's division, was on its way from Arkansas to reinforce him, and that his first work was to attempt to relieve the pressure Grant was putting on Vicksburg, mentioned previously (Pemberton's pleas to Kirby Smith).[1295]

1292. Sprague, H. B., pp. 130, 131.
1293. O.R. Vol. 34/III, p. 333.
1294. O.R Vol. 26/I, p. 12.
1295. Taylor, R., p. 137.

Banks' retreat south would be accomplished by the forming of a provisional brigade,[1296] to be commanded by Col. J. S. Morgan of the 90th New York. It would have the assignment of convoying a train of supplies and refugees back to Brashear City. The brigade included three companies of the 41st Massachusetts Mounted Rifles, the 90th New York, the 52nd Massachusetts, the 22nd Maine, the 26th Maine, Company E of the 13th Connecticut, and Snow's section of Nims' 2nd Massachusetts Battery. Some elements of the 110th and 175th New York regiments also participated.[1297]

Under way from Barre's Landing, on the morning of the 21st, the column was joined on the 23rd by the 114th New York at St. Martinsville. The train consisted of 50 army wagons carrying ammunition and stores, 500 "emigrant" wagons carrying the household goods of the former slave families, 5,000 former slaves, 2,000 horses and mules, and 1,500 cattle. It was almost eight miles in length. Though harassed by guerillas, notably at Franklin, when the rear guard was attacked on the evening of the 25th, it arrived safely near Berwick City on the 26th.

1296. O.R. Vol. 26/I, pp. 40, 41; Irwin, R. B., p. 155, Ewer, J. K., pp. 81, 82; Moors, J. F., p. 145; Maddocks, E. B., p. 37; Pellet, E. R., pp. 80, 81.

1297. Pellet, E. R., p. 79. Pellet mentions the 110th and 175th New York; Irwin does not. Colonel Morgan's report mentions individuals from these units. The statement above is the compromise.

Chapter 9

*Record 6/63; Port Hudson; Demonstrations; Plains Store;
The Wider War; Closing the Ring; May 23rd;
May 24th; May 25th; May 26th; Easy As 1-2-3;
Weitzel Advances; Sherman Advances; Augur Advances; Cease Fire*

Record 6/63
1 MAY – 30 JUNE, 1863, PORT HUDSON, LOUISIANA

MAY 5th Left Barre's Landing Bayou Courtableu, La. & arrived at Stafford's Plantation, La., 70 miles, May 8th - May 11, moved to Webb's Plantation, 4 miles & 12 miles from Alexandria, Red River, La. May 14th broke up camp and took up line of march for Port Hudson via Simmesport, Atchafalaya River. May 24 reached Rebel pickets which were driven in and position taken within 750 yards of the rebel intrenchments on our right centre. Drove in skirmishers fired a storehouse and commenced fortifying. June 14th drawn up for the advance of that day, casualties 2 horses wounded. Held this position up to June 20th. At work upon Rebel artillery, camps, storehouses and other shelter. June 20, Sgt. Becker with one section detached on escort duty, drove the Rebel Artillery from the train & behaved with most Commendable coolness & ability. June 25th took up position on the extreme left in the Redoubt 300 yards from Rebel citadel, operating upon rebel sharpshooters, covering our working and assaulting parties and shelling out the Rebel defenders. June 27th Pvt. Casey mortally wounded by Sharpshooters while at his gun. Rebel colors three times shot away by 1st Sergt. Louis Keller. June 28, Lt. Taylor and two sections detached to Donaldsonville, La, engaged and dispersed the Enemy. June 30, two sections of Battery in Redoubt as before. One section under Sgt. Becker in Redoubt at Donaldsonville, La.

May 24th Pvt. Buckly fatally wounded while cannonading the rebel lines.

(The above has been rewritten by the author, making a narrative by combining the Battery's monthly records for May and June. Details recorded in the two monthly reports were omitted in the muster roll Record, and dates conflicted.)

Henry W. Closson Capt. Commanding Battery and Chief of Artillery, Grover's Div. 19th Army Corps.

Frank E. Taylor	1st Lt. Ass't Comm'y of Musters S.O. no. 16, Hdqrts Dept of the Gulf 19th A Corps, Apr. 9, 1863
Edward L. Appleton	1st Lt.
J. A. Sanderson	2nd Lt. App. to Co. by prom. Vice Gibbs prom. G.O. No. 73 War Dept. A.G.O. Wash, July 4, 1863 (never joined Co.)
Detached: George Friedman	Pvt. On Det. Svc. at N.O. as Artillerist. Left Co. May 24,'62.
Amelius Straub	Pvt. Absent on Ex. Duty as Cook in Gen. Hosp. Baton Rouge since Mar. 14,'63.
Martin Stanners	Pvt. Absent on detached service at Bayou Boeuf, since April 7,'63

At Donaldsonville:

Julius Becker	Sgt.	
William Demarest	Cpl	
William Wynne	Cpl.	
James Beglan	Miles McDonough	Ephriam Orcutt
James Comfort	Daniel Moore	Philip H. Schneider
Clark Dickson	Cornelius McEnearny	Andrew Stoll
Daniel Howard	Christian Meese	Michael Teigh
Benjamin Hughs	John H. Moran	Henry H. Ward
John Kelly	John A. Nitschke	Joseph Wilkison
John Kastenbader	Sholto O'Brien	Thomas M. Wilcox

Strength: 141, Sick: 11 [1 not accounted for]

Sick present: none

Sick Absent: William C. Brunskill, Ft. Hamilton, NY, Left Company Sept. 17, 1861.
       John Casey absent, sick in 2nd Div. Hosp.
       George Chase Brashear City, La., Since April 22,'63
       William Crowley Baton Rouge, Since Mar. 27,'63
       Benjamin O. Hall   "   "   "   "   "
       Joseph Kutschor Brashear City, Since May 4,'63
       Charles F. Mansfield Pensacola, Fla. Since Dec. 24,'62
       Solomon J. Montgomery Baton Rouge, Since June 11,'63
       Wallace D. Wright Pensacola, Fla. Since Dec. 24,'62
       Peter Welsch Baton Rouge, Since June 11,'63

Died: John Buckley Pvt. 30 Sept.'58 New York Of wounds received before Port Hudson, May 24,'63.

Discharged: Franklin W. Richards Pvt. 6 Feb.'61 New York. At Fla. Pickens, FL April 28,'63 After serving 6 mos. confinement. Gen'l Court Martial O. No. 26.

Horses: [Not Listed.]

Deserted: None

In the "Remarks" after each man's name, there is no notation as to who owed what to whom, as was so scrupulously recorded in all earlier rolls. There are no remarks here whatever, save sickness, the promotion of William Wynne to corporal, and those on detached service at Donaldsonville, Brashear City, Baton Rouge, and New Orleans. The record keepers apparently had no time for this nonsense at this busy time. There was no money noted as owed to laundresses, and it is therefore assumed that there were officially none, though many of the officers and groups of the enlisted men throughout the department had by this time hired servants from the population of escaped slaves. The August–October muster roll notes enlisting "colored" cooks, who had been "cooking in the Company since May 20, '63." The enlistment made it official, though they were hired and paid privately until then.

It is noted that though Battery L was present and participated in the shelling during the May 27th assault on Port Hudson, not a word is mentioned here.

Port Hudson

The arrival of Banks' forces at Port Hudson near the end of May would find it weakened but not abandoned, as had been alluded to in one of Grant's messages. On April 30th, after Grant's forces had landed at Bruinsburg on the east side of the Mississippi, the critical moment had come, and the reinforcements for the Confederate force predicted as needed for the defense of Vicksburg and Port Hudson would ultimately not arrive, due to the direct intervention of none other than Jefferson Davis.

In November of 1862, Joseph E. Johnston had been appointed commander of the Confederate department embracing Tennessee, Mississippi, Alabama, and that portion of Louisiana east of the Mississippi; and to whom both Pemberton, E. Kirby Smith, and Bragg reported. Noting the Union buildup of Grant's army (McClernand's recruiting efforts), Johnston had predicted the invasion of Mississippi, and had requested troops from Arkansas, which were never sent[1298] though there were two corps in the Trans-Mississippi Dept. under Holmes at the end 1862.[1299]

In February, before Grant began to pressure him, Pemberton sent Rust's brigade[1300] to reinforce Gardner at Port Hudson. It consisted of two Arkansas regiments, the 12th Louisiana and the 6th and 15th Mississippi, plus three artillery batteries, all of whom had arrived in March. However, in March, Grant's activity had increased. This included the brief threat from the Yazoo Pass Expedition and the necessity of Pemberton constructing and manning his fort near Greenwood.

1298. O.R. Vol. 17/II, pp. 784, 801, 811, 823, 828, 838.
1299. O.R. Vol. 22/I, pp. 903, 904; Johnston, J. E., *Battles and Leaders...* pp. 473, 474. Randolph, the Confederate secretary of war, had directly ordered Holmes in Arkansas to send reinforcements to Pemberton, but it was countermanded by Jefferson Davis. A few days later, Randolph resigned, "unfortunately for the Confederacy," quoting Johnston.
1300. O.R. Vol. 15, pp. 985, 1,005, 1,032, 1,033, 1,035, 1,069.

Now, more recently, the threat was the move of McClernand south to Richmond and New Carthage. Thus, Pemberton ordered Rust back out of Port Hudson on April 4th – a total of 3,400 troops. On May 1st, with Grant now having crossed the Mississippi, Pemberton ordered Gregg's brigade out – about 3,800 troops. Then again, on May 4th, Pemberton ordered Gardner to "come and bring with you 5,000 infantry," including Maxey's brigade.[1301] This would leave only Beall to garrison Port Hudson with about 3,800 troops. The message was in cipher, and Gardner initially could not understand it, delaying any action on it until May 6th, when Gardner and Gregg's brigade left. Pemberton appeared to be on the brink of abandoning Port Hudson as had been implied in a message from Johnston to him on May 1st: "If Grant's army lands on this side of the river, the safety of Mississippi depends on beating it. For that object you should unite your whole force."

Jefferson Davis now entered the picture with a May 7th direct communication to Pemberton, bypassing Johnston. The message began with information, among other things, that the eastern reinforcements for him from Beauregard would be limited to the 5,000 already sent. He then closed with a message devastating to Johnston's plan of uniting the few Confederate forces: "To hold both Vicksburg and Port Hudson is necessary to a connection with Trans-Mississippi."[1302] Naturally, on the next day, the 8th, Pemberton ordered Gardner to return with 2,000 troops to Port Hudson "and hold it to the last." On the 9th, Pemberton notified Johnston that "one brigade, about 5,000 infantry, cavalry, and artillery, at Port Hudson." A careful review of Gardner's returns, noting that Gardner had retained Logan's troops at Olive Branch, some fifteen miles to the east, reasonably agrees with Pemberton's estimate.

The new Confederate secretary of war, Seddon, concerned, but with little control over a situation in which Jefferson Davis had already dictated the fatal strategy, on May 9th, ordered Johnston to personally take the field. Then stationed at Tullahoma, Tennessee, and still recovering from wounds received at the Battle of Seven Pines (when he was in command of the Army of Northern Virginia, and due to his wounds, was succeeded by Lee), Johnston complied, leaving on the first train the following morning.[1303] Arriving at Meridian, Mississippi, on the 13th he was delivered a telegram from Pemberton that described the advance of Grant's forces, which greatly outnumbered him. Arriving at Jackson, Mississippi, that evening, Johnston learned that Gregg's force from Port Hudson had been defeated by Grant (McPherson's 17th Army Corps) at Raymond the day before

---

1301. O.R. Vol. 24/III, pp. 808, 828, 835, 839. On p. 839, a Gardner note dated May 6th appears: "Gregg's division ought to reach Brookhaven next Thursday or Friday." See also Vol. 15, pp. 1,071, 1,074, 1,076.
1302. O.R. Vol. 24/III, pp. 842, 845, 846.
1303. O.R. Vol. 24/I, pp. 215–218; O.R. Vol. 24/III, p. 859; Johnston, J. E., *Battles and Leaders...* p. 478, Raymond, May 12th, 1863; CWSAC No. MS 007; O. R. Vol. 24/III, pp. 870, 876.

and had fallen back to Jackson, Mississippi, accompanied by W. H. T. Walker's men (those sent by Beauregard). Maxey's brigade from Port Hudson was due in, as were 3,000 exchanged prisoners from Van Dorn's defeat at Corinth the previous October. Thus, perhaps, there would be 15,000 troops at Jackson available to reinforce Pemberton. The "perhaps" is added because the exchanged men were not armed and might not soon be able to be.

Johnston had an order hand delivered to Pemberton that evening, informing him of his arrival, and that they should cooperate. Pemberton received the message on the 14th and then described his own plan to attack the Union army at a point southwest of Jackson. In the interval, Johnston had been forced by Grant's advance to evacuate Jackson,[1304] to Vernon to the north, placing the two even farther apart. Calling a "council of war" to discuss the situation with his commanders, Pemberton decided against their opinion to attack the enemy in the direction of Clinton so as to unite with Johnston. Instead, he headed southeast on the Edwards – Raymond Road, "by which this army might endeavor to cut off the enemy's supplies from the Mississippi." He had ignored Johnston and, in Johnston's words, disobeyed him. On the 16th, Pemberton was attacked by Grant, known as the Battle of Champion Hill, and was forced to withdraw toward Vicksburg, only stopping to defend himself at the Big Black River.[1305] The next day, a portion of McClernand's Corps attacked Pemberton again, resulting in his troops fleeing in disorganization to the defenses of Vicksburg.[1306]

On May 17th, Pemberton reported his series of setbacks to Johnston, who replied,[1307] "If you are invested in Vicksburg, you must ultimately surrender. Under such circumstances, instead of losing both troops and place, we must, if possible, save the troops. If it is not too late, evacuate Vicksburg and its dependencies, and march to the northeast" (Johnston's location at Vernon, Mississippi).

Johnston also sent a separate order to Gardner by courier on the 19th, apparently not trusting Pemberton to do so: "Your position is no longer valuable . . . Evacuate Port Hudson forthwith . . ."

Gardner may have received the order or heard of its contents verbally because he is reported, by Confederate Lt. James Freret,[1308] to have evacuated, and to have reached Clinton, yet upon hearing of Augur's advance from Baton Rouge, (see "Demonstrations" below) retreated. The actual copy of Johnston's order arrived at the commander of the Port Hudson outposts, Col. John L. Logan's headquarters at Clinton, on the 25th, but by that time it could not be sent through, Port Hudson having been surrounded. Confirming Freret, in some degree at least, Logan reported

---

1304. Jackson, May 14th, 1863, CWSAC no. MS 008; O.R. Vol. 26/II, p. 9.
1305. Champion Hill May 16th, 1863, CWSAC no. MS 009.
1306. Big Black River Bridge, May 17th, 1863, CWSAC no. MS 010.
1307. O.R. Vol. 24/III, pp. 887, 888, 896, 897; O.R. Vol. 24/I, pp. 222, 242.
1308. Stanyan, J. M., p. 247; Freret was present within the fort during the siege.

that Gardner had intended to cut his way out on the night of the 24th, and had he succeeded, his line of retreat to Johnston would have been so long as to "have been attended with great loss."[1309]

Gardner's "incomplete" return indicates 5,715 for the "aggregate present" at Port Hudson on May 19th, 1863, close to the 5,000 given by Pemberton to Johnston on May 9th, and slightly more than half of Banks' estimate of 10,000 given to Grant on May 12th.[1310]

Some few more souls would be added to the Port Hudson garrison by paroled prisoners. One of the "ironies of war," or so the expression goes, is found in the journal of the *Richmond*, which had been on station below Port Hudson since May 2nd. Its entry for May 11th reads: "At 10:00 a.m., the *Iberville* came up with a flag of truce. She had between three and four hundred rebel prisoners on board. The *Iberville* went up to the batteries at Port Hudson, where the paroled prisoners were landed." Described here as paroled, they would have to have been officially exchanged if they were to legally reenter active service. Regardless of the fine point, under Gardner's dire need for men, the suspicion was that they would be pressed into service. This suspicion is evidenced by a comment regarding the 100 or so prisoners Grierson brought into Baton Rouge. Company G of the 49th Massachusetts was detailed to escort them to New Orleans, "where, I suppose, they will be paroled, and set loose to fight us at Port Hudson."[1311]

Gardner's return for June 30th, 1863, settles the matter at 4,098 "Aggregate present," though 6,273 are listed as "Aggregate present and absent."

Demonstrations

Long before the decision to turn to an attack on Port Hudson, Banks had insisted upon Augur, at Baton Rouge, making "offensive demonstrations every day in the direction of Port Hudson, with the view and effect of deterring him [Pemberton] from weakening his forces there. I desire you to observe closely the movements of the enemy at Port Hudson, especially in the direction of New Orleans."[1312] This sheds light on Banks' thinking regarding his final decision to attack Port Hudson, and not immediately attempting to reinforce Grant. Keeping Gardner bottled up at Port Hudson, he assumed he would quickly dispose of him and manage his own small force so as not to lose New Orleans. His final report, written in 1865,[1313] mentions his worry regarding Taylor reconstituting his force and attacking the

---

1309. O.R. Vol. 26/I, p. 180. Logan's report, written from Gardner's outpost at Clinton, LA.
1310. O.R. Vol. 26/II, p. 10; see also Chapter 8, "Cooperation with Grant."
1311. ORN Ser. I, Vol. 20, pp. 790–804. There had been earlier exchanges; Johns, p. 214; O.R. Ser. IV, Vol. 2, p. 615.
1312. O.R. Vol. 15, p. 704.
1313. O.R. Vol. 26/I, p. 12.

Lafourche, thereby threatening New Orleans, which is what actually happened, and happened quickly, even before the siege of Port Hudson had ended. Noting the latter part of the muster roll record, p. 363, those members of Battery L detached to Donaldsonville were sent there because Taylor had attacked it in June, a relatively short space of time since being "dispersed."[1314]

A part of the planned program of demonstrations relied, once again, on Farragut and parts of his squadron. South of Port Hudson, a naval bombardment involving the Mortar Flotilla, the *Essex*, and the *Richmond*, would commence. Later, Farragut would add the *Kineo* and the *Genesee*, with the admiral himself occasionally visiting from New Orleans on the *Monongahela*. On Farragut's orders of May 5th, the Mortar Flotilla was brought into position near the *Essex* and began shelling the Port Hudson works on the 8th.[1315] A response was made on the night of the 9th by Lieutenant Colonel De Gournay, in command of the left wing of the Port Hudson heavy batteries, who sent a detachment of four guns, the heaviest being a 20 pounder Parrott, to the river at Troth's Landing to attack the mortar fleet. Unfortunately, they used up their ammunition, accomplished no damage to the fleet, and withdrew.

After Port Hudson was invested on May 23rd, the navy shelling would be continued nightly until the surrender on July 8th, 45 days by the reckoning of the commander of the Mississippi Squadron, D. D. Porter. He failed to mention that Farragut had started it 16 days earlier.

Grierson's cavalry[1316] was utilized as a part of these demonstrations as well, Banks noting that his recently constituted "infantry mounted on the horses of the country" had not yet made up for his "deficiency in cavalry." On May 13th, accompanied by the 2nd Louisiana Volunteers, the 30th Massachusetts, the 161st and 174th New York, and Godfrey's Cavalry, Grierson cut the Clinton railroad and the telegraph line to Port Hudson. Dudley, of Augur's 3rd Division, had left Baton Rouge on the 12th and camped on the Merritt Plantation, leaving the 50th Massachusetts to hold the White's Bayou bridge, about ten miles from Baton Rouge. When the regiment left Baton Rouge on that day, "this was the end of camp life . . . so far at least as the 50th Regiment was concerned, the campaign opened which ended in the fall of Port Hudson." They guarded the bridge until the 26th, when they were ordered to the front for the assault of May 27th.

1314. Taylor, R., p. 135.
1315. ORN Ser. I, Vol. 20, pp. 178, 247, 218, 261; Defenders, SHS, Vol. 14, 1886, p. 313
1316. Vol. 15, pp. 409–411, 728, 729; Stevens, W. B., p. 102, 112; O.R. Vol. 26/I, p. 16.

Plains Store

On May 18th, Banks wrote to Halleck,

> Grover's division left Alexandria on the 14th; is now at Simsport. Emory's division marched on the 16th, and is 7 miles to-day from Simsport. Weitzel probably marched on the 17th, and will reach Simsport by the 20th, making a concentration of all our forces at that point. We shall move across the Mississippi, without delay, against Port Hudson, with the best chances of success, and join Grant immediately after. A communication received to-night informs me that this is satisfactory to him, and that he will send re-enforcements to us as proposed earlier, for which, however, we shall not wait . . . [1317] General Augur's forces will move tomorrow toward Port Hudson.

The demonstrations were over. Augur would try to secure as much of the approaches to Port Hudson as possible and await the arrival of the forces from Simmesport via Bayou Sara, and Thomas W. Sherman's forces from New Orleans. The provisional brigade that had marched south to Brashear City would ultimately join them, coming upriver from New Orleans to Springfield Landing.

Quoting from the history of the 49th Massachusetts Regiment:

> Precisely at 5 A.M., May 20th, Col. Sumner led us from camp, and without any noteworthy incident we reached Merrick's [sic] plantation, about sixteen miles from Baton Rouge, where we encamped for the night . . . Save the firing on the river, the night was uneventful . . . The morning of the 21st found us early in line . . . we had marched but a few miles when the battle of Plain's Store commenced.[1318]

Plains Store was at the intersection of the old Zachary Highway and the Port Hudson – Plains road, about three and one-half miles due east of Port Hudson. Here stood a two-story white wood-framed structure, which, typical of the time, consisted of a "drug-store and post-office . . ." with a Masonic Lodge above.

Augur's First and Third Brigades, led by Grierson's cavalry, had advanced to here to discover a Confederate force commanded by Col. F. P. Powers.[1319] The Confederate cavalry pickets were dispersed by Godfrey's cavalry, and the column of Augur's 3rd Brigade, led by the 30th Massachusetts,[1320] continued on until within

---

1317. Vol. 26/I, pp. 492, 493. T. W. Sherman replaced Emory as commander of the 2nd Division. Emory to be in command of the defenses of New Orleans.

1318. Johns, H. T., pp. 228, 230, 235.

1319. O.R. Vol. 26/II, p. 5. Powers was detached from the 14th Arkansas, at Port Hudson, on May 15th; Defenders, SHS Vol. 14, p. 314.

1320. O.R. Vol. 26/I, pp. 120–122; *Passages from the life of Henry Warren Howe*, by Howe, Lowell, Massachusetts, 1899, p. 47; O.R. Vol. 26/I, pp. 179, 137. Pages listed in order of appearance in text.

about three-quarters of a mile from the Plains store, when they were fired on by Abbay's Mississippi battery of light artillery. One section of Battery G of the 5th U.S. Artillery was brought up and joined one section of the 18th New York Battery. They engaged the enemy battery for a half hour and failed to silence it. General Augur then ordered up four pieces of the 2nd Vermont Battery, supported by the 174th New York Infantry. With an additional section of Battery G on the right, supported by the 30th Massachusetts, and a flanking move by the 2nd Louisiana, supported by the 161st New York, this overwhelming force drove Powers' force from their position. The 3rd Brigade then occupied a position near the store, the advance chasing Powers as far as the Clinton Railroad. The fighting tapered off by noon.

In the afternoon, on Gardner's orders, Col. W. R. Miles[1321] with 400 of his Legion and Boone's battery, arrived on the road from Port Hudson to run into the 48th Massachusetts which was stationed in the open, supporting a section of Battery G, 5th Artillery, which had been placed to cover the road. The 48th, a nine-month unit, thrust into its first action, was surprised, overwhelmed, and consequently retreated into and through the 49th Massachusetts, which was coming to its aid. Battery G's guns were briefly taken. Miles then managed to flank and get into the rear of the 49th and the 116th New York, which had followed the 49th. The 116th and the 49th were both then "faced about," putting the 116th in a position to engage Miles. Augur now ordered a charge, to which the 116th responded. A second charge routed Miles and thus ended the Battle of Plains Store. The total casualties on the Union side were 102, the 116th taking the most: 11 killed and 44 wounded. Miles reported a total of 89, though it was incomplete.[1322]

Augur was now in place, holding the ground southeast and east of Port Hudson. Col. John L. Logan, commanding the remainder of Gardner's "outside" troops here, reported that his force was too weak to attempt to attack Augur, but would keep on Augur's right flank, after a move to Clinton.[1323]

T. W. Sherman, now in command of the 2nd Division,[1324] came upriver from Carrolton via Springfield Landing and reported to Augur late on the 22nd. He was directed to deploy his troops to the east and south of Slaughter's and Gibbons'

1321. O.R. Vol. 26/I, pp. 167, 168, 144; ibid., pt. II, p. 10; Johns, p. 235; Clark, pp. 78–80; Irwin, p. 161.
1322. Eighty-nine enlisted and 4 officers *killed*, Defenders, SHS Vol. 14, p. 314; Stanyan, J. M., p. 247
1323. O.R. Vol. 26/I, pp. 179, 180.
1324. Emory took over as the commander of the defenses of New Orleans after Sherman. Weitzel was temporarily assigned to the command of the 3rd Division for one day, May 13th, and was then returned to the command of the 2nd Brigade, 1st Division, plus that of Dwight, plus other cavalry and artillery detachments, to hold Alexandria while the rest of the army marched out on the 17th. Paine took over the command of the 3rd Division. O.R. Vol. 26/I, pp. 486, 492, 493, 500, 501; Irwin, p. 159; Hanaburgh, p. 35; Stevens, W. B., p. 130; Johns, pp. 228–230.

fields and hold the road to Baton Rouge. He moved within sight of the rifle-pits the next day, his cavalry pickets exchanging shots. He then looked to the task of repairing the bridges on the road to Springfield Landing.

At Simmesport, Grover's division was left considerably reduced by the detachment of five regiments, and portions of two others, who had been assigned to the provisional brigade under Chickering and Morgan, which was just getting under way on its forced march to Berwick City. The remainder of the division was ordered to load "two artillery batteries on board the steamers Empire Parish and St. Maurice, with as large a part of his infantry as the two steamers can carry," destination Bayou Sara[1325] (figure 1).

FIGURE 1

One regiment, however, did not go with Morgan. This was the 6th New York, whose term of service having already expired, had been assigned to the 3rd Division, now under Brig. Gen. Halbert E. Paine, and had been doing provost duty at Alexandria.[1326] The 3rd marched from Alexandria on the 19th and arrived at Simmesport on the 21st. Since both Battery L and its old comrades-in-arms were together on the same day, there seems no doubt that there was a chance for some rather stunned goodbyes, the 6th, thanks to Dwight, no longer under the command of its colorful Billy Wilson. Had almost two years passed since the days at Pickens and the sands of Santa Rosa? The war was now a much wider one, and the attention

---

1325. O.R. Vol. 26/I, p. 499; Figure 1 from June 20th, 1863, *Harper's Weekly*, p. 389.
1326. Morris, G., pp. 114–116.

the darlings of the City of New York had gotten while at Fort Pickens had long since faded. Many, many more units had been mustered and sent off. The attention of the city and the state had lately been focused on unpleasant news of events elsewhere. The political scene had changed as well, Seymour was now governor, and his positions against Lincoln on emancipation, military arrests, and conscription had wafted an antiwar scent into the New York ether.[1327] The deplorable consequences of this would not take long to appear.

The 6th was shipped out on a small steamer by way of the Atchafalaya, bound for Brashear City, New Orleans, and New York. The 3rd Division marched as escort to the quartermaster's wagons by way of Morganza, the now dry roads having eliminated the problem of the lack of river transportation that had so convulsed Banks and staff up to just a few days prior. Weitzel's command was to begin its march to Simmesport on the 22nd and await orders.

The Wider War

There was a wider war, with huge armies, other than just that of Grant at Vicksburg. One was Rosecrans' Army of the Cumberland. After the Battle of Stones River, which ended on January 2nd, 1863, Bragg had retreated to Tullahoma. Rosecrans did not pursue. He was still sitting in his camp, using the questionable argument that he was threatening Bragg and thus preventing him from sending reinforcements to Johnston. He was still there at the time of Grierson's raid in April, as was mentioned earlier (chapter 8).

The President and the general-in-chief agreed that Rosecrans was not aiding, but harming the Vicksburg Campaign, as well as that of Hooker in Virginia, by sitting idly by. Lincoln and Halleck both urged Rosecrans to move on Bragg and sent him some 14,000 reinforcements to do so.[1328]

Rosecrans had been in command under Grant at Corinth when Van Dorn attacked in October of 1862. Victorious in the battle, and ordered by Grant to pursue Van Dorn, he insubordinately delayed, and any follow-up advantage was lost. However, details of this behavior were not reported by Grant and were unknown in Washington. Consequently, Rosecrans' battle victory was viewed favorably enough in Washington to cause him to have been reassigned to replace Buell in Tennessee. Incredibly, his promotion was on the same day, October 29th, 1862, that Grant had resolved to relieve him.[1329] Grant is silent on the question as to whether Lincoln or Halleck asked for his advice on Rosecrans. He admits to being "delighted" that Rosecrans was promoted to a separate command "because I still believed that when

---

1327. *Encyclopedia Britannica*, 1911, Vol. 24, p. 755.
1328. Nicolay & Hay, Vol. VIII, pp. 43–45.
1329. Grant, U. S., Vol. I, pp. 416–420. Grant was still under "distrust and suspicion" at Washington at this time; Nicolay & Hay, Vol. VII, pp. 118, 119, 153; Ibid., Vol. VIII, p. 45.

independent of an immediate superior the qualities, which I, at the time, credited him with possessing, would show themselves. As a subordinate I found that I could not make him do as I wished, and had determined to relieve him . . ." Of course, Rosecrans now saw Lincoln as that adversarial superior. The chemistry that resulted was that Lincoln soon realized that he had saddled himself with a virtual clone of McClellan, with one exception: "While in McClellan's case delay was an instinct, in the case of Rosecrans delay seemed to spring from a certain controversial insubordination which appeared to render prompt obedience . . . impossible . . ."

The ring of the proper noun "McClellan" brings us back to the subject of the Army of the Potomac, which continued to be the focus of attention for the largely New England and New York men here in the Gulf. Capt. Homer Sprague of the 13th Connecticut Volunteers, in his diary entry for May 12th, notes: "We were saddened by the report of Hooker's great defeat at Chancellorsville on the 3rd of May."[1330]

Lincoln had replaced Burnside with Hooker, though he freely expressed his many misgivings about him in a personal letter to him after his assignment.[1331] The Battle of Chancellorsville was fought from April 30th to May 6th, 1863 [1332] and was a Union defeat of the first magnitude, resulting in 14,000 Union casualties vs 10,000 Confederate. It had a "deplorable effect . . . on the public mind . . ."[1333] It was a dark hour. The confidence of the Confederacy was raised "to the highest point they ever reached," according to the President's secretaries, Nicolay and Hay. Compare this with the spring of 1862, when recruiting had been discontinued, and the war was assumed to be coming to an end. Based upon the good news, Lincoln had issued his Proclamation of Thanks (Chapter 5), a sour memory indeed. Worse, by the end of 1862, the volunteers that had flooded to the recruiting stations were no longer appearing. The device that Congress had used to draw additional thousands into the service, viz., the extension of the Militia Act, which had supplied Banks' and McClernand's recruiting, had dried up,[1334] and in early 1863, the Congress would at last have no alternative but to face the difficult political prospect of passing a draft law.

The defeat at Chancellorsville came on the heels of news that the Confederacy had recently obtained a loan from private English interests. Gideon Welles' diary[1335] dated April 7th notes, "which would never have been consummated had the English officials disapproved. With these means, which the Englishmen will ultimately lose, the Rebels can purchase vessels, ordnance, munitions, and prolong the war . . . Sumner [Senator Charles, of Massachusetts] thinks the alliance with

---

1330. Sprague, p. 128.
1331. Nicolay & Hay, Vol. VII, pp. 87–109.
1332. CWSAC no. VA 032
1333. Nicolay & Hay, Vol. VII, pp. 197–200.
1334. Only about 87,000 of the 300,000 called for were obtained. Nicolay & Hay Vol. VII, p. 3
1335. Welles, G., Vol. I, p. 263. The loan was for $15 million.

slavery will be so unpopular with the English people as to restrain the Government, but confesses to fearful misgivings."

Yet there was hope and determination, because a turning point was sensed (note Welles' comment about the English investors ultimately losing their money). The Battle of Antietam (Maryland, Sept. 17th, 1862) had prevented Lee from entering the north. The editors of *Harper's Weekly* put it as a "sense of disappointment, which was not childish and crushing, as after Bull Run, but sober and manly, as of men who, if disappointed, are not dismayed, and if repulsed, are neither disgraced nor disheartened."[1336] The war would go on, regardless of the temporary setbacks, not only those of the army but those of the navy as well, i.e., news of Admiral Du Pont having failed in his April 7th, 1863 attack on Charleston.[1337]

Closing the Ring

Banks, with Grover's division, landed after midnight on the 22nd at the remains of the town of Bayou Sara, which "presented a very battered appearance," having been shelled and raided repeatedly by the navy ever since the Battle of Baton Rouge in August of 1862 (figure 2).[1338]

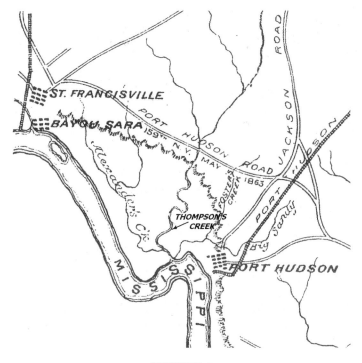

FIGURE 2

1336. Saturday, May 23rd, 1863, p. 322.
1337. O.R. Vol. 14, pp. 240, 241.
1338. Sprague, H. B., pp. 131, 132, 134; Bissell G., (McManus), pp. 43, 44; Willis, H. A., p. 117; figure 2, Tiemann, W. F., facing p. 23, altered.

Resting until morning, they began the march to the north side of Port Hudson. Climbing up the bluff on which stood St. Francisville, then turning south, they encamped near Thompson's Creek that night. During the day, the advance guard had met and engaged Wingfield's 9th Louisiana Partisan Ranger Battalion (the same unit that had fought Grierson at the bridge over the Tickfaw, chapter 8), with Pvt. Thomas Flannery of the 13th Connecticut Volunteers having the honor of being the first man wounded in the army approaching from the north.

As with the advance of Augur from the south, the skirmishing by the Confederate forces was never strong enough to stem the tide of Banks' thousands. In fact, after Plains Store, Gardner seemed committed to slowly retreat to within his defensive works, his only real option, given his limited strength, and Jefferson Davis' dictum. The course of the proceedings at Port Hudson were running parallel, though on a smaller scale, to those that had occurred at Vicksburg only a few days earlier. There, after the battle of Big Black River Bridge, on May 17th, the last of Pemberton's forces had fled into the defenses of Vicksburg.

Halbert Paine's 3rd Division had followed Grover. The 53rd Massachusetts, the last of Paine's troops, landed at Bayou Sara at about 1:00 a.m. on the 23rd. By 5:30 p.m., they had joined the rest of the brigade, which was encamped on the Perkins Plantation, one mile behind Grover's position.

Resuming the march on the 23rd, Grover's troops, though still annoyed by Wingfield's 9th Louisiana Rangers and the skirmishers of the 1st Alabama under Locke, linked up with Grierson's cavalry,[1339] who were the advance of Augur's troops. This was near the junction of the Jackson and Bayou Sara roads, above the Clinton Railroad, to where Grierson had advanced after the Battle of Plains Store. It was about 9:30 a.m.

Gardner had originally felt that the north side of Port Hudson had too many natural obstacles to overcome and that no attack in force would come from that direction. Now that it was obvious that the Yankees were approaching, he had sent a considerable force there, under the command of Col. I. G. W. Steedman of the 1st Alabama. He placed Steedman in command of the whole left wing of the defenses, essentially the area north of the Clinton Railroad, including that portion of the earthworks known as the Priest Cap and Fort Desperate, where Col. Ben Johnson's 15th Arkansas was deployed (figure 3).[1340] The irregular line indicates the prepared Confederate fortifications, which extended from the river in the south to the advanced work, Fort Desperate. Beyond it, following a line curving around south of Sandy Creek, and extending to the swamp above the river, was undefended.

Gardner then ordered Steedman to "observe the enemy and to oppose his advance upon our works, but without risking a serious engagement . . ." This rather

---

1339. Hanaburgh, D. H., p. 36; Sprague, H. B., pp. 136, 137; Stanyan, J. M., p. 220; O.R. Vol. 26/I, pp. 165–167.
1340. Tiemann, facing p. 38, altered. O.R. Vol. 26/I, p. 84, 501, 504.

peculiar directive, in retrospect, may have been Gardner's idea to probe the Yankees for an escape route.[1341]

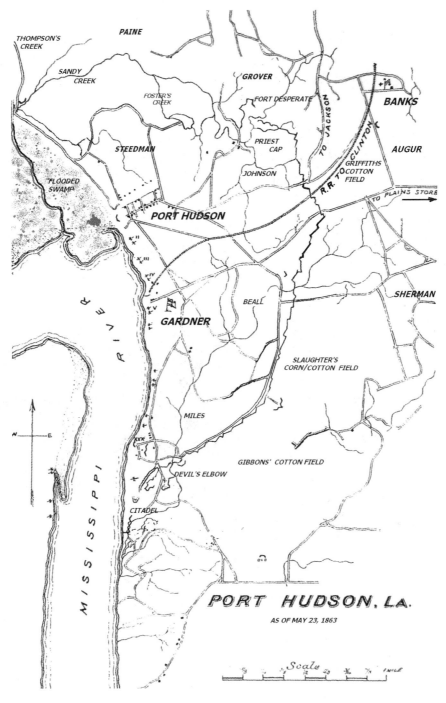

FIGURE 3

1341. Defenders, SHS, Vol. 14, pp. 316–318; Stanyan, J. M., pp. 220, 247, 248.

May 23rd

Figure 3 roughly indicates the positions of both the Union and Confederate troops as of May 23rd, when the Union line closed around Port Hudson. Weitzel was still crossing the Atchafalaya at Simmesport. Paine's troops had crossed Thompson's Creek and there, acting with Prince's regiment of Grierson's cavalry, captured the steamers *Starlight* and *Red Chief*, which, it was feared, could have been used as part of a Gardner escape plan. Paine now covered the right of the Union line from the swampland above the river on the north side of Sandy Creek up to Grover's position.[1342] Grover extended along from the north side of the Sandy to one half mile north of the Clinton Railroad, to Augur's right.

General Banks' Headquarters, near Grover, was on the Riley Plantation.[1343] Sherman, who, as described earlier, had arrived at Springfield Landing on the 22nd, was deployed south of Augur and directed to move to "a position on the Western Port Hudson Road" with pickets within sight of the enemy rifle pits, which he reported he would "carry . . . tomorrow." Others of his troops conducted limited reconnoitering of his flanks and front.

The zigzag Confederate defensive earthworks, lined with heavy guns, ran along a natural prominence overlooking the corn and cotton fields of the Gibbons, Slaughter, and Griffiths plantations. The tortured terrain in the north, which was described as "very peculiar, looking like the skeleton of a huge fish, the backbone representing the long ridge running from the woods towards the fortifications, and the ribs the short ridges . . ." with deep ravines in between.

FIGURE 4

A network of roads ran within the perimeter.[1344] South of the Plains Store road, one such inner road is seen in figure 4 running along the inside edge of the earthworks, down to the Devil's Elbow. Gardner would use these to advantage during both of the failed Union assaults, able to move troops, artillery, and ammunition to points where any attack had concentrated. Today their remnants are grown up with a thick cover.

Hilly and forested areas before the works had been cleared by the Confederates

---

1342. Stanyan, J. M., p. 220; O.R. Vol. 26/I, p. 138, Report of Col. Edward Prince, 7th Illinois Cavalry.
1343. Irwin, R. B., p. 166; *Harper's Weekly*, June 11th, 1863, p. 446.
1344. Stanyan, J. M., p. 226; figure 4 photo by the author.

and the trees left in every conceivable position, making what was termed a "slashing." The slashing opposite Weitzel's and Augur's position appears in figure 5.[1345] Weitzel (Paine's troops under Weitzel), was to face a similar front after Steedman completed his preparations. In areas where "the ground was open and favorable to assault," such as Gibbons' and Slaughter's fields, a ditch had been dug. Described as anywhere from three to four feet deep and five to six feet wide and rumored to be twelve feet deep and fifteen feet wide, it undoubtedly varied and was deeper and wider where natural features helped. From the bottom of the ditch to the top of the parapet was no more than seven or eight feet. About one hundred yards of cleared ground extended out from the ditch, all swept by the fire of the guns on the parapet.[1346]

FIGURE 5

Sherman's front faced Slaugther's field on the edge of the wood opposite the site of the Slaughter house, which was said to be occupied by rebel sharpshooters. Fire from the 1st Vermont Battery was concentrated upon it on the afternoon of the 26th, which drove out the sharpshooters, and it was then burned down by

---

1345. Figure 5, Tiemann, W. F., p. 159 "Scene of Charge, May 27, 1863." The same picture appears in the "Album of the 2nd Battalion Duryee Zouaves" (pages not numbered but approx. p. 49). This was the 165th New York Regiment.
1346. Tiemann, W. F., p. 41; Pellet, p. 85; Clark, O. S., p. 83; Bacon, E., p. 131; Johns, H. T., p. 243; Smith, D. P., p. 42; Woodward, J. T., p. 34. Figure 6, McGregor, C., p. 463.

members of the 128th New York regiment.[1347] Its chimney can be seen to the right in figure 6. Beyond, the "white face of their parapet could be seen zigzaging away to the right and left until it disappeared from view." The artillery in the picture is moving into battery 16, which can be found in figure 14. Today this view has been obscured by an overgrowth of forest, with trees in the field as well as on the earthworks. A visitor can obtain but few clues to the scene as depicted.

FIGURE 6. VIEW FROM SHERMAN'S FRONT, CONFEDERATE PARAPET 1000 YARDS DISTANT

Speaking of change from then until now, even the river, once the western edge of the defenses, has altered its course, and siltation has caused it to recede some two miles or more to the southwest. The eighty-foot high bluffs at what was once the river's edge (see chapter 5, figure 8), are no longer kept free of growth by erosion and are tree covered, obscuring any clear view of the broad plain where there once was the river. The town of "Port" Hudson is a ghost of its former self, and is no longer at the river's edge. Figure 7 is a portion of a 1906 Geodetic Survey map (Bayou Sara gda_5595150) which clearly shows that the siltation process had begun long ago. Compare it with the inset, a portion of Persec's 1858 map.[1348]

The larger map confirms the irregular terrain on the north side of Port

---

1347. McGregor, C., pp. 318, 323, 424, 434, 463; Hanaburgh, D. H., p. 36.
1348. ORN. Ser. I, Vol. 19. pp. 350, 354; historicalmaps.arcgis.com/usgs/.

Hudson, and as well, properly identifies the location of Sandy Creek (Bayou)[1349] called Foster's Creek on some Union maps (see figure 2). Also shown is a portion of the Hermitage plantation on the west side bend of the river, which was ordered to be occupied on the 23rd.[1350] Col. Lewis Benedict of the 162nd New York regiment, commanding the 110th New York, one section of the 6th Massachusetts Battery, and a cavalry company, arrived there on the 24th, thus closing the ring around Port Hudson.

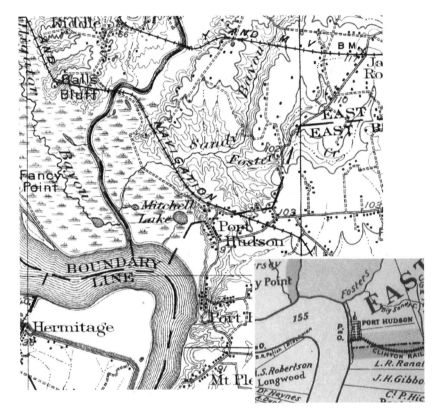

FIGURE 7

May 24th

Having completed the encirclement, a consolidation began which would test and push in the Confederate outlying defensive lines and picket positions. Casualties

---

1349. One local definition of a bayou is a creek or river that flows in different directions during the course of a season. The Sandy is influenced by the level of the Mississippi.

1350. *Massachusetts Soldiers.* Vol. V, p. 412; Irwin, R. B., p. 165; O.R. Vol. 26/ I, p. 502; the remainder of the 162nd was ordered into "Grover's line." From *Historical Sketch of the 162nd New York Infantry*, p. 15. The 162nd was ordered to join Paine at Port Hudson, under Blanchard; its commander, Benedict, absent at Hermitage, or Fausse Point. See also: National Archives M594, roll 131, Compiled Service Records of the 110th New York, and roll 137, 162nd New York.

began to mount, and the ferocity of the skirmishing on Steedman's front grew when Paine advanced. Finally, on the afternoon of the 24th, having observed Paine's advance of about a mile, Steedman was ordered by Gardner to "determine the enemy's strength, if possible, and drive him from my front." With Weitzel not having yet arrived, Gardner may have conceived of a weakness in Paine's 3rd Division line, whereby he could break out, which he was apparently still considering.[1351] Breakout or not, it is clear that Steedman was placed there in urgent desperation because, in Steedman's words: "Up to Monday night, the 25th of May, no works of any description had been thrown up to defend this position, extending from Col. Johnson's advanced work, on the right . . . to a point within five hundred yards of the river on the left . . . about three-fourths of a mile."

Paine confirms that he had advanced a mile on the 24th: "My special duty to-day being to resist any attempt of the garrison to escape through my line . . . Reconnoitered in force, met the enemy, cut the artillery road across the Big Sandy, was ready for an advance." From Paine's comments, it seems clear that he was unaware of the weakness of the Confederate defenses at this part of the front, and that he had no contingency plan to take advantage of it, even if a reconnaissance had discovered it. The whole mind-set was worry about enemy escape. The reason Prince of the 7th Illinois Cavalry had been sent to Thompson's Creek was "to destroy the enemy's means of transportation with the view of frustrating the probable attempt to escape at this point." The two steamers captured, and wisely not destroyed, were, including a "small flat," the only Confederate means of water transport.[1352]

Rev. James K. Hosmer,[1353] detailed as a hospital steward at Springfield Landing, noted, "A great battle might happen at any hour. Already many wounded had been brought in, and dispatched to Baton Rouge, from the preliminary skirmishes; and it was high time for the doctor to complete his preparations . . ." Among the preparations were the construction of icehouses and the pitching of two large "pavilion" tents, with floors, capable of holding 60 wounded "with comfort."

As Grover advanced along the Jackson Road, the first shots of the day occurred at noon, when "sharp skirmishing ensued. A labyrinth of woods, lanes and ravines afforded cover for both offensive and defensive operations . . ." Here, the two sides were close, much closer than at Paine's, Augur's, or Sherman's fronts. Grover was facing a portion of Steedman's troops, the 15th Arkansas, under Johnson, whose line was now forced back to his main work on Commissary Hill (figure 8).[1354]

A relevant part of Battery L's "Record of Events" notes:

1351. O.R. Vol. 26/I, p. 180; SHS, Vol. 14, p. 318; Stanyan, J. M., p. 220.
1352. O.R. Vol. 26/I, p. 506. May 26th report of Banks to Farragut.
1353. Hosmer, J. K., pp. 166–168.
1354. Sprague, H. B., p. 137; figure 8, portion of map "Defense of Port Hudson," from McMorries, E. Y., p. 48.

May 24 Reached Rebel pickets which were driven in and position taken within 750 yards of the rebel intrenchments on our right centre. Drove in skirmishers fired a storehouse and commenced fortifying.

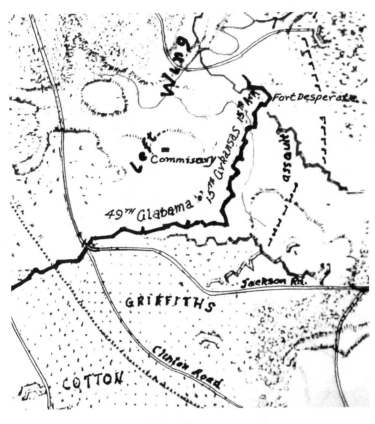

FIGURE 8

Lieutenant Taylor's section of Battery L, with Grover's advance, was the first to come into action, at about 10:00 a.m. Skirmishers, sharpshooters, and artillery on both sides were active; the artillery positions had little or no protection at this time, and Confederate fire resulted in the death of Battery L's Pvt. John Buckley, "fatally wounded while cannonading the rebel lines." Though there were no other casualties in Battery L, the men and animals were exhausted by the constant activity since arriving from Simmesport, their horses in harness for days. They were fortunate to be relieved at the front by the 2nd Massachusetts Battery the next day. The 2nd may have had some rest in the interval, but were likely nearly equally worn out.[1355] Taylor's section later reoccupied the position, remaining near there until June 25th.

In contrast, W. R. Miles, now back in place from the engagement at Plains Store, and sitting on the right wing of the Confederate defensive line opposite

---

1355. Haskin, p. 191, 193; Whitcomb, C. E., p. 48. They were under strength as well. Snow's section was still with Chickering's column.

Sherman, reported "that no attack or menace has been made on my line today. The shelling from guns and mortars has, however, been extraordinarily furious" with the 12th Louisiana Heavy Artillery suffering 3 killed and 3 wounded.[1356] The sound and fury of the nearly constant artillery firing may have exceeded that described so eloquently by Bragg back at Pensacola (chapter 4).

May 25th

Miles' turn came today. He was threatened by two Union advances resulting in a number of Union casualties, compared to none reported by him. Viewing the Yankees removing their dead and wounded under a white flag, Miles complained to Gardner of its "illicit" use, saving those who might have become prisoners.

The rear guard, Weitzel, landed at Bayou Sara and hurried "for it was feared that the Confederate garrison might attempt to evacuate the place and escape. The troops went into position in line of battle, on the Union right, near Foster's Creek."[1357] At this time, Weitzel was named to command the right wing, which consisted of his own troops, the 3rd Division under Halbert Paine, Dwight's brigade of Grover's Division under Van Zandt, and the 7th Illinois cavalry under Prince.[1358]

Commodore Palmer, on the *Hartford*, signaled to Admiral Farragut on the *Monongahela* that General Banks had requested him to shell the west side of Thompson's Creek at midnight "to prevent any attempt of the enemy to escape over that side."[1359]

General Paine wrote:[1360] "25th Crossed the Big Sandy, Dwight's brigade of Grover's division in advance. Drove the enemy steadily through the woods to within a half-mile of his fortifications." Steedman confirms Paine's move: "Monday noon . . . the enemy advanced in heavy force from the direction of Aberger's fields . . . our line slowly retreating until they reached the open space fronting my line of battle . . . This advance, consisting of a heavy line of skirmishers, soon discovered our artillery, and at once took cover behind the numerous trees and began sharp-shooting the artillery horses and cannoneers."

A battle ensued along the whole line, and an attempt was made to overwhelm both Steedman's right and left flank. He was reinforced but notes: "Thus reinforced the right repelled every attack; but in consequence of my inability . . . to extend

---

1356. O.R. Vol. 26/I, p. 168, 169.
1357. Carpenter, G. N., p. 112; O.R. Vol. 26/I, pp. 92, 505, 506; Irwin, R. B., p. 166. An example of the confusion over Sandy/Foster's Creek. There were two Paine's: Br. Gen. Halbert E. of the 4th Wisconsin, commanding Emory's 3rd Division troops, and Col. Charles J, commanding Augur's 2nd Louisiana regiment.
1358. O.R. Vol. 26/I, pp. 505, 506; Stanyan, p. 224.
1359. ORN Ser. I, Vol. 20, p. 209.
1360. Stanyan, J. M., p. 220; Defenders, SHS, Vol. 14, p. 316, 317.

my line to Sandy Creek, the enemy marched a body of troops around the extreme left and seriously threatened our rear." This was the 38th Massachusetts Regiment, supporting Mack's 18th New York Battery, who drove back Wingfield's Partisan Rangers. The skirmish resulted in the 38th reporting two killed and one wounded. One of Wingfield's officers was killed.

In the afternoon, the 1st and 3rd Louisiana Native Guards arrived at Paine's camp and were ordered to join the 38th at its position, which was on the north side of the still flooded Sandy Creek, near where the telegraph road to Bayou Sara had crossed[1361] (see figure 9). Command of the Native Guards was transferred by Paine to Dwight, since his division occupied the remainder of Weitzel's right. The positions of Dwight's troops are indicated by the small rectangles. Note the gap between the position of the Native Guards on the north side of Sandy Creek and the closest of the others, almost three-quarters of a mile. Dwight then assigned Col. John A. Nelson, commander of the 3rd Native Guards, to the command of the two units brigaded for the assault.

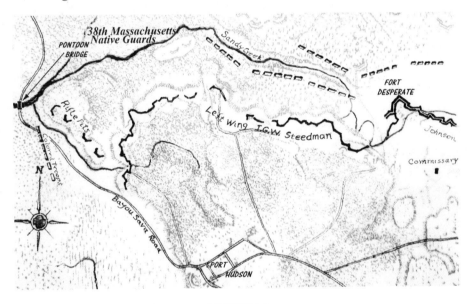

FIGURE 9

Darkness terminated the action, with Steedman withdrawing within his "fortifications," which were, in fact, only begun to be constructed that night, as was alluded to earlier. "The enemy demonstrations on this day convinced me beyond a doubt that he determined to attack our lines in the vicinity of our commissary depot, arsenal, etc. I reported my convictions to the Major-General . . . and he

---

1361. Figure 9, McMorries, E. Y., portion of map, p. 48; Powers, G. W., pp. 90, 91; Stanyan, J. M., p. 222; Bosson, p. 364, 365; O.R. Vol. 26/I, pp. 128, 167. It is instructive to note that the 18th New York was at this time assigned to Sherman, yet they were deep in Paine's area; Defenders SHS, Vol. 14, p. 318.

ordered all the available tools, negroes, etc., to be placed at the disposal of the chief engineer. The work was promptly laid out . . . and ere the dawn of Tuesday, considerable progress had been made."

May 26th

To support any kind of assault by the Native Guards, the Telegraph Road Bridge, earlier destroyed by the Confederates, would have to be replaced. See "Pontoon Bridge" in figure 9. It had crossed the wide swath of the flooded lowland of the Sandy. Company K of the 42nd Massachusetts, serving their non-combat role as required by the terms of their parole, arrived with their pontoon train, and along with 19th Army Corps Pioneers, and elements of the 1st Louisiana Engineers,[1362] began their work. Covered by Mack's battery firing over their heads from the bluff behind, the 280-foot-long span was completed in time for the assault. Phelps' section of the 6th Massachusetts Battery was assigned to remain for the assault, and they were joined by Company G of the 8th New Hampshire, the only mounted company in that regiment, and Company A of the 1st Louisiana Cavalry, under Williamson.[1363]

Orton S. Clark of the 116th New York records: "A council of war was held during the day by General Banks, in which all of the general officers participated, and at which it was determined to at once assault the works.[1364] But, two of the Generals dissented from this determination – Gen'l Auger and Gen'l Weitzel – whose better judgment was, in the fatal result of that assault, recorded, as it were, in blood."

We must pause here to absorb Clark's remarks. The assault was a fatal mistake, hurriedly planned and poorly executed. It was eerily similar to Grant's May 22nd assault on Vicksburg, which we shall see that he admits was a mistake.

Though Clark has the meeting as "during the day," Irwin[1365] says, "When night fell . . . the division commanders met at headquarters at Riley's on the Bayou Sara Road to consider the question of an assault. No minutes of this council were kept and to this day its conclusions are a matter of dispute." The latter is certainly true, as little regarding the meeting has been found in any of the many histories of the regiments there at the time. That little is hearsay. It is reasonable to assume that preliminary orders to prepare for an assault on the 27th had already been issued, and an attack on the 27th was a foregone conclusion. Most of the orders may have

---

1362. Organized by members of the Massachusetts 42nd Regiment, Schouler, W., p. 454. The Pioneers had been originally organized by Major Houston, the chief engineer of Banks' staff, from Co. K of the 53rd Massachusetts Regiment. Willis, pp. 187, 188, 190.
1363. Stanyan, J. M., p. 221; Compiled Records, M594, roll 67; Irwin, R. B., pp. 452, 453, 455; Bosson, C. P., p. 364.
1364. Clark, O. S., p. 84. Grant, U. S., Vol. 1, pp. 530, 531.
1365. Irwin, R. B., pp. 166, 167.

been oral, explaining the disarray that was to characterize the events of the morrow. Irwin, writing[1366] before the publication of his *History of the 19th Army Corps*, notes a feeling of urgency:

> Nothing was known, of course, of the phenomenal success of Grant's operations, nor could it have been surmised, while his precarious position [he crossed the Mississippi and left his supply base behind] in the event of a defeat or even a serious check was obvious enough; the magnitude of the Confederate forces in Mississippi, the energy habitual to their commanders everywhere, added an additional reason against delay. Finally, the troops themselves, elated by their success in the Teche campaign, were in the best of spirits for an immediate attack.

The energy habitual to their commanders, is a salute to Richard Taylor, with real concern about his potential to reorganize after the Teche Campaign. Regarding the troops' spirits, almost every unit history describes how worn out the troops were after marching through the hundreds of hot and alternately dusty or muddy miles of the Teche Campaign. Many of the troops were sick. Johns, in his *History of the 49th Massachusetts Regiment*, notes: "If we have forty regiments before Port Hudson, we are less than twenty thousand strong for each regiment will not average five hundred fighting men. We have cause to doubt the result of this day's work."[1367] The actual numbers were fewer.

Irwin ignores a most serious consideration regarding urgency, the expiration of the militia enlistments. Of the 54 regiments now present, excluding those in the defenses of New Orleans, and at Key West and Pensacola, 21 were nine-months militia conscripts.

Though Banks knew of Grant's successes (which drove Pemberton back into Vicksburg) he was apparently unaware of Grant's rebuff in his first assault there, on the 19th (942 killed, wounded, and missing) or of his bloody failure on the 22nd (3,199 killed, wounded, and missing).[1368] Grant had given a similar argument for being in a hurry. If Banks had Taylor, Grant had Johnston to think about.

If Augur and Weitzel had, in fact, dissented, as Clark alleged, it may have been within the context of a discussion that the character of the ground over which the attack was to be made was relatively unknown, what with Weitzel having been in position for less than a day. Another factor was that roads for direct communication between adjacent commands were "not open,"[1369] a fatal flaw.

There is a chance that T. W. Sherman dissented, as well, given his opinion of

---

1366. Irwin, R. B., *Battles and Leaders*, Vol. III, p. 593; O.R. Vol. 26/I, pp. 529–531.
1367. Johns, H. T., p. 246. We remember that a full strength regiment was nominally 1,000 men – a number seldom achieved.
1368. Grant, U. S., Vol. I, p. 529–531; Fox, p. 545.
1369. Irwin, R. B., p. 167; Hanaburgh, D. H., p. 39.

Banks. Graduated from West Point, class of 1836, he was a veteran of the Seminole War and the Mexican War. He was the commander of the ground forces in the famously successful Port Royal Expedition (see chapter 4, "Confederate Concerns") and was subsequently a division commander in the Army of the Tennessee at Corinth, until reassigned to the Department of the Gulf in September of 1862.[1370] As an experienced professional, he looked down upon the volunteers and Banks. He is quoted as never having forgotten his glorious achievement at Port Royal and as having referred to Banks as "that d–d militia colonel . . ." He was too big a man to be kept "in penal service here under Banks much longer."

Regardless of his sour attitude, there seems to be no hint of mutiny. It was merely a fact, in his professional view, that a frontal assault against Confederate cannon and sharpshooters, entrenched on a parapet with a ditch, fronted by an abatis, was essentially suicide.[1371] His front was the most open, and the advance across it was more than a thousand yards (figure 6). In this situation, the attacker is always at the disadvantage. Sherman may have studied Napoleon at Waterloo.[1372] He began preparations for the worst. A forlorn hope and fascine bearers were called for, as is noted in the history of the 15th New Hampshire regiment.

The situation was similar on Augur's front, though the ground was more broken, he reacted as had Sherman. Henry T. Johns[1373] quotes from a letter he wrote at 9:00 a.m. on the 27th: "Yesterday morning we were aroused to the solemnity of a soldier's life. Volunteers to constitute a 'forlorn hope' were called for. One field officer, four captains, eight lieutenants, and two hundred men were desired from each brigade. We were expected to furnish five from each company. As nearly as we could learn, a part were expected to run from the woods and bridge the ditch in front of the enemy's parapet or breastworks with fascines and then return; the other part to cross the bridge thus made and assault the enemy at the point of a bayonet." Similar preparations were being made in the other of Augur's regiments: the 48th Massachusetts, the 21st Maine, the 116th New York, and the 30th Massachusetts.

The brigades of the right wing, commanded by Weitzel, with the exception of Kimball and Birge, who were under Grover, are shown in figure 10.[1374] The organization was temporary, and the positions are approximate. Dwight commanded the extreme right, i.e., Nelson, Van Zandt, and Thomas. Paine commanded what

---

1370. Cullum no. 859; Bacon, E., p. 101.
1371. Harding, G. C., p. 334.
1372. *Encyclopedia Britannica*, Vol. 28, pp. 378, 379.
1373. Johns, H. T., p. 243; Plummer, p. 36; Woodward, J. T., pp. 31, 32; Clark, p. 84; Howe, H. W., p. 48; McGregor, C., p. 376.
1374. Grover was at the right center. Weitzel, in command of the assault on the "right wing," included Grover's command, though it seems Grover took over command in the afternoon, after Weitzel's assault had failed. Stevens, W. B., p. 146; figure 10, a portion of figure 3.

were formerly Emory's troops: Fearing and Gooding. The regiments of Grover, Paine and Dwight near the Confederate Fort Desperate were intermixed on the morning of the 27th as final movements were made in preparation for the assault, rendering any brigade listing nearly meaningless. The cavalry, and particularly the artillery, were assigned where needed regardless of their division affiliation.[1375]

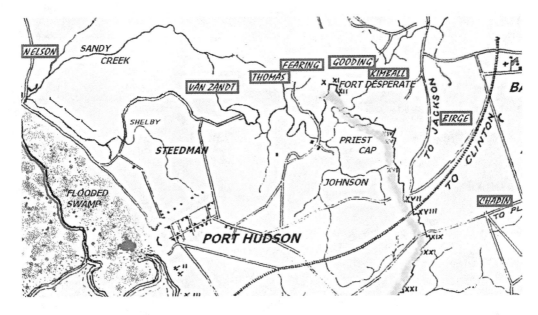

FIGURE 10

The connection of Grover's troops with Augur, who was south of the Clinton Railroad, is indicated by the position of Chapin, a part of Augur's command.

ORGANIZATION FOR THE ASSAULT

DWIGHT'S DIVISION

NELSON - 1st and 3rd Louisiana Native Guards; 6th Massachusetts Battery, Phelps' section; 1st Louisiana Cavalry, Company A; 8th New Hampshire, Company G, mounted.

VAN ZANDT - 1st Louisiana (Holcomb); 131st New York; 91st New York.

THOMAS - (Weitzel's old Reserve Brigade)[1376] 75th New York; 12th Connecticut; 160th New York; 8th Vermont; 6th Massachusetts Battery.

1375. Organization chart of the Department of the Gulf as of April 30th, 1863, O.R. Vol. 15, pp. 712, 713. The 1st Indiana Heavy Artillery, the Native Guards, and some cavalry, were unattached.
1376. The 114th New York had not yet arrived.

PAINE'S DIVISION

FEARING- 8th New Hampshire; (298)[1377] 133rd New York; 173rd New York; 4th Wisconsin, mounted; 162nd New York, nine companies.

GOODING - 31st Massachusetts (300); 38th Massachusetts; 53rd Massachusetts (377).

GROVER'S DIVISION

KIMBALL - 12th Maine, eight companies; 24th Connecticut.

BIRGE - 13th Connecticut; 25th Connecticut; 159th New York.

The remainder of the dispositions for the Union "left center" and left are indicated in figure 11. Note that there was no occupation of the ground south of the Gibbons house, all the way to the river. Security here was left to Grierson.

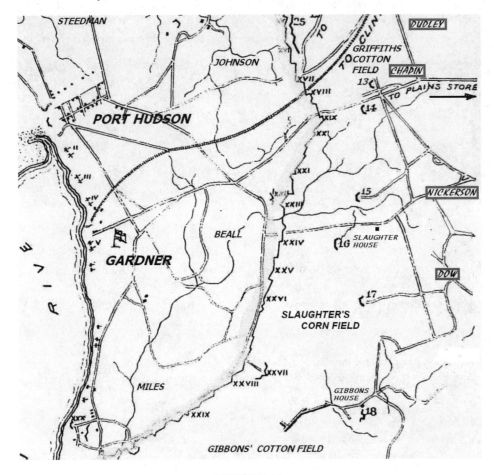

FIGURE 11

1377. The numbers in parentheses are the number of men fit for duty, as stated in the unit's history. Stanyan, J. M., pp. 245, 209; Willis, H. A., p. 158; Johns, H. T., p. 267; 162nd New York, p. 15; Irwin, R. B., p. 203. Figure 11, portion of figure 3.

AUGUR'S DIVISION

CHAPIN - 48th Massachusetts; 49th Massachusetts (233); 21st Maine; 116th New York; 2nd Louisiana; 2nd Vermont Battery.

DUDLEY - 30th Massachusetts; 50th Massachusetts, four companies; 161st New York; 174th New York.

SHERMAN'S DIVISION

DOW- 6th Michigan; 15th New Hampshire (250); 26th Connecticut; 128th New York.

NICKERSON – 14th Maine; 165th New York (350); 177th New York.

RIGHT WING ARTILLERY

WEITZEL - 1st Maine, Morton; 1st US Battery A, Bainbridge.

PAINE - 4th Massachusetts, Briggs; 1st US Battery F, Duryea; 18th New York, Mack.

DWIGHT - 6th Massachusetts, Phelps; 2nd Massachusetts, Nims.

CENTER ARTILLERY

GROVER - 1st US Battery L, Closson; 2nd US Battery C, Rodgers; 6th Massachusetts, Carruth.

AUGUR – 2nd Vermont, Holcomb; 5th US Battery G, Rawles; 1st Indiana, (7 batteries).

SHERMAN – 21st New York, Barnes; 1st Vermont, Hebard; 1st Indiana, (1 battery).

There were 39 regiments actually in place ready for the assault. The few figures available for the numbers of fit men (the numbers in parentheses above) show an average less of than 300 per regiment. Even if 400 fit were assumed for each regiment, the result is a total of 15,600. The department return for May[1378] totals 23,283 for its four divisions, which includes the troops in the defenses of New Orleans, Key West, and Pensacola. Another consideration was the absence of the regiments still returning from duty with Chickering's train to Brashear City, such as the 114th New York and the 28th Connecticut. The 156th New York was present on the 27th but was acting as Banks' headquarters guard.[1379] Grierson's cavalry, and units assigned to him, acting as security, did not participate in the assault.

Though numbers like the 23,000 above are often seen in descriptions of the siege, Banks quotes 13,000.[1380] This number, vs. 6,000 Confederates, nevertheless, met the test of the then current theory that a weight of two to one for an assault on a fortified position was required. However, the details were far more complicated by reasons that were soon revealed.

1378. O.R. Vol. 26/I, p. 528.
1379. National Archives Compiled Service Record for May and June 1863, the 28th Connecticut says, "Joined forces investing Port Hudson same day [26th]. Was engaged in action of June 14th . . ."
1380. O.R. 26/ I, p. 44. Fascines are bundles of sticks variously five to eight feet long., and about a foot in diameter. Johns, pp. 245, 250.

Easy as 1-2-3

Special Orders No. 123[1381] were issued on the night of May 26th. Significant portions are reproduced here:

> III. Generals Augur and Sherman will open fire with their artillery upon the enemy's works at daybreak. They will dispose their troops so as to annoy the enemy as much as possible during the cannonade, by advancing skirmishers to kill the enemy's cannoneers and to cover the advance of the assaulting column. They will place their troops in position to take instant advantage of any favorable opportunity, and will, if possible, force the enemy's works at the earliest possible moment.
>
> V. General Weitzel will, according to verbal directions already given him, *take advantage of the attacks* on the other parts of the line to endeavor to force his way into the enemy's works on our right.
>
> VI. General Grover will hold himself in readiness to re-enforce within the right or left, if necessary, or to force his own way into the enemy's works. He will also protect the right flank of the heavy artillery, should it become necessary.
>
> VII. General's Augur, Sherman, Grover, and Weitzel will constantly keep up their connection with the commands next to them, so as to afford mutual aid and avoid mistakes.
>
> VIII. The fire of the heavy artillery will be opened by General Arnold at as early an hour as practicable, say 6 a.m.
>
> IX. Commanders of the divisions will provide the necessary means for passing the ditch on their respective points of attack.
>
> X. All of the operations herein directed must commence at the earliest hour practicable.
>
> XI. Port Hudson must be taken to-morrow.
>
> By Command of Major-General Banks:
>
> Richard B. Irwin
> *Assistant Adjutant-General.*

Regarding part X, one must make the observation that: "the earliest hour practicable" is not definite, and if given to different commanders not equally situated, the assault will begin at their convenience, given local difficulties. In plain language, it allows for confusion. That said, what actually happened was inexcusable; there was an absence of any "connection" as ordered in part VII, since no connecting paths had been cleared, and as a result, there was little or no knowledge of affairs in the other parts of the line. *No attacks*, as ordered in part V, were initially made by Augur or Sherman, with the result that Weitzel had none to "take advantage of."

Previously having informed Admiral Farragut of the planned assault, Banks sent a final message at midnight on the 26th: "I have ordered the light artillery to

---

1381. O.R. Vol. 26/I, pp. 508, 509; author's italics.

open fire on the enemy's works at daybreak tomorrow morning, and the heavy batteries concentrated on the left center to open at 6 a.m. . . . Your fire should cease as soon as you observe our artillery cease its fire, which will probably be about 10 o'clock, though the time is dependent upon circumstances."[1382]

From the *History of the 8th Vermont Regiment*:[1383] "In accordance with orders, the fleet in the river opened with their guns on the morning of the 27th of May, and rained shot and shell upon the garrison; the land batteries began firing with great spirit and determination; and the ground fairly shook . . ."

Weitzel Advances

Weitzel's troops, awakened at 3:00 a.m., were formed at 5:00 a.m., and finally, at 6:00 a.m., *assuming* that Augur and Sherman had done so, Weitzel ordered Dwight to advance on the Confederate left center, i.e., that portion of I. G. W. Steedman's defensive line commanded by Col. M. B. Locke, which extended west from Fort Desperate for approximately one thousand yards. Paine was to follow. Before reaching the objective, the troops would have to carry an advanced line, about a half mile in front of the fortifications, which occupied a hill beyond the ridge on the north side of Sandy Creek. Locke's line was held by elements of the 15th Arkansas, the 10th Arkansas, the 1st Alabama, and the 1st Mississippi regiments, about 500 troops in total.[1384] Figure 12 shows the area of the attack, which is a portion of the map "Defense of Port Hudson," which appears in McMorries' *History of the First Regiment of Alabama Volunteer Infantry*. However, the copy shown here, which was obtained courtesy of the Port Hudson State Historic Site, bears the personal markings of Colonel Steedman, showing the location of the assault on this part of his front. It is the heavy double-curved pen line at the center. North is to the right, as on the original. Weitzel's dispositions are the dashed lines.

1382. O.R Vol. 26/I, pp. 506, 507.
1383. Carpenter, G. N., p. 114.
1384. The narrative is derived from: Irwin, R. B., pp. 169–184; Hanaburgh, D. H., p. 40, 41; Tiemann, W. F., p. 40–42; 114, 115; Willis, H. A., p. 122; Hall, H & J., *75th History*, pp. 112–117; Babcock, W. M. Jr., p. 30; Defenders, SHS, Vol. 14, Official Report of I. G. W. Steedman, pp. 319–324; Sprague, H. B., p. 139, 140; Powers, G. W., pp. 92–94; Bissell G., (Ellis), pp. 46–48; Stanyan, J. M., pp. 224–226, 229, 230, 248–250, 261; O.R. Vol. 26/I, pp. 157, 163, 166, 509, 510, 551, 626; www.dnma.ny.gov *160th New York Regiment, Clippings*, p. 9; McMorries, E. Y., pp. 62–64; Smith, D. P., p. 63; Haskin, W. L., p. 192; Bacon, E., pp. 160, 161; Johns, H. T., pp. 281, 282.

FIGURE 12

Van Zandt's 91st New York led Dwight's brigade, in column of regiments, with Weitzel's, under Thomas, of the 8th Vermont, following. Paine's division followed in support, Fearing's 8th New Hampshire in front, and Gooding in reserve. Pushing through the dense forest, the men of the 91st New York, with the 131st New York on their left, and the 1st Louisiana on their right, soon ran up against the outer rifle pits that Locke had prepared. They were taking casualties from the raking fire, and they were ordered to lie down.

Thomas had deployed the 12th Connecticut, the 75th New York, the 8th Vermont, and the 160th New York behind Van Zandt, who was now stalled before Locke's riflemen. Thomas was ordered by Weitzel to drive through Van Zandt's line. "His men responded nobly, led by the gallant colonel on foot, for orders had been given for field and staff officers to leave their horses in the rear." Charging "into the fearful storm of missiles," their overwhelming weight of numbers caused Locke to turn to his prearranged line of retreat, slowly and deliberately down the ravine, and into the Confederate works.

As mentioned previously, having had little time to reconnoiter the area, the nature of the ground ahead was unknown. Paine noted: "We had not definite knowledge of the ground over which we were to fight, for the enemy occupied it. The forest was so dense that glasses were useless." Thomas came out on the edge of a hill which overlooked a deep ravine, with Sandy Creek at its bottom, with the Confederate fortifications on the opposite side. The whole area, once covered with pine and magnolia, had been haphazardly "slashed" (figure 5). Locke's sharpshooters still lingered, hidden behind some of the few trees still standing, and sheltered behind a succession of gullies and the fallen timber. Thomas' open position on the hill was swept by fire from the fort, and a decision had to be made whether to retreat back under the cover of the forest, or plunge into the purgatory before them. A single rough road on the left, the wagon road in figure 12, which led into the fort, was covered by a battery of four guns on Commissary Hill, and two guns of Battery B of the 1st Mississippi, in Johnson's 15th Arkansas line at Fort Desperate.

Plunging ahead into the slashing, Thomas' line of battle disintegrated, both from the rebel fire and the confused maze that confronted them. The men were now advancing nearly one by one, and only maintaining cohesion by what little that could be seen of each other in the smoke, or from behind logs or gullies. Their organization had broken down into groups or squads. Their training, which had consisted of a few weeks of close order drill around the fields of Baton Rouge, had not contemplated this. Colonel Thomas and a group broke off to the right, and another group followed the 75th's Colonel Babcock, who was on the wagon road to the left. In a desperate charge, they made it to the protection of a gully about 50–80 yards from the parapet. In Babcock's words: "I reached the most advanced position which we have yet occupied, and saw the rebs running up the hill beyond into their inner line of rifle pits and found myself here with only five or six men, one of whom was Johnny Mathews and another, a boy of the 91st Regt., who was already hit twice."

That Babcock had managed to do so, we must hark back to Irish Bend. The majority of the Confederate defenders there were equipped with old flintlock muskets, with an effective range of forty yards. This was also the case here at Port Hudson. Thus, in the initial part of the assault, the danger had come only from sharpshooters and the enemy's artillery. To use the word "only" is to cringe. The artillery had already proven potently effective, killing and wounding hundreds.

Van Zandt, with elements of the 91st New York, the 131st New York, and the 1st Louisiana, had since flanked off to the right toward the field called the Bull Pen, the Confederate slaughter pen, where there may have been an opportunity to advance, since it looked to be lightly defended, and it was further from the guns on Commissary Hill. From his position on Commissary Hill,[1385] Steedman saw the move, and requested reinforcements from Gardner. The 23rd Arkansas, under Col. O. P. Lyle, arrived in time to check any Federal advance.

The position of Battery L, which had not changed since it first arrived at Port Hudson, but not definitely shown on any map, can only be inferred from the fact

---

1385. McMorries, E. Y., pp. 63, 64; Smith, D. P., p. 71.

that it could pour fire into Steedman's line and cover at least a part of Thomas' advance. They had opened fire since early in the morning, and the battery "was warmly engaged until the coming into action of batteries A and F."

Bainbridge's Battery A, Duryea's Battery F, and Morton's 1st Maine Battery had been on the move since 5:30, following Weitzel's advance in the woods. So little advance preparation had been made that it was necessary for pioneers to chop trees to open their way. They arrived in the rear area into which Paine had driven, with Paine personally directing the placement of Duryea's battery near the wagon road. The 38th Massachusetts, previously ordered to return from its duty with the 42nd Massachusetts and the Native Guards, had "been hunting in the woods for the brigade," when General Paine rode up, and sent it forward to support Duryea. The other two batteries, supported by the 53rd Massachusetts, were deployed several hundred yards farther to the left. "The four batteries now in position soon silenced the guns in this part of the field." They were not in place in time to cover Babcock's advance, and it is noted that the "heavy batteries," those of the 1st Indiana, were not in place until 10:00 and never were a factor in the action of the day.

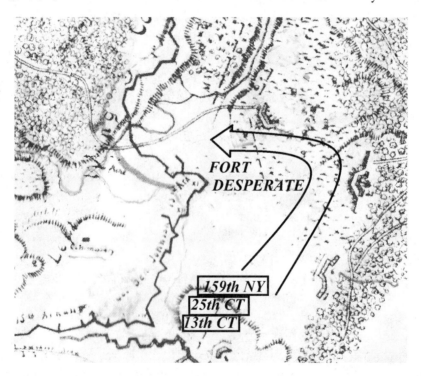

FIGURE 13

With the helpful fire of the newly arrived batteries, and the distraction created by Paine's advance, more and more troops were able to pick their way forward and join their comrades on the slopes. Yet they were stalled, and now their own artillery had to cease firing, "lest its fire should prove fatal to friend as to foe." Thomas fell back to a better cover in the ravine, and reported his position to Weitzel. He was told to hold in place if possible. As to Babcock, he never moved, and it is reported that "the 75th asked leave to charge the works above it on the slope, and penetrate the citadel" – but no order came. Weitzel reported his situation to Grover, and sought the desired permission.

Grover now moved to Weitzel's support. Two of Birge's three regiments, the 159th New York and the 25th Connecticut, were marched out from the slightly advanced positions they had secured on the southeast side of Fort Desperate (figure 13).[1386]

Under the command of Maj. Charles A. Burt of the 159th New York, they attempted to maintain the double-quick, but their path (the large arrow) was made difficult by brush and fallen timber.[1387] In spite of every exertion, they took over an hour to struggle the half mile to the base of the hill on the north side of Fort Desperate, which was the point of the planned assault. They were met by Grover and ordered to charge on the earthworks. Grover gave out the same deranged opinion that he had given the 25th Connecticut at Irish Bend – that there were "hardly any rebels there. Major Burt . . . was told that his regiment alone was able to carry the works and to send back our regiment if it wasn't needed."

A too familiar scenario then played itself out; with the fallen and hidden of Weitzel's command in their path, they advanced out into a "valley . . . filled with felled trees, and heavy underbrush, while thick and black rolled the battle-smoke." Fortunately, the 24-pounder in Fort Desperate was kept quiet by "a handful of brave men firing a stream of bullets at that piece. For six long hours the gunners did not dare approach to load . . . and that wicked looking piece was kept silent."

Finally, Burt's troops reached close to the base of the Confederate works.[1388] "The nature of the ground was such it was impossible to form in battle line . . ." so the attack was made in three columns. They waited "for a few moments with beating hearts . . . for the forward charge. The word came, and with a terrifying yell, we rose to our feet and rushed forward. It was a terrible time, when bounding over the last tree and crashing through some brush, we came out within a short distance of the enemy's entrenchments, and it seemed as though a thousand rifles were cracking our doom. This fire was too deadly for men to stand against. Our brave fellows, shot down as fast as they came up, were beaten back." The Confederate line had been given adequate time to observe the Union advance, and had massed four deep. The front man would fire, turn to the rear to reload, allow the next man to fire, and so on.

A "short time" later, a second charge was made, with the same deadly results. Between the two regiments, there were 80 men killed and wounded. There, within thirty yards of the parapet, the charge was stalled, and they were forced to seek

---

1386. McMorries, E. Y., p. 48, portion, altered.
1387. Irwin, R. B., p. 171; Tiemann, p. 40; Bissell G., (Ellis), p. 46.
1388. Irwin, R. B., p. 172; Bissell, G., (Ellis), p. 47.

shelter. Grover then tried a diversion to allow the attack to regain the initiative, ordering his 12th Maine (the unit in which Lt. Appleton's brother was serving), supported by the 13th Connecticut, to attack the west face of Fort Desperate. It did not succeed.

Irwin relates: "After the first attack [Weitzel's] on the right had wellnigh spent itself, and when its renewal, in *conjunction with an advance on the centre and the left, was momentarily expected*, Dwight thought to create a diversion and at the same time to develop the strength and position of the Confederates toward their extreme left,[1389] where their lines bent back to rest on the river, and to this end he ordered Nelson to put in his two colored regiments." Irwin, of course, here refers to the expected attacks by Augur (the center) and Sherman (the left), which had not yet begun and would not until 2:00 p.m., long after the last attack on the right had failed.

Absent Augur and Sherman, Dwight's plan seemed like a good alternative. The order was given. Colonel Nelson and the Native Guards, accompanied by their artillery and cavalry, were observed to be advancing across Sandy Creek on the pontoon bridge just after 7:00. The 1st Regiment led, with the 3rd following, their total number being 1,080.

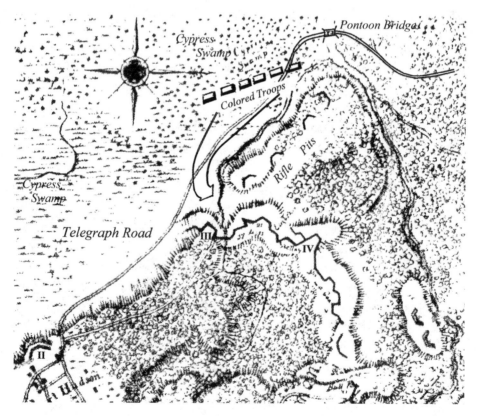

FIGURE 14

1389. Irwin, R. B., p. 175; author's italics.

They were opposed by Shelby's 39th Mississippi Regiment and elements of Wingfield's Battalion, who were arrayed along a detached ridge, which ran for four hundred yards along Telegraph Road and up to within two hundred yards of the bridge (figure 14). Along its sharp crest ran a line of rifle pits. In Shelby's words: "This ridge was a strong position and easily held . . . it was abrupt and inaccessible." Still farther back, along the natural prominence which was Steedman's line, were emplaced Shelby's light gun batteries III, and IV. To the south, a detachment of Company K of the 1st Alabama manned a 24 pounder in battery II.[1390] Backwater from the still-flooded Mississippi filled this end of Sandy Creek, which left a narrow stretch along the road as the only avenue for Nelson's troops to advance. The 6th Massachusetts had just crossed the pontoon bridge and begun to unlimber when they were hit by "rapid and effective fire" from a gun in the Confederate line. Shelby's report: "The enemy's artillery, after firing one gun retreated across the creek." The Native Guards crossed under the same fire and filed to their right "and under cover of the willows formed in line of battle and advanced." They continued to advance at the double-quick, shown by the arrow in figure 14, ". . . until they reached to within about two hundred yards of the extreme left, when ". . . two pieces of light artillery on Col. Shelby's line opened ". . . on them with canister, and at the same time, the infantry (in their anxiety to fire – fired without orders) opened on them, driving them back in confusion and disorder, with terrible slaughter. Several efforts were made to rally them, but all were unsuccessful, and no effort was afterward made to charge the works during the entire day."

The Native Guards, like the 6th Massachusetts Battery, were able to fire but once before falling back. They were raked from the rifle pits as they advanced, and when they had just made it to where they should turn to an assault, they were hit by the three separate batteries of artillery.

After the bloody repulse, one of Nelson's aides was sent to Dwight's headquarters for permission to retire, they being "all cut up." Dwight would hear none of this and ordered, "Charge again, and let the impetuosity of the charge counterbalance the paucity of numbers." The aide left. Dwight had been skeptical about the use of black troops, and allegedly having been drinking since before breakfast, he was showing no sympathy for their fate. Dwight's rant was ignored, in the sense that no further charges were attempted after the regiments had retreated to cover, where they remained under heavy fire for the rest of the day.[1391]

The Federal attack on the Confederate left was now entirely stalled. We turn to Irwin, Banks' adjutant general, for comment:

1390. Defenders SHS, Vol. 14, pp. 321, 322; Stanyan, J. M., pp. 249, 250; Bosson, C. P., p. 364; Smith, D. P., p. 63; figure 13, McMorries, E. Y., p. 48, portion, altered; McMorries, E. Y., p. 61, 62.

1391. Irwin, R. B., pp. 173–175; Stanyan, J. M., p. 229. Grover was senior to Weitzel and, in fact, replaced him as the commander of the right wing that afternoon.

The morning was drawing out when these movements were well spent, and the advanced positions were simply held without further effort to go forward. The hour may have been about 10 o'clock . . . Grover had been ordered to support either the right or the left, or attempt to make his way into the works, as circumstances might suggest. This last he had tried, and failed . . . On his left there was no attack to support.

Riding to meet Weitzel, Grover gave him the "counsel of prudence" and either ordered or convinced him to ask for "fresh orders" before continuing the attack.

Steedman confirms when the attack on the Confederate left had petered out:[1392] "The battle on the left wing . . . was an assault or series of assaults for the first two hours: at the end of that time the enemy had been repulsed signally at every point, and he had withdrawn a short distance and concealed his men under the cover of the trees, logs, ravines, etc., and from this hour, about 11 o'clock, until five o'clock, the firing relaxed and could only be called sharpshooting."

No attack to support? Nothing had been heard from either Augur or Sherman, and it was Banks who now addressed a note to Weitzel. Dated 1:45 p.m. It read:

> General Weitzel:[1393]
>
> General Sherman has failed utterly and criminally to bring his men into the field. At 12 m. I found him at dinner, his staff officers all with their horses unsaddled, and none knowing where to find their command. I have placed General Andrews in command, and hope every moment that he is ready to advance with Augur, who waits for him. Together, they have 5,000 men. I should have sent Augur to you, but thought that Andrews could join sooner he could reach you. We hear that you are supporting your position successfully, and hope it is so. I shall forward another messenger the moment I hear from Andrews.
>
> N.P. BANKS
> *Major-General, Commanding.*

Sherman Advances

Andrews, Banks' chief of staff, rode immediately for Sherman's campsite, in the woods southeast of the entrance road to the Slaughter plantation (figure 15). When he arrived, he found that the whole division had been deployed, with Sherman on horseback, ready to lead the advance.[1394] Andrews handed Sherman a message. Sherman was seen to throw his hat to the ground, "and after some words and excited gestures, he turned to the troops and cried 'Forward! Double Quick! Double

---

1392. Defenders, SHS, Vol. 14, p. 323.
1393. O.R. Vol. 26/I, pp. 509, 510; Irwin, R. B., p. 177.
1394. Hanaburgh, D. H., p. 41.

Quick.'" It was 2:10 p.m.[1395] Andrews deferred from taking over the command but remained to observe the action.

Sherman was able to react so quickly because, regardless of his seemingly careless attitude about the timing of the assault, he had roused his troops, as had Augur, early in the morning, and they had been active in preparations ever since. In the case of the 15th New Hampshire, advanced picket positions on the front had been established since the evening of the 26th, and Companies A and K, along with Companies A and C of the 128th New York, had been skirmishing near the Slaughter house since daybreak. Companies D and E of the 15th were further south, part of a line that extended across the front.[1396] Companies B, G, I, and H were ordered to join the 26th Connecticut in support of one of the batteries, which since early morning had been firing "twenty shots per minute; their shells sound like a distant train of cars." At 9:00, the regiment was drawn up in line of battle, and at 10:30, it was advanced to "half way through the intervening woods" to the site of the Slaughter house. At 12:15, Dow's attack column was formed up. It consisted of the 6th Michigan, the 15th New Hampshire, the 26th Connecticut, and the 128th New York. Nickerson had done the same, his pickets advancing at 9:00, with the 14th Maine acting as skirmishers. His attack column consisted of the 165th New York, the 14th Maine, 24th Maine, and the 177th New York.[1397] Sherman and his entire staff, all "splendidly mounted," were positioned in between the two brigades.

An account from the History of the 15th New Hampshire Regiment:

> The Vermont battery [1st, Hebard, the Gray Horse Battery] moves forward down the front of the Fifteenth . . . Some teams now drive up loaded with heavy poles; negroes shoulder them, two to each, and are placed in front of the skirmish line. Those who volunteered from our regiment are each provided with a 2-inch plank a foot wide and about four feet long, the design being to force the negroes up to the face of the enemy's parapet, and compel them to lay the poles across the ditch in front, the plank carriers then to lay on their planks, and so bridge over. There is a brief wait here. The enemy in our front are ominously silent. But suddenly the bugle call is sounded . . . General Dow wheeled his horse and gave his order in the same old manner as on the parade at Carrolton: "Attention brigade! forward . . . March!" The column moves, and instantly emerges from the wood, when the enemy's artillery reopens with tremendous power; the "gray horse" battery, lashed to its utmost fury, dashes upon the field . . . and pours its thunder in with a deafening roar. As soon as free from the woods double quick is ordered, and in a moment we are in rifle

---

1395. O.R. Vol. 26/I, p. 125; Bacon, E., p. 138.
1396. McGregor, C., pp. 319, 320, 331.
1397. Irwin, R. B., p. 177; McGregor, C., pp. 334–339. The record of the assault, McGregor given in pp. 334–380, is recommended to those interested in the most scrupulously detailed description of any yet found.

range, and the enemy's parapet for more than a mile to the right and left bursts forth in one unbroken sheet of flame.

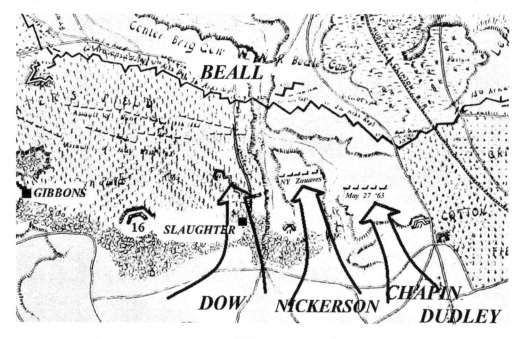

FIGURE 15

Now on the grounds of the Slaughter house, they broke into two wings, one passing to the right and one to the left. They were slowed and their organization disrupted by fences around flower gardens,[1398] and the right fell into a ravine beyond, the left remaining on the cornfield, directly exposed to the "murderous musketry fire that mows all in winrows, and thickly covers with the dead and dying." The advance was stopped, then rallied, with Sherman[1399] directing Lieutenant Colonel Blair of the 15th New Hampshire to "lead them ahead – straight ahead – dead upon the enemy's works." Shortly after, Blair, now at the head of the column, looked back "and hardly anybody but the dead and wounded were in sight. General Sherman was dismounted when I had left him, but pushing forward bareheaded encouraging the men around him . . . I ran back . . . near the edge of the ravine and found him . . . with his left leg shattered."

In figure 15,[1400] the ravine can be seen running to the right of and parallel to the road past the Slaughter plantation. It afforded some cover, and those in the groups that advanced through it were able to reach the most advanced position "but from which all efforts to scale the enemy's works proved futile."

1398. O.R. Vol. 26/I, pp. 123–125.
1399. McGregor, C., pp. 347–350.
1400. Figure 15, a portion of the *Defense* (McMorries) map, labels and arrows added, and altered to

Dow was felled next, Clark of the 6th Michigan was wounded,[1401] and Cowles of the 128th New York, to whom the brigade command fell after Dow was wounded, was killed. The brigade command devolved to Nickerson, who was not notified. Kingsley of the 26th Connecticut was then wounded while trying to rally the men. Leaderless, for a period of time in which no direction was given, Dow's columns ground to a halt.

Nickerson had stepped off on the right of, and at the same time as Dow, with the 165th New York leading the column.[1402] Remarkably, the faint original inscription NY Zouaves can be seen in figure 15, at the head of the superimposed arrow indicating Nickerson's advance. The description of what happened next is left to an extract from the Southern Historical Society Papers:[1403] "While the battle was raging on this [Beall's] part of the line, a New York regiment of Zouaves came dashing out of the swamp on the extreme right of the field, making, with their red breeches and caps (figure 16), a magnificent spectacle. To meet this new danger our troops were thrown rapidly to the right and opened a hot fire on the advancing Zouaves, who, nevertheless, came dashing on, deploying from column into line with the precision of veterans, as they neared our works, we mowing them down by the scores, when they were ordered by their colonel to lie down, who, himself walked back and forward with as much apparent coolness, as if he were giving orders on parade."

FIGURE 16

In a moment more, the ranking officers of the 165th, Col. Abel Smith, and Maj. Gouverneur Carr, had fallen, and many of the men then broke and fled for cover, leaving a great many killed and wounded behind them. Though a few remained behind stumps and logs as sharpshooters, the assault of the Zouaves had been stopped.

As soon as Banks heard the rattle of musketry on the left, and saw from the smoke of the Confederate guns that Sherman was engaged, he ordered Augur forward.[1404]

---

conform to a definition of where the edge of the forest extended, (five hundred yards from the works, near the Plains Store road) per p. 32 of Woodward, J. T., 21st Maine.
1401. Bacon, E., pp. 126, 139. Clark was allegedly stunned by the concussion of a cannon ball, which passed near him. He was unmarked when carried off the field. Bacon accuses him of cowardice; Irwin, R. B., pp. 178, 179.
1402. On Chapin's side, observe the note, which reads, May 27th, 1863.
1403. *Defenders*, SHS, Vol. 14, p. 324. Figure 16 from *History of the Second Battalion Duryee Zouaves*, May 27th, 1905, frontispiece; dmna.ny.gov/historic/reghist/civil/infantry/165thinf/165thinfCWN.htm, p. 4.
1404. Irwin, R. B., p. 179.

Augur Advances

Augur, had also been prepared. As we have seen, on the 26th he had asked for volunteers for a 200 man storming party, a "forlorn hope." and had begun making fascines, which would be used to fill the ditch along the base of the Confederate parapet. Col. James O'Brien of the 48th Massachusetts had volunteered to lead it.

Companies B and G of the 116th New York had been thrown out as skirmishers on either side of the Port Hudson – Plains Store road to a place "only less dangerous than the open field," where they formed a part of the support for Holcomb's 2nd Vermont Battery.[1405] Colonel Chapin, the brigade commander, had been up since daylight, directing its firing. Colonel Dudley, the commander of the 2nd Brigade, was concerned about this being the first time that the 50th Massachusetts[1406] would be under fire and had "routed" them out at 3:00 a.m. for "advice and instruction" before breakfast. The cooks later brought bread up to their position near Hadden's Co. D of the 1st Indiana Battery on the north side of the Plains Store road, where they were sent to protect it.

Before breakfast, Chapin's men had received their orders to assault, and they had been moved to their assault positions in the woods along the Plains Store road (figure 17). Chapin's brigade was to lead, and Dudley's was to support. The 21st Maine was to act as skirmishers to be followed by the forlorn hope, in the advance of the regiments. Lt. Col. James O'Brien's, forlorn hope, with 15 officers and 77 men from the 48th Massachusetts,[1407] 40 from the 49th Massachusetts, 38 from the 21st Maine, 72 from the 116th New York, and 52 from the 30th Massachusetts, was already oversubscribed before 32 more came forward from the 161st New York, Dudley having demanded 30. Assuming Dudley had likewise demanded 30 from the 174th New York, the forlorn hope totaled some 370 men.

At 1:00 p.m., the forlorn hope had formed up in the woods across the Plains Store road, about a mile from the enemy's works, some only with muskets, others with muskets slung and carrying fascines, and some who had stacked their muskets, and carried only fascines.[1408] The fascine bearers were to be in the vanguard. Chapin had addressed the storming party and said, "Remember that you do not go unsupported. My brigade will follow close on your heels."

The regimental lineup had Holcomb's battery on the road, with the 21st Maine to its left, and looking left, the 116th New York, the 49th and 48th Massachusetts,

---

1405. Johns, H. T., p. 249; Plummer, A., p. 36; Clark, O. S., p. 87.
1406. Stevens, W. B., pp. 137, 138, 141.
1407. Plummer, A., pp. 36–38; Bowen, J. P., *Massachusetts in the War*, pp. 648, 652, 653; Woodward, J. J., pp. 31, 32; Clark, O. S., pp. 84, 85; Bowen, J. P., p, 458; dman.ny.gov/ *Clippings, 161st Regiment*, p. 8; Irwin, R. B., pp. 179, 180.
1408. Stevens, W. B., p. 136; Clark, O. S., pp. 88, 89. Clark's quote has been rearranged, a printer error suspected in the original text. The regimental lineup here does not agree with Irwin.

followed by the 2nd Louisiana, and Dudley's brigade. Now they waited.

Shortly after 2:00 p.m., Augur commanded, "Now boys, charge, and reserve your fire until you get into the fort; give them cold steel, and as you charge cheer . . . ! Press on no matter who may fall," (figure 17).[1409] Lieutenant Colonel O'Brien then gave the order: "Come on boys . . ." The storming party emerged from the woods, turned to the right and up the road. "A small belt of timber to our left hid us from our foe."[1410]

FIGURE 17. GRAND ASSAULT OF GENERAL AUGUR'S DIVISION

"The artillery had ceased firing; all was quiet till we passed that small belt and came in full view of the rebels. Then bullets, grape, and canister hurtled through the air, and men began to fall . . . For a few yards the field was smooth, but difficulties soon presented themselves. A deep ditch or ravine was passed, and we came to trees that had been felled in every direction. Over, under, around them we went. It was impossible to keep in line. The spaces between the trees were filled with twigs and branches, in many places knee-high. Foolishness to talk about cheering or the 'double-quick'. We had no strength for the former, aye, and no heart either. We had gone but a few rods ere our Yankee common sense assured us we must fail."

The fascine bearers could not keep up with the rest. "They looked more like loaded mules than men." The forlorn hope and the main forces now became mixed together, the state colors of the 48th Massachusetts "came passing by," wrote Henry

---

1409. *Harper's Weekly*, June 27th, 1863.
1410. Johns, H. T., p. 253-261; Plummer, A., p. 38.

Johns, "and I followed. Soon the standard-bearer was killed; an officer grasped the colors and waved them aloft. In less than a minute his blood had dyed the white silk of the banner."

Johns continues: "We had been there about an hour, and as the fire slackened, Col. O'Brien came springing across the logs, waving his sword, shouting 'Charge! Boys, charge. In half a minute, just ahead of me, he fell dead." He had turned to direct the charge and briefly faced his back to the enemy's fire. He had taken a ball through the back. Examination of his body revealed that the ball had passed through and had flattened against a steel vest he was wearing. Next, it was Chapin, who was at first wounded in the knee, but remained on the field. Then, exactly one year after being wounded while serving in the Army of the Potomac in the Peninsular Campaign, he was killed by a bullet to the brain. Then it was Colonel Bartlett, commander of the 49th Massachusetts, "the only mounted man to be seen"[1411] because while serving in the Army of the Potomac at the Battle of Ball's Bluff, he had lost a leg. Today he was twice wounded, once in the ankle of his remaining leg and in his wrist.

Adj. Joseph T. Woodward of the 21st Maine Regiment[1412] wrote:

> To reach and scale them with the force remaining, exhausted as it was by the effort already made in the terrific heat of the day in the face of a foe admirably protected by fortifications and nearly equal in numbers, was impossible, though some of the stormers reached the ditch, there about six feet deep and ten feet wide, and placed their fascines in it. To retreat was extremely hazardous. On our left fires had started in the underbrush which added to the discomfort and danger. At this juncture, a line of supports came forward which met with the same resistance and secured no greater success. It was then evident that . . . the attack had failed.

The support he mentions was the 2nd Louisiana (black) of Dudley's brigade, "and a noble sight it was to see them bravely advance to our assistance; but it was of no avail."

Cease Fire

They knew not why, but "towards night . . . the bugle called out "cease firing" and immediately all strife stopped. Then commenced carrying off the dead and wounded."[1413]

Major Burt of the 159th New York may have been the savior of the day.

1411. Stevens, W. B., p. 139.
1412. Woodward, J. T., p. 34; Clark, O. S., p. 90.
1413. Stevens, W. B., p. 140; Tiemann, W. F., p. 41; Hall, H. & J., *75th History*, p. 116; Stanyan, J. M., pp. 231, 232; *Defenders*, SHS, Vol. 14, pp. 323–325.

Unauthorized to do so, he called a truce, "which enabled him to bring off his dead and wounded. The display of the white flag was mistaken for some distance along the line . . ." It is said that one Confederate regiment stacked arms on or near the works and fell back to await the surrender. However, when Gardner learned of it, he ordered that hostilities be resumed in half an hour. At least, this had allowed the men on both sides to emerge from their shelter for more than two hours, and no doubt, many lives were saved, particularly those wounded earlier in the day, and had suffered in the sun for hours without water.

Next day, an official truce[1414] was finally effected. Considerable time was wasted by negotiations. It was initially agreed that it was to extend to 2:00 p.m. but had to be revised to 7:00 p.m. because Banks and Gardner had not finished their correspondence until after 3:00 p.m. A part of the negotiating involved Banks having to apologize for Burt's unauthorized truce.

Much delay was caused by Gardner's demand that the Union troops withdraw to no closer than eight hundred yards from the works. Banks refused, but in a subtle concession, he remonstrates: "The wounded men to whom my letter refers are on our left . . ." (where they were the most distant from Gardner). Gardner's reply did not press the issue, and he agreed to a truce. Banks then clarified the situation, saying, "I have been informed that there are also some dead and wounded on my right." All of this negotiation had consumed nine hours. It seems that if either man cared about the condition of the wounded still lying on the field, by now, he would have agreed to almost anything. The final words were from Banks: "I will agree to send all of the killed and wounded of your command that are within my lines or on my front to your lines, by unarmed parties, if you will consent to send the killed and wounded of my command within your lines or on your front to my exterior lines, by unarmed parties."

Such detail has been repeated here to allow the reader to try to grasp why the Native Guards dead and wounded were, in fact, ignored. A Confederate view of this is found in the history of Company K of the 1st Alabama Regiment.[1415] "On the 28th there was a cessation of hostilities . . . for the purpose of burying the dead. Gen. Banks did not deem it worth while to bury the colored troops who 'fought nobly' and their bodies lay festering in the sun till the close of the siege . . ."

In the *History of the First Regiment, Alabama Volunteer Infantry*, the explanation given is: "A brigade of negroes had charged the 39th Mississippi on our left; about half were killed outright on the field, and for the burial of these Gen. Banks never asked a flag of truce. They lay there in the hot sun and putrified and swelled until the stench became so unbearable to Col. Shelby . . . that he asked Banks to

---

1414. O.R. Vol. 26/I, pp. 513–518; McMorries, E. Y., p. 64.
1415. Smith, D. P., p. 66; McMorries, E. Y., p. 64.

allow him to bury them. Banks replied that he had no dead there."

Any reasonable person would be suspect of this explanation, accusing the Confederates of duplicity. Then again, with knowledge of Dwight's foibles, perhaps Banks really had been misinformed.

The truce worked to the particular advantage of the Confederate side. They were able to freely roam the field and collect the Enfields and Springfields left near the ramparts, a feat that they had attempted since the previous evening. Originally attracted to the scene by the cries of the Yankee wounded, they had ventured out of their fortifications to succor them with water. The discovery of the rifles was an important side benefit for the 1st Alabama Regiment, previously only armed with smoothbore flintlocks. "Our men quickly supplied themselves, and after this each man kept two loaded guns, his Enfield for 'long taw' and flint and steel for close quarters."

It was early after dark at Dr. Lilley's hospital station, on the road to Springfield Landing, that the Rev. James K. Hosmer first heard of the "repulse of the storming party; and the surgeons are warned of the approach of a large number of wounded. We hear of the fall of generals and colonels, and rank and file without number; and close upon the heels of the intelligence follow the ambulances, loaded as never before with hastily dressed wounded from the field hospitals in front." The two large pavilion tents can accept no more, and thankfully, the *Iberville* had arrived to transport the wounded directly to Baton Rouge. On board, Hosmer wrote, "I can hardly step among the prostrate and gory company," spread out in the saloon. "At the farther end, just in front of the mirror, lie a Zouave major [Carr], two colonels, and the adjutant of a Maine regiment [Woodward] then the brave and unfortunate colonel of the Massachusetts Forty Ninth [Bartlett]. He lost a leg at Ball's Bluff . . . he meets pain with calm and dignity."

Hosmer's iced tea and wash water having run out, he returned to shore to refill. Now an ambulance with an escort of Zouaves arrives, bearing a famous general. "I catch sight of his agonized face in the moonlight, and recognize him as the same general in whose tent I had sat on one occasion, rather more than a year before, in the camp at Port Royal. I left him groaning and shrieking beneath the awning on the deck of the little steamer" (Admiral Farragut's dispatch steamer, which was to bring T. W. Sherman to New Orleans).[1416]

1416. Johns, H. T., p. 269; Hosmer, J. K., pp. 175–177. Incredibly, as much as Sherman disliked Banks and had felt that he had deserved a better assignment than in the Department of the Gulf, he would return. After being fitted with an artificial leg, he was assigned to the command of forts Jackson and St. Philip on March 16th, 1864. He then went on to replace Arnold as Chief of Artillery, then to command the 3rd Division of the 19th Army Corps, and succeeded Reynolds as Commander of the Defenses of New Orleans. See O.R., Vol. 34/II, pp. 474, 629; O.R., Vol. 34/III, p. 437; O.R., Vol. 34/IV, pp. 294, 295, 406; Cullum no.859.

The day would claim 293 Union killed, 1,545 wounded, and 157 missing.[1417] The heaviest total losses were in Augur's division, no doubt due to the bold charges of the forlorn hope. The heaviest loss, though, for any one regiment, was to Fearing's 8th New Hampshire, which suffered 124 killed and wounded, or 42 percent.

The Native Guards 1st Regiment lost 2 officers and 32 enlisted men killed, and 3 officers and 92 enlisted men wounded (including those mortally). The 3rd Regiment, which followed the first in column, lost 1 officer and 5 enlisted men killed, 1 officer and 37 enlisted men wounded and 1 officer and 2 enlisted men missing.[1418]

On the Confederate side, Beall, who faced Sherman's attack, allegedly reported the incomplete total of 68 killed, 194 wounded, and 96 missing, for a period up to June 1st. Steedman, who faced Weitzel's and Grover's attacks, reported that the totals of killed, wounded, and missing to his command as 10th Arkansas (80), 15th Arkansas (70), and 1st Alabama (75), a total of 225, "or one man out of every four."

There were no casualties in the ranks of the 39th Mississippi and Wingfield's 9th Louisiana Partisan Rangers who had faced the Native Guards.

Note that the reports partially overlap and do not agree. If the 1st Alabama losses, as reported by Steedman, are added to the Beall table, a total of 433 would result for the Confederate side. Clearly, Banks' attack on this fortified position, where the attacker is always at a disadvantage and in such an inept, uncoordinated manner, caused nearly five times as many casualties, 1,995, as were taken by the defenders.

The unique story of black units in battle was set upon by the Northern press and was distorted by all sorts of exaggerations and inaccuracies. For example, the June 20th issue of *Harper's Weekly*: "On 29th an assault was made which was unsuccessful. The Second Louisiana (colored) regiment fought with extraordinary gallantry, losing in killed and wounded 600 out of 900 men."

The inaccurate descriptions grew worse. The June 27th issue of *Frank Leslie's Illustrated Newspaper* displayed a large engraving, spread across pages 216 and 217, which was captioned: "ASSAULT OF THE SECOND LOUISIANA (COLORED) REGIMENT ON THE CONFEDERATE WORKS AT PORT HUDSON, MAY 27TH 1863." The scene, figure 18, is entirely a figment of the artist's imagination, for the simple fact that the Second Louisiana *was never there*. They were stationed at Ship Island.[1419] Also, no hand-to-hand combat, as is shown, took place in the real engagement. The 1st and 3rd Native Guards were repulsed entirely by rifle and artillery fire.

1417. Fox, W., p. 102; Stanyan, J. M., p. 245,
1418. The numbers for the 1st Regiment are taken from Fox, chapter 6, p. 58. Numbers for the 3rd are not published in Fox. O.R. Vol. 26/I, p. 68, agrees with Fox and lists the 3rd. O.R. Vol. 26/I, p. 147; *Defenders*, SHS, Vol. 14, pp. 325, 326; McGregor, C., p. 418.
1419. Dyer, F. H., chapter 16, reg. 154; Stanyan, J. M., p. 230.

FIGURE 18

An honest appraisal of the performance of the Native Guards by an eyewitness, Capt. T. C. Prescott of the 8th New Hampshire Regiment, whose Company G was assigned as a part of the Native Guards' cavalry support, is here quoted: "The two colored regiments . . . acquitted themselves like veterans, standing under heavy fire for hours, and this experiment with that class of soldiers proved their valor and worth . . ."

Chapter 10

The Siege Begins; June 10th; June 14th; Paine's Assault; Weitzel's Assault; Augur's Feint; Dwight's Assault; June 15th; Taylor Again; The Last Days; Finally; Recovery of the La Fourche; "Record" 8/63; The Next Step

The Siege Begins

Having negotiated the terms of the truce, Banks turned his attention to Grant,[1420] who had written him on May 25th, explaining that he had decided to lay siege to Vicksburg because it could not be taken without "a great sacrifice of life." He was worried about a buildup of Johnston's forces, and asked that Grierson be sent back immediately, along with "such force as you can spare." The note was carried by a member of Grant's staff, who was instructed to give "all the particulars of my present situation." Grant even sent two steamers along to carry the requested troops back.

Banks' answer reads almost as if he never understood what Grant had said. The request for Grierson was completely ignored, and Banks closed his response with a postscript, which requested that Grant send him a brigade of 4,000 or 5,000 men. The steamers were sent away empty. Grant tried once more on the 29th, this time notifying Banks that he was sending Charles Dana to make the case. As had so often had happened, the missive from Grant passed down while another from Banks passed up. On the 29th, Banks wrote a less curt explanation of his situation: "My force is far less than you imagine, and, with such detachments from it as would be necessary to protect New Orleans, while Port Hudson, Mobile, and Kirby Smith[1421] are within a few days' movement…" He went on to repeat his request for troops.

Dana started on his mission on the 30th of May.[1422] While passing down the river near Grand Gulf, he met the steamer bearing Banks' reply, and hearing of his latest negative response, Dana returned to Grant's headquarters. There the matter lay.

1420. O.R. Vol. 26/I, p. 520; O.R. Vol. 24/III, pp. 346, 359–360.
1421. Lt. Gen. E. Kirby Smith, commander of the Confederate Trans-Mississippi Dept., at Shreveport; Richard Taylor's superior, and with whom Taylor often clashed.
1422. Dana, p. 81; Irwin, *History*, pp. 186–187. (Subsequent references to Irwin are all from his *History of the Nineteenth Army Corps*.)

In the next few days, the regiments with Chickering and Morgan that had marched to Berwick City were brought up to Port Hudson, and most were returned to their divisions. Entrenching tools were distributed to those assigned to construct improved defenses, and as these were completed, the remainder of Keith's 1st Indiana Heavy Artillery was deployed.

If anything had been accomplished by all of the blood spilled on the 27th, it was that the Union lines had been advanced closer to the Confederate works. "Fort Babcock" was established opposite the 1st Alabama, in Steedman's line. The men of the 75th New York had sheltered there during the May assault, and two fallen trees had provided enough protection to allow them to begin digging.[1423] On June 10th, a battery of four mortars, commanded by Lt. Taylor of the 4th Massachusetts, was completed opposite Steedman's line near the Bennett house. It can be seen at position 3, at the very top of figure 1. According to Confederate reports (also citing Hall), it was fired day and night, which "gave us a great annoyance."

Some reorganization was required in order to fill the impressive number of command positions vacated by those officers killed or wounded. Dwight[1424] was assigned to the command of Sherman's division. Col. Thomas S. Clark, miraculously recovered from the cannonball wind that had knocked him down on the battlefield, replaced the wounded Brig. Gen. Neal Dow in command of the 1st Brigade; Lt. Col. Edward Bacon replaced Clark in command of the 6th Michigan; Lt. Col. James Smith replaced Col. D. S. Cowles (killed) in command of the 128th New York; Capt. Felix Agnus replaced Col. Abel Smith (killed) in command of the 165th New York Zouaves.

In Paine's division, Maj. James P. Richardson replaced Lt. Col. William M. Rodman (killed) in command of the 38th Massachusetts; Capt. William M. Barrett replaced Lt. Col. Oliver M. Lull (killed) in command of the 8th New Hampshire; and Lt. Col. Frederick A. Boardman replaced Col. Sidney A. Bean (mortally wounded) in command of the 4th Wisconsin.

In Augur's division, Col. Charles J. Paine, commander of the 2nd Louisiana, replaced Col. Edward P. Chapin (killed) in command of the 1st brigade. Lt. Col. Charles Everett replaced Paine as commander of the 2nd Louisiana. Maj. Charles T. Plunkett replaced Lt. Col. S. B. Sumner (wounded), after he had replaced Col. Wm. F. Bartlett (wounded) in command of the 49th Massachusetts.

1423. Hall, H. and J., 75th, p. 117; Stanyan, pp. 251–252, Defenders, SHS vol. 14, p. 330. Figure 1 from Irwin, facing p. 192.
1424. O.R. Vol. 26/I, p. 17, 529–532, 632; Irwin, p. 182; Johns, p. 265.

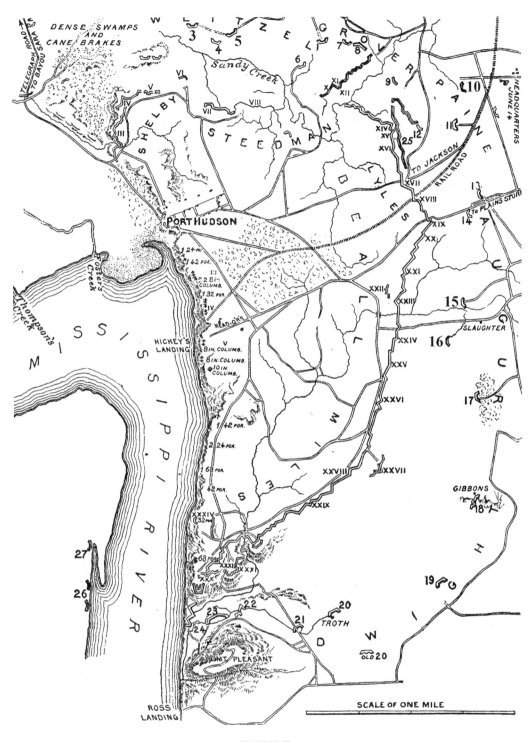

FIGURE 1

Other realignments: Grover got back four of the six regiments he had let go at the close of the Teche Campaign: the 22nd Maine, the 90th New York, the 52nd Massachusetts, and the 26th Maine, though he lost the 41st Massachusetts—now called the 3rd Massachusetts Cavalry—to Grierson. Of course, the 6th New York had gone home. Weitzel fell back into the command of his reserve brigade, to which the 114th New York had returned after the march to Berwick City. Paine lost the 4th Wisconsin (mounted) to Grierson, though he gained the 4th Massachusetts and the 16th New Hampshire. However, the 16th was found to be so disabled from its ordeal at Butte La Rose that it was replaced by the 28th Connecticut, brought up from Pensacola.

June 1st, Monday. From the *History of the 15th New Hampshire*, encamped on the Slaughter plantation:[1425]

> Day mostly clear and pleasant; though at times it threatened rain but none fell…
>
> Regular siege operations are now on foot; heavy guns are brought up; the woods are full of shovels, picks, axes, wheelbarrows, and other tools. Our artillery and the fleet fire constantly on the enemy. There is no picket firing in the immediate front, the enemy for some reason remaining silent. Colonel Grierson is seen around our camp; he looks rough and soiled.

June 2nd, Tuesday. (15th New Hampshire narrative):

> A most beautiful day. Our camp in the woods was shelled last night, and in the morning, just before roll-call five or six ten-inch shells were pitched over which fell right into our midst…

This was "Lady Davis" or the "Old Demoralizer" speaking.[1426] It was a 10-inch Columbiad mounted on the locomotive turntable at the end of the railroad. It could thus turn in any direction. It did little damage, however, as its shells were either empty or failed to detonate.

> At 10 o'clock General Banks, with attendants, comes up to our front and views the situation with a glass.
>
> Thousands of negroes are picking and shoveling, as well as the soldiers, on the disputed open ground between us and the enemy, and gradually advancing the trenches and rifle pits toward their parapet…
>
> Captain Gordon was…on an eminence with some of the 6th Michigan boys, who were using "Henry" rifles; they were provided with telescopes. One of them said, "Look through this glass." The captain looked, and as one of our men fired he saw the bullet strike…and it seemed to go right through [the Confederate soldier foolish enough to have stood on the parapet]…
>
> We are nearly opposite their centre; [referring to figure 1, to the rear of

---

1425. McGregor, pp. 419–422, 427, 434, 436–437, 440.
1426. Sprague, p. 142; Tiemann, p. 43. The gun was mounted on a rail car, able to use the turntable or be moved along the railroad.

Battery 16, near the Slaughter home[1427]] their works may be entirely silent now, and none of their men are to be seen; but their works are manned; the Confederate soldiers lie thick behind them all armed and ready to fire on the instant. Their guns are leveled across their parapet through loop holes formed by three sand bags—two laid side by side a little apart, and one across the top—and thousands of unseen eyes are watching [through] them night and day. Should now our men make a show of advancing in any force, that parapet would burst into flames as if by magic. But within their lines are trees and woods; concealed in them, and perched in the trees are many of their riflemen. Expose yourself now…and…a bullet will whistle by you; another will follow apparently within an inch of your ear. One of their sharpshooters has got your range, and his next shot will drop you unless you seek protection. You don't see this marksman in his butternut and slouched hat, nor do you hear the crack of his rifle, but our hundreds of sharpshooters and advance pickets, who are right in sight before us…watch close to make out the smoke of his gun.

While the 15th New Hampshire toiled, similar activity took place on Weitzel's front.[1428] Navy Lt. Commander Terry and crews from the *Richmond* and *Essex* arrived with their guns at Battery 10, which was described as "748 yards from the enemy's works," (see the upper right in figure 1, and figure 2 from Miller, F.T. Vol. 2 p. 219.)

FIGURE 2. THE NAVY HELPS ON LAND

1427. Union batteries are numbered 1–25. No. 25 was a trench cavalier (an observation tower) and was located next to Battery 12. Confederate batteries are identified by Roman numerals. See table 1.

1428. Stanyan, pp. 251–252; Hall, H. and J., p. 122; ORN 20, p. 257. These references do not enumerate the battery positions exactly, though the *15th New Hampshire History* does, providing a map nearly identical to Irwin's. Many battery positions were not constructed until after May 27th, and almost all of the Port Hudson maps available only show battery positions as of the close of the siege, in July.

June 3rd, Wednesday.

Banks was concerned about Logan's presence to the east, and on June 1st had dispatched Grierson toward Jackson and then Clinton, finally engaging the enemy at Pretty Creek, where Grierson managed to extricate himself from a superior force with 8 killed, 28 wounded, and 15 missing.[1429] Among the killed was the well-known and admired Lt. Solon A. Perkins, of Lowell, Massachusetts, commander of the 3rd Massachusetts Cavalry, Co. C. His was one of three independent cavalry companies raised at the end of 1861 and sent along with the Butler Expedition to New Orleans. Perkins had accompanied the marine detachment first sent into the city by Farragut to raise the flag over the mint. Perkins' death angered Banks, who grew up in Lowell, and he resolved on retaliation. On the 4th, a part of General Paine's 3rd brigade, reinforced by the 52nd Massachusetts and the 91st New York, was added to Grierson's force. Chasing Logan to Clinton, and entering there at daylight on the 6th, they found him to have escaped in the direction of Liberty. Remaining at Clinton, they destroyed the railroad depot, a locomotive, and numerous Confederate stores, then turned back.

They had managed to rescue seven Union prisoners, and captured and paroled, quoting Irwin, "after the useless fashion of the time," 30 rebels. On Friday the 5th, on the return march, they stopped at the same plantation at which they had stopped for water on the way out, and where they had been cursed at by its mistress. They now found eight families, apparently the whole number of the slaves on her plantation, packed and waiting. They had resolved to leave. All but one too old, they fell in with the column. The mistress of the plantation could, of course, do nothing to stop them, and was reduced to selling eggs "at a great price to Gen. Paine's cooks."

No casualties were reported, though Paine wrote: "The extreme heat caused great suffering, my ambulances returned at night loaded with men prostrated by sunstroke." How many of the 8th New Hampshire were affected is not reported. The regiment, which had entered the assault of May 27th with 298 men for duty, and had taken the highest percentage of casualties, were only able to muster 140 for this mission.

Dwight reported the interrogation of three deserters who cited that the condition of the Port Hudson works on the Confederate left, though reported as strengthened, had not been completed. "They are nothing but rail, fence and mud, and no ditch…Artillery would knock them down." The Confederates were short of caps.[1430] Most of the men, being natives of Mississippi, Louisiana, or Alabama, wanted to go home.

1429. O.R. Vol. 26/I, pp. 2, 134–137, 712; Irwin, pp. 190–191. The parole quote is Irwin's; Butler, B. F., *Butler's Book*, p. 370; Powers, pp. 103–104.
1430. O.R., Vol. 26/I, p. 537.

June 5th, Friday.

A battery of "rifled guns" was planted opposite the "slaughter pen" (the Bull Pen field referred to earlier) about 400 yards from the Confederate battery at the Bennett house. Battery 5 falls into this definition. It is found as having four rifled guns in a list of the batteries, see table 1, below.[1431]

BATTERY		BATTERY	
1	(1) 30 pdr. Parrott	16	(4) 3 inch rifled, Bane
2	(2) 12 pdr. howitzers Phelps		(6) 12 pdr. Napoleon, Rawles
3	(4) siege mortars Taylor	17	(4) 8 inch siege howitzers, Rose
4	(1) 30pdr. Parrott, Harrower	18	(4) siege mortars, Hill
5	(4) 6 inch rifled, Healy	19	(6) 3 inch rifles, Hebard
6	(6) 12 pdr. Napoleons, Duryea	20	(4) 20 pdr. Parrotts, Roy
7	(2) 30 pdr. Parrotts, McLaflin	21	(4) 12 pdr. Napoleon, Bradley
8	(4) 12 pdr. Napoleon, Carruth	22	(8) inch siege howitzers, Baugh
	(4) 12 pdr. Napoleon, Bainbridge	23	(1) 10 inch siege mortar, Motte
	(2) 3 inch rifled, Norris	24	(2) 20 pdr. Parrotts, Hartley
9	(2) 12 pdr. rifled, Cox		(3) 24 pdr., Hinkle
10	(4) 9 inch Dalhgren's, Terry USN		(2) 9 inch Dalhgren Lt., Swann USN
11	(6) 20 pdr. Parrotts, Mack		(1) 8 inch howitzer, Lt. Clever
12	(6) 12 pdr. Napoleon, Duryea		(2) 12 pdr Napoleon, Closson
	(1) 20 pdr. Parrott, Duryea		(2) 10 pdr. Parrots, Appleton
13	(3) 24 pdr., Hadden		(3) 30 pdr. Parrots, Grimsley
14	(6) 6 pdr. Sawyer, Holcomb		(2) 10 inch siege mortars, Hamlen
15	(2) 20 pdr. Parrotts, Hamrick	25	Trench Cavalier
	(2) 24 pdr. Parrots, Harper		

TABLE I

June 7th, Sunday.

After working mostly at night, to be safe from Confederate sharpshooters, Battery 15 was ready and Captains Hamrick and Harper of the 1st Indiana were able to move in with their two rifled 20-pounder Parrotts and two 24-pounder Parrotts.

June 8th, Monday. Very hot. (15th New Hampshire narrative):

> One man wounded from the 128th New York. All men working night and day. Lt. Col. Blair, though wounded on the 27th returned, only to find that Dwight had arrested Col. Kingman, so Blair, with his right arm in a sling, and looking "weakened and emaciated," took command. The suspicion was that

---

1431. Atlas, portion of plate 38. Plate 38 was prepared in 1864, hence it shows positions that do not exist at the current time, particularly 20–25. Note Duryea is listed at 6 and again at 12. His position at Battery 6 was on May 27th, and he was subsequently moved to 12. Closson or Appleton will not move to No. 24 until June 25th, and it is noted that no exact position is shown for Battery L prior to that time.

Kingman had been too forthright with Dwight in protesting that the May 27th assault was a futile, rash, and ill-considered affair. No charges were ever brought. Quoting Kingman: "It was a petty, spiteful, and cruel exercise of …authority, which I had no means of resisting or clearing up, as our term of enlistment had nearly expired."[1432]

June 9th, Tuesday (15th New Hampshire narrative, in part): Very hot, dry and dusty; good breeze that shakes the leaves; "Only coffee and hard bread for breakfast after shoveling and picking all night…Considerable bombarding but no one injured near our camp."

June 10th, Wednesday.[1433] Extracts from a letter home, written by Lt. Washington Perkins of the 15th New Hampshire:

> We are building batteries and digging rifle pits all around them, and in a day or two I expect there will be one of the most terrific bombardments that has ever been known. Our rifle pits are within rifle shot of their parapet; we have been at work on them night and day. Their sharpshooters are firing on us all the time, and the balls are whizzing over our heads, but they don't hit many. They give us a shower of shells and grape, but we give them back ten fold. There is scarcely five minutes, day or night, but that we hear the roar of artillery, or of the bursting of shells. A good many deserters come in from the fort, and according to their reports the rebels have about six thousand men, with a good supply of provisions, and plenty of ammunition for small arms, but short of large.[1434] They say also that a great many would leave if they could get away, and that many of the officers are in favor of surrendering. The day that we buried our dead a good many of them came and talked with us and appeared very friendly; shook hands with us when we left, telling us that if they took any of us prisoners they should use us well, and requested us to do the same. The night after the battle some of the wounded were left on the field, and the rebel surgeons went out and dressed their wounds, and told our pickets to bring water and they would not be fired on. One of our rifle pits runs across the battle field. I expect our regiment will go into one of them tomorrow.

1432. The 15th was one of Banks' 22 nine-months regiments. Though organized on Oct. 16th, 1862, they were not mustered into Federal service until Nov. 12th, 1862. Hence, their term of service was due to expire not in July, as they all thought, but on August 12th, 1863. From: *New Hampshire Adjutant General's Report*, Concord, 1865, vol. I, p. xvi, and vol. 2, Concord, 1866, p. 836.
1433. Stanyan, p. 252; McGregor, p. 441, 445–446, 456, 461–462. Perkins does not understand that their time will be counted from their date of muster, which as noted, was nearly a month later.
1434. Gardner was simply conserving. Even after the surrender, Banks reported (O.R. Vol. 26I, p. 55) the capture of 44,000 pounds of cannon powder, and a "good supply of projectiles for light and heavy guns." The conservation efforts extended to rifle ammunition as well. Spent Minie balls, shot into the fort, and lying "thick on the surface of the ground" were picked up, and if in good condition re-used. If deformed, the lead shot were used as canister. Smith, D. P., *Co. K History*, p. 65.

Our time is out July 16, and we expect to get home by that time.

This was a forecast of some trouble. The men calculated their time from when they were organized; the government calculated their time from when they were mustered into the Federal service; which was a month later.

A report of the interrogation of deserters, written by Dwight to Banks, had the Port Hudson garrison as despairing of relief and wishing to surrender. This seemed to confirm an earlier report made by Dwight.[1435]

The men of the 15th were still working on Battery 16, in a position that was very exposed (see figure 1 also Vol. 1, Ch 9, fig 6). When the battery's construction was first commenced, the men had advanced behind cotton bales that they rolled forward into position. Then, once at the desired location, crouching behind them, they began a trench; throwing the dirt up and over the bales.

June 10th

Not waiting for all of these gun positions, rifle pits and engineering work to be completed, a reconnaissance-in-force, of sorts, was ordered by Banks. It was prompted by the fact that Confederate fire had slackened by degrees. During the day, the Yankee sharpshooters were so effective that the Confederates had begun firing only at night. It was becoming difficult to "estimate their available ordnance."[1436] The objects of the reconnaissance (Irwin describes it as a feigned attack) were stated to be: (1) harassment of the enemy, (2) inducing him to bring forward and expose his artillery, and (3) acquiring knowledge of the ground, which would allow pioneers to remove obstructions, if necessary.

The *History of the 75th New York Volunteers* describes the action, which began on the night of the 9th:

> [A] grand bombardment was begun…and kept up for thirty-six consecutive hours. Finding that this maneuver elicited little response, Banks resolved on a feint with infantry along the whole line…The ball opened on the left and the advance and skirmish fire soon became general, and the artillery, which for a short interval had been comparatively silent, now resumed their work…the hills and woods around Port Hudson resounded as they never had done before.

At midnight on the 10th, a continuous line of skirmishers was formed and ordered to sneak forward, in Banks' words, "[to] get within attacking distance of the works, in order to avoid the terrible losses incurred in moving over the ground in front of the works."

1435. O.R. Vol. 26/I, pp. 536–537, 551.
1436. Hall, H. and J., 75th p. 123–124; Irwin, p. 192; O.R. Vol. 26/I, pp. 14, 67, 131–133.

Steedman describes it with a telling opening:[1437]

> On the 10th of June a furious bombardment all day and night indicated to us an approaching attack, and at three o'clock in the morning of the 11th, a show of an assault was made near the centre of our line of fortifications, while, at the same time, the real attack was made on our left in the woods...During the fighting two regiments of the enemy, favored by the extreme darkness, crept up through a gorge among the abattis, penetrating within our lines of defence [sic]. Had they known the ground and been strongly reinforced, this movement might have proved disastrous to us.

As soon as the Confederates were seen to have manned their parapet, and were returning fire, the Union skirmishers were ordered to lie down, the sharpshooters in their rear conducting the return fire over their heads. From the 75th New York: "Toward morning a slow rain set in and the men were ordered to fall back."

The five companies of Weitzel's 12th Connecticut who were involved suffered casualties "greater in proportion to the number engaged than in any other single engagement during the entire siege." The 22nd Maine suffered some casualties. In all, incomplete reports totaled 2 killed, 53 wounded, and 65 missing.

The operation accomplished nothing, with the exception that on Grover's front the 131st New York was able to reposition itself closer to the works.[1438]

June 11th, Thursday.[1439] Very heavy shower, commencing at 2:00 a.m.; showery in the afternoon; cleared in the evening. "Hard bread fritters [hardtack fried in pork fat] for breakfast, Kelly shot through the neck and spine. Twelve hundred men ordered out to finish breastworks and batteries. Thirty or forty loads of cotton were hauled up and used for breastworks."

June 12th. Very pleasant; not quite so hot. Work on the "great cotton battery built by Capt. Johnson...Battery 16," was becoming feverish. "Chief Engineer Bailey[1440] became very nervous, and the men were urged to the utmost exertions; there were many more men on the work besides the Company D boys. It seems that Chief Engineer Bailey's orders were to have the work completed in such season that the battery [Hebard's] could drive into the works before light on the thirteenth."

June 13th. The day "rose in semi-tropical beauty, and during the day the sun shed down his fierce rays with a blinding glare and intolerable and pitiless heat." The work on the "12 gun... battery [16]" was not quite complete, but in the

---

1437. Defenders, SHS used here and in the rest of the volume to abbreviate "Southern Historical Society Papers" vol. 14, p. 326.
1438. O.R. Vol. 26/I, p. 131.
1439. Continuing with the 15th New Hampshire narrative, McGregor, pp. 446, 451, 460.
1440. Capt. Joseph Bailey, of the 4th Wisconsin, was eventually assigned to Banks' staff as acting military engineer of the 19th Army Corps. He was to become renowned for his dam on the Red River. O.R. Vol. 34/I, p. 406; O. R. Vol. 34/II, p. 544; Defenders, SHS vol. 14, p. 326.

morning Hebard's 1st Vermont "with horses lashed to the keen gallop, went in in broad daylight…" They were subjected to a "terrible" fire with two men and one horse killed,[1441] and three men wounded.

At 7:30 a.m., Banks wrote to Farragut, on the *Monongahela*:[1442]

> I shall open a vigorous bombardment at exactly a quarter past 11 this morning, and continue it for exactly one hour. I respectfully request that you will aid us by throwing as many shells as you can into the place during that hour, commencing and ceasing fire with us. The bombardment will be immediately followed by a summons to surrender. If that is not listened to, I shall probably attack to-morrow morning, but of this I will give you notice.

Gardner refused the surrender demand, and at 9:00 p.m. Banks signaled Farragut to commence firing, with mortars only, at 11:00 p.m., and to cease at 2:00 a.m. on June 14th. The second assault was on.

June 14th

A general council was held on the evening of June 13th at Banks' new headquarters, closer to the front, as indicated by the small star in the upper right corner of figure 3. Though preliminary orders for troop dispositions were sent out from headquarters at 8:45 p.m., and the signal to Farragut at 9:00, the final orders were not read and approved until 11:00, and the first copies were not sent out until 11:30. As a result, some regiments did not receive their orders until after they should have begun moving to their assigned positions—not an auspicious beginning.

The main attack[1443] would be under the overall command of Grover, and would take place at the Priest Cap, indicated in figure 3 by the heavy arrow at the top. A second assault would be conducted by Dwight at the Union extreme left, the southern end of the Confederate defenses, as indicated by the heavy arrow at the bottom, and a feint would be conducted by Augur from the Plains Store Road, as shown by the light arrow.

Depending upon the course of events, Augur was to be prepared to reinforce either assault.

1441. McGregor, p. 465. Table 1 lists Bane and Rawles, Battery G, 5th U.S. Artillery. They were later occupants, but at this point it was Hebard.
1442. ORN ser. 1, vol. 20, p. 229–230; O.R. Vol. 26/I, pp. 552–553.
1443. O.R. Vol. 26/I, pp. 554–555. Figure 3, Irwin, facing p. 192 (altered).

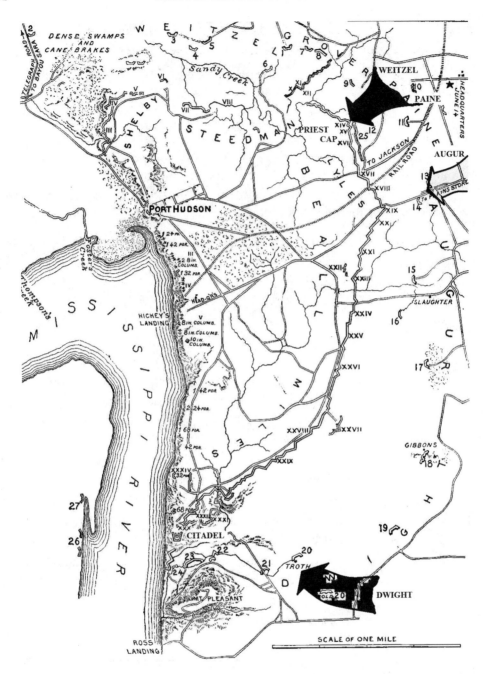

FIGURE 3

The attacks were to begin at 3:30 a.m. in a coordinated manner; with all watches set. The preliminary bombardment would begin at 3:00.[1444] Nothing was

---

1444. If the reader missed Steedman's comment regarding the opening of the June 10th reconnaissance, it was "a bombardment indicated to us an approaching attack…" Every action by Banks had been preceded by a bombardment, and this was no exception. The Confederate garrison would be duly warned.

vague and left to discretion as it had been on the 27th, *except* a caveat: The 3:30 a.m. advance by the skirmishers might be delayed until "as soon thereafter as General Grover may find best." Another flaw related to time should have been evident, in that, there was but little of it allowed for the troops to get into position, particularly those transferred from other regiments. For example: the 48th Massachusetts from their location at Plains Store to Dwight, and the 50th Massachusetts from the Plains Store Road to Dwight. A lesser movement involved Dudley to Grover with the 161st and 174th New York regiments. The rough ground, and darkness, would make it difficult, even for those already in the vicinity, such at the 75th New York, to reach their final assault positions.[1445]

Though Grover was named as in command of the main assault, the concept of the plan is credited to Weitzel, who believed that a concentrated attack on one point would penetrate the line "by a combination of force and stratagem[1446]…A perfect surprise was intended." Ah, but it seems that the senior generals, and Grover in particular, were the ones who laid out the details, and worse, remained to direct. It was to be a deadly repeat of the 27th.

Since neither Weitzel nor Grover made any report after the battle, we have no clue as to whether anyone had argued against the use of a preliminary bombardment. Then again, it was to be general, and would not warn of an attack at a specific location. However, it was still a warning, and Gardner had the ready ability to transfer his troops as required.

Paine's whole division was to attack on the left of the Priest Cap, and be the "chief" assault, figure 4.[1447] Weitzel's brigade, reinforced by the 161st and the 174th New York regiments from Augur (Dudley's 3rd Brigade), with Grover's division in support, was to make an advance on the right through a gully, or "little ravine" which ran between Cox's Battery 9, and Duryea's Battery 12.[1448] It is important to note that on June 12th Gardner had moved the 49th Alabama into place to reinforce Ben Johnson's 15th Arkansas. The 1st Mississippi was also in place near the 49th.

1445. Hall, H. and J., *75th*, p. 125; Plummer, pp. 41–42. The 48th had marched from their bivouac at Plains Store; had worked all the day of the 13th entrenching a battery position on Augur's front, and then at dark, were ordered back to Plains Store. Upon arriving there, they received Banks' order to march to Dwight.
1446. Hall, H. and J., *75th*, pp. 124–125; dmna.ny.gov/*75th New York, Clippings*, p. 1, Letter to *N.Y. Herald*.
1447. Irwin, p. 196.
1448. Hall, H. and J., *75th*, p. 124; McMorries, *Defense* map, portion. The Jackson Road is mislabeled on Irwin's map, and there are no terrain features whatsoever. The general arrangement of the McMorries map seems to better match the description of the attack. Labels have been added. The battery numbers have been changed to conform to Irwin's, and the Federal maps in general. (The Confederate map numbers the Federal batteries less by one, e.g., 12 is 11.) A trench, position No. 25, into which was later constructed a cavalier, has been partially removed, as it was not completed at this time. Defenders, SHS, vol. 14, p. 328.

Griffiths Field, through which Paine was to advance, was described as scrubby undulating ground, a part of which was "formerly...cultivated,"[1449] (refer ahead to figure 5.) These words seem to forewarn of trouble, if not failure. The approach was nearly wide open and unobstructed. But of course, the advance was to be a stealthy surprise, at dark, and Weitzel's attack, not to mention those of Augur, or Dwight, were supposed to divert attention in a coordinated manner.

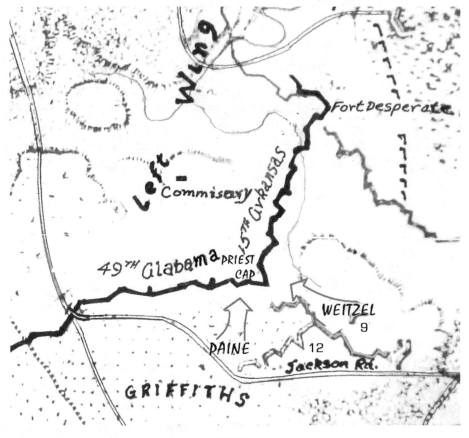

FIGURE 4

The ravine through which Weitzel was to make his approach had at its end a sap (a protected trench dug in the "little ravine" referred to, and shown in figure 4), which ran between batteries 9 and 12. It had been "pushed to within a few rods of the eminence" on which the powerful Confederate bastion stood. Weitzel's plan was to send a force into this passage by night, "which should begin the attack just before daylight." It is hard to imagine even portions of seven or eight regiments passing through a sap, and quietly.

The general formation of the two attacking columns had been settled upon

---

1449. Stanyan, pp. 254, 260; *dmna.ny.gov/Clippings 75th New York*, p. 1, letter to *NY Herald*, describes the distance from the end of the sap to the parapet as one hundred and fifty yards.

by the 11th of June,[1450] and on June 12th Paine issued his General Order No. 64,[1451] which set it straight as to where each of his regiments were to be positioned in his attacking column, and what their job was. The format of the order was as appears below, with the exception that changes to show the actual composition that existed on the morning of June 14th have been made. The hand grenades were percussion-fused, 6-pounder artillery shells, one per man, and the "cotton bags" were sand bags filled with 30 pounds of cotton, *two* per man.

Column of Attack
Front
8th New Hampshire, 4th Wisconsin as skirmishers, at intervals of two paces
Companies A&K, 4th Massachusetts and A, B, E,
& I, 110th New York, with hand grenades.
38th Massachusetts in line of battle
53rd Massachusetts in line of battle
31st Massachusetts and a detachment of 60 men from the 173rd New York, with
400 cotton bags
156th New York
2nd Brigade, Fearing
133rd New York, 173rd New York
1st Brigade, Ferris
28th Connecticut,
50 pioneers, to level parapet
Nims' Battery

No such order of Weitzel's survives, but his column[1452] was nearly identical to Paine's, with the 12th Connecticut and the 75th New York positioned at the head as skirmishers. Next, the 91st New York and 100 men of the 28th Connecticut, with hand grenades, the 24th Connecticut with cotton bags, followed by the 8th Vermont, the 114th New York, and the 160th New York. Grover's 1st brigade, reduced to the 1st Louisiana, 22nd Maine, and the 90th and 131st New York, were to follow. Grover's 2nd and 3rd brigades, with Dudley's 161st and 174th New York, were held in reserve. The 30th Massachusetts was to be initially deployed to support Terry's Battery (No.10).

Battery L and Duryea's Battery F were to be drawn up in the rear of the attacking column, and remain in reserve.

1450. Hanaburgh, p. 54; *dmna.ny.gov/historic/reghist/civil/infantry/156thInf/156thInfCWN.htm*.
1451. Stanyan, pp. 254–256; Willis, p. 131. These two sources differ; Whitcomb, pp. 49–50; Ewer, p. 91; *dmna.ny.gov/historic/reghist/civil/infantry/24thInf/24thInfScribner00Intro.htm*; Powers, p. 105.
1452. Irwin, p. 198; Crofutt and Morris, p. 412; Haskin, p. 193; *Massachusetts Adjutant General's Report*, for the year ending 1863, p. 800.

Paine's Assault

FIGURE 5

Roused a little before midnight, on this clear and cool evening, Paine's regiments began forming on the edge of the woods alongside the Jackson Road (figures 4 and 5)[1453] by 2:00 a.m. They were formed up by 3:00, with the 8th New Hampshire and 4th Wisconsin in front, as planned. The cannonade had begun, the four 9-inch Dahlgrens of Terry's naval battery (10) throwing their 75-pound shells into the Confederate works over the heads of Paine's men.[1454] Immediately to the south, Augur had promptly begun his feint. To the north, McLaflin's Indiana battery (7) had joined in the firing. Weitzel's troops had been on the march since 11:00 the night before, and the head of the column had arrived at its attack position. Today, unlike May 27th, a well coordinated attack was evidently poised to begin. Even a subsequent Confederate report would describe it as "simultaneous." However, that report notes: "The Federals at first pressed heavily on the right where the 49th Alabama was stationed…" This was Paine.

So we have the first intimation that the attack was not quite "simultaneous," and that would prove to be fatal.

1453. Powers, pp. 107, 108; Stanyan, pp. 259, 268; figure 5, *Harper's Weekly*, July 18th, 1863, p. 452. The activity shown is the picking up of the dead on June 17th, presented here to give a general view of the battlefield. The Confederate parapet is in the background; O. R. Vol. 26/I, p. 555.

1454. *Ordnance Instructions for the U.S. Navy*, U.S. Gov't Printing Office, Washington, 1866, p. 90; Bissell, p. 50. Stanyan, pp. 261, 269; Defenders, SHS, vol. 14, p. 328; Irwin, p. 196; Willis, p. 137.

For a time, the front of Paine's column was shielded from the view of the Confederates by the thick hedges of osage orange on the approach, and somewhat by a fog that had developed toward dawn. There was little wind. At about 4:00, the order was given to go forward. They pressed through the wood, and found that the distance to the works was farther than expected, about five hundred yards. It consisted of undulating ground, and a succession of ridges and ravines, in which there were fallen trees, and scrubby bushes and brambles. On the brow of every ridge they would be exposed to the fire of the Confederate riflemen, who by now would have been fully warned. Many men and officers were falling, even before reaching a clearer area. The advance lay checked about ninety yards from the face of the parapet. Paine, seeing that the advance had stalled, but that the first line of skirmishers was holding their positions, came forward from the head of the column of the 38th Massachusetts,[1455] and "as loudly as I possibly could" gave the order to advance "at the first word of which the men sprang forward." Kimball, of the 53rd Massachusetts, repeated the order. Soon, General Paine fell, "... struck, soon after daylight, by a rifle ball... about fifty yards from the enemy's works..."

The statement is significant, since it give us the time – 5:15 – soon after which Paine's assault faltered. It is also significant, in that it confirms the Confederate use of their "long taw," their Enfield rifles, picked from the field after the assault of May 27th. The significant numbers of these long range weapons now in the hands of the defenders no doubt contributed heavily to the high number of casualties in Paine's lead regiments, and was likely an unexpected surprise.

There was a pause in the action in the absence of Paine's commands, and the men simply sought cover. The hand grenades were a failure, many failing to explode when striking the soft earth of the Confederate entrenchments. They were then hurled back at the attackers. Company K of the 4th Massachusetts suffered three officers killed and nine enlisted men wounded, all on a date in time when many of them had reckoned their nine months service was up.[1456]

1455. Stanyan, p. 260–262; Powers, pp. 107–110; Willis, pp. 137–138. *Massachusetts Soldiers, Sailors and Marines in the Civil War*, vol. 4, Norwood, MA, 1932, pp. 1, 620; dmna.ny.gov, *133rd Regiment, Letters, Diary of a Williamsburgh Soldier–The Entrenchments*; Irwin, p. 196–197; Defenders, SHS, vol. 14, p. 328; McMorries, p. 66.

1456. *Massachusetts Soldiers and Sailors*, vol. 1, p. 228. Its companies had been mustered in at various dates in September, varying from the 1st to the 26th. Co. B, was the only one mustered in on the 1st, and both A and K, who were so cut up in the assault, were dated from the 23rd. Quite precisely then, only Company B had a complaint on the 14th of June. The government, i.e., Banks, now pushed their enlistment date as far forward as possible, reckoning that their time was from when their *field and staff officers* were mustered, and that was December 16th, 1862. Compiled records, M594, roll 77. They all were mustered out on August 28th, 1863, having been shipped out of Port Hudson on August 4th. Prior, a handful of the men had refused to do further service. They were arrested and threatened with doing time at Ship Island, but were instead dishonorably discharged.

A few of the 8th New Hampshire and the 4th Wisconsin men had crossed the ditch, which in places was only two feet deep, reached the parapet, went over, and were either immediately shot down or captured, but many lay dead in the ditch. From the "Defenders" article in the *Southern Historical Society Papers*: "The smoke was so thick that nothing could be seen more than twenty steps in advance, and before our troops were aware of it the enemy were pouring into the ditch and scaling our breastworks[1457]...The ground in front of our works was blue with their uniforms..." The skirmish line was decimated; the 4th Wisconsin suffering 140 killed and wounded, or 63 percent, and as it turned out, the most of any regiment that day. The 8th New Hampshire was next, suffering 122 killed and wounded out of 217 present, or 56 percent; a dreadful repeat of May 27th when they lost 124. No regiment lost more at Port Hudson. The 38th Massachusetts had 90 men lying on the field either dead or dying. Next in line had come the 53rd Massachusetts, which now had 86 killed or wounded. The only advantage that accrued from their cotton bags was that the 31st Massachusetts had managed to make a breastwork of sorts at the site of their most advanced position, which they were able to hold, losing only 30 men.

The 133rd New York and the 173rd New York were mixed in with the advanced regiments when Paine fell. Maj. A. Power Galloway of the 173rd having been killed, the troops were rallied by L. D. H. Currie of the 133rd, and then had made a gallant charge. This last attempt to retrieve the situation failed, and left Currie and 58 others of the 133rd wounded, with 9 killed. Of the 173rd, there were 16 killed and an unknown number wounded.[1458] Paine's assault had failed.

1457. Defenders, SHS, vol. 14, p. 328; Powers, p. 108; Willis, p. 138, Stanyan, p. 260. The 173rd New York is the only unit not specifically mentioned in any records of the assault which have been found. One letter home (see *http:// dmna.ny.gov*) refers to: "The 173rd Regiment being in front..." gives evidence that it was with, and remained with, the 133rd. As to specifics regarding Currie's rally, it is only referred to in *The Story of the 38th Massachusetts Regiment*, Powers, p. 108. That the 133rd was in "the thick of it," is proven by a reference in Stanyan's *History of the 8th New Hampshire Regiment*, p. 260, which is from Halbert Paine's diary, and describes when he was hit: "[W]as struck, soon after daylight by a rifle ball, and fell in the midst of many dead and wounded about fifty yards from the enemy's works...Slight ridges of the field which had formerly been cultivated, protected me from the fire of the enemy, which broke out with great fury, as often as the intolerable heat compelled me to move." It was a deep bone of contention in the Union ranks that the Confederate marksmen continued to shoot at the downed wounded, and the stretcher bearers, many of them black, that attempted to remove them.

1458. See *dmna.ny.gov./173rd Regiment*, Table. The table combines May 27th with June 14th for a total of 67 wounded; Croffut and Morris, p. 412. See also Peck, Lewis, p. 1.

Weitzel's Assault

The 75th New York, which was to head the column,[1459] was quietly called to arms at 11:00 on the night of the 13th. After 60 rounds of ammunition had been issued to each man, and a breakfast of coffee and hardtack, they were on their way at midnight. They and the other of Weitzel's regiments in the attack would have to quietly withdraw from their positions along the ridge of the ravine north of the Sandy, skirt Fort Desperate, and then move south to be in position for the attack. They stumbled in darkness; the new moon would not emerge until June 16th.[1460] On this rough, circuitous route through brush and woodland, it took the 75th three hours to get to their rendezvous, the entrance to the sap near Battery 9 (figure 4).

The 12th Connecticut was supposed to join them at the head of the skirmisher column, which was under the command of Col. Babcock of the 75th. Emerging from the sap, the 75th was to deploy to the right of the north of the angle of the Priest Cap, and the 12th to the left. The 91st New York, and 100 men of the 28th Connecticut were to follow with hand grenades, and the 24th Connecticut with cotton bags, to make a crossing of the ditch for the storming party. The rest of the brigade was to follow, the 8th Vermont, the 114th New York, and the 160th New York, all under the command of Colonel Smith of the 114th. The skirmishers and grenadiers, having driven the rebels back from the face of the parapet, would allow the cotton bags to be placed, and then the stormers would be expected to cross, scale the works without pausing to fire or reload, and charge into the works at the point of the bayonet.[1461]

"The batteries of our friends had opened the ball." McLaflin's Indiana battery, (7) had joined in the firing, and it was now 4:00 a.m., exactly one hour before sunrise, the "transparent gray in the atmosphere which was the prelude of dawn, and which obscured objects without concealing them." There was enough light to just see the horizon through the early morning mist that had formed.[1462] There would be only a few minutes before there was enough light for the rebels to aim and fire at the skirmishers who would emerge from the sap—one hundred and fifty yards or so from the ditch and the face of the parapet.

The 12th Connecticut had not arrived,[1463] and after some delay, Colonel Babcock decided against waiting for them. Absent the 12th, there was another considerable delay as the result of having to rearrange the plans for deployment and inform the guides. Finally, the 75th advanced into the sap by double file. About two

---

1459. Hall, H. and J., 75th, pp. 124–125. The 75th eventually headed the column on the right, the 12th Connecticut on the left. O.R. Vol. 26/I, pp. 132–133.
1460. *http://aa.usno.navy.mil/moon phases & sunrise.*
1461. Fitts, James, p. 125.
1462. *aa.usno.navy.mil/*, beginning of nautical twilight for 1863 at Baton Rouge; Pellet, p. 115.
1463. Sprague, p. 148; Fitts, pp. 127–128; Hall, H. and J., *75th History*, p. 125.

hundred yards in length, the sap, "sunken road," or "cut," was only six feet wide and seven feet deep, at its deepest. The skirmishers, the grenadiers, and the bag carriers were expected to crowd through this defile, and deploy at its end with sufficient stealth and speed to accomplish a surprise attack on the entrenched rebels, at least sufficient to drive them away from the face, which would allow three more regiments sufficient time to filter through, mass, and carry the works.

The 12th finally arrived, having been misdirected by its guides, and entered, brushing past[1464] the 91st New York and 28th Connecticut with their grenades, and deployed on the left as originally planned. Everyone then had to wring their hands while the bag carriers struggled through the sap. The 114th New York was just entering the sap when Weitzel's order "Fix Bayonets!" was heard. It was 5:00a.m. – almost an hour after Paine's assault had begun. The delays had ruined the attempt at simultaneity, and the changing light, for 5:00 was sunrise, had ruined the chances for even somewhat of a surprise. Of course, the bombardment would have already awakened the Port Hudson garrison, both literally and figuratively, as we know from Confederate commentary.

The 75th were in, and, the fighting having begun, those near the end of the sap became cautious, slowed, and it became clogged with humanity. "For God's sake, don't stop now; go on and let us get through…We can't, the fighting up front has choked up the road." Finally, the column moved slowly on, though now they had to make way for the stream of dripping wounded, aided or alone, which began to come out, their only safe path to the rear.[1465]

Before the 114th made its way through it was something near 6:00 o'clock, and the ground was strewn with soldiers in blue; dead, dying, and too severely wounded to move. The noise would have prevented any distinction of the fact that on the left, Paine's assault had failed, but the fury of the Confederate fire in front forecast the fate of Weitzel's. The regiments were scattered in "hopeless confusion." Colonel Smith of the 114th was mortally wounded, and one-third of his regiment was disabled. The command now passed to Van Petten of the 160th New York, who ordered a second charge.

The aftermath is described by Capt. James F. Fitts, of Company F of the 114th New York:

> As the troops crowded up from the rear, they were sent forward to join in this bush-fighting; but there was no serious demonstration after the sun was an hour high. The battle was lost and the blood shed before sunrise…

There were some 49 killed or wounded (incomplete report) in the 75th New York, 96 in the 8th Vermont, 84 in the 12th Connecticut, 85 in the 114th New York,

---

1464. O.R. Vol. 26/I, p. 133; Croffut and Morris, p. 412; Hall, H.&J., *75th History*, p. 126.
1465. Pellet, p. 116–119; Fitts, pp. 120, 129–130.

and 59 in the 91st New York.[1466] The assault was stalled.

There was palpable pause.[1467] Sprague, in his history of the 13th Connecticut, illuminates: One of Banks' aides now appeared and informed Weitzel to "force an entrance at once into the rebel works at all hazards." "Yes," replied Weitzel; and then, to a staff officer, "Give my compliments to Colonel Holcomb, and tell him to go in immediately." Weitzel's "cool, yet unsatisfied and discouraged air astonished some of us, who looked for an impetuous charge by the favorite young general." Weitzel may have been discouraged to note that his own troops had failed and that he was now forced to turn to Grover's (Holcomb was temporarily commanding Grover's 1st Brigade.)[1468] Another point could have been that Weitzel simply had concluded that the concept and timing of the assault had not been implemented as planned, and to continue it further would be futile, as was the last charge of the 114th New York.

Nevertheless, in went the 1st Brigade. By now it was 7:00 a.m.:

> [The sap] was obstructed by the dead and wounded, by men carrying stretchers, and by stragglers making their way to the rear. Every available cover behind stumps, logs, or earth, every little depression of the ground that could shelter from the enemy's fire was occupied. Hand grenades were scattered along the path; also muskets, bayonets, cartridge-boxes and belts, gunny-bags filled with cotton, and here and there pools of blood.

Birge's 3rd Brigade, composed of the 13th and 25th Connecticut, the 26th Maine, and the 159th New York, "pressed forward to support Holcomb."[1469] The 26th was either misdirected or uninformed of the sunken road, and charged straight into the ravine to its right and through the rough landscape. Noting the crowded sap, half of the 13th was split off, with five companies plunging forward on its left.

About half of the 3rd arrived in time to hear their old major (Holcomb was chosen from the 13th Connecticut by Butler to recruit the 1st Louisiana at New Orleans in July of 1862) "haranguing" his brigade at the front. The initial rush of the 13th had caused the Confederate firing to slacken, as "a few" of the Confederates were observed to turn and run back from the parapet, which gave a moment's time for Holcomb to roar: "All I ask of you is to follow me! Will you follow me?" "Yes! Yes!" was heard from a handful, the rest remaining silent. The interval also allowed somewhat of a line of battle to be formed by the mixture of the two brigades. Before this could be completed Holcomb, swinging his sword, gave the command, "Forward."

1466. Casualties derived from: Compiled Service Records, 75th NY and 91st NY, M594, roll 125; 12th CT, M597, roll 7; *dmna.ny.gov./History*; Carpenter, p. 124; Pellet, p. 119, *Record of the 114th Regiment*, by H. H. Beecher, pp. 209–210.
1467. Sprague, p. 314; O.R. Vol. 26/I, p. 130.
1468. Compiled Service Record, M594, roll 67, 1st Louisiana; Beecher p. 208.
1469. Sprague, pp. 151–157; Croffut and Morris, p. 413.

The line almost instantly lost any organization. Its center, with Holcomb leading, was exposed to the renewed fire from the parapet and he was shot down at once. It was now 10:00 a.m. None of the commanders present; Burt of the 159th New York, Morgan of the 90th New York, Jerrard of the 22nd Maine, Hubbard of the 26th Maine, or Day of the 131st New York; could agree on a plan, despite the urgings of Banks' staff for more assaults. The words of Col. Day sum up the situation: "It's too damned risky!"

This was clearly "misbehavior before the enemy," the most serious of court martial offenses. However, no such charges are of record – additional assaults, as demanded by Banks' staffers, being regarded as futile and beyond the bounds of common sense. A Confederate view: "Again and again they reformed and charged, but...towards the last of the battle their officers could not get the Federals to leave their own breastworks. They were not cowards, but brave men. They saw no hope of storming our position successfully..." The assault was not renewed.

Though they were in reserve, Battery L was close enough to the firing to have had two horses wounded. They remained in this position until June 20th, firing on "Rebel artillery, camps, storehouses and other shelter."

Augur's Feint

As noted, Augur's troops, reduced to only the 49th Massachusetts, the 21st Maine, the 2nd Louisiana, and the 116th New York, had begun their feigned attack promptly, at about two hours before daybreak.[1470] The 116th crept out from its position in support of Holcomb's battery (14), moved south, and acting with the other regiments, sent half of their companies forward as skirmishers, creeping up through Slaughter's Field as close as possible to the Confederate parapet. They were not met with fire from the Confederate heavy guns, most of them having been disabled by the Union bombardments of the previous days. At the signal, the skirmishers opened up. The reserves were later called in, and they remained on the field for the rest of the day. They were withdrawn at nightfall.

There were light casualties, owing to the absence of Confederate artillery fire, and the fact that no charge upon the works had been made.

Dwight's Assault

Dwight issued his Special Orders No. 32 on June 11th.[1471] Nothing was said about the location of the assault, except that: "The troops will be held in hand, and prepared to move immediately to such point of assault as the Brigadier-General commanding shall designate." The usual details such as bag and fascine carriers

---

1470. Clark, p. 94.
1471. Bacon, pp. 151–157; O.R. Vol. 26/I, p. 549; Hanaburgh, p. 55; Benedict, p. 16.

were outlined, even ordering a detail of pontoniers, and another of engineers, to prepare a way for the entry of the artillery into the works. Two other sections of the orders were first, bizarre, and second, mysterious:

> 5. Colonel Clark will detail fifty picked men of the Sixth Michigan Volunteers… for a sudden attack upon the headquarters of General Gardiner [sic]…
> 6. Colonel Clark will also detail two hundred men of the same regiment, under command of the senior captain,[1472] for an important and decisive movement.

Revealing Dwight's contempt for the nine months units, section 7 ordered that they should lead the advance.

Dwight's troops consisted of his 1st and 3rd brigades, plus two regiments transferred to him on the night of June 13th. His 2nd Brigade had been assigned to the defenses of New Orleans. Col. Thomas S. Clark commanded the 1st Brigade, consisting of his own regiment, the 6th Michigan, plus the 15th New Hampshire, the 26th Connecticut, and the 128th and 165th New York. A temporary 2nd Brigade was commanded by Col. Lewis Benedict, just returned from his assignment with the 110th New York on the west side of the river. This consisted of the 162nd and 175th New York, 28th Maine, and 48th Massachusetts. The reserve consisted of four companies of the 28th Maine, the 177th New York, and the 50th Massachusetts.[1473]

Summoned to Dwight's headquarters, the mysterious details were explained to Col. Edward Bacon, commanding the 6th Michigan. The assault would be two pronged; left, at the river, and right, along the Mt. Pleasant Road. The left would consist of the 50 picked men mentioned, disguised as rebels, and guided by two deserters. Under the cover of darkness, they were to climb into the "citadel," the prominent Confederate fortification at the edge of the river, via steps that had been cut into the clay bank, and known to the deserters. The raiders were to then proceed immediately to General Gardner's headquarters and take him prisoner. The remaining two hundred were to follow, and entering the Citadel, spike the guns. Bacon was to follow with the rest of his regiment, as Dwight had specified "five or six hundred infantry." All of this was to be formalized in later orders.

The right prong was to be the main assault, which would be carried by Clark and Benedict, with the balance of Dwight's regiments approaching along the Mt. Pleasant Road, an extension of which crosses a ravine at a bridge, and enters the fort through a sally port.

As a consequence of the tardy publication and promulgation of Banks' orders, noted earlier, many of the regiments all along the line were not informed of their role until very late. The remote location of Dwight's assault was even worse in this

---

1472. Capt. John Cordon, Michigan Adjutant General's Report, 1863, p. 33.
1473. Compiled Service Records, 28th Maine, M594, roll 71. The remainder of the regiment was at either Donaldsonville or New Orleans; 177th New York, M594 roll 138, *Massachusetts Adjutant General's Report, 1863*, 50th Regiment, p. 440.

respect, though he was given the broad option of moving[1474] "at such time after 3:30 a.m. to-morrow as he may deem most expedient." Thus, either by tardy orders or Dwight's own ineptitude, the assault would go forward in daylight.

For example, the 15th New Hampshire was not directed to begin to move into position until after midnight. The route to their assigned position with Dwight was almost four miles long, running from the woods in the rear of the Slaughter plantation, south to the Mount Pleasant Road. It was a wide circuit, ostensibly for stealth. The latter portion of the route is shown in figure 6.[1475] They made it to the rendezvous near the Mt. Pleasant Road at sunrise, too late, in the minds of the men, for an unseen approach. It didn't matter; Dwight had not yet given his order for the assault. There would be no surprise attack in darkness, as had been anticipated.[1476]

The 6th Michigan, marching toward the rendezvous near the Mt. Pleasant Road, was met by Col. Clark with the late news that the raid on the Citadel was on, and the picked men required must be named. Final orders arrived with an aide who directed the 6th to follow the 14th Maine, which was to follow the picked men, all guided by the two deserters. They headed toward the river, the road curving around Mt. Pleasant their likely path, shown as a dotted line. At the riverbank, they turned right and advanced along the mud and sand until coming within sight of the high bluff, atop which sat the Citadel/Confederate Battery XXXIII. It was now broad daylight, the column had been spotted, and the Confederate alarm had sounded.

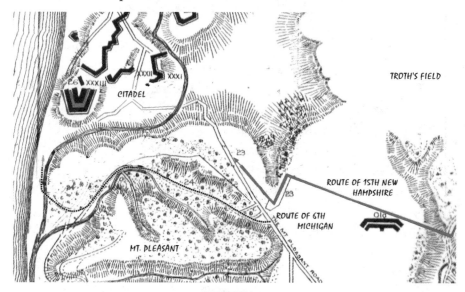

FIGURE 6

1474. O.R. Vol. 26/I, p. 555
1475. Figure 6, a portion of a fold-out map which accompanies the *History of the 15th New Hampshire Regiment*, by McGregor. Batteries shown on the original, which were of later construction, have been removed.
1476. McGregor, p. 473, Bacon, p. 176–177.

Quoting from Bacon:

> Dwight, in broad daylight, and at an hour when he ought to be sober, is about to sacrifice us, to a carry out a scheme devised when he was drunk…
>
> Evidently the rebel officers have been ordering their men to withhold their fire, and are no longer able to enforce complete obedience. First one rifle shot, and the Minie ball comes singing slowly through the air over our heads. Another and another shot. Then a succession of scattering shots. The hiss and whirling, fluttering sounds of some of the bullets are now heard close over our heads, and now right among us. Wounded men are helped back from the front of our column. Sergeant A. Amsden…standing near me, is shot through the thigh, and is borne away. In a few moments more the rebel guns will be raking us, and there will be enough of us killed to make Dwight a great man. Captain Cordon's British common sense gets the better of every other feeling in his soul, and, taking whole responsibility, he says to his detachment, in unmistakable English, "Alt!" and the column never moves again toward the citadel.

As the senior officer, Bacon never countermanded the captain's order.

In the meantime, on the right, the advance of the 1st Brigade was announced by the scattered shots of the sharpshooters of the four companies of the 165th New York. Having learned the hard way on May 27th that wild charges are suicide, they were crawling in on their hands and knees, from stump to stump.[1477] Skirmishers, a detail of 150 men from the 15th New Hampshire and the 26th Connecticut, followed in an attempt to drive in the rebel sharpshooters. The rebels had felt so safe atop their parapet twenty to forty feet above the ravine in front of it, that they had lingered outside their breastworks.[1478]

The 128th New York followed in support, and the remainder of the 15th New Hampshire and the 26th Connecticut followed. They ran up to the edge of the ravine, which had been "entirely unseen and unsuspected until close in its proximity." Flanking left, figure 6, they found the way forward, along the Mt. Pleasant Road, "subjected to the most terrific fire" until "all fell into the ravine where the road makes its steep descent into its dense bottom." The bridge crossing the ravine had long since been destroyed. Now sheltered in the ravine, at least the Confederate fire passed over their heads, though it hit those approaching from behind.

The attack in "disorder,"[1479] Benedict's troops were quickly sent in, led by the 162nd New York. The 175th New York followed, and then came the 48th Massachusetts. The few companies of the 28th Maine present never received the order to

---

1477. *Duryee Zouaves*, 1905, pp. 18–19. The place the Zouaves took is not clearly outlined. They are not even mentioned by Hanaburgh, or McGregor, and the only hint of their being there is in the *History of the 48th Massachusetts Regiment*, p. 43, who define them as the "red clothed fascine bearers." This, at least, puts them up front, as is recorded here.
1478. McGregor, pp. 473–475; Hanaburgh, p. 55; Irwin p. 200.
1479. *Historical Sketch of the 162nd Regiment New York Volunteers*, pp. 16–18.

move, and never participated. The brigade reached the ravine where the 15th New Hampshire had earlier taken cover, and had been ordered by Col. Clark to "desist" from any attempt to storm "the ascent." With the commanding officer of the 175th, Col. Michael K. Bryan, killed, Benedict advanced no further, and ordering his troops to remain under cover, he walked all of the way back to Dwight's headquarters, where he reported "in person…the critical nature of his command." Dwight then ordered that the brigade was to lie where it was "until the darkness of night might favor its withdrawal."

The 177th New York, and the 50th Massachusetts, being in the rear, were never engaged.

It is interesting to note that Grierson had been invited by Dwight to be a part of the assault, and he had met with Dwight to hear the details. A point came in the discussion where Dwight pointed to a map of the Mt. Pleasant Road. Here, Grierson could "charge down this road by twos, at a gallop, and enter the fort." No mention of the destroyed bridge, or what Grierson's horsemen could have done if, in the remotest possibility, they had managed to enter.[1480] Grierson merely left the meeting and was busy elsewhere on the day of the assault, though he had been ordered to detach the 1st Louisiana and Magee's and Perkins' cavalry to Dwight.

One factor that stands out in Dwight's assault is that, having split his force, the numbers at each front were very small. Benedict's brigade only totaled 582 men. The 48th Massachusetts, one of Augur's regiments, had, on June 13th, been ordered to do pick-and-shovel work for General Arnold, the chief of artillery. After marching to Arnold's work site from their bivouac near Plains Store, and working all day, they were ordered the three-and-a-half miles back to Plains Store. Before having the opportunity to cook supper, at 8:45 p.m., orders arrived to report to Dwight. Marching out immediately, it took until the "early morning" of the 14th to rendezvous with Dwight. After all of this running around, the 48th could muster only 175 men fit for the assault.[1481]

Dwight's assault, too feeble or tardy to be of value as a diversion, it nevertheless served one useful purpose; it introduced the generals to the value of Mt. Pleasant as a site for the placing of artillery.[1482] Its northern slope overlooked the

---

1480. Bacon, pp. 156–157. It is easy to dismiss Bacon as a crank, he is so cynical, who clearly despises Dwight. Did he manufacture this story? Evidence that it is true appears in Hanaburgh, p. 55: "The 128th was ordered…to form column and be prepared to follow the cavalry at a double quick." Bacon, and Lt. Col. Porter of the 14th Maine were later arrested by Dwight, Vol. 26/I, pp. 599–600, for "speaking in a discouraging manner of the prospects of this army before Port Hudson, and for habitually using such language as is likely to discourage and dishearten the troops of this division in the event of an assault upon the enemy's works." Apparently "political correctness" was as necessary in the army then as today.

1481. Plummer, pp. 41, 42; Stanyan, p. 274, 358; *dmna,ny.gov*, 114th NY *Clippings*, 114th InfCWN4.pdf, "The Attack and Repulse at Port Hudson," *N.Y. Herald*, p. 40; O. R. Vol. 26/I, p. 554.

1482. Irwin, p. 200.

southern flank of the Confederate defenses, and soon the largest Union battery complex at Port Hudson would be constructed there. Two sections of Battery L among many others, would then occupy it, three hundred yards from the Citadel, on June 25th, and would remain there until the surrender.

June 15th

If ordered, those troops required to be withdrawn from the battlefield did so after dark on the night of the 14th and into the morning of the 15th. As well, at night, the recovery of the dead and wounded could proceed with renewed urgency. Many, many were not able to be removed during the day, as the Confederates had fired on any wounded that moved, and on the stretcher bearers; Halbert Paine's plight being a notable example. He would have to lie on the field for 14 hours, all the day in the blistering sun, witnessing two men killed as they attempted to retrieve him. From his diary:

> Two soldiers, whose names I have not been able to ascertain, attempted to reach me with a stretcher and fell near me. Private Patrick Cohen of the 133rd New York, lying wounded near me, tossed me a canteen cut from the dead body of a soldier. That doubtless saved my life.

It was nightfall before he was carried off. The Confederate sharpshooters continued their firing that night, and many wounded were still on the field by daylight.[1483]

Banks sent a letter to Gardner[1484] requesting him to allow medical supplies to be sent into Port Hudson "for the comfort of my wounded in your hands and of such of your own as you may desire to use them for." Gardner replied in the affirmative, and added details of what was already a disturbing situation: "I take the liberty to inform you (deeming that you are probably ignorant of the fact) that there are a few of your dead and wounded in the vicinity of my breastworks, and I have attempted to give succor to your wounded, but your sharpshooters have prevented it."

Certainly, Banks was preoccupied with other matters, and the stinging defeat of June 14th, added to that of May 27th, would enervate any thinking person. Initially he did not react to Gardner's letter. Instead, General Order No. 49[1485] called for more sacrifice, albeit voluntary. In part, it reads:

> We are at all points upon the threshold of his fortifications. One more advance and they are ours! For the last duty that victory imposes, the commanding general summons the bold men of the corps to the organization

---

1483. Irwin, p. 204; Fitts, pp. 130–131; Stanyan, p. 260.
1484. O.R. Vol. 26/I, p. 557.
1485. Stanyan, p. 270.

of a storming column of one thousand men …

Quoting Irwin: "It was not until the evening of the 16th that Banks could bring himself to ask for a suspension of hostilities for the relief of the suffering and the burial of the dead." Irwin is bending the truth, if evidence from the history of the 8th New Hampshire Volunteers can be counted on:[1486]

> No flag of truce was had until the afternoon of the 17th, and then only in front of our own division. It was raised by the Confederates as they said that the stench was unbearable, and they proposed to deliver our dead and wounded to a certain point.

Beall reported to Gardner on June 17th, that 160 dead and only one wounded man had been delivered.[1487] The one wounded man was Sgt. Charles E. Conant of Company F, 8th New Hampshire, "able to speak, though desperately wounded, who was parched with the dreadful pangs of thirst, and whose face, neck and hands had been completely fly-blown." He survived and was still living in Haverhill, Massachusetts, in 1892, when the *History of the 8th New Hampshire Regiment* was published.

The final tally of the Union casualties for June 14th were: 203 killed, 1,401 wounded, and 201 missing. Undoubtedly the missing were unidentified wounded that had died and were buried in mass graves, though some may have been deserters.[1488]

The total, at 1,805, plus 1,995 for the May 27th assault, is a measure of the price that the attacker had, in that era, to pay for an assault on a fortified position, particularly if poorly executed.

Irwin comments: "The truth is …staff officers …forget that an assault upon an enemy behind entrenchments is not so much a battle as a battue, [the driving of game toward hunters] where one side stands to shoot and the other goes out to be shot…" Comparing Port Hudson with other assaults in history, such as those of Wellington, Irwin notes that: "… the losses of the assailants were in proportion less … than at Port Hudson."

Recruiting for the 1000-man forlorn hope began on June 16th, and went on until June 26th, when 893 officers and men had been accepted, including their leaders, Col. Henry W. Birge of the 13th Connecticut and two staff members.[1489] The stormers were marched to a special encampment where training was to be

---

1486. Stanyan, pp. 265, 283; Irwin, p. 204.
1487. Defenders, SHS, vol. 14, p. 333; Stanyan, pp. 265–267, 271. They had lain there for 60 hours or more. "Fly-blown" means attacked by blowflies and maggot filled; Irwin, p. 203.
1488. Fox, p. 102, Irwin, pp. 207, 208.
1489. O.R. Vol. 26/I, pp. 57–66, lists 976. Banks quotes 850 men (p. 46) several days later. See also Irwin, p. 213. The difference could reflect both sickness and some who dropped out, and the fact that 91 of the 1st and 3rd Native Guards had volunteered, but were not accepted.

conducted, and where special equipment, such as scaling ladders, were to be issued.[1490]

For those who did not volunteer for the storming column, the drudgery of digging more and more trenches, for more and more batteries, was renewed, although aided by ever increasing numbers from the black regiments, both of infantry and engineers, who were being actively organized and equipped. As Henry Closson remembered, "…so far as mechanical ingenuity went, the Pilgrim, as usual, was unsurpassed. He might not be able to fight his way into Port Hudson, but he could dig there…" Saps were extended at three key points.[1491] Two large ones are shown at the top of figure 7, along with lesser trenches connecting the batteries and rifle pits. The third is opposite the Citadel, at the bottom. Refer also to figure 1.

FIGURE 7

From top to bottom, they are: (A) Toward Fort Desperate, from Bainbridge's Battery (8), (B) toward the center of the Priest Cap, from Duryea's Battery (12), with a portion extending along the south side of the parapet, and (C) from Roy's Battery (20), all along the face of Mount Pleasant, which connected to batteries 21, 22, 23, and 24. Rifle pits were also extended at batteries 16 and 18.

Those at (C) were the last constructed, after Dwight's June 14th assault, yet were some of the biggest. From Battery 24, the trench then continued to the riverbank and zigzagged toward the Citadel. It was part of a plan to blow up the Citadel. It was to have been charged with a load of 1,500 pounds of powder. The sap opposite the Priest Cap would also be charged with explosives, which when blown, would ostensibly create an entrance to the fort through which an assaulting column could rush upon a stunned garrison. They had been scheduled to be set off on July 9th.[1492]

1490. Sprague, pp. 163–166; Haskin, p. 365
1491. Irwin, p. 219; Stanyan, p. 287; Figure 7, from McGregor, altered.
1492. Irwin, p. 225. Grant allowed such an operation a year later, at Petersburg. It failed miserably;

On June 20th, one section of Battery L under Sergeant Becker was detached to join the 2nd Rhode Island Cavalry and the 52nd Massachusetts Regiment in escorting a foraging train. The train consisted of some 140 or 150 covered wagons, which intended to gather corn and grain stored on two plantations some fourteen miles east, near Jackson Crossroads.

They were joined a few miles out by another party of 50 wagons escorted by a detachment of 200 cavalry from Grierson's command, also on the lookout for forage. Arriving at the crossroads at about 1:00 p.m. Becker went into battery on elevated ground on the southeast side of the crossing, which commanded a fine view of the plantations on either side of the road.

A Confederate private who had been taken prisoner informed of the presence of Generals Mouton and Hughes with a force of some 2,500 men encamped nearby, the same force that had attacked Grierson near Clinton two weeks before. They lay hidden in the woods and fields. Their attack on the train began within minutes. The panicked teamsters soon became disorganized in an attempt to return to a rear defensive position. As J. F. Moors, of the 52nd Massachusetts describes it:

> Among the many covered wagons in the train, and men and horses about our rendezvous, the Confederate generals had failed to notice the battery. We have only to swing around the muzzles of the guns to get the range, and open fire with shot and shell. This is done promptly, skillfully, and most effectively. The artillerymen do their whole duty, just in the nick of time.

The confederate attack was stunned, and repulsed, allowing a more orderly withdrawal. The train arrived back at Port Hudson late that night, minus some 60 wagons and 200 mules. No one in Battery L was injured, and Sergeant Becker was commended for his coolness in the action.[1493]

Taylor Again

We recollect, from chapter 8, that Kirby Smith had been ordered "to do something" to relieve Pemberton at Vicksburg, and that he had reinforced General Taylor with Walker's Texas division. Taylor first responded by attacking Grant's camps on the west side of the Mississippi, the supply points at Milliken's Bend, on June 7th.[1494] He was driven off by the 29th Iowa and two Black regiments, with the aid of the navy gunboats *Choctaw* and *Lexington*.[1495] Aware of a request from Johnston to

---

as, daresay, this probably would have, as well.
1493. Moors, pp. 193–199, Hosmer, pp. 200–204.
1494. O.R. Vol. 22/II, pp. 854, 856–857, 904; vol. 26/II, pp.41–43; Grant vol. 1, pp. 544–545. Kirby Smith was influenced in his decision by his own need for ordnance, and it now must come from Richmond, his usual supply route from Texas being disrupted by the blockade.
1495. ORN, ser. 1, vol. 25, p. 162.

come to the aid of Port Hudson, Taylor abandoned any further action against Grant, recognizing the "impossibility of approaching *Vicksburg along Drury's point, exposed to Federal gunboats for 7 miles,* from the west bank..." Taylor agreed with Johnston, the problem of Vicksburg was how to withdraw the garrison, not how to reinforce it.[1496]

Taylor's reluctant Vicksburg move gave Banks relief from any real threat until mid-June. By then, Taylor had convinced Smith that an advance on the La Fourche would raise Banks' fear of losing New Orleans, and that he would then reduce or abandon his effort against Port Hudson, possibly allowing Gardner to break out and unite with Johnston.

Thus, Taylor planned a two-pronged attack on Berwick Bay, (A) attacking Brashear City, and (B) coming around to the rear of Brashear City at Bayou Boeuf, some six miles east on the New Orleans–Opelousas Railroad. Positioning the force destined for Bayou Boeuf would involve a cavalry raid. Col. James P. Major's three regiments of cavalry had just arrived at Alexandria from Texas, and to get them to Bayou Boeuf for a planned attack on the morning of June 23rd, would involve moving through a hundred miles of nominally Union controlled territory. Taylor met Major at Morgan's Ferry on the Atchafalaya, east of Washington. They crossed and passed down the Fordoche, to opposite Port Hudson, at Fausse Riviere, (near the Hermitage where Col. Benedict had been in command).[1497]

FIGURE 8

Here, Taylor obtained guides. It would be impossible to sneak through the territory, so Major would conduct a mini "Grierson's Raid" on his way to Bayou Boeuf. Having moved on Waterloo, and made a demonstration on Hermitage, he proceeded down along the Gross Tete, figure 8.[1498] On the 18th, he raided Plaquemine, burning three steamers, two flats, some cotton and taking 87 prisoners.[1499] He then started down the west

---

1496. Taylor, pp. 137–142. Italics added.
1497. O.R. Vol. 26/I, pp. 571, 608.
1498. Figure 8 adapted from plate 156, atlas; O.R. Vol. 26/I, pp. 217–220.
1499. O.R. Vol. 26/I, pp. 216–220. Irwin, p. 214, quotes 23 of the 28th Maine, with 14 of the Provost

bank of the Mississippi, to Bayou Goula, destroying the Federal plantations and recapturing 1,000 of the former slaves working on them. Making a feint at Donaldsonville, but afraid to be detained by attacking Fort Butler, he moved toward Thibodeaux. A force sent forward captured Thibodeaux on the 20th. A stiff fight took place at La Fourche Crossing on June 21st. Remembering his date at Brashear City, Major disengaged on June 22nd and marched east, arriving at Boeuf Station at 4:20 on the morning of June 23rd.

The other half of the attack,[1500] consisting of Gen. Thomas Green's cavalry brigade, and Maj. Sherod Hunter's Texas Cavalry, began their approach on the night of the 22nd. Green dismounted his men, entered an unoccupied Berwick City, and set up his gun batteries on the west side of the bay, facing the Union camp and Fort Buchanan at Brashear, about eight hundred yards across the bay. Forty-eight skiffs and flats had been collected for Hunter's 325 men to use to paddle from the Teche up into Grand Lake, and around behind Brashear City. Leaving on the evening of the 22nd, it took the "mosquito fleet" almost the entire night to quietly paddle the twelve miles around to their destination, reaching the shore at 5:30 a.m.

Green opened artillery fire into the Union encampment at dawn, and though the navy gunboat *Hollyhock* was stationed nearby, it was driven off by Green's guns. During Green's bombardment, Hunter's men approached the rear of Fort Buchanan in the open, upon a point where the low and meager earthworks were unfinished. Observers in the fort mistook the attackers as a part of a group of railroad hands reporting to assist in the defense, and hesitated to open fire. Hunter's men then advanced in a sudden bayonet charge, and without firing a shot entered the campsite. It was all over by 7:30. Seventeen hundred officers and men, 11 heavy guns, and all of the Union supplies were captured. Three men from Battery L, privates George Chase, Joseph Kutschor, and Martin Stanners, who had been left there since the beginning of the Teche Campaign in April, were among the prisoners. Chase and Kutschor had been in hospital, and Stanners on detached service.

Fortunately, arrangements were made for parole of the enlisted men, and on the 27th, 1,360 were sent under guard toward Boutte Station, where they were received into the Union lines on July 3rd. The officers were held as prisoners, and were obliged to march from Brashear City to Alexandria, then to Shreveport, and finally to Camp Groce, in Texas.[1501]

Kutschor and Stanners returned to Battery L, and went back into the lineup. There is no evidence that the terms of their parole were honored, in the sense that paroled men were prohibited from combat.

As we shall see, the parole system eventually fell apart, and Sgt. Michael White,

---

Guard escaping.
1500. O.R. Vol. 26/I, pp. 215, 223–225; ORN, vol. 20, pp. 310–311, 313, 316, 320; Duganne, pp. 112–113; Noel, *Campaign*, pp. 53–55.
1501. O.R. Ser. 2, vol. 7, pp. 493–494; Duganne, pp. 182, 185–190, 203, 251.

captured at the 1864 battle at Pleasant Hill, though gravely wounded, would be marched off to Texas. Chase did not return, and his fate remains a mystery. He is entered on every subsequent muster roll as "sick as Brashear City since April 22, 1863," until April, 1865, when he is dropped. No further record.

It is ironic that on June 21st Bank's AAG, Irwin, had sent an order to Emory, (now in command of the Defenses of New Orleans) to be forwarded to the Commander at Brashear, Lt. Col. Albert Stickney. It read, in part:

> The commanding general does not regard it as important that we should run any great risk to save Brashear. He desires that you will send orders to Brashear to get off everything of value there, and at Bayou Boeuf, including, especially, the guns, and, when pressed by the enemy, to retire on board the transports and proceed to New Orleans.

Emory's message forwarding the information was not sent out until the 23rd, and by the steamer *Crescent*, rather than by telegraph, though a message was clicking in when one of Taylor's men destroyed the machine.[1502] Needless to say, the *Crescent* arrived too late.

Taylor estimated the value of what he had captured, and what should have been saved, at $2,000,000. As to Green, he followed those of the Union garrison who tried to escape east on the railroad. Blocked at Bayou Boeuf by Hunter, 275[1503] more surrendered, along with "four guns, ammunition, small arms, commissary and quartermaster's stores; and about 3,000 negroes." Green promptly moved on to Donaldsonville and attacked Fort Butler, figure 9, located on the Mississippi River at the mouth of the La Fourche,[1504] at 1:30 on the morning of June 28th.

Fort Butler was under the command of Maj. Joseph D. Bullen of the 28th Maine. Its defending garrison consisted of only companies F, G, and a part of H, of the 28th Maine, and 13 men of the 53rd Massachusetts. There were 150 convalescents from other regiments, "only about 130" of whom were fit enough to load and fire a musket.[1505] The remainder of Bullen's men were either at stations in the New Orleans defenses, e.g., Plaquemine, or had been called to Port Hudson to be a part of Dwight's June 14th assault.

A telegram from Bullen received at Emory's headquarters at 8:00 on the morning of June 28th only hinted at the story of a rare and heroic defense, and this from a nine months' unit. "The enemy have attacked us and we have repulsed

---

1502. Taylor, p. 142.
1503. O.R. Vol. 26/I, pp. 216, 219. Depending of which report is quoted, either 275 or 435 surrendered.
1504. Figure 9, Fort Butler, National Archives, Map Room, Drawer 133, Sheet 62, dated Nov. 25, 1863.
1505. Various sources, all listed in the following footnotes, list 180, 200, or 225 men in the fort. Taylor, p. 147, destroys his credibility by saying "…two hundred and twenty-five negroes…"

them. I want more men. I must have more men." Of Green's 1,800 men, only 800 actually assaulted, but they had nearly overwhelmed the defenders.

Fortunately, they were warned; by Green himself. On the 27th Green sent a note to Major Bullen requesting permission to warn the women and children within three miles of the fort to remove, or if Bullen would have them removed.[1506] Bullen had agreed.

According to Green's plan, no assault would be attempted on the land side. The ditch around the fort on that side was twelve feet deep and sixteen feet wide, and faced the open plain, interrupted only by a line of abbatis. Instead, the plan was to approach the fort along the inside of the La Fourche and Mississippi levees.

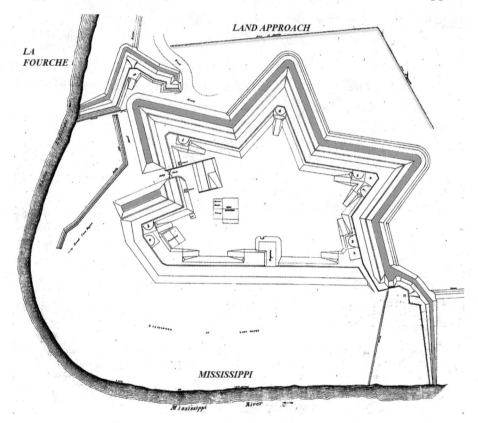

FIGURE 9

Weeds which had grown up along the water's edge, as well as the darkness, would conceal the attackers from both those in the fort, and from the crew of the *Princess Royal*, a navy gunboat stationed in the Mississippi opposite the fort, as they approached the area of the stockade. Hardeman's 4th Texas was to approach along the La Fourche levee, at the left in figure 9, and Shannon with the 5th Texas, along the Mississippi levee, at the bottom in figure 9. They were expected to climb over the stockades, or skirt them at the water's edge. The success of Shannon would

---

1506. O.R. Vol. 26/I, p. 202.

signal a general assault by the remainder of Green's force, Phillips' 3rd Arizona Cavalry, Lane's Partisan Rangers, and Herbert's 7th Texas Cavalry, at the landward side, where they were to "envelope the works, moving up around them to the brink of the ditch, shooting down the cannoneers…on the ramparts at a distance of only 16 or 18 feet."

Contrary to plan, Phillips' 3rd Arizona followed Shannon around to the north, and when their firing was heard, the general advance began. After stumbling in the darkness, and having been discovered by the *Princess Royal*, which opened fire, Shannon's men broke through, or went over and around the stockade. Here, they thought they were inside the fort, but, as reported by Green, they came upon another ditch. In Green's words: "Making their entrance with little or no loss…there was yet a ditch to cross, running in front of and parallel with the river, and no means whatever on hand to cross it." It had not been disclosed to him by his spies.

The attack was stopped here, whereupon desperate hand-to-hand fighting began. With no time to reload, the defenders used their bayonets. The *Princess Royal*, which was joined at about 4:00 a.m. by the *Winona*, were able to hold off Green's storming party for three-and-a-half hours, until the fire of the enemy ceased, at early dawn.[1507] It is clear that fire from the navy gunboats maneuvering offshore measurably aided the defenders, though Green ignores them, blaming his failure on the ditch, and on his spies for giving him "false" information.[1508] The ditch's existence is in question, as none is shown on the original drawing. However, there was a parapet, which is shown, and it fits the description of running parallel with the river. It would have been a considerable barrier, and those trying to scale it would have been exposed to fire from the gunboats, whereas, a ditch would have given the attackers a place to hide.

It is surmised that Green expected to find nothing more than a continuation of the levee behind the stockade. It is also noted that the stockade protected the two entrances to the fort, the road to the sally port on the La Fourche side and another on the north flank at the levee.

Bullen's report stresses the attempts on the entrances, and does not mention a ditch. He first suffered from flank fire from the opposite bank of the La Fourche, which was "driven back in disorder." From Bullen:

> Almost simultaneously with the attack on our left, the enemy made a vigorous assault in front of both entrances of the fort with a large force. On the left they were bravely repulsed…the right entrance…was compelled to withdraw to the inner works…

1507. ORN, ser. 1, vol. 20, p. 357, The log of the *Winona* has its arrival as 4:30. Sunrise was at 5:05, U.S. Naval Observatory data for Donaldsonville, LA, 1863.

1508. O.R. Vol. 26/I, p. 228. Irwin mentions the stockade, p. 244. If it was built in typical fashion (see *A Treatise on Field Fortification*, D. H. Mahan, p. 60, figures 40–41) it would have a ditch behind it.

Green reported that Hardeman's 4th Texas was delayed, and did not attack until near daylight, when it likely took fire from the *Winona*. When opposite the mouth of the La Fourche, it had shelled down the bayou road, which was Hardeman's approach, "causing fearful havoc among the enemy." Lane's regiment waited for a guide that never appeared, and never entered the fight.

Dawn arriving, the frontal attack ceased and those who had entered the front ditch were taken prisoner, even though Bullen reported that "a majority escaped." The casualties in Green's 1st Cavalry Brigade (the 4th and 5th Texas) and Major's 2nd Cavalry Brigade (Phillips, Stone and Lane) are listed in figure 10.[1509] The commander of the 3rd Arizona, Phillips, was among those killed. Figure 10 is a reminder of how small Confederate cavalry regiments were, roughly 135 men each, if their reported total, 800, is correct.

Report of Casualties in the First and Second Cavalry Brigades.

Command	Killed.	Wounded.	Missing.	Aggregate.
4th Texas Cavalry	2	23	3	28
5th Texas Cavalry	12	38	49	99
7th Texas Cavalry	6	35	34	75
Phillips' regiment	19	18	21	58
Stone's regiment	1			1
Lane's regiment				
Total	40	114	107	261

THOMAS GREEN,
Brigadier-General, Commanding.

FIGURE 10

For comparison, the 28th Maine reported 56 of the enemy killed and 130 prisoners, though they could not have accurately known of the enemy wounded. Their own casualties were reported as 8 killed and 14 wounded, with one of the crew of the *Princess Royal* killed, and two wounded. The disparity between the attacker and the defender illustrated here is seen to be similar to that at Port Hudson. The defender has the advantage. Technology would change all that toward the end of the war, when the attacker, the Union, was given the repeating rifle, and the Confederates, now forced into being the defenders, still had muzzle loaders.

Despite the threat and the heroic performance, Emory, in a 9:00 a.m. telegram to Irwin, was reluctant to send any troops to Bullen.

1509. O.R. Vol. 26/I, pp. 49–50, 202–203, 227-230, figure 10 (p. 230); Willis, p.181–183; Taylor, pp. 144–145; Compiled Service Records, M594, roll 71, pp. 1371–1480; Haskin, p. 193; ORN, ser. 1, vol. 20, pp. 325–327, 354. The prisoners were taken on board the *Princess Royal*, the *Kineo* and the *Winona*. The navy counted 124. Irwin, p. 243, notes that Green had a total force of 1,811, the difference being 800 who actually assaulted and the remainder who supported.

Emory's worries were growing, as another part of Richard Taylor's command had advanced along the railroad as far as Des Allemands station, a little more than twenty miles west of New Orleans.[1510] However, Banks' fast response filled the gap, by ordering Gen. Charles P. Stone, newly arrived in the department, and soon to be named as Banks' chief of staff, with the "First Louisiana and two sections of artillery to Donaldsonville." The "two sections of artillery" was a detachment of four guns and 24 men from Battery L, under the command of Lt. Franck Taylor. Though scheduled to arrive at midnight, they finally arrived at dawn on June 29th. Later, the six companies of the 28th Maine previously assigned to Dwight were also sent down.

Immediately upon arrival, the reinforcements were deployed on a line just outside of the town, where they met a remnant of Green's men who had lingered, allegedly to recover their wounded, under a flag of truce. The truce was refused by Bullen, viewed as a ruse to save uninjured men who were still sheltered in the ditch near the fort. In an engagement of about an hour-and-a-half that followed, Green's men were driven off, with no losses to Battery L. That evening, Lieutenant Taylor and two of Battery L's guns returned to Port Hudson, to rejoin the battery at its new position on Mount Pleasant. Sergeant Becker and the detachment of 23 men listed in chapter 9 remained at Fort Butler until after the surrender of Port Hudson.

The Last Days

On June 25th, Battery L, and two of the 9-inch navy Dalgrens that had occupied Battery 10, were moved into Battery 24 at Mount Pleasant. The position would quickly accommodate six other artillery companies, or portions thereof, with a total of 17 guns, see table 1. A representation of it, "The Great River Battery" that appeared in a July *Harper's Weekly*, is shown in figure 11.[1511] The cotton bale construction is clearly visible, as is the Confederate Citadel, in the left background, only a little more than three hundred yards away, but separated by a deep ravine.

On June 26th, 1st Sgt. Lewis Keller's feat of shooting away the Confederate flag three times was noted with satisfaction ("but it was raised no more") by the men of the 15th New Hampshire, who were in the rifle pits in front of Battery 23 (see figure 1). On June 27th, while shelling the Confederate works across the ravine, Battery L's Pvt. John Casey was mortally wounded by a sharpshooter.

1510. O.R. Vol. 26/I, pp.46–47, 141, 216, 621, 630; ORN, ser. 1, vol. 20, pp. 258, 330. Bullen was murdered by a drunken member of the 1st Louisiana on July 6th.
1511. Figure 11, *Harper's Weekly*, July 25th, 1863, p. 476; *Massachusetts Soldiers, Sailors and Marines, 13th Artillery*, vol. 5, pp. 507, 519; *Record of the Massachusetts Volunteers* 1861–1865, Adjutant-General, vol. 1, 1868, pp. 453–458; McGregor, p. 512.

FIGURE 11

Portions of the 13th Massachusetts Volunteer Light Artillery and their ten-inch mortars had been assigned to both Battery 3, apparently in addition to the 4th Massachusetts, as is listed in table 1, at the extreme north end of the line, adjacent to the location of the attack of the Native Guards, as well as to batteries 23 and 24, near Battery L. One of their junior officers was Lt. Charles B. Slack. Their close association with Battery L evidently convinced Henry Closson that Slack, a volunteer, could fill Battery L's current need for another section officer. Slack was transferred to Battery L on July 9th.

Evidence of Slack's close association with Battery L is in signal communications found in the Official Records.[1512] In one, Lt. Bradley of the 2nd U.S Artillery, Battery C, originally at position 21, had been set up on the west shore of the river opposite the Citadel, along with some heavy Parrott rifles. A signal from Bradley to Slack: "Please ask Captain Closson to send me to-day twenty boxes of spherical case and twenty boxes shells."

Additional signals evidently related to the firing of the 10-inch mortars of the 13th Massachusetts battery, from their position on Mt. Pleasant, get comical, revealing an 1863 attempt at artillery spotting which was something less than satisfactory. The Dana here is Lt. John W. Dana, acting signal officer, stationed at Mount Pleasant, "talking" to a lookout in a barn on the opposite shore. The interchange begins on the 28th of June, with: "Can you get over [to] the Point at 11 a.m.?" DANA Sent. "On what part of it?" Received. "Little this side, to find a lookout to direct the fire of our batteries." Sent. "I'll go, but 'tis a fool's errand."

1512. O.R. Vol. 26/I, pp. 96–98.

Next day the fire spotting began:

OPPOSITE FORT HUDSON,
June 29—8 a.m.

Wait a moment. Am awaiting orders.
Sent: From whom?   DANA.
Received: General Dwight. Move a little to the left. How shall the mortars fire to hit the gun on wheels behind the citadel? How many yards to it?
Sent: Three hundred and fifty. The gun is not there.
Received: Where is it?
Sent: Fire 800 yards on the verge of the bank. No; 600 yards.
Received: Is it a rifled gun – about a 62 pounder?
Sent: Yes.
Received: Six hundred yards from here?
Sent: Yes.
Received: Watch a shot fired at it from the mortar. How was that?
Sent: Try it at 500 yards. Neither shell exploded. Fire little to left.
Sent: Splendid range. Fire 100 yards short of last shot.
Sent: That did not explode. Could not see where it fell.
Received: Will try it again; keep watch.
Sent: That fell 100 yards short. Range good.
Received: Did you see that?
Sent: No, did not explode. Can only see shells when they burst.
Received: Will cease firing for the present. Can you see the rebs in the citadel?
Sent: Not in the citadel, but scores of them this side of it.
Received: Direct fire at them.
Sent: All right.

Orders have come to cease firing until further orders. Is it best to remain? The captain commanding the battery will not profit by our instructions. Must see someone in higher authority.

DANA

Today, mortars are still notably inaccurate, being near impossible to aim, as was the case back in 1863. There had been reports of poor quality Confederate powder, but the narrative of three Union shells in a row that didn't explode is not much to celebrate. Of course, the artillerymen were not receptive to having outsiders, that is, the signal corps, directing their fire. They were the experts. The final exchange of signals for the day reveals the insular attitude:

Sent: Will they permit you to direct the fire of one of the Parrotts?
Received: They only bear on the citadel, and all firing has ceased. Shall we go home?
Sent: If you can do nothing with those important artillerists, we will vamose.

Received: I can do nothing. Will send you word if you are to come home. Cease signaling.

Banks wrote a summary of recent events to Halleck on June 29th. Though the enemy now had pushed Emory's forces all the way back to Algiers, Banks calmly related that: "The fall of Port Hudson will enable us to settle that affair very easily[1513]…A few more days must decide the fate of this place."

On July 3rd Emory wrote to Banks that the situation was so dire at New Orleans that he must have reinforcements "immediately and at any cost." Banks advised Emory that he could not send him reinforcements, and in a calm rebuke, said: "I do not think…that the city is in peril." Next day, another message from Emory estimated that the forces threatening New Orleans were 13,000. Emory was correct, only this intelligence was the sum of all of Taylor's forces. Emory's source had failed to mention that, to Taylor's anger and chagrin, Kirby Smith had retained J. G. Walker's division outside of the New Orleans vicinity,[1514] with the result that Taylor had only 4,000 to bring against the New Orleans defenses.

On July 5th, Col. Kilby Smith arrived from Grant's headquarters to give Banks a personal update on events at Vicksburg. The siege there was still grinding on, and Smith noted that he was "particularly struck" by how similar the siege efforts at Port Hudson were to those at Vicksburg. The mysterious inactivity of Johnston and his inability to deter Grant was also a point of discussion.

Confederate Secretary of War Seddon was likewise interested.[1515] On June 21st, he had telegraphed to Johnston:

> There is an almost imperative necessity for action. The eyes and hopes of the Confederacy are upon you. I rely upon you for all possible efforts to save Vicksburg. I can scarce dare to suggest, but might it not be possible to strike Banks first and unite the garrison of Port Hudson with you.

We know of Johnston's long held and forceful opinion that both Port Hudson and Vicksburg should have been abandoned to save the army. Here, he replies that to attack Port Hudson would mean abandoning Jackson, Mississippi, "…by which we lose Mississippi." Johnston had reoccupied Jackson after the battle of May 14th; Grant having moved on to the siege of Vicksburg. Now, after it had fallen, Grant ordered W. T. Sherman to again attack Jackson, and on the 11th of July, Union shelling of the town began. On the morning of July 17th, Sherman's mini-siege ended when it was discovered that Johnston had evacuated during the night.[1516]

1513. O.R. Vol. 26/I, p. 47–53.
1514. O.R. Vol. 26/II, pp. 42, 110–111; Taylor, p. 139. Kirby Smith felt that even if Taylor captured New Orleans, he could not hold it. Taylor had the same doubt as well.
1515. Stanyan, pp. 287–288, 290.
1516. Grant, vol. 1, p. 576; O.R. Vol. 24/I, p. 199.

On July 6th Banks again wrote to Halleck: "The siege has been progressing rather slowly, indeed, but with all the rapidity attainable under the circumstances. Our approaches are pushed up to the ditch at the citadel on our left, and in front of the right priest-cap, where the assault of the 14th was made." That sap was within ten feet of the parapet on July 4th when the Confederates exploded a mine which collapsed it. Mines and counter-mines were being prepared in every approach.

Now, the storming column commanded by Birge was fully organized and ready, on 15 minutes' notice.[1517]

Finally

On the morning of July 7th, the gunboat *General Price* reached Port Hudson with a dispatch from General Grant. It conveyed the news that Vicksburg had surrendered on July 4th, with 27,000 prisoners.

A note was prepared, wrapped around a "clod" of clay, and flung into the Confederate works. It said, "Vicksburg surrendered on the 4th of July." At first, it was regarded as "a damned Yankee lie," but when Gardner saw it, he sent a message asking for Banks' "official assurance" that it was true. By this time, the whole line along the Union side of the front had begun celebrating.

From the History of the 15th New Hampshire:[1518]

> [A]t exactly high noon, by order, rousing cheers were given amid a general discharge of small arms and a grand salute fired by all our fleets and batteries, pouring a terrific iron hail upon the devoted foe within. These were the last shots fired upon Port Hudson.

Gardner, now convinced that the surrender at Vicksburg was true, agreed to an unconditional surrender, with Port Hudson to be occupied by the U.S. Army at 7:00 a.m. on the 9th of July.[1519]

The original time specified for the occupation was 5:00 p.m. on July 8th, but was postponed. This may have seemed innocent enough, but it was a ruse to allow some numbers of the Confederate officers to attempt escape, given the relaxed atmosphere after the cease-fire; a description of which is found in the account of Lt. James Feret, an engineer on Gardner's staff.[1520] As soon as the agreement was signed,

> …the late combatants began to fraternize. Soldiers swarmed from their places of concealment on either side and met each other in the most cordial spirit. Groups of Federal soldiers were escorted round our works and shown

---

1517. Sprague, p. 168; Irwin, p. 226.
1518. Stanyan, p. 554; Tiemann, p. 50, confirms it; McMorries' account, p. 68, says that the note was tied to a hand grenade. How could two sources vary to this degree?
1519. O.R. Vol. 26/I, pp. 52, 54, 625; Hanaburgh, p. 71.
1520. Stanyan, p. 290; Tiemann, p. 50.

the effects of their shots and entertained with such parts of the siege that they could not have learned before. In the same way our men went into the Federal lines and gazed with curiosity upon the work which had been giving them so much trouble, escorted by Federal soldiers who vied with each other in courtesy and a display of magnanimous spirit.

There is ample evidence that a ruse was in operation by one device or another. Confederate Maj. S. L. Knox donned a private's uniform, and by obtaining the parole of a dead man, was able to pass unsuspected through the Federal lines. Simply sneaking out was another obvious option, and it happened to be aided by a heavy thunderstorm that came up that evening. Hence, other officers, as is stated in the *History of the 1st Alabama Regiment*, "after perilous adventure and much suffering from hunger and thirst, effected their escape through the enemy's pickets." There is record of at least two being captured and returned.[1521] The 13th Connecticut intercepted Lt. Col. Lee of the 15th Arkansas, and Captain Hardee of Miles' Legion. They had been two days in the swamps without food.

Capt. C. M. Jackson, Gardner's acting assistant inspector-general, wrote a message addressed to Johnston, dated July 9th, giving the news of the surrender.[1522] This was not a diary entry. It was a report that obviously he intended to deliver. Clearly, either he or a colleague was one of the number who had successfully taken advantage of the ruse. The contents of the first paragraph of his report is of interest:

> Port Hudson surrendered yesterday at 6 a.m. Our provisions were exhausted, and it was impossible for us to cut our way out, on account of the proximity of the enemy's works.

He goes on to note that during the siege there were 200 killed, between 300 and 400 wounded, and 200 died of disease, and at the time of surrender, there were only 2,500 men fit for duty. These casualty numbers are in reasonable agreement with an incomplete surgeon's report, undated, that appears on the same page in the Official Record.

Union records[1523] list the number of Confederate troops surrendered as 5,935 enlisted men, who were paroled and released, and 406 officers, who were held prisoner.

Union casualties for the siege May 23–July 8, were:[1524]

KILLED		WOUNDED		CAPTURED OR MISSING		TOTAL
OFFICERS	ENLISTED	OFFICERS	ENLISTED	OFFICERS	ENLISTED	
45	663	191	3,145	12	307	4,363

A chapter in the parole and release story echoes Irwin's earlier "useless fashion

---

1521. Sprague, p. 171; McMorries, E. Y., p. 69..
1522. O.R. Vol. 26/I, p. 144; Moors, p. 190.
1523. O.R. Vol. 26/I, p. 642.
1524. O.R. Vol. 26/I, p. 70; Fox, p. 545.

of the time" comment, made with regard to the parole of the prisoners taken in the raid toward Clinton. McMorries, in the *History of the 1st Alabama Regiment*, reveals that all of the paroled enlisted men from Port Hudson were subsequently simply declared to be exchanged, the Confederate commissioners of exchange having annulled the exchange cartel. This meant that all of the men, to their disgust, were immediately eligible for military service.[1525]

Regarding exchange, Vicksburg, Port Hudson, and the Battle of Gettysburg (July 1–3) represented a turning point;[1526] the Federal side was now taking more prisoners than the Confederate, quite the reverse of the previous two years. The Confederacy was short of manpower, and it perceived that it would benefit less in a man-for-man exchange, which, in addition, had proven to be slow and bureaucratic. The Confederacy needed men quickly, and so, as seen in this instance, annulled the cartel. The Federal side, having more men, and for the callous lower value they could put on them, no longer had an urgent reason to be interested in the cartel either. Thus, it essentially ceased at this time, though it took until April 14th, 1864, before Grant, who by now had been promoted to lieutenant-general and was the de-facto general-in-chief, rejected it outright.

The officer with the dead man's parole, Knox, would go on to command the reassembled 1st Alabama Regiment, which was to fight at Mobile, and with Johnston's army in Tennessee and the Carolinas, before finally surrendering on April 27th, 1865.

The surrender ceremonies began punctually at 7:00 on the morning of July 9th, figure 12.[1527] They were simple and short. The Confederate troops, "looking ragged and rough," were drawn up in line, their left on the village, facing Banks' chief of staff, General Andrews, who accepted the surrender. The soldiers were ordered to ground arms. Gardner presented his sword to Andrews with the words: "Having thoroughly defended this position as long as I deemed it necessary, I now surrender to you my sword, and with it this post and its garrison." Andrews returned the sword "as a proper compliment to the gallant commander of such gallant troops—conduct that, would be heroic in another cause." To this, Gardner replied with a sour: "This is neither the time nor the place to discuss the cause." The Stars and Bars was lowered from the flagstaff on the bluff, and Old Glory was raised. Duryea's battery fired a salute, and the ceremonies were over.

As far as Banks was concerned, there was not a moment to lose before going after Taylor. As Irwin puts it: "The last echo of the salute to the colors had hardly died away when Weitzel, at the head of the First Division, marched off…and began embarking on board the transports…"[1528]

1525. McMorries, pp. 69–71, 94; Irwin, p. 233; CWSAC PA 002.
1526. Ould, Judge Robert, pp. 34, 44; Duganne, pp. 249–250, 255; Butler, B. F., p. 1043.
1527. Figure 12, *Harper's Weekly*, cover, Aug. 8th, 1863; Irwin, pp. 232; Sprague, p. 171; Stanyan, 293.
1528. Irwin, p. 233; O.R. Vol. 26/I, pp. 626–627.

FIGURE 12

This brief hour of relief was marred by confirmation of the rumor that the bodies of the 1st and 3rd Native Guards had lain on the field since the May 27th assault. Among them, the body of the captain of Company E of the 1st Native Guards, Andre Cailloux, was able to be identified, and it was brought to New Orleans for burial. The arrival of the body brought out an emotional reaction from the many Black civic societies of the city, Cailloux having been a member of the "Friends of the Order." A grand funeral and procession was organized in his honor.[1529] Figure 13 depicts the procession to the St. Louis Cemetery.

Banks' chief of staff, Andrews, was named to the command at Port Hudson, and the 6th, 7th, 8th, 9th, and 10th regiments of the Corps d'Afrique, under Ulmann, were to compose the garrison, along with some nine-months men whose terms were nearly up. After the arguments and threats of mutiny by the 4th and the 50th Massachusetts regiments over their expiration-of-service dates, they, and all of the other nine-months units had agreed to the later time of muster interpreted by Banks. This could have made a difference if Port Hudson had not surrendered as promptly, but now it mattered little. Nine were detached from their divisions and assigned to Andrews. There they would remain close to available transportation homeward.

The final act of significance to Port Hudson history was Banks' July 11th order to General Andrews: "The demolition of all the batteries and works of approach constructed by the United States forces for the recent reduction of Port Hudson

---

1529. Wilson, J. T., pp. 214, 217; *Harper's Weekly*, August 22nd, 1863, pp. 549, 551; O.R. Vol. 26/I, p. 632.

will be commenced without delay…"[1530]

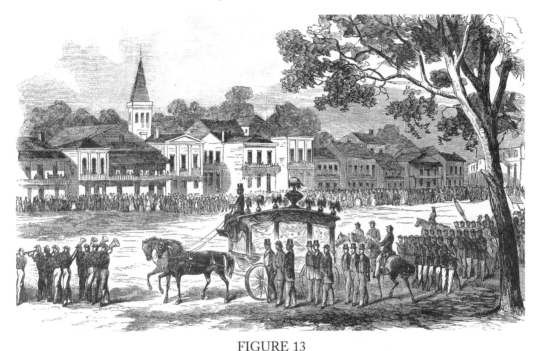

FIGURE 13

Funeral procession for Andre Cailloux at New Orleans, July 29th, 1863

Battery L saw the last of Port Hudson on July 11th, but rather than be transported directly to Donaldsonville with Grover, L was one of six other batteries under Chief of Artillery Arnold that marched. Escorted by the 3rd brigade, 3rd division, they endured the twenty-five miles of mud—it had rained since noon—to Baton Rouge. Here, Sergeant Becker's detachment from Donaldsonville joined them. It was July 15th before the combined company returned to Donaldsonville, thus missing the Battle of Kock's Plantation, which took place there on the 13th.

The three days at Baton Rouge were spent resting and leisurely walking about, in what had become one vast camp "with military garb displayed on every hand."[1531] At Donaldsonville, they remained until the end of the month, then marched to Camp Kearney at Carrolton, and finally to the Apollo Stables in New Orleans. Here they remained until September 15th, after Taylor's forces had been chased out of the La Fourche, and Banks had been given orders from Washington as to what his priorities should be.

1530. O.R. Vol. 26/I, p. 633.
1531. Hanaburgh, pp. 81–82. Likely, all of the river transport available was taken by Weitzel and Grover. Imagine the space seven artillery batteries would occupy. Six guns on limbers, a forge, ammunition wagons, some 80 horses for each—over 90 wheeled vehicles—pulled by nearly 600 horses, if those ridden by the officers is included. O.R. Vol. 26/I p. 660; Whitcomb, p. 53.

The Mississippi was now open, but not altogether due to the fall of either Vicksburg or Port Hudson. Included in the package was the defeat of the Confederate forces under Holmes in Arkansas. In an attempt to re-take Helena, Holmes attacked on July 4th, and was soundly defeated by the Union defenders under Prentiss, and only then was the Confederate threat permanently removed. The combination of the three actually opened the Mississippi, although the action at Helena consumed only one day.[1532] As a symbol of the achievement, the steamboat *Imperial* arrived at New Orleans on July 16th. She had left St. Louis on the 8th and had passed over the whole course without having a shot fired at her. At last, "The Father of Waters" would again go un-vexed to the sea.

Recovery of the La Fourche

Taylor's running rampant in the La Fourche would soon be ended, though for a very brief period he could claim of "brilliant success."[1533] The high-water mark, as it was, involved his bringing up artillery to fire on river traffic below Donaldsonville. On July 3rd, the *Iberville*, a transport, was fired on and disabled. On July 7th, the *New London* and the *Monongahela* had come under fire, and its commander mortally wounded. By July 9th, four batteries had been cut into the levee at Gaudet's Plantation, opposite Whitehall Point, twelve miles below Donaldsonville, as can be seen in figure 14.[1534]

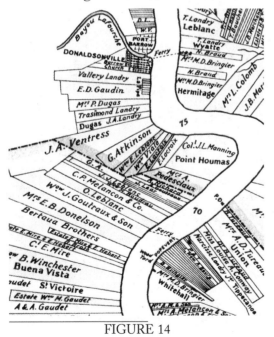

FIGURE 14

For a few days, Taylor's guns had killed and injured some sailors, and caused concern, but if there was a Confederate hope to close the river again, it would never happen. Taylor's artillery consisted of only small field guns. Battery Number 1 had two 3-inch rifled Parrots. Those to the south consisted of a battery of two 6-pounder bronze smoothbores, the next had two 12-pounder howitzers, and the last, one 12-pounder field gun.[1535] The Federal ironclads would be impervious to any of this, and would eventually have put them all out of action. That

1532.   Nicolay and Hay, vol. 7, pp. 323, 327; O.R. Vol. 24/III, p. 492; Selby, p. 12.
1533. O.R. Vol. 26/I, p. 214, 220; ORN, ser. 1, vol. 20, pp. 331, 334–335, 340–341, 363.
1534. Portion of Persac's 1858 Mississippi map.
1535. O.R. Vol. 26/I, pp. 220–222, 230–231, 623.

said, the arrival of Weitzel's troops at Donaldsonville caused Taylor to order these artillery units to abandon their positions on July 10th, in order to support Green and Major. Grover followed Weitzel, all of his troops having arrived by the evening of July 11th.

Green had no idea that Port Hudson had fallen, and thus viewed the Federal force as reinforcements sent there to attack him, and he prepared for battle. Major was posted on the east bank of the La Fourche and Green on the west.[1536]

The purpose, of course, of the arrival of Weitzel and Grover was not only to secure Donaldsonville but to remain in this position, or nearby, and allow the navy time to get gunboats in sufficient force into Berwick Bay. That would close the door of a trap on Taylor. Banks had informed Farragut of the plan, and asked for the light draft gunboats on the very day that Port Hudson surrendered.

After sending pickets out on July 12th, and gaining the opinion that: "The enemy is evidently making preparations to escape if pursued…," Grover began a rather casual advance along the bayou, Dudley on the west bank, and Morgan on the east bank. They were looking for a little more "elbow room" and for forage. In typical Green fashion, it didn't matter what they were up to; they were the enemy, and he attacked. It was a total surprise. Having advanced about six miles, Dudley and Morgan found themselves on the Kock Plantation, typified by a "rank growth of corn, dense thickets of willows, the deep ditches common to all sugar plantations in these lowlands." The hidden enemy jumped on the heads of both columns, and achieving total surprise, caused both to fall back with considerable loss. Morgan's brigade fell back in disorder, which allowed Dudley's flank to become exposed, losing two of the guns of the 6th Massachusetts Battery, before an orderly withdrawal could be effected.

This was an embarrassing, disgusting, defeat, with 2 officers and 54 men killed, 7 officers and 210 men wounded, and 3 officers and 183 men missing, vs. 3 killed and 30 wounded for Green.[1537] Someone was clearly to blame, and it fell upon Morgan, who was charged with disobedience of orders and drunkenness. Banks immediately went to confer with Weitzel and Grover, and it was decided that to try to avenge this "affront" would be unwise, given the wearied condition of the men, the swamps in which they would have to fight, and the overriding consideration of getting the gunboats to Berwick Bay before Taylor.

Farragut started his inquiry as to the light draft gunboats the day after receiving Banks' request, ordering Palmer, the commander of the squadron on the upper

---

1536. O.R. Vol. 26/I, pp. 631–632, 635; Irwin, p. 251; Hanaburgh, p. 82; Noel, *A Campaign*, pp. 59–61.
1537. Irwin, pp. 252–253; O.R. Vol. 26/I, pp. 232, 640. Morgan was eventually tried, found guilty, and ordered to be cashiered, subject to Banks' approval. Banks, ibid., pp. 205–206, did not approve, and after a review, Morgan was restored to duty with the 90th New York Regiment on October 10th, 1863.

Mississippi, to send him the *Estrella*, *Arizona*, and *Sachem*.[1538] Though Farragut had ordered all of them, including the *Clifton* and the *Hollyhock* back to Berwick Bay, the first vessel that was ready, the *Sachem*, did not arrive at Berwick Bay until July 22nd, and it found Brashear City abandoned. As to the army, a detachment of the 12th and 13th Connecticut regiments, under Lt. Col. Frank H. Peck, did not arrive until July 25th.

There were few light draft gunboats available, as was the problem at the beginning of the Teche Campaign, and at this season, the lower water of the Atchafalaya would admit no others. So much had been asked of these few vessels that they were badly in need of overhaul. As a matter of fact, Farragut was concerned about the general condition of his whole squadron, noting that "eleven or twelve" were out of service for repairs.[1539] The *Estrella* reached Berwick Bay on July 23rd, followed by the *Clifton* and the *Hollyhock*.

As might have been expected, General Taylor had news of the trap, and on July 21st evacuated after destroying much of the railroad stock and throwing some of the heavy guns into the bay.[1540] Now, with the ample supplies taken from Brashear City, Taylor moved up the Teche and went into camp.

"Record" 8/63
1 JULY–31 AUGUST, 1863, PORT HUDSON & NEW ORLEANS

The Company remained at Port Hudson, La, until the 11th of July & then proceeded to Baton Rouge, La. arriving at 5 a.m. of the 12th. On the 15th left Baton Rouge and arrived at Donaldsonville, La. Left Donaldsonville. La. on the 29th and proceeded to Carrolton. Arriving on the 1st of August. Left Carrolton on the 9th and took up quarters at the Apollo Stables New Orleans, La. and remained until the present date.

Henry W. Closson	Capt. On furlough since Aug. 9th 1863
Franck E. Taylor	1st Lt. Commanding Battery and Asst. Comm'y of Musters S.O. no. 92 Hdqrts. Dept. of the Gulf 19th Army Corps April 9th 1863.
Edward L. Appleton	1st Lt.
J.A. Sanderson	2nd Lt. Appointed by promotion to Co. vice Gibbs promoted G.O. no. 73 W.D.A.G.O. Washington July 4th 1863 (never joined Co.)
Charles B. Slack	2nd Lt. Joined Co. by assignment S.O. no. 211 Hdqrts. Dept. of the Gulf 19th Army Corps
Detached:	
George Friedman	Pvt. On Det. Svc. at N.O. As artillerist. Left Co. May 24,'62.
Amelius Straub	Pvt. On det. svc. at Baton Rouge as cook in Univ. Hosp. since June 1,'63.
Absent with leave:	
Louis Lighna	Pvt. On furlough left Company August 21st for 14 days.

1538. ORN, ser. 1, vol. 20, pp. 375–376, 379–380; O.R. Vol. 26/I, p. 653.
1539. ORN, ser. 1, vol. 20, p. 378.
1540. Taylor, p. 146.

Absent Without Leave:

William Fudge	Pvt.	Since August 25, 1863
George Harrison	Pvt.	do.
Dennis Moore	Pvt.	
William Mint	Pvt.	
Sholto O'Brien	Pvt.	

Absent in Confinement:

JohnMcKinney	Pvt.	Since August 26, 1863
Hiram Smith	Pvt.	do.
Peter Welsch	Pvt.	

In confinement

John Baker, James Campbell, Patrick Gibbons, John Kelly, James McCarthy, James Mahoney, Frank Morgan, Henry Williams

Deserted:

Michael Breen	Pvt.	At New Orleans	Aug. 27, 1863
William F. Brown	Pvt.	do.	Aug. 19, 1863
James Comfort	Pvt.		Aug. 19, 1863
Patrick Craffy	Pvt.		Aug. 19, 1863
Arthur Flynn	Pvt.		Aug. 19, 1863
Francis Jessop	Pvt.		Aug. 18 1863
George F. Leonard	Pvt.		Aug. 11, 1863
John Lewery	Pvt.		Aug. 10, 1863
John Lowry	Pvt.		Aug. 28, 1863
Christian Meese	Pvt.		Aug. 10, 1863
John H. Moran	Pvt.	Donaldsonville	do.
Michael O'Sullivan	Pvt.	New Orleans	
William Parketton	Pvt.	do.	Aug. 21, 1863
Michael Ranahan	Pvt.	do.	
John Roper	Pvt.	do.	
Henrick Schmidt	Pvt.		Aug. 19, 1863
Morgan L. Shapley	Pvt.		Aug. 21, 1863
Andrew Stoll	Pvt.		Aug. 13, 1863
Owen A. Wren	Pvt.		Aug. 21, 1863
William Wynne	Cpl.		Aug.17, 1863

Discharged:

Edmond Cotterill	Pvt. By reason of reenlistment in the Battery, July 25, 1863
Philip H. Schneider	Pvt. By reason of reenlistment in the battery August 16, 1863

Died:

Bernard Farrell	Pvt. At Baton Rouge, La. July 1863 Cause and date not stated in record with Battery or at Regt'l Hdqrts.
Christopher Foley	Pvt. At Carrollton, La. drowned August 1, 1863
John Murphy	Pvt. do.
John Lanahan	Pvt. At Carrollton, cause and date not known, no record with Battery or at Regt'l Hdqrts.

John Casey	Pvt. From Monthly Return, on June 27th he was "Mortally wounded by Sharpshooters while at his gun." This record notes: Died on July 3, 1863 of wounds received in action at Port Hudson, La.

Joined: July 13, '63 From Detached Svc. at Donaldsonville:

Julius Becker	Sgt.				
William Demarest	Cpl.				
William Wynne	Cpl.				
James Beglan	Pvt.	Miles McDonough	Pvt.	Philip H. Schnieder	
James Comfort	do.	Daniel Moore	do.	Andrew Stoll	
Clark Dickson		Corneilus McEnearney		Michael Tieghe	
Daniel Howard		Christian Meese		Henry Ward	
Benjamin Hughs		John A. Nitschke		Joseph Wilkinson	
John Kelly		Sholto O'Brien		Thomas Wilcox	
John Kastenbader		Ephriam Orcutt			

Strength: 117, Sick: 14

Sick Present: 4 (not recorded) Sick Absent:
William C. Brunskill

Sick at Ft. Hamilton, NY, left Co. Sept. 17, 1861.

Wallace Wright	Sick at Pensacola since December 24, 1862
Charles Mansfield	Sick at Pensacola since December 24, 1862
George Chase	Sick at Brashear City since April 22, 1863
William Crowley	Sick at Baton Rouge, La. since July 13, 1863
Julius Becker	Sick in University Hospital since August 27, 1863
David J. Wicks	do.
William Brooks	Sick at Marine Hospital New Orleans, La. Since August 22, 1863
Henry Champion	Sick at University Hospital since August 27, 1863
John Deering	Sick at Marine Hospital New Orleans since August 28, 1863

The roll gives ample evidence of the battery having endured some rough service, with five deaths, and 14 sick. One man, John Moran, is missing from the list of those joined from service at Donaldsonville, and is listed as a deserter. He did not wait until the company got to New Orleans, but deserted while at Donaldsonville.

Joseph Kutschor was left sick at Brashear City on May 4th, 1863, per the previous muster roll. Though he is not shown as "Joined" in the above list, he appears on the current roll with the remark: "Paroled prisoner of war since June 25, '63." Note that George Chase, also sick at Brashear City, is not listed as a paroled prisoner. His status is unknown. Martin Stanners had been left on detached service at Bayou Boeuf since April 4th, but now is listed as present, without comment. Listed as an exchanged prisoner of war in the next muster roll, he should have been listed here as a paroled prisoner of war, but at least, he, unlike Chase, had managed to return. Both Crowley and Chase will continue to be listed as sick on every roll until April of 1865, when they are dropped. They had been discharged from the service by reason of disability, "date not known."

A sad ending for John Murphy. He had deserted at Fort Duncan in May of 1860 and been apprehended and returned to duty, and had remained in the company without further incident until his drowning. Details of either Murphy's or Foley's drownings are unknown.

Fees appear again, though none are noted for clothing or camp and garrison equipment. For ordnance, each of the following owe:

> James Ahern $0.83, William Fudge $2.30, Benjamin O. Hall $0.83, John Miller $2.26, Hiram Smith $0.83.

The desertion of Corporal William Wynne is of note. It is hard to understand why one of the non-coms, higher paid, and in a respected and sought after position, would do so. He had replaced James Flynn on June 1st, 1863, after Flynn had been reduced to the ranks.

After a stay of two weeks at Donaldsonville, Battery L, Nim's Battery, and the 159th New York, were detailed as guard to a baggage wagon train under the command of Col. Molineaux that was headed to Carrollton. It departed Donaldsonville on July 29th, and proceeded down the east side of the La Fourche, seventy-three miles to Camp Kearny at Carrollton. It arrived on August 1st. The weather was hot and sultry, which exhausted the men and killed two or three horses.[1541]

Capt. Closson was promoted to Brevet Major on July 8th, "For Gallant and Meritorious service at the Capture of Port Hudson, La." On October 4th, he was made chief of artillery of the 19th Army Corps. He would no longer be in command of Battery L on a day-to-day basis. He went on furlough on August 9th, and so did Pvt. Louis Lighna, the same day that the company arrived at New Orleans, where they took up camp at the Apollo Stables. Here, the troops would be given a chance to rest and recover, while Banks carried on correspondence with Grant and the authorities in Washington as to what to do next.

Note that upon L's arrival at New Orleans there were 20 desertions over the course of the month. Three were the very next day. The men had never had the chance to disembark from the *Chi Kiang* and visit the storied Crescent City, even for a few hours, since arriving from Pensacola on Christmas Day of 1862. While at Donaldsonville, on duty with the 1st Louisiana, most all of whom hailed from New Orleans, the members of Battery L undoubtedly had the opportunity to learn about "the shrimp salads, the soft-shelled crabs, and the champagne of Moreau's,"[1542] the gambling, the cock-fights, and more importantly, the best saloons and brothels in town. Having endured the hell of the siege, they simply went on an extended vacation, the army, the war, the government be damned. No doubt, many would return, and would appear on the next roll—wouldn't they?

1541. Tiemann, p. 58; Whitcomb, p. 53.
1542. Haskin, p. 367, Closson's reminiscences; Forman, J. E., pp. 463–479.

The Next Step

There were congratulations all around. At the news of the fall of Vicksburg, it was first, Banks to Grant, on July 7th and then Halleck to Grant on July 11th, though Halleck was still worried by no news, up to then, from Port Hudson.[1543] Then it was Banks to Grant, on July 8th, announcing the surrender at Port Hudson. After some further thought, Banks sent another message asking for 10,000 to 12,000 troops to assist in a move into Texas. This is his first mention of such a thing. Before receiving this, Grant had, on July 10th, sent word that he was assigning a division from his 13th Corps, Herron's, to Port Hudson, but once he received the news of the surrender, he reassigned Herron to occupy Yazoo City.

More correspondence followed, including news from Halleck to Banks that he could "get no more troops to send to you." But he did order Grant to transfer the 10,000 to 12,000 troops Banks desired.

After all, 21 of the nine-months regiments terms of service would expire by August,[1544] leaving Banks with 13,000 men, some 2,500 of whom would have to be returned to Pensacola, Key West, and forts Jackson and St. Philip. Thus, without any reinforcements, he would have only a net moveable force of 8,500.[1545] Grant then sent Herron, and later, the whole reorganized 13th Corps, consisting of four divisions, temporarily under the command of Maj. Gen. C. C. Washburn.

Manpower was of concern everywhere. The spineless action of Congress that had created the nine months regiments was an ineffective stopgap—only about 87,000 men out of a hoped for 300,000 were obtained.[1546] To prosecute a war that was continuing undiminished, Congress had to face up to the necessity of a draft. Arguments for it began early in 1863. In February, the Senate passed a bill for national enrollment, and after much violent rhetoric by prominent Democrats, the House followed on March 3rd. This was the first real draft—ever. It would take time to organize its operation. The law called for the appointment of a provost marshal-general to organize the states into districts, each with enrollment boards. Pushed forward with great energy by Col. James B. Fry as provost marshal-general, the new bureaucracy began enrolling in late May. The operation of the law brought forth many questions and arguments about the assessment of former quotas, etc., even by friendly Republican governors. But, from some Democrats, notably Governor Seymour of New York, there came denunciation. He claimed that it was unconstitutional, and in a peculiar twist, reminiscent of South Carolina's nullification arguments before the war, came across with the argument that it violated the sovereignty of New York.

1543. O.R. Vol. 24/III, pp. 490–492, 498–500, 519; O.R. Vol. 26/I, pp. 619, 624, 626, 644, 665, 709.
1544. Irwin, p. 258; O.R. Vol. 26/I, pp. 3, 603.
1545. Irwin, p. 259.
1546. Nicolay and Hay, vol. 7, pp. 3–5, 9–10, 17–21.

The apparatus for the draft having been completed in New York by the first of July, enrollment could soon begin. In a July 4th address, Seymour said, "The Democratic organization look upon this Administration as hostile to their rights and liberties; they look to their opponents as men who would do them wrong in their most sacred franchises." Newspapers and magazines picked up on the discord, and pretended to quote Seymour in saying that the national government had no right to force anyone in New York "to take part in the ungodly conflict which is distracting the land" without the consent of the state.

On Saturday morning, the 11th of July, enrollment in New York City began. It went on quietly through the rest of the day. The office was closed on Sunday, but the news was spreading. By Sunday night, a mob attacked the enrollment office, and set the building on fire.[1547] The police were inadequate to the task, and the only reliable militia available had been sent to Gettysburg and elsewhere. A scramble for troops resulted in requests for help from even the navy.[1548] Harvey Brown, the one and the same that Battery L had known at Fort Pickens, and now a brigadier general, made the military commander of New York City the previous January, was ordered to send troops to the aid of the National Guard and the police. Mott's 14th New York Cavalry was ordered diverted from its departure to the Department of the Gulf. Two companies of the Invalid Corps were called upon, one from Fort Wood, New York Harbor, and one from Newark, New Jersey.

Losing all logic as to what it was doing and whom it would choose as victims, the out of control mob violence was turned against the Black population. After numerous street beatings and murders, the Colored Orphan Asylum was burned. The office of the *New York Tribune*, a war supporter, was attacked. This went on for three days until an absent Seymour returned to the city, and addressed the mob—his "friends." His fawning attempt at conciliation was useless, and he finally issued proclamations on July 14th condemning the riot, and declared a state of insurrection. The riot was brought near an end on July 15th, when that morning, Mott's cavalry engaged the mob with howitzers at West 32nd Street, and the regulars commanded by Capt. Putnam, of the 12th Infantry, dispersed the rioters in the neighborhood of Gramercy Park that evening. Mott lost 7 men killed and 20 wounded, a surprising measure of how violent and well-armed the rioters were.

Harvey Brown was accused of being uncooperative with General Sandford of the New York National Guard, and at one point refused to serve under him,[1549] which caused confusion and delay in the response to the riot. The old man was swiftly replaced by E. R. S. Canby, by orders from the War Department, on July 15th.[1550] Order was soon restored, and a spotlight was shown on Canby's ability.

1547. O.R. Vol. 27/II, pp. 893, 896–897, 905–906, 914, 916.
1548. O.R. Vol. 27/II, pp. 878–879, 900, 912, 915.
1549. O.R. Vol. 27/II, p. 880; Cullum, vol. 1, no. 185.
1550. O.R. Vol. 27/III, p. 708.

Brown was retired on August 1st, and though officially retired, he was retained as the commander of Fort Schuyler until the war's end.

There were lesser riots in the North End of Boston, and at Troy, Albany, and Buffalo.[1551]

It had been a memorable 4th of July. In addition to the surrender of Vicksburg, Meade had defeated Lee at Gettysburg. Celebrated in the newspapers, Mead's success was met in Washington by mixed joy and despair. Joy for the victory, and a promotion of Meade to a brigadier in the regular army, yet despair that he did not follow Lee, and crush him before he could retreat across the Potomac. Lee was not pursued, at least not vigorously, and on the night of July 14th, the day before the rioting in New York was under control, he successfully crossed the Potomac. Meade's general order after the victory spoke of "driving the enemy from our soil" and Lincoln, upon reading it, exclaimed: "This is a dreadful reminiscence of McClellan...the whole country is our soil."[1552]

It appears that Lincoln never did learn about the details of Halleck's advance on Corinth, or of Banks' on the Teche, or he would have rightfully condemned them both. It was a similar story. A victory was defined as forcing the enemy to retreat. Now, Meade had simply carried on the Halleck tradition. It was all clear to Gideon Welles, who took an eyebrow-raising cynical view. In his diary entry for July 11th he writes:[1553]

> I fear the rebel army will escape, and am compelled to believe that some of our generals are willing it should. They are contented to have the war continue. Never before have they been so served nor their importance so felt and magnified, and when the war is over but few of them will retain their present importance.

Regardless of all of this hand-wringing, the tipping point had been reached, and at least one Confederate officer in Lee's army recognized it. Capt. James Wood of the 37th Virginia Infantry Regiment, Stonewall Brigade, Army of Northern Virginia, later wrote:

> This battle and campaign was the crucial period of the Confederacy. It was an open secret, gained from rumor, that success would bring recognition of her independence by England, and later by France. Other nations would doubtless fall into line, and the blockade of her ports would soon have been raised. Credit and trade relations with other nations, the enlargement of her armies and munitions of war, would follow; and permanent independence would be established. The high tide of Confederate hopes and prospects were

---

1551. O.R. Vol. 27/II, pp. 890, 930.
1552. Nicolay and Hay, vol. 7, pp. 278–279.
1553. Welles, vol. 1, p. 368.

now passed, and on the night of the 4th Lee retired to Hagerstown.[1554]

Returning our narrative to Louisiana, on July 15th Augur was given a leave of absence from which he would never return.[1555] It is revealed, in the *History of the 116th New York Volunteers*, that he, like Sherman, had "stoutly opposed the assault of May 27th… and afterwards was treated in so formal a manner by those at army headquarters that he deemed it best to withdraw as soon as possible." He was later assigned as commander of the defenses of Washington, where his activity there would soon prove to be, once again, a part Battery L's fortunes. Weitzel succeeded him in command.

On July 18th, Grierson was finally ordered back to Grant.[1556]

On July 24th, Halleck wrote to Banks discussing the overall strategy to be taken up next. "While your army is engaged in cleaning out Southwestern Louisiana, every preparation should be made for an expedition into Texas." Mobile was also mentioned. "The navy are very anxious for an attack on the latter place, but I think Texas much the most important. It is possible that Johnston may fall back toward Mobile, but I think he will unite with Bragg."

Grant was in favor of uniting as well—with Banks for an attack on Mobile, while the Confederate forces were in disorder. With Mobile as a base, the Union forces could then threaten Bragg, still opposite Rosecrans in Tennessee. Essentially, with the Anaconda Plan completed, powerful Union forces could be brought to squeeze inland, to where the remaining Confederate armies were concentrated. Texas was outside of the Anaconda ring, and great strategists have to make tough decisions. Though Halleck correctly foresaw Bragg benefitting from the infusion of Confederate troops paroled from Vicksburg, thereby increasing the threat to the Army of the Cumberland, politics interfered. Texas was to be Banks' target. The President was interested in Texas, and on July 29th, he had asked Stanton to see Halleck about organizing an expedition. Great strategy was thus lost to political direction.

Quoting Grant: "The General-in-Chief having decided against me, the depletion of an army…commenced, as had been the case the year before after the fall of Corinth"

As has been chronicled, Texas was not only a source of raw materials and manpower, but it was the conduit for European arms landed in Mexico, which then were smuggled across the Rio Grande, brought to Louisiana, sent up the Red River and crossed into Mississippi. Now, with Union control of the river, this sort of traffic would be shut off, or nearly so. The blockade should have been able to take its toll on foreign ships attempting to drop off arms at the Texas ports. So,

---

1554. Wood, James H., p. 153.
1555. O.R. Vol. 26/I. p. 642; Clark, p. 108.
1556. O.R. Vol. 26/I, pp. 645, 652, 659; Grant, vol. 1, pp. 578–579.

why should Lincoln be concerned about Texas?

The French, under Napoleon III, were still as full of the avarice that characterized the monarchies of Europe before, during, and after the time of our Civil War, and any opportunity would be cynically exploited, regardless of legal or moral considerations. The French army had landed at Vera Cruz in December of 1861, subsequent to threats about financial claims by French interests against the government of Mexico. They had advanced inland, but were checked at the Battle of Cinco de Mayo. However, in September of 1862, their army was reinforced by 30,000 more troops under General Forey. They besieged and reduced Puebla in February of 1863, and entered Mexico City in June. The puppet government formed following the capitulation adopted monarchy, and offered the crown to an Austrian prince by the name of Maximilian.[1557]

It was now Secretary of State Seward's job to make clear to the European courts, monarchies all, that the idea of a monarchy in Mexico, and the French presence there, was viewed adversely by the United States government. Seward foresaw Mexican interference in Texas. Napoleon III was to be warned about any coalition between "the Regency established in Mexico and the Insurgent Cabal in Richmond." A Union presence in Texas would be necessary to add credibility to Seward's message.

1557. *Encyclopedia Britannica*, vol. 18, 1911, pp. 341–342; Nicolay and Hay, vol. 7, pp. 400–402; Grant, vol. 2, p. 545.

Chapter 11

The Sabine Pass Expedition; "Record" 10/63; A Land Route to Texas; The Rio Grande Expedition; "Record" 12/63; The Battle of Grand Coteau; "Record" 2/64; 1864 Roster; "Record" 4/64; The Red River Campaign: Wilson's Farm; Mansfield (Sabine Crossroads & Pleasant Grove); Pleasant Hill

The Sabine Pass Expedition

Mobile was ruled out by Halleck in a letter to Banks on August 12th: "I fully appreciate the importance of the operation proposed by you…but there are reasons other than military why those heretofore directed should be undertaken first. On this matter we have no choice, but must carry out the views of the Government."[1558]

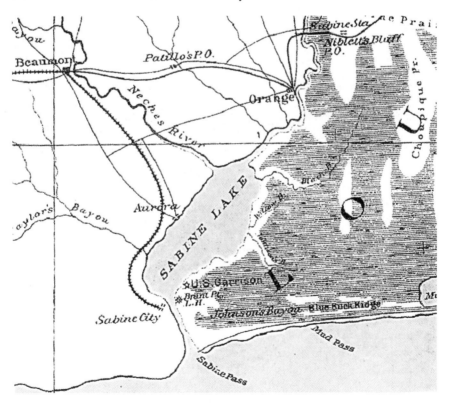

FIGURE 1

1558. O.R. Vol. 26/I, p. 675; figure 1 adapted from Atlas, plate 157.

Thus, Banks was forced into a move that had little or no military value. As Irwin[1559] puts it: "To have overrun the whole state [of Texas] would not have shortened the war by a single day."

General William B. Franklin,[1560] who had arrived in the department in late July, and had been assigned to the command of the 19th Army Corps, was to lead the expedition. It would be his first active role since serving under Burnside at the Battle of Fredericksburg. It would consist of the 1st and 3rd Brigades of Weitzel's 1st Division; Weitzel having succeeded Augur, and the 1st and 2nd Brigades of what was now Emory's 3rd Division. Battery L accompanied the 1st Division, along with the 6th Massachusetts Battery, and the 1st Vermont Battery.[1561] This was a formidable expedition, consisting of 14 regiments, 11 light artillery batteries, and a detachment of the 1st Indiana, with eight heavy Parrotts. All of this was crammed aboard a combination of sailing ships, ocean steamers, and a half-dozen old river steamers, 23 in all, convoyed, or otherwise accompanied by three navy gunboats. The army troops were to be landed in combination with a navy gunboat attack on the fortifications near Sabine City, Texas, on the Sabine River, figure 1, which defines the state line between Louisiana and Texas. It was supposed to be a surprise night approach, and an early morning landing. If successful, more troops would follow, and then move to Beaumont, Galveston, Houston, etc. *Mirabile dictu*, Texas would then fall under Union control.

The troops were loaded into their transports at New Orleans and Algiers on the evening of the 4th of September, and got underway, convoyed by the *Arizona*. Upon reaching the Head of the Passes (the mouth of the Mississippi), on the morning of the 5th it was planned that the expedition would telegraph to Berwick Bay, to allow the *Sachem* and *Clifton* to depart at a time and speed to bring them to a meeting with the transports off the mouth of the Atchafalaya River.

There, the army sharpshooters assigned to the two gunboats could be transferred, and last minute instructions given. The rendezvous took place on schedule, at 7:00 a.m. on the 6th. The other gunboat assigned, the *Granite City*, had left a day earlier, in order to arrive off of the mouth of the Sabine River prior to the arrival of the expedition, to disclose their coming to the ship or ships of the blockading squadron stationed off Sabine Pass, since no prior warning had been given to the blockading squadron. The *Granite City* was to then remain stationed off the pass, and post a signal light for the guidance of the expedition, scheduled to arrive

---

1559. Irwin, p. 264.
1560. *Encyclopedia Britannica*, vol. 11, p. 33; O.R. Vol. 26/I, p. 658. Franklin was graduated from West Point in 1843 at the head of his class. After the Battle of Fredericksburg, where, as a major-general, he commanded two corps, he was accused by his commander, Burnside, of disobedience and negligence, and relieved from duty. Though the charge was later disproved, a cloud hung over him at this time. O.R. Vol. 26/I, pp. 710–711.
1561. O.R. Vol. 26/I, pp. 290–292, 300, 711, 713, 721; Clark, pp. 124–125; Pellet, p. 150.

during the early morning darkness of the 6th. All in readiness, the *Clifton*, *Sachem*, *Arizona*, and the seven transports of Weitzel's force steamed off, at a speed carefully calculated to have them arrive off the mouth of the Sabine River at dark. Then, before dawn of the 7th, the gunboats could run in and achieve a surprise attack on the fort, while Weitzel's troops were landed, and held a position threatening the rear of the fort; until the remaining troops, under Franklin, could be landed.[1562]

The plan fell apart soon. The *Granite City* arrived off the mouth of the pass early on the 6th and found no evidence of the blockading squadron. Not informed of the planned landing, the squadron commander had made no effort to meet or assist it. The blockader, the USS *Owasco*, had left Sabine Pass for Galveston on that morning and the *Cayuga* had been ordered to replace her on station, but did not arrive until the next morning, the 7th. The *Granite City* soon sighted what it thought was a man-of-war. God forbid, perhaps the *Alabama*—and she fled eastward, toward the oncoming expedition. They missed one another. The expedition, led by Captain Crocker in the *Clifton*, passed on in the darkness, to a point that, by their best reckoning, was the mouth of the Sabine. Finding no *Granite City*, and no ship of the blockading squadron, Crocker reckoned that he had passed too far, and reversed course. Thirty miles east, he met the errant *Granite City*, which had fled all the way back to the Calcasieu River, and put a boat ashore, to inquire about conditions on the Sabine. Imagine part of a surprise expedition stopping to inquire about conditions there!

While this drama was unfolding, the transports of General Franklin bypassed Crocker, unseen, and blithely (it was 11 o'clock in the morning) ran up to the Sabine Pass bar. Seeing no evidence of the rest of the expedition, they pulled out, but not far enough to be out from the sight of shore. The attack schedule now in a shambles, with any Confederate on shore having to have been asleep not to know that there was a fleet off of his station. Crocker finally arrived on the scene late in the afternoon.

Considering the loss of surprise, Crocker still preferred to go in immediately, but deferred to Weitzel's idea of postponing the raid until the early morning of Tuesday the 8th. Nothing of the nature of the armaments of the fort being obtained from the *Owasco*, it was agreed that Crocker, in the *Clifton*, at daylight, should cross the bar and make a reconnaissance. This done, and with no response from the fort, even after advancing close to it and shelling it, he signaled, and those transports as indicated in figure 2 entered, though one soon became almost hopelessly aground.

The Confederate fort was armed with six 32-pounders. The attackers felt that they looked "too formidable to warrant an attack by the gunboats alone…and it was determined that the army should assist in the attack."[1563] It was now 10:00

1562. ORN ser. 1, vol. 20, pp. 522, 524, 544–548; O.R. Vol. 26/I, pp. 294–299, 302–303.
1563. ORN vol. 20, p. 545, Crocker's report.

a.m. Weitzel would land and attempt "to advance upon the fort as skirmishers, endeavoring to drive the enemy from his guns..."[1564]

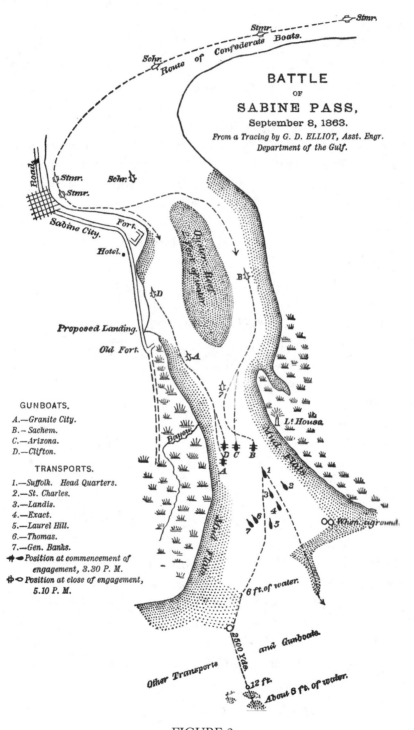

FIGURE 2

1564. O. R. Vol. 26/I, p. 295, Franklin's report; 298–299, Weitzel's report.

There was still no activity from the Confederates on shore, and Crocker, Weitzel, and Franklin were able to reconnoiter the shore in a small boat, concluding that the only place where the shallow marsh would allow boats to come closer than one hundred twenty-five feet from shore was as indicated in figure 2. All of this having taken much time, it was 3:00 p.m. before the attack began.

Since, in Crocker's judgment, the guns of the fort seemed to be trained upon a particular point in the Texas (left) channel, he would have the *Sachem*, followed by the *Arizona*, steam up the Louisiana (right) channel, to cause the guns to be changed in direction. The *Clifton*, followed by the *Granite City*, in the left channel, would steam up slowly to await the turning of the guns, then dash forward upon the battery.

The plan was put into effect at 4:00 p.m. The guns were turned as predicted, and the *Sachem* began taking inaccurate fire. The *Arizona* lagged behind. After about 30 wild shots (the report of Confederate Capt. F. H. Odlum, of Cook's Texas Artillery, commanding Fort Grigsby, as it was called, states that their sixth shot disabled the *Sachem*),[1565] the *Sachem* was disabled, her boiler shot through, and had to anchor to prevent grounding. The *Clifton* kept coming up, and quickly the fort's guns were trained on her. Eventually, with her steering shot out, and grounded, she had her boiler shot through. Both eventually raised the white flag and were captured. At this juncture, Franklin decided to abort. The *Arizona* eventually got free, long after the *Granite City* had departed. The transports made it out as well. A factor in Franklin's decision to pull out was that the landing place was muddy enough to sink troops to their "middle," and another was that the troops and horses had been on board for four days, and were short of water. He mentions nothing of the crowded and filthy conditions, which would have probably motivated the troops to disembark, rather than endure the trip home.

Franklin's reasoning seems weak, and Banks' report on the expedition[1566] only briefly mentions: "In my judgment, the army should not have returned…" In fact, Franklin's orders clearly state: "A landing, if found impracticable at the point now contemplated, should be attempted at any place in the vicinity where it may be found practicable…" Weitzel is reported to have begged to be allowed to take the 8th Vermont, the 12th Connecticut, and the 26th Massachusetts, and charge the fort. If Franklin had deemed the chosen landing site not satisfactory, why did he not object to it during the reconnaissance?

A court of inquiry[1567] was demanded by Gideon Welles, in regard to the captain of the *Owasco* leaving his station without permission, and of the commanding officers of the *Arizona* and *Granite City*, for their behavior "as represented

---

1565. ORN ser. 1, vol. 20, p. 546; O.R. Vol. 26/I, pp. 303, 310.
1566. O.R. Vol. 26/I, pp. 287, 290–291; Carpenter, p. 139; ORN ser. 1, vol. 20, p. 551, River pilot Taylor's report.
1567. ORN ser. 1, vol. 20. pp. 538–539, 554.

in the reports of Major-General Franklin and Brigadier-General Weitzel." The commander of the *Arizona* being accused of not coming to the assistance of the *Sachem* (towing her out) and the commander of the *Granite City* lagging behind and not supporting the *Clifton*. In reading the report of the court, Farragut had to admit that there were grounds for a court-martial of Tibbits, the commander of the *Arizona*, but the difficulty of obtaining witnesses, due to Bank's subsequent moves, forced him to recommend a postponement of any action. Welles did not forget, and finally when Crocker was released from Confederate imprisonment and wrote his final report in 1865, Tibbits had to respond. His excuse that the *Arizona* was grounded at the time the *Sachem* was shot through, seems to have satisfied Welles, and the matter was closed.

Weitzel's report of the casualties is a preliminary, and subsequent reports are incomplete, even in the histories of the regiments that supplied the sharpshooters, namely 75th New York and the 161st New York. The "record" of Battery L is silent, and if it were not for the writings of William L. Haskin, there is only circumstantial evidence that Battery L was even there. Crocker, from his prison camp in Texas, supplied the data for the Clifton: three of the crew killed, four wounded, and 21 missing. As to the 75th New York, who were on board, there were five killed, seven wounded, and seven missing. The Sachem's crew had seven killed, and 10 missing, the 161st New York suffering 30 killed, wounded, and missing.[1568]

The Sabine Pass Expedition was an embarrassment to the navy and a very inauspicious beginning for General Franklin. It was made all the more embarrassing when it was disclosed by the Confederate commander in Texas, Magruder, that Fort Grigsby was garrisoned by only 44 men.

There is a remarkable passage regarding the Sabine Pass Expedition in the diary of Gideon Welles for September 22nd, 1863:[1569]

> Neither General Halleck nor the Secretary of War consulted the Navy in this matter. General Banks appears to have originated it and made a requisition on Commodore Bell, who readily responded in the absence of Farragut, with the light boats built for transporting passengers in the Northern rivers. Admiral Farragut was at the Navy Department when dispatches were received from Commodore Bell, stating that application for cooperation and aid had been made on him, and how he had answered the call. When Farragut read the dispatch, he laid down the paper and said to me: "The expedition will be a failure." The army officers have the impression that naval vessels can do anything; this call is made for boats to accompany an army expedition; it is expected the Navy will capture the batteries, and, the Army being there in force with a general in command, they will take the credit. But there will be no

---

1568. O.R. Vol. 26/I, pp. 299, 303–307; Haskin, pp. 194, 367, 554; Hall, H. and J., *75th*, p. 144; *dmna. ny.gov/historic/reg/hist/civil/infantry/161stInf/161stInf Main.htm*; ORN ser. 1, vol. 20, p. 542.
1569. Welles, vol. 1, pp. 441–442.

credit in this case, as you may expect to hear of disaster. These boats which Bell has given them cannot encounter batteries; they might cooperate and assist the army, but that is not the object. The soldiers should land and attack in the rear, and the vessels aide them in front. But that is not the plan. The soldiers are not to land until the Navy had done the impossibility, with such boats. Therefore there will be disaster.

"Record" 10/63
31 AUGUST–31 OCTOBER, 1863 BARRE'S LANDING, LOUISIANA

The Battery left New Orleans Sept. 15,'63 and proceeded by railroad to Brashear City and crossed to Berwick City, arriving on the 18th. Left Berwick City on the 26th and marched to Vermillion Bayou arriving on the 9th Oct. The Battery in action shelled the enemy. Crossed Vermillion Bayou on the 10th and marched to Barre's Landing, arriving on the 21st and remained there until 31 Oct. 1863.

Henry W. Closson	Capt. On det. Svc. Chief of Artillery 19th Army Corps S.O. no. 13 Hdqrts. 19th Army Corps Oct. 4,'63.
Franck E. Taylor	1st Lt. Commanding Battery and Ass't Comm'y of Musters S.O. no. 92 Hdqrts. Dept. of the Gulf 19th Army Corps Apr. 9,'63
Edward L. Appleton	1st Lt.
J.A. Sanderson	2nd Lt. On det. svc. with Gen. Lee Chief of Cavalry S.O. no. 250 Hdqrts. Dept. of the Gulf Oct.6,'63.
Charles B. Slack	2nd Lt. Joined Co. S.O. no. 211 Hdqrts. Dept of the Gulf Aug. 26,'63.

Attached:
Charles Wheeler	Pvt. Asst. Com'y of musters clerk S.O. no. 20, Hdqrts. 19th Corps Oct. 12,'63.

Detached:
William E. Scott	Cpl. On Det. Svc. Orderly Chief of Artillery
George Friedman	Pvt. On Det. Svc. at N.O. as Artillerist, Left Co. May 24,'63
Amelius Straub	Pvt. On Det. Svc. at Baton Rouge as cook in Univ. Hosp. since June 1,'63.
Thomas Newton	Pvt. On Det. Svc. in Ord. Dept. since Sept. 8, Per S.O. No. 4, Hdqrts. Dept. of Gulf Sept.'63. Due U.S. for Ord. $45.56. For 2nd reenlistment $3.00 per month

Absent with Leave:
Louis Lighna	Pvt. On furlough left Company August 21st for 14 days.

Absent in Confinement:
Michael O'Sullivan	In jail at New Orleans since Sept. 2,'63 (from desertion).

Absent Without Leave:
Joseph Kutschor	Pvt. Exchanged prisoner of war by virtue of G.O. no. 339, A.G.O. War Dept. Wash. Oct. 16,'63

Deserted:
William Fudge	Pvt. Deserted from N.O.	Aug. 25,'63	Due U.S. for ord.	$2.30
Hiram Smith	Pvt. do.	Sept. 10	do.	$7.55
George Kelly	Pvt. do.	Sept. 16	do.	$7.55

John M. Kastenbader	Pvt. from TerreBonne	Sept. 16	do.	$7.55
Clark Dickson	Pvt. from N.O.	Sept. 15	do.	$7.55
Charles E. Deal	Pvt. do.		do.	$7.55
Sholto O'Brien	Pvt.	Sept. 8	do.	$7.55

William Brooks — Pvt. Discharged from hospital and never joined Comp. Due U.S. for Ord. $47.10.

Henry Pelky — Pvt. from N.O. Sept. 15 Due U.S. for ord. $7.00.

William Mint — Pvt. from N.O. Sept. 8,'63 Due U.S. for ord. $7.55

Discharged:

Alexander J. Baby — Sgt. by Promotion to 2nd Lt. Gen'l Banks' bodyguard.

Charles Spangler — Pvt. Expiration of service

Denis Myers — Pvt. Expiration of service

Wallace D. Wright — Pvt. June 10, 1863 at Ft. Pickens, Fla. for disability sick at Pensacola since December 24,'62.

Edward M. Laughlin — Pvt. Sept. 30, 1863 from Berwick City by expiration of service. AWOL since Sept. 24 at N.O.

Died:

John Deering — Pvt. Died at Marine Hosp. Sep. 29, 1863 of dysentery. No notice of decease until this month.

Hiram Hubbard — Pvt. Died in the field near Opelousas, La. Oct. 26, 1863, of congestive fever.

Joined:

John Lowry — Pvt. From desertion at N.O. Sept. 3

Michael O'Sullivan — Pvt. In jail at N.O. since Sept. 2, 1863 Due U.S. for ordnance $43.36

Arthur Flynn — Pvt. From Berwick City Sept. 19, 1863 Due U. S. for ord. $1.63.

John H. Moran — Pvt. do. Sept. 19, 1863 Due U.S. for ordnance $41.63. To forfeit $8.00 of his monthly pay for 4 months pursuant to General Court Martial S.O. no. 3 Hdqrts 1st Div. 19th Army Corps, Sept. 28, 1863.

William F. Brown — Pvt. From desertion at Tarleton Plantation, Oct. 1,'63 Due U.S. for ord. $5.93. To forfeit $10.00 paid Constable for arrest.

Joseph H. Parslow — Pvt. do. Oct. 1,'63

Partick Craffy — Pvt. do. Oct. 2 Due U. S for ord. $1.63 To forfeit $10.00 paid Constable for arrest.

Owen A. Wren — Pvt. Oct. 2 Due U.S. for ord. $2.50. To forfeit $10.00 paid Constable for arrest

Martin Stanners — Pvt. Exchanged prisoner of war by virtue of G.O.339 War Dept. Wash. Oct. 31, 1863

Strength: 108, Sick 5

Sick present: none

Sick absent:

William C. Brunskill — At Ft. Hamilton, Ny, left Co. Sept. 17, 1861.

Henry Champion — At University Hospital since August 27, 1863

William Crowley — At Baton Rouge, La. since July 13, 1863

George Chase — At Brashear City since April 22, 1863

Charles F. Mansfield — At Pensacola since December 24, 1862

Colored Cooks:
Henry Jefferson	31 Oct.'63	Barre's Landing, La. Cooking in Company since May 20, 1863.
Phillip Evens	31 Oct.'63	do.
Virgil Ayres	31 Oct.'63	do.

Why Joseph Kutschor was listed as AWOL and not in the "Joined" is an example of the rather haphazard way some of the muster roll records were kept, entries for the two-month period probably being made before subsequent information made them obsolete. Regardless, both Kutschor and Stanners were lucky men. A declaration of exchange had been issued by the Confederate agent for exchange, Col. Robert Ould, on September 12th, and the notice did not appear in U.S. Army General Orders until October 16th. The page from the O.R. is reproduced here as figure 3.[1570]

GENERAL ORDERS, } WAR DEPT., ADJT. GENERAL'S OFFICE
No. 339. } *Washington, October 16, 1863.*

1. A declaration of exchanges having been announced by R. Ould, esq., agent for exchange at Richmond, Va., dated Seprember 12, 1863, it is hereby declared that all officers and men of the U.S. Army captured and paroled previous to the 1st of September, 1863, are duly exchanged. The officers and men herein declared exchanged will immediately be sent to join their respective regiments. By order of the Secretary of War:

E. D. TOWNSEND,
Assistant Adjutant-General

FIGURE 3

The information only makes the fate of George Chase more of a mystery. He had been sick at a place that fell to the enemy, much like Sgt. Charles Riley, so many months ago, and has not been heard from.

The deserters who came back to the fold were not nearly as numerous as may have been hoped, and almost all of those eight who did, had been apprehended by the authorities. Only Arthur Flynn and Joseph Parslow seem to have escaped punishment. As had been known before, if you turned yourself in, you often escaped severe consequences, much as Francis Hagan, at Fort Duncan.

Fees for ordnance and clothing appear in great number, and only a few examples are given here. Out of 91 enlisted men, a handful owed money for clothing. George Howard owed the largest amount: $32.16. Thirteen owed the U.S. for ordnance, some three or four owed as much as three months' pay. Pvt. Thomas Newton owed the most; he is listed as "Detached," above. See also, John H. Moran, and

---

1570. O.R. Ser. 2, vol. 6, p. 383.

others, in "Joined." Uncle Sam was still a cheap scrooge. Pretty soon, he'd have to pay dearly to keep these men happy enough to reenlist!

Battery L had arrived at New Orleans on August 10th. Since they were to remain until mid-September, it is likely that everyone had a chance to find time to visit the city. While there, there is evidence that they had met members of Farragut's squadron – those who were from ships in port for repairs - the *Gertrude*, *Sciota*, *Kennebec*, *Pinola*, *Virginia*, *Albatross*, and *Arizona* being among them.

Barroom heroes undoubtedly competed with stories of their recent adventures; the sailors in turn regaling their listeners with accounts of prize captures, and of the money shared by the crews. At least one member of Battery L became a believer.

At Pensacola, on December 20th, 1862 (volume 1, chapter 6), when he transferred from the 91st New York Infantry Regiment to Battery L, Enos Deal represented himself to Lieutenant Appleton as Charles. He evidently had decided on a new beginning, and of course, that $100 bounty had helped. However, having experienced the dust and mud of the marches in the Teche Campaign, and the sweaty hell of the Siege of Port Hudson, it was time for a new Deal.

His plan was clear; at the first opportunity, he would desert and join the navy. That time came when Battery L was leaving New Orleans on September 15th. He walked away, and on September 22nd, under the alias of Charles E. Jones, joined to serve as a coal heaver on the USS *Kennebec*.[1571]

The *Kennebec* was returned to service in November, with "Jones" aboard, and in December, she captured the blockade runners, *Marshall J. Smith* and *Grey Jacket*. "Jones" shared in the prize money. Other actions followed, including participation in Farragut's attack on Mobile in August of 1864, which is covered in chapter 13, because of the twist of fate that put Battery L's Commander, Henry Closson into the fray.

The practice of reducing an enlisted man just before his discharge for expiration of service is confirmed by the discharges of Charles Spangler and Thomas Newton. Up to this time, Spangler had held the rank of corporal. The case of Pvt. Thomas Newton is also noted by peeking ahead to the next muster roll. Prior to this month, he had held the rank of sergeant, ever since his reenlistment in Company K of the 1st U.S. Artillery at Fort McHenry, Maryland, on February 12th, 1854.

He was first enlisted into the army on April 12th, 1849, at New York, a fresh immigrant from England. Now, at 35 years of age, and with almost 15 years of service, he had to be one of the most mature and experienced soldiers in the company. The idea of him, with a spotless record, being reduced before discharge and then being charged for ordnance after just going through the combat hell of the Siege of Port Hudson is almost inconceivable. Charges for ordnance, clothing,

---

1571. ORN ser. 1, vol. 20, pp. 510, 627, 652; National Archives, Deal navy pension cert. no. 39985.

or camp and garrison equipment were supposed to be for careless losses, reasonably assumed to be associated with a non-combat situation, although the regulations say nothing about combat.[1572]

The departure of Baby, Newton, Spangler, and Wynne created vacancies which were filled by moving up David J. Wicks and William Demarest from corporal to sergeant, and the promotion of Michael White, Edward Cotterill, Charles E. Walton, and William E. Scott from private to corporal.

The company had accepted three escaped slaves into their midst over the course of May, June, and July. They came into the battery as "hangers-on," as Thomas Newton, the commissary sergeant, described them, willing to work for their "keep," which consisted of their food and cast off clothing. The first to arrive, Philip Ewens, initially acted as a teamster, but later cooked; as did Jefferson and Ayers. This must have made life much easier for everyone, particularly during the siege. No longer did the individual soldier have to cook his own meals or arrange with a voluntary group of messmates to share the job. Once enlisted, the cooks were supposed to be paid ten dollars per month, three dollars of which "may be in clothing." Any money received prior to that time had been "if the men chose."[1573]

The Battery L Record of Events is particularly barren of details for this period. As noted, the fact that the whole Battery, including all of its horses, went on the Sabine Pass Expedition is not even mentioned, and subsequent notes say little about what developed into only a feint on the Sabine by land, our description of which follows.

A Land Route to Texas

Immediately upon return from the Sabine Pass Expedition, portions of Franklin's troops, that is, Weitzel's, including Battery L, and Emory's divisions, were ordered to Brashear City to begin an expedition to Texas by one of the two inland routes available; (a) from Berwick City to Vermilionville, and then west along the plains to Niblett's Bluff, and the Sabine River, or, (b) via the Atchafalaya and the Red rivers to Alexandria and Shreveport, and then west into Marshall, Texas. The shorter southerly route is shown in figure 4.

Franklin's troops were to be followed by Grant's newly arrived 13th Corps. The 13th, having been ordered south from Vicksburg on the 7th of August,[1574] began

---

1572. Revised Army Regulations, 1861, no. 107, p. 22, states: "Ammunition issued will be inspected frequently. Each man will be made to pay for the rounds expended without orders, or not in the way of duty, or which may be damaged or lost by neglect."
1573. The cook positions were authorized by an act of Congress to reorganize the engineer corps. See: 37th Congress, Sess. 3, Ch. 78, dated Mar. 3rd, 1863. See also: Pension Files - Jefferson, Ayers and Ewens; respectively nos. 433110, 433713, and 439866; National Archives.
1574. O.R. Vol. 24/III, p. 581; Grant, vol. 1, pp. 579, 581; Marshall, T. B., pp. 107–108. Figure 4, Atlas, plate 156, portion, altered.

arriving by steamer over the course of the next couple of weeks. On September 4th, Grant made his only visit to Banks' Department of the Gulf. In early August, Halleck, *figure-toi*, having denied him a leave of absence to visit New Orleans and formulate a plan to "move against Mobile," Grant now went on official business, to review the 11,000 men of his 13th Corps.

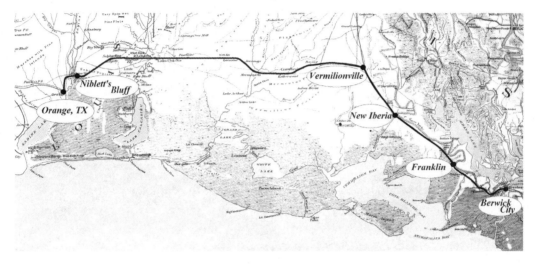

FIGURE 4

The occasion was just before Grant was promoted to the command of the new "Military Division of the Mississippi,"[1575] consisting of the combined departments of the Cumberland, the Ohio, and the Tennessee. It now was everything about Tennessee, and the trouble Rosecrans had gotten himself into at Chattanooga.

It will be remembered that after the Battle of Stone's River, Rosecrans did not pursue Bragg, his ostensible reason being that by threatening Bragg he was helping Grant at Vicksburg; this by preventing Bragg from sending reinforcements to Johnston. Finally, Halleck sent Rosecrans a note that was close to an ultimatum: "After five to six months of inactivity, with your force all the time diminishing[1576] [primarily due to expirations of service, and the draft not going well] and no hope of immediate increase, you must not be surprised that their [Lincoln and Stanton's] patience is pretty well exhausted."

Rosecrans finally started on his Tullahoma Campaign on June 24th. It was a brilliant series of moves that drove Bragg out of Kentucky, across the Cumberland Mountains and the Tennessee River to a refuge in Chattanooga. It was over by July 3rd, 1863, one day before the surrender of Vicksburg, and the same day that the battle at Gettysburg ended. The campaign might have been even shorter had not the weather been exceptionally bad. Rosecrans now repeated his habit. He

---

1575. Grant, vol. 2, p. 26.
1576. Nicolay and Hay, vol. 8, pp. 61, 64–66, 104–105; O. R. Vol. 23/III, p. 592; CWSAC GA004.

stopped and sat at Tullahoma for six weeks, allowing Bragg to tighten his grip on Chattanooga, while the Confederacy began sending the paroled prisoners from Vicksburg to Bragg's aid.

Given a peremptory order to move on the 5th of August, Rosecrans waited ten days, and then began a series of moves that chased Bragg out of Chattanooga, but ended in the frightfully massive and bloody Battle of Chickamauga, which lasted from September 19th to the 20th. There was no clear outcome, except that Rosecrans fell back to Chattanooga, and was left bottled up there, under siege by Bragg. There was the dire prospect of the Army of the Cumberland being starved into surrender. Grant was then summoned to the rescue, and was given the choice of sacking Rosecrans. Grant did not hesitate; he had formulated his opinion a year earlier when Rosecrans had failed to pursue Van Dorn (chapter 9).

Grant's review of the 13th Corps was held on September 4th at Carrollton. A diary entry by a member of the 83rd Ohio captures the event, which serves to confirm the fact that Grant remained in the Department of the Gulf for an extended period of time, much longer than would have been planned.[1577]

> The customary salute was fired and General Grant rode into the field, and was greeted with loud cheers. He rode slowly along the front of each line and galloped back at race track speed. His escort and visitors were strung out far behind, requiring some time for them to catch up and regain their places. There was one naval officer, dressed all in white, who went wherever his horse chose. He was a comical sight...
>
> The general had on his old brigadier coat and was in rather a marked contrast to the well formed and finely dressed General Banks…This was no doubt intended to be his farewell to us, as he had been called east to be the main stay of the great Lincoln, which he most certainly became."

The wild and "vicious" horse Grant had been riding, which he had lost control of during the review, soon shied and fell over, pinning Grant on to the cobbled street at Carrolton. He was injured sufficiently to remain confined at New Orleans until the 13th of September.[1578] The extended period undoubtedly was sufficient time to have raised an inevitable discussion of the failed Sabine Pass expedition, which had already begun when Grant arrived. It ended during his stay. Its failure only points up an expressed opinion of Grant's that Lincoln's wishes could have been fulfilled by not "wasting troops in western Louisiana and eastern Texas, by sending a garrison at once to Brownsville on the Rio Grande." Here he quietly

---

1577. Marshall, T. B., pp. 107–108.
1578. Grant, vol. 1, pp. 582; O.R. Vol. 30/III, p. 594. Grant would go on to a brilliant campaign against Bragg at Chattanooga, resulting in the relief the city, Bragg's retreat, and his replacement by Joseph E. Johnston on December 27th, 1863. Nicolay & Hay, vol. 8, p. 326. This would precipitate the move in Congress to promote Grant to lieutenant general.

suggests the occupation of only a single location in Texas.

Banks recommended a Rio Grande expedition to Halleck on the same day that Grant left,[1579] and at the same time he gave orders to begin Halleck's preferred overland move. Grant's opinions were still ignored, as they had been since the beginning. To the ultimate benefit of the Union, this would finally change, but not for almost another year.

On July 16th, troops were loaded on to cars destined for Brashear City. The ferrying of the troops and equipment across Berwick Bay took up nearly a week,[1580] so that there were considerable numbers of troops in camp on both sides, doing what you do in the army, hurry up and wait. Here, the 19th Corps was joined by the 13th Corps, under the command of Gen. E. O. C. Ord. The easterners had a chance to meet the westerners, most for the first time. The cultural gap was evident. From the 116th New York Regiment: "We soon found it impossible to live in peace with these western men, as they were constantly telling of their prowess, and what *they* would now do in this department if we paper collar soldiers would only let them alone. They were almost destitute of discipline, wore whatever dress they pleased, be it a uniform or not, and considered whatever they could "gobble" [plundering] as their inalienable right. Many hard words ended in harder blows…"

On the bright and clear morning of the 26th of September, what was thought to be the beginning of the march north began. Passing into the country that the 19th Corps had known the previous spring, the lead regiments passed Pattersonville, only to go into bivouac near the Tarleton Plantation. Finally, after waiting here until October 3rd, the march really began. It continued to Franklin, where they now knew enough to take the bypass road at Irish Bend, leading on to "the collection of houses" called New Iberia, occupied by the enemy, which was reached by October 4th. It was not entered until the afternoon of the 7th, after heavy skirmishing.[1581]

Banks left New Orleans and arrived in General Franklin's camp when it was at New Iberia, to be on hand to observe the march to Vermilion Bayou. It was reached on the morning of the 9th. The march was characterized by a lack of water, the army having passed away from the Teche. Their only supply of water was "buffalo holes," stagnant pools unfit for drinking. Here, just as in the spring, the enemy was found on the other side of the bayou, with the bridge destroyed. The artillery, including Battery L, was brought up. The enemy withdrew quickly upon being shelled. Franklin's force now camped, enjoying the fresh water, until a new bridge could be built, which was crossed on the 10th. They then moved on to Carrion Crow Bayou. The 13th Corps, which had been following a day behind, pulled in and camped here also. The entire force under General Franklin was now

---

1579. O.R. Vol. 26/I, pp. 19–20, 289.
1580. Clark, p. 129–131; Billings, pp. 105–106. "Paper collar" was an insult, such a soldier was a "beat" or a "Jonah": an effete shirker.
1581. Hall, H. and J., 75th, p. 148.

about 19,500. It remained here, with Taylor's forces close by, and making daily reconnaissance's,[1582] for nine days.

Banks had seen enough. He had tried Halleck's desired land scheme, and it was not going to work. The difficulties of a lack of water and supplies in the surrounding country, "which had been repeatedly overrun by the two armies, and which involved a march of…400 miles from Berwick Bay, with wagon transportation only…mostly upon a single road…" caused him to abandon the idea of either of the possible land approaches then and there. The enemy would be pushed for a while longer, until a seaborne expedition to Texas had shown some merit. Then Franklin would be ordered to withdraw.[1583]

Franklin's command then marched, the 13th Corps units now in the lead, to Opelousas, skirmishing with Taylor all the way. Two divisions of the 13th Corps occupied the city, and other units spread out to Barre's Landing, where the army would normally be expected to be provisioned by steamer. The low water in Bayou Courtableau would prevent it.[1584] Without this supply route, a withdrawal would have been a foregone conclusion, had it not already been made. It would begin on October 27th, in anticipation of Banks calling for his first reinforcements to Texas. The brief occupation was not all a waste, however; much of it was spent in rounding up all of the horses in the area, to mount, among others, the 75th New York, the 30th Massachusetts, and the 118th Illinois, just as had been done with the 41st Massachusetts and others six months earlier.

The Rio Grande Expedition

As early as October 2nd, Commodore Bell, in Farragut's absence commanding the West Gulf Blockading Squadron, had begun the preliminaries to the expedition, which reveals that Banks was seriously considering this plan, or even had already decided on it, regardless of the conditions of the land route. Bell ordered the USS *Tennessee* to prepare for special service off the Texas coast, and to bring along a captain of the Corps of Engineers to examine "[the] Brazos River, Pass Cavallo, Pass Aransas, Brazos Santiago, and Rio Grande bars…" and the defenses of Brazos Harbor.[1585] The *Tennessee* returned with the information on the 12th, and the *Monongahela*, chosen to convoy the expedition, was ordered withdrawn from blockade duty on the 20th, to report to Bell. The *Owasco* and the *Virginia* would also accompany the expedition. This would be quite a contrast to the Sabine Pass Expedition; these were large heavily armed vessels, incapable of passing into shallow

---

1582. Clark, p. 132; Irwin, p. 274; Hall, H. and J., p. 150–152.
1583. Irwin, pp. 274, 276–277; O.R. Vol. 26/I, pp. 19–20, 367, 771–772, 768. The route to Niblett's Bluff was two hundred miles.
1584. Pellet, p. 155; O.R. Vol. 26/I, pp. 355, 782.
1585. ORN ser. 1, vol. 20, pp. 606–607, 622–623, 636–637, 641, 643.

water. The troops would have to land through the surf.

His decision made, Banks sailed on October 26th, on the transport steamer McCllellan.[1586] He was accompanied by the 2nd Division of the 13th Army Corps, commanded by Maj. Gen. N. J. T. Dana, with detachments of the 13th and 15th Maine regiments, and the 1st and 16th regiments of the Corps d'Afrique–a total of about 4,000 troops. Having encountered a violent "Norther" off Aransas pass, on the 13th, which scattered the fleet, only some had reached Brazos Santiago on the 1st of November, but a landing was made at noon on the 2nd, despite the rough conditions left from the gale. The small force of Confederate cavalry there offered no serious resistance, and a detachment from Company B of the 15th Maine, from the steamer *Clinton*, was the first to plant Old Glory on the shore.[1587]

The next day, the *Monongahela* arrived, and went on to the mouth of the Rio Grande to assist with the landing of troops. Brownsville, figure 5, was occupied by the 94th Illinois Volunteers on the 6th.[1588] The town was in turmoil, the Confederates having set fire to the U.S. barracks, which spread beyond into private property. Banks arrived and made his headquarters there the same day. He was immediately immersed in Mexican politics, many of those opposed to the French having sought refuge in Brownsville. Juan Nepumuseno Cortinas was one, the "marauder" familiar to Battery L in 1860. On November 9th Banks, with justifiable pride, was able to dispatch the following to Lincoln: "Sir: I am in occupation of Brazos Island, Point Isabel, and Brownsville…"

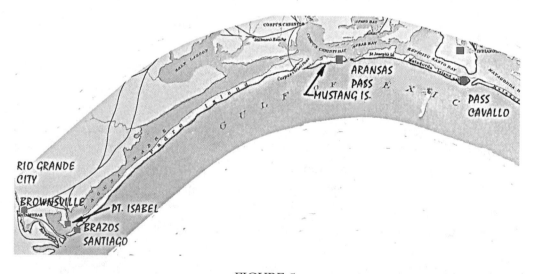

FIGURE 5

Banks left Brownsville for the next phase of the expedition on November 13th. It would be under the command of Brig. Gen. T. E. G. Ransom. After the

---

1586. O.R. Vol. 26/I, pp. 292, 396–398, 428–429, 776, 783; ORN ser. 1, vol. 20, pp. 645–647.
1587. *Harper's Weekly*, Nov. 28th, 1863, p. 754.
1588. O.R. Vol. 26/I, p. 399, 404, 407; Shorey, p. 56. Figure 5 derived from Atlas, plates 156 & 157.

embarkation of the 13th and 15th Maine, the 26th Iowa, the 8th Indiana, and an artillery battery, about 1,500 men, the expedition set off for Corpus Christi Pass, which was reached on the 16th. One transport that held some of the troops was the *Matamoras*, loaned to the expedition by Cortinas, now a friend of the U.S.,[1589] the thought being that its shallow draft would be able to pass over the bar at Corpus Christi. Finding the pass even shallower, the troops were unloaded through the surf and began the twenty-two-mile march along Mustang Island, the target of the expedition being Fort Semmes, which guarded the entrance to Aransas Pass. The fort surrendered without a fight on November 17th. Compare this determined action of Ransom to that of Franklin at Sabine Pass.

After a deserved rest, on November 23rd they were ferried across Aransas Pass to St. Joseph's Island, the objective being Fort Esperanza, which guarded the entrance to Pass Cavallo. Here, Ransom's troops were reorganized into a distinct brigade and were joined by a second, under Col. H. D. Washburn, all under the temporary command of Maj. Gen. C. C. Washburn, the brother of the governor of Maine. Delayed in their march by Cedar Bayou, which separates St. Joseph's Island from Matagorda Island, they were able to make a crossing on November 25th,[1590] and the march was resumed on the 27th. Artillery was placed around the fort and shelling began on the 28th. By the night of the 29th, the Confederate garrison evacuated and blew up the fort. Coincident with the above operations, an expedition was sent up the Rio Grande to Ringgold Barracks (Rio Grande City) on the 23rd, and it was occupied by the 37th Illinois.[1591] As of the end of December, there were troops at Rio Grande City, Brownsville, Pt. Isabel, St. Joseph's Island, Indianola, Matagorda Island, and Decrow's Point, at the tip of the Matagorda Peninsula. It was a brilliant expedition, Banks there in person, undergoing the hardships of the ship's passage in the gale, and in the landing and occupation of Brownsville. It was a swift and decisive operation. Carried out almost entirely by Grant's officers and men, it pointed out their hardiness and their determined behavior, regardless of their sloppy uniforms. Grant had not stinted, he had sent some of those he held in highest regard; Ransom, an example.[1592]

1589. O.R. Vol. 26/I, pp. 405, 409–410. The *Matamoras* was one of three light-draft river steamers placed at the disposal of Banks. Quite a change for the "outlaw" the army was ordered to chase back in 1860–61. Shorey, pp. 58–61.

1590. O.R. Vol. 26/I, pp. 416–425, 446; Shorey, pp. 62–65.

1591. Compiled Records, 37th Illinois Infantry, Microcopy 594, roll 19, p. 1641; O.R. Vol. 26/I, p. 847, 880, 898; Shorey, p. 68.

1592. Grant, vol. 1, p. 573: "Suffice it to say, the close of the siege of Vicksburg found us with an army unsurpassed, in proportion to its numbers, taken as a whole of officers and men. A military education had been acquired which no other school could have given. Men who thought a company was quite enough for them to command properly at the beginning would have made good regimental or brigade commanders; most of the brigade commanders were equal to the command of a division, and one, Ransom, was equal to the command of a corps

While all of this was taking place, as has been noted, Franklin had been ordered to stand by and send reinforcements if necessary, yet make no moves that would indicate a withdrawal. The Confederate forces in the Teche country were to be kept occupied and made to think that the overland attack toward Texas was still the objective, albeit changed to the lower route to Niblett's Bluff. As we have seen, the feint, as it had developed, had worked perfectly. At least up to the end of October, Taylor was not yet aware of the Rio Grande Expedition.[1593]

"Record" 12/63
31 OCTOBER–31 DECEMBER, 1863 NEW IBERIA, LOUISIANA

Nov. 1 Marched from Barre's Landing to Carrion Crow Bayou 14 miles.
Nov. 2   " "   Carrion Crow Bayou to Vermillion Bayou 16 miles.
Nov. 3   " "   Vermillion Bayou to Carrion Crow Bayou 16 miles.
Nov. 4   " "   Carrion Crow Bayou to Vermillion Bayou 16 miles.
Nov. 16   " "   Vermillion Bayou to Camp Pratt 16 miles.
Nov. 17   " "   Camp Pratt to New Iberia 5 ½–Remained until present date.

Henry W. Closson	Capt. Det. svc. Chief of Arty. 19th Army Corps.
Franck E. Taylor	1st Lt. Absent with leave S.O. no. 544 War Dept. Wash. Dec. 28, '63.
Edward Appleton	1st Lt. Absent without leave since Dec. 28, '63.
James A. Sanderson	2nd Lt. Commanding Battery.

Transferred:
Charles B. Slack   2nd Lt. Relieved from Duty with Battery Nov. 8, 1863 S.O. no. 4 Hdqrts. Dept. of the Gulf Oct. 20, 1863.

Attached:
Charles Wheeler   Pvt. Ass't. Com'y of Musters Clerk. Detached from the 8th Reg't Vermont Vols.

Detached:
Edmond Cotterill   Cpl. On Det. Svc. Clerk in A.G.O. Wash. S.O. no. 426, War Dept. A.G.O. Wash. Sept. 23, '63. Left. Co. Nov. 20, '63.
Jeremiah Connell   Pvt. On Det. Svc. Orderly to Chief of Artillery 19th Army Corps. For 1st Re-Enlistment $2.00 per month
George Freidman   Pvt. On Det. Svc. at N.O. as Artillerist. Left Co. May 24, '62
Amelius Straub   Pvt. On Det. Svc. at Baton Rouge as cook in Univ. Hosp. since June 1, '63.

Absent with leave:
William E. Scott   Cpl. Absent with leave since Dec. 29, '63
Terence McGauly   Pvt. Absent with leave since Dec. 29, '63. Due U.S. for ord. $0.67.

Absent without leave:
Joseph Kutschor   Pvt. Deserted
William Brooks   Pvt. At New Orleans, from Marine Hospital, never joined company.

---

at least." From Shorey, p. 60: "During this brief campaign…General Ransom completely captured the affections of the Maine troops, and he and they were ever after close friends."
1593. O. R. Vol. 26/I, pp. 779.

Discharged

Lewis Keller	1st Sgt. Dec. 29,'63 At New Iberia, by order of Gen'l Franklin, S.O. no. 105 Hdqrts. 19th Army Corps Promoted 2nd Lt. 2nd Louisiana Cavalry.
Henry Champion	Pvt. Nov. 20,'63 At New Orleans, from University Hospital, for disability.
Thomas Newton	Pvt. Dec. 13,'63 At Port Hudson, by expiration of service.
Louis Lighna	Pvt. Oct. 15,'63 By expiration of service. Enlisted in 2nd Louisiana Vol. Cavalry.

Died:

James Hanney	Pvt. Nov. 2,'63 At Carrion Crow Bayou, of inflammation of the bowels.
John Baker	Pvt. Nov. 14,'63 At Vermillion Bayou from injuries incurred by a fall.
Hiram Hubbard	Pvt. Oct. 26,'63 At Barre's Landing, of congestive fever.

Joined from Desertion:

James Comfort	Pvt. Oct. 9,'63 At Vermillion Bayou. Due U.S. for ord. $41.63 to forfeit 1 mo. 19 days pay for time to make good to the U.S. time lost by desertion. S.O. # 83, Hdqrts. 19th Corps Dec. 5,'63.
Francis Jessop	Pvt. do.
Christian Meese	Pvt. do.
Michael Breen	Pvt. Oct. 10,'63 Arrested Aug. 26.
Sholto O'Brien	Pvt. Oct. 21,'63 At New Iberia.
Patrick Craffy	Pvt. Date and place not listed.
Joseph H. Parslow	Pvt. do.
Owen A. Wren	Pvt. do.

All of the above were court-martialed at the same time, December 5th, 1863, though most were returned in October, and are thus listed twice. All received forfeiture of pay for time lost, similar to Comfort, but no other penalty, because they returned voluntarily.

James Flynn	Pvt. Absent without leave until Dec. 30,'63. For 1st Re-enlistment $2.00 per mo.
John H. Moran	Pvt. In confinement. Due U.S. for ord. $41.63. To forfeit $8.00 per month from his pay for 4 months. S.O. no. 3 Hdqrts. 1st Div. 19th Corps Sept. 23,'63
John Lowry	Pvt. In confinement.

Colored Cooks: Henry Jefferson, Philip Evens, Virgil Ayres

Strength: 105 Sick: 5

Sick present: none

Sick Absent:

William C. Brunskill	Sick at Ft. Hamilton, NY left Co. Sept. 17, 1861
William Crowley	Sick at Baton Rouge since July 13,'63
George Chase	Sick at Brashear City since April 22,'63
Corneilus McEnearny	Sick in Gen. Hosp. New Iberia, since Nov. 17,'63
Charles F. Mansfield	Sick at Pensacola, Fla. Since Dec. 24,'62

For the first time, an officer, Appleton, is listed as absent without leave. With every other senior officer away for some reason, the command of the company has devolved to the most junior officer, Sanderson, who had arrived only a few weeks ago, an 1862 graduate[1594] of West Point.

Lt. Slack, who was from Massachusetts, was transferred to Nims' Battery, and would be wounded on April 8th 1864, at the Battle of Mansfield.[1595]

Cpl. Edmond Cotterill must have had exceptional skills to have been transferred to Washington.

Among those discharged, Keller had been promoted to the 2nd Louisiana Cavalry, and its unit roster confirms it. No one was immediately named to fill his place. Louis Lighna's record is finally updated. He evidently followed Keller, the 2nd Louisiana Cavalry first being organized on November 25th at New Orleans. Though he never returned to Battery L, Lighna was still serving in the army, in the 1st Regiment of Artillery, Battery A, at Pensacola, in 1875,[1596] where he was commended for his services and untiring zeal, which were "invaluable" during the yellow fever epidemic of that year. He had a son who died in the epidemic who is buried in Barrancas National Cemetery. Henry Champion had been discharged for disability, after being sick since August 27th. Compare this with William Brunskill, still sick at Fort Hamilton, New York, since September 1861.

There were no new deserters that had joined.

Joseph Kutschor, listed as an exchanged prisoner of war in the August–October roll, is now listed as deserted.

The Battle of Grand Coteau

In response to Banks' order to General Franklin to be prepared to send reinforcements to the Rio Grande Expedition, on the 27th of October he withdrew the 1st Division of the 13th Army Corps, under Lawler, from Opelousas to New Iberia.[1597] That left the 3rd Division under McGinnis at Opelousas, and the 1st Brigade of the 4th Division under Burbridge at Barre's Landing. Both, including the 19th Corps, were ordered to pull out on the 31st of October, their march beginning the next day. The first move was to Carrion Crow Bayou, about sixteen miles. McGinnis was to camp on the north side of the Bayou, and Burbridge, coming from the direction of

---

1594. Cullum, vol. 2, no. 84.

1595. O.R. Vol. 34/I, p. 462.

1596. Haskin, p. 387. Requests for Lighna's service records at the National Archives have been returned with the comment "No Record." 2nd Louisiana Regiment history: *www.nps.gov/civilwar/search-rec*; Barrancas National Cemetery Records.

1597. O.R. Vol. 26/I. pp.779, 354, 357, 369. McGinnis was ill and did not participate. The corps commander, C. C. Washburn, was in his place. McGinnis's name has been used only to identify the 3rd Division. Note the hectic moves in the "Record of Events." The description given by Washburn as the position of Burbridge was north of "Muddy Bayou." Subsequently, in Burbridge's report, he describes his position as "3 miles from Carrion Crow Bayou, near the head of a small bayou that runs in the direction of Opelousas"–Bayou Bourbeau.

the Teche, was to camp two miles away. The general location is shown in figure 6.[1598] Weitzel, Grover, and Battery L, were to encamp on the south side.

Having been notified that the enemy was falling back from Opelousas, Taylor ordered Green to pursue and harass. It was Confederate General Thomas Green's cavalry again, the one and the same that had attacked Fort Butler, after having run wild in the La Fourche back in June. He was now reinforced by three regiments of Walker's Texas infantry.[1599]

On the morning of November 2nd, the 19th Corps pulled out, its destination Vermilion Bayou, about eleven miles. The detachments of the 13th Corps under Washburn were left to hold their positions.

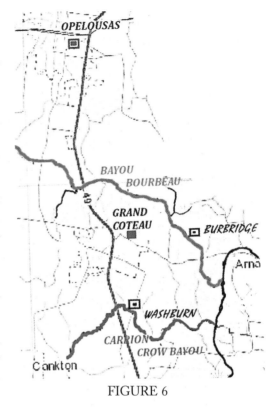

FIGURE 6

Burbridge's 1st Brigade, 4th Division, consisted of the 60th Indiana, 67th Indiana, 83rd Ohio, 96th Ohio, and the 23rd Wisconsin. They were accompanied by Fonda's 118th Illinois Mounted Infantry, the 1st Louisiana Cavalry, and three artillery batteries: the 17th Ohio, a detachment of the 14th New York, and one section of Nims' Battery; the total numbering 1,625 men.[1600] Included with them, as support, was one company of the 6th Missouri Cavalry.[1601] They were camped on the north side of Bayou Bourbeau, with about three miles of open prairie separating them from Washburn.

On November 2nd, Green advanced and tested Burbridge all day long. Washburn sent the 1st Brigade of the 3rd Division out to reinforce Burbridge, but finding the enemy had disappeared, they returned to their camp on Carrion Crow Bayou. However, enough was seen of Green's force for Burbridge to estimate it at 2,500. As it was later learned, Green's tentative moves on November 2nd were only because he was waiting for his infantry to come up, which was marching from Opelousas.

That night, six men from Burbridge's 1st Louisiana Cavalry deserted,[1602] no doubt bringing news of Burbridge's strength and dispositions to Green. On the 3rd,

---

1598. Figure 6, drawing by the author.
1599. Taylor, p. 150, O.R. Vol. 26/I, pp. 369, 393–394.
1600. O.R. Vol. 26/I, p. 360, 364. Note that each regiment averaged only 200 men.
1601. Woods, J. T., p. 40.
1602. O.R. Vol. 26/I, p. 360, 365.

skirmishing began at 10:00 a.m. and then tapered off, allowing Burbridge to think it safe enough to send away the 83rd Ohio on a foraging expedition. The troops were allowed to stack arms. Everyone's attention was then turned to the two paymasters who were in camp. In addition, the 23rd Wisconsin was to vote for state elections.

Their position was exposed, "either in front, flank, or rear..."[1603] and no mention is made of any earthworks having been dug, or any sort of defensive preparations made. Burbridge's concerns were put off by Washburn as nothing but "a scare." The following is taken from the history of the 96th Ohio: "At 12:00 our retreating cavalry gave notice that 'the Philistines were upon us.' The thrilling long-roll called every man to arms. In calm calculated haste, each donned his battle trappings, and with clockwork precision fell into line."

The next quote is from the same page, and it refers to Green's infantry and the Bellevue Road from Opelousas, where his infantry arrived and without "an instant's rest" went into battle.

> Marching directly on the road that turned to the left, close to the right of our camp, the rebel infantry advanced in force, while clouds of cavalry emerged from the woods and deployed on the flanks of their infantry, scattering like wild Commanches [*sic*], and enveloping our camp...our line of battle faces the woods on the right, close to and at right angles to our camp. The 67th Indiana, in open prairie on our left, supports two guns of the 17th Ohio Battery. The 96th Ohio and the 60th Indiana, with the remaining guns, form the centre. The 23rd Wisconsin, a little delayed in reaching their position, forms the right of our line.

Figure 7 represents the battle status at an estimated time of 1:15 p.m., with subsequent movements. The full engagement had started at 12:30, and lasted until 3:00. The line of grey rectangles along the right are Green's infantry, shown deployed in the woods, after arriving from Opelousas. The semicircle of rectangles at the top are Green's cavalry, already drawing around the exposed 67th Indiana, which, in its last-ditch effort, has formed in a hollow square, a tactic left over from the Napoleonic wars.

The numbers are the regiments of Burbridge's troops, with the exception of the 46th Indiana, which is from Cameron's 1st Brigade, 3rd Division.

Hounded by the rebel cavalry, the 83rd Ohio skedaddled home from its foraging expedition, and briefly stopped to support the 17th Ohio Battery. Both were soon flanked, and the 83rd withdrew.[1604] The 60th Indiana, after stubbornly resisting,

---

1603. Woods, J. T., pp. 41–44. A map accompanies the text, p. 48. It is reproduced as figure 6. The quotations are made above to give the reader the exact original initial description of the battle, because other reports refer to "right" and "left" without any frame of reference. After some study, Woods' map was altered and reoriented to conform to the above text. O. R. Vol. 26/I, p. 365.

1604. Marshall, T. B., pp. 112–113; The 83rd history is vague, and the author has added only what reasonably seems to have been their actions. Suffice that they returned, a fact which is ignored

was finally overwhelmed when the 67th Indiana shrunk into its hollow square, which left a gap on the 60th's flank. It then fell back into the 96th Ohio,[1605] as is shown, which made an even bigger gap in the Union line, which fell back into the ravine, and from there into a final defensive line in and along the ravine. About 200 of the 67th were taken prisoner. The 17th Ohio Battery managed to escape with the loss of one gun.

Marland's single section of Nims' Battery, having been abandoned by the infantry, hung on and continued firing, and having expended some 50 shots, it was charged upon from three sides.[1606] It then retreated into the woods, among Green's infantry. Seeing the bridge across the bayou destroyed, they continued, pistols in hand, with one horse killed and two men missing, and succeeded in charging straight through Green's infantry to the open field. They then "made straight for the [46th Indiana] regiment, followed closely by the rebel cavalry."[1607] The 46th Indiana, which was the first unit to respond from McGinnis' division, had just come up from their camp on Carrion Crow Bayou. Most of the rest of the 3rd Division followed, and the enemy attack was finally halted. The stabilized line is represented by the unlabeled rectangles along the ravine. The rebel cavalry briefly attempted to flank Washburn, but three regiments left in the rear drove them off. Figure 8 is a fair representation of the open country in which most of the action took place.[1608]

Washburn's report of the action having arrived at Weitzel's camp, the order was given, late on the evening of Nov. 3rd, for the 1st Division of the 19th Army

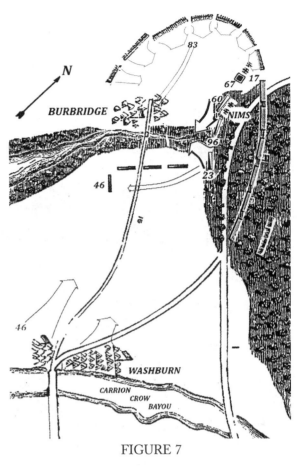

FIGURE 7

---

in almost every other Union report or unit history. O.R. Vol. 26/I, p. 394, Green credited the Union troops as having "most stubbornly resisted."

1605. Woods, J. T., p. 42; Scott, R. B., p. 68.
1606. O.R. Vol. 26/I, p. 371; Whitcomb, p. 56.
1607. Bringhurst and Swigart, p.78.
1608. Figure 8 from Leslie's, p. 492.

FIGURE 8

Corps[1609] to return to Carrion Crow Bayou. Battery L's record of events shows them having already arrived back there on the 3rd, but added detail is absent. After a forced march of five hours, the First Division arrived at 7:00 a.m., on the 4th, to find that all was quiet.[1610] "Subsequent investigation showed that the attack was a shameful surprise, and was declared by General Weitzel "disgraceful to our arms." If the reader remembers the disputes between the easterners and their new western comrades, this now gave the "paper collar" easterners their opportunity to respond to who "knew a thing or two," particularly the daring heroism of Nims' battery contrasted with the huge number of those captured and missing from the ranks of the western regiments. The gallant action that saved the section of Nims' battery resulted in the Medal of Honor being awarded to 1st Lt. William Marland.[1611]

Green submitted a report of his casualties,[1612] which listed 22 killed, 103 wounded, and 55 missing. A revised report of Union casualties had 25 killed, 129 wounded, and 562 (!) captured and missing.

Battery L and Weitzel's division quickly returned to Vermilionville, and remained there until transferred via Camp Pratt to New Iberia, were they remained until the 7th of January, 1864. Banks was still focused on Texas, as well he should be, he now had more than twice as many troops there as in Louisiana. The policies in Louisiana outlined in instructions given to General Franklin in October, were still in effect:[1613] "…hold your position in that quarter, and ascertain as much concerning the country…as possible, and…keep these headquarters well informed…" Though

---

1609. O.R., Vol. 26/I, p. 369; Pellet, p. 129.
1610. Pellet, pp. 156–157. The 114th was a part of Weitzel's First Division, 19th Corps.
1611. *www.history.army.mil/html/moh*. It was not awarded until 1897.
1612. O.R. Vol. 26/I, pp. 359, 395.
1613. O.R. Vol. 26/I, p. 761, 891–892; Clark, pp. 134, 137.

subsequent to these instructions, the Battle of Grand Coteau had taken place, it was initiated by Taylor, not General Franklin. Again, on the 11th of November, a Union cavalry reconnaissance to the Grand Coteau area was forced to beat a hasty retreat.

By the end of December, with the exception of one brigade at Plaquemine, the entire 13th Corps had been shipped to Texas. A defensive stance for the 19th Corps was now a necessity; the 19th Corps, with a total of 8,500 men, including the cavalry, and its recently mounted infantry regiments, was in no position to hold all of this territory as well as to initiate a campaign against Taylor, whose forces were variously estimated at 6,000 or 10,000 depending on whether or not Green had returned to Texas.[1614] Green, with about 3,000 men, indeed had. Another consideration was that the older three-year regiment's terms of enlistment were about to expire in January and February, further reducing Franklin's strength.

The old familiar name, ever since he had been stationed as engineer at Fort Pickens in the summer of 1861, was Godfrey Weitzel. On December 13th, Battery L's association with him would end, when he was replaced by Emory as commander of the 1st Division.[1615] He was transferred out of the Department of the Gulf, and was soon serving, once again, under Butler, his old mentor; after Butler had been given the command of the Department of Virginia and North Carolina.[1616] The entire 19th Corps would be reorganized on February 15th, 1864, and Battery L would then be assigned to Emory.[1617]

"Record" 2/64
31 DECEMBER 1863-29 FEBRUARY 1864 FRANKLIN, LOUISIANA

Marched from New Iberia the 7th of January on route for Franklin, 53 miles. 8th marched 12 miles. 9th marched to Franklin 5 miles and remained there until present date.

Henry W. Closson	Capt. On det. svc. Chief of Arty. 19th Army Corps S.O. no. 13, Hdqrts. 19th Army Corps Oct. 4, '63.
Franck E. Taylor	1st Lt. Commdg. Battery and Asst. Comm. Of Musters, S.O. no. 92 Hdqrts. Dept. of the Gulf 19th Army Corps.
Edward L. Appleton	1st Lt. Commanding Battery
James A. Sanderson	2nd Lt.
Detached:	
Edmond Cotterill	Cpl. On Det. Svc. Clerk in A.G.O. Wash. S.O. no. 426, War Dept. A.G.O. Wash. Sept. 23, '63. Left Co. Nov. 20, '63.
Jeremiah Connell	Pvt. On Det. Svc. Orderly Chief of Artillery

---

1614. O.R. Vol. 26/I, pp. 852, 863, 920; O.R. Vol. 26/II, p. 260, 465; Irwin, pp. 272, 278.
1615. O.R. Vol. 26/I, p. 837.
1616. Butler, B. F., p. 584. We remember that the ever-faithful Lincoln had regretted sacking Butler at the end of 1862. He would soon reinstate McClernand as well.
1617. O.R. Vol. 34/II, p. 333.

George Freidman	Pvt. On Det. Svc. at N.O. as Artillerist. Left Co. May 24,'62.
Amelius Straub	Pvt. On Det. Svc. at Baton Rouge as cook in Univ. Hosp. since June 1,'63.

Absent in Confinement:

Patrick Gibbons	Pvt. At Ship Island serving sentence of G.C.M. no. 18, Hdqrts. 1st Div. 19th Army Corps Dec. 31,'63. Left Co. Jan. 8,'64.
Michael O'Sullivan	Pvt. In jail at N.O. Left Co. Sept. 2,'63.
John Lewery	Pvt. Apprehended as a deserter and confined at New Orleans.

Absent without leave:

Joseph Kutschor	Pvt. Exchanged prisoner of war

Deserted: none

Discharged:

Charles F. Mansfield	Pvt. 10 Jan.'64 on Surgeon's certificate of disability, at Fort Pickens, Fla.
John Tomson	Pvt. 9 Jan.'64 by expiration of service at Franklin
Morris Galavan	Pvt. 14 Jan.'64 by expiration of service at Franklin
Martin Stanners	Pvt. 19 Jan.'64 by expiration of service at Franklin
Daniel McSweeny	Pvt. 11 Feb.'64 by expiration of service at Franklin.

Joined from Desertion:

John Lewery	Pvt. Feb.'64 Apprehended, in confinement at New Orleans.

Strength: 101 Sick: 8

Sick Present: Wm. Creed, Prosper Ferrari, Charles Jackel, Frank Morgan, Daniel Moore

Sick Absent:

William C. Brunskill	Sick at Ft. Hamilton, NY left Co. Sept. 17,'61
William Crowley	Sick at Baton Rouge since July 13,'63.
George Chase	Sick at Brashear City since April 22,'63.

The cooks are not listed.

Appleton had been back in command since January. No explanation for his absence appears in the muster roll record.

Why William Brunskill had not been discharged is of interest, considering that other chronic cases such as Mansfield's, who had been left sick at Pensacola since Dec. 24, '62, was finally dealt with here. Note that Chase is still missing.

As is noted in the "Record," Franklin's troops began their march out of New Iberia on January 7th, and it was abandoned on the night of the 8th, save a number of individuals with smallpox, who had to be left behind in the care of a surgeon.[1618] The move had been delayed due to the freezing rain and sleet on the 6th. Though the rain had stopped, the roads were very muddy. On the 8th, the exceptional cold had frozen the roads so that good progress was initially made. However, the morning sun softened them, making the journey slow and exhausting. Some badly mired horses had to be shot. Finally, on the 9th, they went into winter quarters at Franklin, on the banks of the Teche.[1619] By the 15th, the weather moderated, reminding them

---

1618. O.R. Vol. 34/II, p. 863.
1619. Pellet, p. 166–167.

of early September in the north. One-month furloughs, and bounties were granted to those of the volunteer units that had re-enlisted for three years or the war, and before the end of the month, almost all of the 19th Corps had done so.[1620]

It is noted that Battery L now had 101 men, down from its high of 149 a year before. As a consequence, their number of guns was temporarily reduced to four from six. In fact, all of the reorganized 1st Division artillery units, which included Company A, 1st U.S., the 4th and 6th Massachusetts, and the 25th New York, had only four guns. This was also true of the 2nd Division Artillery. The only artillery company that still had six guns was Nims', with their signature 6-pounder bronze rifles. They, however, had been assigned to Lee's cavalry, which, as will be seen, would put them in extreme harm's way once again.

The two months at Franklin were pleasant, the most pleasant in recent memory. The people seemed friendly, and came out to see the drilling, the parades, and the elaborate decorations that the various regiments built. Emory's selection of their campsite, Camp Emory, was level, green, and "with just enough trees to shade it, but not mar its beauty or interfere…" with the proper layout of the encampment.[1621] Arbors and bowers of evergreens and Spanish moss enhanced the grounds, which "were laid out with exquisite taste."

In the interval, much was discussed between Banks and Halleck, and now, William Tecumseh Sherman, who had taken Grant's place.[1622] The seizure of those points on the coast of Texas did not satisfy Halleck; he still insisted that the Red River was the "best line of defense for Louisiana and Arkansas and as a base of operations against Texas."[1623] Halleck's idea was to unite three forces against Shreveport. One would be sent by Sherman from Vicksburg, a second, from Little Rock, under Steele, the commander of the Department of Arkansas, and the third, that of Banks. The Red River being expected to have its spring rise by the time the plans were to go into effect, Banks' army would be supported by Porter's ironclads. By January 23rd, Banks had agreed with Halleck, and by February 2nd Banks was withdrawing troops from Texas.

It is noted in passing that Lincoln felt the political necessity of healing the wounded pride of Democratic Gen. John A. McClernand (note that in November, Lincoln had reinstated Butler) after his being ousted from command by Grant a year earlier. Here in Texas was a remnant of the 13th Corps, McClernand's old command, which he could perhaps manage, since the defined strategy was to be one of defense only. On February 20th, McClernand was ordered to relieve E. O. C. Ord. One of McClernand's first tasks was to reluctantly evacuate Indianola. This

---

1620. O.R. Vol. 34/II, p. 124, 132.
1621. Clark, pp. 139–140.
1622. Grant, vol. 2, p. 27. Grant had left Mississippi on October 20th.
1623. O.R. Vol. 34/II, pp. 15, 41–42, 45, 133, 215; Irwin, 282–283.

was done on February 28th, bringing along many of its citizens to New Orleans.[1624]

The proposed Red River Campaign was now waiting on the completion of Sherman's expedition to Meridian, Mississippi, which was ordered by Grant to try to break the rail connections there to isolate Mississippi from the east. Having failed in this, or so he thought,[1625] Sherman turned around, and with gusto embraced the Red River Campaign. Unfortunately, Steele, at Little Rock, was full of excuses. His latest message to Banks was that he had to deploy troops to secure the state elections, scheduled for March 14th. He suggested that he could, after that, make a demonstration on the Confederate flank, and if this was done, "they will run to Texas." Having gone to New Orleans to discuss the campaign with Banks, Sherman indicated his impatience with such an excuse, and endorsed Steele's letter by noting: "The civil election is as nothing compared with the fruits of success."

Sherman was one of Grant's men—all business.

A summary memo of the meeting between Banks and Sherman[1626] stated that Sherman would select two divisions for the campaign, about 10,000 men, to rendezvous with Admiral Porter at the mouth of the Red River. Porter would transport Sherman's troops up the river with the goal of meeting Banks at Alexandria on March 15th. Sherman's troops were "designed to operate by water," not having the encumbrances of wagons or horses. The next part of the memo was to prove all governing, and indeed, fateful: "I calculate, and so report to General Grant, that this detachment of his forces in no event go beyond Shreveport, and that you spare them the moment you can, trying to get them back to the Mississippi in thirty days from the time that they actually enter Red River." Grant had planned on Sherman being available by April 15th to begin a move from the Tennessee River into the south, against Johnston and Atlanta.[1627]

Grant was appointed a lieutenant-general on March 2nd.[1628] Only two others had held the rank, George Washington and Winfield Scott, but Grant's victories at Chattanooga, which routed Bragg out of Tennessee for good, and caused Jefferson Davis to remove him from command, had so impressed the Congress that Grant's mentor, Congressman Elihu Washburne introduced a bill to revive the rank. There could now be no doubt that Grant's desires would govern the strategy for the rest of the war, and in fact, the Red River Campaign could be said to be obsolete before it started, because Grant opposed it. It was a creature of Halleck, who was now out-ranked by Grant. Having acted as the habitual "yes man" to Lincoln and

---

1624. O.R. Vol. 34/II, pp. 448–449, 451, 496–497.
1625. Nicolay and Hay, vol. 8, pp. 331–332. As it happened, the Confederate authorities were sufficiently alarmed, thinking that Sherman would attack Mobile, that Jefferson Davis insisted on sending reinforcements there.
1626. O.R. Vol. 34/II, pp. 491, 494, 512. The meeting lasted from Mar. 1st to Mar. 3rd.
1627. Grant, vol. 2, pp. 110, 120.
1628. Nicolay and Hay, vol. 8, pp. 334, 336; Grant, vol. 2, p. 114.

Seward, if Halleck's Red River Campaign had not already been in effect before Grant was promoted, it might have been entirely cancelled. Grant's sole focus was on "Richmond, Lee and his army."[1629] Unfortunately, the campaign was left to limp along, fatally fettered by the required return of Sherman's troops.

Most significantly, the objective of the campaign was *de facto* modified. It was no longer to be an expedition into Texas, if in fact Grant initially understood this, and it seems that he did not. He never even learned of it until February 15th, and then only indirectly.

Finally appraised of the plan, a March 15th memo[1630] written by Grant to Banks stated that under no circumstances could Banks hold Sherman's troops longer than the 30 days agreed to, and that they should be sent back "even if it should mean the abandonment of the main object of the expedition." The main object was then redefined:[1631] "Should it prove successful, hold Shreveport and Red River with such force as you deem necessary and return the balance to the neighborhood of New Orleans."

Lest Banks had misunderstood the March 15th memo, another from Grant on the 31st starkly clarified his orders: first, if the expedition against Shreveport was successful, the defense of the Red River should be turned over to General Steele and the navy, and, secondly: "That you abandon Texas entirely…" Grant was his own man now, conducting the war regardless of Lincoln's previous stance on Texas. Grant wanted to free Banks to go after Mobile, but as Irwin says,[1632] "…it would have been far better to revoke the orders than to trammel their execution with conditions so hard that Banks might well have thrown up the campaign then and there." Unfortunately, absent a clear "no" from Grant, Banks plowed ahead.

Though there were other considerations, Grant initially would have none of them. Halleck had expressed them in early January. Among the many virtues of the Red River, outside of being a route to Texas, it was a shorter and better line of defense for General Steele in Arkansas, and "…moreover, it would open to us the cotton and stores in Northeastern Louisiana and Southern Arkansas." Certainly, the Confederates expected the cotton in Taylor's district to be a target, and gave direction to destroy it if it were in danger of falling into the hands of the enemy.

Of course, Admiral Porter was interested in cotton, so he was in favor of going

---

1629. Grant, vol. 2, p. 146.
1630. O.R. Vol. 34/I, p. 203; O,R. Vol. 34/II, p. 330.
1631. Grant, with his practical knowledge, would have inherently known that forage stations would have to be set up along the route to keep the animals watered and fed if the expedition was to extend into the desert area of Texas. This would take weeks, and the caches would have to be guarded from Confederate destruction. Texas was an inconceivable goal for any 30-day expedition. It would be inconsistent with Grant's plans for the spring campaign. Grant, vol. 2, pp. 559–560.
1632. Irwin, p. 294; O.R. Vol. 34/II, pp. 55–56, 502, 653, 818; O.R. Vol. 34/I, pp. 358–359, 495, 509.

anywhere that he could find it. As a prize of war, in his distorted interpretation of the old navy prize rules, Porter never failed to bring home all that could be loaded on board.[1633] All of the Mississippi Squadron hoped to become rich. As early as March 24th, while off Alexandria, and hardly having begun the campaign, Porter reported having seized 2,021 bales.

BATTERY L 1864 ROSTER
From 31 December 1863–29 February 1864 Muster Roll

1. Henry W. Closson — Capt.
2. Franck E. Taylor — 1st Lt.
3. Edward L. Appleton — 1st Lt.
4. James A. Sanderson — 2nd Lt.

1. Julius Becker Sgt.	12 Oct. '59 New York	1. Michael White Cpl.	7 Oct.'59 Boston
2. David J. Wicks Sgt.	25 Oct. '59 New York	2. Edmond Cotterill Cpl.	12 July '62 New Orleans
3. William Demarest Sgt.	19 Oct. '59 New York	3. Charles E. Walton Cpl.	12 Nov.'62 Pensacola, FL
		4. William E. Scott Cpl.	9 Feb.'60 Boston

1. Ludwig Rupprecht Musician 7 Feb.'60 New York   1. Isaac T. Cain Artificer 4 Oct.'59 Boston
2. Frank Morgan Artificer 14 Nov.'62 Pensacola, FL

Privates

1. Ahern, James	18 Oct.'60 Boston	45. Lowry, John	24 feb.'63 Baton Rouge
2. Anglin, Edmond	19 Oct.'59 New York	46. Mahoney, Thomas	14 Nov.'62 Pensacola
3. Beglan, James	25 Oct.'60 New York	47. Mansfield, Charles F.	16 Jan.'61 Boston
4. Brunskill, William C.	19 Oct.'59 New York	48. McCarthy, James	4 Oct.'60 Boston
5. Brown, William F.	1 Nov.'59 Boston	49. McDonagh, Miles	17 Sept.'60 New York
6. Burke, John	17 Oct.'60 New York	50. McEnearny, Cornelius	16 Dec.'62 Pensacola
7. Bieber, Peter	24 Feb.'63 Baton Rouge	51. McGaley, Terence	18 Sept.'60 New York
8. Breen, Michael	24 Feb.'63 Baton Rouge	52. McGuiness, Angus	14 Nov.'62 Pensacola
9. Campbell, James	15 Nov.'62 Pensacola	53. McKinney, John	14 Nov.'62 Pensacola
10. Card, Rowland	12 Nov.'62 Pensacola	54. Meese, Christian	12 Nov.'62 Pensacola
11. Champion, Henry	12 Nov.'62 Pensacola	55. Meyer, John	1 Mar.'60 New York
12. Chase, George	11 Dec.'62 Pensacola	56. Miller, John	12 Nov.'62 Pensacola
13. Clinton, Thomas	24 Feb.'63 Baton Rouge	57. Montgomery, Solomon J.	14 Nov.'62 Pensacola
14. Comfort, James	12 Nov.'62 Pensacola	58. Moore, Churchill	19 Nov.'62 Pensacola
15. Connell, Jeremiah	14 Sept.'59 Ft. Clark, TX	59. Moore, Daniel	24 Feb.'63 Baton Rouge
16. Cooke, Charles	24 Feb.'63 Baton Rouge	60. Moran, John H	23 Feb.'63 Baton Rouge
17. Coyne, Owen	10 Dec.'60 Ft. Duncan	61. Nitschke, John G.	6 Feb.'60 New York
18. Craffy, Patrick	27 Sept.'60 Boston	62. O'Brien, Sholto	24 Feb.'63 Baton Rouge
19. Creed, William	27 Sept.'60 Boston	63. O'Sullivan, Michael	26 Sept.'60 Boston
20. Crowley, William	17 Nov.'62 Pensacola	64. Olvany, Michael	25 Oct.'60 New York
21. Cummings, Patrick	25 Oct.'60 New York	65. Orcutt, Ephraim	19 Nov.'62 Pensacola
22. Donnely, Patrick	1 Nov.'60 Boston	66. Parks, William	17 Nov.'62 Pensacola
23. Eisle, Joseph	24 Feb.'63 Baton Rouge	67. Parslow, Joseph H.	15 Dec.'62 Pensacola
24. Ferrari, Prosper	22 Oct.'60 New York	68. Pfiffer, George	24 Feb.'63 Baron Rouge

---

1633. O.R. Vol. 34/I, p. 213; ORN ser. 1, vol. 26, p. 35. The ship's captain got the lion's share of the adjudicated value, but the sailors share was enough to make them go after the prize with great enthusiasm.

25. Friedman, George	7 Feb.'60 New York	69. Schneider, Philip H.	16 Oct.'60 New York
26. Flynn, Arthur	12 Nov.'62 Pensacola	70. Shaw, Warren P.	26 Oct.'60 Boston
27. Flynn, James	12 Sept.'59 Ft. Clark, TX	71. Smith, James H.	16 Dec.'62 Pensacola
28. Foote, Edward A.	24 Feb.'63 Baton Rouge	72. Smith, Joseph	11 Oct.'59 New York
29. Gibbons, Patrick	16 Dec.'62 Pensacola	73. Smith, William H.	16 Dec.'62 Pensacola
30. Hadley, George F.	1 Mar.'60 Boston	74. Stewart, William	12 Nov.'62 Pensacola
31. Hall, Benjamin O.	15 Oct.'62 Pensacola	75. Straub, Amelius	8 Feb.'60 New York
32. Harrison, George	25 Dec.'62 Pensacola	76. Thompson, William V.	13 Sept.'60 Rochester, NY
33. Howard, Daniel	24 feb.'63 Baton Rouge	77. Tieghe, Michael	25 Feb.'63, Baton Rouge
34. Howard, George	25 Oct.'60 New york	78. Townsend, Reuben	27 Sept.'60 Boston
35. Hughs, Benjamin	27 Feb.'63 Baton Rouge	79. Ward, Henry H.	8 Nov.'60 New York
36. Jackel, Charles	25 Oct.'60 New York	80. Welsch, Peter	19 Nov.'62 Pensacola
37. Jessop, Francis	12 Nov.'62 Pensacola	81. Wilder, Joshua E.	19 Nov.'62 Pensacola
38. Kelly, John	25 Dec.'62 Pensacola	82. Wilkson, Henry	24 Dec.'60 New York
39. Kenny, Michael	8 Feb.'60 New York	83. Willcox, Thomas M.	15 Dec.'62 Pensacola
40. Kenny, Theodore W.	23 Feb.'63 Baton Rouge	84. William, Henry	28 Sept.'60 Rochester, NY
41. Kilburne, Sirenus	17 Nov.'62 Pensacola	85. Woodruff, Lyman	27 Feb.'63 Barton Rouge
42. Kutschor, Joseph	13 feb.'60 New York	86. Wood, John C.	16 Dec.'62 Pensacola
43. Lashner, Joseph	16 Dec.'62 Pensacola	87. Wren, Owen A.	11 Dec.'60 Boston
44. Lewery, John	14 Nov.'62 Pensacola		

"Record" 4/64
29 FEBRUARY–30 APRIL, 1864 FRANKLIN–ALEXANDRIA, LOUISIANA

March 16th struck camp at Franklin and marched 16 miles on Opelousas road. 17th Marched to Camp Pratt 18 miles. 18th Marched 3 miles beyond Carrion Crow Bayou, 18 miles. 19th Marched to plantation near Washington, 17 miles. 21st Marched 17 miles on Alexandria road. 22nd Marched to Holmsville, 14 miles. 23rd Marched to Cheneyville, 13 miles. 24th Marched to Welles plantation, 17 miles. 25th marched to Alexandria, 13 miles. 28th Marched from Alexandria on Nachitoches road, 18 miles. 29th Marched to Pine Woods, 9 miles. 30th Marched 3 miles beyond Cloutierville, 21 miles. 31st Marched 7 miles and camped on Cane River. 2nd Marched through Nachitoches, 6 miles. 6th Marched 14 miles on Texas road. 7th Marched to Pleasant Hill 22 miles. 8th Marched 10 miles camped for 2 hours, ordered to the front and lay in woods until morning. 9th Marched to Pleasant Hill, Battery in position, went into camp for 2 hours. Battery in action at P.M. 10th Marched 22 miles. 11th Marched to Grand Ecore. 21st Struck camp at 5 P.M. and remained harnessed until 3 A.M., then marched 24 miles and camped for about 4 hours, then marched to Cloutierville. 23rd Marched to pontoon on Cane River, crossed at midnight, camped until 6 A.M. the 24th then marched 16 miles. 25th Marched through Alexandria and remained until present date.

Henry W. Closson	Capt. On det. svc. Chief of Artillery 19th Army Corps S.O. no. 13, Hdqrts. 19th Army Corps OCT. 4,'63.
Franck E. Taylor	1st Lt. Commdg. Battery and Asst. Comm. Of Musters. S.O. no. 92 Hdqrts. Dept. of the Gulf 19th Army Corps.
Edward L. Appleton	1st Lt.
James A. Sanderson	2nd Lt.

Attached: [The 13th Massachusetts Battery was ordered attached on March 1st, by Special Orders no. 60. Seven new recruits joined later. Lincoln, Batson, Bragshaw, Connor, Kingsley, & Welsh joined on May 2nd at Alexandria, and Nichols on May 30th at Morganza. None of the names of the men in the 13th Massachusetts Battery were subsequently integrated into Battery L's Muster Roll. Only exceptions, such as sick, wounded, or killed, were penned in, and appear here in *italics*].

Sias, Chauncy R.	Sgt.	Oct.13,'62 Boston	Carleton, William	Cpl.	Oct. 25,'62 Boston
Lincoln, James M.	Sgt.	Feb. 24,'64 Taunton	Fleming, Daniel H.	Cpl.	Oct. 21,'62 Boston
Merrill, Alfred K.	Sgt.	Nov. 26,'62 Charlestown	Hall, James F.	Cpl.	Oct. 1,'62 Charlestown
Betterton, George	Cpl.	Oct. 20,'62 Newton	Hesseltine, George	Cpl.	Oct. 30,'62
Dubois, Cesar	Musician	Dec. 26,'62 Boston	Hall, Ivory F.	Artificer	Jan. 24,'63 Boston
Berry, Thomas C.	Pvt.	Nov. 17.'62 Boston	Misener, James B.	Pvt.	Oct. 11,'62 Boston
Brown, Stephen E.	Pvt.	Oct. 28,'62 Boston	Mc Donald, John	Pvt.	Nov. 28,'62 Boston
Biaro, Italo	Pvt.	Jan. 21,63 Boston	McCostello, Michael	Pvt.	Mar. 30,'64 Foxboro
Batson, William	Pvt.	Mar. 29,'64 Chelsea	McCarrick, John O.	Pvt.	Mar. 31,'64 Mansfield
Bragshaw, William	Pvt.	Mar. 22,'64 Attelboro	Miller, George	Pvt.	Apr. 27,'64 Abington
Curtin, Patrick	Pvt.	Jan. 27,'63 Foxboro	Kingsley, Amos N.	Pvt.	Mar. 9,'64 Swansea
Connor, James	Pvt.	Mar. 11,'64 Bridgewater	Krall, Bartolomy	Pvt.	Apr. 8,'64 Boston
Connors, Patrick.	Pvt.	Mar. 13,'64 Scituate	Mee, Thomas	Pvt.	Mar. 31,'64 Natick
Dailey, Darby	Pvt.	Dec. 16,'62 Boston	O'Neil, Henry C.	Pvt.	Oct. 13,'62 Boston
Davis, George W.	Pvt.	Apr. 6,'64 Lancaster	Rivers, Harry	Pvt.	Oct. 17,'62 Boston
Edwards, James M.	Pvt.	Dec. 17,'62 Boston	Rivers, James H.	Pvt.	Oct. 22,'62 Boston
Falvey, Michael	Pvt.	Oct. 16,'62 Boston	Piper, Joseph	Pvt.	Apr. 1,'64 Swanzey
Ferguson, John	Pvt.	Oct. 21,'62 Boston	Simonds, John	Pvt.	Oct. 11,'62 Boston
Feeley, William	Pvt.	Nov. 28,'62 Stoughton	Sedgely, Robert	Pvt.	Nov. 28,'62 Boston
Fuchs, Henry	Pvt.	Nov. 25,'62 Boston	Sewall, James	Pvt.	Dec. 29,'62 N. Bedford
Gill, Robert	Pvt.	Oct. 22,'62 Boston	Smith, William	Pvt.	Apr. 8,'64 Lancaster
Graves, Ezekiel	Pvt.	Jan. 26,'63 Falmouth	Stevens, John	Pvt.	Apr. 21,'64 Dover
Hood, Charles	Pvt.	Oct. 28,'62 Boston	Timmins, John	Pvt.	Jan. 24,'63 E. Boston
Hartwell, James A.	Pvt.	Mar. 22,'64 Fitchburg	Thomas, Charles	Pvt.	Jan. 10,'63 Boston
Hesson, Michael	Pvt.	Apr. 25,'64 Arlington	Varner, Harry	Pvt.	Jan. 21,'63 Boston
Hiscock, George	Pvt.	Mar. 22,'64 Somerville	Wilkins, John C.	Pvt.	Oct. 8,'63 Brookline
Lynch, Thomas	Pvt.	Oct. 28,'62 Boston	Welsh, Benjamin C.	Pvt.	Mar. 9,'64 N'buryport
Larrabee, Thomas	Pvt.	Jan. 24,'63 Boston	Redding, George W.	Pvt.	Dec. 30,'62 Boston
Martin, Andrew	Pvt.	Oct. 21,'62 Boston	Roberts, Thomas	Pvt.	Jan. 8,'63 Boston
Mc Laughlin, John	Pvt.	Oct. 22,'62 Boston	Carney, David	Pvt.	May 19,'64 Newton
Murphy, Edward	Pvt.	Dec. 1,'62 Boston	Nichols, Edward A.	Pvt.	Feb. 16,'64 Boston

Detached:
Edmond Cotterill   Cpl. On Det. Svc. Clerk in A.G.O. Wash. S.O. no. 426, War Dept. A.G.O. Wash. Sept. 23,'63. Left. Co. Nov. 20,'63.
Jeremiah Connell   Pvt. On Det. Svc. Orderly Chief of Artillery
Solomon Mongomery Pvt.   do.
George Freidman   Pvt. On Det. Svc. at N.O. as Artillerist, Left Co. May 24,'62.
Amelius Straub   Pvt. On Det. Svc. at Baton Rouge as cook in Univ. Hosp. since June 1,'63.

Absent in Confinement:
Patrick Gibbons   Pvt. At Ship Island serving sentence of G.C.M. no. 18, Hdqrts. 1st Div. 19th Army Corps Dec. 31,'63. Left Co. Jan. 8,'64
Michael O'Sullivan   Pvt. In jail at N.O. left Co. Sept. 2,'63.
John Lewery   Pvt. Apprehended as a deserter and confined at New Orleans.

Absent without leave:
George W. Redding   Pvt. Since April 9th 1864.

Casualties:[1634] April 9th at Pleasant Hill:

Michael White	Sgt. wounded and missing.
Charles Hesseltine	*Cpl. wounded*
John Ferguson	Pvt. wounded
William Parks	Pvt. wounded
Thomas Clinton	Pvt. wounded [from National Archives, M727-5, p. 340. List of Killed Wounded and Missing in Batteries of 1st Div., 19th Army Corps at Battle of Pleasant Hill.]

Died: April 9th at Pleasant Hill

James A. Sanderson	2nd Lt.
Sholto O'Brien	Pvt.
William H. Smith	Pvt.

Strength: 147 Sick:11

Sick Present: Joseph Parslow, David J. Wicks (total 4, remainder of record obscured)

Sick Absent: William C. Brunskill Sick at Ft. Hamilton, NY left Co. Sept. 17,'61

William Crowley	Sick at Baton Rouge since July 13,'63.
George Chase	Sick at Brashear City since April 22,'63.
Charles Jackel	Sick at Franklin, La, since March 12. 1864.
Henry Williams	do.
Churchill Moore	Sick at Franklin since March 12, 1864.
James Connor	Sick since May 8 '64

The cooks are not listed.

The "Record" above gives its usual laconic narrative of a very busy two months in which more men from Battery L were casualties than at any time previous. L's place in the affair was as a member of the 1st Division of a completely reorganized 19th Army Corps.[1635] L itself was reorganized, now having the manpower, it was restored to "full war organization" with six 12 pounders.

The Red River Campaign

Banks' troops for the campaign[1636] consisted of the 3rd and 4th Divisions of the 13th Army Corps, which had been recalled from Texas, under the command of Ransom; the 19th Army Corps under Franklin, consisting of Emory's 1st Division, Grover's 2nd Division, Lee's Cavalry Division, the Reserve Artillery under Closson, and a detachment of the Corps d'Afrique, under Dickey. In all, it totaled 23,000.

Sherman's troops, consisted of the 1st and 3rd Divisions of the 16th Army

---

1634. William H. Smith is reported as killed in action on the Monthly Report. Names have been compared with the 13th Roster as published in: *Record of the Massachusetts Volunteers*, Adjutant-General, Boston, 1868, which indicates Smith as discharged by expiration of service on July 28th, 1865.
1635. O.R. Vol. 34/II, p. 333, 807–808; O.R. Vol. 34/I, p. 406
1636. O.R. Vol. 34/I, pp. 167–168; Irwin, pp. 285–286.

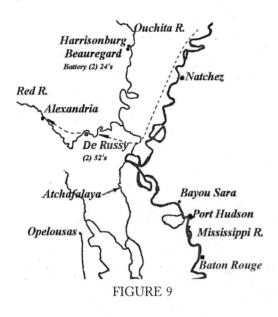

FIGURE 9

Corps, under Mower, a Provisional Division of the 17th Army Corps, under T. Kilby Smith, and Ellet's Mississippi Marine Brigade. All, a total of 13,600, were under the command of Brig. Gen. Andrew J. Smith.

Smith's troops were to be carried south on the Mississippi from Vicksburg to the Red, then to Alexandria, as is roughly shown in figure 9. The transports would remain for the balance of the campaign. In typical Grant fashion, Smith's troops were lightly equipped, and had no baggage wagons. With few horses, they had no worries about forage.

Admiral Porter would meet Smith's troops at the mouth of the Red River, and by March 7th had assembled 19 ironclads there. A March 17th date[1637] was set for all to meet at Alexandria.

A. J. Smith's transports pulled into view on March 11th. They started up the Red on the 12th. With obstructions in the river three miles below Taylor's Fort De Russy, which had been reoccupied, and the danger that the fort itself presented, a plan was made to attack it. A detachment from Porter was sent ahead to clear the obstructions, while the rest, including the army transports, turned down into the Atchafalaya, toward Simmesport, where the army landed and made a thirty-mile march up behind the fort. Late on March 14th A. J. Smith's men reached it and attacked, just before nightfall, carrying it in 20 minutes, with only three killed and 35 wounded. Of about 350 occupants of the fort, 319 were captured, along with 10 guns. It was a stunning victory.

Taylor's commentary on the attack doesn't agree, citing only 185 prisoners taken, but says: "Thus much for our Red River Gibraltar." Back in November of 1862, when he had built the forts; Burton on the Atchafalaya, Bisland on the Teche, Beauregard on the Ouchita, and De Russy on the Red, as he says, "to prevent the passage of gunboats," they had served their purpose, but: "It was not supposed that they could be held against serious land attacks."

Porter's fleet then hurried on to Alexandria, the fastest boats arriving there on March 15th. It was occupied by the advance of Smith's command, General Mower, on the 16th, figure 10.[1638]

1637. O.R. Vol. 34/I. p. 486, 578; ORN ser. 1, vol. 26, pp. 24–27; O.R. Vol. 34/I. p. 306–307; Taylor, pp. 136, 155.

1638. Figure 10, U.S. Navy NH 59089 NR&L(M) 3684. A representation of the scene, but not specific to Mower.

FIGURE 10
UNION TRANSPORTS AT ALEXANDRIA

It was not until March 15th that Emory's 1st Division, with Battery L, finally set off from Franklin. Lee, with the cavalry, had led off the day before. His column, including its supply wagons, being nine miles long, its rear guard did not clear Franklin until the following morning. The start of the march had been delayed by "violent" rains which had made the roads impassable for four days.[1639] An advanced guard from Lee arrived at Alexandria on March 19th, Emory at noon on the 25th, and Ransom on the 26th; Taylor having made no resistance to the march. He had abandoned Alexandria on the 15th, in the direction of Natchitoches, just a few hours ahead of the transports of Mower and the gunboats of Porter.

Vincent's Cavalry, familiar to Battery L from the Battle at Irish Bend, joined Taylor on the 19th, having left Opelousas ahead of Lee. Taylor directed them to Henderson's Hill on Bayou Rapides, about twenty-two miles above Alexandria, and reinforced them with a battery of four guns. Learning of this, A. J. Smith sent Mower forward. It had been a cold and rainy day, and that night, Vincent's men sat by their camp fires. Their visible position and lack of security allowed them to be completely surprised by Mower, and 200 were captured, their four-gun battery included.[1640]

Taylor, with a total force of 5,300 infantry, 300 artillery, and a force of cavalry now reduced to 300 from 500, was desperate for the return of Green from Texas, who had been detached during Banks' Rio Grande Expedition. Taylor would be able to do nothing but continue to fall back ahead of the advancing Yankee columns

---

1639. O.R. Vol. 34/II, pp. 534, 548; Pellet, pp. 171, 181. He notes that it was a delightful day.
1640. O.R. Vol. 34/I, pp. 177–178.

until Green appeared.[1641]

The progress of the march of the combined force now depended on the level of the river. Two miles above Alexandria there were rapids which presented an obstacle to Porter's gunboats unless the river rose.

At Alexandria, a depletion of Banks' force took place. Gen. McPherson requested the recall of Ellet's Mississippi Marine Brigade for the defense of Vicksburg. Since Ellet's transports were not able to cross the rapids, and there had been an outbreak of smallpox among them, they were allowed to return. Thus, 3,000 were lost.[1642] The slow rise of the river, by inches only, predicted that most of the deeper draft vessels would not be able to cross fully loaded, and some, never. Thus, supplies had to be unloaded and brought around the falls. To guard all of the stores and the line of transportation, Grover's division, another 3,000 troops, was detached.

After all of the effort, 13 of the 19 gunboats, and 30 transports, had passed upriver by April 3rd, though the hospital ship *Woodford* was destroyed in the process.

In the meantime, the remainder of the army had departed on March 28th, anticipating Porter's success. They constantly skirmished with Taylor's forces, but no serious engagements were brought on. At Monett's Ferry, on Cane River, near the junction of the old and new portions of the Red River, the road crossed, and then followed the old, or western portion, called Cane River. The order of march had Lee's cavalry in the lead, and he entered Natchitoches on March 29th. On March 31st, the 1st Division had passed through Cloutierville and camped on Cane River. By the 2nd of April, it had reached Natchitoches. The new course of the river, the only navigable route open to Porter, was to the north, called Rigolets de Bon Dieu. Following this, Porter and A.J. Smith landed at a deserted Grand Ecore, about eight miles north of Natchitoches, on April 3rd.[1643]

At Natchitoches, figure 11, the march was halted for three days, waiting for signs that the river would rise sufficiently for Porter and the transports to push further on. The

FIGURE 11

1641. Taylor, pp. 156–157; O.R. Vol. 34/I, pp. 306–307, 511.
1642. O.R. Vol. 34/I, pp. 197–198; Irwin, p. 291; ORN ser. 1, vol. 26, pp. 50–51.
1643. *Record of Events*; figure 11, Ewer, p. 142; Irwin, pp. 292, 295–296; O.R. Vol. 34/I, p. 168; Pellet, p. 192; ORN ser. 1, vol. 26, p. 51.

halt gave a chance for the troops to clean up after the dusty marching, and to visit the oldest settlement in the state. Many of the residences of the town were "almost regal in their splendor," the shift of the river to the east having left the town to survive as a resort for the wealthy. The mostly French inhabitants seemed to be agreeable to the Yankee presence, though "all this a few days later was explained as only their joy that we were being so easily led on to certain defeat."[1644]

On April 6th, Porter finally determined that the river could be trusted only to float the lighter draft transports, including those of the 2,200 men of Kilby Smith's detachment from the 17th Corps, but not A. J. Smith's command. It was then that Banks army resumed its march, now joined by Smith's 9,500 men of the 16th Army Corps. Porter, with half of his ironclads unable to follow further upstream, left on the 7th. He expected to be at Springfield Landing, opposite Mansfield, in two days. There, the plan was for Kilby Smith to reconnoiter in the direction of Mansfield, and seize the bridge across Bayou Pierre.

It is noted that it was from here at Natchitoches that the army diverted from the river, and took the stage road west toward Crump's Hill, and Fort Jesup–the "Texas Road" as is written in the Battery L record. While Banks reports it as "the shortest and only practicable" route, he describes it as passing through "a barren, sandy country, with little water and less forage, the greater portion an unbroken pine forest."[1645] Lee's cavalry had reconnoitered as far forward as thirty-six miles, to Pleasant Hill, on April 2nd, and reported (incorrectly) that Green's cavalry had arrived, (it had been ordered to report to Taylor on March 7th, but did not arrive at Pleasant Hill until April 6th, with about 3,100 men in total).[1646] Prisoners taken at Crump's Hill were reported as from General Price's Arkansas command, which had been ordered to come to the support of Taylor on March 17th.

Thus, Banks knowingly stepped away from supplies on the river, the water in the river (no small item for the horses and mules), and the protection of Porter's guns; straight into a barren country which would soon have the greatest concentration of force E. Kirby Smith could supply to Taylor, who had made his headquarters at Mansfield. Up to now, every advance by Banks had been met with a retreat by Taylor, and the conviction that pervaded the army was that Taylor was destined to retreat into Texas, or would, perhaps, make a final stand at Shreveport.[1647] Little

---

1644. Clark, p. 151.
1645. O.R. Vol. 34/I, pp. 198. This is his final report, written to Stanton, on April 6th, 1865. It is hence in hindsight, but the potential for danger in the conditions of the chosen route should have been obvious at the time.
1646. O.R. Vol. 34/II, p. 1027; O.R. Vol. 34/I. pp. 445, 447–448, 479–480, 524, 552, 579.
1647. Clark, p. 153; O.R. Vol. 34/III, p. 6. This letter, from Chief of Staff General Stone to General Franklin, dated April 1st, contains, in part, the following: "It seems pretty certain that Green's force of cavalry was to have made a junction with Taylor and Walker near Fort Jesup on Wednesday or Thursday, but it is most probable that their intention was to retreat together on

thought was apparently given to the idea that once reinforced, Taylor would stand and fight.

Lee's Cavalry led the long column of the combined army, now under the command of General Franklin, confined as it was, to a narrow road thick with brush on its shoulders, in a dense pine forest. Lee's supply train, consisting of 250 six mule teams, followed immediately behind his 1st, 3rd, and 4th brigades. His 5th,[1648] Gooding's, was detached as guards to the trains. Behind this, came Gen. Ransom's 3rd and 4th Divisions of the 13th Army Corps.[1649] Next, the 19th Army Corps, which now consisted of only Emory's 1st Division, and Dickey's brigade of the Corps d' Afrique–Grover's division having remained at Alexandria. A.J. Smith's detachment from the 16th Army Corps brought up the rear, and as a consequence, did not depart until April 7th. The overall column, including 900 wagon teams, being almost twenty miles long, was of such length that those preceding Smith had not passed out of Natchitoches until then.

The "unusual" placement of the wagon train of the cavalry, immediately behind it, was the subject of some discussion between generals Lee and Franklin, and to the detriment of the entire campaign, this issue was not resolved. Lee essentially wanted his supply train out of his way, considering the distances over which any cavalry often maneuvered. The proper action of the cavalry was, as soon as pressure on it was found to be too strong, not to attempt to hold the front on their own, but to fall back, and let the scattered command consolidate.[1650] Though Lee wanted his train to be behind the infantry, he wanted it ahead of the infantry train. Franklin had disagreed, and if Lee was to move his train to the rear, it would have to be behind the infantry train.

One can describe this as so much petty nonsense, but what was worse, neither Banks nor Franklin seemed to appreciate the criticality of the issue. Banks had fallen into the trap that Lincoln had warned him about in late 1862, when Banks was first assigned to the Department of the Gulf. He had created too much "*impedimenta*"[1651]

---

the road through Mansfield to Shreveport. With the addition to his force of Green's cavalry, Taylor will be enabled to more respectfully cover his retreat than he otherwise could have done."

1648. Lee had 4 brigades: the 1st Lucas, 3rd Robinson, 4th Dudley, and 5th Gooding. O. R. Vol. 34/I p. 171.
1649. O.R. Vol. 34/I, pp. 182, 236–238, 290.
1650. Haskin (Closson), p. 368.
1651. See chapter 7. O.R. Vol. 34/I, p. 241, 454, 458. There are accounts of 250 or more wagons lost, but there were only 200 present. Lee, p. 452, reported 156 lost. The number quoted here is by the acting chief quartermaster. Eleven ambulances and 81 horses were also lost. Regarding "*impedimenta*," the 200 wagons contained 10 day's rations and three days forage, plus ammunition and camp equipage. Lee himself admits that they were loaded "mostly with forage." We marvel that the cavalry horses needed 150 wagons, or more, to haul only three day's forage.

viz., cavalry, which needed forage, a constant headache for the quartermaster to keep supplied in this barren country. Many of the 175 wagons and the 920 mules hitched to them which were lost in the subsequent battle at Sabine Crossroads were loaded with forage. In addition, their mere presence in the narrow road created the fatal danger that they would slow or block an orderly withdrawal.

Wilson's Farm

On April 7th, Lee's cavalry advanced, constantly skirmishing with Taylor's cavalry. They were halted when they encountered a strong force three miles beyond Pleasant Hill, at Wilson's Farm.[1652]

A fight ensued, and Lee's leading 3rd Brigade, (Robinson) was initially pushed back until it was reinforced by the 1st Brigade (Lucas) which dismounted, and charged the enemy. The enemy lines were broken and a pursuit followed, which ended at nightfall at St. Patrick's Bayou, near Carroll's Mill, some eight or ten miles beyond Pleasant Hill. Lee's casualties were 11 killed, 42 wounded and nine missing. From the 23 Confederate prisoners taken, it was determined that they were facing some 3,000 men and a portion of Green's cavalry. The question at this point was whether Taylor could, or would, bring up more.

During the early action, an aide to General Banks who had accompanied Lee was sent back to Pleasant Hill to inform Franklin that, "General Lee was anxious to have a brigade of infantry sent out to his assistance." It was sent, but was inexplicably withdrawn before it arrived, when the firing was heard to cease. Lee was then instructed by Franklin to "proceed as far as possible, with your whole train, in order to give the infantry room to advance to-morrow."

Lee's situation is best explained by his 9:00 p.m. report to General Franklin:

> I am camped with most of my force along the road near this point;[1653] Fourth Brigade [Dudley] is camped on the battleground of to-day. At sundown the enemy was just in our advance, in strong position, with four pieces of artillery, which they used freely. We suffered here somewhat. I am simply holding the ground. I deem it much more expensive to life to fight the enemy in this immediate country with dismounted and, necessarily, somewhat confused cavalry than with infantry. I had intended visiting you to-night, but think I had better not leave. I will, however, with an entire deference to your own judgment, suggest that a brigade of infantry be ordered to the front at an early hour to-morrow morning, to act with me in the conduct of the advance. If a resistance should be obstinate I should like to leave my train with the advance of the infantry. I shall be ready to move at daylight. I find here almost no water.

1652. O.R. Vol. 34/I, pp. 237, 257, 450, 454–455. Banks' report, p. 199, lists 14 killed, 39 wounded and nine missing; obviously, three wounded had subsequently died.
1653. O.R. Vol. 34/I, p. 455. Eight miles beyond Pleasant Hill.

The interrupted movement of the infantry; that is, its failure to come up to Lee's aid; was quickly settled by Banks upon his arrival at Franklin's headquarters at 11:00 that evening, and the 1st Brigade of the 4th Division of the 13th Army Corps, Emerson, was ordered to advance to Lee's support.[1654]

The conflict between Franklin and Banks is thus revealed, and some of the logic, or lack of it, of either's attitude, is also revealed. Franklin wanted to wait for all of Emory's division to arrive at Pleasant Hill. Emory's train had been slowed by a rainstorm which had made the road conditions bad. It did not arrive until late on the morning of the 8th. Then there was A. J. Smith, still further behind. Franklin wanted to try to close up the whole line, at the expense of time. Franklin's original orders to Lee were to attack the enemy wherever he could find him, but not bring on a general engagement. If a general engagement was brought on, unless the troops were within supporting distance of those at the front, they would be beaten in detail. Yet Franklin ordered Lee to keep his train, which would give him no option for maneuver.

Undoubtedly, time was on Banks' mind, it was now only five days from the date he was told by Grant to wrap up the campaign. He wanted to push on and be in Shreveport by April 15th. Surely it was achievable, since they had, thus far – despite the delays at Alexandria – so easily pushed Taylor back.[1655] The opinion was general that there would be no battle.

Mansfield (Sabine Cross-Roads)

Come the morning of April 8th, Col. Frank Emerson and his 1st Brigade, of the 4th Division, 13th Army Corps, accompanied by Col. W. J. Landram, the 4th Division commander, had reported to Lee at sunrise.[1656] Lee quickly pushed forward the cavalry skirmish line, his 1st Brigade under Lucas, and formed the infantry in line of battle. They were successful in driving the enemy back, though with "severe" losses, and by noon, they had advanced some five or six miles, to a hilltop clearing called Honeycutt Hill, a part of the Moss plantations,[1657] about three-quarters of a mile south of the junction of the road from the Sabine River and the road to Bayou Pierre, about three miles outside of Mansfield. The fighting had long since exhausted Emerson's Brigade, and they had run out of water, so a messenger had been sent to the rear to request a relieving force. The advance was halted at the

---

1654. O.R. Vol. 34/I, pp. 264, 290.
1655. O.R. Vol. 34/III, p. 24; O.R. Vol. 34/I, p. 216. Banks received a reminder from Sherman on the 16th that the 30 days was up, by his calculation, on the 10th. It was written on April 3rd; Ewer, p. 144.
1656. O.R. Vol. 34/I, pp. 265, 294, 456–457; Shorey, pp. 81–82; Honeycutt Hill, per display, Mansfield State Historic Site.
1657. Benson, S. F., p. 484; Haskin (Closson), p. 368.

"fine" position they now occupied. Though Emerson had done the complaining, the cavalry were also exhausted, not only from the day's efforts, but by the "alternate pull and chase of the recent campaign, and had reached that pitch when the volunteer thinks he has done enough."

In the meantime, the rear of the column had moved ahead to St. Patrick's Bayou, about ten miles, and by 10:30 a.m., the bayou having been designated as the camping place for the day, had halted, an example of the slow pace ordered by Franklin. It was now about five-and-one-half miles behind Lee's position. The messenger having arrived, the relief force, the 2nd Brigade of the Fourth Division, 13th Army Corps, under Vance, was in motion by 11:00. Though delayed while passing the cavalry supply train, which was halted about one-and one-half miles from the front, it arrived about noon and was deployed on the right, next to Emerson. There would be no relief for Emerson's 1st Brigade, which was ordered to remain in line.

Looking back, Kirby Smith had given Taylor a lukewarm approval to select "a position in rear where we can give him battle before he can march on and occupy Shreveport."[1658] The story of the events for the next couple of hours, on that fateful afternoon of April 8th, is covered in few words in Lee's report, leaving us guessing as to what was going on in Bank's mind.

It was apparent that there was a "heavy force" of the enemy in Lee's front. The 3rd Massachusetts Cavalry had run into Taylor's forces "massed in solid columns." Alerted to the situation, Banks and staff had arrived on the scene sometime after 1:00 p.m. and summoned Lee to report to him.[1659] Lee explained the disposition of his forces vs. that of Taylor, and given the enemy's strength, in his opinion, the Federal army must either "fall back or be heavily re-enforced to advance." Light skirmishing continued on the flanks for some time, while Taylor's forces were observed to be massing on the right, along the road to Bayou St. Pierre, where the skirmishing became "sharp" after 2:30.

Banks took some time to react. The hilltop position from which he could observe the activity of the enemy, looking forward to figure 12, shows that he had a good view of the dispositions Taylor was in the process of making. He could not have been deaf to the clink and thud, or the dust, of the thousands of Green's cavalry moving up, or the redeployment of Randal's brigade from the left of the Mansfield road to the right, to augment Mouton.[1660] Did Banks conclude that it was already too late to make an orderly withdrawal? Did he think back to his 1862 attack on Stonewall Jackson's superior force at Cedar Mountain?[1661] It had caused

---

1658. O.R. Vol. 34/I, pp. 199, 513, 526–528; Taylor, pp. 162–164; Ewer, p. 145; Marshall, p. 128.
1659. Whitcomb, p. 68, gives 3:00 as the time Banks arrived, and goes on to give an account at odds with Lee's statements. Ransom's report, O.R. Vol. 34/I, p. 257, says 3:00, but Lee's report, p. 457, says "about 1:00 p.m."
1660. Woods, J. T., p. 58.
1661. See chapter 6. Taylor, pp. 162, 164; O.R. Vol. 34/I, p. 291.

Jackson to retire. Maybe the right thing to do was attack.

After nearly an hour's consideration, Banks issued the fatal order. Lee was to dispose his troops "so as to advance to Mansfield." Banks makes no mention as to whether he had considered withdrawing, but Ransom put it this way: "It would have been impossible at that time to have retired from the position we occupied…"

He had noted the dangerous Union deployment, within the wings of a "V" where if one unit fell back, it would expose the flank of the defenders on the opposite side.[1662] As later described by Taylor, Banks had put himself in a "vicious" position, and as "we invariably outnumbered the enemy at the fighting point" this was Taylor's cue to make the attack.

In his official report, Lee could not have used the word "shocked" to describe his reaction to Banks' order to advance, but says: "I immediately reported in person to General Banks, representing to him that the troops were already disposed for an advance, but that none could be made without bringing on an engagement. He then directed me to let them remain, and immediately sent an officer to the rear to hasten forward the infantry." This was to be Cameron with the 3rd Division of the 13th Army Corps, and Emory's 1st Division, 19th Army Corps, which included Battery L.[1663] This was the first intimation to Franklin, and those in the rear, of an impending battle.

By bringing up the infantry in piecemeal fashion, Banks had reversed the normally prescribed tactics. He had allowed Franklin to remove the flexibility of the cavalry, seeming not to be able to comprehend its proper function, which was to feel the enemy, disengage, and fall back to a chosen location, at which the infantry and artillery would have been prepared.

The dispositions of the opposing forces are shown roughly in figure 12.[1664] As to Banks' forces, the right;[1665] posted on a narrow, level, but broken plateau, one-fourth of a mile wide by a mile long, along which ran a fence which formed the boundary between two fields of the plantation; was Emerson's tired 1st Brigade, which had been joined by Vance's 2nd brigade. The "dismounted cavalry skirmishers," shown on the right, are the 16th Indiana. The 4th Division artillery, consisting of the Chicago Mercantile Battery and the 1st Indiana Battery, were ordered forward, and though initially sited in a plowed field to the left of the road, were quickly moved

---

1662. O.R. Vol. 34/I, p. 292; *Annals of Iowa*, vol. 7, "Reminiscences of the battle of Pleasant Hill," Henry Childers, pp. 515–518.
1663. O.R. Vol. 34/I, pp. 273, 389–390; Irwin, p. 305.
1664. O.R. Vol. 34/I, pp. 227 (figure 12), 266, 279–280, 293, 298–302; Taylor, p. 163; Marshall, p. 132; Whitcomb, p. 69. The initial order in which the 4th Division regiments were deployed across the front, were the 23rd Wisconsin, to the left of the road; with all others to the right of the road. From left to right, they were: the 67th Indiana, 77th Illinois, 130th Illinois, 48th Ohio, 19th Kentucky, 96th Ohio, and 83rd Ohio.
1665. Woods, J. T., pp. 55, 58, 66; Scott, R. B., p. 71.

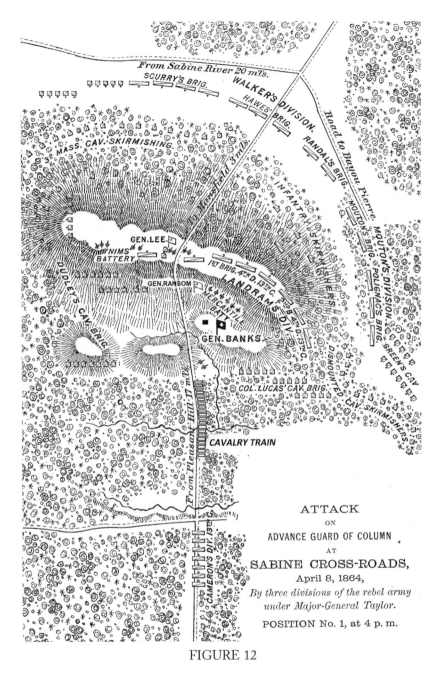

FIGURE 12

behind the 4th Division. The line on the right was extended by Lucas' cavalry acting as skirmishers.

Nims' six-gun battery, supplemented by two howitzers detached from the 6th Missouri cavalry, were assigned to Lee. They were strung across the road at the top of the hill (note the gun symbols in figure 12). They were supported by the 23rd Wisconsin, shown only by a regimental symbol, from Emerson's Brigade, which constituted the extreme left of the defensive line. Dudley's cavalry, consisting of the 2nd New Hampshire, 3rd Massachusetts, 31st Massachusetts, and 2nd Illinois, all acting as skirmishers, covered the flank in the forest.[1666]

At 4:00, Taylor ordered Mouton to open the attack on the Federal right.[1667] At this time, Cameron's 3rd Division had not yet arrived. It had been five-plus miles back, at Bayou St. Patrick, and had received Banks' order forward at approximately 3:00. Though Cameron would bring his whole division, it was under-strength, totaling only 46 officers and 1,247 men, and they would prove insufficient to stem Taylor's tide.

Emory, with the 1st Division of the 19th Army Corps, was seven miles back, and would not receive the order forward until 3:40.

"The initial ardor" of Mouton's Louisianans, (though they may have been lukewarm to the Confederacy, they were "inflamed" by the recent Yankee outrages on their homes, and were concerned by camp rumors that if Banks succeeded, the Confederacy would abandon Louisiana) resulted in severe losses, 64% of the Consolidated Crescent Regiment. Mouton, carrying a regimental flag, was one of the first of the many Louisiana officers killed, having exposed themselves as examples to their men.[1668]

The fierce resistance of Landram's 4th Division, as directed by Gen. T. E. G. Ransom, for a time stopped Mouton's and Polignac's brigades, but, running short of ammunition, the 83rd Ohio, the last of the line on the right, was in danger of being outflanked. Ransom's assistant adjutant-general, sent to order them to retire, was killed, and receiving no orders, they stood their ground. Many, including almost all of the 19th Kentucky, and 143 of the 77th Illinois, were taken prisoner. Adding in the 77th's 28 killed, wounded, and missing; it was left with only 130 on the roll after the battle, a loss of 57 percent.

On the other end of the line, the 23rd Wisconsin and Nims' battery were left nearly alone when the 67th Indiana (decimated at the Battle of Grand Coteau, and subsequently strengthened with non-veterans from the 60th Indiana, but still totaling only about 300 men), on their right, gave way. After having repulsed three successive charges of the enemy, with Nims' battery firing shell and canister, and opening wide gaps in the advancing enemy lines, within 20 minutes the left of Landram's line was ordered to retire. Three of Nims' guns were successfully removed from the hilltop, but three were left, their horses disabled. Lt. Snow was mortally wounded and captured; Lt. Slack was wounded slightly in the neck. The three guns that were removed were again prepared for action, but with the panic

---

1666. Irwin, p. 302. Irwin refers to the 8th New Hampshire, its designation when it was infantry. After conversion to cavalry, it became the 2nd New Hampshire.
1667. O.R. Vol. 34/I, p. 564.
1668. Marshall, p. 132; O.R. Vol. 34/I, pp. 264, 302–303, 451, 462, 568. Mouton's brigade included the 28th Louisiana, Colonel Gray, and the Consolidated Crescent Regiment, including Clack's battalion–first seen at Irish Bend; Whitcomb, pp. 68–69; R. B. Scott, p. 69; Irwin, p. 304; Bentley, W. H., 1883, pp. 276–277; Benson, p. 486.

that overcame the retreat, with the enemy closely pressing, they were placed in the road, which soon became blocked.

Earlier, the wagon teams had been ordered not only to keep closed up to the front, but to remain facing forward. Subsequently, they had received conflicting orders to park on the sides of the road, or to face to the rear.[1669] Now, overcome by the retreating mix of cavalry and a demoralized infantry, an order was received for the wagons to turn and retreat. The process of turning six-mule teams, in a rutted road little wider than the wagons themselves, was necessarily slow under normal circumstances, but now was utterly impossible. Nothing could pass the blockage, at the "slough" or creek, near Carroll's Mill, at which a bridge had been constructed, and over which much of the cavalry train had passed before it was halted. Thus, all of the train ahead of the creek was abandoned to the enemy, including the remaining three of Nims' guns, two guns of the 6th Missouri Battery, all of those of the Chicago Mercantile battery, the 1st Indiana Battery, and two of those of Rawles' Battery G of the 5th Artillery.

Quoting from The Story of the Maine Fifteenth:[1670]

> A wild and utterly indescribable panic here ensued–a veritable "Bull-Run-stampede," excepting that here was infinitely better excuse for such demoralization than the memorable "skedaddle" alluded to. Every man seemed to strike out for himself, eager to reach a safe place in the rear as rapidly as possible…the overturned wagons, the wagons faced to the rear, to the front, and but partially turned about, the fleeing cavalrymen, the frantic and riderless horses, the dead and wounded encumbering the way, the hatless officers, with drawn sabers, endeavoring to check the stampede, and the advancing and jubilant rebel hordes, pouring their hot-shot into the…crowd and rushing upon the "jam" with their glistening bayonets at the charge…

The "jam" is identified in figure 13 as *TRAIN*.

By now, generals Franklin and Cameron, with Cameron's 3rd Division, had arrived.[1671] Cameron had advanced at the "double quick" for about a half-mile through the thick underbrush to the edge of the woods, the position shown in figure 13, where they saw the enemy advancing in "heavy force." Finding the "road so full of teams and stragglers on foot and on horseback as to make it impossible to move any farther" Cameron deployed in line of battle: Flory's 1st Brigade, composed of the 46th Indiana, and five companies of the 29th Wisconsin, on the right of the road, and Raynor's 2nd Brigade, composed of the 24th Iowa, 28th Iowa, and

---

1669. O.R. Vol. 34/I, pp. 238, 267, 279–280, 293, 452, 458–459, 465; Irwin, p. 306.
1670. Shorey, pp. 83–84; Shorey grants Banks the following: "It is but just to say…that at every point of this unfortunate and disastrous affair, Gen. Banks and all the subordinate commanders most gallantly acquitted themselves." Figure 13, O.R. Vol. 34/I, p. 228.
1671. O.R. Vol. 34/I, pp. 228, 268, 273, 282–283; Irwin, p. 305; Cullum, vol. 2, no. 1167.

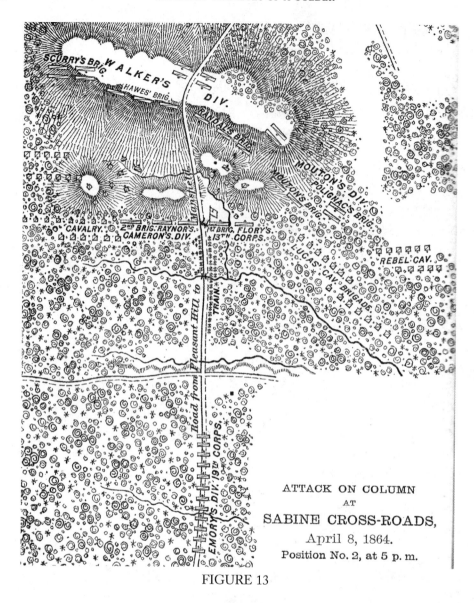

ATTACK ON COLUMN
AT
SABINE CROSS-ROADS,
April 8, 1864.
Position No. 2, at 5 p. m.

FIGURE 13

the 56th Ohio, on the left.[1672] Here they met the "broken troops" of Landram's Division, with the news that both of its brigade commanders, Emerson and Vance, were wounded and taken prisoner, and a wounded General Ransom had been carried from the field.[1673] Riding ahead to where Nims' battery still stood, Franklin described the situation as "discouraging." Hardly a minute later, a volley from Walker's advancing lines wounded Franklin and two of his staff officers, and Franklin's horse was killed. Remarkably, Franklin does not later mention the fact that he was wounded, though he wrote two separate reports of the battle. His leg

---

1672. Bringhurst and Swigart, pp. 88–89; Blake, E. E., pp. 34–35.
1673. Bentley, pp. 257–258; Shorey, pp. 84–86, Irwin, p. 305; O.R. Vol. 34/I, pp. 256–258, 261, 531; O.R. Vol 43/III, pp. 391, 472–474. Ransom later died of complications from his wound.

wound would fester as time passed, much as Admiral Foote's had, and ultimately require him to be replaced by Emory.

Ransom's line had repelled the advance of the enemy twice, but could not prevent an enemy flanking movement around its right rear, and with the 2nd Brigade having been pushed back, exposing the left of the 1st Brigade, and many of its men out of ammunition, it fell back, pursued by the rebel cavalry for a mile-and-a-half, to finally find refuge behind the line formed by Emory's Division,[1674] thus saving the remnant which had not been killed or captured. Those who were prisoners would face captivity at Camp Ford, near Tyler, Texas, and would have to endure a march of 16 days to get there, with little food, and no shelter.

As was earlier mentioned, Emory's 1st Division was seven miles back from Sabine Crossroads, and he did not receive his order forward until 3:40. The order contained the requirement to have his 6,000 troops carry two day's rations. The peculiar reference to the troops carrying rations gave no proper hint of the emergency, and, as Irwin says, if it was not for Emory's personal trait of sensing danger, and "had from the first hour of the campaign been apprehensive of some sudden attack that should find the army unprepared…" the issuance of the rations might have taken an hour, but it was rushed, and only took a "few minutes." Of course, each minute was critical beyond measure by now. Emory's numbers, going forward into line-of-battle at a point subsequently referred to as Peach Orchard or Pleasant Grove, which was about three miles behind the initial battle line, would finally stop Taylor.[1675]

Mansfield (Pleasant Grove)

Leaving Battery L and the 153rd New York to remain with its wagon train, Emory's division, led by the 161st New York, was soon moving forward at the "double quick," and as they moved, the sound of battle became louder, "while demoralized camp followers, black by nature, and almost white from fear, skulking infantry soldiers by twos, and cavalry by squads passed…"[1676] Then it was an ambulance carrying the wounded General Ransom. "It was plain that the most crushing disaster had occurred…" Emory, as angry and "savage as an infuriated bear" ordered the pace of the march increased to the utmost speed; the men of the 161st were ordered to fix bayonets without halting, and to use violence to open a path forward through the jam of fleeing humanity.

They soon came to a fenced farm and orchard, on high ground, which sloped away to a crossroad running parallel to a small stream, figure 14, an original sketch, from the NOAA Historical Maps and Charts Collection, no. 717-04-1864(2).

1674. O.R. Vol. 34/I, p. 257; Bentley, p. 287; Bringhurst and Swigert, pp. 118–119.
1675. Irwin, p, 307; O.R. Vol. 34/I, p. 200, 421, 607; Taylor, pp. 162, 163, Woods, J. T., p. 66.
1676. Clark, p. 155; Woods, J. T., p. 66; O.R. Vol. 34/I, pp. 200; Irwin, p. 308; Shorey, p. 87; Pellet, p. 197; Taylor, p. 164.

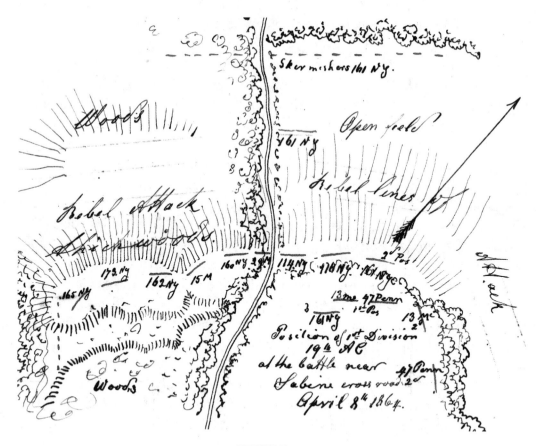

FIGURE 14

Here, Emory halted to deploy his troops. The 161st New York was sent forward as skirmishers "to reconnoiter and check the enemy, until the stampeded cavalry and broken infantry could get to the rear..." and a line of battle could be formed. They had moved nearly across the clearing when Taylor's forces appeared at the far edge of the woods, which forced the 161st into an orderly retreat, loading, halting and firing, before finally reaching the 1st Division line, now formed, where it went into reserve. Emory's line was behind a fence. Most of Benedict's 3rd Brigade was deployed to the left, most of McMillan's 2nd was at the center, and to the right was a mix of Dwight's 1st and McMillan's.

From the history of the 96th Ohio, the last of Cameron's troops to pass within Emory's line:[1677]

> Some of the defeated troops from the front, thrilled with admiration for their comrades who had with such gallantry and soldierly bearing come to their relief, rally and form a line in their immediate rear. The woods before them resound with shouts and musket volleys. The darkness is every where flecked with spectral rifle flashes. It is a weird scene, in which those gallant men [in the

---

1677. Woods, J. T., p. 66.

line] calmly wait…The full brass band of the Nineteenth Corps stands close by the road and pours into the darkness and the ears of the advancing rebels the exhilarating notes of "Hail Columbia"…Time can be counted only by seconds, for the skirmishers, with heavy loss are hurled quickly back, followed instantly by the enemy in three compact columns, one in the road and one on either side.

The first rebel assault was made on the center, the position of the 29th Maine, which in 1862 was designated as the 10th Maine and had fought with Banks at Cedar Mountain. Banks rode across their front, drew up his horse, and shouted: "Men! All depends on you! You can stop these rascals where they are!" To this, the 29th cried out "Shenandoah" "Winchester" "Cedar Mountain" "Cedar Mountain!" "CEDAR MOUNTAIN!"

From the history of the 114th New York:[1678]

> Our whole Brigade line [which had been ordered to lie down, and fire from this posture] waited patiently until the advancing line was clearly visible and then delivered such a volley as is seldom heard. It seemed like the discharge of one piece. Its effect was instantaneous. The line was checked, and put in retreat…The reception was one they had not expected, and the sudden check disconcerted them.

An Elmira, New York, newspaper report for Wednesday morning, April 27th, 1864, under the title: "The Gallantry of the 161st" had it that the troops were ordered by General Dwight to not fire "…till they could see the enemy's eyes." From the 15th Maine: "The rebels, advancing up the slope of the hill, furnished an admirable target from our position, while their shots, for the most part, glanced over our heads and into the adjacent trees."

A second Confederate advance on the Federal right was made at about 6:15 p.m. by Polignac's division, Polignac having taken over the command after Mouton was killed. The 13th Maine and the 47th Pennsylvania had to be moved from reserve to the right of the 116th New York, and finally, the 161st was ordered by Dwight returned into the line to stabilize it, on the left of the 13th Maine. A final determined Confederate attack on the left was then made, and was repulsed.[1679]

No artillery was used by either side, so only the crack of the rifle and the boom of the musket had been heard on this evening. Taylor's artillery could not be brought up for the reason of the wagon jam through which he had advanced, and Emory had purposely left his artillery (including Battery L) and baggage behind, impatient to advance without any possible encumbrances. Though Henry Closson, the chief of artillery, had later ordered Battery L forward, they did not arrive in time for the battle.

1678. Pellet, pp. 197, 198. Shorey, p. 89; Gould, p. 416; O.R. Vol. 34/I, pp. 416, 421–422; Letters, *http://dmna.gov/historic/reghist/civil/ infantry/161stInf/161stInfCWN.htm*
1679. Taylor, p. 163; O.R. Vol. 34/I, p. 392; Irwin, p. 310.

Emory closed this phase of his report on the battle with: "Nothing but the high discipline and morale of my division enabled me to form the line of battle under such discouraging circumstances." He reported 13 officers and 343 men as killed, wounded, or missing, no small number for this relatively small delaying action, which lasted less than 20 minutes. The 161st New York suffered seven killed and 36 wounded.

No single report contains the listing of casualties from the combined actions at Mansfield, that is, the battle at the Crossroads, and at Pleasant Grove, plus the casualties that continued to mount even after the battle, for the reason that Banks decided to precipitately retire from Pleasant Grove. After the close of the battle, Banks reports: "We were compelled, anticipating an attack next morning… either to await the advance of General Smith's corps, or to fall back to meet him. The want of water, the weakness of the position we held, and the uncertainty of General Smith being able to reach the position we occupied at day-break, led to the adoption of the second course."

It may have been well and good that Banks had made this decision, after he had held a "council of war," because Taylor's expected reinforcements, Gen. Thomas Churchill's division, of Price's command, had arrived. But, it was not well for the wounded left on the battlefield, unable to be moved due to a lack of ambulances to carry them. From the history of the 116th New York Volunteers:[1680] "…it was decided to leave *all* our wounded on the field, and surgeons, with such medical supplies as were at hand, were left with them."

Thus, at about 10:00 p.m. orders were given to fall back upon Pleasant Hill, fifteen miles to the rear, and before midnight, with cartridge boxes replenished and under orders to maintain quiet, to the point where orders were whispered, the troops moved out toward Pleasant Hill. As a consequence of the stealth, many in the picket line "did not retire in season to rejoin their commands. Many of these fell into the hands of the enemy, either on the picket line or while on the march… This in a measure accounts for the large number reported as missing."[1681] For example, 27 men of Company C of the 165th New York were left on the picket line, and were taken prisoner.

From this confused picture, the accuracy of the reported Federal losses for the Battle of Mansfield are thrown into doubt. A summary report lists only the combined losses at both Mansfield and Pleasant Hill.[1682] However, separate reports were made for Emory's 1st Division, Cameron's detachment of the 13th Army corps, and Lee. Lee did not differentiate between officers or men, so the table following, which summarizes the casualties, leaves his numbers separate. The total of all killed and wounded shown below is 694, with 1,541 missing.

1680. Clark, p. 159. Italics added by author.
1681. Shorey, p. 91; *History, 2nd Battalion Duryee Zouaves*, 1905, p. 26.
1682. O.R. Vol. 34/I, pp. 258–261, 263–264, 452.

	KILLED		WOUNDED		MISSING	
	OFFICERS	MEN	OFFICERS	MEN	OFFICERS	MEN
Emory & 13th Corps	6	68	27	304	72	1.325
Lee		39		250		144

Taylor claims 1,000 as his total casualties, according to Irwin, though this number has not been corroborated. More questions are raised by Taylor's claim of capturing 2,500 prisoners.[1683] If only 1,541 Union men were missing, this number is hard to justify. Some further evidence of a lower number is found in the history of the 46th Indiana Regiment, where the number that were marched the one hundred forty miles to Camp Ford is stated as 1,250 officers and men, including its seventy-year-old Chaplin, the Rev. Hamilton Robb.

In closing, it is fair to report that the only positive Yankee statement that can be found regarding the Battle of Mansfield was made by Lee:[1684] "The ammunition train was saved." The more common statement would be on the order of: "It is impossible to measure the indignation of this army against Gen. Banks." Regardless of Banks' personal courage, and the brilliant repulse at Pleasant Grove, the disaster at Mansfield still overshadowed all.

Pleasant Hill

Taylor makes no mention of whether he had planned to outflank the Federal army by heading them off at Pleasant Hill, but, at 3:30 a.m., when he discovered that Banks had retired from Pleasant Grove, he ordered Green's cavalry toward Pleasant Hill. They were to be followed by his new reinforcements, Churchill's two divisions of Parsons and Tappan, and then Walker and finally Polignac's weakened brigade.

Emory's troops began to pull in to Pleasant Hill at 7:00 a.m., and occupied the same campground they had left on April 7th.[1685] The strain on the men and animals can only be measured by the fact that after marching ten miles the previous morning, they were ordered at the double quick seven miles forward to the rescue of the rest of the army, fought the Battle of Pleasant Grove, and now had marched all night, for fifteen miles, without stopping. Some were marching in their sleep, or asleep on their horses, and the road was strewn with stragglers and abandoned wagons and equipment. They had not stopped to eat and had only managed to chew down a few pieces of dry hardtack in all of that time.

1683. Taylor, p. 164; Bringhurst and Swigart, pp. 91, 118–119; The 46th Indiana had 86 missing; A. J. H. Duganne, himself a prisoner at Camp Ford, refers to, p. 363, "a first installment of 1186"; Irwin, p. 311.
1684. O.R. Vol. 34/I, pp., 183, 392, 458; Bentley, p. 277.
1685. Taylor, p. 165; O.R. Vol. 34/I, pp. 565, 607, 617; Clark, p. 158; Shorey, p. 91–92; Pellet, p. 207; *Duryee Zouaves*, 1905, p. 26; Haskin's p. 195.

Madison's 3rd Texas Cavalry, the leading element of Bee's cavalry under Green, after riding all night, caught up with the rear guard of Emory's column–which included Battery L—about three miles from Pleasant Hill, at about 9:00 a.m. The sound of whooping, yelling, rattling, and banging gave evidence that the rear was being harassed, and Gooding's cavalry, the only unit of Lee's not engaged at Mansfield, was then deployed to "prevent surprise." An engagement seemed to be a certainty.

Soon after Emory, Gen. A. J. Smith's 16th Corps arrived. A portion of Smith's command, Shaw's brigade, was then assigned to Emory, which relieved McMillan's brigade. McMillan was positioned at the edge of a dense thicket, facing a field dotted with pine trees, through which passed the Mansfield Road. This was beyond Dwight's position, near the old race track, on the northwest outskirts of town.[1686] As Shaw's troops marched into position, Emory's troops stood quietly by, too tired to respond to a revival of some eastern–western insults, manifested by loud taunts, the likes of: "You fellers won't see us coming back…" in reference to their now having been posted at the most advanced position facing the enemy, as well as to the disastrous battle and retreat of the night before.

Bee, having picked off many stragglers, and while skirmishing with Gooding's cavalry, by 9:00 a.m. had driven to within about a mile of Pleasant Hill. Here, he first gained sight of what he described as "a line of battle across the fields in front of the village…The strong front by what was supposed to be a routed and retreating army rendered it prudent to reconnoiter the extent of this line before ordering a charge…" None was made, and soon after, when Green arrived and took command, another "close reconnaissance" resulted in Green doing something extraordinary for Green—he decided to make no move. As it happened, no action was taken until 4:00 p.m. when Taylor finally ordered an attack.

In the Federal ranks, it was learned with some surprise, that the 13th Corps, with a portion of Dickey's brigade of the Corps d'Afrique, and most of the cavalry, (minus a detachment of 1,000 men ordered to report to General Franklin)[1687] had been started to Grand Ecore. The decision to send this portion of the army on to Grand Ecore would seem to indicate that a decision to evacuate Pleasant Hill had been made even before the battle was fought. Heading back to Grand Ecore would leave Porter's fleet without support. A courier was sent to inform Porter of the decision. In fact, three separate messages were sent to Porter on April 19th; one from Banks, and two from Stone, Banks' chief of staff. Banks' message, evidently sent before the battle at Pleasant Hill, is copied here:[1688]

1686. O.R. Vol. 34/I, p. 354.
1687. O.R. Vol. 34/I, pp. 452, 459. The cavalry detachments were from the 1st Brigade, Lucas, and the 5th Brigade, Gooding; ORN ser. 1, vol. 26, p. 60.
1688. O.R. Vol. 34/III, pp. 98, 152–153; O.R. Vol. 34/I, p. 383; ORN ser. 1, vol. 26, pp. 51, 60. Porter's report, made to W. T. Sherman, mentions 20 transports on page 51, and 26 on page

HEADQUARTERS DEPARTMENT OF THE GULF,
Pleasant Hill, April 9, 1864

REAR-ADMIRAL D. PORTER,
Commanding Mississippi Squadron:

The land column that was intended for the movement against Shreveport encountered a superior force 4 miles this side of Mansfield, and, being unable to communicate with the forces from the river, has been compelled to retreat. It is now our expectation to fall back to Grand Ecore. You will make your dispositions accordingly. The fighting was very sharp, but, from the situation of the country, it has been impossible to bring but a portion of our forces against the entire strength of the enemy. The loss of the enemy has been very severe, ours serious. General Ransom has been wounded.

If possible, send a communication to general Steele.

I am, &c.,

N. P. BANKS
Major-General, Commanding

Note that, sticking to protocol, Banks did not order Porter out, since Porter was a separate navy command, cooperating, but not under Banks' authority, though Smith's 17th Army Corps detachment, which was accompanying Porter, was technically under Banks' command. The implication was clear, but Porter was left to make the obvious decision. He was now at Springfield Landing, ten miles south of Shreveport, as is shown in figure 15,[1689] and one hundred ten miles by the "narrow and snaggy" river north of Grand Ecore, with his flagship, the *Cricket*, and five others, the *Fort Hindman, Lexington, Osage, Neosho,* and *Chillicothe*, plus the 20 transports carrying Kilby Smith's command and supplies for Banks' army. He was in peril of losing this portion of his fleet, much as on his near fatal Steel's Bayou Expedition a year earlier, chapter 7. That time, he was rescued by W. T. Sherman, but he felt that Banks, this "political general" might abandon him: "I am not sure that Banks will not sacrifice my vessels now to expediency…"

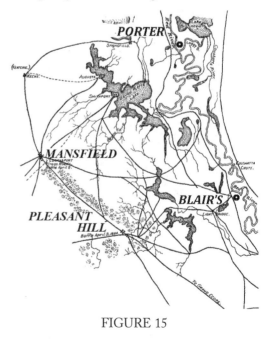

FIGURE 15

---

60. It is 13 pages long.
1689. From ORN ser. 1, vol. 26, p. 44c. Note also the location of Blair's Landing, referenced in the next chapter.

Since Kilby Smith's 17th Corps detachment, 2,237 troops,[1690] was still with Porter, and Grover's division was still at Alexandria, the only troops that would be engaged at Pleasant Hill would be those of A. J. Smith and Emory. Of all of Banks' thousands that had begun the campaign, there were now at Pleasant Hill less than half, or about 15,900. This was hardly the preponderance sought for over Taylor, whose reinforced numbers were now 13,200.

Pleasant Hill, initially founded as a farming community in 1844, was situated on slightly elevated ground, or a plateau, about a mile wide[1691] and two miles long, through which the road from Mansfield to Grand Ecore, about thirty-five miles distant, runs. It boasted about 200 inhabitants, many wealthy, such as the Childers, the Jordans, Chapmans, Davises, Harrels, and Hamptons. The Childers mansion, built in 1859 at the cost of $10,000, was a landmark on the southeast end of town. The village was the home of Pierce and Paine College. It had a hotel, and it was regarded as the "center of refinement and education for miles around."[1692] Such was the luck of this elegant community to be the point where the Federal army would choose to make a stand. The Confederate and Union organizations for the battle are listed in Tables I and II.[1693]

CONFEDERATE

Maj. Gen. John G. Walker's Texas Division

1st Brigade Thomas Waul	12th 18th 22nd Infantry, 13th Cavalry
2nd Brigade Horace Randal	11th 14th Infantry, 28th & 6th Cavalry
3rd Brigade William R. Scurry	16th 17th 19th Infantry, & 16th Cavalry

Brig. Gen. Thomas J. Churchill–2 Divisions:
Brig. Gen. Mosby Parsons (Churchill's) Missouri[1694]

1st Brigade John H. Clark	8th 9th Infantry,
2nd Brigade S. P. Burns	10th 11th 12th 16th Infantry, 9th Bn. Sharpshooters
Brig. Gen. James C. Tappan	1st Div. Arkansas[1695]
Lucien C. Gause	26th 32nd 36th Infantry
H. L. Grinsted	19th 24th 27th 33rd 38th Infantry

Maj. Gen. Thomas Green, Cavalry Corps Commander

1690. O.R. Vol. 34/I, pp. 260, 292, 383; Irwin, pp. 292, 311. The 15,900 is derived by using 6,400 for Emory (his April return, O.R. Vol. 34, Pt. I, p. 168, (which accounts for casualties) 8,500 for A. J. Smith, (less Kilby Smith's 2,200, using his March return, since they had not yet been in battle) and adding the 1,000 cavalry detachment. This agrees with Banks estimate, p. 203. Taylor, p. 162.
1691. Taylor, p. 217; John Scott, p. 202.
1692. Childers, pp. 513–516; Blessington, p. 194.
1693. From map, courtesy of the Mansfield State Historic Site, Scott Dearman; O.R. Vol. 34/I, pp. 169–172.
1694. O.R. Vol. 34/I, p. 601.
1695. O.R. Vol. 34/I, p. 604.

Brig. Gen. Hamilton Bee Cavalry Division Commander[1696]
26th Texas Debray, 1st Texas Buchel, 37th Texas, Terrell
Brig. Gen. James Major Division Commander

Lane's Brigade 1st & 2nd Texas Partisan Rangers, 2nd & 3rd Arizona (Baylor Commanding)
Bagby's Brigade 4th 5th 7th 13th Texas

Brig. Gen. Camille J. Polignac's Division

Col. Henry Gray[4][1697]	28th Louisiana, Consolidated Crescent Regiment
Lt. Col. R. C. Stone	15th 17th 22nd 31st 34th Texas Cavalry (dismounted)
Artillery Maj. J. L. Brent	6th Louisiana, 4th 7th 9th 12th Texas 6th Arkansas Light Batteries

TABLE I

UNION

Maj. Gen. William H. Emory's 1st Division 19th Army corps

1st Brigade Brig. Gen. William Dwight	114th 116th 153rd 161st New York, 29th Maine
2nd Brigade Brig. Gen. James W. McMillan	13th, 15th Maine, 160th New York, 47th Pennsylvania
3rd Brigade Col. Lewis Benedict	30th Maine, 162nd 165th 173rd New York
Artillery Capt. Henry Closson	25th New York Light, 1st United States Battery L, 1st Vermont Light Cavalry (Detachment) 2nd Brigade

Col. Oliver P. Gooding

1st Brigade Col. Thomas I. Lucas	16th Indiana, 6th Missouri, 14th New York
5th Brigade Col. Oliver P. Gooding	2nd New York, 3rd Rhode Island

Brig. Gen. Andrew J. Smith (Detachment) Army of the Tennessee
Brig. Gen. Joseph H. Mower's 1st & 3rd Divisions, 16th Army Corps

1st Div. 2nd Brigade Col. Lucius F. Hubbard	5th Minnesota, 8th Wisconsin, 47th Illinois
1st Div. 3rd Brigade Col. Sylvester Hill	35th Iowa, 33rd Missouri
3rd Div. 1st Brigade Col. William F. Lynch	58th 119th Illinois, 89th Indiana
3rd Div. 2nd Brigade Col. William T. Shaw	14th 27th 32nd Iowa, 24th Missouri
3rd Div. 3rd Brigade Col. Risdon M. Moore	49th 117th Illinois, 178th New York

Artillery Capt. James F. Cockefair
Indiana Light 3rd & 9th Batteries

TABLE II

As earlier related, when Bee arrived at the high ground west of Pleasant Hill, he was surprised by the strength of the army that confronted him, too much for his or Green's cavalry alone, and they then waited for Taylor.

1696. O.R. Vol. 34/I, p. 606.
1697. The Louisiana militia units in Polignac's Division, which was held in reserve, were nominally commanded by Louisiana's Governor Allen. Blessington, p. 194.

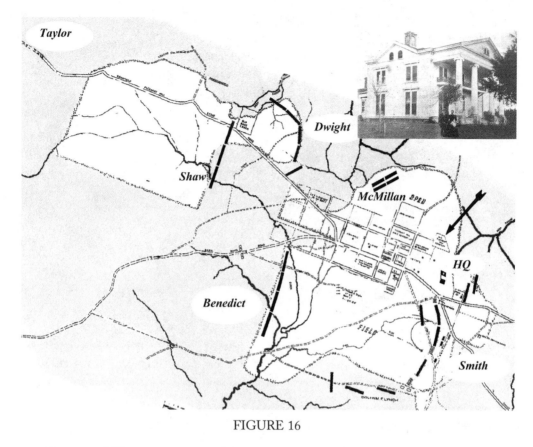

FIGURE 16

Figure 16[1698] interprets what Taylor saw when he arrived; shown are the mid-morning positions of Shaw, Dwight, and Benedict, with McMillan and Smith having deployed in the rear.

From his position on the Mansfield Road, Taylor described the Federal army as "extended across the open plateau, from College Hill on their left, to the right of the road to Mansfield. Winding along in front of this position was a gully cut by the winter rains but now dry, and bordered by a thick growth of young pines, with fallen timber interspersed. This was held by the enemy's advanced infantry, with his main line and guns on the plateau."

Taylor never flinched, despite recognizing A. J. Smith's powerful force as the one "not engaged on the previous day." Shortly "after midday," when Churchill's infantry arrived, he made plans for an attack, allowing the jaded men only two hours' rest, though they had marched forty-five miles. He reasoned that morale was high from the victory of the previous day, and that it was imperative to keep Banks moving, lest he might attempt a junction with Porter.

Like so many other Civil War sites, Port Hudson being an earlier example, the ravages of time have dramatically altered Pleasant Hill. Then, Taylor's view

---

1698. Reproduced from a map obtained by kind permission from the Mansfield State Historic Site, altered by the author.

was clear, today the entire area is overgrown. The map, which we are fortunate to have, shows the location of the village streets. Today, there is no village, and little evidence that there ever was one. The feature most evident to Taylor, the gully, remains, it is shown running from north to south, east of Benedict's (first) position. Another feature which can be found by today's visitor is the old cemetery, which is identified by the arrow. Unlike many other more popular battle sites, there is only one modest private monument, and there are no interpretive trails. Not an original village home remains; including the imposing Childers mansion, which was used as Banks' headquarters, see the inset, and "HQ" near a black square with a flag in figure 16. None of this was due to the war, but the fact that the residents tore down the village long after the war and moved it a few miles into Sabine Parish, so as to be closer to the new railroad.

Figure 17 is an enlarged and more detailed version of figure 16, with the positions of the opposing forces shown as of 4:00 p.m. The Confederate regiments are shown in black, those of Emory's command using the more conventional representation of a black/white slashed rectangle, and those of A. J. Smith's command, in a solid lighter shade. Emory and Smith had traded brigades, McMillan for Shaw, early in the day. Shaw's placement of the 24th Missouri (upper left in figure 17) on a hill next to Battery L was by the approval of General Smith, but Battery L was then called to the rear and put into park, to be replaced in that exposed position by the 25th New York Light Battery; all on the orders of General Emory.

Other units were repositioned during the day, and it is not clear by whose authority. Who was running the show? Banks and Franklin, or was it Emory and Smith? In previous battles, such as Mansfield, the troop dispositions had been made by Banks and his staff, often overriding Franklin, particularly to the detriment of the Battle of Mansfield. Banks' or Franklin's presence on the field is notably not reported; General Stone, Banks' chief of staff, appears to have been doing the supervision on the field, as we remember that Franklin had been wounded.

General Smith then ordered Battery L into position in his line next to the 9th Indiana battery, and the 3rd Rhode Island Cavalry to their picket duty: Perry's troop on the Sabine River Road, and Bicknell and Avery on the other approaches.[1699] This was remarkable cooperation for troops that were fighting together for the first time. However, the hurried arrangements left flaws in the dispositions. Three minutes later *Emory* ordered Appleton's section to report to General Dwight, upon whom the battle had already opened, and the remaining two sections, under Taylor and Sanderson, to the ridge on the dangerous open slope behind Benedict's Brigade, which as shown in figure 17, had now deployed behind the ditch. This was a disastrous mistake. Not only would it take the lives of Lt. Sanderson and privates Sholto O'Brien and William Smith, and wound five others, but it was directly in

---

1699. O.R. Vol. 34/I, pp. 308–309, 318, 342, 354–355, 373, 472–473; Haskin, p. 196; Gould, p. 422.

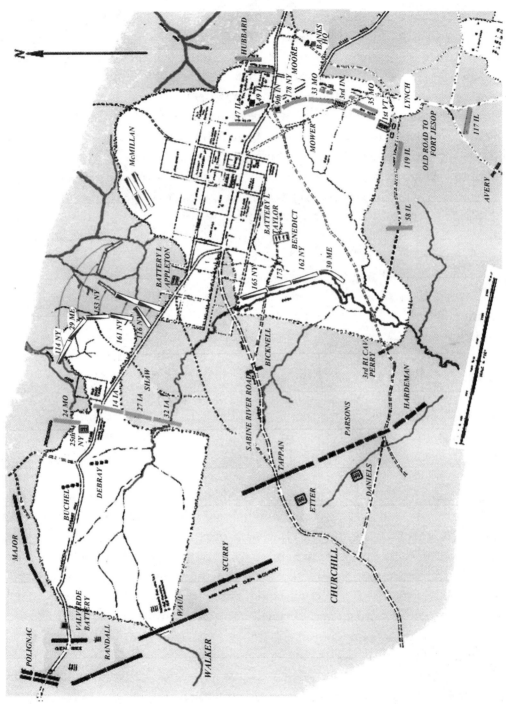

FIGURE 17

front of the field of fire of the 9th Indiana Battery and its supporting 178th New York Infantry, in Mower's line behind them. Neither dared to fire over, or through Battery L until Battery L's position was finally overrun at the point of the bayonet, and was abandoned.

Shortly after "midday" the remainder of General Taylor's troops arrived,

Churchill in the lead. "At a glance," as Taylor says,[1700] "it was clear that the men were exhausted and suffering from the heat," and the attack was postponed for two hours.

As noted, Dwight's brigade was first camped along the edge of the clearing on the north side of the Mansfield Road, across from the old race track, the 114th New York being the right of his line. He did not even know who was in his front, until about 3:00 p.m., when Shaw, in command of the Missouri and Iowa troops deployed there, appeared at his headquarters. The enemy's skirmishers had already begun to flank the right of Shaw's line, and Shaw wanted Dwight to move forward to close the gap between them. He finally found Dwight, "near a house, *in the rear,*" and Dwight agreed to make the changes. An hour later General Stone, of Banks' staff, appeared on the scene, agreed with Shaw, and rode off, apparently to hasten the changes. They were never made. Dwight instead *retired* by swinging around to the temporary positions shown (arrows and partially white symbols) away from Shaw, much to Shaw's disgust.[1701] Shaw's official report pulls no punches: "A few moments after five o'clock the enemy opened heavily on me with artillery… At the same time, General Dwight fell entirely out of my sight to the rear." A line from the history of the 29th Maine confirms the move: "Up to this time we had done nothing except to move a few steps down hill for shelter from the artillery fire and stray musket balls." The 29th was now facing the swamp to the north, with the 153rd New York on its left, and the 114th New York on its right. Dwight would soon be forced to face them about and advance to the road, after Major's dismounted cavalry had driven around and through Shaw—if the reader cares to peek ahead to the depiction of the Confederate advance, shown in figure 18.

Benedict's line is seen along the ditch. Originally positioned in the skirt of woods about three hundred yards to the west (figure 16), Benedict's troops were ordered to this new position at 3:30, and evidently too late to have an additional brigade sent to support their left, *as had twice been requested by Emory.* Having discovered that the ditch had at some previous time been deepened and straightened, and that its banks were covered by switch cane which was tall enough to hide a soldier lying down, the move out of the woods seemed desirable. The troops had a prepared rifle pit. Battery L, hastily placed in Benedict's rear, could then fire over the heads of those in the ditch, or lying near it. However, it would put Benedict far behind Shaw, with a gap similar to that between Shaw and Dwight, yet hung out four hundred yards ahead of A.J. Smith's line. It was only apparent after the battle

---

1700. Taylor, p. 166.
1701. O.R. Vol. 34/I, p. 355; Taylor, pp. 167–168. The time in various reports is often at odds, as has been seen earlier, at Port Hudson, and Fort Pickens, in 1862. Here, the time of the attack, which was "about 4 o'clock" according to the Confederate General X. B. DeBray, of the 26th Regiment of Cavalry, (see *"A Sketch of DeBray's Twenty-Sixth Regiment,"* by DeBray, SHS, vol. 13, p. 158). Taylor says "soon thereafter" referring to 4:30; Gould, p. 422.

had gone awry that the positioning of Benedict and Taylor's section of Battery L was flawed.

Smith's line, consisting of Mower's 1st and 3rd Divisions of the 16th Army Corps,[1702] was basically a reserve position. Compared to the rather straightforward echelon line of General Taylor's dispositions, the Union defense looks peculiar. The right, Dwight, is heavily manned, though a swamp just to the north would have slowed or prevented any attack from that quarter.[1703] It was therefore to be expected that the Confederate attack would be on the center and left of the Union line—if it came at all. There was, in fact, a brief delusion to the effect that it might not.[1704] It is said that Banks, as he dismounted at the Childers Mansion, uttered the words: "There will be no fight today!" He was answered by the opening of Churchill's batteries.

Not Smith nor Emory, but General Stone had placed Lynch's 58th and 119th Illinois regiments hidden in the woods to Mower's left. Newland's 58th was facing southwest, about one-quarter of a mile west of Kinney's 119th, their advanced positions and wide spacing would only slow, but could warn of, any Confederate approach from that quarter (which Taylor, in fact, had intended).[1705] Little could either of these two commanders imagine their almost accidental key role in the upcoming battle. They would be one jaw of a trap which would turn the tide. On the right of Mower, after it was relieved by Shaw, Emory had placed McMillan's brigade in reserve. Redeployed after the battle was initiated, they would be the other jaw of the trap.

At 4:30, it was reported to Taylor that Churchill's troops, ordered to the extreme right to gain the Fort Jesup Road (past the positions of the two Illinois regiments, figure 17), and hence outflanking both Benedict and Mower, were nearly in position to begin their attack. To divert the attention of the Federals, Major Brent was ordered to advance the guns of the Valverde Battery, Moseley's 7th Texas, and West's 6th Louisiana, to open on the 25th New York Battery.[1706] The sound of Churchill's guns signaled that he had begun his attack, and Walker then began his advance.

A projectile screamed over gun no. 2 of the 25th New York, and it returned fire immediately. The 25th was doing "most excellent service" until the two batteries further to the Confederate right opened on them. At this juncture, about 5:00, the 25th fell back.[1707] Seeing this, General Green assumed Shaw's line had

---

1702. O.R. Vol. 34/I. p. 308.
1703. Swamp shown on map of *32nd Iowa History*, Scott, John, p. 288.
1704. Scott, John, p. 203–204.
1705. O.R. Vol. 34/I, pp. 338–342, 344–351, 566.
1706. Taylor, p. 167; Benson, p. 493; O.R. Vol. 34/I. p. 368.
1707. O.R. Vol. 34/I, p. 355, 360, 369, 567, 608. Shaw thought that the battery fell back without orders, prompting Shaw's condemnation in his report. Scott, John, p. 182. Writing about

broken, and ordered Bee's cavalry to charge. As Bee's 350 troopers issued from the woods, Buchel's 1st Texas Cavalry on the north side of the Mansfield Road and De Bray's 26th Texas Cavalry on the south—all west Texas men, superbly mounted and thoroughly disciplined—they made a magnificent spectacle. As they charged across the clearing toward the hillock where the 25th New York had stood, they could not see the skirmishers of the 24th Missouri, posted behind a fence at a right angle to the main line of the 24th Missouri and the 14th Iowa, who were lying on the ground, screened by the woods behind them. Holding their fire until the enemy had approached to within "50 paces," Shaw's troops then let loose a deadly barrage of musket fire which stopped the cavalry in its tracks, the horses and riders almost falling within Shaw's lines. In Bee's words: "The command was literally swept away…" Buchel was mortally wounded, and fell, a prisoner, into the hands of the 14th Iowa.[1708] Bee and many other officers were wounded. DeBray's horse was killed, and fell, injuring DeBray. The cavalry drew back, never to charge again. It was then dismounted, and assigned to Polignac, who was still in reserve.

Walker was now pressing his attack on the 32nd and 27th Iowa regiments, on Shaw's left, south of the Mansfield Road. The fire of the 32nd was so destructive that Walker bypassed it in the gap to its left (south). Col. John Scott of the regiment later reported that the Confederates were "working across the rear of my position, so that in a short time the battle was in full force far in my rear."[1709]

In the meantime, the 14th Iowa and the 24th Missouri felt the repeated attacks of Major's and Bagby's dismounted cavalry, but their resistance was so stubborn that Taylor was forced to call up Polignac's Texas troops. Mouton's old brigade, the 28th Louisiana and the Crescent Regiment, so devastated at Mansfield, and now under the command of Louisiana's Governor Allen, still remained in reserve, and were never used.[1710]

After two hours of fighting,[1711] and repeated charges, Major's Texans gained a position on the right flank of the 24th Missouri. The Missourian's ammunition was running short, and they fell back into the open field behind them, taking heavy casualties. The cross-fire extended to the 14th Iowa, whose commanding officer was killed

---

the incident after the war, Shaw felt he had been too hard on the 25th but, nevertheless, his experience had been that no troops under his command had ever retreated without orders. According to Benson, p. 495, it was the Chief of Artillery who had ordered them back. Benson names Arnold, (Cullum no.1462) who was the Chief of Artillery of the Department of the Gulf *as well as* Chief of Cavalry. Henry Closson had been Chief of Artillery of the 19th Army Corps since Oct. 4, 1863; DeBray, pp. 158–159.

1708. Benson, p. 496. The position of the 24th Missouri skirmishers is shown in figure 17 by a dark rectangle at a right angle to the lighter rectangle representing the 24th Missouri.
1709. O.R. Vol. 34/I, p. 366.
1710. Sliger, J. E., p. 458; Blessington, p. 194, "[P]ast the years of enduring the toils of enduring a soldier's life…" and having taken so many casualties at Mansfield, they were exempted.
1711. O.R. Vol. 34/I, pp. 355–356, 363, 369; Gould, pp. 422–423; Pellet, p. 210.

and its adjutant wounded. At this point, about 5:30, orders from A. J. Smith came to Shaw to retire. So many of the officers of his regiments were either killed or disabled that Shaw could find no one to communicate with, and was compelled to seek out the scattered men individually in the smoke and heavy brush, and order them out. Shaw was not able to reach Col. Scott of the 32nd Iowa, and soon the enemy occupied Shaw's recently vacated positions. Now, the 32nd found itself taking fire on its right, as well as its front and left. Though almost out of ammunition, they were able to hold their position until, at around sunset, an hour later, the tide turned, and the final general advance of Smith's line drove the retreating enemy past them.[1712]

Figure 18 shows these and other movements, but cannot clearly depict the withdrawal of Shaw's troops. They simply melted away, through Dwight's lines, leaving the 32nd an island in a sea of the attackers, and almost ignored. That anyone could survive, and for much time go unseen, is testimony to the condition of the "clear" areas of this portion of the battlefield. They were fallow farm fields, overgrown with brush, and were now clouded with smoke. When the fighting had swept behind the 32nd Iowa, it threatened Dwight, who then repositioned the 153rd New York, the 29th Maine, the 114th New York, and the 161st New York to the south, across the Mansfield Road. The 29th Maine men, as they marched south, were crossed by some of Shaw's retreating troops. Their narrative:

> Just before Shaw's brigade broke, our brigade was ordered toward the center of the field, and how the other regiments got there we cannot tell, but ours came by the right face and filed to the right—our late rear—and in that order (four abreast) went jumping over logs and brushing through the bushes, but whether it was north, south, east or west, who could tell?

From the 114th New York: "The smoke of battle hung over us so densely that the sun was entirely obscured."[1713]

Again, from the 29th Maine:

> We had not gone far before we saw the men of Shaw's brigade coming on the run from our right hand…After Shaw's troops had gone through us we continued to march as before with our flank to the unseen enemy. All this happened in a half cleared field, where from the abundance of bushes we could not see far in any direction; hence we had the least possible knowledge of what was going on around us.

The reader will note that a few faint lines in figure 18 attempt to depict the route of the withdrawal of Shaw's Missouri and Iowa regiments. Though they were scattered, Shaw insists that they were reformed behind Dwight, as is depicted by

---

1712. 6:41 p.m., per the calculations of U.S. naval Observatory for April 9th, 1864. *http://aa.unso. navy.mil/cgi-bin/aa rstablew.pl.*
1713. Pellet, p. 210; Gould, p. 422–423.

the symbols (27 IA, 14 IA, 24 MO) within the old village. Quoting from Shaw's writing years later:[1714]

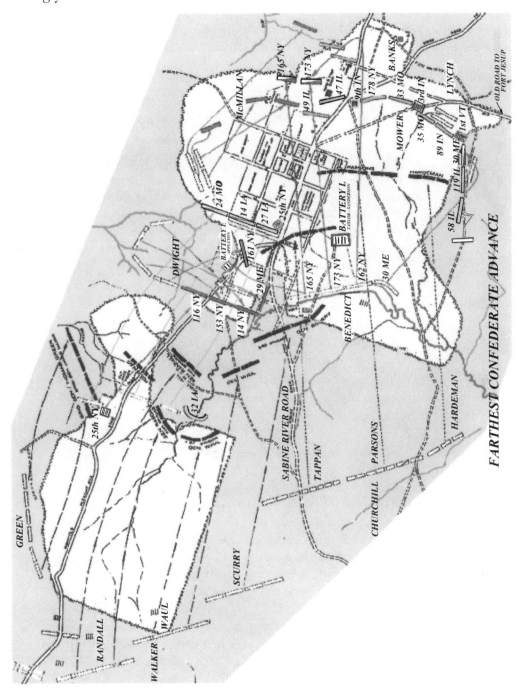

FIGURE 18

About one-fourth of a mile from where my line was first formed I struck

---

1714. Scott, John, p. 183.

General Dwight's brigade just forming across the Mansfield road shown by Emory's map as Dwight's second position. I passed through his lines with the 14th Iowa and 24th Mo., and formed in line of battle within ten paces of Dwight's line. Before I had gotten the 27th Iowa into line, Dwight moved from his position to the rear.[1715]

As the 29th Maine boys came to the Mansfield Road, they spotted an abandoned Napoleon gun. This was clearly one of the two of Appleton's section of Battery L, since the 25th New York, the only other artillery unit in the immediate area, was equipped with 3-inch Southworth rifles.[1716]

Having been assigned to Dwight at the onset of the battle, and since Dwight had found, quoting Appleton, "…no place where we could be of use and told me to take the section back, but directly ordered that it should be halted." Accordingly, it was halted in the road some distance in rear of the infantry, in figure 18, in the road near the 161st New York. From Appleton:

> Soon after, the enemy charged across the open field in our rear and through the woods on the flank of us, and in reversing the pieces in order to get into position, both poles were broken and it became impossible to unlimber them so that they could be fired. The road at that point was very narrow, and the carriage wheels in a ditch. In the mean time, the enemy were advancing on our flank and rear, keeping a hot fire of musketry, and I found it impossible to get the pieces into a position to fire, though the most strenuous efforts were made…I therefore ordered, when the enemy were within a few yards of the guns, the horses to be unhitched and the cannoneers to fall back with them… Shortly after,[1717] the enemy were repulsed and the pieces drawn to the rear… The caisson horses were mostly killed or wounded in the charge; otherwise

---

1715. The last part of this statement, saying Dwight moved to the rear, is a mystery, and is not supported by any evidence in the histories or reports of Dwight's units, except to note, on p. 210 of Pellet, that the 153rd New York was "retired a few hundred yards" to resupply their ammunition. An untitled NOAA map no. 717-04-1864 clearly shows "Smith troops" north of the intersection of the Mansfield Road and the Sabine Pass Road. A 32nd Iowa map also shows: "Shaw's position after the battle" in nearly the same location. Emory's map, O.R. Vol. 34/I, p. 391, shows "Smith's troops" at the intersection. The question of Dwight's withdrawal as alleged by Shaw is open, as on all the maps he is in the same area, though depicted with poor and varying proportion. Our text has to live with these contradictions. There was little doubt that there was no love lost between Dwight and Shaw. Shaw didn't like Banks either. On p. 186 of the 32nd Iowa history, Shaw says of Banks, in reference to the preceding argument: "I might refer to General Banks' report, but it shows such a total want of knowledge of the location of his forces and of the operations of the day, of such a total disregard for truth as to place it beneath criticism."
1716. O.R. Vol. 34/I, p. 406. Figure 18, map copied by kind permission of the Mansfield State Historic Site, altered.
1717. O.R. Vol. 34/I, pp. 411–412.

repairs were easily effected, and the section was ready for action again early in the evening.

Moving south, the next sight that the 29th encountered only hinted at the fate of Benedict's brigade. A spot of bright red, in marked contrast to the dark blood of the dead, was seen beyond Appleton's abandoned gun. It was a dead Zouave, "lying at full length in the sand," clad in the brilliant red pantaloons of the 165th New York,[1718] one of Benedict's regiments. Could this mean that Benedict's troops had broken and withdrawn just as Shaw's had? It was true. Dead Zouaves "like sacred roses, dotted all along the slope from the great ditch where Benedict fell, up to the crest of the hill on which stood the village…" Churchill had attacked Benedict's line, consisting of the 165th, 173rd, 162nd New York, and the 30th Maine, at about 5:00, though this was counter to Taylor's plan. Churchill was supposed to have hit the left flank of Mower's 16th Army detachment, by swinging further south and east as far as the Fort Jesup Road; but he was either misdirected by his guide, or crossing the Sabine River Road, and the road south of it, Churchill had assumed he was already on "the enemy's left."

Bursting from the woods into the clear, Churchill's Arkansas and Missouri troops immediately swept forward, charging down the slope to the ditch, where they fell upon Benedict's 3rd brigade.[1719] The advance is represented in figure 18 by the dashed black arrows. Under orders from Taylor to rely on the bayonet "as we had neither ammunition nor time to waste," a pitched battle briefly took place, the closely mingled troops preventing Battery L from further firing. With Benedict killed and other officers wounded or missing, the lines of the 3rd Brigade were driven back in disorder, the 165th New York broke first, then the 162nd, and then 173rd, which suffered severely for its stand, losing 200 of 400 men. Seeing the others go, and nearly surrounded, the 30th Maine retired, "a portion" landing south

---

1718. Gould, p. 423; The 165th was the only known Zouave unit in the 19th Corps still dressed as such, at this time, Benson, p. 502.

1719. Benson, p. 494; O.R. Vol. 34/I, pp. 431–433, 602, O.R. Vol. 53, pp. 477–478; Sketch, 162nd Regiment, p. 26. A court of inquiry found Col. Peck of the 173rd New York absent from the field at the critical time of the attack, and he was dismissed from the service. However, a later court martial cleared him. This is a measure of the state of confusion at the time of the retreat of Benedict's command. No reports of the incident by the three New York regiments involved are to be found in the Official Records. The only official report is that of Col. Francis Fessenden, commanding the 30th Maine. "Sketch, 173rd Regiment, N.Y.V." By Peck, p. 3, only adds that they lost 200 out of 400 men, which is accurate. From Phisterer, there were 6 killed, 42 wounded–of whom 12 died–and 152 were missing. By comparison, the 162nd lost 106, of whom 40 were missing, the 165th, 49, of whom 34 were missing. Fessenden's report, O.R. 34/I, p. 432, gives numbers varying slightly from these. The large number of missing for the 173rd suggests that it was the regiment that prompted Mosby Parsons, (O.R. 34/I, p. 602) commanding the Missouri regiments of Churchill's divisions, to report: "nearly a whole regiment was captured."

in Mower's line (Lynch's Brigade of the 58th and 119th Illinois), the lower portion of Smith's "crescent", as it has been referred to.[1720] The others were re-formed, though short more than 400 casualties, behind the upper portion of Mower's line in Smith's crescent. The arrows approximate their retreat, and the grey/white slashed symbols indicate where they reformed. The upper portion of the crescent now consisted of McMillan's brigade, which, as noted, had been re-deployed by Emory.[1721]

Walker, on Churchill's left, had moved through the woods, and was "entertained" long enough by Shaw to fail to support Churchill.[1722] In addition, Walker's troops faltered for a time when Walker was wounded and was personally guided from the field by General Taylor. Eventually, his troops slid past the 32nd Iowa, as earlier described, and then appeared behind Dwight, Appleton, and upon a portion of Benedict's line.

Benedict's retreating men can be seen sweeping through Taylor's section of Battery L, leaving it to its fate. Hung out in open space, the two sections, one commanded by 1st Lt. Taylor and the other by 2nd Lt. Sanderson, in spite of the canister which they poured into the advancing foe, the enemy reached forty yards away, and the cannoneers were forced to retreat.[1723] Most of the limber horses had been either killed or wounded, so three of the four Napoleons had to be abandoned. Only then were the guns of the 9th Indiana Battery able to open on Churchill's advancing horde.

The Confederate positions (black) indicate their maximum forward advance. It is instructive to refer to the report of Maj. Thomas Newlan, commanding the 58th Illinois Infantry Volunteers,[1724] which was located at the lower "horn" of Smith's

---

1720. O.R. Vol. 34/I, p. 346. Another specific reference as to where Benedict's troops retreated is found in Benson, p. 494. "They were driven through the 9th Indiana Battery and through the 178th New York in Smith's crescent…"
1721. O.R. Vol. 34/I, p. 566–567; Taylor, p. 167–168. There is a discrepancy between Taylor's official report and his account in *Destruction and Reconstruction*. His official report states: "The Arkansas and Missouri divisions, were sent to the right to outflank the enemy, reach the Fort Jesup road, and attack from the south and west." In *Destruction and Reconstruction*, Taylor says: "The road from the Sabine reached, Churchill formed his line with the two Missouri brigades, General Parsons, on the right and General Tappan on the left…Churchill should have placed his whole command on the right of the Sabine road, and he would have found no difficulty in successfully executing his orders." It is clear from the map that reaching the right of the Sabine road is insufficient to flank Smith, or even Benedict.
1722. O.R. Vol. 34/I, p. 553. This allegation is made by an aide-de-camp of Kirby Smith, Lt. Edward Cunningham: "The Missouri division was to have been supported on the left by Scurry's brigade (Walker's extreme right), but instead of cooperating the two went into action separately, and were whipped in detail. The Missouri division drove back the enemy's line in its front, and came to within 50 yards of their batteries, but having no support on their left, were flanked by the enemy in that direction…" This was McMillan.
1723. Haskin (Closson) p. 196; O.R. Vol. 34/I, p. 410
1724. O.R. 34/I, pp. 340, 350.

crescent shaped line, near the Fort Jesup Road. They had been placed there, facing southwest, expecting to be attacked from that direction. This revelation is at least a salutation to the sagacity with which this portion of the Union defense was planned by General Stone of Banks' staff. It was an exact forecast of Taylor's intent. As Maj. Newlan reports:

> [I]in this position we were not attacked as expected. About 4:00 p.m. heavy skirmishing commenced on our right, and a few minutes afterward the rebels charged Benedict's brigade… [which had been posted about] one hundred and fifty paces to our right…in the ravine, and on the ridge in their rear four guns of a regular battery. [Need it be mentioned that this was Battery L's sections of Taylor and Sanderson]
>
> [Benedict's brigade] delivered one or two volleys and fled in disorder. Being hid by an undergrowth of pine the enemy did not observe us, but passed by our right flank, two hundred yards distant, like an irresistible avalanche, pursuing the retreating brigade toward the center of the crescent. For the briefest moment, the whole field of battle was filled, from where Shaw's line had been, up to the edge of the village, with a great southern army[1725]…But they had gone a little too far, and the tip of the crescent's horn charged their right flank…

This was the 58th Illinois, and Newlan continues:

> Observing this, seeing the battery referred to [Battery L] captured, and fearing that we would be cut off and captured, I fell back about 100 paces, changed front so as to face the enemy's flank, and immediately opened fire with deadly effect. In a few minutes the enemy began to stagger under our fire, and finally broke in disorder.

The 58th charged, and joined by the 89th Indiana, drove the Confederates back to the ditch, capturing many prisoners.

At this point, as A.J. Smith reports:[1726] "Seizing the opportunity, I ordered a charge by the whole line…" A melodramatic Confederate perspective of Smith's charge at least admits that this turned the tide of the battle:[1727]

> Parsons, with the Missouri troops in our centre, were driving everything before them. Just at this juncture, A.J. Smith with his two reserve corps [the 16th and the 17th] arrived. They were thrown against our right and centre, under Churchill. The shock was too great. Ten to one they could not stand; and back they came to be rallied no more that evening.

1725. Benson, pp. 496–497.
1726. O.R. 34/I, p. 309
1727. Noel, T., *A Campaign…* p. 80. Of course, Smith had been there all day, and the 17th Corps had never been; it was with Porter.

Walker's men, seeing themselves flanked, joined in the retreat, and in their confusion, and with the oncoming darkness, a quote from General Taylor defines the end of the battle:[1728] "[A]n idea prevailed that we were firing on each other… At nightfall I withdrew the troops."

A. J. Smith finishes: "We drove them back, desperately fighting, step by step across the field, through the wood and into the open field beyond." From Benson, of the 32nd Iowa: "Rolling like a sea of brown, along the roads west and southwest."

General Taylor's losses are only partially reported. E. Kirby Smith, in an April 11th letter[1729] to General Price, who had been facing Steele in Arkansas, offers: "Our loss has been heavy." Irwin says that Taylor reported 1,500, which cannot be confirmed. Only Parsons and Tappan of Churchill's division wrote reports which include loss figures. Churchill reported seven officers and 58 men killed, with 393 wounded, which is less than the total reported by his two brigade commanders.[1730] His force, at 4,300, represents only about a third of Taylor's total. If it was assumed that Walker's, Major's, Green's, and Polignac's troops took similar percentages of casualties, Taylor's total would calculate to be 1,374.

The losses of the Union army were 152 killed, 859 wounded, and 495 missing, for a total of 1,506. The casualties were about equal between those of Emory, at 725, and Smith at 753. The highest casualties were taken, as may have been expected, by the two most exposed positions on the battlefield, and those which were overrun; namely the brigades of Shaw and Benedict, at 447 and 483 respectively.[1731]

There was some recrimination in the Union ranks, the westerners blaming the easterners. We have already mentioned Col. Shaw of the 14th Iowa, and his disgust with General Dwight. The perceived lack of guts of Benedict's brigade is hinted at in the report of Maj. Thomas Newlan, of the 58th Illinois, when he reports: "Rebels charged Benedict's brigade, which delivered one or two volleys and fled in disorder." Was there anything but prejudice in this attitude?

The position that Benedict's line had been assigned was an advanced one, much as was Shaw's. Neither position was tenable. Normal procedure would dictate a fall back, once seeing that they would be overwhelmed. Shaw was ordered to withdraw, Benedict was killed. No doubt Benedict's command would have, or should have been so ordered. Having seen their commander shot in the head[1732] in the first few moments of the action, was a considerable factor leading to confusion.

The nearly identical losses taken by the opponents, at 1,500 each, leads one to agree with a final assessment of the battle, which was made by Confederate Gen.

1728. O.R. 34/I, p. 568.
1729. O.R. Vol. 34/III, p. 759.
1730. O.R. Vol. 34/I, pp. 604–605. Parsons reported 321, and Tappan, 201; Irwin, p. 322.
1731. Irwin, p. 321; O. R. Vol. 34/I, pp. 260, 313, 413, 432; Phisterer, pp. 3890, 3921, 3966.
1732. Pellet, p. 215; Clark, p. 163; Annals of Iowa, Van Dyke's Narrative, p. 524.

X. B. DeBray:[1733]

> This was, at best, a drawn battle. Both armies held the ground they occupied in the morning, but General Taylor, apprehending a renewal of the contest on the next day, knowing that water was not accessible where his troops stood, determined to fall back to a creek five miles distant, there to select a position. DeBray's and Buchel's regiments were left on the battle-field, with instructions to observe the enemy, and, if necessary, to retire slowly before his advance.

Nightfall found the Federals in control of the battlefield, and thus there was no exact repeat of the situation at Mansfield, where the Union wounded had been outrightly abandoned to the Confederates. Some of the dead were buried, and, at least, some walking wounded did not fall prisoner into Confederate hands. Nevertheless, darkness and the precipitate departure of Banks' army from the scene, at about 2:00 a.m. on April 10th, left an overwhelming number of the wounded, estimated to be 400,[1734] still wandering in the woods, or lying in agony hoping to be recovered to hospital.

And then there were the animals. Rider-less horses, some wounded, were still wandering or dragging themselves around. Remember that most of the limber horses of Franck Taylor's sections of Battery L were either killed or wounded, as were the caisson horses of Appleton. The three limbers and two caissons that were lost were drawn by 30 horses, 27 of whom were wounded or killed. The wounded, left still in harness, some still standing, faithfully waited hours for the slap of the reins and the command to move, though the dead and maimed hitched with them would make it impossible.[1735]

A party of General Taylor's men appeared at the battlefield that morning with a flag of truce, prepared to bury their dead. They were astonished to find only the Union surgeons and the rear guard of Banks' army, Colonel Lucas' cavalry.

Banks's order to abandon the wounded and retire that morning was protested by A. J. Smith, who is said to have favored remaining at Pleasant Hill long enough to care for the wounded, then continuing the advance. He considered arresting Banks, and proposed to Franklin that he take command. Franklin later acknowledged that Smith had approached him, but he avoided the matter of the alleged mutiny, only writing that he opposed the idea of an advance.[1736] He apparently was opposed to the idea of serving any longer under Banks, which was revealed in his response to a letter of inquiry from Col. John Scott, who had commanded the 32nd

---

1733. DeBray, X. B., p. 159.
1734. Benson, p. 503.
1735. Blessington, p. 201. "Dead and maimed horses lie about, some still plunging and endeavoring to drag their broken limbs after them." Battery L Monthly Return, April, 1864, "Horses Lost in Action" 27.
1736. Scott, John, pp. 231–237; Irwin, p. 322; O.R. Vol. 34/I, pp. 184.

Iowa, in Shaw's brigade. Franklin wrote: "The idea of an advance after what I had just experienced under Banks' generalship was odious to me…"

Banks' report of the retreat, written on April 13th, says, in part: "There was not water for man nor beast, except as the now exhausted wells had afforded during the day, for miles around… These considerations…the exhaustion of rations, and the failure to effect a connection with the fleet…made it necessary for the army …to retreat to a point where it would be certain in communicating with the fleet and where it would have an opportunity of reorganization." He was apparently still in contemplation of continuing the campaign, but at this time could offer only the vague, "upon a line differing somewhat from that adopted first and rendering the column less dependent upon a river proverbially as treacherous as the enemies we fight."

As to Battery L, Franck Taylor's official report gives few details of the battle, and does not name his casualties, as he was apparently loath to do. He had filed a separate casualty report that was incomplete, but another, figure 19, was prepared by members of the 1st Division staff,[1737] which contains the casualties taken by Battery L, including members of the 13th Massachusetts Battery, the 25th New York, and the 1st Vermont.

The data for Battery L reads: Killed, Pvt. Sholto O'Brien, and from the 13th Massachusetts Battery, Pvt. William H. Smith. Wounded and missing: 2nd Lt. James A. Sanderson, Sgt. Michael White, Pvt. Thomas Clinton, Pvt. William Parks, and from the 13th Massachusetts Battery: wounded, Cpl. William Hesseltine, Pvt. John Ferguson, and missing, Pvt. J. Redding.[1738]

Lt. Sanderson, known as "Sep" at West Point, had stood by his guns and was horribly mangled by an exploding shell. Though mortally wounded, he remained "between his pieces…still giving his commands." He was later taken to hospital, died that night, and was buried out under the pines.

1737. Figure 19, National Archives *Regimental Returns*, 1st Artillery, January 1861–December 1870, M727-5, p. 318.
1738. There is a George Reading listed in the 13th Massachusetts Battery, (Record of Massachusetts Volunteers, vol. 1, p. 457) who served from December 30th, 1862, until his discharge on July 28th, 1865, by expiration of service. The service dates identify him as the man with Battery L. Absent any other record, he clearly was returned from missing; Haskin, p. 364; Schaff, Morris, pp. 89, 240.

List of Killed, Wounded and Missing in Batteries of 1st Division, 19th Army Corps at the Battle of Pleasant Hill La. April 19th 1864 — Should read April 9th 1864 — See Original List Index 50 ? No. 50, of which this list appears to be a copy. W.H.

Artillery

Name	Rank	Battery	Killed	W'd/M'g
Shott, O'Brien	Private	I	1st U.S.A.	
Wm Smith	"	"	"	Total 2
Sanderson	2d Lieut	"	"	Wounded & Missing
Thos. Clinton	Private	"	"	"
Chas Necettine	"	"	"	"
John Ferguson	"	"	"	"
Wm Parks	"	"	"	"
White	Sergeant	"	"	Wounded & Missing
				Total 6
J. Redding	Private	"	"	Missing
				Total 3
Jesse Laundry	Private	x 1st Vermont	Wounded	x Total 1
Busser ✓	Private	25 N.H. ✓	Killed	Total 2
Nahn	"	"	"	
Diegler	"	"	Wounded	
Wilkinson	"	"	" Missing	
Straw	"	"	" Missing	
				Total 3
Chrtm	"	"	Missing	Total 2
				Total 19

(Total loss 16)

FIGURE 19

Chapter 12

Withdrawal: April 10th; Grand Ecore; Cane River;
Porter's Passage to Alexandria; The Dam at Alexandria; "Record" 6/64;
Marksville & Mansura; Canby; Last Days in the Gulf; "Record" 8/64;
Camp Barry; Politics & Peace Initiatives; Washington Threatened;
The Nineteenth Corps Arrives; After Early; Anecdote

Withdrawal: April 10th

The portion of the "Record" for February–April, which bears upon the bloodiest battle Battery L had ever been caught up in, merely says: "9th Marched to Pleasant Hill, Battery in position, went into camp for 2 hours. Battery in action at P.M. 10th Marched 22 miles."

It gives no hint of the difficulties during the battle, or subsequently. Having had to bury Lt. Sanderson, and privates O'Brien and Smith, someone had to see that a wounded Thomas Clinton was cared for, all the while knowing that White, Hesseltine, and privates Parks and Ferguson were wounded and missing, perhaps prisoners, or perhaps lying unseen in the brush, dying. There was frantic activity, all the while working in the dark to unhitch wounded and dead horses from their limbers and caissons,[1739] and repair broken poles and wheels before their abandoned guns could be removed from the battlefield; all of this, after the stress of a battle, and without proper rest or food since the 8th. Then the order came to march again, after midnight, for twenty-two miles. They were reduced to towing only four guns, after 27 of their horses had been killed and 11 others were unserviceable. It is surmised that lightly wounded horses were coaxed into duty, without any treatment whatever. The severely wounded animals had to be ignored, and for the lack of time to administer a kind pistol shot to the head, they were left to die.

The march continued for several miles in the almost absolute darkness of the chill night. The road was bad; worst of all,[1740] seeing how the campaign had been mismanaged, the men were in a dark mood. The thoughts were for the wounded

---

1739. O.R. Vol. 34/I, pp. 411–412. Appleton had his 12 caisson horses "mostly killed or wounded…" per Battery L's April monthly return; Irwin, p. 323.
1740. Lufkin, E. B., pp. 86–87; Blessington, p. 201; Benson, p. 500; Pellet, p. 215; Clark, p. 163; John Scott, pp. 215–218, 233–236; Heath, pp. 520, 522.

that had been left on the battlefield, now for a second time, yet for a new reason. The medical supply train had been earlier sent toward Grand Ecore with the rest of the wagon train, leaving no facilities available for removal or treatment. Reflecting the opinion of A. J. Smith, a most decided victory had been gained; the disgrace of Mansfield had been wiped away, and the troops had looked forward to chasing the defeated enemy to Shreveport, but that was to be denied.

April 10th was a day of some other significant events. Only two hours after their arrival, that afternoon, near Loggy Bayou, where they were blocked from further ascent of the river by the sunken Confederate steamer *New Falls City*, Porter's gunboats and Kilby Smith's transports were ordered to be turned back downriver.[1741] Almost simultaneously with the fleet's arrival, Banks' messenger had arrived with his verbal order. The written order reached them on the 11th, when they had already descended to Coushatta Chute.

E. Kirby Smith, the commander of the Trans-Mississippi Department, appeared at Taylor's camp after the battle at Pleasant Hill. He had ridden the sixty-five miles from Shreveport on the 9th, but did not reach there in time to witness the battle. Satisfied that Banks was in full retreat, he was concerned that Taylor would not be able to supply his troops in a pursuit. Quoting Smith: "The country below[1742] Natchitoches had been completely desolated and stripped of supplies. The navigation of the river was obstructed, and even had our whole force been available for pursuit it could not have been subsisted below Natchitoches." Incredibly, the *New Falls City*, sunk to block the advance of Porter's gunboats and Kilby Smith's transports, was now operating in the reverse. It would block the shipment of any supplies to Taylor from Shreveport. While discussing their options, Smith convinced Taylor that the better alternative was to break off the "main body of our infantry" and use it to pursue Steele, then at Prairie D'Ane, Arkansas.

In accordance with Halleck's original plan, Steele's 7th Army Corps,[1743] about 7,000 troops, had marched out of Little Rock on March 23rd in the direction of Shreveport, more than two hundred miles distant. At about the same time, another column of about 5,000 under General Thayer left Fort Smith, planning to unite with Steele at Arkadelphia, also a march of more than two hundred miles. Swollen spring streams and bad roads delayed Thayer, and initially Steele marched on alone. As has been mentioned, Steele knew almost nothing of Banks' fortunes and vice versa.

After repeated skirmishes along the road forward, April 2nd at Terre Noir Bayou, April 4th at Elkin's Ford, on the Little Missouri, and on April 10th, an engagement at Prairie D'Ane, about one hundred miles southwest of Little Rock,

---

1741. O.R. 34/I, pp. 204, 380, 381, 385, 388; ORN Ser. I, Vol. 26, p. 51.
1742. O.R. Vol. 34/I, pp. 480, 485; E. Kirby Smith to Jefferson Davis.
1743. Byers, S. H. M., p. 284; O.R. Vol. 34/I, p. 653; Vol, 34/III, p. 39; *www.nps.gov/abpp/battles/* AR012, AR013.

Steele was still more than a hundred miles from Shreveport, yet Kirby Smith viewed him as "in position to march upon our base and destroy our depots and shops…" To this argument Taylor agreed, and requested that he might "accompany" the troops.

The argument was, however, only a portion of E. Kirby Smith's thoughts. His private opinion, as expressed to Jefferson Davis, confirmed the general sentiment of the Union troops that had fought at Pleasant Hill, as well as that of A. J. Smith, viz., that Taylor's force was completely worn out, and should have been relentlessly pursued. Kirby Smith:

> To my great relief I found in the morning that the enemy had fallen back during the night. He continued his retreat to Grand Ecore, where he entrenched himself and remained until the return of his fleet and its passage over the bars, made especially difficult this season by the unusual fall of the river.
>
> The question may be asked why the enemy was not pursued at once. I answer, because our troops were completely paralyzed by the repulse at Pleasant Hill, and the cavalry, worn by the long march from Texas, had been constantly engaged for three days, almost without food or forage. Before we could reorganize at Mansfield and get into condition to advance over the 55 miles of the wilderness which separated the armies, the enemy was re-enforced and intrenched at Grand Ecore…If we could not whip him at Pleasant Hill in a fair fight, it would have been madness to have attacked him at Grand Ecore in his entrenchments, supported by a formidable fleet of gunboats.

Thus, Steele in Arkansas being his boss's preferred target, Taylor detached Walker's Texas division and Churchill's two divisions, Parson's Missourians, and Tappan's Arkansas infantry, who departed Mansfield on the morning of the 14th to march to Shreveport. Taylor would retain his cavalry, already sent in pursuit of Porter's fleet, and Polignac's infantry, which had been sent along on the road to Natchitoches, in support of the cavalry.[1744] Taylor, figuring to accompany his troops on the expedition to reinforce Sterling Price in Arkansas, arrived at Smith's headquarters on the 15th, where he learned that the fight at Prairie d' Ane had forced Steele to divert his march away from Shreveport, toward Camden. Regardless of the fact that Price seemed capable of handling Steele, Smith still wanted to press on with his expedition, and had decided to command it himself. Taylor would remain at Shreveport in nominal command.

In the meantime, the remnant of Taylor's command had pursued the fleet. Bagby to Grand Bayou Landing fifteen miles below Loggy Bayou, and Green to Blair's Landing. On the east side of the river, Gen. Liddell, commander of the

---

1744. O.R. Vol. 34/I, pp. 388–389, 570, 572, 634; Taylor, p. 177; figure 1, ORN ser. 1, vol. 26, pp. 44c (portion), 49–52; Irwin, pp. 325–326.

sub-district of North Louisiana, with Harrison's brigade of cavalry, and two sections of artillery, harassed the fleet almost constantly, following it downriver from the 11th to the 15th. However, Porter labeled Harrison's force as "careful about coming within range" and their effect only slowed the fleet at one point on the 13th.

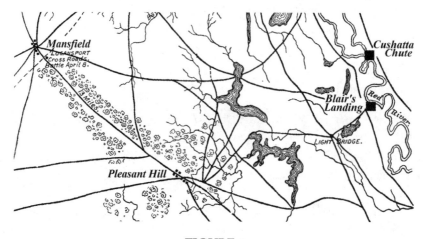

FIGURE 1

The fleet had already passed Grand Bayou Landing, and was fifteen miles beyond, near Coushatta Chute, figure 1, by the time Bagby arrived, so Bagby pushed south on the river road to join Green at Blair's Landing. Arriving on the evening of the 12th, he found that Green had attacked the tail end of the fleet, specifically the *Hastings*, *Black Hawk*, and *Emerald*, at about 5:00 p.m. Green, alleged to have been primed by Louisiana rum, had led Woods' 36th Texas cavalry in a wild charge across an open field toward the gunboats. The gunboat *Osage*, in tow by the *Black Hawk*, then opened on them with canister and shrapnel. Green, who was well in advance, was killed. The *Lexington* soon joined the action, as did the bow guns of the *Rob Roy*, and one section of the 1st Missouri Battery posted on the deck of the *Emerald*. Their combined fire ended the engagement after about 40 minutes, the whole action having taken less than two hours. An estimated 300 of Woods' cavalry were dead or wounded. The casualties among the navy crews and the companies of the 95th Illinois Regiment, Company A, on board the *Black Hawk*, and F on the *Hastings*, was comparatively light.[1745] On the 13th, the fleet received musketry fire and ran a gauntlet of four 12-pounders posted at Vandares by Liddell's band. The pilot houses were the enemy's target. The soldiers on board

---

1745. ORN Ser. I, Vol. 26, pp. 50, 55. Bache, the commander of the *Lexington*, estimated 150. Porter claims 400–500, Selfridge of the Osage, 200, Noel, *Autobiography*, pp. 100, 143, says 300. Casualties on board the fleet are at variance in different reports, but one killed and 18 wounded is totaled from the reports of the 95th Illinois Regiment, with each of its companies on different boats, and the combined reports of the *Osage* and the *Lexington*; O.R. Vol. 34/I, pp. 205, 383, T. K. Smith reports his loss as "incredibly small." W. W. Wood, pp. 102–103.

had put up breastworks of hay, boxes of hard tack, and "every available article," and to this protection is attributed the fact that there were only two casualties. On April 14th, they again endured musketry fire from the east bank, below Campti, twenty miles above Grand Ecore, where they were finally met by a detachment from A. J. Smith, which assured their safe passage to Grand Ecore the next day.

April 10th also was the day that Gen. W. T. Sherman was to have his troops back. So determined was he that he sent Brig. Gen. J. M. Corse on a special mission to visit Banks, with orders for A. J. and T. K. Smith to prepare for "big licks"—the spring campaigns in the east.[1746] To Banks he wrote:

> I beg you will expedite their return to Vicksburg, if they have not already started, and I want them, if possible, in the same boats they used up Red River, as it will save the time otherwise consumed in the transfer to others boats. All is well in this quarter and I hope by the time you turn against Mobile our forces will again act to the same end…General Grant, now having lawful control, will doubtless see that all minor objects are disregarded, and all the armies acting on a common plan.

The earlier initiatives by Halleck in Texas and Red River, were now "minor objects," and were to be cancelled.

These were serious tidings to a man in a deep quandary. The fleet had had trouble grounding in the shallows arriving at Grand Ecore, and the river was continuing to fall. The low level of the river below Grand Ecore and the falls at Alexandria threatened to trap it. There could be no question of an advance unless the river rose, and to that, even the ever-aggressive Porter agreed.[1747] However, as to whether Steele was successful in advancing and ultimately joining with Banks, at this time, it was impossible to say. It had come down to the old problem of communications, always behind by 15 to 20 days. It was easier for Steele to communicate with Sherman and Grant than Banks, and vice versa. Any messages between Steele and Banks would have to pass through enemy territory or else go by the circuitous route of courier to Vicksburg and Memphis, to finally be telegraphed from there. Though Banks had heard nothing from Steele, one point was very clear. On March 27th, Banks received from Grant the fateful March 15th order, mentioned earlier, that said: "Should you find that the taking of Shreveport will occupy 10 or 15 days more time than General Sherman gave his troops to be absent from their command you will send them back at the time specified…*even if it should lead to the abandonment of the…expedition.*" Grant followed up on March 31st, which ordered Banks to turn over the defense of the Red River to Steele and the navy, abandon all of Texas except the Rio Grande, and then prepare to move against Mobile.

1746. O.R. Vol. 34/III, pp. 24–25, 244. Big licks they would be—Sherman's famous march to the sea.

1747. ORN Ser. I, Vol. 26, p. 64; O.R. 34/I, pp. 11, 203, 216.

Curiously, Grant left Sherman to inform Steele of this order, which was not sent until April 7th. In it, Sherman informed Steele of his recall of A. J. Smith, and then said: "Your forces and General Banks' conjoined…would be able to accomplish all that should be attempted this spring. But if General Grant has also recalled Banks' command to be directed on Mobile, as I suppose he has done or will, you will not have enough men to accomplish all that should be done." He went on to say: "I have recommended to General Grant to give you all available forces in Kansas and Missouri…"[1748]

Grand Ecore

It was clear that Banks' campaign was "ruined," as Irwin puts it,[1749] and the only thing to do was to try to wrap it up before May 1st as Grant had directed. The fleet must be extricated from the falling river, and for the moment, at least, Grand Ecore would be fortified to form a defensive line while the fleet passed down. To do this, however, Banks would have to have the security of A. J. Smith's troops, at least until he could recall troops from Texas, and accept the chance of thinning the number of troops defending the rest of the department. McClernand was ordered to leave Texas with nearly all the troops at Pass Cavallo, and four regiments of the 13th Corps at Baton Rouge were ordered to Grand Ecore. Grover's 2nd and 3rd brigades were sent to Grand Ecore. The 133rd New York, serving in the defenses of New Orleans, was sent to report to Grover at Alexandria. Grover's 1st Brigade, under Nickerson, left Carrollton, also for Alexandria.[1750]

A hint of Grant's suspicion and distrust of what was going on in Banks' department was his April 15th order to Halleck to have Major General David Hunter report to him. Hunter was to be sent to look over Banks' shoulder, to "impress upon the general particularly two points": the importance of an advance on Mobile at the earliest possible time, and that Banks detach enough troops for the expedition. "You will remain with general Banks until his move from New Orleans is commenced, and a landing is effected at Pascagoula…"[1751]

On the 16th when Smith reported that his transports had all arrived at Grand

---

1748. O.R. Vol. 34/III, pp. 76, 77.
1749. Irwin, p. 326; O.R.Vol.34/I, p. 174; O.R. 34/III, p. 125, 126–128, 194, 195, 254, 269. The 20th U.S. Infantry (colored), from Port Hudson, was sent to Pass Cavallo to replace those troops of the 13th Corps who were ordered to New Orleans.
1750. Hanaburgh, p. 101.
1751. O.R. Vol. 34/III, pp. 160, 169, 190–192. It is noted that Grant sent this order to Halleck from his headquarters at Culpeper, Virginia. Such details were left to Chief of Staff Halleck. Grant was all business, and notably remained out of Washington, and away from Lincoln and Stanton, where there was a chance that they might interfere with his plans. From p. 123 of vol. 2 of Grant's *Memoirs*: "I did not communicate my plans to the President, nor did I to the Secretary of War or to General Halleck."

Ecore, and that he was ready to respond to Sherman's order to leave, Banks refused.[1752] Smith obeyed, and with the others sent as reinforcements, continued building a defensive line around Grand Ecore, which consisted of two miles of felled trees covered with earth.

The struggle of bringing the transports and Porter's gunboats down to Grand Ecore and then to Alexandria, had resulted in the sinking of the massive *Eastport*, which was alleged to have struck a torpedo on April 15th, eight miles below Grand Ecore.[1753] Attempts to re-float her by pumping had to await the arrival of pump boats. On the 21st she was finally pumped out, bulkheaded, and floated. Towed by the pump boat *Champion No. 5*, she made twenty miles further downstream, where she grounded again. After fifty-seven miles and four more days of dragging her over increasing numbers of sand bars and log jams, her five support boats all the while taking considerable Confederate fire, the *Eastport* became impossibly stuck on a bed of sunken logs, and rather than have her fall into Confederate hands, she was blown up at 2:10 p.m. on April 26th.

The name of Lt. Col. Joseph Bailey, the acting military engineer in the department, is revealed in a later report by Banks, commenting on the *Eastport* affair. Bailey, familiar to almost all of the troops at Port Hudson, where he supervised the construction of many of the gun battery positions, and who was credited with the salvage of the Confederate steamers *Starlight* and *Red Chief*, which were captured in Thompson's Creek, had suggested the construction of wing-dams to raise the level of the river, and thus float the *Eastport* free. Army aid was ignored.[1754] Banks, justifiably sour, writes; "No counsel from army officers was regarded in nautical affairs."

On April 21st, the minute that Banks had heard that the *Eastport* was afloat, he prepared to march out of Grand Ecore, already having waited 10 days for Porter. However, this was shown to be not quite enough time to allow Porter to save the *Eastport*. Banks, marching down the island created by the Cane River and the Red River at the furious pace set by Birge, who was leading a temporary division,[1755] forged ahead of Porter, and left him unsupported—an accidental mini scenario of what Porter had earlier feared regarding his whole fleet while at Loggy Bayou.[1756] Kilby Smith, in a letter to Porter dated April 25th, remarked: "General Smith and I both protest at being hurried away. I feel as if we were shamefully deserting you."[1757]

1752. O.R. Vol. 34/III, p. 175; Beecher, p. 327; Pellet, p. 221; Sprague, p. 192;
1753. ORN ser. 1, vol. 26, pp. 68, 72, 76, 81–82, 84–87, 110, 167, 781.
1754. O.R. Vol. 34/I, pp. 206, 403.
1755. Sprague, p. 193: "Twenty five miles" from 5:00 p.m. on the April 21st to 3:00 a.m. on April 22nd; Hanaburgh, p. 103, Taylor, p, 182. Cloutierville was thirty-two miles, where the army finally halted.
1756. ORN ser. 1, vol. 26, p. 56.
1757. O.R. Vol.34/III, p. 279.

Cane River

Banks' haste was the result of the fact that he had been warned that Taylor had sent troops around from his front at Grand Ecore to his rear. This was either to intercept the passage of the fleet at the mouth of the Cane River, attack Alexandria, or obstruct the march toward Alexandria at Monett's Bluff.[1758] To Richard Taylor, it was all of the above, depending on how events unfolded. After the battle of Pleasant Hill, as previously noted, Taylor had sent Polignac to occupy the vicinity of Natchitoches, five miles from Grand Ecore; Bee and Major to the Cane River Valley; and Vincent's and Bush's cavalry to threaten Alexandria. After his being informed that his presence with E. Kirby Smith's expedition against Steele was not desired, Taylor resolved to join Polignac. Accompanied by Green's replacement, Maj. Gen. John A. Wharton, the pair arrived at Polignac's camp on April 21st, just in time to have word of Banks' preliminary move, which was directing A. J. Smith to march out of Grand Ecore to Natchitoches on the 20th. The move was a feint, designed to look like the beginning of another advance to Shreveport, and as T. K. Smith says: "Up to this time our troops had been encouraged by the belief or direct promise that they were to march directly upon Shreveport. But now it became evident that we were on the eve of making a grand retreat instead of marching against the enemy."[1759] Taylor was not fooled, and was apparently later confirmed in his belief, when some houses were set afire by a citizen of Grand Ecore on the 22nd, thought to be a signal to Taylor that the Federal army was moving out. Taylor warned Bee, who was instructed to fall back, and stand and hold the ferry across Cane River at Monett's Bluff.

As has been noted, Banks was unaware of Steele's status, or that on April 17th Grant had ordered Maj. Gen. David Hunter to travel to Banks' headquarters with further instructions. In a letter introducing Hunter, Grant assumed that Shreveport had fallen, and expressed fear that Banks was planning, or was already in pursuit of Taylor into Texas.[1760] If so, he was ordered to "retrace his steps on receipt of this."

At least, the continuation of the retreat from Grand Ecore to Alexandria had accidentally fallen in with Grant's desires. The river had continued to fall, and there was no prospect for any advance, absent all of the other considerations.[1761]

The retreat brought destruction and devastation in its path. At night, the burning buildings marked the route. The destruction was blamed on the western troops; their memories of atrocities still fresh from earlier in the war—homes looted and burned at the hands of southern sympathizers organized as guerilla bands. General Franklin rather tardily issued an order on April 27th deploring the

---

1758. O.R. Vol. 34/I, p. 190; Taylor, pp. 180–182; O.R.. Vol. 34/III, pp. 235–236.
1759. Smith, W. G., p. 120.
1760. O.R. Vol. 34/III, pp 191–192.
1761. O.R. Vol. 34/I, p. 205.

"incendiarism, disgraceful to the army of a civilized nation." He offered a $500 reward for evidence to convict those found guilty.[1762] The order, only issued after the army had reached Alexandria, suggests that command discipline was breaking down, with a demoralized Franklin's health deteriorating from his wound.[1763] Franklin was only nominally in command. He would be replaced by Emory on May 2nd, and would soon leave the department.

The Battery L "Record" says: "21st struck camp at 5 P.M. and remained harnessed until 3 A.M. 22nd, then marched 24 miles and camped for about 4 hours, then marched to Cloutierville. 23rd Marched to pontoon on Cane River…" It says nothing about the fact that its commanding officer, as the chief of artillery, was a key in the battle at Cane River Crossing, and that it was held in reserve, under his command, standing the whole day, ready to enter the battle.

On April 23rd, about three miles out of Cloutierville, Gooding's cavalry, at the head of Banks' column, met and skirmished with Bee's pickets. Regardless of Birge's fast-paced march, Bee had beaten him to the crossing. Driving Bee's pickets as they advanced, the cavalry approached Burton's Crossing and Bee's artillery opened on them. It was about 4:00 a.m.[1764] Bee's Texans—Debray, Bagby, and Major—had hastily placed batteries on the high bluffs on the south bank of the river. Two batteries, one of seven guns and the other of four, commanded an area of open fields across which Banks' column would have to pass. Emory, now in command, as ordered by Franklin, who was increasingly suffering from his wound,[1765] put a plan into action which consisted of planting his 1st and 2nd brigades, under McMillan, along with the reserve artillery, under Closson, supported by the 116th New York regiment, and parts of the 153rd, in front of the woods facing the enemy positions. Birge, with Emory's 3rd Brigade under Fessenden, and a portion of the 13th Corps under Cameron, were to then gain a ford (top left, in figure 2) out of sight of the enemy, which was about three miles above the ferry. Here they were to cross and advance to attack the flank of the Confederate position held by Debray. A brigade of cavalry was to advance from the opposite direction, making a demonstration, as no suitable ford had been found below.

1762. O.R. Vol. 34/III, p. 307.
1763. O.R. Vol. 34/III, pp. 391, 472; Irwin, p. 330; Ewer, p. 179. He was still "confined" as of May 6th.
1764. O.R. Vol. 34/I, pp. 190, 207–208, 394–397, 406–407, 418–419, 610–612; Pellet, pp. 226, 228; Clark, pp. 169–170; DeBray, SHS, vol. 13, p. 161.
1765. O.R. Vol. 34/I, p. 262, Figure 2, ibid, p. 395, captions added.

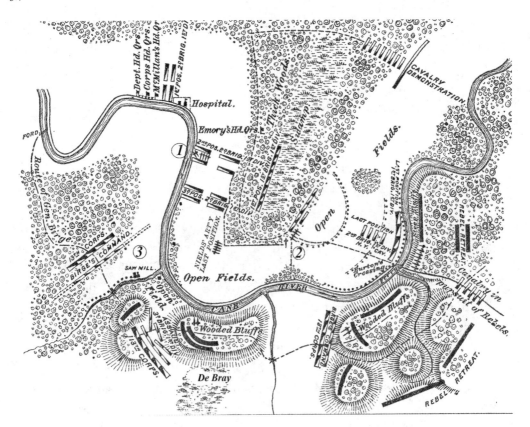

FIGURE 2

To secure McMillan's advance, by 6:00 a.m., Closson had placed two of the 20-pounder Parrotts of the 1st Indiana battery and six of the 3-inch rifles of the 1st Delaware battery, shown at position 1 in figure 2, so as to shell the four guns on the bluffs on the Confederate left.[1766] Initially firing at a range of two thousand yards, the Confederate guns were silenced after about a half hour. Birge had not, as yet, gotten into position to attack Debray at the left end of the Confederate line, and operations were briefly suspended. In the meantime, at Emory's request, five more guns, those from the 1st Indiana, the 25th New York, the 1st Vermont, and the 1st Delaware, were moved—all the while under Confederate fire—through the swampy woods in front to position 2, about one thousand yards from the seven guns above Burton's Crossing, on the Confederate right. After "a good deal of labor" the guns were finally in place by 2:00 p.m, and had opened fire. After 10 minutes of shelling, the Confederate artillery was silenced. At about the same time, Birge's command had made their way through the swamps and almost impenetrable woods to the point of their assault, position 3, and the rattle of their musketry told of its beginning. After repelling two of Birge's attacks, made at the point of the bayonet, Debray was ordered to fall back, whereupon the colors of the 162nd

---

1766. O.R. Vol. 34/I, pp. 406–407.

New York, closely followed by the 30th Maine, were planted on the works.[1767] The 3rd brigade commander, Fessenden, who had replaced Benedict—killed at Pleasant Hill—was wounded during the assault, and Blanchard of the 162nd New York took over the command. In the meantime, the demonstration before Burton's Crossing had been intensified into a full assault, the river was crossed and the hill climbed, only to find, to everyone's astonishment, that while Debray had been retiring, Bagby and Major had fled.

The four regiments involved in the charge against Debray suffered severe casualties, 153 out of 200 for the entire engagement; the 30th Maine, by far the most of all, at 86. Their commander, Lt. Col. Thomas Hubbard, blamed the interference of one of Banks' staff for giving orders for movements that scattered the attackers, and which resulted in a required delay to reform. This had allowed DeBray to withdraw to the wooded bluff to the west, which made the advance of the 30th Maine a half-mile longer, and their taking more casualties as a result.

While the front of the Federal column had engaged Bee, the rear, guarded by Ward's brigade of T. Kilby Smith's detachment, had been attacked by Wharton's 7th Texas Cavalry, supported by Polignac. Wharton, as noted, had joined Taylor as a replacement for Green.[1768] A furious engagement then ensued, which lasted two hours, but Wharton was repulsed. Thus began an almost continuous series of clashes that lasted until the army reached Alexandria.

Porter's Passage to Alexandria

Leaving the *Eastport* on April 26th, the five support boats were attacked by guerrillas as they headed downstream, but repelled them.[1769] However, at a point five miles above the entrance to Cane River, to which point Taylor had ordered the four guns of Capt. F. O. Cornay's St. Mary's Cannoneers, Porter was really cut up. Cornay's battery, remembered from the battle at Bisland and Grover's passage to Irish Bend, was impressive—attested to by the fact that Porter claimed that Cornay had 18 guns, and that the flagship, the *Cricket*, had been struck 38 times. The incident was a memorial to the skill and daring of Cornay, who was killed, and a reminder of Gideon Welles' comment that exaggeration was Porter family "infirmity."

There was another incident on the 27th. Between the two days, Porter's flagship had lost 25 killed and wounded, the *Juliet* lost 15, the *Fort Hindman* 2, the *Champion No. 5*, one killed and all of the crew taken prisoner, and the *Champion No. 3*, whose boiler was shot through and exploded, had four of the crew scalded to death, the cook wounded; and of about 200 contraband passengers, men, women,

---

1767. *162nd New York Infantry*, p. 28; Peck, p. 3, Haskin, p. 370; O.R. 34/I, pp. 434–435, 438–441; Clark, pp. 226–227.
1768. Irwin, p. 329; Wood, W. W., p. 104.
1769. ORN ser. 1, vol. 26, pp. 74–87, 176–177; Taylor, pp. 183–184; Welles, vol. 1, p. 157.

and children—taken from the plantations along the river—there were 100 dead and 87 badly scalded, all of whom died within 24 hours. The *No. 5* was abandoned while on fire. The *No. 3* was captured, repaired and put into service by the Confederates.

Porter makes mention of the Confederates diverting the Red River to speed its drop. Impressive engineering feats were conducted during the war, and we remember many that were used on the Mississippi. Pope had dug the new Madrid Canal to bypass the Confederate guns at Island No. 10, Grant had blasted the Yazoo Pass to try to gain access to Pemberton's rear; he revived the work on the Williams canal to try to bypass Vicksburg; he initiated the Lake Providence scheme, and the Duckport Canal. Later, the Confederates used a diversion to flood False River, to deny Federal passage across that point of land opposite Port Hudson. None of these, however, were calculated to lower the Mississippi, though it technically was a side effect. Porter alleges:[1770] "When the rebels heard we had arrived at Grand Ecore, they commenced turning the source of the water supply off into the lakes, which would have been remedied had the army succeeded in getting to Shreveport." In other words, it was now the army's fault, in addition to Mother Nature, that the Red River was receding. There is, however, no reference to be found as to any such colorful scheme in any of Richard Taylor's writings.

The Dam at Alexandria

As referenced in the Battery L "Record," after the battle at Cane River Crossing had ended, the army continued on its march. Battery L's turn came when, "at 12 midnight, the column crossed Cane River on a pontoon bridge" constructed by the engineer brigade.[1771] They camped until 6 a.m. on April 24th then marched sixteen miles. "25th Marched through Alexandria and remained until present date."

Grant's man, Hunter, arrived on April 27th, eight-and-one-half days out from Washington. It was at the worst possible time—the crisis over the entrapment of the fleet at the rapids at Alexandria, discussed below.[1772] Hunter took little time to reach a judgment. The next day, he reported back to Grant that the situation was "complicated, precarious, and perplexing…" He precipitously recommended destroying the boats, and went on to say: "Why this expedition was ordered I cannot imagine." Of course, it was the creature of Seward and Lincoln, and was endorsed by Halleck.

April 28th was the same day that Grant had received Banks' latest report, dated April 17th. In it, Banks tried to promote the idea of enlarging the campaign, to prevent the enemy from threatening Arkansas and Missouri. He would again

---

1770. ORN ser. 1, vol. 26, p. 69.
1771. O.R. Vol. 34/I, p, 250.
1772. O.R Vol. 34/I, p. 191; Vol. 34/III, p. 316.

advance and capture Shreveport. Grant was unmoved. He wrote to Halleck: "I do not see that better orders can be given than those sent a few days ago...(*retrace your steps, etc.*)...General Banks, by his failure, has absorbed 10,000 veteran troops that should now be with General Sherman and 30,000 of his own that would have been moving toward Mobile, and this without accomplishing any good result." He had already made up his mind to sack Banks,[1773] and asked for the President's concurrence in a telegram dated April 22nd. Grant reveals that he had had a low opinion of Banks for nine months, which would correspond with the time he had spent with Banks at New Orleans. He had had a chance to observe how Banks operated, and was not impressed.

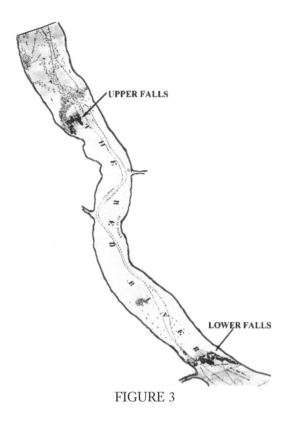

FIGURE 3

As to Porter's gunboats, his troubles while dropping down from Grand Ecore were only the end of the beginning. The rapids at Alexandria began at an upper falls, about a mile above the town, and followed an *S*-shaped channel of solid rock to a lower falls, figure 3. Through these the water was running at a depth of 3 feet 4 inches, and Porter's gunboats required 7 feet. There were 10 in all, the ironclads *Mound City*, *Louisville*, *Pittsburg*, *Carondelet*, *Chillicothe*, *Osage*, *Neosho*, and *Ozark*, plus the tinclads *Lexington* and *Fort Hindman*; all "blockaded" as he put it, above the upper falls.[1774]

Porter was angry, and in a letter to Welles, he blamed Banks' incompetence in managing the campaign. He offers nothing of his own as a plan of action, except to suggest a massive relief effort. "Steps will have to be taken quickly to relieve us from our perilous position, and all this country should be invaded at different points and held as long as the war continues." Of course, this was diametrically opposed to what Grant planned, and was the reason Banks was retreating. "This is a most important part of the Union to us, and it will be the greatest defeat we have met in this war if we have to recede an inch farther." Perhaps Porter could see his

---

1773. O.R. Vol. 34/III, p. 252

1774. ORN ser. 1, vol. 26, pp. 92, 94–95. Figure 3 adapted from NOAA Historical Collection no. TO 1921-05-1864.

legacy of being a naval hero slipping away, as well as his feast at the trough of prize money. He transparently asserts: "I have sacrificed all private interests, all desires of a personal nature…" Here, Porter lets his inner secret come close to the surface. He had visions of making a fortune in prize money, and was scrupulously guarding his potential for making more.[1775] That said, rescuing Porter was essential, the loss of this portion of the Mississippi squadron would be an embarrassment, and vessels worth nearly $2,000,000. could not be left to fall into Confederate hands. Even if they were destroyed, the salvage of their iron would be valuable to the Confederacy.

Aside from constructing defensive deployments around the perimeter of Alexandria, which occupied the next few days,[1776] a plan to dam the river to raise the water level sufficiently to allow the passage of the gunboats took shape. Blasting the solid rock bed of the channel to deepen it was ruled out, given that it was estimated to take 30 days. A dam was judged feasible by the engineering staff, and the supervision of the project was given to Lt. Col. Joseph Bailey, who had earlier proposed a similar solution regarding the *Eastport*.

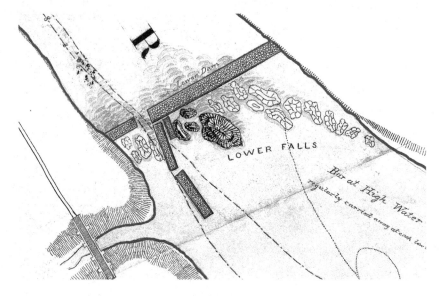

FIGURE 4

The work began on May 1st, and the initial plan, accomplished by some 3,000 men working night and day, was completed on May 8th. It consisted of building a dam across the river at the lower falls, figure 4,[1777] to back up the water level

---

1775. ORN ser. 1, vol. 26, pp. 35, 318, 342, 363, 394, 412, 460, 556. Prize claims were made for captured cotton, molasses, iron, vessels, and horses, among others; Value of gunboats, ibid, pp. 132, 159.
1776. ORN ser. 1, vol. 26, pp. 95, 97–98; O.R. Vol. 34/I, pp. 209; ORN ser. 1, vol. 26, p. 95; Pellet, p. 231.
1777. Portion of figure 3; Irwin, pp. 338–340.

behind it to create a pool which would extend all the way to the upper falls. At the point chosen, the river was 758 feet wide. The longest part of the span extended from the northeast side. It consisted of large trees laid with their tops facing the current, their rooted ends tied with cross logs, and the whole covered with brush, and weighted down with stone and brick, which was obtained by tearing down neighboring buildings. There were fewer trees on the south side, so that portion was constructed of a crib filled with stone, brick, and pieces of machinery collected from sugar houses and cotton gins in the area. To narrow the gap between the two wings, which was about 150 feet, four heavy navy coal barges were sunk in it, which narrowed it, yet left a sufficient gap through which the boats could pass. At completion, the water was found to be pooled to a depth of almost eight feet at the upper falls, the water having risen almost five-and-a-half feet. The three light draft gunboats, the *Osage*, *Neosho*, and *Fort Hindman*, having gotten steam up, soon passed the upper falls and entered the pool created by the dam.

The water level on the dam now was at its maximum, and the velocity of the flow through the narrow opening was tremendous, but the dam held; yet there was no further reaction from the rest of Porter's fleet. This tardy response, which Porter conveniently omits in his reports, soon rendered the hope for the successful passage of the rest of the fleet to be dashed. Early in the morning of May 9th, the surging water swung aside two of the coal barges, leaving a gap 66 feet wide. Warned of the failure by Banks, who personally observed it, Porter is credited with riding north to the upper falls and ordering the *Lexington* to run immediately into the rapids, and through the chute at the dam. After a heart-stopping run through the foam, it was safe below. Seeing the example, the three light-drafts followed; figure 5, from the cover of *Harper's Weekly* of June 18th, 1864.

FIGURE 5

Quickly, it became too late to move the remaining six gunboats and two tugs still above the upper falls. The rush of water out of the dam lowered the pool behind it and the level at the upper falls soon dropped below six feet. Judging that a repair to the lower dam would only wash out as it already had, Bailey rose to the occasion, and proposed a second dam at the upper falls, sufficient to raise the level there to allow the gunboats to pass into the channel of the lower pool and finally through the lower dam. Construction of an upper dam took three more days. It consisted of essentially the same approach that had been taken at the lower dam, though some distance removed from the upper falls. This confined enough water to the channel to raise it to slightly more than six feet, but still insufficient to pass the gunboats without a herculean effort to lighten them. This the navy heartily entered into, having seen the results of the army's earlier effort. Lightened by the removal of guns, cargo, ammunition and plating, the draft of the remaining gunboats was reduced sufficiently to have them hauled through the crooked and narrow channel between the two dams. By the 13th of May all had passed safely south of the lower falls.[1778]

This was the signal for Banks to leave.

"Record" 6/64
30 APRIL–30 JUNE 1864 ALEXANDRIA–NEW ORLEANS, LOUISIANA

May 13th Marched from Alexandria 12 miles. 14th Marched 12 miles. 15th Marched 10 miles. 16th Marched to Marksville 15 miles. 17th Marched to Simmesport 10 miles. 19th Crossed Atchafalaya & marched 3 miles. 20th Marched 10 miles. 21st Marched 18 miles. 22nd Marched to Morganza 3½ miles. Remained until June 28th; proceeded on board S.B. *Universe* to New Orleans, arrived on the 29th.

Henry W. Closson	Capt. Det. svc. Chief of Arty, 19th Army Corps
Franck E. Taylor	1st Lt. Commanding Battery and Asst. Comm. of Musters
Edward L. Appleton	1st Lt. On det. svc. Commanding Battery "C" 2nd US Arty. S.O. no 36 Hdqrts. 19th Army Corps June 11, 1864
Joined:	
George Kelly	Pvt. From desertion, May 19, 1864, at Simmesport. Apprehended at Pensacola and sent under guard to Company.
Andrew Stoll	Pvt. do.
Detached:	
Edmond Cotterill	Cpl. On Det. Svc. Clerk in A.G.O. Wash. S.O. no. 426, War Dept. A.G.O. Wash. Sept. 23,'63. Left Co. Nov. 20,'63.
Solomon Mongomery	Pvt. On Det. Svc. Orderly Chief of Artillery
George Freidman	Pvt. On Det. Svc. at N.O. as Artillerist, Left Co. May 24,'62.
Amelius Straub	Pvt. On Det. Svc. at Baton Rouge as cook in Univ. Hosp. since June 1,'63.
Absent in Confinement:	
Patrick Gibbons	Pvt. At Ship Island serving sentence of G.C.M. no. 18, Hdqrts. 1st Div. 19th Army Corps Dec. 31,'63. Left Co. Jan. 8,'64.
Michael O'Sullivan	Pvt. In jail at N.O. since Sept. 2,'63.
John Lewery	Pvt. Apprehended as a deserter and confined at New Orleans.
John H. Moran	Pvt. In confinement, awaiting sentence.

1778. ORN ser. 1, vol. 26, pp. 130–133; Clark, p. 177.

Peter Welsh	Pvt. In confinement.	

Absent without Leave:
Michael White	Sgt. Wounded and missing since April 9, 1864.
George W. Redding	Pvt. 13th Mass. Since April 9th 1864.
William F. Brown	Pvt. Since June 29, 1864
Joseph Kutschor	Pvt. Since June 29, 1864
John Kelly	Pvt. Since June 29, 1864

Died:
James McCarthy	Pvt. Of typhoid fever at Morganza, June 8, 1864.

Strength: 99 Sick: 9

Present Sick:
Patrick Craffy, Joseph Eisle, Joseph H. Parslow.

Absent Sick:
William Brunskill	Sick at Ft. Hamilton, NY left Co. Sept. 17, 1861.
William Crowley	Sick at Baton Rouge since July 13, 1863.
George Chase	Sick at Brashear City since April 22, 1863.
Charles Jackel	Sick at Franklin since March 12, 1864
Churchill Moore	Sick at New Orleans Left Co. April 20, 1864.
Henry Williams	Sick at New Orleans Left Co. March 12, 1864.

Sgt. Demarest is listed as: "under arrest" no explanation given.

Cooks: Virgil Ayers, Phillip Evens, Henry Jefferson.

The cooks are listed without rank, and in fact they were never given an official rank. They had finally been recruited on October 13th, '63 at Barre's Landing, after serving with the company for more than five months. They were now being paid $6 each per month. Here, there appears the note: "Error on last payroll." No explanation is given.

The May monthly report lists nine men as "transferred to Navy" on May 9th. They were not listed in those of the 13th Massachusetts who were assigned to Battery L, but are listed in the record of the 13th Battery as published in: *Record of Massachusetts Volunteers, 1861–1865*, The Adjutant-General, Boston, Wright & Potter, 1868.

The "Joined" column shows deserters George Kelly and Andrew Stoll as returned on May 19th, at Simmesport, but they had been apprehended at Pensacola. They were part of the large number of men who had deserted, see chapter 10, at New Orleans in 1863; Kelly on August 13th, and Stoll on September 16th. How they managed to remain in New Orleans and Pensacola for eight months is material for a detective story in itself. One factor might have been that they were dropped from the muster rolls for the intervening period—reason unknown. Note that neither appears on the 1864 roster (chapter 11), which is based on the 31 December '63–29 February 1864 roll.

The sick list is remarkably small, as was the 10 sick on the previous muster roll, though the men were worked, fought, and marched to exhaustion. The extended periods of sickness for some of those absent, Brunskill for almost three years, Chase for a year, and Crowley nearly a year, reminds us, again, of the medieval state of medicine in that era. It did not discriminate—remember Admiral Foote, and Col. Charles Ellet, both of whom died of what today would be called minor leg wounds, and now we witness the illness of General Franklin, also with a leg wound.

McClernand's command had arrived at Alexandria from Texas on April 29th, and gone into the defensive line beside A. J. Smith. While there, with all of the attention focused on the dam, the Federal army lay confined behind its works, leaving Taylor free to roam the countryside.[1779] Though there were local skirmishes, no determined effort was made by Banks to destroy Taylor.

Unchallenged, Taylor divided his reduced force to try to block traffic in the Red River below Alexandria and cut off Banks' communication with the Mississippi. He sent Major with about 1,000 men twenty-five miles south to David's Ferry, which Major reached on April 30th. The next day, he captured and sunk the transport *Emma*, and on May 3rd, the *City Belle*, carrying 425 officers and men of the 120th Ohio, many of whom were either killed or wounded. The steamer was then sunk across the channel and the river blocked. On May 5th, the *John Warner*, carrying the 56th Ohio, was captured. In the same action the *Covington* was disabled, then abandoned and set on fire, and the *Signal* was captured and sunk across the channel. The river remained closed for 15 days. With the army pulling out of Alexandria on May 13th, and following the river course until the 15th, it passed the points where Major's batteries had been placed and the river blocked. Major was then forced to flee, though he remained, along with Polignac and Bagby, hovering at the front and flanks of the Federal column.[1780]

As at Grand Ecore, columns of smoke were seen as the army left Alexandria. Banks, in his 1865 report of the campaign, makes note of the fact that a fire was started in a building on the levee, which had been occupied by refugees or soldiers, and that the wind on that day made it impossible to extinguish. The fact that "a considerable portion" of the town was consumed was not intentional. This is corroborated by Lt. Edward Cunningham, Kirby Smith's aide-de-camp, who wrote: "My opinion is that they did not intend total destruction."[1781] In addition, more widespread fires, specifically on 19 plantations, were noted by a member of the 4th Texas cavalry, Theophilus Noel, as he stood on McNutt's Hill twelve miles northwest of Alexandria.[1782] He makes the startling point that these were lit by

---

1779. Irwin, pp. 342–343; Taylor, pp. 185–186; ORN ser. 1, vol. 26, pp. 112, 116–123, 134.
1780. Clark, p. 179; Irwin, p. 344; Taylor, p. 191, Pellet, p. 233; O.R. Vol. 34/I, p. 212; O.R. Vol. 34/III, p. 568.
1781. O.R. Vol. 34/I, pp. 212, 558.
1782. Noel, *Autobiography*, pp. 143–144; figure 6, portion of NOAA Civil War Collection, "Atchafalaya Basin," 1863.

native Louisiana residents "who embraced this opportunity of revenge on the rich planters and their cruel overseers, who had fenced them off from water and had taken their cattle, as did the lords in the feudal days of the dark ages."

Marksville & Mansura

On May 15th, the army left the course of the river and entering Avoyelles Prairie, turned toward Marksville, an easier march to Semmesport (see figure 6, now called Simmesport), per the Battery L record. Here, the advance of Banks' column, Col. Thomas Lucas' 1st and 3rd cavalry brigades, with Battery F of the 1st U.S. Artillery, moved forward at a trot, "pieces and caissons jumping and pounding against the cypress knees until it seemed that much more of such travelling would knock everything to pieces, but finally clear daylight ahead and an open prairie with the village of Marksville in the distance."[1783] Here stood Polignac, with a brigade, who slowly fell back through the village, and for two miles beyond, on the rolling prairie. At sunset, Polignac turned and formed across the prairie, from the swamps and bordering woods on the left to the edge of woods on the right—a line of mounted riflemen extending a mile-and-a-half, all in plain view.

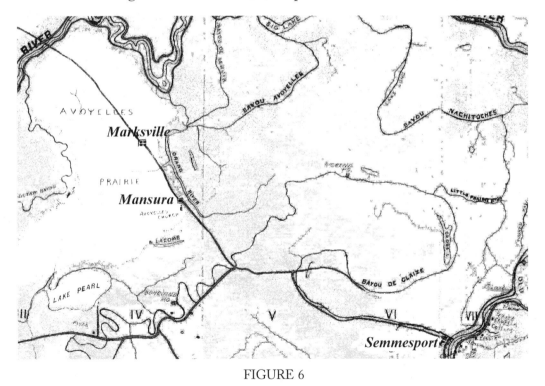

FIGURE 6

A battery of four of Polignac's rifled guns, posted in his center, played upon the approaching Federals. Lucas's brigade then formed up and charged. The

---

1783. Haskin, pp. 555–556.

Confederate line broke, and doubled back into the woods on either side. From Haskin, in command of Battery F: "The whole performance was in plain sight and was one of the most exciting it was ever my fortune to witness." Darkness ended the engagement.[1784]

The main body of the army had encamped two miles back, but now it was hurried up to encamp near the cavalry, and retain the ground gained. On the morning of the 16th, the march resumed, and after several hours of skirmishing on the rolling prairie, the Federal column was confronted by a torrent of projectiles from 10 of Polignac's guns[1785] placed in battery near the village of Mansura. It was a grand and symbolic last stand, taken before the Federal army could pass through on the road to Semmesport. Vastly outnumbered, Polignac traded artillery shots with Lucas' cavalry, and Battery F, at the front, while the Federal army drew up in line of battle, Mower on the right, Emory in the center, and Lawler, now in command of McClernand's troops, on the left. They were all in full view, from flank to flank. As the Federals advanced, Polignac began a steady withdrawal, away to the Federal right, toward Cheneyville. A spectacular scene, on a beautiful clear day, with neither tree nor fence to obstruct the view, as thousands of men in blue moved forward with mathematical precision. Major Henry Closson,[1786] present, and seeing the Confederate artillery fire taking its toll on Battery F as it entered Mansura, sent in the 1st Vermont Battery to its relief, and the engagement ended.

Semmesport and the Atchafalaya were reached the next day; finding the transports and gunboats waiting. Crossing the swollen river, now some six- or seven-hundred yards wide, would have to await the completion of another of Col. Bailey's inventions, a pontoon bridge consisting of steamers lashed together.[1787]

Ever the aggressor, Taylor again attacked, on the rear of the Federal army. This was on May 18th, near Yellow Bayou. A. J. Smith's command, under Mower, had been stationed there to cover the crossing of the Atchafalaya. Mower advanced, and fought one of the sharpest engagements of the campaign. Mower lost 267 in killed, wounded, or missing, and Confederate returns report 452 of theirs as killed or wounded.[1788]

The crossing was made on the 19th, two days short of their crossing a year before, when at the end of the Teche Campaign, they had turned to Port Hudson.

It had been a long and exhausting year; one with satisfaction at the completion of the Siege, and the consequent opening of the Mississippi, but indelibly marred by memories of the Red River Campaign's failure, and of the fruitless

---

1784. O.R. Vol. 34/I, p. 447; O.R. Vol. 34/III, p. 517; Haskin, pp. 198–199, 371.
1785. Irwin, p. 344–345; Clark, pp. 178, 180; Pellet, p. 234; Ewer, pp. 182–183.
1786. Brevet Major Closson had been chief of artillery of the 19th Corps since October of 1863. He still is listed in Battery L records as captain, his permanent rank. O.R. Vol. 34/I, p. 408.
1787. Irwin, p. 346–348; Clark, p. 181.
1788. Irwin, p. 346; Taylor, p. 191.

waste, "this sink of shame," the invasion of Texas. The quote is from Irwin, who, like most in the department, knew that the Texas invasion was Halleck's creation, as had been urged by Seward and Lincoln. Though it had been faithfully carried out by Banks, he was now blamed for it by Grant; and Halleck, now bending in Grant's wind, had quickly turned on Banks. Lincoln was more faithful. He was very reluctant to relieve Banks, which, no doubt, resulted in the awkward creation of a new department—the Military Division of West Mississippi,[1789] to include Steele's Department of Arkansas, and Banks' Department of the Gulf. However, both Steele and Banks had a new boss, Maj. Gen. E. R. S. Canby, who assumed command on May 11th. In fact, Banks was left no command at all, but would remain squeezed between a subordinate, Franklin, and a junior officer, Canby, as his superior.[1790]

From the 114th New York regiment:

> There were many opinions expressed regarding the step, but a majority of the enlisted strength of our army sympathized with the former. But it was only to be expected, and is decidedly "American." A single success is proof of Napoleonic genius; a single defeat, of total incompetency. General Banks was not an exception to the rule.

At least Grant got his wish, avoiding the waste of trying to invade and control vast stretches of under-populated territory in Texas, Louisiana, and Arkansas, which would be meaningless to the outcome of the war.

In Taylor's words: "[On] May 19, 1864, the enemy crossed the Atchafalaya and was beyond our reach. Here, at the place where it had opened more than two months before, the campaign closed."[1791] Not quite, at the rear of the column were A. J. Smith's troops, who only completed the crossing on May 20th, after which the steamboats were unlashed and the "bridge" was no more. It was then that Smith's troops were ordered to Vicksburg by the new commander, Canby.[1792] The remainder of the army continued the march, arriving at Morganza, on the Mississippi, fifty-one miles above Baton Rouge, on May 22nd.

1789. O.R. Vol. 34/III, pp. 490, 543; Pellet, p. 235; Irwin, p. 348.
1790. Canby was promoted to major-general just before taking over the control of the new department, making him equal in rank to Banks, *but*, junior by date. We remember his appointment to quell the New York draft riots. Background on the replacement of Banks can be found at: O.R. Vol. 34/III, pp. 253, 278, 293–294, 331–333, 409, 580, 600, 615, 631.
1791. Taylor, p. 191.
1792. O.R. Vol. 34/I, pp. 212, 645–646, 680, 695; Stanyan, p. 482; Tiemann, p. 78. Canby took over command on May 19th, at Simmesport.

Canby

An experienced old soldier,[1793] he had graduated from West Point in 1839, a classmate of Samuel Dawson. He had seen service in the Florida War and the Mexican War. He came to Louisiana already knowing the territory, like W. T. Sherman, who had been superintendent of the "State Seminary of Learning and Military Academy of Louisiana" at Pineville. Canby had been on an inspection tour of the posts on the Arkansas and Red Rivers, the Mississippi, and the Gulf Coast for some eight months up to July of 1854. Upon taking this assignment, he had reported[1794] to Grant that "no new expedition by the line of the Red River should be undertaken. Its navigation has always been treacherous and unreliable, and even when good the character of its banks is such that gun-boats can be but of little service…" He went on to suggest the same plan that Banks' chief engineer, Maj. D. C. Houston, had recommended to Banks the previous January[1795]—an advance on Shreveport from Vicksburg via Monroe, along the railroad. This would be an extremely time consuming and laborious affair, which was completely out of line with what Grant desired, and makes one wonder how Canby could have so misread his orders, or how vague and misleading his orders may have been.

Canby had been given broad powers, beyond just the command of Banks' and Steele's departments. He was also given control of those of W. T. Sherman's troops that occupied the east bank of the Mississippi.[1796] Thus, he now controlled the 16th and 17th Army Corps detachments under A. J. Smith and T. K. Smith, simply because if they went upriver to Vicksburg or Memphis, they would still be in his realm. Halleck erroneously confided to him that the Mobile expedition was now given up, and that all of the troops so urgently sought after from Banks, just a few weeks earlier, would now be retained in the new Division of West Mississippi. Canby was also authorized to tap the Department of Missouri for reinforcements, provided there were any, which soon became a matter of dispute.[1797]

Rather than sending the troops on new expeditions, they would be concentrated, and be equipped to be as "mobile as that of the rebels."[1798] The 19th Army Corps would be retained at a defensive location where it could be built up and refitted, which would take 30 days, though Canby had to admit that Banks' army was "in better condition than I supposed from the accounts that reached me…"[1799] As mentioned above, Canby requested "4,000 to 6,000" troops from the Department

---

1793. Cullum no. 1015
1794. O.R. Vol. 34/IV, pp. 15–16.
1795. O.R. Vol. 34/II, pp. 126–128; vol. 34/IV, pp.74–75.
1796. O.R. Vol. 34/III, p. 491.
1797. O.R. Vol. 34/III, p. 654.
1798. O.R. Vol. 34/IV, p. 74.
1799. O.R. Vol. 34/III, p. 644.

of the Missouri. This was where Rosecrans had been sent after he was sacked from the command of the Army of the Cumberland (see chapter 11). Rosecrans was still his irascible self, and he refused. Seeming not to comprehend Steele's weak position in Arkansas, Canby asked Steele for troops. Steele also refused.

The issue with Rosecrans became heated, as Rosecrans protested Canby's request on grounds of Canby being junior in rank, not to mention that there were only 2,200 infantry on duty in his department.[1800] This was settled in a heartbeat; Rosecrans' star having fallen far. The Department of the Missouri was added to Canby's command.

The new broom already began to sweep. The army was directed to halt along the scorching lowland next to the levee in the vicinity of the Morgan Plantation, Morganzia. Here it would remain for the next six weeks, under conditions memorable for "its dust and intense heat."[1801] It was chosen by Canby as a suitable place for defense, covering the approaches from the Red River and Opelousas, and was the most suitable place for assembling the troops "designated for service west of the Mississippi," making it clear that Canby considered that he had been called in to continue an aggressive western campaign. It ultimately would prove to be against Mobile, regardless of Halleck's remarks, or Canby's assumptions.

At Morganzia,[1802] figure 7, there was, admittedly, water, and plenty of the muddy stuff, which had to be filtered. The encampment stretched for seven miles beside the levee, below the river level, which shut off any breeze. From Irwin: "The sickly season was close at hand, the field and general hospitals were filled, and the deaths were many." The mosquitoes were at their worst.[1803]

FIGURE 7

Last Days in the Gulf

Something else was underfoot, however, for Battery L. On June 7th it was ordered

---

1800. O.R. Vol. 34/IV, pp. 49–50, 59.
1801. Sprague, pp. 214–215.
1802. Morganzia and Morgansia were used interchangeably, though the latter was the name of the Morgan plantation. Figure 7, a portion of Persec's map.
1803. Haskin (Closson's account) p. 371. The clever troops filtered their drinking water by pouring it through a handful of corn meal. Howe, p. 67, Irwin, pp. 348–349; vol. 34/IV, p. 16. The road to Opelousas left the Mississippi from the Morgan Estate.

to New York, and on June 11th, Lt. Edward Appleton was ordered on detached service, to serve as commander of Battery C, 2nd U.S. Artillery.[1804] Battery L was to be accompanied by three of the other regular batteries in the department: A & F, 1st US, and C, 2nd US. The order for Battery L to leave was perhaps "out of the blue" as it were, because L, with the 13th Massachusetts men attached, was nearly up to strength. Of the other companies, none were in full war organization, something Emory and Canby felt that was needed if they were to remain. They were to be transferred out, for reorganization, on the recommendation of Maj. Henry Closson, the chief of artillery, with the concurrence of Emory.[1805] Closson would remain behind, the 19th Corps still requiring his services as chief of artillery.

Batteries A and F had only 78 and 53 men, respectively, and had been reduced to four guns. Until Appleton was assigned, Battery C had had no officers, their commander, Rodgers, being sick. Battery L was weak, on paper at least, *if* the men of the 13th Massachusetts Battery were discounted. There were 99 regulars and 61 of the Massachusetts men (listed separately) on Battery L's June return. The brief integration of the state volunteers with a regular unit was evidently something out of the ordinary, and perhaps something that the larger system could not accommodate. The Massachusetts men were never listed on any of Battery L's muster rolls while attached to L, except as casualties. In fact, if anyone outside of the Department of the Gulf read the returns of the Regiment, they would have had no clue as to the association of Battery L and the 13th Massachusetts Battery. The combination was apparently a creature of the Department of the Gulf, and may never have been known or officially approved at Washington. That said, on July 1st, the 13th Massachusetts was again made an independent command, when its commanding officer, Capt. Charles Hamlin, returned to Louisiana.[1806]

Though the three batteries in Emory's command had been ordered out, considerations regarding turning over their equipment would delay their actual departure. C was to turn over its equipment to the 21st New York, which was ordered to proceed to Morganza on June 18th. On June 20th, the 4th Massachusetts battery was ordered to Morganza to receive Battery L's guns and equipment. Finally, three days after General Reynolds, commanding the forces at Morganza, had reviewed the newly reorganized 19th Army Corps, the three batteries boarded steamers bound for New Orleans, and arrived there on June 29th. Battery A had already been stationed in the defenses of New Orleans.

However, events in the east, specifically, Grant's Overland Campaign in Virginia, would cause a surprising turn. The very next day, June 30th, a substantial detachment of the 19th Army Corps would be doing the same, boarding steamers

---

1804. O.R. Vol. 34/IV, p. 256, Battery L June monthly return, see "Record," this chapter.
1805. O.R. Vol. 34/IV, pp. 306–307, 333, 358–360.
1806. *Massachusetts Soldiers, Sailors and Marines*, vol. 5, pp. 507–508; Bowen, p. 854; O.R. Vol. 34/IV, pp. 440, 464.

for movement to New Orleans. They also had been ordered east, and the urgency of the matter, combined with the delays in transferring the guns, as noted above, caused the 19th Corps detachment to leave Louisiana before Battery L. The advance of the 19th left on July 2nd.[1807] Battery L and its colleagues would have to await transportation.

Our narrative will here continue with Battery L's transfer, and will later pick up on the story of the 19th Corps, which seems to fit properly in a review of events in the east, including the consolidation of Battery L with another veteran battery, and the reasons behind it.

"Record" 8/64
30 JUNE–31 AUGUST, 1864, NEW ORLEANS, LA–NEAR BERRYVILLE, VIRGINIA

Battery ordered to Fort Schuyler, New York for refit and the mustering of new recruits. The Company left New Orleans on board the steamer Yazoo on July 27th and arrived at New York Harbor on August 4th. Thence ordered to Camp Barry, near Washington, D.C. Left Washington on the 15th and marched to Harper's Ferry, Va. Engaged the enemy on the 28th & 29th near Smithfield, Va. Camped near Berryville, Va. on the 31st.[1808]

Henry W. Closson	Capt. Det. svc. at New Orleans on General Granger's staff.
Franck E. Taylor	1st lt. Commanding Battery
Edward L. Appleton	1st Lt. On recruiting service at New York S.O. 185 Hdqtrs. Dept of the East, New York City Aug. 4, 1864.

Detached:
Edmond Cotterill	Cpl. On Det. Svc. Clerk in A.G.O. Wash. S.O. no. 426, War Dept.A.G.O., Wash. Sept. 23,'63. Left Co. Nov. 20,'63.
William Demarest	Sgt. On recruiting service, S.O. 185 Hdqtrs. Dept of the East, New York City
Benjamin O. Hall	Pvt. do. do.
Michael Teighe	Pvt. do. do.
Rueben Townsend	Pvt. do. do.
Edmund Anglin	Pvt. In Battery G 5th US Artillery at New Orleans.
Arthur Flynn	Pvt. do. do.
Michael Kenny	Pvt. do. do.
John Meyer	Pvt. do. do.
Joseph Smith	Pvt. do. do.
Solomon Montgomery	Pvt. [Previously orderly to the Chief of Artillery, he does not appear on this roll, he reappears on the next roll as a private.]

Absent in confinement:
Patrick Gibbons	Pvt. At Ship Island, serving sentence of Gen. Court Martial S.O. no. 18, Hdqtrs. 1st Div. 19th Army Corps Dec. 31, 1863.

1807. Irwin, p. 353.

1808. The "Record of Events" portion of the on the muster roll is blank. The narrative above is a combination taken from Haskin, p. 199, and the July monthly return.

John Lewery	Pvt. In confinement at New Orleans, La., apprehended as a deserter.

Absent Missing:

Michael White	Sgt. Wounded and missing since April 9, 1864. Deserted:
Henry Wilkson	Cpl. Deserted July 27, 1864 Location not specified.
William F. Brown	Pvt. Deserted July 2, 1864 do.
Benjamin Hughes*	Pvt. do. July 2, 1864 do.
George Harrison	Pvt. do. July 23, 1864 do.
Francis Jessop	Pvt. do. Aug. 11, 1864 Philadelphia
Joseph Kutschor	Pvt. do. July 2, 1864 Location not specified.
John Lowry	Pvt. do. July 23, 1864 do.
Daniel Moore	Pvt. do. Aug. 11, 1864 Philadelphia.
John H. Moran	Pvt. do. July 4, 1864 Location not specified.
Michael Olvany	Pvt. do. Aug. 11, 1864 Philadelphia.

* This man deserted from this organization and enlisted Aug. 5, 1864 under the name of John Wilson (as substitute) in Company M, 1st Missouri Light Artillery Vols. in violation of the 23rd (now 50th) Article of War.

Discharged:

George Friedman	Pvt. By promotion to 2nd Lt. Corps d' Afrique S.O. no. 200 Hdqtrs. A.G.O. Washington June 7, 1864.
William E. Scott	Cpl. By reason of reenlistment in the Battery, July 11, 1864.
Henry Wilkson	Cpl. By reason of reenlistment in the Battery, July 18, 1864.
Owen A. Wren	Cpl. By reason of reenlistment in the Battery July 11, 1864.
Ludwig Rupprecht	Musician do.
James Ahern	Pvt. By reason of reenlistment in the Battery July 18, 1864.
James Beglan	Pvt. do.
John Burke	Pvt. do.
Patrick Craffy	Pvt. do.
Patrick Donnely	Pvt. do.
William Creed	Pvt. do.
Patrick Cummings	Pvt. do.
George Howard	Pvt. do.
Miles McDonough	Pvt. do.
Andrew Stoll	Pvt. do.
Reuben Townsend	Pvt. do.
Henry Williams	Pvt. do.
Prosper Ferrari	Pvt. By reason of enlistment in the Battery, July 19, 1864.
George Hadley	Pvt. do.
Michael Olvany	Pvt. do.
Wm. V. Thompson	Pvt. do.
Henry A. Ward	Pvt. do.

Died:

Michael O'Sullivan	Pvt. In parish prison New Orleans, La., Oct. 2, 1863, of chronic diarrhea.
Joseph H. Parslow	Pvt. Killed in action near Smithfield, West Virginia.

Strength: 86 Sick: 7

Present Sick: none

Absent Sick:
William Brunskill	Pvt. At Ft. Hamilton, NY left Co. Sept. 17, 1861.
George Chase	Pvt. At Brashear City, La., since April 22, 1863.
William Crowley	Pvt. At Baton Rouge since July 13, 1863.
Daniel Howard	Pvt. At Harper's Ferry, Va., since Aug. 25, 1864.
Charles Jackel	Pvt. At Franklin, La., since March 12, 1864.
John McKenny	Pvt. At Harper's Ferry, Va., since Aug. 26, 1864.
Churchill Moore	Pvt. At New Orleans, since April 20, 1864.

Colored Cooks: William Jefferson, Phillip Evens, Virgil Ayers. Paid $12.00 each, with the note: "Error on last payroll."

Note that there are only two illnesses that are recent. Others are the typical long-lasting debilities of the time, William Brunskill being the extraordinary example. What a way to go: Michael O'Sullivan, dead in prison; doubtlessly from unsanitary conditions, poor food, or both—or maltreatment?

It could have been predicted, having not had a roof over their heads for the past year, much less having enjoyed even the most rudimentary comforts of civilization, that what had happened upon their arrival at New Orleans back in 1863 was repeated on August 4th at New York. It meant going out on a "vacation." The number of those who are listed as deserted, at ten, however, is lower in proportion to the number of those who deserted at New Orleans. Then there were 141 listed in the battery, and 20 deserted. Older and wiser? Wiser seems reasonable. Sixty-four had reenlisted since, and were due installment bounty payments. Earlier reenlistments were for a bounty of $100, and only $25. had been paid on installment as of this date. However, the government having become near desperate to retain veterans, the bounty now became $400, and no installment had been paid to date. Another minor point is that four of the men were assigned to recruiting service at New York! Who would desert if they had gotten wind of the potential for that plum?

Yet, Cpl. Henry Wilkson deserted, as did Michael Olvany, just after reenlisting and getting the government's $400 promise. Wilkson may have been influenced by those damned assessments for camp and garrison equipment, and ordinance! He owed $40; though Olvany only owed $3.04. Note that Olvany, Moore, Moran, and Jessop deserted at Philadelphia, while the battery was on its way to Washington. They had not returned by the end of the year.

Another way to get ready money in hand, though, was to become a substitute. The $300 offered a substitute attracted Benjamin Hughes, who illegally, but for a time successfully, deserted and reenlisted, under the assumed name of John Wilson, in the 1st Missouri Light Artillery, as was over-written into the muster roll record—*in 1890*. This was likely when he applied for a pension.

Friedman, discussed earlier, here left the Battery L books forever, promoted to 2nd lieutenant.

Camp Barry–Consolidation with Battery K

The steamer *Yazoo* pulled into New York Harbor on August 3rd with the four artillery batteries.[1809] Reporting at headquarters, Department of the East, they were immediately ordered to the Light Artillery Depot and Camp of Instruction,[1810] also known as Camp Barry, on the Bladensburg Turnpike, northeast of Washington, D.C. Here Battery L was consolidated with Battery K of the 1st U.S. Artillery. In the absence of new recruits from the failure of the draft, consolidating the men of the two batteries was the device chosen to obtain something close to full war organization, though they still had only four guns.

K had been there since the 14th of July, arriving from duty with the Army of the Potomac, where it had served in Grant's spring campaign, the "big licks" designed to end the war. From their new association, Battery L was introduced to the intensive campaign that Grant had begun six weeks earlier, and the fact that Battery K had been severely cut up in the Battle of Ream's Station. Their story will serve to introduce the reader to the recent history of operations in Virginia.

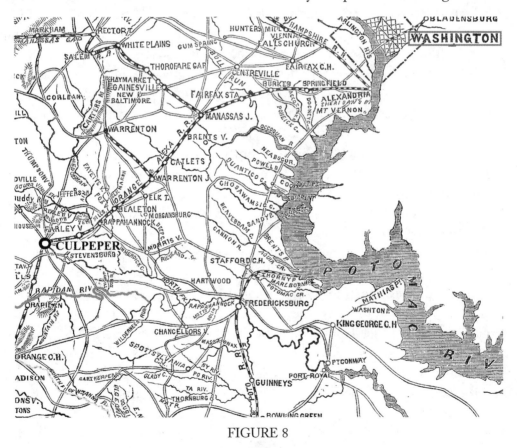

FIGURE 8

1809. The Second Regiment of Artillery, Simpson, *www.history.army.mil/books/R&*, p. 322; Haskin, p. 199.
1810. O.R. Vol. 43/I, p. 975.

Grant's spring campaign plan was never revealed to Lincoln, Stanton, or Halleck.[1811] The annoyance that Grant had with Halleck and Stanton reviewing his orders and often altering them would only grow. In a few weeks Grant would bypass the two entirely.

Grant not only kept the plan of the campaign confidential, but to avoid meddling by anyone, including members of Congress, he did not establish his headquarters at Washington, but at Culpeper, Virginia, some seventy-five miles southeast, on the Orange and Alexandria Railroad, the white circle near the left margin of figure 8. He initially only visited Washington once per week, and when the campaign began, he remained with Meade's army. His plan was only revealed to the participants: Meade, the commander of the Army of the Potomac; Sherman, the Army of the Tennessee; and Butler, the Army of the James.

As defined by Grant, Meade's objective was Lee, who was now south of the Rapidan River; south of Culpeper in figure 8. Butler's objective, from his base at Fort Monroe, was Richmond; Sherman's was Johnston's army in Georgia. All other considerations were subsidiary to the entrapment and defeat of the Confederates in and around their capital. Other commands were ordered to reinforce or support the general move. As already discussed, only one point in Texas, Brownsville, was to be held, and the troops freed up would reinforce Banks/Canby for a move on Mobile, in support of Sherman. Non-strategic points in and around the South Carolina coast would also be abandoned, and the resulting force, under Gillmore, would reinforce Butler. Sigel, launching from West Virginia, was to move toward the Shenandoah Valley, and thus stop supplies from coming to Lee. The Army of the Potomac was to be reinforced by Burnside's 9th Corps, reorganizing at Annapolis.[1812]

Butler had moved out of Fort Monroe, and unopposed, had taken City Point on the James, on May 5th, and on May 6th was entrenching at Bermuda Hundred, across the river, figure 9.[1813] Meade crossed the Rapidan May 3rd–4th with the most powerful army in the east, consisting of more than 100,000 men, and advanced upon the "memorable campaign" as Grant puts it, that was destined to capture Richmond and defeat Lee.[1814] Little did Grant know, it would take nearly a year.

Grant, always present on the field with Meade, first clashed with Lee in the series of battles known as the Wilderness, May 5th–7th. These were immediately followed by multiple engagements, all south of Richmond, near Spotsylvania Court House, from May 8th through the 21st; at the North Anna River from May 22nd–26th, Old Church on May 30th, and Cold Harbor, May 31st–June 12th.

1811. Grant, vol. 2, p. 123, 130–132, 134–135, 141, 146, 317; figure 8, portion of Viasz map of the Virginia Central Railroad, Library of Congress.
1812. O.R. Vol. 33, pp. 657, 729, 795; Grant, vol. 2, p. 136, 140.
1813. Figure 9, portion from *Harper's Weekly*, May 28, 1864; Grant, vol. 2, p. 208.
1814. Grant, vol. 2, p. 177, 290; CWSAC, Gettysburg, PA002.

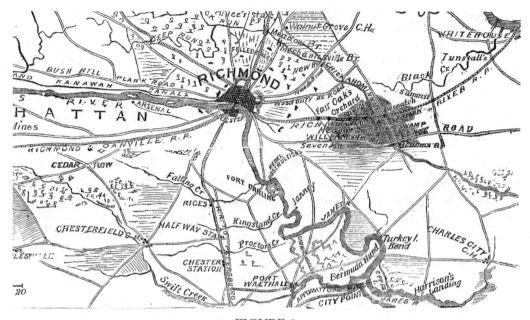

FIGURE 9

The battles of the Wilderness were inconclusive, though as we might have expected, Grant continued to move *forward*, with a new engagement nearly every day. The Spotsylvania clashes were equally inconclusive, and casualties were beginning to mount. By the end of the fighting at Spotsylvania, on May 21st, Union casualties had exceeded those at Gettysburg. There was other discouraging news which was received during the Spotsylvania campaign: Sigel had been defeated at New Market, in the Shenandoah Valley, on May 15th, and was retreating. Nevertheless, Grant continued to press Lee, advancing by the left flank, south along the line of the Fredericksburg Railroad, in a portion of the campaign known as North Anna, May 23rd–26th. Here, repulsed by Lee, Grant withdrew and continued south by the left flank, crossing south of the Pamunkey River, to a line along the Chickahominy.

Meade's army encountered Lee's entrenched position at the crossroads known as Old Cold Harbor, on May 31st, and here he began a series of assaults. At dawn[1815] on June 3rd, Mead's 2nd and 18th Corps made a frontal attack on Lee's line, which formed along a seven-mile front from Bethesda Church to the Chickahominy River. It was all over by 7:30 a.m. with the Union forces repulsed, and with 10,000 casualties. Grant attempts an explanation: "The assault cost us heavily and probably without benefit to compensate; but the enemy was not cheered by the occurrence sufficiently to induce him to take the offensive."[1816] It would have been reasonable for Grant to have avoided such a move, given what we were led to believe that he had learned at Vicksburg. In his memoirs, he confronts the answer honestly, saying:

1815. *http://aa.usno.navy.mil/cgi-bin/aa_pap*. Sunrise at 4:49 AM.
1816. Grant, vol. 2, pp. 270–272, 276–277; Haskin, p. 203.

"I have always regretted that the last assault at Cold Harbor was ever made." This introduces Battery K, 1st U.S. Artillery, which at Cold Harbor suffered two men wounded, and three horses killed.

The two antagonists continued to stare at each other until June 12th, when Grant pulled away. To cover the move, and to draw off the Confederate cavalry, Gen. Philip Sheridan made a raid northwest, on June 11th, which threatened the Virginia Central Railroad.[1817] He was stopped at Trevilian Station, from which he had to withdraw on the 12th. If he had been successful, he would have continued to Charlottesville to aid Hunter, who had replaced Sigel in the Shenandoah Valley.

Continuing south, Grant reached the James River on June 14th, to threaten Petersburg. On the 15th, crossing at City Point, Grant attacked the defenses, but was repulsed. Battery K crossed on the 17th, after being engaged all the day of the 15th at Charles City Court House, covering the passage of the troops. Aggressively using the cavalry, on June 21st, Grant ordered Brig. Gen. James H. Wilson's 3rd Division of Sheridan's[1818] cavalry, of Meade's army, and Kautz's cavalry division of Butler's army, on a raid to destroy the Weldon and Southside Railroads, the major supply routes to Petersburg and Richmond, (figure 10).[1819] Battery K was a "light" battery artillery assigned to Wilson's cavalry.

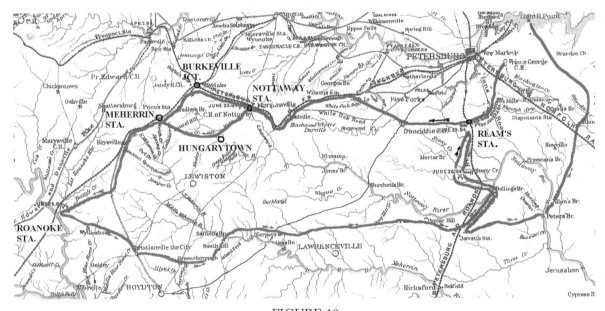

FIGURE 10

Leaving their camp in the vicinity of Prince George Court House (the upper right in figure 10) early on the morning of June 22nd, they reached Ream's Station,

---

1817. Grant, vol. 2, pp. 300, 303; Haskin, pp. 204–207.
1818. O.R. Vol. 36/I, pp. 26, 119, 208–209; O.R. Vol. 40/I, pp. 625–633; Sheridan's *Memoirs*, vol. 1, pp. 438–445.
1819. Figure 10, adapted from Atlas, plate 74; Wilson's Report, O.R. Vol. 40/I, pp. 625–632.

on the Weldon Railroad, destroying it. They then proceeded west, passing though Dinwiddie Court House, to a point on the Southside Railroad about fourteen miles west of Petersburg, where they moved deliberately, tearing up the track toward Nottaway Station. Kautz's division pushed ahead to Burkeville Junction on the Southside Railroad, and proceeded to destroy the depot and track there. The two divisions were now separated. Wilson was attacked by the Confederate cavalry of Fitzhugh Lee near Nottaway Station. Though Lee was driven off, there were some 75 Union casualties. Wilson now moved south, through Hungarytown, striking the Richmond and Danville Railroad at Meherrin Station. Here, Kautz rejoined Wilson. On the morning of the 25th of June, the column proceeded toward the Staunton River, and the bridge near Roanoke Station. That evening, the advance ran up against Confederate batteries and entrenchments on the south bank of the river.

Hoping to reach the bridge in order to burn it, the two divisions were dismounted and the artillery brought to bear. From Haskin: "The disadvantages of the change in the armament of the horse-batteries which was made about the first of June—giving each battery two light twelves and two three-inch rifles instead of four rifles—was now severely felt."[1820] The Confederate batteries posted themselves just out of the range of the Union smoothbore twelves, and practically threw the Union gunners out of the contest. Battery K had one gun disabled, and many horses and men were injured.

Beaten, the column turned to the eastward and took almost a direct line toward Ream's Station, where it expected to find the left wing of Meade's army. Fortunately, Saffold's bridge over the Meherrin River, and the Double Bridges over the Nottaway were intact, and the column reached Stony Creek on the 28th without meeting significant resistance, though Confederate forces were now gathering all around it. Here, a small force of the enemy was found at Stony Creek Depot, which was met and overcome, allowing the wearied column, which had been barely subsisting off the land for the past eight days, to move on to Ream's Station. Crossing Rowanty Creek, the enemy was met again, and fierce fighting ensued. Facing them was Gen. Wade Hampton, with his and Fitzhugh Lee's cavalry. Wilson's column then discovered that two brigades of infantry under Confederate Gen. William Mahone had moved in behind them. By 10 o'clock that night they found themselves surrounded.

Wilson ordered a retreat, back down the road, and across the Nottaway. The movement began at midnight. Re-crossing the Rowanty, the column was attacked at Stony Creek, and the whole rear of the column was thrown into confusion. The only route out was through a wood which obstructed the passage of the guns and wagons, and all 12 guns of the three batteries accompanying Wilson were abandoned. All of Wilson's wagons were lost, and out of 5,500 men in the raid, there

---

1820. Haskin, p. 205.

were 1,800 casualties. The battered and worn column finally reached Light House Point on July 2nd.

As to Battery K, Capt. Maynadier and Lt. Egan went missing; Sgt. McNamara[1821] was wounded and missing, and 35 others were captured or missing, though revised figures show 16 men and officers as prisoners of war. The battery lost 125 horses. On July 11th it was sent to Camp Barry to refit. It had no officers. Capt. William Graham was on detached service at Regimental Headquarters, Concord, NH; Capt. Maynadier, and Lt. Egan were prisoners; 1st Lt. Tulley McCrea was absent with leave, and 2nd Lt. Jacob Counselman had been on detached service since May 14th as a Brevet Lt. Col. of the 2nd Maryland Cavalry.

Regarding the enlisted men, there were 64, but 16 were on detached service, sick, or absent with or without leave, and 15 were prisoners of war; this left but 33 enlisted men for duty.

The scale of the fighting and the casualties in the Army of the Potomac, from the beginning of the Overland Campaign from May 5th until it ended on June 24th, was double that of Gettysburg.[1822] This does not include the casualties in Butler's Bermuda Hundred Campaign, which took place in the same time period.

The huge attrition described above was growing, and it had taken place everywhere. The July strength for Battery L was 90, as listed on the monthly report, but only 74 officers and men were present for duty, double that of Battery K. A relatively new and urgent reason for men to be absent had now appeared. One officer, Appleton, and 5 enlisted men were on detached service, on recruiting duty in New York.

Peeking ahead to the muster roll record for the months of September and October, it is seen that the result of the recruiting efforts were worse than dismal. Only two men were recruited. One was the former first sergeant of the battery, Lewis Keller, who had been discharged on December 29th, 1863, by reason of promotion to Second Lieutenant in the 2nd Louisiana Volunteer Cavalry. The other was a member of the detachment itself, Sgt. William Demarest.

Equally dismal recruiting results were reported by the 116th New York Regiment, soon to arrive in Virginia with the 19th Army Corps. After the end of the siege at Port Hudson, the regiment had detailed a lieutenant colonel, a captain, a lieutenant, and six enlisted men to return home[1823] "for the purpose of bringing to the regiment such conscripts as should be assigned to it." They left on August 12th, 1863, fully expecting the operation of the new draft to fill their needs. They did

---

1821. Regimental casualty list, M727-5, pp. 332–333. Haskin; pp. 207, 562; has 15 men, plus the two officers as prisoners.
1822. Grant, vol. 2, p. 290. CWSAC Battle summaries, Old Church, Trevilian Station, St. Mary's Church, Yellow Tavern, Ream's Station (incl. all in Wilson's Raid), Wilson's Wharf, Haw's Shop.
1823. Clark, pp. 116, 186.

not return to the regiment until it was encamped at Morganzia, in June of 1864. In 10 months, they had not recruited a single soul. We see now the utter failure of the draft, and the reason for the $400 bonus.

The $400 for reenlistment had worked, and most of the five-year regulars, plus the first group of the 300,000 three year volunteers, the veterans, had reenlisted.[1824] However, the Union army was still running short of men. The draft was not producing the men that were expected because its provisions for exemption were lenient enough to allow thousands to avoid service. In the end, the draft only produced 52,068 men and 75,429 substitutes. Upon the payment of a $300 commutation, 86,724 were excused.

The merging of the two batteries, K and L, was the only practical answer. Other batteries in the 1st regiment, E–G, and H–I, had already been consolidated back in April,[1825] and others of the 2nd and 3rd regiments that were destined to serve with them, particularly those horse batteries that were assigned to the cavalry, also had been consolidated.

Politics & Peace Initiatives

There was no increased public outcry to end the war. Those opposed still were. But an article in the *Atlantic Monthly* of July 1864, entitled "The May Campaign in Virginia" concludes with: "The day is approaching when the Army of the Potomac, unfortunate at times in the past, derided, ridiculed, but now triumphant through unparalleled hardship…will plant its banners, on the defences of Richmond, and …crush out the last vestiges of the Rebellion."[1826] Was this article representative of public opinion? The *Atlantic Monthly* was alleged to be less partisan than the likes of the *New York Tribune*, whose editor was Horace Greeley, an ardent Republican and Lincoln supporter; but nevertheless, the question remained, was there now an increased optimism abroad in the land?[1827]

Concluding a discussion of Grant's May campaign, Haskin[1828] says: "At this time the people of the north had become thoroughly accustomed to the war, and nothing shows this more plainly than the fact that, although the army of the James met with losses aggregating over four thousand killed and wounded during this

---

1824. Fox, pp. 526, 532–533.
1825. Haskin, p. 202; O.R. Vol. 43/I, p. 130.
1826. Carleton, p. 132.
1827. Comment on relative partisanship from *Personal Recollections of Abraham Lincoln and the Civil War*, by James R. Gilmore, p. 289; Greeley, *Encyclopedia Britannica*, 11th ed., vol. 12, p. 533.
1828. Haskin, p. 201. Technically Butler was in command of the Army of the James. Here Haskin is assumed to lump it with the Army of the Potomac, which took by far the larger number of casualties.

month of May, less is known generally concerning the operation in which these great losses occurred than of the circumstances of any one of the lesser actions…"

It is suspected that none of the above was universally true, but that for the moment, the country was turning its attention away from battle statistics (perhaps better words would be *distracted from*) and had turned to politics. Lincoln had many critics among his own party, such as Senator Benjamin Wade of Ohio, and Henry Davis of Maryland, who worried that Lincoln would be too soft on the conquered South during reconstruction. The Wade-Davis Bill[1829] on reconstruction policy had passed both houses of Congress near the end of the session, and Lincoln had refused to sign it. Instead, on July 8th, he issued a proclamation defining his plans for reconstruction. Most notably, he would not declare that the free state governments already established by Steele in Arkansas and Banks in Louisiana be "set aside and held for naught" and he asked for the adoption of a constitutional amendment abolishing slavery.

The reader will observe that the heated politics involved *reconstruction* of the South—a concept that had to follow from its *defeat*. Admit it or not, the Union had already assumed that it would be victorious.

The disaffected of the Republican Party and sundry splinter groups had met in Cleveland on May 31st in order to recommend the nomination of John C. Fremont, while they denounced "the imbecile and vacillating policy of the present Administration in the conduct of the war" and its plans for reconstruction. Fremont accepted the nomination. Even more embarrassing was that Democratic newspapers gave the convention's declarations its support.

Regardless of all of the hoopla, the majority of Republicans were in favor of Lincoln for a second term. New Hampshire the "first in the nation" state, did so, on January 6th, and regardless of New Hampshire's claim, Pennsylvania did so on the same date.[1830] As the weeks rolled by into March; New York, Kansas, New Jersey, Connecticut, Maryland, Minnesota, Colorado, Wisconsin, Indiana, Ohio, and Maine had all declared for Lincoln. The Union League Clubs everywhere, even at Vicksburg, declared for Lincoln.

The Republican convention went ahead at Baltimore on June 7th and did little more than announce what had already been shown to be the will of the party: the nomination of Lincoln.[1831]

This accomplished, in July there came an incident that might give sustenance to the Democrats. It was the appearance of two Confederates, Jewett and Sanders, at Niagara Falls, New York, who represented themselves as ambassadors of Jefferson Davis, with full and complete powers to negotiate for peace.[1832] They first

---

1829. Wade, *Encyclopedia Britannica*, p. 226; Davis, p. 866.; Nicolay and Hay, vol. 9, pp. 29–30, 41.
1830. Nicolay and Hay, vol. 9, pp. 51–57.
1831. Nicolay and Hay, vol. 9, p. 63.
1832. Nicolay and Hay, vol. 9, pp. 185–194.

contacted Horace Greeley, with a letter to the President elaborating certain proposals. Greeley forwarded it on July 7th. Lincoln agreed to meet them, provided that their proposals contained two conditions: The restoration of the Union, and the "abandonment of slavery." On the 16th, Greely was given a safe conduct providing Clement C. Clay, Jacob Thompson, James P. Holcombe, and George N. Sanders to travel to Washington. This forced these Confederates to admit that they were not accredited representatives of their Government, but that they could be sent to Richmond armed "with the circumstances disclosed in this correspondence."

Thus was revealed a ruse to make it look like Lincoln had taken the initiative in suing the Confederate government for peace, something that had escaped Greeley. The affair broke up after the Confederates rejected Lincoln's conditions, reiterated in a letter to them on July 18th. The rebel negotiators got no further, but their letter to Greeley expressing their exasperation at "the sad termination of the initiatory steps taken for peace…" was released to the press by Jewett. According to Nicolay and Hay, "It formed a not ineffective document in a heated political campaign."

However, Lincoln knew something that the bogus commissioners did not—another peace initiative was underway, that of Jaquess and Gilmore. A quote from Greeley:[1833] "But happily another negotiation, even more irregular and wholly clandestine, had simultaneously been in progress at Richmond…" It had been fermenting for a long time.

Early in 1863, Col. James F. Jaquess, a Methodist minister commanding the 73rd Illinois Volunteers, "The Preacher Regiment," and a personal friend of Lincoln,[1834] had become convinced that the Confederacy was beaten, and that the war had already "virtually obliterated slavery, and all the prominent questions of difference between the North and the South." He also had the conviction that many southern members of the "old [Methodist Episcopal] church" wished to rejoin their "brethren" in the North, and that, "God has laid the duty upon me" to go to the Confederacy on a mission of peace.

Jaquess repeatedly appealed to his commander, Gen. W. S. Rosecrans, to be allowed. Finally, on May 21st 1863, Rosecrans gave in, and sent a letter to Lincoln asking that Jaquess be given permission to leave his regiment.[1835] Though Rosecrans doubted any useful results, he wrote: "I …believe that a moral force will be generated by his mission that will more than compensate for his temporary absence from his regiment." Lincoln acquiesced, but stipulated that the colonel was on his own, and could not make any official proposals.

Jaquess left the Department of the Cumberland, eventually arriving at Fortress Monroe, were he was allowed through the lines to rebel held Petersburg. He

---

1833. Newlin, p. 546.
1834. Newlin, pp. 7–8, 539–541.
1835. O.R. Ser. 3, vol. 3, pp. 214–215; ser. 2, vol. 7, p. 447.

was there for three weeks, but did not meet with any officials of the Confederacy, only "influential but unofficial personages" who all admitted that they were weary of war, hopeless of success, and ready to give up slavery to end the war. He returned in June, and wrote a report to Lincoln. After waiting at Baltimore for two weeks and receiving no reply, Jaquess returned to his regiment, hurried by the news that Rosecrans, after six months at Murfreesboro, was finally going to march, touched upon in chapter 9, to Tullhoma against Bragg.[1836] We recall that on September 9th, 1863, Chattanooga was taken, subsequently bringing on the Battle of Chickamauga (Sept. 18th–20th). Following Rosecrans' reverse at Chickamauga, Bragg had laid siege to Chattanooga, and the situation had caused the government to call Grant east to command, whence Rosecrans was replaced by Thomas.

The 73rd Illinois and its colonel, being in the midst of all of this (his 14-year-old son, a drummer-boy, was captured at Chickamauga), there was no time for any consideration of such things as peace missions. However, by November 4th, Jaquess was back at it. He sent a letter[1837] to James R. Gilmore, a member of the editorial staff of the *New York Tribune*, offering to renew his peace mission. Why Jaquess sought out Gilmore is not clear, and nothing came as a result of his letter until Gilmore happened to meet Lincoln six months later. Gilmore then asked Lincoln why he had not answered Jaquess back in 1863. Lincoln exclaimed that he had never received the letter, and Gilmore then handed him a copy, whereupon Lincoln briefly reopened the issue. Events, however, again postponed any action, as Jaquess was fighting in Sherman's Atlanta Campaign, and Lincoln was influenced to drop the initiative.[1838]

As it happened, in June 1864, Jaquess was sent by Sherman to Washington to deliver dispatches to Lincoln. Attempting to see Lincoln on the subject of the peace mission, he was rebuffed, and again he fell back on Gilmore. The two met at Baltimore. Jaquess revealed that he had met one of his Methodist colleagues who had, in fact, interviewed Jefferson Davis on June 16th. The essential point brought out was that Davis would never consent to anything other than Southern independence.[1839]

Gilmore's reaction: "It at once occurred to me that if this declaration could be got out in such a manner that it could be given to the public, it would, if… broadcast over the North, destroy the Peace party, and reelect Mr. Lincoln…" The mission was subsequently carried out on this basis—as a device in the Presidential election campaign of 1864.

1836. Nicolay and Hay, vol. 8, pp. 61–73, 119. Rosecrans started out on June 24th; Chickamauga, CWSAC GA004.
1837. Gilmore, pp. 233–236, 276.
1838. Gilmore, pp. 237, 239.
1839. Gilmore, p. 238. It was alleged that Davis then said that he personally would agree to defensive league, for all "external" matters.

Cleared by Lincoln, Gilmore and Jaquess visited Richmond, accompanied by Maj. John E. Mulford, the Assistant Agent of Exchange for Prisoners.[1840] They met with Davis on July 17th, and after much discussion, it was revealed that there could be no agreement. As Gilmore, Jaquess, and Mulford were leaving, Davis' parting remark was: "Say to Mr. Lincoln…that I shall at any time be pleased to receive proposals for peace on the basis of our independence. It will be useless to approach me with any other."

Gilmore returned to Washington and read aloud his report to Lincoln. When he finished, Lincoln asked: "What do you propose to do with this?" "Put a beginning and end to it, sir, on my way home, and hand it to the *Tribune*." Some discussion followed, Lincoln preferring the *Atlantic Monthly* as less partisan, though it would involve some delay. The article appeared in the September issue, entitled "Our Visit to Richmond," written by Gilmore, under the pseudonym of Edmund Kirke.[1841]

As it was, the article was perfectly timed to combat the results of the Democratic convention, held in Chicago from August 29th to 31st, which had nominated George B. McClellan for President[1842] and had adopted a platform that was carefully obtuse, containing such statements as "to preserve the Federal Union and the rights of the States unimpaired…" and that "…immediate efforts be made for a cessation of hostilities, with a view of an ultimate convention of the States, or other peaceable means, to the end that, at the earliest practicable moment, peace may be restored on the basis of the Federal Union of the States."

Could a man in the street, or at the Democratic convention for that matter, tell what this meant? Perhaps the man in the street heard what he wanted to. To Republicans, it was ominous, meaning peace at any price, even if the Union was dissolved.

Washington Threatened

This was not the first threat.[1843] After the first Battle of Manassas, in July of 1861, the defeated Union soldiers fled into Washington, and it was feared that the Confederates would follow. They did not. However, the close proximity of Washington to Richmond, Lee's army, the open country of the Shenandoah Valley,

---

1840. Mulford was known to the Confederate authorities. He was included as an escort to the mission on Lincoln's orders. This gave an air of authenticity to the mission, though Lincoln had given no official sanction to it. Gilmore, pp. 253, 272.
1841. *Atlantic Monthly*, pp. 372–383.
1842. *Official Proceedings of the Democratic National Convention*, Chicago, Times Steam Book and Job Printing House, 1864. McClellan accepted on Sept. 8th, p. 60. He wrote: "The reestablishment of the Union in all its integrity is, and must continue to be, the indispensable condition in any settlement." The platform, on p. 27, made no such firm declaration.
1843. *www.nps.gov/history/his*

and the water routes available to the Confederacy, resulted in an almost constant state of anxiety, especially as the campaigns early in the war resulted in mostly Union defeats. In March of 1862, when the CSS *Virginia*, best remembered as the *Merrimack*, cut loose from Norfolk navy yard and attacked and destroyed the Union frigates *Congress* and *Cumberland*, there was alarm in Washington that it next might come up the Potomac and shell the city.[1844]

Lincoln's fears for Washington often extended far beyond the perimeter of the forts, and rightly so. In 1862, when Stonewall Jackson was ordered by Lee to advance down (north) the Shenandoah Valley, Lincoln's fear for Washington caused him to order troops from McClellan to reinforce those in the Valley. Initially defeated at Kernstown, Jackson remained to defeat Banks' army at Winchester, on May 25th, 1862, and Jackson ultimately gained control of the upper and middle valley. Again, it was the highway of the valley through which Lee retreated after his first invasion of the north, after the bloodiest battle on any single day of the entire war, September 17th, 1862, at Antietam, called Sharpsburg by the Confederacy.

The defeat of Union forces at the Second Battle of Winchester on June 13-15th, 1863 had paved the way for Lee to move down the valley, cross the Potomac, and again invade the north,[1845] resulting in the great battle of Gettysburg. Defeated, Lee abandoned his invasion, crossed the Potomac at Williamsport and retreated to the upper (southern) part of the valley, which remained in Confederate control.

Now, in 1864, came the last, and greatest, threat to Washington. It was precipitated by Grant's spring campaign, and Lee's reaction to it, part of a series of seesaw movements between Grant and Lee that would cause Battery L and a detachment of the 19th Corps to be transferred to Virginia, and ultimately lead to Lee's surrender.

With Butler having failed in his attempt to enter Petersburg[1846] on June 9th, the Army of the Potomac crossed the James River and began moving to support Butler and renew the assault, which began on June 15th. After some initial successes, Lee rushed reinforcements to the defending general, Beauregard, and when the Union 2nd, 5th, and 11th corps attacked on June 18th, they were repulsed with heavy casualties. The siege of Petersburg had begun. Thus, as Grant puts it, "comparative quiet reigned about Petersburg until late July."[1847]

Another part of Grant's spring campaign was his order to Franz Sigel, head of the Department of West Virginia, at Winchester, Virginia, to destroy the Confederate railroad complex at Lynchburg. Advancing down the Valley Pike, Sigel met Maj. Gen. John C. Breckinridge at New Market, and was soundly defeated.

1844. Welles, vol. I, pp. 61–63.
1845. O.R. Vol. 27/II, pp. 313–325.
1846. CWSAC: Antietam, MD003, Valley Campaign VA101-106, Petersburg 1, VA098, Petersburg 2, VA068.
1847. Grant, vol. 2, p. 303.

He was replaced[1848] by Maj. Gen. David Hunter, who took over the direction of the initiative. Moving up from Piedmont, to Staunton, each time he met them, he defeated the enemy. He then moved to his objective, Lynchburg, via Lexington, home of the Virginia Military Institute, which he ordered burned on June 12th, as retribution for their participation in the Battle at New Market.[1849] He reached Lynchburg on June 16th, and attacked on the 17th.

He was repulsed by Ewell's 2nd Corps, commanded by Lt. Gen. Jubal A. Early, who had been sent by Lee from near Gaines' Mill via Charlottesville to strike Hunter's rear.[1850] Running short of ammunition and supplies, Hunter was forced to retreat west to Liberty (Bedford), then through Buford's gap into Salem, and then into West Virginia. This move left the Valley open to Early. Before Lee even knew of the direction of Hunter's retreat, he had ordered Early to move north, "and if opportunity offered, to follow him into Maryland" and threaten Washington,[1851] perhaps the threat would cause Grant to detach troops from the siege of Petersburg.

Hunter "disposed of," Early decided to move north on June 23rd, knowing that Hunter could not stop until he had reached the Kanawha River. Often traveling by two roads; his cavalry on one, and his infantry on a parallel one; Early reached Staunton on June 26th and 27th. Unopposed, he marched rapidly down the valley, the track shown in figure 11,[1852] reaching Winchester on July 2nd. He captured Martinsburg on July 3rd, causing Sigel's[1853] force there to retreat across the Potomac to Shepherdstown, and Weber's garrison at Harper's Ferry to retreat across to Maryland heights. The Confederate cavalry occupied Boonsboro, and a detachment out of McCausland's cavalry drove a portion of the 6th U.S. Cavalry from Hagerstown on July 6th, where $20,000 was levied against the inhabitants. Breckinridge occupied Frederick on the 9th, where the levy demanded was $200,000, "all of which was paid in Federal and Northern money."[1854]

Early met his first real resistance on July 9th. Gen. Lewis Wallace, commanding the Middle Department, headquarters at Baltimore, who had been reinforced by Rickett's Division of Wright's 6th Corps, sent from Grant, had put up a defensive line on the Monocacy River, just east of Frederick. Wallace's hastily formed force of about

---

1848. O.R. Vol. 37/I, pp. 1, 5–6: CWSAC VA110.
1849. O.R. Vol. 37/I, pp. 88, 97.
1850. Early, *Sketch*, pp. 371, 378–379; CWSAC VA064; Grant, vol. 2, p. 304; O.R. Vol. 37/I, pp. 100–101; O.R. Vol. 43/I, pp. 1018–1020.
1851. Sheridan, vol. I, p. 457; O.R. Vol. 37/I, pp. 180–182, 191–196 769; CWSAC #MD007, DC00; Grant, vol. 2, pp. 304–306; Early, *Memoir*, pp. 41–45.
1852. Long, A. L., *General*, pp. 122–123. Figure 11 from Plate 81, map 11; Atlas.
1853. O.R. Vol. 37/I, p. 7, 199, 347, 349. Sigel was assigned as commander of the Reserve Division Headquarters at Martinsburg, after he was relieved from command of the Department of West Virginia.
1854. O.R. Vol. 37/I, pp. 170, 336–337, 349

3,350 were outflanked and defeated by Early's 12,000,[1855] but the delay of about a day allowed reinforcements to reach Washington, possibly saving it from invasion.

FIGURE 11

Early then moved toward Washington via Rockville, and making his headquarters at Silver Spring, his troops pushed along the 7th Street Road, up to the defenses near Fort Stevens, late on the 11th, figure 12.[1856] His troops were exhausted, the weather being "excessively hot…and the dust so dense…" that he had had to slacken his pace, after making thirty miles on the 10th. They were not in a condition to make an attack, and they rested until the next day.

Wallace's action on the Monocacy had delayed Early long enough to allow Wright, with the two remaining divisions of 6th Corps, to arrive near Fort Stevens, and on July 12th, Wright pushed out from the defenses in the face of destructive Confederate fire, and drove Early's pickets out from the house and orchard grove which sheltered them, back about a mile.

1855. Nicolay and Hay Vol. 9, pp. 161, 169; Early, *Sketch*, p. 381, reports 2,000 cavalry, 10,000 of the 2nd Corps, and 2,250 of Breckinridge's command. O.R. Vol. 37/I, p. 191; O.R. Vol. 37/II, pp. 158–159.

1856. Figure 12 adapted from map *Defences of Washington*, no. 88-69074 Nat'l Archives.

FIGURE 12

The President, as usual, was keenly interested in the action, and had ridden out to Fort Stevens on the afternoon of the 11th. When the first of Early's troops arrived he was standing near the parapet, witnessing the action, his tall figure making him a conspicuous target, until he was ordered to withdraw. He returned on the 12th and stood in similar danger, watching as Wright's men moved out. Whizzing bullets mortally wounded an officer standing within three feet of him, and he was again advised by Wright to take cover. The scene was almost surreal, viewed by the President of the United States from the defending side, and by the 1860 Democratic candidate for that Presidency, Gen. John C. Breckinridge, now a division commander in Early's army, from the attacking side.[1857]

The determined action resulted in Wright's troops suffering 280 casualties.[1858]

Early ignores any of these details in his report, and ends his account of the affair with these words: "I determined at first to make an assault, but before it

---

1857. Nicolay and Hay, vol. 9, pp. 172–173.
1858. O.R. Vol. 36/I, p. 28.

could be made it became apparent that the enemy had been strongly re-enforced, and we knew that the Sixth Corps had arrived from Grant's army, and after consultation…I became satisfied that the assault even if successful, would be attended with such great sacrifice as would ensure the destruction of my whole force…"[1859] He then withdrew to Leesburg and planned to retreat up the valley, by "forced marches…toward Richmond." As we shall see, he did not follow his plan.

The Nineteenth Corps Arrives

As it happened, Emory, with the advance of the 19th Corps, consisting of four companies of the 114th New York, and the 153rd New York, had arrived on the steamer *Crescent* at Fortress Monroe on the afternoon of July 12th.[1860] He was immediately ordered to Washington and arrived at Fort Saratoga that night. He then encamped at Camp Barry.

The story of how it came to pass that the 19th Corps would beat Battery L to Washington is of interest. On May 29th, Butler's headquarters had received the news that "Banks has escaped from Alexandria via Simsport." Butler did not hesitate to suggest to Stanton: "In view of the news, as the Nineteenth Army Corps is disengaged, I respectfully suggest that it be sent by water, to land here or at West Point in reach of General Grant. General Weitzel, who so well knows the military situation in Louisiana, concurs…"[1861] This was clear thinking, completely in line with Grant's strategic view that only a minimal force was needed in Louisiana. Yet Grant, at that moment in the midst of his assault at Cold Harbor, apparently didn't want to think of anything new or different, and he disapproved! He had apparently been influenced by Sherman, who wanted to follow through with the expedition on Mobile, which up to then had been Grant's set policy directive, first for Banks, and then for Canby.

It was not long before events caused Grant to change his mind. A factor had to have been the tremendous number of casualties the Army of the Potomac and the Army of the James had taken up to that time, almost as many as in Lee's *entire* army. By June 23rd, Grant's thinking was back on track, saying,[1862] in an order to Halleck:

> The siege of Richmond bids fair to be tedious, and in consequence of the

---

1859. The remaining two divisions of the 6th Corps had arrived on the night of the 11th. O.R. Vol. 37/II, pp. 7, 243; Grant, vol. 2, pp. 303–304. In an addendum to his report, Early says: "The arrival of the Ninth Corps is again reported, and there is a report that a part of Banks' force has arrived, but I do not place much confidence in these reports." Pellet, pp. 243–245.
1860. O.R. Vol. 37/II, p. 243.
1861. O.R. Vol. 36/III, pp. 314, 315; O.R. Vol. 34/IV, p. 185; Irwin, pp. 352–353.
1862. Irwin, p. 352. Up to June 15th Meade's and Butler's losses were 61,142. Lee's army is estimated to have been between 61,000 and 64,000. O.R. Vol. 34/ IV, pp. 514–515. Quoted without omission, as being the definitive policy that remained in place for the rest of the war.

very extended lines we must have, a much larger force will be necessary than would be required in ordinary sieges against the same force that now opposes us. With my present force I feel perfectly safe against Lee's Army, and, acting defensively, would feel so against Lee and Johnston combined; but we want to act offensively. In my opinion, to do this effectively, we should concentrate our whole energy against the two principal armies of the enemy.

In other words, nothing should be attempted, except in Georgia and here that is not directly in co-operation with these moves. West of the Mississippi I would not attempt anything until the rebellion east of it is entirely subdued. I would then direct Canby to leave Smith unmolested where he is; to make no move except such as is necessary to protect what he now holds. All the troops he can spare should be sent here at once. In my opinion the white troops of the Nineteenth Corps can all come, together with many of the colored troops. I wish you would place this matter before the Secretary of War and urge that no offensive operations west of the Mississippi be allowed to commence until matters here are settled. Send the Nineteenth Corps and such other troops as you can from the Department of the Gulf to me.

Halleck issued the orders the next day.[1863] Thus, it was *finis* for Canby's initial consideration of a renewed campaign on Shreveport via the railroad from Vicksburg or any substantial initiatives anywhere. Mobile would escape attack for a little while longer.

After Early

At the height of the tension, on July 10th, as Early was approaching Fort Stevens, Lincoln had appealed to Grant to come to the scene in person. To bolster the defenses, Grant had detached a whole corps, Wright's 6th, from the Army of the Potomac, the 19th Corps was arriving, and appeals had been made for sundry 100 day's militiamen from the city, from New York, from Pennsylvania, and Massachusetts; even a detachment of sailors from the navy yard at New York.[1864] Surprise! This time, Lincoln viewed the city as safe, and he was not urging more defense, but offense. He was proposing that Grant come and supervise a "vigorous effort to destroy the enemy's force in this vicinity. This is what I think, upon your suggestion, and is not an order." The suggestion referred to was Grant's. It was: "Forces enough to defeat all that Early has with him should get in his rear south of him, and follow him up sharply…" Again pure Grant; go *forward*. However, Grant begged off on the idea of his personally coming to the scene. His Pennsylvania Volunteers had nearly finished a mine under the Confederate works before Petersburg, which just might open a new phase in the siege.

1863. O.R. Vol. 34/IV, p. 528; Taylor, p. 192.
1864. O.R. Vol. 37/II, pp. 134, 155–156, 157, 174, 191, 193–194; Grant, vol. 2, pp. 305–307.

In response to Grant's suggestion, Halleck was defeatist as usual, but soon fell into, or was forced into the idea, and he ordered Wright's 6th Corps to not go into the Washington defenses, but to be prepared, as rapidly as possible, for the field.[1865] On July 11th he contacted Hunter who was headed to Harper's Ferry, and ordered him to join Wright at or near Edwards Ferry, figure 13, making a correct assumption as to the direction in which Early would retire.

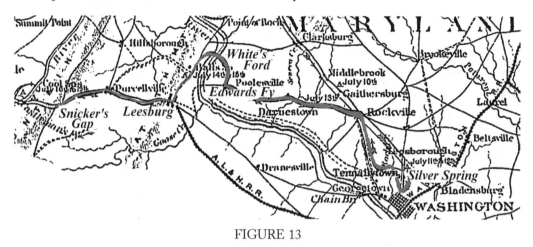

FIGURE 13

Early retired on the night of July 12th,[1866] and on the 13th, Wright, assigned as the commander of the combined forces moving against the enemy, was seen, at 5:00 p.m., at the head of his column moving out on the Rockville Road, passing the burned-out mansion of Postmaster Blair's house at Silver Spring. Rather an auspicious moment.

Charles A. Dana, Grant's old ally, and now assistant secretary of war, wrote to Grant, commenting: "Boldness is all that is wanted to drive the enemy out of Maryland in confusion." As we shall see, Wright, *warned to be cautious by Halleck*, did not present boldness.

Wright's force initially consisted of only about 10,000 effectives of his own, and only 650 of the 19th Corps had arrived, yet none other than the secretary of war had assured him, in a telegram, that: "You can doubtless count on a large part…re-enforcing you in season for a battle, if you need them, and need not delay for want of support." Eventually the 19th Corps detachment would number about 7,000, and with a detachment of about 1,500 from the 8th Corps, Wright's force was larger than Early's, at 10,000 infantry and 2,000 cavalry. But all previous Federal estimates of Early's strength had been so exaggerated that Wright was convinced he was facing a more powerful foe,[1867] and he was cautioned by Halleck to unite with Hunter's West Virginia forces commanded by Crook. Arriving at

---

1865. O.R. 37/II, pp. 207, 210, 258; 37/I, p. 103; figure 13, portion of plate 18, map 11, Atlas.
1866. O.R. Vol. 37/I, p. 348; O.R. Vol. 37/II, pp. 258–261, 264, 284, 285, 287, 345, 547.
1867. O.R. Vol. 37/II, p. 291.

Poolesville, near Edwards Ferry, figure 13, on July 14th, Wright discovered that Early's forces had crossed the Potomac;[1868] the bulk of them at White's Ford. Wright then reported that his troops were "wholly insufficient to justify the following up of the enemy on the other side…I presume this will not be the policy of the War Department, and I shall, therefore, await instructions…" His troops had marched over thirty miles in 24 hours over bad roads, and though the heat was excessive, his action allowed Early to rest and recuperate at Leesburg, safely on the south side of the Potomac.

Grant then entered the calculation with a dictum fatal to the chase. He confided to Halleck that he really wanted Wright and the 19th Corps back with the Army of the Potomac, and though he cautioned Halleck: "I do not intend this as an order to bring Wright back while he is in pursuit of the enemy with any prospect of punishing him, but to secure his return at the earliest possible moment…"[1869] Grant would leave it to Hunter's men from the Department of West Virginia to follow Early. The operations about Washington and Petersburg were only a part of what Grant had to consider. He was worried that Lee would be ordered to detach a force to Johnston to resist Sherman in Georgia, and pressure had to be kept up on Lee's front to prevent it.

Accordingly, on July 15th, Grant ordered that all of the remaining steamers "arriving from the South" should be directed to City Point, i.e., the Army of the Potomac. Rather remarkably, Halleck replied to Wright that the pursuit was to be continued until the receipt of further orders. Only the next day, Grant repeated his desire for the return of Wright's command, leaving Hunter/Crook to follow Early, and remain "always between the enemy and Washington…"[1870]

The pursuit continued to Snicker's and Clark's Gaps, where it was discovered that Early had withdrawn through Snicker's Gap, and had crossed the Shenandoah River, reaching Berryville on July 17th. Wright and Crook were now close, and though they had not quite united, Crook's cavalry had struck the rear of Early's column on the Snickersville Pike. On the 20th, after a sharp action at the river, it was reported that Wright, now united with Crook, had found the enemy retreating toward Front Royal and Strasburg. This was all the excuse that Wright needed, and he promptly made the decision to call off the chase: "Conceiving that the object of the expedition to be accomplished, I at once started back, as directed…" Wright headed for Washington, and Crook for Winchester to unite with Hunter's

---

1868. Early, *Sketch*, pp. 294, 396; O.R. 37/II, p. 315.
1869. O.R. Vol. 37/II, pp. 300, 328–329, 333, 338–339. Wright had been assigned to the overall command of the pursuing force (p. 289). Wright was junior in rank to Hunter, and a clash now ensued. Hunter asked to be relieved. He was assuaged by Lincoln (p. 365), using the device of assigning General George Crook to command those troops detached from Hunter's Department of West Virginia that were serving with Wright. Petty, time wasting nonsense.
1870. O.R. Vol. 37/II, pp. 350, 369, 401, 404–405, 411–413, 417, 422; Early, *Sketch*, pp. 396, 398–399.

cavalry, under Averell. The chase after Early would now be left to Hunter's direction. Wright's departure would seriously reduce Hunter's options, and he predicted that with the size of his force he could not prevent Early's return.

Anecdote

During Early's raid, as he was approaching Frederick, Maryland, Bradley T. Johnson's and Harry A. Gilmor's Partisan Rangers were ordered to make a cavalry raid north of Baltimore to cut the two main railroads, the Northern Central and the Philadelphia, Wilmington, and Baltimore. They advanced to New Windsor, then to Westminster, where the telegraph was seized and the wires cut. Moving to the railroad, where it passes through the village of Cockeysville, only fifteen miles from Baltimore, they burned the bridges over the Gunpowder River. Gilmor, with his 130 men, then pushed on alone, through Towson, and, on the morning of July 11th, as they were approaching the Philadelphia and Baltimore Railroad, near its bridge crossing the Gunpowder River, a passenger train was discovered heading north out of Baltimore. It was stopped, and General William B. Franklin, his aide, and several other army, navy, and marine officers were captured.[1871]

General Franklin, as we know, wounded at the Battle of Mansfield, had been granted medical leave on June 11th. He was now on the last leg of his trip home, having reported at City Point, likely conferring with Grant. Franklin was taken away in a buggy toward Towson. His Partisan Ranger guards, told to wait for the appearance of their commander, halted near the Towson Road rail crossing, at Randalstown. Not having slept the night before, they all fell asleep, and Franklin escaped that morning. General Ord, at Baltimore, informed of Franklin's escape and of his having been safely hidden by Union sympathizers, sent a cavalry escort out to pick him up the next day.[1872]

1871. O.R. Vol. 37/II, p. 349; Gilmor H.A., pp. 191-194, 202, 203.
1872. O.R. Vol. 34/IV, p. 531; vol. 37/II, pp. 193, 302, 314, 322–323; vol. 40/III, p. 86.

Chapter 13

*Sheridan Appointed; The Army of the Shenandoah; First Moves;
The Confederate Partisan Rangers; Sheridan Retreats North; The Public Mind;
Berryville; Smithfield Crossing; "Record" 10/64; Anderson; Winchester*

Sheridan Appointed

Dana, now the assistant secretary of war, and as we know, always free to express his opinion to Grant, on July 24th telegraphed Grant's chief of staff regarding Early's raid, and the defense of Washington: "Wright and Crook accomplished nothing, and Wright started back as soon as he got where he might have done something worth while."[1873] Grant must have been impatient with the progress of things as early as July 18th, when he had suggested to Halleck that the departments of the Susquehanna (Pennsylvania), West Virginia, and Washington be merged. Though he did not name the Middle Department (Maryland), it was clear that one vigorous commander would cut through all of the agonizing communication and ego problems that had hampered the response to Early. Grant had suggested Franklin as the man. The response from Halleck was immediately negative: "General Franklin would not give satisfaction. The President ordered him to be tried for negligence and disobedience of orders when here before, but General McClellan assumed the responsibility of his repeated delays in obeying orders." The reader is left to judge Halleck's response from Franklin's performance in the Department of the Gulf.

On the 25th, Grant tried again. He wrote directly to Lincoln, outlining the same proposal, and explained that he didn't care who was to be placed in command, and mentioned Meade. The "Middle Division" as it would be called, if run by Meade, would be "used to the very best advantage from a personal examination of the ground, and would adopt means of getting the earliest information of any advance of the enemy, and would prepare to meet it." The letter was delivered to the President by Grant's chief of staff, Rawlins, who could convey "more information… than I could give you in a letter." Part of that information was of such a nature that he would "not care to commit to paper…"

Clearly the comment about "personal examination of the ground" referred to Halleck. We have seen evidence of the fact that Halleck never visited the field,

---

1873. O.R. Vol. 37/II, pp. 374, 408, 427, 433.

and the one time that he did was before he became general-in-chief, during the advance to Corinth. Since, he had sat in the War Department relying on telegrams and dispatches, which tended to be several days late for the reason of cut telegraph wires, or the inability of a fighter in the field to promptly put pen to paper.

The rest of Grant's note, the part that he cared to not commit to paper, is hinted at in his *Memoirs*. It evidently referred to long previous and continuing interference from Washington, i.e., both Halleck and Stanton. From his *Memoirs*:[1874] "It seemed to be the policy of General Halleck and Secretary Stanton to keep any force sent there [the Shenandoah Valley] in pursuit of the invading army, moving right and left so as to keep between the enemy and our capital; and, generally speaking, they pursued this policy until all knowledge of the whereabouts of the enemy was lost. They were left, therefore, free to supply themselves with…such provisions as they could carry away…"

The same day, Lincoln responded that he would like to meet with Grant at Fortress Monroe, "after Thursday," which would have been July 28th. This was too quick for Grant, and he begged off, as previously noted, saying: "I am commencing movements for which I hope favorable results." He was referring to the preparations for the explosion of a mine under the Confederate breastworks of Petersburg, and a diversionary raid on Richmond, designed to draw away some of Lee's forces from the front at Petersburg, which has now come to be known as Deep Bottom.[1875] He was already in the process of sending the 19th Corps and several regiments of cavalry back to Washington. Elements of Early's command had skirmished with Averell's cavalry at Stephenson's Depot, about six miles northeast of Winchester, on July 20th (figure 1),[1876] and Early had struck a part of Hunter's command, under Crook, at Kernstown, in force, on the 24th,[1877] handing him a severe defeat. Crook had been flanked, and shaken. Crook doubted, for a while, that he would be able to retreat to Harper's Ferry. Halleck had taken the initiative to send Wright back out, with orders to unite with Hunter's forces, wherever they could be found.[1878] As it happened, Hunter's force was able to get to Maryland Heights and Harper's Ferry.

Circumstances were such that at least two of Grant's earlier suggestions were adopted immediately: (1) a single commander, and (2) a combined command. On the 27th, Stanton, as directed by Lincoln, named Halleck to the command of the defense of the combined Middle, Susquehanna, Washington, and West Virginia Departments.[1879] Grant reveals in his *Memoirs* that he had suggested Sheridan,

---

1874. Grant, vol. 2, p. 317.
1875. CWSAC VA069.
1876. Figure 1, Atlas, plate 27, portion of map 1, altered.
1877. O.R. Vol. 37/II, pp. 408, 436, 445–446, 459; Early, *Sketch*, pp. 398–400; CWSAC VA116.
1878. O.R. Vol. 37/II, p. 456.
1879. O.R. Vol. 37/II, pp. 463, 470, 486, 509, 511, 515, 525, 558; Grant, vol. 2, p. 317; *Encyclopedia Britannica*, 1911, vol. 24, p. 847.

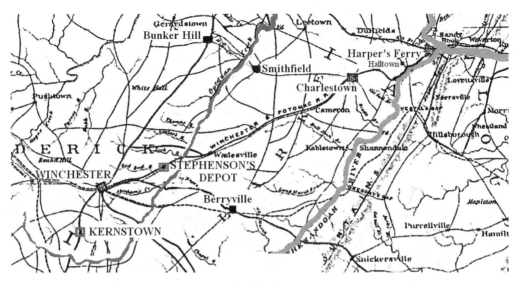

FIGURE 1

but the suggestion was rejected by Stanton on the grounds that Sheridan was too young for so important a command, though he was now 34 and had been in the regular army for 11 years, several at Fort Duncan, as we remember. After Corinth, he had distinguished himself at Booneville, under Halleck, and under Rosecrans at Murfreesboro, Chickamauga, and Chattanooga. On Rosecrans' recommendation, he had risen to brevet major general. He was appointed commander of the cavalry corps of the Army of the Potomac after Grant had taken command, only after Grant had asked Halleck for "an active and energetic man, full of spirit and vigor and life." What more could Stanton have wanted? Perhaps Stanton could not be blamed. After so many other failed generals with whom he had been involved, starting with McClellan, he had earned a right to skepticism.

In the meantime, just as Grant had said, Early was left free to harvest grain and hay in the Shenandoah Valley and run it to Culpeper, Virginia, by train. At this point, Early had knowledge of Hunter's actions in the burning of the houses[1880] of several prominent Confederate officials in the Valley, as well as the Virginia Military Institute. He determined on a retaliatory attack (not to be confused with the earlier attack on Hagerstown and Frederick.) Having control of the territory as far north as Martinsburg, he decided to strike at Chambersburg, Pennsylvania, and beyond, if possible. On the 29th two of his cavalry brigades, one under McCausland and the other under Bradley T. Johnson, crossed the Potomac. Entering Chambersburg on the 30th, McCausland ordered it burned when his ransom demand[1881] for $100,000 in gold or $500,000 in greenbacks, could not be met. He moved

---

1880. Early, *Sketch*, pp. 401–402.
1881. Nicolay and Hay, vol. 9, pp. 176, 177; O.R. Vol. 37/II, pp. 525, 534, 542; Gilmor, p. 209, says $200,000 in gold, or its equivalent in greenbacks. Reference to Hancock, p. 213; O.R. Vol. 37/I, pp. 354–356; O.R. Vol. 43/I, pp. 7–8.

on to Hancock, Maryland, where he demanded $30,000. Not having obtained it, he ordered the town burned. However, Col. Harry Gilmor, a Marylander, commanding the 2nd Maryland Partisan Rangers, objected, and with the permission of Johnson, stationed his own troops so as to prevent it. Averell's arrival shortly thereafter chased them out of the place, and it remained unharmed. McCausland was reported as drunk during most of these proceedings.

Johnson's official report, which includes acts before and after the Chambersburg and Hancock raids, terms the conduct of McCausland's troops as "outrageous."

> Every crime in the catalogue of infamy has been committed, I believe, except murder and rape. Highway robbery of watches and pocket-books was of ordinary occurrence; the taking of breast-pins, finger rings, and earrings frequently happened. Pillage and sack of private dwellings took place hourly. A soldier of an advance guard robbed of his gold watch the Catholic clergyman of Hancock on his way from church on Sunday, July 31, in the public streets… At Chambersburg, while the town was in flames, a quartermaster, aided and directed by a field officer, exacted ransom of individuals for their houses, holding the torch in terror over the house until it was paid. These ransoms varied from $750 to $150, according to the size of the habitation. Thus, the grand spectacle of a national retaliation was reduced to a miserable huckstering for greenbacks.

Chased by Averell, McCausland fell back into West Virginia. Near Moorefield, Johnson was offended that the barbarism had continued. He relates: "A lieutenant knocked down and kicked an aged woman who has two sons in the Confederate army, and after choking the sister locked her in the stable and set fire to it. This was because the two women would not give up horses he and his fellow thieves wished to steal." Here were Confederate soldiers stealing from Confederate sympathizers. What was going on? There was little doubt that the south was suffering and the Confederate soldier was becoming desperate, frustrated, and often barefoot, a condition even the Yankee army occasionally experienced, given the broad scale to which the war had grown.[1882] Most significantly though, many in McCausland's cavalry were former guerrillas, with lawless habits inherited from what had been authorized in the Confederate Partisan Ranger Law, since repealed. This is discussed later.

By the 1st of August, with Early finally driven away by Averell's cavalry, Grant had had enough. His "movements," that he had earlier described to Lincoln for which he hoped "favorable results" had proved to be a "stupendous"[1883] failure. The mine explosion in front of Petersburg was ineptly followed up, the troops

---

1882. O.R. Vol. 33, p. 1275, O.R. Vol. 36/II, p. 821; O.R. Vol. 37/I, pp. 13, 120; O.R. Vol. 43/I p. 558; Pollard, E. A., pp. 332–334; Foote, F. H., SHS, vol. 31, pp. 237–239; Butler, B. F., p. 610.
1883. Grant, vol. 2, p. 315; CWSAC no. VA069, VA070; Grant, vol. 2, pp. 313–314; O.R. Vol. 40/I, p. 563.

entering the massive 175-by-50-foot crater, rather than skirting it, leaving them to be picked off as fish in a barrel, which resulted in almost 4,000 men as casualties or prisoners. In addition, the diversionary raid to Deep Bottom had failed to draw away enough of Lee's force to make a difference. Grant saw the handwriting on the wall, which said: *You have failed, and the stalemated trench warfare in front of Petersburg will continue.* It would do so for another eight months.

Perhaps the necessary action to solve the problem of Early in the Shenandoah Valley was really an opportunity in disguise. After all, it was Lee's breadbasket, and had been his avenue into the north ever since 1862, which, as we have said, resulted in the bloody battle of Antietam, and then, in 1863, the famous battle of Gettysburg. The Shenandoah would not be given up easily by Lee, and as we shall see, Early was soon reinforced. If Early could be decisively defeated in the open country and good roads of the Valley, it would be a major setback to Lee's Army of Northern Virginia, something that now seemed impossible to accomplish, given the stalemate at Petersburg.

Grant now instructed Halleck that he "wanted" Gen. Philip Sheridan put in temporary command of all of the troops in the field, "with instructions to put himself south of the enemy and follow him to the death." This was the first time that Grant had not made a "suggestion." Up to this point, Halleck and Grant had showed great deference to each other's authority,[1884] but this telegram offered no options. Sheridan was named—period.

During Early's invasion, Lincoln had resolutely kept from interfering in any of the decisions made by either Halleck or Grant, and he once again said nothing for or against Sheridan. However, upon reading Grant's telegram, he replied (and here, it is quoted in full, to picture the President's level of despair at the lack of Halleck's decisiveness, and the lack of aggressiveness of those in the field):

> I see your dispatch in which you say "I want Sheridan put in command of all the troops in the field, with instructions to put himself south of the enemy and follow him to the death. Wherever the enemy goes let our troops go also." This, I think, is exactly right as to how our forces should move, but please look over the dispatches you have received from here ever since you made that order, and discover, if you can, that there is any idea in the head of anyone here of "putting our army south of the enemy," or of "following him to the death" in any direction. I repeat to you it will neither be done nor attempted, unless you watch it every day and force it.

The one aspect of Grant's appointment of Sheridan that was not settled was the reaction of Hunter. Prompted by Lincoln's remarks, Grant replied that he "would start in two hours for Washington." Instead, he went directly to Monocacy

---

1884. Nicolay and Hay, vol. 9, pp. 172, 180; O. R. Vol. 37/II, pp. 582, 591.

Station, near Frederick, Maryland, where he found Hunter.[1885]

As had happened earlier, when Wright had been assigned to the overall command of the troops chasing after Early, Hunter offered to resign. Previously, he had been assuaged by his being retained as department commander, having his subordinates, Crook and Averell, in the field. A similar desk job was now offered Hunter, with Sheridan to be in the field, but Hunter "gallantly" declined; he allegedly stated that the greater good was for him to step aside and let Sheridan run his own show. Grant only too quickly said "very well then" and summoned Sheridan from Washington to meet him.[1886] Having met Lincoln and Stanton just before he left, Sheridan was provided with a special train.

The three generals met the next day, August 6th. Though he was to be relieved, Hunter had not hesitated to order the first phase of Grant's written instructions—a concentration of all of his forces at Halltown, southwest of Harper's Ferry. As a result, Monocacy Station was virtually deserted, save Grant, Sheridan, Hunter, and their staffs. Grant, with a few words, handed Sheridan his letter of instructions. It was, in fact, still addressed to Hunter.

By Presidential order, Sheridan was officially made commander of the Middle Military Division on August 7th. The troops in his command, which came to be called the Army of the Shenandoah, would consist of Wright's 6th Corps, Emory's 19th Corps detachment (only two of its divisions, under Dwight and Grover had come north), the Army of West Virginia, under Crook, and a cavalry corps, eventually organized into three divisions, Merritt's, Averell's, and Wilson's, under the overall command of Alfred Torbert. Torbert, Merritt, and Wilson were sent by Grant from the Army of the Potomac, and Averell was transferred from Crook.

Looking back at these events, after the President's prompting, it can be said that this was the point in time when Grant gained full control of the war as general-in-chief.

The Army of the Shenandoah

Sheridan was detached from the Army of the Potomac, where he had commanded the cavalry corps. Almost his whole experience in the war had been with the cavalry, having been promoted to the command of the 2nd Michigan on May 25th, 1862.[1887]

In earlier discussions with Halleck, prior to his appointment to head the

---

1885. Grant, vol. 2, pp. 319–320; Nicolay and Hay, vol. 9, pp. 181–182. The idea that Hunter was gallant in stepping aside is put forward by Nicolay and Hay, and also in Sheridan's *Memoirs*, vol. 1, pp. 465–466.
1886. Sheridan, vol. 1, pp. 464–466, 472–474; O.R. Vol. 37/II, p. 572, 582–583.; O.R. Vol. 43/I, pp. 110–111.
1887. Sheridan, vol. 1, p. 141.

whole Army of the Shenandoah, then assuming he would serve under Hunter, Sheridan had expressed his preference for the cavalry alone. He would not need the 6th Corps. His reasoning was not his inherent love of the cavalry, but his opinion that in the open country of the Maryland and northern Virginia area, with its fine macadamized roads, the cavalry would be most effective. Fortunately, he was given control of the infantry as well, and events would prove that he would need it.

Grover's division, the 2nd, had not yet joined Emory's 1st Division of the 19th Corps, which was now in the vicinity southwest of Harper's Ferry, at Charlestown. Grover had been stationed at Washington. On the 12th he was ordered to join Sheridan.[1888] On August 14th, Augur, in command at Washington, was notified that Batteries K & L, having been consolidated at Camp Barry, and wondering what would become of them, were to form a reserve battery for the cavalry of General Sheridan's command, and were to temporarily join Grover's division, "and proceed with it." This was exciting news; official notification that their place in the scheme of things for the rest of the war was to be with the cavalry. It was the first time ever that Battery L had specifically been assigned to support cavalry.

Though Sheridan had not failed to aggressively begin offensive operations, his full complement was not complete and in close presence until the 19th of August. The march of the column of Grover's Division with Batteries K & L arrived at Berryville on the night of the 16th, and on the 18th, they resumed the march toward Harper's Ferry. On the 22nd, they took up position at Halltown, four miles outside of Harper's Ferry, where the two 19th Corps divisions were united under Emory. Here, Batteries K & L were assigned to the command of Brig. Gen. Alfred Torbert's 1st Cavalry Division, under Brig. Gen. Wesley Merritt. It would be the last of Battery L's association with the 19th Army Corps.[1889]

Merritt's Division had been ordered detached from the Army of the Potomac to the Shenandoah Valley on July 30th and had only reached the vicinity of Harper's Ferry on August 9th. The second of the two cavalry divisions promised by Grant, Wilson's, did not leave until August 4th and arrived on the 19th.

Sheridan would now have a much larger force than that of Hunter and Wright when they made their previously aborted attempts to deal with Early. Sheridan mentions 26,000; Grant mentions 30,000, but of that total, "8,000" were cavalry. However, these declarations are misleading. Both Grant and Sheridan were only thinking of the new detachments from the Army of the Potomac which would follow Sheridan into the Valley. There already was Crook's Department of West Virginia, with 12,436 infantry and Averell's 6,472 cavalry, which are listed in figure 2. There were thousands of others in his new Middle Military Division, but as Sheridan notes: "Baltimore, Washington, Harper's Ferry, Hagerstown, Frederick,

---

1888. O.R. Vol. 43/I, pp. 40, 79, 724, 727, 760–761, 776, 793; Pellet, p. 249.
1889. O.R. Vol. 43/I, pp. 421, 516, 987.

Cumberland, and a score of other points; besides the strong detachments that it took to keep the Baltimore and Ohio Railroad open through the mountains of West Virginia, and escorts for my trains, absorbed so many men that the column which could be made available for field operations was small when compared with the showing on paper."

Abstract from return of the Middle Military Division, Maj. Gen. Philip H. Sheridan, U. S. Army, commanding, for the month of August, 1864.

Command.	Present for duty.		Aggregate present.	Aggregate present and absent.	Pieces of artillery.		Headquarters.
	Officers.	Men.			Heavy.	Field.	
General headquarters	24	120	216	389			In the field.
Department of Washington (Augur):							Washington, D. C.
Staff and infantry	483	18,597	23,076	26,572			
Cavalry	120	3,402	5,752	7,180			
Artillery	218	5,895	7,753	9,854	736	279	
Detachment of Signal Corps	7	68	75	81			
Total	828	27,962	36,656	43,687	736	279	
Department of the Susquehanna (Couch):							Chambersburg, Pa.
Staff and infantry	138	1,872	2,228	3,670			
Cavalry	13	401	427	464			
Artillery	5	181	194	296		12	
Detachment of Signal Corps	2	56	59	66			
Total	158	2,510	2,908	4,496		12	
Middle Department (Wallace):							Baltimore, Md.
Staff and infantry	260	5,067	5,963	8,362			
Cavalry	19	297	347	660			
Artillery	8	219	294	329		6	
Total	287	5,583	6,604	9,351		6	
Department of West Virginia (Crook):							In the field.
Staff and infantry	538	11,898	14,032	23,443			
Cavalry	241	6,231	8,457	14,722			
Artillery	83	2,877	3,521	4,478			
Total	862	21,006	26,010	42,643			
Sixth Army Corps (Wright):							In the field.
Staff and infantry	635	11,333	15,717	29,599			
Artillery	24	623	697	812		24	
Total	659	11,956	16,414	30,411		24	
Detachment Nineteenth Army Corps (Emory):							In the field.
Staff and infantry	657	12,068	14,187	21,081			
Artillery	15	436	458	559		20	
Total	672	12,504	14,645	21,640		20	
Cavalry forces (Torbert):							In the field.
Cavalry and staff	371	7,891	10,347	20,028		32	
Artillery	22	611	701	979		24	
Total	393	8,502	11,048	21,007		56	
Grand total	3,883	90,143	114,501	173,624	736	397	

FIGURE 2

This reminds us of the price to be paid to hold territory. There is no question that holding this particular home ground was a sound and necessary strategy, but think back to the wisdom of Grant wanting Banks to pull out of Texas and most of Louisiana. The war could never be won by trying to occupy those vast stretches beyond the Mississippi.

With Crook and Averell added in, Sheridan had more like 38,500 infantry and 15,000 cavalry. The artillery attached to the cavalry would raise the total force available for use in the field to 57,000; out of a total of 90,000 in the department listed as "present for duty."[1890]

Imagine having 18,500 horses to feed (15,000 cavalry and 3,500 artillery). An absolutely stupendous number to have to supply with grain and forage. The 1862 caution of Lincoln to Banks about the "thousand wagons to feed the animals that draw them…" was still true, but here in the Shenandoah, supply lines were shorter by far than in Louisiana, and the expense of all of the "impedimenta" for such a magnificent cavalry force seems to have never entered into anyone's calculation. Economy had gone out the window. The national purpose was now to win at any cost. We remember the enormous expense of the $400 reenlistment bonuses offered to thousands of veterans this past month. But, it had successfully retained the first volunteers, and what was money when the very substance of the Nation was at stake?

The July 23rd issue of *Harper's Weekly*[1891] ends a long discussion of the military situation with:

> The duration of the war proves quite as much the national purpose as the rebel pluck. If it would have been foolish to relinquish our cause before we had proved our quality, it would be the height of folly to do so when that quality has been established. If it were wrong to cry for quarter before we had taken Paducah, and were not sure of St. Louis, it can hardly be right when we have one hand on Atlanta and the other on Richmond.

The Union was determined to win, expense be damned, because it could now see the light at the end of the tunnel.

The same issue of Harper's also discloses the June 19th sinking, after engaging with the USS *Kearsarge*, of Raphael Semmes' *Alabama*, off the coast of Cherbourg, France. From Gideon Welles: "It does… me good to dwell upon the subject and the discomfiture of the British and Rebels."

Early was also reinforced, in a most peculiar way. On August 6th, Lt. Gen. Richard H. Anderson, commanding the 1st Army Corps, and his staff, was detached

---

1890. Figure 2, O.R. Vol. 43/I, p. 974; Sheridan, vol. 1, p. 475; Grant, vol. 2, p. 321.
1891. Page 467; Welles, vol. 2, pp. 70–71.

from the Army of Northern Virginia, on orders from Gen. Robert E. Lee.[1892] He was given Kershaw's Division, Fitzhugh Lee's Cavalry Division, Cutshaw's Artillery Battalion, who were ordered to *cooperate* with Early. They left Richmond on August 7th, and arrived at Culpeper on the 12th. In the meantime, Lee had decided to send even more troops to Early. On the 11th, Lee promoted Major-General Wade Hampton to the command of the cavalry of the Army of Northern Virginia, and ordered him to report to Anderson. Advised of Lee's movements of reinforcements, Grant played the diversionary raid card once again, and it was once again at Deep Bottom, figure 3, on the James River. Deep Bottom was fearfully close to Richmond, only some twenty miles, and bound to get Lee's attention.[1893]

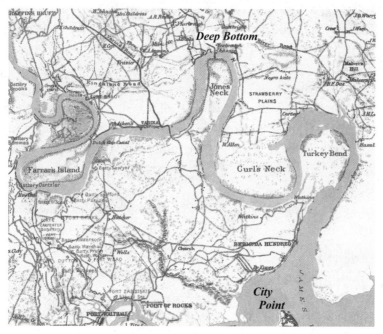

FIGURE 3

On August 12th, Grant ordered Gen. W. S. Hancock, commander of the 2nd Corps of the Army of the Potomac, to prepare, in the utmost secrecy, for a move that would appear as the transfer of his troops to Washington. On the night of the 13th, the 2nd Corps, along with 9,000 men of the 10th Corps, and Gregg's Cavalry, were embarked on steamers and landed on the north side of the river, at Deep Bottom.[1894] Hancock's instructions were to threaten, but not to bring on a battle. In addition, a coordinating attack on the Weldon Railroad, near Petersburg, was made on the 17th by Warren's 5th Corps. After six days, and some sharp fighting, it looked

---

1892. O.R. Vol. 42/I, p. 873 O.R. Vol. 42/III, pp. 1151; O.R. Vol. 42/II, pp. 116, 1170–1173, 1214–1215, 1219.
1893. Figure 3, portion of Atlas, plate 77, map 3.
1894. O.R. Vol. 42/II, pp. 131–132, 135–137, 140–141, 148, 153, 160, 162, 167, 172–173, 210–211; Grant, vol. 2, pp. 321–322.

like Hancock's advance had run up against lines of the enemy that were, even if successfully attacked, deemed difficult to hold, and of no decisive advantage.[1895] News of Warren's success allowed Hancock to be recalled. Hancock's casualties were 95 killed, 553 wounded, and 267 missing, a total of 915. This time, the effect of a Deep Bottom raid was nearly instantaneous. To Hampton from Lee, dated August 14th: "Halt your command and return toward Richmond. Gregg's division is crossing at Deep Bottom…"[1896]

The Deep Bottom raid brings out another point. For a mere raid, we have 915 casualties. This is more than half of the Union casualties taken at Pleasant Hill. The scale of the fighting in the east had always been large, but the concentration ordered by Grant, and his aggressiveness, had pushed up the numbers of casualties for both sides. Unpleasant for the North, the casualties were disastrous for the South. Now Grant had succeeded in concentrating the forces of the Union, and Union victories in faraway places like Vicksburg and Port Hudson had rendered the remaining Confederate forces there ineffective, or of little consequence. Their slave society had been broken up, and, what did it matter now how much war materiel could be smuggled into Texas, if it couldn't cross the Mississippi?

Many things have been written about Grant, and abundant comparisons by contemporary scholars always seem to have Grant standing in Lee's shadow. A quote from Grant during Deep Bottom is put forth[1897] as an example of Grant's clear thinking, and unyielding strategy. There was an opportunity in the Valley, not a problem. Only great generals can analyze certain threats as opportunities. Patton did, after Hitler launched his raid through the Ardennes, known as "The Battle of the Bulge" in World War II.

CITY POINT, VA., *August 19, 1864 - 8 p.m.*
(Received 2.50 p.m. 20th)

MAJ. GEN. H. W. HALLECK:

Fitz Lee's cavalry and Kershaw's division, of Longstreet's corps, have gone from here to the Valley. No other troops have gone, and with the present distribution of troops here the enemy is much more likely to withdraw from the Valley than to send more there. The enemy's loss here this week in killed, wounded and captured cannot fall much short of 4,000, if does not exceed this number. They are now so extended that that they are forced to keep every man on the watch, and from accounts of prisoners are running their men to death shifting them from one place to another. Sheridan has a force about equal to the enemy, and if the latter advances will have him at an advantage.

U. S. GRANT,
Lieutenant-General.

1895. O.R. Vol. 42/II, pp. 226, 250, 301, 326–327; O.R. Vol. 42/I, pp. 216–221; CWSAC VA071.
1896. O.R. Vol. 42/II, p. 1177.
1897. O.R. Vol. 42/II, p. 292.

First Moves

Early, concerned that McCausland would not be able to withdraw from the Chambersburg raid unscathed, and to keep Hunter guessing, moved out on the 4th of August from Bunker Hill, figure 4,[1898] where he had been encamped since the 1st of the month. He sent Breckinridge across the time-worn fords of the Potomac at Shepherdstown, and occupied Sharpsburg, just as Lee had done in 1862. To Williamsport, through which Lee had retreated after Gettysburg, Early sent Rodes' and Ramseur's

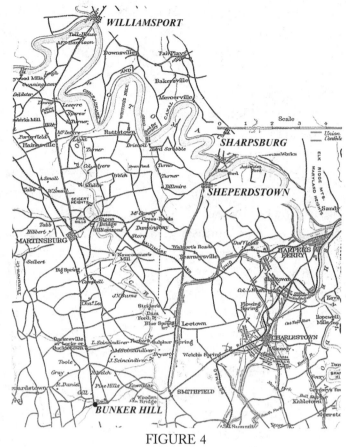

FIGURE 4

divisions. Vaughn's cavalry went on as far as Hagerstown, for the second time, having entered it on July 29th.

These moves did nothing to protect Johnson's and McCausland's brigades from Averell's attack, which routed them, and hearing of the news that Torbert's cavalry had entered the Valley, Early retreated back to Bunker Hill on August 7th.

As ordered by Grant, Hunter had begun the concentration of his forces at the secure defensive position at Halltown before he was replaced. They would be ready for anything Sheridan planned.

Taking only three days to study the situation, Sheridan moved out from Halltown on the 10th of August; even before all of his force had gathered. He subsequently found that he could not safely hold any ground, and in little more than a week was back where he started. Sheridan may not then have understood that he had, in fact, gained something more valuable. His careful initial moves drew Early to the fatally flawed conclusion that Sheridan was merely another one of the timid generals from the Army of the Potomac.[1899]

Sheridan's initial moves are briefly described here to introduce the reader to

---

1898. Figure 4, portion of Atlas, plate 83, map 1, altered; Sheridan's *Memoirs*, vol. 1, pp. 476–478.
1899. Early, *Sketch*, p. 414.

the Shenandoah Valley. Typical of the cavalry, and Battery L was now a part of the cavalry, they were far ranging; and typical of Sheridan, they were ceaseless.

Sheridan sent his 1st Cavalry Division, Merritt's, under the overall command of Torbert, some twenty-five miles south to White Post, southeast of Winchester; the 1st Division's Reserve Brigade, Lowell's, went to Summit, and the infantry, Wright, Emory, and Crook, were placed along a line from Clifton to Berryville,[1900] figure 5, shown by black squares. Informed of Sheridan's moves Early retired to Winchester. Though this was driving the enemy south, per Grant's instructions, Sheridan would have preferred to bring Early to battle quickly—at, or north of, Winchester.

On the 11th, Merritt's cavalry discovered that Early was retreating up (south) the Valley Pike, toward Kernstown. Torbert then moved toward Newtown, to strike Early's flank and harass him. Merritt met Gordon's division of Early's infantry, which held the ground east of Newtown until nightfall. Lowell's brigade, of Merritt's division, followed through Winchester on the Valley Pike, while Crook moved toward Nineveh south of White Post, and the rest of the infantry remained within supporting distance of Crook.[1901]

FIGURE 5

The next morning, Early retired further south from Newtown, through Middletown, to Hupp's Hill, and seeing Sheridan's forces still advancing in much heavier concentration than he had yet encountered, he decided to withdraw to Fisher's Hill, two miles south of Strasburg. Early was now made aware that Anderson had been

---

1900. Grant vol. 2, p. 582; figure 5, Irwin, *History*, facing page 368, altered.
1901. Sheridan, vol. 2, pp. 479–480; Early, *Sketch*, p. 406, Nicolay and Hay, vol. 9, p. 293; figure 5, Irwin, facing p. 368, portion altered.

sent to reinforce him, and with Anderson having arrived at Culpeper on the 12th, Early requested him to move to Front Royal, just east of Manassas Gap, to cover the approaches, and prevent Sheridan from advancing from the east, potentially getting behind him through the Luray Valley.

At Fisher's Hill, Early took up a defensive position with his right resting on the North Fork of the Shenandoah River, and his line extending to Little North Mountain ("Mountains" in figure 5).

It was here that McCausland and Johnson finally joined him with the remnants of their brigades, having been routed, as previously noted, by Averell on the 7th. Escaping from Hancock, Maryland, they were pursued all the way to Moorfield, West Virginia. They then moved on to Mount Airy, west of Middletown, and finally reported to Early at Fisher's Hill. They had lost all of their artillery, a setback which Early later wrote had materially weakened his cavalry[1902] for the rest of the campaign. This was a significant accomplishment for Averell, though he and Sheridan would soon clash and Averell's career would come to an unjustified end.

While at Fisher's hill, Early set up a signal and observation station on Signal Knob, on Three Top Mountain, where the Massanutten range ends. It overlooked the Valley for miles. Early would use it to his advantage in the future.

On August 14th, Sheridan received, through Halleck, a message from Grant, considered of such importance that it was delivered by a full colonel, who was escorted by a regiment of cavalry. It warned of Anderson's corps having been sent by Lee, but mistakenly cited two infantry divisions, instead of one, which was Kershaw's. Grant did not mention Fitzhugh Lee's Cavalry, or Cutshaw's artillery, which were evidently mistaken for the additional infantry division mentioned. Grant had decided that this increase in Early's force would be "too much for General Sheridan to attack."[1903] It now became Sheridan's time to be concerned. He might become trapped and overwhelmed by a superior force. Wilson's cavalry, and Grover's division of the 19th Corps (and Battery K–L) had not yet joined him, and he had had to leave numbers of troops to garrison points taken in his advance up the Valley, including Winchester. The mistake in the message was corrected two days later, stating that the additional division was still on the Petersburg front. Nevertheless, Grant reiterated: "I would not advise an attack on Early in an entrenched position…and if he attempts to move north follow him."

Deciding that there was no defensible ground in the Valley except at Halltown, Sheridan began a withdrawal, which would also allow time for the remainder of his army to join him. On the way north, he had been instructed by Grant to "destroy and carry off the crops, animals, negroes, and all men under fifty years of age capable of bearing arms. In this way you will get many of Mosby's men.

1902. Gilmor, pp. 225–226; Early, *Sketch*, pp. 405, 407.
1903. Nicolay and Hay, vol. 9, p. 293; Sheridan, vol. 2, pp. 482–483, 489; O.R. Vol. 43/I, pp. 792, 811.

All male citizens under fifty can fairly be held as prisoners of war, and not as citizen prisoners. If not already soldiers, they will be made so the moment the rebel army gets hold of them." The Confederate conscription age at this time had been extended to all males from the age of eighteen to fifty-five.[1904]

As to Mosby, he had crossed into the Valley on the 8th of August, and on the 13th had attacked Sheridan's supply train near Berryville, and either captured or destroyed 75 loaded wagons, took 600 horses and mules, 200 cattle, and 200 prisoners.[1905] Mosby was a Partisan Ranger, authorized by the Confederate Partisan Ranger Law, which was passed by the Confederate Congress on April 21st, 1862.[1906] Earlier in this chapter the participation of Gilmor's 2nd Maryland Cavalry in McCausland's raid on Chambersburg was described. They were once Partisan Rangers, and still styled themselves that way, but the term now had little meaning, it was a leftover from the past. The Partisan Ranger Law was repealed on February 17th, 1864. They were now officially the 2nd Maryland Cavalry, a part of the Provisional Army of the Confederacy. However, Mosby remained the lone exception.

The Confederate Partisan Rangers

The Partisan Ranger Law specified that the President could commission any person he deemed proper to organize "bands" of partisan rangers. They were to have the same pay, rations, and quarters as other soldiers, and be subject to the same regulations. Most significantly, they were authorized to be paid in full value for "any arms or munitions of war captured from the enemy…" Plainly stated, they were official privateers. If pecuniary gain was not enough of an attraction, initial recruitment practices under the law made it even more attractive. A conscript could opt out and join the Rangers at any time before he was mustered into the Provisional Army. Other features were that the volunteers in the Rangers were paid by their state and any assignment outside of their state was at their state's option. Also, in many of these bands, the men could elect any of their officers below the rank of captain.[1907]

Confederate Partisan Rangers have been mentioned earlier, particularly those serving in the campaigns in the Gulf. As we earlier saw, General Lovell, after the defense of New Orleans had fallen apart, wrote to General Beauregard at Corinth that he would try to organize some Partisan Rangers, apparently understood to be

---

1904. Pollard, p. 331.
1905. O.R. Vol. 43/I, p. 633.
1906. Lester and Bromwell, *A Digest of the Military and Naval Laws of the Confederate States*, pp. 104–105. Scott, Maj. John, Preface pp, vii–xi, 271–272, 274, 276–277; O.R. Vol. 19/II, p. 682.; Munson, J. W., p. 25.
1907. O.R. Vols. 29/I, p. 917; 25/II, pp. 856–857.

easier to enlist than ordinary soldiers.[1908] Governor Moore was so concerned for his state that he did not wait for Lovell, and he had authorized the raising of a company in Terre Bonne Parish. This was in May of 1862, so soon after the passage of the law that there was no experience with how it would work. In June of 1862, the commander of the Department of the Gulf, Benjamin Butler, on hearing the news, was not fooled. He described the Partisan Ranger Law as the inauguration of guerilla warfare, and had noted that Union or peace-leaning Louisiana leaders from the Baton Rouge area that he had talked with deprecated the idea.

Elsewhere, in May of 1862, since troops could not be sent to reinforce the Confederate Department of Southwestern Virginia, even Robert E. Lee recommended that General Loring, commanding there, raise some Partisan Rangers, as "the most speedy way of increasing your present force…"[1909] Initially, it seemed that the law was a boon.

The idea that a conscript soldier could opt for the Rangers was soon quashed, and anyone of conscript age who had been enrolled as a Partisan Ranger after July 31st, 1862, was declared a conscript, and any connection with the Partisan Rangers was severed. Nevertheless, the Partisan Rangers continued to be enrolled, but only those who were above the conscript age, which at that time was 35.[1910]

Never having more than a few hundred men, mostly mounted, and either wearing no uniforms (sometimes for the lack of the Confederate government's ability to supply them)[1911] or "something gray" they roamed freely, detached from any formal command, and usually attacked by stealth. Only a few months had elapsed before they began to get a bad reputation. The commander of the Confederate Missouri State Guard wrote to Jefferson Davis at the end of June 1862, that "…those that I have seen most anxious to join have been induced to believe that they are to be a band of licensed robbers, and are not men to care whether it be friend or foe… We (*have*) lost many friends and irritated many lukewarm Union men in Missouri, and I have seen it already commenced in Tennessee and Mississippi…"[1912]

At the end of September 1862, General Curtis, commanding the Union Department of the Missouri, described them as bands of men in the garb of private citizens sneaking through the brush, intent on stealing, robbing, and murdering. They deserved no quarter, and no terms of civilized warfare. He ordered that they be pursued and destroyed. Unfortunately, this was easier said than done.

By the end of 1862, there were already Confederate calls for their outright abolition on the grounds that: "Acting alone, they accomplish nothing, and when

---

1908. O.R. Vol. 15, pp. 502–503, 735, 741
1909. O.R. Vol. 12/III, p. 899.
1910. ORN ser. 1, vol. 23, p. 708; O.R. Vol. 9, p. 733.
1911. O.R. Vol. 19, p. 682.
1912. O.R. Vol. 52/II, pp. 325–326.

serving with other troops, hang upon the rear to gather up property, and instead of turning it in to proper departments, spirit it away for speculation." The army got no reward for captured property and to have to witness that a few were allowed this license, injured morale.

On December 23rd 1862, Col. J. D. Imboden, commanding the First Virginia Partisan Rangers was *asked* by the Confederate secretary of war to reorganize his Partisan Rangers out of existence, but, the adjutant-general noted, it would require the "consent of the men now enrolled."[1913] In January his men voted in the affirmative.

At this time, it seems that Robert E. Lee's motive in reorganizing Imboden into the Provisional Army was as much in increasing his force to a brigade—the Partisan Rangers being limited in size to a regiment—as it was in eliminating the Partisan Rangers.[1914] Lee wanted Gen. W. E. Jones, in temporary command of the Valley District (in Stonewall Jackson's absence) reinforced. Lee wanted to keep the Yankees out of the Valley for two reasons: (1) It was a fruitful country filled with supplies, and (2) It was a tempting highway for him to use in a flanking march on Washington, or the invasion of Maryland and Pennsylvania. Remember that this was January of 1863, and Lee was thinking of staging a repeat of Antietam. Gettysburg, of course, took place in early July.[1915]

The Valley was not a strategic objective or even a useful highway for the Union army, because it led away from Richmond. Thus, the Yankees had previously almost conceded the Valley to the Confederacy. In 1864, Grant recognized this, but also recognized the solution—make the Valley untenable. But we digress. The fate of the Partisan Rangers at this time is still hanging in the balance. By the end of February 1863, Imboden had reorganized, and called himself the Northern Virginia Brigade, with a strength of 1,592. Two more regiments were yet to be enlisted.[1916] Clever hypocrisy was used in authorizing their recruitment. Since they were no longer Partisan Rangers, they could enlist persons of conscript age. A rich new source for Imboden's recruiters was also opened up, as many men were enlisted from behind the enemy's lines, or in other areas where the Confederate conscript law could not be enforced.

In March of 1863, Mosby was ordered to convert his Rangers in similar fashion as had Imboden.[1917] He was specifically warned to "ignore the term Partisan Ranger. It is in bad repute." Instead, Gen. Robert E. Lee had suggested "Mosby's Regulars." This was hypocrisy in the extreme, Mosby was to simply go on as before under a new name, and now could recruit men under 35.

1913. O.R. Vols. 21, pp. 1076, 1102; 31/III, p. 849.
1914. O.R. Vol. 21, pp. 1080, 1086, 1109.
1915. Merritt, Wesley, *Battles and Leaders*, vol. 4, p. 500.
1916. O.R. Vol. 25/II, pp. 657, 611.
1917. O.R. Vol. 25/II, pp. 856–858.

In December of 1863, General Ransom, in command of the Confederate District of Southwestern Virginia and East Tennessee, made a recommendation to the secretary of war to abolish the Partisan Rangers.[1918] A few weeks later, the commanding officer of the Valley District, General Rosser, reflected the same thinking in a letter to Lee. The disgust that these high officers expressed proved that the irregular bands, Mosby's included, since "reformed" and by whatever name, had continued in their old habits, which were detrimental to the Confederate army.

Though the Union army had come to revile Mosby, justifiably as his victim, listen to the commentary of a Confederate officer, Rosser:[1919]

> [A] nuisance and an evil to the service. Without discipline, order, or organization, they roam...the country, a band of thieves...They are a terror to the citizens and an injury to the cause. They never fight; can't be made to fight. Their leaders are generally brave, but few of the men are good soldiers, and have engaged in this business for the sake of gain. The effect upon the service is bad...It is bad because:
>
> First. It keeps men out of service whose bayonet or saber should be counted on the field...
>
> Second. They cause great dissatisfaction in the ranks from the fact that these irregular troops are allowed so much latitude, so many privileges. They sleep in houses and turn out in the cold only when it is announced by their chief that they are to go on a plundering expedition.
>
> Third. It renders other troops dissatisfied; hence encourages desertion.

J. E. B. Stuart endorsed Rosser's letter to Lee, noting that Mosby's command was the only efficient one he knew of, though, he had to admit, such organizations, were, as a rule, detrimental to the army at large. Lee forwarded Rosser's letter to the War Department, recommending, "that the law authorizing these partisan groups be abolished. The evils resulting from their organization more than counterbalance the good they accomplish." This, despite the fact that Lee had, just a few weeks before, forwarded reports of Mosby's operations since the first of the year, lauding Mosby's "zeal," and had recommended his promotion to lieutenant-colonel!

On February 17th 1864, the law was repealed, and notice of the fact was sent to the attention of other Confederate commands.[1920] But wait! Seddon, the secretary of war, was given authority to name exceptions to the law. On April 1st, 1864, Lee recommended to the secretary of war that Mosby's command be excepted. It was approved. As a result, our account of Sheridan and Battery K–L in the Shenandoah reports the occasional raids and depredations of the only official Partisan Rangers

---

1918. O.R. Vol. 31/III, p. 849.
1919. O.R. Vol. 33, pp. 1081, 1082.
1920. O.R. Vols. 43/I, p. 811; 33, p. 1083; 32/III, p. 668; 51/II, p. 1060, 1061; O.R. series 4, vol. 3, p. 194.

left in the Confederacy—Mosby's.[1921]

Sheridan Retreats North

At 11:00 on the night of August 15th, Emory set off moving to Winchester. The march was begun at night to try to conceal the withdrawal from Early, who could see nearly every movement from his observation station on Massanutten Mountain. The attempt at secrecy apparently left even Emory in the dark. From his report from Winchester, which he reached at 5:00 a.m. on the 16th, he is disturbed, declaring the place "entirely indefensible." He suggests that the crossing at the Opequan, a creek northeast of Winchester, would be preferable. Not-to-worry, he received orders that night to be prepared to move at 4:00 a.m. on the 17th, though the orders did not say where.[1922]

On the 15th, Wright and Crook were ordered back from their occupation of the heights above Strasburg to the north side of Cedar Creek, and on the 16th, they were ordered to march for Clifton via Winchester. Crook, moving first, was to begin at 8:00 p.m. To avoid any signs that a move was to be made, the troops were cautioned not to strike their tents until after dark, or by "unusual fires after dark."

All of the caution was probably wasted, because it was reported that Mosby, clothed in a blue uniform, with 160 or more of his band, was encountered near Middletown, and that one of his men had penetrated into the camp of the 3rd Brigade of the 1st Division of the 6th Corps. The scuttlebutt regarding the night's march was already being circulated among the men even before the orders had reached brigade headquarters, and it was calculated to be almost certain that Mosby had picked up the information.

At about 2:00 p.m. on the 16th, while Sheridan was moving his headquarters to Winchester, he was informed that Devin's brigade of Wesley Merritt's 1st Cavalry Division had been attacked at Guard Hill near the crossing of the North Branch of the Shenandoah River, on the Front Royal road. It was by General R. H. Anderson, whose troops were the reinforcements which had been sent to Early by Lee.[1923] The engagement was later variously called the Battle of Cedarville, Guard Hill, or Front Royal; not to be confused with a battle fought there between Nathaniel Banks and Stonewall Jackson, on May 23rd, 1862.

Two battles in the same spot were to become common in the Valley, which only underscores how much fighting the Shenandoah had seen up to this time. Most, or all of the earlier engagements had resulted in Confederate victories. In the earlier battle, Banks' troops were driven north to Winchester, setting the stage

---

1921. Mosby, p. 283.
1922. O.R. Vol. 43/I, pp. 814–815.
1923. Sheridan, vol. 1, pp. 488–489; Merritt, p. 502; O.R. Vol. 12/II, pp. 560, 562; CWSAC VA103–Front Royal; CWSAC VA114–Guard Hill.

for the First Battle of Winchester on May 25th, 1862, in which Banks was soundly defeated, and driven north across the Potomac. The record of the Union army here was such that the Valley had come to be called the "Valley of Humiliation."[1924]

In this latest battle, Devin's brigade of cavalry repulsed Fitzhugh Lee's, but Kershaw's infantry was seen moving to cross the river. Custer's brigade, one regiment dismounted and one mounted, were then brought up and posted near the river bank. The combined close range repeater fire—the cavalry carried repeating carbines—of the two brigades cut down the Confederates attempting to wade the river. Some 300 Confederate prisoners were taken. No accurate report of Confederate casualties has been found, though Merritt claimed 500 or 600, depending on which of his two accounts you wish to believe.[1925] Sixty of Merritt's troops were casualties.

A Confederate account of the battle notes that the enemy retreated on the morning of the 17th, burning barns and hay ricks as they went.[1926] If Grant's actions near Petersburg worked out, Lee would call Anderson back. Then would be the time to attack Early.

Emory had left Winchester at daylight on the morning of the 17th. Crook and Wright passed through later the same morning, after arriving from Cedar Creek. Both continued toward Clifton, though Wright left Penrose's 1st Brigade with Torbert. Close on their heels, Wilson's 3rd Division arrived, having passed through Snicker's Gap, and turning south from Berryville, had passed through Millwood. They were followed closely by Early since passing Kernstown.[1927] Merritt, leaving his 3rd Cavalry Brigade at Winchester with Torbert, was ordered back out to White Post.

Observing all of Sheridan's movements from the signal station atop Three Top Mountain, Early quickly moved to attack Sheridan at Winchester. He signaled Anderson to cross the Shenandoah at Front Royal and move towards Winchester.

Wilson, posted so as to cover all of the roads into Winchester from the south, particularly the Millwood, Front Royal, and Valley Pikes, was engaged by Early's advanced skirmishers at 4:00 p.m. and the full force of Wharton, Ramseur, and Gordon fell upon them at 6:00. At nightfall, Wilson and Lowell retired to north of the Opequan, near Summit Point, and Early, united with Anderson, arrived at Winchester on the morning of the 18th.

With the exception of Wilson's cavalry, the position of Sheridan's forces now was essentially the same as it had been on August 10th, occupying a line from Summit to Berryville, and White Post (looking back at figure 5).

Sheridan continued to fall back on the 18th, moving the 6th Corps to Flowing

---

1924. Pellet, p. 269.
1925. Merritt, p. 502–503; O.R. 43/I, pp. 19, 439.
1926. O.R. Vol. 43/I, p. 1024; Sheridan, vol. 1, pp. 483–484.
1927. O.R. Vol. 43/I, p. 516; Early, *Sketch*, p. 408; Sheridan, vol. 1, pp. 489–490.

Spring, two-and-a-half miles west of Charlestown, with Emory two-and-a-half miles south of Charlestown. Emory now had Grover, who had made thirty-three miles on the final 13½ hours of his sixty-nine-mile march from Washington, and had arrived at Berryville at midnight.[1928] Merritt fell back to Berryville, and Wilson was stationed at Summit Point (Summit on the map).[1929] Crook was moved from Clifton to a position outside of Charlestown, next to Emory, on August 20th.

On the 20th, outside of Charlestown, Battery K–L reported to General Torbert. Shortly after, they were assigned to Devin's 2nd Brigade of Merritt's 1st Cavalry Division.[1930]

The name Charlestown had a vaguely familiar ring. Yes, it was here in Jefferson County, then in Virginia, now in West Virginia, that John Brown was held, from October 19th, 1859, until he was hung on December 2nd. So long ago as measured by events, if not time.

The line at Charlestown was attacked by Early on the 21st and Sheridan then pulled back to Halltown, calling in Merritt, who had been attacked by Anderson. Sheridan was now back at the same position he was when he took command on August 7th.

Sheridan's retreat back to Halltown was confusing to the public, and was fodder for the enemies of the Lincoln administration, who made the most of the apparent setback. Of course, it was part of the plan worked out that Sheridan was to act on the defensive until Anderson was recalled by Lee. Grant was to see to that by his move at Deep Bottom and another on the Weldon Railroad, one of Lee's two rail lifelines to Petersburg.[1931] Warren's attack on the railroad, known as the Battle of Globe Tavern, made in coordination with the diversionary raid by Hancock at Deep Bottom, was alluded to earlier, in that it caused Lee to almost instantly recall Wade Hampton. Now, with the Weldon railroad in solid Union possession, and it would remain so for the rest of the war—despite a renewed attempt by Lee to recover it on August 24th and 25th—how long would it be before Lee recalled Anderson? The ruminations in a letter to Early from Lee, dated August 26th, indicate *not long*.[1932] It is copied here:

HEADQUARTERS ARMY OF NORTHERN VIRGINIA
August 26, 1864

GENERAL EARLY:

GENERAL: Your letter of the 23d has been received, and I am much pleased at your having forced the enemy back to Harper's Ferry. This will

---

1928. Tiemann, p. 92.
1929. O.R. Vol. 43/I, p. 44; Sheridan, vol. 1, pp. 490–491; Irwin, p. 375. Middleway was called Smithfield by Sheridan; Redpath, pp. 286, 393.
1930. Haskin, p. 213.
1931. Badeau, A., *The Century*, p. 503; Sheridan, vol. 1, p. 492; CWSAC VA072.
1932. O.R. Vol. 43/I, p. 1006.

give protection to the Valley and arrest the travel on the Baltimore and Ohio Railroad. It will, however, have little or no effect upon Grant's operations, or prevent re-enforcements from being sent to him. If Sheridan's force is as large as you suppose, I do not know that you could operate to advantage north of the Potomac. Either Anderson's troops or a portion of yours might, however, be detached to destroy the railroad west of Charlestown, and Fitz Lee might send a portion of his cavalry to cross the Potomac east of the Blue Ridge, as you propose. I cannot detach at present more cavalry from this army; the enemy is too strong in that arm. I am aware that Anderson is the ranking officer, but apprehend no difficulty on that score. I first intended him to threaten the enemy east of the Blue Ridge, so as to retain near Washington a portion of the enemy's forces. He crossed the mountains at your suggestion, and, I think, properly. If his troops are not wanted there he could cross into Loudon or Fauquier and return to Culpeper. It would add force to the movement of cavalry east of the Blue Ridge. I am in great need of his troops, and if they can be spared from the Valley, or cannot operate to advantage there, I will order them back to Richmond. Let me know.

Very Respectfully,

R. E. LEE,
General,

The actual events regarding Anderson's departure would take a strange twist, which will be described later. It is important to note, however, that he left the Valley, taking with him Kershaw's division and Cutshaw's artillery, before the Battle of Winchester, which was fought on September 19th. Thus, when Early really could have effectively used Anderson's troops, they had left—excellent strategy by Grant and Sheridan.

The Public Mind

The retreat of Sheridan to Halltown was mentioned as having caused concern. This should not be over-stated. Good news soon came in from Alabama and from Georgia. From Mobile, the public[1933] was soon treated to the news that Farragut, in a combined operation with an army force provided by Canby, had on August 5th, made one of his classic daring runs, this time past the guns of Forts Morgan and Gaines, into Mobile Bay. First reports of the feat were known in Washington from Confederate newspapers as early as August 10th, but Secretary Welles did not receive Farragut's report, dated August 5th, until the 23rd. He had captured the formidable Confederate ram, the *Tennessee*, and the gunboat *Selma*. Admiral Buchanan, on board the *Tennessee*, was wounded, and was captured, along with

---

1933. *Harper's Weekly*, August 27th, 1864, p. 547, Welles, vol. 2, pp. 101, 115; ORN ser. 1, vol. 21, pp. 405–407, 414–418, 520–521; figure 6, ORN ser. 1, vol. 21, facing p. 600.

20 officers and 170 of his crew. 90 officers and men of the *Selma* were taken. Two other Confederate gunboats, the *Morgan* and *Gaines*, escaped to the shelter of the guns of Fort Morgan, figure 6.

The cost was great in terms of damage to Farragut's ships, but these details would remain to be disclosed later. The monitor USS *Tecumseh*, leading the fleet into the bay, struck a torpedo and sank, carrying almost all of her crew to the bottom. A revised count of the casualties was 52 killed and 170 wounded.

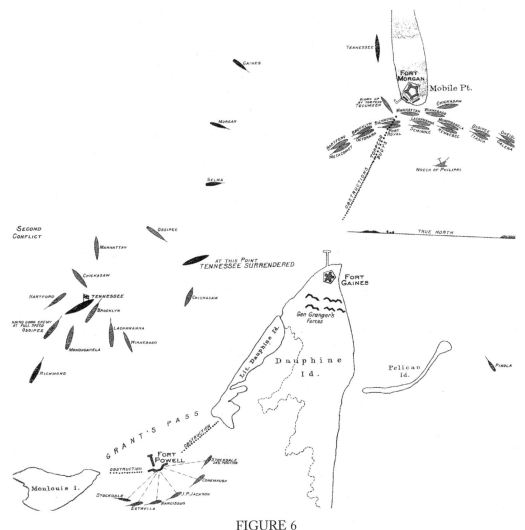

FIGURE 6

During the attack, observing the *Tecumseh* sink, and not understanding the reason for the lead ship, the *Brooklyn*, having slowed, Farragut says: "I determined, at once, as I had originally intended, to take the lead…I steamed through between the buoys where the torpedoes were supposed to have been sunk…but believing that their having been some time in the water, they were probably innocuous, I determined to take the chance of their explosion." Thus, we have the Admiral's modest explanation for what he was famously, and only somewhat erroneously, quoted as ordering: "Damn the torpedoes, full speed ahead!"[1934] According to his son, Loyall, who was aboard the flagship, Farragut had shouted to the *Brooklyn*: "What's the trouble?" and the *Brooklyn* had answered "Torpedoes!" To this Farragut said: "Damn the torpedoes! Four bells! Captain Drayton, go ahead! Jonett, full speed!" And the *Hartford* passed the *Brooklyn*.

The *Tennessee*, almost impervious to Farragut's gunfire, survived the passage of the fleet, and when it was observed to be apparently undamaged in their rear, the fleet turned, with orders to run her down at full speed. The *Monongahela*, freed from the *Kennebec* (we are reminded that Enos/Charles Deal alias Charles Jones, formerly of Battery L was aboard), which had been lashed to her side during the passage of Fort Morgan, struck her first, and though the *Tennessee* may have been injured badly, she remained afloat. Struck again by the *Lackawanna* (the activity shown to the left in figure 6), and taking a broadside of 9-inch solid shot from the *Hartford* at a range of ten feet, she was still not disabled. The *Hartford*, and the three remaining monitors in the fleet again bearing down on her, at 10:00 a.m. she finally surrendered.

Of particular interest to the members of Battery L, was what had become of Henry Closson. Ever since his orders of July 22nd "to take command of his company now awaiting transportation to New York" had been revoked, he had remained in the Department of the Gulf, and had been assigned to the staff of Maj. Gen Gordon Granger, as planning for a raid on Mobile had already begun.[1935]

The troops under Granger consisted of detachments from the 3rd Brigade, 3rd Division of the 19th Army Corps, five regiments of the old 13th Army Corps, two batteries of heavy artillery, two of light artillery, and a battalion of engineers; about 1,500 men. They were to be landed on Dauphin Island, to threaten Fort Gaines, at the harbor entrance, before Farragut was to attempt his run.

They embarked on July 29th from Algiers, arriving at Petit Bois Pass, off the south end of Dauphin Island, on August 2nd, and a portion of the troops began landing that afternoon. Their landing technique was just as primitive as that used at the landings of the 6th and 75th New York regiments at the shallow sandy shore

---

1934. Farragut, Loyall, pp. 416–417.
1935. O.R. Vol. 41/II, pp. 65, 104, 105, 326, 566, 759, 760. As a matter of interest, the remnant of the 19th Army Corps, at Morganza, now commanded by General J.J. Reynolds, and in an apparent clerical error, was listed as the 2nd Division. Thus, there were two second divisions, one commanded by Grover, at Halltown, West Virginia, and the other at Morganza, commanded by Brig. Gen. Elias Dennis. The expedition to cooperate with Farragut at Mobile, had been assigned to Granger-a new man, who had been sent to Canby, at his request, by Halleck. It is consisted of troops from the old 13th Army Corps, which on June 11th, had been temporarily discontinued. See: O.R. Vol 34/IV, pp. 304, 479, 480; McClernand, while in command of the 13th had become ill at Alexandria, after returning from Texas, and was replaced by General Lawler "in the field." McClernand resigned form the army in November, 1864. See: 34/III, pp. 519, 520, 546; Encyclopedia Britannica, Vol. 17, p. 202.

of Santa Rosa Island, a lifetime ago. The men jumped overboard and waded, the artillery pieces were plunged over next, then dragged by hand. The horses were made to jump. Only the lifeboats, stowed full with ammunition, were lowered carefully into the water.[1936]

The landings proceeded until dark, when they were halted by a violent thunderstorm, with the later arrivals left to wait aboard ship until the morning. The next day dawned clear and warm, and the expedition began its advance toward Fort Gaines, at the northeast tip of the island. By evening, their pickets encountered those of the enemy.

By the morning of August 4th, the fort was invested, rifle pits having been dug, and the artillery having been hauled into place. The day was spent advancing the picket line and digging new pits—a regular siege. By 8:00 on the morning of the 5th, led by the monitor *Tecumseh*, the line of Farragut's attacking ships could be seen passing near the torpedo buoys opposite Fort Morgan.

During the fleet action in the bay, Fort Powell was shelled by the gunboats *Stockdale*, *Estrella*, *Narcissus*, *J.P. Jackson*, and *Conemaugh*. At about the same time that Admiral Buchanan surrendered the Tennessee, 10:00, Fort Powell was observed to be being evacuated. That night, Granger's troops occupied little Dauphin Island, and on the morning of August 6th, men from the *Estrella* landed at Fort Powell and found it abandoned and blown up, all of its 18 guns left behind.

By August 5th, a landing site had been constructed close by the besiegers before Fort Gaines, and the heavier guns were begun to be landed, though hampered by rough surf, under the direction of Henry Closson.[1937] On the morning of the 6th, the *Chickasaw* moved into position and shelled Fort Gaines, and Granger ordered the siege guns to open on it.[1938] On the morning of the 7th, Colonel Anderson, Fort Gaines' commanding officer, requested terms from Farragut. The fort was occupied by Union troops the next day, after an unconditional surrender, with 46 officers and 818 men taken as prisoners. Granger then planned to immediately move to the attack of Fort Morgan, on the peninsula opposite. He landed there on August 9th and requested reinforcements. A determined Canby ordered out four more regiments the same day. Canby seems to have outdone himself, but the earlier success justified it. On the 10th, he ordered the 17th Ohio Battery and the 6th Michigan Heavy Artillery to report to Brig. Gen. Richard Arnold, the chief of artillery of the Department of the Gulf, who, on August 13th, was ordered to report to Granger, now at Mobile Point.

On August 24th, Closson, his job done, was ordered to return to "his battery wherever it may be."

1936. O.R. Vol. 41/II, pp. 449, 566; Bentley, 77th *Illinois*, pp. 320–322; ORN ser. 1, vol. 21, pp. 504, 520, 524.
1937. O.R. Vol 52/I, p. 582.
1938. ORN ser. 1, vol. 21, pp. 414, 514, 524; O.R. Vol. 41/II, pp. 592–593, 631, 832.

This was the story of a thrilling victory. It was all pure Farragut, and couldn't have happened without him. The Richmond papers soon knew about it, and by the 11th, Benjamin Butler, so nearby at City Point, was thus made aware.[1939] Butler immediately sent off a congratulatory letter, telling Farragut: "It was like you." He went on to reminisce about the events they both had experienced in Louisiana, and wrote, that as he read the news, he had burst out loud, calling: "Three Cheers for Farragut" which caused a bit a stir to his staff, "who thought their general had gone crazy." He went on to say that those cheers, first by him, "are not done ringing yet, but every hilltop is resounding with them as they are caught up from hamlet to hamlet, city to city, of a grateful nation."

Reports from Sherman were soon to be heard, and combined with Farragut's exploit, it is clear that any story of Sheridan's retreat was sandwiched into a narrow context, which had little impact on the public mind. It was only attempted to be magnified by the likes of the peace Democrats, and the *Richmond Examiner*, which was transparently advising the upcoming Democratic Convention in Chicago that the only chance for it was to propose an armistice.[1940] The Confederacy was in trouble and it knew it, though Jefferson Davis remained intransigent.

Berryville

Here, northeast of Winchester, Battery K–L had gone into bivouac on August 20th, 1864, at the encampment of Merritt's 2nd Brigade, Brig. Gen. Thomas C. Devin commanding. They did not rest for a single day. The next day, Sunday, their brigade was ordered to cover the retirement of Lowell's 3rd Brigade, often referred to as the Reserve Brigade, which had been attacked by Anderson that morning on the Winchester Pike, in front of Berryville, and had been ordered to withdraw to Charlestown. They were followed as far as Summit Point,[1941] figure 7.

On August 19th, Early had moved to occupy Bunker Hill, and now on the 21st, thinking that Sheridan had taken a position at Summit Point, moved from Bunker Hill across the Opequan, through Smithfield, aiming to hit Sheridan's rear. This was coordinated with Anderson, who moved out from Winchester toward Berryville. Early quickly learned otherwise. At Cameron's Depot, about three miles west of Charlestown, he ran up against the first two brigades of Wilson's 3rd Division of cavalry, who, after a sharp fight were ordered to retire. Early then ran into Getty's Division of Wright's 6th Corps, posted at Welch's Spring, about two-and-a-half miles west of Charlestown. Heavy skirmishing ensued, Getty with a loss of

---

1939. ORN 21, pp. 526–527.
1940. *Harper's Weekly*, August 27th, 1864, p. 547; Badeau, p. 503.
1941. O.R. Vol. 43/I, pp. 44, 473; Irwin, p. 375; Early, *Sketch*, p. 408; Merritt, p. 505, figure 7, Atlas, portion of plate 69, map 1, altered.

260 killed and wounded.[1942] That night, the infantry retired to Halltown, Sheridan's defensive strong point, which was covered by the heavy guns on Maryland Heights behind Harper's Ferry.

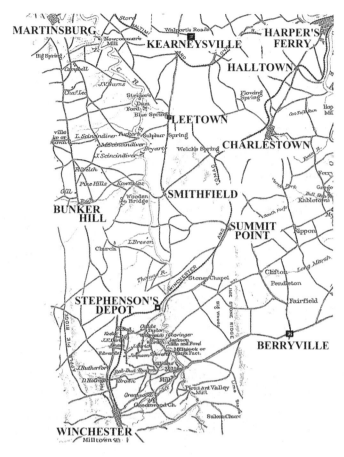

FIGURE 7

On the morning of August 22nd, the cavalry followed through Charlestown toward Halltown. Merritt's division, with Battery K–L, was, however, ordered north, to near Shepherdstown.

Early then pushed up to the position taken by Sheridan at Halltown, and for the next three days probed the defenses, but finding no suitable place to attack, he switched course. He resolved to place Anderson, with Kershaw's division, McCausland's cavalry, and a regiment of Fitzhugh Lee's cavalry, in position before the Halltown defenses, to occupy Sheridan, to mask a move north toward Maryland. On the 25th, Early moved his infantry and artillery through Leetown and Kearneysville to Shepherdstown, while sending the rest of Fitzhugh Lee's cavalry to Williamsport, via Martinsburg.[1943] Early uses the reason he sent Lee's cavalry to

---

1942. O.R. Vol. 43/I, pp. 155, 416; Merritt, p. 504; Sheridan, p. 491.
1943. Early, *Sketch*, p. 409; Sheridan, p. 493; O.R. Vol. 43/I, p. 425; Irwin, p. 375.

Williamsport as "to keep up the fear of an invasion of Maryland and Pennsylvania." This statement would seem to indicate that this was only a diversion, as anyone at this time would recognize that the North would manage to bring to bear enough force to defeat any such a move, just as it had twice before.

From Sheridan's point of view, he had already planned for Early attempting such a move, and had planned to fall on his rear if he did.[1944] We might gain some insight as to why Early began this move, by referring once again to Lee's most recent letter to him:

> I am much pleased at your having forced the enemy back to Harper's Ferry. This will give protection to the Valley and arrest the travel on the Baltimore and Ohio Railroad. It will, however, have little or no effect upon Grant's operations, or prevent reinforcements being sent to him. If Sheridan's force is as large as you suppose, I do not know that you could operate to advantage north of the Potomac. Either Anderson's troops or a portion of yours might, however, be detached to destroy the railroad west of Charlestown, and Fitz Lee might send a portion of his cavalry to cross the Potomac east of the Blue Ridge, as you propose." Fitzhugh Lee would thus be substituted for Anderson, and soon Anderson would be recalled, as Lee discloses that he had originally planned Anderson to be sent east of the Blue Ridge "so as to retain near Washington a portion of the enemy's forces.

Lee's remarks seem to indicate that he thought things were more or less wrapped up in the Valley, with the enemy chased almost out of it, as it had been in 1862, and that it could be retained almost in the status quo, so long as Early remained there as a direct threat to Maryland and Pennsylvania, the operation of the B&O Railroad, the Chesapeake and Ohio Canal, and to Washington. Thus, in this passive assignment, Early could be stripped of valuable troops which could be better used elsewhere. In this, Lee seems to have assumed that the man that was now in control, viz., Grant, was as indecisive or inept as his predecessors in the Army of the Potomac, and that he had assigned an equally passive person in the Valley. Lee seems oblivious to the fact that the war had progressed to a stage where there were now only two main objectives left: his own army at Richmond, and Johnston's in Georgia. He fails, or refuses to recognize, that Grant was now concentrated on these two objectives and was not going to be diverted from them. The Valley would no longer be tolerated as a base of supplies for Lee, or the shortest route for a diversion north of the Potomac.[1945]

Aware that Early had disengaged, Sheridan sent Torbert, with Merritt's and Wilson's cavalry, to Kearneysville with instructions to proceed to Leetown and

---

1944. Sheridan, p. 495.
1945. Sherman, W. T., *The Grand Strategy of the Last Year of the War*, pp. 247, 249; Early, *Sketch*, p. 414.

determine what had become of Fitzhugh Lee. Between Leetown and Kearnesyville, Torbert ran into Breckenridge's infantry, Fitzhugh Lee's cavalry having already passed north. Torbert attacked and was briefly successful at throwing the Confederate force back in confusion, until Early realized that he was dealing only with cavalry, and he brought up the whole of his four divisions, which pushed Torbert rapidly back through Shepherdstown, and across the Potomac.[1946]

Early writes:

> Fitz. Lee reached Williamsport, and had some skirmishing across the river at that place, and then moved to Shepherdstown. On the 26th, I moved to Leetown, on the 27th moved back to Bunker Hill; while Anderson, who had confronted Sheridan during the two days of my absence, with but a division of infantry, and a brigade and a regiment of cavalry, moved to Stephenson's depot.

He also reveals his danger:[1947]

> Had Sheridan, by a prompt movement, thrown his whole force on the line of my communications, I would have been compelled to cut my way through, as there was no escape for me to the right or left, and my force was too weak to cross the Potomac while he was in my rear. I knew my danger, but I could occupy no other position that would have enabled me to accomplish the desired object.
>
> If I had moved up the Valley at all, I could not have stopped short of New Market, [the distance from Kearneysville, WV, to New Market, VA, is more than eighty miles] for between that place and in the country, where I was, there was no forage for my horses; and this would have enabled the enemy to resume the use of the railroad and the canal, and return all the troops from Grant's army to him. Being compelled to occupy the position where I was, and being aware of its danger as well as apprised of the fact that very great odds were opposed to me, my only resource was to use my forces so as to display them at different points with great rapidity, and thereby keep up the impression that they were much larger than they really were. The events of the last month had satisfied me that the commander opposed to me was without enterprise, and possessed an excessive caution which amounted to timidity.

The foregoing hopefully serves to explain to the reader the tiring, and seemingly mindless, moves which had taken place to date. Sheridan's policy of defense only, as ordered by Grant, was working superbly, and the fact that Early withdrew so quickly from the Potomac that Sheridan was unable to attack, only solidified Early's careless contempt for Sheridan's timidity.

1946. Sheridan, vol. 1, p. 494; Early, *Sketch*, pp. 409, 410, 414.
1947. Early, *Sketch*, p. 415.

Smithfield Crossing[1948]

On August 27th, all of Early's infantry was in position in his old camps at Bunker Hill, with his cavalry holding Leetown and Middleway (Smithfield). Anderson was south, at Stephenson's Depot.[1949] Next day, Sunday, the bugles in the three brigades of Merritt's Division that were stationed near Shepherdstown blew reveille at 3:00 a.m., to be ready to go out on a reconnaissance. At daylight, the 1st, 2nd, and Reserve brigades headed south toward Kearneysville. They marched in typical Sheridan fashion, the three brigades abreast; Custer's 1st on the right, Devin's 2nd on the left, and the Reserve Brigade, then commanded by Gibbs,[1950] on the Pike. Outside of Leetown, the advance of the Reserve Brigade, the 2nd US Cavalry, ran into the camp of Harry Gilmor's and portions of Bradley Johnson's Partisan Rangers, on the Smithfield Pike. Supported by the 6th Pennsylvania, they attacked, and pressed the Rangers back to a wood outside of Smithfield, where Early's artillery opened on them. Williston's 2nd US Battery D,[1951] one of the two artillery batteries assigned to Merritt's command at this time—the other being Taylor's Battery K–L—was brought up and placed upon "an eminence" to the left, soon silenced them. Threatened by a move on their left flank by Custer, the entire enemy force then retired down the road and across the turnpike bridge on Opequan Creek. Darkness coming on, the Union cavalry then encamped for the night on the heights on the east side of the creek, within sight of Early's campfires, figure 8.[1952]

At dawn on the morning of August 29th, Custer and his 1st Brigade boldly crossed the creek, and advanced about a mile before running into Early's cavalry, which Custer drove back. But he then ran smack into Early's infantry, Gordon's and Ramseur's, which had already been marching from Bunker Hill. Early had become uneasy that Merritt had possession of the bridge and fords,[1953] and had ordered his troops to the attack. Custer's brigade came swiftly back, some across the covered bridge, and others spurring their horses into making the four-foot jump from the bank into the creek. They then formed on the right of the Reserve Brigade, which was in position to the right of Devin's brigade, (under the temporary command

---

1948. So named in popular references, CWSAC WV015; Smithfield is now known as Middleway; N. Cheney, pp. 214–215; Wm. O. Lee, pp. 98, 99.
1949. Sheridan, vol. 1, pp. 495–496. He refers to Anderson's position as at Brucetown, which is near Stephenson's Depot; O.R. Vol. 43/I, p. 1025.
1950. O.R. Vol. 43/I, pp. 94–95, Gibbs assumed command on August 10th, and Lowell on September 8th.
1951. O.R. Vol. 43/I, pp. 469, 470, 486, 488, 571, 946, 953, 966, 987.
1952. Figure 8, Atlas, portion of plate 82, map 7, altered. Original drawn by Jedediah Hotchkiss, Early's mapmaker.
1953. Gracey, S. L., pp. 292–293. Referring to the map, there are clearly two bridges, and two nearby fords. The upper bridge is assumed to be the covered bridge Custer used as he fell back to the right of the Reserve Brigade. Bowen, J., pp. 220–221; Cheney, p. 215; Haskin, p. 213; Early, *Sketch*, p. 410.

of Col. Louis P. Di Cesnola), which was lined up to face the enemy, dismounted, on the heights just west of Smithfield, as is indicated by the small black positions captioned "Merritt" on the right in figure 8.

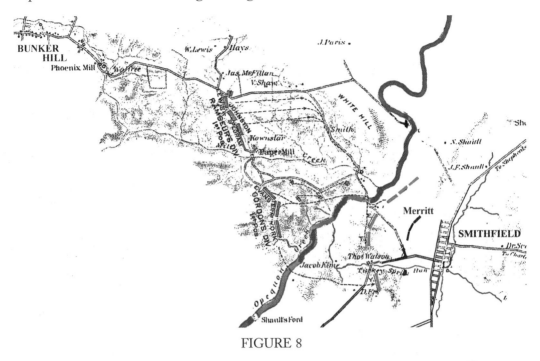

FIGURE 8

At about 10:00 a.m., Early's force, indicated by the positions in grey, and his moves, the dotted lines, appeared on the far side of the creek, and by 11:30, he had artillery in place on either side of the Pike, which began a furious and well-directed fire at Merritt's line.

This was not the type of fight that any cavalry liked to be forced into. They should perhaps have withdrawn immediately, but were directly ordered to make a stand by Merritt, regardless of the fact that the 6th Pennsylvania was out of carbine ammunition. "Use your pistols," he said. Even those regiments still with ammunition were at a disadvantage, due to the fact that the long-range rifle fire of Early's infantry was "far more effective than the cavalry carbines..." whose Sharps and Spencer repeaters, designed for close fast action, were of limited range, compared to the Enfields and Springfields which the Confederates now had appropriated in increased numbers. The cavalry revolvers, handy for multiple shots in furious action while in the saddle, were even more limited in range and accuracy. Of course, their sabers, in this case, were nothing but an obsolescent encumbrance.

The important item that differed here, though, was that Merritt's cavalry had its own artillery, albeit only two batteries, Williston's and Taylor's, and they had been available to promptly respond. Early describes this initial phase of the engagement, with the two sides separated by the creek, as a sharp artillery duel.

At 12:30, Gordon's Division executed a flank movement, by fording the Opequan south of the bridge. Thus threatened, and "notwithstanding the…shells, grape, and canister poured into their ranks by our artillery, on they came like demons." Their regiments then formed in front of the defenders, as is shown in figure 8. Sometime after 2:00 p.m. so many of Merritt's defenders had run out of their carbine ammunition that the three brigades were finally ordered to withdraw. Thus began a slow, deliberate, and appropriate withdrawal, without confusion, the men protecting themselves with their pistols, and, of course, covered by their artillery. Over the space of some three hours they were drawn back through the town, to an open ridge about two miles east of Smithfield. There, at 5:00 p.m. they were greeted by Sheridan. Sheridan and his staff had arrived just before, and as was his custom, he was right there at the front, ahead of the reinforcements; Rickett's 3rd Division of the 6th Corps.[1954] On horseback, in the open, Sheridan's little group was fired upon, and Sheridan's acting medical director was hit by a Minie ball and killed. The retreat was halted, and breastworks of fence rails were hastily constructed, while the enemy occupied the village in heavy force. Now, with something like equal numbers between the combatants, and with infantry against infantry, and cavalry against cavalry, the tide turned, and Early's entire force was quickly pushed back across the Opequan.

Specifics of the participation of Battery K–L in the action are not reported. Any report Franck Taylor may have written has not been found, and Col. Di Cesnola, in temporary command of the 2nd Brigade, only refer to placing his "pieces" and consulting with his battery officers, without naming them. In contrast, the action of Williston's battery in support of the Reserve Brigade is reported in some detail by Col. Gibbs. We only know from the Battery L monthly report that Pvt. Joseph H. Parslow was killed in action in this engagement, and from the regimental casualty report that privates Brown and Jesse W. Smith of Battery K were wounded.

The next day, Col. Charles R. Lowell, at that time commanding Merritt's 3rd Brigade, was ordered to hold Smithfield and the crossing. Those of Merritt's divisions that had fought there were ordered to Berryville, where they joined Wilson's 3rd Division. Thereafter, a lull in most of the action took place, with the exception that, on the 31st, yet another quick attack by Rodes' division was made on the railroad at Martinsburg.[1955] The lull was brief. On the 2nd of September, Early went on a reconnaissance toward Summit Point, and clashed with Averell. Early then retired to Stephenson's Depot and joined Anderson.

"Record" 10/64
31 AUGUST–31 OCTOBER 1864 THE SHENANDOAH VALLEY CAMPAIGN

Battery engaged at the Battle of Winchester, Va. Sept. 19, 1864. In action at Fisher's Hill, Va. Sept. 23. At Mt. Jackson, Va. Sept. 24. At New Market, Va. Sept. 25th. At Port Republic, Va. Sept.

1954. O.R. Vol. 43/I, pp. 469, 489; Parslow death: *"Record"* 8/64, ch. 12.
1955. O.R. Vol. 43/I, p. 1026.

27th & 28th. Engaged in the Cavalry Fight near Strasburg, Va. Oct. 8th & 9th. Pursued the enemy to Woostock, Va. Participated in the battle of Cedar Creek, Va. Oct, 19, 1864. Camped near Middletown on the 20th. Relieved from duty in the field and ordered to Reserve camp in Pleasant Valley, Md. Oct 26th and arrived there on the 29th October, 1864.

Henry W. Closson	Capt. Joined Co. Oct. 25,'64 from absence with leave. Sp. Orders 347 War Dept. A.G.O. Washington Oct. 14,'64.
Franck E. Taylor	1st Lt. Relieved of duty with Battery and assigned to duty as Chf. Arty. & Ord. (in the field) of Cavalry, War Dept. A.G.O. Washington Oct. 14,'64.
Edward L. Appleton	1st Lt. Relieved from duty Gen. recruiting svc. & ordered to join Co. S.O. no. 315, War Dept. A.G.O. Washington, Sept. 22,'64. Absent without leave.

Detached:

Charles Cooke	Pvt. Abs. on det. svc. As orderly for Chf. Arty. of the Cav. Mid. Mil. Div. since Oct. 28, 1864.
Michael Kenny	Pvt. In Battery G 5th US Artillery at New Orleans.
John Meyer	Pvt. In Battery G 5th US Artillery at New Orleans.

Absent in confinement:

Patrick Gibbons	Pvt. At Ship Island, serving sentence of General Court martial S.O. no. 18, Hdqtrs. 1st Div. 19th Army Corps Dec. 31, 1863.
John Lewery	Pvt. Abs. confined in New Orleans, La. Apprehended as a deserter.

Deserted: none.

Discharged:

Julius Becker	1st Sgt. Oct. 12,'64 Strasburg, Va. By expiration of service
Michael White	Sgt. Oct. 7,'64 New Orleans, La. do.
David J. Wicks	Sgt. Oct. 25,'64 Middletown, Va. do.
Edmund Anglin	Pvt. Oct. 19,'64 New Orleans, La. do.
William Brunskill	Pvt. Oct. 19,'64 New York Harbor do.
Issac T. Cain	Artificer Oct. 4,'64 Harrisonburg, Va. do.
Jeremiah Connell	Pvt. Sept. 13,'64 Smithfield, Va. do.
Edmond Cotterill	Pvt. Sept. 18,'64 Washington, DC By order of War Dept., A.G.O.
James Flynn	Pvt. Sept. 13,'64 Smithfield, Va. By expiration of service.
Joseph Smith	Pvt. Oct. 11,'64 New Orleans, La. do.

Died:

Rowland Card	Pvt. Oct. 19,'64 Of wounds received in action at Cedar Creek, Va.

Joined:

William Demarest	Sgt. Oct. 14,'64 Reenlisted in the company while on recruiting duty at New York.
Lewis Keller	Cpl. Oct. 28,'64 From enlistment in New York.
Benjamin O. Hall	Pvt. Oct. 14,'64 From recruiting duty in New York.
Michael Teighe	Pvt. Oct. 14,'64 do.
Rueben Townsend	Pvt. Oct. 14,'64 do.
John McKenny	Pvt. Sept. 18,'64 From sick at new Orleans.

Strength: 76 Sick: 11

Sick Present: none

Sick Absent:

Ludwig Rupprecht	Bugler Oct. 9,'64 Wounded in action at Strasburg, Va.
James Campbell	Pvt. Sept. 19,'64 Wounded in action at Winchester, Va.
George Chase	Pvt. April 22,'63 At Brashear City, La.
Patrick Craffy	Pvt. Sept. 26,'64 At Philadelphia, Pa.
William Crowley	Pvt. July 13,'63. At Baton Rouge, La.
Charles Jackel	Pvt. April 20,'64 At New Orleans, La.
John Kelly	Pvt. Sept. 19,'64 Wounded in action at Winchester, Va.
Churchill Moore	Pvt. April 20,'64 At New Orleans, La.
Warren P. Shaw	Pvt. Oct. 12,'64 (no entry)
Andrew Stoll	Pvt. Sept 25,'64 Wounded in action near New Market, Va.
John C. Wood	Pvt. Sept. 19,'64 Wounded in action at Winchester, Va.

The cooks are listed on the muster roll, though separately from the numbered roster, and are not counted as part of the 76-man strength. Their pay due is listed with the comment, "$13.00, error on last payroll"; their pay finally had achieved parity with that of a private.

Items of note are: 1. Henry Closson finally arrived back from his duty at Mobile, and some additional time on leave. He did not, however, get back in time to participate in any of the battles in the Shenandoah Valley. He was brevetted a lieutenant colonel on August 23rd, 1864: "For Gallant and Meritorious Services at the Battle of Ft. Morgan, Ala."[1956] 2. It was now Franck Taylor's turn to become chief of artillery, but only of the cavalry. 3. Edward Appleton, who had gone to New York on recruiting duty, has been declared AWOL. He had been ordered to rejoin Battery L on September 22nd, more than five weeks earlier. 4. William Brunskill was finally discharged, not on a disability, but by expiration of service. After being taken sick at Fort Pickens on September 10th, 1861, and sent to the Hospital at Fort Hamilton, New York, on September 17th, 1861, he had been in the hospital for more than three years out of his five-year enlistment. Though Michael White's term of service may have expired, his listing here as discharged is rather presumptuous. He is still missing—since the battle at Pleasant Hill.

Anderson

Early had been receiving "loud" calls from Lee, according to Sheridan's memoirs, to return Anderson and Kershaw's division.[1957] There are no records to contradict Sheridan's statement about the force of Lee's remarks, but Early confirms that he had received a letter *requesting* Kershaw and Anderson, and that, after consulting Early, Anderson had decided to return, taking Kershaw and Fitzhugh Lee's cavalry with him. He moved on September 3rd, towards Berryville, intending to cross the Blue Ridge at Ashby's Gap. To cover the move, Early had agreed to move toward

---

1956. Cullum, no. 1638, vol. 2, p. 580.
1957. O.R. Vol. 43/II, p. 862; Sheridan, vol. 1, p. 498; Early, *Sketch*, pp. 410–411.

Charlestown. The fruit of the Grant/Sheridan policy was about to ripen. With Early stripped of his reinforcements, Sheridan could begin an aggressive campaign.

In the meantime, Sheridan had begun a general advance, moving Wright to Clifton, Crook to Berryville, and Torbert to White Post, with orders to reconnoiter as far as the Front Royal Pike. Crook had just gotten into position about an hour before sunset, when firing was heard along his front west of the town. It was Anderson, who had blundered into Crook. The next day, Early came to Anderson's rescue, only to discover that he now faced a whole new line of Sheridan's, which extended all the way to Summit Point. Appreciating Sheridan's strength and position, Early and Anderson then both decided to withdraw back to Winchester and Stephenson's Depot. More reconnaissances were sent out by Sheridan on the several days succeeding, but it was not definitely learned that this incident involved Anderson's and Kershaw's attempt to withdraw from the Valley until they tried again, and succeeded, on September 14th.

On September 5th, news was received of the President's message of September 3rd, giving the national thanks to Admiral Farragut and generals Canby and Granger for the success of the Mobile expedition, and in the surrender of Fort Morgan on August 23rd.[1958] A 100-gun salute was to be fired at the navy yard in Washington on the 5th, and at "each arsenal and navy yard in the United States..." another was to be fired on the 6th. On the 7th, yet another was to be fired at the arsenals in honor of Sherman's occupation of Atlanta on September 2nd. Lincoln also requested that: "In all places of worship in the United States thanksgiving be offered to Him for His mercy in preserving [the Union]."

The news of the victories came at a point in time during and just after the Chicago Democratic Convention, which had opened on August 29th, and had closed on September 3rd. It had nominated George B. McClellan.[1959] The effect of the news, as commented upon in *Harper's Weekly*, was: "There is not a man who did not feel that McClellan's chances were diminished by the glad tidings from Atlanta..." The presidential campaign season had now opened, and Grant understood that the administration was afraid of any setback, hence all of the caution Sheridan had been warned to exercise up to this time was still in effect. Caution involved knowing more about Anderson's plans. If Anderson took Kershaw back to Lee to try to recover the Weldon Railroad, only then would Early be ripe for an attack.

The positions of both Early's forces and Sheridan's remained essentially unchanged from September 3rd until September 17th, though Sheridan's cavalry was employed every day in harassing the enemy. Sheridan purposely remained some six miles back from Early's positions behind (west) of Opequan Creek, and

---

1958. Cheney, p. 217; ORN ser. 1, vol. 21, pp. 538, 543–544; O.R. Vol. 38/I, p. 127.
1959. *Harper's Weekly*, Sept. 10th, 1864, p. 579; ibid., Sept. 17th, 1864, p. 594; O.R. Vol. 43/I, p. 811.

if this expanse could be dominated by Union scouting parties, no enemy pickets would be able to warn of any future general move Sheridan might make.[1960] On one occasion, September 13th, McIntosh's brigade, of Wilson's division, advanced on the Berryville Pike, crossed the Opequan, and when within two miles of Winchester, at Abraham's Creek, captured the entire 8th South Carolina Infantry, a part of Kershaw's division, which decisively proved that Anderson had not yet left. No move on Early would be prudent yet.

Even this reconnaissance did not get the real information necessary: *when* Kershaw and Anderson were planning to leave, if at all. After weeks of inaccurate information, much of it passed on from Washington,[1961] Sheridan felt that he needed a better approach. Up to now, the gathering of information, particularly that of enemy positions or troop movements, had been by reconnaissances, which only incidentally captured prisoners for interrogation. Other methods involved interviewing "doubtful citizens and Confederate deserters." The more detailed information on enemy plans was elusive. Sheridan concluded that his own soldiers who volunteered for specific intelligence gathering duty would be more accurate and trustworthy, and that they should be organized.[1962] They were consequently formed into a battalion, dressed in Confederate uniforms as the occasion required, and were to be paid in an incentive scheme in proportion to the value of the intelligence gathered.

In only a few days, the new scouts had learned of a possible way of getting information out of Winchester. An "old colored man" living near Millwood, southeast of Winchester, had been given a permit by the Confederate commander to pass in and out three times a week for the purpose of selling vegetables. The scouts had "sounded this man, and finding him both loyal and shrewd, suggested that he might be made useful…" Fortunately, General Crook was acquainted with many of the Union people residing in Winchester, and on the 15th of September, Sheridan turned to him to recommend someone to contact. He mentioned Miss Rebecca Wright, a Quaker teacher who ran a small private school, with the caveat that her pro-Union sentiment was well known to the Confederate authorities, and that she was under constant surveillance. Sheridan wasted no time, that same night directing his scouts to bring the old man to his headquarters. The interview convinced Sheridan "of the negro's fidelity." He said that he knew Miss Wright well. After some persuasion, he agreed to carry a letter, wait for any answer, and return. The letter was written on tissue paper, and compressed into a small pellet, which was wrapped in tin-foil, the object being to protect it while it was carried in the old man's mouth. In the event he was stopped, he could swallow it. The message

---

1960. O.R. Vol. 43/I, pp. 24, 46, 87, 427, 517; Early, p. 419. Early began a raid on Martinsburg on the 17th. Abraham's Creek is today referred to as Abram's Creek.
1961. O.R. Vol. 43/II, pp. 18, 21–22; Sheridan, vol. 2, pp. 2, 8.
1962. Sheridan, vol. 2, pp. 2–6; O.R. Vol. 43/II, p. 90.

was delivered to her home the next day. It said:

> I learn from General Crook that you are a loyal lady, and still love the old flag. Can you inform me of the position of Early's forces, the number and divisions in his army, the number and strength of any or all of them, and his probable or reported intentions? Have any more troops arrived from Richmond, or are any more coming, or reported to be coming?
>
> I am, very respectfully, your most obedient servant,
> P. H. Sheridan, Major-General Commanding
> You can trust the bearer.

Upon opening the tin-foil, the message was found to be readable, and the old man departed, telling Miss Wright that he would return later for her reply. She was startled by the perils involved, but after consulting her mother, decided to become involved, though it might put her life in jeopardy. Incredibly, only the night before, a convalescent Confederate officer had visited her mother's house, and in conversation, revealed the fact that Kershaw's division and Cutshaw's batallion of artillery had started to rejoin Lee. She answered:

> September 16, 1864.
> I have no communication whatever with the rebels, but will tell you what I know. The division of General Kershaw, and Cutshaw's artillery, twelve guns and men, General Anderson commanding, have been sent away, and no more are expected, as they cannot be spared from Richmond. I do not know how the troops are situated but the force is much smaller than represented. I will take pleasure hereafter in learning all I can of their strength and position, and the bearer can call again.
> Very respectfully yours,

* * * * *

This finally resolved the conflicting reports and rumors that had gone before. Sheridan decided to bring Early to battle the next day. He had a plan to attack him south of Winchester, at Newtown, and thus seal off his withdrawal up the Valley.

Though Grant and Stanton insisted on caution, and that "only positive success" was acceptable, there were others insisting upon some action which would keep open the Baltimore and Ohio Railroad and the Chesapeake and Ohio Canal. Most of this clamor was directed at Grant.[1963]

On September 11th, Halleck had telegraphed that the continued interruption of the railroad was seriously affecting the supply of provisions and fuel in Baltimore and Washington. If the Chesapeake and Ohio Canal were closed, it threatened a sufficient supply of coal reaching the city before the canal froze, ending the year's navigation. The gas companies were already thinking of shutting down for want of

---

1963. O.R. Vol. 43/II, pp. 83–84.

coal (coal was used to make illuminating gas, as well as for fuel). The lights would go out in Washington.

Either prompted by this, or both this and his own impatience (he mentions no reason in his *Memoirs*), Grant decided to visit Sheridan, with the purpose to have him "attack Early, or drive him out of the Valley and destroy that source of supplies for Lee's army."[1964]

On the 15th, he sent a courier (no telegram, which would be read in Washington) to Sheridan that he was coming, and then left, directly for Charlestown, ten miles south of Harper's Ferry. He avoided stopping at Washington, and he went in person, for the reason that: "I knew it was impossible for me to get orders through Washington to Sheridan to make a move, because they would be stopped there and such orders as Halleck's caution (and that of the Secretary of War) would suggest would be given instead, no doubt contradictory to mine." Grant's telegram reached Sheridan in time to for him call off his planned attack, and "defer action" until he had met with Grant.

In their meeting, Sheridan laid out his plan. It consisted of approaching Early from the south via Newtown, hitting his right along the Valley Pike, his only outlet from the Valley, and his communication with Lee. Cut off, Early would have been compelled to cut his way through, as there was no escape right or left, and to try to escape north across the Potomac was impossible.[1965] Grant was sufficiently impressed with the plan to not question it, and did not disclose his own plan, which he had drawn up on a piece of paper, still in his vest pocket.[1966] The only question that Grant asked, was *when* Sheridan could launch the attack. Knowing that Sheridan's wagon teams and most of his supplies were at Harper's Ferry, Grant asked if he could be ready by the following Tuesday. This was on Friday. Sheridan answered that he could be off whenever the general should say "Go in,"—before daylight on Monday, the 19th, if necessary. So delighted was Grant with this answer that he simply said "Go in!"

Note the careful planning regarding the teams. The horses and wagons were held at their point of supply, so that the horse forage would not have to be delivered to them by yet more teams.

Winchester

Sheridan had reported that once the two armies had drawn up facing each other, Early at Winchester, and Sheridan at Berryville, there were no further substantial movements. One that escaped all of his reconnaissances and scouting was on the 17th. It was then that Early had detached Rodes' and Gordon's divisions, Lomax's

---

1964. Grant, vol. 2, p. 327
1965. Nicolay and Hay, vol. 9, p. 299.
1966. Grant, vol. 2, p. 583; Irwin, p. 377.

cavalry, and Braxton's artillery, all under the command of Breckinridge, to take yet another crack at the B&O Railroad at Martinsville. Next day, while Rodes remained at Bunker Hill, Gordon, with a part of Lomax's cavalry (Jackson's), reached Martinsburg, driving Averell from the town, and across the Opequan. Fortunately, Averell reported the fact to Sheridan at noon.[1967] While there, Early learned from the Union telegraph office that Grant had visited Sheridan, and, as a result, suspected an "early move." He therefore rushed Rodes back to Stephenson's Depot that evening, and ordered Gordon back to Bunker Hill, with orders to return to Stephenson's Depot on the 19th.

Sheridan, now aware that Early had sent off the two divisions, but *not aware* that they had been ordered back, then decided to alter his plan to attack via Newtown. His original orders had been issued on Sunday afternoon. They were cancelled and new ones issued. Instead of heading for Newtown, Sheridan now planned to take advantage of the "disjointed state of the enemy giving me an opportunity to take him in detail…" and planned to go directly west, along the Berryville Pike. Not knowing Early had planned the return of his divisions would *almost* prove fatal to Sheridan. It certainly increased the intensity of the subsequent battle and Sheridan's casualties.[1968]

The plan was for Torbert, on the flank, to advance with Merritt's cavalry, from its location at Summit Point, to carry the crossings of the Opequan at Sievier's and Locke's fords, and form a junction with Averell, who was to advance south from near Darkesville, to where he had returned on the night of the 18th, after Early had driven him out of Martinsburg. Marching south via the Pike, through Bunker Hill, he was to join Torbert near Stephenson's Depot, figure 9.[1969] Sheridan makes no mention of the fact that Merritt was, apparently, instructed to delay those Confederate forces found at the fords, so as to prevent them from freely retiring back to reinforce Breckinridge at Stephenson's Depot.[1970]

Wilson's cavalry was to move west on the Berryville Pike, cross the Opequan, drive in the enemy's pickets, and attack the enemy positions to cover the advance of the infantry. The 6th Corps was to follow, the 19th Corps behind it, with Crook, who was originally to go to Newtown, to be held in reserve.

1967. Early, *Sketch*, p. 419; Sheridan, vol. 2, pp. 9–10; O.R. Vol. 43/I, pp. 25, 46, 518, 554, 1027; O.R. Vol. 43/II, pp. 106–107; R. E. Park, p. 90; Pellet, pp. 252, –253; Early, J.A., *Battles and Leaders* vol. 4, p. 522.
1968. Sheridan, vol. 2, pp. 11–14.
1969. Atlas, plate 85, map 1, portion, altered.
1970. O.R. Vol. 43/I, pp. 444, 455.

FIGURE 9

Regardless of the fact that Early had ordered back his two divisions, only Rodes' division had reached Stephenson's Depot, five or six miles north of Winchester, and Gordon's division, the only one of the two that had entered Martinsburg, had been allowed to stop overnight at Bunker Hill.[1971] Hence, neither were within supporting distance of Ramseur, posted east of Winchester. Gordon, having to march about eight miles to Stephenson's Depot from Bunker Hill, would not even reach there until about 8:00 a.m. Thus, the situation still looked satisfactory enough to Sheridan, at daylight on th 19th, to continue with his "straight in" plan. As we shall see, regardless of the great victory claimed for the outcome of the battle, it was long, difficult, and bloody. Worse, note figure 9, Sheridan had left the door open for Early to escape south, with Crook held in reserve, and subsequently needed at Winchester, rather than driving to Newtown.

Since the cavalry was the arm to which Battery K–L was assigned, its organization for the battle is shown in some detail in figure 10.[1972] Note that the artillery is listed separately, unassigned to any particular brigade. They were intended to be flexibly assigned as required, and in the coming battle, Battery K–L served under both Devin and Custer.

1971. O.R. Vol. 43/I, p. 554; Sheridan, pp. 83 89; Naval Observatory sunrise for Winchester, VA, Sept. 19th, 1864, was 5:58.
1972. Sheridan, vol. 2, pp.11–21; O.R. Vol. 43/I, pp. 107–112. *http://dmna.ny.gov/historic/regthist/civi/cavalry/4thCav/4thCavHistSketch.htm*

CAVALRY: Br.-Gen. Alfred T. A. Torbert. Escort: 1st Rhode Island Maj. Wm. H. Turner, Jr.

FIRST DIVISION: Br.-Gen. Wesley Merritt

FIRST BRIGADE: Br.-Gen. George A. Custer
   1st Michigan, Col. Peter Stagg
   Michigan, Maj. Smith H. Hastings
   6th Michigan, Col. James H. Kidd
   7th Michigan, Maj. Melvin Brewer
   29th New York, Maj. Charles J. Seymour

SECOND BRIGADE: Col. Thomas C. Devin
   4th New York, Maj. August Hourand
   Maj. Edward Schwartz
   6th New York, Maj. Wm. E. Beardsley
   9th New York, Lt.-Col. George S. Nichols
   1st New York Dragoons, Col. Alfred Gibbs
   17th Pennsylvania, Maj. Coe Durland

RESERVE BRIGADE: Col. Charles R. Lowell
   2nd Massachusetts, Lt.-Col. Casper Crowninshield
   1st United States, Capt. Eugene M. Baker
   2nd United States, Capt. Theophilus M. Rodenbough
   Capt. Robert S. Smith
   5th United States, Lt. Gustavus Urban

SECOND DIVISION: Br.-Gen. Wm. W. Averell

FIRST BRIGADE: Col. James M. Schoonmaker
   8th Ohio (det.), Col. Alpheus S. Moore
   14th Pennsylvania, Capt. Ashbell. F. Duncan
   22nd Pennsylvania, Lt.-Col. Andrew J. Greenfield
   7th Michigan, Maj. Melvin Brewer
   29th New York, Maj. Charles J. Seymour

SECOND BRIGADE: Col. Henry Capehart
   1st New York, Maj. Timothy Quinn
   1st West Virginia, Maj. Harvey Farabee
   2nd West Virginia, Lt.-Col. John J. Hoffman
   3rd West Virginia, Maj. John S. Witcher
   Division Artillery: 5th United States, Battery L, Lt. Julian V. Weir

THIRD DIVISION: Br.-Ben. James H. Wilson

FIRST BRIGADE: Br.-Gen. John B. McIntosh
   Lt.-Col. George A. Purington
   1st Connecticut, Maj. George O. Marcy
   3rd New Jersey, Maj. Wm. P. Robeson, Jr.
   2nd New York, Capt. Walter C. Hull
   5th New York, Maj. Abram H. Krom
   2nd Ohio, Lt.-Col. George A. Purington
   Maj. A. Bayard Nettleton
   18th Pennsylvania, Lt.-Col. Wm. P. Brinton
   Maj. John W. Phillips

SECOND BRIGADE: Br.-Gen. George H. Chapman
   3rd Indiana, (2 companies) Lt. Benjamin F. Gilbert
   1st New Hampshire, (batallion), Col. John L. Thompson
   8th New York, Lt.-Col. Wm. H. Benjamin
   22nd New York, Maj. Caleb Moore
   1st Vermont, Col. Wm. Wells

HORSE ARTILLERY: Capt. La Rhett Livingston
   1st US, Batteries K&L, Lt. Franck E. Taylor
   2nd US, Batteries B&L, Capt. Charles H. Peirce
   2nd US, Battery D, Lt. Edward B. Williston
   3rd US, Batteries C&F, Capt. Dunbar R. Ransom
   4th US, Battery C, Lt. Terence Reilly

FIGURE 10

Figure 11 gives an abbreviated organization of the Union infantry. Units on duty elsewhere are omitted.

6th ARMY CORPS, Maj.-Gen. Horatio G. Wright
1st DIVISION, Br.-Gen. David A. Russell
   Br.-Gen. Emory Upton
   Col. Oliver Edwards

2nd DIVISION, Br.-Gen. George W. Getty
3rd DIVISION, Br.-Gen. James B. Ricketts
Artillery Brigade, Col. Charles H. Tompkins
19th ARMY CORPS, Bvt. Maj.-Gen. William H. Emory
1st DIVISION, Br.-Gen. Wm. Dwight
Artillery, Lt. John V. Grant
2nd DIVISION, Br.-Gen. Cuvier Grover
Artillery, Albert W. Bradbury
Reserve Artillery, Capt. Elijah D. Taft
8th ARMY CORPS (THE ARMY OF WEST VIRGINIA)
Bvt. Maj.-Gen George Crook
1st DIVISION, Col. Joseph Thoburn
2nd DIVISION, Col. Isaac Duval
Col. Rutherford B. Hayes
Artillery Brigade, Capt. Henry A. Du Pont

FIGURE 11

Figure 12[1973] gives an abbreviated organization of Early's army.

ARMY OF THE VALLEY, Lt.-Gen. Jubal A. Early
Rodes'   Division II Corps, Army of Northern Virginia (Lee)
Ramseur's   "   "
Gordon's   "   "
Wharton's   "   (Breckinridge)
CAVALRY: Maj.-Gen. Fitzhugh Lee
Lomax's   Division
Lee's   "
ARTILLERY Col. T.H. Carter
Braxton's   Battalion
Nelson's   "
King's   "

Breckinridge had been in command of Gordon's and Wharton's Divisions since June 27.[1974]

FIGURE 12

The battle that is known as 3rd Winchester, or Opequan, began on September 19th, at 2:00 a.m., when Wilson's 3rd Division of cavalry, with McIntosh's 1st brigade in advance, moved to the Berryville Pike, crossed the Opequan, passed through the two-mile-plus long defile, or canyon, through which the road ran, and before dawn, drove in the Confederate cavalry pickets in front of Stephen D. Ramseur's infantry division.[1975] Ramseur's division had been posted to the east of Winchester,

---

1973. O.R. Vol. 42/II, p. 1213, vol. 43/I, pp. 1002–1003, 1011; remainder corroborated by: Garnett, SHS, vol. 31, *Battle of Winchester*, p. 63; Park, p. 25; Early, *Battles and Leaders*, vol. 4, pp. 522, 523.
1974. O.R. Vol. 37/I, p. 768; O.R Vol. 39/II, p. 877. Breckinridge was assigned to the command of the Department of Southwestern Virginia and East Tennessee, on September 27th.
1975. O.R. Vol. 43/I, pp. 518, 574, 1025; Early *Memoir*, pp. 89–90, 415; Haskin, p. 379.

near Abraham's Creek, while Early's three others had been on the raid to Martinsburg, as discussed, and were at, or approaching, Stephenson's Depot, not in position near Ramseur. Reaching the high ground beyond the canyon at about 3:00 a.m., McIntosh's brigade drove Ramseur from his position. It was the same place where McIntosh had captured the 8th South Carolina regiment on September 13th. Wilson then disposed his force so as to hold the ground and the river crossing until the 6th Army Corps and the 19th Army Corps could come into position.

Also at 2:00 a.m., Merritt's 1st Division,[1976] Custer's 1st brigade in advance, had started out from its encampments at Summit Point, intending to reach the crossing of the Opequan at Sevier's Ford, on the Charlestown Road, south of where the railroad crosses, before daylight and unobserved. Custer's march went by the most direct route, cross-country, regardless of roads. Custer arrived first. The other two brigades, Lowell's and Devin's, followed, in the rear of the division train, and did not arrive until soon after daybreak. Custer was then ordered to take Locke's ford, about one-and-a-half miles to the north. Due to a reconnaissance made to the crossings on September 13th, which had captured a Confederate lieutenant and ten privates, Breckinridge's attention had been brought to them, and he had dispatched Wharton's division, consisting of Forsberg's, Smith's, and Patton's brigades, figure 13,[1977] supported by King's battalion of artillery, to the location. Their skirmishers were found to be entrenched on the west side, alert to the Yankee arrival. Thus, all hopes of securing the crossings unopposed were lost, and the attempt at stealth was a waste.

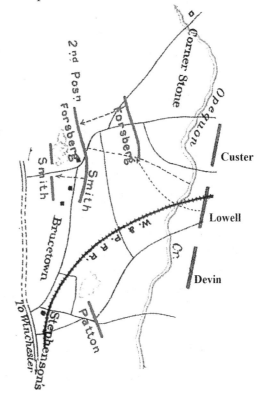

FIGURE 13

At Custer's front, a mounted charge by the 25th New York and the 7th Michigan was organized. It was to dash across the ford and gain the high ground on the other side. It was to be covered by rifle fire from the 6th Michigan, dismounted, which was sent up to occupy the crest of a hill overlooking the ford. Led by the 25th New York,

---

1976. O.R. Vol. 43/I, pp. 443, 454–455, 481–482, 490; Early, *Battles and Leaders*, vol. 4, p. 523.
1977. Atlas, plate 85, map 12. Altered and reoriented to approx. correct north-south. The Union brigade positions, to the east, all originally labeled "CUSTER," have been re-labeled as understood from the reports of Custer, Lowell, Devin, and Merritt.

the charge met heavy fire from well covered rifle pits as it reached the water. The column then gave way, retreating in "considerable" confusion.

Another charge was organized, and this time it was assigned to the 1st Michigan. The first charge having exposed the position of the rifle pits, a detachment of sharpshooters was assigned to "quiet it." The charge of the 1st Michigan had not even begun, before its major, in a shower of whistling bullets, rode up the hill to where the 6th was perched, and complained to its commander that his men were being shot off their horses even before they had begun the charge. The 6th was then ordered to advance, dismounted, to support the charge, and the 7th Michigan was brought up to join the 1st.

By order of General Merritt, one section of Battery K–L, under the command of Lt. John McGilvray,[1978] accompanied by the 4th New York Cavalry as its support, was detached from Devin and reported to Custer. It was directed to a position on the hill formerly occupied by the 6th Michigan. The six-horse teams pulling the guns and caissons had to enter a ravine which ran out at the top of the hill, and then had to turn and negotiate through one hundred to one hundred and fifty yards of plowed ground to the edge of the crest covering Locke's Ford, all the while under enemy fire. Here they "rendered valuable service," according to Devin.[1979] Actually, the enemy suffered little from their fire, being protected as they were by breastworks.

Preparations for this final attack were just about completed when it was discovered that the Confederate skirmishers were withdrawing. With this news, the second charge succeeded, the rifle pits were captured, and a "considerable" number of prisoners taken.[1980] As Custer reports: "The enemy retired about one mile from the ford in the direction of Winchester and took position behind a heavy line of earth-works, protected by a formidable cheval-de-frise."

In the meantime, below, at Locke's ford, Lowell had crossed and established himself on the opposite bank. It had been done "in fine style" by throwing across dismounted men, supported by the 5th US and a part of the 2nd Massachusetts. Then, the 2nd US, led by Capt. Theophilus Rodenbough, made a "brilliant" charge directly up the incline on the opposite side, gained the crest, and captured a body of the enemy, their line having been established in the railroad cut. It was now after

---

1978. Haskin, p. 213; Hall, Besley, and Wood, p. 223.
1979. O.R. Vol. 43/I, p. 482; Denison, F., p. 389. It is a shame that no report by anyone in Battery L or K has been found. We know nothing of whether casualties were taken in this action.
1980. Kidd, J. H., pp. 387–389; O.R. Vol. 43/I, p. 455. We have quoted Custer as to the position to which Forsberg withdrew. Atlas, plate 99, map 1, allegedly to scale, shows less distance. Drawn in 1873, it is of help only in corroborating the time at which the Confederates completely withdrew, which was at 9:00 a.m., per Atlas plate 85, map 12. O.R. Vol. 43/II, p. 113: The Confederate withdrawal was observed by Custer almost an hour later, and reported to Torbert by a member of his escort, Capt. John Rogers, as occurring at 9:50.

sunrise, and as Merritt writes: "The rich crimson of that fine autumnal morning was fading away into the broad light of day when the booming of guns on the left gave sign that the attack was being made by our infantry."[1981]

Custer's brigade now began to consolidate along the ridge in the positions across the creek which had been vacated by the enemy. Custer reports: "Prisoners captured at the ford represented themselves as belonging to Breckinridge's corps... which was posted behind the works confronting us. Deeming this information reliable...I contented myself with annoying the enemy with artillery and skirmishers until the other brigades of the division, having effected a crossing...established a connection with my left."

The connection between Lowell's and Custer's brigades finally made, a combined charge into the face of the enemy defenses was organized. Lowell leading the 2nd US Cavalry and Custer the 1st Michigan, 7th Michigan, and the 25th New York. It failed, as could have been predicted, but the threat of the attack, the artillery firing, and the skirmishing, to this point, had prevented Breckinridge's force from extricating itself and returning to reinforce Early, as he had already ordered.[1982]

Sheridan's personal memoirs mention nothing specifically about using Merritt's cavalry so as to detain Breckinridge, but both Custer and Merritt make a point of it in their reports, and the strategy is recorded in Humphreys' *The History of the 2nd Massachusetts Cavalry*. Sheridan brought on the battle with the knowledge that Early had divided his forces, and holding Breckinridge at the Opequan kept him away from the main field of battle. The trouble was, at some point, who was detaining whom? While tied up with Breckinridge's/Wharton's forces, Merritt was delayed in uniting with Averell. We shall see that Averell's advance from Darkesville was a somewhat similar story, though he was confronted by a much smaller force, as Gordon's division had already left. Averell mentions nothing about enjoining any Confederate force in order to detain it.

At the lines of Custer and Lowell, the artillery firing and skirmishing continued until Custer observed that, unseen, Forsberg had massed his force in the rear and withdrawn, to a "2nd pos'n." as shown in Figure 13.[1983]

At about 11:00, a charge upon this new line was made by the combined forces of portions of the 1st and Reserve brigades, and like the others, was unsuccessful. But time had passed, and Early had finally peremptorily ordered Breckinridge[1984] to: "Move your whole force back toward Winchester and put it on the Martinsburg road about a mile from town." The order had its time of dispatch noted as 11:40 a.m.

1981. O.R. Vol. 43/I, pp. 443, 462, 482; Humphreys, Charles A., p. 158.
1982. Early, *Sketch*, p. 424; O.R. Vol. 43/I, p. 444, 490; Humphreys, pp. 158–159; Sheridan, vol. 2, p. 10.
1983. O.R. Vol. 43/I, pp. 427, 444, 456; vol. 43/II, p. 113.
1984. O.R. Vol. 43/II, p. 876.

At this point, Custer, without orders, advanced, hoping to move beyond Wharton's infantry, and strike him in reverse. At about 1:30 p.m., Torbert gave the order for a general advance, and Devin's Brigade crossed the Opequan without opposition. Joining with Lowell, they moved together toward Winchester along the Charlestown Road. McCausland's brigade of cavalry, and Patton's infantry, which was left with it in support, repeatedly clashed with Lowell and Devin as they advanced.[1985]

As to Averell, at 5:00 a.m. he had crossed the Opequan and headed toward Darksville, driving Imboden's cavalry pickets, the 23rd Virginia Cavalry, under the command of Col. Charles T. O'Ferrall, steadily before him until he reached Bunker Hill, where the Confederate defenders made a determined stand.[1986] Bunker Hill, twelve miles from Winchester, was where Gordon had encamped after leaving from the Martinsburg raid, and here had remained another of Imboden's units, the 62nd Virginia, under the command of George S. Smith. Smith and O'Ferrall couldn't hope to stave off Averell's overwhelming force, and despite their stubborn resistance, Averell pushed through, reaching the area just above Stephenson's Depot into which Torbert/Merritt were pushing Wharton.[1987]

Thus are outlined the actions of Sheridan's 1st, 2nd and Reserve divisions of cavalry on Early's left, and Battery K–L's involvement. These actions took nearly all the morning. Frequent references as to the heavy cannonading[1988] heard from further south, was thought to be proof that a larger battle had been taking place for more than four hours. Actually, the battle was still only developing. Wilson's 3rd division of cavalry had reached the high ground on the west side of the Opequan on which stood the earthworks occupied by Ramseur's division at dawn, and taken possession. Here, Wilson awaited the advance of Wright's 6th Corps. As stated previously, Emory's 19th Corps detachment followed behind the 6th, and Crook's Army of West Virginia, held in reserve, now brought up the rear.

The 6th had been awakened with orders to move since 1:00 a.m., but, preceded by Wilson, it had to wait until 4:30 before marching from camp.[1989] Proceeding directly across the farm fields, led by the 2nd Division, and followed by Ricketts' 3rd Division, with Russell's 1st Division taking up the rear, the 6th Corps arrived at the Berryville Pike about two miles east of the Opequan. There they met Emory

---

1985. O.R. Vol. 43/I, pp.482, 498; Bowen, p. 229, Cheney, pp. 219–220; Altas, plate 99, map 1; Hawkins, pp. 11–12; O.R Vol. 43/I, p. 597, *www.vmi.edu>Archives>*. The Patton referred to here was Col. George S. Patton, of the 22nd Virginia Regiment, who was mortally wounded later in the day. He was the grandfather of the illustrious World War II general, George S., Jr. Grandfather, father, and son all graduated from the Virginia Military Institute.
1986. O'Ferrall, C. T., pp. 89, 94, 96, 114–115; O.R. Vol. 43/II, p. 1247.
1987. Hawkins, p. 153; Early, *Sketch*, p. 424.
1988. Nichols, G. W., pp. 182–183.
1989. Paine, Alanson, p. 256; O.R. Vol. 43/I, pp. 149, 279; O.R. Vol. 43/II, pp. 146–147.

and the 19th Corps, which had already arrived. Emory was told to halt until the 6th Corps had passed, including its ordnance and ambulance trains.

The narrow two-and-a-half-mile long canyon through which the Berryville Pike wound slowed the passage of the 6th Corps, the troops being pressed between the steep sides of the road. It was not until 8:00,[1990] that it finally came forward into the battle area held by Wilson. As they emerged, they were targeted by Ramseur's line, supported by Nelson's artillery. The 6th was not fully deployed until 9:00, and Battery M of the 5th US Artillery, reports that it did not begin to return fire on the enemy until 10:00.[1991]

In the meantime, Emory, as we know, always prompt and ready, had to sit, and watch, and wait. He was "swearing mad." He was angry enough to finally order his lead division, Grover's 2nd, to push forward past and through the 6th Corps train. Nevertheless, it was two hours before the 19th Corps arrived, though it had managed to push up to the rear of the 6th Corps column, and even managed to get in position on the field a little earlier than the 1st Division of the 6th Corps, which had become "mixed up with the artillery and wagon trains." Operations were suspended until all could be fully deployed.

Thus, all that noise which was heard by Merritt, Custer, and Battery K–L, was not a battle, but an artillery bombardment by Ramseur, and the rifles of his skirmishers, while the Federal army struggled to deploy.[1992] The 19th Corps was deployed in two lines to the right of the 6th, all the while closely supervised by Sheridan, who, insisting upon every order being executed to the letter, contributed to even more delay.[1993] It was after 11:00 before the lines were formed as they are depicted in figure 14.[1994]

Note the scope of the battlefield. Ignoring the distant positions of Merritt's cavalry, and Averell who is to the north, the distance from Wilson's position south of Abraham's Creek to the left of Gordon's line on Red Bud Run is almost four miles. Note also that the Berryville Pike, the choke point through which the Federal army took so long to negotiate, is in its rear. It is a point where, if a retreat became necessary, Sheridan could become bottled up, with worse disarray than had occurred during the advance. The potential for Early to strike for the entrance to the canyon and cut Sheridan off was a real possibility. Then Crook could not reinforce, nor could Sheridan retreat. The potential for a situation similar to the Battle of Mansfield was evident. It almost happened.[1995]

1990. O.R. Vol. 43/I, p. 518; Haines, p. 257.
1991. O.R. Vol. 43/II, p. 278; Flinn, p. 177; O.R. Vol. 43/I, p. 318; Early, *Sketch*, p. 421.
1992. *The Story of the First Massachusetts Light Battery*, Bennett, A. J., p. 175.
1993. Clark, p. 219.
1994. Figure 14 from Nicolay and Hay, vol. 9, p. 302, considerably altered, to conform to other texts and maps. See: Atlas, plate 99, map 1; also: F. M. Buffum, facing p. 212.
1995. Sprague, p. 227.

Sheridan's choice of advancing along the Berryville Pike and through the Berryville Canyon had allowed adequate time for Rodes' and Gordon's divisions to fall into line, essentially all of Early's troops save Breckinridge's, rendering Sheridan's strategy of meeting and beating the enemy in detail a failure.

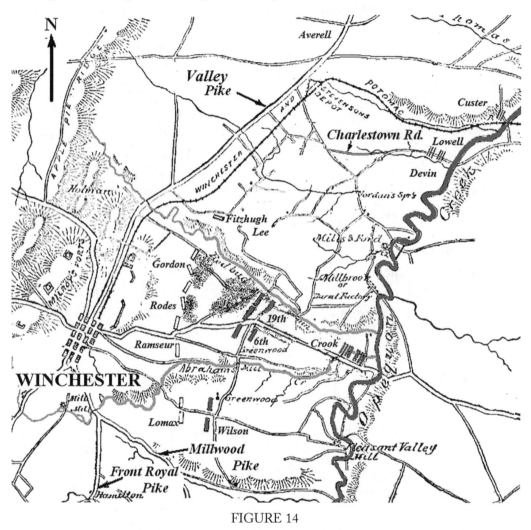

FIGURE 14

In figure 14, the positions of the Union troops are in black, the Confederate positions are uncolored. Wilson is on the south side of Abraham's Creek, a tributary of the Opequan, near the Millwood Pike, to where he moved after the 6th Corps occupied his initial position on the ridge. The 6th Corps positions are, facing west: Getty's division on the Pike, and Ricketts' on the right, several hundred yards west of the gorge. Russell is in reserve to their rear.[1996] The 19th Corps is to the right (north) of the 6th, in an open field behind a heavy piece of woods, Grover in front, Dwight in reserve. Their right rests next to the swampy lowland of Red Bud Run.

1996. Clark, pp. 218–219; Sheridan, vol. 2, pp. 14, 20, 24; O.R. Vol. 43/I, p. 279.

Crook's 8th Corps is seen in reserve, lined up on the Pike, at the entrance to the canyon, in a position to act as a turning column, by advancing towards the Valley Pike south of Winchester. Sheridan was, at this time at least, still hoping to carry out this part of his original plan.

Opposed to Wilson was a part of Lomax's cavalry, consisting of Jackson's and a part of B. T. Johnson's brigades. Opposite the 6th Corps was Ramseur, partially covered by heavy woods, with Nelson's artillery posted on its line. Gordon, who, despite the difficulties of initially missing Early's message to report, had finally arrived from his position at Stephenson's Depot a little after 10:00, and was posted in heavy timber, Red Bud Run on his left, opposite the 19th Corps, with Braxton's artillery. To the north of the Red Bud, was Fitzhugh Lee's cavalry, and a battery of horse artillery.[1997] Rodes, arriving after Gordon, formed on Gordon's right, covered by heavy brush and cornfields.

Strangely, all firing had tapered off, and not a warlike sound could be heard. Finally, at 11:40, Sheridan's bugle call for the advance was heard. Orton Clark of the 116th New York, which was in Dwight's division, behind Grover's, remembers: "All was still as death, to which every man felt he was possibly advancing."

As the two corps lines moved forward, the Confederates opened fire from their hidden positions all along their front. Considerable ground was gained at first. The 6th Corps, the divisions of Getty and Ricketts, guided on the Pike, pressing back Ramseur's infantry, while Wilson, cooperating, faced Lomax's cavalry. The Pike swung gently to the left, and as the lead division of the 19th, Grover's, drove forward into the woods in its front, a separation between the two corps lines began. Grover's division broke into a clearing beyond a wood, and the pace of Birge's brigade was stepped up to reach a second wood in his front, which anchored Early's left, Evans' brigade of Gordon's division. Evans was quickly broken up, and in pursuing him to within range of seven of Braxton's guns, the continuity of Grover's line was lost. This created a gap at the vital point in the Union line where it covered the Pike's entrance to the gorge.[1998]

The success of Grover's advance, by the brigades of Birge and Sharpe, had created an opening for Early. Rodes division having recently arrived, Early ordered Battles' brigade of Rodes' division into Grover's exposed left flank. Under the weight of the fire from Braxton's artillery, Battle's advance, and a terrible flanking fire from Fitzhugh Lee's battery, stationed on an eminence across the Red Bud, not over six hundred yards away, Grover's divisions were compelled to retreat.[1999]

It was here that Lt. Col. Willoughby Babcock of the 75th New York, which was a part of Birge's 1st brigade, was killed. When the news finally was available

---
1997. Haines, p. 258; Early, *Sketch*, pp. 420–422; Sheridan, vol. 2, pp. 21–22; O.R. Vol. 43/I, pp. 150, 222, 266, 279–280, 318–319; Early, p. 422.
1998. Clark, p. 220, O.R. Vol. 43/I, p. 222; Pellet, p. 253; Buffum, p. 212.
1999. Park, p. 90–91; Hall, H. and J., *75th Regiment History*, p. 211.

to those in Battery L who had known him, their thoughts were undoubtedly ones of respect and sadness, but also probably of awe at how long ago it was, or so it seemed in terms of the scale of events, when he was with them as the provost-marshall at Pensacola.

Though *most* of Grover's left was separated from the 6th Corps line, that is, from Ricketts' division, by about five hundred yards, the 156th New York, a part of Sharpe's 3rd Brigade, never lost contact, as Grover points out in his official report.[2000] Ricketts fell back, leaving the 156th stranded, taking all of its 115 casualties there in a few minutes.[2001] Ricketts had taken action to close the gap by ordering three regiments of his 2nd brigade into it, but to no avail. "The bloody but victorious advance was changed into a bloody and ominus [*sic*] retreat."

This was the height of the Union confusion, and was, for them, the most destructive of the day. "Grover's and Ricketts' commands reached the base from which they had advanced in a state of confusion which threatened wide-spread disaster." Emory, Grover, and others, made tremendous efforts to stop the flight,[2002] but 6th and 19th Corps men were crowding together up the Berryville Pike, while to the right and left of it, the fields were dotted with wounded.

On Emory's front, the enemy progress was gradually checked by two small efforts, and a final bloody one that completely recovered all of the lost ground. First, Grover ordered up the 1st Maine Battery, which slowed the Confederates, then the 131st New York, posted by Emory in a wooded ravine, made a flank movement on the advancing Confederate column, and poured such a volley into its backs that it recoiled.[2003] Seizing the opportunity, Grover's 2nd and 3rd Brigades made a second charge, which recovered a large portion of the lost ground. When their ammunition was expended, they were relieved by Dwight's 1st Division, formerly Weitzel's at Bisland and Port Hudson, and Emory's at Mansfield and Pleasant Hill, which had been drawn up in column behind as a reserve. Leading it was the 114th New York, which took 185 casualties out of a total of 315 men present, the highest percentage of any regiment that day, and ranking with the highest in any of the other notorious battles of the war, such as Manassas, Antietam, Gettysburg, or Chickamauga.[2004] As may have been expected, there was controversy over Dwight's behavior during the battle. Grover brought charges against him, among them misbehavior before the enemy. This because he was not seen on the battlefield between noon and 3:30, and was found in the rear "beyond the falling shot of the enemy." This

---

2000. O.R. Vol. 43/I, p. 319.
2001. De Forest, J. W., *Harper's New Monthly Magazine*, vol. 30, New York, 1865, p. 196. De Forest was a captain in the 12th Connecticut Regiment.
2002. Sprague, p. 231.
2003. Hanaburgh, p. 147; DeForest, p. 197; Flinn, p. 182.
2004. Pellett, p. 256; Fox, p. 36; Sheridan, vol. 2, pp. 23, 24; O.R. Vol. 43/I, pp. 150, 300–307; O.R. Vol. 43/II, p. 30.

was in addition to suspicious behavior discovered days earlier, in which movements of the enemy, reported to him, were not forwarded to Sheridan's headquarters. In the end, Dwight survived the controversy.

On the 6th Corps' front, Wright's, the story was similar: Russell's 1st Division, initially in reserve, was ordered up, and Upton's 2nd Brigade fell upon the right flank of the Confederate advance, which together with the action by Emory/Grover, drove them back. Here, Russell was killed. For a period of time the opposing forces were comparatively quiet, rearranging their lines, and preparing for another advance. It was essentially the end of the day's fighting for the 19th Corps, with the exception of some artillery action later in the day, as they were approaching Winchester.

At noon, Sheridan had given up the idea of using Crook as a turning force to try to trap Early south of Winchester, and had ordered him to the front.[2005] The time required to make the two-mile advance through the canyon "so blockaded by ammunition wagons, battery wagons, forges, ambulances and stragglers going to the rear…" was such that he was not in place until about 3:00.

Captain James Garnett, an ordnance officer in Rodes' Division, observed in his diary: "Up to 3 o'clock[2006] we had whipped the enemy well, and but for cavalry we might have held our own against succeeding attacks." Three p.m. would prove to be the turning point.

In the interval that this great infantry battle had taken place, Merritt's cavalry had broken out from its delaying action in front of Breckinridge, as much due to its own actions, or as we have seen, to Breckinridge being ordered to withdraw and come to Early's aid. He did not reach Early until 2:00.[2007] However, essentially freed of entanglement with Breckinridge (only Patton's Brigade had been left behind to aid Fitzhugh Lee in guarding the Martinsburg road) Merritt moved quickly. Custer arrived just outside of Stephenson's Depot at 1:00. Typical of Custer, he reported:

> In the absence of instructions I ordered a general advance, intending, if not opposed, to move beyond the enemy's left flank and strike him in reverse. I directed my advance toward Stephenson's Depot and met with no enemy until two miles of that point, where I encountered Lomax's division of cavalry,[2008] which at that time was engaged with Averell's division, advancing on my right on the Martinsburg Pike. Our appearance was unexpected and caused such confusion…that though charged by inferior numbers, they at no time waited

---

2005. O.R. Vol. 43/I, pp. 361, 280–281; Sheridan, vol. 2, p. 30.
2006. SHS, vol. 31, Richmond, VA, 1903, Garnett, J. M., pp. 62–63.
2007. Early, *Sketch*, p. 424.
2008. Lomax's division was a part of Fitzhugh Lee's cavalry. Lomax, at this time, had four brigades: McCausland's, Imboden's, Johnson's, and Jackson's. O.R. Vol. 43/I, p. 566. The latter two were opposing Wilson, as stated.

for us to approach within pistol range, but broke and fled.

By 2:00 Merritt (Custer, Lowell, and Devin) had linked up with Averell (Schoonmaker and Powell) near the junction of the Charlestown road and the Martinsburg Pike, just south of Stephenson's Depot,[2009] figure 15, where the Federal cavalry is shown arrayed at the top, the opposing Confederate Cavalry, McCausland, and Imboden at the bottom. Here were some 8,000 superbly equipped mounted troops, and counting the artillery that accompanied them, their total made nearly 9,000.[2010] One can only imagine the spectacle that this force presented.

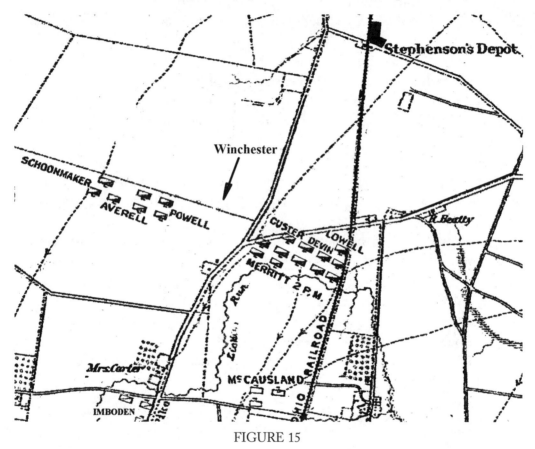

FIGURE 15

Two horses with their riders occupy slightly more space than a modern automobile. Visualize a modern mall or stadium lot with 4,500 cars, and you can appreciate the scale of the overwhelming cavalry force that was descending upon Winchester. Arrayed as they were, each brigade in line of squadron columns, three lines deep,

---

2009. O.R. Vol. 43/I, p. 456; figure 15, Atlas, plate 99, map 1, portion, altered.
2010. O.R. Vol. 43/II, pp. 65, 248. Cavalry returns for September, Torbert, 6,343, Averell, 4,758 present for duty. Wilson's division was not here, as it was posted below Abraham's (Abrams) Creek. Removing his strength, 2,977, results in the quoted total; O'Ferrall, p. 115; Munford, p. 451, claims 11,000.

their front extended more than half a mile.[2011] They advanced at a trot, covered by one continuous and heavy fire of skirmishers, using only carbines. Guidons fluttered (the cover of this book reminiscent), and in the sunlight there was presented one mass of glittering drawn sabers, while the bands played the national airs. James H. Kidd, then a colonel in Custer's 6th Michigan, remembers:[2012] "Officers vied with their men in gallantry and zeal. Even the horses seemed to catch the inspiration of the scene and emulated the martial ardor of their riders." They soon came upon McCausland's cavalry brigade, and Imboden's 18th, 23rd, and 62nd Virginia cavalry, which had taken a position near Mrs. Carter's house. Imboden's was the force which had resisted Averell ever since being pushed back out of Bunker Hill, and Charles T. O'Ferrall, of the 23rd Virginia remembers: "But in the briefest time the Federal cavalry, in a compact mass and powerful in numbers, rushed upon us, and drove us rapidly and in disorder back upon the left flank of Early's infantry line." This Federal horde had pushed the Confederate cavalry to within three miles of Winchester by 3:00 o'clock, the very time that Crook, with his two divisions, the 1st under Thoburn, and the 2nd under Duval, had launched his drive. From the position he had taken on the right of the 19th Corps,[2013] Crook advanced along the north side of the Red Bud, and rapidly drove back Patton's infantry and Payne's brigade of Fitzhugh Lee's cavalry, which had been supporting Patton. Additional elements of Breckinridge's corps, Wharton's were moved by Early, as he writes "in double quick time" to his left and rear, but it would be to no avail.

At about 4:30, Thoburn's left had linked up with Duval, and then had moved on to the Confederate fortifications on the north side of Winchester, where Merritt on the east side of the Pike, confronted Fort Collier, and Averell, on Merritt's right, were confronting Fort Jackson,[2014] in and near which were posted Munford's brigade of Wickham's cavalry, Wickham having succeeded Fitzhugh Lee, see "Federal Line" which the Confederate mapmaker Jedediah Hotchkiss shows in figure 16.

The "fragments of infantry" to the left in figure 16 represent the second line of Breckinridge, Gordon, and Rodes, which was established after their first, opposing Crook's Corps, had to withdraw. Soon, their whole front would give way, retiring south and west through Winchester.

Capt. J. M. Garnett, of General Rodes' Division,[2015] looked at his watch when he saw the Federals enter Winchester. It was 5:07.

2011. Kidd, p. 390; O.R. Vol. 43/I, p. 498; O'Ferrall, p. 115.
2012. Kidd, p. 391; O.R. Vol. 43/I, p. 456.
2013. Sheridan, vol. 2, pp. 25–27; O.R. Vol. 43/I, p. 362; Early, *Sketch*, p. 425; Kidd, p. 391.
2014. Figure 16, Atlas, plate 99, map 1; plate 85, map 16. Figure 16 is presented as it appears in the Atlas, if properly oriented, it would have to be rotated approximately 90° counterclockwise.
2015. SHS, vol. 31, Garnett, p. 67; Early, *Sketch*, p. 426, Sheridan, vol. 2, pp. 26–27.

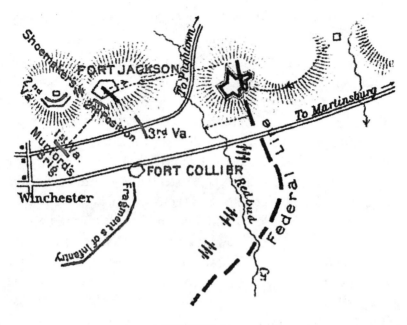

FIGURE 16

Fortunately for Early, Ramseur's line had managed to maintain its organization as it moved south. It checked any attempt by Wilson's cavalry and elements of the 6th and 19th Corps, and even some parts of Merritt's cavalry, to close off Early's escape route. After sunset, which by today's calculations would have been 6:15,[2016] the Valley Pike remained open, and Early withdrew to the area of Newtown, about five miles south, which was not reached until after midnight. Crook reported that he had broken off the pursuit about two miles south.

Sheridan felt it imperative to report the results of the day to Grant, and General Crook conducted him to the home of Miss Rebecca Wright, where he met, for the first time, the lady, who as Sheridan says, "had contributed so much to our success…" Here, at a desk in her school room he wrote his dispatch. It found its way to the telegraph at Harper's Ferry, and was sent out at 11:40 a.m. on the 20th.[2017] It said:

> GENERAL: We fought Early from daylight to between 6 and 7 p.m. We drove him from Opequan Creek through Winchester and beyond the town. We captured 2,500 to 3,000 prisoners, 5 pieces of artillery, 9 battle-flags, all the rebel wounded and dead. Their wounded in Winchester amount to some 3,000. We lost in killed General David Russell, commanding division, Sixth Army Corps; wounded, Generals Chapman, McIntosh, and Upton. The rebels lost in killed the following general officers: General Rodes, General Wharton,

---

2016. *aa.usno.navy.mil*, Winchester, VA; Garnett, p. 66; Nichols, p. 189; Newtown is now Stephens City; O.R. Vol. 43/I, p. 362.
2017. O.R. Vol. 43/II, p. 124; Sheridan, vol. 2, pp. 29–30.

General Gordon, and General Ramseur. We just sent them whirling through Winchester, and we are after them to-morrow.

Passing through Washington, the telegram became known to Stanton and Lincoln, and, it seems, everyone. The last phrase, "whirling through Winchester, and we are after them tomorrow" struck a chord, and it became a household word in a few hours.[2018]

Sheridan fails to mention his casualties, the number of which he must have had an estimate by that time. They were substantial:[2019]

6th Corps : 1,699
19th Corps: 2,074
8th Corps: 794
Cavalry: 451

The total at 5,018, must have been sobering, the huge number being nothing to celebrate. He merely presents them as "about 4,500" in his memoirs.

Battery K–L had 3 men wounded, and since Franck Taylor wrote no official report of the battle, details of where or when are not known.[2020]

James Campbell	Pvt. 15 Nov.'62 Pensacola
John Kelly	Pvt. 26 Dec.'62 Pensacola
John C. Wood	Pvt. 16 Dec.'62 Pensacola

The praise of Sheridan from Washington was effusive, and he was promoted to the permanent rank of brigadier-general of the regular army, and to the permanent command of the Middle Military Department. Grant fired a one-hundred-gun salute from each of his armies at Petersburg and urged Sheridan to "push his success." He had fought what appeared to be a decisive battle and won. This was something that Lincoln had hoped for, but had been afraid of as well, for if Sheridan had gone down to defeat, as had every other Union general in the Valley before him, the news might have caused the administration to be defeated in the November elections.[2021]

None of the Democratic opposition to Lincoln could have quickly had the finer details of the battle, and would not have a chance to analyze it for some time after, even if they then cared. However, we must point out that Early's bitter analysis of it has a ring of truth:

> A skillful and energetic commander…would have crushed Ramseur before any assistance could have reached him, and thus ensured the destruction of *my*

2018. Nicolay and Hay, vol. 9, p. 305.
2019. O.R. Vol. 43/I, pp. 112–118.
2020. Haskin, p. 577, lists five, but the Battery L Monthly Return, from their station at Mt. Crawford, VA, for September lists only 3. The Regimental Return for September, where Battery K is listed, shows no casualties.
2021. Grant, vol. 2, p. 332; Early, *Sketch*, p. 427.

whole force; and later in the day…with the immense superiority in cavalry which Sheridan had…would have destroyed my whole force and captured everything I had.

The losses from the battle of Winchester which Early reported were 3,611, exclusive of those of his cavalry, which were 348 for the period of September 1st to October 1st.[2022] He hints that there were more, saying: "But many were captured, though a good many are missing as stragglers…"

Many of his desperately wounded and dying were left in Winchester when he retreated. The Union Hotel, which had been turned into a hospital, was filled. Other wounded were scattered almost everywhere: the courthouse, in churches, and in private homes; the Confederate surgeons remaining behind.

The attitude of the North, previously analyzed in the section entitled "The Public Mind," concluded that the spirits of the people had been uplifted, almost in the nick of time, by Farragut's exploit at Mobile, and the concern over Sheridan's "retreat" up the Valley had been overshadowed by that news. More good news had followed, upon Sherman's taking of Atlanta, on September 2nd. Now, with the Presidential campaign in full swing, the news of Sheridan's great victory at Winchester came along, and the process of the erosion of support for McClellan had begun.

Of course, the Confederacy was interested in the outcome of the election because in McClellan, there was the chance for a negotiated peace, or at least some softer treatment. Capt. William W. Chamberlain, of Company G, 6th Virginia Infantry, wrote in his memoirs:

> While I was on sick leave [he returned to duty on September 1st] the news from the North led us to believe that the Northern people were anxious to make peace, but a month or two later an entire change of sentiment seemed to have taken place. The Presidential Campaign was then in progress. Lincoln had been nominated by the Republicans, and McClellan by the Democratic Party.[2023]

He also recorded some gossip:

> General A. P. Hill and Mrs. Hill dined one day with General and Mrs. Walker, and in the course of the conversation I heard General Hill say that he hoped General McClellan would be elected, because if it were necessary to surrender, he would prefer to do so to McClellan.

Not only had the sentiment in the north changed, but here, a *corps commander* in Lee's Army of Northern Virginia was openly discussing the possibility of *surrender*.

2022. O.R. Vol. 43/I, p. 555; Park, R. E., pp. 93–95; Haines, A., p. 263.
2023. Chamberlaine, W. W., p. 109.

Chapter 14

Fisher's Hill; The March Up The Valley; Terminated; Tom's Brook/Strasburg/ Woodstock Races; Decisions, Decisions; Sheridan's Ride, Cedar Creek

Fisher's Hill

At daylight on the morning of September 20th, Early continued his retreat, leaving the sides of the Valley Pike strewn with muskets, knapsacks, canteens, and clothing. In the middle of the road were broken-down wagons, their teamsters having cut the harnesses and escaped on the horses. Early was permitted to fall back across Cedar Creek, and he briefly tried to fortify Hupp's Hill, but in the afternoon, he fell back to Fisher's Hill, below Strasburg. Here, he took position on his old defensive line, the one from which he had departed to follow Sheridan north on August 17th. This time, however, he had fewer troops; his line did not extend as far as it had in August, and it was more thinly manned.[2024]

Also at daylight, Merritt's Division, the 1st New York Dragoons in the advance, pushed briskly up the Pike, through Kernstown and Newtown, meeting the enemy cavalry at Middletown, which did not oppose them. Here Devin's brigade and Battery K–L were left to hold the town, and Custer and Lowell continued, arriving at Hupp's Hill, overlooking Strasburg, to discover Early's entrenchments on the south side of Tumbling Run.[2025] No further advance was attempted, pending the arrival of the rest of the army, and of Sheridan making a reconnaissance of the area. At about three o'clock the infantry came up, Emory and Wright marching in the open country on either side of the Pike, with Crook in the rear. Torbert then moved two of Merritt's brigades, Custer's and Lowell's, to the right to join Averell, who had pushed along the Back Road, to the west of, and parallel to the Pike. He was now in position near Cedar Creek, on Early's left. The position to the west of the Pike on Hupp's Hill, which Merritt's brigades vacated, was filled by Wright and Emory to the east. Crook halted to the rear, north of Cedar Creek.

Wilson's cavalry division, when it had reached Middletown, turned toward

---

2024. Denison, Frederic, p. 390; Nichols, p. 189; Early, *Sketch*, p. 429; O'Ferrall, p. 118; vol. 3, Long, A. L., pp., SHS, 118–119; Bowen, p. 239.

2025. Bowen, J. R., p. 239; Sheridan, vol. 2, pp. 33–34; Merritt, p. 510; Haines, p. 264; O.R. Vol. 43/I, pp. 223, 428, 441, 475.

Front Royal, chasing Wickham's cavalry, which Early had directed into the Luray Valley, to a narrow pass at Millwood, to try to prevent a flank attack upon his new position at Fisher's Hill.[2026]

By now, Sheridan had become convinced that any attempt at a frontal assault would be bloody and of questionable success. He resolved upon a flank attack, essentially what he had finally been forced into at Winchester, his frontal attack having taken almost all of the casualties that day. It could have failed, absent the cavalry and Crook. Now, it would be on the right, just as at Winchester, and it would involve Crook, just as at Winchester.[2027] Still cherishing the thought of cutting Early off, which had to be abandoned at Winchester, Sheridan decided to detach Torbert with Merritt's 1st and Reserve brigades to reinforce Wilson's move up the Luray, to ensure that Wickham could be driven out of Luray Pass, and then by crossing the Massanutten Mountain range near New Market, gain Early's rear.

Merritt's 2nd Brigade, Devin and Battery K–L, remained south of Middletown, guarding the rear.

The 21st was spent by Sheridan in reconnoitering the enemy's lines and repositioning his own, by seizing the high bank on the north side of Tumbling Run, which was accomplished by a "brisk fight," and afterwards the work of putting these heights in a defensible condition began. Trees were cleared to facilitate the fire of the artillery, and earthworks were thrown up. These positions, closely opposite Early's, are seen in figure 1,[2028] and are labeled as "SEIZED ON THE 21ST."

Early's defensive line is arrayed all along the high banks on the south (left) side of Tumbling Run. Wharton, now commanding Breckinridge's division, Breckinridge having been ordered to the command of the Confederate Department of Southwestern Virginia,[2029] was on his right, and extending to his left was Gordon, then Pegram commanding Ramseur's old division, then Ramseur, commanding Rodes' division, and at the end of the line, at Little North Mountain, was Lomax's cavalry, dismounted, a mere 300 men.[2030]

Sheridan may have been helped, Early concluding not to retire, by the opinion that he had gained after observing all of Sheridan's activity to establish such a strong position opposite him. Early writes:[2031] "I began to think he was satisfied with the advantage he had gained and would not probably press it further…" Even now, Early seems to have regarded Sheridan as timid. So confident was he that Sheridan would not attack, he had taken all of his ammunition from his caissons

---

2026. Early, *Sketch*, p. 429; O.R. Vol. 43/I, pp. 518–519. Wickham succeeded Fitzhugh Lee, wounded at Winchester.
2027. Sheridan, vol. 2, p. 35; O.R. Vol. 43/I, pp. 428, 441.
2028. Sheridan, vol. 2, p. 39, altered; O.R. Vol. 43/I, p. 152.
2029. O.R. Vol. 43/II, p. 873.
2030. O'Ferrall, p. 118; Sheridan, vol. 2, p. 34.
2031. Early, *Sketch*, p. 430; Sheridan, vol. 2, p. 34; Bowen, p. 239.

and placed them nearby in the breastworks. This also seems to be proof that Early never saw Sheridan's most significant move, that of Crook, until it was too late.

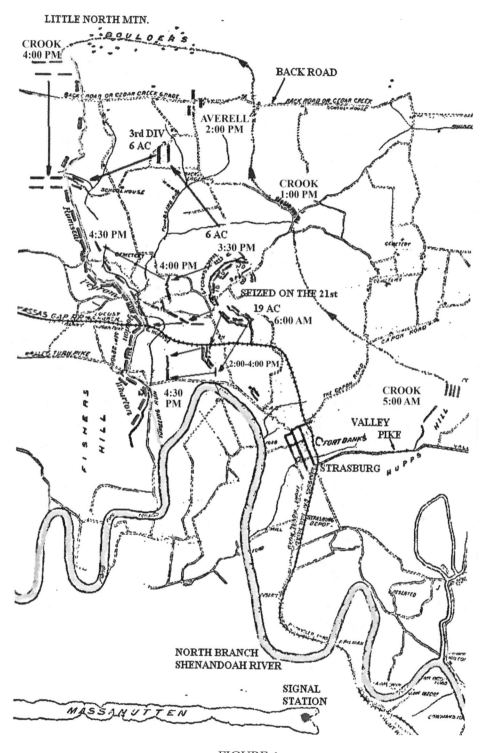

FIGURE 1

Knowing that Early could see every detail of his moves from the observation station on the top of Massanutten Mountain, and learning from a reliable guide that there were forest paths over which an army could move, presumably unseen, to Little North Mountain, Sheridan resolved to put Crook in motion. He waited until the night of September 20th to move Crook into some heavy timber on the far side of Hupp's Hill, near the Valley Pike, where he was ordered to hide all the day of the 21st.[2032] At daylight on the 22nd, he marched around the rear of the 6th Corps, under the cover of the intervening woods and ravines (the dotted trail in figure 1) to a concealed position near Back Road, which he reached by 1:00 p.m.

While this was taking place, Sheridan improved the positions of the 6th and 19th Corps, moving up closer to the Confederate works, which can be seen by the arrows and the times noted in figure 1. In the afternoon, Ricketts' 3rd Division of the 6th Army Corps was pushed out to the far right, near the end of the line of Early's infantry, in the vicinity of Averell's cavalry. While this very visible move occupied Early's attention, Crook completed his move to the base of Little North Mountain.[2033]

Finally, the 19th Corps was moved to a position nearer the Manassas Gap extension of the Virginia Central Railroad, its right resting on the railroad, and the 6th Army Corps was advanced closer still, to within about seven hundred yards of Early's line. It was now 4:00 p.m., and everyone was in position as planned.

Observing Rickett's move, as Early says: "I discovered that another attack was contemplated..." He reacted by giving orders for his line to retire that night, after dark, but it was too late, Crook had begun his move[2034] east from the mountain, along the rear of Early's line. As Crook's cheering men crossed the stretch of broken country between their hidden position and the dismounted cavalry of Lomax, Averell's 1st Brigade, dismounted, also charged forward, and though a piece of Confederate artillery poured grape and canister into them, they were not slowed, and the Confederate resistance began to crumble. Joined by Ramseur, a stand was made on a ridge about a mile from the base of the mountain. Wharton was ordered to the left as well as Pegram. Wharton never arrived, and when Pegram's division joined Ramseur, their lines became disordered. Crook, now united with Averell and Ricketts, then moved along in the Confederate rear with little resistance. The 6th Corps and the 19th then crossed Tumbling Run, and were soon scrambling up the heights, swinging successively into line, and Early was routed, losing 11 guns and whatever property that was in his works.[2035]

Crook followed the retreating Confederates for about two miles, where, in

---

2032. Sheridan, vol. 2, p. 35.
2033. Sheridan, vol. 2, pp. 36–37; Haines, A., p. 265; O.R. Vol. 43/I, pp. 152–153.
2034. O.R. Vol. 43/I, pp. 223, 363–364; O'Ferrall, p. 119; Early, *Sketch*, p. 430; Farrar, S. C., pp. 385, 387.
2035. O.R. Vol. 43/I, pp. 64, 80, 153, 223–224, 283, 364; Sheridan, vol. 2, pp. 38–40, Early, *Sketch*, p. 430.

darkness, he halted, but Ricketts, the rest of the 6th Corps, and the 19th Corps, pursued Early all night, to Woodstock. Averell did not. At midnight, after his 2nd Brigade had guarded Crook's stragglers and captured equipment, he went into camp, and did not move again until daylight.[2036]

At about 5:30 p.m., Sheridan ordered forward the sole remaining brigade of Torbert's cavalry that had not been sent toward Front Royal, Devin's.[2037] To respond to Sheridan's order to chase Early, Devin and Battery K–L, would have to cover the seven miles south to Fisher's Hill before even beginning. Once arriving in the area of Strasburg, his pursuit was slowed by the infantry's presence in the road. Eventually, he says, "with great difficulty" he reached the head of the column, the 19th Corps, with Grover's Division leading. About five miles south of Fisher's Hill, they ran upon a creek, the opposite bank of which had been fortified. It was high, and was covered by woods, in which Early had placed a rear guard of artillery and infantry. The Confederate position was taken and the pursuit was resumed, after, according to Devin: "One section of my battery was placed in position and opened on the enemy's rear." This was Battery K–L, but in the absence of any report by Taylor describing who was involved, it could have been either the section often commanded by Taylor, or the second section, commanded by either of two junior officers from Battery K, W. C. Cuyler or John McGilvray. One section was equipped with Napoleons, and the other with 3-inch rifles.

The pursuit reached Woodstock by 3:00 a.m., and there the 19th Corps went into bivouac, though Devin's cavalry was ordered to continue, and pursue the enemy through to Mount Jackson.[2038] Without rest or breakfast, the pursuit moved on to Edinburg, on the way picking up a number of Confederate stragglers, and finding several burning wagons and an abandoned artillery piece.

Continuing on toward Mt. Jackson, about three miles south of Edinburg, they met Early's cavalry, and drove them through Hawkinsville to within about two miles of Mt. Jackson. Arriving there at about noon,[2039] they discovered a "large force of infantry" bivouacked around the town, and in line of battle. It was Gordon and Ramseur, see figure 2. Early had halted to allow his exhausted troops to rest, and to allow the sick and wounded, and the hospital supplies, all on the slower moving wagons, to be sent on to Staunton.

Battery K–L was ordered into position on a crest on the left of the Pike, and opened on the enemy line. Meanwhile, the 9th New York advanced as skirmishers, with the 6th New York in support, and a warm engagement ensued. At about 2:00 p.m., Averell, who had been following the column, finally arrived and ordered his

---

2036. O.R. Vol. 43/I, p. 499.
2037. O.R. Vol. 43/I, pp. 92, 283, 475; Haskin, p. 213.
2038. Hall, Besley, and Wood, p. 225; O.R. Vol.43/I, pp. 476, 500.
2039. Cheney, p. 223; Hall, Besley, and Wood, p. 226; Nichols, p. 190. Figure 2 is map no. 22, Atlas, plate 85.

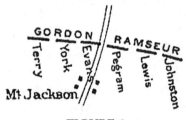

FIGURE 2

two brigades into action, which continued until dark. At that point, Devin, having run out of ammunition, was ordered to retire.

It was here that Sheridan received the news that Torbert had fallen back to Front Royal, and as well, learned that Averell had gone into camp on the night of the 22nd and had left the pursuit to Devin.[2040] Furthermore, Averell had not pressed the action here at Mt. Jackson to Sheridan's satisfaction, Averell preferring to believe the report of a signal officer that a "brigade or division" was confronting him (which we see from figure 2 was true), and as a result, had intended to retire. Sheridan then sent him a note which, in part, said: "I do not advise rashness, but I do desire resolution and actual fighting, with necessary casualties, *before you retire*."

Upon hearing that Averell had literally disobeyed his written order; had retired and had gone into camp near Hawkinsville, Sheridan sacked him. If anyone had been privy to several events leading up to this, it could have been predicted. On September 1st, Grant had sent Sheridan a memo,[2041] which is here quoted in total:

> The frequent reports of Averell's falling back without much fighting or even skirmishing, and afterward being able to take his old position without opposition, presents a very bad appearance at this distance. You can judge better of his merits than I can, but it looks to me as if it was time to try some other officer in his place. If you think as I do in this matter, relieve him at once and name his successor.

To anyone who has been in military service, it is a given that when a superior officer even *hints* at what he desires, it is better to do it. Grant's letter is hardly a hint, and now was the time. Perhaps the unjust part here was that Torbert was not also sacked. In the *History of the 1st New York Dragoons*,[2042] there is found precisely that sentiment. In reference to the Luray Expedition we find:

> Speaking of this fizzle on the part of Torbert, Sheridan says: "I was astonished and chagrined. My disappointment was extreme. To this day I have been unable to account for Torbert's failure." Neither can we account for the keen and discerning Sheridan's appointment and retention of a man so wholly unfitted for the position of chief of cavalry.

Sheridan's situation at Fisher's Hill is reminiscent of Banks' at Bisland. Banks had sent Grover up the Teche, in order to cut off Taylor at Franklin. We know that the plan failed because Grover failed to block the cross road, but at least, Banks had

---

2040. Sheridan, vol. 2, pp. 42–43 (italics added); Early, *Sketch*, p. 432.
2041. O.R. Vol. 43/II, p. 3.
2042. Bowen, J. R., p. 240.

waited. He had held off from making a strong frontal attack on Taylor, to hold him at Bisland, until finally the Clifton had returned with the word that Grover had landed above Irish Bend. Here, in contrast, the impatient Sheridan did not wait to make his attack until some word of Torbert's status was received. Not only should he be angry at Torbert for utterly failing, but at himself for not keeping aware of the situation. This was hardly the sound generalship expected of one of the heroic icons on the war, and Early was allowed to escape once again.

The March Up The Valley

Now began another episode of "the fox and the hounds," or, as Early terms it: "The March Up The Valley." After Averell broke off the engagement at Mount Jackson, Early fell back to Rude's Hill, figure 3,[2043] about two miles south of Mount Jackson, where he camped that night.[2044] On the morning of September 24th, Devin was ordered by Sheridan to push a regiment of his cavalry across the north branch of the Shenandoah and try to flank Early's right, and at the same time, Averell's division, now under the command of Col. William H. Powell, was sent to flank Early's left.

FIGURE 3   FIGURE 4

The 1st New York Dragoons were sent across the bridge, it being intact, figure 4.[2045] Seeing that Early had begun to retreat, Devin deployed the rest of his division, and pressed forward on the trot, coming up on Early's line of battle at New Market, figure 5.[2046] A map of his entire route is shown in figure 6.

2043. Atlas, plate 85, map no. 23.
2044. Early, *Sketch*, p. 432; Nichols, p.190.
2045. Duffey, J. W., p. 9. On October 2nd, when the Partisan Ranger McNeill ordered it burned, the local residents prevented it, fearing that Sheridan would retaliate by burning their homes. Note here the idyllic rural character, the macadamized road surface, and the telegraph poles. O.R. Vol. 43/I, p. 476; Sheridan, vol. 2, p. 46.
2046. Figure 5, Atlas, plate 85, map no. 24.

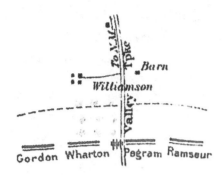

FIGURE 5

Battery K–L was ordered up to the front and placed on a ridge to the right of the road, in the fashion described by G. W. Nichols of the 61st Georgia:[2047]

> They would run cavalry batteries up on top of the hills and shell us severely.

From Devin:

> I opened with shell and spherical case shot, at the same time advancing the First New York as skirmishers. The enemy at once replied with a battery from a hill in my front. I had pressed up to within 500 yards, when the enemy retired precipitately through the town. I charged halfway through the main street, and on the left, but a hot fire from the inclosures [sic] and gardens forced me back. I now dismounted two squadrons of the First New York, cleared the town, charged through with the rest of my command, and found another line formed 300 yards beyond and retiring in excellent order. I again advanced my skirmishers and battery, and again the enemy retired. The chase continued in this manner to a point seven miles south of New Market, the enemy retiring from one position to another, while I pressed them so sharply with my skirmishers and Taylor's battery (I had nothing more) that I was frequently within 500 yards, and the enemy was compelled to retire in line. At dark, I was relieved by the infantry and went into camp…Nothing could surpass the gallantry with which my little force (less than 400 men) continued to press the enemy's line, though at times two miles from support. Lieutenant Taylor handled his guns most efficiently.[2048]

It was in this action that Pvt. Andrew Stoll was wounded.

Devin's men and Battery K–L were on a roll, as Devin rather proudly relates. Early's side of the story agrees, but reminds us of one very significant factor: "As the country was entirely open, and Rude's Hill an elevated position, I could see the whole movement of the enemy, and as soon as it was fully developed, I commenced retiring in line of battle, and in that manner retired through New Market to a point at which the road to Port Republic [the Keezeltown Road] leaves the Valley Pike, nine miles from Rude's Hill [figure 6.]"[2049]

Early could plainly see that following a mile or two behind Devin was a veritable sea of blue, the thousands of the 19th, 6th, and 8th Corps, and though what Devin had done was laudable, he was not driving Early. Early was driven by his, shall we say, "rearview mirror."

2047. Nichols, p. 191.
2048. O.R. Vol. 43/I, p. 476; Early, *Sketch*, p. 432; Sheridan, vol. 2, pp. 46–47.
2049. Atlas, plate 85, Portion of map no. 1, altered; Battery L "September Monthly Report."

On September 25th, Devin was ordered to advance to Harrisonburg, which he did, with the 9th New York in the advance. Though Lomax's cavalry had gone in that direction, he did not find it. However, it was learned that Early had turned off on the Keezeltown Road toward Port Republic, and, though no one then knew it, it was because of Early's intention to join Kershaw, who had been ordered back to the Valley after Lee had heard about the battle of Winchester.[2050] Devin then turned toward the little village of Port Republic.

FIGURE 6

On September 25th, Torbert, with Merritt's two brigades and Wilson's division, finally arrived at New Market. As we have related, he had been ordered to cross the mountains into Front Royal, and with Wilson leading, they had run into Wickham's two brigades at Milford Creek on the 22nd, in a position which Torbert says, "was impossible to turn…" He reported: "Not knowing that the army had made an attack at Fisher's Hill, and thinking that the sacrifice would be too great to attack without that knowledge, I concluded to withdraw…"[2051] He returned to the vicinity of Front Royal, and while there, on the 23rd, he received Sheridan's peremptory order to turn around and advance up to Luray and cross into New Market.

Col. J. H. Kidd, of the 1st Michigan cavalry, remembers: "Torbert made a fiasco of it. He allowed Wickham…with, at most two small brigades, to hold him at bay and withdrew without making any fight to speak of. I remember very well how the Michigan brigade lay in a safe position in rear of the line listening to the firing, and was not ordered in at all. If Custer or Merritt had been in command it would have been different."[2052] As it was, Custer and Lowell led the return trip, and on the morning of September 24th attacked Wickham, scattering his troopers, and the

---

2050. Sheridan, vol. 2, pp. 47–48; O.R. Vol. 43/I, pp. 476–477; Bowen, p. 242; Cheney, p. 223; Haskin, p. 213
2051. O.R. Vol. 43/I, p. 428.
2052. Kidd, p. 396.

way ahead was opened. Kidd adds: "Even then the march was leisurely, and the two big divisions arrived in New Market too late."

Interestingly, Merritt made no official report, and in an article published in *Battles and Leaders*[2053] after the war, he gives little detail, does not explain the expedition's purpose, and abruptly ends the matter, saying: "This design was not accomplished." Wilson's official report was silent on all of the details about the embarrassing withdrawal. Custer made no report. Lowell's was factual, but brief. One statement of his, however, told it all: "September 22,… no attack on the enemy's position was ordered."

We have to conclude that Merritt's and Wilson's reports were an example of doubletalk designed to cover up an event that was embarrassing. Merritt and Wilson were West Pointers, as was Torbert. Lowell, from the 2nd Massachusetts Cavalry, was not a part of the culture, and was not influenced by it.

Credit Sheridan with laconic honesty in a report to Grant on September 25th: "Its operations in the Luray Valley, on which I calculated so much, were an entire failure."

Having arrived, Torbert's divisions were issued rations and forage, and sent on to Harrisonburg. Powell, still in command of Averell's 2nd Division, which had been sent to out to the west, to cover Sheridan's right, also arrived at Harrisonburg, but pushed on to Mt. Crawford.[2054]

On September 26th, not yet knowing of Kershaw's marching back from Culpeper to the aid of Early (Lee had issued the order on the 23rd), and interpreting Early's turn toward Keezeltown as probably caused by Powell's push ahead to gain the Valley Pike at Lacey Springs, which would have flanked him, Sheridan ordered Merritt to catch up with Devin, with orders to advance as far as Port Republic, "to occupy the enemy's attention…"[2055] while Torbert, with Wilson's division and Lowell's Reserve Brigade, were ordered toward Staunton, from where he was to proceed to Waynesboro and blow up the railroad bridge and the tunnel at Rockfish Gap. On his return, he was to drive all of the cattle he could find, and "destroy all forage and breadstuffs, and burn the mills."

Terminated

The key word, "return" was in Torbert's order. Sheridan had begun to think about what to do after Early had escaped him at New Market. Driving Early further, likely to Brown's Gap, would take him across the Blue Ridge Mountains into eastern Virginia, and if he followed, he was certain that he would be urged to pursue further, through Charlottesville and beyond, on a line towards Richmond.

2053. Vol. 4, p. 510; O. R. Vol. 43/I, pp. 490, 519–520.
2054. Sutton, J. J., p. 162; Sheridan, vol. 2, p. 49.
2055. Sheridan, vol. 2, p. 49; O.R. Vol. 43/I, p. 49; O.R. Vol. 43/II, p. 878.

It would pose such a burden on his supply train that a campaign there could not be supported without the opening of the Orange and Alexandria Railroad. (This railroad, and the Virginia Central railroad, would be the subjects of considerable future strategic discussion. The reader may orient himself by looking ahead to the map of figure 11).

To repair and secure the railroad against the guerilla attacks by the likes of Mosby would occupy many men. In addition, he would have to keep secure the gains already made, that of the security of the Baltimore and Ohio Railroad, and the Chesapeake and Ohio canal. There was even the possibility that Grant could not sufficiently hold Lee besieged in Petersburg, who would then detach enough troops to overwhelm Sheridan's then much scattered force.[2056]

On September 26th, Merritt caught up to Devin near Cross Keys, about three miles outside of Port Republic, and took command. Moving on to within two miles of the little hamlet of Port Republic, the 9th New York, in the advance, met and engaged McCausland's cavalry, driving them, without halting, the 3-inch rifles of W. C. Cuyler's section of Battery K–L making some "excellent shots." They arrived in the town just as the rear of Early's wagons were leaving, but Devin's cavalry being far ahead of any of their infantry support, they were not able to capture them. Crossing the South Branch of the Shenandoah, they followed them toward Brown's Gap, into the mountains east of Port Republic.[2057] It was here that Kershaw's men were first encountered. Fitzhugh Lee's and Lomax's cavalry had joined Early,[2058] and Kershaw's division, with Cutshaw's artillery, had crossed through Swift Run Gap, and gone into position below Port Republic on September 25th.

As soon as Devin's Brigade had crossed the river, the second squadron of the 9th New York was ordered to reconnoiter a road that ran along the right bank of the river. One of Early's wagon trains had been seen on the road. About 40 men of the 9th were assembled, and down the road they went. Only too soon they were opened on by Kershaw's men, who had been deployed in some woods on the edge of the road. Just managing to escape with several horses shot, two men captured, and several wounded, they thus confirmed Kershaw's presence the hard way. The rest of the brigade would soon learn that there was a heavy force in their front. Pressed by Kershaw's men, Devin's brigade had to retire away from the woods, to the open country near the river. The "accurate range and splendid execution of Taylor's battery" soon drove the enemy back into the woods, and there, still on the far side of the river, Devin remained encamped.

Sheridan's infantry had halted at Harrisonburg while the cavalry was sent forward on the several reconnaissances described. Having confirmed that Sheridan had halted at Harrisonburg, on September 27th, Early moved out against

---

2056. Sheridan, vol. 2, pp. 53–55; O.R. Vol. 43/I, p. 477; Hall, Besley, and Wood, p. 226.
2057. Cheney, pp. 223–224; Kidd, p. 399, Hall, Besley, and Wood, p. 227.
2058. Early, *Sketch*, pp. 433–434; Sheridan, vol. 2, p. 50.

Port Republic. About noon, the 2nd Division, Powell's, positioned near Weyer's Cave, near Devin, but on the other side of the river, was attacked, and Merritt ordered Devin to withdraw. K–L then marched toward Keezeltown, encamped at Mt. Crawford, near the junction of the road to Cross Keys, and took up a position for battle. Early did not attack, but turned toward[2059] Torbert, using Pegram's division of infantry and Wickham's cavalry to drive him out of Waynesboro on September 28th. Torbert then fell back successively to Staunton, Bridgewater, and Spring Hill.[2060] Early remained at Waynesboro on the 29th and the 30th, and then, on the 1st of October, moved his whole force back on to the Valley Pike at Mount Sidney, opposite Sheridan. In the meantime, Sheridan had sent Merritt back to hold Port Republic, had established the 6th and 19th Corps near Mount Crawford, and thus held a line across the Valley along the North River, extending west to Briery Branch Gap. Crook remained at Harrisonburg.

Merritt, with both the 1st and 2nd divisions, then made a final swing of destruction, leaving Port Republic on the 29th and arriving at Mount Crawford on the 30th.

Though some skirmishing took place in the interval, these positions remained static until the 6th of October. Early's reason for not attempting any move being that he was waiting for Rosser's brigade of cavalry, the "Laurel Brigade," which was on the march from Richmond. Rosser arrived on the 5th. Wickham having resigned, Rosser had been given the command of Fitzhugh Lee's cavalry.[2061] As to Sheridan, he planned only to end the campaign, and retire down the Valley. He was now only waiting for permission to do it.

It was not until the evening of September 29th that Sheridan was able to wire Grant what had happened after New Market, and Grant did not receive the telegram until October 2nd. In the meantime, on the morning of the 29th, Lincoln, with remarkable prescience, had telegraphed to Grant[2062] of his concern that Early would be reinforced, and that Sheridan was in danger. That afternoon, Grant responded that: "I am taking steps to prevent Lee sending re-enforcements to Early by attacking him here." Remarkably, Lee stood firm, not the least moved by Grant's attack, and not only did he not recall Kershaw, but in addition, had ordered Rosser out to aid Early. In fact, Lee urged Bragg[2063] to see to it that everything be done to strengthen Early.

The "steps" that Grant reported to Lincoln was an advance on Richmond. On September 28th, Ord, with the 18th Corps, Birney with the 10th Corps, and Kautz

---

2059. Cheney, p. 225, O.R. Vol. 43/I, p. 442.
2060. Early, *Sketch*, pp. 434–435; Sheridan, vol. 2, p. 50; O.R. Vol. 43/I, p. 477.
2061. Early, *Sketch*, p. 435.
2062. O.R. Vol. 43/II, pp. 209, 879.
2063. Remember that Bragg, following his defeat at Chattanooga and his removal from command (O.R. Vol. 31/I, p. 3), became a military adviser to Jefferson Davis on Feb. 24th, 1864. (O.R. Vol. 32/III p. 3.)

with the cavalry, launched the attack. The 18th Corps captured Fort Harrison, with 16 guns, and took "a good many prisoners." Birney's troops were unsuccessful. Lee responded by reinforcing his position at Fort Gilmer, next door to Fort Harrison, and attempted to retake Fort Harrison. All of Lee's efforts failed, and all that resulted from 394 Union soldiers killed, 1,554 wounded and 324 missing, (more total Union casualties than reported for the entire Battle of Pleasant Hill, chapter 11) was a slight realignment of the siege lines. Another effort by Grant on the 30th was largely unsuccessful in any significant way, and, of course, was a total failure in having any influence on Lee.[2064]

After introducing Grant to his objections to crossing over into east central Virginia in his September 29th telegram, Sheridan grew even more firm, and ended an October 1st report with: "I think that the best policy will be to let the burning of the crops of the Valley be the end of this campaign, and let some of this army go somewhere else."[2065] Later in the day, Sheridan received a dispatch from Halleck which asked about his "push forward to Staunton or Charlottesville."

This caused Sheridan some alarm, already Washington was assuming what he feared, and he immediately sent a lengthy dispatch to Grant, in which he repeated all of his previously announced doubts about a campaign into eastern Virginia. With a supply line of one hundred thirty-five to one hundred forty-five miles, with his present means, he could not accumulate enough supplies to carry him over to the Orange and Alexandria Railroad. He also sent a response to Halleck, in which he proposed to terminate the campaign, and send the 6th and 19th Corps back to Grant, leaving only Crook to hold the Valley.

Here, Stanton stepped in, on October 3rd, not with a disapproval of Sheridan's plan, but, remarkably, with a question as to how to implement it. He wanted an estimate of how quickly the Front Royal Railroad could be repaired, and used to get Sheridan's two corps back to Grant.[2066] Taking this positive cue, Grant asked that the work on the Front Royal Railroad be pushed vigorously, and ordered Sheridan, on the night of October 3rd, to take up a position in the Valley that "you think can and ought to be held, and send all of the force not required for this immediately here."

Sheridan then resolved to move "at least as far as Strasburg," which was duly begun on October 6th. The infantry, passing down the Valley Pike, in rather a reverse of procedure, preceded the cavalry, which, ranging all the way from the Blue Ridge Mountains to the eastern slopes of the Alleghenies, was left to carrying out its orders of destruction.[2067] Henry P. Moyer, of the 17th Pennsylvania Cavalry, after

---

2064. Grant, vol. 2, pp. 333–335.
2065. O.R. Vol. 43/II, pp. 196, 249–250.
2066. O.R. Vol. 43/II, pp. 265–266; Sheridan, vol. 2, p. 55.
2067. O.R. Vol. 43/I, pp. 430, 508; vol. 43/II, pp. 218, 254; Norton, p. 95; Farrar, p. 395; Kidd, p. 396. Custer had briefly replaced Powell in command of the 2nd Division, but with the order

placing a battalion of troops to protect a signal station on a small eminence near Staunton, took a minute to note the scene:

> The view was indeed a grand one, and in anticipation of what was soon to take place left impressions never to be forgotten.
>
> Looking southward…the eye falls on a broad valley…traversed by highways in all directions; towns, villages and churches forming local centers among farms, the improvements upon which were the best in Virginia and possibly in the South. From all points…small bodies of cavalry could be seen, by the aid of field glasses, on every public road, gradually spreading out…giving ample evidence of the thoroughness of their…execution of the order.[2068]

Col. J. H. Kidd, in command of the 6th Michigan, had ordered the startup of several grist mills near Port Republic, thinking to issue the flour to the troops. Having been running since 5:00 a.m. on October 6th, the commissaries were just beginning to issue the flour to their several regiments. But, at about 7:00, Merritt dashed up, and in an angry mood…began to reprimand the colonel for not setting the mills afire. Merritt then pointed west, where "one could have made a chart of Custer's trail where the columns of black smoke… marked it." Merritt was not to be outdone by the likes of Custer.[2069]

With the arrival of Kershaw's infantry, Cutshaw's artillery, and finally Rosser, who either proclaimed himself, or was proclaimed as the "savior of the Valley" with his Laurel Brigade,[2070] Early's strength had been brought back to roughly equal to what he had before the battle of Winchester.[2071] Determined to attack Sheridan, he sent out a reconnaissance on October 5th, only to discover, on the morning of the 6th, that Sheridan had retired. Thus would begin a "stern chase"; Rosser tearing at Custer's heels; Lomax rather tentatively nipping at Merritt's.

Custer, now in command of the 3rd Division, Wilson having been promoted and assigned to General W. T. Sherman in Georgia as his chief of cavalry, took the Back Road; Merritt the Middle Road, and Powell down Page Valley to Luray.

Rosser's men had been eager to be ordered to the Valley; they were in high spirits, optimistic that they could avenge Sheridan's outrages. This, and tales of Rosser's recent deeds of daring apparently having preceded him, he hoped to trade upon them, and garner more recruits as he passed into the Valley. A poster found

---

    to transfer Wilson to Sherman, Custer was moved to the command of the 3rd Division, and Powell again put in command of the 2nd Division; all within the space of a few days. Col. J. H. Kidd, of the 6th New York, then assumed the command of the 1st Brigade, 1st Division, Custer's old "Michigan Brigade."

2068. Moyer, Henry P., p. 215.
2069. Kidd, p. 398.
2070. Fitzhugh Lee, having been wounded at Winchester, was still not able to take the field. T.T Munford, SHS, vol. 13, p. 133; Bowen, p. 244.
2071. Early, *Sketch*, p. 435.

on the door of a grist mill near Port Republic bore this message from the young and dashing leader:

> PATRIOTS OF THE VALLEY: Once more to the rescue of your houses and firesides. Dream not of submission as long as the feet of the Northern vandals desecrate your own native soil. Temporary reverses have befallen our arms in this department; despair not. The government of your choice has declared its speedy redemption paramount to its present and final triumph, and confidently appeals to the patriotic impulses of the masses. Rally. Organize, and report mounted to:
>
> Rosser, Major-general.[2072]

Rosser had just completed participating in Wade Hampton's Great Cattle Raid, which was an enormous embarrassment to the Army of the Potomac. In a three-day expedition, Hampton's men had raided a cattle corral some seven miles below Grant's Headquarters at City Point—obviously well within Union lines. They then successfully drove 2,486 cattle and 304 prisoners back behind Lee's lines. A cattle raid? Though this was cause for Confederate celebration, the desperate need for such a thing was telling. Lee's army[2073] had been on short rations for some time, and unless extraordinary measures such as this were taken, the result would be eventual starvation and surrender. Grant's siege was working.

At dawn on October 7th, Rosser's whole force was in the saddle, and he began his vigorous pursuit of Custer, and as mentioned, left Lomax to follow Devin. Rosser's aggressiveness increased as the miles passed, as they watched the Valley go up in smoke. Many of his men were from the Valley, and Sheridan's acts filled them with rage.[2074] That afternoon, at about 3:00, Rosser made a sudden dash on Custer's wagon train, capturing two forges and several wagons loaded with refugee families. Though Rosser was repulsed, Rosser showed "no mercy to these poor wretches." On the 8th, having bivouacked near Columbia Furnace, at Narrow Passage Creek, Custer continued north on the Back Road, or Cedar Creek Grade, as it was also called. The rear guard was attacked several times on the way. At Forestville, Custer lost seven forges, and several ambulances. After crossing Tom's Brook, about six miles from Fisher's hill, Custer, with Merritt's Reserve and 2nd brigades, which were ordered out to aid him, retaliated in force, doubling back upon Rosser, but Rosser turned back in time to avoid being flanked. According to

---

2072. Moyer, pp. 214–215. At this time Rosser was 28 years old. O'Ferrall, p. 147. It is noted that Confederate cavalrymen were not issued horses, as "report mounted" here implies. They had to supply their own, for which they were given an allowance of 40 cents per day. O.R. series 4, vol. 1, p. 340; series 4, vol. 3, p. 749.
2073. Foote, Frank H., p. 241; McDonald, William N., p. 292.
2074. McDonald, pp. 289–293, 299–301; Boudrye, Louis N., pp. 177–178; Pickerill, W. N., pp. 166–167; Munford, T. T., SHS, vol. 13, p. 136.

the Confederate chronicler, McDonald:[2075] "With a dashing saber charge Custer's column was driven off the Back Road, and the Confederates re-crossed Tom's Brook and went into camp." Custer then pushed on to Fisher's Hill, to within sight of the 19th Corps, before sundown. They then threw pickets back, as far as Tom's Brook, where Rosser had halted, and remained perched on a ridge on its south side.

The same day, Merritt's division having reached Woodstock, on the Valley Pike, the firing of barns and haystacks on the outskirts spread accidentally to the village itself. While the men of two of the Michigan regiments were attempting to douse the flames, they were attacked by Lomax. The 1st brigade, "The Michigan Brigade," under Kidd, then formed to meet it, but Lomax "kept at a respectful distance," while the march moved on, finally approaching Tom's Brook late that afternoon. Here, the Reserve and 2nd brigades were sent to reinforce the beleaguered Custer, and their arrival may have checked Rosser's dashing charge, alluded to above. In turn, the 6th Michigan, leading the 1st and 5th, then chased Lomax back about six miles to near Woodstock.[2076]

It would not have been much of a mystery that Lomax had not energetically attacked, had Kidd observed that Lomax's men were poorly armed. One allegation was that many of his men had no guns, and another more reliable one, was that they were armed only with muzzle loading Enfields, and that fewer than half had sabers. In fact, Lomax later confirmed nearly all of the allegations, reporting that at the coming Battle of Tom's Brook his men had no pistols and no sabers.[2077] It must be remembered that if they all carried Enfields, they were not really cavalry, but mounted infantry, and would have to have dismounted to be able to fire and muzzle-load their weapons, an almost fatal deficiency against the Spencer repeaters of the Michiganders, which could be fired from the saddle, and at that, seven times without reloading.

Tom's Brook/Strasburg/Woodstock Races

That night, while camped on the high ground south of Tom's Brook, Rosser's men found occasion for some sober thought. In fact, some of Rosser's officers tried to persuade him to withdraw during the night, but he was determined to stay, thinking that if pressed, he could withdraw quickly from "an enemy whom he had driven pell-mell for two days."[2078] The numerous campfires of Merritt's division indicated the superior strength of the enemy. In fact, it was overwhelming. If only Merritt's fires were visible, they might have indicated a force of 3,000 to the experienced

---

2075. McDonald, p. 303; O.R. Vol. 43/I, p. 446–447. Here, McDonald seems to have forgotten how poorly equipped the Confederate cavalry was, Lomax having no sabers. Perhaps Rosser had been freshly equipped.
2076. Kidd, pp. 400–401; Whittaker, Frederick, p. 255; O.R. Vol. 43/I, p. 612.
2077. Gilmor, p. 268; O.R. Vol. 43/II, pp. 613, 894; Munford, SHS, vol. 13, p. 140.
2078. McDonald, p. 305.

eye, and Custer's 3rd Division was out of sight, beyond Mt. Olive.[2079] Rosser's total force was about half of that of Custer and Merritt. An accurate estimate of Rosser's force is important to the proper understanding of what took place at Tom's Brook, and it is elusive. A calculation is derived from an incomplete Confederate Strength Report, for October, see figure 7. It has been altered.[2080]

The result is a total that could not have exceeded 2740 officers and men present for duty. Other writers of the time, though none of them quote any authority, quote fewer than what has been derived here. McDonald in *A History of the Laurel Brigade* quotes, "less than 2,000."[2081] Thus, if Rosser had taken the advice of his older and more experienced officers, such as Lomax, West Point class of 1856,[2082] he would have skedaddled. He was about to suffer an ignominious rout.

Command.	Present for duty.		Effective total present.	Aggregate present.	Aggregate present and absent.	Prisoners of war.	
	Officers.	Men.				Officers.	Men.
Lomax's division:							
McCausland's brigade†				670	2,796	40	353
Johnson's brigade		400*		652	2,873		
Jackson's brigade‡	55	386		528	2,559	25	627
Imboden's brigade				356	1,626		
Lee's (Rosser's) division:							
Rosser's (Funsten's, Dulany) brigade	59	754	725	954	2,651		
Wickham's brigade (Munford)		600*		1,505	3,557		
Lomax's (Payne's) brigade¶		600*		662	2,267	36	438
Total	114	2,740*	725	5,327	18,329	101	1,418

FIGURE 7

In this position, Rosser and Lomax were some twenty-five miles ahead of Early's infantry, which was halted at New Market.[2083] Sheridan's infantry, in

---

2079. O.R. Vol. 43/II, p. 248. Torbert's total strength, as of September, including his artillery, is listed as 6,885 officers and men present for duty, exclusive of the 2nd Division (Army of West Virginia) at 4,758, which is listed separately; O.R. Vol. 43/I, p. 965, gives a separate report of Wilson's 3rd Division, for August 30th, which shows 3,355 officers and men present for duty; Whittaker, p. 254, quotes 2,500 each for Merritt and Custer, and 2,000 for the nearby Powell.

2080. Figure 7, O.R. Vol. 43/II, p. 903. Ibid. pp. 556, 559, 612. Lomax cites 800 as the total strength of Jackson's and Johnson's brigades, thus 400 is rationalized as added to the formerly blank "Present for Duty" column for Johnson. Likewise (Early, *Sketch*, p. 435), the remaining blank columns, Wickam's brigade (now commanded by Munford), and Lomax's brigade (now commanded by Payne) has had 600 ascribed to them.

2081. McDonald, p. 305, gives Payne's brigade 300; Lomax reports less than 800 men effective, O.R. Vol. 43/I, p. 612.

2082. Lomax, Cullum, no. 1731. Rosser had attended West Point, and resigned from the class of 1861 at the outbreak of the war. O.R. Vol. 29/II, p. 772. He was a classmate of Custer; Whittaker, p. 258.

2083. Early, *Sketch*, p. 433, Mc Donald, p. 304; Clark, p. 237.

contrast, had moved ahead of its cavalry, whose slow pace was set by the burnings and herding the confiscated sheep, cattle, and hogs.[2084] The infantry had now taken up camp at Fisher's Hill, to where its rear guard, the 116th New York, had finally arrived at 4:00 a.m. on October 8th. For the past two days, the Federal cavalry had always had infantry support ahead of it, and, if needed, and at any favorable place, the infantry could have halted to support Custer and Merritt in an ambush of Rosser, or in an overwhelming counterattack. This did not seem to have dawned upon Rosser, who was convinced of just the opposite. He had extended beyond all hope of succor from his infantry, and the position he had placed himself in was such that if he successfully charged into the Union cavalry, he could not drive them back more than a few miles before running smack up against the encampment of the 19th and 6th Corps, who were now halted, and would remain so, according to Sheridan's plan, which indeed, was to turn on Rosser. Tom's Brook was the perfect place.

It is important to note that nearing Fisher's Hill, the Back Road and the Valley Pike are a little less than three miles apart, looking ahead to figure 9. It would be a perfect place to combine Custer's and Merritt's divisions, and mount an attack.[2085] Annoyed with Torbert since his misadventure in the Luray, Sheridan brusquely dictated that he expected Torbert to "give Rosser a drubbing next morning or get whipped himself" and that the infantry would remain halted until the affair was over. Sheridan also informed him that he would keep an eye on the exclusively cavalry performance from nearby Round Top Mountain.

On the frosty morning of October 9th (there had been snow flurries the day before), Custer's division moved out from its position about six miles north of Tom's Brook at dawn. The advance guard, a battalion of the 5th New York, met Rosser's pickets near Mt. Olive, and after considerable skirmishing, both mounted and dismounted, drove them back to Rosser's established defenses, a line of low ridges running along the south bank of Tom's Brook.[2086] Near the base of these, Rosser had placed a strong line of dismounted cavalry behind stone fences and barricades of rails and logs. On the crest of the ridge there was placed a battery of two guns, strongly supported.

The six miles of skirmishing had taken almost two hours, and it was not until after 8:00 that Peirce's Battery B–L was brought up to shell Rosser. The range from this position to the enemy was apparently too great,[2087] and the relatively ineffective shelling did nothing but cause Rosser to move a group of the led horses of his dismounted skirmishers out of sight. Rosser's guns did not respond at this time.

2084. Bowen, J. R., 243.
2085. Sheridan, vol. 2, p. 56.
2086. O.R. Vol. 43/I, pp. 431, 520; Emerson, E. W., p. 58.
2087. O.R. Vol. 43/I, pp. 520–521, 549. Custer attributes the ineffective fire to defective ammunition; Peirce to high wind. The light twelves in the battery were evidently near their one-mile effective range.

Merritt, already encamped nearer Tom's Brook, moved forward at 7:00; Kidd's 1st brigade, with the 6th Michigan on the right, moved along the north side of the brook to connect with Custer. Devin moved to the center and Lowell to the left, with his left overlapping the Valley Pike.[2088] When formed along the brook, their line of battle extended for more than the nearly three miles between the Back Road and the Pike. As Custer came up, the right of his 1st brigade, Pennington's, overlapped the Back Road, and Custer's 2nd brigade under Wells, was held in reserve behind Pennington, as seen in figure 9.[2089] Martin's 6th New York battery, supported by the 5th Michigan, which was attached to the 1st brigade, was posted adjacent to Custer's left rear, to provide enfilading fire on Rosser.

Facing Custer, his left on the Back Road, was Munford, and behind him was Payne, in support of the artillery. To the right of Munford, was Dulany, in command of the Laurel Brigade. Further along, were Lomax's two brigades, Johnson, and then Jackson, overlapping the Pike, opposite Lowell. The Confederate line was relatively lightly manned in the center, and Rosser's heaviest forces opposed Custer.[2090]

Now, there occurred one of the colorful actions which gave rise to many subsequent fireside stories. Posted to the front, facing Rosser, was Custer, "The Boy General," figure 8, slouch hat in hand, golden braids on his arms, with his golden curls hanging down to his scarlet necktie, and behind him his staff, all identifiable by their scarlet neckties, at the head of the 5th New York.[2091]

FIGURE 8

This could not be missed by Rosser, who looked down from his perch on the ridge. He turned to his staff, and said: "You see that officer down there…that's

---

2088. Bowen, J. R., p. 244; O.R. Vol. 43/I, p.477.
2089. O.R. Vol. 43/I, pp. 520–521; McDonald, p. 305; O.R. Vol. 43/I, pp. 447, 460, 515; Munford, p. 136.
2090. Kidd, p. 402; O.R. Vol. 43/I, p. 612.
2091. Whittaker, p. 254, Boudrye, p. 178; Custer, Elizabeth, title page; Munford, p. 136.

General Custer, the Yanks are so proud of, and I intend to give him the best whipping today that he will ever get, See if I don't."

Custer bowed in a knightly salute to his foe.[2092] He then donned his hat and returned to the line.

Custer's official report mentions none of this, stressing only that he was troubled by the ineffective fire of Peirce's Battery. He then ordered the 5th New York, 2nd Ohio, and 3rd New Jersey to advance as mounted skirmishers, allowing Pierce to be repositioned to within eight hundred yards of the enemy, the position shown in figure 9, where it shelled Rosser's (Thompson's) Battery with "telling" effect, compelling Rosser to withdraw the two guns, after one was disabled.[2093] One of Peirce's light 12 pounders was also disabled, and all of the men of the 7th Michigan who were temporarily supporting the battery were wounded.

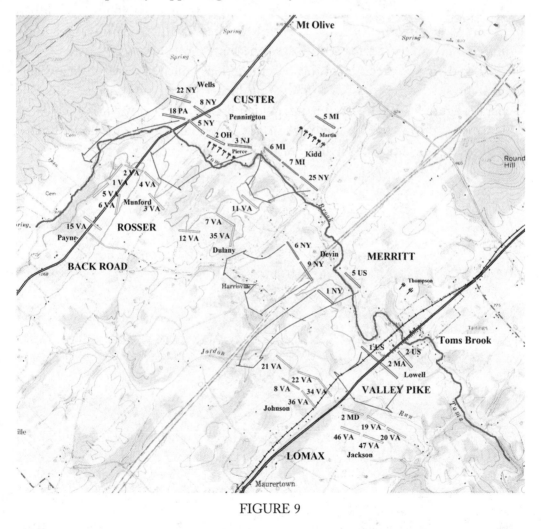

FIGURE 9

2092. Whittaker, facing pp. 258–259; O.R. Vol. 43/I, pp. 520, 549.
2093. McDonald, p. 305; figure 9 drawn by the author.

Seeing the stubborn resistance met by Pennington's skirmishers, Custer ordered the 18th Pennsylvania, supported by the 8th New York and the 22nd New York, to make a flanking move behind the hill upon which Rosser was positioned, figure 9. To support the advanced line, he then ordered Wells' 2nd Brigade, which had been in reserve, forward along the Back Road.

In the meantime, Merritt had gone into position, directing Kidd's 1st Brigade, with Martin's 6th New York battery attached, to connect with Custer's line, and to make a flank attack on the Laurel Brigade, under Dulany.[2094] At the same time, Devin was directed to cross Tom's Brook, and advance in the center, along what is now interstate 81, in between the two concentrations of the Confederate forces, along a ridge midway between the Back Road and the Pike, and into Dulany. Lowell was ordered to advance along the Pike, toward Lomax's two brigades, those of Johnson and Jackson.

Lowell was met by an initial repulse. Seeing it, Merritt ordered Devin to detach two squadrons of the 1st New York Dragoons, while the 5th U.S. Cavalry was hurried from division headquarters to join them, and "curl around" Lomax's left.[2095] It is surmised that Battery K–L's bugler, Louis Rupprecht was wounded at this time.[2096] In the absence of any report by any member of Battery K–L, the only evidence of heavy fighting by any of Devin's commands was that of the 6th New York going after Dulany, and that of the 1st New York Dragoons in support of Lowell.

By now, it was approaching 9:00 a.m. The mounted charge of the 6th, and 7th Michiganders and the 25th New York, of Merritt's (Kidd's) 1st Brigade, aided by the enfilading fire of Martin's battery, had pressured Rosser's right. On his left, the flank move of the 18th Pennsylvania, and the 8th and 22nd New York, had passed unobserved behind the hill to Rosser's left, and pushed rapidly to his rear, near where his hospital and camp of the night before were located.[2097] The bugles then signaled the advance of Custer's line, personally led by Custer, the color bearer of the 5th New York by his side, straight into Rosser's position. Rosser could now hear the yells of the Yankee column in his rear, and on his right, the receding sounds of Lomax's guns. Payne had fallen back, and White's Battalion, on Dulaney's right, fell back. There was no possible chance for Rosser than to move out now, and at a run.

Rosser fell back about a half mile along the Back Road, to a wooded area, where Munford reformed the Laurel Brigade.[2098] Rosser planned to counterattack, but when a Yankee regiment, likely the 6th Michigan, which Col. Kidd reported as "in advance of the other two brigades of the First Division," drew up in full view

---

2094. O.R. Vol. 43/I, pp. 431, 447, 460, 483.
2095. Bowen, J. R., p. 247;
2096. The monthly report only says: "Wounded in action near Strasburg."
2097. Munford, p. 137; Boudrye, p. 179.
2098. O.R. Vol. 43/I, pp. 447, 521.

with drawn sabers, Rosser quailed. To Munford, he confided: "We can't do it." Then Rosser fell back under fire, and after endeavoring to rally several times, reached a point, near Columbia Furnace, where the Yankee pursuit ended.[2099]

As to Devin,[2100] after detaching the 1st New York in support of Lowell, and after Rosser's lines were broken, he gathered up his dismounted skirmishers, and moved out at the trot. Leading the 9th New York, "Uncle Tommy" followed the line of a road west of the Pike.[2101] Reaching "Woodstock with but slight opposition," he then turned on to the Pike, where Torbert ordered him to take the advance and pursue Lomax to Edinburg.

Lowell's advance recovered quickly after being driven back only a "short distance." Lomax had decided to withdraw when he heard "the firing on General Rosser's front retiring rapidly, and stragglers coming from his command with the statement that his force was broken, I withdrew my force slowly, the enemy pressing."

It is noted that Munford and Rosser had decided to withdraw because they had heard the receding sounds of Lomax's guns. No military man likes to admit to deciding to retreat unless forced to, so the conflict remains as to whom exactly withdrew first, Rosser or Lomax. Regardless, Lowell's 1st U.S., 5th U.S. and 2nd Massachusetts, with Devin's 1st New York, followed Lomax's deliberate retreat through the broken and wooded few miles leading up to Woodstock, where Lomax's left was threatened by the appearance of Devin.[2102] The country was now open and unbroken, and Lowell ordered a charge, which fell upon B. T. Johnson's brigade, which, Lomax admits, "was completely broken. I was unable to rally this command." Jackson's brigade was turned to meet Devin, and according to Lomax, "retired in good order." Outside of Edinburg, Torbert having ordered him to take up the pursuit, Devin arrived to find that Lomax had already passed through the town. Taking the 9th New York at the gallop, he pursued Lomax up the Pike, and at Hawkinsburg fell upon him, compelling him to leave one of his two remaining guns. Lomax then managed to throw off Devin at an intersection, sending the 9th down a side road. Learning of his mistake, Devin ordered the 6th New York to take the Pike. The 6th charged clear through Mount Jackson, to the river, where it was

---

2099. Munford, p. 138; O.R. Vol. 43/I. pp. 431, 521. Custer's account and Munford's differ. Here, Merritt's is combined with Munford's. Merritt says beyond Columbia Furnace, Munford infers a point before Columbia Furnace.

2100. O.R. Vol. 43/I, p. 483, 612; Cheney, pp. 227–228; Bowen, p. 247.

2101. This road is mentioned in Cheney, p. 232. It could have been what is now Country Brook Road, or others nearby Saumsville, to Woodstock; Bowen, p. 247.

2102. O.R. Vol. 43/I, pp. 483, 492, 612. Devin never mentions Lomax, and vice versa. Devin is assumed to be the force threatening Lomax's left, though Lomax identifies only an "enemy… column from the Back Road."

learned that a part of Early's infantry was ahead.[2103]

Devin held Mt. Jackson for an hour, while he took stock of the situation. The pursuit had gone on for more than twenty miles, eight miles of that at a gallop, and the horses were beginning to break down. He decided to quit the pursuit and retire, thus ending the "Woodstock Races."[2104]

On returning, Devin learned that the 1st New York had discovered a park of 31 enemy wagons loaded with ordnance and stores. All were burned, according Devin. Others, including six guns, were captured from Rosser by Custer. The guns turned out to be those that were abandoned by the 3rd Brigade, Battery K, at Ream's Station, during Wilsons Raid. The wagons included Rosser's headquarters wagons, which were guarded and sent back intact.[2105] This somewhat settled an old account. Custer got back many of his personal effects which had been captured by Wickham's Brigade at the Battle of Trevilian Station, earlier in June, and now Custer had custody of his old schoolmate Rosser's personal effects. Never failing to be the showman, Custer later appeared at headquarters wearing Rosser's best uniform.

Since Devin was never challenged by any substantial rear-guard action on the part of Lomax, Battery K–L was never called forward to unlimber and shell out any resistance. After Rupprecht was wounded back at Tom's Brook, they had merely gone along for the ride, and only witnessed, "through the eyes of a soldier" one of the great all-cavalry battles of the war. Battery L could, nevertheless, justifiably have "Strasburg" sewn into its battle flag.

Overall, the Union cavalry suffered only 57 casualties,[2106] 48 wounded and 9 killed. Confederate losses were never officially reported, but Sheridan's report of Confederate prisoners said " about 330." Rosser did not call for a report from his subordinates, and it was clear that Early was never fully informed of, as Col. T. T. Munford writes, "the extent of this disaster."

Decisions, Decisions

The Battle of Tom's Brook did nothing to change Sheridan's mind about to leaving the Valley, and the next day the whole army marched away from Fisher's Hill to the north side of Cedar Creek. On October 12th, the 6th Corps, save one brigade stationed at Winchester, was ordered to march to Alexandria, outside of Washington.[2107] Some confusion now resulted from a message from Grant to Sheridan, on the 11th, which, as per the usual flawed procedure, was sent though Washington. Any reasonable person would have assumed that it would then have been forwarded to

---

2103. Early, *Sketch*, p. 436; O.R. Vol. 43/I, p. 484.
2104. Sheridan, vol. 2, p. 59, 431.
2105. Rodenbough, Potter & Seal, p. 112; Crowninshield, B. W., p. 27; Pickerill, p. 167.
2106. O.R. Vol. 43/I, pp. 31, 432; Munford, pp. 134, 139.
2107. Sheridan, vol. 2, pp. 59–61; Early, *Sketch*, p. 437; O. R. Vol. 43/II, p. 346.

Sheridan unaltered. Unfortunately, Grant addressed it to Halleck, who, ever the bureaucrat, *interpreted* the message, rather than forwarding it intact, and sent to Sheridan the "substance" of the message.[2108]

The message from Grant:

City point, Va. *October 11, 1864-9.30 p.m.*

Maj. Gen. H. W. Halleck,
 Washington, D. C.:

After sending the Sixth Corps and one division of cavalry here, I think Sheridan should keep up as advanced a position as possible toward the Virginia Central road, and be prepared with supplies to advance on to that road to Gordonsville and Charlottesville at any time the enemy weakens himself sufficiently to admit of it. The cutting of that road and the canal would be of vast importance to us.

In turn, Sheridan received a ciphered dispatch from Halleck which allegedly relayed Grant's message:

Washington, *October 12, 1864 12M*

Major-General Sheridan:

Lieutenant-General Grant wishes a position taken far enough south to serve as a base for further operations upon Gordonsville and Charlottesville. It must be strongly fortified and provisioned. Some point in the vicinity of Manassas Gap would seem best for all purposes. Colonel Alexander, of the Engineers, will be sent to you to Consult with you as soon as you connect with General Augur.

H.W. Halleck, Major-General

Halleck still evidently fancied himself as the grand strategist at Washington, shaping what Grant wanted into what was a part of Halleck's private strategy, which was to rebuild the Manassas Gap Railroad all the way from Washington to Front Royal, and hold it. From Front Royal, or points along the railroad, an advance up the Valley toward Gordonsville would then be made, step by step, repairing the Orange and Alexandria Railroad as it went.[2109] This was Halleck, still the same as he was at Corinth, and afterward, when he sent Buell east toward Chattanooga, with orders to plod along and repair the railroad as he went.

In any case, though any interpretation of *either* message was contrary to Sheridan's views, the requirement that a strongly fortified position be held, the key item

---

2108. O.R. Vol. 43/II, pp. 339, 343, 345–347, 354.

2109. Grant had become impatient with Halleck, and on the 12th sent him another message asking him to send his first message to Sheridan, (Grant, vol. 2, p. 337, O. R. Vol. 43/II, p. 345). Halleck never did, only responding that "the substance of your dispatch of the 11th was immediately sent to him." O. R. Vol. 43/II, p. 354; Papers of the Military Historical Society of Massachusetts, vol. 6, The Battle of Cedar Creek, by Gen. H. Stevens, Boston, 1907, p. 91.

that Halleck had inserted into the picture, caused Sheridan to abruptly change his mind about sending the 6th Corps away. He responded:

> CEDAR CREEK, Va. *October 13, 1864-9:30 a. m.*
> Maj. Gen. H. W. Halleck, Chief of Staff:
>
> Your telegram dated 12 m. October 12 is received. If any advance is to be made on Gordonsville and Charlottesville, it is not best to send troops away from my command, and I have therefore countermanded the order directing the 6th Corps to march to Alexandria…

Stanton, whether aware of the strategy conflict or not, then stepped into the picture, and, on the 13th, asked Sheridan to come to Washington, saying: "I propose to visit General Grant, and would like to see you first."[2110] Perhaps the whole thing could be set straight.

The same day, Custer, on the Back Road, near Cedar Creek, figure 10,[2111] about four miles north and west of Belle Grove, Sheridan's Headquarters, figure 20, was attacked by Rosser, who succeeded in driving some of Custer's pickets across Cedar Creek. He then advanced about a mile, but was driven off. As a result of this, Merritt's division was moved from the left of the army line to the right (west) going into a position to the left of Custer.

Early had already heard that Sheridan was preparing to leave the Valley, and had moved down, reaching Fisher's Hill that morning. In addition to the thrust by Rosser, he sent a reconnoitering party forward to Hupp's Hill, which overlooked the Federal camp on the north side of Cedar Creek. Soon, a battery was brought forward and began shelling the camp of the 1st Division of Crook's 8th Corps. The 1st and 3rd brigades, under Thoburn, responded, and Conner's brigade of Kershaw's division was then sent forward to meet them.[2112] A "bitter skirmish," as Sheridan calls it, then took place, otherwise known as the Battle of Stickney Farm. It resulted in Thoburn retiring back to the north side of Cedar Creek, and Kershaw retiring to Fisher's Hill. The most significant result of these two encounters was that Sheridan now realized that Early was likely planning to resume the offensive, and writes: "To anticipate such a contingency I ordered the Sixth Corps to return from its march to Ashby's Gap."[2113] This narrative is potentially at odds with the fact that Sheridan had, at

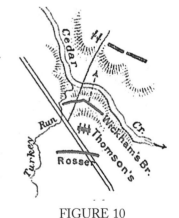

FIGURE 10

2110. O.R. Vol. 43/II, p. 355.
2111. O.R. Vol. 43/I, p. 432; Atlas, plate 85, map no. 35.
2112. Wildes, T. F., pp. 197–199; Sheridan, vol. 2, p. 61, Irwin, p. 406; Early, *Sketch*, p. 437; O.R. Vol. 43/II, p. 365.
2113. Sheridan, vol. 2, p. 61.

9:30 that morning, already telegraphed to Halleck that that he was ordering back the 6th Corps, because of the requirement for more troops in any raid planned to the vicinity of Gordonsville and Charlottesville. The telegram may have been sent after the shelling of the Federal camp had begun, and it had become obvious that Early's full force was present. We cannot be certain, but Halleck's message may or may not have been the reason Sheridan recalled the 6th Corps.

In any case, the 6th Corps arrived back at noon on the 14th, and went into position to the right (west) and rear (north) of the 19th Corps, which held the line along the north bank of Cedar Creek, west of the Pike.

Crook was posted on the left of the 19th Corps, to the east of the Pike, Thoburn's division on a hill overlooking the mouth of the creek where it enters the Shenandoah River. The divisions of Custer and Merritt were placed to the right of the 6th Corps, Custer's left on Cedar Creek, as can be seen, looking ahead to figure 14. Powell covered the roads to Front Royal.

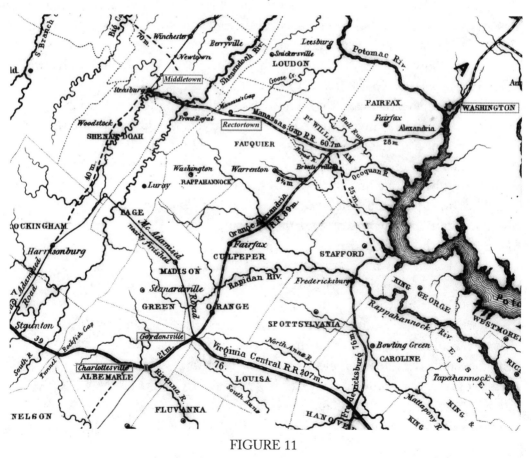

FIGURE 11

Evidence of the urgency that Stanton placed on seeing Sheridan is found in an October 14th telegram sent to General Auger, at Rectortown, then the western terminus of the Manassas Gap branch of the Virginia Central Railroad, out from

Washington, figure 11,[2114] "Has General Sheridan reached you yet?"

On the 15th Sheridan, bound to obey Stanton's summons, rather reluctantly left Middletown, leaving General Wright in command.

Sheridan had been concerned as to whether Early would mount another attack, and had planned to beat him to the punch, as soon as the 6th Corps had returned. However, since Early had withdrawn to Fisher's Hill, Sheridan concluded that he "could do us no serious hurt from there" and deferred the attack, hoping to get to Washington and "come to some definite understanding about my future operations."

As a part of his planned trip, Sheridan would include the raid suggested by Grant. He ordered Merritt's and Custer's divisions to Front Royal, where they would join Powell, and, from there, the entire cavalry force would push toward Charlottesville[2115] to burn the Virginia Central Railroad Bridge over the Rivanna River, near Charlottesville, seen at the bottom of figure 11, while he would go on to Rectortown to take the train to Washington. No doubt, Sheridan knew that one lone railroad bridge in enemy held territory was not of much strategic value unless held, or at least miles of track were torn up as well, for a single bridge could be repaired in a matter of days. To prevent it being rebuilt, the area would have to be held by a substantial force, which Sheridan opposed. Perhaps the raid would divert Early's attention for the interval, and it would signal to Grant that Sheridan was pursuing his wishes. Sheridan makes no explanation in his *Memoirs*.[2116]

On the night of the 16th, upon his arrival at Front Royal, Sheridan received a dispatch and enclosure from Wright:[2117]

> GENERAL,–I enclose you a dispatch, which explains itself. If the enemy should be strongly reinforced in cavalry he might, by turning our right, give us a great deal of trouble. I shall hold on here until the enemy's movements are developed, and shall only fear an attack on my right, which I will make every preparation for guarding against and resisting."
> Very respectfully, your obedient servant,
> H.G. WRIGHT Major-General Commanding

2114. Forsyth, G. A., p. 130; Sheridan, vol. 2, pp. 62–63; figure 11, Viasz map of the Virginia Central Railroad, Ref. LC Railroad Maps, National Archives, only a portion shown, altered.

2115. O.R. Vol. 43/II, p. 363. Grant clarified his position, in this message to Sheridan, dated the 14th. When Sheridan got it is not clear, but Grant now recommended that Sheridan use only a force large enough for a serious threat to the railroad, requiring the enemy to hold a "force equal to your own for the protection of those thoroughfares, it will accomplish nearly as much as their destruction."

2116. Sheridan, Vol. 2, p. 62–63; O.R. Vol. 43/I, p. 508.

2117. Forsyth, pp. 132–133; O.R. Vol. 43/I, p. 51. The message was from Early to Longstreet, a corps commander in Lee's Army of Northern Virginia.

The enclosure read:

> Be ready to move as soon as my forces join you, and we will crush Sheridan.
> Longstreet, Lieutenant-General

The message had been taken down as it was being flagged *from* the Confederate signal station on the top of Three Top Mountain. In cipher, it was translated by Sheridan's signal officers, who knew the Confederate code. What could this mean? Sheridan at first took it as a ruse, but to be on the safe side, he abandoned the cavalry raid toward Charlottesville.

Sheridan, at Front Royal, replied to Wright as follows:

> GENERAL, The Cavalry is all ordered back to you; make your position strong. If Longstreet's dispatch is true, he is under the impression that we have largely detached. I will go over to Augur, and may get additional news. Close in Colonel Powell, who will be at this point. If the enemy should make an advance I know you will defeat him. Look well to your ground and be well prepared. I will bring up all I can, and will be up on Tuesday, if not sooner.

Merritt's and Custer's divisions were then sent back to their original location near Cedar Creek.[2118] Powell's cavalry division had remained since the 13th in the vicinity of Front Royal, his 1st Brigade at Buckton Ford, on the North Branch of the Shenandoah, see figure 14.

Sheridan then proceeded to Rectortown, now only accompanied by the four members of his staff, and his escort, the 2nd Ohio cavalry, of Custer's division.[2119] Arriving at about noon, Sheridan telegraphed Halleck, informing him of the intercepted signal dispatch, and asked whether it was known that any force had been detached from Lee. The answer came back, two hours later, that Grant knew of no troops having left Richmond, and reiterated that if Sheridan could leave his command "with safety, come to Washington, as I wish to give you the views of the authorities here." Having concluded that it was likely that the signal message was of no consequence, since, even if Longstreet had been detached from the Army of Northern Virginia, he could not have reached Early before Sheridan returned. Sheridan then went on, arriving at Washington on the morning of the 17th.[2120]

Early mentions nothing about the ruse in his *Autobiographical Sketch*, but says, "I remained at Fisher's Hill until the 16th, observing the enemy, with the hope that he would move back from his very strong position on the north of Cedar Creek, and that we would be able to get him in a different position, but he did not give any indications of an intention to move, nor did he evince any purpose of attacking

---

2118. O.R. Vol. 43/I, p. 432,509.
2119. Nettleton, A. B., p. 657.
2120. Sheridan, vol. 2, p. 66–72; Forsyth, p. 134–135; Early, *Sketch*, pp. 437–438; O.R. Vol. 43/II, pp. 385–386.

us, though the two positions were in sight of each other."

A careful consideration of the circumstances relating to the receipt of the message would reveal that it was *sent* from the top of Massanutten Mountain, not *received*. Its language is not logical for a received message. Furthermore, the cipher clerk made a note on it, saying: "Longstreet's dispatch reads badly. Cyphers referred to have been repeated. ECKERT."[2121] Sheridan probably never saw the original containing this note, which infers that its content is questionable.

Early finally explained the matter in a private letter to Richard Irwin, the author of *The History of the Nineteenth Army Corps*. Dated November 6th, 1890, Early admits that the signal was instituted by him, and was entirely fictitious; its object was to; "induce Sheridan to move back his troops from the position that they then occupied…"

One can only understand the logic of this thinking by recalling Early's previous commentary regarding Sheridan. Early evidently held such a low opinion of Sheridan's willpower, describing him with such words as "timid," "incapacity," and lacking in "skill or energy,"[2122] that he must have sincerely believed that Sheridan would react in the manner desired.

Thus, we see that it was likely that meddling by Halleck, and a clumsy ruse by Early had caused Sheridan to keep in place a full corps of infantry, and one of the largest and best equipped cavalry forces ever seen in the war, to be ready for the coming battle at Cedar Creek.

Meeting with Stanton and Halleck, Sheridan's objections to operating in eastern Virginia were agreed to, and two engineer officers were assigned to him to scout out a defensive line in the Valley that could be held while the bulk of the army could be returned to Petersburg. The meeting ended at noon. Concerned that he could return as quickly as possible, a special train was provided for his return trip, via the Baltimore and Ohio, to Martinsburg, and a cavalry escort was directed to meet him at Martinsburg. His party arrived there at about dark. Spending the night there, they started up the Valley Pike early the next morning, arriving at Winchester, where the two engineers conducted a survey of the area to determine the "utility of fortifying there."

On the 18th, Sheridan had sent a courier forward to Cedar Creek, with instructions to return with a report of affairs there. The word came back that everything was all right, the enemy was quiet, and that Grover was to make a reconnaissance the next morning. Sheridan writes: "I went to bed greatly relieved, and expecting to rejoin my headquarters at my leisure the next day."

Toward 6 o'clock that morning, the officer on picket duty at Winchester came up to Sheridan's room at the Lloyd Logan Home, figure 12, and reported

---

2121. O.R. Vol. 43/II, p. 386, 699. Major Eckert was assistant superintendent of the U.S. Military Telegraph; Irwin, p. 407–412.

2122. Early, *Memoir*, pp. 75–76; Early, *Sketch* (all subsequent "Early" references are to this), p. 427.

FIGURE 12

that artillery firing could be heard from the direction of Cedar Creek. Asked if the firing was sustained or "desultory," the officer replied, "irregular and fitful." Sheridan assumed that it was Grover's reconnaissance that was heard, and sent the picket officer away.

Not able to return to sleep, Sheridan dressed. The officer returned to report that firing could still be heard. Again questioned, the officer replied that it did not sound like a battle. Regardless, Sheridan requested that breakfast be hurried up, and that the horses be readied. At about a 8:45, Sheridan and his four aides were in the saddle. Riding "at a walk" through Winchester, they arrived at Mill Creek, a mile south, where they met their escort. By now, the sound of the artillery firing was an "unceasing roar."[2123] Moving on, to the crest of a hill, they fell upon the sight of a wagon train, halted, and in disarray; some wagons facing this way and others that. It had been warned to halt, by news from the front that the army had been defeated, and was being driven down the Valley. Moving further along, Sheridan met "hundreds of slightly wounded men" and hundreds of others, unhurt but demoralized, and when accosted, told of the army being broken up, and in full retreat. Sheridan's first reaction was an order to Colonel Oliver Edwards, commander of the 3rd Brigade of the 6th Army Corps, which occupied Winchester, to string his troops across the Valley at Mill Creek, and stop all of the fugitives from passing, though the wagons could be passed through Winchester and parked on the north side.

What to do next? Wait and stop the rest of the whole army at Winchester? Waiting was not something ingrained in Sheridan, and he formulated the idea of riding to the front, to use whatever power his personal presence might accomplish to stop the retreat.[2124]

Sheridan's Ride

The distance from Winchester to Middletown is a little less than twelve miles, and to where the army had been encamped, south of Middletown, about fifteen.[2125] Presently, off dashed Sheridan. He was mounted on the 16-hand Morgan that Capt. Campbell of the 2nd Michigan had given him in Rienzi, Mississippi, after the Battle of Corinth, back in August of 1862, figure 13. He had the distinct advantage of riding

---

2123. Sheridan, vol. 2, pp. 73–77; Forsyth, p. 136; figure 12, Sue Deitz Collection, Stewart Bell, Jr. Archives Room, Handley Regional Library, Winchester, VA.
2124. Sheridan, vol. 2, pp. 77–80.
2125. Forsyth, p. 138.

a horse with great speed and endurance.[2126] His two aides, and the 20 men from the 17th Pennsylvania Cavalry, picked from his escort to accompany him, struggled to follow. The road had become so blocked with wagons, the wounded, and many others unhurt, who simply had fled danger, that they were forced to take to the adjoining fields. Waving his hat, Sheridan shouted: "Turn back, men! Turn back! Face the other way!

FIGURE 13

George A. Forsyth, one of the aides that accompanied him, testifies to the fact that this had but one result: "A wild cheer of recognition, an answering wave of the cap. In no case, as I glanced back, did I fail to see the men shoulder their arms and follow us."

At Newtown, the streets were so crowded that the town had to be bypassed. On this detour, Sheridan met Major William McKinley[2127] of Crook's staff, who agreed to spread the word among the throng. Riding on, south of Newtown, Sheridan saw a body of troops about three-quarters of a mile west of the Pike that he recognized as two divisions of the 6th Corps, but he did not stop, intending to get to the extreme front. Finally, he ran into the rear of the 1st Division of the 6th Corps, Getty commanding, and on the east side of the Pike, Lowell's brigade of Merritt's cavalry, a mile north of Middletown. The army had been pushed back about three miles from the line at Cedar Creek, though it was apparent that the enemy had been checked.

Cedar Creek

When Custer's and Merritt's cavalry returned from Front Royal after Sheridan cancelled the planned raid on the Virginia Central Railroad, Wright returned them to the right, at the end of the infantry line to the west, just as he had stated in his message to Sheridan "…and shall only fear an attack on my right…"[2128]

On October 16th, the indefatigable Rosser reported to Early that his scouts had discovered a campsite of Custer's on the Back Road, near Old Forge Farm, some three miles distant from the main Union line, which allegedly included Custer's headquarters.[2129] It would be an opportunity to "bag Custer." Early gave Rosser

---

2126. Sheridan, vol. 1, pp. 177–178; vol. 2, pp. 81–82; figure 13 from Nettleton, p. 654.
2127. President of the United States 1897–1901, Biographical Directory of the U.S. Congress; Sheridan, vol. 2, p. 82; O.R. Vol. 43/I. p. 194; Forsyth, p. 147.
2128. Sheridan, vol. 2, p. 63.
2129. McDonald, pp. 308–310; Stevens, p. 94; Early, *Sketch*, p. 438; O.R. Vol. 43/I, pp. 580, 605. Old

permission to attack, and a force of 500 picked men, consisting of Rosser's own cavalry, and a mounted brigade of Grimes' North Carolina infantry, of Ramseur's division, set out that night. Unfortunately, Custer's campsite had been moved, and only 30 men of a picket left at the campsite were surprised and captured. It was another of Rosser's failures, and worse, it put Custer and Merritt on the alert. When Early's attack came on the 19th, the cavalry, and as we shall see, Emory's corps, were the only elements of Sheridan's army that were not taken by surprise.

On the morning of the 17th, Early moved all of his troops to the front of his lines to cover the return of Rosser's expedition. He also sent General Gordon, with a brigade of his division, to Hupp's Hill to determine if it was fortified. It was, and Early now was faced with the decision to attack, or move back "for want of provisions and forage." He decided to attack, but not being strong enough for a frontal assault, had to find an approach around "one of the enemy's flanks, and attack him by surprise if I could."

After Gordon's return from Hupp's Hill, Gordon, his chief of staff, Major Robert Hunter, Capt. Jedediah Hotchkiss, Early's topographical engineer, and brigade commander General Clement Evans, were sent up to the signal station on Massanutten Mountain to examine Sheridan's dispositions. Also, General Pegram was ordered to go as near as he could to Cedar Creek, to scout out whether it was practical to make an attack from that flank.

Carefully studying the Union dispositions with a telescope, Gordon writes:[2130]

> It was unmistakably evident that General Sheridan concurred in the universally accepted opinion that it was impracticable for the Confederates to pass or march along the rugged and almost perpendicular face of Massanutten Mountain and assail his left. This fact was made manifest at the first sweep of the eye from that mountain-top. For he had left that end of his line with no protection save the natural barrier, and a very small detachment of cavalry on the left bank on the river, with vedettes on their horses in the middle of the stream. His entire force of superb cavalry was massed on his right…

Gordon was convinced of the potential for success by attacking Sheridan's left. Hotchkiss prepared a map of the proposed route for the attack and presented it to Early that night when they dined together. It was then presented by Early to a meeting of his staff, held at Round Hill, behind Fisher's Hill, the next morning. Though Pegram was in favor of attacking in the direction he had scouted, Early

---

Forge Farm, (listed on the National Register of Historic places) is also referred to as Zane's Furnace, Old Furnace, and Stephen's Fort. It is located at 7326 Middle Road, Middletown, near the intersection of State Route 622 and 628. As the crow flies, it is a little more than four miles west of the Pike.

2130. Gordon, J. B., pp. 333–334.

was already in favor of Gordon's plan.[2131] With the concurrence of the other commanders, Ramseur, Wharton, Rosser, Payne, and Kershaw, plus Carter of the artillery, Gordon's plan was adopted. Gordon, in command of the 2nd Corps, (Evans', Pegram's and Ramseur's divisions)[2132] was to cross the Shenandoah at Fisher's Hill, go around the end of Massanutten Mountain, and again cross the Shenandoah at McInturff's and Bowman's Fords, the route shown by the dotted line in figure 14.[2133] It was so rough that it would have to be prepared by the pioneers of Ramseur's

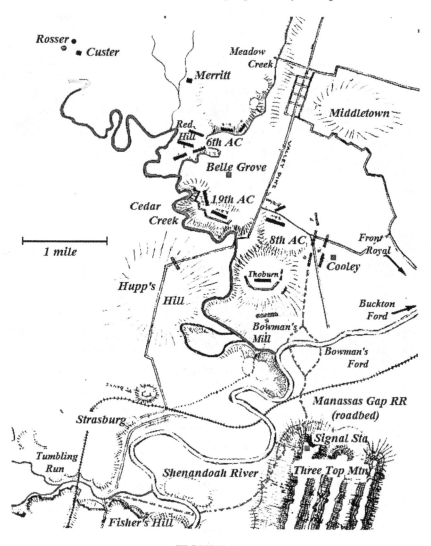

FIGURE 14

2131. O.R. Vol. 43/I, p. 580.
2132. Gordon, p. 335.
2133. Figure 14, frontispiece map from: *The Battle of Cedar Creek*, by Col. B. W. Crowninshield, A Paper Read before the Massachusetts Military Historical Society, December 8, 1879, portion, reoriented north-south, and re-labeled; Stevens, H., pp. 98–99; O.R. Vol. 43/I, pp. 580–581, 613; Early, *Sketch*, pp. 440–441; McDonald, p. 310; Gordon, p. 338.

division prior to the attack. Once across, they would advance past the left flank of Crook's 8th Corps, and press on to the Valley Pike in Crook's rear. Payne's Virginia cavalry was to accompany Gordon, and advance among the disorganized Yankee infantry directly to the Belle Grove House, and capture the commander-in-chief and bring him back as a cavalry "trophy." (Remember Dwight's plan to have Grierson capture Gardner in his headquarters at Port Hudson?)

Kershaw was to move along the Pike through Strasburg, shown by the dotted line to the west of Gordon's track, and at the old railroad crossing, turn off toward Bowman's Mill, crossing Cedar Creek at the ford there, then advance forward to Thoburn's breastworks on the hill opposite, *only when he heard that Gordon had become engaged*. Wharton, followed by the artillery, was to move through Strasburg along the Pike toward Hupp's Hill, hide under the cover of the trees on its edge, and move on the enemy on his front and left, also as soon as Gordon had become engaged.

Rosser was to move on the Back Road, cross Cedar Creek, and engage the Yankee cavalry simultaneously with Gordon's attack. The remainder of Early's cavalry, Lomax's, were to move from the vicinity of Front Royal and support the attack once it had gained the Valley Pike. All watches were set. The attack by Gordon was to begin a little before daylight, at 5:00 a.m.[2134]

Gordon's 2nd Corps and Payne's cavalry began their march to be in position for the attack at 8:00 on the evening of the 18th. No officer was mounted, and none of the men carried canteens or anything that could make noise. Every man had been impressed with the gravity of the enterprise, and everyone spoke only in whispers. Leaving Strasburg,[2135] their guides brought them to the rugged wagon road, and the railroad bed. Finally, they reached the dim pathway the pioneers had prepared along the mountainside, where their long gray line was forced to move single file. Arriving at the two fords on the Shenandoah where their crossing was planned, they waited for more than an hour,[2136] resting on the bank. They could see the Union vedettes sitting on their horses, wholly unconscious of their presence, the low murmur of the river sufficient to mask any whisper.

Meanwhile, after midnight, Kershaw's division, accompanied by Early,[2137] began its march along the Pike to Bowman's Mill Road, which crosses Cedar Creek at Roberts' Ford, figure 15, a little more than a foot deep here, opposite the camp of Crook's 1st Division, commanded by Col. Joseph Thoburn. At 3:30, Kershaw's men were in position within sight of the Union campfires, and were directed by Early to halt, and await the order to cross and advance. (See also the lower left of figure 16.)

Wharton moved along the Pike to Hupp's Hill, with orders to remain hiding

---

2134. Early, *Sketch*, p. 440.
2135. O.R. Vol. 43/I, p. 580; Gordon, p. 336–337. Walker, A. F., p. 134.
2136. Nichols, p. 194. They had all massed on the south bank by 3:00 a.m.
2137. Early, *Sketch*, p. 441–442: O.R. Vol. 43/I, p. 591, McDonald, p. 310; O.R. Vol. 43/II, p. 929.

until the attack began. Carter's artillery was purposely delayed, to avoid the noise of its movement on the macadamized Pike.

Rosser, with the Laurel Brigade, now commanded by Col. O. R. Funsten, of the 11th Virginia, and Wickham's brigade, now commanded by Col. T. H. Owen, of the 3rd Virginia, had moved along the Back Road, to be ready to cross Cedar Creek at Cupp's Ford, opposite Merritt's camp.[2138]

FIGURE 15

Then followed a slight change in the plan; Pegram having observed that a new Federal work was being constructed since the earlier examination of the route Gordon was to take. He had seen the unfinished breastworks being built east of Thoburn by a regiment of Hayes' (the future President) 2nd Division. He recommended that Kershaw's force not wait for Gordon to be in position, which was to be near the rear of Sheridan's line at the Cooley house; Gordon likely to have more difficulty in achieving the position. To this, Early agreed, and Pegram was told to inform Gordon. All of the attacks were now to be simultaneous.[2139]

Waiting on the precipitous bank of the Shenandoah, Gordon writes: "The minute-hand of the watch admonished us that it was time to move in order to reach the 8th Corps flank at the hour agreed upon…" The nearly full moon was still high in the sky, and would provide them with enough light to find their place on Crook's flank, at 5:00 a.m., which was an hour before twilight.[2140] Fortune was with Gordon. A private in the 12th Virginia Cavalry had captured a Yankee picket, who had given him the countersign. With it, the rest of the pickets were approached and captured. There was dead silence, there was no one left to give the alarm. Gordon now gave Payne's cavalry the order to plunge into the river and advance. That done, with Evans' Division leading, Gordon's men rushed into the cold breast-deep current, crossed, and pressed on at the double-quick. No alarm was given by Powell's 1st Brigade, under Moore, stationed a little more than two miles east, at Buckton Ford, though Moore's pickets were supposed to have been

---

2138. McDonald, p. 310; O.R. Vol. 43/I, p. 448.
2139. Early, *Sketch*, p. 442.
2140. http://aa.usno.navy.mil/cgi-bin/aa; Gordon, p. 338; Early, *Sketch*, pp. 442–443; O.R. Vol. 43/I, pp. 372–373, 589–591; Nichols, p. 194. The 12th Virginia was a part of the Laurel Brigade, which was with Rosser not Payne. Why this man was here is not clear, but many of Rosser's men were from the Valley, and he may have been assigned as a guide; Walker, pp. 134–135; Stevens, p. 96.

connected with those of Crook.

Not waiting for the sound of the firing expected from Payne's engagement with Crook's pickets at the river crossing, at 4:30 Early ordered Kershaw to advance.

In the interval, the firing of Rosser, and then Payne, was heard. Early then rode to Hupp's Hill to where Wharton and the artillery had been ordered. He found Wharton's skirmishers being shelled by the only remaining battery of Crook's command, L of the 1st Ohio, which was placed in a position overlooking the bridge at Cedar Creek. Kershaw's artillery was then brought up, and returned fire. Threatened in flank by Gordon's men, and of certain capture by Kershaw, the Ohio battery was forced to retreat down the Pike after only firing a few rounds.[2141]

Rosser's, the remaining arm of the attack, had begun his move at about 4:00. Dismounted, Rosser's men met the pickets of the 7th Michigan Cavalry, of Merritt's 1st Division, who had been posted on the south side of Cedar Creek, near Cupp's Ford.[2142] Driving the Michigan pickets back across the river, Rosser's men initially created a panic in the 7th Regiment. The confusion was aided by a fog which had settled in as the crisp, clear night approached dawn. The 1st Michigan, which was nearby, was roused by the sounds of the scattering shots, and was soon mounted, with Martin's artillery horses hitched. No bugle call had been necessary. As J. H. Kidd of the 1st Michigan, explains it, referring to the two previous raids by Rosser: "The Federal cavalry had recovered from their earlier habit of being 'away from home' when Rosser called. They were…'in' and ready to give him a warm reception. He found that morning that both Merritt and Custer were 'at home.'"

The firing grew heavier, and from the hill where Custer's 3rd Division had camped, three-quarters of a mile away in the direction of Old Forge Farm, the bugle was sounded, telling that their old commander had taken the alarm. The rest of Merritt's 1st brigade was promptly sent to the aid of the 7th. Seeing its deployment, Lowell and the Reserve Brigade arrived on the scene. The night before, they had been ordered by Wright to make a reconnaissance on the Back Road, and were already in the saddle when the attack began.[2143] Rosser did not press the attack. Quoting Kidd: "But contented himself with throwing a few shells from the opposite bank which annoyed us so little that Martin did not unlimber his guns."

The element of surprise which Early would achieve would tend to cast a shadow on Wright, but his precautions had been thorough. On the 18th, Crook was ordered to send out a brigade on a reconnaissance, and it had found no evidence of the enemy in his "old camps."[2144] Crook thus concluded, in an interview with

---

2141. Stevens, H., p. 102.
2142. Isham, Asa, p. 73; Lee, W. O., pp. 100–101; Kidd, pp. 409–411; A much more detailed account is given by McDonald, in the *History of the Laurel Brigade*, p. 310, elaborating some severe fighting, but the fact remains that Rosser halted.
2143. O.R. Vol. 43/I, p. 449.
2144. O.R. Vol. 43/I, p. 158; O.R. 43/I, p. 1042

Wright that evening, that Early had retreated up the Valley. As Wright very graciously reported after the battle: "It should be borne in mind that the destruction of all supplies by our forces between our position at Cedar Creek and Staunton had made it necessary for the enemy to supply his force from the latter place by wagons, and consequently we had been expecting…that he would either attack us or be compelled to fall back for supplies…This view of the matter, which is still believed to be sound, lent the stamp of probability to the [Crook] report…but anxious to place the truth of the report beyond a doubt…" he had ordered Emory to start a division of the 19th Corps to move out on the Pike, up the Valley, and a brigade of cavalry, Lowell's, of Merritt's 1st Division, out on the Back Road, to move parallel to the infantry.[2145] Crook's sloppiness has to have been a factor in the surprise of the Federal army at Cedar Creek.

Though only one division of the 19th Corps, Grover's, was to be involved in the reconnaissance, the apprehensive Emory had given a standing order to the entire 19th Corps to be up, and under arms, that morning. Strange, how when you are cautious, warn others of your concerns, and when nothing happens, you are more than often regarded with disdain, and the inference is that you are a fool. We recall Emory's repeated warnings to Banks about the dangers to New Orleans and the La Fourche while Port Hudson was under siege, and the fact that Taylor had indeed wrought havoc, attacking across Berwick Bay, into the La Fourche, destroying the Federally-worked plantations, and eventually attacking Fort Butler. The situation was eventually saved, though old Emory had initially appeared as an alarmist.

Then, at Mansfield, Chapter 11, Emory was more than justified. He "had from the first hour of the campaign been apprehensive of some sudden attack that should find the army unprepared…" The worst happened, and Emory had been ready to come to the aid of the army in minutes, rather than an hour, and at the double-quick. His action had halted the stampeding retreat of Lee's cavalry and the 13th Army Corps. Now, at Cedar Creek, the worst would happen again, refer to figure 16, an exceptionally detailed map of the battle.

Returning to Kershaw, soon after 5:00, the Georgians of Bryan's brigade, commanded by Col. James P. Simms, without firing a shot, as ordered, had stealthily reached Thoburn's defensive works manned by his 1st and 3rd Brigades. Finally discovered, the attackers were fired upon by the Union pickets. The warning sounds did not give enough time for the 3rd Brigade to properly man the trenches, but it didn't matter. The 1st Brigade, having promptly formed up, and having repelled the initial attack, soon witnessed "the enemy inside the breastwork of the Fifty-fourth Pennsylvania Volunteers [of the 3rd Brigade, on their right], and also over the breastwork of the Fifth New York Heavy Artillery, vacated by the [that] regiments being on picket duty."

2145. O.R. Vol. 43/I, p. 284.

The attackers soon discovered the vacancy—at the very center of the line—that had been assigned to the 2nd Battalion of the 5th New York Heavy Artillery, and charging through, were able to lay enfilading fire in either direction. The entire Union line then collapsed, and the attackers were seen "sweeping," quoting Simms, through Thoburn's camp.

Four officers and 301 men of the 5th were captured, and only about 40 men escaped.[2146] Only two of the 1st Brigade's regiments were able to fall back in good order, and were met at the Pike by Emory, where they joined a new line that Wright and Emory were attempting to form.

The rest of Thoburn's division was driven on in disorder. Simms, pausing only briefly to await the rest of Kershaw's division to close up—Connors, Humphreys, and Wofford's brigades—the four then advanced, as Simms reports: "Driving them like chaff before the wind…"

Thoburn was killed while trying to rally his troops. The fleeing men of the 1st Division now approached the campsite of Hayes' 2nd Division, which had been placed near the Pike as a reserve, about a mile north of Thoburn's line. It had no breastworks, though some were under construction, about three-quarters of a mile to the southeast, the ones that Pegram had noticed.[2147] There were only 1,445 men in camp; one of Hayes' regiments was on picket, and another was guarding cattle south of Middletown. Still another had been assigned to build the breastworks.

Under the direction of Crook, and the supervision of Wright, an attempt was made to form a provisional division, under Kitching, along the Pike on Hayes' left. It was composed of the 1st Ohio Battery, and others like Wildes' 1st Brigade, that had succeeded in fleeing the scene of Thoburn's defeat. It was "early daylight" according to Hayes, something after 6:00 a.m. They were ordered to lie down. The heavy fog concealed anything at a distance, but the firing in their front and on both flanks told them of the advancing foe, Kershaw and Gordon. Soon, fugitives from Thoburn's division were seen streaming by.

2146. Early, *Sketch*, p. 443; O.R. 43/I, pp. 134–135, 379–383, 391–392, 591; Stevens, H., p. 101. Figure 16 from Merritt, *Battles and Leaders*, vol. 4, p. 517, *https://dmna.ny.gov*, (5th Art Table).
2147. O.R. 43/I, p. 403, 417.

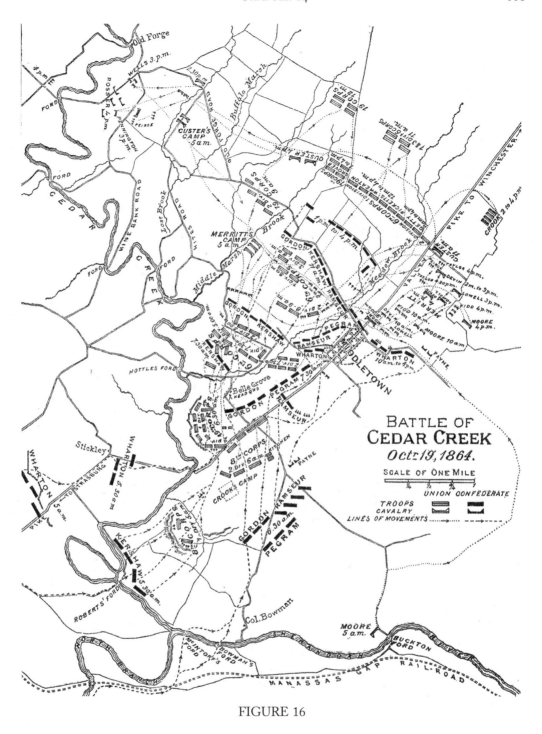

FIGURE 16

When Kershaw had first fallen upon Crook, Emory immediately had headed toward the sounds of the firing.[2148] Though the fog prevented seeing the sweep of Gordon's or Kershaw's advance, he ordered Col. Stephen Thomas' 2nd Brigade of

---

2148. Irwin, p. 418.

Dwight's (McMillan's) 1st Division,[2149] to advance to the left of their breastworks, which faced Cedar Creek. Thomas was to cross the Pike, and advance in a direction (figure 17) to support Crook.[2150] It was here that the slaughter of the Battle of Cedar Creek began in earnest, because here was the first place that any part of Sheridan's army truly made a determined stand.[2151]

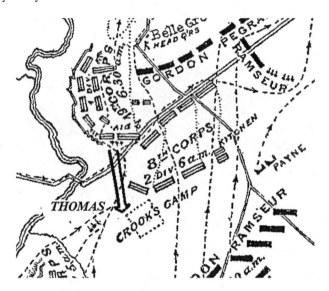

FIGURE 17. DETAIL FROM FIGURE 16

Passing across the Pike, Thomas' brigade plunged into a deep ravine, and a wooded thicket beyond, where they formed up to face both the retreating men of the 8th Corps and the advancing enemy. The intent was to give the men of the 8th Corps a place to form up, but they failed to do so.[2152] In the haste of the slaughter, Thomas' men were unable to reload, and the combat became bayonet and rifle butt against the oncoming horde. The brigade, consisting of the 8th Vermont, 12th Connecticut, 160th New York, and 47th Pennsylvania, was overpowered, and swept back; leaving 85 killed, 246 wounded, and 167 missing. The 8th Vermont suffered 17 killed, 66 wounded, and 23 missing; 103 in all, out of 156 men present, or 67.9

2149. Dwight, as stated in Irwin's *History*, pp. 415 & 432, was present, released from arrest by Sheridan. However, McMillan was in command during the battle. Dwight had been under investigation, accused of conduct unbecoming an officer, from alleged falsehoods in his official report of the Battle of Winchester. Also, he had been charged with misbehavior before the enemy. He was accused of going to the rear, beyond the range of enemy fire. O.R. Vol. 43/I, pp. 300–307. He survived, officially unscathed, by retracting his report, but his reputation as an arbitrary and cowardly officer was merely confirmed in the eyes of his men.
2150. O.R. Vol. 43/I, pp. 284, 308.
2151. O.R. 43/I, pp. 134, 135. The casualty numbers for Thoburn's 1st Brigade total 110 killed and wounded. Compare this with the 498 casualties of Thomas.
2152. O.R. Vol. 43/I, pp. 133, 308, 309; Walker, A.F., p. 137.

percent casualties. This was the seventh highest percentage of any unit in the entire war, though the statistics quoted on the monument to the engagement, see figure 18, differ slightly.[2153] The brigade suffered the highest losses of any other that day. It all had happened in less than half an hour.

Feeling that the improvised line would hold, even though it now faced the combined force of Gordon and Kershaw, Wright had ordered Ricketts, commanding the 6th Corps in Wright's absence, to send forward his 1st and 3rd Divisions,[2154] figuring that it would take them about 20 minutes for them to arrive from their bivouac on Red Hill about a mile to the northwest.[2155] It was not to be. About the time that Wright had given an order to close up the line on the 19th Corps, about a hundred yards to the right, the left of the line, Kitching's brigade was seen to be falling back, flanked, as they were, by Gordon. Soon the fugitives included the remnants of Thomas' brigade.

FIGURE 18

2153. O.R. 43/I., pp. 133, 308, 309; Fox, p. 36. The monument stands where the colors of the 8th Vermont Regiment stood during the engagement. It can be accessed from Claven Lane, off Long Meadows Lane, which leaves the Valley Pike near the entrance to Belle Grove.

2154. O.R. 43/I, p. 158.

2155. Stevens, H., p. 107; Irwin, p. 415.

The enemy now fell upon the 19th Corps' improvised defenses, first striking Grover's Division. The 176th New York, 156th New York, and the 8th Indiana regiments were placed to cover the line facing the southeast, supporting Battery D of the 1st Rhode Island Artillery.[2156] In minutes, they received a random fire from an unseen enemy, which came from the heights formerly occupied by Crook's command. Soon, about one hundred fifty yards distant, the enemy line became dimly visible, extending from Cedar Creek to the left as far as the eye could see. Wharton[2157] had now come up, and joined the combined forces of Gordon and Kershaw—a classic example of an overwhelming force brought to bear at a single point, and with an element of surprise. The enemy swept into the regiments of Grover's 4th brigade, and one gun of the 1st Rhode Island Battery was lost, with all of its horses killed, before it could answer Emory's order to withdraw. Next, the 1st Division, McMillan's, was hit, having gone into a position some four hundred yards to the rear of the struggle on the Pike.[2158] A quote from the history of the 116th New York is instructive: "Bullets began to reach us, but not from the front, and we saw plainly that if we were going to use *this* line of breastworks, which had cost us so much hard work, we must get upon the wrong side of them."

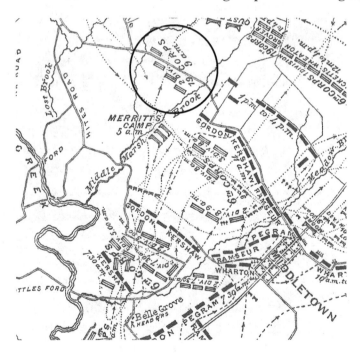

FIGURE 19. DETAIL FROM FIGURE 16

2156. O.R. 43/I, p. 342, 346.
2157. Sumner, G. C., p. 145; O.R. 43/I, pp. 322–323.
2158. Stevens, H., p. 105; Clark, p. 240; O.R. 43/I, pp. 308–309; Irwin, pp. 425–428. Old Forge Road is today called Old Furnace Road.

They were forced to fall back to a position which they soon had to abandon, fleeing past in the rear of the Belle Grove Plantation across Middle Marsh Brook to a position on the right rear of the 6th Corps, which is shown encircled in figure 19.

FIGURE 20

As a matter of interest, the location of Belle Grove, Sheridan's headquarters, is visible at the bottom of figure 19, and a photo appears as figure 20. This also provides a sense of the open country into which the battle now fell.

During this period, Ricketts was wounded, and Getty assumed command of the 6th.[2159] The job of stabilizing the Union line would now fall to him.

Soon after the commencement of the attack, the 6th Corps had been ordered under arms, having no entrenchments, as it was considered a reserve,[2160] it had moved forward and formed on the west side of Meadow Brook. As soon as formed up, the 2nd Division was to have advanced by its left to gain the Pike, and the 1st and 3rd Divisions had been ordered to come forward and join the 19th Corps near the line Wright was forming on the Pike. In Wright's words:

> As the two divisions of the Sixth Corps, ordered from the right of the line to the left, could reach that point within twenty minutes of the time that the line referred to was formed, and as the position taken up was a satisfactory one, there was, in my judgment, no occasion for apprehension as to the result, and I felt every confidence that the enemy would be promptly repulsed. In this

---

2159. O.R. 43/I, p. 159.
2160. O.R. 43/I, pp. 159, 193, 403–404.

anticipation, however, I was sadly disappointed. Influenced by a panic which often seizes the best troops… the line broke before the enemy fairly came in sight, and retreated in disorder down the pike. Seeing that no part of the original line could be held, as the enemy was already on the left flank of the Nineteenth Corps, I at once sent orders to the Sixth Corps to fall back to some tenable position in rear; and to General Emory … that he should fall back and take position on the right of the Sixth.

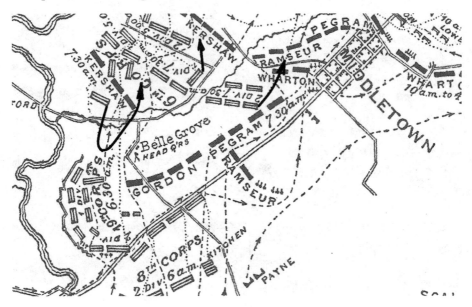

FIGURE 21. DETAIL FROM FIGURE 16

The move is shown by the arrows in figure 21 which reverse direction. Remember that the black symbols are those of the Confederate brigades, and the white are Union. Compare the times.

As can be seen in figure 21, by 7:30, the Confederate line, including Gordon's corps and Wharton's division, had advanced unopposed up the Pike, almost to the outskirts of Middletown. It had pushed back the mix of Wright's defenders several hundred yards across the open country west of the Pike, as far as Belle Grove, which had been the planned objective of Payne's Cavalry. However, the rapid advance of Gordon had completely obviated Payne's assignment.[2161] Kershaw had advanced across Meadow Brook, to a position which faced the old campground of the 6th Corps.

At this point, the losses to the infantry artillery had been substantial. The 1st Maine Battery had to abandon three of its guns, having had 49 horses killed. The 5th New York Battery lost three guns at the crossing of Meadow Brook. All told, the 19th Corps had lost 11 guns, Crook seven, and the 6th Corps, which was to now

---

2161. Carpenter, pp. 208–209.

feel the brunt of the attack, would soon lose six.[2162]

There was no fighting force yet unscathed except the 6th Corps and the cavalry, but Wright could not have known what little impact Rosser's attack had had on them. Wright had decided the next step, and it was withdrawal. With Gordon in control of the Valley Pike, and unopposed on the approach toward Middletown, Wright would soon be flanked on his left and rear. He gave the

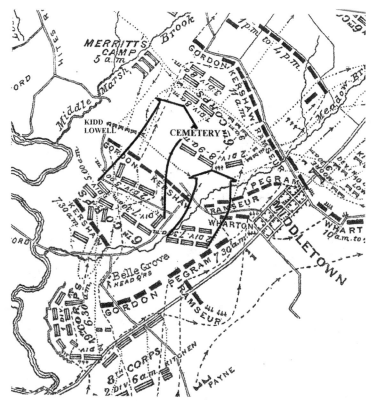

FIGURE 22. DETAIL FROM FIGURE 16

order, the objective point for the withdrawal was the hill upon which the Mt. Carmel cemetery rested, the extension of a ridge of high ground which runs west of Middletown. As it happened, it was adjacent to the camp of Merritt's 1st Cavalry Division. This deliberate withdrawal, done in steps, was completed by the 6th Corps between 8:00 and 9:00, as is indicated in figure 22.

Fortunately for the visitor, both Belle Grove and the cemetery remain today, and are significant points to use to identify the battle area.

Returning to the beginnings of the battle, not long after Rosser had attacked Merritt's camp, he withdrew. An excerpt of Early's Official Report of the battle relates:[2163] "Rosser sent word that when he attacked the cavalry he encountered a part of the 6th Corps supporting it; that a very heavy force of cavalry had massed in his front, and that it was too strong for him, and that he would have to fall back. I sent word to him to get some position that he could hold…"

The "Savior of the Valley" henceforth remained hunkered down for the rest of the morning, of no help to Early. Now, the fully awakened Union cavalrymen found themselves with nothing to do but strain to figure out what was happening

---

2162. Irwin, p. 421.
2163. O.R. 43/I, p. 562.

to the rest of the army. They had not received any orders. Quoting from Col. J. H. Kidd, commanding the Michiganders, i.e., Merritt's 1st Brigade:[2164]

> Colonel Lowell [Charles R. Lowell, Jr., commanding Merritt's Reserve Brigade] informed me that his orders were to support the Michigan men if they needed support. No help was needed at that time. I told him so. The enemy had been easily checked and, at the moment, had become so quiet as to give rise to the suspicion that he had withdrawn from our front, as indeed he had. A great battle was raging to the left, and in response to the suggestion that the army seemed to be retreating, he replied:
>
> "I think so," and after a few moments reflection, said: "I shall return" and immediately began the countermarch. I said to him: "Colonel, what would you do if you were in my place?"
>
> "I think you ought to go, too." he replied, and presently, turning in the saddle, continued: "Yes, I will take the responsibility to give you an order," whereat, the two brigades took up the march toward the point where the battle, judging from the sound, seemed to be in progress. How little either of us realized that Lowell was marching to his death. It was into the thickest of the fight that he led the way, Michigan willingly following.
>
> A startling sight presented itself as the long cavalry column came out into the open country overlooking the battleground. Guided by the sound, a direction had been taken that would bring us to the pike as directly as possible and at the same time would approach the union lines from the rear. This brought us out on a commanding ridge north of Middletown. This ridge…runs to and across the pike. The ground descends to the south a half mile, or more, then gradually rises to another ridge about on a line with Middletown. The Confederate forces were on the last named ridge, along which their batteries were planted, and their lines of infantry [Gordon, Kershaw, Ramseur, and Pegram] could be seen distinctly.
>
> …The full scope of the calamity which had befallen our arms burst suddenly into view. The whole battlefield was in sight. The valley and intervening slopes, the fields and woods, were alive with infantry, moving singly and in squads. Some entire regiments were hurrying to the rear, while the Confederate artillery was raining shot and shell and spherical case among them…Some of the enemy's batteries were the very ones captured from us…but all these thousands, hurrying from the field, were not the entire army…There, between ourselves and the enemy—between the fugitives and the enemy—was a long line of blue, facing to the front, bravely battling to stem the tide of defeat. It was the old Sixth corps—the 'ironsides' of the Potomac army. Slowly, in perfect

---

2164. Kidd, pp. 412–414. The 1st Brigade was called the Michigan Brigade, as it consisted of the 1st, 5th, 6th, and 7th Michigan regiments, though it also included the 25th New York. Kidd here disobeyed Merritt's order to use the 1st Michigan to picket the line against Rosser. O.R. 43/I, p. 449.

order, the veterans…were falling back contesting every inch of the way. One position was surrendered only to take another."

The position which Kidd and Lowell had attained is shown by the line of cavalry symbols labeled KIDD/LOWELL in figure 22.

The successive attacks referred to were by Pegram, and when he was repulsed, another by Wharton, who was sent to fill "a vacancy" in the Confederate line.[2165] Quoting Early: "In a very short time, and while I was endeavoring to discover the enemy's line through the obscurity, Wharton's division came back in some confusion, and General Wharton informed me that, in advancing to the position pointed out to him by Generals Ramseur and Pegram, his division had been driven back by the 6th Corps…The fog soon rose for us to see the enemy's position on a ridge to the west of Middletown, and it was discovered to be a strong one…orders were given for concentrating all our guns on him." The ridge was that upon which stood the village cemetery, figure 22.

Early goes on to disclose the fact that he could see Federal cavalry where it was not expected, on his right, the east side of the Pike: "In the meantime a force of cavalry was advancing along the Pike, and through the fields to the right of Middletown…" This was Moore's brigade of Powell's division, the one that had been stationed at Buckton Ford, just down the river from where Gordon had so stealthily crossed. On his own initiative, Col. Moore had left his position[2166] some time prior to 8:00, and headed north to the sounds of the battle. His circuitous route of some five-and-a-half miles is seen running along the right of figure 16, and a close-up of his final position blocking the Pike is shown encircled in figure 23. The time is 9:30.

Soon after the time that a surprised Early discovered Moore's brigade, the cavalry present on the east side of the Pike would have included two regiments Torbert had placed there on his own initiative. Estimated to be as early as at 7:00, he had ordered his escort, the 1st Rhode Island Cavalry, and Merritt's escort, the 5th U.S. Cavalry, to move to the Pike for the purpose of trying to stem the northward flow of refugees from the 8th Corps. "About this time,"[2167] Devin's 2nd Brigade was ordered to the Pike by Merritt, long before Wright finally ordered "the whole cavalry force" to the left of the army, which was not until after 9:00. The history of the 1st New York Dragoons confirms that Devin "immediately saddled up and moved out without breakfast."[2168] It is interesting to note that by that time, half of the cavalry had already begun their move to the left on their own initiative.

2165. Early, *Sketch*, pp. 444–445; O.R. 43/I, pp. 226, 581; Stevens, pp. 116–117.
2166. O.R. Vol. 43/I, p. 509.
2167. O.R. 43/I, pp. 433, 449.
2168. Bowen, p. 252.

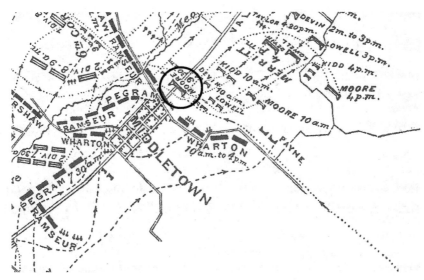

FIGURE 23. DETAIL FROM FIGURE 16

On departure, Devin ordered "Taylor's Battery" to report to Merritt's headquarters, and it was then assigned to the support of the "infantry" which of course was the 6th Corps. After all, the infantry had lost nearly all of its guns. The position that Battery K–L took is assumed to be indicated by the artillery symbols shown in figure 24, alongside the 2nd Division, and the encircled number "1." Successive positions are also shown, the latter two indicating time of arrival. Merritt is quoted in full as to the action:

> On moving to the left General Devin ordered his battery to report to division headquarters, where Lieutenant Taylor, commanding, received orders to advance to an eligible position on the infantry line of battle, and use his pieces on the enemy till such time as it was unsafe to remain there. Great credit is due Lieutenant Taylor for the prompt and efficient manner in which he carried out this order. He was well advanced to the front of battle, without supports from his own command, and none save the thin and wavering line of infantry near his position. The artillery of the infantry had gone unaccountably to the rear, or had been captured by the enemy, and Taylor's was the *only battery* [italics added] for some time on that part of the field. It is thought that his rapid and destructive fire did much toward preventing a farther advance of the enemy on that flank in the early part of the day.

Torbert confirms Merritt's report and adds: "Was the last artillery to leave the front. Too much praise cannot be given to the officers and men of this battery for their coolness and gallantry on this occasion. When the infantry was forced back and was obliged to retire it joined its brigade on the right of the Pike, where it immediately went into action."[2169]

2169. O.R. 43/I, p. 433

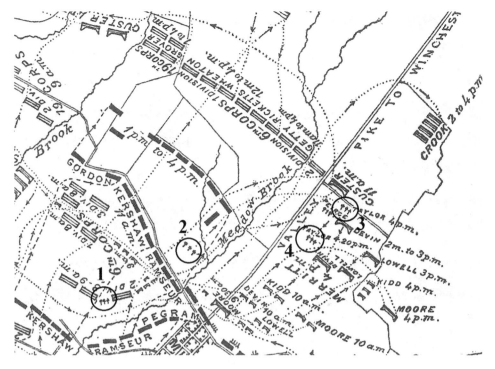

FIGURE 24. DETAIL FROM FIGURE 16

Before 11:00, the infantry had been ordered to again withdraw, and form on and intermediate position along Old Forge Road, on the west side of the Pike.[2170] Taylor was then forced to withdraw, and took a position behind some stone walls that Lowell had seized, which could be position 2 in figure 24, then taking a converging fire from "several" enemy batteries, disabling one three-inch gun, and killing "several men and a number of horses." Later, Devin ordered Battery K–L to move to a more sheltered position on the east side of the Pike, at the end of the final infantry line, number 3. At the time of Sheridan's order to advance, it is shown at number 4, at 4:20 p.m..

Wright finally ordered Torbert to move his "whole force" to the left, which at that time was only Custer's division, the only one that had remained. Here, Torbert used some further initiative, in that he reports that he left "three regiments" back, to cover Rosser. In fact, it was Col. William Wells' 2nd Brigade,[2171] and as he puts it: "To this fact thousands of our stragglers are indebted for their safety, for these brave men held their position at great odds for five hours." His obtuse reference to stragglers was in the context that Custer had remained on the right, until finally ordered to the left at 9:00, and during that time, Custer had deployed a portion of his command to collect and reform infantry refugees, who were rallied and soon

---

2170. O.R. 43/I, pp. 478, 479.
2171. Jackson, H. N., p. 160.

began throwing up defensive works.[2172]

Early was concerned. Wharton's division was ordered to take a position, as Early says, to hold the enemy's cavalry in check. It is the first time that day that he utters a sentence with a tinge of the defensive in it. Discovering that the 6th Corps position on the cemetery ridge could not be assaulted on the left, as its approach was "across an open flat and a boggy stream with deep banks," i.e., Middle Marsh Brook, he then ordered Gordon and Kershaw to attack on the right.[2173] Before the attack took place, the guns of Carter's artillery, 18 or 20 of them, which had been massed on the Pike since 8:00 a.m.,[2174] were put in position on the high ground on the Pike (interpreted to be near where the Cedar Creek Foundation's visitor's center is today), which provided, once the fog lifted, a clear view of the 6th Corps position.

Early's bombardment having commenced, it was time to evacuate, and Wright so ordered both Getty, and Emory.[2175] They were to fall back to the country lane known as Old Forge Road, a place affording no defensive position, but simply a feature upon which to unite the army, and gain time to find a better position further to the rear.[2176] The move experienced some confusion, the brigades losing sight of one another, the 1st and 3rd brigades of the 6th Corps moving a thousand yards further north from where the 2nd Brigade struck the Pike. The 2nd remained at the Old Forge Road position no more than 20 minutes, and then "coolly marched in line of battle a mile further to the rear, when we found a position that General Getty considered suitable to form upon." The was the army's third, and final, position, as can be seen in figure 25.[2177] It was during the course of this move that Sheridan rode past. He notes, as previously quoted:[2178] "Just south of Newtown I saw about three-fourths of a mile west of the Pike a body of troops, which proved to be Rickett's [3rd] and Wheaton's [1st] divisions of the Sixth Corps…" Moving on, he found Getty and the cavalry. The retreat was at an end, and so was Sheridan's ride. It was on a knoll about nine-tenths of a mile from the Middletown line, near what is now called Rienzi Knoll Lane.

Seeing the Union line retreating, Early ordered Gordon, Kershaw, and Ramseur forward as far as (quoting from Irwin) "…the cross-road beyond the cemetery [Old Forge Road]." Continuing, from Irwin:[2179]

> Early had now two courses of action open to him: one was to extricate his

---

2172. O.R. 43/I, pp. 521–522.
2173. Early, *Sketch*, p. 445.
2174. O.R. 43/I, p. 599.
2175. O.R. 43/I, pp. 194–195, 226; Irwin, pp. 425–427.
2176. Stevens, H., p. 122.
2177. Walker, A. F., pp. 144–145; figure 25, Atlas, plate 82, map 9, portion altered.
2178. Sheridan, Vol. II, p. 82.
2179. Irwin, p. 427

army away from its position, with its enemy directly in front and Cedar Creek in rear, before the Union commander could take the initiative; the other was to attack vigorously with all his force before the Union infantry should be able to complete the new line of battle now plainly in the act of formation.

Early did neither. He ordered an attack, but with caveats. Referring to Gordon:

> I ordered him to take position on Kershaw's left, and advance for the purpose of driving the enemy from his new position—Kershaw and Ramseur being ordered to advance at the same time. As the enemy's cavalry on our left[?] was very strong, and had the benefit of an open country to the rear of that flank, a repulse at this time would have been disastrous, and I therefore directed General Gordon, if he found the enemy's line too strong to attack with success, not to make the assault. The advance was made for some distance, when Gordon's skirmishers came back reporting a line of battle in front behind breastworks, and Gordon did not make the attack.

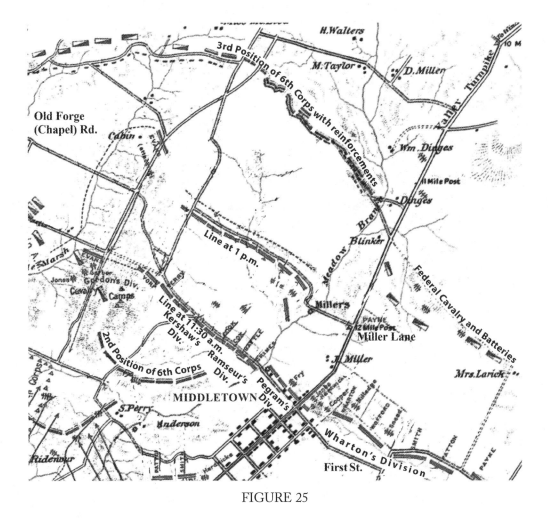

FIGURE 25

The advance referred to was pushed up as far as Miller's Lane; today called

Cougill Road. The Miller house, which still stands; can be seen clearly in figure 25 ("Miller's"), a few hundred yards west of the Valley Pike. The times when the positions were reached are also shown; the Confederate line reached Old Forge Road by 11:30, see "Line at 11:30," and then had advanced to Miller's Lane by 1:00. The Confederates were now stalled.

Early is in error in stating that Gordon did not attack, and Gordon is faulty in skipping over the fact that he halted. This is again referred to below, in conjunction with the description of Sheridan's actions upon his arrival.

The failure to advance further caused recrimination to be expressed in southern literature after the war; Gordon accusing Early of "The Fatal halt at Cedar Creek" with Early and others defending. It is true that the halt allowed time for the Union line to be formed up, allowing the 19th Corps to join it, as well as many of the scattered refugees from the 8th Corps. It would soon be ready to make a stunning and victorious counterattack. However, it is not certain that had the Confederate attack been driven along without the pause that it would have succeeded.

From Gordon:[2180] "The situation was this: two-thirds of Sheridan's army had been shivered by blows delivered in flank and rear. If, therefore, Early's entire army, triumphant, unhurt, and exhilarated, had been instantly hurled against that solitary corps in accordance with the general plan of the battle, it is certain that there would not have been left in it an organized company; and many hours before General Sheridan made his ride, the last nucleus around which he could possibly have rallied his shattered and flying forces would have been destroyed." Of course, Gordon goes on to quote others of his comrades-in-arms who were present that fatal day who agree with him.

From Early:[2181] "It was now apparent that it would not do to press my troops further. They had been up all night and were much jaded. In passing over rough ground to attack the enemy in the early morning, their own ranks had been much disordered, and the men scattered, and it had required some time to re-form them. Their ranks, moreover, were much thinned by the advance of the men engaged in *plundering* [italics added, here again surfaces that controversial word regarding Confederate behavior] the enemy's camps. The delay which had unavoidably occurred had enabled the enemy to rally a portion of his routed troops, and his immense force of cavalry, which remained intact, was threatening both of our flanks in an open country, which in itself rendered an advance extremely hazardous."

Regarding the numbers of the Union troops still capable of opposing Early at that moment, there were about 10,000 cavalry, including their artillery,[2182] and

---

2180. Gordon, p. 356.
2181. Early, *Sketch*, pp. 447–448.
2182. O.R. 43/II, pp. 248, 501. Powell's 2nd Brigade, not present. 8th Corps not included. Estimated 1,000 casualties deducted; Gordon, p. 343. Though Early had estimated he had 8,500 at Winchester, Kershaw's reinforcements were as many as (O.R. 43/II, p. 423) 4,000. Lomax's

the 18,500 infantry of the 6th and 19th corps, with a portion of their artillery. In comparison, according to Gordon, Early had an estimated 10,000 infantry. The numbers speak well in defense of Early. If the notion that his ranks were much thinned by the alleged plundering was true, the advantage Sheridan had over him could have approached three-to-one.

The question about the plundering touched a hot button. For example, a colonel in one of the North Carolina regiments in Grimes' Brigade insisted that none of the hats, blankets, boots, tents, etc., that were scattered about the 8th Corps camp were taken by anyone other than one man who had charges preferred against him.[2183] Grimes himself reports "little plundering…" Certainly, no one would pick up a blanket, to have to carry it throughout the day, but the assertion that no one would search out a canteen, since Gordon's men had taken none, tests credibility.

Here, eschewing any Union reports, or quotes from Union regimental histories, as if they were colored by prejudice, is a quote from Private G. W. Nichols, of the 61st Georgia, in Evans' Brigade of Gordon's Division:[2184]

> We took many prisoners and captured nearly all of their wagons, artillery, ambulances, horses, mules and a great deal of clothing, shoes blankets, tents, etc…We ran in pursuit of them till we had gotten about two miles from their camp, and then everything was halted. A great many of us *went back* to their camp after blankets, shoes, clothing, etc...
>
> It seemed that there were no Yankees in our front. Everything was quiet as death. Some of our boys went to sleep while the others were plundering the camps. I got two nice new tent flies, two fine blankets, a fine rubber cloth, two new overshirts, and two pair of new shoes. In fact, we could get anything we wanted except Yankee money.

While Private Nichols raises a question as to what came first, the halt or the plundering, he leaves no doubt that it happened on a massive scale, and he seems to exempt only those who fell asleep.

The Union line had begun to stabilize at its third and final position at about 11:00.[2185] before Sheridan had arrived; Wright had saved the situation, and members

---

cavalry, estimated by Gordon at 1,700, has been deducted, as they never appeared at the battle; McNeiley, J. S., SHS, vol. 32, 1904, p. 226, gives Early's total infantry and artillery as 12,780; Irwin, p. 437, mentions others who claim 15,000 and up to 22,000.

2183. O.R. 43/I, pp. 600, 608.
2184. Nichols, p.195; Author's italics.
2185. Walker, p. 146; Haines, p. 278; O.R. 43/I, p. 201 Warner, 2nd Brigade, 6th Corps, says: "About 9:30, by direction of General Getty retired slowly and in good order on a line with the First and Third Divisions opposite Middletown. About 10:00 the line was withdrawn to a new position about a mile to the rear." The position is today identified by an historical marker near Rienzi Knoll Lane. Getty reports p. 194, that Sheridan did not *arrive in the field,* until between 11:00 and 12:00. Fair enough, it might not have been until then when he finally was

of his staff have claimed that he issued orders for a planned counterattack. That glory, however, would be remembered as Sheridan's. Upon his arrival, he immediately bought into the moves that Wright had made, though he apparently was unaware, at the moment, that it was Wright that had made them. He established his headquarters nearby.

He then sent his aide, Major Forsythe, to check with Colonel Lowell to see "whether he could hold on there," on the east side of the Pike.[2186] Lowell replied that he could. Sheridan only mentions Lowell, though it must have been obvious to him that nearly his entire cavalry force was there. Satisfied with Lowell's answer, he sent Custer back to the right. Wright was returned to the command of the 6th Corps, and all the others that moved up temporarily were returned to their old slots.

Seeing many of the retreated infantry returning, he directed them to take places in Getty's line. The 19th Corps was directed to take the right, between the 6th Corps and Middle Marsh Brook.

Perhaps two hours had now passed, and at the suggestion of his aide, Sheridan showed himself by riding, hat in hand, along the entire front of the infantry line. The men now knew for sure that he was here, and who was in charge.

Returning to the east side of the Pike see what the enemy "was doing," Sheridan writes that he concluded that Early was preparing for an attack, which came at about 1:00 p.m. on the 19th Corps front. This reference is taken to be the move forward from the Old Forge Road to Miller's Lane by Kershaw, and Evans' Brigade of Gordon's Division, further on the left, on the front of the 19th Corps, which was easily repulsed.[2187] As Sheridan relates: "This repulse…made me feel pretty safe from further offensive operations on their part, and I now decided to suspend the fighting till my thin ranks were further strengthened by the men who were continually coming up from the rear…"

Now, the ever thorough and cautious Sheridan took the time to once again probe the meaning of the mysterious signal from the top of Massanutten Mountain. Was Longstreet's Corps actually with Early? Merritt was ordered to attack an exposed Confederate battery and capture some prisoners. This done, the prisoners confirmed that the only portion of Longstreet's Corps that were present was Kershaw's. As Sheridan relates: "The receipt of this information entirely cleared the way for me to take the offensive."[2188]

The Union line now consisted of the cavalry on the extremes of the right and left. On the east end, across the Pike, was Moore's Brigade of Powell's Division, then Kidd, Lowell, and Devin of Merritt's Division; and on the right was Custer. In

---

able to approach Getty, and later still, Wright; Sheridan, vol. 2, pp. 82–84.
2186. Boudrye, p. 180; Sheridan, vol. 2, pp. 84–85, 89–90; O.R. 43/I, p. 201.
2187. O.R. 43/I, p. 285; Walker, p, 149; Sheridan, vol. 2, pp. 86–87; Stevens, H., p. 130.
2188. A report of Longstreet marching toward Winchester had to be dispensed with as false by Powell. Sheridan, vol. 2, pp. 87–88.

between, from east to west, was the 6th Corps, and the 19th Corps; that is, the divisions of Getty, Kiefer, Wheaton, Grover, and McMillan.[2189] Sandwiched between Getty and Kiefer was a collection of the stragglers from the 8th Corps, under Col. Rutherford B. Hayes, but once the attack was begun, they were withdrawn.

Between 3:30 and 4:00 Sheridan was ready to give the order, which is quoted here in full:[2190]

> Cedar Creek, *October 19, 1864-3p.m.*
> The entire line will advance. The Nineteenth Corps will move in connection with the Sixth Corps. The right of the Nineteenth will swing toward the left, so as to drive the enemy upon the pike.
>
> P.H. SHERIDAN
> *Major-General*

The "swing toward the left" was meant to have the line pivot about its left and close on the Pike, much as a door on its hinge. The intent was to block the Pike, preventing the retreat of the Confederates back to Strasburg and Fisher's Hill. However, what actually happened was that enemy's right gave way after Lowell courageously charged; the charge in which he was killed.[2191] This tore loose the hinge, and the eagerness of the men, with the left insisting upon keeping pace with the right, the line instead advanced along the Pike. The old Union camps at Cedar Creek were regained, and there the infantry halted; but the cavalry were ordered to keep on.[2192]

The country being entirely open, Custer's impressive force of cavalry could be clearly seen by Early bearing down on his left flank, and quoting Custer: "Realizing the necessity of at once gaining the bridge, [across Cedar Creek] the disordered masses of the enemy, now completely panic-stricken, threw away their arms…and sought safety in ignominious flight."[2193] Though exhilarating to observe, the practical matter was that most of Early's army was able to escape, up to this point at least, as Custer admits, with a "small loss in prisoners." Sheridan's tactics had failed to trap Early here, just as it had failed at Winchester.

Some few prisoners were captured by Merritt's cavalry which had, only moments later, arrived at the bridge, and would soon unite with Custer in the chase.[2194] Custer had crossed Cedar Creek at a "difficult" ford, about a mile west of the bridge, and after meeting an enemy line of resistance behind a stone wall about a quarter of a mile beyond, his 1st Vermont and 5th New York broke through, and

---

2189. O.R. 43/I, pp. 227, 284–285, 523.
2190. O.R. 43/II, pp. 33, 416.
2191. Sheridan, vol. 2, p. 90.
2192. Walker, p. 153; Jackson, p. 160.
2193. O.R. 43/I, p. 524, 562–563.
2194. Sheridan, p. 90, O.R. 43/I, p. 525

were able to reach the Pike, though darkness was fast approaching.[2195] Reaching a point about a half-mile beyond Strasburg, they found: "The road blockaded for miles with guns and wagons and ambulances filled with wounded. Whole batteries were captured, with guns, men and horses intact."

Devin, leading Merritt's Division, met the last resistance of the day, one volley, from a line of Confederate infantry on the south side of the Cedar Creek Bridge, before it broke for the woods as the 6th New York charged across the narrow one hundred-and-fifty-foot-long span.[2196] Shortly, they met a group from Custer's cavalry, and were confronted with all of what Custer had captured and left behind. Custer's 1st Vermont and 5th New York continued on through Strasburg, and approaching Fisher's Hill, at nearly midnight, the pursuit was ended.

The result of the battle was the recapture of all of the guns and camp equipage that had been lost earlier in the day, plus 24 guns, 1,200 prisoners, and an immense amount of wagons and equipment. The 1st Division and a brigade of the 2nd Division of the 19th Corps, after two hours rest, were sent out to Strasburg to aid in securing it.

It was rather unabashedly declared a great victory by Sheridan, in his report to Grant, dated the 20th.[2197] Grant duly ordered a shotted (loaded with rounds) 100-gun salute from his armies, which was directed at Petersburg. Lincoln wrote Sheridan a personal note of gratitude, with "the thanks of the Nation." A few weeks later Sheridan was promoted to the rank of major-general in the regular army, having been elevated to brigadier only a month before—after the Battle of Winchester.

	KILLED		WOUNDED		MISSING		TOTAL
	OFFICERS	MEN	OFFICERS	MEN	OFFICERS	MEN	
Sixth Army Corps	23	275	103	1,525	6	194	2,126
Nineteenth Army Corps	19	238	109	1,227	14	776	2,383
Army of West Virginia	7	41	17	253	10	530	858
Provisional Division	1	11	6	66	......	18	102
Cavalry	2	27	9	115	......	43	196
Grand total	52	592	244	3,186	30	1,561	5,665

FIGURE 26

The battle was not without cost. The Union losses totaled 5,665 in killed, wounded, and missing. A breakdown is given in figure 26.[2198] The Confederate losses were reported to Lee from Early, at New Market, on October 21st. He only

---

2195. Jackson, p. 161; Walker, p. 153.
2196. O.R. 43/I, p. 479, 526; Stevens, H., p. 140.
2197. O.R. 43/II, pp. 410, 423–424, 436. O.R. Vol. 43/I, pp. 32–34. A preliminary report was sent out on the night of the 19th, and supplementary ones on the 21st and 25th. Sheridan, vol. 2, pp. 91–92.
2198. O.R. Vol. 43/I, pp. 137, 557, 564.

reports killed and wounded, as "not more than 700 or 800." His *Autobiographical Sketch*,[2199] which so often has been quoted herein, once again gave him the opportunity to reconsider, and he revises the total to 1,860, with "something over 1,000 prisoners."

Again, as at Winchester, Lieutenant Taylor wrote no report, or more precisely, none is found in the Official Records, and the same can be said of Lt. W. C. Cuyler, and Lt. John McGilvray. Though Devin reported three artillerymen killed, only two are in the Battery L "record": Pvt. Perry S. White of Battery K, and Pvt. Rowland Card of Battery L. Pvt. Michael Beckett of Battery K was wounded, and Pvt. Prosper Ferrari of Battery L is listed as wounded in the regimental record of casualties, though there is no record of his being wounded in the Battery L muster roll.[2200]

Sheridan offers no estimate of Early's losses. Gen. Hazard Stevens,[2201] quotes 2,250 for Early's killed and wounded, but offers no source, other than his authority as being present at the battle.

Though a great victory was won, as claimed by Sheridan, the cost was huge, and markedly disproportionate to Early's—even if General Stevens' figure is correct. In fact, 5,665 is more than twice the number of casualties taken by the US 1st and 29th Divisions in the landings at Omaha Beach on D-Day, the 6th of June, 1944.[2202] Only the Union could go on taking these numbers of casualties, because they had twice the number of cannon-fodder. However, even the Union could not take this forever. As we have seen, recruitment was getting nigh impossible and was now down to a trickle.

The losses taken by the 6th and 19th Corps indicates the heroism and determination of their defense, and what can happen in successive assaults on units if taken in detail.

Cedar Creek was the last battle in the Shenandoah for Battery K–L, and eventually would prove to be their last of the war. On the 27th of October, the battery was ordered into Reserve Camp at Pleasant Valley, Maryland. They arrived there on the 29th.

On Tuesday, November 8th, the people went to the polls, and Lincoln won re-election. What specific incident had influenced the election in Lincoln's favor was anybody's guess, maybe the people had always favored him, and all of the speculation was just wasted emotion. Perhaps it was the soldier vote from Ohio, cast in October, the results of which had been revealed. It was 48,000 for Lincoln to 7,000 for McClellan. Speaking to this, *Harper's Weekly* proudly said: "American

---

2199. Early, *Sketch*, p. 450.

2200. Little faith is held in this particular Regimental Record, as Battery L's musician, Ludwig Rupprecht, is also listed as wounded. Actually, it was in the Battle of Tom's Brook, on October 9th.

2201. Ellis, G. H., *The Life of Gen. Hazard Stevens*, p. 12, He was the assistant adjutant-general of Getty's division of the 6th Corps.

2202. www.ddaymuseum.co.uk/d-d

soldiers are not fools."[2203] Nevertheless, the favorable way the war had gone had to have been a factor. Perhaps it was the capture of Atlanta on September 6th, or the Battle of Winchester. However, Cedar Creek was the most recent, and had provided concrete evidence that the South was losing.

On the 9th of November, Sheridan took up a defensive position south of Winchester, at Kernstown, meaning to go into winter quarters. The indefatigable Early, having recovered his bearings, followed as far as Middletown. Torbert was sent out on the 12th and fell upon Rosser, routing him, and though preparations for an infantry attack had been made, on the 13th Early fled back to New Market.[2204]

In mid-November, Early sent back Kershaw to Lee's army.[2205] Nothing could make a better statement about Grant's policy in the Valley than the fact that Lee had removed Early's reinforcements. The Valley was now burned out and of no value—just as he had planned it. The two contending armies had no reason to fight here. Not to be deterred, Rosser found a chink in the armor, attacking the Federal fort at New Creek, West Virginia, on November 28th, and though Sheridan had to send a division of Crook's 8th Corps there, he sent the rest of the 8th to Grant. By mid-December Lee had called back Early's 2nd Corps, leaving only Wharton and Rosser, and Sheridan had sent the 6th Corps to Grant. Only the 19th Corps remained at Kernstown, at what was called Camp Russell; but it would be brief—they left for Stephenson's Depot, the terminus of the railroad from Harper's Ferry, on December 30th. The practical reason for this move was that supplies could reach there by rail without the use of wagon transportation over winter's muddy roads.

Rosser again attacked Beverly, West Virginia, on January 11th,[2206] and was successful at surprising the garrison, but these isolated raids had little bearing on the greater course of Sheridan's plan to dismantle the Middle Military Department.

On the 6th of January, Grover's Division of the 19th Corps was sent on its way to occupy Savannah,[2207] captured by Sherman on December 22nd. There had not come a hint of a new assignment for Battery K–L.

2203. *Harper's Weekly*, Nov. 12th, 1864, p. 722.
2204. Irwin, p. 440.
2205. Early, *Sketch*, p. 454; Sheridan, Vol. 2, pp. 98, 99.
2206. Sheridan, vol. 2, p. 100; Pellet, pp. 280–281.
2207. Irwin, p. 442, O.R. 44, p. 6; O.R. Vol. 43/I, pp. 88–89, 667–668; Clark, pp. 254–255.

Chapter 15

*"Record" 12/64; Mosby, Gilmor & McNeill; "Record" 2/65; 1865 Roster;
Sherman's March; Fort Fisher; The Peace Commissioners;
Sheridan Leaves the Valley; "Record" 4/65; Events of Note; Sherman;
Fort Stedman; Grant Moves; Five Forks; The General Assault; Surrender*

"Record" 12/64
31 OCTOBER–31 DECEMBER, 1864 PLEASANT VALLEY, MARYLAND

Battery quartered in Reserve Camp, Pleasant Valley, Md. during the past two months.

Henry W. Closson	Capt. Abs. on det. Svc. In the field, Va. as Chief of Arty & Ord. of the Cav. of the Mid. Mil. Div. S.O. no. 45 Hdqtrs. Mid Mil Div Oct. 25, 1864.
Franck E. Taylor	1st Lt. Abs. on 20 days leave since Dec.18,'64.
John McGilvray	1st Lt. Battery K, in command.
Edward L. Appleton	1st Lt. Absent without leave.

Detached:

John Meyer	Pvt. On det. Svc. With Battery G, 5th U.S. Artillery, New Orleans, La. since July 24,'64.
Amelius Straub	Pvt. Abs. on det. Svc. As Hospital Attendant since Nov. 22,'64.

Absent in confinement:

Patrick Gibbons	Pvt. At Ship Island, serving sentence of G.C.M. S.O. no. 18, Hdqtrs. 1st Div. 19th Army Corps Dec. 31, 1863.
John Lewery	Pvt. Abs. confined at New Orleans, La. Apprehended as a deserter.

Deserted:

Lyman Woodruff	Pvt. Deserted from Pleasant Valley, Md. Nov. 29, 1864. Apprehended in Frederick, Md. Dec. 1, 1864, and sent under guard to Company. Due U.S. $31. for expenses of arrest & for camp and garrison equipment, 52¢

Discharged:

William Parks	Pvt. At Pleasant Valley, Md. By virtue of S.O. no. 464, War Dept. A.G.O. Washington. Dec. 23, 1864.

Joined:

Charles Cooke	Pvt. Joined Co. from absent on Det. Svc. Dec. 30, 1864
Patrick Craffy	Pvt. Joined from absent sick, Dec. 23, 1864. Due U.S. for transportation $1.70.
Michael Kenny	Pvt. do.

Warren Shaw	Pvt. Joined Co. from abs. sick, on Dec. 30, 1864.
Lyman Woodruff	Pvt. Joined Co. from desertion, Dec. 15, 1864.

Strength: 75   Sick: 11

Sick Present: 3

Benjamin O. Hall	Pvt.
John McKenny	Pvt.
Ludwig Rupprecht	Bugler. Wounded in action near Strasburg, Oct. 9. On 30 days leave. Due U.S. for transportation $3.

Sick Absent: 8

James Campbell	Pvt. Sept. 19,'64 Wounded in action at Winchester, Va.
George Chase	Pvt. April 22,'63 At Brashear City, La.
William Crowley	Pvt. July 13,'63 At Baton Rouge, La.
Charles Jackel	Pvt. April 20,'64 At New Orleans, La.
John Kelly	Pvt. Sept. 19,'64 Wounded in action at Winchester, Va.
Churchill Moore	Pvt. April 20,'64 At New Orleans, La.
Andrew Stoll	Pvt. Sept. 25,'64 Wounded in action near New Market, Va.
John C. Wood	Pvt. Sept. 19,'64 Wounded in action at Winchester, Va.

The cooks are listed, and after each of their names is the remark: "Due cook $12. Error on last payroll." The errors on the cook's payrolls keep going on and on. Eventually, the paymaster will learn that they have been granted equal pay to that of a private.

Note that Henry Closson, though he is now a brevet lieutenant colonel, is still regarded as a captain in his permanent rank as commander of Battery L. He had been promoted on August 23rd, for "gallant and meritorious service during the capture of Fort Morgan."

No doubt the continued absence of Appleton has been the subject of some discussion, and with all of Battery L's officers elsewhere, 1st Lt. John McGilvray, of Battery K, has moved into temporary command.

Note that there are really only two men recently listed as sick, out of the total of eleven. Five are listed from wounds, and four are from lingering diseases contracted while Battery L was in Louisiana. The better health of the whole of Sheridan's army had been noted in a report made by the surgeon-general, for the period from August 27th to December 31st.[2208] He notes: "This low rate of sickness, at a time when the troops were harassed and over-fatigued by repeated battles and skirmishes, can be attributed to the healthfulness of the climate and the quantity of good vegetable food procured solely from the country." At last, an intelligent utterance regarding diet.

His reference to "harassed," no doubt refers to continual skirmishes and major battles, but also to guerilla activity, which was ubiquitous and continuing.

Lyman Woodruff was the lone deserter during this period. He was recruited

---

2208. O.R. Vol. 43/I, p. 145

on February 27th, 1863, at Baton Rouge, from Company E of the 13th Connecticut Volunteers, to serve a term of three years. He had been mustered into the 13th Connecticut on February 5th, 1862. Having served without incident up to November 29th, 1864, when he deserted, his rationale for taking the risk of deserting is a bit of a mystery. Perhaps he was angry that he had not yet been paid the first installment of his $100 enlistment bonus, but many others also had not. His desertion was one of the most unsuccessful ones on record—he remained free only three days before being caught, while, as we have seen, dozens of others had never been caught, or had returned voluntarily and not been charged. It was true that the end of the war was being talked about, and perhaps he felt his job was done. However, he could not have picked a worse time. The war had moved away from this locale, and every petty official, both civilian and military, now had little else to distract them, so when Woodruff was seen at Fredericksburg he was quickly pounced upon. Recall that local police officials were entitled to collect a fee for apprehending a deserter. The fee for the constable or constables who picked up William F. Brown, Joseph H. Parslow, Patrick Craffy, and Owen A. Wren, at the Tarleton Plantation on Bayou Teche, back on October 1st, 1863, was $10. Here, poor Woodruff encountered the full weight of the bureaucracy—he was charged $31. At a general court-martial held on February 24th, he was sentenced to forfeit $10 of his monthly pay for four months. He had been held in confinement awaiting trial ever since he had been returned on December 15th. Two months in confinement satisfied the court, because he was not sentenced to additional jail time.

The pressure of the war having relaxed, at least for Battery K–L, a number of furloughs were granted, as recorded in the December monthly report, "by command of Major-General Sheridan." On December 8th, 1st Sgt. William E. Scott, Cpl. Miles McDonough, and privates James Ahern, John Burke, William Creed, Prosper Ferrari, Henry H. Ward, Henry Williams, and Terence McGauley,[2209] each got 35 days. On the 14th, Sgt. Owen A. Wren, Cpl. George Howard, and privates Patrick Cummings, George Hadley, Reuben Townsend, and William V. Thompson each got 35 days. Cpl. Lewis Keller, and Bugler Louis Rupprecht got 30 days. Promptly on January 12th, 1865 (35 days from December 8th), Wren, McDonagh, Burke, Ferrari, Williams, Cummings, and Thompson were all declared deserters, despite the fact that those who had been given their furloughs on the 14th, Wren, Cummings, and Thompson, still had six days to go! Reuben Townsend was the only one in the latter group who was not declared a deserter until the 23rd of January.

Incidentally, most of those furloughed left for Boston or New York, and a

---

2209. This man's name has a variety of spellings in the various records. To date, it has been left as spelled on the particular record quoted. Here, we defer to the Massachusetts adjutant-general's list of its *Soldiers Sailors and Marines in the Civil War*, Massachusetts having been credited with his enlistment as part of its quota, apparently because his original enlistment was at Lynn, Massachusetts. Actually, he was from Jersey City, New Jersey.

glance at their original enlistment record confirms that in most cases, this was "home." The record-keeping error was apparently recognized in the cases of Keller, and Rupprecht, who are listed without comment in the muster roll ending in February. In fact, for all of the others, the mistake hadn't mattered. Wren, McDonagh, Burke, Ferrari, Williams, and Cummings never were apprehended and never returned. Only Thompson and Townsend were unlucky; they were caught at Ellicott's Mills, Maryland, on February 7th, and returned to stand trial. They were found guilty and fined $10 out of each month's pay for three months, in addition to the $31 for the expenses of their arrest. To understand the harshness of this judgment, the inflation factor, as we have calculated earlier, was about 100. Thus, the two fugitives were fined a total of $6,100, in today's dollars.

The creaking wheels of justice finally turned on May 17th, 1887, when the judgment for Wren, Cummings, and Thompson was removed by the Adjutant-General's Office. The mistake in the original record is duly noted. Unfortunately, the muster roll for 31 December–28 February is in such poor condition that the full notation is unreadable, yet it is clear that the records of other individuals were also reviewed. Wren's record was reviewed again on February 2nd, 1894, and his enlistment was changed to read: "Discharged at Washington, D.C., February 2/94, to date from January 12/65, by order of the Secretary of War and by reason of desertion." This is still rather confusing, as it does not make clear whether his discharge was honorable or dishonorable; if honorable, it would have enabled him to apply for a pension.

Mosby, Gilmor, & McNeill

As soon as Sheridan came into the Valley in 1864 to assume the command of the Middle Military Department, John Singleton Mosby followed, crossing over the mountains on August 8th, though detachments from his band remained[2210] in the vicinity of Washington, as Mosby writes: "To keep Augur in remembrance of his duty to guard the capital." He would remain to harass and carry on his guerilla tactics for the duration, and though wounded and briefly captured, he escaped.

Harry Gilmor, as Sheridan describes him:[2211] "Appeared to be the last link between Maryland and the Confederacy, and whose person I desired in order that this link might be severed," was eventually captured. The exploits of others, like the McNeill's, who were never captured, must also be mentioned.

On August 13th Mosby conducted his first raid on Sheridan, as was mentioned briefly in chapter 13. It was on Sheridan's supply line, the Valley Pike, running from Harper's Ferry south. A train of 325 wagons, at least three miles in length,[2212]

2210. Scott, John, 1867, p. 271; Mosby, pp. 289–292.
2211. O.R. Vol. 43/I, p. 56.
2212. McKinney, E. P., 1922, pp. 126; Scott, Maj. J., p. 279. Scott claims 300 prisoners. O.R. Vol.

had left Harper's Ferry on the 12th, guarded only by the 3rd Maryland Cavalry and two green regiments of "hundred days" men, i.e., those who had been enlisted specifically for the defense of Washington just prior to Early's attack in July. After marching all night, the train had halted at a stream just north of Berryville to water the horses. While waiting for the process to work its way out—each team stopping at the water while the animals drank, while others behind it parked—the infantry guard also halted, laid down, and fell asleep. At this point, Mosby's 250 men, all dressed in blue uniforms, attacked, and the train's surprised defenders scattered, hardly firing a shot. Six hundred mules and horses, 230 cattle, 200 prisoners, and 75 wagons were taken and their contents destroyed or stolen.

The disposition of the spoils is a reminder of the fundamental difference between the Partisan Rangers and the Confederate army. In view of Lee's needs for food, half of the cattle were magnanimously "presented" to Lee, to help feed his army—of roughly 50,000.[2213] This must be put in context by noting that the other half was retained, and used to feed Mosby's command—some 350.[2214] The horses and mules were *sold* to Lee.

The raids continued; some as small as to attack a courier and his escort, or a work detail, and some large bold ones, such as "The Greenback Raid."[2215] On October 14th, 1864, Mosby, with 80 men, struck the Baltimore and Ohio Railroad two miles east of Kearneysville, between Martinsburg and Harper's Ferry. Mosby had been in the vicinity that day, and after roaming around north of Winchester, where they attacked some Federal scouts, they moved that night to the railroad. By removing a rail, the train was thrown off the track. Then the passengers were robbed, and the train burned. Aboard were two Federal paymasters, majors Ruggles and Moore, who were taken prisoner, and their funds, amounting to $170,000, were appropriated. Again, true to their Partisan pirate charter, the funds never went to the Confederate treasury, but were immediately divided among the raiders; each getting $2,100—Mosby allegedly being the exception. According to one of his "delicate notions of honor" he never took a cent—always paying for his expenses out of his own pocket.

The boldness of the Partisan Rangers seemed to know no bounds. On October 3rd, Lt. John R. Meigs, of the Engineer Corps, and serving on Sheridan's staff, was killed near Harrisonburg.[2216] He was the son of Gen. Montgomery Meigs, now the quartermaster of the U.S. Army, the very same officer, then a captain, who was introduced to Battery L as having supervised the ongoing construction at Fort Jefferson in 1861, and who was involved, along with then Capt. David D. Porter,

---

43/I, pp. 484–485, 619–633, 842; 43/II, p. 372.
2213. Bowen, J. J., p. 240.
2214. Mosby, pp. 282–283; O.R. Vol. 46/I, p. 1279; Munson, p. 238.
2215. Mosby, pp. 321–323; Munson, pp. 221–227. A later report indicated that $173,000 was taken.
2216. Sheridan, vol. 2, pp. 51–52.

in Seward's secret expedition to Fort Pickens.

On October 11th, Sheridan's chief quartermaster, Colonel Tolles, and his medical inspector, Dr. Ohlenschlager, were mortally wounded while being escorted from Winchester to the front.[2217]

After the death of young Meigs, Sheridan ordered all the houses in the immediate vicinity of the murder, those which had potentially harbored the guilty, to be burned. Though this was not fully carried out, all of the able-bodied males in the village of Dayton were taken prisoner. Little else was done to react to the depredations during that time, which was leading up to the battle of Cedar Creek, but after the lull in operations in November, Sheridan ordered Merritt to go into the Loudon Valley and clear the countryside of all of its means of subsistence, to deter Mosby's men from being able to be harbored there in the future. It was the only alternative; as Sheridan writes: "Their destruction or capture being well nigh impossible…"

The Loudon Valley is situated in extreme northern Virginia, bordered by the Potomac on its north, from which it extends about ten miles south, into the northern portion of Fauquier County.

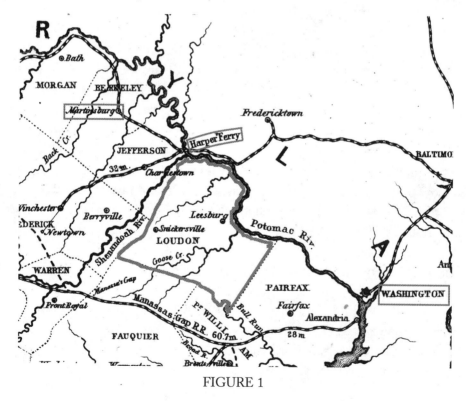

FIGURE 1

The Blue Ridge Mountains border it to the west, and the Bull Run Mountains, on the east, figure 1, which shows Loudon County and other points of Partisan

---

2217. Sheridan, vol. 2, pp. 99–100; O.R. Vol. 43/I, p. 800; 43/II, pp. 272, 351, 374.

activity on, or near, the B & O Railroad.[2218] Note the proximity to Washington, and consider the fact that an area this close to the capital, at the close of 1864, was still a safe hideout for Mosby. He was indeed true to his word, "keeping Augur in remembrance of his duty to guard the capital."

In his orders to Merritt, of November 27th,[2219] Sheridan points to the Loudon Valley as being "the hotbed of lawless bands…To clear the country of these parties, you will consume and destroy all forage and subsistence, burn all barns and mills and their contents, and drive off all livestock. This order must be literally executed, bearing in mind, however, that no dwellings are to be burned, and that no personal violence be offered the citizens."

Well aware of the dismayed reaction to his prior burnings in the Shenandoah, Sheridan adds a reminder about why he is repeating this harsh tactic: "The responsibility for this destruction rests with the authorities at Richmond who have acknowledged the legitimacy of guerilla bands." This was long after the Partisan Ranger Law had been altered by the Confederacy, as discussed in chapter 13; but the loophole in the law allowed Mosby to still exist. The participants in the burning, Merritt's 1st and Reserve Brigades, were repelled by what they were ordered to do, but: "Orders must be obeyed."[2220] Not even the family cow was exempt from the taking of livestock.

Mosby's men seemed to be everywhere, and in fact, they were; either led personally by him, or by other officers in his command. The whole Partisan Ranger issue was confused by how many and varied they were: Gilmor's, the McNeill's—John, and his son, Jesse—and White's, Woodson's, and Harness'.[2221] After a raid, it could often only be speculated as to who the culprits were. Also, Rosser's men were occasional participants with McNeill and Gilmore, and vice versa.

Such was the case at New Creek, West Virginia, mentioned in chapter 14, when the unprepared Union garrison of Fort Kelly was surprised and overwhelmed by Rosser's and Jesse McNeill's men. The location of New Creek, also called Paddytown,[2222] can be seen, on the B&O Railroad, in figure 2. The attack, made on November 28th, resulted in the capture of 700 prisoners, though some 200 to 300

2218. Viasz Railroad Map, portion, revised.
2219. Humphreys, pp. 190–191; O.R. Vol. 43/II, p. 730
2220. Humphreys, p. 192.
2221. O.R. Vol. 43/I, pp. 652–653; 43/II, pp. 522, 542. John McNeill was shot on October 2nd while attacking the camp of the 8th Ohio Cavalry, who were guarding a covered bridge over the North Branch of the Shenandoah, about a mile and half south of Mt. Jackson. A picture of the bridge appears as figure 4 in chapter 14. By the time of the raid on New Creek, his son Jesse had taken over the command., after the elder McNeill had lingered wounded, until his death on November 10th; Duffey, pp. 8–11, 14, 17, 24. At Mt. Jackson, the mix of the two groups, Rosser's and McNeill's, is also of note—one of Rosser's men acted as a guide for McNeill.
2222. Now Keyser.

escaped as they were marched out through the mountains. Also, between 1,200 and 1,500 horses and cattle, more important to Lee than prisoners, were driven off.[2223]

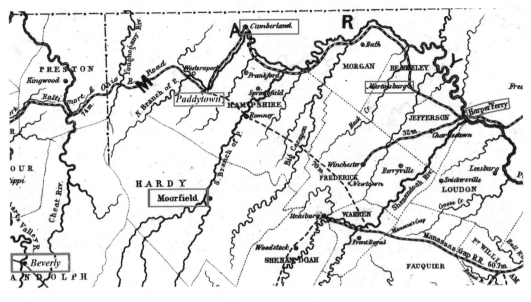

FIGURE 2

On January 11th, Rosser struck again, at Beverly, West Virginia.[2224] He had received intelligence from his scouts that the Federal outpost, some seventy-five miles distant from his base at Staunton, was filled with supplies, and guarded by only 1,000 men. Forage and supplies were the issue, and the remnant of his brigade which had not gone home on winter leave, was, in the words of Capt. William McDonald of the Laurel Brigade, "suffering greatly for the means of subsistence…"

> The country around him was almost famine-stricken. The people had been drained of their substance to support the soldiery. The [Confederate] Government could do little. It was already straining every nerve to maintain Lee's veterans who, in spite of cold, hunger, and Grant's multitudes, formed a wall of defense for the Confederate Capital.

Sheridan's burnings in the Shenandoah Valley had done their job.

Having gained permission to make the raid, in the dead of winter, with deep frozen snow on the ground, Rosser's "volunteers," some 300 in all, some gathered from his own brigade, and others from Munford and Payne, who were rather forced than volunteered,[2225] set out for Beverly. Because Rosser had heard that the route approaching Beverly from the north was less guarded, their march through mountain passes filled with drifted snow, in intensely cold weather, was much longer than

---

2223. O.R. Vol. 43/I, pp. 88, 667–668.
2224. O.R. Vol. 46/I, pp. 447–449; McDonald, pp. 334–340.
2225. SHS, vol. 13, Munford, T. T., pp. 143–144.

seventy-five miles. Finally, on the 10th of January, they camped in Devil's Hollow, to the north of the Federal camp, which was garrisoned by the 8th Ohio Cavalry and the 34th Ohio Infantry.

There is confusion as to how many, if any, sentinels were posted outside the camp, but it is clear that no one expected an attack at this season of the year, and the garrison was completely surprised and overwhelmed. Rosser's men advanced before daylight on the morning of the 11th and in a few minutes the camp was in Rosser's hands. There were only two Confederate casualties, a colonel of the 8th Virginia Cavalry was wounded in the leg, and a private of the 6th Virginia Cavalry killed. They had, however, taken 580 of the garrison prisoner. In addition to their prisoners, the Federal's lost six killed and 32 wounded.

The raid netted Rosser 10,000 rations, 100 horses, and the arms and equipment of most of the Federal prisoners. The prisoners were then forced on a grisly winter march of eighty miles to the Confederate camp at Staunton. As Capt. McDonald of Rosser's Brigade, relates, the march: "Was attended with great suffering both to the troopers and to the prisoners, but particularly to the latter, who were taken many of them without overcoats and only partly clad. The frozen feet and hands of quite a number necessitated amputation."[2226] A senseless act of cruelty which would do nothing to alter the outcome of the war, save adding hundreds to the long list of disabled Union pensioners.

On January 19th, another raid on the Baltimore and Ohio Railroad was made at nearly the same place, Duffield's Depot, between Harper's Ferry and Martinsburg, using the same methods, i.e., by removing a rail, and allowing the train to run off the track. The train was carrying only freight, and for reasons unknown, Mosby's men left the scene after making a failed attempt to set it afire.[2227] The railroad was again hit, and again in almost the same location, on February 3rd.[2228]

After a raid the guerillas would disperse; disappearing into their own homes, or the homes of sympathizers. It was in just such a circumstance that Mosby was discovered and very briefly captured. At dusk of the evening of December 21st, a detachment of the 13th and 16th New York cavalry was seen at Rectortown. Mosby reconnoitered, and assumed that they planned to camp there for the night. Mosby and a companion then stopped near Rector's Cross-Roads, at the house of one Ludwell Lake for supper.[2229] The judgment Mosby had made about the Federal cavalry going into camp was soon proven to be incorrect when the sound of the tramping of horses indicated that their advanced guard was outside, and soon the Yankees were in the room. Shots were fired from the backyard, and one passed through a window, striking Mosby in the lower abdomen. It was a rare occasion,

---

2226. McDonald, pp. 338–339; O.R. vol. 46/I, pp. 447–449.
2227. O.R. Vol. 46/II, pp. 188–189.
2228. O.R. Vol. 46/II, pp. 384, 387; 46/I, p. 455.
2229. Munson, pp. 249–252; O.R. Vol. 43/II, pp. 836, 843–844; Mosby, pp. 335–343, 354.

as Mosby was fully dressed in a new Confederate uniform, complete with the two stars of a lieutenant-colonel. As Mosby describes it, he did everything to distract from his being identified. He covered the stars with his hand, and made a great commotion about being hit. Bullets flying around, there was a stampede to clear out of the room, which knocked over the candles on the supper table, throwing it into darkness. In the interval, Mosby's incriminating garb had been removed, and he was in his shirtsleeves, gushing blood. Only when the commotion had died down did someone strike a light, and Maj. Douglas Frazar of the 13th New York Cavalry, and others, came in to examine the dying "lieutenant."

Convinced that Mosby's wound was mortal, the Yankees took their prisoners, eight in all, and hurried off, already late for a rendezvous at Middleburg, leaving the "lieutenant" to be treated by his own. Mosby was soon bundled up and taken to the house of a neighbor. From there, word was sent to others in Mosby's command. Before morning, friends and two surgeons had arrived, chloroform was administered, and the bullet removed. He was recovered sufficiently by February 25th to return to duty.[2230]

Gilmor was not so lucky, he was captured, unharmed, on February 5th, 1865. It might be considered that "lucky," at this stage of the war, was only a matter of perspective. In Virginia, the war would be over in less than two months, and Gilmor, though a prisoner for a few months more, at Fort Warren, in Boston Harbor, would be a free man by July.[2231]

Gilmor's capture was orchestrated by Sheridan's scouts, the same group who, under Major H. K. Young, of Sheridan's staff, had discovered the "old colored man" involved with Rebecca Wright. Now, the scouts made another discovery. Gilmor was found to be living a few miles outside of Moorefield, West Virginia, which had long since been proven to be a haven for the guerillas. We remember that McCausland, Gilmor, and McNeill had fled to there after the burning of Chambersburg. Recall also, that it was there, back on August 7th, 1864, that General Averell, after following them, had attacked and taken 420 prisoners and 4 pieces of artillery, permanently weakening Early's cavalry for the rest of the war.[2232]

With 20 men dressed in Confederate uniforms, Sheridan's scouts set out for Moorefield on February 4th. They were told to represent themselves to the locals as recruits from Maryland intending to report to Gilmor. They were followed by a detachment of Custer's cavalry in support of the mission; but disguised as allegedly in pursuit of the "recruits." The ruse worked, raising no suspicions along the way, until two men recently recruited by the 8th New York Cavalry were reported as

---

2230. Some reports (O.R. Vol. 46/II, pp. 591, 666) had Mosby back in action as early as February 18th, another by the 23rd.
2231. Gilmor, Preface.
2232. O.R. Vol. 43/I, p. 726; Sheridan, Vol. II, pp. 105–106; O.R. Vol. 43/II, pp. 56, 455–456; Gilmor, p. 278.

deserted. They were southerners, and had been enlisted locally; yet another example of the question that had been asked since the 1861 sell-out of the navy yard at Pensacola: "Whom do you trust?" It was clear that they intended to warn of the Yankee approach, and a race began between them and the 8th New York. Luckily, the large number of horses in the stable at the house of a Mr. Randolph, three miles outside of Moorefield, "excited much suspicion" and when Major Young approached, asking "what soldiers were in the house," a servant, with startled terror, replied: "Major Gilmor is upstairs." The house was surrounded, and Gilmor, and his cousin, late from Baltimore, were surprised while still in bed, and taken prisoner.[2233]

A bold exploit of McNeill's Partisans, the Cumberland Raid, will close our tales of the Partisan Rangers. The raid was alleged to have been hatched because of a grudge that Jesse McNeill had held against General Benjamin F. Kelley, dating back to 1862.[2234] Kelly had then been the Commander of the Railroad District of West Virginia, a part of the Mountain Department, under the command of John C. Fremont, which, on June 26th 1862, was merged into the Army of West Virginia, under John Pope. It was at this time, when the pro-Union western counties of Virginia were resisting the secession of that state, that the Confederate Congress sanctioned partisan guerilla warfare there. Thus, it was General Kelly who denied a passport to McNeill's wife, which she had requested to visit her husband at Moorefield, a place recognized as that where the partisans were collecting.[2235]

Regardless of the romantic nature of the preceding tale, another reason for the raid was to try to force the return or exchange of two of McNeill's rangers who were held in close confinement.

The raiding party consisted of 48 men of McNeill's command and 15 of Rosser's 7th and 11th Virginia Cavalry. All plans complete, the party moved into a position a few miles below Romney, West Virginia. Receiving word that "all was quiet on the Potomac" their guides took them through the snow and ice to the outer picket line at Cumberland, Maryland, where they charged and captured them, forcing them to reveal the password, "Bull's Gap." The password then allowed them through the inner picket line undetected, and they charged forward to the center of town, "where seven thousand sleeping soldiers under generals Crook and Kelley were tucked away under warm blankets, oblivious to all that was going on at three o'clock in the morning…"

Obviously informed of the two generals' whereabouts by local Confederate

---

2233. O.R. Vol. 46/II, p. 442.
2234. Vandiver, W. D., pp. 413–417; O.R. Vol. 12/III, pp. 55, 435, 568. The Second Wheeling Convention, had convened on June 11th, 1862, and the next day declared John H. Pierpont the governor of "Virginia." Virginia now had two governments, one pro-Union, and the other, the seceded pro-Confederate. *Encyclopedia Britannica*, vol. 28, 1911, p. 563. West Virginia was not admitted to the Union until, June 20th, 1863.
2235. O.R. Vol. 12/III, p. 428.

sympathizers,[2236] one squad of the raiders headed to the Barnum Hotel, long since General Kelley's headquarters, as commander of the Department of West Virginia, and the other to the Revere House. Entering the Barnum, the first squad bounded up the stairs to General Kelley's room, and ordered him to surrender. Kelley responded with the question: "To whom?" "To Captain McNeill, by order of General Rosser."

At the Revere House, where General Crook was quartered, the second group played out a similar scene, when James Daily, one of the raiders, and the son of the proprietor of the hotel, ordered Crook to surrender. Crook inquired: "By what authority is this done?" The raider replied: "By order of General Rosser of Fitzhugh Lee's Division." From Crook: "Is General Rosser here?" An answer came back from the stern voice and straight face: "Yes, sir; I am General Rosser."

It had taken no longer than 10 minutes[2237] before the whole group was on its way out of town, another group having secured more horses, including General Kelley's horse, Phillippi. Arriving at the picket line on the south edge of town, they were asked who they were, and without stopping, giving the password, they replied: "We are General Crook's bodyguard."

They were pursued through the ice and snow by two parties of Federal cavalry, one from New Creek, and one from Winchester, all the way to Moorefield, more than sixty miles, where the Federals gave up at the arrival darkness, and at the alleged scattering of the rebels into the mountains. On the second day of their journey southward, the raiders, now in Confederate-held territory, passed Harrisonburg, and arrived at Staunton, where they were introduced to Jubal Early. As to their prisoners, they were soon transported to Richmond, and then paroled. Sent to Grant at City Point, on March 14, 1865, he ordered them to go to their homes, and remain until exchanged.[2238]

The raiders could probably have "harvested" at least two or three other generals who were in camp at Cumberland; one a future president, Rutherford B. Hayes.

"Record" 2/65
31 DECEMBER 1864–28 FEBRUARY 1865 PLEASANT VALLEY, MARYLAND

Battery Quartered at Pleasant Valley Reserve Artillery Camp.

Henry W. Closson	Capt. Commanding Battery. Relieved from det. Svc. in the field, Va. as Chief of Arty & Ord. of the Cav. Mid. Mil. Div. S.O. no. 141, Hdqrts. Cav. Corps. Mid. Mil. Div. Feb'y. 8th 1865.
Franck E. Taylor	1st Lt. Abs. on 20 days leave of absence since February 26th 1865.

2236. Lowdermilk, Wm., pp. 408,420–422.
2237. O.R. Vol. 46/II, pp. 469–470, 515.
2238. O.R. Vol. 46/II, p. 966.

Edward L. Appleton	1st Lt. Relieved from Gen. Recruiting Service and ordered to join his Battery. S.O. no. 315 War Dept. A.G.O. Washington Sept. 25th 1864. Absent without leave.

Detached:

Franck E. Taylor	1st Lt. On detached svc. with Battery K 1st U.S. Artillery.
John Meyer	Pvt. On detached service with Battery G, 5th U.S. Artillery, New Orleans, La. since July 24,'64.

Absent in Confinement:

Patrick Gibbons	Pvt. At Ship Island, serving sentence of G.C.M. S.O. no. 18. Hdqrts. 1st Div. 19th Army Corps Dec. 31, 1863.
John Lewery	Pvt. Abs. confined at New Orleans, La. Apprehended as a deserter.

Deserted:

Owen A. Wren	Sgt. Deserted January 12th 1865, while on furlough.	
Miles McDonagh	Cpl. John Burke	do.
Patrick Cummings	Pvt. Prosper Ferrari	do.
William V. Thompson	Pvt. Deserted January 12th 1865, while on furlough. App. at Ellicott's Mills Md. and sent under guard to camp Feb. 7th 1865.	
Reuben Townsend	Pvt. Deserted Jan. 25th 1865 from Pleasant Valley, Md. App. At Ellicottt's Mills Md. And sent under guard to camp on Feb. 7th 1865.	
Henry Williams	Pvt. Deserted January 12th 1865, while on furlough.	

Discharged:

Joseph Wilkinson	Pvt. Discharged by reason of expiration of service, and final statement given.	
John G. Nitschke	Pvt.	do.
Michael Kenny	Pvt.	do.
Amelius Straub	Pvt.	do.

Joined:

William V. Thompson	Pvt. Join Company from desertion Feb, 7th 1865.	
Reuben Townsend	Pvt. do.	do.

Strength: 65   Sick: 7

Sick Present: none

Sick Absent: 7

James Campbell	Pvt. Sept. 19,'64 Wounded in action at Winchester, Va.
George Chase	Pvt. April 22,'63 At Brashear City, La.
William Crowley	Pvt. July 13,'63 At Baton Rouge, La.
Charles Jackel	Pvt. April 20,'64 At New Orleans, La.
Churchill Moore	Pvt. April 20,64 At New Orleans, La.
Andrew Stoll	Pvt. Sept. 24,64 Wounded in action near New Market, Va.
John C. Wood	Pvt. Sept. 19,'64 Wounded in action at Winchester, Va.

The three cooks are listed, and as usual, are not counted in the "Strength."

Given the fact that Battery L had always been stationed in unhealthful southern climates since it was reorganized in 1854, it seemed that someone was always sick. For the first time in memory, and a search of early regimental records indicates that it may be for the first time *ever* since it was reorganized, that no one present is sick.

The company roster, for the commencement of each year, has been prepared throughout this text from the 31 December–28 February muster roll, thus the 1865 roster status is as of the end of February. Since Wilkinson, Nitschke, Michael Kenny, and Straub had all been discharged during February, they do not appear. Note the relatively few men present in the battery at this time, though we must be reminded that Battery L and Battery K are still officially consolidated, and would remain so until October.

It will be of interest to see if those who transferred to Battery L from volunteer units at Pensacola and Baton Rouge, once it becomes obvious that the war is over, will be tempted to desert. They are likely to forget that their enlistment in this *regular* unit was for three years; not like that of the *volunteer* units, which was for three years *or the war*.

It is hard to understand what those that deserted in January were thinking. All of them had reenlisted on July 18th, 1864, and were entitled to, but had not received, their $400 bounty. It would be gone forever if they did not voluntarily return, and soon.

1865 ROSTER - BATTERY L
From 31 December 1864-28 February 1865
PLEASANT VALLEY, MARYLAND

1. Henry W. Closson Capt.
2. Franck E. Taylor 1st 1st Lt.
3. Edward L. Appleton 1st Lt.

1. William E. Scott 1st Sgt. 11 Jul.'64 New Orleans   1. George Howard Cpl.   Jul. 18,'64 New Orleans
2. William Demarest Sgt.   19 Oct.'59 New York
3. Charles E. Walton Sgt.   Nov. 12,'62 New Orleans
4. Lewis Keller Sgt.   Oct. 11,'64 New York
1. Ludwig Rupprecht Musician 18 Jul.'64 New Orleans   1. Frank Morgan Artificer   14 Nov.'62 Pensacola

Privates

1. Ahern, James	18 Jul.'64 New Orleans	29. Mansfield, Hobart E.	24 Feb.'63 Baton Rouge
2. Beglan, James	18 Jul.'64 New Orleans	30. McGauley, Terence	18 Jul.'64 New Orleans
3. Beiber, Peter	18 Jul.'64 New Orleans	31. Meyer, John	1 Mar.'60 New York
4. Breen, Michael	24 Feb.'63 Baton Rouge	32. Meese, Christian	12 Nov.'62 Pensacola
5. Coyne, Owen	10 Dec.'60 Ft Duncan, TX	33. McKenny, John	14 Nov.'62 Pensacola
6. Craffy, Patrick	18 Jul.'64 New Orleans	34. McGinnis, Angus	14 Nov.'62 Pensacola
7. Creed, William	18 Jul.'64 New Orleans	35. McEnearny, Corneilus	16 Dec.'62 Pensacola
8. Campbell, James	17 Nov.'62 Pensacola	36. Mahoney, Thomas	14 Nov.'62 Pensacola
9. Crowley, William	17 Nov.'62 Pensacola	37. Moore, Churchill	19 Nov.'62 Pensacola
10. Chase, George	16 Dec.'62 Pensacola	38. Miller, John	12 Nov.'62 Pensacola
11. Clinton, Thomas	24 Feb.'63 Baton Rouge	39. Montgomery, Solomon	14 Nov.'62 Pensacola
12. Cooke, Charles	24 Feb.'63 Baton Rouge	40. Orcutt, Ephraim	19 Nov.'62 Pensacola
13. Comfort, James	13 Nov.'62 Pensacola	41. Pfiffer, George	24 Feb.'63 Baton Rouge
14. Donnelly, Patrick	19 Jul.'64 New Orleans	42. Scott, William E.	18 Jul.'64 New Orl;eans
15. Eisele, Joseph	24 feb.'63 Baton Rouge	43. Schnieder, Philip M.	16 Aug.'63 Baton Rouge

16. Flynn, Arthur	12 Nov.'62 Pensacola	44. Shaw, Warren P.	26 Oct.'60 Boston
17. Foote, Edward A.	24 Feb.'63 Baton Rouge	45. Stewart, William	12 Nov.'62 Pensacola
18. Gibbons, Patrick	11 Dec.'62 Pensacola	46. Stoll, Andrew	18 Jul.'64 New Orleans
19. Hadley, George F.	19 Jul.'64 New Orleans	47. Smith, James H.	16 Dec.'62 Pensacola
20. Howard, Daniel	24 Feb.'63 Baton Rouge	48. Thompson, William V.	18 Jul.'64 New Orleans
21. Hall, Benjamin O.	18 Dec.'62 Pensacola	49. Townsend, Reuben	18 Jul.'64 New Orleans
22. Jackel, Charles	26 Oct.'60 New York	50. Teighe, Michael	25 Feb.'63 Baton Rouge
23. Kenny, Theodore W.	23 Feb.'63 Baton Rouge	51. Ward, Henry H.	19 Jul.'64 New Orleans
24. Kilburne, Sirenus	17 Nov.'62 Pensacola	52. Welsch, Peter	19 Nov.'62 Pensacola
25. Kelley, John	17 Nov.'62 Pensacola	53. Wilder, Joshua	19 Nov.'62 Pensacola
26. Kelly, George	16 Dec.'62 Pensacola	54. Wilcox, Thomas	19 Nov.'62 Pensacola
27. Lashner, Joseph	16 Dec.'62 Pensacola	55. Wood, John C.	15 Dec.'62 Pensacola
28. Lewery, John	14 Nov.'62 Pensacola	56. Woodruff, Lyman	27 Feb.'63 Baton Rouge
		57. White, Michael	7 Oct.'59 Boston

Sherman's March

As has been seen, from the time when he first became *de facto* general-in-chief, in March of 1864, Grant had focused on only two basic objectives, one being Lee's army in Virginia, defending the area surrounding Richmond; and the other, the army of Joseph E. Johnston, in Georgia, defending the area surrounding Atlanta. Sherman had been assigned against Johnston; with Meade and Butler, under the supervision of Grant, against Lee.[2239] Grant's earlier initiatives have been summarized in chapter 12. There, Wilson's Raid, as seen through the eyes of Battery K, then in Wilson's 3rd Cavalry Division, was made on the Weldon and Southside Railroads; its purpose being to cut off Lee's supply lines.

Grant's plan for Sherman had progressed to the point where Sherman, who had left Chattanooga on May 6th, had driven Johnston's army back from Dalton to the outskirts of Atlanta. To put this into perspective, on May 6th, Battery L was at Alexandria, Louisiana, awaiting the completion of Bailey's dam so that Porter's fleet could escape from the Red River; and for the previous month, at Nashville, a seeming world away, Sherman was fuming over Banks' failure to return A. J. Smith's command to him, so that "the big licks" could begin.

Jefferson Davis had become dissatisfied with Johnston's strategy in opposing Sherman, which was that of avoiding a major engagement, and the consequent destruction of his army, throughout the more than three months that he slowly fell back. He was replaced by John Bell Hood on July 17th, 1864, just at the time that Sherman was approaching Atlanta.[2240] Looking back, Johnston had always pursued the strategy of preserving his force in the face of impossible odds, versus making heroic and colorful stands that might inspire historic legends, but would practically have the result of killing off his fighting force. We recall, from chapter 9, that Johnston advised Pemberton to abandon Vicksburg "and march to the

---

2239. Grant, vol. 2, pp. 408, 558; O.R. Vol. 32/III, p. 246.
2240. O.R. Vol. 38/V, pp. 885, 889; Grant, vol. 2, pp. 167, 354; O.R. Vol. 38/III, p. 637

northeast" to join him, so that joined, their numbers might have had better options. Recall also, how in the recent Valley Campaign, Sheridan always made it a point to bring to bear superior numbers. Further testing the reader's memory, recall the chapter 6 comment of Willoughby Babcock, while at Pensacola in February of 1862, regarding McClellan's failures: "He has had wonderful means at his disposal, and yet has allowed the enemy to put two men to his one on the point of attack and thus beat him…"

The misguided strategy desired by Davis was an offensive. Hood soon aggressively did so, and as we shall see, his army was soon reduced by half and disbanded. On the 20th of August, he came out from the defenses of Atlanta to attack Sherman. He was driven back. Next day, he again came out, in what became a desperate two-day battle, known as the Battle of Atlanta. He was again driven back behind his defenses, and Sherman began a siege. Atlanta finally fell on September 2nd.[2241] After he had taken the city, Sherman initially thought to fortify and hold it, by making it "a pure Gibraltar," as he reported to Halleck, on September 9th.[2242]

On September 10th, Georgia's governor Brown issued a proclamation[2243] which withdrew the Georgia Militia from Hood's command. They had served during the siege of Atlanta, and were gone from home for more than three months. He reasoned that they needed to "return to their homes and look, for a time, after important interests, and prepare themselves for such service as may be required when another campaign commences against other important points in the State." He had a perfectly legal right to do it. In the Confederacy, the States had independent control over their troops. It brings to mind the condition of the American Colonies, George Washington laboring to conduct our revolution under the Articles of Confederation.

Sherman reported Brown's move to Halleck, and interpreted it as an initiative by Brown and another Georgia man, Alexander H. Stephens, the Confederate vice president, to come to some sort of agreement with him. Lincoln responded with "…great interest…" Sherman answered that he would keep him advised, and that preliminary discussions between Sherman and some local luminaries had led him to believe that:

> [The] people of Georgia are now in engaged in rebellion, begun in error and perpetuated in pride, but Georgia can now save herself from the devastation of war preparing for her only by withdrawing her quota out of the Confederate army and aiding me to repel Hood from the borders of the state…I am fully conscious of the delicate nature of such assertions, but it would be a magnificent stroke of policy if I could, without surrendering a foot of ground or of principle,

---

2241. Grant, vol. 2, pp. 168–169.
2242. O.R. ser. 2, vol. 7, p. 791.
2243. *Harper's Weekly*, October 8th, 1864, p, 643; O,R, Vol. 39/II, pp. 381, 395–396.

arouse the latent enmity to Jeff. Davis…The people say that Stephens was, and is, a Union man at heart…

Brown took no further action. Stephens gave the opinion that the lack of authority to treat, on both sides, would preclude any conference between himself and Sherman. There the issue died.[2244]

Enter Jefferson Davis, who visited Macon and Palmetto. At Macon, on September 23rd, he gave a speech in which he predicted the eventual retreat of Sherman, with disastrous results, much as Napoleon's from Moscow.[2245] He defended his sacking of Johnston, and predicted that Sherman would be driven back beyond Chattanooga. Hearing of Davis' delirious pep-talk, Grant commented that it "exhibited the weakness of supposing that an army that had been beaten and fearfully decimated in a vain attempt at the defensive could successfully undertake the offensive…"[2246]

The speech offered no clue to the thinking which developed Hood's follow-on strategy, and Hood developed his own, as events progressed, in concert with P. G. T. Beauregard, who had just been appointed commander of the Military Division of the West.[2247] With Hood lurking outside of Atlanta, the holding of the railroad to Chattanooga became a burden for Sherman. On October 5th, Hood attacked the railroad, and when viewed from a high point, it could be seen burning for miles (Hood reports ten miles). Leaving a force to defend Atlanta, Sherman pursued Hood, who reported: "Not deeming our army in condition for a general engagement…" withdrew from Lost Mountain[2248] westward, eventually reaching Gadsden, Alabama, on October 20th. In the meantime, Sherman had made a significant decision. It was clear that he could not remain at Atlanta on the defensive, all the while trying to preserve his rail supply line from the north. He telegraphed to Grant his conclusions on October 11th. His businesslike language is worthy of a partial quote here:[2249]

> We cannot remain here on the defensive. With the 25,000 men and the bold cavalry he has, he can constantly break my roads. I would infinitely prefer to make a wreck of the road and of the country from Chattanooga to Atlanta, including the latter city, send back all my wounded and worthless, and, with my effective army, move through Georgia, smashing things to the sea. Hood may turn into Tennessee and Kentucky, but I believe he will be forced to follow me. Instead of my being on the defensive, I would be on the offensive; instead of guessing what he means to do, he would have to guess at my plans. The

---

2244. Nicolay and Hay, vol. 9, p. 471.
2245. *The Papers of Jefferson Davis*, Rice University MS 43.
2246. O.R. Vol. 39/I, p. 27.
2247. O.R. Vol. 39/I, p. 4; Hood, J. B., pp. 425–426.
2248. O.R. Vol. 39/I, p. 802.
2249. O.R. Vol. 38/I, p. 28.

difference in war is fully 25 percent. I can make Savannah, Charleston, or the mouth of the Chattahoochee. Answer quick, as I know we will not have the telegraph long.

Grant approved the "trip to the sea-coast" the same day.

In the event that Hood did not follow, and chose instead to attack the remainder of Sherman's army, that of General Thomas, which had been left at Nashville, Sherman sent his 4th Corps and his Army of the Ohio back to Thomas. Other reinforcements, including A. J. Smith's (finally released by Canby), were sent to Thomas, under Grant's direction, because Grant feared that, indeed, Hood would not follow Sherman to Savannah.[2250] Why Grant felt that way, he does not explain. However, Hood's report makes it plain that he had been waiting for Sherman to divide his force, and when he observed the 4th Corps and the Army of the Ohio leaving, he reported:[2251]

> The enemy for the first time having divided his forces, I had to determine which of the two parts to operate against. To follow the forces about to move through Georgia under Sherman would be to again abandon the regained territory to the forces under Thomas, with little hope of being able to reach the enemy in time to be able to defeat his movement, and also to cause desertion and greatly impair the morale or fighting spirit of the army by what would be considered a compulsory retreat. I thought the alternative clear that I should move on Thomas. If I succeeded in beating him the effect of Sherman's movement would not be great, and I should gain in men sufficiently to compensate for the damage he might inflict. If beaten, I should leave the army in better condition than it would be if I attempted a retrograde movement against Sherman.

Beauregard brought nothing to the party, leaving it optional to Hood what he should do. He even suggested that Hood should divide his forces, sending one after Sherman, and another after Thomas.

What Hood meant about abandoning regained territory is confusing, if not fatuous. There had been no regain of any territory in Tennessee since Bragg had abandoned Chattanooga in August of 1863; and his commentary about the effect of Sherman smashing through Georgia not being great is simply denial. The abandonment of Georgia was just another step toward the end of the war.

It took Sherman nearly a month to destroy Atlanta, gather in supplies, and send useless equipment north, which included reducing his artillery to 65 guns, or 16 batteries, leaving 15 with the infantry and one, the 10th Wisconsin, with the cavalry. As Sherman put it, the artillery was "reduced to the minimum, one gun per 1,000 men."[2252] Nevertheless, these alone would require more than 2,000 horses

---

2250. Grant, vol. 2, pp. 356–358.
2251. O.R. Vol. 39/I, p. 803.
2252. O.R. Vol. 44, pp. 7–8, 20, 22–23, 25.

to pull them and their equipment. One of the fundamentals of this old soldier's experience was what Lincoln had tried to explain to Banks back in 1862 (chapter 7). It would be essential to travel light, and live off of the land. We shall see that the same thoughts were on Sheridan's mind when he finally quit the Shenandoah Valley at the end of February. It is probably the reason that Battery K–L was left behind to sit out the war at Pleasant Valley and Winchester, though Sheridan had an additional reason, the poor winter condition of the roads.

Sherman left a "thoroughly destroyed" Atlanta on November 14th.[2253] He was initially resisted only by the hastily gathered Georgia Militia, a force wholly insufficient to even slow his progress. As at VMI in the Shenandoah that spring, when General Hunter had advanced, the cadets of the Georgia Military Institute were called into action;[2254] as were the inmates of the state prison.

A week into the campaign, the right of Sherman's two wings, under General Howard, was outside of Macon, and the left, under Slocum, was outside of the then state capital, Milledgeville. Along the way, the railroads were torn up; the rails, rather than being thrown aside, where they could be easily salvaged, were laid over piles of burning ties, heating them until red and soft; then they were bent, often around trees, rendering them permanently useless.[2255]

The part of Hood's report in which he had stated himself "with little hope of being able to reach the enemy in time," was proving eminently true; he was far away, and frantic efforts to gather a force to resist Sherman were being made in Confederate circles. Jefferson Davis to Braxton Bragg, at Wilmington, North Carolina, November 22nd, 1864:[2256]

> If the condition of affairs will permit I wish you to proceed via Columbia to Augusta to direct efforts to assemble and employ all available force against the enemy now advancing into Southeastern Georgia. General Hardee and perhaps Taylor and Beauregard are at Macon; Brigadier-General Fry, and perhaps Chesnut, at Augusta. General Lee will telegraph you.

Bragg had been called into service again and assigned to the command at Wilmington, North Carolina, only a month earlier, to defend that key place against an anticipated Union attack.[2257] The worry about an attack was proper, one was indeed planned, and when it was discovered that Bragg subsequently had been called to Geogia, and, in addition, had taken North Carolina troops with him,

---

2253. O.R. Vol. 38/I, p. 29; vol. 44, pp. 7–8; Grant, vol. 2, pp. 356, 361, 363, 365–366; O.R. Vol. 52/I, p. 782.
2254. O.R. Vol. 34/I, p. 20; vol. 37/I, pp. 89–91.
2255. Grant, vol. 2, pp. 362, 365.
2256. O.R. Vol. 44, p. 881.
2257. O.R. Vol. 42/III, p. 1160.

Grant would press it to be made.[2258] Wilmington was one of only two Confederate ports still open to blockade runners on the East Coast. The other was Charleston. Wilmington was regarded by Grant as the most important; it was the closest open port through which supplies to Lee were still passing.[2259]

On the 24th, Sherman's left wing, the 14th and 20th Corps, and his cavalry, moved from Milledgeville to Waynesboro and Louisville, the objective being the Confederate prison camp at Millen.[2260] Arriving outside of Millen on November 26th, they discovered that the prisoners had been moved.

By now, the resistance offered by the Confederates had stiffened; Wheeler, with the Confederate cavalry, about 3,500 strong, had arrived, and a severe engagement with the Federal cavalry ensued, with Wheeler being driven toward Augusta, thus conveying the idea that Sherman was probably headed there.[2261] Regardless, the march continued south, and by the 10th of December it had reached the vicinity of Savannah, when its siege began. By the 13th, Sherman's 2nd Division of the 15th Corps had crossed a bridge constructed across the Ogeechee, and marched down its west bank to Fort McAllister, which was assaulted and taken.[2262] On December 21st Sherman's army occupied Savannah without opposition, General Hardee and his troops having abandoned the city the previous night.

As to Hood, after leaving Gadsden, Alabama, on the 20th of October,[2263] he took up a line of march for the Tennessee River, which, after he was joined by Forrest's cavalry, was finally crossed on the 21st of November. Schofield, assigned by Thomas to watch Hood, fell back successively from Columbia to Spring Hill, and then to Franklin, where, on November 30th the desperate and bloody Battle of Franklin was fought.[2264] Hood's loss was 1,750 buried on the field by the Union victors, with 3,800 wounded in hospital, plus 702 prisoners. Hood reported a total of 4,500. Schofield lost 189 killed and 1,033 wounded, with 1,104 captured and missing.

Despite this loss, Hood continued toward Nashville, and reached its outskirts on December 2nd. Thomas had been preparing for Hood's arrival. Though the bad weather may have been an excuse, Hood did not attack, and Thomas did not come out from his fortifications and engage Hood, despite urgings from Grant. Grant became so impatient with Thomas after repeated orders to attack, that he sent General John A. Logan to replace him. Grant later concluded to go to Nashville

---

2258. O.R. Vol. 44, p. 585. The 10th and 20th North Carolina. Five companies each of the 36th and 40th were also ordered sent on Nov. 22nd, ORN ser. 1, vol. 11, p. 743; O.R. Vol. 38/I, p. 32.
2259. O.R. Vol. 38/I, p. 32.
2260. Grant, vol. 2, pp. 367–368; O.R. Vol. 44, pp. 56–57, 411, 570
2261. Grant, vol. 2, p. 368.
2262. Grant, vol. 2, p. 369; O.R. Vol. 44, pp. 10–12.
2263. O.R. Vol. 45/I, pp. 657, 659
2264. Grant, vol. 2, pp. 377–379; CWSAC TN036; O.R. Vol. 45/I, p. 658.

himself. Before Logan or Grant arrived, Thomas attacked on December 15th. Hood was pushed back, but shortened his lines and remained confident.[2265] The next day, Thomas again attacked, and though initially repulsed at Overton's Hill, General A.J. Smith successfully assaulted Shy's Hill, and seeing the success, the rest of Thomas' command took Overton's Hill and Hood's troops broke and fled. They were chased by the Union infantry and cavalry all the way to the Tennessee River, which Hood crossed on December 27th. His army totaled 30,600 when he crossed the Tennessee in November, and it was now "about 15,000."[2266]

His army then scattered from Tupelo to Meridian, with large numbers furloughed and allowed to go home. On January 23rd, 1865, at his own request, Hood was relieved from command of the Army of Tennessee and replaced by P. T. G. Beauregard.[2267]

Fort Fisher

The ports of Wilmington and Charleston, as noted, were still not in Union hands, despite four years of the existence of Scott's Anaconda Plan. Both were still open to the receipt of goods from blockade runners who regularly operated out of Bermuda and Nassau. Wilmington was by far the most important, because it had not been effectively blockaded, for reasons revealed below. This had been going on since 1862.[2268] Plans to attack Wilmington were actively discussed between the navy and the army in January of 1863, but were finally shelved in May of that year, when Halleck refused to send reinforcements to General J. G. Foster, then the commander of the Department of North Carolina.

The difficulty for the navy was the fact that the shoal waters off the mouth of the Cape Fear River were not deep enough to allow ships of the Hartford class to approach, so that a repeat of the attacks on Port Royal, New Orleans, or more recently, Mobile, could not be made. Recall that when the *Niagara* and the *Richmond* shelled Fort McCree during the naval bombardment at Pensacola, in November of 1862, chapter 4, they had to approach closer than two miles before their gunfire became effective. Though technology had advanced from that time, the navy being equipped with more rifled guns of increased effective range, they alone could not be counted on.[2269] A purely naval attack could not be considered, a joint army-navy expedition was needed, the army to land and seize one, or both, of the two forts which defended the river, Fisher and Caswell.

2265. O.R. Vol. 45/I, pp. 660–661; CWSAC TN038.
2266. O.R. Vol. 45/I, pp. 663–664.
2267. O.R. Vol. 45/II, p. 805; 48/I, pp. 733–734.
2268. ORN ser. 1, vol. 3, p, 189; vol. 8, p. 260, 399–400, 834.
2269. ORN ser. 1, vol. 11, pp. 3, 259. During the first attack on Fort Fisher, 45 men were either killed or wounded by the bursting of navy Parrott guns.

The goods received at Wilmington, twenty-eight miles up the Cape Fear River, and sent on by railroad, figure 3,[2270] had now become critical to the existence of Lee's army in Richmond, and Grant had become ever more impatient to have the port closed. For example, F. G. Ruffin of the Confederate Subsistence Department, notes:

FIGURE 3

> On the 5th of December, 1864, I brought the condition of things to the attention of the Secretary of War, appending a statement of the subsistence on hand, which showed that we had nine days rations on hand for General Lee's army. I quoted General Lee's letter to the Commissary General, that day received, in which he stated that his men were deserting on account of short rations…On December 14, nine days afterward, General Lee telegraphed to Mr. Davis that his army was without meat. Fortunately, disaster was momentarily averted by the timely arrival of supplies at Wilmington."[2271] By January 11th, four days before Fort Fisher was captured, and the port of Wilmington was closed, Lee telegraphed to the secretary of war that he had "but two day's supplies."

Though the navy had been making strenuous efforts to seal the harbor, the efforts had only partial effect.[2272] From Welles: "Blockade-running had by now been systematized into a business, and the ingenuity and skills of Englishmen and the resources of English capital are used without stint in assisting the Rebels."[2273]

Having mentioned shoal water depth, another reason the blockade of Wilmington had been so unsuccessful was ascribed to the fact that the Cape Fear River has two inlets: New Inlet, guarded by Fort Fisher, is on the east coast, and the Western Bar Channel, guarded by Fort Caswell, on Oak Island, is on the southwest side of the river inlet opposite Smith's Island, with Cape Fear at its tip. The shallows of Frying Pan Shoals extend another ten miles. To navigate from one inlet to the other was a

---

2270. Figure 3, ORN ser. 1, vol. 8, p. 848A, portion only, altered.
2271. Bowen, J. J., p. 241
2272. O.R. Vol. 36/I, p. 43; Vol. 38/I, p. 32;
2273. Welles, vol. 2, p. 127.

distance of forty miles. The navy was thus forced to maintain two sets of blockading ships, one for each entrance. For instance, as of November 1st, 1864, there were 13 ships of the North Atlantic Blockading Squadron cruising off Wilmington alone, yet blockade runners were still getting through.[2274] A log from the diary of Col. William Lamb, C.S. Army, commanding Fort Fisher, is illuminating:[2275]

DATE	INBOUND/FROM	OUTBOUND/TO	SEIZED
10/31	Beatrice/Nassau Little Hattie/Bermuda	Annie/Nassau	Annie
11/2		Lucy/Nassau	
11/3		Beatrice Armstrong/Nassau	Lucy
11/4		Little Hattie/Nassau	Armstrong
11/5	Blenheim/Nassau Agnes Fry/Bermuda		
11/7	Banshee/Nassau Talisman/Bermuda		
11/8	Tallahassee (Confederate cruiser)		
11/19	Chickamauga/Bermuda (Confederate cruiser)		
11/20		Banshee/Nassau	
11/23	Little Hattie/Nassau		
11/26		Little Hattie/Nassau	
11/29	Emma Henry/Bermuda Vulture/Bermuda		
11/30	Colonel Lamb/Nassau		
12/1	Wild Rover/Nassau		
12/2	Owl/Nassau		
12/4	Hansa/Nassau		
12/5	Slag/Bermuda		
12/7	Stormy Petrel wrecked on south breakers.		
12/8	Talisman/Bermuda	Wild Rover/Nassau Emma Henry	Emma Henry
12/9		Blenheim/Nassau	

Though Col. Lamb missed one departure of the *Talisman*, he provides us with impressive evidence of the blockade running at Wilmington. Only the *Annie*, *Lucy*, *Armstrong*, and *Emma Henry* were seized by the U.S. Navy during this time period. The *Blenheim* was finally caught on January 25th.[2276]

Gideon Welles had been urging an expedition to capture and close Wilmington

---

2274. ORN ser. 1, vol. 11, p. 40.
2275. ORN ser. 1, vol. 11, pp 740–747. Col. Lamb commanded the defenses of Federal Point, including Fort Fisher, at New Inlet.
2276. *Annie*, *Harper's Weekly*, Dec. 3, 1864, pp. 772–773; see also: ORN ser. 1, vol. 11, p. 31; *Lucy*: p. 44; *Armstrong*, pp. 136–137; *Emma Henry*: pp. 182–183; *Blenheim*: p. 700; *Agnes Fry*: p. 788. Lamb's diary is apparently incorrect regarding the *Armstrong*, and his record of it coming into Wilmington on Nov. 6th has been deleted, as it was seized on Dec. 4th.

"for months" during the summer of 1864.[2277] By the end of August, Welles had begun to consider giving the command of the North Atlantic Blockading Squadron to Admiral Farragut; the current commander, Admiral Lee being "not the man for that," i.e., to plan and control such an important expedition. Furthermore, in talks with Grant, the Assistant Navy Secretary, Fox, learned that Lee was unsatisfactory to Grant. In his memoirs, Grant mentions nothing about these discussions, or of how he derived his opinion of Lee, though it is easy to understand that the apparent lack of success of the North Atlantic Blockading Squadron in dealing with the Wilmington situation would have tarnished the image of anyone who had been in charge.

Farragut, just finished with the attack on the forts at Mobile, declined the appointment.[2278] Welles now had to find another. He reveals some rather incredibly mercenary considerations regarding replacing the commander. The corrupting atmosphere created by the navy prize rules were actually a factor in the choice of an admiral. A quote from Welles' diary:

> I see no alternative but Porter, and, unprejudiced and unembarrassed, I should select him. The movement is secret, and I have no one to confer with but Fox, who is over-partial to Porter…Now, how to dispose of Lee? I think we must send him for the present to the West Gulf, and yet that is not strictly right, perhaps, to others. His harvest of prize money, I think, is greater than that of any other officer, and the West Gulf, should Wilmington be closed, will be likely, if the war continues, to be the theater of blockade-running.

So it was arranged to buy Lee off by sending him to the coast of Texas, the last opportunity for prize money. Lee was assigned on September 27th.[2279]

Porter was interviewed on September 17th, and though he preferred retaining the command of the Mississippi Squadron, he would, if ordered, do anything, including going "over Niagara Falls in an iron pot."[2280] The matter thus settled, on September 19th Welles arranged for Secretary Fox and Admiral Porter to meet Grant, who had just returned to City Point from his visit to Sheridan—the one in which he had approved of Sheridan's plan to move to the attack at Winchester.[2281]

The meeting is not mentioned in Grant's *Memoirs*, and it took place before Porter had taken command of the North Atlantic Blockading Squadron, which was not until October 7th.[2282] Nevertheless, Grant took action, proposing, as General Butler recalls,[2283] that General Weitzel reconnoiter the position of Fort Fisher, to

---

2277. Welles, vol. 2, pp. 127–129, 146–147.
2278. Welles, vol. 2, p. 165; ORN vol. 10, pp. 512–513.
2279. ORN ser. 1, vol. 10, p. 487.
2280. Welles, vol. 2, p. 148.
2281. Grant, vol. 2, pp. 328–329; Welles, vol. 2, pp. 150–151.
2282. ORN, ser. 1, vol. 10, pp. 473, 530; Welles, vol. 2, p. 172.
2283. Butler, p. 774.

act in conjunction with "a fleet that was being prepared by the navy." Weitzel did so on the 26th.[2284]

This was a busy time for Grant. After Sheridan's victory at Winchester, he attacked Early again at Fisher's Hill and again defeated him, chapter 14. After Fisher's Hill, Sheridan began his "March Up the Valley" which was so successful and rapid that Sheridan did not wire Grant what had happened until after New Market, on September 29th, and Grant did not receive it until October 2nd. The reader will recall that Lincoln had become so concerned for Sheridan's safety that Grant had to assure him that steps had been taken to keep Lee in position and not send more troops out to Early.[2285] Grant's "steps" the assault upon Lee's outer defenses were taken by Butler's Army of the James, on the night of the 28th of September, at New Market Heights and Fort Harrison, better known as the Battle of Chaffin's Farm.[2286] On October 1st, Weitzel was assigned as the temporary commander of Butler's 18th Army Corps; he had assumed command during the battle after General Ord was wounded.

At this point, Grant decided that the Wilmington Expedition was more than he could handle; first, there was "a want of disposable forces," though it was first contemplated to send down but 3,000 men. Second, the preparations of the fleet were publicly noticed. The great number of ships gathering at Hampton Roads and Beaufort had created a stir in the newspapers, and it was indicated that it was the largest armada in the world, and that they were headed for Wilmington. There was no longer any hope of surprise.[2287]

At the end of October, an exasperated Welles wrote to the President, describing this "immense force lying idle, awaiting the movements of the army."[2288] He brought up the idea that if the expedition were cancelled, the ships could return to blockade and cruising duty, their present absence being "a most serious injury to the public service." He noted that all of the delay and publicity had prompted the Confederates to send Bragg to Wilmington from Richmond to prepare to meet the attack.

Yet another complication was that it was the time just before the election. New York City was in ferment, and Butler had just been temporarily assigned to take charge of the security of the city. While at Washington, on his way to New York, Butler spoke of hearing of Erith, England, where a gunpowder explosion had caused destruction for miles around, and that possibly "by bringing within four or five hundred yards of Fort Fisher a large mass of explosives…the garrison would be at least so far paralyzed as to enable, by a prompt landing of men, a seizure of the fort." After Butler had returned from New York on November 16th, he discovered

---

2284. ORN, ser. 1, vol. 10, p. 488.
2285. Grant, vol. 2, pp. 332–333.
2286. O.R. Vol. 38/I, pp. 21; CWSAC VA 075; O. R. Vol.42/I, p. 800.
2287. Butler, pp. 774–775.
2288. ORN, ser. 1, vol. 11, p. 3.

that his idea had received favor and that it had been determined that it should be tried. All of this, however, is according to Butler's narrative. At the very least, the proposal had been sent to the Engineer Department, and the report of the chief engineer, General Richard Delafield, was issued on November 18th.[2289] His seven pages of studious logic concluded that the scheme would not work. The major commanding the Washington Arsenal didn't think so either, but he really couldn't be sure.

All of this paperwork was bundled up and sent off to Admiral Porter on November 27th. On December 8th Porter described *his* plan to the senior officer of the blockading squadron. It consisted of loading a shallow draft vessel, eight-and-a-half feet or so, with 350 tons of powder, which would be run up on the beach opposite Fort Fisher and detonated. He ordered the officer to determine how close this boat could be gotten, either from the outside beach or the inside, if she crossed the bar.[2290] The vessel was the USS *Louisiana*, which was to be brought from New York to Hampton Roads, then loaded with powder, and towed to Beaufort.

Learning that Bragg had gone to Georgia, taking forces from Wilmington with him, Grant agreed to support the new expedition and promptly issued his instructions to Butler on December 6th.[2291] Weitzel was to command the land force, which would consist of about 6,500 men. The ultimate sticking point was that Butler, Weitzel's senior, chose to go along, and though Weitzel's orders named him as commander, Butler privately discussed the expedition with Grant, and was allowed to "take the responsibility off General Weitzel."

Coastal storms delayed the army's arrival until December 15th, and the powder boat was not ready until the 18th. Another storm and further delays for coal and water, and it was not until the night of December 23rd that the powder boat was towed, and then finally beached under her own power, about five hundred yards from the shore. The timing mechanism was set, the vessel abandoned, and at about 2:00 a.m. the explosion went off.[2292] It was a non-event, there was no effect whatever on the fort. When asked about what was heard, the commander of Fort Fisher, Col. Lamb, replied "Enemy's gun-boat blown up." Later official Confederate reports of the subsequent attack do not even mention the explosion.

The next day, about 500 men of Weitzel's force, under Generals Ames and Curtis, covered by a dozen gunboats of the navy, landed without opposition about three miles above Fort Fisher.[2293] Curtis headed toward the fort, and Ames turned north, toward Wilmington. Weitzel accompanied Curtis. Ames captured 228 prisoners, and Curtis, advancing upon the fort, pushed up to within a few yards of it,

---

2289. ORN ser. 1, vol. 11, pp. 207–214.
2290. ORN ser. 1, vol. 11, pp. 217–221.
2291. O. R. Vol. 38/I, p. 43; O.R. Vol. 42/III, p. 1254; Butler, p. 783.
2292. Grant, vol. 2, pp. 390–391; O.R. Vol. 42/I, pp. 979, 1003.
2293. O.R. Vol. 42/I, pp. 986–987; Grant, vol. 2, p. 393; O.R. Vol. 36/II, pp. 44–45.

causing the surrender of the garrison of the Flag Pond Battery. Perhaps this was one of the few times in war that the capture of prisoners was unfortunate. To a man, they all admitted being a part of Hoke's division, newly arrived from Richmond, and that the rest of his 6,000 men were not far behind.

Upon hearing this, and a report from Weitzel that the naval bombardment had done little damage to the fort, and in which, for some peculiar reason, Weitzel invoked images of past failed and bloody direct assaults, likely Port Hudson, Butler determined to abort the mission.

The negative attitude of Weitzel here is most peculiar, but it must be noted that he had never been shown Grant's orders, *which were addressed to him*, for the expedition. Butler had intercepted them and had interpreted them as he saw fit.[2294] What Weitzel did not know was what Grant's instructions had made clear:

> The object of the expedition will be gained by effecting a landing on the main land between the Cape Fear River and the Atlantic, north of the north entrance to the river. Should such a landing be effected while the enemy still holds Fort fisher and the batteries guarding the entrance to the river, the *troops should entrench themselves, and, by co-operating with the navy effect the reduction and capture of those places* [italics added.].

Grant offered no options.

Butler used the excuse that the ocean was too rough to land the remainder of his troops and supplies; that a gale had blown up and was worsening, and Porter had informed him that the navy was running out of ammunition, and would have to return to Beaufort for more, leaving him unsupported for up to four days.[2295]

Bizarre it was, that Weitzel and company had been able to walk ashore, look around, and depart unmolested. Bragg had resumed command at Wilmington on December 17th,[2296] and despite recommendations from his subordinates, did little or nothing to interfere with the Butler landing. On December 20th, he requested reinforcements, and Hoke's division was ordered sent from Lee. None of Hoke's troops had arrived by the 23rd, only one brigade by the 24th; and according to Bragg, on the 25th: "They were unable to cover the front."

Porter, after protesting that it was the army that had committed the abandonment, begged for its return, but under another commander. Knowing Porter as we have known him, the cutting up of others to whom he had taken a dislike was a specialty. From Porter:

> It is scarcely worth while to be impatient under these disappointments; the Navy will have to meet them throughout a war like this, where so many incompetent men in the Army are placed in charge of important trusts. General

---

2294. Grant, vol. 2, pp. 603–604.
2295. Butler, pp. 796–797.
2296. O.R. Vol. 42/III, pp. 1278, 1282, 1298, 1302, 1306; O. R. Vol. 46/I, p. 440.

Butler only came here to reap the credit of this affair, supposing that the explosion would sweep the works off from the face of the earth.[2297]

After discussing Porter's report with Lincoln,[2298] on December 29th, Welles was upset enough to literally interpret Lincoln's response, which was: "I must refer you to General Grant." Welles let Fox telegraph directly to Grant, asking what was to be done next. This bypassed the usual protocol, which would have passed the message to Halleck or Stanton first. Next day, Grant asked Porter to "hold on." Grant also wasted little time in requesting Stanton to remove Butler from the command of the Department of Virginia and North Carolina.[2299] He was relieved on January 7th, and General E. O. C. Ord replaced him.

By the 6th of January, General A. H. Terry's troops, the 2nd Division of the 24th Army Corps, (Ames) and the 3rd Division of the 25th Army Corps (Paine, consisting of nine regiments of U.S Colored Troops), essentially the same ones who were with the original expedition, plus an additional brigade, the 2nd, from the 1st Division of the 24th Army Corps (Abbott), and a small siege train, consisting of the 16th New York Battery, and Battery E, 3rd U.S. Artillery,[2300] were all on board their transports, and had sailed from Fortress Monroe. They arrived off Beaufort on the 8th, and unfortunately, met another heavy storm which prevented their landing until the 13th. By 3:00 p.m. the nearly 8,000 men had been landed on the beach, about five miles north of the fort, and after a defensive line facing Wilmington (Paine and Abbott) was thrown across the peninsula, so as to protect their rear, the remainder of the attackers moved south. On the 14th, entrenchments were dug at a position some three miles from the fort, and the artillery was landed. A reconnaissance close to the fort showed that considerable damage had been done to the fort by the navy fire; only nine guns were now evident on the land side, whereas 16 were counted by Weitzel on Christmas day. This, and consideration of the difficulty of landing equipment for a siege, resulted in a decision to risk an assault the next day. The assault would be preceded by a naval bombardment, and it would be continued while the assault was in progress, only diverted to other parts of the work.

In consultation with Porter, an assault of sailors and marines was to attack the northeast bastion, on the seaside, and the army the western land face. All of this was to take place at 3:00 p.m., after a bombardment that would begin at 8:00 a.m. *Seven hours* of bombardment by 57 ships, figure 4.[2301] Note the shoals, which the larger ships have avoided, and the numbered close-in position of the ironclads,

---

2297. ORN, ser. 1, vol. 11, p. 264.
2298. Welles, vol. 2, p. 214; Grant, vol. 2, p. 395; O.R. Vol. 36/I, p. 45.
2299. O.R. Vol. 46/II, pp. 29, 52, 61.
2300. O.R. Vol. 46/I, pp. 43, 394–399, 402–407; Grant, vol. 2, pp. 395–396.
2301. Figure 4, Lamb, W., pp. 644, 649; *www.history.navy.mil/DANFS*. Note the position of the *Colorado*, with a draft of 23' 9", which, it is remembered, Farragut could not get across the Mississippi bar during the expedition to New Orleans.

the *Monadnock*, *Saugus*, *Canonicus*, and the *Mahopac*, all of whom had drafts of less than 14 feet, allowing them to move closer for greater accuracy; their ironclad construction protecting them.

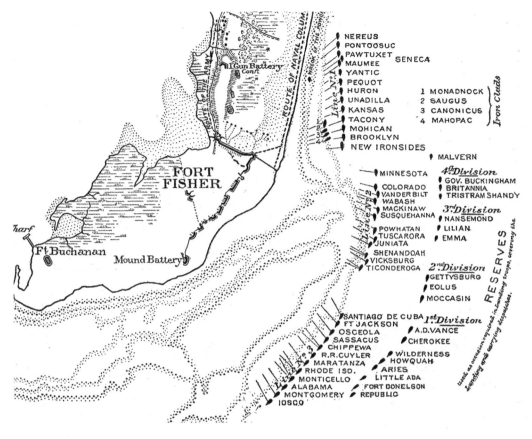

FIGURE 4

The assault by the army was well thought out, and full advantage was taken of the furious naval bombardment, which had caused the defenders to abandon the parapets. Confederate General W. H. C. Whiting, sent to the fort to command the defense, corroborates this, saying: "On Sunday the fire of the fleet reached a pitch of fury to which no language can do justice…The garrison…was not able to stand to the parapets." The naval bombardment was so powerful that before noon on January 15th it had put all of the fort's heavy guns out of action save one. This allowed 100 picked men, 60 of whom were armed with Spencer repeaters, to run up to within one hundred seventy-five yards of the fort and dig in. Though the parapets were subsequently manned after the bombardment was diverted, it would be at the new peril of being picked off by the rapid fire of the sharpshooters. This covered the advance of succeeding waves of troops, who also dug in. At 3:25 p.m. Curtis' brigade was ordered forward in concert with a signal to Porter to change the direction of fire. They reached the palisades, cut through, and reached the parapet.

The navy force, consisting of 1,600 sailors and 400 marines, led by Lt.-Commander Kidder Breese,[2302] was unable to deal with the murderous fire in their front, and had to withdraw. Little credit is given to their sacrifice, except in the reports of Whiting and Bragg, who concede that it caused the garrison to be divided between their right (the sea side), and their left (the river side). In Whiting's words: "The men gallantly repulsed the right column of assault. [The] Portion of the troops on the left had also repelled the first rush…The greater portion of the garrison being, however, engaged on the right, and not being able to man the entire work, the enemy succeeded in making a lodgement on the left flank…"[2303] This lodgment, of Curtis' 1st Brigade, then began the rolling-up of the defenders, as the gun traverses on the land face were carried one-by-one. It was not until nine o'clock that night that the occupation of the fort was completed.

As on Butler's landing, Hoke's troops did little or nothing. They initially faced the considerable force of Paine's and Abbot's total of 14 regiments, but after Abbott's men were ordered to reinforce the attackers, only Ames' colored regiments were left in the north line. At about 4:00 Hoke advanced, and after only a skirmish with Ames' pickets, he withdrew.[2304] The 27th Colored Infantry lost only one man killed and four wounded.

More than 2,000 prisoners were taken, and 700 Confederate dead and wounded were left behind, including General Whiting and Colonel Lamb. The losses taken by Terry's troops were 110 killed and 536 wounded.[2305] Breese's sailors and marines suffered 65 killed and 200 wounded.

Bragg ordered Forts Caswell and Campbell blown up and abandoned on the 16th and 17th.

The dreary predictions of Weitzel and the baffling action of Butler in the first expedition stand in stark contrast to the alacrity and efficiency with which the second expedition did its work, though it suffered almost 10 percent in killed and wounded.

Some salient points regarding military technology and efficiency: Terry's use of sharpshooters armed with repeating rifles to keep the fort's defenders ducked down behind the parapets was clever and well thought-out. The repeater showed its value here, as it had with the cavalry. Breese had intended to use the same strategy, but his marine sharpshooters never got into proper position, and to this he attributes his failure.[2306] Nevertheless, the two attacks were well coordinated, something that was lacking at Port Hudson, and apparently was still coloring Weitzel's thinking almost two years later.

2302. ORN ser. 1, vol. 11, pp. 446–448.
2303. O.R. Vol. 46/I, pp. 415–416, 434, 438–439.
2304. O.R. Vol. 46/I, p. 399, 405.
2305. Grant, vol. 2, p. 399; O.R. Vol. 46/I, pp. 401, 433, 435.
2306. ORN ser. 1, vol. 11, p. 447

The passive behavior of Bragg during the whole affair was demanded to be investigated by General Whiting, who wrote a report to Lee from his prison cell at Fort Columbus, New York.[2307] In it, the general says, in part:

> As soon as lodgment was made…was the time for the supporting force, which was lying idly looking on only three miles off…to have made an attack upon the rear of the assaulting column…General Bragg was held in check by two brigades of U.S. Colored Troops, along a line of no impediment whatever. I went into the fort with the conviction that it was to be sacrificed, for the last I heard General Bragg say was to point out a line to fall back on if Fort Fisher Fell. In all his career of failure and defeat from Pensacola out, there has been no such chance missed, and no such stupendous disaster.

Not all true, but quite a comedown from when, with high hopes, Bragg had entered Kentucky at the head of the Confederate Army of Tennessee in September of 1862, to offer the people their opportunity to join the Confederacy. Now, it seems, after years of tiring struggle, as anyone reading Confederate tea leaves already knew, the war was lost.

The Peace Commissioners

After Lincoln's reelection, Francis P. Blair, Sr.,[2308] editor of the *Washington Globe* from 1830 to 1849, and a long-time Democratic politician, dating back to when he had served in President Andrew Jackson's "Kitchen Cabinet," had formed the belief that his past associations with those men now prominent in the Confederacy might aid in bringing about a cessation of hostilities. If Horace Greeley had failed, and Jaquess and Gilmore had failed, certainly no one had more impressive credentials than Blair. With a clearly faltering Confederacy, there was no more propitious moment for Blair to offer to mediate.

Long before the war, Blair had begun to break away from traditional Democrat beliefs over the issue of slavery. In 1848, he supported the presidential candidacy of Martin Van Buren and the Free Soil Party, which opposed the extension of slavery into the new territories acquired from Mexico. In 1852, he supported the candidacy of the Democrat, Franklin Pierce, against the Whig, Winfield Scott, but Pierce's pro-slavery policies alienated him and he turned away from his former colleagues, and become a founder of the Republican Party. He was a supporter of Fremont in the election of 1856, and of Lincoln in 1860 and 1864. His son, Montgomery, had been postmaster-general in the Lincoln administration from 1861 to 1864.

After Lincoln's reelection, Blair approached him with a proposal to visit

---

2307. O.R. Vol. 46/I, pp. 441–442.
2308. *Encyclopedia Britannica*, 1911, vol. 4, p. 33, vol. 11, p. 87, vol. 21, p. 599.

Richmond. As with Jaquess, Lincoln at first ignored him, then brushed him off, saying: "Come to see me after Savannah falls." It fell on December 22nd, and Blair persisted. Lincoln listened, and on December 28th, 1864, Blair was given a letter which authorized him to pass through the Federal lines, "go South, and return." As Lincoln made clear, Blair had no authority to speak or act for the government.[2309]

In turn, Blair was given permission by the Confederate authorities to visit with Jefferson Davis. In his sessions with Davis, Blair harangued him with a review of Lincoln's December 8th message to Congress, which he managed to weave into a basis for peace. Slavery, he said, no longer remained an insurmountable obstruction to peace. Blair boldly argued: "You propose to use the slaves in some mode to conquer a peace for the South…by risking their lives in the service, the achievement is certainly to be crowned with their delivery from bondage…Slavery, 'the cause of all our woes,' is admitted now on all sides to be doomed. As an institution all the world condemns it." (This is a reference to proposals long since afloat in the Confederacy to enlist the slaves, see "Events of Note" later in this chapter).

"This explanation made, what remains to distract our country?" Blair then reminded Davis of the threat of Maximilian in Mexico. If the Confederacy was successful in somehow negotiating its independence, it could fall victim to the designs of Napoleon III. Southern independence was nothing but a myth; debt and weakness would hold it in bondage to Europe.

The argument given to Davis by Blair, according to Nicolay and Hay,[2310] this former trusted adviser to Andrew Jackson seemed "as though the ghost of the great President had come from his grave in Tennessee to draw him a sad and solemn picture of the ruin and shame to which he was bringing, and had almost brought, the American Republic, especially his people of the Southern States—nationality squandered, slavery doomed, and his Confederacy a supplicant for life at the hands of European despotisms." Ah, but Davis: "Is the fortunate man who now holds the commanding position to encounter this formidable scheme of conquest…" Briefly, if Davis moved to war against Maximilian to restore the Mexican Republic, the South "would complete the work of Jefferson…[by]…delivering Mexico…to our Union and add a new Southern constellation to its benignant sky…"

Insane as all this was, Davis listened. Consulting with Vice President Alexander Stephens, Davis, as Stephens later wrote, "gave the opinion that Washington fully understood the object of Blair's mission…Perhaps such a Convention might be obtained, securing a suspension of hostilities, without committing us to an *active role* in the maintenance of the Monroe Doctrine."[2311]

In summary, the United States and the Confederacy would suspend hostilities

---

2309. O.R. Vol. 46/II, pp. 505–507; Grant, vol. 2, pp. 420–423; Nicolay and Hay, vol. 10, p. 94.
2310. Nicolay and Hay, vol. 10, pp. 102–103. Niclolay and Hay assume that the U.S. would annex Mexico, which is not mentioned.
2311. Stephens, A. H., vol. 2, p. 592.

and unite in a war to drive the French from Mexico. Having entered such an arrangement "the diversion of the popular mind at the North...might result in great benefit..." to the Confederate cause. The Confederacy could slough off (emphasis on the above phrase containing *active role*) and let the Federal forces carry the brunt of the fighting, and perhaps postpone the question of the Civil War. Any scheme was better than what seemed the inevitable catastrophe which was approaching. Davis was willing to appoint a person or persons to talk.

Blair returned, carrying a letter from Davis that indicated that he would either send a commission, or receive one, which might renew the peace effort. Shown the letter, which was dated January 12th, Lincoln replied to Blair on the 18th that he was, "and shall continue to be ready to receive any agent whom he, or any other influential person now resisting the national authority, may informally send to me with the view of securing peace to the people of our common country."

On the 21st, Blair delivered Lincoln's reply to Davis, and in his presence, Davis' only comment was to take issue with the phrase "our common country" instead, correcting it to be understood as "the two countries." It appeared that the initiative had stumbled on Davis' intransigence, until, on the 29th, a telegram was received from the commanding general of the 9th Corps, stating: "Alex. H. Stephens, R. M. T. Hunter, and J. A. Campbell desire to cross my lines, in accordance with an understanding claimed to exist with Lieutenant-General Grant, on their way to Washington as peace commissioners. Shall they be admitted?" They were instructed to await a messenger dispatched from the President. Major Thomas Eckert, an aide to Lincoln, was sent, with instructions to send the commissioners to Fortress Monroe. While Eckert was in transit, the Confederate Commissioners re-wrote their application, and addressed the new one to Grant. It eliminated the sticky "one common country" phrase, and simply said: "To proceed to Washington to hold a conference with President Lincoln upon the subject of the existing war..."

After an initial refusal by Stanton, who appears to have feigned ignorance about Lincoln's dealings with Blair, the commissioners were allowed to proceed to Grant's headquarters at City Point, and were ensconced in comfortable quarters on board the steamer Mary Martin. At this point, Lincoln informed Secretary of State Seward of the commissioners' presence, and ordered him to proceed to Fortress Monroe, giving him instructions as to three points which were "indispensable":

1. "The restoration of the national authority throughout the states."
2. "No receding, by the Executive...on the slavery question..."
3. "No cessation of hostilities short of and end of the war and the disbanding of all forces hostile to the Government."

On the same day, February 1st, Lincoln telegraphed to Grant: "Let nothing which is transpiring change, hinder, or delay your military movements or plans." There was to be no armistice simply because of these discussions.

Enter Eckert, with no knowledge of Grant's receipt of the less strict terms to which the commissioners had agreed, who then denied them permission to proceed. The sticking point was finally resolved by a confidential telegram from Grant, who vouched for the personal integrity of the visitors. (Stephens later wrote that he believed that it was through Grant's intervention that Lincoln consented to appear at the conference.) Lincoln then telegraphed a reply: "Say to the gentlemen I will meet them at Fortress Monroe as soon as I can get there." Lincoln arrived the same night, February 2nd. Nothing would be trusted to Seward alone.

Next morning the commissioners were conveyed to the steamer *River Queen*, where Lincoln and Seward awaited. A four-hour conference ensued.[2312] After reminiscences and small talk, the subject of secession for the cure for sectional differences, brought up by Mr. Stephens, was rejected. Then Stephens moved to Blair's idea of the reunion of the parties on the basis of upholding the Monroe Doctrine and driving the French out of America. Lincoln disclaimed authorizing anything on the subject, and that he would not treat except on the basis of reunion and the abolition of slavery.[2313] Such subjects as the recent action by the Congress to adopt a constitutional amendment to end slavery were disclosed to the commissioners. But, theoretically, if they promptly returned to the Union, they might be able to defeat its ratification. This proposal apparently ignored, it was clear that the end of the conference was at hand, Hunter describing the position of Lincoln and Seward as that of demanding unconditional surrender. Hunter: "Mr. Seward, it is true, disclaimed all demand for unconditional submission. But what else was the demand for reunion and abolition of slavery, without any compensation for negroes or even absolute safety for property proclaimed to have been forfeited?" Here Hunter revealed that money, i.e., the value of their slaves, was still at the root of the war. The elite southern plantation culture had already suffered financially, and the cost of freeing the slaves was so great that all other issues, such as state's rights, or dare to mention, the Monroe Doctrine, shrunk before it. The conference was at an end.

It seems that Hunter's revelation of the Confederacy's attitude regarding the cost of freeing the slaves had made an impression on Lincoln, though he admitted nothing of it to the commissioners. Given two days to think about it, Lincoln disclosed at a February 6th cabinet meeting that he "had matured a scheme which he hoped would be successful in promoting peace."[2314] As Gideon Welles describes it: "It was a proposition for the paying of the expenses of the war for two hundred days, or four hundred millions, to the Rebel States, to be for the extinguishment of slavery…" Welles continues: "It did not meet with favor, but was dropped."

The Hampton Roads Conference, as it became known, had one decisive outcome. After the conference had ended, when Vice President Alexander Stephens

---

2312. Nicolay and Hay, vol. 10, pp. 116–121.
2313. Stephens, pp. 598, 611–615; Hunter, R. M. T., SHS, vol. 3, p. 173, 175–176.
2314. Welles, vol. 2, p. 237.

observed that Davis remained unshaken in his "unaccountable hallucination"[2315] that the war could be continued indefinitely, and would ultimately result in independence, he broke with Davis. He now considered the "Cause utterly hopeless…" He refused to speak at a rally held in Richmond on February 6th and at another a few days later. On February 9th, he abandoned Richmond and returned home to Georgia, where he remained "in perfect retirement" signifying that he had resigned, though apparently no formal resignation was made.

Sheridan Leaves the Valley

The reader will recall that Grant had always been concerned about cutting off supplies to Lee. On October 14th, just before Sheridan fought the Battle of Cedar Creek, Grant had asked him to raid the Virginia Central Railroad and canal, chapter 14. The events preceding the battle caused the cavalry to return to the Valley, and the raid never happened. Again, on the 19th of December, responding to Grant's urging, Sheridan had sent out the cavalry to break up the railroads at Gordonsville and Charlottesville.[2316] The weather was terrible, the roads poor, and worse yet, the movement of the cavalry was closely observed by Early. Custer's division was surprised while in bivouac by his old nemesis, Rosser, at Lacey's Springs, and had to retreat down the Valley. Hearing of Custer's retreat, Wharton was sent to Charlottesville, but Lomax had already checked the remainder of Torbert's force. By the 27th of December, the frostbitten raiders had returned, the raid an utter failure, and the cavalry was put into winter quarters near Winchester.

The advancement of the season, and events further south, where weather had been less of a concern, revived Grant's request. By the 1st of February, Sherman had begun his move north from Savannah.[2317] He captured Columbia, South Carolina, on February 17th. Grant now had the opportunity to put in motion a much larger plan, combining troops from every direction, in which another raid south by Sheridan would play a part. The months since Cedar Creek had changed the whole outlook of the war. Grant's telegram to Sheridan, dated February 20th, 1865, explains the big picture:

Maj. Gen. P.H. Sheridan:

> GENERAL: As soon as it is possible to travel I think you will have no difficulty about reaching Lynchburg with a cavalry force alone. From there you could destroy the railroad and canal in every direction, so as to be of no further use to the rebellion. Sufficient cavalry should be left behind to look after Mosby's gang. From Lynchburg, if information you might get there

---

2315. Bowen, J. J., p. 246; Stephens, pp. 623–626.
2316. Sheridan, vol. 2, pp. 102–104.
2317. O.R. Vol. 34/I, pp. 44–46.

would justify it, you could strike south, heading the streams in Virginia to the westward of Danville, and push on and join General Sherman. This additional raid, with one now starting from East Tennessee under Stoneman, numbering 4,000 or 5,000 cavalry, one from Vicksburg, numbering 7,000 or 8,000 cavalry, one from Eastport, Miss., 10,000 cavalry, Canby from Mobile Bay, with about 38,000 mixed troops, these three latter pushing for Tuscaloosa, Selma, and Montgomery, and Sherman with a large army eating out the vitals of South Carolina, is all that will be wanted to leave nothing for the rebellion to stand upon. I would advise you to overcome great obstacles to accomplish this, Charleston was evacuated on Tuesday last.[2318]

Stoneman[2319] was a part of Thomas' command, and after soundly defeating Hood, Thomas had troops to spare, which Grant quickly made plans for. Schofield's 23rd Corps was sent east to aid in the follow-on attack to take the city of Wilmington after the fall of Fort Fisher. This was accomplished on the 22nd of February. "Tuesday last" in Grant's telegram was February 14th, when Charleston was abandoned as Sherman approached Columbia.

It is interesting to note that Grant advised Sheridan to leave sufficient cavalry to look after Mosby. Proof enough that Mosby, with a few hundred men, had created the need for thousands of security troops. Sheridan would leave behind Powell's whole division.

General Winfield S. Hancock,[2320] formerly in command of the 2nd Corps of the Army of the Potomac, having been made available to command a "veteran volunteer army corps" in November, was now, on February 26th, assigned to head the Department of West Virginia and "temporarily all of the troops of the Middle Military Division not under the immediate command of Major-General Sheridan." The next day Sheridan left Winchester and headed up the Valley Pike. He took with him only Custer's and Devin's divisions, one section of Battery C–E of the 4th U.S. Artillery, and one section of Battery M, 2nd U.S. Artillery;[2321] a total of 9,987 men. Battery M, we recall, was one of the artillery companies that escaped from Texas with Battery L in 1861, chapter 2.

Excepting the artillery, the only other equipment on "wheels" as Sheridan refers to them, were: one headquarters wagon, a supply train with 15 day's rations, eight ambulances, 16 ammunition wagons, and a pontoon train of eight boats.

The weather was bad, and the spring thaw, with heavy rain, had come on, raising the streams to almost higher than could be forded. They reached Woodstock that

---

2318. The number of troops this reference attributes to Canby, at 38,000, apparently included A. J. Smith's command. The number quoted by Grant in his *Memoirs* is 18,000. Grant, vol. 2, p. 409.
2319. O.R. Vol. 34/I, p. 45; Grant, vol. 2, pp. 412–413.
2320. O.R. Vol. 42/I, p. 3; vol. 46/I, p. 2.
2321. O.R. Vol. 46/I, pp. 475, 485, 488; Sheridan, vol. 2, p. 113; McDonald, pp. 359–360.

night. The next day, arriving at Mount Jackson, they found the bridge destroyed, and the first use of their pontoon bridge was made. The third day they made camp at Middle River at Cline's Mills. Though guerillas had been observed, none attacked, but Rosser, who had gathered together about 300 men, had attempted to burn the bridge across North River and had hastily constructed some breastworks near it. Next day, the river was running lower, and two regiments of Sheridan's crossed upstream and hit Rosser in flank. His small force was dispersed, with 30 prisoners and 20 wagons taken, which were destroyed. Nevertheless, Rosser had delayed Sheridan 24 hours, which allowed Early time to move out of Staunton. The next morning, March 2nd, they pressed on to Staunton, despite the incessant rain and consequent mud, arriving to find that Early had retreated to Waynesboro, where he intended to make a stand.

Though Sheridan could have bypassed the last remnant of Early's army, less than 2,000 men, and continued on to Lynchburg, he decided to attack. Custer was ordered to take up the pursuit, and found Early's small force well placed on a ridge covering Waynesboro on the west, and just outside the town.[2322] A reconnaissance convinced Custer that a frontal attack on Early's dug-in position, with the six guns of Nelson's artillery commanding all of the approaches, would be fatal. However, Early's line on his left, Wharton's, did not extend to the river, and a body of woods on its approach would conceal any of the attackers. The gap was the vulnerable point, and without hesitation, Custer ordered three of Pennington's regiments, who were armed with Spencer repeating rifles, to charge. Covered by artillery, and coordinated with an attack on the front, Wharton's men had no choice but to keep their heads down. The surprise of the sudden attack was complete, and Early's men were routed. Quoting Early: "I now saw that everything was lost…I rode to the top of a hill to reconnoiter, and had the mortification of seeing the greater part of my command being carried off as prisoners, and a force of the enemy moving toward Rock-fish Gap."

The battle netted Sheridan 11 pieces of artillery, 200 wagons loaded with subsistence, and 1,600 prisoners. As Jedediah Hotchkiss, Early's mapmaker, noted in his journal:[2323] "The whole army was captured or scattered…" though Rosser's little band escaped, having been ordered to hang on the flanks of the enemy.

Another infamous Confederate that also remained, undaunted, in his haunts near Millwood,[2324] was Mosby.

Early and the party of 15 or 20 with him who escaped capture roamed around and, "watched the enemy for several days while he was at Charlottesville, and

---

2322. Early, *Sketch*, p. 462–464; O.R. Vol. 46/I, pp. 485, 502–503, 516. Though Custer's reconnaissance thought they discovered 10 guns, there were only six, five more were on rail cars at Greenwood, making a total of 11 captured.

2323. O.R. Vol. 46/I

2324. Kidd, p. 445.

while making his way to report to Lee's headquarters outside of Petersburg, was very nearly captured while passing in the vicinity of Ashland."[2325] He then, by way of Lynchburg, headed back to the Valley "to reorganize what was left of my command." While there, news of Thomas marching from East Tennessee was received, and he and General John Echols, head of the Department of Southwest Virginia, went to Bristol, Virginia, on the Tennessee state line. Confirming that "some important move by the enemy was on foot," Early then returned to nearby Abingdon, to try to organize a force to meet Thomas. While there, on March 30th, he received a telegram from Lee notifying him to turn over the command in Southwestern Virginia to Echols, and that of the Valley to Lomax. His career was at an end. Only nine days later, Lee's career would also end.

After the engagement at Waynesboro, with its iron bridge destroyed by heaping railroad ties upon it and setting them afire until the bridge warped and distorted to its destruction,[2326] Sheridan chose to cross over the Blue Ridge Mountains at Rockfish Gap, avoiding Lynchburg, because he had received word that there had been a buildup of the garrison there, and that its fortifications had been strengthened, making its capture "…improbable."[2327] Leaving Waynesboro, he would head to Charlottesville, figure 5, where the crossing of the Blue Ridge Mountains, still covered with snow, would be easier at Rockfish Gap. From Charlottesville, he would head south to destroy the Southside Railroad, which runs east from Lynchburg toward Petersburg, but at a point further east.

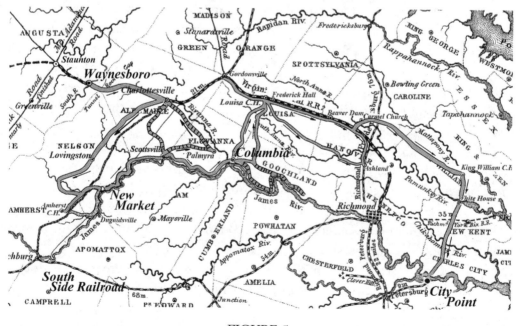

FIGURE 5

2325. Early, *Sketch*, pp. 465–466; O.R. Vol. 46/II, pp. 1041, 1184; Sheridan, vol. 2, p. 121.
2326. Humphreys, pp. 207–208.
2327. Sheridan, vol. 2, pp. 118–119; O.R. Vol. 46/I, pp.477–478, 490–491.

The roads were so bad and the conditions so trying for the horses that they remained at Charlottesville for two days to rest and recuperate. While there, the railroad bridges across the Rivanna River were destroyed, and the Orange and Alexandria Railroad destroyed for fifteen miles in either direction. On March 6th, the expedition was divided into two columns, Custer's and Devin's, shown as dotted lines in figure 5, with Devin and Merritt splitting again, the 1st Michigan going along the Rivanna River to Palmyra, with orders to rejoin the command at Scottsville, and the remainder going directly to Scottsville. The scorched-earth policy that Sheridan had wrought upon the Shenandoah Valley in 1864 was repeated, destroying flour mills, woolen factories, and other manufacturing establishments and tearing up all of the locks and destroying the canal boats on the James River Canal from Scottsville to New Market.

At New Market on the night of the 7th, they encamped, save the 6th Pennsylvania Cavalry,[2328] which was ordered to advance to the bridge at Duguidsville and seize it for the planned crossing to the south side of the James. It was not to be, the bridge was put to the torch as the Yankees approached. Since the bridge at Hardwicksville (Wingina) had already been found burned, Sheridan now had no way to cross; his eight pontoons reaching but halfway into the river.

Custer, the other half of the command, proceeded down along the Lynchburg extension of the Orange and Alexandria Railroad, destroying all of the bridges and trestlework as far as Amherst Courthouse, fifteen miles from Lynchburg,[2329] and then rejoined the command at New Market on the 8th.

Sheridan interpreted the situation as rather an advantage than a loss, since he now finally determined not to try to return to Winchester, and with Lynchburg being too well reinforced for him to attempt an attack, he would join Grant at City Point, something he really wanted anyway, which he now reveals. A glance at figure 5 shows that the shortest route to City Point is via a crossing of the James. As Sheridan put it:[2330]

> Unable to cross until the river should fall, and knowing that it was impractical to join General Sherman…I now decided to destroy still more thoroughly the James River Canal and the Virginia Central Railroad and then join General Grant in front of Petersburg.…I was master of the whole country north of the James as far down as Goochland; hence the destruction of these arteries of supply could be easily compassed, and feeling that the war was nearing its end, *I desired my cavalry to be in at the death*. [Italics added].

2328. O.R. Vol. 46/I, p. 491. The 17th Pennsylvania Cavalry was sent in support. Humphreys, p. 211, includes the 2nd Massachusetts Cavalry, as well.
2329. Gracey, E. H., pp. 321–322; O.R. Vol. 46/I, p. 503.
2330. Sheridan, vol. 2, pp. 119–120; Figure 5, Sheridan, vol. 2, facing pp. 122–123.

Another way of looking at his situation was that he was trapped, and, in addition, he had failed in a primary facet of his mission, which was to get to the rail hub of Lynchburg and destroy its connection with the Southside Railroad. It left Grant the task of having to do it later.

To get to City Point would require the most circuitous of routes. On March 9th, the combined column started eastward along the James River, destroying everything. It reached Columbia on the 10th. From here, Sheridan sent a message to Grant to inform him of his decision to join him, and to request that supplies of forage and rations be made available at the Union depot at White House, on the Pamunkey River. It was absolutely critical that supplies be ready for him at White House, and the device that Sheridan used to get his message to Grant was to send it by two different sets of couriers. One copy was sent overland by a pair of his scouts, Campbell and Rowan, and another was sent downriver in a small boat with another pair of scouts, Fannin and Moore. Of course, the river passes Richmond, and the plan for Fannin and Moore was to join the rebel army as volunteers, in front of Petersburg, and then desert to the Union lines. Both pairs of couriers got through, but Campbell and Rowan arrived first.[2331] It is an education to observe how desperate the Confederates were that they would unquestioningly accept two volunteers that appeared out of nowhere, and that they were able to as quickly desert.

Resting for a day at Columbia, Sheridan noted how wearing the march had been on the mules pulling the wagons. He recalls: "I believe we should have been forced to abandon most of the wagons except for the invaluable help given by some two thousand negroes who had attached themselves to the column; they literally lifted the wagons out of the mud." Here was repeated a scene which Battery L and the 19th Corps had oft experienced in Louisiana; given the opportunity, the slave population would drop everything and follow the bluejackets.

From Columbia, on March 11th, Colonel Fitzhugh's 2nd Brigade, of Devin's division,[2332] was sent forward along the James as far as Goochland Courthouse, the dotted line in figure 5. Along the way they destroyed ten of the canal locks, and 15 canal boats. Sending scouts to within eighteen miles of Richmond, they only had encountered opposition upon entering Goochland, the 7th South Carolina Regiment, which was swept aside. They returned to Columbia that evening.

On the 12th, the command marched north, Custer to destroy the Virginia Central from Frederick's Hall to Beaver Dam Station, and Devin to accomplish the same from Louisa Courthouse to Frederick's Hall. This work continued on March 13th,[2333] and was done as much to ensure that a Confederate force could not be brought from Richmond to attack the column in its flank or rear as for

---

2331. Sheridan, vol.2, p. 120.
2332. O.R. Vol. 46/I, p. 498.
2333. O.R. Vol. 46/I, pp. 478–479, 503; Sheridan, vol. 2, p. 122.

any strategic purpose. Sheridan's scouts had determined that such a force, under Longstreet, was being prepared in Richmond. In addition, they had found that Pickett's division was headed back from Lynchburg on the Southside Railroad. On the 14th, the entire command moved out from the area of Frederick Hall to the vicinity of Ashland, only twenty miles north of Richmond, Devin via the railroad, through Hanover Junction, and Custer down the Negrofoot Road and across the Ground Squirrel Bridge on the South Anna River, to unite with Devin. The object was to divert Longstreet's attention, whose force now included Johnson's and Pickett's divisions of infantry and Fitzhugh Lee's cavalry, and draw them out in that direction, which it did. Leaving Pennington's division to make a show of a continued advance, Sheridan withdrew. The command quickly retraced Devin's steps, and reached Mount Carmel Church on the night of the 15th, where they would ford the North Anna River the next day. The maneuver foiled Longstreet, who gave up the chase. Resuming the march, they reached King William Courthouse on the 17th, and White House on the 18th.[2334] They were tired, dirty, tattered and torn. A measure of the difficulty of the muddy roads is testified to by the fact that they had left 4,000 horses along the way, victims to hoof-rot, grease heel, and leg scratches, caused by repeatedly having to lift their legs in and out of the deep mud. It had rained 16 out of the 20 days of the raid, which had extended over about four hundred miles.

They remained at White House until March 25th, six days, refitting and replacing horses that continued to die from the suffering of the march. Many men were not able to be remounted, and had to be sent to dismounted camp. The march did not end at City Point, as contemplated, but passed on to Harrison's Landing, then along the north bank of the James to Deep Bottom, where they crossed, and were directed into camp at Hancock Station, on the railroad in front of Petersburg. It was now the 27th of March.[2335]

Looking at Early's comments after escaping from Waynesboro, it is noted that he was very nearly captured by Custer near Ashland, Virginia. When Custer arrived at the Frederick's Hall telegraph station, he captured all of the dispatches, one of which was from Early to Lee, warning of Sheridan's approach at Goochland, and that he intended to attack with a force of about 200 cavalry that he had gathered. Custer immediately ordered a regiment after him. It soon scattered Early's little band, capturing two of Early's staff, and most of the rest. Early escaped by swimming the South Anna River.[2336]

2334. Longstreet, James, p. 591; O.R. Vol. 46/I, p. 480; Humphreys, pp. 214–216, 221–222.
2335. Humphreys, p. 224; O.R. Vol. 46/I, p. 480.
2336. O.R. Vol. 46/I, p. 479; Humphreys, p. 215.

"Record" 4/65
28 FEBRUARY–30 APRIL 1865 WINCHESTER, VIRGINIA

The Company left Pleasant Valley, Maryland on the 24th day of April, 1865, and marched to Charlestown Virginia, distance twelve miles. Resumed the march the next morning, and marched to Winchester, Virginia. Joined the Provisional Brigade of Cavalry where the Company is now stationed.

Henry W. Closson	Capt. Commanding Battery.
Franck E. Taylor	1st Lt. Relieved from duty with Battery K 1st U.S. Artillery, and ordered on recruiting service. Orders no. 84, A.G.O. Washington, DC April 1st 1865.
Edward L. Appleton	1st Lt. Absent without leave since Sept. 22nd 1864.

Detached: none.

Absent in Confinement:
Patrick Gibbons	Pvt. At Ship Island, serving sentence of G.C.M. S.O. no. 18, Hdqrts. 1st Div. 19th Army Corps. Dec. 31, 1863.

Deserted:
John Lewery	Pvt. From absent in confinement at New Orleans, to deserted, date not known.

Discharged:
George Chase	Pvt. At Brashear City, for disability, date not known.
William Crowley	Pvt. At Baton Rouge, for disability, date not known.
Charles Jackel	Pvt. At New Orleans, for disability, Oct. 1, 1864.
John Meyer	Pvt. From Battery G 5th U.S. Artillery, New Orleans, by exp. of svc. Mar. 1, 1865.
Churchill Moore	Pvt. At New Orleans, for disability, date unknown.

Died:
James Campbell	Pvt. Oct. 6, 1864. From wounds received at the Battle of Winchester, Va.
John C. Wood	Pvt. Sept. 21, 1864 do.

Strength: 57 Sick: 2

Sick Present: none

Sick Absent: 2
Thomas Clinton	Pvt. Mar. 1, 1865 At Frederick City, Md.
Andrew Stoll	Pvt. Absent wounded since September 24th 1864, near New Market, Va.

With no transfers into it, the number of men in the Battery K–L is insufficient to be sent into action. Battery K at this time had only 45 men. Moreover, neither battery had any horses. According to the regimental return for April, 22 men have been requested from depot for Battery L, and 47 for Battery K. Roughly this same number had been posted on every regimental return since the first of the year. As has been mentioned before, recruitment had been becoming increasingly difficult. In April, there were only 10 recruits sent to the entire regiment, and they all were allotted to Battery C. This, no doubt, is why Lieutenant Taylor has been assigned to recruiting duty, the mysterious disappearance of Lt. Appleton having resulted in no new recruits for the Battery.

There may have been great hopes of being assigned to Sheridan when he left the Valley at the end of February, but this was unrealistic, with no horses and a total of only 102 men. Finally, in March, they were given 140 horses, but these were of no real use in any action, since no new recruits had come in, and as is shown above, the battery was losing men, not gaining them. Nevertheless, now under a well-respected new man, General Hancock, there were some plans for action, and the move out of the reserve camp was a sign. It was Grant's plan to use Hancock in the Valley, or at least east of the Blue Ridge, at Lynchburg, as Grant says:[2337]

> [T]he idea being to make the spring campaign the close of the war. I expected, with Sherman coming up from the South, Meade south of Petersburg and around Richmond, and Thomas's command in Tennessee with depots of supplies established in the eastern part of that State, to move from the direction of Washington or the valley towards Lynchburg. We would then have Lee so surrounded that his supplies would be cut off entirely, making it impossible for him to support his army.

The fall of Fort Fisher and the occupation of Wilmington would seem to have been sufficient to close the supply routes to Lee, but treason on the part of some of those in the North had kept a trickle of supplies flowing in to Lee from yet another direction, the Northern Neck. Smugglers had been using this route since early in the war.[2338]

The Northern Neck was the northernmost peninsula in northern Virginia, between the Potomac River and the Rappahannock.[2339] It consisted of the counties of Lancaster, Northumberland, Richmond, and Westmoreland, an area frequented by Mosby. It was important enough as a source for Lee, even at this late date (March 2nd 1865), that Grant took notice:

> I want an expedition…prepared to send up the Rappahannock as soon as the quartermaster's department can furnish water transportation for them… The object is to break up illicit trade of the Northern Neck, and, if they can, break up the Fredericksburg Railroad.

It had been discovered that supplies were being smuggled in from Philadelphia, collected in the Northern Neck, and then shipped by rail to Richmond. As much as 70,000 pounds of bacon had gone to Richmond in one week in February. Though this was not arms and ammunition, it was sustenance for Lee. The difficulty, of course, was defining what material, other than arms, was contraband when it was

---

2337. Grant, vol. 2, p. 342–343.
2338. O.R. Vol. 5, p. 365.
2339. Ambler, C. H., p. 11; O.R. Vol. 5, p. 365; O.R. Vol. 46/II, pp. 576, 649–650, 666, 790; O.R. Vol. 46/III, pp. 681, 753.

shipped from Northern ports—not by Englishmen running out from Nassau, as in the story of blockade running—but by unscrupulous American profiteers, Southern sympathizers, agents, or a mixture of all shades. As it happened, the 8th Illinois Cavalry, originally assigned to the expedition, was not ready to go until March 20th, and then the expedition had to be temporarily abandoned by order of General Augur on the 22nd.[2340] After Lee had surrendered, on April 9th, the expedition was pointless, but the decision to cancel it was put to Halleck before any such action was taken. Finally, on the 14th of April, the 8th Illinois was assigned elsewhere.

Events of Note

On the 21st of January, Jefferson Davis was informed of "disaffection" in the Virginia Legislature, and more significantly, in the Confederate Congress.[2341] A resolution of no confidence in the chief executive was being informally discussed, and it seemed clear that if a formal resolution was introduced, it would pass by a wide margin. A compromise resulted in the creation, on January 23rd, of the position of general-in-chief of the military forces of the Confederate States, and Robert E. Lee was named. He accepted on February 9th. The intention was to grant Lee with dictatorial power, and that he would make appointments within the army and make other moves as he saw necessary to successfully prosecute the war. He did not. A suggestion soon made to him by Longstreet[2342] was to replace Beauregard in command of the Army of Tennessee, but Lee did not so order it; he merely made a request to the new secretary of war, Gen. John C. Breckinridge, that Joseph E. Johnston report to him. As Longstreet describes Lee: "He made his orders assuming command of the armies, but instead of exercising authority on a scale commensurate with the views of Congress and the call of the crisis, applied to the Richmond authorities for instructions under the new assignment…"

Back on September 26th, 1864, Governor Allen of Louisiana wrote to James W. Seddon, then the Confederate secretary of war,[2343] that the time had come to enlist "every able-bodied negro man as a soldier…I would free all able to bear arms…" The subject was now under active discussion. The November 5th, 1864 issue of *Harper's Weekly* quotes the *Richmond Enquirer* of October 18th as advocating the same, i.e., freedom for service. This had been hinted at in discussions between the peace commissioners and Lincoln. Other proposals included the enrollment of the Indians and Mormons in the west, and diplomatic moves with Mexico to encourage emigration

---

2340. O.R. Vol. 46/III, pp. 84, 681, 754–755.
2341. Longstreet, pp. 582–583; O.R. Vol. 46/II, pp. 1205, 1226
2342. O.R. Vol. 46/II, pp. 1192, 1244, 1245; Longstreet, pp. 588, 589; Cooke, J. E., p. 436; O.R. ser. 4, vol. 3, Breckinridge had replaced Seddon as secretary of war on February 6th, 1865.
2343. O.R. Vol. 41/III, p. 774.

for the purpose of enrollment.[2344] Obviously, desperation finally drove the Confederate Congress to pass, on March 23rd, 1865, an act which authorized the enrollment of the slaves. As might have been expected, it was not a blanket offer of freedom for service; it limited the enrollment to not more than 25 percent of the male slave population between the ages of 18 and 45, and it did not offer freedom. Only the regulations issued under the act specified that: "No slave will be accepted as a recruit unless with his own consent and with the approbation of his master by a written instrument conferring, as far as he may, the rights of a freedman…"

Sherman

On the 18th of January, Sherman transferred the forts and the city of Savannah to General Foster, commanding the Department of the South, and prepared to leave. He aimed to make for Goldsboro, North Carolina, "at one stride," where he could open communication to the sea by the Atlantic and North Carolina Railroad.[2345] On January 19th, all preparations were complete, and orders for the march given, but the flooded condition of the Savannah River had prevented any move. The "real" march began on February 1st.

By February 16th, the head of the column had reached the Congaree River opposite Columbia, South Carolina, and the city surrendered the next day. Gen. Wade Hampton, who commanded the Confederate cavalry rear guard, had ordered all of the cotton moved into the streets and burned. Though generally extinguished by Sherman's men, as he puts it, "the smouldering fires, set by Hampton's order, were rekindled by the wind…" The fires were not brought under control until early the next day. Then, and only then, did Sherman proceed to destroy all property of value to the Confederate war effort: the arsenal, foundries, and the railroad track and bridge.[2346] Columbia, of course, was the capitol of the state that had started the rebellion, and the feelings of some were that utter desolation should be visited upon it as retribution.

Charleston was evacuated by the Confederates without a fight on February 18th, and was garrisoned by General Foster. On the night of the 21st, Bragg evacuated Wilmington, setting afire the Confederate stores. It was occupied by the forces of Generals Schofield and Terry on the 22nd.[2347]

By March 2nd, Sherman's army was at Chesterfield, and entered Cheraw the next day. On the 11th of March, the 14th and 17th corps reached Fayetteville, Confederate General Hardee retreating before them. Three days were spent at Fayetteville destroying the former U.S. arsenal and the "vast amount of machinery which

---

2344. O.R. Vol. 48/I, pp. 1393–1394; O.R. ser. 4, vol. 3, pp. 1161–1162.
2345. O.R. Vol. 47/I, pp. 18–19; Atlas, plate 117.
2346. O.R. Vol. 47/I, pp. 21–23; Grant, vol. 2, pp. 415–416.
2347. CWSAC NC016; Grant, vol. 2, p. 416.

had formerly belonged to the old Harper's Ferry U.S. Arsenal."

On the 15th, Sherman crossed the Cape Fear River, and the march for Goldsboro began.[2348] At the narrow, swampy neck of land between the Cape Fear and the South rivers, Sherman's cavalry, under Judson Kilpatrick, came up against Hardee's infantry on the Raleigh-Smithfield-Goldsboro Road. It was the first real resistance Sherman had met. Hardee's goal was to delay Sherman to allow Joseph E. Johnston, now in command,[2349] to concentrate his forces further down the line. Kilpatrick withdrew and called for infantry support. The 20th Corps, under Slocum, came up during the night. At dawn, the advance division of the 20th Corps turned the first lightly-built parapet of the Confederate line back, and then came up against a second line, which was even stronger. Feeling forward on the left, Kilpatrick's cavalry was attacked and driven back. Late in the afternoon, the Confederates were driven back into their lines again, and according to Sherman, he "pressed him so hard that next morning he was gone, having retreated in a miserable stormy night over the worst of roads."

Though the weather was milder than that during Sheridan's raid, Sherman's army was not exempted from rain, and the going was often slow. After the battle, which has become known as Averasborough, Slocum's command marched on, going into camp on the night of the 18th, five miles outside of Bentonville, and twenty-seven from Goldsboro. General Howard, with the 15th and 17th corps, Sherman's right wing, was south, a few miles away.

On March 19th, Sherman directed Howard to turn directly to Goldsboro, and anticipating news from Schofield, who was coming to meet him from New Berne, and Terry from Wilmington, Sherman then left Slocum, and joined Howard. Slocum continued on, and ran into Johnston's entrenchments outside of Bentonville. Johnston had moved from Smithfield to attack Sherman's left wing,[2350] hoping to take it in detail, as Sherman says, before it could be relieved by its "cooperating columns," i.e., the right wing. Slocum and Kilpatrick fell back, repelling multiple Confederate assaults, until Howard arrived at about noon on the next day. Now Johnston was on the defensive. Sherman saw nothing to be gained by an attack on the enemy parapets, and only skirmishers and artillery were used to press Johnston. By March 21st, Mower's division of the 17th Corps, had nearly worked its way to the Mill Creek Bridge, in Johnston's rear, his only escape route. There followed, as Sherman reports, "Quite a noisy battle…" Mower had demonstrated the weak point in Johnston's defenses, and on the night of March 22nd he withdrew toward Smithfield, ending the Battle of Bentonville.[2351]

2348. O.R. Vol. 47/I, pp. 24–25.
2349. Johnston, J. E., *Narrative*, pp. 371, 382–383. Johnston was ordered to command on February 23rd.
2350. Johnston, *Narrative*, pp. 372, 385, 389–392.
2351. O.R. Vol. 47/I, pp. 26–27.

It was the last one for Johnston's little collection of men, about 5,000 from Hood's Army of Tennessee, and the less than 10,000 left from the Military Division of the West, under Beauregard, since the governor of South Carolina had called home its militia when they entered North Carolina. The outcome was never in doubt, in view of the fact that Johnston initially opposed 30,000 of Sherman's army, and after March 20th, his whole army of more than 60,000. It left Sherman in full possession of Goldsboro and the supply lines to the coast. Sherman's army would then remain in the area to rest and refit. In the meantime, Sherman left to visit Grant at City Point, arriving there on the 27th of March. In their meeting, it became clear that Sherman could not march to join Grant in the grand plan to unite the armies against Lee until April 10th at the earliest.[2352] Here, Sherman learned that Grant had already decided, with Sheridan having returned from his raid, to begin a general advance on the 29th of March, which Grant hoped would result in "terminating the contest…"

Preliminary orders for the campaign were issued on the 14th, which called for a general move to the left (west), and the final orders were issued on March 24th.[2353] The orders read:

> On the 29th instant, the armies operating against Richmond will be moved by our left, for the double purpose of turning the enemy out of his present position around Petersburg, and to insure the success of the cavalry under General Sheridan, which will start at the same time, in its efforts to reach and destroy the South Side and Danville railroad.

FIGURE 6

2352. O.R. Vol. 47/I, p. 29; Grant, vol. 2, pp. 437, 619.
2353. Grant, vol. 2, pp. 616–618; O.R. Vol. 46/II, p. 962; Longstreet, p. 592; O.R. Vol. 47/I, pp. 1141–1147.

The attack was to be made at Five Forks, on the western end of the forty miles or more of the defensive lines in front of Petersburg, figure 6.[2354] With his only remaining lifeline, the Southside Railroad, in danger of being cut off, Grant calculated that Lee would make a great effort to protect it.[2355] By so doing, Lee would weaken his center, where an assault, as Grant says, "might be successfully made."

Fort Stedman

Unfortunately, the smooth narrative of Grant's final plans to defeat Lee were interrupted, however briefly. Lee "gave consent" as Gen. James Longstreet remembers, to a sortie from his line in front of Petersburg, against Fort Stedman, a point where the Confederate and Union lines were the closest together—about two hundred yards. The bold and desperate move, at the opposite end of the line from Five Forks, was planned for gaining time, by forcing Grant to make a longer detour to reach the Southside Railroad, thus allowing Lee time to find dry roads for "our march away, *or for reinforcements to reach us.*" The italics have been added to the last part of Longstreet's remark, to emphasize the irrational hope uttered here. Johnston's army was the only potential reinforcement, and at this time it consisted of less than 15,000 men. Even if it could have been joined with Lee's 43,000 the combination would still pale before Grant's 114,000,[2356] which did not include Sheridan's cavalry.

Gen. John H. Gordon, the author of Early's surprise attack on Sheridan at Cedar Creek, was chosen to plan and lead the raid. Just prior to it, he remembers that Jefferson Davis "was very pertinacious in opinion and purpose,"[2357] and he did not believe that after the Hampton Roads Conference's failure that he could secure peace terms that he could accept. "Neither were the authorities in Richmond ready to evacuate the capital and abandon our lines of defense." A few weeks later, the crushing defeat at Fort Stedman would alter such pertinacity.

Discussing his plan in an interview with Lee, Gordon warned that fully one-half of the army would be required, and ultimately about 18,000 men were collected for the raid. Gordon's plan, much as at Cedar Creek, would rely on stealth and exquisite detail.[2358] In darkness, 50 picked men, carrying axes only, would lead the assault, and would chop through the wooden chevaux de frise, and other obstructions in front of Grant's lines, and enter the fort. They would be closely followed by three 100-man groups, each led by a picked officer. Each officer would be a man who had lived in the area before the war, or who would have a guide

---

2354. Figure 6, Atlas, plate 76, map 5, portion, altered.
2355. Longstreet, p. 596; Grant, vol. 2, p. 440.
2356. O.R. Vol. 46/I, p.62, 386; Gordon, pp. 400, 422.
2357. Gordon, p. 303; Longstreet, p. 593.
2358. Gordon, pp. 402–406; Anderson, John, p. 282.

who was familiar with the local topography. They would also take advantage of orders Grant had issued allowing deserters to cross into the Union lines, taking their arms with them, which were offered to be purchased.[2359] Under these provisions, deserters were coming over and surrendering at the rate of 50 per day. The crossings having become routine, Gordon's pickets could thus advance, pretending to be deserters.

During the week previous to the attack, Gordon had studiously obtained the names of

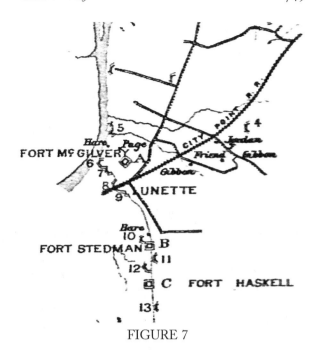

FIGURE 7

the Union officers in the fort, and each of his three picked officers would assume the identity of one of them. The three groups would rush through Fort Stedman while others subdued the garrison, and proceed to the line of the supporting Union infantry behind it. As they advanced, they would yell out that the fort had been overwhelmed, and each would repeat: "The Rebels have captured our works, and I have been ordered by General McLaughlin[2360] to rush back to the fort in rear, and hold it at all hazards."

On March 25th at 4:00 a.m., Gordon stood on the top of the Confederate breastworks, his troops standing in close column, waiting to give the single musket shot that would signal the start of the attack. Gordon ordered the private by his side to fire. The soldier hesitated; he owed the Yankee picket opposite a courtesy warning.[2361]

Gordon recalls that while his troops were gathering at the crossing point, a final clearing of some of the debris of the Confederate obstructions was thought necessary for ease of passage. The work proceeded, but the noise was heard by a Yankee picket, and soon came the inquiry: "What are you doing over there Johnny? What is that noise? Answer quick or I'll shoot." The question conformed to an established understanding between the two sides that they would not shoot each other down except when necessary. As Gordon explains:

2359. Anderson, J., p. 254; Grant, vol. 2, p. 432.
2360. Col. N. B. McLaughlen, per the spelling in the Official Records, was the commander of the Fort Stedman garrison. O.R. Vol. 46/I, p. 70; Anderson, J., p. 263.
2361. Gordon, p. 409.

The call of the Union picket filled me with apprehension, I expected him to fire and start the entire picket line to firing, thus giving the alarm to the fort… The quick mother-wit of the private soldier by my side came to my relief. In an instant he replied: "Never mind Yank. Lie down and go to sleep. We are just gathering a little corn. You know rations are mighty short here."

There was a narrow strip of corn which the bullets had not shot away still standing between the lines. The Union picket promptly answered: "All right, Johnny; go ahead and get your corn. I'll not shoot at you while you are drawing your rations."

Again ordered by Gordon to fire, the private called to his kind-hearted foe and said: "Hello Yank! Wake up; we are going to shell the woods. Look out; we are coming." With that, he fired the signal and rushed off into the darkness. The ruse worked, regardless of the warning given to this single picket, and the axe-men advanced to their task without arousing the rest of the line. The line was successfully breached and the selected 300 advanced, followed by the infantry. The fort was taken and its guns turned in either direction on its flanks, clearing the breastworks on either side. Gordon then assumed command of the fort, taking prisoner its commander, Col. N. B. McLaughlen, of the 57th Massachusetts.

The attack also captured batteries 10, 11 and 12, and threatened Fort Haslkell, figure 7,[2362] but did not succeed in taking it. The tide of Gordon's advance was now stopped. The garrisons of mortar batteries 11 and 12 rallied and re-took them, so that by 7:30 a.m. the raiders were in possession of only Fort Stedman and Battery 10, and were surrounded on three sides by a cordon of Hartranft's 3rd Division of Parke's 9th Army Corps. The remaining space in their rear, where they had crossed in their assault, had now been covered by a cross fire of artillery.[2363] At 7:45 Hartranft advanced and the fort and Battery 10 were retaken. In General Parke's words, the combined artillery and infantry crossfire "deterred many of the enemy from attempting to escape, and caused severe loss among those who made the trial." By 8:00 it was over, the signal sergeant at Walthall Signal Station reporting: "Our line near Fort Stedman just advanced to its old position."[2364]

In Grant's words:[2365] "This effort of Lee's cost him about four thousand men, and resulted in their killing, wounding and capturing about two thousand of ours." In fact, the 9th Army Corps suffered 522 in killed and wounded, and 503 missing. Contrast Grant's mistaken honesty with Lee. Lee's words, here quoted in full, are a report to the new Secretary of War J. C. Breckinridge, dated March 25th:

2362. Figure 7, Atlas, plate 67, map no. 9, portion.
2363. O.R. Vol. 46/I, p. 318; Anderson, J., p. 256.
2364. O.R. Vol. 46/III, p. 119.
2365. Grant, vol. 2, pp. 433–434; O.R. Vol. 46/I, pp. 71, 382–383.

> At daylight this morning General Gordon assaulted and carried enemy's works at Hare's Hill, captured 9 pieces of artillery, 8 mortars, between 500 and 600 prisoners, among them one brigadier-general and number of officers of lower grade. Enemy's lines were swept away for distance of four hundred to five hundred yards to right and left, and two efforts made to recover captured works were handsomely repulsed; but it was found that the enclosed works in rear, commanding enemy's main line, could only be taken at great sacrifice, and troops were withdrawn to original position. It being impractical to bring off captured guns, owing to nature of ground, they were disabled and left. Our loss reported is not heavy. Among wounded is General Terry, flesh wound, and Brig. Gen. Phil. Cook, in arm. All the troops engaged, including two brigades under Brigadier-General Ransom, behaved handsomely. The conduct of the sharpshooters of Gordon's corps, who led the assault, deserves the highest commendation. This afternoon there was skirmishing on the right between the picket lines, with varied success. At dark enemy held considerable portion of the line farthest in advance of our main works.

He even takes the space to close his report with standard army obfuscation, all too common to the U.S. Army as well, congratulating all concerned, thus avoiding the stark truth. Lee's reluctance to convey the fact that the raid was a disastrous failure, which resulted in thousands of casualties, is suspected to be the result of his experience at the futility of being the bearer of bad news to Jefferson Davis. An earlier report about the dire condition of his army had portrayed harsh reality, and was scorned. On February 8th, Lee had reported to Seddon, apparently not aware that he had resigned as secretary of war, that due to the pressure of the enemy, his men had been obliged to be retained in the trenches, without meat for three days, and that all were suffering from reduced rations and scant clothing in the winter rain and sleet; and that the cavalry had to be dispersed for want of forage. He went on to warn that it should not come as a surprise if "calamity befalls us."

Forwarded to Jefferson Davis, the report elicited the following:

> This is too sad to be patiently considered, and cannot have occurred without criminal neglect or gross incapacity. Let supplies be had by purchase, or borrowing, or other possible mode.

Here was the reply of an out-of-touch politician, who had nothing constructive to suggest. The Confederate treasury had only $750,000 in gold left.[2366] It is easy to see why Lee thereafter stopped any attempt at reporting reality.

2366. As of Feb. 19th. Campbell, J. A., pp. 31–32.

Grant Moves

In the end, the attack on Fort Stedman did not for a minute delay Grant's plan to launch his general attack. Preliminary moves were made to position the army for it on March 27th. Ord,[2367] who had relieved Butler in command of the Army of the James, secretly detached three infantry divisions and a division of cavalry from their position east of Richmond, on the north side of the James, and marched them thirty-six miles west, to a position on the extreme left of the Union lines; those positions held by Humphreys' 2nd and Warren's 5th corps, who were then directed to cross Hatcher's run, and extend out toward Five Forks. They would then threaten the Confederate lines along the White Oak Road, figure 8,[2368] and be within striking distance of the all-important Southside Railroad, seen in the upper left corner, and the Danville Railroad, further west. The move, by the 2nd and 5th Corps, which began on March 29th, involved considerable fighting as Lee shifted reinforcements to meet the threat. The fighting, which peaked with a Confederate counterattack on the 31st, became known as the Battle of White Oak Road.

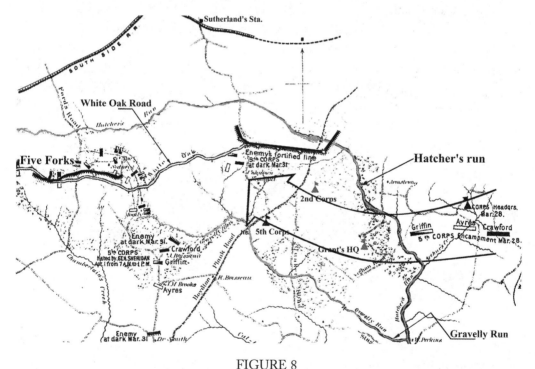

FIGURE 8

2367. O.R. Vol. 46/I, p. 1160, Grant vol. 2, p. 434.
2368. Figure 8, Atlas, plate 66, map 9, altered; CWSAC VA087.

Five Forks

In the meantime, on March 30th, Sheridan was directed by Grant to move via Dinwiddie Courthouse toward Five Forks.[2369] He moved alone, with only his cavalry. On the 31st, north and northwest of Dinwiddie, he was repulsed by Fitzhugh Lee's cavalry and Pickett's infantry, and was driven slowly back to Dinwiddie. In this action Grant gives Sheridan great praise.[2370]

> Here General Sheridan displayed great generalship. Instead of retreating with his whole command on the main army, to tell the story of superior forces encountered, he deployed his cavalry on foot, leaving only mounted men enough to take charge of the horses. This compelled the enemy to deploy over a vast extent of wooded and broken country, and made his progress slow.

As Sheridan remembers, Pickett's move out from Five Forks was the move that Grant was hoping for, a situation where the enemy was outside of his trenches. An immediate follow-up was required. That night, orders were given to Warren's 5th Corps to drop down, cross Gravelly Run, and join Sheridan. Later, Mackenzie's cavalry of Ord's command was added to Sheridan's, and he was given discretionary authority to use his new force as he saw fit. Warren's 5th Corps was expected to get to Sheridan in two hours, or by midnight, but, it not having arrived, Sheridan, feeling that the opportunity would be lost if no attack was made, ordered Warren to move on the left flank of the entrenchments at Five Forks at daylight, while Sheridan moved on the front. Warren did not even begin his move from his bivouac until daylight,[2371] and as a result, owing to more excuses as to the bad condition of the roads, etc., he did not arrive and begin his part in the attack until 4:00 p.m. on April 1st. Regardless of the delays, however, the attack was successful, and the loss drew the Union forces ever closer to the South Side Railroad.

At this point, Grant was worried that Lee would regard the capture of Five Forks as so important that, "he would make a last desperate effort to retake it, risking everything on the cast of a single die," and as soon as Grant got word of its capture, he ordered a general assault on Petersburg—immediately. However, his corps commanders protested that it was so dark that the men could not see to move, so instead the attack was postponed until Sunday, April 2nd.

Lee did as predicted by Grant, on the evening of the 1st, Field's division of Longstreet's command was ordered out of the lines at Richmond to the support of Five Forks. If this had been known by Grant and had been observed by the Army of the James, which was opposite Richmond, i.e., Hartsuff and Weitzel, who was

---

2369. Grant, vol. 2, pp. 439–442; Sheridan, vol. 2, pp. 154, 155.
2370. O.R. Vol. 36/II, p. 56
2371. Sheridan, vol. 2, pp. 157–165; CWSAC VA086. After the battle, Sheridan sacked Warren for his slow behavior.

now commanding the 25th Corps, they could have joined in the general assault, and as Longstreet observes: "Richmond, along with the Confederate authorities, would have been taken before noon."[2372]

One cannot help comparing Sheridan's cavalry with that of General A. L. Lee's at Mansfield, Louisiana, a year prior. Like Sheridan's outside of Five Forks, Lee's dismounted men faced an overwhelming force, yet they ran to their horses and fled. What was different? A proper analysis would require more study, but several thoughts come to mind: 1. Generalship, which Grant credits, i.e., letting your men know what to expect, and conducting it in a clear and cool manner. 2. Training. 3. Experience. 4. Firepower.

Clearly, Sheridan's troops were now hardened veterans, in good health, and superbly equipped. Sheridan's men all had Spencer seven-shot repeating rifles. Seven shots which can be fired in seven seconds is a fatal difference compared to one shot (at best) every 30 seconds for the muzzle-loaders that Lee's men carried back at Pleasant Hill. When Longstreet reported to Robert E. Lee, on his way to Five Forks on the morning of the 2nd, Lee remarked on "the great numbers of the enemy and the superior repeating rifles of his cavalry."

Note that Grant here displayed an alacrity that he had retained through the years. Recall, from chapter 5, when Grant had gone ahead and attacked Fort Donelson without Halleck's permission, feeling that his "15,000 men on the 8th would be more valuable than 50,000 men a month later." Unfortunately, the alleged plodding progress after Grant had taken personal command at Young's point, on January 29th, 1863, leading up to the siege of Vicksburg, had prompted calls from the press that he was idle, incompetent, and unfit to command. Then there was the suspicious Stanton's assignment of Charles Dana to spy on him. Even the gathering-in of the forces of the Union after he became a lieutenant-general and in total command was too slow in the eyes of an impatient American press, and consequently the public. It was never true.

The General Assault

Regardless of darkness, the first moves began at 11:00 p.m. on April 1st, when the troops were ordered to assemble near their assault positions. At about 3:00 a.m. on the 2nd, the assaulting columns began to steal into their final forward positions in complete silence, and at 4:00 a massive artillery barrage was initiated over the heads of the assaulting columns, which lasted until 4:20. At 4:30, there were three quick shots—the signal to advance.[2373]

Parke's 9th Corps on the right, and Wright's 6th in the center, went forward,

---

2372. Longstreet, p. 604.
2373. Embick, M. A., p. 19; Grant, vol. 2, p. 447–449; O.R. Vol. 36/II, pp. 56–57; Longstreet, pp. 602–604; O.R. Vol. 46/I, p. 63.

with Ord's 24th, and Humphrey's 2nd on the left, warned to be ready to take advantage of any weakening in their front.[2374] Wright, the man we know who stopped the retreat at Cedar Creek, now launched an assault as carefully planned as was the Confederate assault on Fort Stedman—axmen and all.[2375] The 6th swept up and over the outer lines, then swung down to the left and reached as far as Hatcher's run. Parke did likewise to the right, but was stalled by the heroic defense made by the 300-man garrison of Confederate Fort Gregg.

Ord and Humphreys, to the west of Hatcher's Run, succeeded in taking the enemy defenses in each of their fronts before Wright reached them, and the outer works of Petersburg were in Union hands. Humphreys' 1st Division then struck north to Sutherland's Station, visible at the top of figure 8, and took possession of the South Side Railroad, Lee's last supply line. Wright also sent a regiment north, which destroyed the railroad closer up to the city. With nightfall, the attack ceased.

Lee was now compelled to withdraw from Richmond and Petersburg. It was 11:00 a.m. when Lee's dispatch reached Davis at Sunday services at St. Paul's Church. The order was out soon enough to have the troops begin the march to the west when night came, but troops were seen evacuating as early as 12:50 p.m. on April 3rd. Learning of this, Grant advised Weitzel to be prepared to assault that morning.[2376] The explosion of the magazine of Confederate Fort Drewry, and the general conflagration of Richmond, which could be seen in the night sky, attested to the activities involved with a general withdrawal and abandonment. At 8:15 a.m. General Weitzel's 25th Corps entered Richmond.

One can only imagine the reaction in Battery L upon hearing the news. Weitzel, the engineer captain with them while they were at Fort Pickens, and the man who had initially refused to command black troops while under Butler in Louisiana, now had entered Richmond in command of the 25th Corps d'Afrique. Yes, all of the 25th Corps was made up of black soldiers. Ironic and moving it was that they were the victors to enter the capitol of an entity devoted to perpetuating their slavery, and under the command of a man who had learned to move beyond his prejudice.

Such place names as Amelia Springs, Jetersville, Rice's Station, Sailor's Creek, Cumberland Church, High Bridge, Farmville, and Appomattox Station adorn the week-long trek of Lee's disintegrating army. Some names were where skirmishes took place, others serious clashes. Sailor's Creek, however, on April 6th, is described by Sheridan as "one of the severest of the war, for the enemy fought with desperation to escape capture, and we, bent on his destruction, were no less eager

---

2374. Grant, vol. 2, pp. 447–448.
2375. O.R. Vol. 46/I, pp. 711–712, 903–904; Longstreet, pp. 605, 607; Grant, vol. 2, p. 456.
2376. Longstreet, p. 608; CWSAC VA091-097; Long, A. L., *Memoirs*, pp. 409–411; O.R. Vol. 46/I, p. 139; O.R. Vol. 46/III, pp. 496, 509.

and determined."[2377] Ewell's corps had been cut off from Longstreet's, the two taking different roads. Sheridan had blocked the road to Rice's Station southwest of Sailor's Creek, and Seymour's and Wheaton's division of Wright's 6th Corps had closed upon Ewell from the northwest, Getty's division arriving last. Seymour's and Wheaton's divisions attacked, simultaneously with Sheridan's cavalry, and to use Sheridan's words, the enemy: "After a gallant resistance, were completely surrounded, and nearly all threw down their arms and surrendered."

Sheridan[2378] also adds:

> The capture of Ewell, with six of his generals, and most of his troops, crowned our success, but the fight was so overshadowed by the stirring events of the surrender three days later, that the battle has never been accorded the prominence it deserves.

The total number of the Confederate command captured that day is given by Gen. A. L. Long, of Lee's staff, as "about 10,000."

On riding up to the scene of the disaster,[2379] as General Mahone recounts: "At this spectacle General Lee straightened himself in the saddle, and looking more the soldier than ever, exclaimed, as if talking to himself, 'My God! Has the army dissolved?'"

Surrender

On April 7th, Lee was approached by "a number of the principal officers" who regarded that the condition of the army, now reduced to 10,000 effectives, was hopeless, "who volunteered to inform him that in their opinion the struggle… should be terminated and negotiations opened for surrender." General Pendleton, Lee's chief of artillery, was designated to deliver the mutinous message. Lee received the communication with: "Oh no, I trust it has not come to that…" He was still harboring the hope that he could break through to link up with General Johnston. Supplies had been deposited at Appomattox Station, and if the retreat reached there, he could push on to the Staunton River and maintain himself behind it until he reached Johnston.

His response, as related by Long, continued, in some regards almost delusional: "The enemy do not fight with spirit, while our boys still do." He was wary of opening any conversations with Grant, lest it be regarded as a sign of weakness, Grant then likely demanding unconditional surrender. He then seems, at least as Long presents it, to wander off subject, in a revealing past tense:

2377. Sheridan, vol. 2, pp. 180–185; Longstreet, p. 429; O.R. Vol. 46/I, pp. 906–909, 914–915, 1107–1108.
2378. Sheridan, vol. 2, pp. 180–181; Long, A. L., *Memoirs*, p. 414.
2379. Longstreet, p. 615; Long 416–417; O.R. Vol. 46/I, p. 1279.

> I have never believed we could, against the gigantic combination for our subjugation, make good in the long run our independence unless foreign powers should…assist us…But such considerations really made with me no difference. We had, I was satisfied, sacred principles to maintain and rights to defend, for which we were in duty bound to do our best, even if we perished in the endeavor.

As it happened, also on April 7th, Lee got a message from Grant,[2380] asking for the surrender "of that portion of the Confederate Southern army known as the Army of Northern Virginia." Undoubtedly relieved that Grant, and not he, had taken the initiative, Lee responded asking for Grant's terms. On the 8th, Grant responded that Lee's army would be disqualified from taking up arms against the United States, until properly exchanged.

Later in the afternoon, when Lee reached the neighborhood of Appomattox Court House, he learned that the supplies that he had counted on at Appomattox Station had been captured.[2381] It was by Custer's cavalry. It was then that Lee agreed to meet Grant "at ten a.m. tomorrow on the old stage-road to Richmond, between the picket-lines of the two armies." Yes, Lee would meet with Grant, but simply because the two were to meet did not signify that a truce had been called. That night, Lee ordered his cavalry commander, Fitzhugh Lee, transferred from the rear to the advanced guard. Then he and General Gordon, commanding the lead, were to march at one o'clock on the morning of the 9th, to try to break out of their position at Appomattox Courthouse.

At 3:00 a.m., Lee rode forward to check on the progress of the breakout, which had not begun. He sent a staff officer to inquire of General Gordon, still in the process of arranging the attack. Gordon's response was: "Tell General Lee I have fought my corps to a frazzle, and I fear I can do nothing unless I am heavily supported by Longstreet's corps." This was of course, impossible, Field's and Mahone's division of Longstreet's corps was the rear guard, and were being heavily pressed by Meade. Then, and only then, did Lee send out a flag of truce, which allowed Sheridan and Gordon to meet, Gordon explaining that: "General Lee asks a suspension of hostilities pending the negotiations he is having with General Grant." Sheridan was miffed.[2382] He responded that he was fully aware of the progress of the negotiations and:

> [T]hink it singular that while such discussions are going on, General Lee should have continued his march and attempted to break through my lines this morning. I will entertain no terms except that General Lee shall surrender to

---

2380. Grant, vol. 2, p. 625.
2381. Sheridan, vol. 2, pp. 189–190, 199; Longstreet, pp. 622–624; Long, A. L., *Memoirs*, pp. 420–422.
2382. Sheridan, vol. 2, pp. 197–198.

General Grant on his arrival here. If these…are not accepted we will renew hostilities. Gordon replied: "General Lee's army is exhausted. There is no doubt of his surrender…"

As it was, Fitzhugh Lee and the cavalry escaped.[2383]

2383. O.R. Vol. 46/III, p. 1394.

Chapter 16

The Remains of the Confederacy Crumbles
"Record" 6/65; Full Circle; The Faithful Few; Two Deserters;
The 1863 Pensacola Recruits; The Three Cooks; Battery L

Jefferson Davis and his cabinet left Richmond on the night of April 2nd, essentially the same time that Lee abandoned the city. They proceeded as far as Danville, Virginia, and remained there for several days, and where, as Davis wrote to Lee, "offices have been opened to keep up the current business…" Davis was still insisting that the Confederate cause was not lost.[2384] At dinner, on Monday, April 10th, Davis was informed of Lee's surrender at Appomattox Courthouse. A cabinet meeting was held, and it was decided that night to leave Danville for Greensboro, North Carolina. At Greensboro, in a meeting with generals Beauregard and Johnston, Davis reviewed Johnston's situation vs. Sherman's, and given the impossible odds of "seventeen or eighteen to one," Johnston represented that: "It would be the greatest of human crimes for us to attempt to continue this war…keeping the field would be, not to harm the enemy, but to complete the devastation of our country and the ruin of its people."[2385] Davis thereupon authorized Johnston to approach Sherman with the proposal for an armistice "to enable the civil authorities to agree upon terms of peace." Johnston wrote Sherman on the 13th, and Sherman promptly replied that he would "undertake to abide by the same terms and conditions as were made by Generals Grant and Lee at Appomattox…"

Johnston met Sherman on the 16th, at a house in Raleigh, midway between the two armies. Here, they both first learned of the assassination of President Lincoln, which took place on the 14th.[2386] Impressed with the necessity of ending the war, the two generals, on the 18th, entered into a memorandum which far exceeded the terms given Lee. It was to be observed in a truce, by both armies, until approved by higher authority. Vice President Andrew Johnson, now duly sworn-in as President, disapproved, and in "great consternation," ordered Grant to

---

2384. Stephens, vol. 2, pp. 627–628; O.R. Vol. 46/III, pp. 1390–1391, 1394; O.R. 47/ III, pp. 774, 816; O.R. Vol. 49/I, p. 370.
2385. Johnston, *Narrative* pp. 396–400; Bowen, J. J., pp. 252–253; O.R. Vol. 47/II, p. 777; O.R. Vol. 47/III, pp. 206–207.
2386. O.R. Vol. 47/I, pp. 33–34; O.R. Vol. 47/III, pp. 838–839; Johnston, *Narrative* pp. 404–415; Grant, vol. 2, pp. 515–517; Duke, *Last Days of the Confederacy*, p. 763.

proceed to North Carolina to take charge. Grant did so, but upon arrival at Raleigh he merely advised Sherman of the President's, as well as Stanton's and the rest of the cabinet's, objections. In a show of respect and as a courtesy to Sherman, Grant then left him "free and untrammeled" to follow the terms stipulated in the truce for notifying Johnston that it had been rejected.

In the meantime, on the 24th, Jefferson Davis, who had fled to Charlotte, and of course unaware of the goings-on in Washington, had, in a telegraph to Johnston, approved of the "convention." However, within the hour, Johnston received Sherman's notice of rejection—hostilities to commence in 48 hours. A telegram to Davis from Johnston informed of the rejection, and asked what to do next. Davis' reply, received on the morning of the 25th, directed Johnston to disband the infantry, with instructions to meet at some appointed place, and to "bring off the cavalry, and all other soldiers who could be mounted by taking serviceable beasts from the trains, and a few light field pieces." There was to be no surrender. Davis was essentially proposing to reconstitute the army elsewhere as an escort for the Confederate government in a flight to some indefinite sanctuary. Johnston refused. Instead, he again approached Sherman, who, urged by Grant, agreed to meet him. On the 26th, they met in the same house as they had before, and finally an agreement satisfactory to General Grant, who was waiting in the wings, was reached; it was essentially those terms given Lee.

Now another, a man who had served the Confederate government since the beginning of the war, stepped forward to end the war, in the total absence of any initiative on the part of Jefferson Davis. From Richmond, on April 11th, Judge J. A. Campbell, the former Confederate assistant secretary of war, one of the commissioners sent by Davis to the Hampton Roads Peace Conference, and who had stood watching as Jefferson Davis packed up and fled Richmond on the night of April 2nd, had written to Grant,[2387] saying:

> The activities of the last few days in my judgment are of a nature to require a cessation of hostilities throughout the Confederate States on the part of those who command their forces. My impression is that the military commanders will adopt the same conclusion. I have prepared a telegram to General Taylor, who is in command at Mobile, acquainting him with the facts, which I request may be forwarded as rapidly as possible…

His telegram gave a synopsis of the conditions of Lee's surrender, and advised that Taylor do the same. It was forwarded on April 13th. Taylor, who had taken over the command of the Department of Alabama, Mississippi, and East Louisiana,[2388] saw little hope of success, Mobile having been taken by Canby on the 12th, but he

---

2387. O.R. Vol. 49,/II, pp. 322, 323, 346; Campbell, p. 38.
2388. O.R. Vol. 39/I, p. 3; Taylor, pp. 221–222, 224, 225; O.R. Vol. 39/II, pp. 347, 440, 481, 531–532, 559, 575; O.R. Vol. 48/II, p. 311.

concluded, "while Johnston was still in arms we must be prepared to fight our way to him." However, Taylor writes, "intelligence of the Johnston-Sherman convention reached us, and Canby and I were requested by the officers making it to conform to its terms until the civil authorities acted." On the 14th, after making an inquiry about the exchange of prisoners, Canby and Taylor agreed to meet. On the 29th, they did so, and agreed to the truce of Johnston and Sherman. However, only the next day, notice of the *disapproval* of the Sherman-Johnston truce reached Canby, and he duly notified Taylor that in 48 hours hostilities would resume, but that he was authorized to offer the same terms as Lee had accepted.

On the 4th of May, Taylor accepted. He had not waited for authorization from Jefferson Davis, or for the news of his whereabouts, his plans, or his status.

As to Davis, upon receiving the news from General Johnston that the authorities in Washington had refused the truce agreement that he and Breckinridge had crafted with Sherman, and that Johnston was now intent upon surrender at any terms offered, Davis resolved to leave Charlotte and attempt to march in the direction of the Confederate Trans-Mississippi Department. There he would join generals Taylor or Forrest, "somewhere" in Alabama.[2389] He would be accompanied by his cabinet, his staff, Gen. Braxton Bragg, and an escort of five brigades of cavalry—the only troops left.

Reaching Abbeville, South Carolina, on May 2nd, Davis held a conference or "council of war" as he characterized it, with the commanders of his escort, brigadier generals Basil W. Duke, S. W. Ferguson, G. G. Dibrell, J. C. Vaughn, and W. C. P. Breckinridge. Also present were his new secretary of war, Gen. John C. Breckinridge and Gen. Braxton Bragg. Davis, who seemed to be in "excellent" spirits, introduced the discussion by saying: "It is time, that we adopt some definite plan upon which the further prosecution of our struggle shall be conducted." At this, he was seen to "smile rather archly" aware of the fact that he was reduced to addressing five brigadiers who now commanded barely 3,000 men and two generals who had no commands left.

After receiving the reports of the condition of the men and equipment of the escort, Davis declared his conviction that the cause was not lost, and that the 3,000 were a "nucleus around which the whole people will rally when the panic that now afflicts them has passed away." He then asked for suggestions in regard to the future conduct of the war.

At first, his amazed listeners were speechless. Breckinridge and Bragg said nothing. Only the five brigadiers finally spoke. They remonstrated that the "whole people" alluded to, were not panic stricken, but broken down and worn out. To continue the war, after all means of supporting it were gone, would be a "cruel

---

2389. Duke, *Reminiscences*, pp. 382–385; Duke, *Last Days of the Confederacy*, pp. 764–765; O.R. Vol. 49/I, p. 372; O.R. Vol. 49/II, pp. 570, 615.

injustice to the South," and that they would be treated as brigands.

Davis then asked why they were still supporting him "in the field." The explanation had to be enunciated that the reason was only out of loyalty to him, and to afford him to avoid the degradation of capture. Their men would risk battle for that purpose, but not to continue the hostilities of the war. The discussion had reached its climactic point, and to speak again, in General Duke's words, "would have approached altercation."

Davis then rose; his spirits transformed. He had become pallid. He bitterly admitted that the cause was lost, and General Breckinridge then helped him from the room.

It was determined to resume the flight, leaving on the night of the 4th for Washington, Georgia,[2390] still carrying the treasure brought from Richmond, which amounted to $500,000 or $600,000 in silver and gold. Before reaching Washington, Davis decided to distribute the silver "pile," about $110,000, to the men of the escort, who received $32 apiece.

Davis then fled with a select group of only 20 men. His purpose in quitting the main body of his troops, as alleged by General Duke, was to allow them to surrender, "before it was too late for surrender upon terms."

Davis was captured on the 10th of May, at Irwinsville, Georgia, by a detachment of the 4th Michigan Cavalry, a part of Gen. J. H. Wilson's cavalry corps—the Wilson who had commanded the raid on the Weldon and Southside Railroads in which Battery K had been so cut-up, chapter 12, and who, after the Battle of Winchester, had been promoted to the command of the cavalry corps of the Military Division of the Mississippi.[2391]

The circumstances of Davis' capture were, indeed, degrading. At dawn, the camp of the Davis party was overwhelmed without a fight, there having been no guards posted, or if there were, they had been asleep. Pvt. Andrew Bee, of Company L, approached one of two wall-tents pitched on the side of the road, and there met Mrs. Davis, who remonstrated, "Please, don't go in there till my daughter gets herself dressed!" In a few minutes a young lady and another person, bent over with age, and carrying a tin pail, appeared and asked to go for water. All three were allowed to pass out toward a "run" at the edge of the woods which bordered the campsite. "But sharp eyes were on the singular-looking 'old mother.' Suddenly…it was discovered that the 'old mother' was wearing very heavy boots for an aged female, when Corporal Munyer, of Company C, exclaimed,—'That is not a woman! Don't you see the boots?'" At the point of a cavalry carbine, the old woman was ordered to remove her shawl, thus revealing Jefferson Davis.

2390. O.R. Vol. 49/I, p. 535.
2391. O.R. Vol. 49/I, pp. 378–380; 534–537; Lawton, G. W., pp. 342–347.

"Record" 6/65
30 APRIL–30 JUNE 1865 WINCHESTER, VIRGINIA

(No entry in Record of Events)

Henry W Closson	Capt. Commanding
Franck E. Taylor	1st Lt. Absent on recruiting svc. Orders no. 84, AGO Washington, DC April 1,'65. Absent Since April 12th 1865

Detached: None.

Absent in Confinement:

Patrick Gibbons	Pvt. At Ship Island, serving sentence of G.C.M. S.O. no. 18, Hdqrts. 1st Div. 19th Army Corps Dec. 31, 1863.

Absent with leave:

Herbert E. Mansfield	Pvt. On furlough, 15 days, since June 20/65.

Dismissed:

Edward Appleton	1st Lt. From absent without leave to dismissed from the service. S.O. no. 219 A.G.O. Washington, DC May 10th 1865

Deserted:

John Lewery	Pvt. (Dropped from roll without explanation.)
Andrew Stoll	Pvt. From Absent Sick in Cuyler Hospital, Germantown, Pa. to Desertion, May 19/65.

Transferred:

George F. Hadley	Pvt. Transferred to Ord. Corps S.O. no. 194, A.G.O. Washington, DC April 29, 1865. Permanently attached to Battery.

Strength: 54   Sick: 1

Sick Present: none

Sick Absent: 1

Thomas Clinton	Pvt. Abs. sick at Frederick, Md. Since Mar. 10, 1865.

The next domino expected to fall was the Confederate west; the Trans-Mississippi Department of Kirby Smith. While Canby dealt with Taylor, Grant asked the Department of the Missouri, now commanded by General John Pope, at St. Louis, (the man whom McClellan managed to have removed from the command of the Army of Virginia by combining it with the Army of the Potomac, back in 1862, chapter 6) to send a representative to Shreveport. On April 19th, Lt. Col. John T. Sprague was ordered to proceed "with the least practicable delay to the most accessible point of the enemy's lines along the Red River and deliver into the hands of General Kirby Smith the enclosed letter."[2392] The letter was a copy of the agreement made between Grant and Lee, and Sprague managed to reach Shreveport and deliver it on the evening of May 8th. Sprague had been advised to mention Lincoln's assassination and the "deep feeling that it has created…which feeling will be heavily visited upon those who continue to resist the authority of the United

---

2392. O.R. Vol. 48/I, pp. 187–194; 48/II, p. 502.

States, to whom the mass of the people in the North attribute, however remotely, the atrocious deed." The response from Smith was instant. He rejected it. He added: "I regret that your communication should have been accompanied with a threat, or that you should have supposed that personal considerations would have influenced me in the discharge of my duties." *But wait!* Sprague was invited to remain, while Smith polled the opinions of the four governors in his department: Allen of Louisiana, Flanagin of Arkansas, Murrah of Texas, and Reynolds of Missouri. Smith proposed that they meet in conference at Marshall, Texas, on May 10th.

The conference refused to surrender on the terms given to Lee, proposing five of its own conditions, viz.: 1. Immunity from prosecution for past acts in the Trans-Mississippi Department. 2. Granting this immunity, all military resistance to the U.S. Government to cease. 3. The Confederate Army be disbanded and its officers and soldiers permitted to return to their homes, transportation to be furnished them as far as possible. 4. Such officers and soldiers be permitted to leave the country, with or without arms. 5. The same permission be granted to citizens.

A glance at the last two rather innocent conditions might have raised a question as to why they were even mentioned. After all, citizens had no restrictions on them as to leaving the country, or returning. Something else was afoot, which was revealed as events unfolded.

An offer to have Governor Allen of Louisiana visit Washington to negotiate a final settlement was rejected by Sprague. The whole affair was thrown into a suspicious light by the testimony of a Confederate officer who expressed the view that Kirby Smith was ready to surrender, but that he was under the control of generals Buckner, Walker, and the governors, who were attempting to secure "all cotton and plunder they can put their hands on." The troops themselves were disaffected and "only kept together by the most despotic of measures." Subsequent to this revelation, the headquarters of the Trans-Mississippi Dept. was ordered on May 13th moved from Shreveport to Houston, though Smith did not arrive there until May 27th.[2393]

On the 17th, at Alexandria: "The fact can no longer be concealed that the whole army and people, with scarce an individual exception, are resolved to fight no more, and to break up the army at all hazards." Given these conditions, General J. L. Brent, in command of the front lines in western Louisiana, was authorized by Kirby Smith to proceed to Baton Rouge to open negotiations preliminary to the surrender the State of Louisiana.[2394] The Louisiana generals, who wanted to surrender, were acting independently of Smith and Buckner, who allegedly were only interested in delay, to enable them time to gather stores and munitions formerly owned by the Confederacy and escape into Mexico. The "Cordova" scheme,[2395]

2393. O.R. Vol. 48/II, pp. 715, 1300, 1310, 1313.
2394. O.R. Vol. 48/II, pp. 538, 558–559, 562–563, 579-581, 603, 648–649, 1314–1315.
2395. O.R. Vol. 48/I, pp. 298, 300, 1258.

better known as the "grand emigration expedition" involving, among others, generals Smith, Buckner, Price, and Magruder, planned to lead a large volunteer force of former Confederates into Mexico, to join the French-supported imperial forces of Maximilian. This news, or simply the fact that Kirby Smith was procrastinating, was of enough concern in Washington that on May 17th, Grant ordered Sheridan to Texas. It was so imperative that he leave immediately that he was not permitted to watch his Army of the Shenandoah pass in the Grand Review, held at Washington on May 23rd and 24th.[2396] He was to "restore Texas, and that part of Louisiana held by the enemy, to the Union in the shortest practicable time..." He would be given all the troops that Canby could spare, as well as 12,000 from Arkansas; the 4th Army Corps from Nashville, and Weitzel's 25th Corps, "now at City Point, Virginia, ready to embark."

News of the June 1st departure of Weitzel's expedition did not appear in *Harper's Weekly* until the June 17th issue.[2397] It probably obtained coverage because of the visible spectacle of a huge fleet of transports leaving Hampton Roads. An engraving depicting the ships as "among the largest and best to a long sea voyage of any known..." appeared in the same issue. News of anything of this sort could not have seemed important compared to the momentous news the Nation had had to endure since celebrating Lee's surrender on April 9th. Only five days later came the news of Lincoln's assassination, and subsequently the news was filled with the details of the funeral, the plot, the capture of the conspirators, and their backgrounds. Then, a month later, there was the news of the capture of Jefferson Davis, his imprisonment, and a discussion of what to do with him. On top of all this, the country had to deal with guessing what policies an unknown, Andrew Johnson, now sworn in as President, would follow.

The *Sultana* disaster, on April 27th, on the Mississippi near Memphis, when a criminally overloaded steamboat's boiler exploded, killing 1,500 returning Union prisoners of war, was also almost crowded off of the news pages.[2398] Sheridan's assignment to the Trans-Mississippi made less impression in *Harper's Weekly* than did Weitzel's expedition; Sheridan was not mentioned until June 24th, in a small article.[2399]

Before Sheridan's troops reached Texas, the charade of surrender, as subsequent events would define it, was carried on by Buckner, Kirby Smith's chief of staff, and Sterling Price. The pair left Shreveport and appeared at Baton Rouge a day after Brent. The three were then transported to New Orleans. Meanwhile, it was learned that General J. B. Magruder, commanding the District of Texas, was interested in opening negotiations for surrender, and that he was dispatching his

---

2396. Sheridan, vol. 2, pp. 208–209; Grant, vol. 2, p. 631, Welles, vol. 2, pp. 307, 310.
2397. Weitzel, *Fleet*, engraving, June 10, p. 372; Sheridan, to Texas, June 24, p. 387.
2398. *Harper's Weekly*, May 13th, 1865, p. 291; May 20, p. 316; O.R. Vol. 49, pp. 721, 836–837.
2399. *Harper's Weekly*, June 17th, 1865, p. 372.

own commissioners on one of the fastest vessels available. That date was May 24th. He announced the fact of the dispatch of the commissioners to the people of Texas on the 26th.[2400]

The Texas commissioners not having yet arrived, General Canby and the trio of Kirby Smith's representatives from Shreveport reached a surrender agreement at New Orleans on the 26th.[2401] Magruder's commissioners did not arrive until May 29th,[2402] and were received by Canby that night. Since the surrender terms were already agreed to, there was nothing to discuss; Canby refused to discuss civil matters, the power of military commanders being limited to things purely military. Nevertheless, the two commissioners insisted that Canby be apprised of "the actual condition of affairs in Texas," which were known to them (from Houston) but not, apparently, by General Smith's commissioners, from Shreveport. By the time they had left Texas, "a large portion of the Confederate troops had actually disbanded themselves…and gone to their homes and before the intelligence of the convention of surrender shall be received the remainder may also have dispersed."

The discussions with Magruder's men completed, Canby arranged to send Gen. E. J. Davis to Texas to confer with Smith about the details of the surrender agreement, and to obtain his signature.[2403] Davis arrived off Galveston on May 31st and sent a note to Smith requesting a time and a place for a meeting. Finally, on Friday, June 2nd, Kirby Smith signed the agreement and the supplemental arrangements for surrender. He had delayed for 24 days. A quote from Grant's final report of the war[2404] illuminates his suspicion of the Smith surrender, and the concern in Washington regarding Texas:

> This surrender did not take place, however, until after the capture of the rebel President…and the bad faith…of first disbanding most of his army, and permitting an indiscriminate plunder of public property.
>
> Owing to the report that many of those lately in arms against the Government had taken refuge upon the soil of Mexico, carrying with them arms rightfully belonging to the United States, which had been surrendered to us by agreement (among them some of the leaders who had surrendered in person), and the disturbed condition of affairs on the Rio Grande, the orders for troops to proceed to Texas were not changed.

A bizarre episode at Brownsville provided confirmation of the turmoil in Texas. Earlier in May, Gen. E. B. Brown had been assigned to the command at Brazos Santiago, the only point in Texas continuously occupied by Union troops

---

2400. O.R. Vol. 48/II, pp. 1319–1320.
2401. O.R. Vol. 48/II, pp. 579–580, 591, 600–602, 604–606.
2402. O.R. Vol. 48/II, pp. 649, 674.
2403. O.R. Vol. 48/II, pp. 620–621, 693, 775.
2404. O.R. Vol. 38/I, p. 51.

since Banks landed there on October 26th, 1863.[2405] From there, Brown sent an expedition to Brownsville, and he occupied it without opposition on the morning of May 31st, 1865. The Confederates did not wait for his arrival, but had abandoned the place the day before. However, Brown's report contained the rather startling information that the rebels had taken the time to sell their six pieces of artillery and other stores "to the Imperialists in Matamoras." This confirmed earlier reports that General Slaughter, in command, was an ally of Maximilian.[2406] The rumors of sympathy with Mexico's dictator now had some credibility, though but few to none of Slaughter's own men agreed with the transaction, and they took him prisoner. He was alleged to have been released by paying them a $20,000 bribe.

Perhaps the last Confederate command to be informed of the formal surrender of the Trans-Mississippi Department was General D. H. Cooper, at Fort Washita, Indian Territory (Oklahoma). The news was not received until June 23rd. Only then were arrangements made for a meeting between the Federal commissioners and the several Indian nations, all allies of the Confederacy, to make a treaty of peace on the 28th.[2407]

The instability on the Rio Grande, which had begun in anticipation of the successful escape of Jefferson Davis and his probable arrival in the Trans-Mississippi Department, then with some 15,000 Confederates joining, or attempting to join, Maximilian, continued. The larger scheme failed after the capture of Davis, but encouraged by the French, numerous bands, numbering a total of 3,000 to 4,000 men, managed to cross the Rio Grande into Mexico, despite the fact that Sheridan had adopted a policy of refusing emigrants to embark from the seaports within his new command.[2408]

Full Circle

As noted above, Brownsville was occupied by Gen. E. B. Brown's troops from Brazos Santiago on May 31st, 1865, without a fight. The last shot fired in the Civil War was in the Battle of Palmito Ranch, Texas, which took place on May 12th and 13th.[2409] A force of about 300 men from the Union outpost at Brazos Santiago attacked the rebel outpost of Palmito Ranch, about fifteen miles from the mouth of the Rio Grande, but the Confederates forced them to withdraw—a Confederate victory.

News that last of the Confederate surrenders had taken place where it had,

---

2405. O.R. Vol. 26/I, pp. 20, 847; 34/II, p. 596; 48/II, pp. 300, 813, 827–828.
2406. O.R. Vol. 48/II, pp. 564–565, 1196.
2407. O.R. Vol. 48/II, p. 1324.
2408. Sheridan, vol. 2, pp. 226–227; Noel, *Autobiography* p. 320; O.R. Vol. 48/I, pp. 298–300; O.R. Vol. 48/II, p. 1258.
2409. O.R. Vol. 48/I, pp. 265–269; CWSAC TX005. Also spelled Palmetto and Palmeto.

in Texas, was undoubtedly of interest to the five batteries F, K, L, and M of the 1st Regiment, and M of the 2nd Regiment, those who had been ordered out of Texas in February of 1861. For Battery M, 1st Artillery, it was striking. Battery L's "sister" company, (as both L and M had been organized at the same time, and both had served together long before the war), M was now one of the four assigned to Weitzel's expeditionary force;[2410] and after its arrival in Texas in mid-June, it was posted to Brazos Santiago. They had come full circle from March 19th, 1861, when they had embarked with Battery L on the steamer Daniel Rusk, destination Fort Jefferson.

The official end of the Civil War was delayed by all of the trouble in Texas, and it was not until August 20th, 1866, that President Johnson issued a proclamation which declared that "the insurrection which heretofore existed in the state of Texas is at an end..."[2411]

The Faithful Few

Of the 83 members of Battery L listed on the muster roll ending in February of 1861, 79 actually left Texas. On the march from Fort Duncan, Sgt. Charles Riley had to be left behind at Fort McIntosh, and privates Francis Hagan and John Bissell had deserted while the battery was at Fort Brown. Lt. James W. Robinson had resigned from the service; he had remained with the battery as a sutler; but could not now be counted as a member. The attrition continued, and brought the number of the "faithful" down to 11 at the close of the war, taken as July of 1865, a month after the last official surrender. Eight men deserted in July, and as usual, some returned later, but cannot be counted as members of the "faithful." Two are mentioned below to round out a picture of the of the battery after the war.

The causes of the attrition have been noted on the summary of each muster roll. As we recall, losses resulted for diverse reasons: killed in action; wounded in action–with subsequent discharge for disability; sickness—with subsequent discharge for disability; prisoner of war; death from disease; conviction by court martial—with subsequent discharge; and desertion. There were, of course, expirations of service—those who chose not to reenlist. Some few in the battery were reassigned, such as Pvt. Edmond Cotterill, sent from New Orleans to Washington to become a clerk in the adjutant-general's office, and of course, all of those who were given commissions as second lieutenants.

A listing of the "faithful" follows. Note that none of the officers of the battery are on it. Capt. Henry Closson, 1st Lt Franck Taylor, and 1st Lt. Edward Appleton were not assigned to Battery L until it was in Florida, and Appleton deserted in October of 1864.

1. James Ahern–18 October, 1860, Boston. This laborer from Boston,

---

2410. 1st Regiment Record for June; Haskin, p. 218.
2411. O.R. Ser. 3, vol. 5, p. 1011.

Massachusetts, joined Battery L as a member of the second group of recruits who arrived from Fort Columbus, New York, on December 5th, 1860. He was one of those who reenlisted under the war provisions of July 1864, and was mustered out at Fort Porter, Buffalo, New York on July 18th, 1867, as a corporal. His widow, Mary, applied for a pension on October 25th, 1889, but a corresponding file for application no. 407,090 has proven to be not available from the National Archives.

2. James Beglan–25 October, 1860, New York. A laborer, he joined Battery L as one of the second group of recruits. Like Ahern, he reenlisted in 1864, and was mustered out, as a private, then age 27, on July 18th, 1867, at Fort Porter.

He got into trouble in Baltimore while the company was stationed at Fort McHenry, and was held there by the "Civil Authorities" from October 1865 until March of 1866. Having returned, in September, he was sentenced by a general court-martial to forfeit one month's pay. Strangely, the whole time he had been AWOL he was not listed as a deserter, and his discharge was not delayed to make up the lost time.

He never married, and existed as a "clerk" in Brooklyn, until at age 60, on September 7th, 1899, he entered the Soldier's and Sailor's Home at Bath, New York. He applied for a disability pension, under the Act of June 27th, 1890. On the basis of a physical examination, he was granted a partial disability pension of $6 per month. At that time, the maximum he could have obtained was $10.

His Pension Record from 1899 onward reflects the changes wrought by new pension laws frequently enacted: May 9th, 1900; July 1st, 1902; February 6th, 1907; May 11th, 1912; and by his new applications, rejections, and appeals. He subsequently applied for a pension increase to the maximum of $10 and it was granted on June 22nd, 1904, after repeated correspondence between his pension lawyer, his examining physician, and the Department of the Interior, Bureau of Pensions. Of course, the Pension Application had to be verified by confirmation at the War Department—the Adjutant General's Office, Commissioner of Pensions. There the records were kept that proved that the applicant had actually served, and where, and for how long, and whether he had been injured or sick. Each time a new application was made, the mountain of paperwork grew, as copies of previous correspondence were forwarded. Of course, all of this was to protect against fraud, and regardless of the good intent of the Congress, bureaucrats made the process slow and arbitrary. An industry had been created, and it lived on into the twentieth century.

On December 11th, 1906, Beglan was given a rate of $12, and on February 1st, 1910, a rate of $15. On May 20th, 1912, it was raised to $25, and on December 26th, 1914, it became $30. He died on July 19th, 1915.

3. Owen Coyne–10 December, 1860, Fort Duncan, Texas. Coyne was not from the groups of recruits enlisted in the east. He was 30 years of age, and this was his second enlistment; he had first served in Company G of the 1st Infantry, into which he had been recruited on July 4th, 1855, at Chicago. He had been discharged, by expiration of service at Fort Chadbourne, Texas, on July 13th, 1860. He then enlisted in Battery L. Because he did not take advantage of the huge reenlistment bonus of July 1864, it is concluded that he felt that at 40 years of age, 10 years of army life was enough, and when his enlistment expired, on December 11th, 1865, he was mustered out as a private, at Fort Schuyler, New York. No further record.

4. Patrick Donnelly–1 March, 1860, Boston. A farmer, he joined from the first group of recruits that arrived in April. At nearly five feet-eleven, he stood taller than most. He must have been a man made of iron. For the entire war years he was never listed as sick, and was never disciplined, save being listed as "in confinement" while a fresh recruit. Finally, this steadfast soldier was promoted to corporal on April 13th, 1865. He had reenlisted at New Orleans in July of 1864, so his three-year term of service extended to 1867, while Battery L was stationed at Fort Porter, New York. There, he met Margaret Moran,[2412] whose family ran a grocery store ten blocks from the fort. His enlistment expired in July, and he was discharged as a sergeant. In August, he reenlisted in Battery L of the 4th Artillery, at Fort Delaware, Delaware City, Delaware. He was appointed a corporal on the same day, and promoted to sergeant the next month.

In December of 1867, Patrick and Margaret were married. His third term of service expired on August 13th, 1870, while he was serving at Fort Macon, Goldsboro, North Carolina. This ended his ten years in the army, and like Owen Coyne, he apparently felt that that was enough. The couple tried farming in Arkansas, but eventually returned to Buffalo, and, as described by his great-grandson, they opened a grocery store in the rough-and-tumble harbor area, near where Margaret's brother operated a saloon. The Donnelly's had six children.

Margaret died on October 4th, 1886. As Patrick's health declined with age, he first applied for a veteran's pension in 1890. Like so many of his comrades, he was at first denied by the bureaucracy, and like so many of his comrades, he would continue to re-apply for years, only to still be denied. In 1897, thoroughly disgusted with the system, he wrote a letter to the commissioner of pensions, which is here partially quoted. He closes a long review of his service, and the legal justifications for his claim, with the following:

> I have come to the conclusion that there is no pension law which covers my case or is of use or benefit to me…I shall go before no more Notary Publics nor Examining Doctors boards. It is evident that as the law stands it makes no difference whether a man served ten years or two months…I shall wait until the Government see the justice of my claim…

In 1899, he was granted a pension of $6 per month. He entered the Soldier's Home in Bath, New York, for two months in 1903, and for four months in 1904,

---

2412. Subsequent information supplied by Paul Callsen, Donnelly's great-grandson.

and each time his health recovered and he was discharged. By 1910, his pension had increased to $15. He died on December 20th, 1910, and is buried at Holy Cross Cemetery, Lackawanna, New York.

His great-grandson, Mr. Paul Callsen, is the only known descendant of anyone in Battery L with whom the author has become acquainted.

5. George F. Hadley–1 March, 1860, Boston. A blacksmith, age 32, he joined from the first group of recruits. By July of 1861, he was assigned on "Extra Duty" as blacksmith, and remained in that position for his entire term of service, though his official title was artificer. As the size of the battery grew, when it was converted, first to a mounted, and then to a light battery, he was joined in that capacity, in the war years of '63 and '64, by Henry Champion and Sirenus Kilburne. He reenlisted in July of 1864. Hadley has a special place in the history of Battery L, as he has been eulogized in Haskin's *History of the First Regiment of Artillery*, in a section which was written by Henry Closson, a portion of which is quoted here:[2413]

> And as I write of battery L there looms up the figure of "Hadley," a typical man of the sturdy rank and file, upon whose faithful shoulders so many generals were borne to honor and success. I seem again to see this honest old fellow, always cheerful, always ready, always at work. He was the company blacksmith, and considered himself responsible for the serviceable condition of the horses, and whenever a halt was made and the labors of other men ceased, Hadley still continued his. Whether sunshine or rain was beating down it made no difference; either found Hadley at it, fastening a nail here, loosening a shoe there, swearing at some careless driver, or petting some restive horse. On the march, he merrily plodded along through the mud or sand, and in camp the most conspicuous object was Hadley's brawny arms and bare head dodging about the horses' feet, and the rat-tat of his hammer was as regular as tattoo itself. And he died as he had lived—in harness—one of the crew drowned with their officer, in attempting, during a storm, off Fort Niagara, to save a drifting boat.

The accident occurred in Lake Ontario, on May 4th, 1870. The "honest old fellow" was 42.

6. Lewis Keller–11 September, 1854, Baltimore, Maryland, butcher, age 21. In 1854–55 the battery was stationed at Key Biscayne, "in the field" in Florida, and he saw service in the Second Seminole War. The battery having been transferred to Fort Brown, Texas, he was stricken with yellow fever during the 1858 epidemic, but survived. He reenlisted on December 1st, 1859, at Newport, Kentucky. As has been noted, he was one of those appointed from Battery L as a 2nd Lieutenant in the newly created 2nd Louisiana Cavalry, one of the Corps d'Afrique units organized by General Banks. He served from November 29th, 1863, was wounded on May

---

2413. Haskin, p. 372.

6th, 1864, and promoted to 1st Lieutenant on May 7th, 1864. The 2nd Cavalry was reorganized in September of that year, and Keller was mustered out. He reenlisted in Battery L on October 11th, 1864.

He was married to Mary Ann Noonan, at Buffalo, New York, on June 2nd, 1867. On May 17th, 1867, he was appointed an ordnance sergeant, which was rather a special position given to veterans who had had at least eight years of service, four of which was in the grade of a non-commissioned officer. This meant he could be assigned as a lone artillery storekeeper at any number of army installations. The assignment was essentially permanent, at the discretion only of the adjutant-general. Keller's assignment was Fort Douglas, Utah.

He continually reenlisted after he left Battery L in 1867, until his last enlistment expired in 1885. During this period, with his wife, he had served for 18 years at Fort Douglas with the 14th Infantry. Upon his retirement, they settled in Buffalo, New York, the location of Fort Porter, and the adopted home of several former members of Battery L. Ever faithful to the army, he was for a time employed as steward at the post exchange. He remained in Buffalo until he died at age 77, on July 10th, 1907.

7. Philipp H. Schneider–17 December, 1853, Lancaster, Pennsylvania, baker, age 33. Schneider claimed prior service in Company A, of the 1st Battalion of New Jersey Mexican War Volunteers, from August 1847 to February 1848. After his first enlistment in Battery L, he reenlisted at Fort Brown, Texas, on October 16th, 1858, and again at Baton Rouge in 1863. His record while serving with Battery L was spotless; all through the war, he was never sick, never deserted, and never disciplined. Though he was never injured in action, as luck would have it, on or about April 1st, 1865, while the battery was at Pleasant Valley, Maryland, he was thrown from his horse, causing injury to his head and back. He is not reported absent, sick, on the Battery L monthly report for April 1865, but is so reported for May. He is not reported sick on the April–June muster roll, a record-keeping deficiency which would, upon his later application for a disability pension, cause him difficulty, and cast doubt on the veracity of his claims. He was, in fact, in the hospital of the Provisional Cavalry Brigade, from May 5th, 1865, to June 10th, 1865.

On May 29th, 1866, while Battery L was stationed at Fort Schuyler, New York, he "went home" to Pennsylvania, and went to work as a baker. Due to his disabled condition, one employer admitted to paying him "two-thirds what I paid full hands because he was needy, but I do not consider him worth what I paid him." Unable to make a living, Schneider surrendered himself at Fort Hamilton, New York, on March 25th, 1868, more than 22 months after he had deserted. He was reassigned to Battery L, and by the intervention of Bvt. Lt. Col. Henry W. Closson, though he was no longer in command of Battery L, it was seen to it that Schneider was restored to duty without trial, for former services rendered, and good behavior. He was promptly discharged on disability, on June 11th, 1868, with an invalid pension of $2 per month.

He first made application for a pension increase on June 30th, 1880, and on a questionnaire from the Bureau of Pensions, he answered "No" to question no. 1, "Have you ever married?" His answer to question no. 5, "Have you any living children?" was "None that I know of." An increase to $4 was not granted him until March 30th, 1887. He, like James Beglan, spent the rest of his days in off-and-on correspondence with his pension lawyer, George Lemon, who charged fees that escalated to as much as $25 to process affidavits and declarations to support increases in his pension (for example, an affidavit was obtained from William V. Thompson, and another from George Kelly, still in the service in May 1885 at Fort Douglas, Utah). Upon his death at age 83, on January 8th, 1904, he was receiving $12.

8. William E. Scott–9 February, 1860, Boston. Clerk, age 24. He arrived at Fort Brown with the first group of recruits from depot. His record is without blemish, and though he was initially reported sick at Fort Brown and at Fort Duncan, and then again at Fort Pickens, after participating in the reconnaissance up Santa Rosa Island, he was never listed as sick again. Perhaps he had become "acclimatized." He was never wounded or injured. He was promoted to corporal on September 8th, 1863. He reenlisted on July 11th, 1864, and was advanced to 1st sergeant on October 25th, 1864. He remained in that capacity until his early discharge, at Fort Porter, New York, for disability (heart) on March 6th, 1867.

On March 17th, 1867, he married Catharine Carson, whom he had met at New York while on furlough in May of 1865. Throughout his entire enlistment, he had used the alias Scott. His marriage license reveals that he was really William Edward Scott Simmonds.

The couple settled in Worcester, Massachusetts, where he was briefly listed as a cigar maker; the offshoot of a government sponsored program to teach disabled veterans a marketable trade. However, he quickly switched to insurance sales. A son, Robert, was born on February 9th, 1870. On May 25th, 1871, he was in a carriage accident, and was thrown to the street. Assured by a doctor that he would be recovered in a few days, he died on May 30th, age 34.

Having survived the entire war, he was killed in a carriage accident—a familiar ring to those students of history who are aware of the fate of Gen. George Patton.

9. Warren P. Shaw–26 October, 1860, Boston. Shoemaker, age 21. He was in the second group of recruits from depot who arrived at Fort Duncan. He is listed as sick, present, at Fort Pickens at the end of 1861 through February 1862, though was never listed as sick again. He did not desert with the party-goers in New Orleans in 1863, or at any other time. He was never disciplined. He declined to reenlist in 1864, and when his enlistment expired he was discharged on October 24th, 1865.

He returned home to Kingston, New Hampshire, to live with his parents and younger brother. He never married. He worked for the rest of his life in one of the many shoe factories in the New England area at that time and died on September 28th, 1893, aged 52.

10. William V. Thompson–13 September, 1860, Rochester, New York. Farmer, age 22. He was a member of the second group of recruits from depot. He was listed as sick, like so many others, at Fort Pickens, in 1861 and 1862. His pension file includes a detailed medical record, unlike many others. On July 31st, 1861, he was treated for "catarrhus" which is hay fever, despite the fact that it does not appear in the muster roll record. On August 9th, 1861, it was "constipation," and on August 18th it was "contusion," on September 6th, "diarrhea;" and on April 3rd, 1862, "conjunctivitis," or pink eye, an inflammation of the eyelid—hardly malaria, scurvy, or some other serious condition. He reenlisted on July 18th, 1864, and his spotless record continued throughout the Shenandoah Valley Campaign. At Reserve Camp, at Pleasant Valley, he was furloughed, and remained AWOL past its January 12th, 1865, expiration date. He was apprehended and returned on February 7th. As was noted in chapter 15, he had not been paid any installment of his $400 reenlistment bonus, and could never have collected if he had remained a deserter. On October 9th through 14th, 1865, he was treated for syphilis, and on February 4th to April 4th, 1866, for gonorrhea, two diseases delicately not mentioned anywhere in the muster roll records for the entire war period, but undoubtedly being cause while the battery was at Pensacola, New Orleans, and elsewhere. He was discharged promptly on July 18th, 1867—evidence that he was not required to make up time lost while AWOL.

He returned to Pennsylvania and became a junk dealer. He married Mary A. Bedow, on March 13th, 1872. They had no surviving children. William applied for a pension under the Act of June 27th, 1890, but was rejected repeatedly for claims of disability due to malaria, and sundry other problems, including piles. He was finally allowed $6 per month on March 9th, 1903. This eventually rose as his situation deteriorated, and he was receiving $50 at the time of his death, on September 9, 1916, age 77.

11. Michael White–7 October, 1859, Boston. Laborer, age 21. Not from the fresh group of recruits, but on his first enlistment. He was only once listed as sick, at Pensacola, in the August–October 1862 roll. He was promoted to corporal on September 8th, 1863, and sergeant on March 2nd, 1864.

He is listed as wounded and missing on the February–April 1864 muster roll. Shot in the left breast, he was stunned and left for dead at the Battle of Pleasant Hill. Found alive by the Confederates, the bullet not having torn through him, but stopped by bone, he was marched off—as a prisoner—to Camp Ford, Texas. There, he got no treatment for his wound, and suffered from exposure for the next 13 months. "I was let live or die."

Exchanged prisoners from Camp Ford arrived at New Orleans on May 27th, 1865. He rejoined Battery L on August 15th, 1865, at Fort McHenry, Maryland, where his accounts were "settled up to that date." His first enlistment had expired on October 7th, 1864, and he was officially discharged. He then reenlisted for three years, serving until August 15th, 1868, when he was mustered out as a sergeant, at Fort Porter, New York. His record is spotless; he never indulged in the "vacations" that many took during the war at New Orleans and elsewhere and there is no record of his having been disciplined for any offence.

Freshly discharged, he left the Buffalo area for Ireland, and remained as a small farmer at Nuke, Arthurstown, County Wexford, for the rest of his life. He married Catharine Power on November 27th, 1872, and they had nine children. On July 16th, 1888, he was awarded a pension of $6 per month, which was raised to $8 on March 14th, 1891, and to $12 on May 10th, 1907. He died on September 16th, 1910, age 73.

In summary, all of the recruits of 1860 had left the Battery by August of 1870, and with the exception of Keller, none on the "faithful" list cared to make a lifelong career out of the army.

Two Deserters

It was mentioned that eight men deserted in July of 1865. Seven would have qualified for the "faithful" list if they had not done so. The fortunes of two, and by association several others, is a study in diverse fortunes.

Patrick Craffy–27 September, 1860, Boston. In the second group of recruits from depot. After the Siege of Port Hudson, when the Battery was stationed in New Orleans, he was one of the 20 members that were so attracted to the delights of the Crescent City that they deserted. After the blood and sweat of the previous months, undoubtedly in their minds it was worth the cost. He left the battery on August 19th, and was arrested on the 27th. He was returned on October 2nd, and was ordered by court-martial to forfeit $10 paid to the constable. A similar penalty was meted out to deserters William Brown and Owen Wren, who also had been quickly arrested. Three more of the 20 re-joined the battery in October, the record not specifying the circumstances of their return. Two were court-martialed, having to forfeit $8 from each month of four month's pay. The third man to be apprehended, Michael O'Sullivan, was held in confinement in the parish prison in New Orleans for an unspecified reason. It was not learned until July of 1864 that he had died there on October 3rd, 1863.

Craffy reenlisted in July of 1864, and deserted again while the battery was stationed at Winchester, Virginia, on July 28th, 1865. He had only been paid $75 of his $400 reenlistment bonus. He evidently returned to the service, though no record has been found. A Patrick Craffy appears in the Massachusetts adjutant general records, which have him as dishonorably discharged, while serving in Texas, on June 24th, 1870.

William Demarest–19 October, 1859, New York. In the first group of recruits to arrive while Battery L was stationed at Fort Brown, on April 15th, 1860. He rather quickly was promoted to corporal on November 25th, 1861, while the battery was at Fort Pickens. He was promoted to sergeant on September 8th, 1863, after the vacancy created by the promotion of Alexander Baby to 2nd lieutenant, who was then transferred out of the battery to General Banks' headquarters, to become a part of Banks' bodyguard.

Mysteriously listed as "under arrest" in the April–June 1864 muster roll, but with no equivalent entry in the May or June monthly Reports, and no disciplinary action noted, he remained as a sergeant. Then, Special Orders no. 185 from Headquarters, Department of the East, New York City, dated August 4th, 1864, were received. They called for men from Battery L for recruiting duty, despite the fact that in its June Returns (both regimental and monthly), the battery had reported that no recruits were required. Headquarters knew something that Henry Closson did not. It was true, the next month, the 13th Massachusetts Battery was separated from Battery L, and L was ordered to New York, and as we know, combined with Battery K, and then sent into service with Sheridan.

Sergeant Demarest, and privates Hall, Teighe, and Townsend, all under the supervision of Lt. Edward Appleton, were detached on August 26th, for recruiting duty in New York. Once they arrived, they were posted, strange as it may seem, at Poughkeepsie. It was there, with Demarest's term of service soon to expire, that he was reenlisted by Lt. Appleton on September 7th, 1864. As has been noted, they failed to recruit anyone else at Poughkeepsie, but having moved back to New York City, they recruited a former member of the battery, Lewis Keller, on October 11th, 1864. As noted, he had originally left the battery due to promotion to 2nd lieutenant in the 2nd Louisiana Cavalry, on December 29th, 1863, and had been mustered out on September 8th, 1864, due to its consolidation with the 1st Louisiana Cavalry on September 7th, 1864.[2414] He was again free to rejoin the battery, and did so, luckily as a corporal.

New York, October 11th, 1864, is the last evidence of the whereabouts of Lt. Appleton, who went AWOL. Demarest, Hall, Teighe, and Townsend all faithfully returned to duty in the Shenandoah Valley.

On April 19th, 1865, Demarest was "reduced to the ranks" i.e., reduced to private, no reason given, but no experienced non-com gets such treatment without a serious offence. He deserted on July 28th, 1865. However, he returned on January 19th, 1866, and served again, still a private. The former sergeant had now reached the bottom; he was assigned as company cook, after the three cooks; Henry Jefferson, Virgil Ayers, and Phillip Ewens; had been discharged by expiration of service on October 3rd, 1866. However, his talent and experience apparently came

---

2414. National Park Service, Soldiers and Sailor's System; Lewis Keller Pension Record.

to the fore, and by the time of the expiration of his service on February 5th, 1871, he was discharged as a sergeant. He reenlisted immediately, and was murdered on July 8th, 1871, while on duty with the battery, which was then stationed at Fort Niagara, New York. He is buried in an unmarked grave in the cemetery at Old Fort Niagara; the record of his burial listed on a separate plaque.[2415]

The 1863 Pensacola Recruits

The sentiment of the recruits that joined the battery from volunteer regiments during the war is indicated by their notable lack of enthusiasm for remaining in the army now that the war had ended. Of the 48 men that enlisted at Pensacola in 1862, only 20[2416] still remained in the battery when their three-year enlistments expired in November and December of 1865. *None* of them reenlisted. Their job was done, and the war was over. When Patrick Gibbons' courts-martial sentence at Ship Island was up, he was dishonorably discharged in December, and he did not reenlist either.

The remarkable rate of attrition, from 48 to 21, was partially from wounds and disease, but primarily from desertion. Card, Campbell, Deering, Hubbard, O'Sullivan, Parslow, William H. Smith, and Wood had died; Crowley, Chase, Champion, and Moore had been discharged on disability, but the remainder, 15 men, had deserted. Some deserted quickly after joining, such as the two Winn brothers at Thibodaux, in May of '63, but many deserted at New Orleans in August and September of '63.

The Three Cooks

Henry Jefferson, Phillip Ewens, and Virgil Ayres, all served out their full enlistments with perfect records. All remained designated as cooks. None were advanced in the ranks. They were all discharged, promptly on schedule, on October 31st, 1866, at Fort Porter, Buffalo, New York. They had come a long way.

Philip Ewens–Called "Phil," or "the lawyer" by the men (for the fact that he questioned everything), he was properly named Phillipe Milton E. Ewens, a French Creole, born into slavery at New Orleans in about 1828. He joined the battery in February of '63, the first of the three, though like the others, was not enlisted until October. After his discharge in October of 1866, he remained in Buffalo, married, and worked as a painter or whitewasher for the next 40 years. He never returned

---

2415. Burial data obtained from the independent research of Paul Callsen.
2416. It is difficult to place an exact number, as some of the deserters returned and were required to serve out time lost while absent, which would push their time of expiration past the records used here. Francis/Frank Jessop is an example, and since he was not discharged until September of 1866, we count 21 in the unit.

to the south. He died on August 5th, 1903, and is buried in Forest Lawn Cemetery.

Virgil Ayres[2417]–Ayers was born on the Wicks sugar plantation, near Franklin, Louisiana, on or about 1835, where he worked as a field hand. He came to the battery in the spring of '63, about six months before he was enlisted, and first served as a teamster. He was described as a "quiet and well behaved fellow" by Sergeant Keller. Like Ewens, after his discharge he remained in Buffalo, marrying and working there until his death in 1896. He is buried in Forest Lawn Cemetery.

Henry Jefferson–Jefferson was born in New Orleans in about 1823, to a slave mother and a French father, and was properly named Henri Louis Gerfie. He spoke only French when he came to Battery L, and as a result of the soft "G" pronunciation of his name, came to be called "Jeff." When enlisted, Lieutenant Appleton assigned him the name Jefferson. He vowed to never return to New Orleans, though he had relatives still living there after the war. He remained in Buffalo and raised a family. He was last recorded as living there in 1901, when he was 78. His place of burial is not known.

Battery L

The last muster roll record we have quoted was while the battery was stationed at Winchester, Virginia, in April of 1865. The story of the war was over. However, as we have seen, some of the faithful remained well beyond the war, to experience the last event involving Battery L that by any stretch could be called a military action. This was the Fenian Invasion of Canada.

The Fenian Brotherhood was an Irish fraternal organization which had existed throughout the time of the Civil War. Naturally, their sentiments centered on the liberation of Ireland from British rule. Since Canada was still ruled by Britain, they felt that now, with all of the training and experience that their members had from membership in the United States Army, plus the arms available to them at the war's end, was the time to strike a blow for the freedom of the Emerald Isle. Even former Confederates who had served under Stonewall Jackson and John Mosby were reported to be involved.[2418] By invading Canada and establishing an Irish Republic, a base for the liberation of the mother country could be established.

One faction of the Fenians, perhaps 500 men, under General Killian, moved on both Calais and Eastport, Maine, in April of 1866. U.S. authorities intervened, and it was observed that British troops were posted in the little town of St. Stephen, New Brunswick, opposite. Not a shot was fired and the event came to a close.

Undaunted, during the month of May, it was observed that a "large body of men" were traveling towards Buffalo, New York. This was under the sponsorship of another faction of the Fenians, those led by Generals Sweeny and O'Neil. On

---

2417. Ayres pension file, National Archives, application no. 642824, certificate no. 433713.
2418. Haskin, pp. 242–245; MacDonald, pp. 23–24; W. C. Chewett, p. 21

June 1st, a force of 1,340 men crossed the Niagara River at Black Rock. During the day, the force grew to some 2,000. They then occupied the Canadian village of Fort Erie, meeting no resistance. They continued on towards Black Creek, but learning that a force of Canadian troops was being gathered at Port Colborne, O'Neil decided to turn to attack them.

They met at the Ridge Road, which bears southwest toward Ridgeway,[2419] and the Canadians were defeated. By now, however, the U.S. authorities had cut off their means of supply, and the whole operation began to break up. Almost all of the invasion force was captured by the U.S. authorities as they attempted to return.

On June 1st, having participated in the ceremonies at the funeral of Winfield Scott at West Point, Battery L was ordered to be ready to move at a moment's notice, and on the 4th left Fort Schuyler for Buffalo. Four other artillery companies had been ordered there, and by the time they had arrived, batteries D, E, H, L, and M were left with nothing more than the duty of escorting the prisoners captured by the USS *Michigan* from its landing place to the jail, and from the jail to the courthouse. They were not called on for further service. While the other batteries eventually were returned to their previous stations, Battery L remained at Fort Porter.

A monument and plaque, figure 1, remembers the defenders.

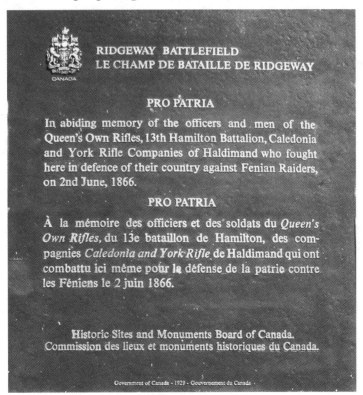

FIGURE 1

2419. MacDonald, pp. 28–32, 38–39; figure 1, monument plaque at Ridgeway Battle site, photo by Paul Callsen.

Though there were later Fenian raids, all of them unsuccessful, Battery L was never again called upon. In 1872 the battery was returned to the Department of the Gulf, as were batteries A and F. By November 26th, the three batteries that had formed the garrison of Fort Pickens during the siege in 1861 had returned.[2420]

All of the alphabetically designated artillery batteries were reorganized under the Act of Congress approved February 2nd, 1901, when Battery L ceased to exist, becoming the 9th Company, Coast Artillery.[2421]

2420. Haskin, p. 259.
2421. Heitman, F. B., p. 61

Appendix

The Fall of New Orleans

Lovell's analysis of the fall was elaborated in a letter to G. T. Beauregard on May 12th, and is here quoted:[2422]

> 1st The carrying away of the river obstructions at the forts by the storm and flood a few nights before the attack [April 11th].
>
> 2d The want of a sufficiency of heavy guns, which I tried in vain to procure from Mobile and Pensacola.
>
> 3d From inefficiency and want of proper co-operation on the part of those who were building and those who were to use the naval defenses when ready. [Here he was referring to the fact that the naval forces were independent of his command, and that the construction of the ironclads, in the hands of the navy department, was seriously mismanaged.[2423]]
>
> ...I have asked for an official investigation. My conscience is clear.

Lovell got his court of inquiry, which lasted from April 4th to July 9th, 1863. He was largely exonerated, even complimented, on most of his efforts. The one complaint was that he had not given clear instructions to General M. L. Smith (who since his promotion on April 11th[2424] had commanded the interior line of defense) for its "retirement." Those few guns of the line that were able to be brought to bear on Farragut's ships were fired until they ran out of ammunition, and only then were the troops withdrawn.[2425] Smith then correctly headed for Vicksburg.

Stephen R. Mallory, the secretary of the navy, did not want the details of the confusion related to the command assignments, or the construction of the ironclads publicized, though the damaging testimony remained in the records of the court. He had earlier threatened that no army court could make conclusions about the

---

2422. O.R. Vol. 6, pp. 889–890.
2423. Ibid., pp. 611, 622–623, 646. C. M. Conrad, the chairman of the Confederate Congressional Committee on Naval Affairs, testified at Lovell's inquiry. He closed his testimony with: "I also felt it my duty...publicly to proclaim in Congress my conviction of the incapacity or inefficiency of the Secretary of the Navy."
2424. Ibid., p. 581.
2425. Ibid., p. 553.

navy.[2426] Nevertheless, the court did so, citing the "non-completion of the ironclads" and the uselessness of the "so-called" river defense fleet.[2427]

2426. Ibid., pp. 612, 613, 617–618, 630.
2427. Ibid., pp. 642.

Sources

Key to Footnotes

A primary reference for this work is *The War of the Rebellion: A Compilation of the Official Records of the Union and Confederate Armies*, published by the U.S. Government Printing Office over a period from 1880 to 1901. It consists of four series and an atlas. Series 1, 53 volumes, consists of Union and Confederate reports, orders and correspondence relating to military operations. Series 2, eight volumes, relates to prisoners; series 3, five volumes, special reports of the secretary of war and others not relating to the first two; and series 4, four volumes, consisting of Confederate papers. The atlas consists primarily of battle maps.

By far the most references used in this book are from series 1, and a typical footnote would be shortened to: O.R. Vol. 34/I, pp. x–xx. Lesser-used references from the remaining three series would read, for example: O.R. Ser. 3, vol. 2, pp. x–xx.

Another significant source is *Official Records of the Union and Confederate Navies in the War of the Rebellion*, published by the U.S. Government Printing Office over a period from 1894 to 1922. There are two series: 1, volumes 1–27, and 2, volumes 1–3. A typical footnote would be abbreviated: ORN ser. 1, vol. 21, p. x.

The framework of the book is based on the service records of Battery L, all available at the National Archives. They fall under RG 391.2.1, Records of the Artillery, 1815–1950:

- Regimental Returns, Microfilm Series 727 - Returns from Regular Army Artillery Regiments
- Monthly Returns, available by special order
- Muster Roll Records, available by special order
- Post Returns, Microfilm Series 617
- Letters Received by the Adjutant General - RG 93
- Letters Sent by the Adjutant General - RG 94
- Civil War Pension Files and Compiled Service Records for units and individual soldiers, available by special order
- U.S. Army Register of Enlistments, Microfilm Series 233
- Complied Military Service Records, Microfilm Publication M594

Bibliography

Adjutant General of the United States Army. Official Army Register, 1891.

Adjutant General, Massachusetts. *Record of the Massachusetts Volunteers, 1861–1865*. Vols. 1–2. Boston: Wright & Potter, 1868.

Adjutant General's Report, Supplement. Lansing, Michigan, 1863.

Adjutant General's Report. *Massachusetts Soldiers, Sailors, and Marines in the Civil War*. Vols. 1–8. Norwood, Massachusetts: The Norwood Press, 1930–1932.

Adjutant General's Report. Vol. 1–2. Concord, New Hampshire, 1865–1866.

Album of the Second Battalion Duryee Zouaves, 165th New York Volunteer Infantry. Veteran Association, 1906. (See also, Duryee Zouaves)

American Missionary. "Leaders." Vol. 50. Aug. 1896.

An Historical Sketch of the 162nd New York Infantry. Albany: Weed Parsons & Co., 1867.

Anderson, John. *History of the Fifty-Seventh Regiment of Massachusetts Volunteers*. Boston, MA: E. B. Stillings & Co., 1896.

Army of the United States, War Dept. *Revised Regulations*. Philadelphia: J. G. L. Brown, August 10, 1861.

Arnold, I. N. *The History of Abraham Lincoln and the Overthrow of Slavery*. Chicago: Clarke & Co., Chicago, 1866.

Babcock, Willoughby M., Jr. *Selections from the Letters and Diaries of Bvt. Brig. Gen. Willoughby Babcock of the Seventy-Fifth New York Volunteers*. University of New York Press, 1922.

Bacon, Edward. *Among the Cotton Thieves*. Detroit: The Free Steam Book and Job Printing House, 1867.

Badeau, Adam. "Leuit.-General Sheridan" *The Century*. Vol. 27, February, 1884.

Ballantine, George. *Autobiography of an English Soldier in the U.S. Army*. New York: Stringer & Townsend, 1853.

Bates, David Homer. *Lincoln in the Telegraph Office*. New York: The Century Co., 1907.

Battles and Leaders of the Civil War. 4 volumes. Edited by Robert U. Johnson and Clarence Buell. Century Press, 1887. (Contains articles authored by numerous participants in the war—refer to individual authors.)

Benedict, G.C. "History of the 7th Vermont Volunteers."Chapter 21 in*Vermont in the Civil War*. Vol. 2. Burlington, VT: Free Press Association, 1888.

Bennett, A. J. *The Story of the First Massachusetts Light Battery* Boston, MA: Deland & Barta, 1886.

Benson, S. F. "The Battle of Pleasant Hill Louisiana." *The Annals of Iowa* Vol. 7, No. 7. Des Moines, IA: State Historical Society of Iowa. October, 1906.

Benson, S. F. Narrative: "Ben Van Dyke's Escape from the Hospital at Pleasant Hill, Louisiana." *The Annals of Iowa* Vol. 7, No. 7. Des Moines, IA: State Historical Society of Iowa. October, 1906.

Bentley, W. H. *History of the 77th Illinois Vol. Infantry*. Peoria: E. Hine, Printer, 1883.

Billings, John D. *Hardtack and Coffee*. Boston: Geo. M. Smith & Co., 1887.

Biographical Directory of the United States Congress. bioguide.congress.gov/

Bissell, George. "Brief History of the Twenty-fifth Regiment, Connecticut Volunteers." *The Twenty-Fifth Regiment, Connecticut Volunteers in the War of the Rebellion*. Includes sections by Ellis, McManus, and Goodell. Rockville, CT: Press of the Rockville Journal, 1913.

Blake, E. E. *A Succinct History of the 28th Iowa Volunteer Infantry*. Belle Plaine, IA, Union Press, 1896.

Blessington, Joseph P. *The Campaigns of Walker's Texas Division*. New York: Lange Little & Co., 1875.

Bosson, C.P. *History of the 42nd Regiment Massachusetts Volunteers*. Boston: Mills Knight & Co., 1886.

Boudrye, Louis N. *Historic Records of the Fifth New York Cavalry* 2nd ed. Albany, NY: S.R. Gray, 1865

Bowen, J. J. *The Strategy of Robert E. Lee*. New York: Neale Publishing, 1914.

Bowen, James P. *Massachusetts in the War*. Springfield: Clark W. Bryan & Co., 1889.

Bowen, James R. *Regimental History of the First New York Dragoons*. Lyons, MI: Published by the Author, 1900.

Bringhurst, T. H., and Swigert, F. *History of the Forty-Sixth Regiment, Indiana Volunteer Infantry*. Compiled by the Regimental Association. Logansport, IN: Wilson, Humphries & Co., 1888.

Brown, J. H., ed. *The 20th Century Biographical Dictionary of Notable Americans*. Vol. 3. Boston, 1904.

Buchanan, James. *Message of the President to the Houses of Congress, 39th Congress*. Part 2. Washington, D.C.: A. O. P. Nicholson, 1854.

Buffum, F. M. *Memorial of the Great Rebellion Being a History of the Fourteenth Regiment of New Hampshire*. Boston: Franklin Press, 1882.

Butler, Benjamin F. *Butler's Book*. Boston: A. M. Thayer, 1892.

Bynum, Tom. *Louisiana Militia Law*. Baton Rouge: Tom Bynum State Printer, 1862.

Campbell, J, A. *Reminiscences and Documents Relating to the Civil War*. Baltimore, MD: John Murphy & Co., 1887.

Carpenter, Geo. N. *History of the Eighth Regiment, Vermont Volunteers*. Boston: Deland & Barta, 1886.

Chamberlaine, Capt. W. W. *Memoirs of the Civil War*. Washington, DC: Press of Byron S. Adams, 1912.

Chase, Salmon P. *Diary and Correspondence of Salmon P. Chase*. Part 4. Letters from George S. Denison to Salmon P. Chase, May 15, 1862, to March 21, 1865. Washington: American Historical Association Annual Report for 1902. (Published in vol. 2, 1903.)

Cheney, Newell. *History of the Ninth Regiment of New York Volunteer Cavalry*. Poland Center, NY: Martin Merz & Son, 1901.

Chewett, W. C. The Fenian Raid at Fort Erie, Toronto. W. C. Chewett & Co., 1866.

Childers, Henry H. "Reminiscences of the Battle of Pleasant Hill." *The Annals of Iowa* Vol. 7, No. 7. Des Moines, IA: State Historical Society of Iowa, October, 1906.

Childs, G. W. *National Almanac and Annual Record for the Year 1863*. Philadelphia: G. W. Childs, 1863.

Clark, Orton S. *History of the 116th New York Volunteers*. Buffalo: Mathews & Warren, 1868.

Cleveland, William. *History of Penobscot County Maine*. Chase & Co., 1882.

Coffin, Charles Carleton. "The May Campaign in Virginia" Boston: *The Atlantic Monthly* Vol. 14. July 1864.

Congressional Globe. 35th U.S. Congress. 1st Session, December 8, 1857. Appendix July, 1861.

Congressional Globe. 37th U.S. Congress. 1st Session.

Cooke, J. E. *Mohun*. New York: F. J. Huntington & Co., 1869.

Crowninshield, B. W. "The Battle of Cedar Creek." A Paper read before the Massachusetts Military Historical Society, December 8, 1879. Cambridge, MA: Riverside Press, 1879.

Crowninshield, B. W. *A History of the First Regiment of Massachusetts Cavalry Volunteers*. Boston, MA: Houghton Mifflin, 1891.

Cullum, George. *Biographical Register of the Officers and Graduates of the U.S. Military Academy, at West Point, N.Y. from its Establishment in 1802 to 1890*. Vols. 1–4. Boston and New York: Houghton-Mifflin, Co., 1891–1910.

Custer, Elizabeth B. *The Boy General*. Edited by M.E. Hurt. New York: Scribner's, 1901.

CWSAC (Civil War Sites Advisory Commission). Battle Summaries. The American Battlefield Protection Program (ABPP). National Park Service.

Dana, Charles, A. *Recollections of the Civil War*. New York: Appleton & Co., 1902.

Davis, Jefferson. *The Papers of Jefferson Davis*. Rice University MS43

Davis, Jefferson. *The Purchase of Camels*. Report of the Secretary of War. Washington: A. O. L. Nicholson, Printer, 1857.

Dawson, Sarah Morgan. *A Confederate Girl's Diary*. Boston: Houghton-Mifflin, 1913.

De Forest, J, W. "Sheridan's Battle of Winchester" *Harper's New Monthly Magazine* Vol. 30. New York, 1865.

DeBray, X. B., *A Sketch of DeBray's Twenty-Sixth Regiment of Texas Cavalry*. Southern Historical Society Papers (SHS), Vol. 13. Richmond, VA: re. J. William Jones, 1885.

Defences of Washington. Map no. 88-69074. National Archives.

Defenders of Port Hudson Association. "Port Hudson – Sketch of its Fortification, Siege and Surrender"– Compiled by the Defenders Association. Southern Historical Society Papers (SHS), vol. 14. Richmond, VA: Southern Historical Society, Rev. J. W. Jones, Secretary, 1886.

Denison, Frederic. *Sabers and Spurs*. Central Falls, RI: The First Rhode Island Veteran Cavalry Association, 1911.

Diary of a Williamsburgh Soldier dmna.ny.gov/historic/reghist/civil/infantry/133rdinf/133rdinfCWN.htm

Duffey, J. W. *McNeill's Last Charge*. Winchester, VA: G. F. Norton Pub. Co., 1912.

Duganne, A. J. H. *Twenty Months in the Department of the Gulf*. New York: J. P. Robens, 1865.

Duke, Basil W. "Last Days of the Confederacy." *Battles and Leaders of the Civil War*. Vol. 4. New York: The Century Co., 1884, 1888.

Duke, Basil W. *Reminiscences of General Basil Duke, C. S. A.* New York: Doubleday Page & Co., 1911.

Duryee Zouaves. *Second Battalion, One Hundred and Sixty-fifth Regt. New York Volunteer Infantry*. Historical Committee, 1905. (See also *Album of the Second Battalion Duryee Zouaves*.)

Dyer, Frederick H. *A Compendium of the War of the Rebellion.* Des Moines, Iowa: The Dyer Publishing Co., 1908.

Early, Jubal A. "Winchester, Fisher's Hill and Cedar Creek." *Battles and Leaders of the Civil War.* Vol. 4. New York: The Century Co., 1884, 1888.

Early, Jubal A., *A Memoir of the Last Year of the War for the Independence of the Confederate States of America.* Toronto: Lowell & Gibson, 1866.

Early, Jubal Anderson. *Autobiographical Sketch and Narrative of the War Between the States.* Philadelphia and London: J. B. Lippincott Company, 1912.

Elliott, E. N. *Cotton is King and Pro-Slavery Arguments.* Augusta, Georgia: Pritchard, Abbott & Loomis, 1860.

Elliott, J. B., *Scott's Great Snake.* Entered according to Act of Congress in the year 1861. Map. Library of Congress.

Embick, M. A. *Military History of the Third Division, Ninth Army Corps.* Harrisburg, PA: Aughinbaugh Printers, 1913.

Emerson, E. W. Life and Letters of Charles Russell Lowell. Boston, MA: Houghton-Mifflin, 1907.

Encyclopedia Britannica. 29 volumes. 1911.

Evans, D. M. *History of the Commercial Crisis 1857-1858.* London: Groombridge & Sons, 1859.

Ewer, J. K. *History of the Third Massachusetts Cavalry.* Historical Committee of the Regimental Association, 1903.

Farragut, Loyall. *The Life of David Glasgow Farragut.* New York: D. Appleton & Co., 1882.

Farrar, S. C. The Twenty Second Pennsylvania Cavalry Pittsburgh, PA: Ringgold Cavalry Association, 1911.

Fenian Raid at Fort Erie, The. Toronto: W. C. Chewett & Co., 1866.

Fitts, James F. "A June Day at Port Hudson" *The Galaxy* Vol. 2, September 15th, 1866.

Flinn, Frank H. *Campaigning with Banks in Louisiana and with Sheridan in the Shenandoah Valley.* Boston, MA: W. B. Clark & Co., 1889.

Foote, F. H. "Recollections of Army Life with General Lee." *Southern Historical Society Papers (SHS) Vol. 31.* Richmond, VA: Southern Historical Society, Rev. J. W. Jones, Secretary, 1903.

Forstall, R. L. *Population of States and Counties . . . 1790-1990,* Dept. of Commerce, 1996

Forsyth, G. A. *Thrilling Days in Army Life.* New York & London: Harper & Brothers, 1900.

Fox, William. *Regimental Losses in the American Civil War.* Albany, NY, 1889

Fullam, G. T. "Our Cruise in the Confederate States War Steamer Alabama." *The South African Advertiser and Mail, Supplement.* Cape Town, Saturday, September 19, 1863. Library of Congress.

Garnett, Capt. J. M. "Battle of Winchester" *Southern Historical Society Papers* (SHS) Vol. 31. Richmond, VA: Published by the Society, 1903.

Gibbon, John. *The Artillerist's Manual.* 2nd Edition. New York: D. Van Nostrand, 1863.

Gilman, J. H. "With Slemmer in Pensacola Harbor." *Battles and Leaders of the Civil War*. Vol. 1. New York: The Century Company, 1887.

Gilmor, Harry A. *Four Years in the Saddle* New York: Harper Brothers, 1866.

Gilmore, James R. (under the pseudonym of Edmund Kirke). "Our Visit to Richmond." *The Atlantic Monthly* Vol. 14, September, 1864.

Gilmore, James R. *Personal Recollections of Abraham Lincoln and the Civil War*. Boston: L. C. Page & Co., 1898.

Gordon, Gen. John B. *Reminiscences of the Civil War*. New York: Charles Scribner's Sons, 1904.

Gould, J. M. *History of the First – Tenth – Twenty-Ninth Maine Regiment*. Portland, ME: Stephen Berry, 1871.

Gracey, S. L. *Annals of the Sixth Pennsylvania Cavalry*. E. H. Butler, Co., 1868.

Grant, U. S. *The Personal Memoirs of U.S. Grant*. Vols. 1–2. New York: J. J. Little & Co., 1885.

Haines, Alanson, A. *History of the Fifteenth Regiment of New Jersey Volunteers*. New York: Jenkins & Thomas, 1883.

Hall, Besley & Wood. *History of the Sixth New York Cavalry*. Worcester, MA: E. H. Blanchard Press, 1908.

Hall, Henry, and James Hall. *Cayuga in the Field: A Record of the 19th N.Y. Volunteers, the 3rd New York Artillery, and the 75th New York Volunteers*. Auburn, NY: 1873.

Hanaburgh, D. H. *History of the 128th New York Regiment*. Poughkeepsie, NY: 1894.

Haney, J. C. *Revulsions in the United States from 1690–857*. New York: 1857.

Harding, Geo. C. *The Miscellaneous Writings of George C. Harding*. Indianapolis: Carlon & Hollenbeck, 1882.

Harper's New Monthly Magazine. Vol. 0022, Issue 129. February, 1861.

Harper's Weekly, 1861–1865.

Haskin, Wm., L. *The History of the First Regiment of Artillery*. Fort Preble, Portland, ME: B. Thurston & Co., 1879.

Hawkins, M. L. "Sketch of the Battle of Winchester" *Sketches of War History*. Cincinnati, OH: MOLLUS Ohio Commandery, P. G. Thomson, 1884.

Heath, Wm. H. "Battle of Pleasant Hill Louisiana." *The Annals of Iowa*, Vol. 7, No. 7. Des Moines, IA: State Historical Society of Iowa. October, 1906.

Heitman, F. B. *Historical Register and Dictionary of the United States Army from its Organization Sept 29, 1798, to March 2, 1903*. Washington, D.C.: The National Tribune, 1890; reprinted U. S. Government Printing Office, 1903.

Henry, Guy V. *Military Record of Army and Civilian Appointments in the United States Army*. Vols. 1–2. New York: D. Van Nostrand, 1873.

Historical Sketch of the 162nd New York Volunteer Infantry. Albany: Weed Parsons & Co., 1867.

Hood, J. B. "The Invasion of Tennessee" *Battles and Leaders of the Civil War* Vol. 4. New York: The Century Co. 1884, 1888.

Hosmer, James K. *The Color – Guard*. Boston: Walker, Wise & Co., 1864.

Howe, H. W. *Passages from the Life of Henry Warren Howe*. Lowell, MA: Courier-Citizen Co., 1899.

Humphreys, Charles A. *Field, Camp, Hospital and Prison*. Boston, MA: G. H. Ellis Co., 1918.

Hunter, R. M. T. "The Peace Commission of 1865." *Southern Historical Society Papers*. Vol. 3. Richmond, VA: Rev. J. William Jones, D. D., 1877.

Irwin, Richard B. "Military Operations in Louisiana." *Battles and Leaders of the Civil War*. Vol. 3. New York: The Century Company, 1888.

Irwin, Richard, B. *History of the Nineteenth Army Corps*. New York: G. Putnam's Sons, 1893.

Isham, Asa. *An Historical Sketch of the Seventh Regiment, Michigan Volunteer Cavalry*. New York: Town Topics Publishing, 1892.

Jackson, H. N. *Dedication of the Statue to Brevet Major-General William Wells*. Burlington, VT: Privately printed, 1914.

James, Marquis. *Life of Andrew Jackson*. Bobbs – Merrill Co., 1938.

Joel. Bible. (King James Version.)

Johns, Henry T. *Life with the 49th Massachusetts Volunteers*. Washington, D.C.: Ramsey & Bisbee, 1890.

Johnson, R., and Brown, J. H., eds. *The Twentieth Century Biographical Dictionary of Notable Americans*. Vol. 3. Boston: The Biographical Society, 1904.

Johnston, Joseph E. "*Jefferson Davis and the Mississippi Campaign*." Battles and Leaders of the Civil War. Vol. 3. New York: The Century Company, 1888.

Johnston, Joseph E. "*Jefferson Davis and the Mississippi Campaign.*" The North American Review. December, 1866.

Johnston, Joseph E. "Jefferson Davis and the Mississippi Campaign." *Battles and Leaders*. Vol. 3. New York: The Century Company, 1888.

Johnston, Joseph E. *Narrative of Military Operations*. New York: D. Appleton & Co., 1874.

Johnston, Joseph E. *Narrative of Military Operations*. New York: D. Appleton & Co., 1874.

Kell, John M. "The Cruise and Combats of the Alabama." *The Century*. April 1886.

Kell, John M. *Recollections of a Naval Life*. Washington, D.C.: Neale Co., 1900.

Kidd, J. H. *Personal Recollections of a Cavalryman*. Ionia, MI: Sentinel Publishing, 1908.

Lamb, Wm. "The Defense of Fort Fisher." Battles and Leaders of the Civil War, Vol. 4. New York: The Century Co., 1884, 1888.

Lawton, G. W. "Running at the Heads." *The Atlantic Monthly*, Vol. 16, September, 1865.

Lee, Wm. O. *Personal and Historical Sketches… of the Seventh Michigan Volunteer Cavalry 1862-1865*. Detroit, MI: 7th Michigan Cavalry Association, 1902.

Leslie, Mrs. Frank. *Frank Leslie's Famous Leaders and Battle Scenes of the Civil War*. New York: Mrs. Frank Leslie Publisher, 1896.

Leslie, Mrs. Frank. *Frank Leslie's Illustrated History of the Civil War*. New York: Mrs. Frank Leslie, Publisher, 1895.

Lester and Bromwell. *A Digest of the Military and Naval Laws of the Confederate States.* Columbia, SC: Evans and Cogswell, 1864.

Library of Congress. Abraham Lincoln Papers.

Library of Congress. Name Authority File, http://id.loc.gov/

Little, H. F. *History of the 7th Regiment of New Hampshire Volunteers.* Concord, NH: Evans, 1896.

Long, A. L. "*General Early's Valley Campaign.*" Southern Historical Society Papers (SHS) Vol. 3. Richmond, VA: Rev. J. Wm. Jones, 1877.

Long, A. L. *Memoirs of Robert E. Lee.* New York, Philadelphia and Washington: J. M. Stoddart & Co., 1886.

Longfellow, Henry Wadsworth. *Longfellow's Poems.* New York and Boston: Houghton, Mifflin, 1882.

Longstreet, James. *From Manassas to Appomattox.* Philadelphia: J. B. Lippincott Company, 1896.

Loudermilk, Wm. *History of Cumberland* Washington, DC, James Anglim, 1878.

MacDonald, John. *Troublous Times in Canada.* Toronto: W. S. Johnston & Co., 1910.

Maddocks, Eldon B. *History of the 26th Maine Regiment.* Bangor, ME: Chas. H. Glass & Co., 1899.

Mahan, D. H. *A Treatise of Field Fortification.* Richmond, VA: West & Johnston, 1862.

Marshall, T. B. *History of the Eighty-Third Ohio infantry.* Cincinnati, OH: Eighty-Third Association, 1912.

McDonald, Wm. N. *A History of the Laurel Brigade.* Edited by B. C. Washington. Baltimore: Mrs. Kate McDonald, 1907.

McGregor, Chas. *History of the 15th New Hampshire Volunteers.* 15th Regiment Assn., 1900.

McKinney, E. P. *Life in Tent and Field.* Vol.1. Boston: R. D. Badger, 1922.

McManus, Thomas P. *Battle Fields of Louisiana Revisited a Second Time.* Hartford, CT: Fowler &Miller. Co., 1897. (See also Bissell.)

McMorries, E.Y. *History of the First Regiment, Alabama Volunteer Infantry, C.S.A.* Montgomery, AL: The Brown Printing Co., 1904.

"Memoirs." *The Galaxy Magazine.* Review of the *Memoirs of General W.T. Sherman.* September 1885.

Merritt, Wesley. "Sheridan in the Shenandoah Valley" *Battles and Leaders of the Civil War.* Vol. 4. New York: The Century Co., 1884, 1888.

Message of the President to the Houses of Congress, 33rd Congress. Part 2. Washington: A. O. P. Nicholson, 1854.

Meyers, Augustus. *Ten Years in the Ranks.* New York: The Sterling Press, 1914.

"Military Training of the Regular Army" *Journal of the Military Service Institute of the U.S.* November 1889.

Miller, F. T., ed., *The Photographic History of the Civil War.* Volumes 1–10. New York: The Review of Reviews, Co., 1911.

Moors, J. F. *History of the Fifty-second Regiment, Massachusetts Volunteers.* Boston: Geo. H. Ellis, 1893.

Morris, Gouverneur. *History of a Volunteer Regiment.* New York: Veteran Volunteer Pub. Co., 1891.

Mosby, John S. *The Memoirs of Col. John Singleton Mosby.* Edited by Charles Wells Russell. Boston, MA: Little, Brown & Co., 1917.

Moyer, Henry P. *History of the Seventeenth Regiment of Pennsylvania Cavalry.* Lebanon, PA: Sowers Printing, 1911.

Munford, T. T. "Reminiscences of Cavalry Operations. - Operations Under Rosser." *Southern Historical Society Papers,* Vol. 13. Richmond, VA: Rev. J. Wm. Jones, 1885.

Munson, John W. *Reminiscences of a Mosby Guerilla.* New York: Moffat, Yard & Co., 1906.

National Archives, Cantonment Duncan, RG 77, Fortification File, drawer 148, sheet 34;

National Archives, LC Railroad Maps.

Nettleton, Gen. A. B. "The Famous Fight at Cedar Creek." *The Annals of the War.* Philadelphia: The Times Publishing Co., 1879.

New York Adjutant General. *Registers of the 91st NY Infantry.*

New York Infantry. *An Historical Sketch of the 162nd Regiment N.Y. Vol. Infantry.* Albany: Weed Parsons & Co., 1867.

New York Infantry. Duryee Zouaves. *Second Battalion, One Hundred and Sixty-fifth Regt. New York Volunteer Infantry.* Historical Committee, 1905. (See also *Album of the Second Battalion Duryee Zouaves.*)

New York Press, Members of. *A Brief Popular Account of All the Financial Panics and Commercial Revulsions in the United States from 1690–1857.* New York: J. C. Haney, 1857.

New York Times. January 6, 1858.

New York Times. July 14, 1861.

Newlin, W. H. *A History of the Seventy-Third Regiment of Illinois Infantry Volunteers.* Springfield, IL: Reunion Association, 1890.

Nichols, G. W. *A Soldier's Story of His Regiment (61st Georgia).* Jesup, GA: 1898.

Nicolay, John G., and & John Hay. "Lincoln in Congress and at the Bar." *The Century.* February 1887.

Nicolay, John G., and John Hay. *Abraham Lincoln, A History.* 10 volumes. New York: The Century Co.; 1886, 1890, 1904.

NOAA (National Oceanographic and Atmospheric Administration). Historical Map Collection.

Noel, Theophilus. *A Campaign from Santa Fe to the Mississippi of the Old Sibley Brigade.* Shreveport: Shreveport News Printing, 1865.

Noel, Theophilus. *Autobiography and Reminiscences of Theophilus Noel.* Chicago: Theophilus Noel Co., 1904.

Noel, Theophilus. *Autobiography and Reminiscences of Theophilus Noel.* Chicago: Theophilus Noel Co., 1904.

Northup, Solomon. *Twelve Years a Slave.* Auburn, NY: Derby & Miller, 1853.

Norton, Henry. *Deeds of Daring, or History of the Eighth N.Y. Volunteer Cavalry.* Norwich, NY: Chenango Telegraph Printing House, 1889.

O'Ferrall, Chas. T. *Forty Years of Active Service.* New York and Washington: Neal Publishing, 1904.

Official Proceedings of the Democratic National Convention Chicago, IL: Times Steam Book and Job Printing House, 1864.

Ould, Judge Robert. "The Exchange of Prisoners." *The Annals of the War.* Philadelphia, PA: The Times Publishing Co., 1879.

Paine, Alanson. *The Fifteenth Regiment of New Jersey Volunteers.* New York: Jenkins and Thomas, 1883.

Papers of Jefferson Davis. Rice University MS 43.

Park, Robert E. "Sketch of the Twelfth Alabama Infantry." *Southern Historical Society Papers* Vol. 33. Richmond, VA: Published by the Society, 1905.

Pellet, E. P. *History of the 114th Regiment New York State Volunteers,* Norwich, NY: Telegraph & Chronicle Power Press Print, 1866.

Persec, A., B. M. Norman, and J. H. Colton. *Chart of the Lower Mississippi River.* Library of Congress.

Phisterer, Frederick. *New York in the War of the Rebellion.* Third edition. Albany: J.B. Lyon Co., 1912.

Pickerill, W. N. *History of the Third Indiana* Cavalry. Indianapolis, IN: Aetna Printing Co., 1906.

Pirtle, J. B. *The Battle of Baton Rouge,* Southern Historical Society Papers (SHS). Vol. 8.

Plummer, Albert. *History of the Forty-Eighth Regiment, M.V.M.* Boston: Press of the New England Druggist Co., 1907.

Pollard, E. A. *Life of Jefferson Davis,...* Philadelphia, Chicago, St. Louis, Atlanta: National Publishing Company, 1869.

Porter, David D. *Incidents and Anecdotes of the Civil War.* New York: D. Appleton & Co. 1885.

Powell, W. H. *Army List.* New York: L.R. Hamersly & Co., 1896.

Powell, W. H. *Records of Living Officers in the U.S. Army.* Philadelphia: L.R. Hamersly & Co. 1890.

Powers, G. W. *The Story of the 38th Regiment of Massachusetts Volunteers.* Cambridge: Dakin & Metcalf Press, 1866.

Redpath, James. *The Public Life of Capt. John Brown* Boston: Thayer & Elgridge, 1860.

Rodenbough, T. F. *The Army of the United States.* Edited by T. F. Rodenbough and W. L. Haskin. New York: Maynard, Merrill & Co., 1896.

Rodenbough, T. F., Potter, Henry C., Seal, Wm. P. *History of the Eighteenth Regiment of Cavalry Pennsylvania Volunteers.* New York: Wynkoop, Hallenbeck Crawford Co., 1909.

Rodenbough, T.F. *The Army of the United States.* Edited by T.F. Rodenbough and W.L. Haskin. New York: Maynard, Merrill & Co., 1896.

Russell, William H. *My Dairy North and South.* Boston: T. O. H. P. Burnham, 1863.

Sanger, G. P., ed. *The Statutes at Large, Treaties, and Proclamations of the United States of America.* 18 volumes. Boston: Little, Brown and Company, 1789–1873.

Schaff, Morris. *The Spirit of Old West Point.* Boston and New York: Houghton-Mifflin, 1907.

Scharf, Thomas. *History of the Confederate States Navy from its Organization to the Surrender of its Last Vessel.* New York: Rogers and Sherwoods, 1887.

Schouler, W. B. *A History of Massachusetts in the Civil War.* Boston: Dutton & Co., 1868.

Schwartz, Stephen. *Twenty-Two Months a Prisoner of War.* St. Louis: A. F. Nelson Co., 1892.

Scott, John. *Story of the Thirty Second Iowa Infantry Volunteers.* Nevada, IA: John Scott, 1896.

Scott, Maj. John. *Partisan Life with Mosby.* London: Sampson, Low and Marston, 1867

Scott, R. B. *The History of the 67th Regiment Indiana Infantry Volunteers.* Bedford, IN: Herald Book and Job Printing, 1867.

Scott, Winfield. *Memoirs of Lieut.-General Scott.* New York: Sheldon, 1864.

Selby, P. *The Lincoln-Conkling Correspondence.* Springfield, IL: Illinois Historical Society, 1908.

Semmes, Raphael. *The Cruise of the Alabama and Sumter.* New York: Carleton, 1864.

Sheridan, P. H. *Personal Memoirs of P.H. Sheridan.* Vols. 1–2. New York: C.L. Webster & Co., 1888.

Sherman, William T. "The Grand Strategy of the Last year of the War." *Battles and Leaders of the Civil War,* Vol. 4. New York: The Century Co., 1884, 1888.

Sherman, William T. *Memoirs of General W. T. Sherman.* Second edition. New York: D. Appleton & Co., 1886.

Shorey, Henry A. *The Story of the Maine Fifteenth.* Bridgeton, ME: Bridgeton News Press, 1890.

Simpson, W. A. "The Second Regiment of Artillery." The Army of the United States, Edited by T. F. Rodenbough and W. L. Haskin. New York: Maynard, Merrill & Co. 1896.

Sliger, J. E. "How General Taylor Fought the Battle of Mansfield." *Confederate Veteran,* Vol. 31. Nashville: E. A. Cunningham, October, 1923.

Smith, Daniel P. *Company K First Alabama Regiment.* Prattville, AL: Burke & McFetridge, 1885. Reprint, Jackson County Genealogical Society, 1990.

Smith, W. G. *Life and Letters of Thomas Kilby Smith.* New York and London: G. P. Putnam's Sons, 1898.

Sprague, Homer B. *History of the 13th Infantry Regiment of Connecticut Volunteers.* Hartford, CT: Case, Lockwood & Co., 1867.

Stanyan, John M. *History of the Eighth New Hampshire Volunteers.* Concord, NH: I.C. Evans, 1892.

Stephens, Alexander. *A Constitutional View of the Late War Between the States.* 2 vols. Philadelphia, PA: National Publishing Co., 1868.

Stephenson, N. W. *An Autobiography of Abraham Lincoln.* Indianapolis: Bobbs-Merrill Co., 1926.

Stevens, General H. "*The Battle of Cedar Creek*" A Paper read before the Military Historical Society of Massachusetts, *December 8, 1879*. Cambridge, MA: Riverside Press, 1879.

Stevens, General H. *A Brief Sketch of the life of General Hazard Stevens*. Boston, MA: G. H. Ellis Co., 1908.

Stevens, Wm. B. *History of the Fiftieth Regiment of Infantry, Massachusetts Volunteer Militia*. Boston: Griffith-Stilling Press, 1907.

Sumner, G. C. *Battery D First Rhode Island Light Artillery in the Civil War*. Providence, RI: Rhode Island Printing Co., 1897.

Sutton, J. J. *The History of the Second Regiment West Virginia Cavalry Volunteers*. Portsmouth, OH: 1892.

Table dmna.ny.gov/historic/reghist/civil/infantry/173rdinf/173rdinfTable.htm

Taylor, Richard. *Destruction and Reconstruction*. New York: D. Appleton & Co., 1879.

Tenny, F. A. *War Diary of Luman Harris Tenny*. Cincinnati, OH: Evangelical Publishing House, 1914.

Tiemann, Wm. F. *The 159th Regiment Infantry New York State Volunteers in the War of the Rebellion*. Brooklyn, NY: Wm. F. Tieman, 1891.

Townsend, L. R. *History of the 16th Regiment, New Hampshire Volunteer*. Washington, DC: N.T. Elliot, 1897.

U.S. Census, Ft. Duncan, Eagle Pass Post Office. August 4, 1860.

U.S. Congress. *Annals of the 50th U.S. Congress*. 1890.

U.S. Navy. *Ordnance Instructions*. Washington: U.S. Government Printing Office, 1866.

U.S. War Department. *Revised Regulations for the United States Army*. 1861.

Union Army, The, A History of Military Affairs in the Loyal States, 1861-1865. 8 Vols. Madison, WI: Federal Publishing Co., 1867. (Ref. vol. 2: 133rd New York Regiment).

Urquart, David. "Bragg's Advance and Retreat." *Battles and Leaders of the Civil War*. Vol. 3. 1888.

Van Vleck, George. *The Panic of 1857*. New York: Columbia University Press, 1943.

Vandiver, D. D. "*Two Forgotten Heros.*" The Missouri Historical Review. Vol. 21, April, 1927.

Walke, Henry. "Battles and Leaders of the Civil War, Operations of the Western Flotilla." *The Century Magazine*. January 1885.

Walker, A. F. *The Vermont Brigade in the Shenandoah Valley*. Burlington, VT: The Free Press Association, 1869.

Watkins, Sam R. *Co. "AYTCH."* Chattanooga: Times Printing Co., 1900.

Welles, Gideon. "Admiral Farragut and New Orleans." *The Galaxy Magazine*. November 1871.

Welles, Gideon. *Diary of Gideon Welles*. Vols.1–2. Boston: Houghton-Mifflin, 1911.

Wheeler, Joseph. "Bragg's Invasion of Kentucky." *Battles and Leaders of the Civil War*. Vol. 3. New York: The Century Company, 1887.

Whitcomb, Caroline E. *History of the 2nd Massachusetts Battery*. Concord, NH: The Rumford Press, 1912.

Whitcomb, Caroline E. *History of the Second Massachusetts Battery of Light Artillery 1861-1865.* Concord, NH: The Rumford Press, 1912.

Whittaker, Frederick. *A Complete Life of General George A. Custer.* New York: Sheldon & Co., 1876.

Wilds, T. F. *Record of the One hundred and Sixteenth Regiment Ohio Volunteers.* Sandusky, OH: L. F. Mack & Bro., Printers, 1884.

Willis, Henry A. The Fifty-Third Regiment Massachusetts Volunteers. Fitchburg, MA: Blanchard & Brown, 1889.

Wilson, Gen. James H. *Reminiscences of Grant. The Century Magazine.* October 1885.

Wilson, J. T. *Black Phalanx.* Hartford, CT: The American Publishing Co., 1890.

Wilson, James Grant, and John Fiske, eds. *Appletons' Cyclopedia of American Biography.* 6 volumes. New York: D. Appleton & Co., 1887–1889.

Wood, J. H. *The War.* Cumberland, MO: The Eddy Press, 1916.

Wood, Wales W. *History of the Ninety-Fifth Regiment Illinois Infantry Volunteers.* Chicago: Tribune Co., 1865.

Woods, J. T. *Services of the Ninety-Sixth Ohio volunteers.* Toledo: Blade Printing, 1874.

Woods, W. B. *Cases Argued and Determined in the Circuit Court for the Fifth Judicial Circuit.* Vol. 1. Chicago: Callaghan & Co., 1875.

Woodward, Joseph T. *Historic Record and Complete Biographic Roster Twenty-First Maine Volunteers.* Augusta, Maine: Charles Nash & Sons, 1907.

Woodward, Joseph T. *Historic Record and Complete Biographic Roster Twenty-First Maine Volunteers.* Augusta, Maine: Charles Nash & Sons, 1907.

Additional Sources Online

For more information, the following web sites are among many available:

http://aa.usno.navy.mil/ moon phases & sunrise
http://bioguide.congress.gov
http://dmna.ny.gov/historic/reghist/civil/infantry
http://memory.loc.gov
www.arlingtoncemetery.net/
www.census.gov/history
www.dhr.virginia.gov
www.gpoaccess.gov
www.history.army.mil
www.history.navy.mil
www.nps.gov.archive
www.nps.gov/history/hps/abpp (See also CWSAC.)
www.sos.louisiana.gov/Home/Museums
www.srrb.noaa.gov
https://historicalcharts.noaa.gov/
historicalmaps.arcgis.com/usgs/
https://ngmdb.usgs.gov/topoview/

Index

Page numbers in *italics* indicate illustrations or maps. Notes are indicated by "n".

A

A. W. Baker (steamer), 288
Abbay, George F., 371
Abbeville, S. C., 761
Abbott, Joseph C., 728, 730
Abercrombie Plantation, 137
Abingdon, Va., 738
Abraham's Creek, 629, 633–634, 638n2010
Adams, Henry A., 71–73, 85, 106
Adams, S., 25
Adams, Wirt, 353
Adams Hill, Tex., 48
Agnus, Felix, 412
Ahern, James, 6, 10, 41–42, 78, 95, 126, 140, 194, 256, 461, 496, 564, 703, 714, 768–769
Ahern, Mary, 769
Alabama, CSS, 237–239, 265, 265n1013, 266, 269n1031, 469, 595
Alabama Infantry, 1st, 156, 376, 393, 409, 453
Alabama Infantry, 1st, Company K, 399, 407–408
Alabama Infantry, 7th, 123
Alabama Infantry, 20th, 132
Alabama Infantry, 23rd, 132
Alabama Infantry, 49th, 423
Albatross, USS, 303–304, 356–358, 476
Alden, James, 240, 347
Alexandria, La., 290, 337, 347, 357–361, 370, 372, 477, 494, 497, 500–502, 504, 506, 520, 544–547, 550, 552, 554, 556, 581, 764
Alexandria, Va., 665
Allegheny Mountains, 655
Allen, H. A., *113*, 119, 527, 744
Allen, James A., 297
Allen, James H., 243, 256, 308–309
Allendorf, Christian, 194, 243
Ames, Adelbert, 726, 728, 730
Amherst Courthouse, 739
Amite River, 354
Amsden, A., 435
Anaconda Plan, *85*–86, 88–90, 131, 143, 145, 153, 465, 721
Anderson, Charles, 50, 611
Anderson, J. Patton, 103
Anderson, James, 4, 6
Anderson, Joseph R., 25
Anderson, Richard H., 103–104, 106–107, 120, 128–129, 595–596, 599–600, 606–608, 612–613, 616, 618, 620–623
Anderson, Robert, 29, 74–75
Andrew, John A., 102, 236, 340
Andrews, George L., 400–401, 453–454
Anglin, Edmund, 4, 6–7, 41, 94, 126, 140, 256, 496, 563, 619
Annie (blockade runner), 723
Apalachicola, Fla., 31
Apollo Stables, New Orleans, La., 455, 458, 461
Appleton, Edward L., 109–110, 125–126, 139–140, 185, 189, 194, 243–244, 254, 256, 307, 318, 321, 364, 458, 473, 476, 484–485, 491–492, 496–497, 523, 530–532, 535, 554, 562–563, 571, 619–620, 701–702, 713–714, 742, 763, 768, 776, 778
Appleton, John, 110
Appomattox Court House, 757, 759
Appomattox Station, 756–757
Aransas Pass, 482, *482*–483
Ariel, USS, 238
Arizona, USS, 313, 316, 336, 342, 357–358, 458, 468–469, 471–472, 476
Arizona Cavalry, 2nd, 521
Arizona Cavalry, 3rd, 445–446, 521
Arkadelphia, Ark., 540
Arkansas, CSS, 199–200, 209–211, 213, 269n1031
Arkansas Infantry, 10th, 393, 409
Arkansas Infantry, 15th, 376, 382, 393, 395, 409, 423, 452
Arkansas Infantry, 23rd, 395
Arkansas Infantry Regiment, 1st, 520
Arkansas Light Battery, 6th, 521
Arkansas River, 268

Armstrong (blockade runner), 723
Armstrong, James, 60, 62, 64–65
Army Corps, 1st, 595
Army Corps, 2nd, 596, 736, 752
Army Corps, 4th, 718, 765
Army Corps, 5th, 596, 752–753
Army Corps, 6th, 578–579, 581–583, 592–593, 605, 618, 625, 629, 632–637, 640–641, 646–647, 650, 655, 660, 665, 667–669, 672–673, 683, 685–690, 692, 695–700, 754, 756
Army Corps, 7th, 540
Army Corps, 8th, 583, 641, 650, 667, 677, 682, 689, 694, 697, 700
Army Corps, 9th, 567, 750, 754
Army Corps, 10th, 596
Army Corps, 13th, 274, 462, 477–481, 491, 493, 504, 516, 518, 544, 547, 610
Army Corps, 13th, 1st Division, 486
Army Corps, 13th, 2nd Division, 482
Army Corps, 13th, 3rd Division, 486, 499, 508
Army Corps, 13th, 4th Division, 499
Army Corps, 13th, 4th Division, 1st Brigade, 486–487, 506–507
Army Corps, 14th, 720
Army Corps, 15th, 274, 419, 720, 746
Army Corps, 16th, 350, 504, 518, 521, 526, 531, 560
Army Corps, 16th, 1st Division, 499
Army Corps, 16th, 3rd Division, 499
Army Corps, 17th, 279, 500, 503, 519–520, 533n1727, 560, 746
Army Corps, 18th, 654–655, 725
Army Corps, 19th, 258, 386, 420n1440, 461, 468, 480, 486–487, 491, 493, 499, 527n1707, 560, 562–563, 571, 577, 581–584, 588, 592–593, 600, 625, 629, 632–634, 636–637, 639–641, 646–647, 650, 655, 658, 660, 679, 683–686, 694–700
Army Corps, 19th, 1st Division, 489, 499, 504, 508, 510, 521
Army Corps, 19th, 2nd Division, 499
Army Corps, 19th, 3rd Division, 610
Army Corps, 20th, 720, 746
Army Corps, 23rd, 736
Army Corps, 24th, 728
Army Corps, 25th, x, 728, 754–755, 765
Army of Northern Virginia, 591, 596, 642, 670, 757
Army of Northern Virginia, 2nd Corps, 578
Army of Tennessee, 721, 744, 747

Army of the Confederate States, 46
Army of the Cumberland, 350, 373, 465, 478–479, 561
Army of the James, 297, 567, 581, 725, 752–753
Army of the Mississippi, 180, 268, 271
Army of the Mountain Department, 711
Army of the Ohio, 88, 157, 180, 718
Army of the Potomac, 16n33, 89, 97, 145, 153, 156, 159, 191, 205, 219, 235, 286, 322, 374, 405, 566–567, 571–572, 572n1828, 577, 581–582, 584, 589, 592–593, 596, 598, 614, 657, 736, 763
Army of the Shenandoah, 592–593, 765
Army of the Southwest, 228
Army of the Tennessee, 157, 175, 180, 184, 207, 222, 268, 349, 388, 521, 567
Army of the West, 209
Army of Virginia, 207, 219, 235, 763
Army of West Virginia, 592, 632, *698*, 711
Arnold, Lewis G., 30, 54–56, 78, 105–106, 106n358, 118, 137–139, 187, 191–192, 194, 408n1416
Arnold, Richard, 392, 436, 455, 611
Ashby's Gap, 620
Ashland, Va., 741
Astor, John J., 87
Atchafalaya River, 228, 231–233, 289, 306, 311, 357, 359–360, 378, 441, 458, 468, 477, 500, 558–559
Atlanta, Ga., 72, 236, 350, 494, 621, 642, 700, 715–719
Atlanta Campaign, 575
Atlantic, USS, 78
Atlantic and North Carolina Railroad, 745
Augur, Christopher C., 258, 292, 294–295, 297, 299, 311–312, 354, 367–371, 376, 378–379, 382, 384n1357, 386–389, 391–393, 398, 400–401, 403–405, 409, 412, 421, 423–424, 426, 432, 436, 465, 468, 593, 668, 670, 704, 707, 744
Augusta, Ga., 31
Augusta, USS, 238
Austrian rifles, 271
Averell, William, 585, 588, 590, 592, 595, 598, 600, 618, 625, 631–633, 637–639, 643, 646–649, 652, 710
Avery, Robert, 523
Avoyelles Prairie, La., 557
Ayres, Virgil, 475, 477, 477n1573, 485, 555, 565, 776–778

B

Babcock, Willoughby M., Jr., 135–138, 188, 206, 395–397, 429, 635, 716
Baby, Alexander J., 4, 41, 110, 112, 126, 140, 256, 474, 477, 776
Bache, A. D., 90
Back Road (Va.), 656–658, 660–661, 663, 667, 673, 676–679
Bacon, Edward, 412, 433, 435, 436n1480
Bagby, Arthur P., 521, 527, 541–542, 547, 549, 556
Bailey, Joseph, 420, 420n1440, 545, 552, 554, 558
Bailey, R., 118
Bailey, Theodore, 172
Bainbridge, Edmund C., 391, 396
Baker, Edward D., 108
Baker, Eugene M., 627
Baker, John, 243, 256, 308, 459, 485
Baltic (steamer), 123
Baltimore, Md., 4, 623, 769
Baltimore and Ohio Railroad, 594, 608, 614, 623, 625, 653, 671, 705, 707, 709
Banks, Nathaniel P., 88, 175, 215, 217n842, 219–220, 231, 235–240, 242, 246, 249, 252, 254, 258–261, 263, 265–266, 270, 285–286, 288–290, 292–295, 297, 297n1122, 299–300, 303–305, 311–312, 314–315, 322–324, 327, 329, 337–339, 339n1238, 340–343, 345–349, 359, 361–362, 365, 368, 370, 374–376, 378, 384, 386–388, 391–392, 399–400, 403, 407–408, 408n1416, 409, 411, 414, 416, 418n1432, 419, 421, 423n1445, 432–433, 437–438, 441, 443, 447, 450–451, 453–455, 457, 462, 464–465, 467–468, 471–472, 478, 480–483, 486, 490, 493–495, 499, 503–508, 510, 515–520, 522–523, 530n1715, 535–536, 540, 543–547, 549, 551, 553–554, 556–557, 559–560, 567, 573, 577, 581, 595, 606, 648, 719, 767, 771, 776
Barnard, J. G., 90, 159, 168, 231
Barnes, James, 391
Barnum Hotel, 712
Baron De Kalb, USS, 274, 276, 278
Barrancas Barracks, Fla., 3, 31, 59–60
Barre's Landing, Bayou Cortableau, La., 307, 343, 345, 358, 362–363, 473, 486, 555
Barrett, Richard, 317–318, 321
Barrett, William M., 412
Barron, Samuel, 77
Bartlett, William F., 406, 408
Bates, Edward, 74
Baton Rouge Barracks, La., x, 31
Baton Rouge, La., 145, 177–178, 184, 191, 198–199, 204–205, 211–215, 242, 247–249, 254–256, 258, 263, 291–292, 294–295, 298, 300, 303, 306–307, 312, 342, 346, 354, 368–369, 455, 458, 764–765
Batson, William, 498
Battery L, 1st Regiment of Artillery. *See* United States Artillery, 1st, Battery L
Battle, Cullen, 635
Battle at Cane River Crossing, 546–550
Battle at New Market, 578
Battle of Antietam, 219, 375, 577, 591
Battle of Atlanta, 716
Battle of Averasborough, 746
Battle of Baton Rouge, 375
Battle of Belmont, 143, 146, 221
Battle of Bentonville, 746
Battle of Bethesda Church, 568
Battle of Big Cypress Swamp, x, 4
Battle of Cedar Creek, 619, 677–700, 706, 735
Battle of Cedar Mountain, 219
Battle of Cedarville/Guard Hill/Front Royal, 605
Battle of Chaffin's Farm, 725
Battle of Champion Hill, 349, 367
Battle of Chancellorsville, 374
Battle of Chickamauga, 479, 575
Battle of Cinco de Mayo, 466
Battle of Cold Harbor, 567–569
Battle of Corinth, 672
Battle of Drewry's Bluff, 297
Battle of Fisher's Hill, 643–649, 651
Battle of Fort Fisher, 721–731
Battle of Franklin, 720
Battle of Fredericksburg, 220, 468, 468n1560
Battle of Gettysburg, 453, 464, 478, 577, 591
Battle of Globe Tavern, 607
Battle of Grand Coteau, 486–491
Battle of Helena, 456
Battle of Irish Bend, 23, 336, 501
Battle of Iuka, 184
Battle of Kock's Plantation, 455
Battle of La Fourche, 441–446, 455–456
Battle of Manassas, 576
Battle of Mansfield, 486, 513–517, 523, 540, 585, 633
Battle of Memphis, 287n1091

Battle of North Anna River, 567
Battle of Old Church, 567
Battle of Palmito Ranch, 767
Battle of Pea Ridge, 209
Battle of Pittsburg Landing, 156–157
Battle of Plains Store, 371
Battle of Pleasant Hill, 517–537, 539, 541, 620, 774
Battle of Port Royal Sound, 122
Battle of Ream's Station, 566
Battle of Ridgeway, 779
Battle of Sabine Crossroads, 506–513, 516
Battle of Sabine Pass, *470*–471, 505
Battle of Sailor's Creek, 755–756
Battle of Shiloh, 156–157, 180, 182, 186, 221
Battle of Smithfield Crossing, 616–618
Battle of Southwest Pass, 111–112, 164
Battle of Spotsylvania Court House, 567–568
Battle of Stickney Farm, 666–667
Battle of Stones River, 373, 478
Battle of Stony Creek, 570–571
Battle of Tom's Brook, 657–665, 699n2200
Battle of Trevilian Station, 665
Battle of Weldon Railroad, 569–570
Battle of Westport, 129
Battle of White Oak Road, 752
Battle of Williamsburg, 313
Battle of Winchester, 608, 618, 624–642, 651, 656, 682n2149, 698, 700, 762
Battles of the Wilderness, 567–571. *See also* Overland Campaign
Baylor, John R., 34, 36
Bayou Boeuf, La., 441, 443, 460
Bayou Bourbeau, La., 486n1596, 487
Bayou Cortableau, La., 307, 343, 345, 358, 362–363, 481
Bayou des Allemandes Station, La., 229
Bayou Goula, La., 442
Bayou Pierre, La., 503, 506–507
Bayou Plaquemine, La., 293
Bayou Rapides, La., 501
Bayou Sara, La., 228, 347, 360, 370, 375–376, 384
Bayou Teche, La., 306–307, 311–312, 316–319, 323–336, 338, 487
Beall, L. J., 403, 409, 438
Bean, Sidney A., 412
Beardsley, William E., 627
Beaufort, N. C., 728
Beauregard, P. G. T., 69, 81, 133, 149, 151, 158, 160, 176, 181–182, 186, 197, 208, 366, 577, 601, 717–719, 721, 725, 744, 747, 759, 781
Beaver Dam Station, 740
Becker, Julius, 4, 41, 110, 119, 125–126, 140, 185, 256, 308, 364, 460, 496, 619
Becker, Sgt., 440, 447, 455
Beckett, Michael, 699
Bedow, Mary A., 774
Bee, Andrew, 762
Bee, Hamilton, 518, 521, 527, 546–547, 549
Beeler, Andrew J., 4, 41, 109, 117, 119, 125–126, 139, 140n477
Beglan, James, 6, 10, 41, 126, 140, 256, 364, 460, 496, 564, 714, 769, 773
Beiber, Peter, 714
Bell, Henry H., 198–199, 472–473, 481
Belle Grove Plantation, 676, 685, *685*–687
Belle Grove, Va., 667
Bellevue Road, 488
Benedict, Lewis, 381, 433, 435–436, 514, 521–523, 525–526, 531–534
Benedict's Brigade, 436, 523, 531, 533–534
Benjamin, George, 4, 6
Benjamin, Judah P., 66, 123–124, 132, 134, 166, 174
Benjamin, William H., 627
Bennett, Thomas W., 283
Bennett House, 412, 417
Benson, Solon, 534
Benton, USS, 203, *203*
Bentonville, N. C., 746
Bermuda Hundred Campaign, 571
Berry, Thomas C., 498
Berryman, O. H., 61–62, 64–65
Berryville, Va., 584, 601, 606–607, 612, 618, 620–621, 624, 705
Berryville Canyon, 634
Berryville Pike, 622, 625, 628, 632–636
Berwick Bay, La., 231–232, 259, 262–263, 293, 311, 313–314, 361, 441, 457–458, 468, 480–481
Berwick Bay (steamer), 288
Berwick City, La., 231, 310, 340, 362, 372, 412, 414, 473, *478*
Betterton, George, 498
Beverly, W. V., 700, 708
Biaro, Italo, 498
Bicknell, George F., 523
Bieber, Peter, 255–256, 496
Big Black River, 367, 376
Biloxi, Miss., 124

Birge, Henry, 327, 330, 334, 388, 390, 397, 431, 438, 451, 545, 547–548, 635
Birney, William, 654–655
Bisland Plantation, 316, 648–649
Bissell, John, 4, 6–8, 41–42, 44, 768
Bissell, Josiah W., 271
Black, Jeremiah S., 22, 51
Black Bayou, 280
Black Creek, 779
Black Hawk, USS, 542
Black River, 272, 289, 347
Blackburn, William D., 354–355
Blackwater Bay, Fla., 134, 138
Blair, Francis P., Sr., 731–734
Blair, Henry W., 402, 417
Blair, Montgomery, 74, 731
Blair's Landing, 519n1689, *519*, 541–542
Blake, Homer C., 265
Blanchard, A. G., 227
Blanchard, Justus W., 549
Blenheim (blockade runner), 723
Bliss, Zenas, 48–49
Blue Ridge Mountains, 652, 655, 706, 738
Blunt, Mathew M., 56, 115
Boardman, Frederick A., 412
Boeuf Station, 442
Boggs, W. R., 356
Boone, R. M., 371
Boonsboro, Md., 578
Boston, Mass., 4, 6, 102, 313
Boutte Station, La., 228–229, 232, 442
Bowling Green, Ky., 146, 148–149, 151
Bowman's Ford, 675
Bowman's Mill, 676
Bradbury, Albert W., 628
Bradley, Theodore, 448
Bragg, Braxton, 69–73, 75, 79, 81, 85, 96–98, 103, 107–108, 110, 112, 119–124, 128–134, 143, 156–157, 161, 163–164, 174, 176n663, 183, 186, 206, 208–209, 234, 268n1022, 286, 350, 373, 465, 478–479, 479n1578, 494, 575, 654, 654n2063, 719, 725–727, 730–731, 745, 761
Bragshaw, William, 498
Brannan, John M., 30, 52–53, 190
Brashear City, La., 311–314, 343, 345, 362, 370, 391, 441–443, 458, 460, 473, 477, 480
Braxton, Carter M., 625, 628, 635
Brazos Harbor, Tex., 481
Brazos Island, Tex., 482
Brazos Santiago, Tex., x, 2, 32, 37, 40, 42–43, 482, *482*, 766–768
Breckinridge, John C., 22, 157, 212, 214–215, 577–578, 580, 598, 615, 625, 628–629, 631, 634, 637, 639, 644, 744, 750, 761–762
Breckinridge, W. C. P., 761
Breen, Michael, 255–256, 459, 485, 496, 714
Breese, Kidder, 730
Brent, J. L., 521, 526, 764
Brewer, Melvin, 627
Briery Branch Gap, 654
Briggs, Joseph B., 391
Brinton, William P., 627
Bristol, Va., 738
Broady, Elias H., 73
Brook, Thomas, 4, 41–42, 78, 94–95, 99, 109, 125–126, 139, 185, 190, 194
Brooklyn, USS, 67–68, 71–72, 81, 89, 171, 176–177, 199–200, 609–610
Brooks, William, 255, 474, 484
Brosenham, John, 187
Brown, E. B., 766–767
Brown, George, 289–290
Brown, Harvey, 16, 74, 77–81, 83–86, 89, 92–93, 98, 100–101, 103, 103n347, 105–107, 110, 112, 117–122, 128, 136–137, 160, 463–464
Brown, I. N., 275
Brown, John, 607
Brown, Joseph E., 716–717
Brown, Stephen E., 498, 618
Brown, William F., 4, 41–42, 78, 95, 126, 140, 194, 256, 459, 474, 496, 555, 564, 703, 775
Brown's Gap, 652–653
Brownsville, Tex., 1–2, 43, 482–483, 567, 766–767
Bruce, William, 194, 243
Brunskill, William C., 4, 41–42, 94, 99, 109, 125, 139, 185, 190, 194, 243, 254, 256, 308, 364, 460, 474, 485–486, 492, 496, 499, 555–556, 565, 619–620
Bryan, Michael K., 436, 679
Bryan's Brigade, 436, 679
Bryant, George, 350
Buchanan, Franklin, 264–265, 608, 611
Buchanan, James, 11, 22–23, 25, 28–29, 51, 65–67, 74, 259
Buchanan, Thomas, 232–233
Buchell, Carl, 521, 527, 535
Buckley, John, 41, 109, 126, 140n477, 257, 364, 383

Buckner, Mrs. Simon, 201
Buckner, Simon B., 146, 764–765
Buckton Ford, Va., 670, 677, 689
Buell, Don Carlos, 29, 146–149, 151–153, 157, 182–183, 204, 207, 209, 666
Buffalo, N.Y., 4, 769–770, 772, 775, 777–779
Bull Run Mountains, 706
Bullen, Joseph D., 443–447, 447n1510
Bunker Hill, W. V., 598, 612, 616–617, 625–626, 632, 639
Burbridge, John Q., 486, 486n1596, 487–488
Bureau of Pensions, Dept. of the Interior, 769, 773
Burey's Point, 199
Burke, John, 6, 41, 126, 140, 257, 308, 496, 564, 703–704
Burkeville Junction, Va., 570
Burns, S. P., 520
Burnside, Ambrose, 130, 220, 286, 292n1108, 374, 468, 468n1560, 567
Burr's Landing, La., 290
Burt, Charles A., 397, 407
Burton's Crossing, 547–548
Bush, William M., 546
Butler, Andrew, 226–227
Butler, Benjamin F., 88, 89n285, 91–92, 102, 138, 144–145, 158, 160, 165, 167–168, 172–174, 177, 179, 184, 190–191, 197–199, 204–205, 211, 215–218, 220, 223–231, 233–236, 236n923, 239–242, 251–253, 259–260, 264, 292–293, 310n1149, 341, 491, 491n1616, 567, 569, 571, 572n1828, 577, 581, 602, 612, 715, 724–728, 730, 752
Butte-la-Rose, La., 262, 293, 316, 357, 414
Byrne, Charles C., 245

C

Cahill, Thomas W., 213
Cailloux, Andre, 454–*455*
Cain, Isaac T., 4, 41, 94–95, 126, 139, 140n477, 255–256, 308, 496, 619
Cairo, Ill., 146–147, 151, 153, 174, 205, 220–221, 236, 266, 285
Cairo, USS, 90
Calais, Me., 778
Calcasieu River, 469
Calhoun, John C., 15, 21
Calhoun, USS, 233, 264, 313, 336, 342
California Road, 17
Callsen, Paul, 771, 777n2415

Cameron, Robert A., 488, 508, 510–511, 514, 516, 547
Cameron, Simon, 74–75, 87–88, 102, 252
Cameron's Depot, W. V., 612
Camp Alburquielas, Tex., 39, 42
Camp Barry, Washington, D. C., 566, 571, 581, 593
Camp Briggs, Mass., 252
Camp Brown, Santa Rosa Island, 103–105
Camp Colorado, Tex., 45
Camp Cooper, Tex., 31, 44–45, 245
Camp Emory, Franklin, La., 493
Camp Ford, Tex., 513, 517, 774
Camp Groce, Tex., 442
Camp Hudson, Tex., xi, 45
Camp Jackson, Fla., 140, 140n477, 141
Camp Kearney, La., 232, 455, 461
Camp Moore, Tangipahoa, La., 163, 198
Camp on Rio Grande, 45
Camp Parapet, La., 191, 260, 301
Camp Pratt, La., 490
Camp Russell, Va., 700
Camp Stevens, La., 234, 264
Camp Sumter, Andersonville, Ga., 297
Camp Verde, Tex., xi, 32, 34–35, 45, 49–50, 245
Camp Walton, Fla., 141
Camp Weitzel, La., 265
Camp Wood, Tex., 45
Campbell, J. A., 733
Campbell, James, 243, 257, 459, 496, 620, 641, 672, 702, 713–714, 740, 742, 777
Campbell, John, 100
Campbell, John A., 760
Canby, E. R. S., 463, 559, 559n1790, 560–562, 567, 582, 608, 611, 621, 718, 736, 760–761, 763, 765–766
Cane River, 502, 545–550
Canonicus, USS, 729
Cape Fear River, 721–722, 727, 746
Capehart, Henry, 627
Card, Rowland, 257, 496, 619, 699, 777
Carleton, William, 498
Carlisle Barracks, Penn., 13
Carney, David, 498
Carondelet, USS, 156, 209, 280, 551
Carr, Edward, 4, 6
Carr, Gouverneur, 403
Carrion Crow Bayou, 480, 486–487, 489–490
Carroll, Patrick, 41, 126, 140n477, 189
Carroll's Mill, La., 505, 511
Carrollton, La., 163, 232, 260, 458, 461, 479

Carruth, William W., 391
Carson, Catharine, 773
Carter, J. W., 628, 675, 677, 692
Casey, John, 4, 41, 140, 257, 364, 447, 460
Casey, Patrick, 126
Cash, John C., 72
Cass, Lewis, 22
Castle Pinckney, Charleston, S.C., 27n56
Cavalry Corps of the Middle Military Division, 110
Cayuga, USS, 172, 469
Cedar Bayou, 483
Cedar Creek Grade, 657
Cedar Creek, Va., 643, 665, 667–668, 670–674, 676–699, 706, 735, 748
Chalmers, James R., 103–104, 350
Chalmette Regiment, 169, 169n629, 172
Chamberlain, William W., 642
Chambersburg, Penn., 589–590, 598, 602, 710
Champion, Henry, 243, 255, 257, 460, 474, 485–486, 496, 771, 777
Champion No. 3 (pump boat), 549–550
Champion No. 5 (pump boat), 545, 549–550
Chapin, Edward P., 389, 391, 404, 406, 412
Chapman, George H., 627, 640
Charles City Court House, 569
Charleston, S. C., 721, 736, 745
Charlestown, W. V., 593, 607, 612–613, 621, 624, 742
Charlottesville, Va., 569, 578, 652, 668–670, 735, 737–739
Chase, George, 243, 257, 308, 364, 442–443, 460, 474–475, 485, 492, 499, 555–556, 565, 620, 702, 713–714, 742, 777
Chase, Salmon P., 74, 225, 285
Chase, William H., 62, 64–65, 68, 71
Chattanooga, Tenn., 153, 156, 182–183, 204, 207, 209, 350, 478–479, 479n1578, 575, 717–718
Che Kiang (steamer), 242, 246, 248, 461
Chesapeake and Ohio Canal, 623, 653
Chesnut, James, 719
Chesterfield, S. C., 745
Chicago Mercantile Battery, 508, 511
Chickahominy River, 568
Chickasaw, USS, 611
Chickering, Thomas E., 372, 383n1355, 391, 412
Childers mansion, 520, 523, 526
Chillicothe, USS, 274, 276–278, 278n1055, 279, 281–282, 519, 551

Chilton, R. H., 97
Choctaw, USS, 440
Christy, David, 12
Churchill, Thomas, 516, 520, 522, 525–526, 531–532, 532n1721, 534, 541
Cincinnati, Ohio, 4
Cincinnati, USS, 202, 280
Citadel/Confederate Battery XXXIII, 433–434, 437, 439, 447–449
City Belle, USS, 556
City of Vicksburg, CSS, 288–289
City Point, Va., 585, 657, 712, 724, 733, 739–741, 747, 765
Clack, Franklin, 321, 326, 329, 339
Clark, George W., 433
Clark, John H., 520
Clark, Orton S., 386–387, 635
Clark, Thomas S., 403, 412, 433–434, 436
Clark's Gap, W. V., 584
Clarksville, Tenn., 152, 201
Clay, Clement C., Jr., 66, 574
Clay, Henry, 21
Clifton, USS, 313, 315n1160, 316–317, 317n1171, 324, 342, 357, 458, 468–469, 471–472
Clifton, Va., 621
Clinton, La., 416
Clinton, Thomas, 255, 257, 496, 499, 536, 539, 714, 742, 763
Clinton, USS, 482
Clinton Plank Road, 297, 299
Clinton Railroad, 369, 371, 376, 378, 389
Closson, Henry W., 92, 109–110, 112, 114–116, 119–120, 125–126, 139–140, 140n477, 141, 185, 188–189, 191–194, 243, 247, 254, 256, 294, 307–309, 318, 333, 338, 363, 391, 439, 448, 458, 461, 473, 476, 484, 491, 496–497, 499, 515, 521, 527n1707, 547–548, 554, 558, 562–563, 610–611, 619–620, 701–702, 712, 714, 742, 763, 768, 771–772, 776
Cloutierville, La., 547
Coast Artillery, 9th, 780
Cobb, Howell, 22
Cockefair, James F., 521
Cockspur Island, Ga., 31
Cohen, Patrick, 437
Cold Harbor, Va., 567–569
Coldwater River, 273–274, 276
Colorado, USS, 98, 111, 168
Columbia, S. C., 735, 745

Columbia, Va., 740
Columbia Furnace, Va., 664, 664n2099
Columbus, Ky., 143
Comfort, James, 243, 257, 364, 459–460, 485, 496, 714
Comite River, 354
Conant, Charles E., 438
Concord, N.H., xii
Conemaugh, USS, 611
Confederate Army of Tennessee, 731
Confederate batteries, 82, 91–92, 128, 199, 417, 570, 696
Confederate command, 121, 240, 304, 342, 350, 472, 604, 622, 756, 767
Confederate Congress, 601, 744–745
Confederate Department of Southwestern Virginia, 602, 644, 738
Confederate District of Southwestern Virginia and East Tennessee, 604
Confederate government, 46, 48, 65–66, 69, 132, 136, 160–161, 189, 209, 228, 234, 237, 574, 602, 708, 732–733
Confederate gunboats, 201, 289, 342, 609
Confederate guns, 79, 117–118, 271, 301, 357, 403, 548, 550
Confederate Missouri State Guard, 602
Confederate Partisan Rangers. *See* Partisan Rangers
Confederate States, 46–48, 65, 68, 83
Confederate Subsistence Department, 722
Confederate sympathizers. *See* Southern sympathizers
Confederate Trans-Mississippi Department, 761
Confederate War Department, 25, 69, 96, 122–123, 132, 160–161, 164–165
Congress, USS, 577
Connecticut Infantry Regiment, 6th, 242
Connecticut Infantry Regiment, 9th, 197, 199, 211, 213
Connecticut Infantry Regiment, 12th, 231, 233, 242, 322, 389, 394, 420, 425, 429–430, 458, 471, 682
Connecticut Infantry Regiment, 13th, 216, 231, 233, 241, 295, 309, 317–322, 327, 331–332, 335, 361–362, 374, 376, 390, 398, 431, 438, 452, 458, 703
Connecticut Infantry Regiment, 23rd, 242, 263
Connecticut Infantry Regiment, 24th, 241, 314, 339, 390, 425, 429
Connecticut Infantry Regiment, 25th, 241, 314, 319, 321, 327–332, 332n1215, 334–335, 390, 397, 431
Connecticut Infantry Regiment, 26th, 241, 391, 401, 403, 433, 435
Connecticut Infantry Regiment, 28th, 242, 246, 391, 414, 425, 429–430
Connell, Jeremiah, 41, 126, 140, 257, 484, 491, 496, 498, 619
Conner, James, 667, 680
Connor, James, 498–499
Connors, Patrick, 498
Conroy, Elizabeth, 4, 40, 122
Conroy, Thomas, 3–4, 40–41, 109, 119, 122
Conscription Act of April 16, 1862, 189
Consolidated Crescent Regiment, 521
Cook, Charles, 255, 257
Cook, Joseph J., 471
Cook, Philip, 751
Cooke, Augustus P., 342
Cooke, Charles, 496, 619, 701, 714
Cooley house, 677
Cooper, D. H., 767
Cooper, S., 33, 158
Cooper, Theodore, 117
Cordon, John, 433n1472, 435
Cordova Scheme, 764–765
Corinth, Miss., 131, 133, 149, 156–160, 174–175, 178–186, 204, 206–208, 222, 227, 350, 367, 373, 388
Cornay, Florian O., 316–317, 329, 331–332, 549
Cornie, CSS, 336
Corps d'Afrique Regiment, 1st, 482
Corps d'Afrique Regiment, 6th, 454
Corps d'Afrique Regiment, 7th, 454
Corps d'Afrique Regiment, 8th, 454
Corps d'Afrique Regiment, 9th, 454
Corps d'Afrique Regiment, 10th, 454
Corps d'Afrique Regiment, 16th, 482
Corps d'Afrique Regiment, 25th, 755
Corps d'Afrique Regiments, 499, 504, 518, 771. *See also* Louisiana Native Guards
Corpus Christi Pass, 483
Corse, J. M., 543
Cortinas, Juan Nepumuseno, xi, 1, 482–483
Cotterill, Edmond, 41, 126, 140n477, 243, 254, 257, 459, 477, 484, 486, 491, 496, 498, 554, 563, 619, 768
Counselman, Jacob, 571
Coushatta Chute, 540, 542, *542*
Covington, USS, 556

Cowles, David S., 403, 412
Cox, Chambers, 423
Coyne, Owen, 10, 41, 126, 140, 257, 496, 714, 769–770
Craffy, Patrick, 6, 41–42, 126, 140n477, 257, 459, 474, 485, 496, 555, 564, 620, 701, 703, 714, 775
Craven, Thomas, 71, 171, 176
Creed, William, 6, 41, 95, 126, 140, 257, 492, 496, 564, 703, 714
Creighton, John, 105–106
Creole (steamer), 191, 195
Crescent (steamer), 443, 581
Crescent Regiment, 510, 527
Cricket, USS, 519, 549
Crimean War, 11–12
Crittenden, George B., 146
Crocker, Frederick, 469, 471–472
Crook, George, 583–584, 584n1869, 587–588, 592, 595, 599, 605–606, 621–623, 625–626, 628, 632–633, 635, 637, 639–640, 643–647, 654–655, 667–668, 673, 676–682, 684, 686, 700, 711–712
Cross Keys, Va., 654
Crowley, William, 243, 257, 308, 364, 460, 474, 485, 492, 496, 499, 555–556, 565, 620, 702, 713–714, 742, 777
Crump's Hill, 503
Crusader, USS, 53, 55, 71, 81
Cullum, George W., 149, 151–152, 179
Culpeper, Va., 566–567, 589, 652
Cumberland, Md., 711
Cumberland, USS, 577
Cumberland Raid, 711–712
Cumberland River, 90, 144, 146–147
Cummings, Patrick, 6, 41–42, 78, 94–95, 99, 126, 140n477, 257, 496, 564, 703–704, 713
Cunningham, Edward, 532n1722, 556
Cunningham, Peter, 6
Cupp's Ford, 677–678
Curran, Robert, 41, 95, 109, 126, 140, 185, 194
Currie, L. D. H., 428, 428n1457
Curtin, Patrick, 498
Curtis, Newton M., 726, 729–730
Curtis, Samuel R., 602
Custer, George A., 616, 626–627, 629–630, 630n1980, 631–633, 637–639, 643, 651–652, 655n2067, 656, 656n2067, 657–659, 659n2079, 660, 660n2087, 661–663, 664n2099, 665, 667–670, 673–674, 678, 691, 696, 698, 710, 735–737, 739–741, 757
Cutshaw, Wilfred E., 596, 600, 608, 623, 653, 656
Cuyler, W. C., 647, 653, 699

D

Dailey, Darby, 498
Daily, James, 712
Dalrymple, W. C., 44
Dalton, Ga., 350
Dana, Charles, 225, 280, 282–283, 285–286, 411, 583, 587, 754
Dana, John W., 448–449
Dana, N. J. T., 482
Daniel Rusk (steamer), 768
Daniel Webster (steamer), *43*–44, 53n148
Danville, Va., 759
Danville Railroad, 747, 752
Darrow, Caroline B., 34–35
Dauphin Island, *609*–611
David's Ferry, 556
Davis, Charles H., 90, 197, 199–205, 210–211, 228
Davis, E. J., 766
Davis, George W., 498
Davis, Henry, 573
Davis, Jefferson, 5, 46, 65–66, 70, 77, 85, 134, 161, 165–166, 209, 234, 310n1149, 365, 365n1299, 366, 494, 494n1625, 541, 573, 575–576, 602, 612, 654n2063, 715–717, 719, 722, 732–733, 735, 744, 748, 751, 755, 759–762, 765, 767
Davis, Theodore, 82–83
Dawson, Samuel K., xi, 2–3, 17, 20, 39, 41–42, 56, 94, 99, 109, 560
Dawson, Sarah, 240, 341
Day, Nicholas, 319, 432
De Gournay, Paul F., 369
De Kalb, USS, 278n1055
De Soto (steamer), 289
Deal, Charles/Enos, 244, 257, 474, 476, 610
DeBray, X. B., 521, 525n1701, 527, 535, 547–549
Decrow's Point, Tex., 483
Deep Bottom, 588, 591, 596, *596*–597, 607, 741
Deer Point, Fla., 134–135, 138
Deering, John, 243, 255, 257, 460, 474, 777
Delafield, Richard, 726
Delaware Battery, 1st., 548
Demarest, William, 4, 41, 126, 140, 185, 256,

364, 460, 477, 496, 555, 563, 571, 619, 714, 776–777
Democratic Party, 22, 88, 91, 93, 165, 216, 235, 573, 576, 612, 641, 731
Denison, George S., 225–227
Dennis, Elias, 610n1935
Department of Alabama and West Florida, 186
Department of Alabama, Mississippi, and East Louisiana, 760
Department of Arkansas, 493, 559
Department of Cairo (Ill.), 146, 285
Department of Mississippi, 208
Department of Mississippi and East Louisiana, 227, 274
Department of North Carolina, 721
Department of Southern Mississippi and East Louisiana, 184, 209
Department of Texas, 46n116, 162n592
Department of the Cumberland, 574
Department of the East, 566, 776
Department of the Gulf, 175, 191, 236, 241, 249, 251, 254, 270, 304, 341, 388, 408n1416, 463, 478–479, 491, 504, 559, 562, 587, 602, 610–611, 780
Department of the Mississippi, 157, 183, 209
Department of the Missouri, 145, 560–561, 602, 763
Department of the Ohio, 145, 478
Department of the Potomac, 145
Department of the South, 216, 217n843, 252, 745
Department of the Susquehanna, 587–588
Department of the Tennessee, 222, 478
Department of the Trans-Mississippi, 337, 540, 763–765, 767
Department of the West, 90
Department of Virginia and North Carolina, 728
Department of Washington, 587–588
Department of West Virginia, 577, 584, 587–588, 593, 712, 736
Des Allemands station, 447
Desertions, viii, ix, 6–10, 17, 39, 42, 44, 78, 98, 122, 141, 156, 182, 206, 270, 297, 308–311, 313, 337–338, 416, 418–419, 433–434, 438, 459, 461, 473–476, 485–487, 565, 702–704, 714, 722, 740, 742, 749, 768–769, 772–777
Detroit, Mich., 4
Devil's Hollow, 709
Devin, Thomas, 605–607, 612, 616, 626–627, 629–630, 632, 638, 643–644, 647–651, 653–654, 657, 661, 663–664, 664n2102, 665, 689–691, 696, 698–699, 736, 739–741
Devine, Thomas J., 34
Di Cesnola, Louis P., 617–618
Diana, CSS, 311, 324–325, 331, 333–334
Diana, USS, 233, 264, 312n1153, 336
Dibrell, G. C., 761
Dickey, William H., 499, 504, 518
Dickson, Clark, 255, 257, 364, 460, 474
Dimick, Justin, xii, 49
Dinwiddie Court House, 570, 753
District of Texas, 765
Division of West Mississippi, 559–560
Dix, John A., 48
Dobie, J. H., 105
Dodge, Charles E., 4, 6
Dodge, Grenville, 350
Donaldsonville, La., 228, 232–233, 307, 312–313, 369, 442–443, 447, 455–458, 460–461
Donnelly, Patrick, 4, 10, 41–42, 126, 140, 257, 496, 564, 714, 770–771
Double Bridges, 570
Douglas, Stephen A., 22
Dow, Neal, 189, 195, 391, 401, 403, 412
Dry Tortugas, Fla., 54
Du Pont, Henry A., 628
Du Pont, Samuel F., 90, 122, 375
Duane's Engineer Company, 78
Dubois, Cesar, 498
Duckport Canal, 550
Dudley, N. A. M., 369, 391, 404–406, 423, 457, 505, 509
Duffey, T., 118
Duffield's Depot, 709
Duffy, Thomas, 4, 6
Duganne, A. J. H., 239
Duke, Basil W., 761–762
Dulany, R. H., 661, 663
Dumas, F. E., 219
Duncan, Ashbell F., 627
Durland, Coe, 627
Duryea, R. C., 115, 395, 423, 425, 453
Duval, Isaac, 628, 639
Dwight, William, 303, 312–313, 316–317, 327, 333–335, 339, 339n1238, 349, 358–359, 372, 384–385, 388–389, 391, 393–394, 398–399, 408, 412, 416–419, 421, 423, 423n1445, 424, 432–436, 436n1480, 439,

447, 449, 514–515, 518, 521–523, 525–526, 528, 530, 530n1715, 532, 534, 592, 628, 634–637, 682, 682n2149

E
Eagle Pass, Tex., 19
Early, Jubal A., 578–580, 581n1859, 582–585, 587–593, 595–596, 598–600, 605–607, 612–618, 620–626, 628–629, 631–635, 637, 639–647, 649–654, 656, 659, 665, 667–671, 673–674, 676–679, 687, 689, 692–697, 699–700, 705, 710, 712, 725, 735, 737–738, 741, 748
Eastport, Me., 778
Eastport, USS, 545, 549, 552
Eaton, S. M., 359
Ebel, Christopher, 94–95, 99
Echols, John, 738
Eckert, Thomas, 733–734
Edwards, Oliver, 627, 672
Edwards Ferry, 583
Edwards James M., 498
Egan, John, 571
Eisele, Joseph, 255, 257, 308, 496, 555, 714
Elkin's Ford, Ark., 540
Ellen (steamer), 343
Ellet, Alfred, 202, 210–211, 228, 287, 287n1091, 356–357, 502
Ellet, Charles, 90, 200, 202–203, 210n808, 287n1091, 556
Ellet, Charles Rivers, 288–290
Elliott, W. L., 181–182
Ellis Bluffs, Miss., 199
Emancipation Proclamation, 251–252, 254
Emerald, USS, 542
Emerson, Frank, 506–509, 512
Emma, USS, 556
Emma Henry (blockade runner), 723
Emory, William H., 258, 292, 297, 299, 311–312, 314–315, 323–324, 326, 338, 341, 370, 370n1317, 371n1324, 389, 443, 446–447, 450, 468, 477, 491, 493, 499, 501, 504, 508, 510, 513–514, 516, 518, 520–521, 523, 525–526, 530, 532, 534, 547–548, 558, 562, 581, 592–593, 599, 605–607, 628, 632–633, 636, 643, 674, 679–681, 684, 686, 692
Enfield rifles, 228, 330, 617, 658
Engineer Regiment of the West, 271
Enrica, SS, 237
Epps, Edwin, 358–359

Epps Plantation, 358–359
Era No. 5 (steamer), 289
Erben, Henry, 62
Erie Railroad, 11–12
Erving, John, xii
Escambia River, 137
Essex, USS, 210, 210n813, 211, 213, 228, 240, 269n1031, 299, 301, 369, 415
Estrella, USS, 233, 264–265, 313, 317, 336, 342, 357–358, 458, 611
Evans, Clement A., 635, 674–675, 677, 695–696
Evens, Phillip, 475, 477, 477n1573, 485, 555, 565
Everett, Charles, 412
Ewell, Richard S., 578, 756
Ewens, Philip, 776–778
Ewens, Phillipe Milton E. *See* Ewens, Philip
Ewing (steamer), 104

F
Fair Play, CSS, 228
False River, 550
Falvey, Michael, 498
Fannin, Dominick, 740
Farabee, Harvey, 627
Farragut, David G., 138, 145, 158, 160, 166–170, 173–175, 177–179, 197–200, 203–205, 210–211, 213, 228, 231, 234, 240–241, 260, 265, 287, 292–295, 299–305, 345–346, 346n1254, 347, 356–359, 369, 384, 392, 421, 457–458, 472, 476, 608–612, 621, 642, 724, 781
Farragut, Loyall, 610
Farragut and Butler expedition, 160, 167–179
Farrand, Ebenezer, 61–62, 62n179, 64
Farrell, Bernard, 5, 41–42, 126, 140n477, 194, 257, 459
Fayetteville, N. C., 745
Fearing, Hawkes, 389–390, 394, 409
Feeley, William, 498
Fenian Brotherhood, 778–780
Fenian Invasion of Canada, 778–780
Feret, James, 451
Ferguson, John, 498–499, 536, 539
Ferguson, S. W., 761
Ferrari, Prosper, 6, 41, 126, 140, 257, 492, 496, 564, 699, 703–704
Fessenden, Francis, 531n1719, 547, 549
Field, Charles, 753, 757
First Battle of Winchester, 606
First Confiscation Act, 96–98, 136

Fisher's Hill, Va., 599–600, 618, 643–644, 648, 651, 658, 660, 665, 667, 669–670, 674–675, 697–698, 725
Fiske, Stuart W., 316–317
Fitch, G. N., 160, 200–203
Fitts, James F., 430
Fitzhugh, Charles L., 740
Fitzpatrick, Benjamin, 66–67
Five Forks, Va., 748, 752–754
Flag Pond Battery, 727
Flanagin, Harris, 764
Flannery, Thomas, 376
Fleming, Daniel H., 498
Flint, Charles A., 6, 41, 94, 126, 140, 243, 254, 257, 308–*309*
Flint, Sarah, 308
Florida, CSS, 237
Florida Infantry Regiment, 1st, 103
Flory, Aaron, 511
Floyd, John B., 16, 22–25, 28–30, 151, 151n524
Flynn, Arthur, 244, 257, 459, 474–475, 497, 563, 715
Flynn, Emily, 4, 40
Flynn, James, 3–4, 40–41, 126, 140, 256, 461, 485, 497, 619
Flynn, Mary, 4, 40
Flynn, Patrick, 5–6, 8
Flynn, Thomas, 4, 40
Foley, Christopher, 5, 41–42, 78, 126, 140, 185, 257, 459
Fonda, John G., 487
Foote, A. H., 71, 90, 130, 147–151, 151n524, 152–154, 156, 159–160, 166, 174, 179–180, 200–201, 203, 207, 225, 556
Foote, Edward A., 255, 257, 308, 497, 715
Ford De Russy, 500
Forey, Élie Frédéric, 466
Forney, J. W., 23n45
Forney, John H., 186
Forrest, Nathan Bedford, 350n1272, 720, 761
Forsberg, Augustus, 629, 630n1980, 631
Forsyth, George A., 673, 696
Fort Babcock, Md., 412
Fort Barrancas, Fla., 31, 59–62, 71, 79, *79*, 116, 118, 156, 185, 187, 249
Fort Beauregard, Bay Point, S.C., 122
Fort Beauregard, La., 261–262, 500
Fort Bisland, La., 246, 259, 261–263, 311, 316, 500
Fort Bliss, Tex., 45–46
Fort Breckinridge, Ariz., 46

Fort Brown, Brownsville, Tex., x, xi, 1–2, 8, 14, 16–17, 32, 37, 42, 44–45, 768, 771–773, 776
Fort Buchanan, La., 442
Fort Burton, La., 261, 342, 500
Fort Butler, La., 263n1001, 442–445, 447
Fort Campbell, N. C., 730
Fort Caswell, Wilmington, N. C., 721–722, 730
Fort Chadbourne, Tex., 45, 47, 770
Fort Clark, Brackettville, Tex., xi, 1, 34, 45
Fort Clark, N.C., 92
Fort Collier, Va., *640*
Fort Columbus, N.Y., x, 4, 13–14, 731, 769
Fort Dallas, Miami, Fla., x
Fort Davis, Tex., 45
Fort Delaware, Del., 770
Fort DeRussy, La., 261–262, 287, 289, 289n1098, 290, 343, 357–359
Fort Desperate, La., 376, 393–398, 429, 439
Fort Donelson, Tenn., 130, 132, 146, 148–152, 221, 754
Fort Douglas, Utah, 772–773
Fort Drewry, Va., 755
Fort Duncan, Eagle Pass, Tex., xi, 6–7, 17–20, 27, 32, 37–41, 44–45, 461, 475, 589, 768–769, 773
Fort Erie, Canada, 779
Fort Esperanza, Tex., 483
Fort Fillmore, N.M., 46
Fort Fisher, Wilmington, N. C., 721, 721n2269, 722, 724–731, 736, 743
Fort Foote, Tenn., 221
Fort Gaines, Dauphin Island, Ala., 31, 108, 608, 610–611
Fort Gilmer, Va., 655
Fort Gregg, Va., 755
Fort Grigsby, Tex., 471–472
Fort Hamilton, N.Y., 44, 78, 86, 772
Fort Harrison, Va., 655
Fort Haskell, Va., *749–750*
Fort Heiman, Ky., 146–149
Fort Henry, Tenn., 130, 132, 146–151, 221
Fort Hindman, Ark., 268
Fort Hindman, USS, 519, 549, 551, 553
Fort Independence, Boston, Mass., 30, 54
Fort Inge, Tex., 45
Fort Jackson, Ga., 31
Fort Jackson, La., 31, 161, 163, 166, 168–172, 246, 260, 408n1416
Fort Jackson, Va., 639–*640*
Fort Jay, N. Y., 13n24

Fort Jefferson, Tortugas, Fla., 30, 42, 51, 53–56, 76, 78, 89, 294, 705, 768
Fort Jesup, La., 503
Fort Jesup Road, 526, 531, 532n1721, 533
Fort Kelly, Va., 707
Fort Lancaster, Sheffield, Tex., xi
Fort Leavenworth, Kans., 2, 16
Fort Macomb, La., 31, 176, 260
Fort Macon, Goldsboro, N. C., 770
Fort Mason, Tex., 45
Fort Massachusetts, Ship Island, Miss., 31
Fort McAllister, Ga., 720
Fort McCree, Fla., 31, 51n140, 59–60, 62–63, 80, 92, 111, 116–117, 119–120, 133, 168, 186–187, 721
Fort McGilvery, Va., *749*
Fort McHenry, Baltimore, Md., xii, 77, 769, 774
Fort McIntosh, Laredo, Tex., 17, 40, 45, 245–246, 768
Fort Monroe, Va., x, 2, 15–16, 86n273, 88, 91, 156, 205, 236–237, 567
Fort Morgan, Mobile Point, Ala., 31, 60, 108, 608–611, 621
Fort Moultrie, Charleston, S.C., xii, 21, 27n56, 29–30
Fort Niagara, N. Y., 771, 777
Fort Pemberton, Miss., 277–278, 280–281
Fort Pickens, Pensacola, Fla., xii, 3, 30, 51, 57, *57*–76, 78–79, 81–82, 84, *84*–87, 89, 92–95, 106n358, 107–109, 111–114, 114n379, *114*, 116–118, 120–121, 125–126, 128, 131, 132n448, 136–139, 141, 160, 168, 185, 187, 491, 620, 706, 773–774, 776, 780
Fort Pike, Rigolets, La., 31, 176, 260
Fort Pillow, Tenn., 153, 159, 166, 179, 200–202
Fort Porter, Buffalo, N. Y., 769–770, 772–773, 775, 777, 779
Fort Powell, Ala., 611
Fort Pulaski, Ga., 31, 186
Fort Quitman, Tex., 45
Fort Randolph, Tenn., 153
Fort Saratoga, Washington, D. C., 581
Fort Schuyler, N.Y., 10, 464, 770, 772, 779
Fort Semmes, Tex., 483
Fort Smith, Ark., 161, 540
Fort St. Philip, La., 31, 161, 163, 166, 168–172, 246, 260, 408n1416
Fort Stedman, Va., 748–750, 752, 755
Fort Stevens, Washington, D. C., 579–580, 582
Fort Stockton, Tex., xi, 45

Fort Sumter, Charleston, S.C., 22, 29–30, 47, 59, 65, 67, 67n193, 68, 73–75, 79, 81
Fort Taylor, Key West, Fla., 2, 30, 44, 51–53, 76, 78, 89, 188
Fort Walker, Hilton Head, S.C., 122
Fort Warren, Boston, Mass., 48, 710
Fort Washita, Indian Territory (Oklahoma), 767
Fortress Monroe, Va., 574, 581, 588, 728, 733–734
Foster, J. G., 721
Foster, James P., 277, 279, 281–282
Foster, John G., 745
Fox, Gustavus, 74–75, 77, 144–145, 287, 724, 728
Frank, R. T., 49
Franklin, La., 312, 321–322, 325–327, 330, 333–334, 337, *478*, 491, 493, 497, 501, 778
Franklin, Tenn., 720
Franklin, William B., 468, 468n1560, 469, 471–472, 477, 480, 483–484, 486, 490–492, 504, 506–507, 511–512, 523, 535–536, 546–547, 556, 559, 585, 587
Frazar, Douglas, 710
Frederick, Md., 578, 585, 592
Frederick Hall, 740–741
Fredericksburg Railroad, 568, 743
Free Soil Party, 235, 731
Fremont, John C., 90, 95, 97–98, 144, 252, 573, 711, 731
French, William H., 2, 39–40, 43, 53, 78, 225
Freret, James, 367
Friedman, George, 5, 41, 126, 140, 185, 189–190, 194, 243, 254, 257, 308, 364, 458, 473, 484, 492, 497–498, 554, 564–565
Front Royal Railroad, 655
Front Royal, Va., 606, 621, 647–648, 651, 668–670, 673, 676
Fry, James B., 462, 719
Frying Pan Shoals, 722, *722*
Fuchs, Henry, 498
Fudge, William, 244, 257, 459, 461, 473
Fuller, Edward W., 336
Funsten, O. R., 677

G

Gabaudan, Edward C., 305, 345–346, 346n1254, 359
Gadsden, Ala., 717, 720
Gaines, CSS, 609

Gaines' Mill, Va., 578
Galavan, Morris, 95, 126, 140, 257, 492
Galloway, A. Power, 428
Galveston, Tex., 43–44, 240–241, 293, 469, 766
Gantt Plantation, 344–345
Gardner, Franklin, 258, 300–301, 304, 350, 365–368, 371, 376–378, 382, 384, 395, 407, 421, 423, 433, 437–438, 441, 451–453
Gardner, La., *390*
Garnett, J. M., 639
Garnett, James, 637
Gause, Lucien C., 520
General Meigs, USS, 187
General Price, USS, 451
General Quitman, CSS, 290
General Rusk (steamer), 44, 53
Genesee, USS, 301–302, 369
Georgia Infantry Regiment, 5th, 104, 132
Georgia Military Institute, 719
Georgia Militia, 719
Georgia Volunteers, 61st, 650, 695
Gerfie, Henri Louis. *See* Jefferson, Henry
Gertrude, USS, 476
Getty, George W., 612, 628, 634–635, 673, 685, 692, 695n2185, 696–697, 699n2201, 756
Gettysburg, Pa., 464
Gibbons, Patrick, 244, 257, 459, 492, 497–498, 554, 563, 619, 701, 713, 715, 742, 763, 777
Gibbons Plantation, 378, *390*
Gibbs, Alfred, 616, 618, 627
Gibbs, J. S., 109, 125
Gibbs, T. K., 109, 125–126, 139–140, 185
Gilbert, Benjamin F., 627
Gill, Robert, 498
Gillmore, Quincy Adams, 567
Gilman, J. H., 60, 60n171, 61, 64
Gilmor, Harry A., 585, 590, 602, 616, 704, 707, 710–711
Gilmore, James, 574–576, 731
Gilroyd, Thomas, 41, 126, 140n477, 185, 189
Gist, William H., 53n147
Glynn, James, 68, 71
Godfrey, John F., 354, 369–370
Golden, James, 5, 41, 56, 95
Goldsboro, N. C., 745–747
Goochland Courthouse, 740–741
Gooding, Oliver P., 323–324, 389–390, 394, 504, 518, 521, 547
Gordon, George C., 414
Gordon, John, 606, 616–617, 624–626, 628, 631–635, 639, 641, 644, 647, 674–677, 680–681, 683–684, 686–689, 692–696, 748–751, 757–758
Gordon's Landing, 289–290, 358
Gordonsville, Va., 668, 735
Gorgas, Josiah, 82
Graham, William, 571
Grand Bayou Landing, 541–542
Grand Coteau, *487*
Grand Duke, CSS, 316, 358
Grand Ecore, La., 518–520, 540–541, 543–546, 550–551, 556
Grand Gulf, 199, 346–349, 353, 357, 411
Grand Lake, 293, 307, 311–312, 314–316, 325
Granger, Gordon, 610, 621
Granite City, USS, 468–469, 471–472
Grant, John V., 628
Grant, Ulysses S., 13, 96–97, 130, 132, 143–144, 146–152, 157–160, 175, 180, 182–185, 204, 207–208, 220–222, 227, 266–274, 276, 278–279, 281, 283–286, 288, 304–305, 311, 340, 345–346, 346n1254, 347–350, 353, 355–357, 359, 361, 365–368, 373, 387, 411, 440, 450–451, 453, 462, 465, 477–479, 479n1578, 480, 483, 483n1589, 493–495, 495n1631, 506, 543–544, 544n1751, 550–551, 559, 566–569, 572, 575, 577, 581, 583–584, 587–592, 595–597, 600, 606–608, 614–615, 621, 623–625, 640–641, 648, 652–655, 657, 665–666, 666n2109, 667, 669, 669n2115, 670, 698, 700, 708, 712, 715, 717–718, 720–722, 724–725, 727–728, 733–735, 739–740, 743, 747–749, 752–753, 755–758, 760, 763, 765–766
Gravelly Run, 753
Graves, Ezekiel, 498
Gray, Henry, 330–334, 521
Great Cattle Raid, 657
Greeley, Horace, 572, 574, 731
Green, Thomas, 326, 338, 442–446, 446n1509, 447, 457, 487–491, 501–505, 507, 517–518, 520–521, 526, 534, 542
Green Lake, Tex., 45–47
Green Plantation, 298
Greenback Raid, The, 705
Greenfield, Andrew J., 627
Greenleaf, Halbert S., 344–345
Greensboro, N. C., 759
Greenwood Plantation, 234
Gregg, David M., 596–597

Gregg, John, 366
Grey Jacket (schooner), 476
Grierson, Benjamin, 347–350, 352–355, 368–370, 373, 376, 378, 390–391, 411, 414, 416, 436, 440, 465
Grierson's Raid, 350–355, 373
Griffiths Field, 424
Griffiths Plantation, 378
Grimes, Bryan, 674, 695
Grinsted, H. L., 520
Gross Tete, 441
Ground Squirrel Bridge, 741
Grover, Cuvier, 215, 240–242, 258, 292, 294, 297–300, 303, 307, 311–317, 319–328, 330, 333–340, 343–344, 358, 360–361, 363, 370, 372, 375–376, 378, 381n1350, 382–384, 388–392, 397–398, 399n1391, 400, 409, 413, 420–421, 423, 425, 431, 455, 455n1531, 457, 487, 499, 502, 504, 520, 544, 592–593, 600, 607, 628, 633–636, 648–649, 671–672, 679, 684, 697, 700
Gulf Blockading Squadron, 98, 111–112, 124, 138, 168
Gunboat No. 7, 240
Gunpowder River, 585
Gwathmey, Washington, 72

H

Hadden, Jesse, 404
Hadley, George, 5, 10, 41, 95, 126, 140, 255, 257, 497, 564, 703, 715, 763, 771
Hagan, Francis, 3, 6, 8, 41–42, 44, 475, 768
Hagerstown, Md., 578
Hall, Benjamin O., 244, 254, 257, 308, 364, 461, 497, 563, 619, 702, 715, 776
Hall, Ivory F., 498
Hall, James F., 498
Halleck, Henry W., 144, 146–155, 157–160, 174, 179–185, 191, 200–201, 204, 206, 208, 216, 218, 220–222, 225, 236, 239–240, 250, 258, 264, 266–267, 272, 285–286, 292–293, 305, 310, 340, 346, 359, 370, 373, 450–451, 462, 464–465, 467, 472, 478, 480–481, 493, 495, 540, 543–544, 544n1751, 550–551, 559, 561, 567, 581–584, 587–589, 591, 597, 600, 623–624, 655, 666, 666n2109, 667–668, 670–671, 716, 721, 744, 754
Hallett, Joseph L., 299, 303
Hallonquist, James, 104
Halltown, Va., 592–593, 598, 600, 607–608, 613
Hamill, Henry, 339
Hamilton, Andrew J., 237–238, 240
Hamlin, Charles, 562
Hammond, J. A., 12
Hampton, Wade, 570, 596–597, 657, 745
Hampton Roads Conference, 733–735, 748, 760
Hampton Roads, Va., 204, 287, 725–726, 765
Hamrick, James W., 417
Hancock, Md., 590, 600
Hancock, Winfield S., 596–597, 607, 736, 743
Hancock Station, 741
Hanney, James, 95, 126, 140n477, 257, 485
Hanney, Michael, 109, 119
Hanover Junction, Va., 741
Hardee, William J., 157, 452, 719–720, 745–746
Hardeman, William Polk, 444, 446
Hare's Hill, Va., 751
Harkins, James, 6, 41, 94–95, 99
Harness, G. S., 707
Harper, William, 417
Harper's Ferry, Va., 578, 583, 588, 592–593, 613, 624, 640, 700, 704–705, 709
Harriet Lane, USS, 75, 172, 187, 240, 260, 290–291
Harrington, James R., 255, 257, 308–309, 313
Harrington, Michael, 243
Harris, Isham G., 157
Harrison, George, 244, 257, 459, 497, 564
Harrison, John, 5–6, 254
Harrison, Thomas, 542
Harrisonburg, Va., 651–654, 705, 712
Harrison's Landing, 741
Hartford, USS, 171, 177, 179, 199, 203, *203*, 299, 301, 301n1131, 303–304, 345, 347, 356–357, 359, 384, 610
Hartranft, John F., 750
Hartsuff, George L., 753
Hartwell, James A., 498
Hartz, Edward L., 49
Haskin, William L., 43n97, 51n140, 60n171, 472, 558, 570
Hastings, Smith H., 627
Hastings, USS, 542
Hatch, Edward, 350, 354
Hatcher's Run, Va., 752, 755
Hatch's Ranch, Nev., 46
Hatheway, John S., ix
Hatteras, USS, 265, 265n1012, 266, 269n1031
Hatteras Inlet, N.C., 91–92

Hay, John, 374
Hayes, Rutherford B., 628, 677, 680, 697, 712
Haynes, James, 6
Haynes Bluff, Miss., 273, 305, 350
Head of the Passes (Mississippi River), 468
Heartland Campaign, 209
Hebard, George, 391, 400, 421
Hebert, Paul O., 161–162, 162n592
Hehn, Henry, 39
Helen (steamboat), 186
Helena, Ark., 456
Hemphill, John, 66
Henderson, USS, 274
Henderson's Hill, 501
Henry, William, 139
Henry Lewis, USS, 124
Herbert, Philemon, 445
Hermitage Plantation, 381, 441
Herron, Francis J., 462
Hesseltine, Charles, 499
Hesseltine, George, 498
Hesseltine, William, 536, 539
Hesson, Michael, 498
Heuberer, Charles E., 118
Hey, Louis, 41, 109, 122
Hildt, John, 105, 112–*113*, 116n383, 118
Hill, A. P., 235, 642
Hill, Bennett H., 2, 43
Hill, D. H., 48
Hill, Sylvester, 521
Hiscock, George, 498
Hoffman, John J., 627
Hoke, Robert, 727, 730
Holcomb, Richard E., 216, 233, 263n1001, 316, 318, 389, 391, 404, 431–432
Holcombe, James P., 574
Holland, John, 41–42, 126, 140, 194
Holly Springs, Miss., 266–267
Hollyhock, USS, 442, 458
Holmes, Philip, 332
Holmes, Theophilus H., 456
Holt, Joseph, 24, 29–30, 32, 51, 68
Honeycutt Hill, 506
Hood, Charles, 498
Hood, John Bell, 715–721, 736, 747
Hooker, Joseph, 286, 373–374
Horace, USS, 48
Hosmer, James K., 317n1171, 320n1181, 382, 408
Hotchkiss, Jedediah, 639, 674, 737
Hourand, August, 627

Houston, D. C., 560
Houston, Sam, 34, 38, 38n91, 44
Houston, Tex., 764
Howard, Daniel, 255, 364, 460, 497, 565, 715
Howard, George, 6, 41, 127, 140, 257, 475, 497, 564, 703, 714
Howard, Oliver O., 719, 746
Hubbard, Hiram, 244, 257, 474, 485, 777
Hubbard, Lucius F., 521
Hubbard, Nathan H., 432
Hubbard, Thomas, 549
Hughes, Benjamin, 255, 257, 354, 364, 440, 564–565
Hughs, Benjamin, 460, 497
Hull, Walter C., 627
Humphreys, J. M., 680, 752, 755
Hunt, E. B., 78, 81
Hunt, Henry J., 3, 16, 16n33, 53
Hunter, David, 138, 144, 217n843, 252, 544, 546, 550, 569, 578, 583–584, 584n1869, 585, 588–589, 591–593, 598, 719
Hunter, M. T., 733–734
Hunter, Robert, 674
Hunter, Sherod, 442–443
Hupp's Hill, Va., 643, 646, 667, 674, 676, 678
Hutchin's Point, 316

I

Iberville (steamer), 368, 408
Illinois, USS, 78–79
Illinois Cavalry, 2nd, 153, 509
Illinois Cavalry, 6th, 350, 370, 378
Illinois Cavalry, 7th, 350, 354, 382, 384, 391
Illinois Cavalry, 8th, 744
Illinois Infantry Regiment, 17th, 274
Illinois Infantry Regiment, 37th, 483
Illinois Infantry Regiment, 47th, 521
Illinois Infantry Regiment, 49th, 521
Illinois Infantry Regiment, 58th, 521, 526, 532–534
Illinois Infantry Regiment, 77th, 508n1664, 510
Illinois Infantry Regiment, 94th, 482
Illinois Infantry Regiment, 95th, 542, 542n1745
Illinois Infantry Regiment, 117th, 521
Illinois Infantry Regiment, 118th, 481
Illinois Infantry Regiment, 119th, 521, 526, 532
Illinois Infantry Regiment, 130th, 508n1664
Illinois Mounted Infantry, 118th, 487
Illinois Volunteer Infantry, 73rd, 574–575
Imboden, J. D., 603, 632, 638–639
Imperial (steamboat), 456

Indiana Battery, 7th, 426, 429
Indiana Battery, 9th, 523–524, 532
Indiana Cavalry, 16th, 521
Indiana Heavy Artillery, 1st, 300, 324, 391, 396, 404–405, 412, 417, 468, 508, 511, 548
Indiana Infantry Regiment, 8th, 483, 684
Indiana Infantry Regiment, 16th, 508
Indiana Infantry Regiment, 21st, 197, *212*, 230, 232, 241–242, 263
Indiana Infantry Regiment, 46th, 489, 511, 517
Indiana Infantry Regiment, 60th, 487–489
Indiana Infantry Regiment, 67th, 487–489, 508n1664, 510
Indiana Infantry Regiment, 69th, 283
Indiana Infantry Regiment, 89th, 521, 533
Indianola, Tex., 37–40, 45–47, 71, 483
Indianola, USS, 289–291, 293
Invalid Corps, 463
Iowa Cavalry, 2nd, 181, 352
Iowa Infantry Regiment, 14th, 521, 527, 530, 534
Iowa Infantry Regiment, 24th, 511
Iowa Infantry Regiment, 26th, 483
Iowa Infantry Regiment, 27th, 521, 527, 530
Iowa Infantry Regiment, 28th, 511
Iowa Infantry Regiment, 29th, 440
Iowa Infantry Regiment, 32nd, 521, 527–528, 530n1715, 532, 534, 536
Irish Bend, La., 311–312, 316, 326–327, 339, 361, 480
Iroquois, USS, 177–178
Irwin, Richard B., 294, 304, 315, 335, 386–387, 392, 398–399, 409, 443, 446, 452, 468, 517, 534, 671
Irwinsville, Ga., 762
Island No. 10, 154–156, 202
Itasca, USS, 169, 178
Iuka, Miss., 184
Iverson, Alfred, 66

J

J. A. Cotton, CSS, 234, 259, 262–264, 311, 316
J. D. Clark, CSS, 357
J. P. Jackson, USS, 611
Jackel, Charles, 6, 41, 119, 127, 140, 257, 492, 497, 499, 555, 565, 620, 702, 713, 715, 742
Jackson, Andrew, 21, 28–29, 731–732
Jackson, C. M., 452
Jackson, John K., 104
Jackson, Miss., 359, 366–367, 450
Jackson, Richard H., xii, 39, 41–42, 56, 94, 99, 105–106, 109, 112–*113*, 119, 139–141, 187, 245
Jackson, Stonewall, 184, 205–206, 219, 235, 577, 635, 778
Jackson, William L., 659n2080, 661, 663–664
Jackson Road, 426
Jaecke, Daniel, 5, 7
James rifles, 115, 119
James River, 569, 577, 739–741, 752
James River Canal, 739
Jaquess, James, 574–576, 731–732
Jeanerette, La., 246
Jefferson, Henry, 475, 477, 477n1573, 485, 555, 565, 776–778
Jerrard, Simon G., 432
Jessop, Francis, 244, 257, 459, 485, 497, 564–565, 777n2416
Jewett, William, 573–574
John Warner, USS, 556
Johns, Henry T., 388, 406
Johnson, Andrew, 759, 765, 768
Johnson, Benjamin W., 376, 382, 395, 423
Johnson, Bradley T., 585, 589–590, 598, 600, 616, 635, 659n2080, 661, 663–664
Johnson, Reverdy, 217n839, 224
Johnson, William A., 741
Johnston, Albert Sidney, 123, 130, 132, 143, 156–158, 164
Johnston, Joseph E., 208, 349–350, 356, 365–368, 373, 411, 440–441, 450, 452, 479n1578, 494, 567, 582, 584, 715, 717, 744, 746–748, 756, 759–761
Jones, Charles E. (Enos Deal), 476
Jones, Samuel P., 129–130, 133–134, 141, 176, 186
Jones, Thomas M., 133–134, 141
Jones, W. E., 603
Joseph Whitney (steamer), 54–55
Judah (schooner), 98, 103, 110, 168
Juliet, USS, 549

K

Kanawha River, 578
Kastenbader, John M., 255, 257, 364, 460, 474
Katahdin, USS, 200, 213
Kautz, August, 569–570, 654
Kearneysville, W. V., 613–616, 705
Kearsarge, USS, 595
Keezeltown Road, 650–652
Keifer, J. Warren, 697

Keith, John A., 412
Kell, John M., 238
Keller, Lewis, 3, 10, 41, 94, 119, 126, 140, 256, 363, 447, 485–486, 571, 619, 703–704, 714, 771–772, 775–776, 778
Kelley, A. D., 165
Kelley, Benjamin F., 711–712
Kelley, John, 460, 715
Kelly, George, 244, 257, 473, 554–555, 715, 773
Kelly, John, 244, 257, 364, 459, 497, 555, 620, 641, 702
Kennebec, USS, 169, 200, 476, 610
Kennedy, John A., 24
Kenny, Joseph, 7
Kenny, Michael, 5, 41, 109, 127, 140, 257, 308, 497, 563, 619, 701, 713–714
Kenny, Theodore W., 255, 257, 497, 715
Kentucky Infantry Regiment, 19th, 508n1664, 510
Kernstown, Va., 643, 700
Kershaw, Joseph B., 596–597, 600, 606, 608, 613, 620–623, 651–653, 656, 667, 675–681, 683–684, 686, 688, 692–693, 696, 700
Key Biscayne, Fla., x, 771
Key West, Fla., 2, 30, 44–45, 51–55, 60, 71, 78, 92–93, 118, 131, 136, 190, 225, 387, 390
Keyes, Erasmus, 76
Kidd, James H., 627, 639, 651–652, 656, 656n2067, 658, 661, 663, 678, 688–689, 696
Kilburne, Sirenus T., 244, 255, 258, 497, 715, 771
Killian, Bernard D., 778
Kilpatrick, Judson, 746
Kimball, John W., 427
Kimball, William K., 327, 388, 390
Kineo, USS, 213, 302, 369, 446n1509
King, D. W., 233
King William Courthouse, 741
Kingman, John W., 417–418
King's artillery battalion, 628–629
Kingsley, Amos N., 498
Kingsley, Thomas G., 403
Kingston, N. H., 773
Kinney, Joseph, 5
Kinney, Thomas J., 526
Kinsman, USS, 233, 264
Kirby, Edmund, 99, 109–110
Kirke, Edmund. *See* Gilmore, James
Kirkwood, Samuel J., 223

Kitching, J. Howard, 680, 683
Knox, S. L., 452–453
Kock Plantation, 455, 457
Krall, Bartolomy, 498
Krom, Abram H., 627
Kutschor, Joseph, 5, 41–42, 94, 127, 140, 190, 258, 364, 442, 460, 473, 475, 484, 486, 492, 497, 555, 564

L

La Fourche Crossing, 442, 444–446, 455–456
La Grange, Tenn., 350–351, 355
Lacey Springs, Va., 652, 735
Lackawanna, USS, 610
Lafourche, La., 292, 294, 312
Lafourche Campaign, 218
Lafourche Militia Regiment, 233
Lafourche River, 313
Lake, Ludwell, 709
Lake Providence, 283, 305, 345–347, 550
Lamar, G. B., 24–25
Lamb, William, 723, 723n2276, 726, 730
Lanahan, John, 95, 127, 140n477, 258, 459
Lancaster, USS, 202, 356
Landram, W. J., 506, 510, 512
Lane, Walter P., 445–446
Langdon, Loomis L., 2–3, 17, 107, 112, 118
Larrabee, Thomas, 498
Lashner, Joseph, 244, 258, 497, 715
Laughlin, Edward M., 474
Laurel Brigade, 656, 661, 663, 677, 677n2140, 708
Laurel Hill (steamer), 307, 312–313, 317, 317n1171
Lawler, Michael K., 486, 558, 610n1935
Lay, George W., 29
Leaf River, 353
Lee, Albert L., 499, 501–502, 504–509, 517–518, 754
Lee, Fitzhugh, 570, 596–597, 600, 606, 613, 615, 620, 628, 635, 637, 637n2008, 639, 653, 741, 753, 757–758
Lee, Paul Lynch, 452
Lee, Robert E., 17, 46, 46n116, 134, 186, 206–207, 219, 375, 464–465, 567–568, 577–578, 582, 584, 591, 596–598, 600, 602–604, 606–608, 614, 620, 623–624, 642, 651–655, 657, 670, 698, 700, 705, 708, 715, 720, 722, 725, 731, 735, 738, 743–744, 747–748, 750–751, 754–761, 763–765

Lee, Samuel P., 177, 724
Leesburg, Va., 581, 584
Leetown, W. V., 613–616
Lemon, George, 773
Leonard, George F., 255, 258, 459
Lewery, John, 244, 258, 459, 492, 497–498, 554, 564, 619, 701, 713, 715, 742, 763
Lewis, John L., 173
Lexington, USS, 440, 519, 542, 542n1745, 551, 553
Liddell, John R., 541–542
Lighna, Julia, 40
Lighna, Louis, 3, 40–41, 126, 140n477, 258, 458, 461, 473, 485–486, 486n1596
Lighna, Louis, Jr., 40
Light House Point, 571
Lilley, Dr., 408
Lincoln, Abraham, 22, 28, 42, 47–48, 70–77, 79, 82, 87–88, 96–98, 145, 181, 206–207, 216–217, 220–221, 223, 236n923, 240, 251–253, 259, 373, 464, 466, 479, 482, 491n1616, 493, 504, 550, 559, 567, 573–577, 580, 582, 587, 590–592, 595, 607, 641, 654, 698–699, 716, 719, 725, 728, 731–734, 759, 763
Lincoln, James M., 498
Lincoln administration, 51, 74, 97, 221, 223, 253
Little Missouri River, 540
Little North Mountain, 644–646
Little Rock, Ark., 494, 540
Livingston, Alexander, 6–7
Livingston, Rhett, 627
Llano Estacado, x
Locke, M. B., 376, 393–395
Locke's Ford, 630
Loeb, Sigmund, 194, 243
Logan, John A., 720–721
Logan, John L., 367, 371, 416
Loggy Bayou, La., 540–541, 545
Lomax, Lunsford L., 624–625, 628, 635, 637, 637n2008, 644, 646, 651, 653, 656–659, 661, 663–664, 664n2102, 676, 735, 738
Lomax, Tennant, 62
Long, A. L., 756
Longstreet, James, 670–671, 696, 741, 744, 748, 753–754, 756–757
Loring, W. W., 277, 602
Loudon Valley, Va., 706–707
Louisa Courthouse, 740
Louisiana (map), *253*

Louisiana, CSS, 163, 166, 168, 172, 199
Louisiana, USS, 726
Louisiana Artillery, 241–242
Louisiana Battalion, 8th, 176
Louisiana Battery, 6th, 526
Louisiana Cavalry, 1st, 340, 370, 487, 776
Louisiana Cavalry, 1st, Company A, 242, 386, 389
Louisiana Cavalry, 1st, Company B, 231, 242
Louisiana Cavalry, 1st, Company C, 231, 241
Louisiana Cavalry, 1st, Company E, 297
Louisiana Cavalry, 2nd, 316–317, 486, 771–772, 776
Louisiana Cavalry, 2nd, Company B, 263
Louisiana Cavalry, 6th, 521
Louisiana Cavalry, 9th, 353
Louisiana Engineers, 1st, 386
Louisiana Field Battery, 2nd, 371
Louisiana Heavy Artillery, 1st, 190
Louisiana Heavy Artillery, 12th, 384
Louisiana Infantry, 1st, 425
Louisiana Infantry Regiment, 1st, 161, 190, 216, 231, 233, 242, 316–318, 321, 335, 389, 436, 447n1510, 461
Louisiana Infantry Regiment, 1st, Company K, 121
Louisiana Infantry Regiment, 2nd, 161, 216, 241, 369, 371, 391, 412, 432
Louisiana Infantry Regiment, 3rd, 161
Louisiana Infantry Regiment, 4th, 161
Louisiana Infantry Regiment, 5th, 162
Louisiana Infantry Regiment, 6th, 162
Louisiana Infantry Regiment, 7th, 162
Louisiana Infantry Regiment, 8th, 162
Louisiana Infantry Regiment, 9th, 162, 215
Louisiana Infantry Regiment, 11th, 162
Louisiana Infantry Regiment, 12th, 162, 365
Louisiana Infantry Regiment, 13th, 162
Louisiana Infantry Regiment, 14th, 162
Louisiana Infantry Regiment, 15th, 162
Louisiana Infantry Regiment, 27th, 176
Louisiana Infantry Regiment, 28th, 330, 332, 521, 527
Louisiana Native Guards. *See also* Corps d'Afrique Regiments
Louisiana Native Guards, 1st, 160, 165–166, 190, 217, 217n842, 218–219, 232–233, 242, 263, 264n1004, 385–386, 389, 394–395, 398–399, 407, 409, 448, 454
Louisiana Native Guards, 1st, Company E, 454

Louisiana Native Guards, 2nd, 217, 219, 242, 263, 264n1004, 405–406, 409
Louisiana Native Guards, 3rd, 217n842, 242, 263, 297n1122, 385–386, 389, 398–399, 409, 454
Louisiana Native Guards Heavy Artillery, 1st, 217, 217n842
Louisiana Partisan Ranger Battalion, 9th., 376, 385, 409
Louisiana Volunteer Cavalry, 2nd, 501, 571
Louisville, Ga., 720
Louisville, USS, 280, 551
Lovell, Mansfield, 121n404, 133, 162–166, 168, 172–173, 176, 176n663, 186, 198, 209, 225, 261, 601–602, 781
Lovell, W. S., 120–121
Lowell, Charles R., 599, 606, 612, 618, 627, 629–632, 638, 643, 651–652, 661, 663–664, 673, 678–679, 688–689, 691, 696–697
Lowry, John, 255, 258, 459, 474, 485, 496, 564
Lucas, Thomas J., 505, 509, 521, 535, 557–558
Luckett, Phillip N., 34
Lucy (blockade runner), 723
Lull, Oliver M., 412
Luminary (steamer), 87
Lundenberg, Henry, 39
Luray Valley, 600, 644, 651–652
Lyle, O. P., 395
Lynch, Thomas, 498
Lynch, William F., 521, 526, 532
Lynchburg, Va., 577–578, 735, 737–741, 743

M
Macedonian, USS, 68, 71
Mack, Albert G., 386, 391
Mackenzie, Ranald S., 753
Maclin, Sackfield, 35, 49
Macon, Ga., 717, 719
Madison, George T., 518
Madrid Canal, 550
Magruder, John B., 2, 205, 240–241, 260, 765–766
Mahone, William, 570, 756–757
Mahoney, James, 459
Mahoney, Thomas, 243, 258, 496, 714
Mahopac, USS, 729
Maine Battery, 1st, 231, 242, 323–324, 391, 396, 636, 686
Maine Infantry Regiment, 10th, 515
Maine Infantry Regiment, 12th, 110, 241, 314, 339, 390, 398
Maine Infantry Regiment, 13th, 242, 482–483, 515, 521
Maine Infantry Regiment, 14th, 241, 391, 401
Maine Infantry Regiment, 15th, 191, 193, 242, 255, 482–483, 511, 515, 521
Maine Infantry Regiment, 15th, Company B, 482
Maine Infantry Regiment, 21st, 388, 391, 404, 406, 432
Maine Infantry Regiment, 22nd, 241, 318, 321, 362, 413, 420, 425, 432
Maine Infantry Regiment, 24th, 401
Maine Infantry Regiment, 26th, 240–241, 297, 302, 327, 330, 332, 335, 339, 362, 431–432
Maine Infantry Regiment, 28th, 433, 435, 443, 446–447
Maine Infantry Regiment, 29th, 515, 521, 525, 528, 530–531
Maine Infantry Regiment, 30th, 521, 531, 531n1719, 549
Major, James P., 441, 446, 457, 521, 527, 534, 546–547, 549, 556
Mallory, Stephen R., 66–67, 67n193, 68, 163, 166, 193, 195, 781
Malvern Hill, 205–206, 322
Manassas, CSS, 111n373, 112, 117, 163–164, 166, 168, 171, 199
Manassas Gap, 646
Manassas Gap Railroad, 666, 668
Mansfield, Charles F., 94–95, 127, 140, 190, 194, 243, 254, 258, 308, 364, 460, 474, 485, 492, 496
Mansfield, Herbert B., 255–256, 763
Mansfield, Hobart E., 714
Mansfield, La., 503, 506–508, 513–516, 518–520, 522–523, 525, 527–528, 530, 535, 541–*542*
Mansura, La., *557*–558
March up the Valley, 649–652, 725
Marcy, George O., 627
Maria Wood, USS, 140, 187
Marksville, La., 557, *557*
Marland, William, 489–490
Marshall, Tex., 477, 764
Marshall J. Smith (schooner), 476
Martin, Andrew, 498
Martin, Joseph W., 663, 678
Martinsburg, W. V., 578, 629, 631–632, 671, 705, 709

Martinsburg Pike, 638
Mary (steamboat), 186
Mary Keene (steamer), 275
Mary Martin (steamer), 733
Mary T, CSS, 316, 342, 358
Maryland Cavalry, 2nd, 571, 602
Maryland Cavalry, 3rd, 705
Maryland Partisan Rangers, 2nd, 590
Massachusetts, USS, 92
Massachusetts Battery, 2nd (Nims'), 197, 199, 199n756, 200, *200*, 211–212, 241, 254, 294, 297, 300, 314, 327, 333, 335, 338–339, 362, 383, 391, 425, 461, 486–487, 489–490, 493, 509–512
Massachusetts Battery, 4th, 199n756, 242, 391, 493, 562
Massachusetts Battery, 6th, 198–199, 199n756, 200, 231, 242, 381, 386, 389, 391, 399, 457, 468, 493
Massachusetts Battery, 13th, 497–498, 536, 536n1738, 776
Massachusetts Cavalry, 2nd, 228, 231, 340, 630, 652, 664, 739n2328
Massachusetts Cavalry, 2nd, Company A, 241
Massachusetts Cavalry, 2nd, Company B, 242
Massachusetts Cavalry, 3rd, 341, 414, 507, 509
Massachusetts Cavalry, 3rd, Company C, 416
Massachusetts Cavalry, 31st, 509
Massachusetts Infantry Regiment, 4th, 414, 448, 454
Massachusetts Infantry Regiment, 4th, Company A, 425, 427n1456
Massachusetts Infantry Regiment, 4th, Company B, 427n1456
Massachusetts Infantry Regiment, 4th, Company K, 425, 427, 427n1456
Massachusetts Infantry Regiment, 13th, 313, 448, 555, 562
Massachusetts Infantry Regiment, 26th, 242, 413, 471
Massachusetts Infantry Regiment, 27th, 297
Massachusetts Infantry Regiment, 30th, 197, 199, 210, 242, 369–371, 388, 391, 404, 425, 481
Massachusetts Infantry Regiment, 31st, 198, 241, 323, 390, 425, 428
Massachusetts Infantry Regiment, 38th, 295, 324, 385, 390, 396, 412, 425, 427–428
Massachusetts Infantry Regiment, 41st, 236, 241, 297n1122, 316, 339–340, 344, 413, 481
Massachusetts Infantry Regiment, 42nd, 240, 290, 386, 386n1362, 396
Massachusetts Infantry Regiment, 47th, 271, 297
Massachusetts Infantry Regiment, 48th, 371, 388, 391, 404–405, 423, 423n1445, 433, 435–436
Massachusetts Infantry Regiment, 49th, 246–247, 252, 368, 370–371, 391, 404, 406, 408, 412, 432
Massachusetts Infantry Regiment, 50th, 354, 369, 391, 423, 433, 436, 454
Massachusetts Infantry Regiment, 52nd, 241, 299, 314, 320n1181, 344, 362, 416, 440
Massachusetts Infantry Regiment, 53rd, 324, 376, 390, 396, 425, 427–428, 443
Massachusetts Infantry Regiment, 57th, 750
Massachusetts Mounted Rifles, 41st, 362
Massachusetts Unattached Cavalry, 2nd, Company B, 241
Massachusetts Volunteer Light Artillery, 13th, 448
Massanutten Mountain, 600, 605, 644, 646, 671, 674–675, 696
Matagorda Bay, 47–48
Matagorda Island, Tex., 483
Matamoros, Mexico, 1, 767
Matamoros, USS, 483, 483n1589
Mathews, Johnny, 395
Mattie Cook, USS, 274
Maverick, Samuel A., 34
Maxey, Samuel B., 366–367
Maximilian, Emperor of Mexico, 466, 732, 765, 767
Maynadier, William, 25, 571
McCarrick, John O., 498
McCarthy, James, 6, 41–42, 78, 127, 140, 194, 256, 459, 496, 555
McCausland, John, 578, 589–590, 598, 600, 602, 613, 632, 638–639, 653, 710
McClellan, George, 88–89, 89n285, 97, 144–149, 151, 153, 156, 159, 180–181, 184, 205–207, 219–221, 235, 236n923, 286, 374, 576–577, 587, 589, 621, 642, 699, 716, 763
McClellan, USS, 111–112, 482
McClernand, John, 147, 185, 220–223, 235–236, 266–269, 269n1027, 272, 283–284, 346, 366–367, 491n1616, 493, 544, 556, 558, 610n1935
McCostello, Michael, 498

McCoy, Daniel, 6, 41, 95, 127, 140, 194, 254, 256, 308
McCoy, James, 42, 78
McCrea, Tulley, 571
McCulloch, Benjamin, 33, 36–37
McCulloch, H. E., 45, 47
McDonagh, Miles, 6, 41, 95, 127, 140, 256, 364, 460, 496, 564, 703–704, 713
McDonald, John, 498
McDonald, William, 708–709
McEnearny, Cornelius, 243, 256, 364, 460, 485, 496, 714
McFarland, George F., 112–*113*
McGauley, Terence, 6, 41, 127, 140, 256, 484, 496, 703, 714
McGilvray, John, 630, 647, 699, 701–702
McGinnis, Angus, 244, 254, 256, 489, 496, 714
McGinnis, George F., 486, 486n1596
McIntosh, John B., 622, 627, 629, 640
McInturff's Ford, 675
McKean, William, 110, 110n372, 111–112, 117, 119, 122, 138
McKenney, John, 244, 565, 619, 702, 714
McKenzie, James, 7
McKerrall Plantation, 328
McKinley, William, 673
McKinney, John, 256, 459, 496
McLaflin, Edward, 426, 429
McLaughlen, N. B., 750
McLaughlin, Edward, 41–42, 95, 127, 140, 256, 308
McLaughlin, John, 498
McMillan, J. W., 230, 514, 518, 521–523, 526, 532, 532n1722, 547–548, 682n2149, 684, 697
McNamara, Edward F., 571
McNeill, Jesse, 707, 707n2221, 711–712
McNeill, John, 649n2045, 704, 707, 707n2221, 710–711
McNutt's Hill, 556
McPherson, James B., 502
McRae, CSS, 172
McSweeney, Daniel, 95, 127, 140n477, 256, 492
McWaters, James, 41, 94–95, 127, 140, 189
McWilliams Bridge, 318
McWilliams Plantation, 318
Meade, George Gordon, 464, 567–570, 715, 743, 757
Meadow Brook, 685–686
Mee, Thomas, 498

Meese, Christian, 243, 257, 364, 459–460, 485, 496, 714
Meherrin River, 570
Meherrin Station, 570
Meigs, John R., 705–706
Meigs, Montgomery C., 54–55, 75–76, 80–81, 705
Memphis, Tenn., 89, 132, 156, 159–160, 179, 203–204, 236, 266, 268
Mercer, Samuel, 77
Meridian, Miss., 494
Merle, Francis, 7
Merrill, Alfred K., 498
Merrimack, USS, 72, 205
Merritt, Robert B., 188
Merritt, Wesley, 592–593, 599, 605–607, 612–614, 616–618, 625, 627, 629, 631, 633, 637–638, 640, 643–644, 651–654, 656, 658–659, 659n2079, 660–661, 663, 667–670, 673–674, 677–679, 687–690, 696–698, 706–707, 709, 739
Merritt Plantation, 369–370
Mervine, William, 98, 110n372
Mexican War, 11, 16
Mexico, 465–466, 731–733, 744, 764–767
Mexico City, Mexico, 466
Meyer, John, 41–42, 78, 95, 127, 140n477, 257, 496, 563, 619, 701, 713–714, 742
Meyers, David, 78, 95
Michigan, USS, 779
Michigan Brigade, 688n2164
Michigan Cavalry, 1st, 631, 651, 678, 739
Michigan Cavalry, 2nd, 181, 592, 672
Michigan Cavalry, 4th, 762
Michigan Cavalry, 6th, 629–630, 639, 656, 658, 661, 663
Michigan Cavalry, 7th, 629, 631, 662–663, 678
Michigan Heavy Artillery, 6th, 611
Michigan Infantry Regiment, 6th, 177, 212n820, 213n822, 241, 263, 361, 391, 401, 403, 412, 414, 433–434
Middle Department, 578, 587–588
Middle Marsh Brook, 685, 692, 696
Middle Military Division, 587, 592–594, 641, 700, 704, 736
Middle Road, Va., 656
Middleburg, Va., 710
Middletown, Va., 643–644, 669, 672–673, 680, 686–690, 692–*693*, 700
Middleway, W. V. *See* Smithfield, W. V.
Miles, W. R., 371, 383–384

Miles' Legion, 452
Milford Creek, 651
Military Division of the Mississippi, 478, 762
Military Division of the West, 747
Mill Creek, 672, 746
Mill Springs, Ky., 146
Milledgeville, Ga., 719–720
Millen, Ga., 720
Miller, George, 498
Miller, John, 243, 257, 461, 496, 714
Miller's Lane, 693–694, 696
Milliken's Bend, La., 356, 440
Millwood Pike, 634
Minnesota, USS, 81
Minnesota Infantry Regiment, 5th, 521
Mint, William, 255, 257, 459, 474
Misener, James B., 498
Mississippi (steamer), 167
Mississippi, CSS, 163, 166, 168, 173
Mississippi, USS, 168, 171–172, 211, 301–302, 303n1138
Mississippi Infantry Regiment, 1st, 393, 423
Mississippi Infantry Regiment, 6th, 300, 365
Mississippi Infantry Regiment, 9th, 103, 130, 132
Mississippi Infantry Regiment, 15th, 365
Mississippi Infantry Regiment, 27th, 134
Mississippi Infantry Regiment, 39th, 399, 407, 409
Mississippi Light Artillery, 1st, 371
Mississippi Light Artillery, 1st, Battery B, 395
Mississippi Marine Brigade, 304, 356–357, 502
Mississippi rifle, 23
Mississippi River, 89–90, 95, 143, 145, 153, 155, 163, 166, 168–174, 177–178, 197–201, 203–205, 210–211, 214, 222–223, 228, 236, 246, 248, 260, 266–271, 273–274, 280, 283, 285, 290, 349, 355–356, 360–361, 456, 500, 550, 558
Mississippi Squadron, 496, 724
Missouri Battalion Sharpshooters, 9th, 520
Missouri Battery, 1st, 542
Missouri Battery, 6th, 511
Missouri Cavalry, 6th, 487, 509, 521
Missouri Infantry Regiment, 8th, 520
Missouri Infantry Regiment, 9th, 520
Missouri Infantry Regiment, 10th, 520
Missouri Infantry Regiment, 11th, 520
Missouri Infantry Regiment, 12th, 274, 520
Missouri Infantry Regiment, 16th, 520
Missouri Infantry Regiment, 17th, 274
Missouri Infantry Regiment, 19th, 520
Missouri Infantry Regiment, 24th, 520–521, 523, 527, 527n1708, 528, 530
Missouri Infantry Regiment, 26th, 520
Missouri Infantry Regiment, 27th, 520
Missouri Infantry Regiment, 32nd, 520
Missouri Infantry Regiment, 33rd, 520–521
Missouri Infantry Regiment, 36th, 520
Missouri Infantry Regiment, 38th, 520
Missouri Light Artillery, 1st, Company M, 564–565
Mobile, Ala., 204, 211, 236, 411, 465, 494n1625, 495, 543–544, 561, 567, 581–582, 621, 642, 724, 760
Mobile and Ohio Railroad, 181, 352
Mobile Bay, 608
Mohawk, USS, 55, 71
Molineaux, E. L., 297, 299–300, 332, 461
Monadnock, USS, 729
Monett's Bluff, 546
Monett's Ferry, 502
Monitor, USS, 72, 205
Monocacy River, 578–579
Monocacy Station, 592
Monongahela, USS, 294, 302, 369, 384, 421, 481–482, 610
Monroe, La., 560
Montgomery, Ala., 48, 60, 65
Montgomery, Solomon V., 243, 257, 364, 496, 498, 554, 563, 714
Moon Lake, 273–274
Moore, Alpheus S., 627, 677, 689, 696
Moore, Caleb, 627
Moore, Churchill, 243, 257, 496, 499, 555, 565, 620, 702, 713–714, 742
Moore, Daniel, 255, 257, 364, 460, 492, 496, 564
Moore, Dennis, 459
Moore, Edwin L., 705
Moore, Frederick, 740
Moore, Risdon M., 521
Moore, Thomas Overton, 53n147, 133, 160–161, 165–166, 227–228, 229n897, 234, 253, 602, 777
Moorefield, W. V., 590, 600, 711–712
Moors, J. F., 314, 440
Moran, John H., 255, 257, 459–460, 474–475, 485, 496, 554, 564–565
Moran, Margaret, 770
Moreno, Francesco, 250
Morgan, CSS, 169, 609

Morgan, Frank, 243, 255, 257, 459, 492, 496, 714
Morgan, J. S., 362, 372, 412, 457
Morgan, Sarah, 215
Morgan Plantation, 561
Morgan's Ferry, 441
Morganza, La., 360, 559, 561–562, 572, 610n1935
Morning Light, USS, 312
Moro (steamer), 288
Morris, Gouverneur, 47
Morris, Henry W., 357
Morris, John, 5, 7
Mortar Flotilla, 369
Morton, John E., 392, 396
Morton, Oliver P., 223
Mosby, John S., 600–601, 603–605, 653, 704–707, 710, 736–737, 743, 778
Moseley, B., 526
Moss Plantation, 506
Motts, Thaddeus P., 463
Mound City, USS, 202, 280, 551
Mount Carmel Cemetery, 687
Mount Carmel Church, 741
Mount Crawford, 652, 654
Mount Jackson, 647–649, 664–665, 707n2221, 737
Mount Pleasant, La., 433–436, 447–448
Mount Sidney, Va., 654
Mount Vernon, Ala., 31
Mouton, Alfred, 233, 262–264, 323, 326, 334, 346, 440, 507, 510, 527
Mower, Joseph A., 500–501, 521, 524, 526, 531–532, 558, 746
Moyer, Henry P., 655
Mulford, John E., 576
Mumford, William, 224–225, 310n1149, 639
Munford, Thomas, 661, 663–664, 664n2099, 665, 708
Munyer, Corporal, 762
Murphy, Edward, 498
Murphy, John, 5, 7–8, 41, 127, 140, 257, 459, 461
Murphy, Michael, 5, 7, 39, 44
Murrah, Pendleton, 764
Murtaugh, John, 3
Mustang Island, Tex., 483
Myers, Denis, 41, 127, 140, 185, 254, 257, 474
Myers, John, 5
Mystic (brig), 48

N

Narcissus, USS, 611
Nashville, Tenn., 133, 151–152, 158, 720
Nassau, USS, 195
Natchez (steamer), 249
Natchez, Miss., 177–178
Natchitoches, La., 502–504, 540, 546
Neaffie (steamer), 104, 106, 116, 116n384
Negrofoot Road, 741
Nelms, CSS, 116
Nelson, George, 628, 633, 635, 737
Nelson, John A., 385, 388–389, 398–399
Nelson, William, 628, 633, 635, 737
Neosho, USS, 519, 551, 553
Nerson's Woods, 327, 333
New Carthage, La., 283, 346, 355, 357, 366
New Creek, W. V., 700, 707, 712
New Falls City, CSS, 540
New Hampshire Cavalry, 2nd, 509, 510n1666
New Hampshire Infantry Regiment, 8th, 232–233, 242, 326, 340, 390, 394, 409, 412, 416, 425–426, 428, 438, 510n1666
New Hampshire Infantry Regiment, 8th, Company F, 438
New Hampshire Infantry Regiment, 8th, Company G, 386, 389, 410
New Hampshire Infantry Regiment, 15th, 241, 246, 270, 388, 391, 401–402, 415, 418, 433–436, 447, 451
New Hampshire Infantry Regiment, 16th, 241, 342–343, 349, 414
New Iberia, La., 338–339, *478*, 480, 484, 486, 490, 492
New Jersey Cavalry, 3rd, 662
New Jersey Mexican War Volunteers, 1st, 772
New London, USS, 260
New Madrid Canal, 199
New Madrid, Mo., 154, 156
New Market, Va., 577–578, 649–652, 654, 659, 698, 700, 725, 739
New Orleans, La., 145, 158, 160–167, 169, 172–174, 176, 179, 186, 190, 197, 199, 204, 211, 215, 223–228, 231–232, 234, 238, 240–241, 246–247, 252, 258, 260–263, 285, 291, 293, 306, 312, 341–342, 357, 368–369, 411–412, 441, 447, 450, 456, 458, 460, 494–495, 544, 554–555, 563, 565, 601, 721, 765–766, 774–775, 777–778, 781
New York Battery, 5th, 686
New York Battery, 6th, 663

New York Battery, 14th, 487
New York Battery, 16th, 728
New York Battery, 18th, 241, 297n1122, 371, 385–386, 391
New York Battery, 21st, 391
New York Battery, 25th, 493, 526–527, 527n1707, 530, 536, 548
New York Cavalry, 1st, 664–665
New York Cavalry, 2nd, 521
New York Cavalry, 4th, 630
New York Cavalry, 5th, 660–663, 697–698
New York Cavalry, 8th, 710–711
New York Cavalry, 9th, 664
New York Cavalry, 13th, 710
New York Cavalry, 14th, 463, 521
New York Cavalry, 25th, 629, 631, 663
New York Dragoons, 1st, 643, 649–650, 663, 689
New York Heavy Artillery, 5th, 679–680
New York Heavy Artillery, 6th, 698
New York Heavy Artillery, 9th, 647, 651, 653
New York Infantry Regiment, 6th, 92–93, 104–106, 106n358, 107, 117–118, 121, 128, 187–188, 193, 195, 241, 304, 312, 316, 318, 321, 335, 372–373, 414, 610, 647
New York Infantry Regiment, 6th, Company D, 139, 141
New York Infantry Regiment, 6th, Company G, 105
New York Infantry Regiment, 6th, Company K, 139, 141
New York Infantry Regiment, 8th, 663
New York Infantry Regiment, 12th, 463
New York Infantry Regiment, 21st, 562
New York Infantry Regiment, 22nd, 663
New York Infantry Regiment, 70th, 313
New York Infantry Regiment, 75th, 123, 128, 135, 187, 191, 231, 242, 264, 322–323, 389, 394–395, 412, 420, 423, 425, 429–430, 472, 481, 610, 635
New York Infantry Regiment, 90th, 362, 413, 425, 432
New York Infantry Regiment, 91st, 188, 190, 193, 241, 244, 246–247, 255, 309, 389, 394–395, 416, 425, 429–431, 476
New York Infantry Regiment, 110th, 241, 362, 381, 433
New York Infantry Regiment, 110th, Company A, 425
New York Infantry Regiment, 110th, Company B, 425
New York Infantry Regiment, 110th, Company E, 425
New York Infantry Regiment, 110th, Company I, 425
New York Infantry Regiment, 114th, 239, 241, 322, 340, 358, 362, 391, 414, 425, 429–430, 515, 521, 525, 528, 559, 581, 636
New York Infantry Regiment, 114th, Company F, 430
New York Infantry Regiment, 116th, 263, 295, 371, 386, 388, 391, 404, 432, 480, 516, 521, 547, 571, 635, 660, 684
New York Infantry Regiment, 128th, 242, 380, 391, 401, 403, 412, 433, 435
New York Infantry Regiment, 131st, 241, 318–319, 321, 339, 389, 394–395, 420, 425, 432, 636
New York Infantry Regiment, 133rd, 241, 390, 425, 428, 428n1457, 437, 544
New York Infantry Regiment, 153rd, 513, 521, 525, 528, 530n1715, 547, 581
New York Infantry Regiment, 156th, 241, 391, 636, 684
New York Infantry Regiment, 159th, 241, 254, 297, 317–318, 327, 332, 335, 340, 360, 390, 397, 407, 431–432, 461
New York Infantry Regiment, 160th, 241, 263, 322, 389, 394, 425, 429, 521, 682
New York Infantry Regiment, 161st, 241, 369, 371, 391, 404, 423, 425, 472, 513–516, 521, 528, 530
New York Infantry Regiment, 162nd, 241, 381, 381n1350, 390, 433, 435, 521, 531, 531n1719, 548
New York Infantry Regiment, 165th, 242, 324, 391, 403, 412, 433, 435, 516, 521, 531, 531n1719
New York Infantry Regiment, 173rd, 241, 297n1122, 390, 425, 428, 428n1457, 521, 531, 531n1719
New York Infantry Regiment, 174th, 241, 369, 371, 391, 404, 423, 425
New York Infantry Regiment, 175th, 297n1122, 323, 362, 433, 435–436
New York Infantry Regiment, 176th, 239, 684
New York Infantry Regiment, 177th, 242, 391, 401, 433, 436
New York Infantry Regiment, 178th, 521, 524
New York Light Artillery, 25th, 521, 523
New York National Guard, 463
New York, N.Y., 4, 6

Newlan, Thomas, 532–534
Newland, Abraham, 526
Newport, Ky., 4, 6
Newton, Ann, 4, 40
Newton, Mary, 4, 40
Newton, Thomas, 3–4, 40–41, 119, 126, 140, 194, 256, 473, 475–477, 485
Newtown, Va., 625–626, 640, 643, 673, 692
Niagara, USS, 111–112, 117, 120, 721
Niagara River, 779
Niblett's Bluff, 477–*478*, 484
Nichols, Edward A., 498
Nichols, G. W., 650, 695
Nichols, George S., 627
Nichols, W. A., 40
Nickerson, Frank S., 391, 401, 403, 544
Nicolay, John, 374
Nims, Ormond F., 391
Nims's Battery. *See* Massachusetts Battery, 2nd. (Nims')
Nitschke, John G., 5, 41, 127, 140, 254, 257, 364, 460, 496, 713–714
Noel, Theophilus, 337, 556
Noonan, Mary Ann, 772
North Anna, Va., 568
North Atlantic Blockading Squadron, 723–724
North River, 737
North Star, USS, 252
Northern Central Railroad, 585
Northern Column, 144–145, 153, 156, 160, 174, 179, 200, 235, 266
Northern Neck, Va., 743
Northern Virginia Brigade, 603
Northern Virginia Campaign, 206, 219
Northrup, Solomon, 358–359
Nottaway River, 570
Nottaway Station, 570

O

Oak Island, N. C., 722
Oaklawn Manor. *See* Porter Plantation
O'Brien, James, 403, 405–406
O'Brien, Sholto, 255, 257, 364, 459–460, 474, 485, 496, 499, 523, 536, 539
Ocean Queen, SS, 191
Ocmulgee (whaler), 237
Odlum, F. H., 471
O'Donnell, Edward, 39
O'Ferrall, Charles T., 632, 639
Ogeechee River, 720
Ogelthorpe Barracks, Ga., 31

Ohio Battery, 1st, 678, 680
Ohio Battery, 17th, 487–489, 611
Ohio Cavalry, 2nd, 662, 670
Ohio Cavalry, 8th, 707n2221, 709
Ohio Infantry Regiment, 34th, 709
Ohio Infantry Regiment, 48th, 508n1664
Ohio Infantry Regiment, 56th, 512, 556
Ohio Infantry Regiment, 83rd, 479, 487–488, 508n1664, 510
Ohio Infantry Regiment, 96th, 487–489, 508n1664
Ohio Infantry Regiment, 120th, 556
Ohio River, 4, 89–90
Ohlenschlager, Emil, 706
Old Cold Harbor, 568
Old Forge Farm, 673, 674n2129, 678
Old Forge Road, 691–692, 694, 696
Old Fort Niagara, N. Y., 777
Olvany, Michael, 6, 41, 99, 125, 127, 140n477, 185, 257, 496, 564–565
Oneida, USS, 177–178
O'Neil, Henry C., 498
O'Neil, John, 778–779
Opelousas, La., 307, 340, 346–347, 358–359, 481, 486–488, 561
Opequan Creek, 616, 618, 621–622, 625, 628–629, 631–632, 634, 640
Orange, Tex., *478*
Orange and Alexandria Railroad, 567, 653, 655, 666, 739
Orcutt, Ephraim, 243, 254, 257, 364, 460, 496, 714
Ord, E. O. C., 184–185, 480, 493, 585, 654, 725, 728, 752–753, 755
Oreto, CSS, 237
Osage, USS, 519, 542, 542n1745, 551, 553
O'Sullivan, Michael, 6, 41–42, 78, 127, 140, 257, 459, 473–474, 492, 496, 498, 554, 564–565, 775, 777
Ould, Robert, 475
Overland Campaign, 562, 571. *See also* Battles of the Wilderness
Overton's Hill, 721
Owasco, USS, 469, 471, 481
Owen, T. H., 677
Ozark, USS, 551

P

Paddytown, W. V. *See* New Creek, W. V.
Paducah, Ky., 146
Page Valley, 656–657

Paine, Charles J., 216, 384n1357, 412, 728, 730
Paine, Halbert, 215, 324, 326, 371n1324, 372, 376, 378–379, 381n1350, 382, 384, 384n1357, 385, 388–391, 393–394, 396, 412, 414, 416, 423–428, 428n1457, 430, 437
Palmer, James S., 177, 384, 457
Palmito Ranch, Tex., 767
Pamunkey River, 568, 740
Park, John, 203
Parke, John G., 750, 754–755
Parketton, William, 6, 41–42, 78, 127, 140, 257, 459
Parks, William, 243, 257, 496, 499, 536, 539, 701
Parrott rifled guns, 112, 115, 139, 193, 336
Parslow, Clarissa, 308
Parslow, Joseph, 244, 257, 309, 474–475, 485, 496, 499, 555, 564, 618, 703, 777
Parsons, Mosby, 520, 531n1719, 532n1721, 533–534, 541
Partisan Ranger Law, 590, 601–602, 604, 707
Partisan Rangers, 445, 521, 585, 590, 601–605, 616, 705–711
Pascagoula, Miss., 544
Pascagoula River, 123
Pass Cavallo, Tex., *482*–483, 544, 544n1749
Pattersonville, La., 480
Patton, George S., 629, 632, 637, 639
Pawnee, USS, 75
Payne, William, 639, 659n2081, 661, 663, 675–676, 678, 686, 708
Peach Orchard, 513
Peck, Frank H., 458
Peck, Lewis M., 531n1719
Pegram, John, 644, 646, 654, 674–675, 677, 680, 688–689
Peirce, Charles H., 627, 660, 660n2087, 662
Pelky, Henry, 244, 257, 474
Pellet, Elias P., 358
Pemberton, John C., 227, 266–268, 274, 277, 304, 350, 355–356, 365–368, 376, 440, 550, 715
Pendleton, William, 756
Peninsular Campaign, 153, 156, 159, 184, 205–206, 223, 322
Pennington, Alexander C. M., 661, 663, 737, 741
Pennsylvania Cavalry, 6th, 739
Pennsylvania Cavalry, 17th, 655, 673, 739n2328
Pennsylvania Infantry Regiment, 6th, 616–617

Pennsylvania Infantry Regiment, 18th, 663
Pennsylvania Infantry Regiment, 47th, 515, 521, 682
Pennsylvania Volunteers, 54th, 679
Penrose, William H., 606
Pensacola, Fla., 3, 30, 59–60, 80–81, 83, 86, 138–139, 161–162, 174, 176, 185, 187–192, 194, 216, 246, 249, 555, 774, 777
Pensacola, USS, 168, 211
Pensacola Bay, 3, 57, 249
Pensacola Harbor, 28, 60
Pensacola occupation, 186–189
Perkins, Solon A., 416
Perkins, Washington, 418
Perkins Plantation, 370
Perry, Madison S., 66
Perry, Raymond H., 523
Petersburg, Va., 577–578, 584, 588, 590–591, 596, 600, 606–607, 641, 653, 698, 738, 740–741, 747, *747*–748, 753, 755
Pfiffer, George, 255, 257, 496, 714
Phelps, John F., 386, 389, 391
Phelps, John W., 217
Phelps, S. L., 228
Philadelphia, Penn., 4
Philadelphia, Wilmington, and Baltimore Railroad, 585
Phillips, John W., 627
Phillips, Joseph, 445–446
Pickett, George, 741, 753
Piedras Negras, Mexico, 19
Pierce, Franklin, 731
Pierce and Paine College, 520
Pierpont, John H., 711n2234
Pillow, Gideon, 143, 151
Pinola, USS, 177, 476
Piper, Joseph, 498
Pittsburg Landing, Tenn., 156–159, 180–181
Pittsburgh, USS, 156, 280, 551
Plains Store, La., 370–371, 378, 404, 421, 423, 423n1445, 436
Plaquemine, La., 441, 491
Pleasant Grove, La., 513–517
Pleasant Hill, La., 503, 505, 516–518, 520–523, 539, 541–*542*
Pleasant Valley, Md., 699, 714, 719, 742, 772, 774
Plunkett, Charles T., 412
Pocahontas, USS, 75
Point Isabel, Tex., 482–483

Polignac, C. J., 510, 515, 521, 527, 534, 541, 546, 549, 556–558
Polk, Leonidas, 157, 234
Poole, Thomas, 41–42, 78, 109, 122
Pope, John, 153–156, 159–160, 174, 179–183, 200–201, 207, 219, 221, 225, 235, 550, 711, 763
Port Gibson, Miss., 353
Port Hudson, La., 90, 175, 199, 214, 228, 258, 260–261, 263, 265, 288–294, 297, 299–305, 307, 311, 341, 343, 345–349, 352, 354, 356, 359–361, 363, 365–371, 376–381, 381n1350, 382–390, 391n1379, 392–402, 404–409, 411–413, 419, *422*, 428, 430, 437–438, 440–441, 443, 446–447, 449–458, 461–462, 522, 550
Port Isabel, Tex., 2, *43*, 44n99
Port of Saluria, Tex., 48
Port Republic, Va., 650–651, 653–654, 656–657
Port Royal, S.C., 91, 721
Porter, Alexander, 320
Porter, David Dixon, 76–77, 80–81, 145, 168–170, 172, 175, 187, 191, 197, 200n759, 204, 228, 267–269, 269n1031, 271–276, 279–283, 286–291, 294, 305, 345–347, 355–359, 369, 439, 493–496, 500–503, 518–520, 522, 540–543, 545, 549–553, 705, 724, 726–729
Porter, F. J., 53
Porter, James, 320
Porter, John, 43–44
Porter, Mary, 307, 318–321, 327
Porter, Thomas W., 436n1480
Porter, W. D., 210–211, 213, 269n1031
Porter Plantation, 307, 318–321, 325, 328
Portsmouth, USS, 211, 260
Potomac River, 584, 589, 598, 614–615, 706, 743
Poughkeepsie, N. Y., 776
Powell, William, 638, 649, 652, 654, 655n2067, 656, 656n2067, 668–670, 677, 689, 696, 736
Power, Catharine, 775
Powers, F. P., 370–371
Powhatan, USS, 75–77, 80–81
Prairie D'Ane, Ark., 540–541
Pratt, John, 229n897
Prentiss, Benjamin, 456
Prescott, T. C., 410
Pretty Creek, 416
Price, Sterling, 184, 503, 516, 534, 541, 765

Pride, G. G., 283
Priest Cap, La., 421, 423, 439
Prince, Edward, 350, 382, 384
Prince George Court House, 569
Princess Royal, USS, 444–446, 446n1509
Profit's Island, La., 301
Provisional Army of the Confederacy, 602
Provost, William Y., 254
Purington, George A., 627
Putnam, Henry R., 463

Q

Queen of the West (ram), 202, 210–211, 287–291, 316, 336, 357
Queen's Own Rifles, Hamilton Battalion, 13th, *779*
Quinby, I. F., 202
Quinby, Isaac N., 279–280, 305
Quinn, Timothy, 627
Quinnebaug, USS, 314

R

Railroad District of West Virginia, 711
Raleigh, N. C., 759–760
Raleigh-Smithfield-Goldsboro Road, 746
Ramseur, Stephen, 598, 606, 616, 626, 628, 633, 635, 640–641, 644, 646–647, 674–675, 688–689, 692–693
Ranahan, Michael, 244, 257, 459
Randal, Horace, 520
Randolph, George W., 134, 166, 365n1299
Ransom, Dunbar R., 627
Ransom, T. E. G., 482–483, 483n1589–484n1589, 499, 501, 508, 510, 512–513, 604, 751
Rapidan River, 567
Rappahannock River, 219, 743
Rawles, Jacob B., 391, 511
Rawlins, John, 279, 285, 587
Raynor, William H., 511
Reading, George, 536n1738
Ream's Station, *569*–570, 665
Rectortown, Va., 668–670, 709
Red Bud Run, 633–635, 639
Red Chief, CSS, 378, 545
Red River, 166, 175, 212, 214, 223, 236, 261, 272–273, 287–291, 294, 304–305, 343, 345, 349, 357–358, 360, 477, 493–495, *500*, 502, 543, 545, 550–554, 556, 561, 763
Red River Campaign, 494–495, 499–537, 558

Redding, George W., 498, 555
Redding, J., 536
Reedy, Michael, 41, 109, 122
Reeve, Isaac V. D., 48–49
Reilly, Terence, 627
Reily, James, 316, 321, 325–326, 329
Renshaw, Francis B., 61–62, 62n179, 240–241
Republican Party, 22, 66, 88, 95, 216, 223, 235, 573, 642, 731
Reserve Brigade, 231–232, 414, 599, 612, 616, 618, 627, 631–632, 644, 652, 678, 688, 707
Revere House, 712
Reynolds, J. J., 562, 610n1935
Reynolds, Thomas C., 764
Rhode Island Artillery, 1st, 684
Rhode Island Cavalry, 1st, 689
Rhode Island Cavalry, 2nd, 440
Rhode Island Cavalry, 2nd, Company F, 297n1122
Rhode Island Cavalry, 3rd, 521, 523
Rice's Station, 756
Richards, Franklin W., 95, 127, 140, 243, 257, 364
Richardson, James P., 412
Richmond, La., 283, 346, 355–356, 366
Richmond, USS, 111–112, 117–118, 120, 240, 294–296, 301, 303n1138, 345, 347, 357, 368–369, 415, 721
Richmond, Va., 48–49, 88, 97, 108, 161–163, 165, 205–207, 220, 310, 567–*568*, 576, 588, 596–597, 603, 652, 654, 707, 712, 715, 722, 727, 735, 740–741, 743, 747–748, 752, 754–755, 759, 762
Richmond and Danville Railroad, 570
Richmond rifle, 25
Ricketts, James B., 578, 618, 628, 632, 634–636, 646–647, 683, 685, 692
Ridgeway, Ontario, 779
Rienzi Knoll Lane, 692, 695n2185
Rigolets de Bon Dieu, 502
Riley, Charles, 5, 39–42, 47, 56, 94, 99, 109–110, 125, 127, 139, 185, 190, 194, 243, 245–246, 310, 338, 342, 475, 768
Riley Plantation, 378
Ringgold Barracks, Tex., 2, 17, 42, 45, 47, 245, 483
Rio Grande, viii, 1–2, 8, 19–20, 32, 43–44, 131, 482–483, 543, 767
Rio Grande City, Tex., *482*–483
Rio Grande Expedition, 480–484, 486

Rivanna River, 669, 739
River Queen (steamer), 734
Rivers, Harry, 498
Rivers, James H., 498
Roanoke Island, N.C., 130
Roanoke Station, 570
Rob Roy, USS, 542
Robb, Hamilton, 517
Roberts, Thomas, 498
Roberts' Ford, 676
Robertson, Felix H., 105
Robertson, J. M., 115, 116n383
Robeson, William P., Jr., 627
Robinson, Harai, 505
Robinson, James W., 2–3, 17, 20, 39–42, 56, 768
Robinson, William, 39
Rochester, N.Y., 4
Rockfish Gap, 652, 737–738
Rockville, Md., 579
Rodenbough, Theophilus M., 627, 630
Rodes, Robert E., 598, 618, 624–626, 628, 634–635, 637, 639–640, 644
Rodgers, John, 89–90, 294, 318, 321, 334, 391, 562
Rodman, William M., 412
Rogers, James H., 34
Rogers, John, 630n1980
Romney, W. V., 711
Roosevelt, James I., 24
Roper, John, 6, 41, 127, 140n477, 185, 257, 459
Rosecrans, William S., 184–185, 286, 350, 373–374, 465, 478–479, 561, 574, 589
Ross, Leonard F., 274, 276–277, 279, 282
Ross Landing, La., 299
Rosser, Thomas L., 604, 654, 656–657, 657n2072, 658–659, 659n2082, 660, 662–665, 667, 673–677, 677n2140, 678, 687, 691, 700, 707, 707n2221, 708–709, 711–712, 735, 737
Round Hill, Va., 674
Round Top Mountain, 660
Rowand, Arch, 740
Rowanty Creek, 570
Rowland, Card, 243
Rude's Hill, Va., 649, *649*–650
Ruffin, F. G., 722
Ruggles, Daniel, 162, 212, 214, 258
Ruggles, David C., 705
Rupprecht, Ludwig, 5, 41, 127, 140, 256, 496, 564, 620, 663, 665, 699n2200, 702–704, 714

Russell, David A., 627, 632, 634, 637, 640
Russell, John H., 98–99
Russell, William, 82–86, 174
Rust, Albert, 299, 365–366
Ryan, James, 5, 7

S

Sabine, USS, 71–73, 81
Sabine City, Tex., 230, *467*–468
Sabine Crossroads, 506–513, 516
Sabine Lake, *467*
Sabine Pass Expedition, 467, 469–473, 477, 479, 481, 483
Sabine River, 468–469, 477, 506
Sabine River Road, 531, 532n1721
Sable Island, La., 172
Sachem, USS, 301, 357, 458, 468–469, 471–472
Sailor's Creek, Va., 755–756
Saint Mary (steamer), 275, 318–319
Salado Creek, Tex., 48
Saluria, Tex., 49
San Antonio, Tex., 31, 33–37, 39–40, 46, 48
Sanders, George, 573–574
Sanderson, James A., 194, 243, 254, 256, 307, 318, 364, 458, 473, 484–485, 491, 496–497, 499, 523, 532–533, 536, 539
Sandford, Charles W., 463
Sandy Creek, La., 354, 376, 378, 381, 385–386, 393, 395, 398–399
Santa Rosa Island, Fla., 57, 69, 76, 79, 81, 86, 92, 98, 100, 103–105, 111, *115*, 134, 139–140, 611, 773
Saugus, USS, 729
Savannah, Ga., 700, 718, 720, 745
Savannah River, 31, 745
Saxton, Rufus, 137, 217, 217n843, 218, 252
Schaffer, William, 94–95, 109, 125, 127, 139, 140n477, 185, 194
Schlatter, Robert E., 7
Schmidt, Heinrick, 6, 41, 127, 140, 257, 459
Schneider, Philip H., 10, 41, 127, 140, 257, 364, 459–460, 497, 772–773
Schnieder, Philip M., 714
Schoenfeld, Charles, 5, 7
Schofield, John, 720, 736, 745–746
Schoonmaker, James M., 627, 638
Schwartz, Edward, 627
Sciota, USS, 178, 476
Scott, John, 527–528, 535
Scott, Thomas A., 91, 148, 153, 157, 179, 225
Scott, William E., 5, 10, 41–42, 127, 139–141, 194, 257, 473, 477, 484, 496, 564, 703, 714, 773
Scott, Winfield, 27–30, 32, 38–39, 52, 60, 65, 70–71, 74–77, 80, 85, *85*–86, 88–91, 97, 179, 721, 731, 779
Scottsville, Va., 739
Scurry, William R., 520
Second Battle of Winchester, 577
Second Confiscation Act, 137
Second Seminole War, 771
Second Wheeling Convention, 711n2234
Seddon, James, 366, 450, 604, 744, 751
Sedgely, Robert, 498
Seeley, F. W., 115, 116n383, 116n384, 119
Selma, CSS, 608–609
Semmes, Raphael, 89, 238, 265, 266n1015, 326, 331, 333–334, 336, 595
Semmesport, La. *See* Simmesport, La.
Sevier's Ford, 629
Seward, William H., 74–77, 220, 223–225, 259, 285, 466, 495, 550, 559, 706, 733–734
Sewell, James, 498
Seymour, Charles J., 627, 756
Seymour, Horatio, 462–463
Shannon, Denman W., 444–445
Shapley, Morgan S., 94–95, 127, 140n477, 257, 459
Sharpe, Jacob, 635–636
Sharps repeating rifles, 331
Sharpsburg, Md., 598
Shaw, Warren P., 6, 10, 41, 109, 125, 127, 140, 257, 497, 620, 702, 715, 773
Shaw, William T., 518, 521–523, 525–526, 526n1707, 527, 527n1707, 528–529, 530n1715, 531–534
Shelby, W. B., 398–399, 407
Shenandoah River, 584, 600, 605–606, 649, 653, 670, 675–677, 707n2221
Shenandoah Valley, 567–569, 577, 588–589, 591, 595, 598–600, 605–608, 614, 620–621, 623–624, 641–642, 699–700, 708, 719, 735, 739, 776
Shenandoah Valley Campaign, 206, 618, 699, 716, 774
Shepherdstown, W. V., 613, 615–616
Sheridan, Phillip H., 19–20, 181, 569, 588–589, 591–595, 597–601, 604, 606–608, 612–616, 618, 621–626, 631–635, 637, 640–649, 649n2045, 651–657, 660, 665–666, 666n2109, 667–669, 669n2115, 670–674, 677, 682, 682n2149, 685, 691–692,

694–695, 695n2185, 696–700, 702–708, 710, 716, 719, 724–725, 735–741, 743, 747–748, 753–757, 765, 767, 776
Sherman, John, 269n1027
Sherman, Thomas W., 122, 195, 258, 292, 294, 312, 340, 370, 370n1317, 371, 371n1324, 378–380, 382, 384, 387–388, 391–393, 398, 400–403, 408, 408n1416, 409
Sherman, William T., 153, 159, 221–222, 266–269, 269n1027, 271, 274, 280, 283–284, 350, 450, 465, 493–494, 494n1625, 495, 499, 519, 543–545, 551, 560, 567, 575, 581, 584, 612, 621, 642, 656, 656n2067, 700, 715–720, 735–736, 739, 743, 745–747, 759–761
Sherman's March, 715–720
Shiloh, Tenn., 156–159, 174, 180, 182, 186, 221
Ship Island, Miss., 102, 124, 129, 161–162, 168, 237–239, 409, 777
Shipley, Alexander N., 98, 105, 118
Shorter, John G., 124
Shreveport, La., 477, 493–495, 506, 519, 540–541, 543, 546, 551, 560, 582, 763–766
Shubrick, W. B., 180
Shy's Hill, 721
Sias, Chauncy R., 498
Sibley, Caleb C., 47–49, 245
Sibley, Henry H., 322–324, 336, 346
Siege of Port Hudson, 411–456, 476, 775
Sigel, Franz, 567–569, 577–578, 578n1853
Signal, USS, 556
Signal Knob, 600
Silver Spring, Md., 579, 583
Silvey, William, xii, 2–3, 17, 20, 39, 41–42, 56, 94, 99
Simmes, Mrs. Bennet Barton, 361
Simmesport, La., 348–349, 359–360, 370, 372, 378, 500, 557, *557–558*
Simmonds, Robert, 773
Simmonds, William Edward Scott. *See* Scott, William E.
Simms, James P., 679–680
Simonds, John, 498
Simonds, William E., 332, 332n1215
Slack, Charles B., 448, 458, 473, 484, 486, 510
Slaughter, James E., 767
Slaughter Plantation, 378, 400–402, 414–415, 432, 434
Slemmer, Adam J., 30, 60, 60n171, 61–65, 68, 71, 73, 86, 100, 136
Slidell, John, 66–67, 77

Slocum, Henry W., 719, 746
Smith, Abel, 403, 412
Smith, Andrew J., 500–504, 518–523, 525–526, 528, 530n1715, 532–533, 533n1727, 534–535, 540–541, 543–545, 556, 558–560, 715, 718, 721
Smith, Caleb B., 74
Smith, Charles F., 146–148, 201
Smith, E. Kirby, 123, 304, 310n1149, 337, 348, 355–356, 411, 411n1421, 440–441, 450, 450n1514, 503, 507, 516, 532n1722, 534, 540–541, 546, 556, 763–766
Smith, Elisha B., 429–430
Smith, George S., 629, 632
Smith, Hiram, 244, 257, 459, 461, 473
Smith, J. M., 34
Smith, James H., 244, 257, 412, 497, 715
Smith, Jesse W., 618
Smith, Joseph, 5, 41–42, 127, 140, 185, 308, 497, 563, 619
Smith, Martin L., 161–163, 165, 176, 178, 781
Smith, Robert S., 627
Smith, Sooy, 350
Smith, T. Kilby, 450, 500, 503, 519–520, 540, 543, 545–546, 549, 560
Smith, Watson, 274–276, 278–279, 282
Smith, William H., 244, 257, 497–499, 499n1634, 523, 536, 539, 777
Smithfield, W. V., 616–618
Smith's Island, N. C., 722
Snicker's Gap, Va., 584, 606
Soldiers and Sailors Home (Bath, N. Y.), 769–771
South Anna River, 741
South Carolina Regiment, 7th, 740
South Carolina, USS, 92
South Carolina Volunteers, 1st, 218
South Carolina Volunteers, 8th, 629
South River, 746
Southern sympathizers, 30, 75, 77–78, 152, 546, 590, 709, 712, 744
Southside Railroad, 569–570, 715, 738, 740–741, 747–748, 752–753, 755, 762
Southwest Pass, 111–112, 164, 168
Spangler, Charles, 41, 119, 126, 140, 256, 474, 476–477
Spencer repeaters, 617, 658, 729, 737, 754
Spotsylvania, Va., 567–568
Sprague, Homer, 86n274, 320, 335, 374
Sprague, J. T., 49, 763–764

Springfield Landing, La., 371–372, 378, 408, 519
Springfield rifle, 23, 25, 331, 617
St. Augustine, Fla., 31
St. Charles Courthouse, La., 228
St. Francis River, 153
St. Joseph's Island, Tex., 483
St. Louis, Mo., 4, 763
St. Louis, USS, 81
St. Martinsville, La., 338
St. Mary's Cannoneers, 329, 331–332, 549
St. Mary's, USS, 232–233, 313–314, 320n1181
St. Patrick's Bayou, 505, 507, 510
St. Stephen, New Brunswick, 778
Stafford Plantation, 363
Stagg, Peter, 627
Staked Plain, West Texas, xi
Stanners, Martin, 94–95, 127, 140n477, 257, 308, 364, 442, 460, 474–475, 492
Stanton, Edwin M., 22, 82, 89, 137, 144–145, 157, 181–183, 202, 206–207, 217, 225, 231, 259, 282, 285–287, 342, 567, 581, 588–589, 592, 623, 641, 655, 667–669, 671, 733, 754, 760
Star of the South (steamer), 92
Star of the West (steamer), 47, 65, 275
Starlight, CSS, 378, 545
Staunton, Va., 656, 679, 708–709, 712, 737
Staunton River, 570, 756
Steedman, I. G., 376, 379, 382, 384–385, 393, 395–396, 399–400, 409, 412, 420, 422n1444
Steele, Frederick, 493–495, 534, 540–541, 543–544, 546, 559, 561, 573
Steele's Bayou, 279–280, 283, 305, 357, 519
Stephens, Alexander H., 716–717, 732–735
Stephenson's Depot, Va., 588, 618, 621, 625–626, 629, 632, 635, 637–638, 700
Stevens, CSS, 338
Stevens, Hazard, 699
Stevens, John, 498
Stevenson, C. L., 268n1022
Stewart, William, 244, 257, 497, 715
Stickney, Albert, 443
Stockdale, USS, 611
Stoll, Andrew, 6, 41, 56, 94, 127, 140, 257, 364, 459–460, 554–555, 564, 620, 650, 702, 713, 715, 742, 763
Stone, Barton W., 446
Stone, Charles P., 447, 518, 523, 525–526, 533
Stone, R. C., 521

Stone, Richard, 5, 7
Stoneman, George, 736
Stony Creek Depot, Va., 570–571
Stowe, Harriet Beecher, 358
Strasburg, Va., 643, 655, 665, 676, 697–698. *See also* Battle of Tom's Brook
Straub, Amelius, 5, 40–41, 127, 140n477, 257, 308, 364, 458, 473, 484, 492, 497–498, 554, 701, 713–714
Straub, Margaret, 40
Streight's Raid, 350
Stringham, Silas H., 74, 92, 162
Strong, George C., 145n491
Stuart, J. E. B., 604
Sultana (steamboat), 765
Summit Point, W. V., 606–607, 612, 618, 621, 625, 629
Sumner, Charles, 259, 370, 374
Sumner, S. B., 412
Sumter (ram), 210–211, 237
Supply (steamer), 60, 62, 64
Sutherland's Station, 755
Sweeny, Thomas, 778
Swift Run Gap, 653
Switzerland, USS, 202, 356–357
Syracuse, N.Y., 4
Szymanski, Ignatius, 169n629

T

Taft, Elijah D., 628
Talisman (blockade runner), 723
Tallahatchie River, 273, 275, 277, 350
Tansill, Robert, 48
Tappan, James C., 520, 532n1721, 534, 541
Tarleton Plantation, 480, 703
Taylor, Franck E., 105, 112, 119, 125–126, 139–140, 185, 189, 194, 243, 254, 256, 307–308, 318, 364, 383, 412, 447, 458, 473, 484, 491, 496–497, 523, 526, 532–533, 535–536, 554, 563, 616–620, 627, 641, 647, 650, 653, 690–691, 699, 701, 712–714, 742, 763, 768
Taylor, Franck, Sr., 125
Taylor, Richard, 70, 125, 162, 227, 227n890, 228–231, 233–234, 260–262, 274, 287, 289, 292, 304, 310n1149, 311–312, 316, 321, 323–326, 329–339, 346, 348, 355–356, 361, 368, 387, 440–441, 443, 447, 450, 450n1514, 453, 455–458, 481, 484, 487, 491, 495, 500–508, 510, 514, 516–518, 520–526, 531–532, 532n1721,

533–535, 540–541, 546, 549–550, 556, 558–559, 649, 719, 760–761, 763
Taylor, Zachary, 70
Teche Bayou. *See* Bayou Teche
Teche Campaign, 305, 345–346, 348, 356, 361, 387, 413, 442
Tecumseh, USS, 609, 611
Teighe, Michael, 255, 257, 364, 460, 497, 563, 619, 715, 776
Tennessee, CSS, 608, 610–611
Tennessee, USS, 177, 481
Tennessee Infantry Regiment, 1st, 157
Tennessee Infantry Regiment, 48th, 149
Tennessee Infantry Regiment, 51st, 149
Tennessee River, 90, 130, 146–147, 153, 156, 494, 720–721
Tensas Bayou, 272
Terre Noir Bayou, Ark., 540
Terrell, Alexander, 521
Terry, Alfred H., 728, 745–746, 751
Terry, Edward, 415, 425–426
Terry, US Transport, 155
Texas Artillery Battery, 7th, 526
Texas Cavalry, 1st, 241–242, 521, 527
Texas Cavalry, 3rd, 518
Texas Cavalry, 4th, 332, 337, 442, 444, 446, 521, 556
Texas Cavalry, 5th, 444, 446, 521
Texas Cavalry, 7th, 445–446, 521, 549
Texas Cavalry, 9th, 521
Texas Cavalry, 12th, 521
Texas Cavalry, 13th, 229–230, 520–521
Texas Cavalry, 15th, 521
Texas Cavalry, 17th, 521
Texas Cavalry, 22nd, 521
Texas Cavalry, 26th, 521, 527
Texas Cavalry, 31st, 521
Texas Cavalry, 34th, 521
Texas Cavalry, 36th, 542
Texas Cavalry, 37th, 521
Texas Heavy Artillery, 1st, 471
Texas Infantry, 2nd, 487
Texas Infantry Regiment, 2nd, 277
Texas Infantry Regiment, 5th, 326
Texas Infantry Regiment, 12th, 520
Texas Infantry Regiment, 18th, 520
Texas Infantry Regiment, 22nd, 520
Texas Mounted Rifleman, 1st, 33
Texas Partisan Rangers, 1st, 445–446, 521
Texas Partisan Rangers, 2nd, 521
Thames (steamer), 239

Thayer, Henry B., 5, 7
Thayer, John M., 540
Thibodeaux, La., 442
Third Battle of Winchester, 628–642
Thoburn, Joseph, 628, 639, 667–668, 676, 679–680
Thomas, Charles, 498
Thomas, George H., 146, 575, 718, 720–721, 736, 738, 743
Thomas, Lorenzo, 38, 50, 71
Thomas, Stephen, 229, 388–389, 394–396, 681–683
Thompson, Jacob, 22, 574
Thompson, John L., 627
Thompson, William V., 6, 10, 41, 99, 109, 125, 127, 140, 257, 497, 564, 703–704, 713, 715, 773–774
Thompson's Creek, La., 376, 378, 382, 384, 545
Three Top Mountain, 600, 606, 670
Tibbits, Howard, 472
Tilghman, Lloyd, 149
Time (steamer), 103, 116, 116n384, 133
Timmins, John, 498
Tolles, Cornelius, 706
Tompkins, Charles H., 628
Tom's Brook, 657–665
Tomson, John, 95, 127, 140, 190, 257, 492
Torbert, Alfred, 592–593, 598–599, 606–607, 614–615, 621, 625, 627, 630n1980, 632, 638n2010, 643–644, 647–649, 651–652, 654, 659n2079, 660, 664, 689–691, 700, 735
Totten, Joseph G., 52
Toucey, Isaac, 67–68
Tower, Zealous B., 30, 60, 69, 107
Town Creek, Ala., 350
Townsend, E. D., 475
Townsend, Reuben, 6, 41, 94, 127, 140, 194, 257, 497, 563–564, 619, 703–704, 713, 715, 776
Towson, Md., 585
Tredegar Iron Works, Richmond, Va., 25n54
Trevilian Station, 569
Tullahoma Campaign, 478
Tumbling Run, 643–644, 646
Turner, William H., 627
Tuscarora, USS, 237
Twiggs, David E., 27n57, 28–29, 32–37, 40, 45, 102, 133, 161–162
Twohig, John, 17
Tyler, Tex., 513

Tyler, USS, 90, *90*, 210

U

Ullmann, Daniel, 342, 454
Union Defense Committee, 87
Union sympathizers, 133, 250, 585
United States Artillery, 1st, Battery A, 2, 67, 71, 105, 106n358, 122, 242, 263, 391, 396, 486, 780
United States Artillery, 1st, Battery C, 241, 742
United States Artillery, 1st, Battery D, 2, 779
United States Artillery, 1st, Battery E, 572, 779
United States Artillery, 1st, Battery F, 17, 32, 53, 92, 106n358, 242, 245–246, 338, 391, 396, 425, 557–558, 572, 768, 780
United States Artillery, 1st, Battery G, 3, 60, 69, 86, 572, 769
United States Artillery, 1st, Battery H, 109, 572, 779
United States Artillery, 1st, Battery I, 572
United States Artillery, 1st, Battery K, 4, 17, 32, 37, 53, 476, 566, 569–572, 593, 600, 604, 607, 612–613, 616, 618, 626, 632–633, 641, 643–644, 647, 650, 653–654, 663, 665, 690–691, 699, 701–703, 714–715, 719, 742–743, 762, 768, 776
United States Artillery, 1st, Battery L, vii, viii, ix, x, xi, 1–10, 12–14, 16–20, 32, 38–44, 53, 56, 86–87, 90, 92–95, 99–101, 103–104, 106n358, 109–110, 112, 117, 119, 122, 131–132, 139–141, 170, 175, 188, 190, 192, 241, 244–249, 251, 254–256, 294, 297, 300, 308, 310–314, 318, 327, 333, 335, 338, 342–343, 360, 364–365, 369, 372, 382–383, 391, 395, 425, 432, 437, 440, 442, 447–448, 455, 461, 465, 468, 472, 476–477, 480, 482, 486–487, 490–491, 493, 498–499, 501, 503, 508, 513, 515, 518, 521, 523–526, 530–533, 535–536, 539–540, 547, 550, 554–557, 561–566, 571–572, 577, 581, 593, 599–600, 604, 607, 610, 612–613, 616, 618, 620, 626, 632–633, 636, 641, 643–644, 647, 650, 653–654, 663, 665, 690–691, 699–700, 702–703, 712–715, 719, 742–743, 755, 768–780
United States Artillery, 1st, Battery M, viii, ix, 2, 32, 43–44, 53, 768, 779
United States Artillery, 2nd, 16, 493
United States Artillery, 2nd, Battery A, 78, 92, 106n358
United States Artillery, 2nd, Battery C, 54, 106n358, 112, 294, 391, 448, 562
United States Artillery, 2nd, Battery D, 616
United States Artillery, 2nd, Battery H, 78, 105, 242
United States Artillery, 2nd, Battery K, 78, 106n358, 242
United States Artillery, 2nd, Battery M, 32, 37, 43–44, 78, 92, 736, 768
United States Artillery, 3rd, Battery E, 728
United States Artillery, 3rd, Company C, 105
United States Artillery, 4th, Battery C-E, 736
United States Artillery, 4th, Battery L, 770
United States Artillery, 5th, Battery G, 242, 371, 391, 511
United States Artillery, 5th, Battery M, 633
United States Artillery, 27th, 483
United States Cavalry, 1st, 599, 605, 607, 664, 687
United States Cavalry, 2nd, 616, 630–631
United States Cavalry, 2nd, Company D, 44–45
United States Cavalry, 2nd, Company H, 44–45
United States Cavalry, 3rd, 632, 715
United States Cavalry, 5th, 630, 663–664, 689
United States Cavalry, 6th, 578
United States Cavalry, 7th, 369
United States Colored Heavy Artillery, 10th, Company F, 190
United States Colored Infantry, 20th, 544n1749
United States Colored Infantry, 27th, 730–731
United States Colored Infantry, 77th, 190
United States Infantry, 1st, 32
United States Infantry, 1st, Battery A, 562
United States Infantry, 1st, Battery F, 562
United States Infantry, 1st, Company G, 47
United States Infantry, 1st, Company H, 44–45
United States Infantry, 1st, Company K, 47
United States Infantry, 3rd, 122
United States Infantry, 3rd, Battery B, 32
United States Infantry, 3rd, Company A, 47
United States Infantry, 3rd, Company C, 32, 44, 78, 98, 106n358
United States Infantry, 3rd, Company E, 32, 44, 78, 105, 106n358, 112
United States Infantry, 3rd, Company F, 47
United States Infantry, 3rd, Company I, 47
United States Infantry, 8th, 48, 290
United States Infantry, 8th, Company A, 47
United States Infantry, 8th, Company B, 46
United States Infantry, 8th, Company D, 47
United States Infantry, 8th, Company E, 46

United States Infantry, 8th, Company K, 46
United States Infantry, 14th, 772
United States Infantry, 19th, 109
United States Infantry, 75th, 122
Upton, Emory, 627, 637, 640
Urban, Gustavus, 627
Urbana, USS, 48

V

Valley District, 603
Valley Pike, 635, 640, 643, 646, 650, 652, 654–655, 658, 660–661, 663–664, 668, 671, 673, 676–677, 679–680, 682, 683n2153, 684–687, 689–692, 694, 696–698, 704, 736
Valverde Battery, 526
Van Buren, Martin, 731
Van Dorn, CSS, 203
Van Dorn, Earl, 46, 48, 124, 132, 184–185, 200, 206, 209, 212, 214, 227, 267–268, 373
Van Petten, John, 430
Van Zandt, Jacob, 384, 388–389, 394–395
Vance, Joseph W., 507–508, 512
Vanderbilt, USS, 92
Varner, Harry, 498
Varuna, USS, 169
Vaughn, John C., 598, 761
Vera Cruz, Mexico, ix
Vermilion Bayou, 480, 487
Vermilionville, La., 477–478, 490
Vermillion Bayou, 473
Vermillion River, 307, 338–340
Vermont Battery, 1st, 241, 379, 391, 401, 421, 468, 536, 548, 558
Vermont Battery, 2nd, 371, 391, 404
Vermont Cavalry, 1st, 521, 697–698
Vermont Infantry Regiment, 7th, 195, 198, 211–*212*, 231–232, 242, 255
Vermont Infantry Regiment, 8th, 199, 228–229, 232–233, 242, 263–264, 322, 389, 393–395, 425, 429–430, 471, 682, 683n2153, *683*
Vicksburg, Miss., 49, 174–176, 176n663, 177–178, 198–200, 204–205, 210–212, 214, 222–223, 228, 236, 246, 266–271, 273–274, 277, 281, 283–288, 290–293, 304, 346–347, 349, 355–358, 361, 365–367, 373, 376, 440–441, 450–451, 453, 456, 462, 464, 478–479, 500, 502, 543, 559–560, 715, 754, 781
Vicksburg II, 197–200, 216, 233

Vicksburg River Expedition, 267–269
Villepigue, John B., 119–120
Vincennes, USS, 111, 111n373, 138, 187
Vincent, William G., 316–317, 320–321, 323, 329, 501, 546
Vinton, D. H., 35
Virginia, CSS, 577
Virginia, USS, 476, 481
Virginia Cavalry, 3rd, 677
Virginia Cavalry, 7th, 711
Virginia Cavalry, 8th, 709
Virginia Cavalry, 11th, 711
Virginia Cavalry, 12th, 677, 677n2140
Virginia Cavalry, 18th, 639
Virginia Cavalry, 23rd, 632, 639
Virginia Central Railroad, 569, 646, 653, 668, 673, 735, 739–740
Virginia Central Railroad Bridge, 669
Virginia Infantry Regiment, 6th, 642
Virginia Infantry Regiment, 37th, 464
Virginia Military Institute, 578, 589
Virginia Mounted Infantry, 62nd, 632, 639
Virginia Partisan Rangers, 1st, 603
Virginia Volunteer Cavalry, 11th, 677
Vodges, Israel, 67, 67n196, 68–69, 71–72, 74–75, 81, 86, 86n273, 105, 118
Voltiguer (barque), 239

W

Wade, Benjamin, 573
Wade-Davis Bill, 573
Waite, Carlos A., 32, 35, 37–40, 45–46
Walke, Henry A., 64
Walker, James, 642
Walker, John G., 278, 282, 356, 440, 450, 512, 520, 527, 532, 534, 764
Walker, L. P., 46, 69, 78n244, 81, 129, 160
Walker, W. H. T., 367
Walker, W. S., 68, 71
Walker's Texas Division, 440, 487, 520, 541
Wallace, Lewis, 578–579
Waller, Edwin, 229, 229n897, 230, 326
Walsh, Richard, 7
Walton, Charles E., 244, 257, 477, 496, 714
War Department, 3, 16, 23, 29–30, 32, 46, 49, 82, 121, 158, 182–183, 202, 227, 237, 286, 310, 315, 339, 342
Ward, Henry A., 42, 94, 257, 460, 497, 549, 564
Ward, Henry H., 109, 127, 364, 703, 715
Warner, Alexander, 361
Warren, Gouverneur, 596–597, 752–753

Warren, James, 297
Warrington, Fla., 59, 62, 65
Washburn, C. C., 462, 486n1596, 487–489
Washburn, H. D., 483
Washburne, Elihu, 222, 267, 494
Washington, D. C., *566*, 577, 579, 581, 584, 587, 623–624, 641, 666–667, 670, 707
Washington, Ga., 762
Washita (Ouachita) River, 272
Watson, Josiah, 64
Waul, T. N., 275, 277
Waul, Thomas, 520
Waynesboro, Ga., 720
Waynesboro, Va., 654, 737–738, 741
Webb, CSS, 289–291, 342
Webb Plantation, 363
Weber, Max, 578
Weir, Julian V., 627
Weitzel, Godfrey, xii, 114n379, 132n448, 145n491, 231–234, 259–261, 263–264, 264n1004, 292, 294, 311, 313, 315, 321–324, 329, 338, 358–359, 370, 371n1324, 373, 378–379, 382, 384–389, 391–394, 396–398, 399n1391, 400, 409, 414–415, 420, 423–426, 429–431, 453, 455n1531, 457, 465, 468–472, 477, 487, 489–491, 581, 724–727, 730, 753, 755, 765, 768
Welch's Spring, W. V., 612
Weldon Railroad, 569–570, 596, 607, 621, 715, 762
Welles, Gideon, 67, 72–74, 76–77, 89–90, 110, 144–145, 174, 191, 199–200, 205, 207, 210, 213, 220, 223, 228, 231, 237–238, 269, 269n1031, 271, 276, 281–282, 286–287, 290, 292–294, 357–358, 374–375, 464, 471–472, 549, 551, 595, 608, 722–725, 728, 734
Wells, William, 627, 663, 691
Welsch, Peter, 244, 257, 364, 459, 497, 715
Welsh, Benjamin C., 498
Welsh, Peter, 555
West, John, 526
West Florida (British schooner), 230
West Gulf Blockading Squadron, 138, 167, 293, 481
West India Squadron, 237
Westfield, USS, 240, 260
Wharton, Gabriel C., 606, 628–629, 631–632, 639–640, 644, 646, 675–676, 678, 684, 686, 689, 692, 700, 735, 737
Wharton, John A., 546, 549

Wheaton, Frank, 692, 756
Wheeler, Charles, 473, 484
Wheeler, Joseph, 720
White, Elijah V., 663, 707
White, Michael, 5, 10, 41, 127, 140, 194, 257, 442, 477, 496, 499, 536, 539, 555, 564, 619–620, 715, 774–775
White, Perry S., 699
White Hall Plantation, 361
White House, Va., 741
White Oak Road, 752
White Post, Va., 606, 621
Whitehall Point, *456*
White's Ford, 584
Whiting, W. H. C., 729–731
Whitley, R. H. K., 35
Wickham, John, 639, 644, 651, 654, 665, 677
Wicks, David J., 5, 41, 119, 126, 140, 256, 460, 477, 496, 499, 619
Wicks Plantation, 778
Wigfall, Louis T., 66
Wilcox, Thomas M., 254, 258, 364, 460, 715
Wilder, Joshua E., 244, 254, 257, 497, 715
Wildes, Thomas F., 680
Wilkins, John C., 498
Wilkinson, Joseph, 5, 41, 127, 140, 257, 364, 460, 713–714
Wilkson, Henry, 42, 127, 140, 257, 497, 564–565
Willcox, Thomas M., 497
Williams, Alpheus, 235
William(s), Henry, 6, 41, 95, 127, 140–141, 258, 459, 497, 499, 555, 564, 713
Williams, James, 7
Williams, Thomas, 172, 177–179, 197–200, 204–205, 210–211, 212n820, 213, 216, 271, 703–704
Williams Canal, 282–283, 288, 305, 550
Williamsburg, Va., 205, 313, 322
Williamson, H. F., 386
Williston, Edward, 616–618, 627
Wilmington, N. C., 719–728, 736, 743, 745
Wilmington Expedition, 725
Wilson, Henry, 23n45
Wilson, James H., 222, 273–274, 276–279, 282, 569–570, 592–593, 606–607, 612, 614, 618, 622, 625, 627, 632–635, 638n2010, 640, 643–644, 651–652, 656, 656n2067, 762
Wilson, John (Benjamin Hughes), 564–565
Wilson, Thomas W., 244

Wilson, William "Billy," 93, 104n350, 106, 193, 195, 312–313
Wilson's Farm, 505
Wilson's Raid, 715
Winchester, Va., 578, 584, 588, 599–600, 605–606, 612, 621–622, 624, 626, 628–629, 631–632, *634*, 637, 639–642, 644, 671–672, 699–700, 705–706, 712, 719, 725, 735, 739, 742, 763, 775, 778
Wingfield, J. H., 385, 399, 409
Winn, Abram F., 244, 258, 308–311, 313, 777
Winn, Joel T., 244, 258, 308–311, 313, 777
Winn, Mary, 311
Winona, USS, 169, 178, 299, 445–446, 446n1509
Wisconsin Cavalry, 4th, 358, 390
Wisconsin Infantry Regiment, 4th, 177, 199, 210–211, 215, 241, 324, 340, 412, 414, 420n1440, 425–426, 428
Wisconsin Infantry Regiment, 8th, 521
Wisconsin Infantry Regiment, 12th, 350
Wisconsin Infantry Regiment, 23rd, 487–488, 508n1664, 509–510
Wisconsin Infantry Regiment, 29th, 511
Wisconsin Light Artillery Battery, 10th, 718
Wissahickon, USS, 177–178
Witcher, John S., 627
Withers, Jones M., 108, 124
Wofford, William, 680
Wood, James, 464
Wood, John C., 258, 497, 620, 641, 702, 713, 715, 742, 777
Wood, Sterling A. M., 123
Woodford (hospital ship), 502
Woodruff, George A., 94, 99, 109–110, 497
Woodruff, Lyman, 255, 258, 701–703, 715
Woods, John C., 244
Woods, Peter C., 542
Woodson, Charles, 707
Woodstock, Va., 647, 658, 664–665
Woodstock Races, 665. *See also* Battle of Tom's Brook
Woodward, Joseph T., 406, 408
Wool, John E., 91
Worcester, Mass., 773
Worden, John L., 72–73
Wren, Owen A., 42, 127, 140, 258, 459, 474, 485, 497, 564, 703–704, 713, 775
Wright, Horatio, 578, 580, 582–584, 584n1869, 585, 587, 592, 599, 605–606, 612, 621, 627, 643, 669–670, 673, 678–680, 683, 685–687, 689, 691–692, 695–696, 754–756
Wright, Rebecca, 622–623, 640, 710
Wright, Wallace D., 39, 41, 56, 95, 127, 140, 243, 254, 258, 308, 364, 460, 474
Wyandotte, USS, 60–62, 64, 72, 81
Wynne, William, 41, 95, 127, 140, 243, 258, 364, 459–461, 477

Y

Yalobusha River, 273, 275, 277, 279
Yates, Richard, 223
Yazoo, USS, 566
Yazoo City, Miss., 462
Yazoo Pass, 273–274, 280–281, 305, 356–357, 550
Yazoo River, 199, 209–210, 271, 273–274, 277, 279
Yellow Bayou, 558
York Rifle Companies of Haldimand, *779*
Yorktown, Va., 156
Young, H. K., 710–711
Yulee, David L., 66–68

Z

Zouaves. *See* New York Infantry Regiment, 155th; New York Infantry Regiment, 6th

About the Author

Robert C. Simmonds received a BS degree in Mechanical Engineering from Worcester Polytechnic Institute in 1958. After service in the army (he notes that ROTC was "the thing expected of us"), he began employment in machinery research and development.

He received an MS in Mechanical Engineering from Northeastern University in 1967. That was the year Benjamin Braddock (Dustin Hoffman) in the movie *The Graduate* received the advice: "There's a great future in plastics." As it happened, that same year, the author's employer, USM Corporation, went on an acquisition binge—acquisitions including manufacturers of plastics processing machinery. Soon, the author's research lab was assigned to support their R&D. It was the beginning of an immersion into packaging, consumer goods, and, finally, the automotive industry, that would continue for the rest of his career. Time puts a rosy glow on the past, but the author remembers that: "In all candor, it was stressful."

He enjoyed piloting his Grumman Tiger and was a longtime member of the Experimental Aircraft Association. Now, however, his interests have come down to earth—to his classic boat and cars, and, of course, his family.

Retirement has meant travel and a rather fateful step into genealogy, which led to the writing of this book.

His great-grandfather served in Battery L before, during, and after the Civil War.

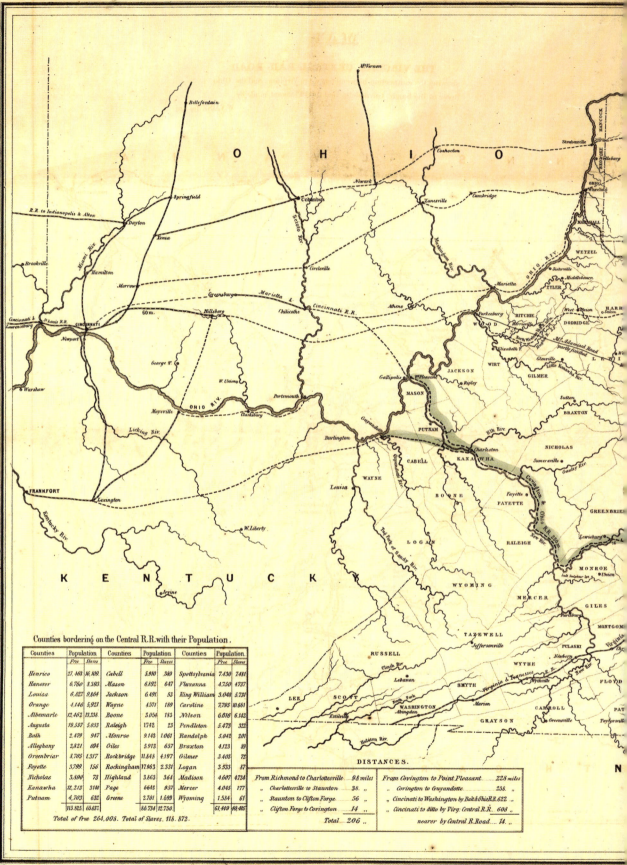